BL
2525
.C354
2012
v.1

THE CAMBRIDGE HISTORY OF RELIGIONS IN AMERICA

VOLUME I

Pre-Columbian Times to 1790

The three volumes of *The Cambridge History of Religions in America* trace the historical development of religious traditions in America, following both their transplantation from other parts of the world and the inauguration of new religious movements on the continent of North America. This story involves complex relationships among these religious communities as well as the growth of distinctive theological ideas and religious practices. The net result of this historical development in North America is a rich religious culture that includes representatives of most of the world's religions.

Volume I extends chronologically from prehistoric times until 1790, a date linked to the formation of the United States as a nation. The first volume provides background information on representative Native American traditions as well as on religions imported from Europe and Africa. Diverse religious traditions in the areas of European settlement, both Christian and non-Christian, became more numerous and more complex with the passage of time. Tension and conflict were also evident in this colonial period among religious groups, triggered sometimes by philosophical and social differences, other times by distinctive religious beliefs and practices. The complex world of the eighteenth century, including international tensions and conflicts, was a shaping force on religious communities in North America, including those on the continent both north and south of what became the United States.

Stephen J. Stein received his Ph.D. from Yale University in 1970 and subsequently taught in Indiana University's Department of Religious Studies for thirty-five years. He has received numerous grants and fellowships, including two from the National Endowment for the Humanities. In 1994, he served as the President of the American Society of Church History. In 1995, Stein received the Tracy M. Sonneborn Award for Excellence in Teaching and Research at Indiana University. He edited three volumes in *The Works of Jonathan Edwards* and *The Cambridge Companion to Jonathan Edwards*. Stein's volume, *The Shaker Experience in America: A History of the United Society of Believers*, was awarded the Philip Schaff Prize by the American Society of Church History in 1994. He is a coeditor of the journal *Religion and American Culture*.

THE CAMBRIDGE HISTORY OF RELIGIONS IN AMERICA

Edited by Stephen J. Stein, *Indiana University*

EDITORIAL ADVISORY BOARD

Dennis C. Dickerson, *Vanderbilt University*

R. Marie Griffith, *Washington University in St. Louis*

Christopher J. Kauffman, *Catholic University of America*

Jonathan D. Sarna, *Brandeis University*

Richard Hughes Seager, *Hamilton College*

Jane I. Smith, *Harvard Divinity School*

Jace Weaver, *The University of Georgia*

THE CAMBRIDGE HISTORY OF RELIGIONS IN AMERICA

VOLUME I

Pre-Columbian Times to 1790

Edited by

STEPHEN J. STEIN
Indiana University

Hiebert Library
Fresno Pacific University
Fresno, CA 93702

CAMBRIDGE UNIVERSITY PRESS
Cambridge, New York, Melbourne, Madrid, Cape Town,
Singapore, São Paulo, Delhi, Mexico City

Cambridge University Press
32 Avenue of the Americas, New York, NY 10013-2473, USA

www.cambridge.org
Information on this title: www.cambridge.org/9780521871105

© Cambridge University Press 2012

This publication is in copyright. Subject to statutory exception
and to the provisions of relevant collective licensing agreements,
no reproduction of any part may take place without the written
permission of Cambridge University Press.

First published 2012

Printed in the United States of America

A catalog record for this publication is available from the British Library.

Library of Congress Cataloging in Publication data
The Cambridge history of religions in America / [edited by] Stephen J. Stein.
    p. cm.
    Includes bibliographical references and index.
    ISBN 978-1-107-01334-6 (set) – ISBN 978-0-521-87110-5
(volume 1: hardback) – ISBN 978-0-521-87109-9 (volume 2:
hardback) – ISBN 978-0-521-87108-2 (volume 3: hardback)
    1. United States – Religion. I. Stein, Stephen J., 1940–
    II. Title: History of religions in America.
    BL2525.C354   2012
    200.973–dc23   2011026109

ISBN 978-0-521-87110-5 Volume I Hardback
ISBN 978-0-521-87109-9 Volume II Hardback
ISBN 978-0-521-87108-2 Volume III Hardback
ISBN 978-1-107-01334-6 Three-Volume Hardback Set

Cambridge University Press has no responsibility for the persistence or accuracy of URLs
for external or third-party Internet Web sites referred to in this publication and does not
guarantee that any content on such Web sites is, or will remain, accurate or appropriate.

CONTENTS

Contributors	page xi
Editor's Introduction STEPHEN J. STEIN	xiii

SECTION I. BACKGROUND ON RELIGIOUS TRADITIONS – PRE-1500s

1 Native American Religion RAYMOND D. FOGELSON	3
2 Roman Catholicism circa 1500 MEGAN C. ARMSTRONG	28
3 Protestant Traditions in Western Europe on the Eve of North American Colonization ROBERT D. LINDER	52
4 Religious Traditions in Great Britain on the Eve of Colonization PETER LAKE	73
5 Some Notes on African Religious Traditions from the Fourteenth Century Onward JACOB K. OLUPONA	96

SECTION II. RELIGIONS IN THE POST-COLUMBIAN NEW WORLD – 1500–1680s

6 Iroquoian Religion during the Seventeenth Century NEAL B. KEATING	113
7 Mississippian Religious Traditions DAVID H. DYE	137

8 The Anasazi   156
   JACE WEAVER

9 Spanish Catholicism in the Era of Exploration
   and Early Colonization   177
   PABLO GARCIA AND KATHLEEN ANN MYERS

10 French Catholicism in the Era of Exploration
   and Early Colonization   200
   DOMINIQUE DESLANDRES

11 English, Dutch, and Swedish Protestantism in
   the Era of Exploration and Early Colonization   219
   JAMES D. BRATT

SECTION III. RELIGIOUS PATTERNS IN COLONIAL AMERICA – 1680s–1730s

12 Spanish Catholicism in the Caribbean, New Spain,
   and the Northern Frontiers   241
   STAFFORD POOLE

13 French Catholicism in New France   263
   LUCA CODIGNOLA

14 Congregationalist Hegemony in New England,
   from the 1680s to the 1730s   282
   MICHAEL P. WINSHIP

15 The Middle Colonies, 1680–1730   303
   THOMAS D. HAMM

16 Religion in the Southern English Colonies, 1680s–1730s   328
   CHARLES H. LIPPY

SECTION IV. RELIGIOUS DIVERSITY IN BRITISH AMERICA – 1730s–1790

17 Religious Ferment among Eastern Algonquians and
   Their Neighbors in the Eighteenth Century   349
   AMY C. SCHUTT AND CHRISTOPHER VECSEY

18 African Slave Religions, 1400–1790   369
   SYLVESTER A. JOHNSON

19 Colonial Judaism   392
   JONATHAN D. SARNA

20 Roman Catholicism in the English North American
   Colonies, 1634–1776   410
   TRICIA T. PYNE

21 Anglicanism and Its Discontents: Protestant Diversity
   and Disestablishment in British America   429
   DANIEL VACA AND RANDALL BALMER
22 Protestant Evangelicalism in Eighteenth-Century America   451
   THOMAS S. KIDD
23 Sectarian Communities: Religious Diversity in British
   America, 1730–1790   467
   ETTA M. MADDEN
24 Liberal Religious Movements and the Enlightenment   489
   LEIGH E. SCHMIDT
25 Folk Magic and Religion in British North America   510
   RICHARD GODBEER

SECTION V. AMERICAN RELIGIONS IN THE EIGHTEENTH-CENTURY INTERNATIONAL CONTEXT

26 Religion and Imperial Conflict   531
   JON SENSBACH
27 Evangelical Awakenings in the Atlantic Community   550
   RICHARD P. HEITZENRATER
28 Religion and the American Revolution   570
   FRANK LAMBERT
29 The Religious Landscape: From the Revolution
   to the New Nation   588
   PATRICIA U. BONOMI
30 Religion in Canada, 1759–1815   610
   MARK A. NOLL
31 From Religious Nationalism to Political Consciousness:
   The Bourbon Reforms in Spanish America, 1750–1790   634
   ANA MARÍA DÍAZ-STEVENS AND ANTHONY
   M. STEVENS-ARROYO

SECTION VI. THEMATIC ESSAYS

32 Religious Thought: The Pre-Columbian Era to 1790   663
   E. BROOKS HOLIFIELD
33 Piety and Practice in North America to 1800   686
   ERIK R. SEEMAN
34 Sacred Music in Colonial America   708
   STEPHEN A. MARINI

35 Religious Architecture   728
    PETER W. WILLIAMS

36 Religion and Visuality in America: Material
    Economies of the Sacred   748
    DAVID MORGAN

37 Religion and Race   781
    PAUL HARVEY

38 Religions and Families in America: Historical Traditions
    and Present Positions   804
    KEVIN J. CHRISTIANO

39 Religious History   825
    EUAN KERR CAMERON

    Index   851

CONTRIBUTORS

MEGAN C. ARMSTRONG, McMaster University
RANDALL BALMER, Columbia University
PATRICIA U. BONOMI, New York University, Emerita
JAMES D. BRATT, Calvin College
EUAN KERR CAMERON, Union Theological Seminary
KEVIN J. CHRISTIANO, University of Notre Dame
LUCA CODIGNOLA, Universitá di Genova
DOMINIQUE DESLANDRES, Université de Montréal
ANA MARÍA DÍAZ-STEVENS, Union Theological Seminary
DAVID H. DYE, The University of Memphis
RAYMOND D. FOGELSON, University of Chicago
PABLO GARCIA, University of West Virginia
RICHARD GODBEER, University of Miami, Florida
THOMAS D. HAMM, Earlham College
PAUL HARVEY, University of Colorado
RICHARD P. HEITZENRATER, Duke University
E. BROOKS HOLIFIELD, Candler School of Theology
SYLVESTER A. JOHNSON, Indiana University
NEAL B. KEATING, SUNY College at Brockport
THOMAS S. KIDD, Baylor University
PETER LAKE, Princeton University
FRANK LAMBERT, Purdue University
ROBERT D. LINDER, Kansas State University
CHARLES H. LIPPY, University of Tennessee, Emeritus
ETTA M. MADDEN, Missouri State University
STEPHEN A. MARINI, Wellesley College
DAVID MORGAN, Duke University
KATHLEEN ANN MYERS, Indiana University
MARK A. NOLL, University of Notre Dame
JACOB K. OLUPONA, Harvard Divinity School
STAFFORD POOLE, The Vincentian Studies Institute

TRICIA T. PYNE, St. Mary's Seminary and University Associated Archives
JONATHAN D. SARNA, Brandeis University
LEIGH E. SCHMIDT, Washington University in St. Louis
AMY C. SCHUTT, The State University of New York, Cortland
ERIK R. SEEMAN, The State University of New York, Buffalo
JON SENSBACH, University of Florida
ANTHONY M. STEVENS-ARROYO, Brooklyn College, Emeritus
DANIEL VACA, Columbia University, doctoral candidate
CHRISTOPHER VECSEY, Colgate University
JACE WEAVER, University of Georgia
PETER W. WILLIAMS, Miami University, Ohio
MICHAEL P. WINSHIP, University of Georgia

EDITOR'S INTRODUCTION

STEPHEN J. STEIN

The history of American religions does not begin on the North American continent. On the contrary, it is a complex tale of the transplantation, interaction, and transformation of diverse imported religious traditions that hailed from a host of geographical locations on the Asian, European, and African continents alongside new religious movements that arose in the context of the Americas. This complexity creates a challenge for all who wish to understand the religious world in the United States, which is an astonishingly diverse, complex, and powerful reality in the opening decades of the twenty-first century. What follows is an anticipation of some of the insights that authors of the essays in this first volume of *The Cambridge History of Religions in America* provide regarding the early history of American religions.

Native American religions, for example, scattered across the full expanse of the American continent, functioned centrally for their adherents many centuries prior to European exploration and colonization in the New World. Native Americans came from elsewhere too, namely, from Asia. The continuities between Native American and Asian religious traditions were evident in the spiritualities manifest in tribal rituals at sacred sites as well as in the organization of daily life. The role of the shaman also was central in transformative rites, accessing diverse spiritual powers for both individuals and tribes.

In the Iroquoian religion, which existed for more than five thousand years in the Northeast Woodlands, the tradition of ceremonial dance was a means of achieving diverse ends, from healing, to success in the hunt, to victory in war. Spirits and spiritual forces were evident in soul travel and in dreams. Mississippian religious traditions, present in the Midwest and Southeast after 1000 C.E., involved a complex cosmology in which there were diverse deities, including Earth Mother, a female life-giving force. Mississippian shamans gained access to power by fasting and visions. The Anasazi, ancestors of today's Pueblo nations, lived in the Southwest beginning around 1200 B.C.E., first in underground chambers and then in surface dwellings. Their world included abundant spirits and deities, including the rain god Tlaloc, a critical deity for their planting and harvesting of corn and squash. Another god, Tanama – half god, half human – gave them fire, clothing, and housing.

The Christian hegemony evident in early modern Europe was over time exported to America. Beginning in the sixteenth century, Roman Catholicism was carried to America by the members of Spanish religious orders. The spiritual conquest of New Spain – the Caribbean, New Mexico, and South America – was carried out by monastic communities including the Franciscans, Dominicans, and Jesuits. Catholic theological and devotional emphases included transubstantiation in the Eucharist, the cult of the Virgin Mary, penance and purgatory, and relics of the saints. Conversion of the native population, however, often involved reciprocal misunderstanding. As a result, despite Catholic arguments against indigenous religiosity, native elements were added to Catholic rituals; Roman Catholicism was often mixed with preconquest religious practices. New devotions also were added to the tradition, including one triggered by the appearance of the Virgin Mary to the Indian convert Juan Diego in 1531. The resulting image of the Dark Virgin – the Virgin of Guadalupe – reinforced the commitment to Catholicism of the natives whose own dark color was shared by the Mother of God. Convents flourished in New Spain, where the majority of nuns were creoles, persons of mixed ancestry. Franciscan missions were highly successful in Alta California.

The Catholic Church was also a primary agent in the early colonization of New France. Samuel de Champlain (1567–1635), the founder of Quebec, devoted himself to converting Amerindians both to French civilization and to Christianity. Conversion of the Native Americans to Christianity, however, was more successful than "Frenchification." There were never, however, enough priests for the tasks at hand. The number of nuns, by contrast, did expand. Indian missions were left primarily in the hands of religious communities such as the Jesuits, Sulpicians, and Recollets. One unintended legacy of all the colonial enterprises was disease brought to the new land for which Native Americans had no immunity. The results were devastating for the native population.

Protestant traditions from the European continent – Lutheran, Calvinist, and Anabaptist – arrived in America under varying circumstances and at different times during the colonial era. Lutheran doctrinal emphases included justification by grace through faith and the authority of scripture. The Calvinist or Reformed tradition underscored the sovereignty of God and the doctrine of election or predestination. Anabaptists were restorationists, calling for a direct return to New Testament patterns, including the notion of the church as a "gathered society." Anglicanism arose on the British Isles over conflicts regarding royal succession and the sacraments, as the sequence of English monarchs sought authority over both church and state. The resulting Church of England valued tradition and change, episcopacy and conformity, sacramentalism and ceremony. One religious result of the reign of Queen Elizabeth was the emergence of Puritanism, a dissenting Reformed movement defined by its rejection of bishops, popish ceremonies, and a national church as well as by its positive accent on the proclamation of the Word and the doctrine of election.

Africans carried to the Americas in bondage as slaves brought with them diverse African religions in which deities, spirits, and ancestors played a role. African indigenous religions enabled participants to manipulate numerous spirits or forces by means of rituals. Power or magic in these traditions was exercised by witches and sorcerers. Proper relationships with one's ancestors, who resided in the underworld, were religiously important. Monotheism was also present on the African continent in its Christian and Islamic forms long before the beginnings of the slave trade to America.

The nature, place, and function of religion in the English colonies on the Atlantic seaboard during the seventeenth century varied dramatically, from the New England Puritan colonies of Massachusetts and Connecticut, where religion functioned centrally in a prescribed and controlled manner, to Virginia and New Netherland, where founding religious patterns changed with the passage of time and therefore played a more modest role. The most persistent commitment to religious liberty during the period was in the colony of Rhode Island; in other colonies, the very category of "liberty" was redefined in accord with the view of the controlling parties.

In the decades surrounding the turn of the eighteenth century, religion in New England continued to be dominated by Congregationalism, a Christian polity in which the minister and the laity shared power in a single congregation, bound together by a covenant that spelled out mutual obligations and was renewed periodically. With the passage of time, other Christian groups came on the scene in New England in limited numbers – Presbyterians, Anglicans, Baptists, and Quakers. Native Americans and African slaves were also part of the growing religious diversity in the region.

The Middle Colonies were the most ethnically and religiously diverse region in the English colonies on the Atlantic seaboard. The nationalities present in significant numbers included the English, Dutch, French, German, Swedish, Scottish, Irish, and Welsh, as well as Native Americans and African slaves. The religious traditions present in varying strength included the Reformed, Lutheran, Mennonite, Presbyterian, Baptist, Congregational, Huguenot, Roman Catholic, and Jewish traditions. Many of these traditions held dramatically different views regarding the rights of the state over religion and over the individual conscience. The diversity in this region anticipated the subsequent ethnic and religious pluralism characteristic of later periods in American history.

Religion in the southern colonies had a prominent Anglican caste to it. Priests ordained in England served as the spokesmen for the Church of England in a land and in circumstances far removed from the homeland. They were challenged by the multiracial task of relating their gospel to both African slaves and Native Americans, as were also other religious communities in the South. The social and religious situations were highly complex. The colony of Maryland was an exception to the Protestant caste of the English colonies. The Act of Toleration in 1649 created in Maryland a religious situation in which Protestants and Catholics existed side by side. In Carolina, the religious diversity in the colonial period included Huguenots, Jews, Quakers, Lutherans, and Baptists. The stage was therefore clearly set for more diversity with the passage of time.

In all of these regions of English settlement, another kind of religious belief exercised substantial influence over many of the colonists. Folk beliefs in the power of the supernatural were widespread. The common judgment was that occult forces could be controlled and exercised by those who had knowledge of the same or astrological insight. Belief in the power of magical techniques that could be passed from generation to generation existed on both sides of the Atlantic. Magic could be employed for the purpose of healing sickness, protecting from harm, predicting the future, and telling personal fortunes. Witches and those who were able to manipulate these secret powers occupied a special place in colonial society. Belief in the occult was widespread throughout colonial America, even among groups very active in the established religious communities. The most striking evidence of this belief existing side by side with orthodox Christian establishments was the witchcraft craze that swept Salem Village in Puritan New England in 1692, an episode that ultimately led to the execution of some twenty persons, males and females, linked to witchcraft.

In the years prior to the Revolutionary War, which led to the formation of the new United States, Native American societies in British America were under assault as European settlers continued to advance into their homelands. These years were, for example, a time of religious ferment for members of the Eastern Algonquian tribe located in the New England and mid-Atlantic regions. They were also times when boundaries were crossed by religious persons in both cultures seeking spiritual renewal and reform. Dreams and visions were powerful among Native Americans, as was belief in guardian spirits. Manitou, or spiritual power, was accessed by them through diverse rituals and ceremonies; success in the hunt and personal health were also obtained in this manner. Perceived correspondences between certain indigenous rituals and Christian religious practices facilitated a measure of evangelical Protestant success among some Native Americans in this period. Others, however, were suspicious of the Christian missionaries because of the history of injustices against the natives.

The Spanish, French, and British brought African slaves to their American colonies. Slave religion, as it evolved in America, blended African religious expression – dancing, jumping, shouting – with the diverse forms of Christianity. Concern among the slaves with healing and divination, ancestors and spirits, remained central in these African slave religious traditions. Among Protestant communities, evangelicalism, with its focus on the workings of the Spirit, resonated positively with African slaves at revival meetings because of the parallels with African religious expressions. Anglicanism, with its more structured and staid liturgical worship, was not successful among the slaves. The First African Church, a Baptist evangelical community, was founded after the American Revolution by Andrew Bryan, himself an African American, in Savannah, Georgia. Islam, which had significant African adherents, was also transferred to America by slaves. Its presence in the colonial period is difficult to document because of the absence of organized communities.

Jews, expelled from Spain and Portugal in the 1490s, saw the New World as a possible refuge from the Inquisition and from the widespread hostility they experienced in Europe. Conversos practiced their Judaism in secret because of the sustained hostility directed against Jews. In North America, the Dutch colonies allowed Jewish activity, and as a result Jewish refugees from Brazil settled in New Amsterdam in 1654. The majority of Jews in early America were Sephardic, with roots on the Iberian Peninsula, by contrast with Ashkenazic Jews from Germanic lands. Many Jews in this time period lived in port cities. The first Torah scroll arrived in Savannah in 1733; by contrast, the first permanent rabbi in the United States did not arrive until 1840. Cantor readers assumed leadership functions in the communities, which often worshipped in private homes, where the Torah was read. The primary belief of the Jewish tradition was belief in one God. Male circumcision was a defining religious ritual. In the colonial period there were synagogues in New York and Newport, Rhode Island. Jews were standardly denied voting rights in the colonies.

The power and influence of the primary religious traditions legally established in specific English colonies – Anglicanism, Congregationalism, Roman Catholicism, and Quakerism – did not deter the introduction of numerous other new religious communities over the course of the eighteenth century. Some of the latter imported from abroad were for a time confined more or less to the immigrants carrying the traditions to America.

The Dunkers, or Taufers, for example, later the Church of the Brethren, came from Germany to Germantown, Pennsylvania. Other new communities were offshoots or parties that separated from religious traditions already present in the English colonies, often over some particular theological or practical issue. The Separate Baptists in New England departed from Congregationalism over the question of infant baptism. Still other communities were founded by individuals who were influenced by an existing religious tradition, but who set out to create a new and different community. Mother Ann Lee, the founder of the Shakers who immigrated to New York, was shaped in some measure by her experiences with a group in England identified as "Shaking Quakers." It is often difficult to categorize many of these new groups because of their religious creativity and striking diversity.

Religious liberalism in North America owed its origins largely to those influenced by the moderate to radical Enlightenment. Among the members of the founding generation of the United States, deism was a powerful influence, cultivating both civic virtue and moral benevolence. Following the American Revolution, the new nation made a constitutional commitment to the principle and practice of religious liberty and to the separation of church and state. This revolutionary step was achieved with relative ease despite the history of religious establishments in the British colonies and the presence of contrary proposals. From this time on, the voluntary religious principle was in place. The architects of this new way of handling religion were James Madison and Thomas Jefferson, political thinkers influenced by the Enlightenment who held high views of human nature and who were sharply critical of religious enthusiasm. They also equated Calvinism with unreason. This generation established a strong foundation for the emergence of liberal religion in the first half of the nineteenth century.

Canadian religion in the late eighteenth century bore some similarities to religion in the British colonies, but there were also major differences from the religious situation developing in the new United States. The French-speaking Catholics and the English-speaking Protestants were successful in working out a system of living together. The Catholic Church was a powerful organization in Quebec. The American Revolution produced a wave of Protestant Loyalists who moved to Canada. Over time the Maritimes became the seat of an aggressive evangelicalism. Methodists also enjoyed success in Upper Canada. Despite the presence of both Catholics and Protestants, Native American religions continued with remarkable success throughout Canada, in some cases with substantial mingling of Christian and native religious patterns.

In the period from 1750 to 1790, religion continued to play an important role in the Spanish colonies on the continent. The presence of Catholic diversity was evident in different spiritualities or ways to live out the faith, including powerful traditions followed by the religious orders and diverse patterns of lay spirituality. Catholic religious life was reflected by attention to patron saints, celebration of holy days, and participation in diverse patterns of lay spirituality. European political and intellectual developments had a direct impact on Catholic religious life in the Spanish colonies, resulting in such diverse developments as the expulsion from the region of the Society of Jesus to the impact of Enlightenment ideas on religious activity. It would be difficult, however, to overestimate the impact of Roman Catholicism on life in the Spanish colonies.

Settlers coming to the New World imported diverse theological traditions, religious and devotional practices, and sacred music. Religious leaders in the colonies addressed social and political issues including gender and race as well as tensions within and conflicts among denominations. Residents in the colonies expressed their religious commitments through daily activities, including acts of piety and traditional religious practices as diverse as Algonquian vision quests, Puritan Sabbath routines, Morning Prayer in Anglican Virginia, and African practitioners of obeah engaged in healing disease among the slave population.

One set of essays in this volume not confined chronologically to the early period of American history deals with art, architecture, family, and race, respectively, ranging across the full time period from colonial America to the present. These topics invite wide-ranging temporal reflection as well as consideration of the specific roles of diverse religious traditions. For example, art forms – from the rock imagery on the Columbia Plateau to santos or holy images in New Spain, and from the Lakota winter count on a buffalo hide to a Jacob Lawrence painting of an African American hanging from a tree – were powerful religious statements. Similarly, religious structures, including the hogans of the Navajos, Bruton Parish Church in colonial Williamsburg, Temple Beth Elohim in nineteenth-century Charleston, and the Mother Church of Christian Science in Boston, reflected the religious values of the traditions they housed. Family life also often mirrored a relationship to religion. Witness, for example, patriarchal patterns in Puritan New England and nineteenth-century Catholic families modeled after the Holy Family. In recent times too, family patterns and values have been imported from around the world – from Confucian, Buddhist, Muslim, or Hindu traditions – as well as crafted by new religious groups, from the Mormons to the Unification Church. Another issue heavily influenced by diverse religious judgments is the concept of race. Over the course of

American history, negative racial identities have been assigned to Native Americans, Africans, slaves, Negroes, Jews, and most recently Asians – judgments often reinforced by implicit religious teachings.

The essays in *The Cambridge History of Religions in America* present striking evidence of an astonishing range of teachings and beliefs professed by diverse religious communities on the North American continent from the earliest recorded times down to the present, the opening decades of the twenty-first century. Religious historians often frame the past in ways that make sense to the world that is contemporary with them. Religious history has also commonly been a tool employed by opposing parties in theological conflicts, moving the genre toward apologetics because of partisan and confessional uses. The professionalization of religious history in the nineteenth and twentieth centuries has reduced that use somewhat. In the opening decades of the twenty-first century, religious history is often in dialogue with the traditions it sets out to describe. In the diverse essays in this and the two following volumes, the manifold forms of religious history are evident, and they are therefore highly suggestive for those who wish to join the unending task.

Section I

BACKGROUND ON RELIGIOUS TRADITIONS – PRE-1500s

I

NATIVE AMERICAN RELIGION

RAYMOND D. FOGELSON

Native American "religion" may be a misnomer for many traditionally oriented Native Americans, as well as for some academic scholars. Native Americans frequently associate religion with a rigidly organized orthodoxy and orthopraxy anchored by sacred scriptures and an established ecclesiastical hierarchy. In point of fact, the vast majority of Native Americans today are true believing Christians who clearly embrace a religion and subscribe to its basic tenets. However, Native American traditionalists with at best a nominal tie to Christianity often prefer to use the term "spirituality" to refer to their sacred belief systems and related practices.

The idea of spirituality invokes indigenous conceptions of a fluid, unwritten sense of profound power ordering the visible and invisible universe. Such power infuses the worldviews of traditionalists; it goes under various names but can also operate as an unnamed category. It is manifest in sacred sites, and it can be activated by ritual publicly performed during collective ceremonial periods or in privately practiced rites by individuals during times of personal crisis.

Spirituality claims a timeless authenticity seamlessly interwoven within distinctive cultural patterns. These patterns extend far into the past, embody the present, and project into the near and distant future. Native spirituality was closely connected to prophecy. From a traditionalist viewpoint, prophecy was history and history was prophecy. Linear temporality alternated with nonlineal time and with a sense of eternity. These alternative systems of time may be best exemplified by various forms of divination. Divination is concerned not only with prophetic prediction about future outcomes, but also with "postdiction," in an effort to reveal the factors leading up to the present situation. Also significant in divinatory practice is "syndication," referring to events or conditions occurring simultaneously elsewhere, beyond immediate perception.

The etymologies of the terms religion and spirituality deserve attention. The *Oxford English Dictionary* suggests two Latin roots: *religare*, "to bind," and *religere*, "to read over."[1] The former meaning, referring to a "rebinding" or "binding back," is usually cited by religious scholars in suggesting a unifying function for religion. This would be consistent with the Durkheimian notion of collective solidarity.[2] The root may also refer to bonding to a particular religious association, or a rebonding to or reaffirmation of particular deities; to spiritual bondings; or to the source of some metaphysical power. These occasions may occur at critical junctures in the life cycle, as in vision questing at or before puberty with the acquisition of spirit animal protectors. The second etymology for religion, "to read over," resonates with the repetition or incessant rehearsal characteristic of ritual. This derivation would fit well with theories, such as that of Robertson Smith,[3] that view religion as based primarily on ritual action rather than on mythical belief.

Spirituality, of course, is linked with the Latin root *spiritus*, whose basic meaning relates to breath and breathing and by extension to air, life, and the idea of a soul or souls. Some of these associations are clearly present in Native North America, as with the conception of a supreme being or author of life, breath, and consciousness, who, not coincidentally, was referred to as "the Master of Breath" among many Muskogean-speaking groups in the Southeast. Spirit, or in French, *espirit*, can also denote courage, vigor, or morale. The adjective "spiritual" generally relates to matters of the soul or intellect and is sharply contrasted with the physical body and materiality. The noun, "spiritualism," has taken on certain negative connotations in popular usage. The term "spirituality" is less encumbered than spiritualism with psychic pseudoscience and instead is associated more with alternate religious beliefs and practices frequently derived from individual exotic, non-Western sources. Spirituality features an affinity to nature bordering on worship.

To summarize, Native Americans clearly possessed what we recognize as religious institutions. Many examples of indigenous religious institutions can be noted, including Pueblo ceremonialism, Creek rituals, the Longhouse religion of the Iroquois, ancestral rites such as the potlatch on the Northwest coast, and Navajo and Apache traditions. The list could be enlarged by mentioning religious revivals and revitalizations among many other tribes.

An increasing number of Native Americans see a continuing vitality in what they consider their traditional beliefs and practices. They feel that the rubric "spirituality" more closely captures their inherent traditions

---

[1] *The Compact Edition of the Oxford English Dictionary* (Glasgow, 1971), 2.

[2] Emile Durkheim, *The Elementary Forms of Religious Life,* trans. Joseph Ward Swain, 1909 (New York, 1965).

[3] William Robertson Smith, *Religion of the Semites: The Fundamental Institutions, 1889* (New York, 1956).

than the term "religion," which they associate with externally imposed Christian assumptions, however ecumenicalized and compromised.

Native American spirituality not only appeals to traditionalists and to such serious native intellectuals as Vine Deloria, Jr., but also has attracted an enthusiastic following among New Agers, Green movement advocates, and Neopagans. These ideological movements have appropriated such indigenous features as a belief in a layered universe, an earth island floating on a turtle's carapace in a primal sea, mystical circles and medicine wheels, multicolored directionality indicators, divining crystals and dream catchers, tobacco sacrifices and sweat baths, native herbal remedies and the purifying smell of sweet grass, stone effigies, and a solemn belief in the redeeming power of Mother Earth. These elements have been stripped of whatever meaning and validity they may once have claimed in the context of native cultures and have passed uncritically into the realm of popular culture.

This brings us to issues of authenticity and questions of what is meant by tradition. Scholars today write about invented or reinvented traditions.[4] They cast doubt on the authenticity of particular beliefs and practices. Tradition is generally recognized as the intergenerational handing down of stories, beliefs, and customs. Traditions are usually transmitted orally in native cultures. Although literacy and written texts are sometimes taken to be the hallmark of the so-called Great Religions, oral traditions also figure prominently in their foundations

Traditions can persist covertly from ancestors to descendants, from generation to generation. However, the continuity of traditions can be threatened by outside pressures. Thus, because the potlatches of the Northwest coast and the Sun Dance of the Great Plains were considered barbarous and as obstacles to the civilizing efforts of the missionaries, they were duly outlawed by governmental agents. However, memories of these rituals continued, and when the political climate finally moderated, they reemerged fully formed as recollected traditions.

In some cases the specific traditional forms are altered owing to memory lapse and cultural loss, but the idea and spirit of the ritual remains alive in the collective imagination. Alternative versions of the traditional custom may be introduced from elsewhere and be adjusted to fit the local cultural pattern. A case in point is the recent pan-tribal diffusion of the sweat bath. Most tribes once had a version of this sudatory rite, but its practice had often died out. This was the situation with the Eastern Cherokees and with the Mississippi Choctaws until recently, when Lakota variants of the sweat

---

[4] Eric Hobsbawn and Terence Ranger, eds., *The Invention of Tradition* (Cambridge, UK, 1983).

bathing ritual were adopted. Traditions have careers. They may sometimes go into abeyance, but they have the capacity to be regenerated through memory and diffusion.

As cultural process has ebbs and flows, religions and spiritualities have similarly undergone continuities and discontinuities. The archaeological record of the Americas reveals changes in the treatment of the dead in memorial structures and in accompanying symbolism, all of which suggests concomitant changes in religious ideology and spiritual practices. Interment in individual and collective burials, as well as the position and orientation of skeletal remains, appeared to have religious significance, as did the quality and quantity of grave goods. In the Eastern Woodlands, burial mounds going back to late Archaic times (c. four thousand years ago) were prototypical. In the Northern Plains, wrapped corpses were suspended on scaffolds; and in the Northwest, a certain incidence of tree inhumations, as well as cremations, occurred. In some regions of the Subarctic, the graves of shamans were oriented with the head pointing to the west, while the general population faced east, toward the rising sun. In Nova Scotia, buried skeletons were sprinkled with red hematite, perhaps indicating revivification or rebirth. Perhaps this latter practice represented a union of white skeletal material, symbolic of males and semen, with the symbolic birth or menstrual blood of female procreation and fertility.

The practice of double burial, first conceptualized by Robert Hertz, was widespread in Native North America.[5] Death rituals, mourning, condolence, and the initial disposition of the corpse might, after a prescribed period of time, be followed by a relocation of the mortal remains and a briefer, less emotionally charged set of rituals. Not only were life cycles punctuated by rites of passage, but cycles of death were also marked. Thus for many Native Americans, death was less of an event than a continuous process indicated by several transformative junctures. Physically, the death cycle involved the progressive decomposition of the material body and the release of spiritual essences. Often this process was conceived of as a separation of flesh from bone. When this process of cleansing the skeleton of decaying flesh was completed, often through exposure of the corpse to the upper world, as in scaffold burials, or to the lower world, in temporary interment, the skeletal remains were deposited in a more permanent location, as an ossuary, tomb, or burial mound. Even so-called totem poles sometimes featured carved boxes that contained the charred remains of the cremated ancestral chief in whose memory the pole was erected.

---

[5] Robert Hertz, *Death and the Right Hand,* trans. R. and C. Needham, 1907 (New York, 1960).

The aforementioned means of disposing of the corpse varied with different societies. Moreover, there could be alternate forms of burial within a particular society depending on the circumstances of death, the status of the deceased individual, or such other factors as gender or age. Additional variables surrounded the treatment of the deceased. How was death ascertained? Who handled the corpse? Was the body publically displayed, as it was among the Tlingits, or was the dead person feared and avoided, as among the Apache and Navajo? How was the property of the deceased passed on? Were there direct rules of inheritance of property and status, or were personal belongings of the deceased distributed to the winners of the hand game that was played during the funerary rites among the Shuswap of British Columbia? The type and amount of grave goods was again highly variable. Burials might include offerings of food as provisions for the arduous journey to the afterlife, such as the pots of parched corn that accompanied proto-historic Wampanoag burials. Wealth objects and utilitarian items, as well as the souls of slain sacrificial animals, also might be ticketed to accompany the dead to their ultimate destination.

The ideas behind double burials and grave goods offerings bespeak native ideas of eschatology and the fate of the soul, or better, souls, because most native metaphysical theories were premised on multiple souls. The term "souls" may mask what may be better translated as "living essences." Native understandings of life processes and vitality more closely resembled the pre-Socratic ideas of particular humors than the Christian notion of a unified soul. These living essences were imparted to the body from various sources during procreation and took their sequential leave from the body at different junctures of the death cycle. Indeed, some Native American theories of death stood in a reciprocal relationship to theories of birth. This linkage of birth and death could be extended to incorporate ideas of rebirth and reincarnation that prevailed in many metaphysical belief systems, the Wet'suwet'en of British Columbia being an exemplary case.[6]

The limen between life and death was often blurred in native North America. Oral narratives are replete with accounts of people who returned from the land of the dead with vivid imagery of what life, or death, is like in the otherworld. Orpheus and Eurydice motifs pervaded many North American bodies of myth,[7] and we have many historical accounts of people taken for dead suddenly regaining consciousness before the final funerary

---

[6] Antonia Mills and Richard Slobodin, eds., *Amerindian Rebirth: Reincarnation among North American Indians and Inuit* (Toronto, 1994).

[7] Åke Hultkrantz, *The North American Indian Orpheus Tradition: A Contribution to Comparative Religion*. The Ethnographical Museum of Sweden, Monograph Series, Publication No. 2 (Stockholm, 1957).

rites were performed. Indeed, most Native American prophets and shamans endured near-death experiences in connection with their spiritual revelations. A deathlike episode or fatal illness was often a prerequisite for becoming a shaman or a medicine person.

Ghosts loomed large in the behavioral environments of Native America. Death was rarely regarded as a natural event in native reckoning. If the cause of death was not addressed, the spirit of the deceased would haunt the living in an attempt to exact revenge. But not all visits of spirits from the otherworld were vengeful. In many groups it was expected that deceased members of the community would rejoin their living relatives on ceremonial occasions. Thus the Tulelo adoption ceremony made provision for the attendance of deceased kin.[8] Pueblo Katchinas were impersonations of the souls of dead kinsmen who resided half the year in the nearby mountains as controllers of rain and who returned to the pueblo in the other half of the year, where they participated in ceremonies through the agency of masked performers.

It can be seen that the relations between the living and the dead among Native Americans involved both separation and inclusion. In many instances, the intention of death rituals was to create space between the living and the dead. However, on other occasions, especially celebratory ones, the spirits of the deceased were reincorporated into the living community. In all cases, the boundaries between life and death were at best tenuous. Understanding some of the metaphysical beliefs concerning death and the serious manner in which funerary rites were conducted helps us appreciate the sensitivities that most, but not all, Native Americas felt toward eschatology and the death cycle. Implicit in these views was the deep-seated belief that bones, though separated from flesh, still contained real and symbolic power. Skeletal material retained some degree of living vitality and had a potential for regeneration. Bones could be likened to seeds planted in the ground; they also served to claim a birthright, if not deathright, to the land and its history. Disturbance of graves and removal of bones therefore were conceived by some as a source of affliction.

The notion that bones possess vital qualities presupposed belief in souls that transcend death and have at least a potential for reincarnation. One of the acknowledged fathers of modern cultural anthropology who engaged these issues was Sir Edward Burnett Tylor (1832–1917). Tylor had only minimal field exposure as a tourist in Mexico, but he was an encyclopedic researcher of early documents containing ethnological data. These sources comprised reports by missionaries, soldiers, explorers, and colonial officials

---

[8] Frank G. Speck, *The Tutelo Reclothing and Spirit Adoption Ceremony* (Harrisburg, PA, 1942).

who observed the manners and customs of indigenous peoples around the world, including Native Americans. Tylor was what we would recognize today as an armchair cultural evolutionist, but perhaps he can more accurately be considered a universal historian interested in the stages of human culture history and the regularities of human cultural development. In staking out his subject matter, he coined a valuable omnibus definition of culture that still commands respect today. Tylor was interested in the general direction of human history, with its attendant philosophical and theological debates about the idea of progress and perfectibility versus theories of cultural decline and degeneration from a hypothetical golden age. In systematizing and analyzing his extensive material, Tylor paid particular attention to social institutions and their sequential development.

Tylor's magnum opus, *Primitive Culture* (1871),[9] laid out his use of the comparative method to deduce the uniformitarian upward progress toward an eventual goal of civilization. In this work, Tylor was especially concerned with the origins and subsequent development of religion. Many of his contemporaries viewed primitive cultures as devoid of genuine religion; the development of these simpler societies was impeded by reliance on superstitious beliefs and magical thinking. Tylor, on the other hand, argued that religion was a human universal and proposed a minimum definition of religion as a belief in spiritual beings, or what he called "animism."

"Animism" is a term that Tylor rescued from the early eighteenth-century theory of vitalism, as posited by Georg Stahl.[10] According to the latter, living beings possess *anima*, or life properties, that operate differently from the laws of chemistry or physics as applied to inert materials. Stahl contrasted *anima* with another substance, *phlogiston*, which was the combustible element in inert matter that could burn off or oxidize at different rates. Tylor might have chosen the term "spiritualism" to encompass his minimum definition of religion, but that term already possessed unwanted connotations of mysticism. Tylor was, if nothing else, a strict rationalist, even though his Quaker background seems to have stimulated an enduring fascination with the uncanny.

Tylor's theory of animism as a belief in spiritual beings involved a logical deduction of the survival of souls from the prevalence of dreams about the deceased. That the soul could take semipermanent leave of the living body seemed evident in cases of mental derangement. More temporary soul loss could occur in sudden fright or sneezing. Survivals of these primal beliefs were embedded in linguistic usage: as "I was beside myself," or "I

---

[9] E. B. Tylor, *Primitive Culture*, 2 vols., 1871 (London, 1913).
[10] Graham Harvey, *Animism: Respecting the Living World* (New York, 2006).

was scared out of my wits," or with formulaic phrasings accompanying sneezing, yawning, or temporary paroxysms.

Tylor's influential theory of religion as originating from common individual experience was severely criticized by others. Durkheim and his followers saw religion as emanating from collective rather than individual experiences. Religion, thus, was not so much a psychological as a sociological phenomenon or, perhaps better, had a social-psychological basis in the collective effervescence manifested in, for example, Australian aboriginal corroborees or Native American ghost dances.

Tylor's rationalism also diminished the importance of the emotional impact of religion. For theorists like Durkheim, Freud, William James, and other strange bedfellows, religious experience was of primary significance in both the phylogenetic and ontogenetic origins of religion. The hyperrationality of Tylor's formulation of animism also troubled other theorists, such as Lucien Lévy-Bruhl,[11] who suggested that what he called the Law of Participation, characteristic of primitive thinking about the self and its extensions, did not conform to Western logical assumptions, like the Law of Contradiction, and operated on different, culturally specific systems of logic.

A development derived from Tylorian animism was the theory advanced by one of his students, R. R. Marett (1866–1943).[12] Marett postulated a pre-animistic conception based on a belief in impersonal notions of power that may have preceded a belief in spiritual beings. He labeled this preanimistic religious stage as animatism. Marett was influenced by the discoveries of Bishop R. H. Codrington[13] in the South Pacific, where he found a native concept of *mana*. *Mana* referred to a kind of disembodied power that could be resident in things, winds, places, times, and a human elite who were closely aligned with the gods and shared some of their divine substance and characteristics. *Mana* defies precise translation but has been compared to energy and likened to electricity; it can also be related to good fortune or luck. Soon after Codrington's book became widely circulated, ethnographers began to describe similar native conceptions in far-flung corners of the world. Thus in North America, J. N. B. Hewitt recycled a Huron term, *orenda*, to encompass Iroquoian concepts of power.[14] The Crows had a notion of power called *maxpe*;[15] the Lakotas and other Siouan speakers had highly

---

[11] Lucien Lévy-Bruhl, *How Natives Think*, trans. L. C. Clare, 1910 (London, 1926).

[12] R. R. Marett, *The Threshold of Religion*, 1900, 4th ed. (London, 1929).

[13] Robert H. Codrington, *The Melanesians: Studies in Their Anthropology and Folklore* (Oxford, 1891).

[14] J. N. B. Hewitt, "Orenda and a Definition of Religion," *American Anthropologist* 4 (1902): 33–46.

[15] Robert H. Lowie, *The Crow Indians* (New York, 1935).

differentiated notions of *wakan*;[16] the Algonkian concept of manitou was often translated, perhaps wrongfully, as power,[17] while in the Northwest, Salish speakers spoke of *sulia* and Chinookan peoples viewed *tamanous* as a form of power. In many other groups, power was an unmarked category, yet an effective force in social relations and religious life.

Power concepts are highly variable in meaning and extensiveness and therefore must be understood in their cultural context. Contra Marett, ideas of power need not be taken as logically a priori to animistic beliefs in souls or personified spiritual beings. Indeed, a closer reading of Codrington's classical account of *mana* reveals that the winds, often assumed to be an almost prototypical example of diffuse, disembodied, impersonal power, were usually addressed by kinship terms and thus personalized by the natives. And the manitous of the Algonkian Ojibwa, although frequently associated with winds and directionality, were usually anthropomorphized as deities.[18]

Ideas of power, however, may be embedded at deeper levels of what we regard as animism. The aforementioned Ojibwas and related Algonkian speakers provide a case in point. In the 1830s, in the process of learning the language, Henry Rowe Schoolcraft[19] discovered that Ojibwa lacked gender distinctions in classifying nouns, unlike Indo-European languages (excepting English, which lost the gender distinction over time). Instead, Schoolcraft postulated an animate/inanimate means for Ojibwa noun classification. Although this distinction, which attributes "life" to some nouns and "inertness" to others, accommodates most Algonkian nouns, it is still an externally imposed grammatical construction that may mask more fundamental Ojibwa associations. Students of Algonkian languages have been bedeviled by anomalies that seem to contradict the animate/inanimate distinction. Certain body parts may be classed as inanimate, as elbows or knees; some berries are animate, and others are inanimate, as strawberries and raspberries.

Probably, the most puzzling anomaly in Ojibwa noun classification concerns rocks.[20] Indeed, rocks under some conditions may move. It is believed

---

[16] James R. Walker, *Lakota Belief and Ritual,* ed. Raymond J. DeMallie and Elaine A. Jahner (Lincoln, 1980).

[17] William Jones, "The Algonkin Manitu," *Journal of American Folklore* 18 (1905).

[18] A. Irving Hallowell, "Ojibwa Ontology, Behavior, and World View," in Stanley Diamond, ed., *Culture in History: Essays in Honor of Paul Radin* (New York, 1960).

[19] Henry Rowe Schoolcraft, *Algic Researches, Comprising Inquiries Respecting the Mental Characteristics of the North American Indians.* First Series. Indian Tales and Legends (New York, 1939).

[20] Mary B. Black, "Ojibwa Power Belief System," in Raymond D. Fogelson and Richard N. Adams, eds., *The Anthropology of Power* (New York, 1977).

that in the past, or possible future, some rocks may have possessed qualities of life. Past or potential animation gets us closer to resolving the seeming dilemma. But for Ojibwas, some rocks could be talked to and were considered to be persons who possess autonomy and volition in their dialogue with human beings. Pushing the analysis further, we must inquire about the source of this capacity for movement, this animation, this personhood. Again, we must posit some underlying *mana*-like energy that Ojibwas and other Native Americans frequently conceive of as medicine power. Some rocks, plants, or other objects have it, and some do not.

This medicine power, like *mana*, can be changeable and transient. Trees in most Algonkian languages were considered inanimate. Although they may grow over time, sway in the wind, and change appearance seasonally, trees do not display much inherent mobility. Yet for some Algonkian speakers like the Fox, the bark of an elm tree was transformed from an inanimate to an animate state when it was used to cover a wigwam. In effect, it became the skin of a living domicile, which was energized by the fire from a central hearth (or "heart"). Among many Plains Algonkians, a tree in the forest may be inanimate, but when it was cut down, stripped of its bark, and erected in a consecrated area as a Sun Dance pole, the pole was enlivened and became animate.

Power can also be inherent in certain objects. We consider skeletal material to be dead and inanimate after being separated from living flesh and blood by undergoing a process of mineralization. However, many Native Americans considered bones as retaining living power and thus animate. Animism or animatism ultimately may prove to be fundamental to our understanding of Native American spirituality and, perhaps, as Tylor intended, essential to all religions.

Another concept indigenous to North America also attracted the attention of many prominent scholars interested in tracing the origins of religion. That concept is totemism, derived from the Ojibwa stem *–do.de m*.[21] It was first described in an account by John Long, a late eighteenth-century fur trader. The stem root that was nominalized as "totemism" probably referred to a local settlement of related members. The curious feature for Europeans was the naming of these various totems after wild animals. These animals, or more rarely particular plants or natural phenomena like storms or lightning, were more than just eponyms. It was believed that an individual or group had a special relationship to the totemic animal through

---

[21] Raymond D. Fogelson and Robert Brightman, "Totemism Reconsidered," in William L. Merrill and Ives Goddard, eds., *Anthropology, History, and American Indians: Essays in Honor of William Curtis Sturtevant.* Smithsonian Contributions to Anthropology, 44 (Washington, DC, 2002).

descent or affiliation. In the case of descent, there was a belief that the totemic animal was a direct ancestor. People who shared the same totem were members of the same descent group, be it a lineage, clan, phratry, or moiety. As such, individuals were prohibited from marrying totemic kin. Totemism thus framed kinship relations and legal usages.

Totemism had strong religious associations. Various taboos obtained between an individual and his or her totemic animal. Mythic narratives became the property of a totemic clan that controlled their recitation, and much of the work of ritual was organized according to clan.

Scholars of totemism have regarded it to be primarily a social or collective phenomenon. However, there was also a form of individual totemism by which a supplicant acquired a guardian spirit, usually in the form of an animal, through a vision quest experience. Vision quests tended to be more common in the northern reaches of North America, areas where hunting was the dominant form of subsistence, and they became more attenuated in horticultural economies.

Vision quests for boys were normally taken at or before puberty.[22] The young boys, and in some areas young girls, were separated from their families and dispatched to the wilderness to seek a vision. This ordeal might include fasting, vigorous exercise, and sensory deprivation enhanced by highly charged powers of suggestion from previous exposure to mythic knowledge conveyed by tribal elders. These preconditions could help induce an alternate state of consciousness through vivid dreaming or hallucinatory trances in which a spiritual being, often a mythic being from primordial times, might appear to the receptive vision seeker. Trance states and dreams were semantically undifferentiated. The dream-seeker might become possessed by the spirit animal, and through imagined encounters, sacred knowledge might be revealed.

In most instances, vision quest experiences could best be conceived of as the establishment of a partnership with a spirit animal or with an other-than-natural being that involved enduring reciprocal rights and duties. The vision quester must observe certain taboos respecting the animal spirit. Often instructions were given to collect various objects and keep them hidden in a special pouch as a medicine bundle. This bundle was more than an iconic means of remembrance of the encounter in the wilderness; it also acted as a means of communication with the individual totem. The spirit animal could also present the human partner with a special song that could serve to summon divine aid in times of crisis. For the Beaver Indians in northern British Columbia, the melodic lines of these songs

---

[22] Verne Ray, *Cultural Relations in the Plateau of Northwestern North America*. Publications of the Frederick Webb Hodge Anniversary Publication Fund (Los Angeles, 1939), 3.

were likened to trails reaching to heaven.[23] In most cases, successful vision quests reflected a kind of empowerment, giving one special skills and confidence in adjusting to the demands of adulthood.

Among many plateau groups, the kind of power one obtained determined one's reputation or future career. Thus one person might gain special talent as a fisherman, a second might become a great hunter, a third might be a lucky gambler, a fourth could become a fierce warrior, and a fifth could become an infamous lover. Women might obtain special gifts from isolation at or around puberty. These could include exceptional talent as a basket-weaver, knowledge of herbal curatives, or ability as a midwife. In some groups in the Northwest, the vision quest experience might be so traumatic that the dream encounter was repressed, only to return suddenly to consciousness in later life, often during winter spirit dancing ceremonies. Retroactively, the powers that one obtained at puberty were thought to be confirmed.

There was considerable cultural variation in vision quest practices among Native Americans. The time spent seeking visions varied from a few days to several months, from a single night to multiple efforts to make contact with a spirit animal extending over several years, or from a formative experience around puberty to repeated vision quests in later life. Plains Indians, in particular, might seek power from a spirit being at any stage of the life cycle. These vision quests entailed great abnegation marked by groveling pleas for pity, as well as self-mutilation in the form of bodily scarification or amputation of fingers. In northern California, Yurok aristocrats would climb the mountains of the Siskiyou Range to commune with spirits through a special language.[24] Among ranked societies in the Northwest coast, the person seeking visions usually obtained the type of spirit appropriate to someone of his status. With Great Lakes tribes, one could seek and sequentially acquire associations with several different spirit animals. However, obtaining too many spirit guardians among the Ottawa or Winnebago was considered greedy and might result in a power outage.[25]

For many scholars, sociological totemism and individual totemism were separate and unrelated phenomena. However, examination of early accounts of North American totemism suggests that a closer generic relation may once have existed. In a headlong rush to get at the essential source

---

[23] Robin Ridington, *Trail to Heaven: Knowledge and Narrative in a Northern Native Community* (Iowa City, 1988).

[24] Thomas Buckley, *Standing Ground: Yurok Indian Spirituality, 1850–1990* (Berkeley, 2002).

[25] Paul Radin, "Some Aspects of Puberty Fasting among the Ojibwa," *Museum Bulletin of the Canada Geological Survey* (1914): 2.

of totemism, theorists simplified and overschematized both the fragmented North American data and fuller ethnographic accounts of Australian aboriginal totemism to create a reified totemic complex that never existed in pure form. The dissolution of this supposed complex was attributed to the acute comparative analysis of Alexander Goldenweiser, published in 1910.[26] As a result, the subject of totemism fell into abeyance for more than a half century, only to be partly revived by the brilliant reinterpretation by Claude Lévi-Strauss.[27] Lévi-Strauss eschewed traditional functional explanations that attempted to rationalize its seemingly bizarre features by endowing totemic practices with practical utility. Instead, he viewed totemism as a cognitive device used for classifying social groupings based on analogies with native classifications of their natural worlds, especially in light of the distinctions between different animal species.

Lévi-Strauss' influence has been potent in encouraging efforts to comprehend the richness and sophistication inherent in native systems of ethnoscience.[28] However, the structural approach that he developed too easily devolved into arid logic and bloodless intellectual exercise that ignored the emotional metaphysics in the mystical associations between totemic people and their animal familiars. A strong identification of personhood obtained between human beings and totemic animals, be they clan totems or guardian spirits. Part of this sympathetic relationship was due to the belief that animals, like human beings, possessed sensitive souls that required respect, sincere supplication, and continuing reciprocity. Thus, for the Cree of Manitoba, as described by Robert Brightman,[29] game animals succumbed not so much to the technical prowess of the hunter as to his spiritual attributes in following correct ritual procedures and dream connections that resulted in the prey voluntarily surrendering its corporal life to the human predator. The animal gave up its flesh but was assured that its living essence, or soul, would survive in another realm or re-enter this world through reincarnation.

The idea of metamorphosis is relevant here. In some Northwest coast societies, a human could be transformed through ritual into a totemic being by donning the external skin of that animal; conversely animals might shed their external cover to reveal their basic, undisguised humanity. Where we recognize the principle of the conservation of matter whereby matter ultimately can be neither created nor destroyed, many hunting peoples in

---

[26] Alexander Goldenweiser, "Totemism, An Analytic Study," *Journal of American Folklore* (1910): 23.
[27] Claude Lévi-Strauss, *Totemism Today*, trans. Rodney Needham, 1962 (Boston, 1963).
[28] Claude Lévi-Strauss, *The Savage Mind*, trans. John and Doreen Weightman, 1962 (Chicago, 1966).
[29] Robert Brightman, *Grateful Prey: Rock Cree Human-Animal Relationships* (Berkeley, 1993).

Native America recognized an analogous principle whereby souls or living essences of both humans and animals could be removed, re-embodied, and recycled. Many Native American cultures seem engaged in something resembling a "soul exchange" in which vital essences could be accumulated, spent, and reinvested.

The dark side of totemism was often revealed in native theories of witchcraft and sorcery. Soul dislodgement and capture were implicit in many such nefarious activities. A witch was a being (or nonbeing) that lacked a sense of true personhood. A witch might impersonate a human being but in metaphysical reality was a pseudo-person existing outside the human community. Through metamorphosis or shape-shifting, the witch might transform itself into other pseudo-beings. Animals frequently associated with witchcraft and illfare included such nocturnal beings as owls, particularly screech owls, as well as bats, various felines, stiff-legged bears, moles, and other night-stalking creatures. Although Iroquoian speakers were known to create witches by isolating infants (a practice known as "down fending") and denying them the breast by substituting herbal decoctions for the "milk of human kindness," most other groups viewed witches as belonging to another order of creation and, as such, as a permanent part of the existential landscape. Witches could be associated with a wide repertoire of monstrous beings who were often regarded as vestiges of previous mythic eras. Frequently such malevolent monsters were defeated by a beneficent culture hero and banished to the underworld or to the outermost rim of the earth island.

However, monsters could be ambivalent figures. Anthropophagous stone giants who roamed the Eastern Woodlands when the world was young were overcome by superior spirits and often sang their medicine songs to future generations of shamans and bequeathed their ice-crystal hearts to humankind as divining instruments. The Iroquois Falseface spirit, who had his nose smashed in a power contest with his culture hero brother, Sapling, was exiled to the forest, where he and his kind could cause troubles for disrespectful wayward travelers in their domain. However, these same Falsefaces participated in Longhouse rituals and could be summoned into domestic dwellings to perform curing ceremonies for certain types of illnesses.

Witchcraft conventionally served as a means of explaining misfortune. Usually witches were believed to come from outside the local community. However, as with the case of Iroquoian down fending or in Pueblo societies like the Hopi, where inmarried men might be targeted as possible witches, witchcraft could arise from within the local group and reveal stress points in the social structure.

Witchcraft accusations were used as a scapegoating mechanism in many otherwise tightly knit native communities. Although providing convenient explanations for tragic events, witchcraft accusations could also increase tensions within a society and lead to factional strife and to paranoid outbreaks that frequently resulted in the killing of vulnerable people. Witchcraft accusations could serve as a barometer of social anxiety. Iroquois dystopic anomie, for example, might be measured by the amount of native tobacco (*Nicotiana rustica*) thrown in the fire to dispel any witches lurking in the vicinity.

Like the Iroquois, most Native American societies employed elaborate procedures for defending against witches. Witches usually had to make direct contact with their intended victims and thus were often susceptible to anti-witchcraft techniques. One line of defense was to solicit the services of a sorcerer. A sorcerer, unlike a preternatural witch, was a person who had acquired various powers through a divine calling, a religious experience tempered and domesticated through tutelage with a knowledgeable wisdom keeper. Trained sorcerers could counter the destructive powers of a witch, but they did so by spells and instrumental machinations that could be activated and manipulated from afar. Witches literally, as well as metaphorically, preyed on the human community, feasting on the livers, hearts, flesh, and souls of their victims. Cherokee witches added the unexpired life terms of their victims to their own; longevity was both honored as a manifestation of power and feared as possible witchcraft. Sorcerers, in contrast, served clients. Between the practitioner of sorcery and his client it was decided whether, when, and how to initiate action, and when to terminate it. Whereas witchcraft was amoral and uncontrollable, sorcery had some ethical dimensions and control mechanisms.

Durkheim considered sorcery and witchcraft to be antisocial and thereby excluded such phenomena from his eufunctional definition of religion. However, the data from North America indicate that such separation was artificial at best. The metaphysics of sorcery and witchcraft appear intimately entwined with native spirituality and religion.

Closely related to the concepts of animism and totemism was the phenomenon of shamanism. Shamanism can be considered a third type of classic essentialist theory that attempts to account for the origins of religion. The work of Mircea Eliade accorded primacy to shamanism in the history of religions.[30] Eliade and others viewed the shaman as the first religious specialist, a virtuoso who is a master of "archaic techniques of ecstasy." This supposedly fundamental form of religion was first identified and described among the native peoples of Siberia. The word "shaman" is derived from a Tungusic term and refers to a person who can control out-of-body experiences in which the free or noncorporeal soul escapes the body and ascends

[30] Mircea Eliade, *Shamanism: Archaic Techniques of Ecstasy*, 1951 (Princeton, 1964).

to the upper world or descends to the lower world under the earth or sea and returns to the body with new knowledge obtained from its psychic journey. Eliade was careful to eschew any idea of a pure or primordial form of shamanism, yet he insisted that shamanism was most fully developed in Siberia, its *locus classicus*, and had connections to other parts of Asia, as well as to Australia, northern Europe, and North and South America, and might be embedded in proto-Indo-European and Paleolithic religious systems.

Shamanism was clearly part of a northern pan-Boreal complex, which includes, among many other items, Bear Ceremonialism; the Earth Diver mythic motif; large decorated, single-headed hand drums; and a mastery over fire manifested in the handling of hot coals and in metallurgy. This complex was evidenced in northern Scandinavia among the Sami, throughout northern Eurasia to Siberia, and across the Bering Straits to the Yupik and Inuit cultures of Arctic North America. The shamanic complex remained more or less intact with Northwest coast peoples, with northern Athapascan and Algonkain hunting bands, and with desert foragers of the Great Basin. Many Californian groups also had recognizable shamans. Shamanic practices tended to fade out among horticultural peoples, although herbalists, diviners for weather and other prognostications, and sorcerers or conjurors may still be found. In South America, shamanism reappeared, but rattles replaced drums as percussive instruments to help induce alternate states of consciousness, and there was great knowledge of hallucinogenic plants to bring about a trance state.

It is worth noting that the vast majority of the world's hallucinogens were first discovered by Native Americans, even though in most cases analogous plants were available in the Old World. It seems as if the first peoples of the New World were oriented to searching out mind-altering botanicals. Indeed, at one of the earliest dated sites in South America – Monte Verde – Thomas Dillehay found evidence of the use of quint, a known hallucinogen.[31]

Shamanism was premised on and situated within a particular view of the world. The shamanic worldview was inseparably connected to native cosmology. This world was not preexistent, but for many groups was created as an island floating in a primal sea. In some cosmogonic narratives, this island rested on the back of a turtle, giving rise to the expression "Turtle Island." In the Iroquoian version of cosmogenesis, a timeless upper world populated by primal beings was located above the celestial firmament. The pregnant bride of the sky world chief fell, or was pushed, through a hole made by an uprooted tree and descended toward the watery world below.

---

[31] Thomas D. Dillehay, ed., *Monte Verde: A Late Pleistocene Settlement in Chile*, 2 vols. (Washington, DC, 1989–97).

Her fall was broken by a team of sea birds, who placed her on the carapace of a giant sea turtle called up from the depths of the sea. In some versions, she brought seeds from the upper world under her fingernails; in others, she was provided with a miniature corn mortar and other essential supplies by a fire dragon or meteor as their paths crossed in the sky. After she alighted on the turtle's back, there was still no land, so various small animals took turns diving to the bottom of the sea to bring up some dirt. Finally, it is said, the muskrat succeeded in returning from the deep with some grains of sand in his paws. The woman who descended from the sky took these grains of sand and walked in a counterclockwise direction to magically create and expand the earth island. This mythic theme, the Earth Diver, is widespread in North America and can also be traced back to Siberia.[32]

In this process of unfolding cosmogenesis, a three-tiered universe was revealed. It was comprised of a primary upper world, a residual underworld, and an intervening middle world. This middle world, or Turtle Island, was seeded and first populated from the upper world but fertilized and energized by forces from the underworld. This world had a beginning and an imagined end, when it would sink back into the murky depths from which it had originally emerged. The earth island was quadrisected by the four cardinal directions: the east was oriented toward the sunrise and associated with spring, birth, and beginnings; its polar opposite, the west, indicated sunset, death, and darkness; the north symbolized midnight, winter, and old age; and the south was associated with noon, summer, and maturing youth. These orientations were connected by a "sun-wise," or counterclockwise, directional rotation, or its opposite. This implicit structural model thus encompassed the diurnal cycle, the yearly or seasonal cycle, and the life-death cycle.

A fifth reference point was the intersection of the four cardinal directions at the center or middle, often marked by a monumental pole, a sacred tree, a sacred fire, or a geyser. This center point, or axis mundi, became the permanent or ritually empowered center of the world. This intersection indicated not only the conjunction of the four lateral directions, a magical place where horizontal directionality was temporarily suspended, but also a point through which a vertical axis possessing an apex and nadir passed. The upward thrust connected this world with the upper world, whereas downward movement provided a symbolic path to the underworld. The upward journey retraced the trip of the woman who fell from the sky, whereas the journey to the underworld retracked the descent of the Earth Diver.

[32] Anna Birgitta Rooth, "The Creation Myths of the North American Indians," *Anthropos* (1957): 52.

These routes represent the itineraries taken by shamans in their soul journeys to other worlds. Sometimes in a dreamlike ecstatic trance, the free soul of the shaman ventured on a journey to obtain vital information or blessings for his beleaguered clients from spiritual beings of the upper world. This trip might be marked by increasingly higher levels of ascension representing different degrees of power. Thus Cherokee medicine people recognized seven celestial levels. The shaman's soul might also travel to the underworld in the interests of an individual client or the whole community. The routes to the underworld might pass through springs, geysers, or riverheads, or through pits, tunnels, or cave mouths. Inuit shamans visited the underwater goddess Sedna, the mother of sea mammals, to placate her anger over human taboo violations and to convince her to release her offspring for human consumption.[33] One might also gain access to these other worlds by venturing to the ends of the earth, a liminal space where land, sea, and sky merged.

However, powerful shamans might also summon spiritual helpers to come to them from afar. These spiritual beings might visit ceremonial sites to bestow their blessings, to cure the sick, or to impart valuable information about the future. In these instances, it seemed as if the shaman did not so much beseech or propitiate superior beings from a position of inferiority, but rather commanded them in a hortatory fashion to do his bidding. It is as if the shaman had domesticated his spirit familiars. Such goings and comings might be reflective of economic transformation, from dependence on hunting, gathering, and fishing, to pastoralism and the management of animal herds and, perhaps, minimal horticulture.

Some of these macrocosmic features of the shamanic worldview were replicated microcosmically in ceremonial structures and domestic dwellings. Thus, the sacred fire represented the focal center of the human world, with fire acting as a transformative agent that sent plumes of smoke up above and to the four quarters in the form of exhaled tobacco smoke from a ceremonial pipe. In enclosed ceremonial centers and domestic dwellings, the roof often symbolized the sky vault perforated by a smoke hole that afforded access to the upper world. A fire hearth dug into the earthen floor might be sacralized by burying sacred objects into its base and by offering sacrifices of meat, corn, or tobacco to "feed" the fire. With the Muskogeans, the butt end of logs in the square ground were pointed toward the cardinal points, whereas smaller logs and kindling might be arranged in a radial pattern in the indoor semi-subterranean council house, or "hot house."

---

[33] Franz Boas, *The Central Eskimo*. Sixth Annual Report of the Bureau of Ethnology (Washington, DC, 1884–85, 1888).

In the underground kivas of the Pueblo peoples, a hole, or *shipapu*, functioned like an umbilical cord, or earth navel. The *shipapu* connected this fourth world with the three lower worlds from which their ancestors were believed to have emerged. In the Northwest coast and northern California, cosmic and bodily symbolism was also frequently found in portals oriented to the east and often modeled after mouths. The term for rafters was sometimes cognate with the word for ribs, and the outside covering of the framed structure was regarded as skin, even if the covering material was bark, woven mats, or sod. In sum, ceremonial structures and secular dwellings were considered to be living beings and to incorporate aspects of the shamanic worldview.

Shamans in North America were not only diagnosticians of disease and curers of ailments, but they were also diviners who could predict game movements based on the weather and other factors. They could recover missing objects, including lost souls. They served as psychopomps who guided the souls of the deceased to their postmortem destination. They were literally masters of ceremonies and were a source of creativity in native communities. Shamans gave dramatic public performances in a theatrical mode to demonstrate their powers. They were often skilled musicians, ventriloquists, jugglers, acrobats, metallurgists, and masters of the sleight of hand.

The shamanic calling often was announced by an extended illness or by dreams and visions and predicated by the presence of inborn propensities. The potential shaman suffered greatly as he or she (or both) confronted various tests and ordeals and encountered a variety of spirits who might embody known and unknown plants, animals, landscapes, and living persons, or represent ghosts of the departed. During this liminal period of psychic travail, the shaman-to-be had direct exposure to the realm of the sacred. Special powers would be instilled in the novice after recovery from the illness and near-death experience. The whole encounter with the spirit world and its aftermath constituted a symbolic death and resurrection. On returning to this world, the new shaman had to learn how to control his newly acquired powers, usually under the tutelage of an established medicine person. This learning period might take years and still more time before he emerged as an acknowledged accomplished shaman. As one who had experienced death and rebirth, the shaman knew the way to the spirit world, but he had to ensure he had a roundtrip ticket.

The powers possessed by the shaman could be dangerous and ambivalent. Unsuccessful shamans could become vulnerable targets of a wrathful community, and a shaman always had to be wary of the powers of rival shamans. The well-intended measures of a shaman might quickly devolve into perceived sorcery and witchcraft.

Shamanic gender was frequently indeterminate. Although the majority of Native American shamans were men, some were bisexual, and women shamans were not unknown. In northern California among the Yurok, Hupa, Karuk, and Shasta, the shamans were usually women. These women suffered "pains" from introjected, paired disease objects sent through dreams by spirit guardians. The shaman so afflicted had to learn to control her "pains" through extensive discipline, after which she became a successful curer. Sucking and massage were the principal techniques employed to expel harmful entities that had invaded the patient's body. Whereas death and resurrection stood metaphorically for the activities of male shamans, pregnancy and birth seemed to be symbolized in the midwife-like actions of these female shamans in northern California. It is important to note that for both male and female shamans recovery from the type of disorder that they would later treat was a prerequisite for shamanic practice.

This discussion of Native American religion has revolved around three essentialist positions regarding the original bases of religion – animism, totemism, and shamanism. Each theory had its early champions and detractors. However, none of the three theories existed in pristine form as an independent complex. Rather they were all interrelated. Their advocates failed to appreciate the fact that these three concepts, two of which bear indigenous names, are, nevertheless, examples of Western-imposed categorical thinking that fell short of grasping native understandings or the extent of inter- and intracultural variation. However, a critical review of these controversial, one-size-fits-all universal theories does provide at least a blurry lens through which to view the wider spectrum of Native American religion and spirituality.

In disentangling the intertwined roots of Native American religion and spirituality, it is also possible to employ a direct historical approach by utilizing archaeological data, as well as information from early contact narratives. The widespread presence of mounds in eastern North America leaves a religious marking on the landscape. Mounds dating back almost to the end of the Archaic period (c. 3,500 years ago) were used as burials. These gravesites contained varying types and quantities of grave goods that suggest developed beliefs in an afterlife. Earthen effigy mounds were built in the shape of mythic animals whose outlines could only be discerned in their full detail from the gaze of the resident celestial beings of the sky above. In the Mississippian period (commencing about 700 C.E.), mounds were enlarged and served as platforms for temples and other sacred enclosures. Clearly in Mississippian times we encounter divine rulers and elaborate priesthoods overseeing a highly complex ceremonial system. As reconstructed from a variety of objects ranging from shell gorgets to woven designs, iconic sculpture, and petroglyphs, a highly developed symbolic system is revealed. The structure and semiotics of this symbolic system were first identified by Waring and Holder[34] and were thought to reflect the diffusion of a so-called Southern Cult. Further studies by later scholars relabeled this phenomenon as the Southeastern Ceremonial Complex and have narrowed the gap between the Mississippian period and ceremonial usage among historic tribes.[35]

Other areas of Native North America show similar patterns of continuity between the archaeological past and the ethnographic present. In the Southwest, connections between prehistoric remains and contemporary Pueblo peoples are well documented. These small-scale theocracies were remarkably perduring in their settlement patterns, architecture, pottery, social structures, and religious rituals and ideology. Large, freestanding totem poles were absent in the Northwest coast before metal tools became available. Nevertheless, familiar Northwest symbols and designs were found carved in house posts and etched on stone surfaces long before the arrival of the white man. Spiritual beliefs in native California and in the Great Basin also testified to considerable antiquity.

Documents written by early European contact agents often ignored evidence of native religion and spirituality, or they dismissed native beliefs and practices as idolatry, devil worship, or benighted superstition. However, a close reading of some of these texts can produce insights into native spirituality and religiosity. Because the Spaniards, with the exception of some silent Scandinavians, were the first Europeans to penetrate into what they called the "New World," two early Spanish sources warrant examination.[36]

The first source is Juan Rogel's account of the Calusa. The Calusa, a paramount chiefdom in southwestern Florida, had already experienced several years of Spanish military contact when the Jesuit missionary Father Juan Rogel arrived in their midst in 1567. Rogel was strongly dedicated to his mission to convert the Indians to Catholicism. He preached the Christian

---

[34] Antonio J. Waring, Jr., and Preston Holder, "A Prehistoric Ceremonial Complex in the Southeastern United States," *American Anthropologist* (1945): 47.

[35] James H. Howard, *The Southeastern Ceremonial Complex and Its Interpretation*, Memoir 6, Missouri Archaeological Society (Columbia, 1968); and Robert L. Hall, *An Archaeology of the Soul: North American Indian Belief and Ritual* (Urbana, 1997).

[36] See Daniel G. Brinton, trans., "Rogel's Account of the Florida Mission (1569–70)," *The Historical Magazine, and Notes and Queries Concerning the Antiquities, History and Biography of America* 5:11 (1861); and John H. Hann, ed. and trans., *Missions to the Calusa* (Gainsville, FL, 1991). The most up-to-date and comprehensive sketch of Calusa culture is William H. Marquardt, "Calusa," in Raymond D. Fogelson, ed., *Handbook of North American Indians, Southeast* (Washington, DC, 2004), 14: 204–12.

doctrine of the oneness of God, a universal, omnipotent Lord who created heaven and earth and the first man and woman, as well as the possession of an immortal soul. He told the natives about an afterlife of rewards and punishment based on conduct in this world.

Rogel's information about the natives came from observations and interviews mediated by translators of informant testimony. The Calusa accepted the doctrine of the oneness of God and regarded it as secret knowledge passed down through their priests and royal lineages. They even adjusted to the seeming paradox of the unity of the Trinity and the trinity of the unity by avowing that those who govern the world were three persons: first, the universal God of the heavenly movements and seasonal changes; second, the person who rules human government; and third, the person who helps in wars, that is, the war chief and/or the war priest.

The Calusa had more difficulty accepting the unity and immortality of the Christian soul. They believed in the existence of three souls. The first was located in the pupil of the eye and remained within the body. The other two souls were manifested in one's shadow and in reflected images of the self. These latter two souls permanently departed at the individual's death. The corpse was greatly feared, but after burial it was believed that one could communicate with the deceased and gain information of divinatory significance. Illness was often equated with soul loss, and it was thought that the soul returned through the nape of the neck. On death, the soul or souls might enter some animal or fish. When the animal was killed or the fish caught, the soul(s) would transfer to lesser beings. Gradually the souls became reduced to nothing. This idea of ultimate soul destruction was incompatible with Christian concepts of soul immortality and resurrection and with notions that deeds in this life were subject to rewards and punishments in the next life.

Father Rogel was appalled at the Calusa worship of idols, their practice of infanticide and human sacrifice, and sodomy, all of which he saw as the evil work of the devil. Rogel met resistance in his insistence that the idols be destroyed. The Calusa argued that the idols protected them from ever-present maleficent spirits and that the idols were handed down by their forefathers from the beginning of time. They were more fearful of the immediate evil spirits than of a distant, otiose, universal God. They wanted to continue their traditions and be left alone. One native critic questioned whether their worship of idols differed in principle from Christian adoration of the cross.

There were other matters of dispute. The Calusa challenged the idea that God was invisible. They claimed that their ancestors saw God at their burials, after many days of fasting and strenuous running (presumably inducing an alternate state of consciousness). Rogel rejected these traditions out of hand by insisting that their Calusa ancestors were deluded and saw the devil rather than God.

At daybreak, seated in the arbors of their square grounds, the Calusa chief and his retinue discussed these and other spiritual matters. Father Rogel realized that if his evangelical efforts were to succeed, he would first have to convert the chief and the rest would then follow. However, there were other stumbling blocks. Calusa chiefs not only had multiple wives, but also engaged in brother-sister marriage to consolidate divinely derived power. Conversion to Christianity would undermine traditional social structure and distribution of power.

The few baptisms that Father Rogel performed were the result of fear, coercion, bribery, and hope for a short-term advantage. The converts soon reverted to their previous "heathen" ways after Rogel's departure. Nevertheless, some of the Christian seeds he planted took root in the next century, before the Calusa, as a distinct ethnic group, disappeared from ongoing human history by the 1750s. Despite the mutual misunderstandings present in Rogel's encounter with the Calusa, it is, nevertheless, possible to capture some glimmerings of the nature of Calusa spirituality and its underlying premises. Paradoxically, Father Rogel's inflexible adherence to Catholic orthodoxy illustrated native differences in broad relief.

A second interesting early Spanish document (1649) depicts a ritual among the north-central Mexican Coahuiltecan Indians that involved the use of peyote. Peyote had been condemned by the church as an evil substance and was the subject of many inquisition trials. Most of these cases involved the use of peyote as an instrument of divination.[37]

The Coahuiltecan peyote ritual was originally described by Alonzo de Leon as follows:

> The Indian men and women begin to dance in one or two circles around the fire ... until the night is already dark, singing in their fashion whatever words they want, without having meaning, only harmony, and they sing them so harmonically that one is not discordant from another, but it seems a single voice. Everyone who wants to joins in this group, sometimes a hundred, at other times more or less. They drink the peyote ground up and dissolved in water; this drink intoxicates in such a manner that it makes them lose consciousness and they remain from the movement and the wine, on the ground like dead persons. They choose among two or three of such as these, and with some beaks from a fish called *aguja* ... they scratch them from the shoulders to ankles and to the wrists, from whence flows a quantity of blood, and with it they smear it all over their bodies. They leave them in this condition until they are over their drunkenness.[38]

[37] Omer C. Stewart, *Peyote Religion: A History* (Norman, OK, 1987), 24.

[38] *Ibid.*, 25–26; and Rudolph C. Troike, "The Origin of Plains Mescalism," *American Anthropologist* (1962): 64.

This ritual bears an uncanny resemblance to corn ceremonies in the Southeast and Southwest. Some of the common elements include the mixed-gender, nocturnal, circular dancing around a fire; the "meaningless" song verses; the drinking of a botanical decoction to induce a trance state; and the ritual scratching of the body. In the Southeast, the medicine imbibed was the so-called black drink, brewed from macerated leaves of *Ilex cassina*, which, while mildly hallucinogenic owing to its high caffeine content, principally served as a purgative to induce vomiting to cleanse the internal body. Ritual scratching with a sharp object, sometimes garfish teeth, was also a bloody accompaniment to green corn ceremonies. In sum, de Leon's account can almost be seen as a descriptive template for more widespread Native American ritual patterns.

As with the analyses of these two early Spanish accounts, it is also possible to reconstruct spiritual beliefs and religious practices by mining other early Spanish, French, Dutch, Scandinavian, English, and Russian texts to trace rich veins of information, to unearth priceless nuggets of data on indigenous religion, and finally to seem to hit a solid baseline of bedrock.

The search for pure, unrefined, pre-Columbian "religious gold," before it became tarnished by European colonization and tainted by Christian exposure, is not only a daunting task, but also a foolish one. The presupposition made by too many scholars and even more popularizers of Native America assumes that there once existed a cultural stability and timeless eternity before Columbus and his successors destabilized this delicately balanced equilibrium. The picture of the past derived from archaeology, from early contact history, and from native narratives portrays a much more fluid and dynamic world. Resistance movements, cultural decline and revitalization, and the evolution, diffusion, and syncretism of the spiritual beliefs and practices so characteristic of the post-Columbian world were already well evidenced in the long ago pasts of the not-so-New World societies.

The singularity of New World religions and spiritual beliefs and practices and their uniformitarian trajectory through time were an illusion projected by Europeans. The path to a Native American religious or spiritual past is not clear; it is obstructed by a tangled bank of intertwined roots and branches.

SUGGESTIONS FOR FURTHER READING

Benedict, Ruth. *The Concept of the Guardian Spirit in North America*. Memoirs of the American Anthropological Association, 29. Menasha, WI, 1923.

Hultkrantz, Åke. *Conceptions of the Soul among North American Indians*. The Ethnographical Museum of Sweden. Monograph Series, Publication No. 1. Stockholm, 1953.

———. *Native Religion of North America: The Power of Visions and Fertility*. New York, 1987.

Irwin, Lee. *Coming Down from Above: Prophecy, Resistance, and Renewal in Native American Religions*. Norman, OK, 2008.

———. *Native American Spirituality*. Lincoln, 2000.

Sullivan, Lawrence E., ed. *Native Religions and Cultures of North America: Anthropology of the Sacred*. New York, 2000.

Tedlock, Dennis, and Barbara Tedlock, eds. *Teachings from the American Earth: Indian Religion and Philosophy*. New York, 1975.

Tooker, Elisabeth, ed. *Native American Spirituality of the Eastern Woodlands: Sacred Myths, Dreams, Visions, Speeches, Healing Formulas, Rituals and Ceremonials*. New York, 1979.

2

ROMAN CATHOLICISM CIRCA 1500

MEGAN C. ARMSTRONG

Decades of scholarship reconsidering the nature of the early modern Catholic Church has yet to erase popular perception of this institution as a rattling, decrepit hulk, one groaning under the weight of overfed monks, bejeweled cardinals, and ignorant indolent parochial clergy. To be sure, this perception reflects in part the influence of early Protestant historiography. For Martin Luther and many of his Protestant contemporaries, informed by the apocalyptic sensibilities of their age, the Church by 1521 was in its final days. Its imminent destruction was part of a divine plan leading to the return of Jesus and the final judgment of the quick and the dead. The Church was irredeemably corrupt, and its leader, the pope, was the Antichrist. Luther certainly had good reasons to complain about the Church of his day, but he proved incorrect in predicting its imminent destruction. Indeed, by 1600 the Catholic Church still presided over the single largest religious tradition in Western Europe, even managing to reassert its spiritual authority in some formerly Protestant regions while extending its reach to the New World. If we are to appreciate its remarkable resiliency in the face of Protestant challenges, and more pertinently its influence in shaping cultures across the Atlantic after 1500, we have to view the Church through multiple lenses, of which only one is the Protestant Reformation. This broader perspective brings into the foreground an institution that was by any measure a great international power. The Church was, furthermore, a heterogeneous body, an amalgamation of religious beliefs, practices, and institutions, all governed loosely by an ambitious and centralizing papal administration. Such a complex institution defies easy analysis, all the more so because it was changing. The Church that gazed across the Atlantic in 1500 was not the same one that produced the crusades three centuries earlier, and nor would it remain unchanged in the wake of its experience with the New World cultures, Ottoman Empire, and religious division. As John O'Malley argues, early modern Catholicism was itself a distinct phase in the history of the Church.

This essay makes no claims to universal coverage but rather sets out critical facets of church governance, organization, and spirituality that will help us understand the religious mindset of Catholic Europeans on the eve of their Atlantic encounters. The underlying argument is a general one: the Catholic tradition was the single most important ideological and cultural force shaping Western European societies prior to the Reformation. Moreover, it would remain the most important one for three of the colonial nations that would play a pivotal role in the Atlantic during the sixteenth century: France, Portugal, and Spain.

First, however, we must confront the slippery usage of the term "Church." Do we mean the administrative body that presides over the faithful, in other words, the clergy and the hierarchy of offices they fulfill, or do we mean the Catholic Church in a broader sense, as a religious culture? The short answer is that contemporaries and modern historians alike define the Church in both senses, and they rely on context to explain their particular intent. For the sake of clarity, I am going to use the term Church when discussing the administrative body and institutions, and "Catholic tradition" when discussing the Church as the manifestation of particular beliefs and practices.

CHURCH ORGANIZATION

For most Western Europeans in 1500, the known world was Christian. Travel literature exposed them to the existence of other important religious traditions such as Islam, Judaism, and Buddhism, just as it would soon inform them about New World beliefs. With the exception of those living in the Iberian Peninsula and around the edges of the northern Mediterranean, however, most Europeans only saw, heard, and touched, in other words, experienced, a Christian culture. The vast reach of the Christian tradition itself was matched by an enormous and highly visible institutional structure. In kingdoms such as France, the clergy might comprise 5 percent of the population, but religious institutions collectively controlled as much as 25 percent of the land. For contemporaries, the size and potency of the Church was manifested particularly through its physical marking of the landscape of Europe. Travelers expected to find churches and cathedrals, monasteries, chapels, shrines, and cemeteries along their journeys, as well as the colorful sight of religious men and women dressed in their distinctive monastic habits. The seeming ubiquity of the Church as a material presence in medieval society was the end product of an institution that found itself one of the last remaining Roman administrative structures binding the former empire after 500 C.E. Following the legalization of Christianity in 313 C.E., churches quickly began appearing openly in every diocese of the empire, beginning with the city of Rome itself in Italy. The term "diocese" is just one of many legacies of the Roman political administration to the Church, referring initially to the administrative districts of the empire. The Church continued to organize its mission according to these administrative units even after the empire itself disappeared. The spread of Christianity resulted in the fragmentation of each diocese into much smaller administrative units known as parishes, all under the jurisdiction of the bishop. By 1500, dioceses varied dramatically in size and wealth, ranging from the relatively poor, rural ones in such regions as Galicia in Spain to the large and wealthy ones found in the large urban centers of Paris, Nuremburg, and Seville. The oldest and most powerful of these was the diocese of Rome, of which the pope was bishop, hence the term "papa" or "father" of the Church. The bishop of Rome acquired this title by the fifth century to reflect his primacy among all bishops. The complex weave of religious institutions so characteristic of the Catholic Church from the first century onward spawned an equally complex administrative organization. Scholars tend to differentiate between the "secular" – in other words, the diocesan – and the "monastic" structures, because the history and orientation of each was substantially different. The term "secular" reflects the primarily pastoral, and thus "secular," focus of this part of the church administration. This structure was hierarchical in nature, linking parochial religious life through the mediation of the office of bishop with the papacy itself.

THE SECULAR CHURCH

By 1500, the assumption of the church hierarchy was that every Christian lived in a parish and every parish had a priest. The voluminous work we have on early modern parishes shows that parishes, like dioceses, varied dramatically in size both in terms of geography and population. Part of the problem lay in the inflexibility of medieval geographic divisions that failed to account for population shifts over time. A parish holding several hundred people in 1300 might have a dozen two centuries later, once the effects of plague and warfare took their toll. Conversely, the rapidly growing urban centers of the fifteenth century saw many parishes grow dramatically in size during this time. Such administrative inflexibility no doubt contributed to mounting criticism of Church neglect in many parts of Europe even before the Reformation. The distribution of priests in many instances did not reflect the true distribution of European populations. The Church was, nevertheless, equally guilty of favoring the wealthier parishes with more and better trained priests than the poorer ones. Generally speaking, the wealthier parishes were in the cities. Whereas a populous parish such as Saint-Jacques-de-la-Boucherie in Paris might have four or more priests to fulfill its various pastoral functions, the peasants embroiled in the Peasants' War of Reformation Saxony (1524–25) complained of sharing their own priest with other parishes. Emmanuel Le Roy Ladurie's famous study of late medieval Montaillou attributes the lingering appeal of the Cathar heresy in the mountainous regions of southwest France to the absence of properly trained Catholic priests.[1] For the people of Montaillou, the Cathar *perfecti* provided an active and viable alternative to priestly authority, and certainly a present one.

Such variance aside, most Christians likely knew their priest personally and relied on him to perform a variety of spiritual functions. Above all, the priest was responsible for administering the Sunday service (Mass) and the seven sacraments. The sacraments lay at the center of parochial spiritual life, designed to aid the spiritual journey of the individual from birth through to death. The first and most important was baptism, signaling an infant's inclusion in the spiritual community of the Church. The catechetical formation of the teenage Christian (confirmation), marriage, and death (extreme unction) were also critical moments requiring priestly sanctification. Following the Lateran Council of 1215, Christians were also required to participate in the Eucharist and give confession to their priest once a year, usually at Easter time. The Eucharist was one of the two earliest and most important sacraments, marking the moment in the Mass when the bread and wine used to celebrate the Last Supper was transformed into the body and blood of Christ. The seventh sacrament, holy orders, was restricted to priests because this sacrament bestowed on its recipient the spiritual authority left to Saint Peter by Christ. It was the priest alone who had the authority to administer the sacraments, because he alone had the formal theological and liturgical training, and more importantly, the calling, to give them efficacy. The Church's claim to special priestly authority was soon to be challenged by Martin Luther, among other church reformers, who found no scriptural basis for this assertion. Luther's doctrine of the priesthood of all believers effectively removed priests as spiritual intermediaries between the believer and God and in doing so challenged the very foundations of the Church's claim to sacramental authority. In 1500, however, Luther's challenge was still unvoiced, and Europe remained largely united as a Christian community. Ordinary believers accepted the essential role of the clergy in their pursuit of salvation.

BISHOP

The parish clergy were ultimately responsible to their bishop for the spiritual care of their flock. To be sure, some bishops were much more diligent

---

[1] Emmanuel Le Roy Ladurie, *Montaillou, village occitan de 1294 à 1324* (Paris, 1975).

than others. Accusations of corruption and malfeasance among the clergy, including the episcopacy, were gaining momentum in many church quarters already by the time of the Council of Constance in 1415. The Parisian theologian and outspoken critic of the Church Jean Gerson (1363–1426) was among those who accused bishops of appointing poorly trained priests and refusing to visit parishes on a regular basis. At the foundation of these accusations lay the explicit charge that many, if not most, bishops favored the political, "worldly" facets of their office over its religious function. Certainly by 1500, noble families across Europe competed to place sons in this prestigious office because of its political and economic importance as an ecclesiastical office. Bishops were, for one thing, a frequent source of political recruitment by medieval monarchs. Bishops were used as ambassadors and advisors. In France and England, bishops along with other high-ranking ecclesiastics claimed seats in particular organs of medieval governance such as the Estates General (France) and the House of Lords (England). Beyond service to the crown, bishoprics were themselves lucrative offices for the noble elite. The very wealth and political influence of the bishopric explains why the most important ones went invariably to great noble families and might be held for generations. The Gonzaga family, for example, occupied the episcopacy of Mantua for more than a century, beginning in 1466. Many bishops, nevertheless, did take their spiritual responsibilities seriously, even if at times these took a backseat to more pressing political concerns. Their spiritual authority was, to say the least, extensive. The locus of episcopal authority was the cathedral, and it was from here that the bishop and his administrators supervised the performance of the clergy, enacted church policy, and administered diocesan temporal affairs.

MONASTICISM

This territorial organization reflected the mandate of the Church to provide ideological formation and spiritual solace to stable, settled communities of ordinary believers. It formed, nevertheless, only one part of a much more complex and convoluted geography of religious institutions that emerged over the centuries. Monastic institutions in particular challenged a parochial structure, insisting that greater spiritual perfection was secured through a life lived in isolation from all worldly temptations. Monks and nuns sought a more rigorous, often ascetic and contemplative, model of spiritual reform in communities of like-minded devouts. Especially early on, such communities favored isolated locations in deserts, on mountaintops, or in forests and enforced the practice of claustration. Cloistered communities forbade contact between members and the community outside of monastic walls without the permission of religious officials in order to minimize their spiritual contamination. Certainly by the Lateran Council of 1215, claustration was so ubiquitous a practice among many communities that the central administration of the Church came to see it as a mark of true monasticism. It was a particular hallmark of female monasticism, reflecting medieval concern about female capacity for sin.

By 1500, the expanding population of Europe made physical isolation more difficult to achieve in many regions, but also less a specific objective for many of the newer traditions. By 1500, one was likely to find numerous communities of monks, friars, nuns, canons regular, and other kinds of monastic traditions jostled together within the walls of urban centers, praying for the dead, providing charity, or preaching moral reform in the streets according to their own rule (*regula*), or constitution. This coexistence of religious institutions was at times a source of tension, because each represented a different interpretation of spiritual perfection within the Catholic tradition. The reorientation of monasticism to urban centers was, nevertheless, only one of the most striking developments that accompanied the proliferation of new traditions. The formation of the mendicant orders (Franciscan, Dominican, Carmelite, and Augustinian) after 1200 was perhaps the single most important alteration to the monastic landscape of late medieval Europe. The term "mendicant" reflects the rejection by these medieval reformers of the material world, above all, wealth. The early constitutions (*regula*) of the four orders, in fact, prohibited the ownership of individual and communal property. The name "friar" (*frater*), the wearing of coarse habits and sandals, and restrictions on diet were just some ways in which these religious modeled their understanding of religious purity. More importantly for our understanding of New World Catholicism, it was these clerics who would first cross the ocean from Iberia and France to convert indigenous cultures. In addition to producing famous preachers, the mendicant orders were also active and effective missionary traditions that could point to three hundred years of spiritual engagement in distant frontiers, including Asia and Africa, by the time they first encountered the Aztec and Inca peoples. Viewed from their perspective, one can understand why the mendicants viewed the sixteenth-century Jesuits as latecomers on the missionary scene.

By the fourteenth century, other new traditions emerged that reflected a particular desire for a more mixed model of monastic life. The Spanish order of Santiago aided the conquest of the Moors in the Iberian Peninsula, participating in a similar "crusading" spirit as its Templar forbearer. It was, however, a new form of communal life. Whereas the friars were to stay at home and pray for the conversion of the Moors, their lay noble members (who could marry) would pursue a more militaristic role. This model of order, mingling lay and fully cloistered brethren, proved popular among men and women who either could not afford the pension to join a traditional order or were unwilling to renounce all facets of their secular existence. More controversial was the Beguine/Beghard tradition, communities that steadfastly rejected claustration throughout the late medieval period, only to succumb later on. For the most part a phenomenon of the Netherlands, these communities of lay individuals pursued a more intensive and enthusiastic devotional life in urban centers. Beguinages (communities of laywomen) mingled elements of the monastic and lay devout life with daily worship and communal work (i.e., textile industry). That some Beguines earned reputations for reading the scriptures and teaching doctrine, and that a few were even considered mystics, explains why church authorities were very concerned about the orthodoxy of these lay communities. Medieval society viewed women as temperamentally unsuited to clear rational thought and the control of their bodily desires. Contemporary women could blame this perception on the role of Eve in the Christian tradition, but credit must also be given to the growing influence of classical scholarship during the Renaissance. The combined influence of these intellectual traditions was to make female claims to spiritual authority of any kind a matter of suspicion. Such concern, however, did little to undermine the remarkable popularity of the Beguinages in northern Europe as an alternative model of communal religious life for women seeking a more rigorous religious life but one less defined by claustration and contemplation.

This mixed religious life was influential, but so too were the observant reforming movements percolating in many of the older monastic traditions, including the Benedictine, Cistercian, and mendicant orders. These "observant" movements varied both in nature and intensity, but in general terms one can say that they shared a deep concern about restoring what they believed to be the original purity of their own tradition. Moreover, they proved to be catalysts for growth. The new impulses rejuvenated each order, and, although often divisive, spawned new communities without displacing the older ones. At times, this diversity took on a regional character. Within the Franciscan tradition alone, we find Colettan communities in France, Recollets in Spain, and the Riformati and Capuchins of Italy, to name a few. To differentiate among themselves, members of the traditions that gained recognition by the central administration wore variations of the traditional habit and introduced their own regulations.

PAPACY

Presiding over this complex weave of religious institutions was the papacy, the central administration of the entire Catholic Church. Scholars generally agree that the papacy was no longer as powerful an institution in 1500 as it had been in its thirteenth-century heyday. Legal and political challenges to its spiritual and temporal authority by European dynasties, most famously in the form of the Babylonian Captivity (1303–78), and also conciliarism, saw papal authority steadily diminish after its peak under Innocent III (1198–1216). By the time of European expansion into the New World, European monarchs knew that their nominations for the highest ecclesiastical offices would likely receive papal acquiescence, just as did their demands for subsidies from ecclesiastical institutions in their own lands. In their own kingdoms, the rulers of Europe had long since absorbed many powers once claimed by the papacy. As Pope Julius III told Henry II of France in a letter dated 1551, "You give elective benefices which I do not ... you place tithes on the churches as you please. You order the cardinals and bishops as you think fit ... you are more than pope in your kingdoms."[2] Even within the body of the Church, papal authority was by no means absolute. Similar to other medieval governments, the corporatist sensibility of the Church ensured that papal authority over its clerical body was perpetually mitigated by the particular constitutions and regulations of its varied ecclesiastical constituencies.

To say that its power diminished, however, is not to say that the papacy became an impotent, let alone irrelevant, European authority. Paolo Prodi is one in a succession of historians who views the fifteenth and sixteenth centuries as transformative periods in the evolution of this institution. What constituted its transformation remains a matter of some debate. At the very least, one can say that for the fifteenth-century popes and their cardinals, retaining Church spiritual authority increasingly became tied ideologically to political and economic independence. These popes transformed the city of Rome into a showcase of papal power, putting Renaissance artists to work beautifying ecclesiastical spaces, developing elaborate imperialistic ceremonials, and employing humanist scholars as papal historians, biographers, and poets. They also focused attention on tightening control and expanding the boundaries of the Papal States, the slice of lands in central Italy and the basis of the temporal authority of the papacy. To be sure, the aggressiveness with which Alexander VI (1492–1513) and Julius II (1503–13), in particular, pursued the expansion of papal dominions did little to assuage growing concern about the pastoral mission of the crown on the eve of the Protestant Reformation. Julius II would forever be immortalized as the warrior pope barred from heaven in Desiderius Erasmus's famous satire, *Julius Excluded from Heaven* (1514). These popes,

---

[2] Cited in Paolo Prodi, *The Papal Prince: One Body Two Souls: The Papal Monarchy in Early Modern Europe,* trans. Susan Haskins (Cambridge, UK, 1987), 168.

nevertheless, did succeed in increasing the wealth and political power of the papacy after a long period of decline.

This focus on papal ceremonial and territorial power went hand in hand with the development of a larger, more centralized, and unified bureaucracy, one capable of facilitating the expansion of papal authority both within and without Italy. This bureaucratic growth would continue throughout the early modern period, but already by the end of the fifteenth century the papal government was considered one of the largest and most sophisticated of its time. At the heart of this administration was the College of Cardinals (curia). The cardinals were the highest officials in the Church, and also its chief administrators. It was from this body that each new pope would be chosen. The prestige and power enjoyed by the cardinals made this office highly sought after among European powers. It was, however, an office largely controlled by the great noble families of Rome. Roman noble control of the cardinalate meant that we do find cases of men promoted solely on the basis of their familial connections. It would be inaccurate to say, however, that this reflected the majority. With a few exceptions, cardinals were drawn from men already in holy orders. High-ranking bishops and archbishops, the heads of the religious orders, and at times even prominent theologians at the universities would earn the cardinal hat. By the end of the fifteenth century, the Church had also more clearly defined the office of cardinal as a jurisdictional one that was distinct from those found in other parts of the secular hierarchy. In contrast to the bishop, for example, whose power was tied to his diocese, the cardinal enjoyed jurisdiction that extended across the church body.

The curia presided over all facets of church administration, most importantly, justice and foreign policy. The organs of justice were already elaborate by 1500. The Roman Inquisition would not be instituted for a few more decades to govern matters of religious orthodoxy. Already well-tested, however, were the courts of the Rota and Audience. The Church also had its own jurisprudence, known as canon law. Papal justice was expensive, and it could be slow, but it was highly regarded as a sophisticated judicial system. In consequence, papal justice was very much in demand among the elite of Europe and their rulers on all matters regarded religious in nature. Beyond the provision of justice and foreign relations, the curia also managed internal church affairs, including the provision of benefices and the formulation of church legislation. At the heart of the entire administration was the chancery, the largest organ of the curia. J. A. F. Thomson links the growth in papal business to the quadrupling in size of this organ during the fifteenth century. It was the chancery that drafted papal decrees known as bulls (*bullus*).[3]

---

[3] J. A. F. Thomson, *Popes and Princes, 1417–1517: Politics and Polity in the Late Medieval Church* (Sydney, 1980), 97.

CHURCH REFORM, REJUVENATION, AND RESTORATION

The increasing attention given by fifteenth-century popes to the expansion of papal political authority did not pass unnoticed. Early modern Europeans gave greater latitude to the secular engagement of religious institutions than we understand today. Martin Luther's criticism of the Catholic Church as too preoccupied with secular matters, however, resonated powerfully in many quarters of Europe. The main question concerned not whether the Church was worldly, but whether it was too worldly. What were the limits to papal and clerical authority? How wealthy should the Church be? Concern about fiscal and moral abuse, in particular, was percolating long before Luther appeared on the scene, stirring widespread concern about the state of the only Christian institution in the West. Conciliarism emerged within the ecclesiastical hierarchy itself during the fourteenth century, as many theologians, bishops, and cardinals jointly called for internal reform. The term "reform" had different meanings during the medieval and early modern periods and so requires some clarification. Conciliarists demanded not only a cleansing of fiscal abuses from the entire structure of the Church, but also the better training of parish priests and a rigorous enforcement of clerical discipline. Reform, in other words, meant not a radical uprooting of the existing hierarchy, as proposed by Luther, but a restoration of the existing Catholic tradition to an earlier state of purity. Although they never succeeded in securing papal recognition of the supremacy of the ecumenical councils in spiritual matters, conciliarist reformist agendas with regard to pastoral care and clerical abuse would eventually penetrate even the papacy itself. They would shape, in particular, the decrees of the Council of Trent (1545–63), the most influential general church council of the early modern period.

Conciliarism coincided with many other reforming impulses, including observant monastic reform and the classically informed scholarly tradition known as Christian humanism. Their collective influence explains why early modern historians have in recent years come to challenge the term "Counter-Reformation" when describing the sixteenth-century papacy. The term continues to enjoy currency, but Hubert Jedin and John O'Malley, among others, insist that such a designation inaccurately situates the early modern Church as simply reactive to Protestantism.[4] Counter-Reform has also become indelibly associated with the more aggressive, intolerant

---

[4] John O'Malley, *Trent and All That: Renaming Catholicism in the Early Modern Era* (Cambridge, MA, 2000); and Hubert Jedin, "Catholic Reformation or Counter-Reformation," in David M. Luebke, ed., *The Counter-Reformation: The Essential Readings* (Malden, MA, 1999), 19–45.

measures such as the Roman Inquisition and the Index of Forbidden Books. For these reasons many scholars now lean toward "Catholic Reform" or "early modern Catholicism" as terms that better embrace the complex nature and broader context of the Catholic tradition at this time. It goes without saying that this approach has the simultaneous effect of carefully delineating the novel nature of Lutheran reform. Viewed within the broader context of Catholic history, Luther's radical break with the Catholic Church is still extremely important, but the ideas propelling it owed substantially to earlier debates over the nature of the Christian faith.

CHURCH AND SOCIETY

As the previous discussion has already shown, the Catholic Church was a powerful and present fixture in late medieval and early modern Europe. It was also in the throes of serious internal examination at the time Europeans began encountering New World cultures. Even during this time of questioning, however, one cannot ignore the degree to which the Catholic tradition and its governing institution informed the character of early modern culture. Much of the authority of the Christian tradition lay in its ubiquity. It was not simply that religious institutions dotted the landscape of Europe. It is that Christian beliefs informed how early modern individuals understood their role as citizens, wives, and husbands, and even neighbors. Church ritual life, furthermore, contoured their daily existence. The calendar of feast days largely dictated when one worked, rested, married, and baptized children. Feast days, and there were many of them in the Catholic calendar, were also occasions to socialize with one's neighbors and families, perform charitable acts, and pray to the honored saint. Lent added ideological weight to the restriction of certain foods such as meat that were difficult to obtain in the winter. This imposed forty days of "suffering" was spiritual preparation for the most important liturgical moment in the calendar, Easter. Easter signaled the sacrifice but also the resurrection of Christ, and it simultaneously marked the move from winter to spring, from austerity to fertility. The very landscape inhabited by early modern Catholics similarly bore the ideological hallmarks of the Catholic tradition in ways that were taken for granted by contemporaries. Shrines, monasteries, churches, and cemeteries delineated spaces considered sacred either through the presence of a community of devout or the physical remains of a holy person (saint). Consecrated by church authorities, these spaces bore witness to the regular operations of divine authority on earth. There were other spiritual markers: crosses found along rural roads and sculptures of the Virgin Mary located at the corner of urban streets provided spiritual protection for travelers. Early modern Catholics expected the peal of church bells to call them for Sunday service or to mark the commencement of monastic devotions, and they would have found familiar the chanting of penitents as they processed through the streets on the way to religious service at one of the monastic or parochial churches. The advent of Renaissance culture after 1300 gave Catholicism a different pictorial look as the prophets, Christ, and the Virgin Mary found themselves garbed in classical robes, but it did little to "secularize" early modern culture. Even as the printing press expanded the range of subjects available to readers in Europe after 1470, scholars show that the lives of saints and devotional texts remained the most popular.

This imbrication of the Catholic tradition in early modern European society extended to its social and political ordering as well. Medieval political theories assigned a critical role to the clergy in their conceptions of a prosperous and stable state. Influenced by theological discussions of the Christian community as the body of Christ (*corpus christianorum*), medieval theorists by the fourteenth century increasingly described the state in terms of the human body, as one organism dependent on its aggregate parts for survival. Medieval society comprised three mutually dependent parts or "orders." The third order (the legs) comprised the majority of people whose role was to provide the labor and sustenance necessary to support the work of the other orders. The nobility, their protectors, formed the second order (the arms). The clergy – those who "prayed" – were the first and most important order (the heart) and protected societal purity. Finally, the monarch was *de natura* the head of the Christian body.

Theorists argued that the monarch was not divine per se, but he was divinely appointed. His role was to enforce God's law on earth in part by ensuring that each order fulfilled its natural function. As Ernst Kantorowicz shows, increasing desire on the part of royalist theorists to promote monarchical authority both within and without the state during the late Middle Ages spawned the notion of the king's two bodies.[5] Heralds announced the death of a monarch with the well-known phrase, "The king is dead, long live the king," to underscore that only the earthly body of the monarch had passed away. The anointing of the newly crowned king similarly served to mark this transition of the spiritual body. These practices reminded contemporaries that the divine body lived on in his successor, forever attached to the state. Royal theorists had in mind papal insistence on its supreme authority as stated in the bull *Unam Sanctam* (1302). Claiming divine appointment placed the king on an equal playing field with the pope, at least within his own kingdom.

---

[5] Ernst Kantorowicz, *The King's Two Bodies: A Study in Medieval Political Theology* (Princeton, 1957).

The degree to which this conception of an orderly society permeated popular consciousness becomes clear when examining paintings of late medieval and early modern civic processions. Almost invariably, the local clergy as the first order took precedence, followed by the other orders. Medieval perception of the spiritual value of the clergy as a foundation of a stable society also explains the many privileges granted religious institutions within European states. Certainly in France, religious institutions were exempt from property tax, although secular monarchs found other ways to extort money from its clergy. Monastic institutions were also frequently exempt from customs duties on such staples as wine and salt. More importantly from the perspective of ecclesiastical independence, the clergy as a body was considered outside the bounds of secular juridical jurisdiction except in the most serious cases of disorder, such as treason, homicide, and heresy. The inclusion of heresy as a secular crime might at first seem unusual, but contemporaries had little difficulty accepting it as such. Heresy was a form of spiritual error, one that naturally divided its proponent from the rest of the Christian body. There could only be one true faith, just as there was only one king and one kingdom. Heresy, in other words, was a form of treason because it set the heretic in opposition to the divinely constituted order and thus the authority of the king. Secular and church authorities feared the spread of this spiritual "disease" or "pollution." Like a cancer, heresy could gradually take over the entire body and corrupt it, disturbing the political as well as the religious order in the process. It was such logic that explains why anxious authorities urged the eradication of such error, by force if necessary.

For clerics, falling prey to false teachings was a particularly serious crime. Religious institutions might protest but were generally known to cooperate with secular authorities if the crime was considered well proven. In such cases, the cleric in question was generally defrocked – in other words, ritually deprived of his clerical status – prior to his execution. This was the ritual, for example, performed for clerics found guilty of converting to Protestantism in the sixteenth century. Secular punishment of clerics was, however, relatively rare in the decades prior to the Reformation. For the most part, the clergy knew that they were only responsible to their own hierarchy of officials. Indeed, the Catholic Church supervised quite an extensive ecclesiastical court system in each kingdom, one based in the diocese. For the most part concerned with the regulation of diocesan religious life, the episcopal courts operated under the authority of the bishop and were administered by the canons regular. These courts frequently sat in judgment on cases involving such spiritual crimes as blasphemy and adultery and lay accusations against priests, as well as cases that would today be considered civil matters, such as marital property. In such matters as these, however, the lines between secular and ecclesiastical jurisdiction became quite murky. Always savvy, early modern men and women frequently shopped their disputes to both civil and ecclesiastical courts in pursuit of a favorable decree. The two legal systems, in other words, were never neatly distinct in practice, even if they were in theory.

BELIEF AND PRACTICE

The foundational role played by the Catholic tradition in shaping early modern values, social structure, and even its political order is impossible to ignore, and it explains why it would be anachronistic to look to this time for signs of modern scepticism. As Lucien Febvre acutely points out in his study of the sixteenth-century author Rabelais, atheism was simply not a possibility for early modern people.[6] With the notable exception of Spain, furthermore, where both Islam and Judaism flourished for centuries, no other religious tradition emerged to challenge Christian hegemony in Western Europe after the fall of the Roman Empire. European men and women consequently grew up within cultures that were heavily informed by Christian spirituality, but they also were very much conscious of their membership in the larger Christian community called Christendom. The Latin culture of the Church only encouraged this perception of a unified and extensive Christian culture, ensuring that core Christian rituals were immediately recognizable to travelers regardless of their spoken language. This was the tradition that accompanied Columbus and his followers to the New World and that would soon be called Catholicism, following the fragmentation of Christendom after 1520.

The fact that not all Christians became Protestant after this time tells us that the appeal of the Catholic tradition was more durable than many early Protestant reformers assumed. Scholarship over the last thirty years suggests quite strongly, furthermore, that to define Catholic faith only in terms of orthodox doctrine misrepresents its nature. One was no less a Catholic for believing in the existence of ghosts or magic. Catholics could and did differ over matters of belief, and they differed even more frequently in the practice of their faith. Religion from this perspective is by nature a cultural product, informed by the particular concerns and values of its practitioners that were not simply theological in nature. To appreciate the nature, appeal, and indeed the influence of the Catholic faith, we have to embrace it in all its complexity, diversity, and seeming contradiction.

---

[6] Lucien Febvre, *The Problem of Unbelief in the Sixteenth Century, the Religion of Rabelais*, trans. Beatrice Gottlieb (Cambridge, MA, 1985).

What, first of all, did early modern Catholics believe? And how did they manifest these beliefs?

THEOLOGY

The Catholic Church enforced certain doctrines that it considered unassailable tenets of the true faith. These tenets were drawn substantially from the scriptures, both the Old and New Testaments. Centuries of commentary on the part of leading church theologians and the deliberations of church councils also played a critical role in the formulation of a set of orthodox beliefs. The major tenets of Catholic doctrine were firmly delineated by the time of the meeting of the fourth Lateran Council (1215). Catechetical texts formulated for parochial instruction of young children paid attention, in particular, to the doctrine of the Trinity, original sin, the crucifixion and resurrection of Christ, transubstantiation, and purgatory. The doctrine of the Trinity asserts the coterminous existence of God, the Holy Spirit, and Christ as three aspects of one being also known collectively as God. God was all-powerful, all-knowing, and eternal. Christ, even in his incarnate (human) form, shared fully in God's potency. Catholics considered Christ the Son of God, sent in human form to seek their salvation. Christ's death on the cross at the hands of Roman authorities was the ultimate sacrifice, an exchange of his life for the eternal salvation of good Christians in atonement for Adam and Eve's fall from a state of grace. Their fall marked the fate of all Christians, because God's punishment was to ensure that they were born in a state of sin. Christ's resurrection three days later was a moment of triumph, reflecting the power of God over the material world and even death. For Catholics and Protestants alike, this salvific mission of Christ lay at the heart of their understanding of the path to eternal happiness. To live a good life on earth meant living in accordance with the laws of God, just as Christ did while in human form. To do otherwise was to sin – in other words, to embrace evil and thus earn disgrace and eternal damnation. Salvation thus involved the active engagement of the individual in the pursuit of perfection (free will), but salvation was ultimately a gift from God (grace). It was, in part, on this notion of the role of human will as an agent of reform that Protestant and Catholic theologians would divide after 1520.

Although Luther and Calvin never entirely eradicated the role of the will, they significantly reduced its significance. More troublesome to these reformers were Church claims to special spiritual authority over the binding and loosing of souls. Generations of Christians learned that the first bishop of Rome, Saint Peter, received the spiritual authority of Christ. This transference of authority underpinned clerical claims to an intercessory role, including not only the administration of the sacraments but also the authority to excommunicate sinners on earth and even reduce their time in purgatory. Other facets of Catholic doctrine would also become a source of contention after 1520, but for the most part Catholic teaching would remain unchanged throughout the early modern period. What is important to understand is that these orthodox beliefs existed within a much larger ideological framework that also informed the religious perspective of early modern Catholics. This framework pivoted, importantly, on a dualistic understanding of the cosmos, a profound preoccupation with the nature of sin, the immanent nature of the supernatural, the spiritual efficacy of devotional practices, and a syncretic sensibility.

THE COSMOS: GOOD AND EVIL

By 1500, a binary understanding of salvation in terms of good and evil had come to shape European conceptions of the cosmos. Whether late medieval Europe can be fairly labeled an "apocalyptic" culture is a matter of some debate among scholars. Such an assertion requires widespread belief in the imminent coming of Christ and the last judgment as prophesied in the Book of Revelation. It is certainly true that Christ's adjudication of the saved and damned was one of the most iconic scenes in the salvific narrative, frequently found carved in the central portals of medieval European churches. It was also quite common to find late medieval treatises reading into the calamitous events of the age signs of the earthly conflict between Christ and his nemesis, the Antichrist, which preceded the final judgment. Such fear of imminent end to the known world was, however, episodic rather than persistent, gaining momentum during times of crisis only to subside thereafter. Perhaps it is more accurate to say that late medieval Catholics assumed the routine, active presence of both good and evil supernatural powers in their daily lives. Drout, untimely death, and the spread of heresy were serious enough signs of disorder to warrant the perusal of the scriptures for spiritual guidance. God could bless the virtuous with good health, wealth, and peace, but he was also quick to chastise the errant with misfortune. Unfortunately for early modern Catholics as well as Protestants, the devil was no less present in their lives. Martin Luther's conviction that the devil "thudded around in the storage room" of his monastery to get his attention shows vividly that even the Protestant reformers believed in an active maleficent force bent on snatching their souls.[7] Witches existed, men and women who worshipped the devil and used his power (black magic) to do harm on earth. Indeed, early modern

---

[7] Heiko Oberman, *Luther: Man between God and Devil* (New Haven, 1989), 107–8.

Catholics and Protestants both accepted the existence of two eternal rival kingdoms, each vying for domination of the human race. Whereas God promised eternal happiness in his beautiful kingdom in the heavens, the devil and his nefarious minions lured weak-willed Christians to sin in the hopes that they would spend their eternity tortured in the fiery pits of an earth-bound hell. This battle was vicious and destructive, but apocalyptic texts promised the ultimate triumph would go to God. It was in this moment of victory that Christ would return as judge on earth, to determine who would go to heaven or hell for their final resting place.

THE SEVEN DEADLY SINS

This binary understanding of the cosmos is the necessary context for understanding the nature and significance of sin in the Catholic tradition. The Ten Commandments have long been considered the foundation of the Christian moral code. It is worthwhile noting, even so, that Catholic preachers and confessors, the primary instructors of Catholic doctrine, were much more likely to use the Seven Deadly Sins as a vehicle for spiritual guidance. The origins of the Seven Deadly Sins as a religious concept remain murky. At the very least, one can say that the concept's rise to prominence in Catholic teachings during the early Middle Ages reflected growing anxiety over the nature of sin and demand for a penitential model of piety. On one level, the seven sins – anger, lust, gluttony, sloth, pride, envy, and hate – were the antithesis to the teachings of Christ as found in the New Testament. Christ emphasized brotherly love, charity, selflessness, and eschewing material possessions and physical desires, as well as compassion and forgiveness. The pervasiveness of the seven sins in sermons, devotional treatises, and art along with vivid depictions of the tortures of hell convinced the historian Jean Delumeau that late medieval Europe was obsessed with and fearful of sin. Delumeau overlooked equally strident discussions about the loving nature of God in many of the same treatises that significantly mitigate his assertion of a fearful culture. It is, nevertheless, true that Catholics were preoccupied with sin and sinning, and their Protestant counterparts were no different. Sin was a natural, albeit dangerous, facet of the human condition, a product of their earth-bound existence. The soul was a small sliver of spiritual perfection, but it was trapped in a material mass that was by nature imperfect, changeable, and corrupting. The human body, with all of its sensations, naturally yearned for satisfactions that, if gratified, only further distanced the Christian from the delights of heaven. Sin was the enemy of God, and thus must be the enemy of the good Christian. To make war on sin, one must wage war against the temptations of one's own flesh. The ideal model of Christian virtue was, of course, the incarnate Christ.

The fifteenth century would see the proliferation of devotional treatises dedicated to lay reform through the imitation of his life. The best known and perhaps most influential was that of Thomas à Kempis (d. 1471), but it was by no means alone. Safely ensconced in their own homes, laymen and laywomen could pursue their own spiritual perfection through daily devotions that focused on important moments in Christ's life and teachings. Saints' lives offered other alternative models. It is no surprise, for example, that confraternities dedicated to the reform of prostitutes frequently took Mary Magdalene as their patron saint. The cult of the saints grew in importance during the medieval and early modern periods, in part, because these holy individuals collectively reflected the range of human experience, and consequently the capacity for all Christians to find salvation.

Such models of perfection, however, were difficult to follow even for the most well-intentioned Catholics. Atoning for one's sins became an expected practice, one that recognized the importance of human will in the pursuit of salvation. Penance was an act of atonement, assigned by the confessing priest to the sinner. It took many forms, depending on the severity of the spiritual crime. For the less serious sins, such as lustful thoughts, the Christian might simply say a few prayers, whereas adultery could incur the mortification of the flesh through self-flagellation, or perhaps an arduous pilgrimage. Charity was a particularly common way to make amends, and it could be given in the form of money, property, or agricultural goods. Penance, moreover, was not simply a mortal affair. Located midway between hell and heaven, purgatory was a penitential kingdom where Christians who failed to atone for all their sins while on earth toiled away to do so in preparation for the ascent to heaven. The punishments in purgatory often rivaled those in hell, but Christians welcomed a sojourn there because it meant escaping the eternal punishment of hell. The purgatorial fires were meant to do just that – purge them of sin, whereas the fires of hell were punitive. Purgatorial fires, in other words, were finite. Protestants would later challenge Catholic insistence on the existence of purgatory as well as the efficacy of "good works" in securing salvation. It remains, nevertheless, true that the rapid spread of the Catholic tradition and the visual transformation of the European landscape throughout the medieval and early modern periods owed a great deal to the generosity of well-meaning patrons who viewed the funding of the Catholic ministry as a pious and spiritually reformative act.

AN INTIMATE PIETY

The preceding discussion shows that Catholics believed that devotional rites were spiritually efficacious. Through such practices, believers proved their devotion to God with the hope that they would earn his favor and atone for their own, or society's, sins. Such practices underscore an intimate relationship between the believer and God. God was not only present in this world; he and his saints were responsive to the requests of his followers. Virginia Reinburg shows that early modern Catholics often described this relationship in terms that were familiar to them in their own feudal society: that of patron and client, or great lord and vassal. God was all-powerful, but as a beneficent patron his role was to take care of the faithful in his household. The client – the good Christian – in turn, owed his or her loyalty to God in the form of virtuous behavior. This intimate relationship could take a decidedly material form, most powerfully shown in the eucharistic rite. Protestants would call belief in transubstantiation cannibalistic because it meant that Catholics willingly feasted on the body of Christ. For Catholics, however, this literal incorporation of Christ's flesh and blood into their own was important for their own spiritual transformation. As in the case of the relics of the saints, Christ's presence in the bread and wine brought his spiritual potency fully to bear on those who ingested him. With the spread of the cult of Corpus Christi during the fourteen century, this appearance of Christ in the parish congregation became all the more important to worshippers who eagerly sought direct access to the Son of God. Priests encouraged this, enveloping the Eucharist in increasingly elaborate ritual that peaked with the ringing of a bell and the elevation of the transformed host (bread) before the assembled parishioners. Miri Rubin shows that by the fifteenth century simply to gaze on the Eucharist at the moment of transformation was sufficient for most Catholics.[8]

This Christocentric piety that we find intensifying by the fifteenth century in many parts of Europe took other forms as well, the most extreme expression perhaps being that of the mystical encounter. Mysticism posited an ecstatic union with God brought about through ardent prayer. Mystics frequently described the experience as transcendent and intensely emotional, as well as physical. The late Middle Ages saw a growth spurt in the spread of mysticism among women in particular, much of it focused on God in the form of Christ. Church authorities were rarely comfortable with these claims to direct communication with divinity, perhaps because it challenged their own authority as spiritual mediators, but also because they worried about heresy. It was not unheard of for mystics to claim a role for themselves as a vehicle of divine authority. For this reason, church authorities, and usually the bishop, rigorously scrutinized all claims to mystical experience. Only those claims that proved orthodox and showed genuine signs of miraculous intervention could escape church censure. Legitimate

---

[8] Miri Rubin, *Corpus Christi: The Eucharist in Late Medieval Culture* (Cambridge, UK, 1992), 63–5.

mystics could become enormously influential and attract devoted followers. Even ordinary believers, however, could feel privileged with the favor of God. The explorers Christopher Columbus and Hernán Cortes certainly wrote of their special calling to convert "heathens" in their letters to the king and queen of Spain; they were convinced of their special destinies.

A similar intimacy to that of Christ and believer also marked the piety surrounding the cult of the saints. Catholic theology insisted that saints also could work miracles, even after death. The very physical remains of holy individuals, clothing, and even the space they inhabited bore the imprint of their spiritual perfection – a perfection that could be harnessed on behalf of the devout believer. By the sixth century, collecting saints' relics had already become a matter of serious international competition among bishops, popes, and rulers. Indeed, Phillip II of Spain built the austere Escorial palace in part as a depository for his enormous collection of relics.[9] That he placed the relics in a crypt directly underneath his own bedchamber testifies to early modern conviction in the spiritual potency of these saintly remains and their accessibility to human intercession. Catholics sought saintly intercession for many reasons: to atone for their sins or to bring good fortune, political influence, or even a healthy crop. By the late Middle Ages, scholars such as Rudolph Bell and Donald Weinstein find a marketplace of possibilities for the would-be pilgrim, as certain cults gained reputations for specialized services or particular interests.[10] Anyone suffering from stomach ailments might pray to St. Elmo. But sailors and merchants also found him useful during storms at sea. Midwives might turn to St. Margaret of Antioch in times of need, whereas Francis of Assisi was a popular intercessor for peasants worried about sick livestock. Without question, the most popular of all cults was that of the Virgin Mary. Marian shrines mushroomed during the late Middle Ages, and they would quickly spread to the New World after 1500. Mary's popularity was no doubt aided by the promotion of certain missionary orders, including the Franciscans. As the mother of Christ, she was, even so, a natural focus of devotion for men as well as women. Her proximity to Christ enhanced her influence as an intercessor, while as a mother, virgin, and faithful follower she offered women a multitude of reasons for emulation.

DEVOTION AND COMMUNITY

As much as the cult of the saints underscores a desire for an intimate experience of the holy, it was no less important to medieval and early modern

---

[9] Carlos Eire, *From Madrid to Purgatory: The Art and Craft of Dying in Sixteenth Century Spain* (Cambridge, UK, 2002), 266–72.
[10] Rudolph M. Bell and Donald Weinstein, *Saints and Society* (Chicago, 1986).

conceptions of community. Whereas Protestant thinkers would come to see the dead as irretrievably gone from the Christian community, their souls departed for heaven or hell, Catholics saw no such temporal division. For Catholics, death was another dimension of existence, one easily transgressed by both the living and the dead. The spirits of the dead could walk the earth, just as devout Christians could use ritual action to facilitate the spiritual reform of their ancestors. This transgressive conception of Christian community accounts for the migration of cemeteries from outside the walls of Roman cities to their urban centers, as the new faith took hold in the late Roman Empire. Clustered around parish churches, cemeteries brought the dead into direct communion with their living relatives and former neighbors. By the fourteenth century, early modern Catholics, even of a modest status, would have also expected their sons and daughters to fund masses on the day of their death at a local, favored monastic institution. As an act of charity, these masses said by devout men facilitated a speedier transit through purgatory. It was even so an act of filial loyalty, marking the continuity of families from one terrain of existence to the next.

The bonds of family continued after death in the Catholic tradition, but for John Bossy, among others, the Catholic tradition played just as critical a role in forging communal bonds among the living. His path-breaking study of the Mass as a social rite emphasized its peacemaking and unifying function among local members of the community.[11] Civic and parochial processions similarly served multiple spiritual functions, one of which was to inculcate communal identity within a spiritual framework. Social historians note that these processions invariably reflected contemporary conceptions of an orderly society, one that was hierarchical and paternalistic by nature but also centered on the local community. Participants walked with members of the same status or trade, their location in the procession determined by their perceived importance in the local community. Religious processions were distinctive, even so, because of their spiritual agenda. Whether organized to recognize the feast day of an important saint or to seek divine assistance during a time of crisis, these processions paraded local relics around the perimeters of the town or village and through its streets and fields to mark its sacral character. Participants believed that the spiritual potency of the relic infused the community, helping to protect it from spiritual corruption while strengthening the commitment of its members to God. Confraternal members also processed, one important indication that Catholic sociability was defined in myriad ways, including that of family and civic community. Frequently organized around a

---

[11] John Bossy, "The Mass as a Social Institution, 1200–1700," *Past and Present* 100 (1983): 29–61.

particular trade or social group, confraternities clearly served to intensify economic, political, and familial relations among members of the same strata. However, they took a form that gave its members a special spiritual purpose. They met on defined days for communal worship, intent on fostering a more intensive devotional experience. They were also an important source of charity and patronage for religious foundations, giving money to fund private chapels for their services, pay for the burial of members in confraternal crypts, and also support the sick and poor, among others. Confraternities, finally, defined a new kind of community alongside the other Christian communities to which their members belonged, one that also transgressed the boundary between the living and the dead.

RELIGIOUS SYNCRETISM AND THE EXPANSION OF THE EARLY MODERN CHURCH

The communal nature of devotional life, its emphasis on an intimate relationship with divinity, and the possibilities for self-perfection through good works helped to give the Catholic tradition its distinctive character. To understand its spread outside of Western Europe after 1500, however, we also need to consider its syncretic nature. Scholars working on the formation of New World Catholic traditions have been particularly effective at illuminating their unique incorporation of European and indigenous cultural elements, but the Catholic tradition always had syncretic tendencies, mixing and mingling local cultural practices and concerns with its own. This historic mutability of the Catholic tradition explains, for example, why many of the oldest Christian churches were built on ancient pagan sites. Perhaps church authorities sought to eradicate the pagan tradition, but it is equally likely that local people had long recognized that particular space as sacral. A shared cultural sensibility may also explain the visceral depictions of the crucified Christ found in the Mediterranean regions of late medieval Europe. In the wine region of Burgundy, Mack Holt finds the vintners taking liberty with the eucharistic liturgy, giving themselves a central role in it as preparers of the Lord's wine. Even the neighboring villages in William Christian's study of rural religious life in early modern Spain point to highly developed "local" expressions of the spiritual.[12]

The point to be made here is that the Catholics who left Iberia and France for the New World brought with them their own regional understandings of the Catholic tradition. If we only compare the two colonial

---

[12] Mack Holt, "Wine, Community and Reformation in Sixteenth-Century Germany," *Past and Present* 138 (1993): 58–93; and William Christian, *Local Religion in Sixteenth-Century Spain* (Princeton, 1981).

powers of France and Spain, we can already see significant differences. The most notable example is the Spanish Inquisition. A religious tribunal introduced in 1478 under the direct authority of the monarchs of Spain, the Inquisition was first instituted to uproot any religious recidivism among formerly Jewish (converso) and Muslim (*morisco*) communities. It was, in other words, a product of the unique history of the Iberian Peninsula, where for centuries Muslims, Christians, and Jews coexisted. By 1500, two centuries of Christian "reconquest" of the peninsula had created a culture that was wary of any signs of deviance from orthodox Christian beliefs and practices. Unfortunately for the New World cultures, the Inquisition was exported across the Atlantic. French Catholics, in contrast, had little if any direct experience of other faiths prior to arriving in the New World. Until the Wars of Religion made religious division impossible to ignore, French Catholics accepted the words of their preachers and royal theorists that France was the most Catholic of kingdoms. Even after their own experience of religious division following the spread of Calvinism (post-1555), French Catholics found it useful to criticize the Spanish Inquisition as tyrannical. It was one more way to differentiate their brands of colonial authority. These colonial powers, however, were not the only bearers of distinct Catholic traditions. Each missionary order brought along its own understanding of spiritual perfection. Moreover, they also carried with them a well-honed mandate to spread their understanding of the true faith, even if it entailed some negotiation. Church authorities were not always comfortable with diversity, but discussions between the New World missionaries and their European superiors show that many found the mingling of cultural elements essential for winning indigenous acceptance of their teachings. It may be in these cultural negotiations that we can come to understand the growth of the Catholic tradition outside of Europe even as it faced serious opposition at home.

SUGGESTIONS FOR FURTHER READING

Armstrong, Megan. *The Politics of Piety: Franciscan Preachers during the Wars of Religion, 1560–1600*. Rochester, 2004.

Burkhart, Louise. *The Slippery Earth: Nahua-Christian Moral Dialogue in Sixteenth-Century Mexico*. Tucson, 1989.

Christian, William. *Local Religion in Sixteenth-Century Spain*. Princeton, 1981.

Delumeau, Jean. *Sin and Fear: The Emergence of Western Guilt Culture, 13th–18th Centuries*. New York, 1990.

Duffy, Eamon. *The Stripping of the Altars: Traditional Religion in England, 1400–1580*. New Haven, 1992.

Kamen, Henry. *The Spanish Inquisition: A Historical Revision*. New Haven, 1999.

Prodi, Paolo. *The Papal Prince: One Body Two Souls: The Papal Monarchy in Early Modern Europe*, Trans. Susan Haskins. Cambridge, UK, 1987.

Rubin, Miri. *Corpus Christi: The Eucharist in Late Medieval Culture*. Cambridge, UK, 1992.

Taylor, Larissa. *The Soldiers of Christ: Preaching in Late Medieval and Reformation France*. New York, 1992.

3

PROTESTANT TRADITIONS IN WESTERN EUROPE ON THE EVE OF NORTH AMERICAN COLONIZATION

ROBERT D. LINDER

By 1550, most Europeans believed that the Protestant Reformation would engulf the entire continent. By 1600, this was no longer a self-evident truth. The Roman Catholic Church had rallied its forces and held off the Protestant advances in Western and Central Europe and regained lost ground in the East. The Oratory of Divine Love, papal reform, the Council of Trent, the Jesuits, and the various coercive devices associated with the Index of Prohibited Books and the Roman Inquisition all contributed to Catholic renewal by the end of the sixteenth century.

By 1600, confessional loyalties had begun to harden among the various strands of the Protestant Reformation. Moreover, recent Reformation historians believe that they had detected not one Protestant reformation, but four: Lutheran, Calvinist, Anglican, and Radical. The fifth reformation of the sixteenth century is, of course, the Catholic Reformation. This essay will deal with the Protestant reformations that originated on the continent – Lutheran, Calvinist, and Radical – and their identity on the eve of the colonization of North America.

Almost all immigrants to North America in the early seventeenth century had a religious allegiance, and most were serious about their religious commitment. Those who came after them in the next century may have been less committed, but the first generation of newcomers to the American wilderness from the European continent were mostly firm believers whose religious experience reflected one of the three great Protestant traditions: Lutheran, Reformed, or Anabaptist.

Those who embarked for North America in the seventeenth century did not make lightly the decision to leave Europe. The Atlantic Ocean, the second largest in the world, was a formidable obstacle, and the three-month, 3,000-mile trip across its treacherous waters was a life-threatening and life-altering experience. The vast distance from the homeland in terms of both space and time eventually would modify, but not basically change, the worldview of the various Christian communities who migrated to the

American wilderness. Therefore, the initial wave of Europeans to reach American shores brought their religious baggage with them.

THE LUTHERANS

Lutherans, of course, were the original Protestants. Martin Luther, the founder of the Lutheran Church, called his new branch of Christianity "Evangelical," meaning those who proclaimed the "evangel" (i.e., the gospel) or "the good news" of salvation in Christ. In a very real sense, Luther was the Father of Protestantism in that he established the main doctrines shared by all Protestant believers from the sixteenth century onward: biblical authority, justification through faith in Christ alone, the priesthood of the believer, and the two sacraments (or ordinances) of baptism and the Lord's Supper. Luther's doctrines, therefore, became the lingua franca of the Protestant Reformation.

The first Lutherans to arrive on American shores were from Sweden and settled at Fort Christina (later Wilmington) in Delaware in 1638. Because Lutheranism in Europe was closely tied to the state, the first Lutherans came to North America as part of a political colonizing effort. Ultimately, the Lutherans would drop their established church mentality and become the third-largest body in American Protestantism, which, in turn, embraced Luther's legacy of a common Protestant theology.

All of the Protestant reformers followed Luther in his belief in biblical authority and consequently in his rejection of the authority of the Roman Catholic Church and its penitential system. Lutherans brought this high view of the Bible and dislike of Catholicism with them to the New World. Luther had become a prolific reader of the Bible while he was in monastic orders, before his break with Rome, and he had developed his Reformation breakthrough from his intense study of scripture in the years before 1517, when he nailed his Ninety-Five Theses to the church door at Wittenberg. This breakthrough led to his doctrine of justification by faith alone (*sola fides*) based on scripture alone (*sola scriptura*). Luther, who had been deeply troubled by his inability to find reconciliation with God through the means prescribed by the Church of Rome, finally found peace for his troubled soul by discovering the biblical doctrine of justification by grace through faith in Christ alone. This was for Luther and all later Protestants the key to salvation and peace with God that involved faith in Christ rather than doing good works. Luther described how his new understanding of the Bible transformed his life and reoriented his soul:

> There I began to understand that the righteousness of God is that by which the righteous lives by a gift of God, namely by faith. And this is the meaning: the righteousness of God is revealed by the gospel, namely, the passive

righteousness with which merciful God justifies us by faith.... Here I felt that I was altogether born again and had entered paradise itself through open gates. There a totally other face of the entire Scripture showed itself to me.[1]

It was this recovery of New Testament teachings that energized Luther and his followers and led them to make the final break with Rome in 1521. This break, in turn, plunged Europe into civil and religious turmoil as new loyalties struggled against old and deeply entrenched traditions. Many Lutherans would try to escape the ensuing upheaval by immigrating to the colonies of British North America.[2]

Nevertheless, Luther did not countenance upheaval and turmoil but rather counseled law and order. He believed that church and state operated in separate spheres, but that the minister and the magistrate could and should cooperate in maintaining order and in establishing reform in the church. However, Luther taught that if the magistrate or prince were not Christians, then separation would be the obvious recourse. In any event, Luther rejected theocracy, on the one hand, and servility on the part of the church to the magistrate, on the other, and believed that in most instances the minister was commissioned to be the mentor of magistrates and princes. Most important, if the magistrate and the minister agreed, then the establishment of a state church was not only possible but also permissible. Therefore, various states and principalities of Germany as well as the kingdoms of Denmark, Norway, Sweden, and Finland established official state churches in the sixteenth century that required adherence to Lutheranism.

As far as the governance of the various Lutheran state churches was concerned, Luther left this up to the areas in which Lutheranism spread. Because he had no rule concerning church polity, Lutheran churches in different parts of Europe adopted one of the three basic ecclesiastical systems: episcopalism, presbyterianism, and congregationalism. Episcopal church government was basically a monarchical form of polity that involved a church run by bishops, presbyterianism was essentially a republican form of governance that rested on elected representatives, and congregationalism was the practice of direct democracy in church affairs. Some Lutherans eventually adapted to the more democratic procedures that developed in the United States, but most of their churches in the New World did not influence the development of democratic government by modeling such procedures.[3]

---

[1] Lewis W. Spitz, ed., *Luther's Works*, 55 vols. (Philadelphia, 1955–86), 34: 37.
[2] This was especially true during the Thirty Years War (1618–48) and during the many wars along the border between France and the various German states in the following years.
[3] Sydney E. Ahlstrom, *A Religious History of the American People* (New Haven, 1972), 245–59; and Martin E. Marty, *Martin Luther* (New York, 2004), 191–4.

Lutherans thus brought with them to the New World their Reformation doctrines and practices. The Augsburg Confession of 1530 and the Formula of Concord of 1580 theologically united them. However, they also brought with them a certain amount of theological bickering stemming from quarrels that erupted in Europe following Luther's death. On the one hand, their different languages in the New World were somewhat of a problem, as Swedish-speaking and German-speaking Lutherans, even though initially theologically united, held forth in their different tongues. On the other hand, the common denominator of the German language strengthened the ethnic bond between German Lutherans and German Reformed churches in places like Pennsylvania in the first century following settlement. In this latter case, Germans found solace and strength in their common ethnicity, which led to widespread cooperation between Germans – Lutheran and Reformed. Because the quarrels within Lutheranism in Germany and of second-generation Lutherans with the Reformed churches founded by John Calvin were preceded by a remarkable degree of friendliness between Luther and Calvin, there were ample grounds for cooperation and even intermarriage in the New World.[4] Generally speaking, Calvin maintained a positive attitude toward Luther, disagreeing with his position on the Lord's Supper, but revering him as a godly man and a pioneer in the restoration of the gospel.[5] After a disconnect in the years following the death of the two great reformers, American followers of Luther and Calvin resumed more friendly relations in the New World. Furthermore, the Lutherans enjoyed this era of relative theological tranquility in the seventeenth and eighteenth centuries because they were not wracked by controversies over revivalism such as troubled most of the other Protestant denominations in the New World during the First Great Awakening.

Lutherans also brought with them their hymnody and love of music, fostered by Luther, an accomplished musician, and furthered by his successors.[6] Most North American Protestants soon embraced with great enthusiasm Luther's magnificent hymn, "A Mighty Fortress Is Our God," and the practice of congregational singing.

THE CALVINISTS

John Calvin was the most dynamic and widely read theologian of the Protestant Reformation. Among his many theological writings, the

---

[4] Eric W. Gritsch, *A History of Lutheranism* (Minneapolis, 2002), 1–178.
[5] Robert D. Linder, "The Early Calvinists and Martin Luther: A Study in Evangelical Solidarity," in Jerome Friedman, ed., *Regnum, Religio et Ratio* (Kirksville, MO, 1987), 103–16.
[6] Lutheran music undoubtedly reached its height in the work of Johann Sebastian Bach in the eighteenth century.

Institutes of the Christian Religion has been the most influential and enduring. Originally designed as a manual for new believers, it was enlarged and revised over the years until by its final formulation in 1559, shortly before Calvin's death, the *Institutes* had grown into a sophisticated theological work that dealt in significant detail with some of the most complex doctrines of the faith. Thousands of copies in several languages, including English, were published in the sixteenth century, and it is still widely reprinted today. The *Institutes* became the most important theological treatise of the Reformation era and is the primary expression of Calvin's ideas.

Those ideas had a profound impact beyond the specific churches that Calvin founded. On the eve of colonization, they provided the theological foundation for the majority of America's first European settlers: Puritans; Presbyterians; the Reformed churches of the Netherlands, Germany, and France; many Anglicans; and a number of Baptists.[7]

Calvin's theology contained a strong emphasis on the guiding hand of Providence, the sovereignty of God (belief in the absolute authority of God as eternal lawgiver and judge whose will is law), human sinfulness, and the idea of elect individuals and elect nations. In terms of personal salvation, Calvin believed that God elected whom he willed to eternal salvation. The Holy Spirit through the Word of God at God's pleasure induced faith, according to Calvin, and when that happened humans could not reject it. When individuals believed, they feared the penalty for their sins, which in turn led them to repent, to look to Christ in faith for salvation, and to believe in his redemptive work on the cross. After that, on the basis of New Testament promises, they were assured that they were elected to salvation. This Augustinian view of salvation and predestination, however, did not lead to fatalism because Calvinist believers were confident that God had elected them. Moreover, they believed that their election was demonstrated by their confession of faith in Christ, regular participation in the sacraments, and consistent godly living. This produced a dynamic form of Christianity that gave the Calvinists their sense of destiny and that the Roman Catholic Church believed made Calvinism its most formidable rival.

Calvinist intellectuals in the various countries of Europe where the Calvinist Reformation had spread eventually developed the concept of a covenant theology that in due course became important in American political life. Covenant theology was a system that explained the relationship between God and humankind in terms of a compact or covenant. It is

---

[7] David W. Hall has emphasized the impact of Calvin and his followers on colonial America in his recent book *The Genevan Reformation and the American Founding* (New York, 2003).

based on biblical themes, especially God's covenant with Israel as recorded in the Old Testament. Although an ancient concept, an overall systematic covenant theology grew out of the Protestant Reformation. The reformers understood the concept of a "covenant" to mean a compact between two or more parties by which they solemnly obligated themselves to one another to accomplish a particular task. This concept was utilized as a theological construct especially by Calvin's Reformed churches in the sixteenth and seventeenth centuries and beyond.

Reformed covenant theology taught that God offers grace and salvation to humanity. To those who by faith accept God's offer of eternal life in Christ, he most assuredly grants salvation. Although there are several variations, Reformed theologians have discerned three covenants in the Bible. There is the covenant of works, offered to Adam, which he failed to maintain; the covenant of grace, offered after the fall of Adam, again to Abraham, and renewed in Christ; and, according to some theologians, the covenant of redemption, the eternal promise of God's salvation underlying the covenant of grace for the elect.

By the seventeenth century, Calvinist believers had extended the covenant theory into the secular world. Just as God had covenanted with humankind in salvation and in gathering churches, so groups within society were to covenant with one another as they carried out their ordinary affairs. In fact, the seventeenth century was an age of compacts, contracts, and secular covenants through which the public's business was transacted. Theological and social-political covenants sprang out of the same milieus in America and often overlapped one another. The Mayflower Compact of 1620 founded the first settlement in Massachusetts, Roger Williams established Providence in Rhode Island in 1636 by a compact, and the Fundamental Orders of Connecticut in 1639 created a government by covenant. In fact, the first Puritan settlement in New England was based on a covenant with God and with one another. In Puritan understanding, the founding of America was a mission to establish a model Christian commonwealth based on a covenant. As John Winthrop declared, "Thus stands the cause between God and us; we are entered into Covenant with him for this work.... We shall be a City upon a Hill."[8]

A Reformed understanding of the covenant inspired Calvin's followers to attempt to establish Christian communities that included church-state cooperation. Calvin advocated the separation of church and state, but not in the later American constitutional sense. He believed that the church should be separate and independent of state control, but that church and state should operate like an interlocking directorate with the same basic

---

[8] John Winthrop, *Papers*, ed. A. B. Forbes, 5 vols. (Boston, 1929–47), 2: 29.

personnel in charge of both institutions. That is, Calvin held that all actors in both ecclesiastical and civil government should be genuine Christian believers.[9]

Covenant theology was one of several important ingredients in the development of the American ideal of political compact and contract so prominent in its great public documents. Talk of covenants and compacts saturated Puritan New England, prompting theologian H. Richard Niebuhr to suggest the likelihood of an enduring connection between "the Idea of Covenant and American Democracy."[10] Moreover, the idea of a covenant in a secularized form became a cornerstone of the United States' civil religion and fed the American sense of mission in the world.[11]

There are several other aspects to the political legacy of Calvin and his followers. Calvin taught and his followers believed that the sovereignty of God entailed that universal human rights should be protected and must not be surrendered to the whim of tyranny. He also believed that these fundamental rights, which are always compatible with God's law, were the basis of whatever public liberties humans enjoy. Further, his followers taught that mutual covenants between rulers and God and between rulers and subjects were binding and necessary. Moreover, his followers held that the sovereignty of the people followed logically from the mutual obligations of these covenants. Finally, Calvin and many of his followers believed that the representatives of the people were to be the first line of defense against tyrants and tyranny.

But Calvinism's two greatest contributions to political thought on the eve of the colonization of North America were republicanism and the right of revolution. Calvin seldom intervened in the internal politics of other countries. Instead, he dealt with whatever type of political polity was in power. However, he clearly had republican preferences in both secular and ecclesiastical government, and he supported the elective political process in Geneva and in his Reformed and Presbyterian churches. In his own terminology, he preferred a "mixed government" in which power is shared by many different individuals. Nevertheless, it would be stretching things to claim that Calvin was a progenitor of modern democracy. "Democracy" was still an unacceptable term among the thinkers of the sixteenth century. However, there is evidence of democratic thought among his followers, even in the sixteenth century, such as in the thinking of his friend Pierre

---

[9] Philip Benedict, *Christ's Churches Purely Reformed: A Social History of Calvinism* (New Haven, 2002), 88–98.

[10] H. Richard Niebuhr, "The Idea of Covenant and American Democracy," *Church History* 23:2 (June 1954): 129.

[11] Richard V. Pierard and Robert D. Linder, *Civil Religion and the Presidency* (Grand Rapids, 1988), 48–64.

Viret and in the mind of his more prickly follower Jean Morely. In any case, it is clear that by the time North American settlement began, most Calvinist believers promoted republican and democratic church government (presbyterianism and congregationalism), and many held republican principles.[12]

Calvin and many of his colleagues and followers authorized resistance to established authority if that authority proved to be hostile to preaching of the gospel, provided that they were led in their resistance by duly constituted lesser magistrates.[13] Calvin himself was careful to limit this right of resistance to a core of lesser civil officials under highly qualified circumstances. However, his followers in the sixteenth and seventeenth centuries gradually extended that right of resistance until it covered all sorts of ecclesiastical tyranny. Thus, there is a history of the right of resistance from Calvin and many of his sixteenth-century followers like Viret, Theodore Beza, François Hotman, Lambert Daneau, the French Huguenot author of the *Vindiciae Contra Tyrannos*, William of Orange, Johannes Althusius, John Ponet, Christopher Goodman, John Knox, William Whittingham, and George Buchanan, down to seventeenth-century Samuel Rutherford and the Westminster Divines.[14] By the time of the American Revolution, the religious component of the Calvinist principle of the right of resistance had been diluted but was still recognizable. Thus, when former British member of Parliament Horace Walpole learned that the Rev. Dr. John Witherspoon, a Presbyterian minister and the president of the College of New Jersey (later Princeton University), had signed the Declaration of Independence, he observed, "Cousin America has run off with a Presbyterian parson."[15]

Many historians believe that Calvin's greatest contribution to Western and therefore American thought was in the realm of economics. Calvin's fondness for I Corinthians 10:31, "So whether you eat or drink or whatever you do, do all for the glory of God," and his insistence that all work should be a calling from God helped to highlight the importance of hard work and the dignity of all labor in the life of the elect. He also preached

---

[12] John Calvin, *Institutes of the Christian Religion*, ed. John T. McNeill, trans. Ford Lewis Battles, 2 vols. (Philadelphia, 1960), 2: 1518–21; and Robert M. Kingdon, "Calvinism and Democracy," in John H. Bratt, ed., *The Heritage of John Calvin* (Grand Rapids, 1973), 177–92.

[13] The modern terminology would be "the right of revolution." However, in the sixteenth and seventeenth centuries, "revolution" referred to a turning around or rotating, as on an axis, and was applied mostly to the turning of a heavenly body in its orbit.

[14] Robert M. Kingdon, "Calvinism and Resistance Theory," in J. H. Burns, ed., *The Cambridge History of Political Thought*, 6 vols. (Cambridge, UK, 1988–2006), 1: 193–218.

[15] George P. Donehoo, ed., *Pennsylvania History*, 9 vols. (New York, 1926–31), 1: 1069.

what later became known as middle-class virtues, each backed by biblical authority: reverence, chastity, sobriety, frugality, industry, and honesty. These concepts were foundational to worker productivity.[16] A combination of these various emphases helped produce what historians have called "the Protestant work ethic," with its emphasis on industriousness in all fields of human endeavor. Although hardly unique to Calvinism among the various Protestant communities, Calvin seems to have articulated the work ethic's biblical base more clearly than any other Protestant thinker.[17]

Further, according to the prominent twentieth-century sociologist Max Weber, it was Calvin and, more particularly, Calvin's English Puritan followers who were the source of modern investment capitalism. The fact that Calvinism produced a group of productive and reliable people led Weber to formulate his well-known thesis concerning the connection between Calvinism and capitalism. In his classic essay, *The Protestant Ethic and the Spirit of Capitalism*, Weber argued that the Calvinist ethic played an important part in the rise of modern capitalism.[18] Of all the expressions of Reformation Christianity, Weber maintained, Calvinism inculcated in its followers an austere, ascetic work ethic that systematically suppressed the pursuit of pleasure. However, in contrast to medieval Catholicism, this "worldly asceticism" encouraged believers to work hard, discipline themselves, and find their meaning in life in their secular calling. Among other things, Weber claimed, this attitude tended to inspire economic productivity and generate income that was not spent for "frivolous purposes," but instead turned into savings or investment capital. Moreover, rejecting medieval strictures on usury and allowing Christians to participate in money lending helped to stimulate economic activity among believers.

There has been almost endless controversy over the validity of Weber's thesis, with various critics pointing out its flaws and finding the origins of modern capitalism in various other religious movements of the early modern period. Nevertheless, it is intriguing to note that not only were English Puritans inclined to act this way, especially in the seventeenth century, but additionally so were many other Calvinists in places like the Netherlands and Germany. It is interesting to note, for example, that although the first Dutch Reformed settlers who came to New Amsterdam in 1628 were deeply religious people, they came primarily to represent the Dutch West India Company and to establish villages and trading posts

---

[16] Georgia Harkness, *John Calvin: The Man and His Ethics* (New York, 1958), 157–77.

[17] André Biéler, *Calvin's Economic and Social Thought*, ed. Edward Dommen, trans. James Greig (Geneva, 2006), 365.

[18] Max Weber, *The Protestant Ethic and the Spirit of Capitalism*, intro. Anthony Giddens (Gloucester, 1988).

along the Hudson River. In any case, they immediately founded Reformed churches in the area and tried to keep other non-Reformed Christians at bay. By 1660, six Dutch Reformed ministers had arrived in the Dutch New World, and by 1700 some twenty-six Dutch Reformed churches dotted the landscape of the Middle Colonies. Similar observations could be made of the many German Reformed Christians who brought their entrepreneurial skills to Pennsylvania in the early eighteenth century. They came primarily to escape the devastation of their lands in the Rhineland and the Palatinate by marauding armies, but at the same time they brought with them their devoutly Calvinist ways.[19]

Calvin and his followers also stressed that society should be economically just. Living in Geneva, then and now a center of trade and banking, meant that Calvin's environment required him to think carefully about economic and social issues. He warned that "social disorder is first and foremost disdain for the poor and oppression of the weak." André Biéler, the noted Genevan economist, maintains that Calvin taught his followers to be sensitive to issues of economic justice because all occupations should be based on God's calling. He pointed out that Calvin taught that believers were not to exploit the work of others, especially the weak, the poor, and strangers. Calvin also warned the rich against abusing power, and he promoted laws that protected ordinary people against such misuse of power. He also advocated "fair wages" for the laboring man and just prices in the marketplace. He argued for wage agreements and arbitration and supported laws that regulated usury. Calvin believed that consumption loans, that is, those to help out the consumer, should be made without interest because humans, after all, are ultimately only the trustees of any wealth that God has given them. However, he believed that loans for purposes of enterprise, which were to be used as a means of production, should be made at a fair rate of interest. On balance, Calvin and his followers agreed that the ideal was a fair and just economy, and they tried to introduce that kind of society wherever they held sway, whether that was Geneva, Edinburgh, or Boston. In any case, if any religious movement of the sixteenth century and after was world affirming, it was Calvinism. Calvin's followers in their many manifestations brought this attitude with them to the New World.[20]

This was certainly true of the members of the French Reformed Church, popularly known as Huguenots, who came to the New World. Clusters of French Huguenots settled in Massachusetts, New York, and South Carolina

---

[19] Edwin S. Gaustad and Philip L. Barlow, *New Historical Atlas of Religion in America* (New York, 2001), 46–8.

[20] Biéler, *Calvin's Economic and Social Thought*, 35–403; and Alister E. McGrath, *A Life of John Calvin* (Oxford, 1990), 219–45.

in the late seventeenth and early eighteenth centuries. Most of them were merchants, bankers, lawyers, artisans, and shopkeepers. Interestingly enough, the majority of these Huguenots eventually became members of the Church of England. It has been suggested that they switched from the Reformed family of faith for various reasons, including financial advantage, social acceptance, and political power, as well as for religious reasons related to gratitude to the English for allowing them to settle in North America and a growing fondness for Anglican ways. In any case, these Huguenot refugees contributed names like Paul Revere, John Jay, and Francis Marion to the annals of American history.[21]

Calvinism also left its mark on education and intellectual life through the insistence by Calvin and his followers on the value of education for all believers, women included. Calvinists stressed the education of ministers in particular and provided institutions of higher learning for that purpose, beginning with the Academy of Geneva in 1559, followed by universities and colleges like Leiden, Heidelberg, Harvard, Yale, and Princeton. Moreover, Calvin promoted scholarship for the glory of God and provided a model for his followers as a scholar-pastor.[22]

THE ANABAPTISTS

Whereas the Lutherans and Calvinists who began to stream to North America in the seventeenth century represented churches founded by well-educated theologians and on sophisticated confessional schemes, the Anabaptists who soon joined them came from a movement of common people whose existence was as simple and as straightforward as their theology. Moreover, these children of the Radical Reformation were undoubtedly the most misunderstood of all the immigrants from the continent. By "radical," historians mean that this cluster of believers wanted to get back to the root or origin of Christianity and restore the primitive church of the first century. Therefore, they were "restorationists" rather than "reformers" like the Lutherans, Calvinists, and Anglicans. Whereas magisterial Protestants like Luther and Calvin relied on the assistance of secular rulers and officials to help reform the old Church, the Radicals shunned any intervention by magistrates. Instead they wanted to discard the traditional Church of the day and go directly back to what they believed to be the New Testament

---

[21] Robert M. Kingdon, "Why Did the Huguenot Refugees in the American Colonies Become Episcopalian?" *Historical Magazine of the Protestant Episcopal Church* 49:4 (Dec. 1980), 317–35; and Jon Butler, *The Huguenots in America: A Refugee People in New World Society* (Cambridge, MA, 1992).

[22] Bruce Gordon, *Calvin* (New Haven, 2009), 56–7, 98, and 298–303.

pattern, when governments had no part in the spread and maintenance of the faith.[23]

Although historians include Spiritualists, Unitarians, millenarians, rationalists, and various individuals who rejected conventional Christianity in the ranks of the Radical Reformation, the Anabaptists constituted by far the largest segment of that movement. Likewise, the Mennonites were the largest subgroup of the Anabaptist movement. When the first Mennonites settled in Germantown, Pennsylvania, in 1683, secular authorities everywhere in Europe – except the Netherlands and a few small German states – were still persecuting Anabaptists.

Why were the Mennonites so unpopular? They were persecuted for various reasons, but mostly because Catholic and Protestant authorities perceived them as endangering the social order by their repudiation of the old order and their insistence on a free church separate from the state. However, the initial appearances of the Anabaptists in German-speaking Switzerland, where they defied Ulrich Zwingli's Protestant state church in Zurich in the early 1520s; in central Germany, where many Anabaptists followed the unstable millenarian preacher Thomas Müntzer during the Peasants' War of 1524–25; and in Münster in Westphalia, where many Anabaptists cast their lot with the fanatical kingdom of Jan Mattys and Jan van Leyden in 1534–35, all involved defiance of lawfully established civil authority. The Anabaptists of Zurich quarreled with Zwingli over the issues of baptism and state control of religion. However, in Germany the main problem was that many early Anabaptists believed that Jesus' second coming was imminent, and they followed millenarian fanatics like Müntzer, Mattys, and van Leyden. When these millenarians later revealed themselves as on the far margins of Christianity, many Anabaptists perished with them as their millennial vision failed and their short-lived "kingdoms" collapsed. More important, the bizarre behavior of a relatively few Anabaptists during these millennial outbreaks allowed Catholic and Protestant leaders to stigmatize all Anabaptists as dangerous fanatics who were a threat to social order.

A former Catholic priest named Menno Simons rescued the shattered remnants of the Anabaptist movement at the very time when they were being most fiercely persecuted. Simons, who became a Protestant sometime in the early 1530s and who then had embraced Anabaptist views only after the most severe soul-struggle, began to gather the scattered Brethren (as they called themselves) in the Dutch lands and, beginning in 1536, formed them into a more peaceful group. He persuaded them to look more closely at the New Testament and to embrace the basic

---

[23] George H. Williams, *The Radical Reformation*, 3rd ed. (Kirksville, MO, 2000), xxvii–xxxvi and 1–21.

teachings of Jesus rather than to follow the charismatic millenarian fanatics who had won their allegiance in the previous decade. Moreover, he based the movement squarely on biblical authority and other generally accepted Protestant doctrines. However, Simons' doctrine of the church radically separated him and his followers from the mainline Protestants and traditional Catholics alike.[24]

The Roman Catholics and Protestants continued the medieval pattern in which the church encompassed the whole of society. In contrast, Anabaptists aimed to restore the New Testament understanding of the church as a "gathered society" separate from the wider society. Anabaptists were persecuted not only because they refused to conform to the state churches of their day, but also because they rejected participation in government, war, oaths, and courts of law. Therefore they were seen as a threat to the accepted understanding of church and society, and thus were condemned by the churches as heretics and by civil governments as outlaws. The official reason for persecution, however, was that they "rebaptized" people who had already been baptized by the official state churches, a capital crime under the Roman law that underlay most European legal systems. However, the name "Anabaptist" (literally "rebaptizer"), given to them by their enemies, was unfair because the Anabaptists rejected infant baptism as invalid. Therefore when they baptized adult believers only, they did not consider it a second baptism. It mattered little because most of the civil governments of Europe were glad to have a legal reason to eliminate Anabaptists. Although the persecution had died down by the time of the settlement of British North America, Anabaptists still were not welcome in most of Europe.

Toward the end of the sixteenth century, the Dutch Anabaptists happily accepted the common name of "Mennonites" in place of the much-hated term "Anabaptists," for obvious reasons.[25] However, the term Anabaptist as applied to Mennonites and Baptists persisted well into the eighteenth century. In any case, by the turn of the seventeenth century, the Mennonites had worked out the basic theology that informed their churches world over. Foundational to their theology was the belief that the Bible should be their only creed and interpreted according to a commonsense literalism. Moreover, they believed that faith in Christ led to a "new birth" that was the key to a life lived according to the ethics of Jesus. Simons called on those who were "born again" to follow the teachings of Christ literally. As

---

[24] Franklin H. Littell, *The Anabaptist View of the Church*, 2nd ed. (Boston, 1958).

[25] At about the same time, another large group of Anabaptists embraced the name "Hutterites." Mennonites and Hutterites came to accept most of the same fundamental beliefs, except that the Hutterites based their way of life on communalism.

noted, they also rejected the idea of an official state religion and instead embraced the view that only religious freedom guaranteed by a separation of church and state was biblically correct. Otherwise, it was impossible for individuals freely to place their faith in Christ and thus avoid the curse of nominalism (being Christians in name only) that had plagued the church since the days of Constantine I in the fourth century. Religious freedom was necessary in order for faith to be genuine; therefore, the Anabaptists became the first champions of the liberty that became part of the new nation's First Amendment rights.

Also, unlike the established Protestant churches, the Mennonites emphasized the importance of the community of faith and the priesthood of the believer within that community. In fact, they carried Luther's belief in the priesthood of the believer to its logical conclusion in that Mennonite polity deemphasized the role of an ordained ministry and stressed congregational autonomy and shared governance. They believed that salvation was individual, but that the local church was a community of baptized believers who participated in the decision making and in the development of the spirituality of its members. They also believed that within their community of faith there should be no need. Balthasar Hubmaier, an early Anabaptist leader in southern Germany, captured this aspect of their faith when he stated:

> Concerning community of goods, I have always said that everyone should be concerned about the needs of others, so that the hungry might be fed, the thirsty given to drink, and the naked clothed. For we are not lords of our possessions, but stewards and distributors. There is certainly no one who says that another's goods may be seized and made common; rather, he would gladly give the coat in addition to the shirt.[26]

Finally, the Mennonites maintained their peace witness by renouncing violence and promoting the theme of nonviolence found in the teachings of Jesus. In America, they would be joined in this peace witness by the English Quakers and later by continental cousins in the faith such as the Amish, the Hutterites, and the Church of the Brethren.

The early Mennonites thought of themselves as neither Catholic nor Protestant, and they behaved accordingly. They saw little essential difference between so-called Christian and non-Christian governments in their political roles. They resolved to obey legitimate governments as long as they did not require disobedience to their fundamental beliefs. For the most part, the governments of the various British North American colonies welcomed the industrious Mennonites because they believed that they

---

[26] Quoted in P. J. Klassen, *The Economics of Anabaptism* (The Hague, 1964), 32.

should glorify God through hard work. Therefore, except during wartime, they were viewed as good citizens.

The Mennonites also brought with them to the New World their rich heritage of singing their faith. Many of their hymns kept alive the memories of the severe persecutions of the sixteenth and seventeenth centuries that they had left behind. They also continued to give women a prominent place in their church and community life. Moreover, they passed some of their basic beliefs along to the early English Baptists during that group's sojourn in the Netherlands in the early seventeenth century. In particular, when those first Baptists returned to England in 1612, after contact with the Dutch Anabaptists, they took with them a fervent belief in religious liberty and separation of church and state. The Baptists, in turn, brought those views with them to North America later in the century.[27]

PIETISTS AND MORAVIANS

Although latecomers when compared to the Lutherans, Calvinists, and Mennonites, the Pietists and Moravians also became an important part of the continental immigration to North America in the seventeenth century. Pietism began as a reaction against the religious indifference, the moral laxity, the tendency toward cultural accommodation, and the inter-confessional bickering prevalent in the various Protestant state churches in the late sixteenth and early seventeenth centuries. Therefore, it emerged within the established state churches of Germany, the Netherlands, and Scandinavia, rather than outside of and in opposition to them. It laid stress on the new birth, that is, on the religious renewal of the individual, which was lived through a life of piety and good works. Pietists embraced a literal interpretation of the Bible governed by common sense, stressed the inner-directedness of faith, promoted a revival of Christ-centered piety, and emphasized Christian fellowship across confessional, national, and ethnic boundaries. From these few simple beliefs, they developed a pietistic lifestyle in conscious opposition to the shallow nominalism that characterized the religious establishments of their day.

Kaspar von Greyerz notes that church historian Johannes Wallmann dates Pietism's beginnings from the work of Johann Arndt in the early seventeenth century, with the movement first coming to fruition with the work of Philipp Jakob Spener in the latter part of the century in the Lutheran Church in Germany. Beginning in 1691, August Hermann Francke established the academic center of Lutheran Pietism at Halle in Saxony, infused it with its penchant for charitable endeavors, and gave it a vision of a world

---

[27] W. R. Estep, *The Anabaptist Story*, 3rd ed. (Grand Rapids, 1996), 267–306.

in need of vital Christianity. In time, Pietism influenced every facet of world Protestantism: its theology, hymnody, style of worship, and church life. It encouraged the devotional study of the Bible in churches as well as in homes, stimulated the desire to establish charitable and educational institutions, held out the hope for better ecumenical relations, and opened the way for more lay participation in the established churches.[28]

Some of Pietism's basic emphases bear the marks of Anabaptist thought and practice. Anabaptists and Pietists often lived near each other in Germany and seemed to share certain beliefs, such as a stress on an intimate, primitivist church fellowship; a markedly individualized biblical interpretation; and a rigorous search for a vital Christian life through personal moral rejuvenation. Further, both Pietists and Anabaptists held to privileged experiential Christianity over liturgical formalities and theoretically subordinated formal theological inquiry to its expression in daily life. In 1708, Alexander Mack and seven followers melded Pietism with Anabaptism to establish the Church of the Brethren (also known as Dunkards and German Baptist Brethren) in Schwarzenau, Germany. The entire congregation immigrated to Pennsylvania in 1723.

From the early eighteenth century onward, large numbers of German immigrants swelled the ranks of American settlers, many with a Lutheran background. Because of a shortage of clergy, the Lutherans in America appealed to various charitable societies in the home country to supply them. The most generous response to these requests came from Halle. Consequently, many Lutheran congregations were soon shepherded by Halle-trained pastors.

Dutch Reformed and German Reformed Pietism in the Middle Colonies began to take root early in the eighteenth century. Theodore J. Frelinghuysen, a confirmed Pietist, arrived in America and took up work in the Raritan Valley of New Jersey. His fervent preaching produced a large-scale revival that attracted the attention of Presbyterian minister William Tennant, Sr., and his sons, which infused the Pietist impulse in that denomination.[29]

Several strands of the Reformation, including Lutheran Pietism, combined to form the modern Moravian Church. The roots of the Moravian faith reach back to the Unity of the Brethren (*Unitas Fratrum*, also known

---

[28] Kaspar von Greyerz, *Religion and Culture in Early Modern Europe, 1500–1800* (Oxford, 2008), 83–5. Pietist scholar F. Ernest Stoeffler sets the date of the beginnings of Pietism even earlier, in 1590. See Stoeffler, *The Rise of Evangelical Pietism* (Leiden, 1965), 201–5.

[29] Ahlstrom, *A Religious History of the American People*, 236–44; and Hartmut Lehmann, "Pietism in the World of Transatlantic Religious Revival," in Jonathan Strom, Hartmut Lehmann, and James Van Horn Melton, eds., *Pietism in Germany and North America, 1680–1820* (Farnham, 2009), 13–21.

as the Bohemian Brothers, or simply the Brethren), one wing of the Hussite movement in fifteenth-century Bohemia. The Brethren were followers of the Czech reformer Jan Hus, who was martyred for his theological opinions in 1415. The Brethren organized in 1457 as a separatist and pacifist branch of Hus' evangelical movement. In 1517, the year Luther inaugurated the Protestant Reformation by posting his Ninety-Five Theses on the church door in Wittenberg, the Unity of the Brethren numbered at least two hundred thousand with more than four hundred parishes. They were all but destroyed in Czech lands during the Thirty Years War (1618–48) and through the repressive measures of the Roman Catholic Church. After several decades of clandestine existence, a handful of Brethren refugees from Moravia found religious freedom in 1722 on the estates of the wealthy Count Nicholas Ludwig von Zinzendorf in lower Saxony. Their village of refuge, which they named Herrnhut – meaning "The Lord's Protection" – integrated religious, civic, and economic life, and it soon attracted other Protestant dissenters.

Powerfully moved by the spirit of German Pietism, the Herrnhut group decided to renew the old Unity of the Brethren movement. When its ministry was restored in 1735, the group became popularly known as the Moravians, and the pietistic Lutheran Zinzendorf became increasingly involved with the Herrnhut group. He regarded the Moravians as an ecumenical renewal movement within the church at large. Although he never officially broke with the Lutheran Church, Zinzendorf became a "bishop" of the Herrnhut Moravians in 1737.[30]

Generally evangelical in theology and practice, Moravian religious thought and church polity developed in certain unique ways over the years following the reconstitution of the Unity of the Brethren in 1735. Like all evangelicals, the Moravians embraced biblical authority and belief that salvation was achieved by grace through faith in Jesus Christ as Savior. They not only believed in the priesthood of the believer, but also stressed the communal aspects of biblical Christianity by building Moravian communities in Germany and elsewhere in the eighteenth century. They endorsed the Augsburg Confession of 1530 but did not require formal subscription to the historic Lutheran creed. Like the Pietists, they emphasized faith and emotion and the interior life of the spirit as the foundation of their spirituality. They observed three sacraments: baptism, communion, and foot washing (the latter abandoned in the twentieth century), and they

---

[30] John R. Weinlick discusses Zinzendorf's rescue of the remnants of the Unity of the Brethren and of his unusual dual relationship with the Lutheran Church and the Moravians in *Count Zinzendorf: The Story of His Life and Leadership in the Renewed Moravian Church* (New York, 1966).

celebrated a love feast in preparation for communion. Early Moravianism was characterized by a great deal of mystical devotion and celebrated the blood and wounds of Christ to a degree unusual in the eighteenth-century Protestant world. As church historian Philip Schaff once noted concerning seventeenth-century Moravians, "They prefer the chiaroscuro of mystery and the personal attachment to Christ to all scientific theology."[31]

The Moravians followed a strict discipline in their churches and glorified hard physical labor. They offset these emphases with a belief that piety was encouraged by love for music, social refinement, and a gender-neutral program of education. Their church polity was a kind of episcopal presbyterianism under the supreme legislative power of synods and an executive administration of an elective board of bishops and elders called the Unity's Elders' Conference.

Zinzendorf himself visited North America in 1741–43. Arriving in Philadelphia late in 1741, he presided over an interdenominational Christmas Eve observance. While in America he served as interim pastor of a Lutheran congregation in Philadelphia, preached widely in eastern Pennsylvania, made three missionary journeys among the Native Americans, and unsuccessfully urged ecumenical unity.[32]

A prolific hymn-writer, Zinzendorf left texts for some two thousand hymns. His personal religious experience led him to focus on the pietistic theology of the individual experience of the Savior and shaped his mission theory that guided the early work of the Moravians. He spent his life after 1743 in Moravian ministry in Germany and England, and he met with John Wesley on several occasions. Historians have noted the Moravian influence in Wesley's own highly influential ministry. Moreover, the emphasis of Zinzendorf and the Moravians on Christianity's global vision in terms of ecumenism and missions greatly influenced American religion. American Protestants in general eventually embraced Zinzendorf's global missionary vision with extraordinary enthusiasm. The Moravians also promoted ecumenical cooperation among the Protestant denominations. They often reached out to the various ethnic groups, such as the Native Americans, without attempting to gather them into Moravian churches. Instead they directed fresh converts into already-existing evangelical churches in the area.[33]

---

[31] "The Moravians," http://www.ccel.org/ccel/schaff/creeds1.x.ix.html (accessed 14 Sept. 2009).
[32] Ahlstrom, *A Religious History of the American People*, 241–3.
[33] A. J. Lewis, *Zinzendorf the Ecumenical Pioneer: A Study in the Moravian Contribution to Christian Mission and Unity* (Philadelphia, 1962), 98–115; and Arthur J. Freeman, *An Ecumenical Theology of the Heart: The Theology of Count Nicholas Ludwig von Zinzendorf* (Bethlehem, 1998).

CONCLUSIONS

By 1660, the churches of the continental Reformation were well represented in British North America. If one includes Calvin's theological offspring – Congregationalists, Presbyterians, and some Anglicans – as well as the Anabaptist/Baptist churches, then they represented the overwhelming majority of the religious population of the colonies. By 1780, these same clusters of churches numbered approximately 2,520 of the 2,745 churches in the land. Even if one limits the numbers to those who came directly from continental Protestant churches, they still are representative of a significant share of the religious market at the time of the American Revolution. Adherents of these various churches also represented a significant portion of the total American population of nearly 2,400,000 people in 1780.[34]

What did these Lutherans, Calvinists, Anabaptists, and Moravians bring with them to the New World? First, they brought with them a reverence for the Bible as the authoritative Word of God. All of the continental Protestants could agree on this central fact. It was the basis of their discussions and arguments about "true religion" in the years following European settlement in the seventeenth century. But because they considered it authoritative, they could appeal to it to settle their arguments and to persuade others to their positions. It also gave them a common idiom for not only religious disputes but also discussion of moral, social, and cultural issues as well.

Second, they brought with them an emphasis on the individual. Lutherans, the Reformed, Anabaptists, and Moravians all agreed that salvation was an individual and not a collective event. This point led these groups and those in their cultural orbits to focus on the individual as the central feature of religious, political, and social life in the colonies. All of these groups contained elements of community emphasis in their theologies and were not void of emphasis on the communal aspect of the Christian faith. Both the Anabaptists and Moravians stressed these matters in their theology and thus mitigated individualism to some extent in their churches. But when all was said and done, Protestant individualism was an enormous fact of life in British North America.

Third, all of these groups highlighted the dignity of manual and mental labor and stressed hard work as a part of their religious ethic. No group did this more emphatically than the Calvinists. However, Lutherans,

---

[34] Gaustad and Barlow, *New Historical Atlas of Religions in America*, 7–10; and Evarts B. Greene and Virginia D. Harrington, *American Population Before the Federal Census of 1790* (Gloucester, 1966), 7.

Anabaptists, and Moravians also praised work as a gift of God and urged believers to do all that they did, including work, to the glory of God.

Fourth, the Anabaptists brought with them their belief in religious liberty and separation of church and state. Because they were an exceedingly small group and dedicated in the early years to survival and self-sufficiency, they did not make as significant an impact on the life of the colonies as did their spiritual cousins the Baptists, who held almost identical views concerning church and state. In any event, the Anabaptists maintained their faithful witness to religious liberty until the Baptists became the third-largest denomination in the fledgling United States. With that growth, Baptists became an increasingly more important player in constitutional politics. The Baptists, Anabaptists, Quakers, and Presbyterians joined with the Founders and other Enlightenment intellectuals to deliver the religious liberty clauses of the First Amendment to the American people in 1791.[35]

It is true that the religious beliefs and practices of the Old World were tested in a New World that was three thousand miles and many weeks distant from the European continent. A view of space and time that was different from that to which they had been accustomed in Europe certainly played an important part in the religious and secular history of colonial America. This difference allowed the Americans to develop their basic theology and their basic spirituality in a new historical and geographical context that led to changes in the way that they practiced their faith. However, core beliefs remained the same, even as they cooperated and argued with and influenced one another in new ways and directions. In this new context in a new world, most continental Protestants and their theological children clung to their biblical faith, their individualistic approach to religion, and their adherence to a hard-driving work ethic. They also flavored religion in British North America with a new outlook on church-state relations. All these religious factors would deeply affect the course of American history in the seventeenth century and after.

SUGGESTIONS FOR FURTHER READING

Brecht, Martin. *Martin Luther*. 3 vols. Minneapolis, 1985–91.

Heinz, Rudolph W. *Reform and Conflict: From the Medieval World to the Wars of Religion, AD 1350–1648*. Grand Rapids, 2005.

Lindberg, Carter. *The European Reformations*. 2nd ed. Oxford, 2009.

Linder, Robert D. *The Reformation Era*. London and Westport, 2008.

---

[35] William R. Estep, *Revolution Within the Revolution: The First Amendment in Historical Context, 1612–1789* (Grand Rapids, 1990), 97–179; and Steven Waldman, *Founding Faith: Providence, Politics, and the Birth of Religious Freedom in America* (New York, 2008).

McGrath, Alister. *Reformation Thought: An Introduction.* 3rd ed. Oxford, 1999.
Parker, T. H. L. *John Calvin: A Biography.* Philadelphia, 1975.
Stoeffler, F. Ernest. *The Rise of Evangelical Pietism.* Leiden, 1965.
Wiesner, Merry. *Christianity and Sexuality in the Early Modern World.* New York, 2000.

4

RELIGIOUS TRADITIONS IN GREAT BRITAIN ON THE EVE OF COLONIZATION

PETER LAKE

In a period as actually or potentially unstable as the post-Reformation era, it would probably be a serious (albeit common enough) mistake to speak of religious traditions as though they were stable and unproblematic features of the religious, cultural, and political scene. Rather we should think of the period as one in which various traditions were under construction and reconstruction, as a number of different groups and factions sought both to accommodate themselves to and to shape the course of events. On both sides of what by the latter part of the sixteenth century had become the confessional divide between Catholics and Protestants, the issue was how to explain the past and exploit the present. The resulting processes of tradition building were dialogic and even dialectical in nature, as each group and subgroup reacted to and played off the claims and counterclaims of others. The result was a complex series of dialogues and exchanges not only between Protestants and Catholics, but also between various subgroups or factions located within the two great confessional coalitions or syntheses. It is a situation that positively demands a chronologically organized, diachronic recounting, as well as a rather more static, synchronic, and analytic approach.

Let us start with the group whose relationship to tradition ought to have been the least problematic – the Catholics. Theirs, after all, was the "old religion," and yet there has long been a debate among historians of English Catholicism about the extent to which the English Catholic community that emerged over the course of Queen Elizabeth's reign represented continuity or change. As is the case with many such debates, there is much truth to be found on both sides of the argument. Thus it is not the case that the English Catholic community had to be created ex nihilo by Catholic missionary priests trained on the continent and reintroduced into England in the 1570s and 1580s. Rather Catholic religion was kept alive by priests ordained under Mary or even Henry VIII and driven from their parish livings by the Elizabethan settlement. By these means in some areas Catholicism may have persisted as something like the communal norm well into the mid-Elizabethan period. To that extent, emphasizing continuity makes sense. Moreover, many of the leading players had seen the Edwardian and Marian regimes collapse like a pack of cards on the unexpected or premature death of the monarch. What had happened before might well happen again; after all, if Elizabeth were to die childless, she would in all probability leave her kingdom to the Catholic Mary Stuart, and if she were to marry, it would almost certainly be with a foreign prince, very probably a Catholic. Thus, for some Catholics and in some areas, the experience of continuity and the expectation of a return to a communally sanctioned Catholic "normal" may have been the norm. And it is certainly the case that there were strong correlations between the areas of strongest Catholic feeling in the 1560s and the areas with the most recusants in the 1570s, 1580s, and 1590s.

So much, then, for continuity. But things did not turn out as many Catholics must have hoped in the 1560s and 1570s. Elizabeth neither died nor married; the Protestant regime assembled around her strengthened its hold on power and, after the crises of the early 1570s, started to define itself against the threat of popery and gradually to intensify its repressive efforts against Catholicism. The refusal of reality to return to anything recognizable as a Catholic normality meant that even in those areas where Catholicism was strongest, change was inevitable, as the central sites of communal religion – the parish church, the publicly accredited versions of the liturgical year, and the life cycle – fell into alien heretical hands. If we accept the picture of pre-Reformation Catholicism produced by Eamonn Duffy, this was a religion defined by the observances, the holy places, times, objects, and observances of the parish church.[1] That is not to say that this was a religion of merely outward forms composed entirely of public communal observances and gestures, but it is to say that even the most private and introspective aspects of this religious style had been structured by an intensely public round of religious observance. All that the Elizabethan settlement had taken away; in most places this did not happen at a stroke, but it happened gradually, as the queen refused to either marry or die, and was all but complete by the 1590s.

All this placed considerable stress on what it meant to be a loyal subject of the English crown and a Catholic, and over time debates opened up among English Catholics about how to conduct themselves under heretical rule. Should Catholics become recusants, refusing ever to attend the heretical

---

[1] Eamon Duffy, *The Stripping of the Altars: Traditional Religion in England, c. 1400–c. 1580* (New Haven, 1992).

services of the national church and consequently suffering the legal and financial consequences as a form of religious witness, even of martyrdom, for their faith? Or should they attempt to accommodate themselves to the status quo, finding ways to stave off the worst effects of the law, offering the authorities low-grade gestures of conformity while continuing to act and present themselves as Catholics before God and their coreligionists?

If Catholics took the determinedly recusant path, refusing ever to darken the doors of their parish church again, they were cutting themselves off entirely from the central Christian observances, the formerly holy places and times defined by the practices of the national church. Their priests were now marked men; from the 1580s their very presence in the realm branded them as traitors, and any Catholic who was caught harboring one was guilty of a felony. The terms of Catholic existence came to depend almost entirely on whether and how the relevant statutes were enforced, and that was a function of a number of factors: of the capacities and limitations of the early modern English state, of the politics of the moment, of the social standing and connections of particular Catholics, and of the good or ill will of their neighbors and the local authorities. But even in the best of times, the religion of English Catholics had perforce to become in some basic sense private, rooted in the household, or wherever the services of a Catholic priest, or the company of other Catholics, might be obtained; Catholicism was entirely cut off from the national church.

The Catholics who took the so-called church papist route and conformed, at least to some extent, in order to escape the perils of the law might be thought to have retained a foothold in the national church, but they did so only on terms that rendered their Catholicism if anything even more compartmentalized and furtive than that of their recusant brethren. For if their identity as Catholics was going to be preserved, their contact with the national church had to be interpreted by both themselves and their coreligionists as a merely secular gesture of obedience to the authority of the crown. Denuded of any religious significance, it could do nothing to reattach them to the exercise of public religion in England. If in some places "Catholics," that is to say, church papists, sometimes managed to be buried, and even to erect rather prominent tombs, in their local parish churches, that was as much a gesture of ownership and inclusion directed to a view of the Catholic past and perhaps to the prospect of a Catholic future as it was an affirmation of a current reality.

Divergent views of the relationship of English Catholics to England and the English Catholic Christian past began to develop among Catholics both at home and in exile. There was a long-running dispute about the legitimacy of church popery and the necessity of recusancy. From the 1580s, rigorist ideologues like Nicholas Sander and Robert Parsons stressed the need to remake the English Catholic community on the basis of the sufferings of its martyrs, the witness of its most obdurate and defiant recusant members, and the evangelical efforts of the seminary-trained missionary clergy. This was to stress discontinuity. Both Sander and Parsons upbraided past generations of Catholics, for their lack of backbone in the face of heresy (under Henry VIII and Edward VI), for their lack of zeal in the face of opportunity (under Mary), and for their resignation before various (both lay and ecclesiastical) vested interests and institutional inertias. Other Catholics reacted very badly to such claims, coming to blame the insurgent zeal of the clergy, and particularly of the Jesuits and their allies, for attracting the hostile attentions of the regime and, in so doing, undermining the myriad tacit accommodations and trade-offs whereby the majority of English Catholics managed to square their identities as Catholics and as loyal English subjects in ways that left both their consciences and estates intact. And yet as some Catholics made a play to the regime about their own loyalism, they inevitably defined themselves against the disloyalty of at least some of their coreligionists. Similarly, while certain rigorists wrapped themselves in the flag of ideological purity, they inevitably cast aspersions on the claims to true Catholicism of at least some of their more conformable colleagues.

These differences achieved perhaps their highest, that is, their most coherent and polemically charged, level of expression at the very end of Elizabeth's reign in the archpriest controversy. The details of the dispute need not detain us. Suffice it to say that it became the site for a struggle between two very different visions of English Catholicism, with the "appellants" canvassing a vision of a traditional, hierarchical Catholic religion, at peace with itself, devoid of political ambitions, and in some sense politically loyal to the regime and therefore capable, under the right circumstances, of coming to an accommodation with it. Their opponents, the Jesuits and their supporters, identified with a more insurgently missionary vision of the Catholic cause, were impatient of traditional hierarchies, and (to their enemies at least) were arrogant and dismissive in their attitude to other religious orders, and indeed to any other locus of social, religious, and political authority. Moreover, (again at least to their opponents) their commitment to the ambitions of the Spanish throne, support for the infanta, and opposition to James VI as the next successor to the English throne rendered them positively un-English. The regime actively intervened in the dispute, covertly facilitating the polemical outpourings of the appellants in an effort to exploit the internal divisions of the Catholics and to foster the production of loyalist sentiments from within the English Catholic community.

What the controversy shows is the difficulty, perhaps even the impossibility, of constructing and maintaining a unitary Catholic tradition in the face of the political, ideological, and practical strains imposed on English Catholics by the experience of religious change and heretical rule. Nor did these fault lines disappear with the end of the controversy and the accession of James VI and I. On the contrary, even after the ultimate provocation of the Gunpowder Plot, through the oath of allegiance, the regime continued to play on these intra-Catholic divisions, and many of the same issues are to be found attaching themselves to later disputes during the 1620s about the appointment of a Catholic bishop for England.

If even the Catholics had trouble establishing and maintaining a stable and coherent English Catholic tradition, the problems faced by the Protestants were obviously far greater, for one of the standard Catholic polemical charges against the Protestants was the novelty of their religion. The question, "Where was your church before Luther?" bulked large in Catholic polemic. Consequently, Protestants put a great deal of intellectual energy into constructing a version of church history that identified the Church of Rome with the Antichrist and traced the true church through a series of more or less underground groups of true believers, their status as such vindicated by the fact that they had been persecuted as heretics by the false Church of Rome. These efforts culminated in that great martyrological church history, John Foxe's *Acts and Monuments*, popularly known as his "Book of Martyrs." This was tradition building on the grand scale, and for decades Foxe's book represented the dominant version of the English Protestant tradition.

The vision of the true church developed by Foxe to connect the current Church of England with a vision of the Christian past untainted by popery had little or no role for bishops and princes. Rather it turned on groups of true believers united by the truths of right doctrine brought to them through the unvarnished Word of God. More often than not, the hierarchies of church and state, the bishops and their agents and even the Christian prince and his deputies, had been on the wrong side, their persecution of the saints of God providing a crucial clue to the identity of the true and of the false churches. Foxe got around these difficulties by emphasizing that in Queen Elizabeth the English church was now enjoying the protection and rule of a second Constantine, a truly Christian prince, who had restored to the church the saving doctrine of true Protestant, indeed reformed, religion and the right administration of the sacraments.

As for the structures of government and outward worship of the church, they were indifferent; that is to say, because there were no direct scriptural injunctions governing such matters, no blueprints either for ecclesial government or for divine worship under the gospel, such issues were left to the relevant human authorities to decide according to general rules of expedience and edification, which *were* laid down in scripture. In the English case that meant that they were left to the Christian prince, and the ordinary members of the church, who were also her subjects, were under a scriptural injunction to do what they were told in such indifferent matters.

Such an account provided a formal justification for the Elizabethan church as it had come into being in 1559. But it left great swathes of the national church, the entirety of its government and most of its liturgy, devoid of any direct scriptural warrant or positive religious charge. These were outward matters left indifferent by God to be arranged by the relevant human authorities in whatever way seemed expedient and in greatest accord with the demands of edification. Much turned on the meaning of that word, "edification"; not a mere synonym for morally improving instruction, for Protestants it referred to the process whereby the spiritual temple of the true church was constructed out of the lively stones of true Christian believers converted to a true Christian faith by the Word of God, both read and more particularly preached. For most English Protestants, preaching remained the ordinary means of salvation, and it was the job of the visible church to bring as many of its actual or potential members to such true belief as possible.

The urgency of this task was considerable, and it was based on theoretical and practical, religious and political, factors. Theologically, of course, this was a matter of spiritual life and death; souls were at stake, and in the great struggle with the Antichrist, the clouds of popish error could only be dispelled by shining the light of the gospel into the dark corners of the land through the preaching of the Word. Except, of course, there were nowhere near enough trained and committed preaching ministers to do that. Politically, the residual conservatism, if not the actual Catholicism, of the mass of the population represented a considerable threat to the stability and perhaps to the very existence of the Protestant regime. For much of her reign, the queen's most likely successor was Mary Queen of Scots, and should Elizabeth die suddenly, such people might very well flock to Mary and then the (Protestant) game would be up. Protestant anxiety on this issue was considerably heightened by memories of what had happened to the Edwardian regime, whose sudden collapse was widely ascribed to the failure of the English to respond with the requisite zeal to the promptings and blessings of the gospel. Indeed, the popish tyranny of Mary Tudor was often presented as a divine punishment, visited on God's people because of that fatal lack of zeal. And, of course, precisely such a providential visitation could happen again, if, having been given a second bite at the cherry by a just but also a merciful God, the English did not learn the lessons of the recent past and again failed to respond to the blessings of the gospel.

On this account, the Church of England needed to be judged as a proselytizing machine, an engine designed to bring the saving message of the Word to the mass of the English people as quickly and effectively as possible. But, judged by such criteria, the early Elizabethan church was something of a bust. With as many as a third of its benefices left empty and lumbered with many ministers ordained under Henry VIII or Mary and thus entirely uncommitted to anything like a Protestant agenda, the Elizabethan church lacked the cadre of trained preaching ministers necessary to bring true religion to a population still sunk in popish error. Not only that, but to meet the chronic shortfall in clerical manpower, the bishops resorted to the ordination of all sorts of entirely unqualified persons – unqualified, that is, according to the fairly exalted standards that defined the person of the godly preaching minister.

Herein, then, lies the origin of what subsequently became known as Puritanism. By the time we reach the moment when emigration to New England was about to start, it is quite licit, even necessary, to talk of a Puritan tradition. But we should not assume the existence of such a tradition from the outset or conceive of its emergence as anything like inevitable. For it is important to remember that dissatisfaction with the current state of the church and in particular with its performance as an actively proselytizing, almost missionary, church was not a characteristic distinctive of a self-consciously oppositional group dedicated to root-and-branch reform of the church. On the contrary, many of the men who found themselves recruited to the Elizabethan episcopate shared the same impulses that were shortly to prompt Puritan schemes for further reformation.

What produced the emergence of Puritanism first as a movement to reform the church and then as an increasingly distinctive style of divinity, a form of religious practice and belief and a style of subjectivity, was the failure of various attempts, many of them pseudo-official, to reform the church. Those failures were politically contingent, produced at the most basic level by the intransigence of Queen Elizabeth and her refusal to give ground to the reforming impulses even of some of her most intimate advisors and counselors, not to mention many of her bishops. Here is not the place to recount the political fortunes of the cause of further reformation – the emergence, activities, and suppression of what Professor Collinson termed "the Elizabethan Puritan movement."[2] Suffice it to say that despite the best efforts of a whole series of both insiders and outsiders; of privy councilors, their clients, and "men of business"; of bishops like

---

[2] Patrick Collinson, *The Elizabethan Puritan Movement* (London, 1967).

Edmund Grindal; and of Puritan divines and their lay patrons and allies, both moderate and radical, further reformation was not achieved.

The Elizabethan settlement, the church as it had been reestablished in 1559, had been regarded by many at the time – indeed, even by some of the first Elizabethan bishops and leading Elizabethan councilors – as an opening gambit, even as a somewhat unsatisfactory compromise, that in the years to come would be fashioned into something better. However, the queen's intransigence ensured not only that this did not happen, but also that members of the establishment became embroiled in the defense of policies and the enforcement of rules and regulations that, left to their own devices, they would have either not adopted in the first place or reformed out of existence at the first opportunity. They were obliged to do this by their supervening obligation to obey the queen as the supreme governor of the church, and therefore to enforce policies about things indifferent that lay entirely within the legitimate purview of royal authority, even if they did not themselves particularly approve either of the policy itself or of the consequences of its enforcement.

All this could not but lead to hurt feelings and increasingly bitter mutual recriminations, as those on the receiving end of the bishops' enforcement of royal policy accused them of having checked their Protestant principles at the door of their episcopal palaces, and those doing the enforcing accused their accusers of irresponsibility, disobedience, and "popularity." This last was a peculiarly heinous offense involving playing to the popular gallery by denouncing the ceremonies as simply unlawful rather than accepting and even defending them as inherently indifferent, and by attacking the bishops as persecuting, lordly prelates, and all to enhance the popular reputation of the Puritans for superior godliness and zeal. Thus while, according to the Puritans, the bishops were selling out the cause of true religion by turning on their brethren and enforcing the use of popish ceremonies, according to the bishops, the Puritans were misleading the people and dividing the godly party over trifles.

It is perfectly possible to trace the peaks and troughs of Puritan and conformist confrontation during the reign of Elizabeth and in so doing to tell a story of Puritan radicalization, as objections to various aspects of conformity – to popish remnants in what Bishop Jewel termed the "scenic apparatus" of the church – turned into a full-scale presbyterian repudiation of the episcopal structure of the church as simply popish. This led ultimately, among small groups of separatists, to the denunciation of the national church as a false church and to calls for withdrawal from it into gathered churches of true believers wedded to a gospel purity in church government and worship that was to be achieved without tarrying for the magistrate.

Such a tale has often been told, and there remains much truth to it, but it is far from being the only story that can be told about Puritanism. For while that dynamic of radicalization and fragmentation was produced by the failure to achieve any formal change in either the government or the worship of the church, there was another process afoot, one of integration and burgeoning influence and status. Here was a relative success story, predicated on a piecemeal reformation wrought by the Word preached and the influence of myriad godly ministers and magistrates, operating within and through the structures of the national church to spread the gospel among the people. Here is Puritanism conceived not so much as a coherent "movement" for reform of the church, but rather as a form of "voluntary religion," a style of divinity, which sought to spread the gospel and edify the godly community through the exercise of true religion in the church and the household, both in the public face of the congregation and in the private meeting or conventicle. Puritanism taken in this sense, far from being opposed to the Church of England, saw itself as the essence of that church, providing the saving remnant that served to validate the national church as a true church, and to buttress the Elizabethan regime in church and state against the popish threat.

As Puritanism of this sort established itself in various parts of the country, even ministers and laypeople with serious qualms about conforming fully to the ceremonies of the church developed a very real stake in at least a version of the status quo. Not only were the ministers' livelihoods at risk in disputes over conformity, so too was their capacity to continue to further the cause of true religion, to build and sustain the godly community, and to dispel the clouds of popish error that still – in the eyes of the godly at least – enveloped so many of the people. The evangelical Protestant agenda being pursued by such men was shared by many, if not most, of the bishops, many of whom conspired to allow Nonconformist ministers to keep their livings. Elaborate casuistries were developed to reconcile the precise yet subtle consciences of many ministers to the various forms of modified subscription and conformity on offer from the more sympathetic of the bishops. Here then was Puritanism as but the leading edge, the shock troops, of wider bodies of evangelical Protestant thought and feeling. And with, if not the collapse, then certainly the eclipse of the Elizabethan Puritan movement in the last decade of the sixteenth century, it was this aspect of the Puritan impulse that came to the fore.

The flurry of activity in favor of further reformation that greeted the accession of James VI and I culminated in the damp squib of the Hampton Court Conference. That letdown was followed in quick succession by a renewed campaign for subscription and conformity and a renewed outbreak of public disputation and agitation about conformity and further reformation. Thereafter, the relative absence, during the central years of James' reign, of public argument or agitation over such issues arguably aided the practical integration of many Puritans into the structures of the national church. So too did various changes if not in the formal structures then certainly in the practical realities of the church. More and more graduate clergy and qualified preachers were churned out by the universities. In some dioceses a graduate clergy had become the norm by the turn of the sixteenth century. A strenuous preaching ministry became a more and more prevalent feature of English life. The values of true religion spread through the ruling class and local elites, penetrating quite far down the social scale in certain areas of the country. In some areas Puritan religion became hegemonic, even constituting something like the communal norm. On this account then, even by James' reign, we should beware of thinking of Puritanism as a clear-cut, free-standing "religious tradition," entirely distinct from the "Anglican" culture and norms of the national church. Rather we should conceive of an emergent Puritan tradition as merely the logical continuation or product of the English Protestant tradition tout court.

That was certainly how things appeared from the inside looking out, that is to say, to the Puritans themselves, who habitually saw themselves as "the godly," that is, the most zealous, pious, and loyal of her majesty's subjects, persons marked off from their contemporaries only by the purity and zeal of their profession of true religion. But it was by no means always how things looked from the outside looking in. Here we need to remember that the word "Puritan" was in origin a term of abuse, first coined by Catholics and then adopted for the conduct of intra-Protestant dispute. Gradually, in the course of the various controversies about conformity, ceremony, and church government, a language of anti-Puritan vituperation and stereotype was developed. Although it would be going too far to suggest that "Puritanism" as a distinctive style of divinity or identity was simply invented in and through this process of polemical labeling, derision, and excoriation, it is certainly the case that, as Patrick Collinson among others has argued, the phenomenon of Puritanism cannot be understood outside of the often-harsh polemical, satirical, and libelous exchanges in which the term was first deployed and defined by contemporaries.[3]

This labeling process took place at a number of different cultural levels and was conducted through a number of different media or genres. At the

---

[3] Patrick Collinson, "Ecclesiastical Vitriol: Religious Satire in the 1590s and the Invention of Puritanism," in J. Guy, ed., *The Reign of Elizabeth I: Court and Culture in the Last Decade* (Cambridge, UK, 1995).

highest level of discourse, anti-Puritan stereotyping owed its existence to the polemical activities of the various conformist divines who had taken it upon themselves to defend the ecclesiastical status quo from Puritan assault. Here a crucial role was played by John Whitgift, the future archbishop of Canterbury and the great opponent of Thomas Cartwright, the leading ideologue of English presbyterianism. It was Whitgift who first established the correlation between Puritanism and popularity and who attacked the Puritan laity for their sacrilegious greed in using the prospect of reformation as a pretext to seize the remaining landed wealth of the church.

The same process of stereotyping was continued by Whitgift's protégé, Richard Bancroft, the future bishop of London, and then under James I, the archbishop of Canterbury. Even more than Whitgift, Bancroft was a gifted polemicist, and in the early 1590s he continued the processes (initiated by Whitgift in the 1570s) whereby Puritanism was associated, on the one hand, with a popular and subversive political agenda and, on the other, with a grandstanding hypocrisy. Bancroft was also up to his neck in sponsoring and perhaps even coordinating a pamphlet campaign designed to reply to the notorious Marprelate tracts, scurrilous Puritan squibs dedicated to the furtherance of presbyterian reform through the ribald ridicule of the bishops. The resulting tracts, written by the likes of Anthony Munday and Thomas Nashe – denizens of the London literary demimonde – represented elaborated exercises in anti-Puritan satire and stereotype. Here the disreputably popular outpourings of the pamphlet press met the far more respectable efforts of university-educated divines, of future bishops and archbishops, to produce an emergent tradition of anti-Puritan invective and stereotype.

For anti-Puritan libel and squib had never been limited to the elite and learned world of anti-presbyterian polemic, nor even to the world of print – however popular or low. Although the godly might take themselves to be simply that, godly Protestants and loyal subjects of exemplary religious zeal and moral austerity, to at least some of their neighbors and contemporaries – the butts of the Puritans' religious admonitions and moral reproaches and the objects of their attempts at moral reformation – they were anything but. As the cultural reach and the social and political clout of the godly spread, the result was a certain reaction, a moral and cultural pushback, which often took the form of libelous poems, songs, and ballads designed to out the godly as self-serving and self-righteous hypocrites who used a veneer of godliness to hide the pursuit of material, carnal, or fleshly self-interest. These different strands of anti-Puritan discourse met and mingled in the tracts produced (at Bancroft's behest) by the likes of Nashe and Munday to counter Marprelate. The Puritan also became a feature of the popular stage, with various playwrights from Shakespeare to Jonson producing a variety of alternately absurd and sinister bearers of quintessentially Puritan characteristics. (One thinks, for instance, of Angelo in *Measure for Measure*, Malvolio in *Twelfth Night,* or Zeal-of-the-land-busy in *Bartholomew Fair*.) Because the popular stage had long been the object of intermittent excoriation, much of it conducted through pulpit and press by Puritan or Puritan-sounding polemicists, this development represents a perfect example of the dialogic, indeed, of the positively dialectical, cultural forces and relations that produced anti-Puritanism and thus, to a certain extent, Puritanism itself.

By the turn of the sixteenth century, it is not going too far to see the emergence of a tradition of anti-Puritan discourse that if it did not rival certainly paralleled the tradition of anti-popery that had long provided the Protestant tradition with its defining other, its negative image of the false, persecuting church of the Antichrist against which the true church of the Protestants could define itself. It was their opposition to popery in all its myriad forms that underpinned the Puritans' self-image as the most loyal of the Christian prince's subjects and the staunchest of the true church's stays and supports. Thus, Presbyterians, and even Separatists, saw themselves as bringing to the realm of church government and worship the same radical, purging scripturalism that had already removed the last vestiges of popery from the doctrine of the English church and would now do the same for its government, if only the authorities would give them a fair hearing. Now, with the emergence of anti-Puritanism, at least some of the enemies of the godly started to claim that the Puritans represented just as serious a threat to the Church of England as the papists. That remained an extreme position, one enthusiastically canvassed by various Catholic polemicists who had long sought to exploit the divisions among English Protestants by describing the Puritans and the Protestants as two separate religions and presenting the Puritans as epitomes of the most extreme forms of what they took to be typically heretical (Calvinist) zeal and political radicalism. Compared to the Puritans, the argument went, English Catholics were models of loyalism and obedience.

Perhaps unsurprisingly, relatively few Protestants would endorse such views; even committed defenders of the church from Puritan criticism and relatively willing enforcers of conformity held that the Puritans were brethren, albeit brethren in error, and as such crucial allies in the struggle against the real threat of popery. Others, Bancroft and crucially James VI and I, used the equivalence of the popish and Puritan threats to make distinctions between and among different sorts of papists and Puritans, claiming that the most extreme Puritans – Presbyterians and sectaries – and the most extreme, papalist Catholics – a group typified and led by the

Jesuits – with their shared addiction to resistance theory and shared rejection of the power of Christian princes over the church, did indeed represent an equivalent threat to monarchical government rule. Having made these claims, the idea was that other more moderate Puritans and papists, anxious to avoid such labels, would proceed to repudiate their erstwhile coreligionists and come to some sort of accommodation with the crown. Just as he had in Scotland, James I sought to personally favor and even to employ loyalist Catholics and crypto-Catholics, sometimes at the highest levels of government, as a counterbalance to the godly.

The significance of all this for Puritan identity formation can be traced through the relation of those stigmatized as Puritans to the word itself. On the one hand, throughout the period down to the English Civil War, the objects of this style of vituperation denied that they were any such thing and denounced the term as a slur and a libel, implying as it did that they regarded themselves as somehow purer than others when it was well known that no one was more sensitive to the taint of original and actual sin than they. No, they were members of no sect, but simple Christians, professors of the true religion. On the other hand, from the later sixteenth century on, some of the godly came almost to own the term, indeed to wear it as a badge of pride, because they claimed that the use of "Puritan" as a term of abuse was a sure sign that the user him- or herself was a member of the ungodly, anxious to tar the professors of true religion with the brush of singularity and sedition, and that the target of the abuse could be taken to be a member of the godly indeed. Thus was the negative and denunciatory usage of the term inverted. Certainly, by the second and third decades of the seventeenth century we can find Puritan authors using the term almost as a value-free self-descriptor.

The emergence of Puritanism as an increasingly distinctive, almost freestanding religious identity was further helped by the activities of their enemies, which were not limited to the realm of polemical name-calling, crude stereotyping, and satirical caricature. We return here to the paradoxical nature of tradition building in a period of rapid ideological change and conflict like that of the post-Reformation. The Protestant tradition that developed to legitimate the Church of England as the continuation of the underground church of true believers persecuted by the false church of the Antichrist produced a vision of the Christian community, indeed in many ways of the true church, as a gathered group of true believers, even, as Catharine Davies has it, as "a poor persecuted flock of Christ."[4]

---

[4] Catharine Davies, "'Poor Persecuted Flock' or 'Commonwealth of Christians'; Edwardian Protestant Concepts of the Church," in Peter Lake and M. Dowling, eds., *Protestantism and the National Church in Sixteenth Century England* (London, 1987).

Not only was such a vision not best suited to the realities of a comprehensive national church; it also had the paradoxical effect of consigning to the dustbin of history many of the institutional, liturgical, and physical aspects of the English church that most lent themselves to demonstrating continuity with the pre-Reformation church, because those aspects – the church's episcopal structure, forms of government, and canon law – were associated with the repressive forces of the false church used, as recently as the early sixteenth century (not to mention Mary's reign), to persecute the members of the true church in England. Some of those aspects of continuity were so deeply tainted with idolatry and false religion that they needed extensive purging before they could be appropriated for truly Protestant purposes; hence the very considerable iconoclasm that attended the Elizabethan settlement, despite the best intentions of the queen herself. Others, insofar as they were retained, had to be stripped of any positive religious charge or role in order to be rendered acceptable to Protestant sensibilities; hence the insistence that various ceremonies and institutions, up to and including episcopacy itself, were indifferent, their adoption and continuation rendered acceptable only by the exercise of the royal will in retaining them.

Under the initial impact of Puritan assault, conformist defenders of the status quo had been constrained by these limits. Their case had remained essentially a negative one that denied that scriptural blueprints could be found for the government of the church under the gospel, asserted the inherent indifference of the institutions and ceremonies under dispute, and then assaulted the Puritans for disobedience, popularity, and self-serving error. The impulse to fight fire with fire, to counter the scripturalism of the Puritans with a counter-scripturalism of their own, was however considerable. By the late 1580s conformist defenders of the church can be found making what would rapidly become *iure divino* arguments in favor of episcopacy, arguments that used certain passages in the New Testament to assert that episcopacy was in fact of apostolic foundation.

What was happening here was something of a clericalist reaction against what was coming to be seen in certain circles as an excessive lay dominance of religious policy and church affairs, and a move toward justifying the basic lineaments of the national church, not to mention the status and wealth of the clerical estate, on *iure divino*, scripturalist grounds. *Iure divino* claims about episcopacy were followed soon after by *iure divino* claims about tithes, a subject even more controversial with large sections of lay opinion, and particularly common lawyers. It was no accident that Bancroft was at the forefront of both of these movements, for there was more than an element of clericalist reaction about his style of anti-Puritanism, which saw the presbyterian discipline as, among other things, the product of a corrupt alliance between greedy laymen with designs on the remaining wealth of the church and ambitious and seditious ministers desperate to arrogate to themselves as much power and status as possible. Such views of Puritanism were countered, on the other side, by accusations that the bishops and their hangers-on and clients were corrupt, evil councilors, desperate to perpetuate the status quo because of the wealth and status that their positions within it conferred on them, and thus willing to sacrifice myriad potentially savable souls on the altar of their own greed and ambition.

The 1590s were a crucial decade for the development of more ideologically aggressive versions of conformity, and the most daringly innovative and aggressive figure at work in that decade was Richard Hooker. Hooker redefined the relationship of the Church of England to the Catholic past, and in the process produced a novel version of the English Protestant tradition that placed a positive value on the continuity of the English church's structures and practices with the pre-Reformation church. Far from something to be sloughed off and played down, these links were now to be gloried in; they showed that the Protestant church had diverged from only those aspects of Catholicism that were genuinely corrupt and for the rest relied on the traditions of the church as the highest expression of the collective wisdom of Christians.

By thus revalidating the role of tradition, Hooker was able to attribute a more exalted religious role in the life of the church to ceremonies and practices, now, on his account, not only indifferent to but also underwritten by tradition. Hooker also reordered the balance between public prayer and public worship, preaching and the sacraments, in the life of the church and then used the resulting recalibrated account of the Christian life and its relation to the public ordinances and observances of the church to create a genuinely broad-bottomed vision of the Christian community, a vision he juxtaposed against the narrowly restrictive views of the self-selecting "godly." In short, Hooker was offering a vision of true religion and the national church that was very different from what had passed for orthodox or normative among the majority of committed English Protestants (both Puritan and conformist). Certainly, had his account of the English national church and its relation to Christian tradition been widely accepted, it would have entirely ruled out of court Puritan claims to represent the leading edge, the logically necessary culmination, of the Protestant tradition. And that, of course, was precisely what his position was designed to do, relegating the Puritans from their self-chosen role as the shock troops of further reformation, the epitome of both Protestant zeal and political loyalty, to the status of bearers of a profoundly mistaken and potentially subversive view not merely of church government, but of true religion tout court.

The ironies at work here were considerable. For because Hooker's version of and insistence on the role of ecclesiastical tradition was at variance with what had passed as the English Protestant tradition since at least the reign of Edward VI, what rendered his thought aggressively novel, in the immediate context in which it was first written and consumed, was precisely its self-conscious traditionalism. We return to the paradox of tradition building in an age of change and conflict, when any number of different groups and factions were seeking to find, in different versions of tradition, a legitimating warrant for their own current views and agenda.

Hooker, of course, was something of a maverick; if his thought represented by far the most systematic assault on Puritanism conceived both as a platform of ecclesiastical reform and as a style of divinity and vision of the Christian life and community, on a number of crucial issues, he was scarcely at one with the other leading conformist thinkers of the day. He was no fan of *iure divino* episcopacy, and his political thought – most of which remained unpublished in his lifetime – was sharply divergent from the increasingly absolutist views of men like Richard Bancroft, Matthew Sutcliffe, and Hadrian Saravia, the other leading anti-presbyterian ideologues of the 1590s. But for all his eccentricity, Hooker can be taken as in some way representative of a wider ideological moment in which, during the 1590s, a variety of different conformist divines were working their way toward newly exalted versions of and justifications for if not quite the ecclesiastical status quo then certainly what they took to be the true being or essence of the Church of England, or to put it another way, what they thought the English church should and would become once it was freed from its current Puritan-infested and lay-dominated state.

Hooker was careful never to let his own views come into direct conflict with the Reformed or Calvinist theology of grace that passed for orthodox among most of his contemporaries, that is to say, among conformists like Whitgift and Bancroft as well as among Puritans like William Perkins, Laurence Chaderton, or Andrew Willett. However, others, braver, more ambitious, or more foolhardy than he, tried to use the opportunity presented by the virulently anti-Puritan tenor of the times to shift the doctrinal goal by attacking Calvinist predestinarianism as well. Lancelot Andrewes and Samuel Harsnet led the way in London and at court, only to be followed in Cambridge by William Barrett and Peter Baro. In Oxford, John Howson sought to establish a positively Hookerian relocation of the sacred within the observances, the holy times and places, of the national church, as defined by ecclesiastical tradition and authority. All these efforts ended in inconclusive controversy. The theological disputes in Cambridge ruined the careers of the anti-Calvinist principals Barrett and Baro, but they also left the doctrinal issue formally unresolved. Indeed, the decidedly

Calvinist formula designed by none other than Archbishop Whitgift to control further discourse on the subject was left hanging because of the personal intervention of the queen. Both Whitgift and Bancroft, however, did their best to reestablish the theological status quo ante through other means.

The accession of James VI and I occasioned a rising of expectation among Puritans and Catholics. Both groups had reason to put their hopes in James, who, after all, was the king of a still-presbyterian country, but also the son of Mary Queen of Scots. Moreover, in the years immediately prior to Elizabeth's death, James had given as many people as possible reason to think that they might have something to gain from his rule. However, once established in power, after a period of initial confusion, with overt petitioning and maneuvering on all sides, James did little or nothing to change the status quo. He refused the lure of symbolic alterations in the outward observances of the church to appease the Puritans, and he denied the Catholics even the de facto toleration that his initial suspension of the recusancy laws had appeared to offer them. But even in the face of the ultimate provocation of the Gunpowder Plot, he resisted the temptation to conflate all Catholics with the radical minority and continued to play radicals and moderates with both Puritans and Catholics, offering favor to those who would defer to his divinely ordained authority as a Christian prince and head of the church.

Avant-garde conformists like Lancelot Andrewes, John Overall, Samuel Harsnet, or Richard Neile, all of them veterans of the anti-Puritan and anti-Calvinist putsch of the 1590s, found themselves on the Jacobean episcopal bench, some of them (like Andrewes and Neile) enjoying the personal favor of the king. But so too did evangelical Calvinists like George Abbott, who succeeded Bancroft as archbishop of Canterbury in 1610; John King; and James Montague, a peculiar favorite of the king and editor of his works. The ideology of the Jacobean church was founded on the doctrine of divine right, picturing a church presided over by a divine-right king and bishops whose office in the church was taken to be of directly apostolic origins. Bancroft continued to push the idea that tithes were due to the clergy by divine right as well, and eventually the claim that the observance of the Sabbath was a directly scriptural ordinance achieved official standing. As for the doctrinal position of the church, that was taken to be in line with Reformed orthodoxy, something that James himself seemed to confirm when he sent a delegation to the Synod of Dort to collaborate in the condemnation of Arminianism in 1618.

For Puritans, the impact of James' regime was uneven. As Michael Winship has shown, for radical Puritans, like William Bradshaw, the dashing of their hopes for further reformation merely confirmed them in their fears that an episcopally driven and, in effect, popish conspiracy of evil counsel had taken hold of the state.[5] Some were pushed over the edge into separatism; others like Bradshaw himself held back, adopting a version of the classically moderate Puritan via media by seeking to occupy a middle ground located somewhere between separation and even limited conformity. Thanks to the patronage of the godly Redich family, Bradshaw managed to do all that, not in exile in the Low Countries, but while exercising a ministry within, but perhaps not quite of, the national church. Others, after the initial shock of the enforcement of the 1604 canons had worn off, found the Jacobean church a relatively comfortable place to be. Even Nonconformists as uncompromising as John Cotton managed to forge some sort of modus vivendi with sympathetic bishops, in his case John Williams, and to maintain themselves in a parochial ministry. John Dod and Arthur Hildersham slipped in and out of trouble with the authorities but again through the patronage of sympathetic gentry families – in Dod's case, the Knightleys – managed for the most part to keep a toehold in the ministry.

Other more formally moderate souls were able to accommodate themselves with relative ease to the demands of conformity Jacobean-style, which often meant a combination of an insistence on subscription, that is, a formal acknowledgment that the Prayer Book and all that it entailed was "lawful," with a certain amount of leeway about the actual performance of conformity. This could prove entirely compatible with a distinctively Puritan style of ministry, on the basis of the symbiotic relationship between the voluntary religion practiced by the godly – various forms of household religion, sermon gadding, conventicle keeping, the repetition of the heads of sermons, private fasts – and a public worship centered on those three uniquely scriptural ordinances: the word preached, the sacraments, and a strict observance of the Sabbath.

How easily such accommodations were to establish and maintain depended to a large extent on both local circumstance and the course of national and sometimes even international and dynastic politics. If the local diocesan was some sort of evangelical Calvinist, like John King, the Abbott brothers, or later John Davenant or Joseph Hall, or even a politique anxious to keep in with the local godly, like John Williams at certain stages of his career, all might be relatively plain sailing. If he was an avant-garde conformist or hardened anti-Puritan, like Neile or Harsnet, things might not go as well.

---

[5] Michael Winship, "Freeborn (Puritan) Englishmen and Slavish Subjection: Popish Tyranny and Puritan Constitutionalism, c. 1570–1606," *English Historical Review* CXXIV (2009): 1050–1074.

The ebb and flow of royal policy as interpreted by and mediated through such local agents was determined by wider events. When James was pursuing a dynastic match for his two sons with Catholic powers, Spain or Savoy, the impulse to be nice to Catholics while cracking down on Puritans became all but irresistible. At the height of the negotiations over the Spanish match, much turned on the readiness of the pope to grant a dispensation to allow the marriage to go ahead, and to get that, the regime had to create the impression that Catholics in England were no longer subject to "persecution." That led to the suspension of the recusancy laws and to a considerable amount of semipublic activity on the part of English Catholics. That, in turn, led to a concomitant alarm among those members of the English church – Puritans certainly, but not only Puritans – most exercised by the imminence of the popish threat, a threat rendered all the more real by the events in Central Europe that were to culminate in the outbreak of the Thirty Years War.

As opposition to the Spanish match rose in court and country, and indeed in parliament, James I became more and more susceptible to the anti-Puritan views of the more avant-garde conformist or Arminian of his bishops and, indeed, of the crypto-Catholic Spanish faction at court, who were increasingly able to portray those who opposed the match as bearers of a populist, disobedient, and potentially antimonarchical Puritanism. It was this political juncture that led to the so-called rise of Arminianism. In many ways this was a more concerted repeat of the anti-Puritan and anti-Calvinist putsch of the 1590s. The aim was, once again, to use the rabidly anti-Puritan mood of the moment, particularly in the circles around the king, to persuade James that the problem was not merely Puritanism as he had conventionally defined it, that is, as a propensity to flout the royal will in matters of outward conformity and as a linked series of subversive beliefs about church government, resistance theory, and the powers of the Christian prince. Rather the real problem lay with the Calvinist doctrine of predestination itself, which, it was claimed, underpinned Puritan populism and disobedience, fractured the unity of the Christian community, and thus threatened both the integrity of the church and order in the state.

Here is not the place to recount in detail the alarums and excursions that attended the proclamation by Richard Montague of a vision of the English church undermined from within by all sorts of Puritans and Calvinists passing off their own erroneous and dangerous private doctrinal opinions as the official doctrine of the church. Nor is it the place to retell the essentially political story of the rise to power in the church of Laudianism, a one-step-forward, two-steps-back process, much complicated by the political crisis of the 1620s and not completed until the early 1630s. Suffice it to say that the rise to dominance in the church and in the ecclesiastical – but not only the ecclesiastical – counsels of the king of men like William Laud, who formally succeeded Abbott as archbishop of Canterbury in 1633, having effectually assumed the leadership of the church years earlier, transformed the ideology hegemonic in the Church of England.

Whereas by "Arminianism" I refer to a movement defined by its opposition to Calvinist predestinarianism and by the articulation of a theology of grace, and particularly of election, predicated on foreseen faith, by the term "Laudian" I refer to the wider religious program pursued by Archbishop Laud and others during the Personal Rule. While both sedulously anti-Puritan and concerned with denouncing the deleterious spiritual and political effects of the doctrine of absolute predestination, Laudianism's positive program consisted not so much in the espousal or dissemination of an Arminian theology of grace, but rather in a vision of the nature and mission of the visible church centered on a series of holy times and holy places, on the outward worship of God, and on the distribution of sacramental grace by a sacerdotal priesthood rather than by a more conventionally Protestant ministry of the Word. Along with all this came a heightened concern with the beauty of holiness, that is, with both ritual observance and outward ceremony, and with the physical condition and decoration, often with images and pictures, of the actual church itself. These trends were perhaps best typified by a renewed emphasis on bowing at the name of Jesus and to the altar, and by an insistence that communion be received not only kneeling, but kneeling at the rails of a newly elevated and railed-in altar. All this was combined with, and indeed constitutive of, a newly assertive clericalism. Along with all that, most notably in the University of Cambridge, came a doctrinal and a liturgical avant-garde willing to experiment with all sorts of new ideas and ritual practices that to persons of a traditionally Reformed, let alone Puritan, caste of mind could not seem anything but popish. (The poster boy for the resulting reaction, which portrayed all these developments as innovations totally at odds with the preceding English Protestant tradition, was William Prynne.)

This movement bears Laud's name not because he invented any of the major constituent parts of the ideological synthesis in question. The really creative and original work had been done years earlier by the likes of Hooker and Lancelot Andrewes. Later, the Laudian avant-garde was led by the likes of John Cosin, in matters liturgical; of Thomas Jackson, in more formally theological matters; and of the poet Crashaw, in questions of religious sensibility or subjectivity. In the 1630s the ideologues who both legitimated and drove forward the Laudian agenda tended to be younger men on the make or on the rise like Peter Heylin, Christopher Dow, or

Robert Skinner. Laudianism derives its name from Laud because it was in large part through Laud's influence in church and state that the vision of Hooker and Andrewes was given practical shape.

To return to the notion with which we started, one way to look at Laudianism is as an extended exercise in tradition building. Notions of institutional continuity came to the fore, with the church conceived not as a succession of groups linked both together and to the true church of the apostles by their common profession of right doctrine, but rather as a visible succession of sacred spaces, places, and persons. On certain versions of the *iure divino* argument for episcopacy, bishops came to be viewed as not only of apostolic but of directly divine origin, the first bishops being not Timothy and Titus, who were appointed by the apostles, but the apostles themselves, who were appointed by Christ. Thus episcopal ordination became essential for the exercise of the ministry or rather priesthood, and possession of bishops became equally essential for the being of a true church. All this involved a total recasting of the Church of England's relation both to its own Catholic past and with the present Church of Rome. If the Church of England did represent some sort of via media, to the Laudians that middle ground was located between Rome and Geneva. But just as in the current climate a Puritan-induced sacrilege represented a far more pressing threat to the church than any sort of idolatry, so the affinities of the Church of England with the catholicity of Rome were far greater than any links it might retain with Geneva or the foreign Reformed churches, churches that the Laudian insistence on apostolic succession and *iure divino* episcopacy all but unchurched. Accordingly, Laudians like Peter Heylin produced an account of the post-Reformation Church of England centered on the most conservative aspects of the Prayer Book. Indeed, Heylin actually went so far as to prefer the 1549 version to that of 1552. Such accounts saw any contact with foreign Reformed influence as corrupting, and more often than not as the product of lay attempts to undermine the independence and wealth of the church and the standing of the clergy. Puritanism became the misshapen spawn of this malign coupling of indigenous greed with sinister foreign influence. Thus, viewed from a Laudian perspective, the various forms of Puritan voluntary religion, which the godly saw as both supplementing and feeding off the public ordinances of the national church, and hence as entirely compatible with full membership of that church, became sinister signs of sectarianism, indeed of de facto separation.

Viewed from the inside out, Laudianism was the quintessence of orthodoxy and moderation, nothing more or less than an attempt to realize the true essence of the Church of England in the practice and outward appearance of every church in the land, an end to be achieved by purging that church of the Genevan doctrinal errors, the profane Puritan practices, and the sacrilegious neglect with which decades of Puritan infiltration and lay influence had polluted it. However, viewed from the outside looking in, to those committed to versions of the English Protestant and Reformed traditions that, until the rise of Arminianism and Laudianism in the 1620s and 1630s, had been viewed by many as normative or hegemonic within the Church of England, Laudianism was anything but moderate or orthodox. Rather it represented an ideologically aggressive attempt to highjack the national church and move it from the Protestant orthodoxy it had espoused since the Elizabethan settlement back toward something that looked uncomfortably like popery. Such impressions could only have been confirmed by the fact that to certain Catholics Laudianism looked like confirmation that the Catholics had been right all along. Puritanism was indeed synonymous with the worst aspects of Genevan heresy, and Puritanism and Protestantism were indeed two entirely distinct and incompatible religions. The Catholics involved were, in effect, the ideological heirs to the appellants. They wanted a Catholic episcopal hierarchy reestablished in England to restore order and obedience to the English Catholic community and to defeat what they continued to see as the Puritan-like threat represented by the insurgent evangelism of the Jesuits. From their perspective, Laudianism looked like several steps in the right direction, if not simply toward Rome, then certainly toward a rapprochement between a Laudian Church of England and their (Gallican) vision of English Catholicism. Their fan letters to Laud went unanswered for obvious reasons; because he was being accused by the likes of William Prynne of popery, the last thing Laud wanted or needed at such a moment was Catholic admirers.

By repudiating the Reformed orthodoxy that had underwritten the Church of England's status as a true church, by suppressing crucial aspects of that church's scriptural worship – and here the Laudian assault on what Puritans took to be the proper observance of the Sabbath bulked large – and by enmeshing others in practices that bordered on idolatry, Laudianism fatally undermined those features of the national church that had underpinned the Puritans' continued commitment to that church. This was no accident. The Laudians wanted to violate the sensibilities of the godly; they wanted to drive what they regarded as a sinister fifth column of insincerely conforming Puritans out into the open, thus forcing them to either leave the church altogether or buckle down and fully and finally conform.

All of which could not but have a radicalizing and a divisive effect on the godly, some of whom moved to outward defiance and others of whom were forced to defend their conformity to a national church that looked, at least to them and their Puritan friends, entirely different from anything they had signed onto under Elizabeth or James or indeed during the 1620s.

Confronted by the rise of Arminianism; the creeping influence of the likes of Montague, Laud, and Neile; and what appeared to be the abandonment by the Caroline regime of the Protestant cause abroad, some Puritans decided to go into exile, not merely in the traditional bolt-holes on the continent but in the New World, where they could found both a church and a commonwealth according to what they took to be almost entirely scriptural first principles. It might be tempting to see in that decision the final move to an entirely freestanding Puritan tradition, but in fact it was a move that presaged decades of further furious debate about the nature of that tradition and its relation to various versions of the national church. But that is quite another story.

SUGGESTIONS FOR FURTHER READING

Collinson, Patrick. *The Elizabethan Puritan Movement*. London, 1967.

Como, David R. *Blown by the Spirit: Puritanism and the Emergence of an Antinomian Underground in Pre-Civil-War England*. Stanford, 2004.

Duffy, Eamon. *The Stripping of the Altars: Traditional Religion in England, c.1400–c.1580*. New Haven, 1992.

Fincham, Kenneth, and Nicholas Tyacke. *Altars Restored: The Changing Face of English Worship, 1547–c.1700*. Oxford, UK, 2007.

Lake, Peter, and Michael C. Questier. *The Antichrist's Lewd Hat: Protestants, Papists and Players in Post-Reformation England*. New Haven, 2002.

Milton, Anthony. *Catholic and Reformed: The Roman and Protestant Churches in English Protestant Thought, 1600–1640*. Cambridge, UK, 1995.

Walsham, Alexandra. *Providence in Early Modern England*. Oxford, UK, 1999.

5

SOME NOTES ON AFRICAN RELIGIOUS TRADITIONS FROM THE FOURTEENTH CENTURY ONWARD

JACOB K. OLUPONA

In the absence of significant archival materials, it is difficult to reconstruct the exact nature of precolonial sub-Saharan African religions. Current understandings about early African religious practices are based on accounts written by missionaries during the colonial period and date primarily from the nineteenth century. Nevertheless, ethnographic research can help contemporary scholars envision the religious traditions that existed prior to European contact. Indeed, the cosmogonic structures and general praxis found in the colonial and postcolonial eras emerge from a preexisting polytheistic worldview that had been heavily influenced by newer monotheistic traditions. This essay seeks to outline the nature and structures common to many African belief systems prior to 1800. Surprisingly, long before the transatlantic slave trade, these belief systems contained elements not only of traditional African religions, but of Islam and Christianity as well.

An inquiry into African religions requires an understanding of the African contexts in which these religions developed. Human species have walked the continent for at least two million years.[1] Archeological finds since the early twentieth century verify the existence of hominids in Africa during this period. Thus Africa, we understand, was the human beings' initial home. As *Homo sapiens* migrated, new ethnic groups and cultures emerged. The San and Khoi Khoi, among the earliest groups, inhabited the Kalahari Desert, a thirstland stretching across Namibia and Botswana that sustains water-retaining vegetation such as the tsamma melon and the gemsbok cucumber.[2] Astonishingly, the Kalahari also supports an ecosystem in which game such as eland, gemsbok, wildebeest, hartebeest, and

---

[1] Joseph O. Vogel, "Search for Human Origins in Africa: A Historical Note," in Joseph O. Vogel, ed., *Encyclopedia of Pre-Colonial Africa: Archaeology, History, Languages, Cultures, and Environments* (Walnut Creek, CA, 1997), 84–90.

[2] Laurence Bartman, Jr., "Southern African Foragers," in Vogel, *Encyclopedia of Pre-Colonial Africa*, 190.

porcupine became critical food sources for the San and Khoi Khoi.[3] As this essay will show, geographical and environmental surroundings, as well as political, economic, and even existential exigencies, inform the people's cosmology.

According to Christopher Ehret, the Bantu migration from West Africa to rainforests in central Africa, which began as early as fourth millennium B.C.E., coincided with oil-palm cultivation.[4] Ehret explains that technology such as stone axes would have accompanied these agriculturalists. A Bantu subgroup, the Ubangian people, traveled further eastward and settled in the African savannah.[5] Archeological and anthropological evidence suggests the Mahariki, an eastern Bantu group, migrated to the Great Lakes region, where they settled and quickly expanded into Uganda and as far south as Kwa-Zulu Natal in South Africa.[6] These various migrations of African peoples across the continent are the main reason for Africa's tremendous ethnic diversity. This diversity lends itself to the continent's various religious cosmologies. This array encourages one to speak about these worldviews in the plural, "African religions," the latter word indicating the divergences in religious practices. Nevertheless, the approach taken by scholars for decades has been to describe the commonalities among these religions prior to the transatlantic slave trade. On this basis, I submit that there is a general cosmological worldview expressed in African mythology, narratives, and stories that explores the origins of the human universe. These same oral traditions lay out the structures of human life.

A three-tiered universe characterizes most African cosmologies. The sky, the first tier, belongs to the Supreme Being and to spirits. Human beings dwell on earth, the middle tier; yet a porous boundary between it and the heavens enables spirits to interact with human beings on a quotidian basis. An equally porous border exists between the underworld, where the ancestors reside, and earth. Thus ancestors often interact with their progeny via rituals conducted by their descendants. An ancestor's manifestation in a descendant's dreams is also common. As a rule, in indigenous African religions, deities, spirits, and ancestors remain active in and upon the human world.

Myths from across the continent often depict a passive or distant Supreme Being whose role in the universe's creation varies. For instance, in a narrative among the San, the cosmos, earth, animals, plants, insects, and humans

---

[3] Ibid.
[4] Christopher Ehret, "African Languages: A Historical Survey," in Vogel, *Encyclopedia of Pre-Colonial Africa*, 165.
[5] Ibid.
[6] Ibid.

exploded from Tutumbolosa's body on her death.[7] The goddess's sacrifice of self seems the only causation behind the world's formation. Conversely, oral tradition among the Bassari of Guinea recounts how Unumbotte, a creator god, seems disinterested at first but later assists his creation. In the myth, Unumbotte fashions a human being, a serpent, and an antelope. The Creator places these living beings on unrefined earth and furnishes them with a pack of seeds. A fruit-bearing tree grows from these seeds, and Unumbotte consumes the fruit, while the human, antelope, and snake remain hungry. Finally, the snake convinces the human and the antelope to eat some of the fruit. This surprises Unumbotte, but the Creator opts not to punish them. Rather, Unumbotte satisfies each creature's desires: the antelope lives out its days eating grass as it prefers; the human being receives new food: yams, sorghum, and millet; and the serpent receives venom. Because of the resemblance between this story and the Genesis narrative, it is fascinating to learn that it has existed among the Bassari since long before Europeans arrived in West Africa.[8]

In addition to Supreme Beings, African cosmogonist myths speak about numerous divinities, intermediaries between human beings and the Creator. The Yoruba and Fon, groups from what are now Nigeria and the Republic of Bénin, respectively, established elaborate pantheons. According to the Fon creation myth, Mawu-Lisa, the creator couple, birthed several sets of twins. Ogu, Heviosso, and Sakpata became the strongest deities in the Fon pantheon. As in Yoruba cosmology, Ogu is the god of iron and technology; Heviosso ("Sango" in Yoruba) rules over thunder, lightning, and rain; and Sakpata ("Obaluaye" in Yoruba) is the god of medicine. Interestingly, a cherished Yoruba cosmogonist myth recalls how Olodumare, the Supreme Being, charged seventeen divinities with the responsibility of ordering the earth. Osun, the beautiful goddess of wealth and fertility, was the youngest among them. As such, the other gods excluded her from their meetings. When they struggled to implement their plans, they returned to Olodumare to complain. The Creator noticed Osun's absence and instructed them to consult her. On doing so, their plan succeeded. Osun permitted the rivers to lie in their places. She also populated the earth with her children. The story demonstrates the agency attributed to divinities and their interaction with the Supreme Being: the Creator remains powerful, but the divinities are involved more directly in earthly affairs.

---

[7] Lewis J. Murphy, *Why Ostriches Don't Fly and Other Tales from the African Bush* (Englewood, CA, 1997), 14–17.

[8] Clyde W. Ford, *The Hero with an African Face: Mythic Wisdom of Traditional Africa* (New York, 1999), 171–5.

African religion is defined in reference to specific ethnic groups; their names define people's identity (e.g., BaKongo, Yoruba, Nupe, Nandi) and inform their cultural mores. In the period before the transatlantic slave trade, some of the largest ethnic enclaves interacted with different groups in their regions and exchanged and borrowed cosmological ideas, divination techniques, and ritual practices. For example, the Fa divination of the Fon in Benin (Dahomey) came from Ifa of the Yoruba. Fa became a religious and political apparatus to aid the king in governing.

Precolonial African religions involved beliefs in a human being's ability to manipulate the sacred and, consequently, amend natural phenomena and human events. "Magic" remains a problematic term for this concept, because in Africa people find such human power quite credible, whereas Western notions of the term "magic" suggest a lack of credibility. Men and women who use this power for malevolent ends are deemed sorcerers and witches. The Kgaga, a Xhosa-speaking ethnic group, believe that witches inherit their power matrilineally and thus possess innate abilities. Sorcerers, they claim, use nefarious medicines.[9] A common belief among the Bakweri of Congo is that both men and women may become witches, garnering an ability to decimate victims by devouring their shadows.[10] Interestingly, consumption is a common theme among African beliefs about witchcraft. Victor Turner notes that the Lozi of Zambia claim that witches and sorcerers consume flesh from their victim's cadaver in order to augment their powers.[11]

A sorcerer's ability to reorder events and alter outcomes is the same skill healers apply to their clients, the difference being one's benevolent intentions for the subject. In either case, magic, a spiritual enterprise aimed at altering human circumstances, was integral to precolonial African religions because it allowed Africans to respond to a physical world imbued with both malevolent and benevolent events. In an African worldview, no event transpires without either a spiritual or natural cause. As such, the proper ritual or sacrifice has the power to change circumstances in the world. Rainmaking among the Ihanzu of Tanzania, for instance, involves anointing rainstones with oil and sacrificing a goat while praying to the Supreme Being.[12] It aims to alleviate drought through spiritual means.

---

[9] W. D. Hammond-Tooke, *Boundaries and Belief: The Structure of a Sotho Worldview* (Johannesberg, 1981), 95–103.

[10] Edwin Ardener, *Kingdom on Mount Cameroon: Studies in the History of the Cameroon Coast 1500–1970*, ed. Shirley Ardener (Providence, 1996), 246–9.

[11] Victor W. Turner, "The Lozi Peoples of North-Western Rhodesia," *Ethnographic Survey of Africa: West Central Africa Part III* (London, 1952), 51–2.

[12] Todd Sanders, *Beyond Bodies, Rainmaking and Sensemaking in Tanzania* (Toronto, 2008), 125–38.

Similarly witches and sorcerers may annihilate someone they envy by conducting a ritual to send sickness or misfortune to that person. In this way, precolonial Africans negotiated not only the world around them, but also their social interactions.

Ancestor veneration, by far, is the most ubiquitous component of African religions. Those who have departed from the clan and who have lived to a fairly old age assume status as ancestors. To be recognized as an ancestor, an individual must have died a "good death," one not resulting from disease or accident. Candidates for ancestral veneration were usually elders and community leaders. On transcending into the next life, they are seen as possessing a supernatural force and as being capable of beseeching the gods on behalf of their living descendants. Ancestor veneration, though a ubiquitous practice, varies across the continent. On the one hand, in some groups, only men may achieve this revered status. Some matrilineal groups, on the other hand, honor female ancestors in addition to their forgone patriarchs. In either case, the deceased community members act as intermediaries between the world of the spirits and the world of the living because they possess human characteristics but dwell in a spiritual realm. Their need for food and water requires ancestors to depend on their progeny for offerings. At the same time, an ancestor's access to the spirit world and its power means the living depend on them for blessings. For this reason, people pray to them when there is calamity in order for them to assist with restoring the universe to its proper balance.

Sacred authority, another trait defining precolonial African religions, involves the divine action of kingship, priests, diviners, healers, and sorcerers. African ethnic communities such as the Nyamwezi of Tanzania believe their king holds sacred power and associate his welfare with the rains. According to Serge Tcherkézoff, if the king maintains a healthy relationship with the ancestors, adequate rainfall will follow. If the preliminary rituals fail, then the Nyamwezi beat the king to tears. The traditional belief is that his tears will evoke water from the sky, water controlled by ancestors.[13] In this sense, not only does the king have the most important spiritual connection with the ancestors, but also his body seems to represent the cosmos. If water falls from his eyes, then water will also fall from the sky. Similarly, the Kafa, Seka, and Bosa from the Ethiopian highlands compare the king's body to the cosmos. His welfare determines the community's wellness. These indigenous groups consider the king to be a second sun. Werner Lange's ethnographic research reveals the king eats only after sunset because dining during the day would represent two

---

[13] Serge Tcherkézoff, *Dual Classification Reconsidered: Nyamwezi Sacred Kingship and Other Examples*, trans. Martin Thom (Cambridge, UK, 1983 / Paris, 1983), 69–85.

risen suns.[14] This would defy the world's natural order. Essentially, sacred kingship as a religious trope points to a divine connection between the community and the cosmos and manifests in the king's physical and spiritual well-being.

Priests and diviners function as sacred authorities in indigenous African religions because they hold access to divine oracles and, in some cases, serve as spirit mediums who deliver messages from the spirit world. Often the responsibilities of these roles overlap. Priests usually conduct important ceremonies for various divinities and lead the community in calendrical rites and specific feast days for the deities. Diviners deliver and decode sacred knowledge to intercede on an individual's or a community's behalf. For example, Yoruba *babalawo* cull meaning from the proverbs, poems, and stories embedded in the *odu*, the oral chapters of Ifa poetry. The *odu* are concrete patterns that appear when the diviner tosses a divining chain or set of cowries. These patterns are considered divine words; the remedies and moral teachings become the divinity's will for the client. Effectually, precolonial African cosmology suggests that spirit beings can explain the *why* behind disasters. It is the diviner's responsibility to discern sacred knowledge and elucidate its pertinence to the client's situation.

Numerous divinatory methods characterize indigenous African religions. Chadic-speaking people of the Jos Plateau in southeastern Nigeria such as the Ngas, Mupun, and Mwaghavul practice Pa divination. It resembles Ifá divination, but as Umar H. D. Danfulani's extensive research demonstrates, important differences exist between the two systems. Both Ifá and Pa use specific tools. Pa divination requires a tortoise shell filled with thirty river pebbles. According to indigenous beliefs, river spirits enable these stones to reveal hidden information. Daily washings with river water maintain the stones' potency. Like Ifá, binary visual codes generate concretized patterns produced throughout the divination process; if one stone falls when cast, the diviner makes a single indentation in a special powder. When two stones fall, he makes two strokes. The impressions are made by holding the index finger and the middle finger together. Pa requires multiple sets of hands; therefore two or more diviners collaborate during consultations: one to cast the stones and record results, and another to interpret the outcomes. Confirmation of the diviner's interpretations occurs away from the consultation session. The patient confesses her or his misbehavior to a confidant. If the diviner is skilled and effective, these confessions will confirm his interpretations of the sacred knowledge revealed through casting the

---

[14] Werner Lange, *Dialectics of Divine "Kingship" in the Kafa Highlands*. Occasional Paper no. 15 (Los Angeles, 1976), 3–4, 25–33.

pebbles. It is standard for each remedy to involve either herbal prescriptions or sacrificial rites, which the diviner will prescribe to the client.[15]

Mediumistic divination, as is practiced among the Yaka in southwestern Democratic Republic of Congo, relies on the diviner's clairvoyance. Rather than interpret a sacred body of knowledge, the medium's validity depends on her or his ability to name the cause, moment, and perpetrator of the client's problem. This must happen without any clues from the client. As René Devisch explains, in the Yaka worldview, family members can stanch an individual's life flow. In other words, sorcery begins at home. Ancestors are also subject to these accusations. It is not uncommon for a Yaka diviner to claim that a maternal great-granduncle holds malicious intentions against the client.[16]

For the Nyole of eastern Uganda, mediumistic divination takes place via three-way conversations between the spirits, the diviner, and the client. Susan Reynolds Whyte has written extensively on how the diviner calls forth spirits of deceased maternal greatuncles who then speak through the diviner to the client, using the medium's mouth and body to communicate. Information travels between the client, the diviner, and the supernatural beings in order to generate a resolution. Clients in disagreement with the results may opt not to pay the diviner, choosing to seek consultation elsewhere.[17]

Rituals are the weft on the cosmological warp that is African religions, reifying the sacred values contained in myths. Rituals occur on calendrical cycles, determining when community members must honor a particular divinity or observe particular taboos. Yearly festivals for deities and ancestors involve sacrificial animals, libations, and specific foods. These events recharge the connections between humanity, ancestors, the Supreme Being, and other deities. Indeed, they enable communication between the human world and the world of spirits, engendering blessings of longevity, children, and sustenance. Rites aimed at persuading the gods to deliver rains and successful harvests exemplify communal rituals. Nevertheless, some events remain specific to sacred authority figures that are able to interact with consecrated ritual icons.

---

[15] Umar Habila Dadem Danfulani, "*Pa* Divination: Ritual Performance and Symbolism among the Ngas, Mupun, and Mwaghavul of the Jos Plateau, Nigeria," in Jacob K. Olupona, ed., *African Spirituality: Forms, Meanings and Expressions* (New York, 2000), 87–111.

[16] René Devisch, "Yaka Divination: Acting Out the Memory of Society's Life-Spring," in Michael Winkelman and Philip M. Peek, eds., *Divination and Healing: Potent Vision* (Tucson, 2004), 243–6, 252–5.

[17] Susan Reynolds Whyte, "Knowledge and Power in Nyole Divination," in Philip M. Peek, ed., *African Divination Systems: Ways of Knowing* (Bloomington, 1991), 153–72.

African rites of passage are well known among anthropologists and ethnographers from various disciplines. These events denote personal transitions and coincide with birth, naming, circumcision or coming-of-age rituals, marriage, old age, and death. Each ceremony indicates a transition from one rank in society to another. Coming-of-age rites mark the crossing from childhood to adulthood, when elders transfer ancestral knowledge to younger society members. Seclusion characterizes these events; the initiants usually gather in a natural space (forest, grasslands, etc.) beyond the community's perimeter. They dwell in this new locale for a process that can take up to several months. Above all, a rite of passage is a spiritual affair dependent on prayers to the Creator and supplications to ancestors and deities for the children's good fortune.

So far I have outlined elements and features of what in the absence of a better term is often called "indigenous African religions." However, it is a mistake to assume that Africans did not participate in other religions that came from outside. On the contrary, Islam and Christianity, two powerful monotheistic traditions, began to penetrate into the continent almost at the dawn of the two traditions from their places of origin in the Middle East. In 1990, when I returned to the United States to accept a teaching appointment, I worked with African American students who were passionate about African history. They knew quite a bit about ancient Egypt, which they often regarded as the home of their black ancestors, but they knew very little about what scholars often refer to as the western Sudanese empires of ancient Ghana, Mali, and Songhai that existed between the ninth and the sixteenth centuries. This is a curious gap in their understanding, given that their more immediate heritage is often derived from West Africa, one of the sources of the transatlantic slave trade. This area was home to many of the polytheistic religions whose traditions are described previously. But West Africa was also home to an ancient Islamic culture.

As early as the eleventh century, Arab geographers, including Abu Ubayd Abd Allah-Bakri, write of West African and central Sudanese towns being inhabited by Muslims. Islam first penetrated the elite classes, and the kings of Takrur (Senegambia) and Gao (Niger Bend) had already converted to Islam.[18] It appears that although these kings now adhered to Islam, they still sought to hold on to their political and judicial mechanisms, which incorporated aspects of traditional religious practice. For them, Islam was a way to engage the then "global" trade community, which they perceived to be Islamic. In this period, it was also politically and financially beneficial to be associated with Islam. Ralph A. Austen uses the records of pilgrimages to Mecca and Medina made by men like Mansa Musa (1324) and

---

[18] Ralph A. Austen, *Trans-Saharan Africa in World History* (Oxford, UK, 2010).

Askia Muhammed of Songhai (1496) and mosques that were built during this time to document the extent of Islamic practice and presence in West Africa. In particular, Mansa Musa, the legendary ruler of the Mali Empire, has often been viewed by African historians as the figure who succeeded in penetrating the iron curtain of color prejudice that for centuries had barred black Africans from engaging in global commerce. During his pilgrimage, he impressed the rest of the Muslim world with his extravagant display of wealth, thus drawing the attention of the Mediterranean world to the massive gold deposits found in Mali. His pilgrimage created prestige, however momentary, for black Africans and illustrates the fact that complex religious traditions in which traditional religious practices were overlain by the monotheism of Islam existed in parts of West Africa as early as the fourteenth century.

Austen posits that it was Juula traders from among the Mande-speaking peoples that first began penetrating these regions and establishing small Islamic merchant communities, dating back to the ninth century. It was not until the sixteenth century that these communities gained more of a following, as contact with Islamic learning centers in Egypt increased and scholars traveled back and forth. The form of Islam they practiced, the Suwarian tradition, was not as rigid as the Maliki tradition, which was more popular in North Africa, and they did not directly interfere with the religious activities of non-Muslims. Muslims of the Suwarian tradition engaged in the study of *batin*, which involved sewing the words of the Koran into amulets, or soaking handwritten verses to make a potion from the water, practices that resonated with already-existing indigenous religious practices[19] and were readily adopted by many non-Muslims. Indeed, *batin* may have been useful in drawing people to Islam, as they could view conversion to the faith as a means of broadening their religious and spiritual repertoire.

Islam first came to Sudan in the fourteenth century and would eventually become the religion of choice for the ruling class and the trading classes in the empires of Ghana, Songhai, and Mali. But it was not until the eighteenth century that Islam began to penetrate populations outside of the urban centers.[20] The forest zones of West Africa took much longer to accept Islam than the coastal and Sahara-border empires, cities, and towns. The jihads that began in the late eighteenth century were responsible for bringing Islam to many non-Muslim areas and ethnic groups. Mervyn Hiskett informed us that Islam was essentially nominal in Hausaland in

---

[19] According to Austen, "Some forms of batin even used local plants and other substances in much the same manner as the healers and diviners of indigenous societies" (95).

[20] Roberto O. Collins, *Problems in African History: The Pre-Colonial Centuries* (Princeton, 2005), 143.

northern Nigeria until the Uthman Dan Fodio's jihad.[21] Rulers and traders took Islamic titles and may have attended Friday mosque, but they still practiced traditional religion, keeping a few indigenous Muslim scholars around as symbols of prestige. Certain Islamic practices, such as styles of storytelling and divination, trickled down to the masses, infusing already-existing practices. But in Hausaland, slaves captured before the eighteenth century would have been at least nominally Muslim.

What was the consequence of this form of Islam on the transatlantic slave trade and the new culture of the Americas that Africans helped build? Africans' forced migration to the New World involved a transfer of a mixed form of religious traditions, material cultures, and values that reflected their preslavery religious culture. Islam, then, was part of the black religious mosaic that traveled to the New World.

Many of the major slave rebellions in Bahia, Brazil, were begun by Hausas, who seem, from the evidence provided, either to be Muslim or to use Muslim rites or sacred objects in their spiritual worship or practice. For instance, amulets like those described by Austen in the *batin*[22] practice were found on executed slaves after the rebellion was quelled,[23] as were "papers with prayers and passages from the Koran."[24] Names of slaves recorded by the police were often variations on the Hausa term for Muslim – *malomi, malam, mu'allim*.[25]

Austen notes that some of the most salient markers of difference between the trans-Saharan slave trade and that of the Atlantic were the facts that more females than males were taken and that the women often ended up working as domestics in wealthy houses or became concubines.[26] A large number of the men worked on cotton farms in Egypt during a cotton boom, or they were inducted into the military. As Muslims are required to acknowledge their children even from their slaves, some children born to slave women achieved great political influence, Mawlay Ismail, the Moroccan sultan of the seventeenth century, being one example. He is also known for having a large army of black soldiers. The level of records for trans-Saharan slavery is minimal in comparison to those for transatlantic slavery. It is estimated that between 800 and 1900, about ten million slaves were driven across the Sahara.[27]

---

[21] Mervyn Hiskett, *The Sword of Truth: The Life and Times of Shehu Usuman dan Fodio* (New York, 1973).
[22] Collins, *Problems in African History*, 143.
[23] João José Reis, *Slave Rebellion in Brazil: The Muslim Uprising of 1835 in Bahia* (Baltimore, 1993), 93.
[24] *Ibid.*
[25] *Ibid.*, 47.
[26] Austen, *Trans-Saharan Africa*, 31.
[27] *Ibid.*, 32.

Although Islam predated Christianity in the West African region, the story of religion in the central African region, a major hub and corridor of transatlantic slave trade, differs significantly from the West African story. Here Christianity played a more significant role than in West Africa.

In *Africa and Africans in the Making of the Atlantic World, 1400–1800*, John K. Thornton suggests that "only a limited number of slaves (mostly Central Africans) were actually Christians before they arrived in the New World."[28] However, due to missionary efforts in West and central Africa, many slaves were familiar with Christianity. Thornton explains that conversion to Christianity would have begun in Africa and continued in the New World as Africans were enslaved. Africans were able to accept Christianity because they found its revelatory character appealingly reminiscent of indigenous divination practices. Adherence to Christianity did not bring an end to Africans' beliefs in traditional religious systems; rather Africans incorporated these new ideas into what they already believed. In Kongo, for example, the success of Christianity was aided by the belief that many kings and leaders in the region received revelations from various Christian icons. In the late fifteenth and early sixteenth centuries, two Kongo nobles dreamed of the same woman imploring them to convert to Christianity. When an unusual black stone was found near one of their homes, this was interpreted by the Christian clergy as a sign that the Virgin Mary was imploring the Kongolese to convert. The king accepted this interpretation and thus began a series of conversions and religious revelations among the Kongo rulers.[29]

Revelation has been emphasized as the key to establishing a Christian tradition among the people of the Kongo. Christian converts could continue to value revelation, a concept that was already present in traditional religion. But now revelation was to be regulated by missionaries, who decided whether someone's revelation or possession was valid or the work of the devil.[30] Thornton recounts descriptions of slave religious leaders who were condemned during inquisitions as evidence of Christianity's contact with slaves in the New World during the seventeenth century. These leaders were condemned for, among other things, including Jesus Christ and the Virgin Mary in the opening of their religious prayers or using Christian religious symbolism on their clothing or amulets. Some even claimed that their powers came from Christian saints.[31] Although this does not prove

---

[28] John K. Thornton, *Africa and Africans in the Making of the Atlantic World, 1400–1800* (Cambridge, MA, 1998), 254.
[29] *Ibid.*, 257–8.
[30] *Ibid.*, 260–2.
[31] *Ibid.*, 266–7.

that these slaves practiced Christianity in the conventional sense, it does show that there was at least contact and a conscious effort to incorporate Christian figures and icons into indigenous religious practice. It is possible that the slaves' effort to engage Christianity was also a way to hide their African identity or to gain legitimacy with the white slave owners.

In another publication, "Religion and Cultural Life in the Kongo and Mbundu Areas, 1500–1800," Thornton reiterates that in 1491 the king of Kongo had converted to Christianity. The Portuguese, from whom the primary records detailing their practice come, tended to depict the Congolese as not quite Christian enough, because they had incorporated some of their traditional religious practice into the worship and because they still regarded their own king as the holy leader instead of the European pope or his priestly representative. Asserting that the Congolese were not entirely Christian was also a way of justifying the continued need for funding to continue colonial endeavors in the Kongo. This was in spite of the fact that a Dutch observer said that "the king of Congo and his people are Roman Catholics."[32]

Thornton says that it was the children of the urban elite who were taught in Catholic schools who would eventually become responsible for spreading Catholicism, as they would go to the rural areas and lead large prayers and "perform a few spiritual exercises."[33] King Afonso I (1509–42) is credited with giving the institutionalization of Christianity a great push due to his vision of St. James Major, which helped him to win a battle against his pagan brother. Saint days were celebrated, but they were also days on which the Kongo people revered their ancestors. Church officials tolerated this because they did not want to jeopardize their hold on the territory they had gained. Afonso was even given a bull of crusade so that any expansion he achieved would be sanctioned and recognized by the Holy Church. The penetration of the territories south of the Kongo, such as Ndogo or Imbangala, by Portuguese Christians came through military force. It was not until the 1620s that they arrived at these hinterland communities with their religion, and in the case of Queen Njinga's state, Christianity did not become an official religion until 1655.[34] The priests wisely incorporated indigenous religious terms for the gods and ancestors, *nkisi* and *kiteke*, into the catechism and other religious practices. They also conducted prayers and masses in the native languages.

Overall, Christianity was more widespread in the Kongo and northern territories such as Loango, Ngoyi, and Kakongo, but much of it was largely

---

[32] Thornton's essay appears in Linda Heywood, ed., *Central Africans and Cultural Transformations in the American Diaspora* (New York, 2002). See p. 83.
[33] Ibid., 84.
[34] Ibid., 87.

syncretic. In *Central Africans, Atlantic Creoles, and the Foundation of the Americas, 1585–1660*, Thornton and Heywood provide even greater detail about how the Portuguese used the *soba*, or kings, of the various nations as instruments of conversion and condemnation of the indigenous religion. They recount the experience of the baptism of *soba* Songa, whose territory was close to the kingdom of Kongo, in 1581. This is after the continual campaign of the Portuguese to establish themselves and their religion beyond the kingdom of Kongo and their close neighbors. This *soba* was an in-law to the king of Ndongo (Angola), which was, at this point, resistant to the Portuguese. After his baptism, the king went throughout his territory with the Port priest, "planting crosses in key locations and identifying and burning 'houses of idols' or the shrines dedicated to the *kilundas*."[35] People would bring their idols to these shrines to be destroyed.

Soon another local *soba* sought to be baptized, and his baptism also included a celebration of the recapture of a relic of the Virgin Mary, which was then placed in one of the local shrines as an "object of devotion."[36] The emphasis here is on the "Atlantic creole" culture that was being created in the Kongo region. Much of the discussion centers around how the Port clergy, the Jesuit priests, and even Kongolese secular clergy attempted to spread Christianity throughout protected territories, first through converting the chiefs and elites and then through establishing schools and having people baptized in mass baptisms. They do mention frequently, however, that many of the priests lamented what they thought to be the slowness with which the people abandoned their traditional religious practices. Many of them had to be content with the fact that the people professed themselves to be Christians, adopting Christian names and being baptized. For Thornton and Heywood, in this Atlantic creole culture that they created, leaders would at times discuss which elements of Christianity to adopt and which elements of their traditional religion to abandon.[37]

As the preceding narratives make clear, by the time of the transatlantic slave trade, religions in West Africa and central Africa were poised to make a significant impact on the Americas. When they were forcibly removed from their homelands, Africans had already adopted forms of religious pluralism that enabled them to mix indigenous religious practices and beliefs with monotheistic faith in Islam and Christianity. And just as Africans had knowledge of Islam and Christianity during this period, so were the agents

---

[35] Linda M. Heywood and John K. Thornton, *Central Africans, Atlantic Creoles, and the Foundation of the Americas, 1585–1660* (New York, 2007), 100.
[36] *Ibid.*, 101.
[37] *Ibid.*, 103–4.

of Islam and Christianity privy to the existence of the slave trade, in some cases even aiding and abetting it.

SUGGESTIONS FOR FURTHER READING

Austen, Ralph A. *Trans-Saharan Africa in World History.* Oxford, UK, 2010.

Collins, Roberto O. *Problems in African History: The Pre-Colonial Centuries.* Princeton, 2005.

Ford, Clyde W. *The Hero with an African Face: Mythic Wisdom of Traditional Africa.* New York, 1999.

Murphy, Lewis J. *Why Ostriches Don't Fly and Other Tales from the African Bush.* Englewood, CA, 1997.

Olupona, Jacob K., ed. *African Spirituality: Forms, Meanings and Expressions.* New York, 2000.

Sanders, Todd. *Beyond Bodies, Rainmaking and Sensemaking in Tanzania.* Toronto, 2008.

Thornton, John K. *Africa and Africans in the Making of the Atlantic World, 1400–1800.* Cambridge, MA, 1998.

Section II

RELIGIONS IN THE POST-COLUMBIAN NEW WORLD – 1500–1680s

6

IROQUOIAN RELIGION DURING THE SEVENTEENTH CENTURY

NEAL B. KEATING

The early colonial period of the sixteenth and seventeenth centuries was a time of trauma and devastation for Iroquoian peoples and territories. The historical record of that period is as dramatic and stunning as it is flawed. From the time of first direct contact with Europeans in the 1530s, Iroquoians have been subjects of interest to European writers, largely for reasons of power. In the early seventeenth century a large body of writing about the Iroquoians began developing under the pens of French Jesuit missionaries, whose aims were to destroy Iroquoian and other indigenous religions. Known collectively as the *Jesuit Relations*, in subsequent centuries these writings became the primary source documents for knowing and understanding Iroquoian life in the seventeenth century. Important English and Dutch sources exist as well, but they are far smaller in size and scope. The *Jesuit Relations* were compiled and translated in the early twentieth century into seventy-three volumes. Other important sources for Iroquoian religion during the seventeenth century include indigenous oral traditions, archaeology, linguistics, and later ethnographic research from the nineteenth and twentieth centuries.[1]

The famous "League of the Iroquois" included five different indigenous nations that were united into a permanent league or confederation, arranged through an Iroquoian set of principles known as Gayanashagowa, the "great law of peace." The names of these nations are usually given as the Mohawk, Oneida, Onondaga, Cayuga, and the Seneca. In the early eighteenth century, a sixth nation was added, the Tuscarora. It was the French who used "Iroquois" as a name for these peoples. The English usually referred to them as the League of the Five Nations, and after 1722, the Six Nations. Their name for themselves often was (and still is) a variation of

---

[1] Ruben G. Thwaites, ed., *The Jesuit Relations and Allied Documents: Travels and Explorations of the Jesuit Missionaries in New France, 1601–1791*, 73 vols. (New York, 1896–1901). Hereafter *JR*.

Haudenosaunee, "people building a longhouse." Despite the new stressors introduced with European contact, the Haudenosaunee/Iroquois league resisted colonization and became one of the strongest and most enduring political forces in eastern North America, remaining largely sovereign and self-determining peoples for some three centuries after colonization began. Haudenosaunee power was facilitated through inclusive sociopolitical organization, intersocietal diplomacy, competitive exchange, and strategic military maneuvering, all of which was articulated through religious discourse emphasizing the importance of maintaining good relations with a multidimensional range of human and other sentient persons, and performed through ceremonies of thanksgiving, condolence, dreaming, and healing.[2]

The Haudenosaunee Iroquois are, however, part of a larger linguistic family called "Iroquoian," which includes the Susquehannock, Nottoway, Meherrin, Erie, Wendat/Huron, Neutral, Wenro, Petun, Laurentian, and Cherokee languages, in addition to the six languages of the Haudenosaunee. There are multiple names for all of these groups, and linguists vary in terms of how they subdivide the different languages. These other Iroquoians shared many cultural aspects with the Haudenosaunee Iroquois. In addition to a shared linguistic history, Iroquoian peoples generally shared certain sociopolitical tendencies, an emphasis on ceremonial exchange, mixed horticultural economies, and shared religious discourses and practices. During the seventeenth and eighteenth centuries, along with many Algonkian peoples, all of these other Iroquoian peoples were absorbed into or dispersed by the Haudenosaunee/Iroquois confederacy, except the Cherokee.[3]

In the seventeenth century, there were two regions of the Eastern Woodlands where Iroquoian-speaking peoples lived, one in the South and a larger region in the North. Surrounding the two Iroquoian regions were many different groups of Algonkian-speaking peoples. Most of the Iroquoian-speaking peoples lived in the northern region, which divides into three smaller subareas, including the eastern Great Lakes area (Huron/Wendat, Neutral, Wenro, Petuns, and Eries), the upper St. Lawrence River valley (Laurentians), and the area today known as upstate New York and northern Pennsylvania (Susquehannock and the Haudenosaunee/Five Nations). The Tuscarora, Nottoway, Meherrin, and Cherokee peoples lived

---

[2] Lewis H. Morgan, *League of the Hau-de-no-sau-nee, or Iroquois* [1851] (New York, 1962); Elizabeth Tooker, *An Ethnography of the Huron Indians, 1615–1649* (Syracuse, 1991); and Tooker, *The Iroquois Ceremonial of Midwinter* (Syracuse, 1970).

[3] Floyd G. Lounsbury, "Iroquoian Languages," in Bruce G. Trigger, ed., *Handbook of North American Indians*, vol. 15, *Northeast* (Washington, DC, 1978). Volume 15 is a comprehensive source of Iroquoian ethnology. Hereafter *HNAI* 15.

in the southern region around the piedmont area of North Carolina. In the case of the Haudenosaunee peoples, their geopolitical reach extended well beyond their traditional territories: west throughout much of the Great Lakes region, east to the Atlantic coast, and south as far as Georgia and Mississippi.

The etymology of "Iroquois" is not fully confirmed, but current scholarship posits its origin in a sixteenth-century pidgin Algonkian-Basque language that developed on the Atlantic coast as "hilokoa," which is glossed as "killer people." It is likely that Iroquois is the French version of this earlier Algonkian-Basque name. Without attempting to resolve this nomenclative opacity, the usage of the term Iroquoian is here intended as a general reference to Iroquoian-speaking peoples, and more specific names (Haudenosaunee, Huron/Wendat, Mohawk, etc.) will be used for particular referencing.[4]

PRE-CONTACT SITUATION

At the time of contact, Iroquoian societies were socially organized through matrilineal kinship relations, with mixed foraging and horticultural economies and egalitarian politics. Iroquoian religion reflected these relations, economies, and politics insofar as it was not a hierarchical or dogmatic institution; nor did Iroquois religion support the concentration of power. Iroquoian religion was an open system that more closely fit the shamanic paradigm of religion than it did the stratified religions of agricultural states and empires. Spiritual power was considered to be widely available to all people, varying according to ability and luck.[5]

The development of Iroquoian religion should be understood as emerging within a context of long-distance exchange networks of foraging and horticultural peoples, which have ebbed and flowed in the North American Eastern Woodlands for more than five thousand years. These networks constituted a world system in which the exchange relationships between different societies were important sources of social change within societies. In the Eastern Woodlands world system, the main logic animating these exchange relations was kinship. Archaeological evidence conservatively suggests that such exchange networks began developing in the Woodlands during the late Archaic mast forest adaptation, circa 3000 B.C.E. Over time, the objects exchanged included shells, stones, metals, tobacco, cultigens,

---

[4] Peter Bakker, "A Basque Etymology for the Word 'Iroquois,'" *Man in the Northeast* 40 (1990): 89–93.
[5] See Michael Winkelman, *Shamanism: The Neural Ecology of Consciousness and Healing* (Westport, 2000).

and other materials, much of which was ceremonial and nonutilitarian. Religious ideas, discourses, and languages must have also accompanied these exchanges of materials, including ideas about death, power, the sky, and transformation.[6]

The topography of the Woodlands world system can be envisioned as a well-watered, forested region punctuated by a chain of mountains within which networks of trails connected villages, clusters of villages, and temporary or seasonal camps. The trails were both physical and informational media. Historical evidence supports that many of these trails were lined with visual expressions painted by indigenous people as they traveled. These expressions included painted narrative pictures that were legible to other indigenous travelers, regardless of linguistic differences. The best explanation for such shared comprehension is that the artist-creators of these "tree paintings" used a kin-based visual grammar that was generally understood within the Woodlands world system. It was widely understood because the principles on which it was based were common elements in the lives and societies of the different peoples that constituted the Woodlands system. Interestingly, these tree paintings were usually not legible to Europeans, who required the assistance of indigenous interpreters. Europeans were generally enculturated in an entirely different kinship system.[7]

In the Northeast, the earliest material evidence of clearly circulating religious-like information dates to circa 3000 B.C.E. and consists of a widespread occurrence of red paint in mortuary ceremonialism. Although the maritime region contains the earliest known use of red ocher, it occurs soon after in other late Archaic and early Woodland sites from both sides of the Great Lakes, and it is interpreted as a key component of an "ancient northeastern burial cult." Along with red ochre, the burials typically include various tools and implements, many of which appear to have been intentionally broken or killed. In the late Archaic burials, the remains were commonly cremated, a practice that would fit the cultural logic of nomadic foraging peoples.[8]

---

[6] Richard F. Townsend, ed., *Hero, Hawk, and Open Hand: American Indian Art of the Ancient Midwest and South* (Chicago, 2004); Michael S. Nassaney and Kenneth E. Sassaman, eds., *Native American Interactions: Multiscalar Analyses and Interpretations in the Eastern Woodlands* (Knoxville, TN, 1995); Timothy G. Baugh and Jonathan E. Ericson, eds., *Prehistoric Exchange Systems in North America* (New York, 1994); Randall Collins, "The Geopolitical and Economic World-Systems of Kinship-Based and Agrarian-Coercive Societies," *Review* 15:3 (1992): 373–88; and Christopher Chase-Dunn and Thomas D. Hall, *Core-Periphery Relations in Precapitalist Worlds* (Boulder, 1991).

[7] Neal B. Keating, *Iroquois Art, Power, and History* (Norman, OK, forthcoming).

[8] See Warren K. Moorehead, "The Red Paint People of Maine," *American Anthropologist* 15:1 (1913): 33–47; and James A. Tuck, "Regional Development, 3000 to 300 B.C.," in *HNAI* 15 (1978), 42.

Starting around 100 C.E., red paint mortuary ceremonialism continued to spread and was elaborated in a number of regions in the Woodlands, now associated with horticultural societies. This is particularly the case in the Ohio valley, where peoples known archaeologically as Adena built elaborate earthworks that served a number of different purposes, including large, multilayered burial mounds in which the remains were accompanied by an amazing volume and quality of objects, including representations of multinatural beings. Some Adena earthworks were apparently created for geometrical astronomical alignment, whereas others were gigantic power animal effigy mounds, like horned serpents, which may also have served astronomical purposes. They can be read as constructed cultural landscapes in which a synergistic association between humans, earth, and sky was produced. Such landscapes continued to be built in the Ohio valley during the middle and late Woodland phases by peoples archaeologically known as Hopewell. The emblematic combination of art and earthworks of Adena-Hopewell culture extended eastward into the northern Iroquoian territories. Farther south, in the Mississippi River system, earthwork construction reached yet another level during the later Woodland sequence, resulting in colossal truncated pyramids atop which political power could be symbolically concentrated and administered to large, urban populations, such as that of Cahokia.[9]

Throughout the Woodland sequence, cultigens originating in Mesoamerica and South America spread northward, most notably varieties of corn, beans, squash, and tobacco. It is likely that new religious discourses accompanied them, for example, ideas about the alignment of stars and farming practices. In the Northeast at the time of contact, it was Iroquoian peoples who had adapted to economies that were no longer based entirely on foraging, but included substantial cultivation of these plants. The peoples living in the region south of Lake Erie and just east of the Adena-Hopewell region were Iroquoian-speaking peoples, known as the Eriehronon, or Erie peoples. Furthermore, a number of the personas in the stories of Iroquoian oral traditions, such as horned serpents, correspond with the imagery of Adena-Hopewell artworks. So too does some of the key symbolism of Haudenosaunee ritual, such as the ceremonial deer antlers of office that are taken up by the Haudenosaunee league *royaaner*, "peace chiefs," on their appointment. All of these correspondences suggest

---

[9] The multinatural perspective is discussed in the following, drawing on Eduardo Vivieros de Castro, "Cosmological Deixis and Amerindian Perspectivism," *The Journal of the Royal Anthropological Institute* 4:3 (1998): 469–88. For discussion of Adena-Hopewell culture expanding into Iroquoian territories, see "Champlain Site" in Edmund S. Carpenter, *Two Essays: Chief and Greed* (North Andover, MA, 2008).

exchange relations existed between different peoples, including Iroquoian, Adena-Hopewell, Mississippian, and Mesoamerican peoples.[10]

The northern Iroquoians appear to have developed at least two large political leagues or confederacies at the time of contact, one in what is now Ontario and the other in what is now New York State. The Wendat/ Huron peoples formed a confederacy on the east side of Lake Huron, by the Georgian Bay, which in the 1630s included four Iroquoian nations: the Attignawantan, Attigneenongnhac, Arendahronon, and the Tohontaenrat. The Haudenosaunee peoples formed the other confederacy, also known as the Five Nations League of the Iroquois. Some have argued that the league formed as a post-contact response to the behavior of the Europeans and to the rapid development of the fur trade. More have argued that the confederacy originated prior to European contact in response to local pressures, such as those circulating within an indigenous world system. Haudenosaunee oral traditions support a pre-contact confederacy formation, as does the general archaeological sequence of changing settlement patterns in New York State during the late Woodland phase, possibly in the twelfth century (C.E.).[11]

The Five Nations of the Haudenosaunee league physically existed as five clusters of villages or towns, each surrounded by large expanses of resource territories for farming, hunting, fishing, gathering, and so on, through which people cycled on a seasonal basis. The populations of settlements varied, from several hundred people to well over a thousand. Multifamily residential units consisted of bark and sapling longhouses of variable lengths, ranging from 25 to more than 300 feet. The number of longhouses per settlement varied, containing anywhere from five to twenty or more longhouses.[12]

A kinship-based mode of production prevailed in these societies in which the division of labor followed lines of gender and age, and the general principle of reciprocity was the normative frame of reference. The organization of households and settlements generally operated through bifurcated

---

[10] Lynn Ceci, "Watchers of the Pleiades: Ethnoastronomy among Native Cultivators in Northeastern North America," *Ethnohistory* 25:4 (1978): 301–17; Marian E. White, "Erie," in *HNAI* 15 (1978), 412–17; James B. Griffin, "The Iroquois in American Prehistory," *Papers of the Michigan Academy of Science, Arts, and Letters* 29:4 (1944): 357–73; and Miguel Covarrubias, *The Eagle, the Jaguar, and the Serpent: Indian Art of the Americas* (New York, 1954).

[11] The Wendat confederacy is enumerated in *JR* 16: 227. For the post-contact confederacy formation hypothesis, see George T. Hunt, *The Wars of the Iroquois: A Study in Intertribal Trade Relations* (Madison, 1940). For a nuanced argument for pre-contact confederation, see Georges E. Sioui, *Huron Wendat: The Heritage of the Circle* (Vancouver, 1999).

[12] For discussion of longhouse architecture, see Dean R. Snow, *The Iroquois* (Cambridge, MA, 1994).

merging networks of kinship that emphasized matrilineal families, known in Mohawk as *owachiras,* and more commonly referred to as the clan system. Oral traditions suggest *owachiras* were created by the people as a way of dividing themselves into more manageable subgroups that could then assist one another in times of mourning and for other religious ceremonies. Through their organization of families, marriages, and alliances, *owachira* networks not only organized the internal structure of society, but also provided mechanisms for integrating new members within the group, as well as developing new relationships with other, more distant groups. The residential longhouse was typically a multifamily dwelling, which in times of relative stability housed families related to one another through *owachiras.* Some have argued that entire villages at one point were organized within a single *owachira,* although it is more likely that each village contained multiple lineage groups.[13]

Villages and towns were periodically shifted over time, usually ten to twenty years, depending on environmental and/or political factors. The larger settlements were generally located within proximity to rivers and/or lakes. Immediately surrounding the villages were cultivated fields of corn, beans, and squash. Beyond these were diverse hardwood and mast forests of oak, hickory, chestnut, beech, elm, basswood, ash, birch, pine, cedar, linden, alder, and willow, among others. The main material products of Iroquois culture were cultigens, and the primary producers of these were generally women, who in addition to cultivating plants also gathered wild plants and fruits. Hunting was largely a male practice. Fishing was perhaps less gendered but was also an important contribution to the economy.[14]

CONTACT SITUATION

The earliest direct contacts between indigenous peoples and Europeans in northeastern North America took place on the Atlantic coasts, probably starting in the 1480s. After this, new information and European trade goods began to circulate through the Woodlands world system, much faster

---

[13] William N. Fenton, "Iroquoian Culture History: A General Evaluation," *Symposium on Cherokee and Iroquois Culture, Bureau of American Ethnology Bulletin* 180 (1961): 253–77; Heidi Bohaker, "Nindoodemag: The Significance of Algonquian Kinship Networks in the Eastern Great Lakes Region, 1600–1701," *William and Mary Quarterly* 63:1 (2006): 23–52; and Thomas Porter, *Clanology: Clan System of the Iroquois* (Akwesasne Mohawk Nation Territory, 1993).

[14] For a general description, see William Englebrecht, *Iroquoia: The Development of a Native World* (Syracuse, 2003). Gender is discussed in Barbara A. Mann, *The Gantowisas* (New York, 2001), and in William N. Fenton, "Northern Iroquoian Culture Patterns," in *HNAI* 15 (1978), 296–321.

than did Europeans themselves. By the 1520s, European iron and copper were moving through western Haudenosaunee communities.[15]

The first documented direct contact between any Iroquoian peoples and Europeans took place in the St. Lawrence River region in 1534 during Jacques Cartier's first voyage to the "new world." The initial encounter proved to be a sneak preview of what was to come. There, in the Bay of Gaspé, Cartier kidnapped two young Iroquoian men named Dom Agaya and Taignoagny. They lived to return with Cartier during his second voyage in 1535. On this voyage Cartier traveled farther up the St. Lawrence River to the large Iroquoian towns of Stadacona and Hochelaga. Stadacona later became the site of Quebec City, and Hochelaga became Montreal. In his departure, Cartier kidnapped more than two dozen Iroquoian people from Stadacona, including one of the leaders of Stadacona, named Donnacona. As far as is known, none of them ever returned home. Cartier returned once more in 1541; there is little record of that voyage, but enough to suggest that the Iroquoians this time attacked Cartier's group and forced them to leave in 1543. For the next sixty years there is no documented evidence of further direct Iroquoian-European contact. In 1603, Samuel Champlain retraced Cartier's voyages; by then Stadacona and Hochelaga were abandoned.[16]

Between Cartier's and Champlain's arrivals, it is estimated that the northern Iroquoian population overall was about 95,000, with 22,000 of them Haudenosaunee. If we include the Laurentian Iroquoians of Stadacona and Hochelaga, the pre-contact Iroquoian population was likely well over 100,000 people. Cartier's arrival heralded a new period of disease, death, war, contestation, and upheaval. Iroquoian peoples were not at all passive in their response. They entered into numerous relationships with the colonizers, and at least in the case of the Haudenosaunee Iroquoians, they successfully maintained a relatively high degree of autonomy in terms economic, religious, political, territorial, and visual.[17]

Daniel K. Richter argues that during the early colonial era, Iroquoian culture was importantly transformed by four "ordeals" that Iroquoian

---

[15] Basques, Bretons, and other European fishermen were actively fishing in the Grand Banks region during this time (Englebrecht, *Iroquoia*, 133).

[16] Jacques Cartier, *The Voyages of Jacques Cartier* (Toronto, 1993). Cartier's third voyage is interpreted in Barbara A. Mann and Jerry L. Fields, "A Sign in the Sky: Dating the League of the Haudenosaunee," *American Indian Culture and Research Journal* 21:2 (1997): 105–63. See also *The Works of Samuel de Champlain*, ed. Henry P. Biggar, 6 vols. (Toronto, 1922–36 [1626]).

[17] Estimates are based on Snow, *Iroquois*, 88. See also Daniel K. Richter, *The Ordeal of the Longhouse: The Peoples of the Iroquois League in the Era of European Colonization* (Williamsburg, 1992); and Matthew Dennis, *Cultivating a Landscape of Peace* (New York, 1993).

peoples underwent, which dramatically altered the political demography of the Northeast. These ordeals included massive depopulation from imported disease, a rapid slide into economic dependence on trade with Europeans, ensnarement in the imperial struggles of powerful French and English colonizers, and eventually, direct incursions on Iroquoian territories and sovereignties. These ordeals were by no means unique to Iroquoians; what is unique in the historical record is the demonstrated Haudenosaunee capacity to withstand and survive these ordeals. Almost all the other tribal nations in the Northeast were destroyed by them. The reasons for this likely center on two cultural advantages that Richter analyzes: the extensive Haudenosaunee practice of adopting and integrating war captives, refugees, and others into Haudenosaunee society; and the political-spiritual discourse of the Gayanashagowa, which provided a basis for extensive intersocietal diplomacy. In both adoption practices and political discourses, the key is the *owachiras* – the dynamic kinship networks – within which newcomers were incorporated, and from which the political structure of the confederacy originated.[18]

Contact with Europeans led to repeated waves of disease epidemics that killed many Iroquoian peoples. The most deadly of these diseases were smallpox, typhus, and measles. Not only were Iroquoian peoples new to these diseases, but their settlement patterns of relatively large and densely populated towns provided ideal vectors for rapid spread of these pathogens. The first of these epidemics may have begun in the sixteenth century, following Cartier's initial contact with Iroquoians at Stadaconna and Hochelaga; this is one of the leading hypotheses about why these two large towns were depopulated sometime between 1536 and 1603. It is difficult to confirm this because the documentary record for European disease epidemics in Iroquoian populations does not begin until a century later, in the 1630s. The estimates of mortality for Iroquoian peoples during the 1630s and 1640s are very high, ranging from 84 to 95 percent. Reports of intermittent epidemics in different Iroquoian settlements continue throughout the seventeenth century.[19]

In addition to massive depopulation by disease, post-contact Iroquoian societies were chronically stressed by the political struggles for domination introduced by competing European polities; by the new economies of fur, beads, iron, and guns; and by the presence of Jesuit missionaries in their territories and communities. In the face of these stressors, many

---

[18] Richter, *Ordeal of the Longhouse*, 2–3.
[19] William A. Starna, "The Biological Encounter: Disease and the Ideological Domain," *American Indian Quarterly* 16:4 (1992): 511–19; and Richter, *Ordeal of the Longhouse*, 59 n313.

indigenous societies collapsed, fragmented, or disappeared altogether. However, the Haudenosaunee response was different. The Haudenosaunee responded by engaging in aggressive campaigns to repopulate their nations through "absorbing" other peoples, such as the Wendat/Huron and other Iroquoians, as well as Algonkians. This was achieved through a variety of different means of persuasion and coercion, including raids, wars, councils, charisma, and invitation. *Rotihshennakéhte,* "they carry the name," is a Mohawk term used to refer to the category of adoptees and indicates a key dynamism of the *owachira* system, its flexibility to incorporate new members within subgroups. By "absorption" it is meant that those who survived the process were adopted into Haudenosaunee *owachiras* and became *rotihshennakéhte*. By 1650 it is likely that approximately 75 percent or more of the Haudenosaunee were *rotihshennakéhte*. According to an Iroquoian oral tradition, more than 150 different nations of indigenous peoples were "brought into" or absorbed into the Haudenosaunee confederacy during the seventeenth and eighteenth centuries. That a political and cultural structure such as the Haudenosaunee could endure through such enormous demographic transitioning suggests that there must have been something very enigmatic about the ideas on which it was based.[20]

IROQUOIAN ONTOLOGY

As in many other Woodlands traditions, seventeenth-century Iroquoian ontology posited the universe as three different worlds: a sky world above, a water world below, and an earth world in the middle. The creation of the earth is a result of interactions between beings in the sky world and the water world. *Orenda* is a generic Iroquoian term for power that suffuses the entirety of the universe. Humans and other persons make variable use of this power in their lives to achieve desired outcomes. Given its correspondence with many other similar theories from indigenous societies around the world, it is likely that the theory of *orenda* has its roots in a paleo-shamanic hunter-gatherer adaptation. The Jesuit chroniclers of the seventeenth century apparently never noticed or wrote about *orenda* as an indigenous ontology, but it can be read out from their excoriations of Iroquoian ceremonies of healing and well-being. For example, there are numerous tirades in the *Jesuit Relations* about Iroquoian "sorcerers, witches, demons, and soothsayers"; the most commonly recorded Iroquoian names

---

[20] For "absorption," see Francis Jennings, *The Ambiguous Iroquois Empire: The Covenant Chain Confederation of Indian Tribes with English Colonies from Its Beginnings to the Lancaster Treaty of 1744* (New York, 1984). *Rotihshennakéhte* is described in Porter, *Clanology*. Oral tradition from James Sky, *Cayuga Faithkeeper* (1999).

for these shamanic practitioners was *arendiouwane*, translated as "his *orenda* is great / one whose *orenda* is great."²¹

It was not until the turn of the twentieth century that the first documented linguistic analysis of *orenda* terminology was made. On the basis of linguistic data collected from living Iroquoian speakers, J. N. B. Hewitt described *orenda* as a "mystic potence" or a "magic power" that permeates the natural world, and the existence of *orenda* as a fundamental postulate not only for Iroquoians, but for all those peoples he described as "savage" and "primeval." The general theory is that through ritual actions, persons can access and use *orenda*, either for health and well-being (*kariwiio* in modern Mohawk, or "good mind") or for destructive and deadly purposes (*otgon*, "witchcraft"). Hewitt made a direct correlation between *orenda* and other related indigenous theories, such as those represented by the Siouan term *wakan* and the Algonkian term "manitou"; he argued that all are animistic philosophies, that is, they presume the universe is alive. The term "animism" came into modern usage with Edmund B. Tylor in 1871 as a category of religion characteristic of so-called savage society. For Tylor, animism is the idea that nature is populated by conscious sentient beings, and that this "belief in spiritual beings" originated as a result of human consciousness engaged with the human predicaments of death and dreaming. Tylor's formulation was that of a continuum: the less evolved a culture, the more animist it was; primitive culture was more animist than civilized culture. But his was a continuum of error, because any belief in spirits was for Tylor incompatible with the scientific viewpoint that spirits do not really exist. This view is problematic because it objectifies indigenous theory and further suggests the theory is erroneous.²²

The religious perspective of pre-contact and early contact Iroquoian peoples accommodated many different kinds of spirits and spiritual forces and so has been consistently classified as an animistic religion. A more process-based understanding of how *orenda* existed and operated in Iroquoian culture requires thinking beyond Tylor's "belief in spirits," and also considering the pragmatic relations between humans and nature, and between humans and other humans. Underlying these relations are ontological presumptions about personhood and the body. Iroquoian ontologies of bodies and persons were quite different from those of the Europeans, on

---

[21] John N. B. Hewitt, "Orenda," in *Handbook of American Indians North of Mexico*, ed. Frederick W. Hodge. Bureau of American Ethnology Bulletin, 2:30 (Washington, DC, 1912): 178.

[22] John N. B. Hewitt, "Orenda and a Definition of Religion," *American Anthropologist*, new series 4:1 (1902): 33–46; Edward B. Tylor, *Primitive Culture* (New York, 1958 [1871]) I: 424; and Nurit Bird-David, "'Animism' Revisited: Personhood, Environment, and Relational Identity," *Current Anthropology* 40 (1999): 567–91.

the basis of the high frequency with which the Jesuit missionary-writers denounced them.

Recently, the idea of "multinatural perspectivism" has been advanced as a more phenomenological approach to the understanding of animism, and as one that can help to develop a more nuanced understanding of *orenda*. This theory is an analytical improvement on the Tylorean conception of animism, for it posits indigenous theory about spirits as a valid ontology of subjective personhood. The perspectivist model suggests that all human experience of reality is subjective, that indigenous experiences of reality are no less inaccurate than those of Europeans, and that what is grouped into "the savage slot" as animism has in general served as a highly successful strategy of human adaptation. It suggests that we consider non-, extra-, or metahuman beings or spirits as sentient persons who experience their subjective selves much as humans do. This upends the conventional Western view that generally presumes the existence of one nature, and many cultures. Instead it suggests one culture from which emerge multiple bodily natures.[23]

The multinatural perspective is evident in the *Jesuit Relations*, which suggests that the way in which Iroquoian persons regularly experienced their subjective selves was that each body was a multiplex consisting of two or more different kinds of indwelling entities or souls, what some referred to as the sensitive soul (*khiondhecwi* in Wendat/Huron) and the thinking soul (*endionrra*, or *oki andaérandi*). The Jesuit Brebeuf translated *oki andaérandi* as "like a demon, counterfeiting a demon." The contexts in which *okis* were described are related to *orenda*, and they suggest that an *oki* was a personification of the general energy of *orenda*. Thus people who stood out from the crowd through special ability or charisma were sometimes called *okis*. In at least one case, *oki* is used to reference an advanced level of shamanic development. Ihongwaha was a Wendat/Huron dreamer in 1636 who through fasting reportedly transformed into an *oki*, which was understood as a more powerful status than an *arendiwane*, or healer. In another account of transformation from Iroquoian oral tradition, the grandson of Skywoman, Iouskeha, was said to have on one occasion changed into an *oki*, a horned being named Tehonrressandeen. At other times *okis* are described as distinct beings that dwell within the bodies of *arendiwane* healers, enhancing their abilities to diagnose and treat illness. As indwellers of humans, *okis* were sometimes described as the persons who reveal the hidden desires of the other soul within the body. *Okis* are also mentioned in nonhuman contexts, as indwellers of lucky fishing nets, certain rocks, the

---

[23] Vivieros de Castro, "Cosmologial Deixis."

sky, particularly strong animals, and loud thunder.[24] What is common in all these different usages is the association with unusual agency and power; *okis* are entities who as indwellers provide their variable hosts with their effective force, and as stand-alone entities are persons of great power, usually greater than that of human healers. But like humans, *okis* are receptive to gifts of tobacco. Of course, the Jesuits rejected *okis* as satanic devils and demonized them in the bilingual prayers they taught to their Iroquoian neophytes. Yet on at least one occasion, an Iroquoian speaker used the term *oki* to reference the Christians' god.[25]

Another aspect of the multiplex self in seventeenth-century Iroquoian ontology was the potential capacity of person-souls to travel, to leave their bodies, to go into other existing bodies (human or nonhuman), or to transform into new bodies. This capacity to travel, combined with the cohabitation of different souls within the body, meant that life was experienced in a distinctive way. Considering that other animals and beings experienced their selves as multiplex human animals do, one can begin to understand why the maintenance of good relationships was emphasized in Iroquoian ceremony. A successful adaptation to this kind of complex multinatural environment would require developing the perceptive capacity to relate to these other beings, and to create and maintain good relations with them. To simply reject such ontologies as animistic delusions in no way clarifies how such a worldview might actually have served an adaptive advantage as a type of embedded ecology.[26]

Other examples of Iroquoian multinatural perspectivism are evident in the pan-Iroquoian epic tradition of world creation, and the specifically Haudenosaunee epic tradition of the founding of the Great League of Peace. Neither of these traditions are strictly chronological linear histories,

---

[24] See *JR* 10: 49 for *khiondhecwi, endionrra,* and *oki andaérandi,* and for gifted people; *JR* 10: 199 for the account of Ihongwaha; *JR* 10: 135 for Tehonrressandeen (probably a horned serpent); *JR* 39: 21 for indwellers in *arendiouannens*; *JR* 17: 155 for *okis* revealing hidden desires, known as *ondinoc*; *JR* 17: 199 for *okis* in fishing nets; *JR* 10: 167 for *oki ca ichikhon* (rock); *JR* 10: 161 for the sky *oki*; *JR* 39: 25 for strong animals; *JR* 10: 195 for *onditachiaé* (thunder *oki*). Also see John N. B. Hewitt, "The Iroquoian Concept of the Soul," *The Journal of American Folklore* 8:29 (1895): 107–16.

[25] E.g., from a prayer taught to Wendat converts: *serrewa itondi; din de Oki esoniatoata ondayee d'okiasti,* "and the wicked ones who through poison cause death, turn them away also" (*JR* 10: 71). See *JR* 15: 49 for reference to the Christian God as an *oki*.

[26] Within environmental studies, indigenous perspectivist ontologies are receiving new attention as worldviews of the relational nature of life on earth. See Alexandre Surrallés and Pedro G. Hierro, eds., *The Land Within: Indigenous Territory and the Perception of Environment* (Copenhagen, 2005); and *Animism: Respecting the Living World* (New York, 2006).

but that should not lead to their rejection as valid understandings of the past. As a way of repatriating these epics, Anthony F. C. Wallace suggested that many societies produce "historias" rather than linear histories. By "historias," Wallace referred to cosmogonic frameworks of time that are not based on linear chronology, but are based on key events that generally answer several fundamental questions of existence: where we come from, what we are like, and where we are going.[27]

In the Iroquoian oral traditions of the creation of the world, animals and spirits are people who collaborate in creating the earth on the back of a turtle. These traditions have been documented intermittently, starting in the early seventeenth century, and they continue to circulate in the twenty-first century. More than forty versions have been recorded, starting with Gabriel Sagard's Huron/Wendat version dating to 1632. There is a demonstrable structural continuity in the different versions over close to four centuries, so much so that it has led some ethnohistorians to assure readers that this pattern of continuity is no mere ethnological freak specimen, but an indication of substantial cultural survival within Haudenosaunee societies.[28]

The Iroquoian creation epic fits into the archetypal category of the Earth Diver myths, which are distributed around the world. A general synthesis of the account is as follows. The places that already exist in the beginning are in the sky and in the water. The beings that lived in the sky lived and looked much like Iroquoian peoples. The beings that lived in the water lived as animals, but with full communicative ability, much like people. Although the explanatory details vary, ultimately a tree is uprooted in the sky world, leaving a hole in the ground through which a woman from the sky world descends toward the water world below. In the seventeenth century, she was known as Aataentsic in Wendat/Huron, Iage^n'tci in Seneca, and Eia'tage^n'tci in Onondaga, translated as "Mature Flowers" or "Fertile Flower." She became known as Skywoman in the twentieth century. As she descended from the sky, water birds (usually geese, sometimes ducks or seagulls) flew up and caught her and brought her down gently to rest on Turtle's back. At the same time, a number of different animals attempted to reach the bottom of the water world to bring up some mud to spread on Turtle's back. One of them, usually a muskrat, finally succeeded. When Aataentsic landed, she then spread out the mud, and it began to grow. She

---

[27] Anthony F. C. Wallace, "The Consciousness of Time," *Anthropology of Consciousness* 16:2 (2008): 1–15.

[28] George M. Wrong, ed., *The Long Journey to the Country of the Hurons by Father Gabriel Sagard* (Toronto, 1939 [1632]). See Snow, *Iroquois*; and William N. Fenton, "This Island, the World on the Turtle's Back," *Journal of American Folklore* 75:298 (1962): 283–300.

created a giant island on Turtle's back. It became the earth world, known in Wendat/Huron as Wendat Ahen, "this old island."[29]

In many versions Aataentsic is pregnant during all of this, and she gives birth to a daughter on Turtle Island. When her daughter matures, she becomes mysteriously pregnant with twin boys. She dies during childbirth, the result of one of her sons deciding to come out through her armpit rather than through the birth canal. This son was named Tawiskaron, "flint," and the other was named Iouskeha, "sapling," or Tharonhyawakon, "skyholder." Unlike the twin boy-gods in the Mayan Popul Vuh, Iouskeha and Tawiskaron do not work together but instead fight each other. Eventually Iouskeha vanquishes his brother, but in the course of their turbulence, they modify the earth and create the different animal populations. In twentieth-century versions, it is explained that Iouskeha created the humans and animals like deer, birds, and fish and tried to create a world that was pleasant for the humans, whereas Tawiskaron cared not for humans, instead preferring to make their life as difficult as possible. Tawiskaron made the poisonous snakes, spiders, black flies, and other dangerous and irritating animals. In the seventeenth century, Iroquoian traditions state that Iouskeha became the sun, while his grandmother Aataentsic became the moon. All of these persons have great *orenda*.[30]

Another key oral tradition in Iroquoian culture is that of the founding of the Haudenosaunee Great League of Peace. As with the creation tradition, the league tradition provides narrative evidence of how *orenda* is understood, although in this tradition *orenda* is used by humans for achieving human goals: putting an end to war and cannibalism, and establishing a framework for extending peace among nations through confederation. There are multiple versions of the tradition. Although the earliest recorded narrative account of the league tradition was not made until 1743, references to the league are contained in documents as early as 1634, including its name, written as *kanosoni*, "extended house." In 1654 the Jesuits recorded the league's name as Hotinnonchiendi, "the completed cabin."[31] As with the creation tradition, the league tradition continued to be salient in Haudenosaunee communities during the later centuries, and it remains culturally relevant in the twenty-first century.

---

[29] Alan Dundes, "Earth Diver: Creation of the Mythopoetic Male," *American Anthropologist* 64:5 (1962): 1032–51; and Arthur C. Parker, "Fundamental Factors in Seneca Folklore," *New York State Museum Bulletin* 253 (1924): 49–66.

[30] *JR* 10: 129–33; Parker, "Factors," 52; Hewitt, "Iroquoian."

[31] For *kanosoni*, see Charles T. Gehring and William A. Starna, eds., *A Journey into Mohawk and Oneida Country 1634–1635, By H. M. van den Bogaert* (Syracuse, 1988). For Hotinnonchiendi, see *JR* 41: 87.

The league tradition centers on an Iroquoian visionary prophet and culture hero named Dekanawida (also known as Peacemaker), whose prophetic vision of peace was accepted by the Five Nations and became the basis of the league. In most accounts, Dekanawida possesses much *orenda*, and like the twins in the tradition of creation, he is the product of a multinatural marriage between a Wendat/Huron woman and an undetermined male spirit person. He was born on the north side of Lake Ontario. His childhood was filled with passages of trials, culminating in his departure in a white stone canoe, in which he crossed the great lake and then made his way into Mohawk territory. In the tradition, Dekanawida uses *orenda* to make peoples' minds work well, to help them process and work through grief and sorrow, to regain mental clarity, and to develop the capacity to unite with other clear minds.

The tradition states that before the coming of the league, the Five Nations were locked into a growing cycle of internecine violence, which many have described as "mourning wars," wars in which one group (A) raids another group (B) in response to prior raids by group B on group A. The motives of revenge and replacement are driven by the mourning and grieving over the loss of family members. Dekanawida's vision was that of putting an end to such violence. One of the main antagonists in the league tradition was the Onondaga personage of Tadodaho, who embodied the condition of all-out war; he too had powerful *orenda*, but he used it for *otgon*, "maleficent witchcraft." Furthermore, he was a cannibal, and rather than hair on his head, Tadodaho had snakes. Tadodaho represented the opposite of what Dekanawida symbolizes. The imagery of snakes coming out of Tadodaho's head, combined with his stated proclivity for cannibalism, suggests to some that Dekanawida's plan was opposed by factions within the Five Nations, including a cannibalistic snake cult. The tradition states that Dekanawida met with much opposition. A key moment in this tradition is when Dekanawida combed out the snakes from Tadodaho's head/mind. Yet were it not for some key allies, Dekanawida's plan might not have worked.[32]

Hiawatha (or Aionwatha) is another important figure in the league tradition, who in most accounts joins with Dekanawida to deliver the Gayanashagowa to the nations. Aionwatha was usually portrayed as an Onondaga leader, and unlike either Dekanawida or Tadodaho, fully human by birth. He was himself a victim of *otgon*, possibly at the hands of Tadodaho himself. Through witchcraft, his seven daughters were murdered, causing Aionwatha to leave his home and wander off into the woods, insane with grief. In his travels he created an effective means of condoling and

---

[32] Mann and Fields, "Sign in the Sky."

overcoming intense grief and mourning brought about by death, using strings of shell beads as a primary medium for conveying and visually supporting spoken words of condolence. As he developed the ceremony, Dekanawida stepped forward and performed the first condolence ceremony on Aionwatha himself, after which Aionwatha became clear-minded again and became the leading spokesman for Dekanawida's plan. The use of shell beads in association with spoken words of condolence became a key ritual mechanism for extending the new social order suggested by the Gayanashagowa, itself a manifestation of *orenda*.

IROQUOIAN CEREMONIAL PRACTICE

The Jesuits regularly denounced indigenous cosmology and its related ceremonial practices, so much so that a basic reading strategy for decolonizing the past they documented is to determine what practices and theories the Jesuits most regularly condemned during the seventeenth century and then presume those were key components of Iroquoian religiosity. Although certainly not foolproof, it seems to work in the case of the Jesuits, for they were rather direct and consistent in their assessment of what got in the way of successful Christian proselytization of Iroquoians; it was "their dreams, dances, sweats, and feasts." With the exception of sweats, these often went together. Tooker argued that Iroquoian ceremonies in the seventeenth century generally followed a basic four-part structure: (1) thanksgiving speech, (2) performance of the specific ceremony, (3) thanksgiving speech, and (4) feasting. Although the Jesuits thought them to be without merit, in these ceremonies it appears the Iroquoians' general objective was that of returning thanks and maintaining reciprocal relations within a multinatural world. In that way they can be thought of as ceremonies of communication in which the performance constitutes the information and its transmission. Through such communication, Iroquoians self-managed their health and well-being, thought to heavily depend on the maintenance of good relations with other spirit beings.[33]

Dreaming and dream enactment are very clear examples of this. Seventeenth-century Iroquoian ceremonies associated with dreams were described at length in the *Jesuit Relations*. In addition to the practice of dreaming itself, related ceremonies included dream interpretation and dream enactment, ceremonies known generally as *ononharoias*, "turning the brain upside down, or festival of dreams." The *ononharoia* was a flexible

---

[33] Le Mercier, writing in 1638, *JR* 15: 127. See Tooker, *Midwinter*, 7. It seems that sweats were part of Wendat/Huron culture, but not part of Haudenosaunee culture (*JR* 6: 189; 29: 157; 68: 73).

community ceremony aimed at interpreting the meanings of dreams and then enacting those dreams as closely as possible. It often involved dance, song, and feasts.[34] Dreaming was another experience of existence, as real and as valid as the experience of existence in an awakened state of consciousness. The Iroquoian experience of dreams utilized a theory of mind that in many regards resembles that of contemporary mainstream psychology, in which dreams are interpreted as the secret desires of the soul. In the Jesuits' opinions, Iroquoian peoples treated their dreams as if the dreams were divine gods, that is, as if they had to be obeyed.[35]

In the Iroquoian theory, it is through dreams that the secret desires of the soul are made known. In Wendat, the desirous part of the soul was named *gonennoncwal,* "the soul desiring, wanting," and the actual desires or wishes were called *ondinonc* or *ondinnonk*; thus one might have said, *ondayee ihaton onennoncwat,* "that is what my heart says to me, that is what my appetite desires." The fulfillment of these desires/*ondinnonk* was important not just for the individual dreamer, but also for the well-being of the community. According to Hewitt's analysis, the connection between dreams and cosmology is evident insofar as the secret wishes/*ondinnonk* inside the soul were considered expressions of Iouskeha, planted there by Iouskeha's agentive *oki*. Therefore the proper interpretation and fulfillment of dreams is vital to the maintenance of good relations with a most powerful person, Skyholder. Successful fulfillment of the *ondinnonk* promoted well-being, whereas failure to fulfill or properly interpret the dream meant illness and possibly death, as the frustrated soul would likely revolt against the body.[36] *Ondinnonk* varied from objects to actions. They might be desires for particular things, or else for certain kinds of dances, feasts, or other ceremonies. On at least one occasion, an Iroquoian dreamer's *ondinnonk* called for an *andacwander* rite, which was described by the Jesuits as "a mating of men with girls." In this particular *andacwander*, the dreamer called for twelve girls, and a thirteenth for himself.[37]

More commonly, *ondinnonk* called for dances. Although dances were performed for social pleasure, many Iroquoian dances were motivated by ceremonial reasons, including religion, healing, protection, war, and success. In 1536, during the first recorded contact between an Iroquoian and a European, the Iroquois leader, Donnaconna, initiated the meeting with

---

[34] As translated in JR 10: 173. In 1895 Hewitt offered a different translation for *ononharoia*, which he spelled as *ka-nen-hwa-ro-ri*, "literally a driving or propelling of the brain, but meaning laterally to roar or mumble" (Hewitt, "Iroquoian," 111).

[35] Anthony F. C. Wallace, "ND Dreams and Wishes of the Soul: A Type of Psychoanalytic Theory Among the Seventeenth-Century Iroquois," *American Anthropologist* 60:2 (1958): 234–48.

[36] *JR* 10: 141; 17: 155; 33: 191; and Hewitt, "Iroquoian."

[37] *JR* 17: 147.

Jacques Cartier via a shamanic-type performance combining dance and singing, probably intended to assess the natures of Cartier and company. The first in-depth description of Iroquoian dancing is from Gabriel Sagard's 1623/24 visit to the Wendat/Huron; he reported that Huron dancing was usually carried out for several reasons: to contact spirits, to welcome someone, to rejoice, or to heal illness. As a quick index of Sagard's estimation of the efficacy of Iroquoian dance (and ritual more generally), consider his chapter title: "Their Dances, Songs, and Other Silly Ceremonies."[38]

The Jesuit Brebeuf reported the existence of at least twelve different ceremonial dances that were performed in Wendat territory during the 1630s. There were probably many more than that. Such dances were often community-wide or multicommunity events that involved extensive preparations, including body modification through fasting or decoration, feast preparation, and spatial rearrangement. The two dances that Brebeuf described were both clearly ceremonial and were likely related to recent outbreaks of French-borne smallpox epidemics. He wrote that in the dance called Akhrendoiaen, "those who take part in this dance give poison to one another." The other dance he described was called Otakrendoiae, in which dancers supposedly attempted to kill each other by throwing "charms" at each other, "composed of Bears' claws, Wolves' teeth, Eagles' talons, certain stones, and Dogs' sinews." A Wendat name for charms was *ascwandies*, which was translated as both charms and "familiar demons." What were poisons and charms to the Jesuits were to the Iroquoians most likely medicines that were being danced to increase their *orenda*, and thus their ability to protect Iroquoians from the strange and deadly illnesses that were suddenly sweeping through their towns.[39]

Feasting also had strong ceremonial connotations, associated with powerful healing outcomes, including the power to restore life to the dead. A seventeenth-century Iroquoian tradition explained that a long-tailed lionlike animal named Ontarraoura once resuscitated a murdered hunter in the course of a giant feast, perhaps a reference to the powerful Iroquoian medicine known as "the little water medicine." This constituted a strong symbolic association between feasting and spiritual healing. Brebeuf claimed that all of the different kinds of feasts could be reduced to four different types. These are Athataion, "the feast of farewells"; Enditeuhwa, a feast "of thanksgiving and gratitude"; Atouront aochien, "a feast for singing as well as for eating"; and Awataerohi, "for deliverance from a sickness." However, he provided no additional explanations about these feasts.[40]

---

[38] Cartier, *Voyages*; Wrong, *Sagard*, 115.
[39] *JR* 10: 205–7; 17: 159.
[40] *JR* 10: 177.

RELIGIOUS LEADERSHIP

Religious leaders in Iroquoian societies were generally healers working in a variety of different areas, including divination, diagnosis, and treatment of illness. Some of the Jesuits attempted to distinguish different kinds of healers. The most commonly recorded name for healers is *arendiouane* (Wendat, plural: *arendiouannens*). The Mohawk cognate is *agotsinnachen*. Other Wendat names for healers included *ocata* or *saokata* and *ontetsans* or *aretsan*. In addition to the diagnosis and treatment of illness, *arendiouannens* reportedly practiced weather control and clairvoyance. In diagnosing human illness, successful *arendiouannens* were able to successfully interpret dreams and determine patients' *ondinnonk*.[41] Perhaps no other Iroquoians came under as harsh a critique by the Jesuits as did the *arendiouannens*, who appear to have been the main competition for the Jesuits. The *arendiouannens* occupied the social status that the Jesuits coveted – that of spiritual leader. This disregard appears to have been mutual. Not only did the *arendiouannens* also sense the status competition, but from their multinatural perspective they also regarded the Jesuits as metahuman agents of death. A common Iroquoian name for the Jesuits was *genherontatie*, "the dead or dying man who walks."[42]

One fairly well-documented and recursive scenario in which this competition played out was in the disputes between the Jesuits and the *arendiouannens* over the Jesuit practice of displaying large crosses in Iroquoian territories. For example, in one account from 1636, a Wendat *arendiouane* named Tehorenhaegnon publicly denounced Brebeuf's erection of a large red cross in the Wendat community, charging that the cross was interfering with the weather and preventing it from raining. According to Brebeuf, Tehorenhaegnon explained to the people that the Jesuits were there in order to kill the Wendat, and that the cross had to be taken down. Although the Jesuits disagreed, it seems that Tehorenhaegnon's argument was more persuasive at the time. Brebeuf noted that some of the youths subsequently began shooting at the cross with their bows and arrows, while others began to verbally denounce the Jesuits' god with what he called "horrid blasphemies."[43]

Arendiouannens shared a multinatural perspective with other healers around the world working within a general shamanic paradigm, namely, that the capacity to heal depends on the learned skills of the healer in

---

[41] *Arendiouane, JR* 8: 123; *ocata* or *saokata, JR* 17: 211 and 33: 193; and *ontetsans* or *aretsan, JR* 17: 213, 215.
[42] *JR* 64: 83.
[43] *JR* 10: 37.

negotiating and manipulating multiple dimensions, natures, and persons of power and force. The new crowd-type illnesses brought by the Europeans undercut the abilities of the *arendiouannens*, as they had little experience with smallpox and influenza.[44]

ARTISTIC EXPRESSION

Iroquoian visual expression varied considerably and entailed a number of different representational strategies, including painting, carving, tattooing, weaving, and ceramics. Media included paints made from pigments of different colored minerals, berries, charcoal, and plant roots, mixed with binders such as bear fat and other oils. The surfaces utilized for paintings included human bodies and faces, animal skins, the trees along the trails that linked villages together, the posts and poles erected within villages, houses, sections of bark, hides, wooden clubs, sticks, and boards. The forms that these expressions took included tree paintings, wampum belts, smoking pipes, bowls and spoons, house markers, marked bodies, masks, and more.[45]

With the exception of smoking pipes, hair combs, and ceremonial masks, the subject matter in Iroquoian art was usually humans and their relationships and adventures, as well as pragmatic accounts of reality, experience, travel, alliance, and identity, that is, cultural realism. Typical subjects included individuals (warriors, hunters, or captives), corporate collectivities (represented by the *owachira*/clan), and tribal nations (represented as fires and councils). Although the most frequently mentioned colors are black and red, there appear to have been no restrictions on color. In speaking of Iroquoian media in 1656, a Jesuit remarked, "The most vivid scarlet, the brightest green, the most natural yellow and orange of Europe pale before the various colors that our Savages procure from roots." The sources suggest a wide range of hues was used. When they became available, native painters made use of European materials as pigments, including lampblack, leadwhite, ink, and in the eighteenth century, watercolors.[46]

The practice of tree painting in the Eastern Woodlands generally consisted of removing the bark of a tree and applying color and line, sometimes incised, on the smooth exposed surface of living wood beneath. Although sometimes they were painted near the village entrances, most tree paintings were created in the forested passages between villages. Some of the busier passages were reportedly lined with tree paintings, as were encampments,

---

[44] *JR* 15: 137.
[45] Keating, *Iroquois Art*.
[46] *JR* 43: 259.

that is, clearings in the woods where travelers might rest. In discussing this media environment of open trails, Paul A. W. Wallace concluded that "he who runs may read." Tree painting was widespread throughout the Eastern Woodlands during the seventeenth and eighteenth centuries and was especially pronounced among Iroquoian peoples. Tree paintings were a widespread form of public art that could only have been practiced within a context of autonomy and unrestricted movement. The paintings required a geography of open trails between villages, along which native people could travel in relative freedom.[47]

The subjects of tree paintings were often narrative cycles of war parties and hunting excursions, and also representations of *owachira*-based identities. In some accounts, tree paintings also served to territorialize the land by visually indicating boundaries. The creator-artists of tree paintings were usually male warriors. Warrior narrative art was also created on wooden posts in villages and towns, on boards that were hung inside their longhouses, and on richly decorated wooden war clubs often left behind after a successful raiding party as a kind of calling card. A similar iconography informs all these different forms: *owachira* identities and the summary of the particular outcomes, including the number and quality of warriors, hunters, captives, and casualties.[48]

Equally widespread throughout the Eastern Woodlands was the practice of body painting. Both permanent and non-permanent techniques of Iroquoian body painting are described at length by the Jesuits, most of whom were, of course, opposed to such practices. Body painting was not gender-specific but could include women and children, as well as men. Just as the ancient red paint peoples made a direct connection between paint, death, and the afterlife of the spirit world, so too did Iroquoian peoples during the seventeenth century.[49]

Painting the face with black paint or charcoal seems to have been a widespread practice relating to mourning and fasting. Other styles of body painting using different colors served a variety of purposes. At times the Jesuits reported an aesthetic function to Iroquoian body painting – making their bodies more beautiful and presentable, or alternately striking fear into an enemy. Some reported a pragmatic function – protecting their bodies from cold or insects. Others have proposed a spiritual

---

[47] Keating, *Iroquois Art*. See William M. Beauchamp, "Aboriginal Uses of Wood in New York," *New York State Museum Bulletin* 89, Archeology 11 (1905): 87–272; and Paul A. W. Wallace, *Indians in Pennsylvania* (Harrisburg, PA, 1961), 125.

[48] Keating, *Iroquois Art*.

[49] *JR* 72: 335; and J. F. Lafitau, *Customs of the American Indians Compared with the Customs of Primitive Times* (Toronto, 1977). Originally published as *Moeurs des sauvages américains, compares aux moeurs des premier temps* (Paris, 1724).

function – as a means of preparing to die and crossing the threshold into the land of the dead.[50]

Although Iroquoian peoples did not practice writing in the European sense of an alphabetic script, they did make use of a metonymic system of notched sticks, which operated along a similar principle regarding beads strung together; namely, they served as repositories of memory and information, and with proper focus of the mind these repositories could be accessed. This is now recognized as a kind of writing system. The most booklike of all the metonymic texts produced by Iroquoians consisted of shell beads strung together to form what became known as wampum belts or porcelain collars. There were two general categories of Haudenosaunee wampum belts: those that recorded individual treaty events with other indigenous groups and with European groups, and those that commemorated the founding of the league. A third category of wampum usage by Haudenosaunee peoples was in the form of ceremonial strings of wampum beads, which were used in condolence ceremonies to "wipe away the tears" of the grieving moiety.[51]

By the end of the seventeenth century, ceramic Iroquoian smoking pipes were no longer being produced. They were replaced by cheaper mass-produced clay pipes from Europe. One of the more distinctive traits of Iroquoian pipes was the style of creating the pipe bowl into the face of a being that gazes back at the smoker. The association of tobacco with the sky world, combined with the mental effects of the plant, suggests strongly that this style was informed by a multinatural perspective, and that the faces on the pipes were those of indwellers or other spirits. The only other areas of expression in which spirit beings are visually represented are on hair combs that accompanied burials and in the carving of ceremonial masks that embodied powerful spiritual beings that were used in particular ceremonies.[52]

Among the visual novelties introduced by Europeans during the seventeenth century were Jesuit-made pictures of various Christian themes that were circulated and used for the purpose of Christian proselytization. These often included pictures of hell and damnation, which appear to have had mimetic effects in the oft-epidemic-ridden communities. Also new was the practice of treaty signing. During the colonial period, declarations of land cessions, treaties, deeds, and other "agreements" – always written in the

---

[50] Keating, *Iroquois Art*.
[51] P. Williams, "Wampum of the Six Nations Confederacy at the Grand River Territory: 1784–1986," in C. F. Hayes III, ed., *Proceedings of the 1986 Shell Bead Conference: Selected Papers* (Rochester, 1989), Research Records Number 20.
[52] Englebrecht, *Iroquoia*.

language of the colonizer – were produced on surfaces of parchment and vellum, on which Iroquoian people produced their signatures, often in the form of their *owachira* symbol. By the early nineteenth century, this style of signature was replaced by the more anonymous "X" mark.[53]

CONCLUSION

Iroquoian religion changed dramatically as a result of contact with Europeans. The Catholics and other Christian missionaries were ultimately very successful in converting the majority of Iroquoian peoples to Christianity. However, they did not completely destroy the indigenous religion that had developed in the Woodlands world system over the *longue durée*. Some of the information of Iroquoian religion continues to circulate in the twenty-first century global world system, to a great extent because of the efforts of past and present Haudenosaunee visionaries.

SUGGESTIONS FOR FURTHER READING

Englebrecht, William. *Iroquoia: The Development of a Native World*. Syracuse, 2003.

Keating, Neal B. *Pictures and Power: Haudenosaunee and Iroquoian Visual Expression from the Seventeenth Century into the Twenty-First*. Norman, OK, forthcoming.

Richter, Daniel K. *The Ordeal of the Longhouse: The Peoples of the Iroquois League in the Era of European Colonization*. Williamsburg, 1992.

Sioui, Georges E. *Huron Wendat: The Heritage of the Circle*. Vancouver, 1999.

Thwaites, Ruben G., ed. *The Jesuit Relations and Allied Documents: Travels and Explorations of the Jesuit Missionaries in New France, 1601–1791*. 73 vols. New York, 1896–1901.

Vivieros de Castro, Eduardo. "Cosmological Deixis and Amerindian Perspectivism." *The Journal of the Royal Anthropological Institute* 4:3 (1998): 469–88.

Winkelman, Michael. *Shamanism: The Neural Ecology of Consciousness and Healing*. Westport, 2000.

---

[53] Keating, *Iroquois Art*. See François-Marc Gagnon, *La Conversion par L'Image: Un Aspect de la Mission des Jésuites Auprès des Indiens du Canada au XVIIe Siécle* (Montreal, 1975).

7

MISSISSIPPIAN RELIGIOUS TRADITIONS

DAVID H. DYE

Mississippian religion was a distinctive Native American belief system in eastern North America that evolved out of an ancient, continuous tradition of sacred landscapes, shamanic institutions, world renewal ceremonies, and the ritual use of fire, ceremonial pipes, medicine bundles, sacred poles, and symbolic weaponry. Mississippian people shared similar beliefs in cosmic harmony, divine aid and power, the ongoing cycle of life and death, and spiritual powers with neighboring cultures throughout much of eastern North America. Although similarities in religious practices and rituals existed throughout the Mississippian world, individual polities possessed divergent trajectories of religious thought that over time resulted in differing paths of belief and ritual.

Above all, Mississippian people were logical, pragmatic, and rational in their religious beliefs, and their observations and thoughts about the world around them were reflected in their views of the spiritual world. Their rituals and sacred narratives embodied abstract meanings, archaic language, complex symbolism, and esoteric metaphors. The numerous and widespread Mississippian polities gave rise to a remarkable tradition of religious beliefs and practices. Their religious system flourished for more than half a millennium as a meaningful and vibrant set of beliefs.[1] Identifying the circumstances, complexity, and nature of Mississippian religion is a major focus of current research among a number of scholars, including anthropologists, archaeologists, ethnohistorians, folklorists, and historians. Although scholars debate various points of religious belief, there is general agreement on the overall religious traditions.

Mississippian people grounded their beliefs on those of the pre-Mississippian societies, especially Woodland cultures, with their elaborate

---

[1] Robert Hall, *An Archaeology of the Soul: North American Indian Belief and Ritual* (Urbana, 1997); and Garrick A. Bailey, ed., *The Osage and the Invisible World: From the Works of Francis La Flesche* (Norman, OK, 1995).

mortuary rituals and monumental earthwork constructions. The rich heritage and legacy of Woodland cosmology became a catalyst for the flowering of Mississippian religion, with its distinctive ancestor shrines, iconography, mortuary patterns, and sacred monumental complexes. Incorporating religious institutions from the pre-Mississippian era, these transformations found expression in new forms of architecture, customs, leadership, ritual, and worldview.[2]

Mississippian culture appeared over a wide swath of the Midwest and Southeast after 1000 C.E., heralded by widespread domestic, economic, political, and religious changes. Chiefly offices, priestly institutions, and shamanic societies accompanied population increases and the adoption of field agriculture. Fortified ceremonial and political complexes appeared along the major river systems and their tributaries throughout much of the Eastern Woodlands. These sedentary, kin-based polities cultivated beans, corn, squash, and sunflowers, in addition to minor crops including tobacco, and depended heavily on fishing, gathering, and hunting. Mississippian societies were aggressive and competitive. A warrior ethos was deeply embedded in the political and social fabric. Religious leadership was grounded on war honors and success in warfare.

These chiefdoms, ranging from simple to complex regional polities, were governed by hereditary chiefs and their priestly councils. Each level in the hierarchically ranked system was composed of potentially non-hierarchical groups. Ruling elites traveled widely in their world, but the average person remained close to home, living in a relatively small- to moderate-sized community as a member of a ranked social system. Religious leaders were also farmers, hunters, and warriors and did not represent a distinct social class.

Spreading out from the Midwestern prairies between 1000 and 1200 C.E., Mississippian towns began to appear along the major waterways of the Eastern Woodlands, especially the Mississippi River and its tributaries, and the rivers flowing along the lower Atlantic and Gulf Coastal plains. An early, grand political and religious center was founded near the confluence of the Mississippi and Missouri Rivers at the Cahokia site in west central Illinois.[3] By the end of the first millennium C.E., Mississippian religion had crystallized at Cahokia and neighboring polities in the Midwest. Cahokia influenced a vast region, with its complex religious ideas expressed

---

[2] Adam King, ed., *Southeastern Ceremonial Complex: Chronology, Content, Context* (Tuscaloosa, AL, 2007); and David G. Anderson and Robert C. Mainfort, Jr., *The Woodland Southeast* (Tuscaloosa, AL, 2002).

[3] Timothy R. Pauketat and Thomas E. Emerson, eds., *Cahokia: Domination and Ideology in the Mississippian World* (Lincoln, 1997).

in exquisite crafting of exotic materials, including copper, marine shell, mica, and various stones and minerals that were exchanged throughout eastern North America. Skilled crafting immortalized a spiritual world of creators, culture heroes, and tricksters in sacred art that in turn chartered cultic institutions; political, social, and religious behavior; priesthoods; and sacred societies.

Mississippian leadership was expressed through shamanic and priestly practices that accessed the various spheres of the cosmos. Mississippian shamans worked as individuals or collectively in religious sodalities, including medicine societies, in which internally ranked membership was restricted to those who experienced appropriate dreams or visions. These shamanic societies effected cures on behalf of the sick by recovering lost souls through dramatic performance, guardian animal aid, magical flight, and shamanic transformation. Ritual plants, such as tobacco (*Nicotiana rustica*); various forms of deprivation, including sleep and food; dancing; drumming; purifying drinks brewed from button snakeroot (*Eryngium yuccifolium*) and yaupon (*Ilex vomitoria*); and ceremonial paraphernalia were associated with attaining altered states of consciousness. Mississippian shamans extracted magically inflicted foreign objects from their patients and crossed cosmic boundaries to retrieve the souls of the sick from the realm of the dead and then return with them to the world of the living. Shamans restored balance, health, harmony, and order to the community and to individuals suffering from various illnesses.[4]

Shamanic cults, with their emphasis on healing through retrieval of souls, empowered members by teaching otherwise restricted esoteric knowledge, hosting ritual events, and scheduling ceremonial performances. Mississippian religious cults were primarily concerned with life and death and the maintenance of a balanced, cohesive, and harmonious world. As an exclusive community of religious worship and ritual, the cult's focus often centered on a single deity or spirit and possessed distinctive dances, esoteric knowledge, pipes, regalia, rituals, sacred bundles, and songs.

Power and authority in Mississippian polities resided with the chiefly advisory council. Priests, distinguished from one another through a ranked system, represented their respective clans in these councils. Clan organization took on a variety of forms, within which religious beliefs and practices were embedded. Priesthood membership was often restricted, being based on achieved war honors, the acquisition of esoteric ritual knowledge, appropriate visions, and the ability to host feasts and ceremonies. Priests acted as intermediaries between humans and spirits and manipulated the

---

[4] Thomas E. Emerson, "Materializing Cahokia Shamans," *Southeastern Archaeology* 22:2 (2003): 135–54.

relationship between cosmos and polity. The chief, on the other hand, was the foremost priest, the person most closely connected and related to divine spiritual forces. Mississippian rituals, especially public religious events, including world renewal ceremonies, were coordinated and controlled by these formal priesthoods, each of which was associated with distinctive ritual knowledge and paraphernalia.[5]

Chiefly political organization transformed previously existing Woodland religious practices into non-hierarchical and hierarchically based religious systems that gave rise to new ideological forms, practices, and structures. Chiefdoms in general were politically fragile and short-lived, with complex forms often collapsing into less integrated political and religious systems. Direct administrative political control was limited to relatively small areas separated from their enemies by buffer zones. Mississippian political and social organization was expressed in the differentiation of elites and commoners within principal towns. Ranking was manifested among political-religious communities, with smaller settlements being subservient to some degree to larger religious precincts or towns. Some early Mississippian centers served primarily mortuary functions and were occupied by ruling elites and a small resident population of priests and their families.

Mississippian elites acquired their authority by descent from previous leaders, often through matrilineal lines, and this relationship was symbolized by the chiefly ancestor shrine that held the reposed elite dead. Political authority resided more on sacred, cooperatively based forms of authority than coercive power. In keeping with a ritual-based political authority, a chief's primary sources of power rested on ownership of the ancestor shrine, effective leadership in councils, a strong ideological foundation, limited control over the economy, and an effective chiefly militia.

Mississippian religion was centered on several basic tenets: achievement of balance, harmony, and order; belief in souls; attainment of sacred power; creation of a sacred landscape; renewing the world through ritual; and supplication for divine aid and power.[6] World renewal embodies the belief that the present world can be maintained, renewed, and vitalized through ritual acts that re-create the past, often through dramas that reenact events from the time of creation by actors who impersonate spirits and employ the ritual paraphernalia of deities. Mississippian world renewal rituals embodied beginnings that emphasized balance, harmony, and purity. For example, ritual cleaning took place on plaza surfaces or mound summits by removing polluted debris and replacing it with clean layers of sand or other variously colored and textured sediments, resulting

---

[5] Bailey, *The Osage*.
[6] Charles M. Hudson, *Elements of Southeastern Indian Religion* (Leiden, 1984).

in the periodic rebuilding of earthen mounds. Rekindling the sacred fire as part of the green corn ceremony also had a cleansing function, as did ritual sweating in special lodges and vomiting after consuming specially prepared elixirs such as the black drink and various war medicines. World renewal ceremonies ritually reconciled cosmological tensions and conflicts to achieve balance and harmony. These ceremonies were dramatized before an axis mundi, typically a striped cedar pole that drew, concentrated, and mediated solar power to earth.

Mississippians believed a person possessed two souls, which stood in opposition to each other – the free soul and the life soul. The life soul kept the body alive and active. Priests reasoned that the free soul could be renewed, requickened, or revitalized through appropriate rituals, thus ensuring a long line of descendents. The free soul, able to leave the body, especially in death, dreams, and visions, could journey to the realm of the dead. Because of this ability to travel, the free soul could be "recycled" as it journeyed to the land of the dead and then returned to the living. In addition, the free soul might be "lost" due to illness or stolen by malevolent persons or spirits. The shaman was then required to retrieve the soul and bring it back to the land of the living.[7]

Through fasting, employing guardian spirits, and seeking visions, Mississippian people were granted special powers and gifts by spiritual beings. Dances, guardian spirits, esoteric knowledge, medicine bundles, sacred narratives, plants, rituals, songs, and symbolic objects could be bestowed on a person through fasting and supplication. This transfer of knowledge, power, and sacred objects to the supplicant hinged on special relationships, typically kinship, between humans and transcendent beings that appeared to the seeker in dreams or visions. Deprivation, including fasting and deprivation of sleep and sex; narcotics, especially nicotine and other drugs; physical and social isolation; and ritual cleansing through bathing, scratching, sweating, and vomiting promoted success in visions. Guardian spirits were instrumental in vision quests and might visit a person during dreams, illnesses, or visions. Interpretations of dreams or visions were rendered by elders or priests.

Formal religious beliefs explained only certain components of the cosmology; therefore many aspects of the world remained unexplained. Thus, the average person also believed in conjurers, ghosts, little people, prophets, sorcerers, and witches. These everyday lived beliefs and practices reflect a complex religious and spiritual world.[8]

---

[7] Åke Hultkrantz, *Conceptions of the Soul Among North American Indians: A Study in Religious Ethnology* (Stockholm, 1973).

[8] Bailey, *The Osage*.

MISSISSIPPIAN COSMOLOGY

Earth Maker brought the great cosmos into being, structured the world, and placed people, plants, and animals on earth. Mississippian religious leaders sought to invigorate, re-create, renew, manipulate, and symbolize this spiritual world in architecture, art, built landscape, dance, drama, material culture, narrative, ritual, and song. The primary structure and organization of the cosmos was based on dual, opposed layers.[9] The bottom layer, the beneath world, comprised a vast body of water, whereas the above world included the majestic expanse of sky. The middle world, where humans, plants, and four-legged animals resided, floated as a massive disk on the watery beneath world that rotated each evening, revealing the path of souls in the night sky. The middle world lay between the bound but opposing forces of the beneath world and the upper world. As residents of the middle world, humans not only renewed the world, but also mediated tensions between these two cosmic realms through ritual and religious practice. Mississippian religious leaders were mindful of the oscillations between chaos and order in the world, and they counteracted these shifting tendencies whenever necessary.

The basic dualism of the Mississippian cosmos was expressed not only in the concept of the beneath world and the upper world, but also in the oppositions of enemy and friend, kin and non-kin, life and death, old and young, female and male, and day and night. Mississippian art revealed this balanced and opposing structural duality in a wide variety of media, including copper, pottery, shell, and stone. The cosmos was a set of contradictions that had to be stabilized through ritual propitiation and iconographic representation. Thus, tensions inherent in the natural world were balanced against the spiritual world and reconciled through ceremonial forms and practice and the aid of sacred beings.[10]

In addition to the basic dual nature of the cosmos, a tripartite division of the cosmos was manifested not only in the above world and the beneath world, but also in the middle world. The three-field cosmic structure held special significance for Mississippian people and is seen in the recurring pattern of design motifs in balanced and opposed triads. Art motifs often reflect the tripartite cosmology as an axis mundi, with sacred forces or powers descending from the upper world or ascending from the beneath

---

[9] Charles Hudson, *The Southeastern Indians* (Knoxville, TN, 1976).

[10] F. Kent Reilly, III, "People of Earth, People of Sky: Visualizing the Sacred in Native American Art of the Mississippian Period," in Richard F. Townsend and Robert V. Sharp, eds., *Hero, Hawk, and Open Hand: American Indian Art of the Ancient Midwest* (New Haven, 2004), 125–38.

world. Animals, such as birds and raccoons, and plants, especially tobacco, were often associated with the vertical movement of divine beings, power, and prayer. Figural imagery of celestial travelers transcending these cosmic zones portrays the use of sacred, stripped poles adorned with magical aides, including raccoon-pelt bindings.

Finally, the cosmos also included a quadripartite pattern reflected in art motifs, dance patterns, four-sided platform mounds, plazas, ritual recitations, and sacred songs. The concept of a four-sided world was basic to Mississippian religious thought. Earthen mounds were "earth-islands," and specific animals, such as birds or serpents, anchored the earth quarters. Art motifs reflect this quadripartite principle of balanced, opposed, and reversed figures and elements in a wide variety of media, especially ceramic and shell art.[11]

Mississippian ideology was materialized through sacred cultural landscapes, public ceremonial events, and symbolic objects, and it hence offered opportunities for political control by ruling elites.[12] Public events, including feasts, dramatic performances, and rituals, comprised the stage for religious events that acted to acculturate individuals into appropriate forms of political, social, and religious behavior and beliefs. Public ceremonials, because they were prescribed in form, participation, and sequence, provided ruling elites varying opportunities for authority by their ability to control, fund, muster, schedule, or restrict ritual participation. The demands of leadership and the costs associated with sponsoring ritual events were prohibitive for the average person, so prestigious and wealthy kin groups tended to host and schedule important public rituals and thus gain honor and authority through opportunities for leadership roles.

Leadership of some degree was necessary to coordinate and finance ceremonies by marshaling resources from the group. Orchestration of public ceremonies was achieved by restricting the participation of religious specialists to those who occupied offices earned through various degrees of exacting criteria. These ritual specialists owned interlocking and mutually interdependent components of ceremonies, dances, regalia, sacred narratives, songs, and symbolic objects. Ritual performances, such as the green corn ceremony, required not only specific knowledge, skills, and symbolic objects, but also the authority, prestige, and wealth to attract sufficient numbers of people to witness ceremonial events.[13]

---

[11] George E. Lankford, "World on a String: Some Cosmological Components of the Southeastern Ceremonial Complex," in Townsend and Sharp, *Hero, Hawk, and Open Hand*, 207–18.

[12] Vernon J. Knight, Jr., "Mississippian Ritual" (Ph.D. diss., University of Florida, 1981).

[13] John Witthoff, *Green Corn Ceremonialism in the Eastern Woodlands* (Ann Arbor, 1949).

Portable symbolic objects, including ceremonial paraphernalia and regalia, were important means for communicating and displaying political and religious status. These publically viewed icons communicated coded information to large groups of people at ceremonial gatherings. Such items included carved stone; embossed copper plates; engraved marine shell cups and gorgets; engraved, modeled, and painted ceramic vessels; and knapped flint. Mississippian symbolic objects signified political positions and social relationships and communicated and reaffirmed a body of shared religious beliefs in the context of ceremonial events.

Construction of public monuments and sacred landscapes was central to the emergence and perpetuation of Mississippian chiefly lineages. Mississippian earthen mounds, earth lodges, and partitioned plazas took shape from the organization of mobilized social labor and contributed to a sacred landscape that communicated religious as well as political statements about authority, ideology, power, practice, prestige, and wealth. Public monuments, as stages for ceremonial performances, also required coordination, finance, and leadership to organize labor and resources.

MISSISSIPPIAN DEITIES

Mississippian deities dwelled in the above world as well as the beneath world and bestowed special or sacred gifts and chartered medicine bundles and rituals to supplicants. They also granted special powers to humans who sought their aid through solicitation. Religious specialists, including priests and shamans, acted as intermediaries between deities and humans. Mississippian divinities could be seen in the day and night sky as celestial figures. Through such celestial portals, shamans visited the otherworld, often accompanied by powerful animals or spirits who acted as guardians, guides, and helpers.

Deities often manifested themselves as celestial bodies and became astronomical indicators for seasonal rituals and other religious events. Mississippian sacred beings sometimes had special kinship relations with humans, especially with leaders, priests, or shamans. The rank order and affinal connections among these spiritual beings reflected the kinship relationships evident in Mississippian polities. Spiritual beings, including Birdman, Earth Mother, Great Serpent, and the Twins, for example, were manifested in multiple forms throughout eastern North America and the Mississippian world, and this diversity of conceptualization was a key concept for Mississippian religion, especially considering the bipartite, tripartite, and quadripartite structure of the cosmos.

These deities, including creators, culture heroes, and tricksters, brought the world into being, established a moral code, and set up basic relationships among animals, humans, and plants. In short, Mississippian spiritual beings created and set into motion the natural and social worlds of the Mississippian people. But tensions were generated among these "other-than-humans" on the basis of their symbolic oppositions, and humans attempted to mediate these cosmic struggles through prayer, ritual, and supplication.

Creators brought into existence humans, the natural world, and the cosmos. The creation of the world took place by the activities of a creator figure surrounded by preexisting preternatural beings and other creators who had the ability to actualize themselves and restore the dead to life. Culture heroes, on the other hand, bestowed religious institutions and sacred knowledge and gifts to humankind. As founders who provided important institutions and rituals to the Mississippian world, they were memorialized in iconography and oral narratives, and their deeds recapitulated in dramatic acts and public ceremonies.

Tricksters, as bawdy, comical, and contrary deities, provided an entertaining commentary on the moral world of humans. Although tricksters were creators of a sort, they personified the dark side of humans and the opposites of human cultural rules by expressing opposition to social mores by parodying sanctioned values. During rituals they were exempted from the social rules that charted normal human behavior. Oftentimes the roles of creators, culture heroes, and tricksters overlapped, especially as religious ideas were diffused, reworked, and remodeled over time and space.

EARTH MOTHER

The powerful, renewing, female side of the Mississippian spiritual force stood in balanced opposition and dynamic equilibrium to the destructive male life force. The Mississippian conception of the universe was based on logically patterned beliefs and tenets. Women brought forth life through childbirth and planting; men took life through warfare and hunting. Mississippians exercised great care in avoiding any disturbance of the natural order and balance of the world and the powerful female and male forces through gifts, prayers, rituals, and supplication to spiritual beings.

The female aspect of this all-permeating, invisible life force was personified in a powerful deity who was manifested and depicted in various iconographic forms. She was known as Cloud Mother, Corn Mother, Corn Woman, Earth Mother, First Woman, Grandmother, Old Woman, and Old-Woman-Who-Never-Dies.[14] There is a large corpus of cosmological

---

[14] James R. Duncan and Carol Diaz-Granados, "Empowering the SECC: The 'Old Woman' and Oral Tradition," in Carol D. Granados and James R. Duncan, eds., *The Rock-Art of Eastern North America: Capturing Images and Insight* (Tuscaloosa, AL, 2004), 190–215;

knowledge, iconography, and religious concepts and practice associated with beliefs in the Earth Mother. She was the mythical mother of humans and plant life, bestowing to humans agricultural crops, including beans, corn, gourds, squash, sunflowers, and tobacco. She brought forth seeds from the beneath world in sacred containers, such as bundles, gourds, and packs, and gave plants to humanity with specific instructions and taboos for their care and propagation. Earth Mother mediated the critical connective link between the life-giving forces of the above world, personified in the Birdman, and the life-taking forces of the beneath world, symbolized in the Great Serpent, her consort and protector.

The entrance to the beneath world may have been symbolized as Earth Mother's vulva, a portal to the realm of the dead as seen in the night sky, perhaps the Orion constellation. From her, life originated in birth, and to her, life returned in death. Whereas the Great Serpent took lives, she returned the life force to humanity in the recycling and revivification of souls and the renewal of life by capturing the life-giving force from the above world, especially the sun. Many life forms originated in the beneath world and emerged onto the middle world, the earth's surface. Just as animals emerged from the earth and seeds brought forth new life upon planting in the spring, so too were souls of selected dead "recycled" by burial beneath the earth's surface. Shamans, in particular, were believed to have been reincarnated. The basis for the cyclical life, death, and rebirth themes in Mississippian cosmology was predicated on Earth Mother's retrieval of souls from the realm of the dead in sacred containers, which were then placed into the adopted, reborn, or revived person. Through Earth Mother, humans defeated death, life sprang forth, and souls were reborn to continue their cycling. She also enabled shamans to cure the sick by their searching for souls that had gone to the realm of the dead.

Mississippian people revered and respected Earth Mother. Supplications were offered her through rituals and prayers for her continued bestowal of beneficence, descendents, fecundity, and longevity. She was a guardian for people who respected her and abided by her rules, but she dispensed punishment to those who broke her taboos, brought about disharmony and imbalance in the world, and violated prescribed rules.

Earth Mother is portrayed in a variety of artistic media, including ceramic vessels, rock art, and stone statuary. The primary visual metaphor for Earth Mother is the ogee or vulvar motif. The frequency of the ogee on pottery

---

George E. Lankford, "A Maze of Maize Myths," in George E. Lankford, eds., *Looking for Lost Lore: Studies in Folklore, Ethnology, and Iconography* (Tuscaloosa, AL, 2008), 24–69; Guy Prentice, "An Analysis of the Symbolism Expressed by the Birger Figure," *American Antiquity* 51:2 (1986): 239–66.

vessels, rock art, and shell engravings attests to the devotion and respect accorded her in the rituals of daily life throughout the Mississippian world. In western Mississippian rock art, for example, vulvar motifs are oriented along the daily solar path to ensure life-sustaining sunlight that fertilizes the earth. Earth Mother's intercourse with the solar deity provided a continuous cycle of births and a long line of progeny, especially humans. Her vulva, a metaphor for the earth, was the recipient and receptacle of the life-giving force and the sun's generative power.[15]

Religious belief in Earth Mother continues among some Mississippian descendents. For example, the Osage Big Moon peyote ceremony centers on an altar that represents the Earth Mother. In the peyote Greeting the Sun ceremony, a sacred fire is lit inside the vulva-form altar.[16]

THE GREAT SERPENT

One of the major Mississippian cosmic powers was the master of the beneath world, the denizen of the realm of the dead and protector of Earth Mother and her progeny. This spiritual being had many names: Great Horned Water Panther, Great Panther, Great Serpent, Horned Water Serpent, Master of the Beneath World, Protector of the Realm of the Dead, Underwater Monster, Underwater Panther, and Winged Serpent. As was the case with other spiritual beings, the Great Serpent was rarely called by name, for fear of conjuring him forth. In addition to the plethora of names, he also possessed a multitude of forms, ranging from serpentlike to pantherlike. In some instances, the Great Serpent possessed a combination of avian, feline, and serpent attributes or manifestations to symbolize his embodiment of the above, middle, and beneath worlds.[17]

The Great Serpent incorporated the powers of the beneath world and was the master of the beneath world spirits, especially those that dwelled in the water. The Great Serpent was not a single creature so much as the incarnation of many powerful underworld spirits. One of the functions of the Great Serpent was serving as protector and guardian of the Earth Mother and the souls of the beneath world. Evidence of the Great Serpent was seen in the dangerous waves on lakes and in treacherous rapids and

---

[15] Duncan and Diaz-Granados, "Empowering the SECC."
[16] Daniel C. Swan, *Peyote Religious Art: Symbols of Faith and Belief* (Jackson, 1999).
[17] Thomas E. Emerson, "Water, Serpents, and the Underworld: An Exploration into Cahokia Symbolism," in Patricia Galloway, ed., *The Southeastern Ceremonial Complex: Artifacts and Analysis* (Lincoln, 1989), 45–92; George E. Lankford, "The Great Serpent in Eastern North America," in F. Kent Reilly III, and James F. Garber, eds., *Ancient Objects and Sacred Realms: Interpretations of Mississippian Iconography* (Austin, 2007), 107–35.

perilous whirlpools in rivers, all believed to be caused by its thrashing tail. Drownings were usually attributed to the Great Serpent, and so tobacco was offered as a gift prior to traveling on lakes or rivers. In addition, animals or people venturing near water might be subject to capture and seizure by the Great Serpent. It was in perpetual conflict with the Birdman, or more typically, Thunderbirds. Their mutual antagonism reflected the fundamental interlocked and balanced opposition between the above world and beneath world forces.

The beneath world and realm of the dead were potentially dangerous places. Shamans who possessed the requisite knowledge and spiritual power were the only ones who dared visit or communicate with the resident beneath world spiritual beings. In dreams and visions shamans journeyed to the lodge of the Great Serpent, where they received religious instruction, personal power, ritual paraphernalia, and sacred bundles. Sacred narratives, especially the Eastern Woodland version of the Orpheus story, provided a model for shamanic encounters with the Great Serpent and served as a charter for those who sought his power.

As a deity who rose from the waters of the beneath world in summer and flew low in the night sky as the Scorpio constellation, the Great Serpent was the guardian of the realm of the dead at the southern end of the Milky Way or Path of Souls. One of his major functions was aiding those in search of lost souls. The Great Serpent was depicted as a rattlesnake when engraved on ceramic bottles and bowls and marine shell cups, which were employed for medicinal drinks consumed in purification rituals. When the Great Serpent resided in the night sky, he was marked iconographically by the addition of feathers or wings. Crosshatching, as a widespread artistic convention, symbolized renewal based on the earthly serpent's ability to shed its skin.

THE BIRDMAN

The male procreative life force in Mississippian religion was represented by an aggressive above world deity who confronted and engaged the masters of death in the beneath world through deadly combat or contest.[18] This other-than-human person was a central figure in Mississippian religion because he played a key role in ensuring that life triumphed over death and that the life force of humans continued to prosper. He was instrumental in rebirth and world renewal by bestowing the life force that descends from the sun to the earth. This allegorical figure was symbolized by and

---

[18] James A. Brown, "On the Identity of the Birdman within Mississippian Period Art and Iconography," in Reilly and Garber, *Ancient Objects and Sacred Realms*, 56–106.

responsible for the emergence of daylight from darkness each day. In other words, he was a metaphor for the continued renewal of the world and the revitalization of human life.

This major above world deity was known to Mississippian people under several guises: Birdman, He-Who-Gets-Hit-with-Deer-Lungs, He-Who-Wears-Human-Heads-as-Earrings, Morning Star, and Red Horn. In his avian identity he was recognized as the falcon or hawk. The Birdman's cosmological adversary was the Great Serpent. As a heroic warrior and player in a deadly game, he engaged in cosmic confrontation with the forces of the beneath world through one-on-one mortal combat that tested his skill and luck. In these matches he fought death, and was sometimes defeated and beheaded, but was ultimately rescued by a compatriot who restored him back to life. It was a relation – often a nephew to Birdman in the sacred narratives – who defeated death, retrieved Birdman's head, and revived him. The relation of nephew to uncle (mother's brother) was a special one, particularly in Mississippian matrilineal societies, because the two belonged to the same clan and had reciprocal duties, obligations, and responsibilities to each other.

Mississippian iconography reflects this basic allegorical narrative in numerous works of art, especially in embossed copper and engraved marine shell. These dramatic tableaux vividly illustrate the "junior" Birdman carrying the head of the defeated heroic warrior. The protagonist is strikingly attired in ritual regalia and adorned with ceremonial accoutrements. He prominently wields a raised war club, proclaiming his victory in mortal combat over the forces of the beneath world by besting his opponent and revitalizing his kinsman and compatriot. Various eye and mouth treatments, especially the forked eye surround derived from the peregrine falcon, are a visual metaphor for the Birdman and are found on numerous works of art.

Mississippian people extended prayer, respect, and supplication to Birdman because of his exploits on their behalf, and in return he bestowed important gifts: health, longevity, power, and a long line of descendents. This last gift was crucial, because the ultimate victory in the defeat of death resides in the ability of a person's life force to survive through their progeny. The theme of life's triumph over death through one's descendents had its counterpart for Mississippian people in individual martial combat and ritual games of chance and skill, such as lacrosse or stickball and chunkey.

The nature of the sacred falcon/morning star allegory with its celebration of the triumph of life force over death, had an appeal that was transferable from egalitarian to hierarchical societies but was also retained in post-contact polities. The Birdman cult arose in the eastern prairies of the

Midwest at the end of the first millennium C.E., with the falcon or hawk as its central figure. In the eleventh century, religious figural art representing Birdman intensified as new Mississippian religious practices flourished in the regional polities and great towns. By the fifteenth century, Birdman cult imagery had diminished considerably, but among Mississippi valley and prairie-plains groups, the hawk continued to be an important religious focus. The most compelling disjunction in the Birdman complex took place in the late nineteenth century, when eastern prairie polities surrendered their political autonomy and no longer pursued intertribal warfare. In recent times the Birdman has been replaced by the Thunderbird, who continues to hunt and devour underwater serpents and bestows to the worthy supplicant the gifts of healing, knowledge, medicine, and power.

THE TWINS

The sacred Twins were principal Mississippian above world deities who possessed extraordinary and miraculous powers associated with sacred bundles used to access the beneath world and to revitalize the dead. Paul Radin referred to the Twins narrative as "the basic myth of the North American Indians."[19] The Twins were known by many names: Children of the Sun, Little Men, Lodge Boy and Spring Boy, Lodge Boy and Thrown Away, Lightning Boy and Thunder Boy, and the Thunder Twins.[20]

One boy was "civilized" and adhered to the basic tenets of society, whereas the other, "uncivilized" sibling opposed society through contrary behavior. The Twins were created by the above world deities to correct an imbalance of power in the world. In part they accomplished this task by slaying the primordial monsters, presumably beneath world spirits, who were killing humans. Once the Twins restored the world to balance and established harmony and order, they underwent an apotheosis as stars or thunder beings, and as such they continued to bestow humans with knowledge and special gifts. The primary protagonist of the Twins story is the "wild" brother and his beneath world powers, which include the shamanic principles of transformation and revivification of the dead.

The Twins repeatedly demonstrated their remarkable spiritual powers by battling and defeating otherworld monsters and spirit-powers. They possessed remarkable transformational abilities. With the use of magical arrows, they outdistanced their pursuers by propelling themselves as

---

[19] Paul Radin, "The Basic Myth of the North American Indians," *Eranos-Jahrbuch* 17 (1949): 359–419.

[20] James R. Duncan and Carol Diaz-Granados, "Of Masks and Myths," *Midcontinental Journal of Archaeology* 25 (2000): 1–26.

arrows, and they could change into feathers to float wherever they wished. The boys could also transform themselves into stars or weather powers, especially storms, bringing about lightning and much-needed rain. Their magical arrows were stored in the sacred Thunder Bundles employed in healing and revivifying the dead. Through these bundles the Twins brought each other back to life after having been killed. In one narrative episode, the wild Twin is decapitated and replaces his head with a rattle. In another instance he replaces his brains with pebbles. The Twins are often represented by rattle-head ceramic effigies, especially in the Mississippi valley, and by dual, opposed figures in Mississippian religious art.

The Twins' ritual death and revival were an important Mississippian religious theme, based on the power of the sacred Thunder Bundle and the Twins' use of the bundle to achieve success in warfare and healing and to revivify the dead through magical arrows. Religious practitioners used the bundles to reincarnate select persons and to call on powerful deities. For example, reincarnation was the central theme of adoption ceremonies, in which the symbolic resurrection of the dead was associated with the renewal of the earth. In this case, when the wild Twin impersonator symbolically raised the deceased through the Thunder Bundle, he also represented the earth being reborn in the spring, and through him the polity was rejuvenated.

That the Twins were important to Mississippian people is demonstrated by their portrayal on ceramic vessels, on marine shell cups and gorgets, and as components of the ritual regalia in the form of long-nose god maskettes. Perhaps most importantly, they reopened the Orion constellation, the portal to the realm of the dead, thus allowing human souls to continue to be recycled. They killed the great monsters that harassed humans, and they created the Thunder Bundle and the dances, prayers, and songs that accompanied it. Those who received a dream or vision from the Twins became members of the Thunder Bundle society. The Thunder Bundle instructed shamans in healing and magical power. The welfare of the Mississippian people depended on the outcome of the conflict between the above world and beneath world deities, and the Twins were crucial in mediating these powerful forces.

MISSISSIPPIAN RELIGION AND CULTURE CHANGE

A number of discontinuities or disjunctions over time altered, modified, and shaped Mississippian religion. Numerous changes can be seen in the archaeological record in the centuries following emergence of Mississippian culture, including natural disasters that brought significant disruptions and reorientation in political, religious, and social systems. For example, climate change in the form of mega-drought events had major bearings on Mississippian societies between 900 and 1700 C.E.[21]

Perhaps in conjunction with droughts and other climatic changes, major changes took place in the late fourteenth century, when a regionwide deterioration in political power, skilled crafting, subsistence patterns, and religious organization took place. The drastic decline in craft production, especially decorated ceramics, embossed copper, engraved marine shell, and sculpted stone statuary, is evidenced throughout the Mississippian world as centralization waned.

European contact precipitated further widespread depopulation, culture change, population relocation, and increased conflict and violence, with the intrusion of expeditionary forces and traders into the interior and the establishment of European colonies along the Atlantic and Gulf coasts. Devastating pandemics raced across the North American interior in a series of waves beginning in the sixteenth century, resulting in the loss of specialized knowledge and ritual practitioners who staffed religious offices. Depopulation was especially damaging to the routine transference from one generation to the next of esoteric rituals, religious knowledge, and sacred chartering narratives, causing significant changes to the Mississippian belief system.

The onslaughts of slaving expeditions, initiated from the English plantations near Charleston in the late seventeenth and early eighteenth centuries, had devastating and profound effects on the interior populations, especially the institution of chieftainship and associated ruling elites. The foundation of chiefly authority resided in the mortuary shrine and the paraphernalia stored within, especially the seated human sculptures. Slaving brought about the collapse of these chiefly institutions and the demise of the mortuary shrines.[22]

The impacts of ethnocentric Christian missionaries were particularly debilitating to Eastern Woodlands religious traditions. Missionaries were antagonistic and hostile toward shamanic practices, especially mortuary rituals and beliefs that emphasized resurrection or revivification of the dead, soul loss, multiple souls, and iconographic veneration, especially temple statuary. Native religious systems – and associated iconography, sacred narratives, and shamanic drama, flight, and transformation – were reworked over time according to biblical texts. Remodeled sacred, oral

---

[21] Larry V. Benson, Michael S. Berry, Edward A. Jolie, Jerry D. Spangler, David W. Stahle, and Eugene M. Hattori, "Possible Impacts of Early-11th-, Middle 12th-, and Late-13th Century Droughts on Western Native Americans and the Mississippian Cahokians," *Quaternary Science Review* 26 (2007): 1–15.

[22] James A. Brown, *Human Figures and the Southeastern Ancestor Shrine* (Carbondale, IL, 2001).

narratives chartered new political, religious, and social roles. The upper world and beneath world opposition and their respective deities gradually assumed features of Christian theology, with its emphasis on a heaven-and-hell dichotomy. The Great Serpent, in particular, took on the connotation of Satan, and ritual activities associated with the beneath world were thus tagged "devil worship."

Political and religious autonomy gradually faded with resettlement onto bounded reservations to the west. For many polities, forced removal began in the early nineteenth century and continued for several decades. Small pockets of holdouts, however, remained in various areas; particularly, the Cherokee in western North Carolina, the Choctaw in east central Mississippi, and the Muskogee/Seminole in south Florida retained elements of Mississippian religion. Over time the ancient sacred narratives ceased to function in the face of new political realities, being stripped of their sanctity and original meanings. The power-chartering and status-confirming functions of the narratives lost their sanctity, to be recorded later as simple cautionary, etiological, explanatory, or humorous folktales. The once-powerful and sacred narratives became "just so" stories popularized in children's books by the nineteenth century.

Forced resettlement also prevented men from attaining war honors, which had provided critical political and social criteria for ambitious men to progress through the various ritual grades within medicine societies or priesthoods. Interpolity combat and war achievements had been a major currency for male status advancement and for attainment of religious and social positions. Without demonstrated military honor and valor, men had difficulty marrying into desirable clans that would have, in turn, endowed them with prestigious political and religious offices.

In a society based on oral sacred narratives, the survival of religious beliefs and knowledge depended primarily on two factors: the number of people who embodied and taught religious knowledge, and the ability of these religious practitioners and personnel to relay that knowledge to their successors. Religious doctrine became endangered when the transmission of sacred lore was threatened. Death of the knowledge bearers was a primary cause of the destruction of esoteric and specialized lore, especially religious knowledge. Religious change had been ongoing throughout the Mississippian era, as the belief system was remodeled and reworked through domestic, economic, political, and social change brought on by a variety of factors, including climate change, depopulation, population movement, and interpolity conflict. However, Western contact accelerated and exacerbated many of these already ongoing changes in the Mississippian religious system.

Whereas external forces, such as European contact, brought about major, if not catastrophic, religious change, revitalization movements had an internal focus. Revitalizing and purifying the remaining components of the old social and religious order in the face of drastic social change necessitated the destruction of former religious leaders, who became identified as witches and vilified as the sources of societal ills. Traditional religious leaders, the bearers of religious knowledge, were seen as the enemy by their own people and became scapegoats for the rampant social and political problems caused by European contact, especially the introduction of alcohol, the fur and skin trade, slaving, and virgin soil pandemic diseases. With the destruction of their religious leaders, Eastern Woodland people suffered rapid acceleration in the reduction and transformation of religious knowledge and ritual practices.[23]

Some groups remained relatively autonomous due to their isolation on the eastern plains until after the Civil War, but over time they became increasingly egalitarian in their political, religious, and social systems.[24] Religious ideology maintained its focus on multiple souls, revivification of the dead, and mythic combat of life against death in the post-chiefdom world. In some ways these egalitarian polities resembled that time prior to the rise of Mississippian chiefdoms when polities were relatively egalitarian.

Elements of Mississippian religion survive today, among western Mississippian descendents, such as the Osage and Quapaw, and many Southeastern groups, including, but not limited to, the Alabama, Caddo, Cherokee, Chickasaw, Choctaw, Koasati, Muskogee, and Yuchi.[25] The green corn ceremony, for example, with its emphasis on purification and renewal, continues to be performed at dance grounds within the old Mississippian homeland as well as in Oklahoma, where the descendants of the Mississippian people continue a transformed but ancient religious tradition.[26]

[23] George E. Lankford, *Looking for Lost Lore: Studies in Folklore, Ethnology, and Iconography* (Tuscaloosa, AL, 2007).
[24] Brown, "On the Identity of the Birdman"; Joel W. Martin, *Sacred Revolt: The Muskogee's Struggle for a New World* (Boston, 1991).
[25] Jason B. Jackson, *Yuchi Ceremonial Life: Performance, Meaning, and Tradition in a Contemporary American Indian Community* (Lincoln, 2005); David Lewis, Jr., and Ann T. Jordan, *Creek Indian Medicine Ways: The Enduring Power of Mvskoke Religion* (Albuquerque, 2002); J. T. Garrett and Michael Garrett, *Medicine of the Cherokee: The Way of Right Relationship* (Rochester, 1996); James H. Howard, *The Southeastern Ceremonial Complex and Its Interpretation* (Columbia, MO, 1968).
[26] I wish to thank F. Kent Reilly III, who initiated and has organized the annual gathering of scholars at the Mississippian Iconographic Workshops at Texas State University (San Marcos) since 1995. The workshop discussions, both formal and informal, and conference papers and publications resulting from the meetings helped inspire and shape many of the ideas presented herein. A draft of this chapter was reviewed by James Brown, Deborah Dye, Adam King, Robert Hall, George Lankford, Kent Reilly, George Sabo, and Patty Jo Watson. To them I owe thanks and appreciation for their constructive criticism and suggestions.

SUGGESTIONS FOR FURTHER READING

Hall, Robert. *An Archaeology of the Soul: North American Indian Belief and Ritual.* Urbana, 1997.

Hudson, Charles M. *Elements of Southeastern Indian Religion.* Leiden, 1984.

Jackson, Jason B. *Yuchi Ceremonial Life: Performance, Meaning, and Tradition in a Contemporary American Indian Community.* Lincoln, 2005.

King, Adam, ed. *Southeastern Ceremonial Complex: Chronology, Content, Context.* Tuscaloosa, AL, 2007.

Lankford, George E., F. Kent Reilly, III, and James F. Garber, eds. *Visualizing the Sacred: Cosmic Visions, Regionalism, and the Art of the Mississippian World.* Austin, 2010.

Martin, Joel W. *Sacred Revolt: The Muskogee's Struggle for a New World.* Boston, 1991.

Reilly, F. Kent, III, and James F. Garber, eds. *Ancient Objects and Sacred Realms: Interpretations of Mississippian Iconography.* Austin, 2007.

Townsend, Richard F., and Robert V. Sharp, eds. *Hero, Hawk, and Open Hand: American Indian Art of the Ancient Midwest.* New Haven, 2004.

8

THE ANASAZI

JACE WEAVER

We do not even know what they called themselves. Certainly, they did not call themselves Anasazi. That is a name that the Athabaskan-speaking Navajo, who moved into their homeland and saw the monumental ruins of their settlements, gave to them. It is a term tinged with more than a hint of hostility. It is often translated "ancient strangers," but it is more precisely rendered "ancient enemies" or "enemy ancestors" (*annasázi*, from *anna'* = enemy/stranger, and *bizází* = ancient/ancestor). They were the ancestors of the modern-day Pueblos. Their descendants most often call them simply "the ancient ones." The Hopi, one of the tribal nations descended from them, term them *hisatinom*, "the ones who came before." Understandably, given the etymology of the term "Anasazi," contemporary Pueblos consider the term offensive. Today it is considered more precise and correct to refer to them as "Ancestral Puebloans" or "Ancient Puebloans."

Despite the pejorative connotations of their most familiar appellation, no indigenous people in the Americas has been more romanticized than the "Anasazi." Given this and the fact that they disappeared before the coming of Europeans to North America, is it possible to say anything about their religious beliefs and practices? The answer is a definite (but cautious) "Yes."

There are thousands of years of Native American habitation in the Americas prior to European contact that can only be known in two ways: archaeology and oral tradition. For groups like the Ancestral Puebloans, there is only archaeology and the oral tradition of others. Archaeology is excellent at helping us discover the material world. It can tell us what a given people's houses were like, what they ate, their level of health, and many other tangible things. It becomes more speculative when it attempts to determine what a people believed or did, on the basis of physical evidence. Fortunately, we also have the traditions and stories of their descendants, the Pueblos, establishing a continuity, albeit imperfect. And we have the oral traditions of the Athabaskan Navajo and Apache, who migrated into the area circa 1400 C.E.

Who then were the Anasazi or Ancestral Puebloans? These ancestors of contemporary Pueblos occupied the Colorado Plateau and the Four Corners area, the region around where the states of Colorado, Utah, Arizona, and New Mexico intersect, from around 1200 B.C.E. to circa 1425 C.E., when the last holdouts abandoned their settlements. They first emerged as a culture that we know as the Basketmakers, who flourished between approximately 1000 B.C.E. and 750 C.E. and who are divided by archaeologists by period into Basketmaker II and Basketmaker III.[1] In actuality, they were not a single people. Like the Mississippians in the East, they were separate groups living in separate communities that shared a religious complex, political affiliations, and similar customs and cultural practices that marked them as more similar to one another than to other tribal groupings. According to Dennis Slifer, a petroglyph specialist with the New Mexico Museum of Indian Arts and Culture, "There was significant regional variation within Ancestral Pueblo culture, and this is reflected in their distinctive cultural remains, including pottery, architecture, and rock art."[2]

These Ancestral Puebloans emerged on the Colorado Plateau out of peoples of the Archaic period. During the early Basketmaker II period, roughly from 1200 to 1000 B.C.E. to 50 C.E., they lived seasonally in small groups in camps or caves. It was during this period that corn and squash agriculture began. By late Basketmaker II (50 C.E. to 500 C.E.), small groups began to be linked to larger polities. They arrived in the Four Corners region around 200 C.E. Shallow pit houses came into use. Religious structures began to emerge. During Basketmaker III (500 C.E.– 750 C.E.), the pit houses became both deeper and more prevalent. The bow and arrow supplanted the atlatl (a spear-throwing device) as a hunting tool. Crude pottery made its appearance, and with it the cultivation of beans. Other staple foods included piñones and amaranth. Also, it was probably during this period that Ancestral Puebloans domesticated the turkey. In rock art, one sees evidence of a turkey cult, with humans depicted with turkey heads.[3]

Eminently suited to their desert environment, pit houses were warmer in the winter and cooler in the summer. Between 700 and 750 C.E., however, the Ancestral Puebloans moved aggressively to build aboveground dwellings. They retained their former homes as sites for the performance

---

[1] Kendrick Frazier, *People of Chaco: A Canyon and Its People*, rev. ed. (New York, 1999), 80.

[2] Dennis Slifer, *Kokopelli: The Magic, Mirth, and Mischief of an Ancient Symbol* (Salt Lake City, 2007), 67.

[3] Frazier, *People of Chaco*, 89.

of ritual. These underground ceremonial chambers are known as *kivas*. They serve the dual purpose of keeping the rituals held there hidden from public view and of providing a climate-controlled environment for their performance. They became linked to the creation myth of the Ancient Puebloans.

Based on the available evidence, we may safely assume that at some point the Ancestral Puebloans, like their descendants, evolved an emergence myth. In such a myth, the people dwelt inside the earth. From there, they emerged through a hole onto the surface. It is a particularly female protology. It is an image of creation as birth, with the people coming out of the womb of the earth. Because people tend to mythologize the practical, over time entering the kiva came to be thought of as reentry into the place of emergence, the place of creation. In the case of the Ancestral Puebloans, of course, this is both symbolically and literally true, because they left their pit houses for surface dwellings: they came out of the earth.

Kivas are entered by descending a ladder through a hole in the roof. Inside the kiva is a hearth. The entrance also serves as a smoke hole. As a ceremony participant climbs down the ladder, he is bathed in smoke from the fire inside, a ritual purification.

All available evidence – archaeology, rock art, and the oral tradition – indicate that the Ancient Puebloans had a rich pantheon of spirits and deities. Religion also permeated everyday life. Grave goods and petroglyphs reveal that there were rituals for quotidian activities like hunting and curing and for specialized actions like success in warfare, weather control, combating witchcraft, and divination.[4] For the agriculturalist Ancient Puebloans, most rituals were undoubtedly part of an annual ceremonial cycle related to the agricultural cycle.

According to Slifer, "Unlike many of their neighbors who shared common Desert Archaic [period] origins and lifeways, the Ancestral Pueblo culture exhibited a tendency for radical change throughout its history. Their culture became more complex with time, perhaps due in part to the well-documented contacts with the cultures of Mexico across the desert to the south."[5] What Slifer states about Ancient Puebloan culture in general is particularly true for their religious traditions. The pantheon, like that of the Aztecs, seems to have been both flexible and fluid.

The contacts with Mexico are not to be minimized in the process of cultural change. Time and again in piecing together the Ancestral Puebloans'

---

[4] Michael O'Hara, "The Magician of Ridge Ruin: An Interpretation of the Social, Political, and Ritual Roles Represented" (unpublished paper, 28 Mar. 2008); David Roberts, *In Search of the Old Ones: Exploring the Anasazi World of the Southwest* (New York, 1996), 219–20.

[5] Slifer, *Kokopelli*, 67.

story, one is drawn to a Mexican connection. Their principal crops – corn, beans, and squash – were all Mexican cultivars that had made their way north. In addition, pottery, bow and arrow, cotton agriculture and loom weaving, and irrigation appear to have arrived from Mexico – if not directly, at least through Ancestral Puebloan contact with the Hohokam or Mogollon.[6] The Mogollon to the south, for instance, were making pottery two centuries before those of Basketmaker III.[7]

After the advent of corn and squash agriculture, appropriate rituals were developed in conjunction with the cycle of planting and harvesting. Slifer writes:

> Summer ceremonies celebrate the fecundity of the earth and often center on corn – the dietary staple but also a profound symbol of fruitfulness. Corn lies at the center of Pueblo religious beliefs, myths, and art – it is synonymous with their identity. Pueblo ceremonies are based on knowledge of the seasons, especially sun and moon cycles, and this knowledge makes it possible to cultivate corn in a harsh arid land with risky growing seasons.[8]

The Ancestral Puebloans therefore acquired a great deal of astronomical knowledge. At the great ceremonial center of Chaco Canyon, there were no fewer than five observatories. One of these in particular, the so-called Sun Dagger on Fajada Butte, is constructed and oriented such that, at noon on the summer solstice, a shaft of sunlight bisects a spiral petroglyph carved on the cliff face.[9] The spiral, a common feature in Ancient Pueblo rock art, "symbolized energy, renewal, wind or breath, water, and the cycles of time since the Paleolithic period."[10] Similarly, the winter solstice, marking the rebirth of the sun, remains an extremely important time of Pueblo ceremonial dances, a new year's rite in which the entire community participates.[11] Stephen Trimble quotes Lea Pinto of Zuni Pueblo, writing, "During winter solstice we bring in all our seeds and pray that those seeds will be reborn. It teaches you about growth – the seed that you are, the seed that you are becoming. Your prayer, even if only one, will help the environment, giving respect to what makes us survive as a people."[12] And scientist William Calvin has demonstrated that other Ancestral Puebloan structures were aligned, not with the cardinal directions, but in a northeast-southeast-southwest-northwest fashion, reflecting sunrise and sunset

---

[6] *Ibid.*
[7] Roberts, *In Search of the Old Ones*, 215.
[8] Slifer, *Kokopelli*, 96.
[9] Jake Page, *In the Hands of the Great Spirit* (New York, 2003), 81–2.
[10] Slifer, *Kokopelli*, 118.
[11] Alfonso Ortiz, *Tewa World: Space Time, Being and Becoming in a Pueblo Society* (Chicago, 1972), 102.
[12] Stephen Trimble, *The People: Indians of the American Southwest* (Santa Fe, 1993), 47.

on the solstices.[13] Nora Naranjo-Morse of Santa Clara Pueblo states, "The older people spent time talking to the sun and wishing it well. They had a strong grasp that it was just *okay*."[14] Still other Ancestral Puebloan structures were oriented on the basis of lunar cycles.

One of the most significant ancestral deities carried over to contemporary Pueblo culture is Kokopelli, the hump-backed flute player. Kokopelli is also controversial and much debated. Certainly, much of what is said about this figure in popular culture in what is today the American Southwest is fanciful and spurious. Some scholars also speculate that the image, very common in Ancient Puebloan petroglyphs, represents itinerant traders, who played the flute to announce their arrival – because flute playing took both hands, demonstrating that they were not enemies sneaking up and carrying weapons. Today, Kokopelli is a Puebloan fertility deity with associations with creation. Among the Zuni, he is associated with rain. For the Hopi, he carries unborn children on his back and gives them to young women. In one telling of the Acoma Pueblo emergence myth, it is Kokopelli playing his flute, Pied Piper-like, who leads the people from the world below into this one, although this mytheme is absent from the oldest recorded versions and may thus be a recent interpolation.[15]

The association of Kokopelli with fertility is manifestly ancient. As mentioned previously, his image is prevalent in Ancestral Puebloan rock art. He is often depicted as having an oversized erect priapus, a literal symbol of reproduction, and sometimes in coital scenes. He is sometimes represented playing to animals or to plants. It seems apparent therefore that he was responsible for abundance of game and crops and of human offspring as well. In at least two instances, in ancient kivas in Colorado, he was carved into the floor of the kiva, which was then covered over by a prepared surface. As Slifer states, "These two subfloor figures, being hidden from view, evidently had an esoteric, magico-religious purpose intended to enhance the horticultural and human fertility of the pueblo. Perhaps this was especially important at a time when prolonged drought caused fertility rates to diminish."[16]

Another rain/fertility deity currently much discussed in Ancestral Puebloan studies circles is Tlaloc, the rain god of the Tolteca, later adopted by the Aztecs. His imagery even predates the Toltecs, appearing in the culture of Teotihuacan. Tlaloc, according to David Carrasco, was "the

---

[13] William H. Calvin, *How the Shaman Stole the Moon* (New York, 1991), 79.
[14] Trimble, *The People*, 47.
[15] Diane Reyna, dir., *Surviving Columbus: The Story of the Pueblo People* (Public Broadcasting Service, 1992).
[16] Slifer, *Kokopelli*, 81–3.

most popular and widespread deity in central Mesoamerica." Depicted with characteristic large "google" eyes, his imagery in Mexico dates back to 800 B.C.E., "making it the oldest recognizable religious complex in the Americas."[17] A fertility/fertilizing deity, Tlaloc was a god over many aspects of the world and life. Not unlike Kokopelli, he was the god of rain, thunderstorms, water, agriculture, and abundance. As naturalist Craig Childs puts it in his book *House of Rain*, "The deity Tlaloc encompasses a variety of related themes: mountains, clouds, mists, rain, drought, caves, springs, a watery underworld, crops, fertility, and renewal." Although, as a god of water, he is associated with the sea, he is most associated with caves and mountains.[18] A water deity, he is also a powerful earth spirit: Tlaloc (or Tlalloc) means "he who has the quality of earth," or "he who is made of earth," or "he who is the embodiment of earth."[19] Tlaloc is thus a deity tailor-made for the desert Southwest and its agricultural peoples.

The Mogollon occupied a vast territory south of the Ancient Puebloans that encompassed parts of Arizona, New Mexico, and West Texas and extended southward deep into the present-day Mexican states of Sonora and Chihuahua. More than other prehistoric desert Southwestern peoples, they left a record of their religious beliefs in stone. Slifer notes that "the near-universal appearance of moisture-associated elements," like crested serpents and clouds, "suggests that the rock art was placed, in part, to ensure adequate rain and good harvests in this harsh desert land. Other water-loving figures found in Jornada Style [Mogollon] sites are fish, tadpoles, turtles, and dragonflies." Tlaloc imagery is commonplace.[20] There are tantalizing clues that the Tlaloc cult might have been the seed from which katsina religion germinated among the Ancient Puebloans and their descendants.

Contemporary Puebloans vehemently object to the idea that their religion has origins in Mexico. Trimble writes succinctly, "The Pueblo people do not think of their spirit beings 'migrating' from anywhere; for them, katsinas have been here from the beginning."[21] There is, however, a consensus among scholars that contemporary Pueblo katsina religion had its beginnings in Mexico and was imported into what is today the American Southwest relatively late in the Anasazi period.

The katsinas are ancestral spirits who act as messengers and intermediaries between the Pueblo people and their deities. Tlaloc resided in the

---

[17] Johanna Broda, David Carrasco, and Eduardo Matos Moctezuma, *The Great Temple of Tenochtitlan* (Berkeley, 1989), 141; Craig Childs, *House of Rain: Tracking a Vanished Civilization Across the American Southwest* (Boston, 2007), 459.
[18] Broda, *Great Temple of Tenochtitlan*, 25, 91; Childs, *House of Rain*, 459.
[19] Broda, *Great Temple of Tenochtitlan*, 102.
[20] Slifer, *Kokopelli*, 63–5.
[21] Trimble, *The People*, 45; see also Ortiz, *Tewa World*, 18.

mountains and mountain caves. The katsinas live in the clouds that gather around mountain peaks. Like Tlaloc, a principal function of the katsinas is to bring rain, and like him, they also bring fertility and health. When a Pueblo person dies, he or she is reborn as a katsina and helps assure the survival of the people by participating in the bringing of life-giving rain. Like their descendants, the Ancient Puebloans carved statues of katsinas. These statues are at once representations of the spirit, dwelling places for the spirit, and embodiments of that spirit. Likewise, they carved masks to be worn by dancers during ceremonies. Jake Page describes the scene:

> Their impersonators come in season to the village plazas, where they are given the opportunity to perform dances and are fed spirit food (cornmeal). In return for these pleasures, they are told that the people have been leading proper lives and the katsinas are obliged to tell the deities that they should allow the rains to come. These ceremonies are not prayers in the sense of pleas – instead they bespeak a reciprocal arrangement, a sacred deal between people and spirits.[22]

In Mexico, Tlaloc was accompanied by the *tlaloque*, "the host of small servants ... who were supposed to assist him in producing the rains." Craig Childs points out the obvious: "Katsinas are very similar to Mesoamerican Tlaloques, which are the rain god Tlaloc's children and family: feathered long-haired spirits said to brew rain, to pound on drums and create thunder." He concludes his discussion on the subject by stating, "Both the symbolic and practical aspects of Tlaloc religion are very similar to those of the Pueblo katsina religion still practiced in the Southwest."[23]

Mogollon territory – where Tlaloc images were abundant – was to the immediate south of that of the Ancestral Puebloans and sat between the homeland of the latter and their trading partners, the Toltec. Religious ideas could have been transmitted directly from Tollan (the Tolteca capital) to the Four Corners via traveling merchants or, as science writer Kendrick Frazier suggests, by "down-the-line" trade. Down-the-line trade "is a more natural and modest means of conducting exchange than the idea of trade emissaries traveling long distances. In down-the-line trade, there are a whole series of exchanges, like a bucket brigade, between adjoining regions. Each trades with its neighbors. Extensive travel is minimized, yet goods and information can move considerable distances."[24] Either way, new religious concepts could have easily traveled up the line.

There is a related element here that brings us back to the oral tradition. In researching *House of Rain*, Craig Childs was struck by repeated bulky

---

[22] Page, *In the Hands of the Great Spirit*, 87.
[23] Broda, *Great Temple of Tenochtitlan*, 73; Childs, *House of Rain*, 420, 459.
[24] Frazier, *People of Chaco*, 169.

T-shapes he saw at Chaco Canyon, Mesa Verde, Aztec ruins, and elsewhere. This form was found primarily in the shape of doorways. On first seeing it at Pueblo Bonito, he assumed it served some ordinary, everyday function, perhaps "allowing people to enter with loads on their backs or facilitating the movement of air into deeper recesses of the great house." It is also found in petroglyphs, in wall niches, painted on walls, and in designs on baskets, textiles, and pottery.[25]

Scholars and other sources Childs consulted were divided and unsure as to the purpose and meaning. Working at Spruce Tree House in 1891, Gustaf Nordenskiöld, the first trained scholar to study Mesa Verde, believed the T-shaped doorways denoted public spaces. Archaeologist Beth Bagwell told Childs, however, that she thought they demarcated "preferred living spaces." She also believed that they were "probably a sort of symbol," but was unsure as to what kind. Rock art specialist Joe Pachak believes the shapes to be representations of points of emergence, "sipapus in the architecture." He told Childs, "People would have been reminded of their story daily, going in and out of the house, emerging into the world, then going back inside." Charles Di Peso, the distinguished archaeologist who excavated Paquimé in Chihuahua, sees T-shaped doors and carvings (as well as a T-shaped public space he believed to be a religious arena) as representing Tlaloc. Childs writes, "He wrote in his notes that passing through one of the doorways, you would have been passing through the very eye of Tlaloc. Inside you would reach the legendary seat of this rain god, a fabled underground lake. Perhaps cool air flowing through the T-shaped doorways was like the moist air that ushers from caves, the breath of Tlaloc."[26]

Most of these theories advanced are not intellectually mutually exclusive, and all may have a degree of truth. It appears, however, that Di Peso hits closest to the heart of it. Childs asked a Hopi man about the T-shapes. The anonymous consultant replied, "I believe the T shape is a mountain underground.... I think it symbolizes an inverted mountain, a mirror of what is aboveground. The mountain aboveground gathers clouds and rain. The mountain below draws rainfall into an underground lake.... The shape of the T is a mountain upside down. Its stem leads into the underworld where there is water." Commenting on the Hopi's story, naturalist Childs states:

> Of course, I thought, pre-Columbian people knew the hydrological cycle, the way in which water transfers from the atmosphere to the ground and back. Living in the Southwest for thousands of years, people would have

---

[25] Childs, *House of Rain*, 50, 459.
[26] *Ibid.*, 138, 217, 417–18; Jay W. Sharp, "Paquime: The Last Great Center of Puebloan Influence," http://www.desertusa.com/ind1/ind_new/ind13.html (accessed 25 June 2008).

been keenly aware of the rhythmic relationship between precipitation and spring flows. They would have known how many years of good rain it would take to fill an underground lake, an aquifer, able to predict chances of survival and calculate how soon a migration might need to begin.[27]

Childs' linking of oral tradition to TEK (traditional environmental knowledge) makes sense.[28] He concludes his discussion, "Even modern hydrologists cannot adequately explain the direct correlation between climate shifts and water table fluctuations. Sitting at the man's wooden table, I thought, perhaps they cannot explain it because they have not had to live and die by it for thousands of years. They are unaware that Tlaloc is breathing."[29]

One other spirit figure deserves individual discussion: Tanama, a figure common among the indigenous peoples of the desert Southwest under various names – and, like Kokopelli, Tlaloc, the origin of the katsina religion, and practically everything else in the discussion of Ancient Pueblo religion, controversial. The fullest explication of him appears in the 1924 work *Children of the Twilight: Folk-Tales of Indian Tribes,* by travel writer and amateur ethnographer Emma-Lindsay Squier, who pieced together a cycle of stories about him from Apache, Navajo, Havasupai, Hopi, and Taos Pueblo sources.[30] She calls the myth she records "The Trembling God." Of her multiple tribal informants, she writes, "Each one will give you a different version; there will be wide gaps in the tale, and vague inconsistencies. But all of them know – yet rarely speak of – this legend of the desert, a legend of those mysterious peoples who built their pueblos high on inaccessible cliffs."[31] This then is a story of the Ancestral Puebloans. For Squier, the fact that she found versions among five different tribes lends credence, although given the close geographic proximities involved, diffusion is more than possible. She also saw in her travels in Arizona the topographic feature of the title, a toppled slab of tapered granite that had once been naturally balanced upright on one end: it had been known to Euro-American immigrants as "Balanced Rock" but was called the "Trembling God" by Indians, hence the myth.

---

[27] Childs, *House of Rain*, 420–1.
[28] See also Duane Good Striker, "TEK Wars: First Nations' Struggles for Environmental Planning," in Jace Weaver, ed., *Defending Mother Earth: Native American Perspectives on Environmental Justice* (Maryknoll, NY, 1996), 144–52.
[29] Childs, *House of Rain*, 421.
[30] See "Of Trembling Gods and Moon-Eyed People: Ruminations on the Limits of Ethnography," in Jace Weaver, *Notes from a Miner's Canary* (Albuquerque, 2010). My wife, Laura Adams Weaver, also has found a version among the Tohono O'Odham in Arizona.
[31] Emma-Lindsay Squier, *Children of the Twilight: Folk-Tales of Indian Tribes* (Cleveland, 1924), 55.

Squier does not identify the cliff dwelling where she saw the rock, but from her description and details of the trip and the location, it appears to have been Montezuma Castle. The story is that of Tanama, a hero who was half god and half human.

At the beginning of the world, Tanama came among the People and saw that they had next to nothing and no skills whatsoever. Acting as a culture hero, he gave them fire. He taught them how to make clothing and housing. He taught them to build dams and grow crops. He gave them the corn dance and the snake dance. He spent years among the People, instructing and helping them. Everywhere he went, he counseled purity. As Squier tells it, he preached, "Keep your honor clean; do not mingle with other people; let your sons marry in their pueblos. If you do this, you will always be a strong people. If you welcome strangers among you, it will bring ruin upon you."[32]

At length, however, the thunder god became jealous of Tanama and his connection to the People. He was angry that the hero had not taught the People to honor him. He lured Tanama up to the mesa rim and turned him to stone. The People could find no trace of Tanama after his encounter with Thunder, but they saw the new balanced stone, which vibrated ever so slightly. In a dream, Tanama made known to the priest that the peculiar rock was he and that he was still with the People to protect and teach them. He repeated his purity admonition and, according to Squier, declared, "As long as I shall stand erect, so shall your strength and glory endure. But if I fall, then let your children weep. For the red man shall perish with my going."[33]

The myth then shifts. Many years have passed. One day, a remnant of the Toltecas arrives, saying that they have been displaced by "a fierce and bloodthirsty people." They had decided to leave rather than submit. For seven years, they journeyed ever northward, until they arrived at this place. They request that they should be permitted to stay and "join forces with the people of the cliff pueblos, should live with them in peace and amicability, and that the two tribes should combine their might against the roving desert savages." There ensue many discussions as to whether the People should honor the request of the migrants, but at length they agree. The war chief, Nanoomi, however, is uneasy. He dreams of Tanama, who tells him in his vision,

> Send them away.... Nothing but evil will come of this tribal union. Behold, the nation of the Toltecas was rotten like a melon that has lain too long in the sunshine. The foot of the invader crushed it because it was soft and

---

[32] Ibid., 64.
[33] Ibid., 65–6.

offered no resistance. Bring not the rottenness of a conquered people into the high places of desert men. Send them away, lest your tribe become polluted, lest they forget the things which I, Tanama, gave my life to teach. Send them away, lest your people perish![34]

The war chief and his doubts do not carry the day. The southerners are made welcome and integrate into the life of the People. Unfortunately, the prophecy proves correct. The newcomers bring deceit, treachery, and infidelity among the People. The Trembling God topples himself in order to prevent a grievous assault on the People. He resurrects himself to his previous promontory a year later, only to reveal the evidence of the attempted crime (precipitated among other things by the cuckolding of Nanoomi by the Toltec band, Coatzil). Squier notes that the Trembling God collapsed a second and final time in the nineteenth century as Euro-Americans displaced the natives.

This lengthy summary of the myth Squier relates is still inadequate to capture its drama. Although it obviously has been romanticized by the writer in her retelling, it nevertheless bears markings of orature. In evaluating it, I come down on the side of authenticity, at least in its basic elements.

A granite slab standing alone, precariously upright on a tapered point and vibrating or trembling has "personality," that is to say, it is an oddity. It was thus likely to become a sacred site and as such would merit an explanation.

I believe the reason Squier had to piece the myth together was that she actually encountered a cycle of stories, common among indigenes for trickster figures and culture heroes. The reason the story veers so widely in both time and tone from the early contributions of Tanama to the People, to his inevitable departure (all culture heroes depart), and to the much later story of acceptance and betrayal is that Squier has stitched multiple myths together in a desire for coherence. She notes gaps and inconsistencies.

There are several elements that need analysis. The plotline about the Toltec might at first blush seem preposterous. The Ancient Puebloans' main partner in the turquoise trade – and their only large customer – was the Toltec. If some Toltecas did decide to depart, north might not seem an improbable destination. The Azteca entered the Valley of Mexico in the mid-thirteenth century. Tenochtitlan was founded in 1325. According to Alfredo López Austin, the Toltec capital fell in 1350, and in 1371 the political equilibrium of the region collapsed, and the barbaric (to Toltec lights) northern invaders allied themselves with the equally aggressive Tepanecs.[35]

---

[34] *Ibid.*, 68.
[35] Alfredo López Austin and Leonardo López Luján, *Mexico's Indigenous Past* (Norman, OK, 2001), 186, 207.

Any remnant Toltec exodus would therefore logically be between 1350 and 1371. If the seven-year time frame cited by Squier approximates reality, that would put the arrival of the wandering band among the Ancestral Puebloans between 1357 and 1378. If, in turn, I am correct in my identification of the site of the Trembling God at Montezuma Castle, then the cliff dwelling was built by the Sinagua. The location was one of the last holdouts, inhabited until circa 1425. So, temporally, this element of the myth is plausible.

The fact that Squier lists Hopi as one of the sources for the story is significant. The Hopi regard themselves as ancestrally related to the Sinagua and to Montezuma Castle. That the chronicler cites the Apache and Navajo is potentially more problematic, because it is commonly assumed that these Athabaskan migrants, after departing what is today western Canada, entered the Southwest only around 1400 C.E. This would not automatically negate, however, Squier's culture hero as Ancient Puebloan.

In his *Anasazi America*, published in 2000, anthropologist David Stuart writes:

> Navajo oral tradition may help us learn something about the enemies of the Mesa Verdeans. One series of ancient and remarkable Navajo tales tells of a poor beggar woman and her son who went from Chacoan great house to great houses seeking food. Several great houses such as Pueblo Bonito, Wijiji, and Aztec are referred to by name, and the kinds of food and specific events at each (such as plucking turquoise offerings from the cliff behind Pueblo Bonito) are recounted. In the tale, Keet Seel, White House at Canyon de Chelly, and another cliff house (probably Jacquet) near Farmington are mentioned. All these sites contain Mesa Verde black-on-white pottery, so we know they were inhabited during the 1200s, in Mesa Verdean times.[36]

Stuart admits that such stories are not "absolute proof" of Navajo presence while the great houses, such as Pueblo Bonito, were occupied, but he finds them "strongly suggestive." Although the scholar believes that the Dine (i.e., Navajo) myths will be independently confirmed, he acknowledges, "The Navajo, of course, are not waiting for confirmation from us. They hold these tales to be true, and obviously so. After all, how else would their ancestors have known who lived at the great houses and what food they offered or refused the beggar woman and her sons?"[37]

Stuart posits that perhaps the Navajo stories are reflective of the known Mesa Verdean reoccupation of Chaco between 1050 to 1260 C.E. He notes that recent excavations date some Navajo hogans to the fourteenth century. He writes, "That leaves the archaeological gap between Mesa Verdean

---

[36] David E. Stuart, *Anasazi America* (Albuquerque, 2000), 135.
[37] *Ibid.*

reoccupation at Chacoan great houses and Navajo settlement in the Four Corners at just a century, not the four or five that most textbooks report."[38] Even if Navajo and Apache arrival did occur at the later date on the cusp of the fifteenth century, that would still fall within the period of occupation of Montezuma Castle, making possible Navajo and Apache firsthand knowledge of the Ancestral Puebloans. In fact, the myth itself seems to suggest that the two Athabaskan-speaking peoples might be "the roving desert savages" against whom the Toltec suggested they and the cliff dwellers join forces for mutual protection.

This brings us to the final great issue concerning the Ancestral Puebloans and the role of religion – specifically the katsina religion – in their lives. Like everything else pertaining to the subject, it is highly contested, contentious, and uncertain. Although there is still much we do not know, there is also a great deal that we do know and more that we can infer with a degree of certitude. The question is that of the collapse of Ancestral Puebloan civilization. It is known as the Great Abandonment, and to adequately understand it, one must backtrack all the way to the beginning of the so-called Anasazi Pueblo I period.

Prior to 800 C.E., only a small group of Basketmakers lived in arid Chaco Canyon in the Four Corners area, in what is today Arizona. Between 800 and 850, the Ancient Puebloans began a massive building campaign in the canyon, erecting a great ceremonial and trade center. At the height of the classic period, circa 1100 C.E., there were fifteen great multistory settlements, accounting for a population of five thousand persons. Trees for roof timbers of the pueblos were brought from forests a hundred miles away. Broad highways radiated from Chaco, bringing in pilgrims, merchants, and shoppers from all points of the Ancestral Puebloan Empire and beyond. Toltec traders would have regularly arrived from Tollan (Tula). Chaco completely controlled the mining of turquoise. The aquamarine semiprecious stone became a principal medium of exchange, and it helped draw Puebloan people to the great religious centers, like Pueblo Bonito, of Chaco Canyon.

Even though there were five thousand inhabitants of the great houses of Chaco, and although the classic period represented one of the wettest cycles climactically in the history of the North American West, the arable land adjacent to these towns could support only about two thousand individuals. Thus, like the great Mississippian ceremonial and trading center at Cahokia, Chaco was dependent on farmers in the greater surrounding area to supply it with the wherewithal for survival. By about the year 920, Chaco Canyon, like Cahokia, had developed a system of outlier agriculturalists to

---

[38] *Ibid.*, 136.

provide it with food. In this, of course, it was no different than modern metropolitan centers. How much food does New York, or Paris, or Beijing produce to sustain itself?

According to Native American studies scholar Karen Strom,

> Some 2500 outlying Anasazi abandoned rural farm villages of single-family pit and adobe homes have been found. Turquoise, the medium of exchange, was one thing that pulled their inhabitants into Chaco for the large religious festivals and trade fairs, packing all they could carry of surplus food (such as dried corn, beans, squash rings) on their backs, for there were no burden-bearing animals and no wheeled vehicles. Outlying farmers could exchange surplus food for turquoise, a permanently-storable wealth, which could be traded later, if necessary, for food and craft goods from the center or locally. Turquoise thus functioned for all the people of this civilization as money – wearable, beautiful, spiritually enhancing, and religiously iconic, but practical, too.[39]

The era when this picture of Chaco's dominance was literally true was relatively brief. The peak of Chacoan power lasted only from about 1020 C.E. until 1130 C.E. As David Stuart points out, however, even by 1050, Chaco was already under stress "as health and living conditions progressively eroded in the southern district's open farming communities" that supplied the urban centers and provided surpluses to be stored in the great houses.[40] More shocks were to come.

According to Strom, "Chaco governors tightly controlled the turquoise mines at Cerillos [New Mexico]. Raw stone was brought to Pueblo Bonito to be cut into small tiles, which the merchant-traders took back to Tollan for use in jeweled and tiled creations." But new mines opened in present-day Nevada and Arizona, breaking the Puebloan monopoly on supply and creating a competitive market. As Strom correctly characterizes the situation, with more turquoise in circulation, prices fell and a kind of inflation was created. Then, in 1100, civil unrest in the Toltec Empire disrupted the turquoise market.[41]

This created the first major disruption of Chacoan society. The collapse of its turquoise monopoly appears to have broken the power of Chaco's elites over religious observance. Archaeologist Lynne Sebastian has pointed out "that large religious gatherings did not take place in Chaco Canyon after 1100." Analyzing Sebastian's findings, Stuart writes, "Clearly, the elites' economic and religious power over an entire region had been destroyed,

---

[39] Karen Strom, "Pueblo Bonito: Turquoise Trade Capital," http:www.kstrom.net/isk/art.beads/boninto. html (accessed 22 June 2008).
[40] Stuart, *Anasazi America*, 67, 122.
[41] Strom, "Pueblo Bonito," n. 39.

never to be reestablished. After 1100, ritual leaders could exercise power only over small competing groups of followers.[42]

Stuart says the crisis caused the elites to respond "with the sacred formula – more roads, more rituals, more great houses." At this moment there was a major proliferation in construction of kivas, pointing, he says, "to a ritual life that had stopped nurturing open communities and had grown increasingly demanding and obsessive." He concludes, "I also find it ironic that the greatest Chacoan building projects were, like many of the CCC and WPA projects of our own Great Depression, the desperate economic reactions of a frightened and fragile society."[43] Although there is undoubtedly some truth to Stuart's assessment, especially as it pertains to public buildings and roads to nowhere, from a religious point of view, I see the marked increase in kivas somewhat differently. It simply represents the breakdown in religious domination, in the same way that economic competition did in the turquoise monopoly. It represents new, competing religious sects – new congregations, if you will.

Decreasing rainfalls between 1080 and 1100 C.E. had contributed to the farm crisis, but the rains revived in the early twelfth century. By then, however, these other dislocations added to the stresses on Chaco society. Finally, in 1130 the rains stopped yet again, ushering in a fifty-year drought. Chaco's outlier system fell apart in 1140. Although the canyon towns struggled on for another decade, in 1150 Chaco itself collapsed and its residents dispersed. They migrated to Hopi, Zuni, and other communities in the Four Corners area and beyond. As Chaco Canyon spun people out centrifugally, Mesa Verde ascended as the major center of Puebloan culture. Beginning around 1200 C.E., construction of high cliff dwellings began at places like Mesa Verde, Keet Seel, and Montezuma Castle, supplanting flatland pueblos and indicating a society under some kind of threat.

The twelfth and thirteenth centuries saw the gradual desertion of Ancestral Puebloan centers. Puebloan trade seems to have imploded entirely around 1250 C.E. There was a refulgence of occupation of Chaco, but it lasted only about two decades. Another drought struck in 1276 and lasted until 1299. By 1300, the Ancient Puebloans had abandoned the Four Corners and Colorado Plateau.[44]

In his discussion of his Hopi consultant's story, Craig Childs ties TEK to migration and thus to the Great Abandonment. It has long been assumed that climatic shifts and drought led the Ancestral Puebloans to leave their homes. Geographer Jared Diamond, in his book *Collapse: How Societies Choose*

---

[42] Stuart, *Anasazi America*, 143.
[43] Ibid., 122–3.
[44] Roberts, *In Search of the Old Ones*, 150–1.

to Fail or Succeed, follows the contemporary trend among scholars of eschewing "single-factor" explanations.[45] Already cited previously are the multiple shocks to the system that the Ancient Puebloans had to absorb: the loss of their turquoise monopoly, the resultant inflation, recurrent droughts, and the collapse of their trade markets and outlier farming support system. Ultimately, for some reason or constellation of reasons, the Ancestral Puebloans abandoned the Four Corners and, in a reversal of the Toltecs of the Tanama myth, migrated south, where they reconfigured themselves. Archaeologist William Lipe states,

> For most of this century, archaeologists focused on environmental causes for the abandonment: drought, famine, arroyo cutting, and the like. Or they talked about wars with the nomads. They saw the abandonment only in terms of push. But we're coming to see that it takes a pull as well as push. Something immensely attractive or compelling must have been going on to the south and east, and up on the Colorado Plateau they got wind of it. More and more, we're coming to believe that the pull was the Kachina Phenomenon.[46]

The "Kachina Phenomenon" can also be thought of as katsina religion. Interestingly, Lipe and others are coming to see the missing piece of the abandonment puzzle as this new religious movement, which remains the religion of the descendants of the Ancestral Puebloans to this day.

Regardless of whether it can be linked directly to the Tlaloc cult, katsina religion was, as already discussed, another cultural phenomenon that, according to anthropologists, migrated northward from Mexico. Like the possibility of its Mesoamerican origins, the exact timing of its advent is much debated. Reflecting the commonly accepted timeline, Stuart writes, "The early 1300s were the years when masked rain gods and the kachina cult, thought to have originated west of the Zuni area, began to penetrate the eastern pueblos and displace many older religious customs." For years, it was stated that the earliest evidence archaeologists could find for the new religion dated from circa 1325. Leigh Jenkins, the cultural preservation officer for the Hopi, told Roberts, however, "If you look at the rock art, you can verify that the kachinas were around. There is no doubt that they were around at the time of migration." And opinion has begun to swing in Jenkins' direction. Scholars are, in fact, pushing the date of this religious upheaval even farther back. Lipe states, "The late 1200s was a time of substantial, political and religious ferment and experimentation."[47]

---

[45] Jared Diamond, *Collapse: How Societies Choose to Fail or Succeed* (New York, 2004), 137.
[46] Roberts, *In Search of the Old Ones*, 149.
[47] John Fox, "Religion May Be Hidden Motive Behind Anasazi Migration, http://archives.cnn.com/2000/NATURE/03/28/america.quest.day17/index.html (published 28 Mar. 2000; accessed 20 June 2008); Stuart, *Anasazi* America, 150; Roberts, *In Search of the Old*

The question has become so central to Ancestral Puebloan studies that speculation has at times run somewhat wild. *New York Times* science writer George Johnson notes, "Other archaeologists see evidence of an evangelical-like religion – the forerunner, perhaps, of the masked Kachina rituals, which still survive on the Hopi and Zuni reservations – appearing in the south and attracting rebellious northerners." Archaeologist Bruce Bradley of the University of Exeter has gone even further, suggesting that the entire Chacoan revival "was driven by a single charismatic figure, a Christ type, if you will." He explains, "In any event, the Chacoan revival lasts only fifteen or twenty years, before it falls apart. Then the great drought of 1276 to 1299 hits. They kill their leaders – all through Sand Canyon we found bodies showing signs of violent death. They burn their kivas, perhaps to exorcise the trauma of the violence. Then they abandon the Colorado Plateau." In Bradley's theory, the new katsina religion they found in the south provided them with a way to reconstitute themselves and survive as the Pueblos for seven hundred years.[48]

Despite more spectacular speculations, did religion play a central role in the Great Abandonment? There are logical reasons for believing that it did, and there are tantalizing clues leading in that direction.

Bradley's vision of a messiah and a religious revolt aside, he is correct that as Ancestral Puebloan societies became more complex socially, politically, and religiously, they also became more interdependent. As Lipe says, "You can't have a situation where it just happens that hundreds of local communities for their own individual, particularistic reasons decide to either die or get up and move. There had to be something general going on." His colleague at Washington State University Timothy Kohler concurs, stating, "You can't peel off a lineage here and a lineage there and have them go their own way. These parts are no longer redundant. They are part of an integrated whole." George Johnson summarizes, "Pull one thread and the whole culture unwinds."[49] For a society under severe stress from drought and possible conflict, either internal or external, the new movement might have provided precisely Lipe's "pull" southward. According to him, "With its focus on rain, fertility, and peace the kachina religion offered a new vision of hope to the Anasazi as it drew them south in search of a better place."[50] Santa Clara Pueblo historian Rina Swintzell puts it philosophically, "There is an easy flow of life. Build up this community,

---

Ones, 102; George Johnson, "Vanished: A Pueblo Mystery," http://www.nytimes.com/2008/04/08/science/08anasazi.html_r=1&sq=Anasazi&st=nyt&orefslogin (published 8 Apr. 2008; accessed 24 June 2008).

[48] Johnson, "Vanished"; Roberts, *In Search of the Old Ones*, 151–2.
[49] Johnson, "Vanished".
[50] Fox, "Religion May Be Hidden Motive."

something happens, time to go, move on to the next place, leaving the pot sitting there, walking away from it, without any need to pack it and take all your possessions with you. The thing that you took with you was creative capability, and that was all you needed."[51]

Historian Leigh Jenkins ties the religious impulse for the Great Abandonment to the oral tradition. He states, "We had a spiritual covenant with our guardian deity, Maasaw. The covenant required us very literally to place our footprints over the Fourth World. This was the cause of the migration of the Hopi clans."[52]

The Fourth World is this one, the current world onto which the Hopi emerged after inhabiting three previous worlds underground. Maasaw is their omnipresent, tutelary deity.[53] Depicted as a skeletal figure, he is both the god of the underworld and the original proprietor of the Fourth World. As Arlene Hirschfelder and Paulette Molin summarize in *The Encyclopedia of Native American Religions*, he is

> in charge of the underworld and the earth's surface, as well as death, fire, fertility, creation, darkness and war. As the ruler of the underworld, Masau'u is the spirit of death. He stands at the entrance to the underworld mediating between the living and the dead. He has the power to cause the metamorphosis of nature and takes many forms. He is the deity responsible for teaching Hopis about using fire.[54]

Ekkehart Malotki of Northern Arizona University, the foremost scholarly authority on Maasaw, amplifies,

> In the entire pantheon of Hopi mythological figures none is more important than the god Maasaw. His complexity and wealth of associations within the Hopi scheme of the world is immense.... While regarded as the god of death and ruler of the underworld, he is also believed to be ... the owner of fire and crops, and the maker of all things animal and vegetal. Furthermore, he is venerated as the caretaker of life, the defender of Hopi ways, and as a powerful war deity.[55]

Although, according to Malotki, Maasaw today has risen "to the status of a near-monotheistic divinity," he began as a relatively minor trickster figure.[56] Maasaw appears in petroglyphs dating from the Ancestral period.[57]

---

[51] Trimble, *The People*, 45.
[52] Roberts, *In Search of the Old Ones*, 102.
[53] Ekkehart Malotki, *Stories of Maasaw, a Hopi God* (Lincoln, 1987), vii.
[54] Arlene Hirschfelder and Paulette Molin, *The Encyclopedia of Native American Religions* (New York, 1992), 169–70.
[55] Ekkehart Malotki, *Maasaw: Profile of a Hopi God* (Lincoln, 1987), 3–4.
[56] *Ibid.*, 3.
[57] See, e.g., William M. Eaton, *Odyssey of the Pueblo Indians* (Paducah, KY, 2002), 52.

If he begins in Hopi mythology "at a rather low level," as is "still traceable in a few surviving stories," it seems certain that this reflects his original Ancestral Puebloan function. Over time new roles were accreted, and perhaps he was repurposed.

Speaking about the Great Abandonment and Maasaw's role, Leigh Jenkins continues, "There are old stories about the clans becoming a little too complacent. The stories say some clans were sternly reminded by natural phenomena that they had to move on. The natural phenomenon was a kind of sign: 'Look, you're getting a bit lazy.'"[58] Migration is thus part of the people's original instructions and a chastisement. The Hopi were enjoined to plant their feet over the entire earth. Some clans were failing to live up to their responsibility, and Maasaw used environmental change to prod them along.

The Spanish colonial experience presents a problem, however, when examining Southwestern oral and performed traditions. Spaniards harshly suppressed Pueblo religion, forcing it underground. Although, as has been the case with religious persecution at all times and in all places, this undoubtedly increased the strength of individual adhesion, it also disrupted the natural chains of cultural transmission. By the time of the Pueblo Revolt of 1680, which at least temporarily halted the process, much had already been lost. After the *reconquista* in 1692, the onslaught of evangelical violence began anew. So disruptive were the Spanish efforts that Polly Schaafsma of the Museum of New Mexico says that "what we know today of kachinas is essentially a 'relic population' of a once grander phenomenon."[59]

Archaeologist Paul Reed writes,

> Our list of "unknowns" regarding Chacoan ceremonialism is substantial. We cannot specify accurately the nature of Chacoan ritual and ceremony. We do not know what ceremonies were like or how they were conducted. We have no information on the words that were spoken, the songs that were sung, and the music and drumming that probably occurred during ceremonies. More specifically, we do not know the names of the deities important to Chacoan religion.[60]

Alhough Reed speaks specifically of Chaco Canyon, what he says is equally true of the Ancestral Puebloans generally. It should be noted that the names of the deities discussed in this essay were not those necessarily employed by the ancestors themselves but are rather the names invoked by their historical descendants.

---

[58] Roberts, *In Search of the Old Ones*, 102.
[59] *Ibid.*, 150.
[60] Paul F. Reed, *The Puebloan Society of Chaco Canyon* (Westport, 2004), 86–7.

George Lankford, at the beginning of his book *Looking for Lost Lore: Studies in Folklore, Ethnology, and Iconography*, quotes British writer L. P. Hartley: "The past is a foreign country; they do things differently there." Lankford elaborates, "When the problem of 'doing history' is shifted from societies that commit everything to paper, whether contemporary or past, to societies that left only objects in the ground and oral traditions among their descendants, the foreignness of the country becomes truly daunting."[61]

Although there is unquestionably a degree of truth in the assessments of Reed, Hartley, and Lankford, we must be equally careful not to overstate their case. The past may be a foreign country, but it is not another planet. Although remote from us temporally and although evidence about them may at times be scant, groups like the Mississippians and the Ancestral Puebloans are not completely alien to us. In *Looking for Lost Lore*, Lankford seeks the mythology of groups, including the Mississipians, that are no longer extant. And Reed acknowledges that Ancestral period ritual artifacts found by archaeologists are similar enough to contemporary objects to "suggest ceremonial practices that were at least similar to those of the modern Pueblos." He continues,

> Ritual is, in fact, believed by many Chacoan archaeologists to be the primary raison d'etre for the rise of Chacoan society in its unique form. We can say unequivocally that ritual and ceremony were important factors in its evolution. Archaeologists are confident that ritual specialists, whom we might call priests, were responsible for conducting ceremonies, for maintaining ritual artifacts and paraphernalia, and for tracking the ritual calendar and scheduling events.[62]

The past may be a foreign country, but it is not Hamlet's unknown country. The Ancestral Puebloans are not dead to us. They are not unknowable intellectually. They are part and parcel of the human story.

SUGGESTIONS FOR FURTHER READING

Childs, Craig. *House of Rain: Tracking a Vanished Civilization Across the American Southwest*. Boston, 2007.

Frazier, Kendrick. *People of Chaco: A Canyon and Its People*. Rev. ed. New York, 1999.

Malotki, Ekkehart. *Maasaw: Profile of a Hopi God*. Lincoln, 1987.

———. *Stories of Maasaw, a Hopi God*. Lincoln, 1987.

Malotki, Ekkehart, and Paricia McCreery. *Tapamveni: The Rock Art Galleries of Petrified Forest and Beyond*. Tucson, 1994.

---

[61] George E. Lankford, *Looking for Lost Lore: Studies in Folklore, Ethnology, and Iconography* (Tuscaloosa, AL, 2008), 1.

[62] Reed, *Puebloan Society of Chaco Canyon*, 86.

Roberts, David. *In Search of the Old Ones: Exploring the Anasazi World of the Southwest.* New York, 1996.

Slifer, Dennis. *Kokopelli: The Magic, Mirth, and Mischief of an Ancient Symbol.* Salt Lake City, 2007.

Stuart, David E. *Anasazi America.* Albuquerque, 2000.

9

SPANISH CATHOLICISM IN THE ERA OF EXPLORATION AND EARLY COLONIZATION

PABLO GARCIA AND KATHLEEN ANN MYERS

The centuries-long effort to reclaim the Iberian Peninsula from North African Muslim invaders known as the *reconquista* ended in 1492 with the fall of the last Moorish stronghold, the city of Granada. In the same year, Fernando of Aragon and Isabel of Castile, known as the Catholic Kings for their service to Christendom, embarked on the transatlantic venture that would bring the crusading spirit and sense of providential entitlement of the *reconquista* to the New World. From the outset, the spread of Roman Catholicism was an immediate and pressing concern. The faith provided not only an identity for the budding Spanish Empire, but a legal and moral justification for the conquest and colonization of what was generally referred to as Las Indias (the Indies). There, being Spaniard was synonymous with being Christian, and no expedition set forth without at least one priest, whose task it was to minister to the troops and convert the natives. Saying that the sword went hand in hand with the cross has become a truism.

CONQUEST AND CONVERSION

The inextricable tie between the Church and the state is one of the most salient features of the Spanish evangelization efforts in the Indies. In a series of bulls issued in 1493, Pope Alexander VI granted possession of the newly discovered territories to the Spanish crown. In 1501, another bull assigned the tithes obtained from the territories to the crown for the purpose of founding and endowing new churches. The crown's authority over the American Church was further enhanced in 1508 when Pope Julius II bestowed the *Patronato Real* (Royal Patronage), which granted Spanish kings the right to nominate church officials – whether directly or through obedient overseas officials – and a decisive role in the establishment and delimitation of dioceses in the Spanish territories. Later attempts by the Vatican to regain control from the crown were mostly ineffectual. In 1622, Pope Gregory XV established the Sacra Congregatio de Propaganda Fide, a curial office intended to oversee missionary work. However, the Consejo de Indias (Council of the Indies), instituted by Charles I in 1524 to manage transatlantic affairs, including ecclesiastical ones, would not allow any interference from Rome and suspended the establishment of new dioceses for the next 155 years, until 1777.[1]

The American Church served the imperialist will of the crown as an instrument of expansion, an indirect means of control, and an agent of cultural transformation. The rapid spread of a missionary presence throughout the continent coincided with the conquering endeavors promoted by individuals who sought personal fortune and fame and, at least nominally, the salvation of Indian souls. Their victories over the indigenous groups brought about the imposition of new civil and religious structures. Whenever possible, missionaries and colonial administrators alike took advantage of preexisting structures that could facilitate colonial reorganization. This was especially true in central Mexico and Peru, where the Nahua (Aztec) and the Inca had well-established political and administrative systems. Elsewhere, the establishment of *reducciones*, ad hoc communities intended to facilitate evangelization, also brought the indigenous populations under colonial control. Numerous factors account for the receptivity or resistance to Spanish impositions, including religion. The violence and ravaging plagues brought by the conquistadors must have made a profound impression on the indigenous population, driving many to seek refuge in the more powerful religion of their vanquishers. Likewise, persistence of pre-Hispanic customs and beliefs varied greatly depending on the circumstances of evangelization.[2] Over time, however, the systematic attack on traditional religious systems, added to demographic and social upheaval, transformed indigenous cultures in radical ways, often to the point of annihilation.

The Caribbean was the point of departure for both the military and spiritual conquest of the New World. After the aborted mission of Fr. Bernal Boyl as apostolic vicar to the New World, evangelization began in earnest around 1500, when Franciscan missionaries landed on the island of Hispaniola and founded the first church in the Indies. The first three dioceses were created on Hispaniola and Puerto Rico in 1511. Three years after the founding of the first continental settlement, the diocese of Santa María del Darién was established in 1513. In 1524, three years after the conquest of Mexico, twelve Franciscans arrived in New Spain, where the first diocese

---

[1] J. Lloyd Mecham, *Church and State in Latin America: A History of Politico-Ecclesiastical Relations* (Chapel Hill, 1966).

[2] Stafford Poole, "Observations on Mission Methods and Native Reactions in Sixteenth-Century New Spain," *The Americas* 50:3 (1994): 337–49.

was created the following year in Tlaxcala. Cuzco, the former capital of the Inca Empire, became the first diocese in South America in 1537. Not all the sees succeeded in equal measure. Some of the early establishments were abandoned or relocated; dioceses in poorer districts were unable to support large-scale churches, a diversity of ecclesiastical offices, or numerous parishes. As with other colonial enterprises, dioceses prospered more rapidly in areas with larger populations and dynamic economies.[3] Santo Domingo, Mexico City, and Ciudad de los Reyes (Lima) gained archdiocese status in 1546. In the second half of the sixteenth century, a number of important provincial councils in Lima and Mexico set the policies that, once approved by the Consejo de Indias, would govern the colonial Church. Also at this time, the Office of the Holy Inquisition was formally established and started policing the orthodoxy of the colonizers and their offspring in the New World. In 1620, two new dioceses were created at the edges of the empire, Buenos Aires in the south and Durango in the north, bringing the total number of American dioceses to thirty-five. By the early seventeenth century, the colonial Church had acquired its lasting institutional structure.[4]

THE EVANGELICAL ENTERPRISE

During the decades of exploration and conquest, roughly 1500–42, missionary work was left mostly in the hands of the regular orders. The Franciscans were the first to be granted access to the Indies in 1500, followed by the Dominicans (1509), the Mercedarians (1514), the Augustinians (1533), the Jesuits (1565), and finally the Capuchins (1657). Generally, each order established its own areas of influence, claiming territories as it arrived. Thus the Franciscan order was the first and most influential in central New Spain, where one of its members, Juan de Zumárraga, served as first bishop of Mexico. Likewise, the Dominicans played a key role in the evangelization of Peru, with Vicente de Valverde, who had participated in Francisco Pizarro's conquering expedition, appointed as the first bishop in Cuzco. As late arrivals, Jesuit missionaries were especially active in the southern and northern reaches of the empire, although they also gained prominence in colonial centers as scholars and teachers. The number of regular missionaries grew throughout the colonial period, with new members coming from Spain, but also increasingly from the criollo population of locally born

---

[3] A. C. van Oss, "Comparing Colonial Bishoprics in Spanish South America," in idem, ed., *Church and Society in Spanish America* (Amsterdam, 2003), 61–102.

[4] Johannes Meier, "The Organization of the Church," in Enrique Dussel, ed., *The Church in Latin America, 1492–1992* (Tunbridge Wells, 1992), 55–65.

Spaniards. This was also the case with the secular clergy. By the end of the seventeenth century, there were seventeen Franciscan, nine Dominican, and eight Mercedarian provinces, while the Augustinians and the Jesuits each had seven. Even so, there were never enough clergy, whether regular or secular, to match the scope of the evangelical enterprise, and many remote communities remained at the margins of their labors. The relatively rapid spread of the Catholic Church in Spanish America was not necessarily proportional to the success of its evangelical aims.

Each order brought its own missionary ideals and methods to the New World. In the sixteenth century, the Franciscans and the Dominicans were the most influential. The first Franciscans were driven by a millenarian vision that sought to re-create a purer, so-called primitive, church in America as the final preparation for the thousand-year reign of the Spirit, which would be followed by the Apocalypse. Their zeal led them to conduct mass baptisms and to imbue indigenous symbols with new Christian meanings. According to the Franciscan chronicler Fr. Juan De Torquemada, soon after their arrival in New Spain, the missionaries felled a holy tree associated with the worship of the rain god Tlaloc, made it into a cross, and planted it in the middle of their church's courtyard.[5] Such practices were criticized by the Dominicans, who had more orthodox views and less confidence in the spiritual capacities of the Indians.[6] Early on, the Franciscans also became instrumental in the education of the indigenous population. Their most radical educational experiment was the school of Santa Cruz de Tlatelolco. Founded in 1536 near Mexico City, the school's original intent was to create an indigenous clergy – an effort steadfastly opposed by the Dominicans, and even by some Franciscans. But by the following year, enthusiasm for the project had waned, and not long after, the various provincial councils decreed that Indians were not to be admitted into the priesthood or even as regular lay brothers. Before becoming entangled in endless administrative problems, the school produced a number of well-rounded Nahua scholars who became invaluable assistants to the order's linguists and ethnographers.[7] The Franciscans conducted extensive studies of indigenous languages and cultures. For example, in the second half of the sixteenth century, Bernardino de Sahagún and his research team

---

[5] Solange Alberro, *El águila y la cruz: Orígenes religiosos de la conciencia criolla, México, siglos XVI–XVII* (Mexico City, 1999).

[6] John Leddy Phelan, *The Millennial Kingdom of the Franciscans in the New World*, 2nd ed. (Berkeley, 1970); and Robert Ricard, *The Spiritual Conquest of Mexico: An Essay on the Apostolate and the Evangelizing Methods of the Mendicant Orders in New Spain, 1523–1572* (Berkeley, 1982).

[7] José María Kobayashi, *La educación como conquista: empresa franciscana en México* (Mexico City, 1985).

compiled an encyclopedic work that remains the main primary source for Nahua culture and religion. In the Yucatan, Diego de Landa was a careful student of Maya religion. However, he was also a heavy-handed persecutor of idolatries and destroyed many Mayan texts and artifacts.[8] One of the great ironies of the evangelization process is that much of what is known about pre-Hispanic religious theory and practice comes from people intent on its disappearance.

Mastery of indigenous languages allowed the regular orders to produce vocabularies and catechetical materials, in particular, doctrinal and confessional manuals, which were among the first books to be printed in the New World. They were intended to not only facilitate the conversion process, but also monitor their native flocks' spirituality. For a time, the regular orders' cultural and linguistic expertise granted them a monopoly over indigenous communities that on occasion set them against colonists, civil and ecclesiastic authorities, and even other religious orders. Before more stringent requirements for parish priests were put in place in the late sixteenth century, knowledge of local languages also provided the regulars with a significant advantage over the secular clergy, who could not minister effectively to the native population and whose sphere of action was therefore limited to the settler minority.

In general, the regular orders were better suited to the demands of transatlantic evangelization. Their organizational structure allowed small groups to operate independently. This capacity was officially recognized in 1522 by Pope Hadrian VI in a bull known as the Omnimoda, which granted complete freedom of religious activity, including administration of the sacraments normally reserved for bishops, to regular clergy more than two days' travel away from a diocesan center.[9] Although contrary to both canon law and the provisions of the Council of Trent (1545–63), this prerogative was reaffirmed several times over the next few decades and became a continuous source of conflict between the regular and the secular clergy regarding jurisdiction. In 1573, when Pope Gregory XIII attempted to rescind their privileges, the Franciscans invoked the authority of the crown over the Church to defend their self-sufficiency. In this context, the Franciscan scholar Fr. Juan de Focher argued that they were beyond the authority of local bishops by virtue of the fact that their mission to the New World issued directly from the Spanish kings' "Royal Vicariate" and not from Rome.[10]

---

[8] Inga Clendinnen, *Ambivalent Conquests: Maya and Spaniard in Yucatan, 1517–1570* (Cambridge, UK, 1987).
[9] John Frederick Schwaller, "Introduction," in John Frederick Schwaller, ed., *The Church in Colonial Latin America* (Wilmington, DE, 2000), xi–xxiii.
[10] Johannes Meier, "The Religious Orders in Latin America: A Historical Survey," in Dussel, *The Church*, 375–90.

OBSTACLES TO THE ENTERPRISE

The establishment of Catholicism in the New World faced many obstacles. The first was the unprecedented nature of the transatlantic mission. The diversity of environments, peoples, languages, and beliefs present in the New World constantly called for improvisation. The great distances, both geographical and experiential, that often separated legislators from executors also created discrepancies between de jure and de facto governance, between the letter of the law and its implementation by local agents under particular circumstances. The success of the missionaries depended in large measure on their ability to adapt themselves and their message to each situation as it arose. Although the crown's investment in the missionary effort guaranteed support and funding for the colonial Church, it also created tensions between the material aims of the former and the spiritual aspirations of the latter.

Another obstacle faced by the colonial Church in the New World was the medieval nature of the popular Christianity brought by conquistadors, clergymen, and colonizers in general, which habitually challenged Catholic orthodoxy through a combination of ignorance, prejudice, and superstition. Moreover, as critics of the conquest repeatedly pointed out, the conquistadors' actions systematically belied the spirit of the religion they claimed to represent. Christianity's association with violence impeded the dialogue between the indigenous populations and the missionaries, many of whom may have regarded themselves as agents of salvation but were perceived, often quite accurately, as agents of colonial oppression.[11] The missionaries were well aware of this incongruity and sought to distinguish their mission from the rest of the Spanish enterprise, often by assuming a critical stance toward the colonists' exploitative labor practices. They also fought vehemently to keep their indigenous flocks from pernicious communication with the Spanish population at large by attempting to limit contact with colonists or through the exclusive use of indigenous languages.

STATUS OF *LOS INDIOS*: SEGREGATION AND SUBJUGATION

At first, the strict separation between the República de Indios, comprised of the indigenous population, and the República de Españoles, which

---

[11] Robert Haskett, "'Not a Pastor but a Wolf': Indigenous-Clergy Relations in Early Cuernavaca and Taxco," *The Americas* 50:3 (1994): 293–336; Patricia Lopes Don, "Franciscans, Indian Sorcerers, and the Inquisition in New Spain, 1536–1543," *Journal of World History* 17:1 (2006): 27–49; and Brian Sandberg, "Beyond Encounters: Religion, Ethnicity, and Violence in the Early Modern Atlantic World," *Journal of World History* 17:1 (2006): 1–26.

would have included people of Spanish ancestry, all manner of mestizos (mixed-bloods), and African slaves, seemed a practical solution for the civil administration and religious indoctrination of the indigenous populations. For a time, the special legal provisions associated with República de Indios status may have allowed some indigenous communities to preserve a measure of autonomy in material as well as spiritual matters. However, in all but the most inaccessible communities, the segregation policy was soon overwhelmed by the ongoing miscegenation that blurred racial categories, by vagrants who sought to take advantage of the exemptions granted to the República de Indios, and by land-encroaching settlers. Paradoxically, the statutory divide was also undermined by the concrete demands that the colonial regime imposed on the Indians. Economic, civil, and religious obligations entailed regular and ever-increasing interaction between the Indian and Spanish republics. Finally, the system in general was challenged by the indigenous peoples themselves, who, vanquished and diminished as they may have been, still sought to have a say about their place in their new colonized reality. Although the laws regarding the separation of the two republics were never formally rescinded, they became increasingly unenforceable.

The status of the Indians in the colonial regime presented the most vexing problems for both the crown and the Church, and because the two were inextricably intertwined by virtue of the *Patronato Real*, the endless debates around the "question of the Indian" always had both juridical and theological implications. In 1532, a series of lectures presented at the University of Salamanca by Dominican Francisco de Vitoria established that the sole justification of the conquest was to save Indians' souls. Theoretically, violent conquest could only occur in specific circumstances, such as impeding acts of cannibalism.[12] The intensity and impact of these debates on legislation attests to the Spanish crown's ongoing preoccupation with the spiritual well-being of its transatlantic subjects. However, in the colonies, practice seldom reflected theory, and the laws intended to protect the Indians from abuse were often acknowledged only to be disregarded.[13] Nonetheless, the official priority of conversion served as the platform to either support or criticize Spain's colonial venture in the Americas.[14]

The treatment of the natives by the colonizers was at the heart of the dispute between defenders of the Indians, a role consistently assumed

---

[12] Lewis Hanke, *The Spanish Struggle for Justice in the Conquest of America* (Philadelphia, 1949).
[13] Luis N. Rivera, "The Theological-Juridical Debate," in Schwaller, *The Church*, 3–26.
[14] Vicente L. Rafael, *Contracting Colonialism: Translation and Christian Conversion in Tagalog Society under Early Spanish Rule* (Ithaca, 1988).

by members of the regular orders, and their detractors. The first public protest came from the Dominican Antonio de Montesinos, who lambasted the white population of Hispaniola in a Sunday sermon delivered in 1511. Soon after, Bartolomé de las Casas began his lifelong struggle to curtail the violence brought on the Indians by the conquistadors. Las Casas, who joined the Dominican order in 1524, ceaselessly proposed legislative reforms and alternative methods for attracting indigenous populations to Christianity. His influence in the shaping of policy regarding Native Americans cannot be overstated. Las Casas' advocacy contributed to the introduction of the New Laws in 1542, which sought to limit the *encomienda*, the practice of granting conquistadors the labor or tribute of a group of Indians in exchange for a Christian education. Promoted as a benign agency of acculturation, the *encomienda* in practice constituted a quasi-feudal means of systematic exploitation. As with other laws issued in the same spirit, the key provisions of the New Laws were soundly rejected by the colonists. The failure of his efforts seemed to galvanize Las Casas, who went on to challenge the justice of the Spanish conquests in the famous debate against Juan Ginés de Sepúlveda that took place in Valladolid between 1550 and 1551.

The core issue of the Valladolid debate was whether subjugation was a legitimate and necessary first step in order to establish Christianity in the New World. Each side based its argument on an interpretation of indigenous religiosity, with examples taken mainly from the Nahua system, which was considered the most sophisticated but also the most disturbing because of its well-documented practices of human sacrifice and ritual cannibalism. Las Casas saw a deep spirituality that, however misdirected, was superior to the beliefs and rituals of pagans in ancient Europe. Even human sacrifice was evidence of a profound spirituality, because life was the most precious gift a people could offer in worship to a god, albeit a false one. For Las Casas, this constituted further proof of the Indians' civility, reason, and, most importantly, capacity for nonviolent conversion to Christianity through the use of understanding. Sepúlveda disparaged indigenous civilization in general but found sodomy, human sacrifice, and cannibalism most heinous and sufficient cause to justify violent conquest. There was no question on either side that conversion was a justified end of colonization; at issue were the appropriate means to achieve it. The debate itself was inconclusive, as the panel of judges never returned an opinion.[15] Las Casas managed to block publication of Sepúlveda's treatise on the issue. However, negative or ambiguous attitudes toward the indigenous populations prevailed in secular and religious spheres on both sides of the Atlantic.

---

[15] Benjamin Keen, *The Aztec Image in Western Thought* (New Brunswick, 1971).

ASSIMILATION: AN UNFINISHED TASK

After the fierce excesses of New Spain's first inquisitor, Fr. Juan de Zúmarraga, in the late 1530s, which culminated with the burning at the stake of the Texcocan noble Don Carlos Ometochtzin, the Church officially categorized Christianized Indians as neophytes and placed them beyond inquisitorial jurisdiction. Nevertheless, they still required strict supervision in view of their intellectual deficiencies as well as their vulnerability to sin and the wiles of Satan. Clergy often explained the uncanny similarities between the Christian sacraments and some indigenous rites as the devil's attempts to mimic the true Church. Even those willing to recognize the many achievements of pre-Hispanic civilization, such as the Jesuit José de Acosta or the Franciscan Juan de Torquemada, portrayed native religions as satanic. Moreover, despite the optimistic expectations of the first missionaries, by the middle of the sixteenth century it was increasingly clear that the Indians had failed to fully assimilate Christian doctrine.[16]

Even though indigenous religious leaders had been displaced by Christian clergy, ritual specialists remained active in the practice of daily religion. An early seventeenth-century treatise on heathen superstitions in New Spain prepared by the secular priest Hernando Ruiz de Alarcón exposes the persistence of private rituals and a folk cosmology based on traditional notions of the natural and supernatural worlds. Alarcón's inquiries also reveal the incorporation of Christian elements, such as rosary beads and Latin phrases, into native rites. In one example, he describes native methods for seeking beehives: propitiatory incantations must be recited to the bees, and honey-hunters must exhibit a peaceful and joyful state. According to Alarcón's native informants, bees are divine beings that dislike worry and deserve reverent treatment because they make wax that will burn before God. The attribution of divinity to animals or the ritual use of hallucinogens was worrisome evidence of the Indians' failure to observe Catholic orthodoxy. Religious authorities considered such idolatrous inclinations as evidence of Indians' limited moral and spiritual capacity as well as of the malignant influence of the devil.[17] Suspicions of contamination by or even reversion to pre-Hispanic beliefs and rituals resulted in periodic campaigns intended to extirpate idolatry. Systematic efforts to unearth and eliminate unorthodox practices and beliefs were carried out with inquisitorial zeal and violence

---

[16] Fernando Cervantes, *The Devil in the New World: The Impact of Diabolism in New Spain* (New Haven, 1994).

[17] Hernando Ruiz de Alarcón, *Treatise on the Heathen Superstitions that Today Live among the Indians Native to This New Spain*, 1629, J. Richard Andrews and Ross Hassig, eds. (Norman, OK, 1984).

among the Maya in the mid-sixteenth century and in the Andes throughout the seventeenth century and beyond.[18]

The widespread survival of pre-Hispanic religious structures and patterns is not necessarily a symptom of sustained resistance to Christianity. Rather it reveals mutual adaptation processes that depended on any number of regional variables. Some of these, such as the intensity of the missionary effort, the distance from a colonial center, or the number of Spanish settlers, were a corollary to colonization. Others related to existing religious patterns, such as the flexibility of a local pantheon and specific modes of devotion. In New Spain, where a rich iconographic tradition existed, the missionaries developed pictorial catechisms by combining European-style images with Nahua glyphs. A European ladder might be used to indicate ascent toward heaven, whereas the heart could be represented by the corresponding Nahua sign. Sometimes images converged: the entrance to hell was drawn as a monstrous mouth, typical of medieval illustrations, but stylized to conform to the glyph for cave.[19] On the other hand, the native population enthusiastically embraced Christian images. Locally painted or sculpted reproductions became a staple for domestic altars that had been used for family devotions since pre-Hispanic times. The images' aesthetic employed indigenous conventions that clergy often disparaged as the result of artistic ineptitude or condemned as evidence of idolatrous confusion. Several attempts to curb their proliferation were unsuccessful. As were other aspects of Catholicism, Christian imagery was inevitably rendered through an indigenous prism.[20]

The process of conversion involved reciprocal miscommunication as much as calculated misinterpretation on the part of the would-be converts, who asserted their own indigenous spirituality. Missionaries methodically used local languages to explain the tenets of the faith or to administer confession. In so doing, their message, more or less unintentionally, became infused with local categories of thought, allowing for a certain degree of continuity between old beliefs and the new creed. Religious drama, which the regular orders, and the Franciscans in particular, employed as an exemplary means of evangelization, provided an opportunity for native translators to co-opt the meaning of the plays. *Holy Wednesday*, the translation into Nahuatl of *Lucero de nuestra salvación*, a Spanish play published in the

---

[18] Kenneth Mills, "The Limits of Religious Coercion in Midcolonial Peru," in Schwaller, *The Church*, 147–80.

[19] J. Eric S. Thompson, "Systems of Hieroglyphic Writing in Middle America and Methods of Deciphering Them," *American Antiquity* 24:4 (1959): 349–64.

[20] Serge Gruzinski, *The Conquest of Mexico: The Incorporation of Indian Societies into the Western World, 16th–18th Centuries* (Cambridge, UK, 1993).

early 1580s, may be read as a commentary and even a critique not only of the original text, but of Christian values and Spanish colonialism. The play dramatizes a farewell scene between Mary and Jesus, who is soon to be arrested and crucified. In the translated version, Mary possesses more authority and knowledge, and her son treats her with more deference than in the original. The prominent role of ancestors, whose demands determine Jesus' behavior, and the significance granted to past events that disrupt the linear thrust of the play, are in the spirit of Nahua morals and cosmology. The dislocation of the family structure as well as the impending violence and injustice of Christ's treatment by Roman officials and soldiers could potentially stand as a symbol of the Nahua's oppression at the hands of Spaniards. Once translated, the play appropriated Spanish Christian discourse in ways that defied the doctrinal intent of the missionaries.[21]

Although certain elements of pre-Hispanic religion remained operational in some regions, a more or less orthodox version of Christianity eventually became part of the corporate identity of most indigenous groups subject to colonial civil and religious rule. One expression of popular Catholicism that was readily appropriated in the New World was the cult of saints. Saints were the most visible religious expression of the colonists' religiosity, and they served as a catalyst for the religious and administrative reorganization of existing and new indigenous settlements. Pre-Hispanic notions of divine intermediaries who could be propitiated through rites of worship were compatible with the medieval devotion to saints that missionaries transplanted in the Americas. Saints had affective power to perform miracles through images that had a life of their own: many were known to move, bleed, or weep. The widespread practice of hollowing out saints' images in order to secrete local gods inside possibly contributed to a smooth transition between the old faith and the new. Thus the cult of the saints promoted by colonial authorities easily lent itself to adaptation by indigenous communities seeking to reestablish the religious base of their worldview and their social solidarity in the colonial context. As the basis of pilgrimages, for which there may also be pre-Hispanic precedents, and *fiestas patronales* (feast days in honor of a town's patron saint), the devotion to saints became a fundamental form of religious mediation, especially in more rural areas. *Fiestas patronales* were usually funded by the *cabildo* (municipal council) and a dedicated *cofradía* (religious brotherhood), with members' dues collected for such religious expenses, or by a *mayordomo* (steward) who sought the social prestige and the opportunity for service associated with the relatively onerous charge. In parishes underserved by

---

[21] Louise M. Burkhart, *Holy Wednesday: A Nahua Drama from Early Colonial Mexico* (Philadelphia, 1996).

the clergy, confraternities and *mayordomos* served as sponsors and enforcers of religious obligations; they also helped consolidate a town's identity around its patron saint. The festivals included public ceremonies, church services, processions, floral decorations, costumes, food, and drink. Native elements, such as traditional dress, song, and dance, added to Catholic rituals and lent local color to the festivities.[22] Indeed, these *fiestas patronales* became so ingrained in local tradition that they persist to this day.

In contrast, parish centers with a more racially diverse population tended to celebrate festivals that corresponded to the liturgical cycle of the Catholic Church. Yet, like the *fiesta patronal*, these religious festivals also provided opportunities for indigenous populations to display a Christian piety that incorporated pre-Hispanic symbols. Often the display was a strategic way of co-opting power within the colonial system. In seventeenth-century Cuzco, the procession on the feast of Corpus Christi, which included members of the indigenous nobility, was an occasion to exhibit the triumph of the Catholic faith as well as the colonial power structure in the old Inca capital. Although the participation of Inca nobles in traditional costume confirmed a subordinate status, subtle manipulations of traditional attire helped them secure a privileged position within that structure. Contemporary paintings of the procession show the inclusion of Andean royal insignia into the Christian pageantry of Corpus Christi. The *maskapaycha*, the scarlet fringe that traditionally adorned the Inca rulers' headdress, was adopted by members of the elite seeking recognition from their peers, the colonial authorities, and indigenous peasants. Other aspects of this legitimizing tactic involved employing indigenous symbols, such as a rainbow or a snake, together with Christian mottoes like "Ave Maria," in European-style coats of arms. In so doing, the elites projected European concepts of Christianity and royalty onto their ancestry.[23]

The same strategy was employed in a number of sophisticated historiographical works produced in the early 1600s by indigenous and mestizo authors, such as Fernando de Alva Ixtlilxochitl in New Spain and the Inca Garcilaso de la Vega and Felipe Guamán Poma de Ayala in Peru. These authors, all of whom claimed descent from prestigious native lineages, projected Christianity onto the pre-Hispanic past and assigned their enlightened ancestors a crucial role in preparing for the advent of the Catholic

---

[22] Charles Gibson, *The Aztecs under Spanish Rule: A History of the Indians of the Valley of Mexico, 1519–1810* (Stanford, 1964); Manuel M. Marzal, "Daily Life in the Indies (Seventeenth and Early Eighteenth Centuries)," in Dussel, *The Church*, 69–80; and James Lockhart, *Nahuas after the Conquest: A Social and Cultural History of the Indians of Central Mexico, Sixteenth Through Eighteenth Centuries* (Stanford, 1992).

[23] Carolyn Dean, *Inca Bodies and the Body of Christ: Corpus Christi in Colonial Cuzco, Peru* (Durham, 1999).

faith in the New World. Such creative revisions of history illustrate how the imposition of Spanish Catholicism in America radically affected not only contemporary indigenous reality, but also indigenous memory, by triggering a reinterpretation of the past in light of new experiences and pressures.[24] They also exemplify the great resourcefulness and skill with which indigenous peoples were able to adapt the Old World creed to their cultural environments. Just as Catholicism changed indigenous cultures, the diversity of indigenous realities and memories reshaped Catholicism in countless local variations.

SYNCRETISM AND AUTONOMY

The introduction of a new spiritual power resulted in ritual manifestations that are often described as syncretic because they appear to mix disparate elements from different religious traditions. However, it is impossible to gauge any faith's true character from its outward expressions alone. The impact of Catholicism differed widely by region, and although some common strategies existed, there was no standard indigenous response. Native ritual elements that did not explicitly contravene Church doctrine were generally allowed by the missionaries, whereas others, like singing and dancing, were even encouraged. In some instances, they ceased to be an expression of pre-Hispanic belief and became an integral part of popular Catholic devotion. However, they may also signal the persistence of pre-Hispanic spiritual and ritual structures beneath a Christian surface.[25] In other cases, the transitory coexistence of Christian and pre-Hispanic concepts and values may have caused internal conflict and self-doubt among the new converts regarding that which could be salvaged and that which should be discarded.[26] The process of selective addition and deletion was never static and was often riddled with contradictions and inconsistencies. In terms of belief, rather than a mixture, there appear to have been countless reconfigurations, driven by particular attitudes and specific circumstances that continued to evolve in the long and complex process of religious conversion.[27] In general usage, the term "syncretism" fails to properly account for the dynamic processes and the idiosyncrasies that lie behind countless unorthodox expressions of common Catholic beliefs. Moreover, the notion

---

[24] Louise M. Burkhart, *The Slippery Earth: Nahua-Christian Moral Dialogue in Sixteenth-Century Mexico* (Tucson, 1989).
[25] *Ibid.*, 188.
[26] Sabine MacCormack, *Religion in the Andes: Vision and Imagination in Early Colonial Peru* (Princeton, 1991), 11.
[27] Enrique D. Dussel, *A History of the Church in Latin America: Colonialism to Liberation (1492–1979)* (Grand Rapids, 1981), 68.

generally tends to obscure the violent and traumatic aspects of conversion by directing attention exclusively to mostly superficial features of its outcome. A city in Mexico, Cholula, exemplifies the persistence of this process – and the inadequacy of the term "syncretism" – even today. Built on top of the huge pyramid devoted to the god Quetzalcoatl and the most sacred site in pre-Hispanic Mesoamerica, the Church of Nuestra Señora de los Remedios purportedly houses the statue of the Virgin Mary carried by Hernán Cortés during the massacre of the city's religious leaders. This "Conquest Virgin" is the focal point of religious celebrations in Cholula today. But as the lay steward in charge of the celebrations and church explains, the strength of the devotion to the Virgin originates from the deity "behind her," the deity of their pre-Hispanic ancestors.[28]

Evangelization produced a diversity of outcomes in the different regions of the New World. In the Caribbean, where the indigenous population was decimated, the influx of black slaves eventually produced a distinctive religion that can be accurately described as syncretic because it blended many Christian elements into a distinctive theology that, nevertheless, remained firmly rooted in the African tradition from which it sprang. On the continent, Nahua groups, whose homeland was rapidly and heavily settled by Spanish colonists, integrated the new creed, or at least its outward manifestations, with relative speed. Nahua religion also had practices, such as state cults with a regimented priestly structure, that may have eased the transition to Christianity by providing a sense of continuity. In other cases, there may have been a convergence of beliefs, as indigenous populations attempted to reconstruct their cosmos within a Christian framework. In the end, however, the sustained efforts of the Church, together with the persistence of colonial structures in central New Spain, generally resulted in a thorough identification with the major tenets of Catholicism.

In the Andes, the internal strife among the Spanish leadership delayed the consolidation of colonial institutions both civil and religious. Moreover, Andean traditional religious beliefs were especially resilient because of their abstract nature as well as their association with the physical landscape, a sacred topography that stayed outside the boundaries of church regulation. Andean specialists conducted their rituals on mountaintops, near streams, or inside caves, *huacas* (holy spots) where religious power had always resided. The mythic and historical activities of deities and dead ancestors, whose *mallquis* (mummified remains) were safeguarded from extirpators, also retained their importance in daily community life.[29] Among the Maya,

---

[28] Gilberto Munoz Galicia, as quoted in Kathleen Ann Myers, *In the Shadow of Cortes: From Veracruz to Mexico City* (forthcoming).

[29] MacCormack, *Religion in the Andes*, 411.

where the colonial establishment as a whole was persistently challenged, missionaries lacked the numbers and the influence to effectively institute Catholic orthodoxy; the result was the development of distinct varieties of Maya Christianity. In the case of the Tzeltal Maya, pre-Hispanic notions that include animal-soul companions, sacred mountains, and the demanding spirit of the Holy Earth came to be placed under the aegis of a single omnipotent God.[30] In regions where the colonial Church had a consistent presence, local religious idiosyncrasies were periodically investigated and persecuted, sometimes with great brutality. In some instances, these campaigns may have effectively contributed to the disappearance of traditional practices; in others, the assault may have only succeeded in driving them deeper underground, where they lived on as a form of resistance and continued to influence the development of indigenous Christianities. Areas that were less populated, more difficult to reach, or unattractive to settlers remained relatively isolated from colonial impositions, and, consequently, the conversion process and its impact were temporarily deferred or never completed.

AFTERMATH: CONSOLIDATION OF THE RELIGIOUS ESTABLISHMENT

By the end of the sixteenth century, evangelical fervor had faded in view of the only partial success of the conversion efforts, and evangelization leveled off in keeping with the slowing pace of exploration and colonization in the Americas. Rather than set up new outposts, the regular orders focused on filling the gaps between existing monasteries and consolidating their areas of influence.[31] This may have exacerbated competition among the regular orders, as well as between the regular and the secular clergy. At the same time, there was increasing conflict within the ranks of the different orders, as growing numbers of American-born friars challenged the predominance of peninsular-born cadres. All these factors cast doubt on the regulars' motives, goals, and efficacy. Moreover, although in the early days regulars were generally considered to be more virtuous and better prepared than seculars, the overall quality of the latter improved, owing to the provisions of the Ordenanza del patronazgo. Issued by King Phillip II in 1574, the Ordenanza instituted a competitive examination process for

---

[30] Eugenio Maurer Ávalos, "The Tzeltal-Maya-Christian Synthesis," in Gary H. Gossen and Miguel León Portilla, eds., *South and Meso-American Native Spirituality: From the Cult of the Feathered Serpent to the Theology of Liberation* (New York, 1993), 228–50.

[31] A. C. van Oss, "Mendicant Expansion in New Spain and the Extent of the Colony (Sixteenth Century)," in idem, ed., *Church and Society*, 103–23.

prospective parish priests and included indigenous-language proficiency. In addition, the Ordenanza offered job security and a guaranteed income, which encouraged capable candidates to join the ranks of the secular clergy. In 1622, Pope Gregory XV finally revoked all exemptions that contradicted the Tridentine decrees, and over the course of the seventeenth century the secular clergy increasingly dominated the organization of religious life in the Indies. Nonetheless, the regulars, especially the Jesuits, continued to play significant roles as educators and as missionaries in peripheral areas where evangelization was in its infancy.[32]

Whereas in the sixteenth century clergy crusaded for the spiritual conquest and integration of indigenous populations, by the beginning of the seventeenth century, the growing numbers of Spanish and criollo colonizers were donating vast sums of money to build and maintain churches, monasteries, and convents in their towns. People of Spanish ancestry seized the opportunity to create a New World paradise for Christianity in criollo cities, such as Puebla de los Angeles and Cuidad de los Reyes (Lima), as well as in former Nahua and Inca centers, such as Mexico City and Cuzco. Monastic life beyond evangelization blossomed and now included convents for women. The first convents for women in New Spain and South America were built in the mid-sixteenth century, but by the late seventeenth century dozens of convents had been founded by many religious orders, including, among others, the Augustinians, Capuchins, and Carmelites. In seventeenth-century Lima, for example, about one in four women lived in a religious institution.[33] The first religious institutions for women began in the early sixteenth century with *recogimientos* (refuges) and *beaterios* (saintly houses) that followed monastic-like daily schedules of prayer and work but required no profession of the religious vows of poverty, chastity, and obedience. The early *recogimientos* were either refuges for women who had been abandoned by husbands, a fairly common situation during the conquest, or a sort of penal institution for *malas mujeres*, fallen women. Later, *beaterios* developed for virtuous women who wanted to dedicate themselves to a religious life but could not enter a convent. To profess as a nun, considered the highest ranking position for a woman in colonial society, required a hefty dowry, legitimate birth, and "pure" Spanish ancestry. Although the requirements could be waived (especially the first two),

---

[32] Meier, "The Religious Orders," 379; John Frederick Schwaller, "The Ordenanza del Patronazgo in New Spain, 1574–1600," in Schwaller, *The Church*, 49–69.

[33] Luis Martin, *Daughters of the Conquistadores: Women of the Viceroyalty of Peru* (Albuquerque, 1983), 176–80; and Nancy E. Van Deusen, *Between the Sacred and the Worldly: The Institutional and Cultural Practice of Recogimiento in Colonial Lima* (Stanford, 2001), introduction.

in general the system created a class- and race-based religious hierarchy in which *mestizas*, *indias*, *mulatas*, and black Africans were servants or slaves, while the black-veiled nuns served as the administrators and prayers who sought God's goodwill on behalf of the community. It was only in the late colonial period when convents were founded for indigenous women. But even then, sometimes candidates had to demonstrate noble birth.[34]

Within this broadly defined religious life, convents differed greatly depending on whether a convent observed a regular or reformed rule. At the height of their popularity in mid-colonial society, a regular convent generally housed hundreds of women. Although only a few score women generally professed as black-veiled nuns, the nuns were joined by white-veiled *donadas*, servants, and slaves to create huge cloistered communities that could occupy up to three or four city blocks, such as the Convent of Santa Catalina in Arequipa, Peru. The Counter-Reformation Church, eager to circumscribe gender roles for women, required nuns to take a vow of perpetual enclosure in addition to the monastic vows of poverty, chastity, and obedience. But the interpretation of the monastic vows and rule was often lax, especially that of the vow of poverty. Nuns in these large convents lived in their own multiroom quarters furnished with personal belongings. They enjoyed plays and other cultural events within the cloister. Reacting to the laxity of rule in these large convents, the reformed orders, following St. Teresa of Ávila's reforms for the Discalced (Barefoot) Carmelites, generally limited the number of professed nuns to a couple dozen and observed strictly all religious vows and canonical hours for prayer. They lived in small individual cells, ate communal meals, owned no personal possessions, and prayed every few hours in the pursuit of spiritual perfection. Area communities supported the convents, and in return the convents offered the assurance of almost continual prayer on the behalf of their benefactors.

Intended by colonists and clergy as the spiritual heart of a New World Christian paradise, the convents ultimately became like any large institution. The archives are filled with documentation of all manner of disputes with the outside world and within the convent. In 1665, when the new commissary general of the Franciscan order, Hernando de la Rua, arrived in New Spain, he ordered Franciscan nuns in several convents to reduce the number of servants they had living in the cloister to one servant per nun. But the Convent of San Juan de la Penitencia in Mexico City decided to fight the order. The battle lasted more than a decade, with the viceroy of New Spain, the Audiencia, and the crown ultimately weighing in on the

---

[34] Asunción Lavrin, *Brides of Christ: Conventual Life in Colonial Mexico* (Stanford, 2008); Mónica Díaz, *The Indias of Corpus Christi* (forthcoming); and Kathryn Burns, *Colonial Habits: Convents and the Spiritual Economy of Cuzco, Peru* (Raleigh, 1999).

matter. In their fight to keep servants, the convent contracted a lawyer and refused to obey the commissar, even when he excommunicated the abbess and appointed a new one. There is no evidence that in the end the nuns conceded. In the late 1760s, the issue resurfaced as part of the struggle to reform the observance of convent rule.[35]

Although entire convents and communities could become engaged in conflict, individual nuns could be caught in private struggles with authorities as well. New Spain's most renowned poet, Sor Juana Inés de la Cruz (1648–95), took the veil at the large convent of San Jerónimo in Mexico City. She sought a place to ensure the salvation of her soul and the time to pursue her studies. Within her two-story "cell," Sor Juana amassed an extensive library and wrote both secular and sacred verse and drama. She was published in her own lifetime, but by the end of her life she had been censured by the proceedings of a secret trial initiated by the archbishop, who ultimately obliged Sor Juana to dismantle her library and renounce her literary career.[36] The convent offered a space for women's spiritual and cultural development, but always under the watchful eye of Church superiors.

Lay holy people, *beatas*, also played an important role in the spiritual landscape of colonial Spanish America, even though the Church considered this a more treacherous spiritual path. Lacking the requirement for entrance into a monastic institution or the desire to be enclosed, *beatas* lived as hermits, visionaries, and spiritual guides outside of the limits of monastic rule. They often became the focus of popular devotion and the target of questioning by the Inquisition. When the *beata* Catarina de San Juan, a Hindu slave brought to Puebla, died in 1688, people lined up for days to view the visionary's corpse. Soon a cult began to develop around her. But the Inquisition curtailed it by prohibiting the display of Catarina's portrait and banning her biography.[37] Women, in particular, became more prominent in the mid-colonial Church because the spread of mysticism, inherited from Spain, and such popular mystics as St. Teresa of Ávila (1515–82), affected women more than men. Considered to be more prone to emotional states, women were seen as natural conduits of divine will. One colonial priest referred to these women as mystical *conquistadoras* because of their power to move Christians toward God.[38] As a result of the building of numerous convents and of the visionary roles allowed for

---

[35] Lavrin, *Brides of Christ*, 162–5.
[36] Sor Juana Inés de la Cruz, in Electa Arenal and Amanda Powell, *The Answer/La respuesta* (New York, 1994); and Kathleen Ann Myers, *Neither Saints nor Sinners: Writing the Lives of Women in Spanish America* (New York, 2003), 93–115.
[37] Myers, *Neither Saints*, 44–68.
[38] *Ibid.*, 6.

women in the seventeenth century, a certain feminization of the Spanish American Church occurred – although women were always circumscribed within the patriarchal, post-Tridentine hierarchical Church structure.

Even in rural areas far removed from the spiritual activity of colonial cities, owners of haciendas sought to create centers for area community religious life. Traveling clergy celebrated Mass at on-site hacienda chapels, and family life often included nightly prayer and recitation of the rosary. Indeed, family libraries sometimes contained only devotional books on methods of prayer and the lives of the saints, because eight out of ten books published in Mexico and Peru during this period were religious books.[39] A seventeenth-century Mexican nun and mystic, María de San José (1656–1719), once described how her family's reading of the lives of the saints inspired her and an Indian house servant to build a hut in the garden, where they engaged in long hours of prayers and penances. But these devotional exercises practiced far from the monitoring of a spiritual director became the center of controversy. María's family debated whether her intense spiritual practices, which had led to an active visionary life, were the work of the divine or the devil. After years of criticism from her family, María took refuge as a nun in the cloister. Later, she became one of the founders of a new convent and published a mystical work on the Virgin Mary.[40]

HOLINESS AND HERESY

The extreme limits of spiritual life set by the Catholic Church – the saint and the heretic – took on exceptional importance in mid-colonial Spanish America. A saint brought fame and legitimacy to the founding of Spanish rule in the Americas; a heretic threatened its newfound Christian identity. The post-Tridentine Church, eager to control the faithful by redefining orthodoxy in reaction to Martin Luther's reform movement, had codified the norms for good Christian behavior and emphasized the importance of active participation in the sacraments and obedience to the Church. If an individual demonstrated saintly heroic virtue, a quality of living that was similar to Jesus Christ, a confessor might initiate the long, formal process of canonization to sainthood. Beginning with the Council of Trent and throughout the following century, canonization became more bureaucratic and centralized in Rome. As Spanish Americans sought spiritual legitimacy, they eagerly identified dozens of holy people living in their midst

---

[39] *Ibid.*, 14.
[40] Kathleen A. Myers and Amanda Powell, *A Wild Country out in the Garden: The Journals of a Mexican Nun* (Bloomington, 1999).

and sent extensive documentation to Rome in order to canonize their local saints. In 1671, the first American saint, Rose of Lima (1586–1617), was canonized. Named "Patron of the Indies," Rose of Lima was heralded as a symbol of divine favor in the New World. Rose had modeled her life on that of the medieval saint Catherine of Sienna and lived outside the cloister as a lay holy woman associated first with the Franciscans and later with the Dominicans. According to legend, Rose's ability to seek divine intervention through prayer had saved the newly founded city of Lima more than once from pirate attacks and malaria. Not content with a saint from Peru, colonists in New Spain actively sought a saint for their viceroyalty; they sent case after case to Rome, but none received approval at the highest rank of sainthood.[41] During three centuries of Spanish colonial rule, no other American saint was canonized.

The line between holiness and heresy, however, could often shift. The Inquisition once questioned Rose of Lima, without incident, but soon after her death, the Holy Office persecuted Rose's followers.[42] In their zeal to create a unified Christian reign, the Catholic Kings had revived the Holy Office of the Inquisition to examine suspects for evidence of heretical practices, such as Judaism, Lutheranism, and Illuminism (*alumbradismo*), as well as for religious fakery (*falsas beatas*). Soon after the conquest, tribunals of the Inquisition were established in Mexico City and Lima. In the early decades of its existence in Spanish America, the Inquisition ruthlessly prosecuted both Spaniards and Indians. The excesses culminated under the command of Episcopal Inquisitor Fray Juan de Zumaraga (1536–43). Fearing a popular uprising after such incidents as the burning at the stake of an Indian noble from Texcoco, the crown called for the removal of Zumaraga and initiated a hiatus in the activities of the Inquisition. By the time the Inquisition was reactivated fully in 1571, Indians were exempt from the institution, and many of the accusations of unorthodox practices in the rest of the population were never prosecuted. In contrast to Spain, the geographical expanse of the Spanish Empire in the Americas made close monitoring of individual behavior impossible. Nonetheless, the Inquisition succeeded in limiting the influx of heretical books placed on the Index of Prohibited Books and in instilling a self- and community-based monitoring system that repressed unorthodox behavior before it reached the chambers of the Inquisition.[43]

---

[41] Antonio Rubial, *La santidad controvertida* (Mexico City, 1999).

[42] Ramón Mujica Pinilla, "El ancla de Santa Rosa de Lima: Mística y política en torno a la patrona de América," in José Flores Araoz, ed., *Santa Rosa y su Tiempo* (Lima, 1995), 54–215.

[43] Richard Greenleaf, *The Mexican Inquisition of the Sixteenth Century* (Albuquerque, 1969); and Ruth Behar, "Sex and Sin, Witchcraft and the Devil in Late-Colonial Mexico," *American Ethnologist* 14:1 (1987): 34–54.

New World criollos also promoted holy apparitions to distinguish themselves from their peninsular peers and to dignify their *patria* (homeland). In New Spain, the pursuit of an autonomous Catholicism was categorically validated by the Virgin of Guadalupe, who allegedly appeared to an indigenous peasant named Juan Diego in 1531. She instructed him to convey her desire for a temple to be built and dedicated to her on that site. At first the bishop of Mexico was skeptical, but he was finally convinced when the image of the Virgin miraculously appeared on Juan Diego's cape (*tilma*). The image, which is still kept at the Basílica de Guadalupe in Tepeyac, adheres to the iconographic conventions of sixteenth-century apocalyptic Madonnas; the story corresponds to the European tradition of the shepherds' cycle. The original adaptation possibly dates to the mid-1600s and may have been intended to ascribe a miraculous origin to an existing image, perhaps painted by an indigenous artist. However, about the same time, criollo clergy eagerly embraced the legend after an account published in 1648 by Miguel Sánchez, a criollo priest, lent a patriotic interpretation to Mary's apparition: it demonstrated her affinity with the land and the people of New Spain. Sánchez equated the Virgin of Guadalupe with the woman of Revelation, clothed with the sun and the moon at her feet, who is granted eagle wings to escape from the serpent. This identification also connected the Virgin of Guadalupe with local antiquity: according to legend, the prophetically designated site of Mexico-Tenochtitlan had been signaled by an eagle devouring a snake. Downplaying the indigenous elements of the original story, Sánchez simultaneously appropriated the Virgin of Guadalupe and the pre-Hispanic past on behalf of New Spain's criollos. Henceforth, Mary's exceptional favor, which constituted a heavenly and historical endorsement of their Mexican identity, would be a recurring theme in criollo patriotic expressions.[44]

INTEGRATION OF RELIGIOUS AND COMMUNITY LIFE

In addition to founding monastic communities and promoting local saints and apparitions of the Virgin, colonizers in the mid-colonial period imported from Spain the practice of lay *cofradías* (confraternities). These sodalities, which in theory required episcopal sanction and supervision, reflected the colonial socioeconomic structure, as they tended to be exclusively Spanish,

---

[44] Jacques Lafaye, *Quetzalcóatl and Guadalupe: The Formation of Mexican National Consciousness, 1531–1813* (Chicago, 1976); Louise Burkhart, "The Cult of the Virgin of Guadalupe in Mexico," in Gossen and Portilla, *South and Meso-American Native Spirituality*, 198–227; and Stafford Poole, "The Woman of the Apocalypse," in Schwaller, *The Church*, 209–43.

Indian, or African. Confraternities proliferated throughout Spanish America and ensured the regular involvement of all sectors of the population in religious life. Even women, generally marginal in the daily operation of the Church, were active participants in the *cofradías* at all levels of the organization, up to the governing council. Some *cofradías* were open exclusively to women.[45] In general, confraternities provided a kind of spiritual insurance. Dues and donations were collected to pay for members' burial expenses and for masses to be said on their behalf; living members were required to attend the funeral services of their brethren. Depending on their means, brotherhoods could also contribute to the welfare of their members' souls by performing acts of charity, sponsoring and participating in processions and festivals, paying for the construction and adornment of chapels and churches, and buying ritual paraphernalia. For Indians and slaves in particular, membership in a confraternity provided an officially sanctioned way to maintain distinct corporate and spiritual identities.[46]

By the mid-colonial period, Catholicism was an integral part of all aspects of life. There were great opportunities as well as pitfalls in following a spiritual path during the colonial period. As the Mexican scholar Edmundo O'Gorman notes,

> New Spain is a period in which a nun's spiritual flight, a terminally ill person's miraculous cure, a sinner's repentance, or a holy woman's vaticinations [prophecies] are more important news than the rise in prices in business or the imposition of a sales tax; a period in which a spiritual journey to the interior of the soul is more momentous than the expeditions to California and the Philippines.[47]

The year was marked by the liturgical calendar, and religious festivals involved the whole community, with individuals enjoying the prestige associated with serving as a *mayordomo* or participating in an exclusive *cofradía*. Rural areas were peppered with chapels and crosses. In every town, the main church building occupied a predominant place in the central square, right next to the seat of civil power. In major Spanish centers the cityscape was suffused with religious architecture; besides impressive cathedrals, cities boasted numerous churches and convents. The clergy dominated the

---

[45] Susan Migden Socolow, *The Women of Colonial Latin America* (Cambridge, UK, 2000), 110.

[46] Paul Charney, "A Sense of Belonging: Colonial Indian Cofradías and Ethnicity in the Valley of Lima, Peru," *The Americas* 54:3 (1998): 379–407; Brian Larkin, "Confraternities and Community: The Decline of the Communal Quest for Salvation in Eighteenth-Century Mexico City," in Martin A. Nesvig, ed., *Local Religion in Colonial Mexico* (Albuquerque, 2006); and Gibson, *The Aztecs*, 127–32.

[47] As quoted in Myers, *Neither Saints*, 4.

field of education, and most of the cultural and artistic production revolved around the Church. Every member of colonial society was subject to constant supervision of Church representatives, whether missionary, parish priest, or inquisitor. Competing religious expressions – so-called idolatry, witchcraft, and crypto-Judaism – were systematically persecuted.

Nevertheless, the imposition of Spanish Catholicism in the New World was a long and all-encompassing process filled with challenges, conflicts, and uneasy accommodations as well as successes. The conflation of conquest and colonization with evangelization had comingled the power of state and Church, creating a colonial system permeated by Catholicism. By the last decades of the seventeenth century, Catholicism had left its imprint in most regions. But the daily practice of Catholicism, the understanding of the tenets of the faith, and the organization of Church structures varied throughout Spanish America. Much like the adaption of Catholicism in other regions of the world, Spanish American Catholicism was both transnational and local. It served as the major catalyst for the creation of a wide range of New World identities and cultures, which followed an official Christian template but also included varying degrees of local indigenous adaptations. The spiritual conquest of America heightened the cultural and demographic catastrophe brought about by war, exploitation, and disease, and yet it also helped to defend indigenous rights and often allowed for traces of indigenous culture and identity to continue in new forms.

SUGGESTIONS FOR FURTHER READING

Burkhart, Louis M. *The Slippery Earth: Nahua-Christian Moral Dialogue in Sixteenth-Century Mexico*. Tucson, 1989.

Dussel, Enrique D., ed. *A History of the Church in Latin America: Colonialism to Liberation (1492–1979)*. Grand Rapids, 1981.

Lafaye, Jacques. *Quetzalcóatl and Guadalupe: The Formation of Mexican National Consciousness, 1531–1813*. Chicago, 1976.

Lavrin, Asunción. *Brides of Christ: Conventual Life in Colonial Mexico*. Stanford, 2008.

MacCormack, Sabine. *Religion in the Andes: Vision and Imagination in Early Colonial Peru*. Princeton, 1991.

Mills, Kenneth. *Idolatry and Its Enemies: Colonial Andean Religion and Extirpation, 1640–1750*. Princeton, 1997.

Ricard, Robert. *The Spiritual Conquest of Mexico: An Essay on the Apostolate and the Evangelizing Methods of the Mendicant Orders in New Spain, 1523–1572*. Berkeley, 1982.

Schroeder, Susan, and Stafford Poole, eds. *Religion in New Spain*. Albuquerque, 2007.

Schwaller, John Frederick, ed. *The Church in Colonial Latin America*. Wilmington, DE, 2000.

10

FRENCH CATHOLICISM IN THE ERA OF EXPLORATION AND EARLY COLONIZATION

DOMINIQUE DESLANDRES

France's claim to have discovered Brazil is doubtless a legend, but it seems that the French did indeed explore the Brazilian coastline before 1500. Nevertheless, Captain Binot Paulmier de Gonneville, who spent six months in Brazil in 1503, brought home the son of a Tupinamba chief, called Essomericq, whom he had baptized and to whom he bequested his fortune. Essomericq, who married into the Gonneville family, founded a line and died in 1583. A century and a half later, one of his heirs, Jean-Pierre Paulmier de Courtonne, canon of Lisieux, became an ardent promoter of a mission to the "savages" he claimed to be his ancestry, publishing his *Mémoires touchant l'établissement d'une mission Chrétienne dans le troisième Monde, ou la Terre Australe, par un ecclésiastique originaire de cette même terre*.[1] It is to be noted how easily the Brazilian convert integrated into French society and how entitled his heir felt to boast about his mixed origins.

Throughout the sixteenth century, stories of assimilation followed the same pattern and paved the way for the charter of the Company of the Hundred Associates – created in 1627 by Cardinal Richelieu for the colonization of Canada – which stipulated that baptized Amerindians would become *naturels français* and enjoy the same privileges as those born in the mother country.[2] Although showing a propensity toward relative racial openness on the part of the French, this policy equated becoming Catholic with becoming French. It aimed not only to establish an alliance with foreign peoples, but also to favor, through demographic growth, French expansion in America. Guided by these principles, French America reached from the Caribbean islands to Newfoundland, with the Great Lakes linking the St. Lawrence Valley to that of the Mississippi. This particular aspect of

---

[1] Paris, 1663. Jean-Pierre Paulmier de Courtonne, *Première découverte du Monde Austral, par Binot Paulmier Gonneville, en 1504*, in Jacques-Philibert Rousselot de Surgy, ed., *Suite de l'Histoire générale des voyages* (Amsterdam, 1746–1801), 17: 448–54.
[2] *Mercure François*, Paris, 1611–48, vol. XIV (1628), part II: 245 (art. 17).

the colonization of America is often overlooked. Most colonial-era histories still equate colonialism in America with the English Protestant experience and omit the other contact scenarios that unfolded in the New World, such as the different ways in which French Catholics dealt with the American realities in the sixteenth and seventeenth centuries.

Contrary to the English, who established agricultural seaboard colonies, the French chose first to set up *comptoirs* – commercial settlements – administered by chartered companies and merchant associations, which implied an alliance with the natives and their evangelization. After a series of failed colonization attempts in the sixteenth century, France gained a permanent foothold in America. In 1603, merchant commander François Gravé du Pont (c. 1554–c. 1629) and King Henri IV's special envoy Samuel de Champlain (c. 1567–1635) smoked *petun* (tobacco) at Tadoussac on the St. Lawrence River with a hundred Montagnais, Algonquin, and Etchemin Amerindians. This official ceremony, presided over by Montagnais chief Anadabijou, whom Champlain introduced as "the Great Sagamore of the Savages of Canada," sealed the alliance that allowed the French to settle in the area and expand elsewhere on the continent. At its peak in 1712, the French continental territory in America stretched from the Atlantic coast of Canada to the Rocky Mountains and from Hudson Bay to Louisiana.[3]

Distinct colonies were established within New France. *Acadia* (Port Royal, 1604), comprising the present-day provinces of Nova Scotia and New Brunswick and part of the state of Maine, constituted a strategic buffer against New England. *Canada* included the whole St. Lawrence Valley (Quebec City, 1608; Trois-Rivières, 1634; Montreal, 1642) and the Great Lakes region (Detroit, 1701). Small *Placentia* (1660) took root in difficult conditions in Newfoundland. *Louisiana* stretched to the Rockies from the upper Mississippi basin, which the French explored during the last quarter of the seventeenth century and called the "Illinois country," and down to the Gulf of Mexico in 1699 (New Orleans, 1718). This continental expansion through waterways was marked by strong but uneasy proximity with the Amerindians, intense merchant activities, and the powerful agency of the Church.

Although at the heart of New France, Quebec City remained a simple fur-trading post for many years. Missions, trading posts, and forts were scattered along the banks of the Saint Lawrence River and the shores of the Great Lakes. Raids by the Iroquois Five Nations against the French and their Amerindian allies were frequent. From 1615 on, Recollect friars – a reformed branch of the Franciscan order – and Jesuit priests started missions

---

[3] Henry Percival Biggar, ed., *The Works of Samuel de Champlain*, 6 vols. (Toronto, 1922–36), I: 98–103; II: 376; III: 314–15.

around Quebec City for the nomadic people, referred to as Algonquians by modern anthropologists, who traded fur with the settlers. Further west and south of Quebec City, the missionaries soon discovered semisedentary peoples, the Huron of the Iroquoian family, who constituted the central axis for the fur trade and whom they felt were the most promising prospects for conversion to Christianity.

From 1632 to the establishment of the Quebec bishopric in 1658, the Jesuits' religious monopoly in New France was almost total. Terrible epidemics, however, quickly decimated the Amerindian populations who lacked immunity to European diseases. This led the Church to devote most of its missionary foundations between Quebec and Montreal to the French settlers. The situation remained difficult in New France, beset, as it was, by epidemics, warfare, dangers of the fur trade, and scarce immigration from France. It was only after royal government replaced company rule in 1663 that French settlements began to develop, but real growth was secured only after the Great Peace of Montreal was signed with thirty-nine Amerindian nations in 1701.

Throughout the period, and despite its wealth and diversity, New France remained secondary in the French crown's colonial scheme, which favored the Caribbean (Santo Domingo, Martinique, Guadeloupe, Saint Christopher, etc.) and Guiana. In the Caribbean from the 1620s on, while fortified garrisons and plantations established France's tropical empire on the fringes of the Spanish and Portuguese possessions, the all-too-frequent rivalries between missionaries, as well as their involvement in slavery, wrote some of the Catholic Church's darkest pages.

FRENCH RELIGIOUS PRAGMATISM IN THE SIXTEENTH CENTURY

During the sixteenth century, the bulk of contact between the French and Native Americans was dictated by religious pragmatism and based mainly on seafaring, trade, and disastrous colonization attempts, in marked contrast to the Spanish, who, already settled, were focusing on labor extraction. Officially an essential part of the Spanish conquest, conversion was placed low among the invaders' preoccupations and mainly was used to subdue native people to secular rule. The English made no attempt at conversion, even though the Anglican clergy urged Queen Elizabeth to make it a colonial objective. Among the French, missionary activities were thought to be desirable by both the Huguenots and the Catholics, but there was little systematic attempt by either group to convert Indians to Christianity.

Decades before Columbus's official discovery of America, the Normans, Bretons, and Basques plied the waters of the Grand Banks of Newfoundland for cod, whale, and walrus, reached Cape Breton, and even entered the mainland. Their regular expeditions allowed the French fishing industry to grow considerably. France remained focused, however, on the Mediterranean, becoming an ally with the enemy of its enemies, the all-powerful Ottoman Empire. But Magellan and El Cano's circumnavigation proved it was possible to avoid the trade monopoly exerted by these difficult allies. Therefore, in 1523–24, the French king commissioned Florentine Giovanni da Verrazano to find a new route to Asia. Verrazano reconnoitered the American coastline from Florida to Cape Breton without finding any breach, but he confirmed the existence of a whole continent that a map of 1529 named "Nova Gallia." Its inhabitants, he wrote, apparently devoid of religion, displayed an eagerness to acquire the mariners' faith, for "everything they saw us Christians do with regard to divine worship [they did] with the same fervor and enthusiasm that we had."[4]

Sent to claim the new lands for his king in 1534 and in 1535, Jacques Cartier (1491–1557) explored the gulf and the river of the St. Lawrence, still looking for the passage that would open up the continental barrier. No real religious motives animated him and his men. Their faith was typical of pre-Counter-Reformation-Catholicism: a spiritual pragmatism relying heavily on propitious rituals and devotional objects that gave baptism a central role in Christian identity. Proselytism was incidental and a means to consolidate alliances. Thus the planting of a 30-foot cross embossed with three fleurs-de-lis on 24 July 1534, to be sure a religious gesture, was above all a political one, aimed at taking possession of the country for the "most Christian King" Francis I. And this was how Donnacona, the leader of the Iroquoian Amerindians present at the ceremony, understood it: He pointed "to the cross and making the sign of the cross with two fingers; then he pointed to the land all around us, as if to say that all the land was his, and that we should not have planted the cross without his leave."[5] Cartier quelled this protest by explaining that the cross was only a landmark and, to force Donnacona into cooperation, had his two sons captured and brought to France.

On his second voyage in 1535, about a thousand people from the fortified town of Hochelaga greeted Cartier "with wondrous joy," obviously mistaking him for a medicine man. Cartier played the game, reciting

> the Gospel of St. John, namely "In the Beginning," etc. making the sign of the cross over the poor sick people.... Then the Captain took a prayer-book and read out, word for word, the Passion of our Lord, that all who were

---

[4] Giovanni Verrazano, *Relatione* in Giovanni Battista Ramusio, *Delle navigationi et viaggi: nel quale si contiene le navigationi al Mundo Nuovo, a gli antichi incognito* (Venice, 1606), 350–9; Lawrence C. Wroth, ed., *The Voyages of Giovanni Da Verrazzano, 1534–1538* (New Haven, 1940), 141.

[5] Henry Percival Biggar, ed., *The Voyages of Jacques Cartier* (Toronto, 1993), 26–7.

present could hear it, during which all these poor people maintained great silence and were wonderfully attentive, looking up to heaven and going through the same ceremonies they saw us.[6]

Cartier's hasty departure "for fear of any misadventure" shows that he realized the limits of his healing powers.[7] In falling into the trap of acting like a shaman to "pacify" the natives, Cartier was no different than Nuñez Cabeza de Vaca, who recalled in 1542, "our method was to bless the sick, breathing upon them, and recite a Pater-Noster and an Ave-Maria, praying with all earnestness to God our Lord that he would give health and influence them to make us some good returns," or Anglican Thomas Harriot, who in his *Briefe and True Report* of his sojourn on Roanoke Island in 1585–86 reported how he and his companions were considered to have miraculous powers.[8]

Cartier observed that his hosts had "no belief in God that amount[ed] to anything," but they appeared willing to learn about Christianity. They even asked en masse for baptism, which the cautious Cartier refused: "We did not know their real intention and state of mind and had no one to explain to them our faith." Many misunderstandings about religion came from the Amerindian's inability to conceive of an exclusive religion and the French's incapacity to think otherwise. The Amerindian wanted to benefit from whatever rituals the French could teach, such as the ones they performed during the epidemic of scurvy in the winter of 1535. One Sunday a procession was organized, and a Mass recited and sung before an image of the Virgin propped up against a tree. Cartier vowed to make a pilgrimage to Roc Amadour if God should "grant him grace to return to France." Ironically, it was the Amerindian ritual of *annedda,* a curative drink made of common white cedar, that saved Cartier and his men. "As soon as they drank it they felt better, which must clearly be ascribed to miraculous causes; for after drinking it two or three times they recovered health and strength and were cured of all the diseases they had ever had. And some of the sailors who had been suffering for five or six years from the French pox [syphilis] were by this medicine cured completely."[9] Cartier's conviction that a miracle had occurred may explain why the cure for scurvy fell afterwards into oblivion.

In 1541, Francis I commissioned his Huguenot friend Jean-François de La Rocque de Roberval (1500–60) to establish a colony in these lands

---

[6] *Ibid.*, 63–4.
[7] *Ibid.*, 66.
[8] Alvar Nuñez Cabeza de Vaca, *Relation (1527–36),* in David B. Quinn, ed., *New American World: A Documentary History of North America to 1612* (New York, 1979), I: 32; Thomas Harriot, *Briefe and True Report,* in *ibid.*, III: 152.
[9] Biggar, *Cartier,* 68, 78–9, 80.

"of Canada and Ochelaga and others around and about them ... in all lands beyond and bordering the seas uninhabited or not possessed by any Christian prince," where a goodly number of gentlemen and others "both men-at-arms and of the populace, of each sex and every liberal and mechanic art ... were to converse with these foreign peoples" and to build "towns and forts, temples and churches for the communication of our Holy Catholic faith and Christian doctrine" as well as to institute the French system of laws in order that the colonists and these peoples live "with reason and order in the fear and love of God." That a Protestant was given the care of promoting Roman Catholicism in America was not a contradiction to the French authorities, who wanted at all costs to please the papacy and thus gain the right to join the race to exploit the New World. But no missionary was among the seven hundred colonists who came in 1541 and 1542. The settlement built near the Iroquois village of Stadacona (present-day Quebec City) did not last.

Plagued by scurvy, a severe winter, and the impossibility of trade with the natives who soon distrusted the French, the colony was repatriated in 1543.[10] The crown shifted its colonial interests to more amiable regions of the New World, financing Huguenot settlements in Brazil in 1555–57 and Florida in 1562–68. Both ended tragically under the antiheretic swords of the Portuguese and the Spaniards.[11] All other attempts implied strong Huguenot participation, as did the short-lived colonies of Marquis Troïlus de La Roche de Mesgouez at Sable Island (southeast of Nova Scotia) in 1598, of merchant Chauvin de Tonnetuit at Tadoussac on the St. Lawrence River in 1599, and of Pierre du Gua de Monts in Acadia in 1604–14. Thus the very first French colonial enterprises had a strong Protestant imprint. Even Catholic-led activities in the seventeenth century depended on Huguenots' commercial networks and savoir faire. Despite Cardinal Richelieu's banning of the Protestants from all the colonies in 1632, Huguenots came and even settled in French America. Moreover, in 1685, following the revocation of the Edict of Nantes, some three thousand Huguenots took refuge in Massachusetts, Rhode Island, New York, and South Carolina, giving birth to a second French America.

---

[10] Henry Percival Biggar, ed., *A Collection of Documents Relating to Jacques Cartier and the Sieur of Roberval* (Ottawa, 1930), 43–4 and 141–2, 207.

[11] André Thévet, *Singularitez de la France antarctique* (Paris, 1558, 1557); Jean de Léry, *Histoire d'un voyage fait en la terre du Brésil* (Geneva, 1594, 1578); "Narrative of the First Voyage of Jean de Ribault" (1562), in Benjamin Franklin French, ed., *Historical Collections of Louisiana and Florida*, 2nd ser. (New York, 1875), 159–89; Nicolas Le Challeux, *Histoire mémorable du dernier voyage aux Indes, lieu appelé la Floride* (1565), in Benjamin Franklin French, ed., *Historical Collections of Louisiana* (New York, 1851), III: 203–22; René de Goulaine de Laudonnière, *L'histoire notable de la Florida* (Paris, 1586).

CONVERSION AND/OR FRENCHIFICATION

In the sixteenth and early seventeenth century, for most French, Huguenots and Catholics alike, religion cemented political alliance, social solidarity, and pacification. Conversion amounted to extending the French nation. For a country like France, which was the most populated in Europe – and numbers meant power – this was a comfortable way to increase the base of its nationals without depopulating its home territory. Numbers were the key to colonization and could only be attained by unification with the colonized through baptism and intermarriage. It would be all to the benefit of the mother country. This inclusive principle was soon coupled among Catholics with the universalist principle of the Roman Church post–Council of Trent. Whereas one aimed to win souls – all the souls – the other aimed to win nationals. Since the 1570s, the missionary orders, including the Capuchins, the Recollects, and the Jesuits, had already been at work within the French countryside. Their aim was to unite, under the same cross and the same crown, the lukewarm and almost pagan peasants. These missionaries were the same ones who went to the New World. Sometimes their zeal turned fanatic.

Historically, the missionaries were the avant-garde of French discovery of America. Jesuits, in particular, became renowned explorers, cartographers, ethnographers, and translators; often they were authoritarians, sometimes they were diplomats, but most of the time they were spoilsports in that their utopian aims clashed with those of the merchants. In the early years they adopted the idea of mixing together French and Amerindians, and they worked hand in hand with the colonial authorities.

In 1610, secular priest Jessé Fleché's attitude toward the Micmacs of Port Royal in Acadia reflected the principles that guided previous colonizers: the Amerindian would be easy to convert, and once baptized, the good example given by the French would suffice to lead them to civilization and Christianity. This less-than-burning conception of the evangelization was doubtless most widespread among the French. However, it was not that of Jesuit Pierre Biard and Ennemond Massé.[12] These agents of the Catholic Reformation pursued the high ideals of the Council of Trent and insisted in 1611 on proper instruction of the neophytes and tough examination of their belief before baptism. This required the missionaries to learn the natives' languages. With them, Trent's rigor came to Acadia, not for long, however, as their mission was destroyed by a Virginian raid in 1613. But it did set a pattern. From then on, any missionary attempt would have to be under the sole control of the clergy reformed by the Council of Trent.

---

[12] Pierre Biard's letter, in Reuben Gold Thwaites, ed., *The Jesuit Relations and Allied Documents,* 73 vols. (Cleveland, 1897), 1: 139–83 (Biard, 1611). Hereafter *JR.*

At the same time, there was also a mission of the Capuchins – an austere reformation of the Franciscan order – in Maranaho (north of Brazil). Known by the written records of the fathers Claude d'Abbeville and Yves d'Evreux, it resembled the Acadian Jesuit mission. Like the Jesuits in Acadia, the Capuchins ran into the language barrier; like them, they tried to evangelize the natives, the Topinambas, who lived around the French "habitation," in accordance with the rules of the Council of Trent. Although it lasted longer than that in Acadia, the Brazilian mission ended in like fashion: a Portuguese raid annihilated the colony. Six catechumens were brought to Paris to be baptized. The event carried a positive image of the Amerindians but subordinated their conversion to their "Frenchification": on the engraving illustrating their devotion, they looked eminently French.[13]

In 1615 Champlain hired the Recollects, another reformed branch of the Franciscan order, to evangelize the Amerindians. The fourteen years the Recollects spent in the St. Lawrence Valley convinced them, too, that Christianization was inseparable from "civilization": the Amerindians had to be "humanized" – made French – prior to conversion. These missionaries, helped by the Jesuits from 1625 on, saw their efforts ruined in 1629, when the English forced Quebec to surrender.[14] It was only in 1632, when England gave the colony back to France, that the missionary endeavors resumed, this time for good. Cardinal Richelieu entrusted Acadia to the Capuchins' care, and the St. Lawrence Valley to that of the Jesuits.

Samuel de Champlain had become by then an ardent advocate of colonization, to the dislike of the merchants, who saw rivals in the settlers and fought the monopolies granted by the crown to support the settlements. Siding with the Church, Champlain carried out his project to merge the people by converting the Amerindians to the Christian faith and French civilization, thus teaching "those peoples, along with the knowledge of God, the glory and triumphs of your Majesty, so that with the French speech, they may also acquire a French heart and spirit."[15] Each time Champlain encountered a new Amerindian nation, he promoted the same idea of union. For example, in 1633 he explained to the Hurons, "'when that great house shall be built, then our young men will marry your daughters, and we shall be one people.' They began to laugh, answering: 'Thou

---

[13] Claude d'Abbeville, *L'arrivée des Pères Capucins en l'Inde nouvelle* (Paris, 1612); and *Histoire de la mission des P. Capucins en l'Ile de Maragnan* (Paris, 1614). Arsène de Paris, *Dernière lettre* (Paris, 1613); Yves d'Évreux, *Suite de l'Histoire* (Paris, 1615); Engraving *Le Baptesme de Trois Sauvages ou Touopinambous* (1613), Cabinet des Estampes, Bibliothèque nationale de France.

[14] Gabriel-Théodat Sagard, *Le grand Voyage au pays des Hurons 1632*, 2 vols. (Paris, 1865); and *Histoire du Canada 1636*, 4 vols. (Paris, 1866).

[15] Biggar, *Champlain*, III: 6.

always sayest something cheering to rejoice us. If that should happen, we would be very happy.'"[16] Paul Le Jeune, the superior of the Jesuit mission at Quebec, wrote in 1636:

> Some say to us: "Do you think you are going to succeed in overturning the Country?" Thus do they style the change from their Pagan and Barbarous life to that is civilized and Christian.... Monsieur de Champlain and Monsieur the General du Plessis Bochart rendered us great service last year, by exhorting the Huron in full council to embrace the Christian Religion, and by telling them that it was the only means not only of being some day truly happy in Heaven, but also of cementing in the future a very close alliance with the French – who, if this were done, would readily come into their Country, marry their daughters, teach them different arts and trades, and assist them against their enemies.[17]

MISSIONS TO THE AMERINDIANS

Uniting the French settlers and the Amerindians was also the aim of the Capuchins. Their missions in Acadia and the French Antilles developed simultaneously from the 1630s on. In Acadia, the Capuchins established residences at Port Royal, Saint John, Pentagouet, La Hève, Miscou, Canseau, and another in Maine, everywhere trying their best to convince the Amerindian to settle close to the French and to send their children to schools, such as the one Madame de Brice founded in Port Royal in 1644.[18] In Guiana and the West Indies, the Capuchins quarrelled with the Dominicans and Jesuits over jurisdictions and property rights, while the Amerindians who had not been decimated by war or epidemics resisted evangelization. Before long these religious orders turned to the exclusive care of the colonists.[19]

In North America, the Jesuits managed different types of missions. The itinerant missions were the most successful. In allowing a missionary to follow a tribe during the hunting season or to meet the nomads at a special time and place during the year, not only did these missions

---

[16] *JR* 5: 211 (Le Jeune, 1633).
[17] *JR* 10: 27 (Le Jeune, 1636).
[18] Ignace de Paris, "Relation de 1656," in Candide de Nant, *Pages glorieuses de l'épopée canadienne* (Paris, 1827), 305–11.
[19] Jacques Bouton, *Relation de l'establissement des François depuis l'an 1635 en l'isle de la Martinique* (Paris, 1640); Pacifique de Provins, *Le voyage de Perse et Brève Relation des Iles de l'Amérique* (1646), ed. Godefroy De Paris and Hilaire de Wingene (Assisi, 1939); Mathias Du Puis, *Relation de l'établissement d'une colonie françoise dans la Gardeloupe* [sic] (Caen, 1652); Pierre Pelleprat, *Relation des missions des PP. de la Compagnie de Jésus dans les île* (Paris, 1655); Jean-Baptiste du Tertre, *Histoire générale des Antilles*, 3 vols. (Paris, 1667–71); Jacques François Artur, *Histoire des colonies françoises de la Guianne* (c. 1734), ed. Marie Poldermann (Matoury, 2002).

open to the French the regions of Lac Saint-Jean, Gaspésie, New England, and the West, but they also created a nomadic and durable Amerindian Church. The sedentary missions aimed to facilitate the settlement of the nomads by providing them with a whole welfare system: school-convent, hospital, and "réduction" modeled on the Indian communities run by the Jesuits in Paraguay. In the réduction of Sillery, founded near Quebec City in 1637, results were mixed, even though everything was done to attract and keep them there. French colonists were specially hired by the Jesuits to clear the land for the Amerindians to farm, whereas others set up fortifications around the converts' village. The chiefs elected by the converts – for the greater part Montagnais and Algonquin – maintained social order and a great fervor among the residents, called *domiciliés*. But most of them left, especially during the winter hunting season, or moved to avoid the Iroquois, who never ceased to threaten them. Alcoholism also caused ravages. In the 1660s, the *Jesuit Relations* recorded only laconically matters concerning Sillery, which was not even Amerindian anymore.

The French also attempted to settle the Amerindians – Algonquin, Attikamegue, Iroquet, and Montagnais – in Trois-Rivières. Epidemics, incessant tribal moves, and difficult relationships with the Amerindian converts and nonconverts made for painful beginnings. But by the 1650s the Christianized had grown in number, and the Amerindian village, where "never has greater peace been remarked, or more calm and piety," was included in the French village.[20] But the experiment did not last. After 1660, the *Jesuit Relations* do not mention it anymore, as the Amerindians had moved to Cap-de-la-Madeleine, where a new converts society was created. Some ten years later, it moved away. A third mission involving settlement of the Amerindians was planned in Montreal as early as 1642, but because Montreal was "an advanced post toward the Iroquois," the natives did not want to stay there. Thus French and Amerindian cohabitation "under the same discipline, in the exercise of Christian Life" did not come true.[21]

The missions to the Huron were much more promising. Their country, situated on the southern banks of Georgian Bay, was key to the western trade. A handful of Jesuits established missions in various villages, as well as a missionary center called Saint Mary among the Huron. In sixteen years, they managed to baptize some ten thousand. It is difficult, however, to estimate the number of true converts. On the one hand, Jesuit policy held that only those who could prove their constancy in the faith were baptized, forming the pivotal axis of a very strong Christendom. On the

---

[20] *JR* 36: 195 (Ragueneau, 1650–51).
[21] *JR* 35: 207 and *JR* 36: 201 (Ragueneau, 1649–50 and 1650–51).

other hand, the missionaries, who did not want to lose a soul, baptized the terminal ill after little or no Christian instruction.

After 1647, there was a fast increase in baptisms, due to the weakening of the Huron traditionalists, who proved unable to counteract fatal epidemics and Iroquois attacks. The Iroquois eventually destroyed the Huron nation in 1649 and murdered eight missionaries who, already considered martyrs by their contemporaries, were canonized in 1930. Some refugees scattered among the western tribes, others followed the Jesuits in Quebec, and still others were taken prisoner by the Iroquois. When Jesuit Simon Le Moyne went to evangelize the Iroquois nations after the 1653 truce, he discovered about a thousand former Christian Huron, who formed a "captive Church" that welcomed him "like an angel from heaven."[22] Le Moyne's mission eventually expanded so much that a missionary center, called Saint Mary among the Iroquois, was built on the Huron model. It came to an abrupt end when the truce was broken in 1658.

The fragmentary evidence that exists of Amerindian views of the French shows that the missions were the source of gross misunderstandings. The association of baptism with death, for example, placed the missionaries in the category of evildoers and sorcerers and put their lives in danger. Moreover, the missionaries failed to understand that the Amerindian eagerness for alcohol was not so much for its taste, but to produce intoxication as a means of stimulating visionary experiences. Finally, if most of the French noticed the centrality of dreams and visions in Amerindian beliefs, they failed to consider them legitimate. As Jean de Brébeuf wrote, "The dream is the oracle that all these poor Peoples consult and listen to, the Prophet which predicts to them future events, the Cassandra which warns them of misfortunes that threaten them, the usual Physician in their sicknesses, the Esculapius and Galen of the whole Country – the most absolute master they have."[23] Indeed, in the missions two religious conceptions of life and death were seen to collide.

THE POLICY OF FRENCHIFICATION

Because the new territory was understood as an extension of the mother country, the French intending to settle in New France were invited to live with the natives and to marry converts who had been properly Frenchified. But the process was only one-way: the Jesuits highly opposed "Frenchmen who had hitherto married in the country" and whose "purpose had been to become barbarians, and to render themselves exactly like them." They explained to the Huron, "We, on the contrary, aimed by this alliance to

---

[22] *JR* 41: 37 (Le Mercier, 1653–54).
[23] *JR* 10: 169–71 (Brébeuf, 1636).

make them like us, to give them the knowledge of the true God, and to teach them to keep his holy commandments, and that the marriages of which we were speaking, were to be stable and perpetual." The superior of the Huron mission, François Le Mercier, reflected, "These brutal minds gave but little heed to the spiritual considerations; the temporal were more to their taste, and of these they wished to have very definite assurances." The Huron came back with very precise demands concerning marriage and the duties of man and wife. "All these questions show that they had thought over the matter."[24]

In 1642, relayed by the Sulpicians in 1657, the pious founders of Montreal also expected that Frenchification and intermarriages would result in mass conversions, a marked increase in the colonial population, and a rapid development of the agricultural potential of the St. Lawrence lowlands.[25] This assimilation plan was often reiterated, as in 1666–67, when Jean-Baptiste Colbert, Louis XIV's minister of finances, remarked that although the Algonquin and Huron of New France had "long been submitted to the authority of the King, ... little [had] been done to stir them away from their savage customs and to compel them to follow ours." He instructed New France intendant Jean Talon that "the most useful way to achieve it would be to try to civilize the Algonquin, the Huron, and the other Savages who have embraced Christianity; and to persuade them to come to settle in a commune with the French, to live with them, and educate their children in our mores and our customs." Thus the intendant, missionaries, and nuns were "to attract these peoples, especially those who embraced Christianity in the vicinity of our habitations, and if possible to have them live there so that after some time, having one law and one master, they may form one same people and one same blood."[26]

AN ORIGINAL WELFARE SYSTEM

This insistence on the Church's agency in this matter illustrates a specificity of New France colonization. The French crown never had the financial

---

[24] *JR* 14: 13–21 (Le Mercier, 1637). For other encouragement of mixed marriage see *JR* 9: 217–19; 10: 27–9; 14: 263; Pierre de Sesmaisons, *Raisons qui peuvent Induire Sa Sainteté à permettre aux Français habitant la Nouvelle France d'épouser des filles Sauvages quoique non baptisées ny mesme encore beaucoup instruictes à la foy chrestienne* (c. 1636), in Lucien Campeau, ed., *Monumenta Novæ Franciæ*, 9 vols. (Rome/Quebec, since 1967), III: 36–9.

[25] Elie Laisné de La Marguerie, *Les Véritables Motifs de Messieurs et Dames de la Société de Notre-Dame de Montréal*, (n.p. 1643), 107; François Giry, *La Vie de M. Jean Jacques Olier* (Paris, 1687), 98–9.

[26] Jean-Baptiste Colbert to Jean Talon, 5 Jan. 1666, in Pierre-Georges Roy, ed., *Rapport de l'archiviste de la Province de Québec pour 1930–1931* (Quebec, 1931), II: 45; Colbert to Talon, 5 Apr. 1667, *ibid.*, II: 72.

means for its expansion policy. The Company of the Hundred Associates, soon out of money, never attained Richelieu's objective. It was the Church that acted for more than thirty years as the principal agent of colonization, giving roots to Canada's welfare state system. The Church, the biggest colonial landowner, controlled all the educational and charitable institutions; its influence was thus considerable, and with the missionaries, it was everywhere.

The powerful position of the Catholic Church is not surprising, because it was already playing a leading role in the reconstruction of France after forty years of civil and religious wars, the end of which coincided exactly with the building of the New France in the New World. From the reign of Henri IV to that of Louis XIII and Ann of Austria's regency, the issue at stake was not only the rebuilding of the foundations of the French monarchy – law divine and absolute – but also the imposition of moral, political, social, and of course religious discipline in order to regain control over the French people. At a time when one of the most famous missionaries, Vincent de Paul, peacefully affirmed, "What is orderly is according to God, and, what is not is not according to God," the remolding of French society would be realized through the infrastructures of the Church, mainly its missionaries.[27] What has been called the "French school of spirituality" molded the precepts of the Council of Trent to the Gallican temperament and rights, while new or reformed religious orders and congregations busied themselves to infuse these precepts in all souls of France by means of missions in the countryside, predications, controversies with the Protestants, schools and colleges, and charitable works. In a huge wave of religious enthusiasm, they set up the foundations of a lasting welfare system.

Women were everywhere in this process. Female moneylenders, founders of hospitals and convents, agents of change, and inspirers of reform were to be found in all levels of the social hierarchy. As often in times of rebuilding, female agency, ideas, and resources made a significant contribution. In this context, a religious feminism emerged in which the first principle was to affirm gender equality to underline the Christian duties of both sexes in the general mobilization. A burgeoning culture of action thus acknowledged that men and women were under the same obligation "to use time" and to "render oneself useful to the public good" while escaping idleness, that is, to study, to be charitable, and to work. Through religion, French Catholic women were given the possibility to fully participate in the foundations of a civil society in which charity, education, and health constituted the pillars of a welfare system that was literally transplanted

---

[27] Vincent de Paul, *Entretiens spirituels aux missionnaires*, ed. André Dodin (Paris, 1949), 1024.

in America. This is why the first women to arrive in New France came not to make babies, but to participate in the conversion and unification of the people. In 1639, Jesuit Le Jeune wrote, "Here are four great works bound together by a single tie – the settlement of the Savages, the Hospital, the Seminary for little Savage boys, and the seminary for the Savage girls."[28] He was describing the Sillery réduction; the Hôtel-Dieu, which was run by Augustine nuns, and the Ursulines' convent (both created in 1639); and the Jesuit college founded in 1635, one year before Harvard University. Women *devotes*, like Jeanne Mance for the Hôtel-Dieu and Marguerite Bourgeoys for the Congrégation Notre-Dame, were actively involved in the foundation of God-ridden Montreal in the 1640s. Education, health care, and charity were to be the "bait covering the hook of faith."[29]

According to the promoters of assimilation, it was only a matter of time and education before the natives, who were perceived as a *tabula rasa*, became French – that is, were educated in the Catholic faith and brought to civility.[30] However, the missionaries soon expressed concern about the outcome of contact between natives and settlers; they noticed the bad influence of the former on the latter, especially in terms of alcohol consumption and loose behavior. So they counteracted this collateral damage first by segregating the Amerindians and the French. And because the danger that the French would yield to the seduction and freedom of life in the wild was great, the clergy carefully controlled who was allowed to contact the Amerindians in the fur trade and in the missions.[31] But they could not stop the growing number of interactions between French colonists and Indian communities, and experience made them more and more reluctant to promote assimilation. When the crown asked for results in the 1660s, the missionaries admitted the failure of Frenchification, but not of conversion.[32] As Jesuit Claude Dablon proclaimed in 1672, "Not only are there true Christians among these savage peoples, but also there are many more in proportion than in our civilized Europe."[33] By the 1680s, the Ursulines had

---

[28] *JR* 15: 33 (Le Jeune, 1639).
[29] Marie de l'Incarnation, *Correspondance*, ed. Guy-Marie Oury (Solesmes, 1971), 49 (letter to Raymond de S. Bernard, 1635). Hereafter MI.
[30] Biggar, *Champlain*, IV: 320–1; Denys Jamet's letter of 1615, in Odoric M. Jouve, *Les franciscains et le Canada: L'établissement de la foy, 1615–1629* (Quebec, 1915), 65–6; Chrestien Le Clercq, *Premier Établissement de la Foy dans la Nouvelle France*, 2 vols. (Paris, 1691), I: 98–9, 264–5.
[31] Gabriel-Théodat Sagard, *Grand Voyage du Pays des Hurons* (Paris, 1632), 178, 185; *JR* 14: 13–21 (Le Mercier, 1637); MI, 221 (letter to her son, 1644); Nicolas Perrot, *Mémoires sur les mœurs, coutumes et religion des sauvages de l'Amérique septentrionale* (1717), ed. J. Tailhan (Leipzig, Paris, 1864), 131.
[32] MI, 809, 828 (letters to her son, 1668).
[33] *JR* 58: 85 (Dablon, 1673–74).

Frenchified only seven or eight Amerindian girls who married Frenchmen, but along with the Hospitalières, they did help bring about the conversion of hundreds of women and girls who remained constant in the Catholic faith. For the missionaries there was no need for Amerindian converts to adopt French manners.

Eventually the colonial authorities acknowledged the problem of cohabitation. In 1685, the new governor, Denonville, claimed that close contacts with the Amerindians were a threat to the orderly society wished by the king: "Instead of familiarizing themselves with our laws, I assure you that they communicate very much all that they have that is the worst, and take likewise all that is bad and vicious in us." This was particularly evident in the behavior of the *coureurs des bois,* the Frenchmen who preferred to trade fur with Amerindians rather than to settle down and cultivate the land, who adopted "a savage way of life which consists of doing nothing, in being restrained in nothing, in pursuing all one's urges, and placing oneself beyond the possibility of correction."[34]

FRENCH CATHOLICISM AND SLAVERY

Slavery existed in all French colonial regions. In Canada, slaves were the property of government officials, religious communities, military officers, and merchants. Slavery remained urban and domestic. Generally, as the fur trade did not necessitate enslavement, the trend was to convert and free enslaved Amerindians – *panis* or war captives – whereas the rare black slaves who happened to come with the wealthier settlers were Christianized but kept in bondage. In Louisiana, slave labor developed along the same pattern as in the Antilles plantations, where Africans were deported to work in the sugar industry. But the Africans were never a missionary priority in the eyes of the various religious orders, themselves slaveholders and benefiting from the institution of slavery. It was only when they faced the resistance and decimation of the Amerindians that some missionaries turned to the evangelization of the bondmen.

None of the religious orders questioned the institution of slavery. If several missionaries denounced its abuses and recommended mild treatment of slaves, their aim was not to overthrow slavery but to Christianize it. According to the Christian rationale of the time, slavery was to help save souls.[35] As a missionary stated, "I admit that the condition of the slaves is

---

[34] Jacques-René de Brisay de Denonville, "Lettre du 13 Novembre 1685," quoted by Guillaume Aubert, "'The Blood of France': Race and Purity of Blood in the French Atlantic World," *William and Mary Quarterly* 61:3 (July 2004): 439–78, at 455.

[35] Bouton, *Relation,* 102; Pelleprat, *Relation,* 55–6; Du Tertre, *Histoire,* II: 469, 483–4, 494, 501; Jean-Baptiste Labat, *Nouveau voyage aux îles de l'Amérique,* 4 vols. (The Hague, 1724), II: 38.

extremely rough, ... but all these disgraces are for them the opportunity of an inestimable happiness, because in their slavery, they enjoy the freedom of the children of God."[36] Overall, however, the number of converts remained small: not only did slave owners everywhere oppose the evangelization of slaves, but also the slaves themselves hardly considered beneficial a religion that promoted their submission.

It is remarkable that the French policy of creating a new and united people in the New World never extended to African slaves. In fact, the authorities were forced to tolerate sexual liaisons between white free men and black women slaves because of the lasting absence of French women. Discourses and practices regarding the moral implications of these liaisons, rarely officialized by marriage, and the status of the offspring of interracial couples remained ambiguous and rather inconsistent, even with the imposition of the Code Noir in 1685. For example, in Martinique, mulatto children were declared free when they reached their majority, whereas in Guadeloupe, they stayed in bondage all their life.[37] By the end of the seventeenth century, the increasing numbers of free blacks and mulattoes on the islands led to a reversal of the officials' tolerance of French-African liaisons, and their racist concerns echoed those developing in New France regarding Amerindians.

THE CHURCH OF THE SETTLERS

Epidemics and warfare ultimately decimated the Amerindians, whereas slaves required only a handful of devoted missionaries. As a result, the religious foundations, such as the schools and hospitals, were reoriented toward the sole care of the settlers. In the St. Lawrence Valley from the 1660s on, several waves of emigration – mainly soldiers and indentured servants, as well as the *filles du roi*[38] – changed the face of the colony. For the first time the French were more numerous than the Amerindians. This contributed to strengthening the Church of the colonists.

The main objectives of the Church's agents had been to establish in the colony "a Jerusalem blessed of God, composed of Citizens destined for Heaven."[39] Thus the religious standards were very high for the time, and the religious orders were very motivated to maintain them. They had played

[36] Pelleprat, *Relation*, 49.
[37] Du Tertre, *Histoire*, I: 117 and II: 511; "Extrait des avis de Mrs de Blénac et Patoulet sur divers objets d'administration que le roi avoit fourni à leur discussion par sa lettre du 30 avril 1681, 3 Décembre 1681" and *Mémoire de M. de Ruau Palu, agent general de la Compagnie des Indes*, 30 Nov. 1673, quoted by Aubert, "The Blood of France."
[38] *Filles du roi* was the name of about eight hundred to a thousand single French women sponsored by the king to find a husband in New France.
[39] *JR* 7: 273 (Le Jeune, 1635).

a crucial role in the colony, which afterward was considered exaggerated. The Jesuits, for example, were the spiritual directors of the governors, and they saw their influence strengthened when their superior was appointed to the council of the colony. Jesuit financial investments, which made up about 20 percent of the colonial budget from 1626 to 1655, helped the development, even the survival, of the French settlement. However their spiritual and temporal monopoly came to an end in 1658, when François de Montmorency-Laval (1623–1708) arrived. Named Bishop of Petrea *in partibus infidelum* and vicar apostolic to ensure his dependence on Rome, Laval had trouble getting his subjects to recognize his authority, because for more than twenty years the very Gallican archbishop of Rouen continuously claimed jurisdiction over New France. Things eventually turned in favor of Laval, who was named bishop in 1674.

Until then, the spiritual jurisdiction in New France was not clear. For example, the churches in Quebec, Trois-Rivières, and Montreal were considered by the colonists as parish churches where the sacraments were administered by any available priests – the Jesuits and, after 1657 in Montreal, the Sulpicians. But these were not yet parish churches as such, because there was no bishop to define their boundaries and appoint priests. Laval's arrival clarified the situation. He set up the structures of the colonial Church. At the top of the hierarchy stood the bishop, appointed by the king and approved by the pope; at the bottom were the parish priests, in direct contact with the faithful. In theory, the bishop's power was immense: not only did he have a hand in every question concerning faith and morality, but as a member of the council he participated in civil administration. In practice, however, things were different. Laval waged a long and bitter struggle to prohibit the brandy trade with the Amerindians, to institute adequate tithing, to hold off the canonical erection of parishes until they became self-sufficient, and to introduce higher moral standards and pious practices among the settlers.

Laval's appointment as bishop coincided with the decline of the Church's influence in the colony and the rise of that of the state. From 1663 on, Louis XIV and Colbert reorganized the entire colonial administration – trade, justice, and religion – and through subsidies reduced the Church everywhere to a handmaiden of the state. The first intendant was instructed to "hold in just balance the temporal authority, which resides in the person of the King, and in those who represent him, and the spiritual authority which resides there in the person of the said Bishop and Jesuits, in such a manner nevertheless that the latter always be inferior to the former."[40]

---

[40] Quoted in Cornelius C. Jaenen, *The Role of Church in New France* (Ottawa, 1985), 3.

THE RELIGION OF THE SETTLERS

In the beginning, the Jesuits often praised the settlers' small communities on the St. Lawrence River. "Peace, love and good understanding reign among our French people; we are living here in a golden age." In Montreal, "an earthly Paradise for both the Savages and the French, were it not for the terror of the Iroquois," the governor's devotion had kept the settlement at peace and in the fear of God. In Trois-Rivières, the French, under Iroquois attacks, attributed their survival to "the extraordinary recourse that they had to the blessed Virgin in whose honor a small oratory was established in each house." And in Quebec City, the cult of the Virgin Mary "has banished enmities and coldness; it has introduced pure discourse in the place of too licentious language; it has revived the custom in families of publicly praying to God, evening and morning; it has given desires for purity to some persons in marriage." The Jesuits collaborated actively with this religious ambiance, frequently visiting the settlers' homes. "Most of those who are in this country admit that nowhere else in the world have they found more instruction, more assistance for their salvation, or a more tender and more ready care for their consciences."[41] It seems that most of the settlers conformed to the Jesuits' rigorous guidance, at least until the 1660s, when emigration and decline in the clergy-to-faithful ratio changed the picture.[42] But for most of the French, religion remained a living environment as well as an explanation of the world. Many daily acts were accompanied by prayers and offerings – from time to time recourse was made to superstition and even sorcery.

In general, throughout this early period of French colonization, the settlers were practicing Catholics. They attended church, respected feasts and Sundays, participated in processions and pilgrimages, observed fasts and abstinence, and gave to charitable institutions. The odd few on occasion refused to comply: some rebelled and refused to or delayed in paying tithes; others sold alcohol to Amerindians, even though they incurred excommunication; still others criticized the priests. But most remained attached to the Church and its institutions.

SUGGESTIONS FOR FURTHER READING

Belmessous, Sahila. "Assimilation and Racialism in Seventeenth- and Eighteenth-Century French Colonial Policy." *American Historical Review* 110:2 (2005): 322–49.

---

[41] *JR* 18: 83–5 (Le Jeune, 1640); *JR* 36: 167–9 (Ragueneau, 1650–51); see also *JR* 5: 83 (1633); 6: 101 (1634); 9: 149–450 (1636); 11: 73–5 (1637); 18: 81, 123 (1640); 23: 269 (1643), etc.

[42] MI: 667–8 (letter to her son, 1661); Marie Morin, *Histoire simple et veritable: Les Annales de l'Hôtel-Dieu de Montréal, 1659–1725*, ed. Ghislaine Legendre (Montreal, 1979), 51.

Boucher, Philip P. *France and the American Tropics to 1700: Tropics of Discontent?* Baltimore, 2008.

Deslandres, Dominique. *Croire et faire croire: Les missions françaises au XVIIe siècle.* Paris, 2003.

Greer, Allan. *The People of New France.* Toronto, 1997.

Litalien, Raymonde, and Denis Vaugeois, eds. *Champlain: The Birth of French America.* Montreal, 2004.

Rushforth, Brett. "'A Little Flesh We Offer You': The Origins of Indian Slavery in New France." *William and Mary Quarterly* 60:4 (2003): 777–808.

Trigger, Bruce G. *The Children of Aataentsic: A History of the Huron People to 1660.* 2nd ed. Montreal, 1987.

Trudel, Marcel. *The Beginnings of New France, 1524–1663.* Toronto, 1973.

11

ENGLISH, DUTCH, AND SWEDISH PROTESTANTISM IN THE ERA OF EXPLORATION AND EARLY COLONIZATION

JAMES D. BRATT

In 1682, seventy-five years after its first permanent settlement was planted at Jamestown, England's empire on the North American mainland consisted of thirteen colonies with some 160,000 inhabitants. The vast majority of that population lived in New England and the Chesapeake colonies of Virginia and Maryland. Carolina was barely ten years old, the territory of New Jersey was being split by its investors into two parts, and William Penn was newly arrived to found Philadelphia. Great changes in rule and demography were in the offing, but at the moment the colonies were more English and less entrammeled by English rule than they would ever be again. The slave-labor system and the African American population were just beginning their course of rapid growth. Gender ratios in the Chesapeake were only then coming into close enough balance to make the majority of the white population there native-born for the first time, opening the prospect of sustained institutional development. Only in New England were institutions old enough to be threatened – in some people's perception – with the prospect of atrophy. All this is to say that the study of religion in the English colonies over the first eighty years of the seventeenth century is in most instances a study in small numbers, embattled beginnings, and fitful development – but also in bold experimentation and what proved to be some definitive shaping of the future.

The major exception to the generalization about spare beginnings was New England, of course, where religion was foundational to the settlement process and pervasive in all this era's developments. For a long time historians were too ready to drape New England's mantle over the other mainland colonies, exaggerating the role of religion in early America. That should not lead to the opposite mistake of dismissing it, however, for religious declarations mark (and sometimes top) the list of reasons that authorities gave for founding a colony and of their prescriptions for how life should be conducted there. Richard Hakluyt the elder put the formula bluntly: England needed to pursue colonization "1. To plant Christian religion.

2. To trafficke [i.e., trade]. 3. To conquer."[1] The piety in such statements might have been window dressing or an idealistic intention that quickly broke on the rocks of Western Hemisphere realities, but the felt necessity to make the rhetorical gesture is telling in its own right. More to the point, religion, geopolitics, and economic prosperity were inextricably intertwined in this era when, after all, the central event on the European continent was the Thirty Years War, and the governing perception about the Atlantic world upon which the Protestant countries embattled in that war lifted their colonizing eyes was the hegemony, oppression, and bounteous profit taking exercised there by Catholic Spain. Put briefly, Protestant countries viewed the world in the first half of the seventeenth century through the lens of religious-national anxiety at least, and imminent peril at worst. In that context, nothing religious was window dressing.

Still, invoking God for strategic purposes and "laying Christ at the foundation" of things, as zealous Puritans pledged to do, were two different enterprises, and the proof of the matter came out in the practices adopted in each colony. We can distinguish four general patterns. In Anglican Virginia and Calvinist New Netherland, religion held a real if subsidiary place in the colony's founding but came to play only a fitful role in its evolution. Separatist Plymouth and Catholic-friendly Maryland, on the other hand, were founded in hopes of giving refuge for people marginalized in England's religious conflicts, but the refugees' faith proved to have limited power in shaping the life of the colony as a whole. In Puritan Massachusetts and Connecticut, no such limits obtained, so that the central religious motivation that characterized the colony's origins persisted through all the complications of the subsequent half century of development. Finally, filtering into several of these places but particularly concentrated in West Jersey and Rhode Island, Quakers and Baptists from off the radical edge of Puritanism generated unwitting laboratories in the possibilities and challenges of living collectively as dissenters. Each of these patterns would be altered by the trials of the 1680s, but each would also endure into the long future of the nation being seeded in this epoch. We shall take them up in turn, but for once treat New England's Puritans last instead of first.

VIRGINIA AND NEW NETHERLAND: FITFUL ESTABLISHMENTS

The "adventurers" who planted Virginia in 1607 brought to their enterprise the typical mixture of patriotism, piety, and profit seeking, as well as

---

[1] Quoted in Alan Taylor, *American Colonies: The Settling of North America* (New York, 2001), 119.

considerable practice at conquest and colonization in Ireland over the previous century. Moreover, in the second half of its first decade, from 1611 to 1616, Virginia was officially governed by "The Lawes Divine, Morall and Martiall" instituted by Governor Thomas Dale, which provided "virtually the outline for a Holy Commonwealth" on the order of those later established in Massachusetts and Cromwell's England.[2] The colony's chaplain in these years was Alexander Whitaker, whose sermon *Good Newes from Virginia* (1613), while acknowledging the ill discipline that Dale's regime had inherited, invoked the divine plan to unfold "true religion" on the continent amid pagan Indians and against Catholic New Spain. Whitaker's theme was a favorite of his father, William Whitaker, Regius Professor of Divinity at Cambridge University, who was a stark predestinarian even by the measure of Puritan theologians.

As it turned out, a different destiny awaited Virginia, and it was prefigured in 1616, when Whitaker drowned in the same waters of the James River that bore in a new strain of tobacco from the West Indies, and with it the colony's economic salvation. Along with high profits, tobacco cultivation dispersed settlement along Virginia's rivers and redoubled the demand for the disposable labor provided by indentured servitude, thus triggering calamitous Indian wars in 1622 and 1644 and continuing the marked skewing of male over female percentages in Virginia's population. The long-term consequence was a decentered, hierarchical, unstable society built on competitive individualism and requiring constant replenishment by fresh immigrants. Because New England would show nearly the opposite patterns, we can conclude that whatever chances the Puritan impulse once had in Virginia died for lack of proper social nutrient at the hands of demography, topography, and the tobacco economy.

That conclusion might be extended to cover *any* faith, for it took thirty years from Whitaker's death before another religious regime began to emerge. This was a royalist type of Anglicanism instituted by William Berkeley during his first term as governor (1641–52; his second ran 1660–77), dedicated to prescribed order and the extirpation of Nonconformity. The punitive side of the plan worked; by the end of the 1640s, scores of Puritan-inclined families had left Virginia for the more tolerant climes of Maryland. Yet the Anglicanism that took hold in Virginia diverged notably from that in England, most of all because in the absence of a resident bishop, functional authority in the church devolved to parish vestries that were dominated by the same elites that ran local politics. These were jealous lords who tended to keep such clergy as were available on short tenures and low salaries. In consequence, Virginia became a place

---

[2] Sydney E. Ahlstrom, *A Religious History of the American People* (New Haven, 1972), 186.

where "a religiously tepid constituency" was served by "an equally tepid ministry."[3] The situation began to turn only with the arrival in 1685 of the Rev. James Blair, who became commissary for Virginia for the bishop of London, and with the chartering of the College of William and Mary under Blair's auspices in 1693. With these, the institutional power of the Church of England could start pushing back against the powers of local gentry.

Even so, the fabric of Anglicanism had difficulty stretching to keep up with the growth and dispersion of Virginia's population. Nor would Nonconformists be equal to the challenge, until the outburst of evangelical revivalism in the 1740s. For the seventeenth century there is no recorded presence of Baptists or Presbyterians on the Virginia scene. Only the Quakers, with their quietism and household polity, managed to spread between the cracks of the Anglican establishment. To his pleasant surprise, Quaker leader George Fox found "many large gatherings" assembled to hear him speak on his 1672 tour of the colony. Yet his journal's account of his arduous trek across the Virginia landscape "explains why Anglican and Nonconformist churches alike tended to be small, poorly supported, and isolated" there.[4]

The planting of New Netherland would have seemed to be more religiously auspicious. In 1609, the same year that Henry Hudson sailed up the river that would bear his name, Spain effectively ceased its attempts to thwart Dutch independence, and the new country awarded official privileges to the Reformed religion that had been crucial in building and sustaining the morale of resistance. Further, the steps by which New Netherland was founded (a fur-trading post – Fort Orange – near present-day Albany in 1614 and a town there in 1624 and at Manhattan in 1626) straddled the meetings of the Synod of Dort (1618–19), in which the Dutch Reformed Church supported the cause of predestinarianism against the Arminian stance of the losing Remonstrants. Because the cities that would invest in the Dutch West India Company (WIC) generally supported the cause of orthodoxy, the chartering of the WIC and the renewal of the holy war against Spain – both in 1621 – might have augured a colony of Calvinist zeal on the Hudson. As it happened, the site turned out to be the least lucrative of the WIC's far-flung ventures, and the company's recurrent attempts to find a formula to land people and extract profits put religious quality far lower on the list of operational priorities than it held in official documents.

Until its first minister, Jonas Michaelius, arrived in 1628, New Netherland was left religiously to the care of a chaplain (*ziekentrooster*).

---

[3] *Ibid.*, 189.
[4] *Ibid.*, 193.

When Michaelius departed in 1632, New Amsterdam was still ten years away from having its own church building; the loft of a flour mill served instead. The new pastor, Everardus Bogardus, saw to the building project but otherwise fell into stormy relations with the WIC. He was finally replaced in 1649 by Johannes Megapolensis (Jan van Mekelenburg), who arrived from a seven-year stint as the pioneer pastor at Fort Orange, where the faithful had gathered for worship in a converted storehouse. University trained, sacrificing considerably for the cause, as did the other dominies to follow, Megapolensis found much that was disheartening in his new charge: a town of fewer than two hundred houses, a fort in disrepair, a church unfinished – and thirty-five flourishing taverns. As the historian of the colony's churches concludes, it was "obvious that the austerity, hard work, and high moral principle preached by the stern Calvinist ministers had only a limited effect on the inhabitants of New Netherland."[5]

The colony's population finally began to take off in the 1650s, when the WIC gave up its monopoly, along with the quasi-medieval patroon system that had succeeded it, and opened farming and the fur trade to all comers. One result was a marked increase in ethnic and religious pluralism. In 1664, when the English took over, probably fewer than half of New Netherland's inhabitants were actually Dutch. Ten percent were enslaved Africans, and twice that number were English settlers on Long Island. Walloons and Jews of differing provenance were present in number, as were the harbingers of the large Huguenot migration still to come. No wonder that Jesuit missionary Isaac Jogues famously reported hearing eighteen languages spoken in the streets of New Amsterdam. By official policy he would have seen no public worship by any but the Reformed, however, for Governor Pieter Stuyvesant, who ruled 1647–64, a zealous son of the Calvinist manse, enforced the policy of religious exclusivism that had always been on the colony's books but had largely been honored in the breach. Thus in 1655 Stuyvesant turned away a Dutch Lutheran pastor who had been duly called by a body of some 150 families on Manhattan, whereas Megapolensis fulminated against the tide of Jewish refugees that arrived after the Portuguese reconquest of Brazil in 1654. At this point the colony's two lines of authority came into conflict, for although the WIC was religiously accountable to the Classis of Amsterdam, which encouraged Stuyvesant's policy, the company held most of the other cards and wanted religious tolerance for the sake of trade and growth. It reminded Stuyvesant that no one was to be disturbed in household devotions or "private" gatherings.

---

[5] Gerald F. DeJong, *The Dutch Reformed Church in the American Colonies* (Grand Rapids, 1978), 43.

In any case the church was challenged enough to keep up with its own flock, which had spread across the East River onto Long Island, across the Hudson into New Jersey, and by 1664 up the Hudson to Esopus (Kingston). Ministers were hard to come by, not least owing to the congregations' poor facilities and pay; Gideon Schaats literally had to live in Albany's (still unoccupied) poorhouse for the first years of his remarkably dedicated tenure there (1652–94). More ominously, the land hunger associated with population growth sparked deadly conflicts with the Algonquian Indians on the lower Hudson. (The Iroquois around Albany, by contrast, were placated at all costs because of their control of the fur supply.) In a series of four wars – 1644–45, 1655, 1659–60, and 1663–64 – the colonists eliminated the native presence in the area. Like the Virginians, they had never pretended to heed whatever evangelizing pretensions had been sounded about the colony before settlement began. Megapolensis had indeed executed a pioneering study of the Mohawk during his time at Fort Orange, but his conclusions were hardly kind: the natives were "entirely savage and wild, strangers to all decency, yea, uncivil and stupid as garden poles."[6]

Stuyvesant and the WIC also turned aggressively against the settlements that had been erected along the lower Delaware River under the banner of Sweden beginning in 1638. This was even less Swedish a colony than New Netherland was Dutch, for half its settlers were Finns, and half of the partners in the controlling trading company, itself a copy of the WIC, were Dutch. When the fur trade and tobacco cultivation proved disappointing, the Dutch sold their interest, and the colony started moving toward the farmer-settler model. After 1648, however, with the Thirty Years War concluded and the Dutch no longer in need of a Swedish alliance, the Netherlands asserted its claims on the Delaware territory, finally invading in 1655 with a force of three hundred men under Stuyvesant's lead. They found four hundred souls being served by three Lutheran churches under the mandate of New Sweden's royal charter to provide "a true and due worship ... to the Most High God in all things" in accordance with "the Unaltered Augsburg Confession."[7] That worship often did not have the benefit of officiating clergy. Among the pastors who came and went, only one, Lars Lock, remained on-site from before the Dutch conquest through the succeeding English one, until his death in 1688. Neither the Dutch nor the English tried to extirpate Lutheran worship, although their tolerance was tried by Lock, who proved as flinty toward outsiders as he was faithful to his flock.

---

[6] Quoted in Taylor, *American Colonies*, 252.
[7] Quoted in Israel Acrelius, *A History of New Sweden*, trans. William M. Reynolds (Ann Arbor, 1966), 39.

In 1664 the hunter turned prey as New Netherland fell to an English war fleet commissioned by James Duke of York. Stuyvesant blustered about mounting military resistance, but with the fort in disrepair and little in the way of a defense force on call, the Dutch pastors prevailed on him to accede to the inevitable. Among other provisions, the English allowed unimpeded conduct of Reformed worship – and of every other type of devotion onsite. Protection of minority religious rights was in keeping with the interests of the Catholic James, but it was also recognized that Anglicans for the foreseeable future could have no more pretense to being an established church, for social harmony and growth in trade could not prosper by official exercise of religious preference. In any case, for the duration of James' rule – first as duke, then as king – New York imitated the policy earlier established in Maryland, where Catholic authorities instituted genuine religious toleration. The most successful administrator in New York's case was the Catholic layman Thomas Dongan (governor 1683–88); the end of his term by virtue of James' deposition also inaugurated an eclipse of Catholic rights that would last for another century.

MARYLAND, PLYMOUTH, AND RHODE ISLAND: HAVENS OF REFUGE

Roman Catholics fared much better in Maryland, which, under Charles I's policy of relieving the religious out-parties in his realm (or relieving the realm of them) via colonization, was separated from Virginia and given to the Catholic Calvert family as proprietors. From the first landing of English settlers in 1634, Maryland saw a role-reversal of the motherland, with a largely Protestant labor force under the political and economic control of a Catholic minority. This relationship endured through a series of tempests and temporary reversals until the Glorious Revolution reached Maryland in 1689, after which a Protestant regime was permanently ensconced and ended Maryland's most significant contribution to colonial religious history, a policy of religious toleration emerging from the traditionalist end of the contemporary theological spectrum. The 1639 instructions of Cecilius Calvert Lord Baltimore mandated freedom of conscience for the colony, although it urged Catholics to "worship as privately as may be" so as not to offend Protestants.[8] After an aggressively Puritan interlude (1642–47) when Baltimore's agent fled to Virginia, the re-seated proprietor joined with the colonial assembly to formalize customary practice in the Act of Toleration (1649). No Trinitarian Christian might be "molested or discountenanced for or in respect of his or her religion nor in the free

---

[8] Quoted in Ahlstrom, *Religious History*, 331.

exercise thereof."[9] Yet the future would not leave this prescription unmolested. Dissenters fleeing Governor Berkeley's Anglican purge of Virginia sharpened the Protestant edge in Maryland, leading to a Puritan takeover in 1655; that in turn accelerated a Catholic flow from Maryland into the northern neck of Virginia. The restoration of the monarchy in England in 1660 brought back the old regime to Maryland, but it did nothing to reverse the demographic tide – by the mid-1670s Catholics constituted less than 10 percent of the colony's twenty thousand inhabitants.

Ministering to this flock were Jesuit missionaries and priests who settled, and they supported themselves as ordinary planters rather than as state- or order-subsidized clergy. By 1640 they were operating five parishes as well as (befitting their order) mission efforts among the native Piscataway people. Andrew White, as leader of this enterprise, composed an Algonquian grammar, dictionary, and catechism, becoming the pioneer in all the English colonies at putting a native language into written form. The Indian mission would fall to the familiar forces of white land hunger; pastoral care of the settlers struggled to keep up with the dispersion that fed that hunger. With fewer than ten of their number typically on-site, and with their order resisting the introduction of secular clergy, the Jesuits undertook a type of circuit riding later made legendary by Methodists. Most of these services occurred in private homes and encouraged the cultivation of domestic devotions to tide the faithful over until the next visitation. The result was a regime of "quiet and reserved piety" far removed from the baroque splendor of the contemporary European scene.[10] Religious schools came and went in the colony, and the Catholic elite (like their Virginia counterparts) typically sent their sons abroad for education. The Catholic public presence in Maryland was therefore minimal. Ordinary believers relied on their leaders to protect their interests, and the leaders prospered as gentlemen among their Protestant peers.

Plymouth colony stood opposite Maryland on the theological spectrum but resembled it as a refuge for an alienated group that constituted only a minority in its new abode, with a modest religious public culture. The Separatists at Plymouth were so called because they had formally disowned the Church of England, a step that also entailed psychological disjunction from the home country and some distance from their Puritan siblings who would move in next door. By the time the Separatists landed at Cape Cod in 1620, their other name, Pilgrim, was also well earned, because a good number of them had been sojourning in the Netherlands since 1607.

---

[9] Quoted in *ibid.*, 334.
[10] James Hennesey, *American Catholics: A History of the Roman Catholic Community in the United States* (New York, 1981), 45.

Pilgrims they would remain in the sense that Plymouth colony never aimed for power or influence on world affairs – rather, it sought to give its people of generally modest means a place where they could pursue their lives, spiritual and temporal, in peace and fidelity to their own lights. Thus although their Mayflower Compact sounded all the notes of covenanted community that the Puritan colonies would amplify to no end, the Separatists' modest ambitions, together with their status as a numerical minority amid people recruited for their economic or military skills, gave them more the classic profile of the "quiet in the land." Few men of learning joined them; they had no minister until 1629, and arguably no formal church until then; and the ten towns that were established in the first generation were more often without than with a pastor. For fifty years Plymouth had no public school, sent no one to university, and returned the same small band of leaders to office in church and state year after year. Their common commitment to Reformed theology and congregational polity kept them more united than were the dissenters to their south in Rhode Island, but the numerical and institutional strength of Massachusetts Bay exerted a gravitational pull that absorbed Plymouth into that colony uneventfully in 1691.

Rhode Island, a third colony of refuge, was unique in providing harbor for dissenters from dissenters – that is, for people fleeing from the ostracized Puritans who had become a new establishment in New England. This further step of dissent had no unitary direction. Some of Rhode Island's founders, like Roger Williams and Anne Hutchinson, can be seen as ultra-Puritans so compelled by certain of that movement's original convictions as to leave behind the rest, or to reject the civic and/or theological compromises that Puritans in power deemed necessary. Other founders, like William Coddington and Samuel Gorton, represented Quaker (or Quaker-like) rejections of the sum of Puritan measures. These four leaders' agreement on what they opposed was stronger than any positive consensus that they shared outside of a resolute commitment to freedom of conscience – that is, to genuine and total religious liberty rather than religious toleration only. Politically they observed a robust localism that allowed each of their towns (Providence, Portsmouth, Newport, and Warwick) to go its own way, even if that did not prevent sharp rivalries and suspicions among them. Williams became the elder statesman in the group, securing a patent from Parliament in 1644 to protect all the towns' claims, then promoting their confederation under a representative assembly in 1647. Williams also did the colony's distinctive principal honor in publishing his two great tracts, *The Bloudy Tenent of Persecution for the Cause of Conscience Discussed* (1644) and, a rejoinder to his critics, *The Bloudy Tenent Yet More Bloudy* (1651). By the late 1650s the colony's besetting factionalism had largely subsided, and in 1663 it entered into a more stable future under a new royal charter, the restored Charles II appreciating Rhode Island's anti-Puritan stance and economic value.

Indeed, well before the founding of Pennsylvania, Rhode Island demonstrated the affinity of minimal religious constraints with maximal economic pursuits. The conjunction was clear already among the adherents of Anne Hutchinson in Boston, and after her exile, although she moved on to Long Island, the mesh of radical spirit with commercial ambition made Newport a leader in both Quaker religion and the Atlantic trade. The disposition toward individual liberty and initiative, on the one hand, and nonviolence and non-coercion, on the other, together with the Quaker diaspora's transoceanic networks, accounts for the rise and effectiveness of the pattern. At the same time, acute theological disagreements persisted, most notably in Roger Williams' rejection of Quaker positions. His religious individualism arose out of a fierce loyalty to scripture as written revelation over against Quaker teachings of an "inner light." Likewise, his suspicion of religious institutions, not to mention state-dictated religious measures, reflected his anticipation of an imminent millennial restoration of the pure system of the original gospel, rather than a progressive step into a modern future. Such disparate sources, nonetheless, worked together to produce a colony whose public culture, especially in its religious dimension, was as weak as its tenacity for individual liberty was strong. The two sowed perennial factionalism into Rhode Island's future. The revocation of the 1663 charter by the Dominion of New England sent the colony back into virtual anarchy for a time, and long after that was redressed, Rhode Island remained one of the most difficult places to govern, as it was the most inviting clime for belief.

QUAKERS AND BAPTISTS: THE RADICALS

That Quakers proved to play the most stabilizing role in Rhode Island politics is testimony not just to its fractiousness, but to unexpected dimensions of a faith founded in radical dissent and aversion to the sword. Emerging off the left flank of Puritanism in the agitations and, finally, disappointments of Cromwell's Commonwealth, the Society of Friends gathered people convinced that the kingdom of God must come by peaceable means as well as toward peaceable ends, that the Puritan reduction of the old Roman Catholic hierarchy and sacramental system had not extended far enough, and likewise that the Protestant principle of individual conscience needed to be taken to its logical conclusion. The result was as antiformal a fellowship as possible, one without sacraments, ordained clergy, creedal subscription, or prescribed liturgy. Its theological distinctive, which taught an unmediated revelation of Christ to the soul, and its ethic of nonviolence, which in theory foreswore use of oaths, arms, and tax payments in support thereof, struck the Friends' opponents as subversive of all authority and order, in church and society. Early Quakers returned the favor by holding disruptive, sometimes scandalous, demonstrations against religious establishments, particularly those of their erstwhile Puritan cousins in dissent, and they felt compelled to proselytize ("publish") their cause despite (or precisely because of) prohibitions to the contrary. Their arrival in New England, then, provoked the most deadly controversy in early American religion prior to the Salem witch craze.

The first Friends to come ashore in Boston, in 1656, were summarily seized, jailed, and shipped out; the next year they began filtering in across the border from Rhode Island and met a similar fate, with whippings added. The spiral reached its peak from 1659 to 1661 as Massachusetts Bay authorities hanged four Quakers, desisting only on the edict of the restored King Charles II. Eventually the Friends' strategy turned from confrontation to more general dissemination, epitomized by their founder George Fox's tour of the colonies in 1672. His witness was effective in Virginia and especially in Carolina, where, with virtually no other fellowships in place before 1680, Quakers probably constituted a religious majority in the future North and a substantial minority in the future South Carolina. The center of the movement on the colonial mainland remained Rhode Island, however, where the regular discipline supplied by the Friends' system of mutually accountable "meetings" (congregations) supplied some of the best sinews of order in the colony. Eminent Friends, who were also eminent merchants, soon held more than their numerical share of public offices in Rhode Island, which required some compromise with the pacifist principle for purposes of establishing an armed defense, although they provided generous allowances for conscientious objection.

When control of West Jersey went over to a Quaker consortium led by William Penn in 1674, the Friends' heartland began to shift south toward its ultimate center in Pennsylvania. Concerted immigration pushed West Jersey's English population by 1682 to 1,400 souls, who were arranged in well-regulated meetings centered in the capital at Burlington. As with its counterpart in Maryland, the Quaker colony of refuge – and opportunity – quickly took on a conservative shape headed by an aristocracy of elite families, which were in turn strengthened by the Quaker mandate of endogamy, the group's only effective mode of boundary maintenance. They superintended a society libertarian in theory but suffused with a Quaker ethos in practice. The success and travail of that arrangement in the context of religious pluralism awaited the merger of West with East Jersey in 1702 under a regime that accorded official toleration to all Protestant Christians.

Baptists are so numerous on the current American scene that their relative paucity in the early colonial era might seem anomalous. The puzzle can be explained by theological and geographical reasons. As to the first, Baptist departures from Puritan orthodoxy, though not trivial, were moderate compared to those of the Quakers. General Baptists, who followed the Separatist trek of exile to Holland before migration to North America, espoused Arminian concepts of human initiative and free will in the way of salvation. Particular Baptists hewed to the Calvinistic line on these matters and so differed from the Puritans principally in restricting baptism to (adult) "believers" rather than including their infant children as well. With the coming of mass revivalism in the next century, these issues would become experientially compelling; for now, if it was dissent one wanted, the Friends offered a stouter option. Then too, Baptists did not dominate any territory in this era as did Quakers but tended to filter into quiet spaces where they would attract less notice. Prior to 1680 they had little presence on the mainland from Virginia south. In the New England core colonies they formed fugitive congregations, reaching significant numbers along the Rhode Island-Connecticut border. Their most notable convert was Henry Dunster, the first president of Harvard College, who had to resign his post in 1654 on refusing to submit his fourth child for baptism. Even at their center in Rhode Island, they did not especially prosper. Roger Williams' later fame as the "first Baptist" obscures the fact that he professed that position only briefly before renouncing all church membership and declaring himself to be a permanent "seeker" after gospel purity. The most concerted of Rhode Island Baptists' energies went into the contest between the Particular and General theological positions. The former, losing, faded away to reemerge later in Pennsylvania in the ranks of Welsh immigrants. Their battle won, General Baptist congregations in Rhode Island tended to atrophy.

NEW ENGLAND PURITANS: DISSENTERS AS ESTABLISHMENT

"Puritanism" has been the subject of so many studies and competing definitions that any summary treatment of its role in early American religion risks partiality, in both senses of the term. It serves best to understand it as a movement that, grounded in certain common convictions and matured over half a century of struggle in England, found unprecedented opportunity to implement its program in America – and to discover the tensions that lay at its heart. The Puritan movement aimed first of all at thorough reform of the Church of England according to the example of the Reformed churches on the continent; this reformation, being frustrated under the reigns of Elizabeth I and James I, generated new, distinctive commitments to congregational polity and anti-formal liturgy. To sustain their program in the face of resistance without leaving the church (thus, as "non-separatists"), Puritans in England developed unofficial networks of friendly parish churches and conventicles. There they focused on the thorough reformation of their own hearts and behavior, a purified self and fellowship, if not a purified nation, being deemed possible. This devotional reformation, with its ascetic "precisianism" and pronounced introspection, was borne along to New England among the twenty thousand souls that constituted the Great Migration of 1629–42.

Although many in that number might not have been fully committed to its program, the Puritan party controlled the rules, offices, and ethos of the colonies established at Massachusetts Bay (1629), Hartford (Connecticut, 1634), and New Haven (1638; absorbed into Connecticut in 1662). In this their heartland, New England Puritans had a unique opportunity to carry out the project not just of ecclesiastical reformation, but also of recovering the covenant that God had made with England but that the home country had putatively forfeited. Their efforts toward that end were as institutionally thick as their dissidents' settlements in Rhode Island were institutionally thin. The Puritan colonies were town- (not manor-, farm-, or plantation-) centered as nowhere else in British North America, each town being formed by formal covenant among its freemen, providing a church from the start and, by laws soon passed in Massachusetts, mandated to support a school as well. Clergy, magistracy, parents, and educators were strictly separated as to office but continuously cooperative in working to uphold a "holy commonwealth." It was only natural, then, that Massachusetts' first crisis, in 1636, came from the antiformal and anti-institutional position of Roger Williams, and that he was exiled forthwith.

Other tensions surfaced quickly as well. Was it New England's purpose to restore the primitive purity of the apostolic church, or to give families squeezed by the home country's economic straits new opportunities, or to build on these shores a model society to be reexported to England once God's judgment had descended with refining fire? The answer was "yes," meaning that the colonists pursued not altogether compatible goals into the indefinite future. It was the task of the clergy (and one they accomplished tolerably well) to harmonize and re-strike the balance between these tensions as times and circumstances changed. A fundamental conflict in the church, however, was not so soluble. It came to a head the year after Williams' banishment around the teaching of the eminent laywoman and midwife Anne Hutchinson and her clerical brother-in-law, John Wheelwright. Wheelwright in his pulpit and Hutchinson in her home Bible studies espoused one strain of traditional Puritan theology, namely, that the works of pious reflection, ascetic discipline, and civic responsibility that the *other* strain of Puritanism emphasized counted as nothing toward salvation or ethical merit in the eyes of God – worse, that they tended to displace the free grace of Christ and inward assurance of the Spirit that alone constituted the substance and consequence of salvation. Their opponents, led by Cambridge pastor Thomas Shepard and Hartford pastor Thomas Hooker, labeled this "antinomianism," that is, an attack on the rightful place of the law in prodding ("preparing") people to conversion and guiding their Christian walk thereafter. Each side had its political allies, and the Hutchinson-Wheelwright camp garnered particular support from the merchant interest besides, but Massachusetts governor John Winthrop was hostile to their cause and held the initiative. As a result, in 1638 first Wheelwright and then Hutchinson were banished, the first to New Hampshire, and the second to Rhode Island. Thereafter, a preparationist model of piety and a high respect for law reigned unrivaled in New England.

Its theology remained resolutely Calvinist (Calvin himself had valorized the "third use" of the law as a guide to holy living), but one step taken beyond Calvin by the Massachusetts regime heightened the perennial Reformed concern with election and predestination. That addition (defined in 1635) was to make a personal experience of conversion required for full church membership – such membership being, besides, a necessary qualification for voting rights in colony-wide elections. But because conversion amounted to the inward conviction of divine election in one's own case, and because God was understood to be both fairly parsimonious and secretive in this decision, the achievement of assurance could be as daunting as it was significant. The clergy responded by publishing manuals of spiritual guidance that described the steps through which one could expect to pass on the way to conversion; that process in turn established a template for one's future spiritual life. Puritan devotionalism thus came to celebrating union with Christ while expecting heights and valleys in the saint's ongoing experience. Dogged persistence or sweet meltings – the prime issue was vigilance.

If some consensus was built around this spirituality, disagreement over its civil effects was worked out by various measures. One was the formation of separate colonies. Connecticut under Thomas Hooker required neither experiential conversion for church membership nor church membership for civil enfranchisement, but that was a double laxity in the eyes of the followers of the Rev. John Davenport, who disapproved of Boston ways for the reason opposite of Hooker's and set up a stricter regime at New Haven. His followers were seeking economic independence as well and appreciated the opportunities provided by the Long Island Sound. Such permissible variations, along with the need to coordinate a common defense and regular trade, made the New England colonies (and Plymouth too) into a system of cooperative enclaves with both leeway and sufficient buffers for a people born in dissent. Consensus was further sustained by highly participatory politics. Local matters in Massachusetts (and colony-wide affairs as well in Connecticut) were regulated by annual elections in which men of fairly modest means could vote. If the "democracy" of the famous New England town meeting did not resemble later versions in aiming not to poll between discordant opinions but to establish communal consensus, participants could go to extraordinary lengths to achieve that goal without coercion. In addition, geography kept economic inequality low by the standards of the day. Largely unsuitable for plantation agriculture, New England generated instead a thick commercial nexus of small farmers and artisans in which nearly everyone participated. The modest scale of that commerce, however, along with suspicions of covetousness and luxury constantly reiterated from the pulpit, kept market exploitation under control and made the achievement of material prosperity as much a cause for introspection as for self-congratulation. It would be left to later, more secularized and individualistic generations to provide grist for Max Weber's mill.

The real pressures of the day rose from remarkable fertility rates that historians ascribe to the region's healthy climate and the relatively equal sex ratios that marked Puritan settlements from the start. Constituting only 5 percent of seventeenth-century immigrants to British North America, by the end of the century New England claimed 40 percent of the non-Indian population there. One consequence was a constant "hiving out" of new towns from old: forty by 1640, ninety by 1675. Clergy might spy covetousness and disunity at work in the phenomenon, but other leaders welcomed the growth it brought, and the young pioneers themselves observed the old practice of covenanting in starting a new town. A deadlier consequence would come in the form of perhaps the costliest warfare in all of American history, discussed further in the following. For now the churches strove to keep order, especially in view of the chaos attending the civil wars back in England. The synod that met at Cambridge, Massachusetts, in 1648 set a theological standard by "attesting to" the scriptural soundness of the confession and catechisms just passed by the Westminster Assembly in England – that is, strict and consistent Calvinism. In polity it affirmed the congregational over the presbyterian (local instead of federal) system, the issue that was then roiling the English church scene. Finally, although claiming strong moral authority for itself and similar church councils, the synod did not claim binding powers over doctrine or life; it assigned those instead to the magistrates as "nursing fathers" of the church.[11]

The Cambridge synod came a bit early to address the most troubling religious consequence of population growth: the disinclination of young people to claim full church membership via profession of conversion experience. Another decade on, however, enough of these children of the founding generation were themselves having children whose status pressed hard against Massachusetts' standards. Their parents not being full members, these grandchildren of the founders did not qualify for baptism. Would the elderly saints thus allow them to fall outside the covenant? Would the clergy entertain the prospect of a rapidly decreasing share of the population belonging to a church that claimed established status? The situation also raised alarms about the passing of New England's promise, all the more poignant in light of the collapse of the Commonwealth (i.e., the failure of the Puritan project) back in England. At stake, then, were the status of souls, the purity of the church, and the purpose and future of their collective enterprise, issues each potent enough in itself but arguably lying athwart one another. Argue the clergy and laity did. The former, by decision of the Massachusetts Bay Synod of 1662, offered a new, tempered standard for baptism; some of both parties but especially the latter disparaged this as a "halfway covenant." (In this case, as with antinomianism, the epithet endured as a descriptor.) The new rule permitted parents who evinced knowledge of Christian truth, a moral pattern of life, and submission to church rules but no conversion experience to present their children for baptism. In Connecticut this was of little consequence, as the stricter standard had never been set. New Haven, merged into Connecticut at just this moment, was riven with dissent. One of its pastors, Abraham Pierson, hived off a new colony in New Ark, East Jersey, to avoid the scheme. New Haven's founding pastor, John Davenport, tried to staunch the tide by moving to First Church in Boston, only to see proponents of the new plan separate and form Third Church there. In any case, because synodical decisions were advisory and not binding, each congregation decided things for itself, and for a good while most did not adopt the new provision. Far from a mark of "declension," as traditional historiography put it, the controversy demonstrated the continuing power of the founders' zeal. Only after mortal crises struck New England and the founders passed from the scene was the new measure widely installed, and with that the region conformed to the model of Reformed churches elsewhere.

[11] Quoted in Ahlstrom, *Religious History*, 156.

The first crisis exploded in 1675 with an Indian military assault that carried deep into the New England heartland. Facing the Indians' shrinking place in the regional economy, on top of long-standing grievances against inequitable dealing and land encroachment by whites, Metacom/King Philip led a pan-tribal attack on more than half of New England's towns, destroying twelve and forcing the abandonment of thirty. Massachusetts, Plymouth, and Connecticut fought back together with their own Indian allies to wreak devastation virtually unparalleled in American history: half of the native population died, including three-fourths of the Indian converts that the Puritan missionary effort had gathered into "praying towns." The clergy weighed in with their own weapons, unleashing a "tidal wave of printed and spoken words" that sought to bring a renewed sense of purpose out of the conflagration.[12] The established genre of the jeremiad spread, bewailing the covenant nation's sin but holding out hope in God's continuing faithfulness. The new genre of the captivity narrative, by which individual "redemption" from the "slavery" of Indian seizure became a type for the region's own trial, became immensely popular. Election-day sermons and histories of the founders cast up a noble origin to which the present generation was called to return. Solidarity, identity, and piety were thus smelted into one.

The second crisis came from abroad in the mid-1680s abrogation of the charters of Massachusetts, Connecticut, and Rhode Island. The three were consolidated along with New York and the Jerseys into a newly declared Dominion of New England under centralized royal rule, the king being the Catholic James II in the bargain. His governor, Edmund Andros, arrived accompanied by regular army troops. Bad enough for New England's politics, the new regime dissolved its religious establishments as well and challenged freehold property claims dating back to the original settlement. A more perfect provocation could not have been devised, so that the Glorious Revolution was hailed in New England with even less equivocation than in the home country. Yet the ensuing negotiations carried on by colonial leaders led by Boston pastor Increase Mather could not win back all their old ways, even with the Reformed prince of the Netherlands, William of Orange, now on the throne of England. The new charter restored Congregational preeminence but instituted broader religious toleration and set the civil franchise on the basis of property, not piety. The agenda, and controversies, of New England's religious future would involve blending these new departures with old markers of loyalty into the formation of a stalwart Protestant place in a divinely blessed empire.

---

[12] Joseph Conforti, *Saints and Strangers: New England in British North America* (Baltimore, 2006), 103.

CONCLUSION

One of the oldest myths of America's origins is that its founders fled here as religious exiles seeking a land of liberty and had the blessings of democracy, unity, and prosperity added unto them. In the first seventy-five years after the planting of Jamestown, this was nowhere true in England's North American colonies. Religious liberty was an unmitigated intention only in the case of Rhode Island and West Jersey, and there unity and democracy paled. In more places religion played but a modest part in motivating, guiding, or sustaining settlement. Sometimes, in Maryland and New Netherland, when it was meant to, it faded. Other times, especially in the Puritan core colonies, it succeeded, but at the deliberate cost of "liberty" as we understand it. For Puritans, religious liberty meant doing things not any old way but God's way, as they detected it. Prosperity, meanwhile, came and went as a wild card, an ally of colonies that in religious terms were diametrically opposed: Massachusetts and Rhode Island, New Netherland and Virginia.

What did happen was more interesting and predictable than the myth, if more complex in its nuanced iterations. These colonies became unwitting laboratories in which intentions wrought in the home country met the opportunities and challenges presented by a new geography and unfamiliar neighbors, resulting in consequences that no one had entirely planned, that few would entirely endorse – and that few would entirely reject. Many people of European, mostly English, origins worked this new earth under a stronger or weaker sense of living under heaven's eye. Some sought to implement God's will exactly, some wanted it as a comfort or consideration on the side. Some wanted a holy society, some a holy self, some both in full, some in moderation. In this variety of plans and the results to which they gave rise, the early colonies remain a distant, yet clear and sometimes uncanny anticipation of their American future and our American present.

SUGGESTIONS FOR FURTHER READING

Bond, Edward L. *Damned Souls in a Tobacco Colony: Religion in Seventeenth-Century Virginia*. Macon, GA, 2000.

Bozeman, Theodore D. *To Live Ancient Lives: The Primitivist Dimension in Puritanism*. Chapel Hill, 1988.

Foster, Stephen. *The Long Argument: English Puritanism and the Shaping of New England Culture, 1570–1700*. Chapel Hill, 1991.

Hall, David D. *Worlds of Wonder, Days of Judgment: Popular Religious Belief in Early New England*. New York, 1989.

Hall, Timothy L. *Separating Church and State: Roger Williams and Religious Liberty*. Urbana, 1998.

Knight, Janice. *Orthodoxies in Massachusetts: Rereading American Puritanism.* Cambridge, MA, 1994.

Krugler, John D. *English and Catholic: The Lords Baltimore in the Seventeenth Century.* Baltimore, 2004.

Stout, Harry S. *The New England Soul: Preaching and Religious Culture in Colonial New England.* New York, 1986.

Section III

RELIGIOUS PATTERNS IN COLONIAL AMERICA – 1680s–1730s

12

SPANISH CATHOLICISM IN THE CARIBBEAN, NEW SPAIN, AND THE NORTHERN FRONTIERS

STAFFORD POOLE

The story of Spanish Catholicism in the Caribbean and New Spain from the 1680s to the end of the colonial period falls easily into two clearly distinguishable parts. The first runs to 1713 and is characterized by the perfection and consolidation of the Habsburg system of church-state relations. The second begins with a change of dynasty, the Bourbons replacing the Habsburgs, and the introduction of a far different form of government. Strongly influenced by the ideals of the Enlightenment, the new rulers completed the state's domination of the Church and centralized their rule as a form of "Enlightened Despotism."

The Catholicism in the Spanish Caribbean in the latter half of the colonial period has not been intensively studied. It thus becomes difficult to describe it in the various islands that made up Spanish possessions in that area. The disasters of the early period of discovery and colonization, especially European diseases and exploitation, had left the Caribbean area all but depopulated of native races. As time went on, they were replaced by African slaves who were imported to work on the sugar plantations. These Africans tended to retain many of their ancestral religious beliefs and practices. Because the islands were main ports of entry and exit for Spanish treasure fleets, they became the objects of attacks by pirates.

In general the area was characterized by great poverty, small populations, and lack of good priests. The latter had little incentive to migrate to the islands, where opportunities for advancement were few. The Jesuits and Dominicans attempted to carry on educational work, often under difficult circumstances. It is not clear what kind of religious service was given to slaves. The situation was further complicated by changes in colonial rulers. The island of Guadaloupe came under French control in 1763, as did the western half of the island of Española (modern Haiti) in 1697. Jamaica was confirmed as an English possession in 1670 and Trinidad in 1797.

In Cuba, the Jesuits undertook educational work but encountered many obstacles. The most notable educational institution in colonial Cuba was the Royal and Pontifical University of San Jerónimo. It was founded in 1728 with authorization from Pope Innocent XIII and King Philip V of Spain. It had a direct impact on the Church through the number of priests it educated. The university still exists, although under the name of the University of Havana. By the mid-eighteenth century Cuba had some 90 churches, 309 diocesan priests, and 399 religious priests.[1] Most of the clergy were well educated, the majority of the diocesans having graduated from the University of San Jerónimo.

NEW SPAIN

Culture and Society

At one time it was common for historians of Mexico to dismiss the late colonial period as a cultural or intellectual backwater. The derisive phrase "Colonial Siesta" was used to describe the period from the 1680s to independence. Such a view is no longer tenable. New Spain had a thriving culture, and given the circumstances of the time, it is understandable that Catholicism played a major role in it.

One of the important musical composers of the time was Ignacio de Jerusalén, who was born in Italy about 1710 and migrated to New Spain. He is best known today for his Matins for the Feast of Our Lady of Guadalupe. Another outstanding figure was Manuel de Zumaya (c. 1678–1755), a mestizo, or perhaps of mixed Spanish-Indian blood. He served as chapel master of the cathedral of Mexico. He was the first person in the New World to write an opera, *Partenope*, unfortunately now lost.

Of literary figures in New Spain in this period, undoubtedly the most famous was the nun, Sor Juana Inés de la Cruz (1651–95), known as "the Tenth Muse."[2] Another notable literary figure was the savant Carlos de Sigüenza y Góngora (1645–1700). He was a poet, historian, mathematician, and astronomer. Among his other works was a poem about the Virgin of Guadalupe, "Primavera Indiana." The Jesuit Francisco Javier de Clavijero was a noted historian whose major work was the *Historia antigua de México*, still an important source. Not surprisingly, a majority of the books published at this time were of a devotional or theological nature. Notable among these was Miguel Sánchez's *La Virgen Madre de Guadalupe* (1648), which made public for the first time the story of the apparitions

---

[1] Figures in León Lopetegui and Félix Zubillaga, *Historia de la Iglesia en la América Española desde el Descubrimiento hasta comienzos del siglo XIX* (Madrid, 1965), 775.

[2] Her life and career have been described in the essay by Garcia and Myers earlier in this volume.

of the Virgin of Guadalupe. A large proportion of this devotion literature was published sermons, often given on special occasions or feasts by noted local preachers.

The outstanding painter of the colonial period was Miguel Cabrera (1695–1768), a native Zapotec born in Oaxaca. He was an extremely popular painter, often in demand for his portraits of the rich and upper classes. He also painted many religious pictures, including a fictional portrait of Juan Diego, the visionary of the Guadalupe tradition, which was labeled an authentic portrait (*verdadero retrato*). He was also noted for his paintings of the various racial groups (*castas*) in New Spain. He painted several versions of the Virgin of Guadalupe and was one of a team of experts allowed to examine the image. He founded the second academy of painting in Mexico.

There is a dispute among historians as to whether the economy of New Spain in the seventeenth century was depressed or thriving. Some have seen it as a century of depression, whereas others have called it a "silver age." The economy was dependent on silver, livestock, commerce (including imports from the Orient), and sugar. The Jesuits were known for their sugar mills (*ingenios*), which were profitable enterprises.

Wealthy creoles spent large sums endowing churches and paying for lavish architecture and decorations. One of the most notable examples is the cathedral of Santa Prisca in Taxco, endowed in 1759 by José de la Borda, a wealthy silver miner. It was built in churrigueresque style, an extravagant form of the baroque. Such endowments not only helped to ensure the patron's salvation but were a proud status symbol for the founder and the city.

Racial Divisions

New Spain was divided into two "republics," that of the Spaniards and that of the Indians. The Spaniards considered themselves to be people of reason (*gente de razón*). In Mexico City the Spaniards and creoles, Europeans born in the New World, were segregated from the Indians and *castas* by the *traza*, which literally meant a drawing or outline, but in this context meant a boundary. In peaceful times the borders were rather porous, but in times of civil unrest, the civil authorities enforced them more strictly. Then after a period of time they would become porous again.

Spaniards born in the mother country stood at the peak of society. They monopolized the highest positions in church and state, such as viceroys or archbishops. In general they looked down on the creoles, whom they considered to be inferior. It was believed that the local climate and proximity to the sun rendered them feeble, inconstant, and lazy. Despite the fact that the only difference between Spaniards and creoles was their place of birth, creoles were clearly second-class citizens. Very few were ever appointed archbishops or viceroys of Mexico. On the other hand, they tended to dominate the lower echelons of the Church, such as canons of cathedral chapters, university and seminary teachers, chaplains, and similar offices.

The status of the Indian in the last half of the colonial period was fixed. In Spanish law they were considered to be minors, on their way to incorporation into Spanish society, but not yet there. In outlying villages, life often went on as it had before the conquest. Local government, customs, and languages remained more or less intact. A basic reality was that the economy and society of New Spain depended almost entirely on the labor of the Indian. This often kept them in a subservient position, although some became artisans and craftsmen of the first order.

The native races have often been pictured as helpless, passive victims. Recent research, especially into native language sources, is changing that view. The indigenous peoples negotiated their place in society, especially through their manipulation of the legal system. In the 1570s the crown had established the *Juzgado general de indios* (general Indian court), whose proceedings were conducted in the native languages. The Indians soon learned how to prolong lawsuits, often for generations, to their benefit.

The same was true of religion. Here, again, the natives negotiated their status. Although they were exempt from the Inquisition, they learned to use that tribunal as a way of ridding themselves of unpopular pastors, for example, by accusing them of sexual irregularities. Passive-aggressive techniques were used to retain old customs and practices. Thus, despite all ecclesiastical prohibitions to the contrary, native dances and songs continued to be used throughout the colonial period. The Mayas of southern Mexico in a special way tended to hold on to their old ways, as they still do today.

There was another class of persons, the *castas*, persons of mixed ancestry. In the beginning this referred almost exclusively to mestizos, persons of Spanish-Indian parentage. This term usually implied a Spanish father and a native mother, and it carried a connotation of illegitimacy. In the last half of the colonial period, the system was both more complex and more fixed. It included mulattoes, persons of white/black ancestry, and various other groupings. Some of these had their own *cofradías* or religious confraternities, which helped to give them an identity and sometimes financial help.

According to the law of the Church enunciated by the Third Mexican Provincial Council of 1585, Indians and *castas* could not be ordained to the priesthood. The wording of the law was rather garbled, in part because of objections by Rome, so there were loopholes. Undoubtedly, in practice many of these peoples were ordained, but it is impossible to say how many or what proportion.

Religious Practice

Religion in the last half of the Habsburg reign (1680s–1713) assumed the form that had begun in the earlier colonial period. Religion in this context, of course, means Roman Catholicism. In New Spain, as in the mother country, this was primarily local in character. In the larger cities, with a more educated clergy and laity, religious devotion tended to be more dogmatic and cultural. In outlying villages, devotion centered around patron saints. In both places it was often mixed with superstition or mingled with preconquest practices.

Saints had two functions. One was as models of sanctity to be imitated, the other as intercessors who pleaded one's cause before God. As intercessors they were advocates for entire communities as well as individuals. "The principal function of these celestial protectors was to attend to the necessities of the faithful united beneath the insignia of a corporation."[3] Among the saints, the predominant one, of course, was the Virgin Mary. She was venerated under a variety of titles, such as Remedios, Ocotlán, and Zapopan. The paramount devotion came to be that of the Virgin of Guadalupe. She was the preferred devotion of the creoles, whereas Remedios was that of the peninsular Spaniards.

Very significant for the Spaniards was devotion to San Hipólito, on whose feast day the city of Tenochtitlan fell to Fernando Cortés. San Nicolás de Tolentino was invoked against earthquakes, San Bernardo against epidemics, and San Antonio Abad against fires.[4] In native Catholicism these saints were often identified with or replaced preconquest deities, such as Tlaloc, the rain god of the Aztecs.

The Impact of the Council of Trent

The strongest influence on colonial Mexican religion was the Council of Trent (1545–63). The council had defined Catholic dogma and regularized devotion and discipline to a remarkable degree. It also imposed a great deal of uniformity throughout the worldwide Church. It was the inspiration for the work of the Third Mexican Provincial Council (1585), which adapted

---

[3] Antonio Rubial García, "Icons of Devotion: The Appropriation and Use of Saints in New Spain," in Martin Austin Nesvig, ed., *Local Religion in Colonial Mexico* (Albuquerque, 2006), 50.

[4] *Ibid.*, 51.

its decrees to the local scene. Part of this adaptation was the strengthening of the diocesan church structure at the expense of the religious orders. By the late colonial period, the independence of the orders had been severely limited. In the early seventeenth century there was a bitter dispute between the bishop of Puebla, Juan de Palafox y Mendoza (1600–59), and the two orders of the Franciscans and Jesuits. The Franciscans had a strong power base among the natives and resisted giving up any of their missions to diocesan clergy. The Jesuits had a strong impact on the intellectual and academic life in New Spain. In addition they had accumulated great wealth through their business enterprises. Palafox lost his battle, but ultimately the state won the war.

Tridentine Catholicism strongly emphasized law. The religious life of the average person was closely regulated as a means of compensating for human fickleness. Churchmen of the seventeenth and eighteenth centuries had a low opinion of human nature and human capabilities, and they sought to compensate through law. It was a highly legalistic age in both church and society.

Catholicism under the Habsburgs was baroque in character. Baroque art was inspired in part by the Council of Trent and the Catholic Reformation as well as by a reaction to the Renaissance. The baroque was exuberant and emotional. As mentioned previously, this was seen in church architecture, with its florid embellishments and unrestrained decorations. Ceremonies were equally elaborate and were sometimes described as the court ceremonial of a great king. Vestments were ornate and rich, and there was abundant use of incense. Music was a vital element in worship. Sermons were long and complex, often using the strained similes and figures of the literary style known as *gongorismo*. Pilgrimages played an important role in popular religion. The whole purpose of the baroque and its offshoot, the churrigueresque, was to waft the mind and heart to God and to the supernatural level. Early missionaries in New Spain were wont to say that Christianity came to the natives through their eyes.

Church and State

In the Spanish system church and state were so closely intertwined that it can be said that the Church was a department of state. Churchmen sometimes acted as civil officials, and there were instances of bishops, and even friars, acting as interim viceroys. This did not mean that relations between churchmen and civil officials were always harmonious. On the contrary, there was a long-standing antagonism between the archbishops of Mexico and the viceroys. One cause of this was the overlapping jurisdictions of the two offices, so favored by the Spanish crown as a form of checks and balances. In 1624 the antagonism between Archbishop Juan Pérez de la Serna and the Viceroy Diego Carrillo de Mendoza y Pimentel, marqués de Gelves, contributed to a major urban riot in that year.

Financial Support

The financial support of the Church's mission came from a variety of sources. Foremost among these was the tithe. This was a tax, theoretically 10 percent, on all produce of the earth. It was collected by royal officials and then "redonated" according to a complex formula. Withholding these temporalities was a method of keeping recalcitrant bishops and priests in line. Other income came from endowed chaplaincies, alms, and fees for various ecclesiastical services. The Church and its various organizations also acted as moneylenders in the absence of a banking system.

The Inquisition

From the time of the conquest until 1571, inquisitorial functions were in the hands of individual bishops. They were called "inquisitors ordinary" because this authority came with their offices. The Spanish Inquisition was an entirely distinct tribunal, founded in 1478 by Pope Sixtus IV at the request of Fernando and Isabel, the Catholic monarchs. Although its higher personnel consisted of bishops and priests, it was a department of state, governed by its own supreme council in the Habsburg administration.

This tribunal was not established in the New World until 1571. The first inquisitor was Pedro Moya de Contreras, later the third archbishop of Mexico. The new tribunal was a part of a program of centralization and increasing control of the Spanish dependencies on the part of the crown. Perhaps surprising to modern readers is that it was not a welcome foundation. It upset a delicate balance of special interest groups and local power structures. Bishops were unhappy to lose their inquisitorial authority. The viceroy did not like yielding legal cases to the intrusive tribunal. Diocesan clergy were angered that Inquisition officials were given canonries for their support that should have gone to them.

In its early days the Inquisition in New Spain dealt with cases of English and French pirates. It also regulated publications and religious art. Toward the end of the sixteenth century, it began to deal with crypto-Jews or Catholics of Jewish background (conversos) who were thought to be secretly practicing Judaism. In later years it concentrated on moral lapses such as bigamy and blasphemy and, among the clergy, solicitation in the confessional. The Inquisition did not deal with witchcraft (considered a delusion) and consensual adult homosexuality. The Indians, considered minors and incapable of heresy, were exempt from the Spanish Inquisition, although not from the episcopal one.

In the last half of the colonial period, the picture is not always clear. One school of thought holds that the Inquisition in New Spain had become corrupt and inefficient, and even intimidated by local elites and power structures, such as publishers of books. Another school considers it to have been active, with a smothering effect on local intellectual life, imposing an obscurantist worldview on a subservient population. The fact of the widespread diffusion of Enlightenment thought in New Spain, including among the clergy, seems to support the first view.

Nuns and Convents

In Spanish society the position of women was defined by convention, law, religion, and prejudice. There were basically two alternatives: marriage or a convent. Both required dowries, and the question of providing adequate dowries was a pressing one. Marriages were usually arranged by families on the basis of social or financial advantage. In the sixteenth century, the Church strongly supported the freedom of marital choice, without which a marriage would be considered invalid. In cases in which young couples wanted to marry against their parents' wishes, ecclesiastics often gave shelter and performed their marriages. This situation began to change in the seventeenth century when civil authorities grew reluctant to enforce ecclesiastical verdicts, and the weight of convention began to favor parental authority.

In colonial Mexico the term "convent" (*convento*) was used for establishments of both male and female religious. Convents of nuns were important social as well as religious institutions. They had a civic importance because they added prestige to the cities or towns where they were established. They were centers of prayer and spiritual uplift, not just for themselves but for the entire urban area – they were located primarily in cities. The convents were cloistered, that is, they had no ministries, such as nursing and teaching. The convents were supported by individual patrons, endowments, and the dowries of the nuns. As their funds increased, they moved into the purchase of urban real estate. Because there was no banking system as such, the convents and other ecclesiastical institutions functioned as moneylenders, and as such had a significant impact on the local economies. It was commonly expected that the principal on such loans would not be repaid, and thus the interest payments constituted a sort of annuity. By the eighteenth century, monasteries and nunneries had come to dominate the real estate market in Mexico City itself and were a powerful economic factor.

Recruitment or commitment to a convent was quite different from later times. The concept of a vocation as a freely chosen response to a call from God was not common. Men entered the Church as part of a career choice or because they were younger children in a family, and women could enter convents without any real suitability for such a life. However, stories of upper-class families using convents as dumping grounds for surplus daughters are exaggerated, if only because of the expense of dowries and subsequent support of the nuns. Some nuns, because of family wealth or connections, lived comfortably, accompanied by servants or slaves, and subject to minimal discipline. They were also able to have personal funds called *reservas*, which were sometimes invested through legal representatives. Theatrical and musical presentations offered recreation, and the convent often provided the only accessible means of achieving an education. The majority of nuns were creoles, and there were very few convents that accepted native women.

Confraternities

Another institution of importance in New Spain was the *cofradía* or confraternity. These were organizations of men who shared a trade, craft, or even, in the case of Indians or blacks, race. Each one had a charter granted by ecclesiastical or civil authority, which delineated its purpose, nature, functions, and officers. Among the common functions were arranging the funerals and burials of its members and giving financial aid to their widows. Others included financing churches, chapels, and hospitals; the organization of festivals, especially of patronal feasts; and works of charity. The members, in turn, enjoyed certain privileges, such as burial places or indulgences. The *cofradías* were an important source of group identity and economic benefits. Like the convents and similar institutions, they were sometimes quite wealthy and acted as moneylenders, especially to their members, rather like a modern credit union.

Guadalupe

By the end of the seventeenth century, devotion to the Mexican Guadalupe was firmly established. According to a tradition, the Virgin Mary appeared to an Indian neophyte named Juan Diego at the hill of Tepeyac, north of Mexico City, in December 1531 and directed him to carry a message to the bishop (actually bishop-elect) of Mexico, the Franciscan Juan de Zumárraga. He was to build a chapel at that site where she could show her love and care for the native population. Juan Diego did as he was told but met with initial skepticism. He reported the failure of his mission to the

Virgin, who encouraged him to persevere with his commission. This time the bishop-elect told him to bring some sign of the truth of his account. Juan Diego's uncle was very ill and asked his nephew to bring a priest to prepare him for death. Juan Diego tried to avoid seeing the Virgin again, but she accosted him and assured him that his uncle was well. She directed him to go to the top of the hill and collect the flowers he would find there as a sign for the bishop-elect. This was at a time when flowers did not grow there. Juan Diego did as he was told and returned to the bishop's palace with the flowers in his cloak. After explaining what had happened, he opened his cloak, the flowers fell to the floor, and imprinted on the garment was the picture now venerated at Guadalupe. Zumárraga, in tears, asked pardon for his skepticism and began the construction of a chapel at Tepeyac.

The story is beautiful and poignant and has charmed generations of believers and nonbelievers alike. It follows closely the standard apparition accounts to be found in Spain and the New World at that time. The Virgin is a compassionate and loving mother who comes to the aid of the oppressed and marginalized in society. Therefore it is all the more surprising that the devotion was stronger among creoles than it was among the natives. Creole interpretations of the tradition saw it as a manifestation of the special destiny of the Mexican people, or *americanos,* as they called themselves. Mexico City was viewed as another Jerusalem or Rome. Other cities had miraculous images, but only Mexico had one painted by the Blessed Mother herself. On seeing a copy of the image in 1752, Pope Benedict XIV is supposed to have quoted Psalm 147, *"Non fecit taliter omni nationi"* ("he has not done the like for any other nation"), words that eventually became the motto of Guadalupe.

The Virgin of Guadalupe was credited with delivering the city from an epidemic in 1736. In the following year both the civil and ecclesiastical officials of Mexico took an oath by which Guadalupe became the patron of the city. After this, the devotion spread beyond the city of Mexico, as far south as Guatemala. In 1746 Guadalupe was proclaimed the patron of all New Spain, and in 1754 the papacy recognized the patronage and granted a special feast day, 12 December, and a proper Mass. In 1750, following years of complex negotiations, the church at Tepeyac was given a collegiate chapter. In 1757 the devotion was officially spread to all Spanish dominion.

In recent years the truth of this account has been the subject of intense historical debate. The fundamental problem is that in the years 1531–1648, there is no mention of the apparition story or of Juan Diego. The story was first made known by a Mexican priest named Miguel Sánchez in a book published in 1648 called *Imagen de la Virgen Maria, Madre de Dios de*

Guadalupe (Image of the Virgin Mary, Mother of God of Guadalupe). The reaction of his contemporaries was that no one had ever heard the story prior to his book. In the following year, another priest, Luis Laso de la Vega, published a more detailed account in Nahuatl, *Huey tlamahuiçoltica* (By a Great Miracle). The actual narrative of the apparitions is called the *Nican mopohua* (Here is recounted), from its opening words. Devotees of the apparitions seek to date this to the early sixteenth century, although it clearly was the work of Laso de la Vega and his native assistants.

In 1794 a Spanish priest-historian, Juan Bautista Muñoz, delivered a strong critique of the traditional account, much to the ire of the creoles. The devotion became the storm center of a bitter controversy in the late nineteenth century. The great Mexican historian, Joaquín García Icazbalceta, wrote a letter at the request of the archbishop of Mexico in which he gave a point-by-point explanation of the difficulties involved. This controversy was renewed in the late twentieth and early twenty-first centuries with the beatification and canonization of Juan Diego.

The Northern Missions

In the late sixteenth century a new form of missionary structure emerged, the presidio/mission system. It was first used on the northern frontier and soon established itself as the standard form. It consisted of a mission with enough soldiers to protect the missionaries. It also used settlements of indigenous Christians to act as a liaison or leaven with the non-Christians. This was especially true of the Tlaxcalans, who had been Fernando Cortés' chief allies in the conquest. This system relied heavily on the mendicants and Jesuits as missionaries. In a policy called *congregación*, the natives were brought together in involuntary isolation from the Spaniards and, in addition to religion, were taught European arts, crafts, and agriculture. In that age there was no concept of culture shock or the fact that the gathering of nomadic Indians into larger groups made them susceptible to epidemics. This system continued throughout the colonial period and is perhaps best exemplified in the Franciscan missions of Alta California.

By the late seventeenth century the Spanish missionary effort had expanded to the north, then to the American Southwest, including Texas, Arizona, and New Mexico. It began as a two-pronged campaign. The Jesuits and Franciscans were the primary missionaries. While the Jesuits pushed up through central and northwestern New Spain, the Franciscans evangelized the eastern and northeastern areas.

Expansion to the north was sporadic and irregular, and so, as a consequence, was the missionary enterprise. Until the mid-sixteenth century, it was regarded as a desert area, inhabited by nomadic and warlike Indians, but unsuitable for Spaniards. This view was changed by the discovery of large silver deposits in the Zacatecas areas around 1545. It led to a rush to the new riches and to the settlements of San Luis Potosí, Jalisco, and Durango. It also brought the Spaniards into contact with the Chichimecas, who fiercely and successfully resisted the intrusion. The government made increasing use of the mission-presidio method. The system proved successful, especially with the aid of Jesuit missionaries, and peace returned to the northern settlements in the early seventeenth century.

From the Chichimeca frontier, the Jesuits moved further northward to what is present-day Sinaloa. By the early seventeenth century, the process of conversion was fairly well advanced. By the time the Jesuits were expelled from the Spanish dominions (1767), there were twenty-one missionaries working among approximately thirty thousand people. By that time their missionary work included the modern areas of Guanajuato, San Luis Potosí, Nuevo León, Jalisco, Zacatecas, Nayarit, Coahuila, Durango, Chihuahua, Sinaloa, Sonora, Baja California, and southern Arizona.

There were two groups of Indians who resisted both Spanish intrusion and conversion: the Tarahumara and the Yaqui. Because of the unsettled frontier conditions, work among the Tarahumara did not begin until about 1630, and even then a number of native revolts resulted in the deaths of missionaries. The missions to the northern Tarahumara in the modern state of Chihuahua were more successful. After their restoration, the Jesuits returned to the Tarahumara, and they work among them today. Less successful were the missions to the fiercely independent Yaquis. These had barely begun when the Society was expelled from New Spain.

Kino on the Frontier

The most famous of all Jesuit missionaries in northern New Spain and the American Southwest was, and probably still is, Eusebio Kino. He was born in northern Italy in 1645 and joined the Society of Jesus in 1665. He was ordained to the priesthood eleven years later. In 1678 Kino was part of a group assigned to the Mexican and Chinese missions. He set out for New Spain the following year, but because of a delay in Spain did not arrive at Veracruz until 1681. He served as cosmographer — he was an expert mapmaker — and Jesuit superior on an unsuccessful expedition to explore and evangelize California in 1683. Adverse conditions forced the abandonment of the mission in 1685.

Toward the beginning of 1687 his superiors sent him north again, this time to the Pimería Alta, the region with which his name will always be associated. This area included present-day Sonora and southern Arizona and was home to the Pima, Papago, Sobaipuri, and (farther north) Yuman peoples. He undertook the evangelization of the Pimas, promoted cattle raising, and engaged in geographic exploration and cartography. In 1689 he was named superior of the mission, and he arranged for missionaries to visit the towns that had been only partially evangelized.

In 1691 Kino was joined by an almost equally famous missionary, Father Juan María Salvatierra. An Italian like Kino, Salvatierra had come to New Spain in 1675 and later to the Primería Alta as a Jesuit *visitador*. He and Kino quickly became a formidable missionary team. Salvatierra's presence helped to ensure the permanence of a mission threatened by native uprisings. One of the most dangerous of these occurred in 1695, sparked in part by harsh Spanish reprisals for the murder of a missionary. The Pimas rose in rebellion and destroyed several of the mission centers. Kino strove to restore peace, which was finally accomplished in August 1695. He rode horseback to Mexico City, some 1,200 miles, to prevent the abandonment of the mission.

Kino was responsible for the return of the Jesuits to Baja California in 1697, when Manuel Díaz, joined by Salvatierra, began missionary work in the area of present-day Guaymas. In 1700, eight years after Kino first explored the area, he established the famous mission of San Xavier de Bac outside the present city of Tucson. In 1702, in two more expeditions, he attempted to reach Alta California by land but was unsuccessful.

Kino died at the mission at Magdalena in 1711. By the time of his death, the missions of Sonora and the Pimería were already suffering, partly because of economic problems caused by war in Europe. There were also conflicts with civil authorities, some of whom were more interested in their own personal wealth than in the good of the natives. More and more mission outposts were abandoned or remained static. Dolores itself, Kino's headquarters, had no missionaries after 1738. Jesuits continued to work in the area, and even farther north, until the expulsion of 1767, but the enterprise lacked its former vigor and extension. After the expulsion, the Franciscans took over the missions of both Baja and Alta California.

Kino was, and still is, a controversial figure. He found himself in conflict with some of his superiors who did not understand either his missionary situation or his lifestyle. Accusations of hasty baptisms and failing to live a proper religious life were leveled against him. He and his neophytes were remarkably successful as ranchers and shipped large quantities of livestock to various missions and villages. He was also responsible for introducing the cultivation of wheat into the area. Kino was regarded by many, including fellow Jesuits, as individualistic and unrealistic. Their view was that the area was desert, sparsely populated by hostile natives, and a poor missionary prospect.

The Franciscans in Northern New Spain

The Franciscans, for their part, concentrated on the eastern coast. At the end of the sixteenth century, Francisco Urdiñola established a colony of Tlaxcalans at Saltillo in order to stabilize the frontier and help in conversions. The real missionary work began in the latter part of the seventeenth century, when the Franciscans entered Nuevo León and Coahuila. The Indians of that area, still called Chichimecas by the Spaniards, were warlike and fierce. The Franciscan work was helped by the establishment in that century of missionary colleges in Querétaro and Zacatecas, which prepared missionaries for work that made different demands than the challenges previously undertaken.

An outstanding figure in the history of this missionary work was Fray Juan Larios, who is sometimes called the Founder of Coahuila. He was born in Jalisco in 1633 and joined the Franciscans at the age of eighteen. He was ordained to the priesthood in 1657. Although his actual stay in Coahuila was brief – only three years between 1673 and 1676 – he accomplished a great deal. The crown had tried to evangelize and pacify the area with Tlaxcalan Indians, but they had been massacred. Larios entered the hostile territory, which had already cost some Franciscan lives, and apparently explored as far north as the Rio Grande. He earned a reputation as a defender of the Indians. He died in 1676. Unfortunately, neither Larios nor the Franciscan missions in northeastern Mexico have been given the historical study they deserve.

NEW MEXICO

The Spanish conquest of New Mexico tended to bypass the areas between Mexico City and New Mexico. There were a number of reasons for this. The missionaries who had accompanied the Coronado expedition (1540–42) were impressed by the receptiveness and character of the Pueblo Indians. The area also seemed to hold promise of mineral wealth. The crown authorized an expedition as early as 1583, but there was no follow-up. Finally, Juan de Oñate, a member of a leading Zacatecas mining family, was appointed to lead an expedition to New Mexico in 1595.

The difficulties of the colony and the bickering of the colonists caused Oñate to resign in 1607. Two years later Pedro de Peralta was named governor of New Mexico. He moved the capital to Santa Fe in order to be closer to the Indian population centers. Tlaxcalan Indians were brought from New Spain at an early date to help with the physical labor of construction and to advertise the benefits of Christianity and European life. Although such use of the Tlaxcalans was common in New Spain – they had been Fernando Cortés' staunchest allies in the conquest – this appears to be the only incident of it within the borders of the present-day United States.

The Spanish presence grew gradually, and even though towns soon dotted the area, they were sparse. As late as 1670 there were only 2,800 Spaniards in the colony, mostly in the area of Santa Fe. The Franciscans' missionary efforts, by contrast, were more successful. By the 1630s there were 25 missions, serving 50,000 Indians. As in other mission areas, there was a great deal of conflict between the friars and the civil authorities, mostly over control of the Indians.

The Spanish settlement and evangelization of New Mexico came to a halt with the ferocious revolt of the Pueblo Indians in 1680. New Mexico was never really prosperous and depended on agriculture and livestock, especially sheep. Because of their precarious situation, the Spaniards increased their demands on the Indians. The Franciscans seem to have lacked some of the fire of their predecessors in New Spain. In addition, as throughout all New Spain, later generations of Franciscans did not learn the native languages or become closely identified with the natives. Ironically, one reason for this was pressure from the Spanish officials who feared that the Franciscans' identification with the Indians weakened royal control. At the same time, pre-Hispanic religious ideas were not dead; many Indians found mission life confining, and the native medicine men were agitating against the Christians. One of them, Popé, devised a plan to purge the entire region of the intruders, and he won a large number of chiefs to his side.

The uprising was carefully planned to begin in the entire area at the same time. The Indians had the advantage of surprise and caught the Spaniards totally off guard. At least 400 Spaniards, including 32 friars, were killed – 21 Franciscans in one day. The Indians laid siege to Santa Fe and cut off its water supply. Taking advantage of Indian complacency, the Spaniards were able to escape. The Indians seemed content to let them go and did not make a serious attempt to exterminate the survivors. Approximately 2,400 refugees fled to El Paso del Norte on the Rio Grande (present-day El Paso, Texas), where they laid the basis for a civilian settlement in what had been until then a military garrison.

Subsequent attempts to probe or reconquer New Mexico were unsuccessful. Finally, in 1688, Diego de Vargas, a farsighted and diplomatic man, was named governor. He began the reoccupation in 1692. With a total force of only one hundred, including three Franciscans and forty professional soldiers, he won over the Pueblos with a combination of diplomacy, psychology, and firmness. By the end of the year, he secured the allegiance of the majority without bloodshed. By the time he set out with a larger, colonizing expedition in 1693, however, the Indians had again become restive. Vargas decided that only a military venture would succeed, while at the same time trying to use diplomacy. The ensuing war was sporadic and slow. By 1696 most of New Mexico had been recovered, although the Zuñi and Hopi continued to be both independent and hostile.

Far from the capital, New Mexico tended to develop in relative isolation. As a result there was a continuity in family generations that was lacking elsewhere and a greater sense of relationship to the past. To this day, a significant part of the Hispanic population of New Mexico regards itself as Spanish, not Mexican. Even more noteworthy is the fact that some of the original families came from converso or crypto-Jewish backgrounds. They fled to the farthest reaches of New Spain to avoid the Inquisition in more populous areas.

The missionary enterprise in northern New Spain and the borderlands proved more formidable and trying than it had to the south. Conditions were harsher, and the natives more hostile and tenacious of old ideas. The distances were enormous, and only the hardiest missionaries, like Kino, Salvatierra, and Larios, could cope with the challenge. Despite numerous setbacks, the missionaries did have a measure of success. In some places, like New Mexico, this required the support of Spanish arms. In others, like the Pimería Alta, there was less reliance on force.

A Change of Dynasty

At the conclusion of the War of the Spanish Succession (1701–13), a new dynasty came to the throne of Spain, the French Bourbons. They brought with them a drastically different approach to government. Under the influence of the Enlightenment, they liberalized the economy and reformed the inefficient forms of government. Whereas Spain under the Habsburgs was a corporate state consisting of competing special interest groups, the Bourbons centralized authority in the monarch. It was a system that came to be called "benevolent despotism."

The Bourbon attitude toward religion was also influenced by the Enlightenment. There was an attempt to suppress baroque religious practices and curtail the independence of the *cofradías* and religious orders. The vows of religion were regarded as unnatural, and the orders themselves were effectively tamed. Under the Habsburgs, the Church was a department of state, but it was an important voice and influence in society. The Bourbon monarchs retained control over the Church but sought to lessen its public and even private role. In a later context, their policies would be called anticlerical.

One important aspect of this was an intense hostility toward the Jesuits. This had begun in the seventeenth century, even before Bourbon rule. The

Society had become wealthy and powerful. In addition to their educational and missionary work, they were involved in various commercial transactions, especially sugar production. Their independence of established civil and ecclesiastical authority made them suspect in the eyes of officials in both church and state. In addition, they were often involved in politics, particularly in their roles as royal confessors. The Bourbons were determined to put an end to what they considered to be a state within a state.

In 1766 the Jesuits were blamed for a series of riots in Spain against an unpopular minister. In the following year, secret orders were sent out to all the Spanish dominions that the Jesuits were to be expelled. This was done suddenly and with ruthless efficiency. They were deported to the Papal States and other parts of Europe. The impact on the Church's mission was devastating. Missions and schools had to be abandoned or given to others. The northern missions were transferred to the Franciscans, but that did little to blunt the damage. Partisans of the Society rioted against this attack, not only on the Church, but also on criollo society. These riots were brutally suppressed.

THE AMERICAN SOUTHWEST

Texas

One of the northern areas that Spain now sought to protect was Texas. As in other areas, the method used was to be a combination of missionary work and military force. The first move into the area was at the end of the seventeenth century to counter the threat of French expansionism from Louisiana. In 1689 an expedition led by Alonso de León left Monterrey for Texas to locate the French intrusion. With it went a Franciscan, Father Damián Massanet, who left an account of the expedition. It was discovered, however, that the settlement the French had made in Texas had been destroyed by the Indians. Massanet attempted to work among the Hasinai Indians but found them too hostile. Another expedition in 1690 went to northeast Texas and established two missions on the Neches River. Texas was made a frontier province the following year, but because there were no further signs of French intrusion, it was abandoned in 1693.

The French threat was renewed in the early eighteenth century when the French governor of the lower Mississippi Valley initiated expeditions to the west, partly in hope of opening up trade with Spanish settlers. The Spaniards reacted with alarm and in 1715 made plans to occupy east Texas. An expedition was launched in the following year with eight Franciscan priests and three lay brothers from the missionary college of Querétaro. The friars were under the leadership of Fray Isidro Félix Espinosa and Fray

Francisco Hidalgo. The latter had worked among the Hasinai when Texas was still the short-lived frontier province. These friars were later joined by one of the greatest of the borderland missionaries, Fray Antonio Margil de Jesús.

Margil (1657–1726), who had joined the Franciscans in Spain in 1673, was ordained to the priesthood in 1682. He came to New Spain in 1683 and in the following year assumed direction of the missionary college of Querétaro, which had been founded the year before by Antonio Llinás. Its purpose was to train mobile missionaries to work with Indians who were dispersed over a wide area and to bring new methods to bear on the task. Margil also developed two other missionary colleges, Cristo Crucificado in Guatemala City (1701) and Our Lady of Guadalupe in Zacatecas (1708). He also worked personally on missions in New Spain and Central America. He was famed for his holiness and zeal, and the cause of his canonization has been introduced.

The Spaniards established a presidio along the Neches and then four mission stations. The Franciscans soon added two more among the Adai and the Ais, both tribes that were close to the farthest limits of the French penetration. In 1718, at the suggestion of Fray Antonio de San Buenaventura Olivares, who was impressed by the location and the docility of the Indians, a mission and presidio were established at San Antonio. The Franciscans worked zealously in east Texas, but progress was slow, primarily because the Indians were nomadic. The Spaniards were not strong enough to enforce *congregación*, and the results remained meager for the next century.

Alta California

Alta California was the last major area to be colonized and evangelized by the Spaniards. Again, the reasons were based on military as much as religious motives. The Russians were beginning to establish posts in the Northwest, and the British were showing interest in the area. In 1769 José de Gálvez, the visitor-general of New Spain, ordered the occupation of California to forestall these intrusions. Gaspar de Portolá was appointed captain and Fray Junípero Serra (1713–84), a Franciscan from Mallorca, was appointed the president of the future missions. In 1769 a presidio and mission were founded at San Diego, although the establishment remained precarious for a number of years because of illness and the difficulty of bringing supplies. Within a year another expedition was sent from San Diego to lay claim to Monterey Bay and to protect it from Russian or British intrusion. Soon after, a land party discovered a magnificent bay to the north, where in 1776 Juan Bautista de Anza established the mission and presidio of San Francisco. Spanish expansion to the north eventually ran into a determined wall of British resistance.

The Franciscan missions in Alta California were classic examples of the mission system first devised by the friars in the sixteenth century. It required all natives to live in the missions. Those who refused were forcibly congregated, whereas those who ran away, a not infrequent occurrence, were brought back and punished. The regimen was paternalistic, and in fact in 1773 Viceroy Antonio María de Bucareli decreed that the Franciscans held the place of parents over the natives. There was also a military presence, centered in the presidios of San Diego, Monterey, San Francisco, and Santa Barbara. This often hindered the missionary endeavor, because of the behavior of the soldiers toward the natives. Serra and his successors had difficulty in controlling bored soldiers and intrusive bureaucrats, and as a result conflicts were frequent.

Serra died in 1784 and was beatified by Pope John Paul II in 1988, a move that aroused a great deal of controversy. He is, of course, the best known of the mission founders, but his successor, Firmín de Lasuén (1736–1803), may be equally important. Born in Vitoria, Spain, he joined the Franciscans in 1751. A volunteer for the New World missions, he served in a variety of places in New Spain, Baja California, and Alta California. He personally founded nine missions, bringing the total to eighteen. During his administration the missions of Alta California reached a high point in numbers and effectiveness.

The California missions have been romanticized far more than any other Spanish enterprise. They came at the end of Spanish expansion and evangelization. They were a very small part of the overall picture and were fewer than those that the Spanish had once had in Texas and the American Southeast. Recent controversies surrounding the beatification of Serra have also added to the isolated view of these missions. Unfortunately, they have also overshadowed the work of Lasuén, who deserves as much credit as Serra for the work of the California missions.

THE AMERICAN SOUTHEAST

In the sixteenth century the term "Florida" included not only the modern state, but also most of Georgia, Alabama, and North Carolina. Both military conquest and missionary activity were slow because of the warlike nature of the native tribes. The first missionaries were Jesuits, who founded ten mission stations between Miami and Jamestown in modern Virginia. After numerous setbacks, the Jesuits abandoned the mission, and because the area produced no precious metals, the Spanish lost interest. In 1573 the Franciscans inaugurated their own missionary effort, but it was very precarious. Spain almost abandoned Florida in 1607, but at the pleas of the Franciscans decided to remain.

The most productive period of the Franciscan missionary activity was between 1612 and the end of the seventeenth century. The situation, however, was not stable. Some of the native tribes proved very resistant to Christianity, and there was a smoldering discontent with Spanish rule. The English presence to the north of Florida began to have an impact. The English were able to exploit the natives' hostility to the Spanish. The Treaty of Paris (1763), which ended the Seven Years War, transferred Florida to English rule. Most of the Spanish population left, and Catholicism in Florida effectively came to an end. The return of Florida to Spanish rule after the American Revolution did not alter the situation.

Although these missions seemed to be models of successful evangelization, this success was superficial. The natives had no genuine attachment to Catholicism, and most abandoned it at the first opportunity. The oppression and exploitation of the Spanish authorities and settlers exacerbated an already unstable situation.

THE ACT OF CONSOLIDATION

The wealth of the Church and organizations such as convents, confraternities, and religious orders rather naturally aroused the greed of secular officials. After the expulsion of the Jesuits in 1767, the crown confiscated their extensive holdings. Bourbon government was particularly hostile to the confraternities, "frowned upon as being economically retrograde, perhaps politically questionable, certainly overfond of ostentatious fiestas."[5]

In the period of the French Revolution and the Napoleonic wars, the Spanish crown desperately needed money for pay for these wars. In 1804 it sequestered all ecclesiastical funds, netting some forty million pesos. Most of these were in the form of loans and mortgages on which it was thought that the principal would never be paid. "The measure was, in effect, a massive foreclosure, which required the Church's debtors (mostly landlords, miners, and merchants) to pay off outstanding loans over a ten-year period."[6] The act had a devastating impact and fostered a dangerous discontent among the creoles, including the clergy.

OVERVIEW

The Spanish missionary enterprise in the New World was one of unprecedented magnitude and scope. At its height it extended from the tip of

---

[5] Alan Knight, *Mexico: The Colonial Era* (Cambridge, UK, 2002), 265.
[6] *Ibid.*, 245.

Argentina to northern California. Such an undertaking demanded enormous resources in personnel and finances. In approaching this daunting task, the missionaries had little tradition or experience to fall back on. The first missionary endeavors were improvisations, creative responses to peoples, languages, and cultures that were entirely new to the missionaries. That they were able to develop programs, pursue language and ethnographical studies, and achieve what success they did is a tribute to their zeal, intelligence, and creativity. These programs were not universally successful. The results of the missionary endeavor varied widely from one geographical area to another and from one people to another.

One lasting contribution of Roman Catholicism in the areas studied in this article was in the field of education. Even today some of the universities founded by churchmen and religious orders are still functioning. Unfortunately, the beneficiaries of this educational system were mostly Spaniards and creoles. For the most part the natives and the *castas* remained outside the system, at least for the period of this study. As has been seen, New Spain was not an intellectual and cultural backwater.

Another unhappy reality is that by the seventeenth century the humanitarian and pro-Indian movement, if not entirely dead, had certainly run out of steam. The place of the natives in colonial society had become fixed, especially under the Bourbons. Their seething resentment would explode in the revolution of 1810.

In the light of recent events, an important and controversial question is that of the impact of the missions and missionaries on the natives. The mission system, once romanticized, is now criticized for uprooting the native cultures and exposing the natives to European diseases. Likewise the system has been criticized for exploiting native labor and for the use of harsh punishments.

Although the level of these criticisms has been intensified by the political correctness of modern times, it is beyond doubt that to a great extent they are justified. Europeans, especially Spanish Christians, were convinced of the innate superiority of their culture and religion. The missionaries sincerely believed that without Christianity the natives were condemned to eternal damnation. Europeans of that age were oblivious to the impact of culture shock and the disruption caused by the jolting transfer from one society to another.

An additional factor was a change in the missionaries themselves and in Spanish colonial policies. In sixteenth-century New Spain, the Franciscans had dedicated themselves in a special way to the study of native languages and cultures. In the following century, the Jesuits took the lead in these studies. One result was that the missionaries often came to have a deep sympathy and understanding for the natives' outlook and cultures. The picture was different in the late seventeenth century and until the wars of independence. The Bourbons were hostile to the missionaries' use of native languages because of their perceived sympathy with the natives. The Franciscans in New Mexico and Alta California either did not know or made little effort to learn the native languages, in part because they were too numerous.

At the same time, it must be remembered that the natives, at least in central New Spain, proved adept at adapting to the new society and religion. They negotiated their place in both and manipulated the legal system to their own benefit. The idea of native victimhood is coming more and more under revision by contemporary scholarship. It should be kept in mind that for the Indians in independent Mexico, the worst period was under the liberal government of the mid-nineteenth century and even more under the rule of Porfirio Díaz (1872–80; 1884–1911). In 1910 "the millions of rural Mexicans who found themselves in dying villages or subsisting as *peones* on the nation's haciendas were worse off financially than their rural ancestors a century before."[7] For the natives in Alta California the decline began with the arrival of gold-hungry Americans after 1848. They left the missions, but without having a place to go or a support system to sustain them.

SUGGESTIONS FOR FURTHER READING

Brading, D. A. *Church and State in Bourbon Mexico: The Diocese of Michoacán 1749–1810*. Cambridge, MA, 1994.

Lavrin, Asunción. *Sexuality and Marriage in Colonial Latin America*. Lincoln, 1989.

Nesvig, Martin Austin, ed. *Local Religion in Colonial Mexico*. Albuquerque, 2006.

Ricard, Robert. *The Spiritual Conquest of Mexico: An Essay on the Apostolate and the Evangelizing Methods of the Mendicant Orders in New Spain: 1523–1572*. Trans. Lesley Byrd Simpson. Berkeley, 1966.

Schroeder, Susan, and Stafford Poole, C. M., eds. *Religion in New Spain*. Albuquerque, 2007.

Sherman, William, Michael Meyer, and Susan Deeds. *The Course of Mexican History*. 7th ed. New York, 2003.

Taylor, William B. *Magistrates of the Sacred: Priests and Parishioners in Eighteenth-Century Mexico*. Stanford, 1996.

Weber, David J. *The Spanish Frontier in North America*. New Haven, 1992.

---

[7] William Sherman, Michael Meyer, and Susan Deeds, *The Course of Mexican History*, 7th ed. (New York, 2003), 460–1.

13

FRENCH CATHOLICISM IN NEW FRANCE

LUCA CODIGNOLA

In New France, the European community consisted of a single body of lay Catholic men and women who were held together, under God's guidance, by the sacraments administered by the clergy. The latter comprised a number of secular priests and the male and female members of the regular orders. The male members of the regular orders were ordained priests who had also pledged themselves to some special vows. In principle, the same description applied in France. The relationship between Church and crown, the role of the Church within the crown, and the crown's obligations toward its Catholic population were the same on both sides of the Atlantic Ocean.

In the early days of French expansion (1608–59), there had been two major differences between France and New France. The most significant one was that the small Catholic community of New France lived side by side with the Indian nations. Although the Indians vastly outnumbered the French, it was then believed that the Indians could become part of the overall Catholic community by way of religious conversion.

Until 1659, the second major difference was the absence of a bishop, that is, a member of the clergy who was not only in a hierarchical superior position, but who also possessed some spiritual faculties that allowed him to administer certain sacraments that simple priests – secular or regular – could not administer, such as the power to ordain new priests or to confirm lay members of the community. When toward midcentury the majority of the population began to be born and raised in New France, this became a potential problem of no easy solution.

There was a third difference between France and New France. This was the absence in the latter of a system of canonically erected parishes, such as existed in France. There, a resident parish priest (*curé*), appointed by the bishop, looked after the community of faithful, alone or with the assistance of a vicar (*vicaire*) and of other priests. Although historians have insisted on this difference, the absence of full-fledged parishes was one of little practical significance, as spiritual services to the faithful were provided anyway. The churches in Quebec, Trois-Rivières, and Montreal were regarded by the people as their parish churches because the sacraments of baptism, communion, and matrimony were provided to the community by whomever was there available, mostly by members of the Society of Jesus (a regular order) and the Société de Saint-Sulpice (a congregation of secular priests). In fact, although the first Canadian parish, Notre-Dame-de-Québec, was erected in 1664, its registers were inaugurated as early as 1616. By 1659 four parish registers were in use, although no parish had yet been canonically erected. Between 1660 and 1674 another eleven registers were added. By 1688, when Jean-Baptiste de La Croix de Saint-Vallier (1653–1727) began his mandate as bishop of Quebec, thirty parish registers were active throughout the St. Lawrence Valley (Canada) and another fifteen parishes had been erected. In 1714 there were thirty-seven parishes and sixty-five open registers.[1]

François de Laval (1623–1708) was appointed vicar apostolic of Canada (not bishop of Quebec) in 1658 and took office in 1659. This compromise solution was used elsewhere in territories administered by the Sacred Congregation "de Propaganda Fide," the Holy See's department in charge of missions. Laval's appointment signaled the fact that the Canadian church was on its way to becoming just like any other church in the territory of France. Its distance from the metropolitan centers of power and its being surrounded by a non-Catholic population were not elements peculiar to the church of New France. These features also applied to a number of French churches located in the southern mountain districts or close to Protestant areas.

LAVAL AND SAINT-VALLIER: CONTINUITY WITHIN THE CHURCH

In the period from 1674 to 1727, the Canadian church was led by two bishops, Laval (1674–88) and Saint-Vallier (1688–1727). If we take into account Laval's initial mandate as vicar apostolic (1659–74), the two prelates ruled for an astonishing sixty-eight years. Almost invariably, historiography has emphasized the difference between the two men. On the one side, there was the innovative Laval. He succeeded in organizing a new church while reducing the Jesuits' overpowering influence; he delayed the erection of proper parishes in order to use the priests of the Séminaire de

---

[1] Alain Laberge, "L'implantation de la paroisse dans la vallée du Saint-Laurent aux XVIIe et XVIIIe siècles," in Serge Courville and Normand Séguin, eds., *La paroisse* (Sainte-Foy, 2001), 15–17.

Québec (a community of secular priests) as a missionary task force; he stood firm against crown officials on the issue of the sale of alcoholic beverages to the Indians (a practice later dubbed as "brandy trade" in English). On the other side was the haughty Saint-Vallier. He reshaped the Canadian church after the French model. He disempowered the Séminaire de Québec and implemented the parish system. He fully espoused the crown's attempt to transform Canada into a viable French province. As recently as 1992, Saint-Vallier's forty-year rule was described as a long "dark night" and the man as "the most detested and resented of New France's episcopal leaders."[2] Yet the difference between the two prelates has been overemphasized.

Both prelates were appointed at around thirty-five years of age. Laval was ready for the Orient when he was picked for Quebec. Saint-Vallier was the result of Laval's own recommendation (1685), although the latter soon regretted his choice. By then Laval was a wary and tired veteran with thirty years of experience in the Canadian mission who found himself confronted by a young and zealous reformer without any field experience, except for an eighteen-month-long visitation of Canada and Acadia (present-day New Brunswick and Nova Scotia) performed in 1685–86. Saint-Vallier had returned home disgusted with the state of religion in the colony and particularly so with the destitute state of the Indian missions and of the churches located in rural areas. Many years later, when in 1713 he returned to Canada after a thirteen-year absence, Saint-Vallier too had become a tired sixty-year-old priest, more willing to devote his last years to his personal fulfillment in God through reconciliation and poverty rather than to making Canada the exemplary diocese of his early days.

The two bishops were personally irreproachable and lived exemplary lives. In both of them, however, the utopian dream of a pristine Christian community in a new world subsided with experience. Unsolved material problems and constant bickering within the Church were not extraneous to their preoccupations. In fact, they spent an inordinate amount of time in France trying to secure overall visibility, court approval, and economic viability for their diocese. Laval was away for twelve years, Saint-Vallier for a staggering seventeen years, including five years (1704–09) of forced detainment in England. Laval, who had resigned in 1688 but continued to live in Quebec, was addressed as Monseigneur l'Ancien and de facto replaced Saint-Vallier during his absences. Furthermore, both Laval and Saint-Vallier continued to believe in the Church's superiority over the crown and in the clergy's right and duty to lead their faithful, although

---

[2] Robert Choquette, "French Catholicism Comes to the Americas," in Charles H. Lippy, Robert Choquette, and Stafford Poole, eds., *Christianity Comes to the Americas 1492–1776* (New York, 1992), 201.

neither could realistically conceive of a system in which Church and crown did not rule over society as mutually beneficial partners.

Much has also been made of the fact that Laval favored communalism and created a system whereby his priests would be sent to their destinations and removed at the bishop's will, something that ran counter to French practice. The Séminaire de Québec was meant to be the focal point for all ecclesiastical personnel of the diocese, from training to assignment to retirement, as well as for its financial resources. Yet Laval had called for the erection of new parishes as early as 1667 and only required that parishes be established after sufficient revenue had been secured for the parish priest. For his part, confronted by the fact that when he arrived tithes paid by the population consisted in less than 30 percent of what was due,[3] Saint-Vallier proceeded rather slowly himself, as only seven new parishes were erected during the first twelve years of his mandate (1688–1700). The truth is that both bishops proceeded rather tentatively in all directions and often had to compromise.

Aside from the parish issue, both bishops had to deal with the spirit of competition and jealousy that more often than not pitted one ecclesiastical community against another, an attitude that had already been typical of the pre-1659 era. They were also similarly confronted by the animosity that most communities, fearing for their independence, showed against their bishop. The Sulpicians represented a constant thorn in the bishop's side. The Jesuits showed a measure of independence with regard to the Indian missions. The priests of the Séminaire de Québec were at first curbed in their power by Saint-Vallier, but then used by him against the Jesuits in Upper and Lower Louisiana. The Recollets of the province of Saint-Denys (Paris) of the Order of Friars Minor, whom the crown allowed back into New France in 1669 as a counterweight to the Jesuits (the first Recollets arrived in 1670), waged a long procedural battle against both bishops. In the West, but particularly so in Louisiana, traditional lack of cooperation between competing religious communities was compounded by conflicting jurisdictions between the Jesuits, the Capuchins (another branch of the Order of Friars Minor), the Discalced Carmelites, and Séminaire de Québec. The two bishops also experienced difficulties with the nuns belonging to the Religieuses Hospitalières de Saint-Joseph, the Augustines Hospitalières de la Miséricorde-de-Jésus of the Hôtel-Dieu of Quebec, and the Filles Séculières de la Congrégation de Notre-Dame.

In sum, neither Laval nor Saint-Vallier was able to steer the colonial church, let alone the society of New France, in the direction of their early

---

[3] Daniel A. Scalberg, "Religious Life in New France under the Laval and Saint-Vallier Bishoprics: 1659–1727" (Ph.D. diss., University of Oregon, 1990), 318.

wishes. Both were confronted by two major problems that they were unable to solve. The first was the scarcity of ecclesiastical personnel in relationship to the population. The second was the uneven distribution of these personnel throughout the diocese. Before addressing both issues, recall that, after Saint-Vallier's death (1727), a long hiatus of some fourteen years elapsed before the arrival in 1741 of another effective bishop of Quebec, Henri-Marie Dubreil de Pontbriand (1708–60). The Capuchin Louis-François Duplessis de Mornay (1663–1741) was appointed in 1727 but never went to New France. His replacement, Pierre-Herman Dosquet (1691–1777), was appointed in 1733 but spent only one year in Canada. Finally, François-Louis de Pourroy de Lauberivière (1711–40), appointed in 1739, died twelve days after his arrival in Quebec. None left any significant trace on the history of New France or of its church.

NUMBERS: PRIESTS ARE NEVER ENOUGH

As for the scarcity of ecclesiastical personnel, in spite of the constant increase of the population of European origin of Canada (6,600 in 1670, 14,100 in 1700, 51,900 in 1750), the number of the ecclesiastical personnel remained constant or actually diminished in absolute figures at the beginning of the eighteenth century. The average growth rate for priests went from 4.2 percent (1665–85) to 3.6 percent (1685–1700), and from 0.2 percent (1700–15) to 0.9 percent (1715–55). Priests numbered 148 in 1696, 168 in 1711, and 148 again in 1713. If in 1675–79 there was one priest for every 71 faithful, this rate varied from 1:59 in 1700–05 to 1:76 in 1725–29. Comparisons are difficult to make, but one may note that in Rome, until 1740, there was one priest for every 15 persons or so; in Lower Canada in 1790 the ratio had dropped to one in 1,400; in Ireland in 1800 each parish priest was responsible for an average of 2,676 parishioners. In the period from 1665 to 1724, the clergy remained at a stable percentage of 1.4 percent to 1.7 percent of the population at large. (A steady decrease started in 1725–29.)[4] The majority of the priests active in Canada were diocesan priests, that is, priests who did not belong to any regular order or community and as such were directly submitted to the jurisdiction of the bishop. Others belonged to regular orders, such as the Jesuits (in Canada 1633–1800) and the Recollets (1670–1849), as well as the few Discalced Carmelites who were active in Louisiana (1720–23). There were also two congregations of secular priests. One was the Society of the Priests of Saint-Sulpice, whose home was the Montreal seminary. The other secular

---

[4] Louis Pelletier, *Le clergé en Nouvelle-France: Étude démographique et répertoire biographique* (Montreal, 1993), 18–41.

congregation was the Frères Hospitalières de la Croix et de Saint-Joseph of Montreal (est. 1692, also known as Frères Charon), who mainly devoted themselves to hospitaler duties.

A large percentage of the priests active in New France came from overseas, most of them from France. As a rule of thumb, the higher one's role in the hierarchical ladder of the Church, the more one was likely to be French-born, not Canadian-born. All the bishops of Quebec were born in the Old World, but so were most of the superiors of all the men's and women's congregations. This trend continued throughout the French regime for such groups as the Jesuits and especially the Sulpicians. With regard to diocesan priests and Recollets, the percentage of Canadian-born priests grew steadily over time. Young Laval had fully shared the Propaganda Fide's missionary dream of distant churches manned by an "autochthonous clergy," in his case, by young Indians who in time would have become priests and ministered to their own kind. The unsuccessful attempt to enroll Indian students at the Petit Séminaire, together with the post-1674 marginal role of the Indian community within the Church, shattered that dream.

The key problem, however, was that Canada did not produce enough new priests to meet the needs of the growing colony. (The first Canadian priest was ordained in 1665; as for Acadia and Louisiana, only four and one priests respectively originated from those regions during the French regime.) The erection of the bishopric of Quebec in 1674 did not have much influence on the fact that the Canadian church largely depended on personnel and material support from the Old World, mainly France. The dearth of priests was evident to church and crown officials alike. In 1683 Intendant Jacques de Meulles (d. 1703) complained that three-quarters of the Canadians did not hear mass more than four times a year, and that as a whole they had little access to sacraments and acquired a poor understanding of Christian religion, an opinion that was shared by Governor General Louis de Buade, comte de Frontenac et de Palluau (1622–98). In 1701, Governor General Louis-Hector de Callière (1646–1703) and Intendant Jean Bochart de Champigny (c. 1674–1703) pleaded for more clergy to be sent from France. The inhabitants of distant rural areas enjoyed fewer opportunities to partake in the life of the Church and to be reminded of God's presence on earth.

Nuns did not follow the negative trend of their male counterparts. Their number grew throughout the French regime, and Canadian vocations proceeded accordingly. In the years from 1640 to 1700, women's communities expanded by an average rate of 5.5 percent a year, whereas from 1700 to 1725 that rate was still a rather high 2.3 percent. Nuns numbered

89 in 1681 and 256 in 1727, almost all of them born in New France.[5] Regular orders of European origin included the Ursulines of Quebec (est. 1639) and Trois-Rivières (1702), the Augustines Hospitalières de la Miséricorde-de-Jésus of Quebec (1639), and the Religieuses Hospitalières de Saint-Joseph in Montreal and the outlying region (1659). Women's communities that were original to Canada were the Sisters of the Hôpital-Général (1701) in Quebec and the Congrégation de Notre-Dame (1658) in Montreal. All these communities were allowed to establish de facto uncloistered communities in New France on account of the crucial social and educational tasks they performed. Overall, in 1670 the clergy still represented the majority of the ecclesiastical personnel of Canada (55 percent, or in absolute numbers 58 priests to 48 nuns), but in 1730 their proportion had changed (43 percent, or 189 to 252). Furthermore, Canadian recruits became more numerous than foreign immigrants as early as 1690 (55 percent).

In spite of their overall scarcity, there is little or no evidence of misbehavior on the part of the Canadian clergy and nuns. Comparisons can only be made with the ecclesiastical personnel of contemporary European Catholic countries. There clerical standards were known to be very low and instances of moral shortcomings were common knowledge in France as well as, for example, in Ireland. Intendant Jean Talon (1626–94) was convinced that New France's clergy was overly strict and guilty of imposing standards that were too high for their flock. Both Laval and Saint-Vallier chastised men who delighted in horse racing, dancing, theater, masquerades, and the game of cards, and lashed out against women who, in their view, enjoyed the vanity of fashion, curled their hair, and dressed indecently, baring their arms and shoulders. In the eighteenth century the high standards of the previous century deteriorated among the clergy in line with what happened in European society at large.

UNEVEN DISTRIBUTION: RURAL POPULATION, ACADIA, THE WEST, AND LOUISIANA

With regard to the distribution of this personnel throughout the diocese, Canada's main urban centers – Quebec, Trois-Rivières, and Montreal – were well endowed with the spiritual, educational, and social services that their residents expected from the combined effort of Church and crown. There were parishes, churches, chapels, schools, hospitals, insane asylums, hospices (*hôtel-dieu*), and poor boards that allowed people to be baptized,

[5] *Ibid.*, 38–40.

to be instructed in the Christian doctrine, to attend Mass, to receive the sacraments, to improve their knowledge or learn a trade, to be cured when ill, to be taken care of when invalid or old, and to register births, marriages, and deaths. Overall, the standards of these services were better than those available to residents of urban France. The smaller size of the Canadian urban centers, together with the good quality of the Canadian clergy, helped. Although relatively few Canadians took advantage of them, Quebec was also well endowed with educational facilities. These comprised the Jesuit College (an institute of higher education), the Séminaire de Québec, the adjoining Petit Séminaire, the Jesuit elementary school, and the boarding and day school operated by the Ursulines. Instruction was also provided in Montreal by the Sulpicians, the Frères Charon, and the Congrégation de Notre-Dame, and in Trois-Rivières by the Recollets and the Ursulines.

Similar facilities, however, were not available to the rural population. Geographically, the diocese of Quebec was immense, stretching from Acadia on the Atlantic Ocean, to the Pays-d'en-Haut (Upper Country) around the Great Lakes, down south to the Illinois country (or Upper Louisiana) all the way to Louisiana. Even putting aside the manning of the Indian missions (a challenge in itself that in principle required voluntary and specialized personnel), in Canada in 1706 there were 41 parishes in the Quebec region, serving 13,000 faithful; 28 in the Montreal region, serving 8,000; and 13 in the Trois-Rivières region, serving 2,000. Whereas by 1713 the priest-to-people ratio stood at 1:83 in the urban centers, this ratio was as low as 1:289 in the countryside, the latter a figure that was much lower than contemporary French standards.[6] In fact, by the 1730s in four-fifths of the 100 parishes, service was provided by nonresidential priests who were charged with multiple assignments. On account of the fact that during the Saint-Vallier years only 20 percent of the clergy took care of the rural population, the people developed a measure of self-reliance – they baptized their own children and did not show any haste in going to the church official to have their infants registered.[7]

The population of Acadia and of the Great Lakes region suffered from the absence of any significant urban center and from distance from Quebec. The bishops of Quebec were well aware of the spiritual needs of their distant flocks, but confronted with the scarcity of priests at home, they would not spare any to meet their needs. Moreover, priests occasionally sent to Acadia or the Great Lakes would normally be charged with responsibility

---

[6] Terence A. Crowley, "The French Regime to 1760," in Terrence Murphy and Roberto Perin, eds., *A Concise History of Christianity in Canada* (Toronto, 1996), 41–42.

[7] Dale Miquelon, *New France 1701–1744: "A Supplement to Europe"* (Toronto, 1987), 233.

for both the faithful of European origin and the local Indians, but in the distant regions the latter invariably took precedence.

In 1671, after its return to France following the Treaty of Breda (1667), Acadia had some 500 inhabitants, a number that grew to 1,400 in 1707 and 5,500 in the 1720s. Aside from other occasional presences, religious service to the Acadian settlers was provided by the Recollets, who settled in Port Royal, the Gaspé Peninsula, Baie-Française (present-day Bay of Fundy), and the region of the Saint John River of New Brunswick (1672–78). They were followed by some secular priests, starting with Louis Petit (1629–1709), a priest of the Séminaire de Québec sent by Laval in 1676, and by the Jesuits, who in 1687 with Jacques Bigot (1651–1711) resumed their activity in the southern part of Acadia. The Congrégation de Notre-Dame established a school for girls in 1685. This was followed by a school for boys that Claude Trouvé (c. 1644–1704), a Sulpician, established in 1686. In the eighteenth century the Recollets returned to Port Royal (1702–26) and, after the British conquered it and then secured peninsular Acadia by the Treaty of Utrecht (1713), they tried to convince the Acadians to move to Île Royale (present-day Cape Breton Island) and Île Saint-Jean (present-day Prince Edward Island), or to remain actively loyal to the French crown even in their new capacity as British subjects. The treaty contained a clause concerning the Catholic religion. Ambiguous as it was, this in practice tolerated its exercise in the former French territories. The building of Louisbourg (started in 1718) substantially altered the human outlook of Île Royale. The fortress soon became one of the major urban centers of the North Atlantic coast. Recollets from the province of Saint-Pierre (Bretagne) were in charge of the spiritual well-being of the Louisbourg community (1713–59). Their quality was rather poor, and the bishop of Quebec, who had final jurisdiction, was frequently at odds with them. Acadia was also served by the sisters of the Congrégation de Notre-Dame (from 1727) and by the Frères de la Charité de l'Ordre de Saint-Jean-de-Dieu (from 1716). As no parish system was established, the costs of all religious establishments were met by the crown and voluntary donations.

Between 1698 and 1702 two forts were established near present-day Biloxi and another one at Mobile. So began the new colony of Louisiana, where New Orleans (est. 1718) became the administrative center in 1722, with a population of one thousand by 1729 to which religious institutions and services were provided. Louisiana expanded north along the Mississippi and Alabama Rivers. In the 1720s small farming was complemented by some large plantations that employed a significant number of African slaves (4,000 by 1739). Saint-Jean-Baptiste-des-Natchitoches (1713), Fort Rosalie (present-day Natchez, Mississippi, 1716), and Fort

Toulouse (present-day Montgomery, Alabama, 1717) were built in the process and became the settlements of Upper Louisiana. Meanwhile, in the Great Lakes region, Fort Pontchartrain was established at Detroit in 1701, and from there French expansion moved further west but especially south, along the Ohio and Mississippi rivers. Although commercial posts, with or without a military garrison, dotted the French American West, this vast territory was still Indian land, peopled by large and often conflicting Indian nations. The very few priests in the area normally lived in or close to French settlements, where they had a small chapel and quarters of their own. They offered their services to the population of European origin and to the Indians who demanded them and moved around when the season or security allowed it.

CHURCH AND CROWN: A STRICT ALLIANCE

The direct rule (1661–1715) of king of France Louis XIV (1643–1715) coincided with the attempt on the part of the crown to make Canada a French territory organized along the same lines as any province in continental France. This attempt also applied to the Church and resulted in the establishment of the bishopric of Quebec (1674) and in the end of the Jesuit yearly reports (relations), regularly published each year from 1632 to 1672. Although the process of Frenchification was not entirely successful, its ideology affected most measures taken with regard to the colony, including the instructions prepared for Talon by Minister Jean-Baptiste Colbert (1619–83). These made it clear that it was "absolutely necessary to hold in just balance the temporal authority [i.e., the crown representatives in the colony] ... and the spiritual authority [the bishop and the Jesuits]" so that "the latter be inferior to the former."[8] Much has also been made of the hostility shown toward the Church by Frontenac, who was twice governor general of New France (1672–82, 1689–98). On the one side, it is a fact that, although the role of the Church did not change substantially, the reign of Louis XIV signaled the decline of its influence in the colony.

On the other side, however, disputes between members of the Church and royal officials were numerous in New France, as they were in France, but these never challenged the complementary roles of Church and crown and were mere squabbles between conflicting personalities. It must also be emphasized that, in a society as small as Canada that possessed only three significant urban centers, personal dislikes certainly played a role, but so did the daily interaction of elite members. Personally or through members

---

[8] Louis XIV and Hugues de Lionne to Jean Talon, 27 Mar. 1665, in "L'Intendant Jean Talon," *Rapport de l'Archiviste de la Province de Québec* (1930–1): 5.

of their natural or acquired family networks and linkages, these elite members were often keen on avoiding personal confrontation and on favoring compromise and accommodation whenever possible. When it existed, conflict was normally related to symbolic issues, of paramount importance during the ancien régime, such as the order of dignitaries in a procession, or who was to use a pew closer to the altar, or who was first to receive communion. The 1700 quarrel between Intendant Champigny and the king's lieutenant at Quebec, the Marquis Antoine de Crisafy (d. 1709), about whose prayer desk (*prieu-Dieu*) should be placed closer to the altar, is typical in this regard. Also, Governor Frontenac directed his hostility against the bishop of Quebec and the Jesuits, who opposed the brandy trade and his fur-trading ventures, but he got along very well with the Recollets, who sided with him and took advantage of his protection. The only significant issue on which the two parties took opposite views was the brandy trade, which was opposed by the Church (for humanitarian reasons) and upheld by the crown (as a passport to trade).

If anything, the complementarity of crown and Church must be emphasized, so much that, "to a considerable degree," at times the clergy can be described as "agents of the Crown."[9] In New France this was particularly true of the 1674–1727 years, when the utopian missionary dreams of the early Church were long past and the transformation of the whole colony into a military compound was not fully realized. The Church was expected to perform various basic functions that the crown could not perform by itself. Its primary responsibility was to minister to the spiritual needs of the people by praying, preaching, administering the sacraments, setting a personal example of piety and temperance, instructing the young, and policing and raising the standards of public morality. Furthermore, the Church was expected to keep accurate vital statistics and to take care of all human beings who were not provided for by their families (the sick, the poor, the aged, the derelict, abandoned children, etc.). Finally, the Church provided ideological justification for the cult of kingship, preached obedience to authority, fostered subordination and docility, emphasized the basic roles of the patriarchal family, and confirmed that belonging in a social order and one's place in society came with birth and could not be undone. By fulfilling its overall role, the Church served to bind society firmly together and to maintain social order. Overall, the role of the Church did not differ substantially in France and New France, except in the latter the Church was also entrusted with keeping the Indians in the French alliance.

---

[9] William J. Eccles, "The Role of the Church in New France," in William J. Eccles, *Essays on New France* (Toronto, 1987), 29.

In France, the crown recognized the Church's role in society by endowing it with land and substantial sums of money variously allocated. During Saint-Vallier's episcopate, the crown manifested its satisfaction with the role fulfilled by the Church in New France by raising its financial contribution. The episcopal palace was built on crown's money (1693–97), together with more hospices (Montreal, 1688; Quebec, 1692), hospitals (Quebec, 1639; Montreal, 1642; Trois-Rivières, 1702), and houses for the poor (1688). In the eighteenth century, crown subsidies amounted to somewhere between 30 and 40 percent of all church revenues. (In Louisiana the Church was entirely financed by the crown.) None of these subsidies constituted a right to which the Church was automatically entitled. Negotiations were constant and lengthy, disbursements were made occasionally, delays were all too frequent. The last word was always the crown's.

Aside from crown subsidies, the balance of the Church's revenues was provided by gifts from French devouts, agricultural profits derived from land granted to the bishop or to the religious communities, ecclesiastical benefices such as those derived from the Méobec and Lestrées abbeys in France, and, in the case of the Sulpicians and the Jesuits, the regular transfer of money from their mother houses in France. The Canadian faithful were meant to contribute to the material well-being of their parish through the disbursement of occasional fees due for a number of sacred functions and practical obligations (weddings, funerals, masses, the selling of pews, Sunday collections, etc.), as well as for the civil functions performed by the parish priest in his capacity as the crown's official (such as the keeping and issuing of official records), and through the regular payment of an ecclesiastical tax called tithe (*dîme*). Laval introduced this European practice in Canada (but not in Acadia) in 1663, but this measure elicited more controversy than revenue. Its rate was often changed (from one-thirteenth to one-twentieth to one-twenty-sixth of one's presumed income). The products on which it was calculated also varied, from all the produce of human labor to wheat only. Yet the results were always the same: the faithful did not pay, and the Church complained. In 1717 Saint-Vallier threatened to refuse absolution to those who did not comply, but the crown refused to intervene harshly in support of the Church. Yet in a colony where inhabitants were not required to pay taxes and the enforcement of any regulation was problematic, people simply took the clergy for granted and felt they could get away without paying, as in fact they did, in spite of clerical threats of withholding sacraments or the intendant's occasional interventions.

The result was that the Church as a whole was neither rich nor poor – the immense wealth of bishops and cardinals in France and the extreme poverty of some rural parish priests were unknown in New France. However, its revenues were not equally distributed. The Sulpicians of Montreal and the Recollets of the Maritimes fared best, whereas hospitals and hospices were in constant deficit, the Séminaire de Québec was in debt, and the nuns were often on the verge of poverty. Moreover, both Laval and Saint-Vallier, who received some 10,000 livres a year from the crown, spent a considerable amount of their own personal patrimony in performing their functions. The income of parish priests varied. Normally a priest who lived in an urban area or in a very productive *seigneurie* would receive more from his parishioners than his counterpart in a poor or underpopulated region. Whereas in the late 1670s Laval and Intendant Jacques Duchesneau de La Doussinière et d'Ambault (d. 1696) had agreed that parish priests could live on 500 livres a year, in the eighteenth century this presumed figure was raised to 1,000 livres a year. In the same period in France, annual incomes varied from 700 to 3,000 livres, the former being considered a very low figure.

INDIAN MISSIONS

Although the process was already in place during Laval's times as vicar apostolic (1659–74), the erection of the bishopric of Quebec (1674) completed the transition of the Canadian church from a missionary institution, whose main task was to make the salvation of the Indians possible, to a *routinière* institution providing services to the population of European origin. Indians were not forgotten, but, in practice, given the scarcity of ecclesiastical personnel, rarely did the bishop send any priest among them unless urged by the crown. Indian missions were then mostly left to religious communities such as the Jesuits, the Sulpicians, the Recollets, the Capuchins, and the Séminaire de Québec. The dozens of mission posts that dot maps of French expansion in North America convey a deceiving image of presence and strength. The opposite was true. These posts were few and far between, distant in space as they were in time, poor in human and financial resources, and extremely weak when compared to the strength of the western Indian nations. Aside from a providential hope that eventually Indian nations will be brought into the Church, there was no real plan for their evangelization. The success and the very existence of missionary initiatives depended on an haphazard combination of elements – the availability of missionaries and of funds, individual ability and stamina, political support and sometimes prompting on the part of the crown, a welcoming attitude on the part of the Indians, and a state of relative peace among both Indian and European nations. One element that was almost always missing was cooperation among religious communities; if anything, competition and hostility were the norm. Although all communities wished and asked to be left alone, in all regions different groups were active at the same time. In Louisiana the sharing of space created more problems than elsewhere.

After 1665, the Jesuits moved in three directions. The first direction was west, toward Lake Superior and the Mississippi River, home to the Ottawas and to a number of Algonquian nations formerly living around Lake Erie and Lake Ontario. Jesuit initiatives were supported by Laval but strongly opposed by Governor Frontenac, who tried to undermine their position by using the Recollets as a counterweight against them and the bishop. The exploring and fur-trading expedition that René-Robert Cavelier de La Salle (1643–87), a commercial partner of Governor Frontenac's, led into the Mississippi and Louisiana regions caused such a turmoil among the Indians that the Jesuits abandoned their missions there. Similarly, the western commercial initiatives of Antoine Laumet, better known as Lamothe Cadillac (1658–1730), the commander at Detroit, created such a havoc in the region that the Jesuits abandoned any hope of success and in 1705 burned their own mission of Saint-Joseph at Michilimackinac (present-day Mackinaw City, Michigan), the center of their activity since 1670. Some Jesuits, however, remained in the West and also moved down from the Great Lakes toward the Illinois country and Louisiana. Saint-Vallier confirmed their spiritual powers among the Illinois in 1690, but the arrival of the priests of the Séminaire de Québec in 1699 made them move to Kaskaskia (1701). Further south, the Capuchins, with whom there had been a long jurisdictional battle, agreed to leave the Indian missions to them as late as 1726.

The second direction taken by Jesuit initiatives was south, toward the Iroquois of the province of New York, who in the late 1650s and early 1660s had undergone a period of relative tranquillity. Renewed Iroquois hostility later in the decade, however, made the Jesuits abandon their missions in their midst. Some of the Iroquois who had embraced Catholicism, mainly from the Oneida and Mohawk nations, fled their own country and in 1668 established themselves south of Montreal, at the Saint-François-Xavier-des-Prés mission, the precursor of what later became the Kahnawake community. The third direction was Acadia, where missions were established with the Penobscot and the Kennebecs. In 1694 Sébastien Râle (1652–1724) founded a mission at Norridgewock, Maine, and Vincent Bigot (1649–1720) founded another one at Pentagouët (present-day Castine, Maine). In 1701 another mission was established at Meductic, New Brunswick. After the Treaty of Utrecht (1713), the Jesuits assisted the Acadians and tried to win them to the French cause. Râle was killed when, during Dummer's War (1722–27), the Penobscot mission was destroyed.

The Sulpicians, who arrived in Canada in 1657, from their Montreal seminary in 1669 sent exploring expeditions in the direction of the Lake Erie region with an eye to possible western missions. From 1668 to 1680 they had a mission serving Kenté (Quinté) Bay on Lake Ontario and its neighborhood. Given their poor results in evangelization, the Sulpicians then concentrated their efforts in the Montreal area, where they established the La Montagne mission (1671–94). As they attributed the slow progress of evangelization and the ravages of alcoholic consumption among the Indians to proximity to the French settlement, they moved the mission first to Sault-au-Récollet, another location within the island of Montreal (1696–1722), and then to Kanesataké (Oka), further away from Montreal (1722). In 1685 the Sulpicians accepted Saint-Vallier's offer to assist in the missions of Acadia. The projected Port Royal seminary was never built, but between 1686 and 1696 they were active in Port Royal and the Bay of Chignecto. They were also in Île Saint-Jean from 1720 to 1723. Their activity, however, was mainly devoted to the Acadian population, and they met the Mi'kmaq only occasionally.

The Recollets returned to New France in 1670 and took part in missions with the Iroquois at Fort Frontenac and Fort Niagara (1670–80), with the Mi'kmaq and the Malecite in the Gaspé Peninsula and Nova Scotia (1689–1701, 1713–31), and with the Illinois (1673–75). The most significant Recollet mission was led by Chrestien Leclercq (c. 1641–post-1700) in the Gaspé Peninsula and south of it in 1675–86. Leclercq was one of the missionaries, and often the only one, serving the local Mi'kmaq.

In 1722 the members of the Capuchin province of Champagne were entrusted with the evangelization of Louisiana. Their jurisdiction extended from New Orleans to Fort Rosalie. Aside from New Orleans, where they had their convent, the Capuchins lived deep in Indian territory in times of significant Indian hostility. They were, however, attached to the French settlements and did not perform any missionary work. The Discalced Carmelites, who had preceded them in the area for a short time (1720–23), acted in the same fashion.

In 1698, Saint-Vallier issued special letters patent to allow the priests of the Séminaire de Québec to engage in missionary activity in the Mississippi region, where the Jesuit mission had been confirmed eight years earlier. The seminary priests took charge of the Sainte-Famille mission (present-day Cahokia, Illinois) with the Tamarois, an Illinois nation. Indians were very numerous, but the results of evangelization were deceiving. The seminary priests then moved down toward Louisiana (1707), before returning to Tamaroa once again (1713). By 1688 the Séminaire de Québec also had two missionaries in Acadia. Although most of the seminary priests in the region devoted themselves to the Acadian population, between 1717 and 1720 Antoine Gaulin (1674–1740) succeeded in bringing together a great number of Mi'kmaq in the mission of Antigonish within British territory but close to the French Île Royale.

Louis XIV's new imperial policy, devised toward the end of the seventeenth century, included the establishment of Louisiana, the creation of a chain of forts connecting Louisiana to Canada via the Mississippi and the Illinois country, and the strengthening of the western commercial posts. Acadia too lost its image of the useless backcountry of an insolvent colony in favor of a new role as a military outpost of crucial importance. In this new strategy, the Church and its missionaries were assigned a new role. They were to maintain the allegiance of the old Indian allies and to help win new nations to the French side. Furthermore, when the Treaty of Utrecht transferred a good many Acadians under the British crown, missionaries became outright crown agents in enemy territory, providing French officials with information and keeping pro-French sentiment alive among not only the Acadians, but also the Indians, whom the Treaty of Falmouth (1726) had granted the right to practice the Catholic religion. Although not all missionaries favored the same methods and solutions, especially in Acadia, all believed that a more perfect union of Church and crown interests would have enhanced the chances of salvation for faithful and heathen alike.

Well-known problems relating to contact between Europeans and Indians, such as the spreading of illnesses and the devastating influence of alcoholic beverages among the Indians, did not derive from the presence of missionaries among the Indians. Conversely, one issue with which the missionaries had to come to terms, together with the Indians they tried to convert, was that of mixed marriages. These were a direct consequence of the fact that everywhere in New France, except in Canada, Indians outnumbered the Europeans. On this issue, as on another number of practices that touched on a faithful's path toward salvation, the Church had the final word. According to canon law, marriages were only permitted between two Catholics, so that the non-Catholic partner (here always an Indian woman) had first to be brought into the faith. However, only seventeen intermarriages took place in New France between 1644 and 1700, the reason being that many Indian women simply chose to cohabit with their European partner.[10] Indeed, mixed unions were never a major factor in Canada, but in the frontier conditions of the Illinois and Louisiana settlements, where French women were scarce and relations with the Indians an everyday occurrence, intermarriages were very common.[11] In the eighteenth century, French authorities tried to stop these unions, but the clergy recognized that such unions did exist and that to refuse the marriage sacrament would

---

[10] Cornelius J. Jaenen, *The Role of the Church in New France* (Toronto, 1976), 28–9.

[11] Charles E. O'Neill, S.J., *Church and State in French Colonial Louisiana: Policy and Politics to 1732* (New Haven, 1966), 253.

simply favor concubinage and profligacy. In Louisiana, marriages between the Indians and the French were soon outnumbered by illegal liaisons between the French and the black slaves, manumitted or not. In 1724 the Capuchin Raphaël de Luxembourg (c. 1663–1734) lamented that nothing was done for the latter, although they would have welcomed baptism and instructions, had they been given a chance.

RELIGIOUS STANDARDS

Catholics believed they could be saved from an eternity in hell and be given access to heaven, but that in order to achieve their salvation they were expected to pray at various times during the day; to visit their church periodically; to abstain from eating meat at appropriate times during the year; never to be avaricious, drink to excess, blaspheme, or lead an irregular sexual life; to behave properly toward their neighbors and their relatives; and to forgive their enemies. All these rules were based on God's Ten Commandments. However, contrary to a number of Protestant denominations, Catholics believed that a saintly life could be led only by a handful of men and women – not necessarily only members of the clergy – and that worldly success would neither prove nor guarantee salvation. They also admitted that salvation was not possible without the personal intervention of the ordained clergy. Whereas this general framework applied to all Catholics throughout the world, there was ample room for variations based on the location of the community, on the period, and on the social standing and age of the individual. To what extent were these general beliefs and expectations reflected in New France's society?

In New France, all year long, and throughout any given day, residents – especially those of the more populated areas – were reminded of their duties toward God. The sound of the church bells, the ornate carved woodwork of the church interiors, the smell of incense, the gold and silver accoutrements of the altar, the processions, the clerical garb, the priest's sermon from the pulpit, the Roman liturgy, the Latin language used in most rituals, the Gregorian singing of the choir, the music of the organ, the stations of the cross that visualized Christ's agony – all these were a constant appeal to the faithful's senses and a physical reminder of the afterlife. The relationship between the clergy and the laity was not limited to church attendance or to the diffusion the rules and regulations derived from the Council of Trent (1545–63). The influence of the Catholic Church was much more pervasive and not limited to the spiritual domain. Baptismal, marriage, and death certificates, for example, were issued by the clergy on behalf of the crown and had to be used and shown on a variety of occasions during one's lifetime. Those aspiring to high office under the crown, such as a judge, had to provide a certificate from the clergy declaring their good moral character. Attendance at Mass and communion was compulsory at least once a year, usually around Easter Sunday, and both were certified by the parish priest. Priests acted as royal notaries in remote rural parishes. Civil authorities used Mass and other religious gatherings to make announcements and read decrees. Banns announcing a forthcoming marriage were published and read aloud to the faithful on three successive Sundays in order to ensure that there were no known impediments, such as a former marriage in France. Instruction was invariably given by the clergy members of the various orders. In entering hospitals and almshouses, the unfortunate individual expected to be assisted, for the sake of his or her body and soul, by members of the Church.

It is impossible to say what religion meant to colonists, as most did not discuss or write about religious matters. Tenets of religion were taken for granted, unity of religion avoided disputes, and all we can glean is from clergy's complaints and visitors' comments. In general terms, especially in the seventeenth century, available sources seem to show that the educational and moral standards of the Canadian faithful were far superior to those of the French church. Even fur traders, so much feared by the clergy for their bad example, keen as these people were to adopt the liberal sexual customs of the Indians, remained practicing Catholics.

The eighteenth century witnessed the lowering of moral standards and an increasing secularism. Blasphemy became more common, fewer people possessed religious objects or books, and charitable bequests and voluntary offerings declined.[12] As the priest-to-person ratio diminished in Canada and Acadia, religious instruction dropped and the literacy rate with it. Premarital sexual liaisons increased, together with the birthrate of illegitimate children, which had been low in the previous century. This general trend, however, was not peculiar to New France and was not due to any growing anticlericalism. In fact, religious and civil authorities alike complained about the growing lack of respect for the Church and the clergy. The absence of important urban centers and the total absence of French immigration limited this negative tendency in Acadia. Conversely, Louisiana was notorious for the deep immorality and disorderly behavior of its population.

SUGGESTIONS FOR FURTHER READING

Codignola, Luca. "The Holy See and the Conversion of the Indians in French and British North America, 1486–1760," in Karen Ordahl Kupperman, ed. *America in European Consciousness, 1493–1750*. Chapel Hill, 1995, 195–242.

---

[12] Crowley, "French Regime," 50.

Crowley, Terence A. "The French Regime to 1760," in Terrence Murphy and Roberto Perin, eds. *A Concise History of Christianity in Canada*. Toronto, 1996, 1–54.

Johnston, A. J. B. *Control and Order in French Colonial Louisbourg, 1713–1758*. East Lansing, 2001.

Laberge, Alain. "L'implantation de la paroisse dans la vallée du Saint-Laurent aux XVIIe et XVIIIe siècles," in Serge Courville and Normand Séguin, eds. *La paroisse*. Sainte-Foy, 2001, 14–25.

Miquelon, Dale. *New France 1701–1744: "A Supplement to Europe."* Toronto, 1987.

O'Neill, Charles E., S.J. *Church and State in French Colonial Louisiana: Policy and Politics to 1732*. New Haven, 1966.

Pelletier, Louis. *Le clergé en Nouvelle-France: Étude démographique et répertoire biographique*. Montreal, 1993.

14

CONGREGATIONALIST HEGEMONY IN NEW ENGLAND, FROM THE 1680S TO THE 1730S

MICHAEL P. WINSHIP

The founders of New England's Congregationalism in the 1630s had an ambitious agenda. Their churches would be islands of sectarian purity, each one covenanted with God and restricted in adult membership to people testifying to conversion. Power in each church would be shared between ministers and laity; each church would police its members with strict communal discipline, and the churches would be united voluntarily, not coercively. The churches would work closely with the secular authorities, all church members, who would protect the churches' religious monopoly, morally supervise the general population through strict laws, and see that the region's youth were indoctrinated. Success in this hegemonic project would bring God's blessings on New England; failure would bring his wrath.

By the start of the 1680s, signs of God's wrath were mounting: crop failure, a devastating Indian war, the irrepressibility of Baptists and Quakers, and in 1684 the most severe punishment of all. Massachusetts' charter, which for half a century had allowed the heartland of Congregationalism to act virtually independently of the English government, was vacated in an English court. There was no barrier between Massachusetts and King Charles II, increasingly authoritarian and increasingly hostile to the Nonconformist heirs of the Puritans. The situation ominously resembled the one that had driven the Puritans to New England initially, and it grew even worse when James II, an open Catholic with an even more expansive understanding of the monarchy's powers, assumed the throne in 1685.[1]

Fifty years earlier, when threatened by the crown, Massachusetts responded by boosting its defenses until the crisis passed. But the expanding Atlantic economy had brought immigrants who had no interest in New England's religious idiosyncrasies; there was no shortage of timid

[1] See Richard R. Johnson, *Adjustment to Empire: The New England Colonies, 1675–1715* (New Brunswick, NJ, 1981), for the political narrative of the following paragraphs.

and/or realistic colonists who thought that compromise was necessary with an English government increasingly able and determined to exercise control over its colonies; and colonists with worldly ambitions were well aware that the most reliable road to wealth and power in the Atlantic world ran through London. Internal divisions meant that when the crown in 1686 sent a royal governor, Edmund Andros, who exercised dictatorial powers over all of New England, he met little political resistance.

All that Congregationalists could do against Andros was pray, but this they did with vigor. In the middle 1670s, during the devastating King Philip's War, some ministers had revived a dormant Congregational collective ritual, the covenant renewal. A church would hold long days of fasting and prayer, during which its minister warned them that they had failed miserably in living up to their covenant obligations and that their only recourse for themselves and for New England was to repent and implore God to give them the strength to carry out their duties with the necessary piety and fervor. After the church had been whipped up into an appropriate intensity of guilt and repentance, it would hold a public service and pledge to live up to its covenant obligations. The covenant renewal ceremonies were a way of rejuvenating religious fervor and also a way of reaffirming the churches' centrality to New England at a time when the region's political institutions were slipping out of local control. Covenant renewals spread widely during Andros' rule and remained a standard ceremonial practice in the eighteenth century.[2]

Andros was overthrown in 1689 after word reached Boston of the Glorious Revolution. James II had been deposed, William and Mary were the new monarchs, and England had been saved for Protestantism, liberty, and limited monarchy. Connecticut, less than half the size of Massachusetts, and tiny Rhode Island got their self-governing charters back. In 1691, Massachusetts had to accept a charter that gave it an unusually strong House of Representatives, but also a franchise based on property, not church membership, as well as an appointed royal governor and toleration for all Protestants. The Massachusetts House of Representatives salvaged as much as it could of the old theocracy by requiring that every town pay for an orthodox minister. The arrangement ensured that Congregationalism remained the de facto religious establishment, but it also meant that churches had to allow all town voters, no matter how ungodly, a say in ministerial selection. The tiny royal colony of New Hampshire devised a similar arrangement, as did Connecticut.

---

[2] Stephen Foster, *The Long Argument: English Puritanism and the Shaping of New England Culture, 1570–1700* (Chapel Hill, 1991), 223–9, 239; Harry S. Stout, *The New England Soul: Preaching and Religious Culture in Colonial New England* (New York, 1986), 176–7.

New Englanders were well aware that both their region and their religious preferences were small parts of England's fast-growing empire. The empire's endless wars against France ravaged their frontiers, and its cosmopolitan diversity penetrated their seaports. In 1722, Boston, the largest town in British North America, had – alongside its seven Congregational churches – Anglican, Baptist, and Huguenot churches and a Quaker meeting; furthermore, by the end of this period, deism and other opinions that would have gotten their proponents exiled or hanged in earlier decades circulated openly. Nonetheless, the residents of the region, having tasted the alternative with Andros, could be, and were, proud to belong to an empire of Protestantism and liberty. From ecumenical aspirations to eschatology to moral reformation, they learned to adapt to these new contours of the international Protestant struggle against the forces of the Antichrist.[3]

Yet on a Sunday in the early eighteenth century, it might have seemed that little had changed. The vast majority of the population continued to attend their Congregational churches. Attendance was not compulsory, but strict Sabbath laws ensured that there was little else to do. Many ministers continued to preach jeremiads, telling their audiences, albeit with slowly diminishing intensity, that their ancestors were paragons of piety, that God had led those ancestors across the Atlantic, protected them, and stirred them to establish the purest Christianity in the world. New Englanders were fortunate, the preachers claimed, to live in a region like ancient Israel because of its churches and because of the predominance of God's people in it, but their degeneration from ancestral standards was alarming, and they could expect God's wrath if they did not reform.[4]

The continuity of alarmist rhetoric in this period existed in part because of a continuity of alarming problems. The self-selected religious zealots who fled England in the 1630s had good reason to believe that their churches could serve both as a religious establishment and as oases of sectarian purity. Perhaps as many as 70 percent of adult immigrants by the mid-1640s had passed the stiff membership requirements. Yet even in that decade, it became obvious that society and the churches were moving in separate directions. New England was beginning a demographic boom

---

[3] Robert J. Wilson III, *The Benevolent Deity: Ebenezer Gay and the Rise of Rational Religion in New England, 1696–1787* (Philadelphia, 1984), 66; Thomas S. Kidd, *The Protestant Interest: New England after Puritanism* (New Haven, 2004); Richard F. Lovelace, *The American Pietism of Cotton Mather: Origins of American Evangelicalism* (Grand Rapids, 1979), ch. 7, 219–24.

[4] Perry Miller, *The New England Mind: From Colony to Province* (Cambridge, MA, 1953), 183–5; Stout, *New England Soul*, 172–4; Michael P. Winship, *Seers of God: Puritan Providentialism in the Restoration and Early Enlightenment* (Baltimore, 1996), 84, 141–6.

that would cause its English population to double roughly every twenty-five years. The increasingly youthful population often lacked the fervency and spiritual self-confidence to stand in front of a congregation and testify to their conversion. Failure to bring the children in not only left them outside the spiritual and moral watch of the churches to the peril of their immortal souls. It also meant that the churches and society were drifting apart, risking divine destruction for both.[5]

In the mid-seventeenth century, Congregationalists split over the problem of the children. "Large" Congregationalists (the term used at the time) argued that the baptismal covenant bond with a church never ceased. By "owning the covenant," adults could claim its benefits – moral supervision of the church and the right to baptize their own children. However, they could not enjoy full communion, which gave participation in the Lord's Supper and male voting rights, until they testified to conversion. "Strict" Congregationalists argued that members' covenants did not extend to their unconverted adult children and that neither the churches nor those children had any responsibilities to each other. In 1662, a Massachusetts synod supported the large Congregationalists. After a decade of tumultuous clashes, both sides accepted that they would have to live with each other. Revivalists of strict Congregationalism in the 1760s gave the opposing position the sneering title that it has carried ever since, the "halfway covenant." Although some churches continued to resist large Congregationalism until well into the eighteenth century, by 1690 less than a quarter of the churches in Massachusetts were practicing strict Congregationalism.[6]

But adjusting terms of membership did not in itself produce a rush to the churches, and this period was marked by a stream of innovations to attract members. Covenant renewal sometimes had the happy effect of stirring up sufficient feelings of guilt, responsibility, and urgency in adult children of the church that they would return in large numbers. Ministers who were especially gifted at hellfire and brimstone preaching sometimes had "awakenings," times when their preaching captured their listeners, especially the young adults, leading to a sharp and sudden influx of members.[7] The most extensive and dramatic awakening took

---

[5] Alison Games, *Migration and the Origins of the Atlantic World* (Cambridge, MA, 1999), 140; Foster, *Long Argument*, 180–3.
[6] John Gorham Palfrey, *History of New England during the Stuart Dynasty*, 3 vols. (Boston, 1865–70), 3: 428; Robert G. Pope, *The Half-Way Covenant: Church Membership in Puritan New England* (Princeton, 1969), passim, 8n2.
[7] Michael J. Crawford, *Seasons of Grace: Colonial New England's Revival Tradition in Its British Context* (New York, 1991), 70–8, 105–14.

place in the Connecticut River Valley from 1734 to 1735. Centered around Northampton, Massachusetts, and the preaching of its minister, Jonathan Edwards, the awakening spread, in large or small measure, to more than thirty other communities.[8]

Another way to pull the larger society into the churches was simply to jettison the hindering elements of Congregationalism. Those hindering elements could be small. Churches increasingly allowed all applicants to waive a public account of their spiritual experiences. They could now communicate in writing or often privately before the minister. Or the change could be more dramatic and fundamental. Large Congregationalists had originally argued that they were defending the true meaning of the original church covenants, not diluting it. But in the 1680s, ministers began to find even this expanded covenantalism too confining. They started to baptize children whose parents were reputable, but not church members. By 1719, it was claimed that a hundred ministers in Massachusetts would baptize the child of any parent who appeared Christian.[9]

This increasingly aggressive outreach worked. Church membership numbers stopped declining and at least in some churches returned to figures approaching the midcentury. Most families in a town would have at least one church member, whereas large numbers of children were connected to the local church through baptism. Congregational churches had successfully reestablished themselves as more or less spiritually serving their entire communities.[10]

But there was a dramatic change in the new membership numbers. Most of these members, half to three-quarters or more, did not move on to full communion. In Wrentham, Massachusetts, in 1739, an extreme example, only two people were eligible for the Lord's Supper.[11]

Why the reluctance? In part, it reflected lay assessment of the respective value of the sacraments of baptism and the Lord's Supper. Baptism did not

---

[8] George M. Marsden, *Jonathan Edwards: A Life* (New Haven, 2003), 152–69; Thomas S. Kidd, *The Great Awakening: The Roots of Evangelical Christianity in America* (New Haven, 2007), 16–21.

[9] David D. Hall, *The Faithful Shepherd: A History of the New England Ministry in the Seventeenth Century* (New York, 1972), 205; E. Brooks Holifield, *The Covenant Sealed: The Development of Puritan Sacramental Theology in Old and New England, 1570–1720* (New Haven, 1974), 182–6.

[10] Pope, *Half-Way Covenant*, ch. 8, 273; Mark A. Peterson, *The Price of Redemption: The Spiritual Economy of Puritan New England* (Stanford, 1997), 105.

[11] Pope, *Half-Way Covenant*, 234–5; Paul R. Lucas, *Valley of Discord: Church and Society along the Connecticut River, 1636–1725* (Hanover, NH, 1976), 134; David D. Hall, "Introduction," in idem, ed., *The Works of Jonathan Edwards*, vol. 12, *Ecclesiastical Writings* (New Haven, 1994), 36.

save a child, but it placed the child within the "external" covenant of God. Baptized children, ministers stressed, were closer to salvation than those who were not, and loving parents would want church membership for the sake of their children.[12] In many cases, this family level of church membership was a satisfactory match to people's level of zeal, and they had neither the time nor inclination to push further to full communion. The Lord's Supper, by contrast, was a problematic sacrament. It did not convert; it offered a chance to strengthen faith through communion with Jesus. Yet the Bible warned that unworthy participants ate and drank their own damnation. Fear of the awful consequences of inappropriately taking the Lord's Supper haunted at least some people who held back from full communion.[13]

Males were a majority of those members holding back; most full communicants were women. The ratio of women to men in a church could be 2:1 or even greater, another change from early Congregationalism. Women, ministers suggested, were less entangled with the cares of secular business than men and had to contemplate their own deaths on a regular basis during the perils of childbirth. Historians have suggested that men, once the initial zeal of settlement had passed, were more uncomfortable with the total self-abnegating submission to Christ insisted on by the ministers and less interested in the increasingly minister-dominated church environment.[14]

One trait that men and women members shared was that they tended to make their church commitments at times of major life transitions like marriage and childbirth. Momentous social events could also engage this episodic piety. Edwards' Northampton awakening kicked into gear with the deaths of two popular young people. The largest awakening before his took place in 1727, when an earthquake shook the region. There was a major increase in memberships during Andros' reign. Death and other significant reminders of vulnerability were scattershot substitutes for the sustained English cultural, political, and religious crisis that filled the first New England Congregational churches. Even in the 1630s, prescient

---

[12] Anne S. Brown and David D. Hall, "Family Strategies and Religious Practice: Baptism and the Lord's Supper in Early New England," in David D. Hall, ed., *Lived Religion in America: Toward a History of Practice* (Princeton, 1997), 41–68; Holifield, *Covenant Sealed*, 189–92.

[13] Holifield, *Covenant Sealed*, 206; David D. Hall, *Worlds of Wonder, Days of Judgment: Popular Religious Belief in Early New England* (Cambridge, MA, 1990), 157–61; James F. Cooper, Jr., *Tenacious of Their Liberties: The Congregationalists in Colonial Massachusetts* (New York, 1999), 135.

[14] Lucas, *Valley of Discord*, 139; Gerald F. Moran and Maris A. Vinovskis, *Religion, Family, and the Life Course* (Ann Arbor, 1992), 85–101; Amanda Porterfield, *Female Piety in Puritan New England: The Emergence of Religious Humanism* (New York, 1992).

ministers worried that in the absence of that crisis, American Puritans would not be able to sustain their zeal.[15]

The piety of this period may have been generally less intense than previously, an inevitable consequence of Congregationalism's routinization, but its forms were familiar. Men and women continued to take notes at sermons, keep journals, watch over their neighbors, meet for prayer and study, and faithfully practice family religion: prayer, psalm singing, scripture reading, and exhortation. They worried that family illnesses and setbacks were proofs of God's anger at them, but they also were attentive to when he answered their prayers. They engaged in strenuous self-examination to distinguish between true and false repentance, and they could worry intensely about whether or not they were among the saved. Jonathan Edwards' uncle Joseph Hawley in 1735 surrendered to an old Puritan temptation when his despair over his salvation drove him to slit his throat, ending both his life and Northampton's awakening. More conventional dying continued to be a teaching process, as friends and family anxiously studied dying persons to see how intensely they were experiencing the truths of Calvinism and how they were assessing their own prospects on the threshold of eternity. Dying people, in turn, exhorted family and friends, and their words were sometimes written down and preserved. The practice of piety had geographic variations: an old settled region had many more social and material resources than a frontier town made up of young families who were strangers to one another and too poor to afford a minister.[16]

The relaxation of strict Congregationalism also reflected the slow penetration of the wider world. Congregationalism had little appeal for most English Puritans. It created artificially high barriers to church membership, they felt; it gave insufficient power to synods; and it gave too much power to the people at the expense of the ministers. Most English Nonconformists were Presbyterians. The majority of Presbyterians would have returned to the Church of England if there had been some adjustments, great or small, to its episcopal government and ceremonies. English Presbyterians were similarly likely to show greater flexibility in their Calvinism than the Congregationalists and greater engagement with non-Calvinist Anglican divines. The much more dogmatic Scottish Presbyterians did not mix well

---

[15] Marsden, *Jonathan Edwards*, 154–5; Stout, *New England Soul*, 177–9; Pope, *Half-Way Covenant*, 209; Michael P. Winship, *Making Heretics: Militant Protestantism and Free Grace in Massachusetts, 1636–1641* (Princeton, 2002), 72–3, 76.

[16] Hall, *Worlds of Wonder*, 128–9, 199, 201–2, 267, chap. 5; Erik R. Seeman, *Pious Persuasions: Laity and Clergy in Eighteenth-Century New England* (Baltimore, 1999), chs. 1, 2; Marsden, *Jonathan Edwards*, 163–4; Stout, *New England Soul*, 175–6; Peterson, *Price of Redemption*, 7–95, 112–19; Richard Rogers, *Seven Treatises* (London, 1603), 42.

either with New England Congregationalism or with New England ethnocentricity, and most Ulster and Scots immigrants avoided the region.[17]

The first important English Presbyterian to come to Massachusetts was the pedagogue Charles Morton in 1686.[18] Morton became a Fellow of the Harvard corporation and the mildly unconventional (for Massachusetts) minister of the Charlestown church. He attracted a circle of young would-be Presbyterians, some of whom became Harvard tutors and started modernizing the curriculum, using Morton's works. They also encouraged the students to read Church of England authors, most notably John Tillotson, a reasonable, tolerant, unemotional, heavily moralistic preacher who, like most Church of England clergy, rejected Calvinist predestination for Arminian free will. Tillotson was especially attractive to Nonconformists because he attempted (albeit unsuccessfully) to modify the government and ceremonies of the Church of England in order to entice Nonconformists back into the church. Soon the students at Harvard were reading Tillotson and other Anglican preachers on their own while being taught theology from the texts of early seventeenth-century scholastic Calvinists.[19]

The combination would seem unstable, yet younger New England preachers managed the feat of emulating Tillotson's tone while still professing their ancestral Calvinism. They cultivated reasonableness, toleration, and moderation and tended to look on the customary piety of New England, with its emphasis on the anxiety-laden process of conversion, as old-fashioned, irrational, and morbid. Attraction to this new piety was part of a larger cultural shift toward "politeness," a shift in which witchcraft, supernatural signs and wonders, and religious gloom were dismissed as unreasonable, unscientific, superstitious, and not worth the attention of learned gentlemen, however much the common people and women might

---

[17] James G. Leyburn, *The Scotch-Irish: A Social History* (Chapel Hill, 1962), 236–42. For Congregationalists, "tell the church" meant tell the body of the church; for Presbyterians, it meant tell the ruling elders. For the resulting difference in practice, see the Cambridge Platform in Cotton Mather, *Magnalia Christi Americana*, 2 vols. (Hartford, 1853), 2: 222–23, and the quasi-official collective statement of English *jure divino* Presbyterianism, *Jus Divinum Regiminis Ecclesiastici* (London, 1646), 185. See also the Massachusetts Presbyterian Solomon Stoddard's expression of frustration with Congregationalism, *An Examination of the Power of the Fraternity*, appended to his *The Presence of Christ with the Ministers of the Gospel* (Boston, 1718); Dewey D. Wallace, *Puritans and Predestination: Grace in English Protestant Theology, 1525–1695* (Chapel Hill, 1982) 179–82.

[18] Dewey D. Wallace, Jr., "Morton, Charles," in *Oxford Dictionary of National Biography* (Oxford, 2004).

[19] Norman Fiering, *Moral Philosophy at Seventeenth-Century Harvard: A Discipline in Transition* (Chapel Hill, 1981), 22–42; idem, "The First American Enlightenment: Tillotson, Leverett, and Philosophical Anglicanism," *New England Quarterly* 54 (1981): 307–44.

still be attached to them. By the end of this period, a few ministers were flirting – very quietly – with Arminianism, whereas others were losing the traditional Calvinist horror of it, and yet others were growing increasingly worried that the new emphasis on reason and morality was undermining the great responsibility of the clergy to preach Christ and conversion. But it was only when the charismatic itinerant preacher George Whitefield came to the region in 1740, denouncing Tillotson as knowing no more of true Christianity than Mohammed, that incipient theological fault lines among the ministry began to come into the open.[20]

Differences about ecclesiology emerged much sooner than theological differences. In 1696, the president of Harvard College, Increase Mather, responded to the Harvard Presbyterian sympathizers by warning that the college was in danger of sliding into apostasy. That warning and other provocations prompted Presbyterians to secretly organize their own church, the Brattle Street Church, in 1699. The Brattle Street Church denied the church covenant, left it to the pastor to admit or refuse new members without requiring conversion accounts, and allowed noncommunicants to vote for the minister. Only in Massachusetts could these be considered innovations; they would have met with widespread approval among English Puritans in the 1630s. In 1700, Mather found himself quarreling in print with the Boston Presbyterians and with an older Presbyterian from Northampton, Massachusetts, Solomon Stoddard, who also argued that the Lord's Supper was not just for the saved but could bring about conversions. In the crowning indignity for conservative Congregationalism, Increase Mather, who had a wide range of political enemies, was pushed out of the Harvard presidency in 1701. The college thereafter stayed in the hands of more broad-minded Congregationalists and Presbyterian sympathizers. Harvard's accelerating drift toward ecumenical Calvinism may have helped spur the founding of Yale College in Connecticut in 1701.[21]

It was perhaps due to Presbyterian influence that by the end of this period, a few Massachusetts churches had waived the requirement of evidence of conversion for communion. Otherwise, Massachusetts Presbyterianism had limited impact. When Presbyterians did assume local pulpits, churches denied them the powers they desired. Stoddard's own Congregational

---

[20] John Corrigan, *The Prism of Piety: Catholick Congregational Clergy at the Beginning of the Enlightenment* (New York, 1991); Wilson, *Benevolent Deity*, 62–7; Winship, *Seers of God*, 80–1, passim; George Whitefield, *Three Letters* (Philadelphia, 1740), 1–11.

[21] Mather, *Magnalia*, 2: 77; Williston Walker, *The Creeds and Platforms of Congregationalism* (New York, 1893), 473–82; Samuel Kirkland Lothrop, *A History of the Church in Brattle Street* (Boston, 1851), 20–6; Richard Warch, *School of the Prophets: Yale College, 1701–1740* (New Haven, 1973), 19.

church took up his Presbyterian ideas only slowly and incompletely. The Brattle Street Church had no successors.[22]

Yet Congregationalist ministers were not immune to Presbyterianism's appeal. In Congregationalist theory, a minister acquired his spiritual authority through his church. Outside the bounds of this covenant, a minister had no special spiritual authority. The first generation of New England ministers, who hammered out that theory, enjoyed a great deal of prestige and authority, despite being, in some sense, the creations of their churches. Their stature came from a mixture of sources – previous bonds with their church members from England, formidable personal piety, sacrifices for and leadership in the Puritan cause, and their status as graduates from England's two universities.[23]

The ministers who succeeded them were young men from a provincial school with nothing special in their personal backgrounds that obviously entitled them to salaries putting them in the wealthiest 15 percent of colonists. Some ministers griped vociferously about the laity's lack of respect for them, and ministers increasingly tended to emphasize the formal importance and autonomy of their office. Their increasing willingness to baptize children outside their church, for example, was not simply an evangelical technique; it was the assertion of ministerial power alien to the first generation. Likewise, ministers increasingly emphasized the significance of ordination for creating their ministerial status over the calling they received from their church. By the eighteenth century, in a complete reversal of the earliest practices, when a new church was formed, the church gathering might be conducted in private. The ordination of the new minister by neighboring ministers was the central focus of the public ceremony, and it was the minister's induction into the fellowship of the ministry that was emphasized. Ministers were at the forefront of efforts to end the church office of ruling lay elder, an office that required them to share their power with a layman. Even so ancestor-worshipping a minister as Increase Mather's son Cotton Mather approved these trends, in spite of writing hagiographies of the first generation of ministers in his massive church history of New England, *Magnalia Christi Americana*.[24]

Cotton Mather participated in an organization probably started at the instigation of Charles Morton in 1690, called the Boston Association, which was a regular meeting – the first in a very long time – of Boston-area

---

[22] Pope, *Half-Way Covenant*, 200; Lucas, *Valley of Discord*, 134, 158, 193–5; Cooper, *Tenacious*, 173, 181–4; Peterson, *Price of Redemption*, 216.

[23] Hall, *Faithful Shepherd*, 181–2.

[24] Cotton Mather, *Ratio Disciplina Fratrum Nov-Anglorum* (Boston, 1726), 9, 25, 124; idem, *Magnalia*, 2: 239–40; Hall, *Faithful Shepherd*, 95; William T. Youngs, Jr., *God's Messengers: Religious Leadership in Colonial New England, 1700–1750* (Baltimore, 1976), 97.

ministers for shop talk. Other clerical associations soon followed. In 1705, their representatives issued a set of proposals, which they circulated among the churches for their approval. The Proposals recommended that the associations license preachers, and that a standing council of ministers and laity investigate and resolve church disputes, with the ministers having a deciding vote. The council's decisions would be binding, and churches that rejected them would be disowned by the Massachusetts communion of churches.[25]

In Connecticut, where Presbyterianism had long been a presence, the Proposals were received positively. Connecticut was something of a backwater, with around thirty thousand people in 1700, less than half of Massachusetts' population, and lacking a major commercial center like Boston. Unlike Massachusetts, it still elected its governor, and there was strong sentiment to create some form of legal oversight of the churches. In 1708, a government-ordered synod convened at Saybrook and issued the Saybrook Platform, calling for a system of oversight councils that drew heavily on the Proposals. The legislature passed it into law that same year. Different local church councils gave the Saybrook Platform more of a Presbyterian or Congregational slant in practice, depending on their own leanings, and some churches rejected it altogether. The peculiar ecclesiastical situation of Connecticut has been called "Presbygationalism."[26]

In Massachusetts, on the other hand, the Proposals clashed with longstanding Congregational tradition and escalating traditionalist concerns. One of the formative anxieties behind Congregationalism was the fear that ministers could easily be seduced into attempting to become clerical lords domineering over an ignorant population, like, it was believed, the bishops of the Church of England, and ultimately like the pope over the Catholic Church. Congregationalism was a way to curb that incipient lust for power. In seventeenth-century Massachusetts, accusations of tyranny regularly accompanied local disputes between ministers and their congregations. Increase Mather and a handful of other ministers and some of the laity reacted to the Proposals much as the first generation would have: the Proposals were a corrupt clerical scheme to drive Massachusetts Congregationalism down the very same road as the Catholic Church. In the face of this opposition, the Proposals formally came to nothing. The suspicions they stirred up, however, remained for decades, while in the absence of institutional change, the clerical associations spread and

---

[25] Walker, *Creeds*, 486–90.
[26] Evarts B. Greene and Virginia D. Harrington, *American Population before the Census of 1790* (New York, 1932), 4; Walker, *Creeds*, 500–15. Lucas, *Valley of Discord*, 189–93.

increasingly took on informally many of the tasks envisioned for them in the Proposals.[27]

Lay and ministerial critics of this new clericalism had little to offer by way of resistance except reaffirmation of the founders' 1648 Cambridge Platform of church government and the reinstitution of ruling lay elders. A few churches took up both ideas.[28] Yet this resistance treated the symptoms, not the disease. A routinized church establishment could not be transformed back into intense godly communities committed to the onerous tasks of mutual watch and protection of church purity by the invocation of old formulas.

The goals of traditionalists and would-be Presbyterians alike were complicated by the reality that many of the laity were willing to abandon their covenanted obligations, but they were reluctant to surrender any of their church liberties. In the eighteenth century, church discipline grew more difficult and less frequent. Members and aggrieved groups, instead of bowing to their churches' will, were more willing to call for church councils when they did not approve of their churches' decisions. There were more than three times the number of serious church disputes from 1721 to 1740 than from 1680 to 1720. In this contentious atmosphere, discipline proved more trouble than it was worth, and churches shied away from tackling difficult cases. In the late 1720s, a few churches started to turn disciplinary responsibility over to a small, select group of laity. Contention also increased between ministers and their congregations, mostly over salaries, which often fell far behind inflation. Ministers were not as prosperous by the end of this period as they had been at its beginning. With New England's expanding economy making more room for lawyers and doctors, a steadily smaller percentage of college graduates turned to the ministry, and those who chose it came from less socially prestigious families.[29]

Congregationalism by the end of this period was frayed both as a coherent theoretical system and as a communion of vital Christian communities. Nevertheless, almost all the churches in Massachusetts and a majority of the churches in Connecticut still retained the founding sectarian ideal of a pure inner church of visible saints.[30] Most ministers continued to stay with a single church for their entire careers. Although the links between

---

[27] Youngs, *God's Messengers*, 72–6; Cooper, *Tenacious*, 124, 131, 146; Michael P. Winship, "Freeborn (Puritan) Englishmen and Slavish Subjection: Popish Tyranny and Puritan Constitutionalism, c.1570–1606," *English Historical Review* 124 (2009): 1050–74.
[28] Cooper, *Tenacious*, 172, 193–4, 203. Youngs, *God's Messengers*, 97–102.
[29] Moran and Vinovskis, *Religion*, 193–4, 196–7; Cooper, *Tenacious*, 132.
[30] Christopher Grasso, *A Speaking Aristocracy: Transforming Public Discourse in Eighteenth-Century Connecticut* (Chapel Hill, 1999), 43n22.

politics and religion had weakened, Congregationalists dominated the governments of all the colonies except Rhode Island, and they promoted Congregationalism as much as they could within the new imperial constraints. For the Congregationalists, New England remained a land of light, its people were collectively the people of God, and the French on New England's borders were enemies not simply as imperial competitors, but as agents of the Antichrist and his tyranny.[31]

Congregationalism, in other words, as a hegemonic system was still operative and relatively cohesive. Had the region not been shortly visited by George Whitefield, with his compelling, violently divisive, pastorally irresponsible preaching style, New England would not have had its convulsive Great Awakening, and the Congregational system, as Stephen Foster has argued, perhaps would have "held together ... until it gradually lost meaningful definition in the successive cultural upheavals of the nineteenth century."[32]

In 1674, on the eve of the catastrophe of King Philip's War (1675–76), it was estimated that, thanks to the work of a handful of English missionaries and Indian converts, Plymouth colony and the islands of Martha's Vineyard and Nantucket had around 2,500 Indians with regular exposure to preaching. To the west of Boston, the missionary work of the Roxbury pastor John Eliot had led to fourteen Praying Indian towns and 1,100 persons as converts or auditors. That totaled about a third of the Indians in southern New England.[33]

King Philip's War devastated the Indians far more than the whites. Southern New England's Indian population shrank 40 to 50 percent. Most of the Indian tribes living in and around the Plymouth colony and Massachusetts were reduced to scattered bands of refugees. Fortunately for the survival of Indian Christianity, its major centers, Cape Cod and the islands, were relatively untouched by the war. A few English ministers and laymen and Indian lay preachers and schoolteachers expanded the mainland missionary work. In the late 1680s, Martha's Vineyard's Wampanoags launched a vigorous mainland campaign to extend and reinforce Indian Christianity, sending preachers and schoolteachers. In 1695, the ruling elders of the Wampanoag Martha's Vineyard church ordained the officers of a new mainland church without the participation of English missionaries.[34]

---

[31] Stout, *New England Soul*, 235–8; Moran and Vinovskis, *Religion*, 194.
[32] Foster, *Long Argument*, 290.
[33] William Kellaway, *The New England Company, 1649–1776: Missionary Society to the Indians* (London, 1961), 116.
[34] David J. Silverman, *Faith and Boundaries: Colonists, Christianity, and Community among the Wampanoag Indians of Martha's Vineyard, 1600–1871* (New York, 2005), 112, 117;

The New England Company, an English charity, continued to provide the financial foundation of Indian Christianity. It paid for Indian preachers and schoolteachers, provided books and other material support, and tried, mostly without success, to interest young white would-be preachers in learning Algonquin, which was the language of Indian Christianity in the region.[35] In 1698, a New England Company survey found that the number of Indians exposed to preaching in what had become southeastern Massachusetts had risen by almost a third since 1674, to around 3,500. By contrast, there were only about 200 Indians under the gospel left in the remnants of Eliot's Praying Indian towns, whereas church membership in Eliot's most important town of Natick had dropped to a handful of people.[36] Shortly thereafter, the church ceased. It was regathered in 1729 with a white Harvard graduate who spoke no Algonquin as pastor, and with a majority of white founding males.[37]

The New England Company's support, vital though it was, was not adequate to Indian need. Indians were widely dispersed, and their preaching was of widely variable quality. Indians living on the islands had relatively easy access to the sacraments and discipline, but Indians on the mainland did not. In 1698, there was only one mainland Indian church with ordained officers besides the expiring Natick church, and no Indians are recorded as members of neighboring English churches in the region. Literacy rates, unsurprisingly, were far lower than among the English, and there were severe shortages of schoolteachers and books in Algonquin. Only slightly more than a third of the Indians around Plymouth were literate in 1710, and perhaps more than 50 percent, in Martha's Vineyard.[38] The English, even with the best of intentions, doled out only enough of their religion to get the Indians entangled in the English spiritual economy, and not enough to allow them to rise easily or often out of their newly defined spiritual poverty.

Delores Bird Carpenter, *Early Encounters: Native Americans and Europeans in New England, from the Papers of W. Sears Nickerson* (East Lansing, 1994), 173–85; Douglas L. Winiarski, "A Question of Plain Dealing: Josiah Cotton, Native Christians, and the Quest for Security in Eighteenth-Century Plymouth County," *New England Quarterly* 77 (2004): 368–413; Mather, *Magnalia*, 2: 433.

[35] Kellaway, *New England Company*, ch. 9.
[36] Grindal Rawson and Samuel Danforth, "Account of an Indian Visitation, A.D. 1698," *Massachusetts Historical Society Collections* 1st ser., 10 (1809): 129–34. Daniel R. Mandell, *Behind the Frontier: Indians in Eighteenth-Century Eastern Massachusetts* (Lincoln, 1996), 30–41.
[37] Kellaway, *New England Company*, 238.
[38] Winiarski, "Question," 386n22; Rawson and Danforth, "Account," 132; Experience Mayhew, *Experience Mayhew's Indian Converts: A Cultural Edition*, ed. Laura Arnold Leibman (Amherst, 2008), 388; Silverman, *Faith and Boundaries*, 215–16.

Nonetheless, despite the shortage of resources, it was possible for well-situated Wampanoags in this period to pursue lives of cradle-to-grave piety in many ways indistinguishable from those of their English Congregationalist neighbors. Families, some of whom were Christians for three generations, and friends engaged in prayer, scripture reading, psalm singing, spiritual discussion, counseling, and exhortation. Edifying deaths might be written down for posterity, and one woman's apparition appeared to her father after he failed to transcribe her dying exhortations, as she had requested. Zealous Indians testified against sin in their communities, sometimes as godly Indian magistrates, and this testimony could be resented by their neighbors.[39] Some Indians, male and female, were especially admired for their praying abilities, and Indians noted when God appeared to answer their prayers. Literate Indians wrote comments and reflections in godly books that had been translated into Algonquin. Some Indians attended sermons with their Bibles to check their preachers' proof texts. Indians fortunate enough to be within a church community and wanting to apply for full communion had to give an account to the entire congregation of their conversion process, as in the earliest Massachusetts churches. It was reported that they did this with much emotion and at length. Like the English, many apparently genuine Christian men and women hesitated to offer themselves for communion out of fear that they were not worthy. Out of the 155 Indian families on Martha's Vineyard in 1720, about 110 adults were communicants at the church.[40]

The Indians' piety had its own cultural inflections. In the absence of a learned ministry, rising in church ranks was a matter of communal approbation. Indian churches chose their clergy with input from the New England Company, but they did not hesitate to ignore that input. On Martha's Vineyard, and probably elsewhere, churches celebrated days of thanksgiving by communal feasts sponsored by the most affluent Indians, whereas on days of fasting, leading laymen, not just the pastor, prayed. At least on Nantucket, when a service was over, the Indians would pass a pipe of tobacco around and say, "I thank you."[41]

---

[39] Mayhew, *Indian Converts*, 155.

[40] Mayhew, *Indian Converts*, passim, 131, 135, 141, 144, 155, 158, 163, 188, 195, 199, 212, 249, 258, 274, 287, 298, 300, 324, 384, 385; Douglas L. Winiarski, "Native American Popular Religion in New England's Old Colony, 1670–1770," *Religion and American Culture* 15 (2005): 156–7, 161–2; idem, "Question"; Ives Goddard and Kathleen J. Bragdon, *Native Writings in Massachusetts*, 2 vols. (Philadelphia, 1988), 1: 375–471; Cotton Mather, Increase Mather, and Nehemiah Walter, *A Letter about the Present State of Christianity, among the Christianized Indians of New England* (Boston, 1705), 7, 8.

[41] Kellaway, *New England Company*, 241; Mandell, *Behind the Frontier*, 108–9; Mayhew, *Indian Converts*, 135, 187; Obed Macy, *The History of Nantucket* (Boston, 1835), 268–9.

Not all Christian Indians were Congregationalists. The schoolmaster Peter Folger introduced Baptist ideas on Martha's Vineyard, was expelled from the island in 1662, and went to Nantucket. By the 1690s, there were Wampanoag Baptist churches on both islands. Wampanoag Baptists and Congregationalists disagreed among themselves about how much toleration they should show each other.[42]

As with the English, the Indians' commitment to strict doctrinal Christianity varied. Some who considered themselves Christians undoubtedly continued with healing, fortune-telling, and ritual practices not strictly compatible with their church Christianity. Others acknowledged the English deity on their own terms, like the shaman who accepted him as the most powerful god and encouraged his Christian wife in her religious practices, but who would not abandon his personal god because he had been good to him. Christianity made no inroads among the Indians of western Rhode Island and Connecticut during this period.[43]

Christianity in this period served as a means of cultural and social cohesion to replace the tribal world of New England's southeast that it had helped to shatter. Traveling Indian preachers helped to create new religious networks and new shared sets of rituals. New intertribal Indian communities coalesced around the practice of Christianity, and Christianity provided Indians with the active support of a handful of influential colonists.[44] Yet even where it was most vigorous, Christianity provided only a fragile bulwark against the staggering problems Indians faced in New England in the years after King Philip's War: poverty, debt, widespread alcoholism, internal political turmoil, and demographic collapse.

Fortunately for historians, whites had powerful ideological and financial incentives to record the Christianization of the Indians. There were no such incentives for recording the Christianization of the African slaves who started arriving in significant numbers toward the end of the seventeenth century. They never rose to more than 3 percent of the population in the eighteenth century, and they were concentrated along the seacoast and in certain farming areas. In 1708, 75 percent of Massachusetts' 550 slaves lived in the city of Boston. The thickening of African slavery across the region produced only a sprinkle of religious objections. Anglican missionaries in Rhode Island reported that many slaves requested baptism,

---

[42] Silverman, *Faith and Boundaries*, 55; Mayhew, *Indian Converts*, 145; Mather, *Magnalia*, 2: 432–3; Isaac Backus, *A History of New England with Particular Reference to the Baptists*, 2 vols. (Newton, MA, 1871), 346–7.

[43] Winiarski, "Native American," 154, 166–7; Mather, *Magnalia*, 2: 445–6; William DeLoss Love, *Samson Occom and the Christian Indians of New England* (Boston, 1899), 26–32.

[44] Silverman, *Faith and Boundaries*, 117; Mandell, *Behind the Frontier*, 48–57, 59.

but that their masters frequently would not consent. More religiously conscientious slave owners regarded their Christian duty fulfilled by treating their slaves humanely, providing them with religious instruction, and making sure they attended church on Sunday, where they often sat in galleries reserved for them in the back. At least in Boston, slaves organized their own religious meetings, where, like the English, they prayed, read sermons, sang psalms, and reviewed and censured one another's conduct. Cotton Mather admired his own Christian magnanimity in visiting those societies once every three months to pray and preach. Some slaves became full church members, but accounts of their conversions do not survive. In 1700, about 75 percent of the slaves were foreign-born, and many slaves must have picked and chosen their way around the novel forms of English Christianity. Boston town selectmen repeatedly complained about the disorderliness of black funerals. Cotton Mather complained in 1706 that "very many" slaves worshipped devils with "Devilish Rites" or maintained a "magical conversation" with them.[45]

Rhode Island at the start of this period was a semi-anarchic group of towns with a population of perhaps ten thousand around 1700. Uniquely in New England, there was complete religious liberty and no state support of any church. Some Jews lived in the colony briefly in the late seventeenth century, although next to nothing is known about them. The colony in this period started to create functional formal institutions, as did its two largest religious groups, the Baptists, who composed around a fifth of the population in 1714, and the Quakers, who composed around a quarter. People who practiced no formal religion made up a sizable amount of the rest of Rhode Island's population.[46]

Baptists were starting to add meetinghouses for worship instead of private homes, to practice better record keeping, and, sometimes, to employ a learned, salaried clergy. It was a mark of rising Baptist respectability that Increase and Cotton Mather ordained the Harvard-educated minister of the Boston Baptist church in 1718. Many Baptists disapproved of the ordination. They had theological differences among themselves, but their deepest

---

[45] Lawrence Towner, "The Sewall-Saffin Dialogue on Slavery," *William and Mary Quarterly* 3rd ser., 21 (1964): 40–52; Arthur J. Worrall, *Quakers in the Colonial Northeast* (Hanover, NH, 1980), 156–9; Raymond W. Albright, *A History of the Protestant Episcopal Church* (New York, 1964), 58; Mather, *Ratio*, 194; idem, *The Negro Christianized* (Boston, 1706), 15; William Dillon Piersen, *Black Yankees: The Development of an Afro-American Subculture in Eighteenth-Century New England* (Amherst, 1988), 6, 51, 78.

[46] Sydney V. James, *The Colonial Metamorphoses in Rhode Island: A Study of Institutions in Change*, ed. Sheila L. Skemp and Bruce C. Daniels (Hanover, NH, 2000), 109; Edwin S. Gaustad, *George Berkeley in America* (New Haven, 1979), 5.

source of conflict in the early eighteenth century was over how much charity to extend to the Congregationalists who were wrong on baptism and had whipped and exiled their predecessors. By 1740, there were twenty-seven Baptist churches in New England, attended, at a very high estimate, by perhaps ten thousand people.[47]

Quakers, or the Society of Friends, as they called themselves, were scattered along the New England coast, from Rhode Island to Maine (at the time, a part of Massachusetts). Quakers in this period were mostly inward looking and focused on building sustaining institutions. They created a pyramid of male and female business and oversight meetings, culminating in a great yearly meeting at Newport, Rhode Island, one of six in America. The American meetings looked to the London Yearly Meeting for advice and direction. Transatlantic unity was further reinforced by male and female ministers who embarked on long and short travels throughout the transatlantic Quaker community.[48]

Institutionalization came at the expense of expansion. Quakers abandoned the fiercely confrontational evangelism of the early decades in favor of nurturing their existing communities.[49] Quaker growth did not outstrip New England's general population growth, save in a few localities.[50] Quaker principles still sometimes led to clashes with neighbors. Rhode Island accommodated Quakers in their refusal to take oaths, as did New Hampshire to a limited extent. In Massachusetts, that principle kept them out of public offices and juries, except in the few towns where local sentiment would allow them to serve without swearing. Rhode Island was willing to accommodate Quaker pacifism, whereas in the other colonies, Quakers risked jail for refusing military service in wartime.[51]

Quakers and many Baptists opposed state-supported religion on principle and resisted paying the religious taxes that were mandatory outside Rhode Island. By the mid-1730s, they had gotten statute relief from most religion-related taxation, although zealous local tax collectors still

---

[47] Greene and Harrington, *American Population*, 4; James, *Colonial Metamorphoses*, 178–80; William G. McLoughlin, *New England Dissent, 1630–1833*, 2 vols. (Cambridge, MA, 1971), 1: ch. 16, 279.

[48] Jean R. Soderlund, "Women's Authority in Pennsylvania and New Jersey Quaker Meetings, 1680–1760," *William and Mary Quarterly* 3rd ser., 44 (1987): 722–49; J. William Frost, *The Quaker Family in Colonial America* (New York, 1973), 4–5, ch. 3; Worrall, *Quakers*, ch. 4; Rebecca Larson, *Daughters of Light: Quaker Women Preaching and Prophesying in the Colonies and Abroad, 1700–1775* (New York, 1999).

[49] Carla Gardina Pestana, "The Quaker Executions as Myth and History," *Journal of American History* 80 (1993): 441–69.

[50] Worrall, *Quakers*, 71–3.

[51] Ibid., chs. 6, 8.

sometimes harassed them. Their relief came about, in part, because of the effectiveness of their lobbies in London and, in part, because they were joined in their lobbying by a fast-growing religious group new to the region with a very different perspective on state support of religion: the Church of England.[52]

Unlike Quakers and Baptists, Church of England partisans were keen to challenge Congregational hegemony. Either their church or none in New England, they felt, should be state supported, and throughout this period they eagerly anticipated the first alternative. Their church was the only legal church in England. Although the penalties of the laws forbidding other English Protestant churches were suspended in 1689, the laws themselves were not repealed. Baptists, Congregationalists, Presbyterians, and Quakers remained second-class citizens. Many members of the Church of England viewed even that limited toleration as a threat to the moral and spiritual health of the realm.[53]

Because the Church of England and the monarchy were still intimately bound together, establishing crown control over the colonies and establishing the Church of England were, for many colonial royal officials, both part of the same imperial policy. The minister of the first permanent Anglican church in the region, King's Chapel in Boston, founded in 1686, came over on a British warship. The second church, Trinity, in Newport, Rhode Island, was created in 1698 at the clamoring of local Anglican merchants and with the encouragement of royal officials as part of an unsuccessful effort to place the colony's government under royal control.[54] After 1701, almost all the Anglican clergy in New England, except self-supporting King's Chapel, had their salaries paid from England by the Society for the Propagation of the Gospel in Foreign Parts (SPG), a well-funded, private charity that worked closely with the government. The SPG's mission was to send Church of England clergymen to those parts of the British Empire lacking an orthodox minister and public religion; and in the eyes of many of the SPG's members, and to the resentment of many New Englanders, New England Congregational towns lacked both.[55]

New England held a special attraction for the partisans of the imperial Church of England. Creating an Anglican beachhead in this Puritan and

---

[52] McLoughlin, *New England Dissent*, 1: chs. 2–4.
[53] George Every, *The High Church Party, 1688–1718* (London, 1956).
[54] Henry Wilder Foote, *Annals of King's Chapel from the Puritan Age of New England to the Present Day*, 2 vols. (Boston, 1881), 1: chs. 2, 3; James B. Bell, *The Imperial Origins of the King's Church in Early America, 1607–1783* (Basingstoke, 2004), 34; James, *Colonial Metamorphoses*, 174.
[55] Foote, *Annals*, 1: 252–3; Bell, *Imperial Origins*, ch. 7.

excessively democratic region represented unfinished intertwined secular and religious business left over from the Puritan-led rebellion that led to the beheading of King Charles I in 1649. The critical component for the Anglican suppression of schism and democracy would be an American bishop. English politicians looked on the plan for an American bishop as creating more political problems than it was worth, and it never got off the ground. But that failure appears more inevitable in historical hindsight than it did at the time to extremely nervous Congregationalists.[56]

The Church of England had a natural constituency in royal officials and in immigrants who came to New England because of the growing transatlantic economy. It could appeal to others for a variety of reasons: its sonorous ceremonies, its apparent stability, the easy accessibility of the sacraments and absence of discipline, the cachet of being connected with England's state church, and the prospect of going off the religious tax rolls and getting religion almost for free – Anglican congregations, with a few exceptions, tended to be poor and could not afford to support a minister on their own.[57]

Yet the Church of England also faced formidable obstacles. In New England, it was still widely regarded as little better than the Catholic Church, while memories of its persecution were still fresh. The ancient battle between Anglicans and Puritans picked up again, with cries of "papist" against Anglican missionaries, vandalizing of Anglican churches, and ferocious printed debates. The Church of England initially made little headway. Connecticut got its first parish only in 1722. By that year, Anglicans in Massachusetts had added churches only at Braintree, Marblehead, and Newbury, with the Newbury church being the product of an out-of-control Congregational feud.[58]

The Congregational world was shattered in 1722 by the "Yale Apostasy." Yale's rector Timothy Cutler and several current and ex-tutors announced they were traveling to England to become Anglican priests, having concluded that they could not be real ministers without episcopal ordination. One of the new Anglicans, Samuel Johnson, proved an extremely effective

---

[56] Foote, *Annals*, 1: 250; Bruce T. McCully, "Governor Francis Nicholson, Patron 'Par Excellence' of Religion and Learning in Colonial America," *William and Mary Quarterly* 3rd ser., 39 (1982): 310; Stephen Taylor, "Whigs, Bishops and America: The Politics of Church Reform in Mid-Eighteenth-Century England," *Historical Journal* 36 (1993): 331–56.

[57] Bruce E. Steiner, "New England Anglicanism: A Genteel Faith?" *William and Mary Quarterly* 3rd ser., 27 (1970): 122–35.

[58] Foote, *Annals*, 1: 109, 253–7, 271–310; Peterson, *Price of Redemption*, 181–4; James B. Bell, *A War of Religion: Dissenters, Anglicans, and the American Revolution* (Basingstoke, 2008), chs. 1, 3.

missionary in Connecticut, which had nine Anglican parishes by 1738, whereas the much larger Massachusetts only had six. This was not much when put against New England's 450 Congregational clergymen and their usually much larger churches, yet it was the start of an acceleration in Anglican growth that kept the ancient Puritan alarm over bishops boiling until it helped kick off the imperial crisis of the 1760s.[59]

SUGGESTIONS FOR FURTHER READING

Cooper, James F., Jr. *Tenacious of Their Liberties: The Congregationalists in Colonial Massachusetts.* New York, 1999.

Foote, Henry Wilder. *Annals of King's Chapel from the Puritan Age of New England to the Present Day.* 2 vols. Boston, 1881.

Lovelace, Richard F. *The American Pietism of Cotton Mather: Origins of American Evangelicalism.* Grand Rapids, 1979.

McLoughlin, William G. *New England Dissent, 1630–1833.* 2 vols. Cambridge, MA, 1971.

Silverman, David J. *Faith and Boundaries: Colonists, Christianity, and Community among the Wampanoag Indians of Martha's Vineyard, 1600–1871.* New York, 2005.

Stout, Harry S. *The New England Soul: Preaching and Religious Culture in Colonial New England.* New York, 1986.

Worrall, Arthur J. *Quakers in the Colonial Northeast.* Hanover, NH, 1980.

---

[59] Warch, *School*, ch. 4; Raymond W. Albright, *History of the Protestant Episcopal Church* (New York, 1964), 51; E. Edwards Beardsley, *The History of the Episcopal Church in Connecticut, from the First Settlement to the Death of Bishop Seabury* (New York, 1874), 110; Stout, *New England Soul*, 186; Bell, *War of Religion*, 211–17.

15

THE MIDDLE COLONIES, 1680–1730

THOMAS D. HAMM

More than a generation ago Carl Bridenbaugh, summing up the religious experience of the colonists on the Hudson and the Delaware, wrote, "In a region of so many nationalities – Dutch, Swedes, Finns, French, Germans, English – toleration was vital."[1] In contrast to the colonies to the north and south, which were largely ethnically homogeneous before 1730, with powerful established churches, Congregationalism in New England and Anglicanism in the South, the Middle Colonies – for the purposes of this essay New York, New Jersey, Pennsylvania, and Delaware – presented a diverse array of faiths and peoples. All of the following found homes there: Dutch and German Reformed; French Huguenots; Swedish and German Lutherans; Scottish, Irish, and English Presbyterians; Welsh and English Baptists; English Congregationalists; and German, English, and Welsh Quakers, not to mention a variety of other sects. Roman Catholics also achieved grudging toleration there, and by 1730 most of North America's tiny Jewish population lived in New York. Living near them, of course, were Native Americans whose religious relationship with Europeans was often uneasy. And arriving involuntarily were growing numbers of enslaved Africans, who would be a source of both missionary labor and uneasy conscience for some of their European neighbors.

This essay presents an overview of the diversity of the religious experience of the inhabitants of the Middle Colonies between 1680 and 1730, largely in terms of denominations broadly defined. It examines not only "high" matters of theology and leadership, but also elements of faith closer to the experience of the masses of worshippers. In a world in which political leadership was firmly in male hands, it looks at how these religious groups incorporated women into their communities. It also explores how these groups envisioned their relationships with the larger world around

---

[1] Carl Bridenbaugh, *Mitre and Sceptre: Transatlantic Faiths, Ideas, Personalities, and Politics, 1689–1775* (New York, 1962), 116.

them – fellow believers in Europe, Native Americans, Africans, and those of different faiths – particularly on the issue of the rights of the state over religion and individual conscience.

Such an understanding is vital because in many ways the experience of the Middle Colonies between 1680 and 1730 presaged what would become the United States. Religious disestablishment, pluralism, and a complicated intertwining of ethnicity and faith would be the rule in the new nation. Moreover, the roots of the identities of many religious groups were largely laid in the Middle Colonies in this half century.

DUTCH REFORMED

The first permanent European settlement in the Middle Colonies was New Netherland. By 1664, when an English fleet took possession of the colony and changed its name to New York, Dutch settlers had settled along the Hudson River from New York City to Albany. The Dutch Reformed Church was the first organized religious body in the Middle Colonies.[2]

The Dutch Reformed faith was Calvinist, with doctrine defined by a series of international synods of divines, especially the Synod of Dort in 1618. It emphasized the absolute sovereignty of God and the utter helplessness of humans to bring about their own salvation. An omnipotent God, from the foundations of time, had willed that only a small proportion of humanity would be saved. Church members were those who could give evidence that they were among this elect. The Dutch Reformed Church emphasized theological education and learning; a university degree was expected for ordination as a minister. The church structure was hierarchical, with ultimate authority possessed by the classis, or synod, in the Netherlands.[3]

By 1680, the Dutch Reformed faced multiple challenges. One was adjustment to an alien government and a growing non-Dutch population; another was maintaining theological uniformity. By the late seventeenth century, Dutch Calvinists, like other continental Protestants, were becoming divided over the growing pietist movement within their churches. Finally, given the realities of geography, the Dutch Reformed tried to establish new structures of ecclesiastical authority that would allow them to resolve problems without waiting for a decision from Amsterdam. By

---

[2] Russell Shorto, *The Island at the Center of the World: The Epic Story of Dutch Manhattan and the Forgotten Colony That Shaped America* (New York, 2004).

[3] See, generally, Philip Benedict, *Christ's Churches Purely Reformed: A Social History of Calvinism* (New Haven, 2002).

1730, Dutch Reformed churches had resolved some of these problems but in the process had created new ones.

The English conquest of New York divided its Dutch inhabitants. Many, especially the well-to-do whose fortunes were based on trade, saw advantages in becoming part of the British Empire. In many cases they intermarried with English and Scottish immigrants. Others of less wealth and political influence held more stubbornly to a distinctive Dutch culture, which included a fierce loyalty to the Dutch Reformed faith. Between 1685 and 1688, the policies of the Roman Catholic king, James II, inflamed fears that Protestantism in the colony was in danger. The Dutch, with long memories of their struggle for freedom against Catholic oppression, particularly resonated to them. Thus when word reached the colony early in 1689 that James II had been overthrown by William and Mary, James' Dutch son-in-law and daughter, the stricter Dutch Reformed, led by merchant Jacob Leisler, proclaimed the new government. Their actions divided New York. When a new governor arrived in March 1691, Leisler initially refused to yield control. This became the basis of his conviction for treason and execution later that year.[4]

This political uprising had religious consequences. Supporters of Leisler boycotted services at churches whose pastors, or dominies, had opposed him, and in some cases they joined other denominations. Randall Balmer concludes that although population pressures would have encouraged migration from the island of Manhattan and Long Island regardless of these developments, the settlers who established a significant Dutch Reformed presence in New Jersey after 1690 were disproportionately Leislerians. They embraced a pietist faith that would, after 1730, identify with the evangelical currents that historians label the Great Awakening.[5]

The number of Dutch Reformed churches in New York and New Jersey grew steadily between 1680 and 1730. In 1680, fifteen Dutch Reformed congregations existed in North America – one in Delaware, one in New Jersey, and the rest in New York, mostly around New York City but with outposts at Albany, Schenectady, and Kingston. By 1730, this number had tripled, to forty-three. Twenty-nine new congregations had formed, fifteen in New York and fourteen in New Jersey.[6]

In the 1690s, Leisler and anti-Leisler factionalism helped determine attitudes toward growing English cultural domination of New York. By

---

[4] Randall Balmer, *A Perfect Babel of Confusion: Dutch Religion and English Culture in the Middle Colonies* (New York, 1989), 3–45; Michael Kammen, *Colonial New York: A History* (New York, 1975), 119–26.
[5] Balmer, *Perfect Babel*, 55–69.
[6] Ibid., 157–8; Kammen, *Colonial New York*, 149.

1700, the Dutch were a minority in the colony. At first, conservative clerics like Henricus Selyns in New York City tried to work with the English governors. But their achievements were limited. In 1695 the Dutch Reformed church in New York won a charter of incorporation, solidifying its legal status, but two years earlier the Anglican Church had been legally established in New York City and three adjacent counties. Dutch Reformed citizens found themselves taxed for the support of Anglicans. Several governors worked tirelessly to advance the Church of England at the expense of the Dutch Reformed, requiring licenses of schoolmasters, trying to impose Anglican priests on Dutch Reformed congregations, and interfering in internal disputes over calling of ministers. By 1710, Dutch Reformed who were previously well inclined toward English authority had become skeptical, and thus they turned their energies toward preserving a distinctive faith that emphasized ministers trained in the Netherlands, educating their children in the Dutch language, and upholding the authority of the classis in Amsterdam.[7]

The Dutch Reformed churches also faced problems of ecclesiastical government that usually centered on the call of ministers. Traditionally, ministerial authority came through appointment by the Classis of Amsterdam. Because few Dutch ministers were willing to go to the New World, there was always a shortage, and it became customary for ministers to serve multiple congregations in America. For example, in 1700 one pastor served all five churches in Kings County. Alternative sources of authority existed, however. Governors tried to appoint clergy, and increasingly, individual congregations asserted the right to call ministers. Other ministers struggled to preserve some standards by using colonial associations to discipline and even remove incompetent, heretical, or immoral colleagues. A good example of the confusion this could cause was in Kings County, where the Dutch Reformed churches became embroiled in bitter controversy between 1703 and 1714 between two ministers, one called by one of the congregations but asserting pastoral authority over all, and the other appointed by the classis.[8]

Most divisive for the Dutch Reformed, however, would be doctrinal and theological controversy. The driving force was the pietist movement. Like many religious movements, it began as a protest against the perceived declining piety and moral laxity of the churches. It had a powerful impact on many Dutch Reformed churches. Randall Balmer provides a succinct overview of the differences that distinguished pietists from their more

---

[7] Kammen, *Colonial New York*, 136–8; Balmer, *Perfect Babel*, 89–90.
[8] Balmer, *Perfect Babel*, 73–8, 93–4.

traditional, orthodox counterparts. Pietists tended to be socially marginal, whereas the orthodox were established and elite. Pietism was ecstatic and informal, whereas orthodox faith was restrained. Orthodox membership was based on baptism and saw the sacraments as a means of grace and central to religious life. Pietists based membership on proof of conversion and reserved the sacraments for the saved. The orthodox looked to tradition and Old World authority, whereas pietists favored autonomous congregations and immediate religious experience. And whereas the orthodox saw their clergy as an educated, professional elite, pietists emphasized proof of salvation and an individual call to preach.[9]

These differences came to a head in controversy over the ministry of Theodorus Jacobus Frelinghuysen, the most influential Dutch Reformed cleric in eighteenth-century America. Born in Westphalia in 1692, Frelinghuysen was educated at the University of Lingen, "a hotbed of pietism." In 1719, he accepted a call to pastor the churches in New Jersey's Raritan Valley. With a commission from the Classis of Amsterdam, Frelinghuysen arrived in America early in 1720.[10]

From the moment of his arrival, Frelinghuysen distinguished himself with his bluntness in judging the spiritual states of others. Invited to the home of the senior minister in New York City, Frelinghuysen condemned him for owning a mirror and told another colleague that he lacked true piety. Once installed in New Jersey, Frelinghuysen provoked more controversy. He announced that the churches there required stricter ecclesiastical discipline, and he limited communion to those he judged to show signs of regeneration. He culminated his campaign by excommunicating some of his loudest critics. Opponents responded to Frelinghuysen's pietist campaign by bringing in other Dutch Reformed ministers and the Classis of Amsterdam. By 1730, the Dutch Reformed churches were badly divided, not only theologically, but also by social class. Surviving evidence indicates that Frelinghuysen got his most enthusiastic support from those who were, in his own words, "poor and of little account in the world." His critics tended to be well-to-do. In 1730, the classis tried to settle the controversy by judging that both sides had been uncharitable and by lifting the excommunications. Frelinghuysen remained unbowed, however, and after 1730 his supporters would forward the revival movement that historians label the Great Awakening.[11]

---

[9] *Ibid.*, 107.

[10] *Ibid.*, 108–9. For the standard account of Frelinghuysen, see James Tanis, *Dutch Calvinistic Piety in the Middle Colonies: A Study in the Life and Theology of Theodorus Jacobus Frelinghuysen* (The Hague, 1967).

[11] Balmer, *Perfect Babel*, 111–16.

JEWS

The Jewish presence in colonial America was tiny, far less than 1 percent of the population. Between 1680 and 1730, that presence was confined almost entirely to New York.[12]

The first Jews in what would become the United States arrived in New Amsterdam in 1654, refugees from Brazil. The Dutch government, mindful of a powerful Jewish community at home, ordered them to be allowed to worship unmolested. When the English seized the colony in 1664, they continued this policy. By 1680, New York Jews had a burying ground and possessed Torah scrolls that they used for private worship. The Torah was vital. "The presence of a Torah scroll served as a defining symbol of Jewish communal life and culture, of Jewish law and lore."[13]

A landmark event for New York City's Jews came in 1703 or 1704, when they opened their first synagogue, Kahal Kadosh Shearith Israel, or "Holy Congregation Remnant of Israel." (Some historians believe that this may have taken place as early as 1695, but records date from the early eighteenth century.) The Portuguese ancestry of the members was reflected in prayers and records kept in Portuguese. The Jews of Shearith Israel saw ritual as vital to their lives as Jews, and they eschewed innovation: they saw their duty as "to imitate our forefathers." Authority lay in the laity – there was no resident rabbi or *haham*. The president of the congregation led prayers and occasionally preached, as did an occasional visiting rabbi. Power lay in the hands of a small group of well-to-do men. Men and women worshipped separately.[14]

By 1730, New York's Jews were confident enough to build their own synagogue, the first in the mainland British colonies. Their numbers remained tiny, perhaps three hundred by 1750. They were also on the verge of establishing a presence in Philadelphia, where, despite Quaker toleration, few Jews had settled. Nevertheless, the Jews of New York and Philadelphia had become the first non-Christian European presence in the colonies.[15]

ANGLICANS

Anglicans entered the Middle Colonies with a position of privilege. They were members of the church "established by law" in England, and they could look for support from royal governors. On the other hand, they faced

---

[12] Jonathan D. Sarna, *American Judaism: A History* (New Haven, 2004), 375.
[13] Ibid., 1–11.
[14] Ibid., 12–15.
[15] Ibid., 17–19.

engrained hostility from dissenters who associated them with repression. Nevertheless, the power and influence of Anglicans in the Middle Colonies, especially in New York, grew between 1680 and 1730.

In 1680, Anglicanism was limited to New York, and there it was relatively weak. As late as 1695, one Anglican reported that of 3,525 families in the province, only 90 were Anglicans. In 1693, however, Governor Benjamin Fletcher procured an act for taxes to support "a good and sufficient Protestant minister" in the counties of New York, Queens, Richmond, and Westchester. Theoretically, the support could go to any Protestant minister, and Presbyterians and Dutch Reformed attempted to secure the tax funds for their choices. Anglican governors, however, aided by sympathetic judges, systematically interpreted the law to favor the Church of England, and it amounted to a de facto Anglican establishment.[16]

Anglicans lacked even this legal endorsement in the other Middle Colonies, and their development was initially slow. In 1700, they had only two churches in the Delaware Valley. After 1700, in all four colonies, Anglicanism grew steadily, partly because of Anglican immigration, partly through the work of the Society for the Propagation of the Gospel in Foreign Parts (SPG).[17]

The SPG was founded in 1701 to proselytize in the colonies. Significantly, its focus was not on "heathen" Indians or Africans, but on colonists outside the Church of England. Its activities in areas already settled with churches caused considerable tension with other denominations, but its accomplishments were real. By 1727, it had established thirteen churches in New Jersey, Delaware, and Pennsylvania, and Anglicanism had grown at a similar rate in New York. Moreover, Anglicanism held an increasing attraction for colonial elites. By 1730, Christ Church in Philadelphia and Trinity Church in New York City were strongholds of status, growing through the accession of converts from Quakers, Presbyterians, and Dutch Reformed.[18]

Still, Anglicans faced problems. One, common to other denominations, was lack of clergy. Anglican ordination could be only at the hands of a bishop, and because there were none in North America before 1784, this meant either that candidates must travel to or be sent over from Great

---

[16] William Warren Sweet, *Religion in Colonial America* (New York, 1942), 209; Bridenbaugh, *Mitre and Sceptre*, 117–21.

[17] Jon Butler, *Power, Authority, and the Origins of American Denominational Order: The English Churches in the Delaware Valley, 1680–1730* (Philadelphia, 1978), 65. Hereafter *Power, Authority*.

[18] *Ibid.*, 69; Brendan McConville, *Those Daring Disturbers of the Public Peace: The Struggle for Property and Power in Early New Jersey* (Philadelphia, 2003), 71–3; David Hein and Gardiner H. Shattuck, Jr., *The Episcopalians* (Westport, 2004), 18.

Britain. Pulpits often went unfilled. Competition from richer Anglican parishes in Maryland and Virginia added to the clerical shortage. Parishioners, who perceived the wealthy SPG as the logical source of support, were often unwilling to pay salaries.[19]

A second problem was related: Anglicanism was by definition episcopal. Anglican priests were responsible to their bishops, but there was no American bishop. The colonies were under the jurisdiction of the bishop of London. When problems arose involving unsuitable clergy, internal congregational disputes, or empty pulpits, Anglicans could only appeal to the distant SPG or the bishop in London. And their favored solution, an American bishop, inevitably brought ferocious criticism from dissenters. Anglicans, then, were caught up in the contradictions of being an episcopal church without the episcopacy that was essential for its success.[20]

HUGUENOTS

Huguenots were French Calvinists who came to Boston, South Carolina, and New York in significant numbers in the late seventeenth century, particularly after King Louis XIV ended toleration of Protestantism in France in 1685. In New York, Huguenots established significant communities on Staten Island, in New York City, and in New Rochelle. Yet, because of internal battles and outmarriage, they had nearly disappeared as a separate group by the time of the American Revolution. These trends were already apparent by 1730.

A few French Protestants had settled in New York before 1685. Theologically, they were similar to the Dutch Reformed. English policy was to welcome French Protestant refugees, and those who arrived in New York flourished. By 1700, they included some of the city's wealthiest merchants. At New Rochelle and on Staten Island, they formed prosperous farming communities that tried to maintain a distinctive French cultural and religious life.[21]

By 1710, however, Huguenot life in New York was clearly under siege. Huguenots divided along class lines during the Leisler controversy between 1689 and 1691. In 1708, the church at New Rochelle voted narrowly to become Anglican, although a dissenting group split off in the 1720s and

---

[19] Butler, *Power, Authority*, 69–72.
[20] *Ibid.*, 70–5.
[21] Jon Butler, *The Huguenots in America: A Refugee People in a New World Society* (Cambridge, MA, 1983), 146–54. For a detailed examination of New World Huguenot culture, see Neil Kamil, *Fortress of the Soul: Violence, Metaphysics, and Material Life in the Huguenots' New World, 1517–1751* (Baltimore, 2005), 711–923.

reinstituted French worship. The church on Staten Island survived until 1734, but it regularly opened its pulpit to Anglican clergy and catechists. Marriage to Dutch and English spouses accelerated after 1700, and many of those who married thus joined Dutch Reformed or Anglican congregations. Internal strife also divided the New York City congregation. Many members were scandalized in 1713 when its minister, Louis Rou, married a fourteen-year-old girl, and they attempted to force him out. Rou responded with an appeal to the governor, who ordered Rou's reinstatement. Many opponents left in disgust.[22] By 1730 Huguenots had not vanished from the Middle Colonies, but they were clearly on the decline.[23]

QUAKERS

The Quakers, or Society of Friends, rose in England in the 1640s and 1650s. At the heart of their theology was continuing revelation, the conviction that God, through the Holy Spirit, still spoke to humans as in biblical times. Closely connected was belief in the Inward Light, the idea that all people have within them a certain portion of the Light of Christ that, if heeded, would lead them to salvation. Friends rejected an ordained, pastoral clergy. Although they recognized that some Friends, whom they called "Public Friends," had a gift for preaching or ministry, they saw this as a gift of God with no human validation or education necessary. Quaker worship was starkly unritualistic. Friends gathered and waited in silence, confident that if God had a message for the meeting, then he would inspire someone to speak. Particularly radical was the Quaker conviction that women had as much right to preach and speak in worship as men did. Friends also set themselves apart through certain practices that they saw as simple obedience to scripture: refusal to use courtesy titles like "your excellency" or "milady," refusal to bow before social superiors, refusal to take oaths, and, increasingly, refusal to bear arms, even for self-defense.[24]

In their first decades, Quakers were aggressive proselytizers. Quaker missionaries traveled not only over the British Isles, but also to continental Europe and even the Ottoman Empire. After 1660, however, this edgy zeal declined. Faced with persecution, Friends increasingly turned inward, focused on preserving their message and members.[25]

---

[22] Butler, *The Huguenots*, 186–94.
[23] *Ibid.*, 199.
[24] For early Quakerism, see Hugh Barbour, *The Quakers in Puritan England* (New Haven, 1964); and Rosemary Moore, *The Light in Their Consciences: The Early Quakers in Britain* (University Park, PA, 2000).
[25] Hugh Barbour and J. William Frost, *The Quakers* (Westport, 1988), 61–72.

The first Friends came to the Middle Colonies in 1657 when English Friends arrived on Long Island. Friends won a foothold there among English colonists in Flushing and adjacent towns. In 1695 they formed a yearly meeting. Quakers found a new territory in 1675, when a syndicate of English and Scottish Friends purchased the rights to what would become known as New Jersey. By 1680, Quakers had settlements on the Delaware at Salem and Burlington and on the Atlantic coast at Shrewsbury.[26]

The Delaware Valley became the great center of American Quakerism because of Pennsylvania. It was the project of William Penn (1644–1718). The son of an admiral, Penn emerged as one of the sect's leading preachers and writers. King Charles II owed considerable money to the Penn family, and William suggested that repayment take the form of a grant of land in the New World.[27]

Penn saw Pennsylvania as an opportunity to realize Quaker ideals of enlightened but godly government, a "holy experiment." Most importantly, Penn also guaranteed broad religious liberty to "all persons living in this province who confess and acknowledge the one almighty and eternal God to be the creator, upholder, and ruler of the world." To what extent Penn and the Quakers who joined him in Pennsylvania before 1690 envisioned the colony as welcoming people of all faiths is unclear. "The laws made few allowances for those who did not believe in the distinctive customs of Friends. The outsiders who came in were expected to conform to Quaker usages, possibly because the settlers saw their habits as not peculiar to Friends but important for all Christians." On the other hand, the Quaker peculiarities, such as referring to the months of the years by numbers rather than by their "heathen" names, and marriage without ordained ministers, were hardly oppressive. Laws that punished gambling, fornication, adultery, drunkenness, and profanity were typical of all of the colonies. Most controversial were the lack of provision for a provincial militia and the use of affirmations rather than oaths in court.[28]

Penn himself sailed to America in 1682, and in the 1680s thousands of Friends emigrated to the Delaware Valley from England, Wales, and Scotland. Pennsylvania was the most popular destination, but many found homes on the east bank of the Delaware in what was called West Jersey, and others settled in the Three Lower Counties, what is now Delaware. They

---

[26] *Ibid.*, 73–4; Hugh Barbour et al., *Quaker Crosscurrents: Three Hundred Years of Friends in the New York Yearly Meetings* (Syracuse, 1995), 7–15.

[27] Edwin B. Bronner, *William Penn's "Holy Experiment": The Founding of Pennsylvania, 1681–1701* (New York, 1962), 6–30.

[28] *Ibid.*, 36; J. William Frost, *A Perfect Freedom: Religious Liberty in Pennsylvania* (New York, 1990), 10–17; Sally Schwartz, *"A Mixed Multitude": The Struggle for Toleration in Colonial Pennsylvania* (New York, 1987), 12–80; Barbour and Frost, *The Quakers*, 76.

reproduced the ecclesiastical order that George Fox and other "weighty" Friends had established in England in the 1650s and 1660s.[29]

Friends referred to their individual congregations as meetings; like most dissenters at the time, they reserved "church" for the buildings of the established church. The basic business unit for Friends was the monthly meeting, which consisted of one or more congregations. It had the authority to receive and disown, or expel, members; collect money for the use of the meeting; and approve marriages. Two or more monthly meetings made up a quarterly meeting. Quarterly meetings dealt with tasks that transcended monthly meeting boundaries. The ultimate authority for Friends was the yearly meeting, which made rules for discipline and acted as a final authority in membership disputes. Friends in the Delaware Valley held their first yearly meeting in Burlington, New Jersey, in 1682. Although the yearly meeting alternated between Burlington and Philadelphia, it soon became known as the Philadelphia Yearly Meeting. By 1685, it was no longer subordinate to the yearly meeting held in London, although it remained tightly bound to it through correspondence and the visits of both British and American ministers across the Atlantic.[30]

Although Friends did not have an ordained clergy, it is clear that they looked for leadership to a relatively small group of Public Friends who were recognized as ministers. Friends also followed the English model in establishing separate meetings for ministers, charged with oversight of Public Friends, at the local, quarterly, and yearly meeting levels. Admission to such meetings was formal acknowledgment of ministerial standing, the only one that Friends provided.[31]

Although Friends prided themselves on harmony and good order, in the 1690s the most serious schism to affect New World Quakerism before 1827 took place in Philadelphia. The precipitant was the ministry of George Keith, a Scot reared as a Presbyterian, who was one of a handful of Friends with a classical education. Scottish Friends were few, but in Keith and Robert Barclay they produced two of the most sophisticated theological thinkers of the second generation of Quaker leaders. Keith came to New Jersey in 1685 with an appointment as the colony's surveyor-general.[32]

In 1688, Keith moved to Philadelphia. He quickly emerged as one of the new yearly meeting's leading ministers. By the time he arrived in

---

[29] Barbour and Frost, *The Quakers*, 74–7; Butler, *Power, Authority*, 27–9. See also Barry Levy, *Quakers and the American Family: British Settlement in the Delaware Valley* (New York, 1988).
[30] Barbour and Frost, *The Quakers*, 76–9.
[31] Butler, *Power, Authority*, 29.
[32] Ned C. Landsman, *Scotland and Its First American Colony, 1683–1765* (Princeton, 1985), 170–4.

Philadelphia, however, Keith found himself increasingly troubled by what he perceived as the unorthodox drift of the Quaker ministry. He mourned what he saw as widespread ignorance of the Bible among many Friends and condemned what he saw as a tendency to minimize the centrality of the historical Christ. The implication was that the Philadelphia Friends were not placing sufficient emphasis on salvation through the blood of Christ shed on the cross. Early in 1690, Keith prepared and circulated among leading Friends a manuscript, titled "Gospel Order Improved." He proposed drawing up a creed to which all Public Friends would be required to subscribe. New members would be required to subscribe as well. They would also demonstrate their fitness for membership by giving "a more imposing demonstration of their orthodoxy by describing their experiences with God," a narration of "their convincement and what God hath wrought in them."[33]

Faced with such a critique of their spiritual state, other leading Philadelphia Friends hesitated to respond to Keith, delaying a formal discussion of his proposal until the autumn 1691 yearly meeting. By that time, however, public controversy had erupted. The issue was an ambivalent Quaker Christology. "Keith asserted that the Bible required a belief in the bodily resurrection of Christ, the bodily ascension, and a bodily sitting at the right hand of God the Father." Many Friends saw Keith's emphasis on the physicality of Christ as derogating the centrality of the Inward Light.[34]

The stage was now set for an open rupture. It came in the spring of 1692, when Keith's supporters in Philadelphia began to meet for worship separately from their opponents. Keith added fuel to the flames by publishing a pamphlet justifying his conduct. He claimed that leading Friends were guilty of "most Gross and Unchristian Errors against the Fundamental Doctrines of the Christian Faith, ... that render them altogether unqualified for the Ministry, and to uphold or tolerate them is to bring Reproach to Truth and our holy Profession." "Keith's behavior tore at the heart of Quaker order."[35]

Keith's course cost him most of the sympathy he had previously had among ministers in the yearly meeting, and they counterattacked ferociously. In June, the yearly meeting of ministers issued a statement in which they concluded, "That he trampled the judgment of the Meeting under His Feet as Dirt." They disowned him as a member and as a minister and ordered that he cease to preach until he was reconciled with the Friends. When the whole yearly meeting gathered in September, it affirmed

---

[33] Butler, *Power, Authority*, 32–3.
[34] J. William Frost, ed., *The Keithian Controversy in Early Pennsylvania* (Norwood, PA, 1980), x.
[35] *Ibid.*, xiii–xiv; Butler, *Power, Authority*, 36; Frost, *Keithian Controversy*, 72–3, 79–81.

the judgment. Keith's followers, perhaps a quarter of the yearly meeting, followed him in forming a separate Keithian group.[36]

Both sides looked to Friends in London as the ultimate arbiters, and they tried to be conciliatory and even-handed. Although finding fault on both sides, the English Friends asked Keith to cease his attacks. Convinced of the correctness of his course, however, Keith persisted, and in September 1695 the London Yearly Meeting pronounced its judgment: Keith was no longer a Friend.[37]

The split's effects lingered long after Keith left Philadelphia. Within a decade, however, Keithian Quakerism had ceased to exist. Keith himself took orders as an Anglican priest. Many supporters followed him into Anglicanism. Others found homes in Presbyterian or Baptist congregations. Some returned to the larger body of Friends. The presence of ex-Quakers in Anglican congregations probably worsened relations between the two groups for generations. Meanwhile, Friends in the Delaware Valley, with the support of Friends in the British Isles, moved to tighten and elaborate their disciplinary structures. In 1695, the Philadelphia Yearly Meeting ordered that each monthly meeting appoint two Friends to act as overseers, charged with reporting moral failures or other lapses from grace by individual Friends. The goal would be restoration, but if offenders would not condemn their misconduct and convince the monthly meeting of their repentance, they would lose their membership. The yearly meeting issued exhortations against behaviors that were considered breaches of good order. These included not only offenses that all denominations condemned, such as drunkenness and fornication, but peculiarly Quaker transgressions ranging from marriage to non-Friends, to erecting tombstones in graveyards, or to wearing clothing that was considered "worldly." In 1715, the yearly meeting expanded the meetings of ministers to include weighty Friends who did not speak in meeting but were considered leaders in other ways. They became known as elders and were charged with oversight of the ministry, encouraging Friends who showed aptitude to speak and discouraging those who did not. By 1730, Friends had constructed an order whose main features would prevail for a century.[38]

BAPTISTS

Baptists today form the largest Protestant group in the United States. Their numbers in the Middle Colonies between 1680 and 1730 were small,

---

[36] Butler, *Power, Authority,* 37–8; Frost, *Keithian Controversy,* xvi–xvii, 4–5.
[37] Butler, *Power, Authority,* 38–9.
[38] *Ibid.,* 40–1; Frost, *Keithian Controversy,* xvi–xx, 371–5.

however, and limited records leave many unanswered questions about their experiences.[39]

Middle Colony Baptists in this period were nearly all Welsh and English. Most were Calvinist in theology, holding to tenets of predestination and the perseverance of the saints, namely, that those God had predestined for salvation could not permanently fall from grace. What set them apart from other Calvinists such as Presbyterians and the Dutch Reformed was their insistence on adult baptism as the rite of entry for church membership.[40]

The first Baptist minister in the Middle Colonies was Thomas Dungan, who came from Rhode Island to Bucks County, Pennsylvania, and organized a short-lived church at Cold Spring by 1685. Four other Baptist congregations were organized before 1700, but these numbers are misleading, because a congregation could include far more than one group of worshippers, what has been called "a congregation of many parts." This distinction would prove a problem for the group.[41]

Baptists faced three major problems. The first was the matter of ministers and their relationship to congregations. The second was the relationship of the various Baptist congregations to one another, whether they would remain autonomous or associate in some way. Finally, they faced problems of doctrine, determining how expansive their fellowship would be. At times, all three melded.

Although seemingly obscure today, the question of the "particular" status of the worshipping groups absorbed Baptists before 1700. All agreed that believers became members of the church through baptism, and that such baptism must be by a regularly ordained minister. Because Baptist clergy were few, however, they traveled among scattered groups of believers. In 1688, the Baptists at Pennepek, north of Philadelphia, recorded in their minute book that "wee [knew] not ... whether we were a particular Church ... or whether all the Brethren in the two provinces [Pennsylvania and New Jersey], made but one body, or particular church." Elias Keach, the preaching minister at Pennepek, had baptized small groups of believers in other places. Did this make them part of the Pennepek congregation? Pennepek's conclusion after considerable debate was that it did.[42]

The second question was closely related to the first: how autonomous were the Baptist churches? This became more important after 1700 with the migration of large numbers of Welsh Baptists into Delaware and Pennsylvania. In 1707, the Baptist congregations in Pennsylvania and New

---

[39] Bill J. Leonard, *The Baptists* (New York, 2005), 2.
[40] *Ibid.*, 7–12.
[41] Butler, *Power, Authority,* 43–4.
[42] *Ibid.*, 44–5.

Jersey sent representatives to a meeting in Philadelphia to confer about matters of doctrine and their relationship to one another. This formed what would become the Philadelphia Baptist Association, the first such Baptist organization in North America. By 1730, it had become the rule-making body for Baptists in the Delaware Valley, establishing standards for ordaining and recognizing pastors and acting as an adjudicatory body for disputes within and between churches. It made attempts to promote the education of ministers, and it advised congregations on questions of doctrine and worship.[43]

Finally, Baptists in the Middle Colonies found themselves regularly facing doctrinal disputes. In 1687, the issue was whether "laying on of hands" was a necessary element of baptism. In the 1690s, they debated whether to receive into membership supporters of George Keith, the former Quaker. Especially controversial was a Keithian Quaker named William Davis, whose ideas about the nature of Christ caused disputes that dragged on for years. Finally, they moved to strengthen ministerial authority. Like many religious groups, Baptists often found themselves without regular ministry, and before 1720 depended on laymen to preach and teach. By the 1720s, however, they discouraged such practices.[44]

Thus by 1730, the Middle Colonies had become central to the future of the Baptist churches in North America. Although its members were numerically few, the Philadelphia Baptist Association would be the spiritual ancestor of most contemporary Baptists in the United States.

CONGREGATIONALISTS AND PRESBYTERIANS

The relationship between Congregationalists and Presbyterians is complicated, as they differed on certain points of theology and were often in competition with each other. Nevertheless, their histories in the Middle Colonies were inseparable. Both developed in the British Isles in the late sixteenth and early seventeenth centuries. Congregationalists were Puritans who rejected episcopacy and all other human authorities beyond the individual congregation. Those congregations, in turn, were to be composed of "visible saints," those who could give assurance that they were predestined to salvation. English Puritan Congregationalists dominated immigration to New England before 1700. Presbyterians were more diverse. They included some English Puritans drawn to the Presbyterian plan of church government in which congregations were part of a presbytery,

---

[43] *Ibid.*, 49–52.
[44] *Ibid.*, 49–51.

an association that helped them preserve doctrinal purity. Two or more presbyteries, in turn, made up a synod, the ultimate authority.[45]

The roots of Middle Colony Congregationalism lay in Connecticut. As early as the 1640s, Puritans from Connecticut moved across Long Island Sound. In the 1660s other Connecticut Puritans, joined by sympathizers from Massachusetts, settled in New Jersey. Similar migrations brought Connecticut Congregationalists into the Hudson Valley. Association with Presbyterians in New York and New Jersey steadily moved these Congregational churches into Presbyterianism, a process that was almost complete by 1730. A number of early Presbyterian ministers were graduates of Harvard and Yale, and a New England influence was strong in Middle Colony Presbyterianism before 1730.[46]

The early makeup of Middle Colony Presbyterianism was more complicated. One current consisted of Scots, drawn especially to East Jersey by the Scottish background of its proprietors. Although most of these immigrants before 1690 were Quakers or Anglicans, by 1730 they had affirmed a distinct Scottish identity by becoming Presbyterians. Some English Presbyterians also found their way to the Middle Colonies. Increasingly important, however, would be ministers and laity from Ulster, many descendants of Scots. These Scots-Irish, as they became known, would be a critical influence not only in the Middle Colonies, but for the larger development of American Presbyterianism.[47]

In 1706, seven Presbyterian ministers met in Philadelphia to form what they called the Presbytery of Philadelphia. Francis Makemie, a widely traveled minister who had served churches in several places, was apparently the moving spirit. Unfortunately, the loss of the opening pages of the meeting's records make it impossible to know just what authority it saw itself asserting. Over the next quarter century, however, as Congregational churches in New York and New Jersey adopted Presbyterian governance and as immigration, especially from Ulster, swelled membership, two new presbyteries in New York and Delaware were formed, and in 1716 they formed a synod. Member ministers now numbered twenty-five. By controlling admission to its meetings, the synod effectively controlled the call of ministers to its member churches.[48]

---

[45] Jon Butler, *Awash in a Sea of Faith: Christianizing the American People* (Cambridge, MA, 1990), 25–8; John Spurr, *English Puritanism* (New York, 1998), 28–45, 94–130.
[46] Ibid., 22–6, 34; McConville, *Those Daring Disturbers*, 73–9.
[47] Landsman, *Scotland and Its First American Colony*, 163–91; Patrick Griffin, *The People with No Name: Ireland's Ulster Scots, America's Scots Irish, and the Creation of a British Atlantic World, 1689–1764* (Princeton, 2001), 1–98.
[48] Leonard J. Trinterud, *The Forming of an American Tradition: A Re-Examination of Colonial Presbyterianism* (Philadelphia, 1949), 29–31, 34–5.

In the 1720s, Middle Colony Presbyterians found themselves in sharp conflict. Several ministers faced charges of immoral conduct, and even when the synod found them guilty, it disagreed on how harsh their punishments should be. Sometimes conflicts were local. New York City Presbyterians spent a decade fighting over whom to blame for cost overruns in building their church and split by calls to ministers. Others were imported from the British Isles.[49]

Between 1710 and 1730, Presbyterians in England, Ireland, and Scotland divided over the question of "subscription," whether ministers should be required, as a condition of ordination, to profess agreement with certain doctrinal statements, usually the Westminster Confession of 1645. Some saw this as a way of preserving doctrinal purity. Others criticized it as replacing the authority of the Bible with human creeds. By 1722, it had embroiled the synod in Philadelphia, as some ministers urged such a requirement. They generally came from Scottish and Irish backgrounds. Opposed were ministers whose roots were in New England. In 1729 the synod reached an uneasy compromise. It required ministers to subscribe to the Westminster Confession in "all the essential and necessary articles" but also allowed candidates for ordination to voice "any scruple." So long as it did not concern an "essential" article of faith, ordination might proceed.[50]

By 1730, the basic cast of colonial Presbyterianism had formed in the Middle Colonies. Divisions over subscription would continue for the rest of the century. Scottish and especially Scots-Irish Presbyterians would become increasingly central. They brought with them not only disputes that divided Presbyterians at home, but also cultural practices, such as communion festivals – "holy fairs," in the words of one historian, that would lay the foundation for that central institution of American evangelicalism, the camp meeting.[51]

THE GERMAN CHURCHES: LUTHERANS, REFORMED, MENNONITES, AND BRETHREN

The Middle Colonies, especially Pennsylvania, became the center of German immigration in the eighteenth century. Germany, of course, did not exist as a nation-state at this time, and a significant number of German-speaking immigrants came from Switzerland or France. Although most German

---

[49] Butler, *Power, Authority*, 56–63
[50] *Ibid.*, 63–4; Trinterud, *Forming of an American Tradition*, 38–52.
[51] Leigh Eric Schmidt, *Holy Fairs: Scotland and the Making of American Revivalism* (Princeton, 1989).

immigrants to the Middle Colonies arrived after 1730, the religious foundations were laid in the previous half century.[52]

Although the overwhelming majority of Lutherans in North America were Germans, the first to arrive were Swedes and Finns, part of the Swedish attempt to plant a colony on the Delaware in 1638. By the time the area fell under William Penn's control, perhaps one thousand Swedish and Finnish Lutherans were there in two churches: Holy Trinity in Wilmington and Gloria Dei in Philadelphia. Continuing support from the Swedish Lutheran church helped them maintain an existence separate from German Lutherans. Similarly, New York was home to a small body of Dutch Lutherans with churches in New York City and Albany, which resisted absorption into the growing numbers of Germans after 1710.[53]

The central figure in Lutheran growth in New York after 1700 was Justus Falckner, who between his ordination in 1703 and his death in 1722 ministered to scattered Lutherans in New Jersey as well as New York. An estimated two thousand Germans arrived in New York in these years, nearly all of them Palatines, and perhaps a third of them Lutherans. By 1730 Lutheran churches existed not only in New York City and the Hudson Valley, but also west of Albany in the Mohawk and Schoharie Valleys.[54]

Although Germans had begun to arrive in Pennsylvania in 1683, the first German Lutheran congregation in the colony was not organized until 1703. Two more had come into existence by 1730. A handful of itinerant ministers served them, but it would not be until 1742, with the arrival of Henry M. Muhlenberg, that Lutheran faith in Pennsylvania achieved real dynamism.[55]

The German Reformed Church would be, by the time of the American Revolution, the second largest German denomination in the colonies. Before 1730, it was confined mainly to Pennsylvania; one estimate had fifteen thousand potential adherents in the colony. Given their common theology, German Reformed often formed ties with the Dutch Reformed and Presbyterians. German Reformed ministers, for example, accepted ordination from Dutch Reformed colleagues, and the first attempt at a congregation of German Reformed in Pennsylvania, at Whitemarsh near Philadelphia, passed through Dutch Reformed and then Presbyterian connections.[56]

[52] A. G. Roeber, *Palatines, Liberty, and Property: German Lutherans in Colonial America* (Baltimore, 1998), 95.
[53] Sydney E. Ahlstrom, *A Religious History of the American People* (New Haven, 1974), 251–3.
[54] E. Clifford Nelson, ed., *The Lutherans in North America* (Philadelphia, 1975), 13–14, 22–4.
[55] *Ibid.*, 28–30.
[56] Ahlstrom, *Religious History*, 246–7; H. M. J. Klein, *The History of the Eastern Synod of the Reformed Church in the United States* (Lancaster, 1943), 5–6.

By 1730, several Reformed congregations existed among Germans both in the Mohawk Valley of New York and around Philadelphia. Lack of clergy plagued them. When the first German Reformed church in the colonies was built in Germantown, Pennsylvania, in 1719, it lacked a minister. The two central leaders in Pennsylvania before 1730 were schoolmaster John Philip Boehm and "the pious tailor" Conrad Templeman. Despite his lack of ordination, Boehm served as pastor to three congregations. When George Michael Weiss, an ordained minister who founded the German Reformed church in Philadelphia, arrived in 1727, he found the situation intolerable, and an acrimonious dispute broke out that was resolved only when Boehm was ordained in 1729. Nevertheless, the foundation for future growth of German Reformed churches had been laid.[57]

Mennonites represented the most radical branch of the Reformation in Germany. They were Anabaptists and pacifists in Switzerland and the Palatinate, and they often faced fierce persecution. In response, they developed a strong sense of community and group discipline.[58]

A few Mennonites appeared in New Amsterdam before 1660, but American Mennonite history before 1730 is confined almost entirely to Pennsylvania. In 1683, a group of German Quakers from Krefeld in the Palatinate sailed for Philadelphia, accompanied by at least one Mennonite family, that of Jan Lensen. They settled at the aptly named village of Germantown. Over the next two decades, other Mennonites were drawn to Germantown, some from Holland and a few from New York, but most directly from Germany. German Quakers who had sided with George Keith joined them. In 1702, after receiving advice from Mennonites in Germany, they organized a congregation and elected two preachers. Six years later, they elected a bishop, Jacob Godschalk, and held their first communion service. Later the same year they built their first meetinghouse in Germantown. In the next five years, another Mennonite community, consisting largely of Swiss Mennonites, formed farther west at Skippack.[59]

Mennonites arrived steadily in Philadelphia over the next two decades. For many, immigration was facilitated by the Dutch Commission on Foreign Needs, organized to aid refugee and persecuted Mennonites. One form of assistance was payment of ship's passage to Pennsylvania. Mennonite migration was often intentional, with groups carefully formed to include both farmers and craftsmen who could supply a variety of necessary skills

---

[57] Klein, *Eastern Synod*, 6–15.
[58] The magisterial overview is still George Huntston Williams, *The Radical Reformation* (Philadelphia, 1962).
[59] Richard K. MacMaster, *Land, Piety, Plenty: The Establishment of Mennonite Communities in America, 1683–1790* (Scottsdale, 1985), 35–49.

in new settlements. They also benefited from wealthy brethren who purchased large tracts of land and made it available to fellow Mennonites on easy terms. By 1730, Mennonites were settling in Lancaster County, which would become a stronghold of German sectarianism.[60]

Similar to Mennonites in many ways – sometimes finding common ground, sometimes competing fiercely with them – were the Brethren, often referred to as Dunkers. They represented a marriage of Pietism and Anabaptism that rose early in the eighteenth century in Germany, particularly in the county of Wittgenstein. Members of Reformed churches there, concluding that their churches were corrupt, decided to follow the model of the early Christian church by forming a new fellowship. Led by Alexander Mack, in the summer of 1708 they symbolized their new commitment by baptizing each other in the Eder River. They described themselves simply as Brethren. Their central tenet of public adult baptism caused others to label them Dunkers or Dunkards. Although sharing Mennonite views on nonresistance and separation from "the world," they saw Mennonites as one of the "fallen" churches that they had to repudiate. Over the next decade, they won several hundred converts among Reformed and Mennonites, especially in the Palatinate.[61]

The first Brethren arrived in Pennsylvania in 1719, led by the minister Peter Becker, drawn by reports of hospitable conditions and probably by a bitter split among Brethren at Krefeld over a member's marriage to a Mennonite. These Brethren did not settle together, however; and, scattered across southeastern Pennsylvania, they did not meet for worship for three years. Not until December 1723 did Becker perform his first public baptism. Another hundred Brethren emigrated in 1729, led by Alexander Mack himself. A third large group arrived in 1733. By 1730, five congregations had been established. Immigration from Europe was complete, and future growth would depend on natural increases and conversions.[62]

The most radical manifestation of German religion in the Middle Colonies, and the first attempt at intentional community, began in Pennsylvania in 1694, when a group of radical pietists led by Johann Kelpius formed the Society of the Woman in the Wilderness. The name comes from Revelation, and the members, all men, devoted themselves to study of religion and astrology and worship, influenced by an eclectic mix

[60] *Ibid.*, 50–78.
[61] Carl F. Bowman, *Brethren Society: The Cultural Transformation of a "Peculiar People"* (Baltimore, 1985), 1–6; Donald F. Durnbaugh, "The Brethren in Early American Church Life," in F. Ernest Stoeffler, ed., *Continental Pietism and Early American Christianity* (Grand Rapids, 1976), 227–31; William G. Willoughby, *The Beliefs of the Early Brethren, 1706–1735* (Philadelphia, 1999).
[62] Bowman, *Brethren Society*, 8–9.

of Hermeticism, Rosicrucianism, and Kabbalism. Avowedly millenarian, they had come to Pennsylvania because of a prediction that the world would end in 1694, and they wished to witness it from the wilderness, per Revelation. Kelpius died in 1708, after which the group declined and had disappeared by 1720.[63]

ROMAN CATHOLICS

Perhaps no Christian group faced such widespread and enduring hostility in the colonies between 1680 and 1730 as Roman Catholics. Viewed by Protestants as the bloody-handed, persecuting agents of a foreign power, Roman Catholicism was illegal in most colonies. Intermittent warfare between England and France from 1689 to 1713 also had religious implications. Particularly in New York, Roman Catholics were enemies who encouraged Indian attacks on the frontier. Outside of Maryland, which was founded under Catholic auspices, only in Pennsylvania had Roman Catholics found a haven by 1730.[64]

A few Roman Catholic Irish indentured servants were in Pennsylvania by 1690, and by the early eighteenth century Anglicans in Philadelphia worried that "this city is very much infested with Popery." The first attempts to minister to Pennsylvania Catholics, however, did not come until 1706, when Jesuits from Maryland traveled into the colony. The first Mass was said in Philadelphia in 1708, much to the chagrin of even tolerant Quakers. By 1729, Philadelphia had a resident priest, Father Joseph Greaton, who four or five years later opened a tiny chapel. The Catholic population was still small, perhaps forty in number.[65]

The Roman Catholic presence in New York was fleeting. Because its proprietor, the Duke of York, later King James II, was a Roman Catholic, before 1689 Catholics served as officials, the most notable of whom was Thomas Dongan, an Irishman who became governor in 1683. Protestant feelings rose after the overthrow of James in 1688, however, and in 1700 a new law subjected any Catholic priest entering the colony to life imprisonment. No organized Roman Catholic life would revive in New York until after the American Revolution.[66]

---

[63] Julius Friedrich Sachse, *The German Pietists of Provincial Pennsylvania* (New York, 1970); Catherine L. Albanese, *A Republic of Mind and Spirit: A Cultural History of American Metaphysical Religion* (New Haven, 2007), 79–80.

[64] Carla Gardina Pestana, *Protestant Empire: Religion and the Making of the British Atlantic World* (Philadelphia, 2009), 162–3.

[65] James Hennesey, *American Catholics: A History of the Roman Catholic Community in the United States* (New York, 1981), 49–50.

[66] *Ibid.*, 52–4, 340–1.

WOMEN IN THE CHURCHES

Nearly all of the faiths in the Middle Colonies subordinated women in church government. With the exception of the Friends, the idea of women as ministers or preachers or having a role in church government was almost unthinkable. Anglican vestries, Presbyterian sessions, and other institutions of congregational life were entirely male. Although women were seen as having a vital role in nurturing piety within the family, that role was perceived as private. And although we have accounts of women challenging male authority in the churches later in the eighteenth century, if such challenges took place at this time, they went unrecorded.[67]

Studies of New England in this period have found that women became the majority of church members in the eighteenth century, but such a pattern is not clear for the Middle Colonies. In congregations without resident ministers or in which ministerial authority was weak, the sexes tended to be evenly balanced. But when ministerial authority was strong, women often dominated the membership rolls. Historians have speculated this reflects the unwillingness of laymen to accept passive roles under strong pastors.[68]

Friends gave women rights in church business unknown in other denominations. From the beginning, a parallel structure of monthly and quarterly meetings of men and women was established. Philadelphia Friends, moreover, broke with the English model in setting up a women's yearly meeting, something not done in London until 1784. The separate business meetings were charged with the oversight of members of their own sex, and they gave some women the experience of serving in official capacities and on committees. Still, women were not completely equal. Property matters were in male hands, and although men could disown members without the concurrence of the women's monthly meetings, women required male approval to exclude or receive members. Meetings appointed equal numbers of male and female overseers, and women served as elders. Most visible were female Public Friends or ministers who not only preached in Quaker meetings, but traveled widely and sometimes held meetings among non-Quakers.[69]

---

[67] A. G. Roeber, "'The Origin of Whatever Is Not English among Us': The Dutch-Speaking and German-Speaking Peoples of Colonial British America," in Bernard Bailyn and Philip D. Morgan, eds., *Strangers within the Realm: Cultural Margins of the First British Empire* (Chapel Hill, 1991), 229.

[68] Patricia U. Bonomi, *Under the Cope of Heaven: Religion, Society, and Politics in Colonial America* (New York, 1986), 111–15.

[69] Rufus M. Jones, *The Later Periods of Quakerism* (London, 1921), 115–16; Rebecca Larson, *Daughters of Light: Quaker Women Preaching and Prophesying in the Colonies and Abroad, 1700–1775* (New York, 1999).

AFRICANS

The first Africans in the Middle Colonies, and the overwhelming majority between 1680 and 1730, were slaves. Dutch colonists early became involved in the slave trade, and other colonists eagerly embraced slave labor. They showed little concern for the spiritual welfare of their chattels. The conclusion of one missionary in 1730 was, "The Negroes were much discouraged from embracing the Christian religion."[70]

Africans brought with them a mixture of religious faiths. Some were Muslims, others followed a variety of West African faiths, and a few were Roman Catholics. In the colonies, they often syncretized Christianity with African faiths. The best example is Pinkster, the Dutch Reformed celebration of Pentecost. One historian describes it as creating "a temporary community among Africans and Dutch." One of its features was the experience of a "Holy Wind," when the Holy Ghost descended on believers, white and black, male and female, and inspired some to "speak in tongues."[71]

Dutch Reformed and Quakers showed little interest in converting slaves to Christianity in this period, even though slaveholding was common among them. The only systematic effort was Anglican. They began evangelizing slaves in New Jersey and New York in the 1680s. In 1703, Elias Neau, a Huguenot convert, opened a school for blacks in New York City in which they were catechized and taught the Apostles Creed and the Ten Commandments. Perhaps most important, he made literacy part of the instruction. Neau did not question the institution of slavery; indeed, he was instrumental in securing legislation specifying that baptism as Christians did not mean freedom for blacks. An abortive slave revolt in New York City in 1712 dampened Anglican ardor, partly because it appeared that some slaves were combining Christian theology with African concepts to aspire to liberty. Despite exhortations from London and the SPG, after Neau's death in 1722 Anglican clergy showed little enthusiasm for work with black people. Lutherans made a few black converts and were willing to admit them to full membership and even give them responsible positions in the church. In Pennsylvania, no church showed much interest in making black converts before 1730.[72]

---

[70] Graham Russell Hodges, *Root and Branch: African Americans in New York and East Jersey, 1613–1863* (Chapel Hill, 1999), 53.

[71] Graham Russell Hodges, *Slavery and Freedom in the Rural North: African Americans in Monmouth County, New Jersey, 1665–1865* (Madison, 1997), 29–31.

[72] Hodges, *Root and Branch*, 54–9, 84–7; Gary B. Nash, *Forging Freedom: The Formation of Philadelphia's Black Community, 1720–1840* (Cambridge, MA, 1988), 16–20; Leslie M. Harris, *In the Shadow of Slavery: African Americans in New York City, 1626–1863* (Chicago, 2003), 34–5.

Although Quakers showed little interest in proselytizing among blacks, they were the first to question the justice of slavery. As early as 1688, Friends at Germantown, Pennsylvania, sent the yearly meeting a protest against Friends holding slaves. George Keith was also an articulate critic of slavery. A succession of Friends in Pennsylvania and New Jersey published statements condemning slaveholding as irreconcilable with Quakerism and Christianity. Yet they had little effect on Friends. The Philadelphia Yearly Meeting, beginning in 1696, did "caution" Friends against purchasing imported slaves and urged Friends to educate those in their care. Yet it refused to consider those who purchased or held slaves as offenders against good order. Nevertheless, the seeds had been planted that would yield a stronger Quaker witness against slavery.[73]

EURO-AMERICANS AND NATIVE AMERICANS

The colonists lived in close proximity to diverse Native American groups. In this period, they showed limited interest in proselytizing, but religious attitudes did affect relationships. Pennsylvania's Quakers probably took more pains than any other colonists to preserve good relations with Native Americans. They tried to regulate alcohol sales and negotiate land purchases fairly. Nevertheless, the pressures for expansion because of white population growth were inexorable. Friends were willing to take decisive action against whites guilty of violence against Indians. When two Welshmen killed three Indians without provocation in 1728, they became the first whites in the colonies hanged for murdering Native Americans.[74]

In New York, a few efforts were made at evangelizing Native Americans. Thomas James, a Congregationalist, attempted to convert Indians on Long Island before his death in 1696, with limited results. Godfrey Dellius, a Dutch Reformed minister, claimed to have made two hundred Mohawk converts by 1693, but he soon turned his attention to land speculation. The SPG sent several missionaries to the Iroquois – in 1710 it resolved to spend half of its income on converting the Mohawks – but they were hindered by their own convictions that Indians were doomed to extinction, by their limited knowledge of Native American languages, and by Iroquois resistance.[75]

---

[73] J. William Frost, ed., *The Quaker Origins of Antislavery* (Norwood, PA, 1980), 69–122; Jean R. Soderlund, *Quakers and Slavery: A Divided Spirit* (Princeton, 1985), 17–26.

[74] Amy C. Schutt, *Peoples of the River Valleys: The Odyssey of the Delaware Indians* (Philadelphia, 2007), 60–93; Carla Gerona, *Night Journeys: The Power of Dreams in Transatlantic Quaker Culture* (Charlottesville, 2004), 98–9.

[75] Allen W. Trelease, *Indian Affairs in Colonial New York: The Seventeenth Century* (Ithaca, 1960), 200–2, 327–30; Kammen, *Colonial New York*, 226–7; Bridenbaugh, *Mitre and Sceptre*, 57–8; Daniel K. Richter, *The Ordeal of the Longhouse: The Peoples of the Iroquois League in the Era of European Colonization* (Chapel Hill, 1992), 229–35.

By 1730, the Middle Colonies had become the most religiously diverse region of British North America. Anglicanism grew, but the Anglican church establishment was remarkably weak, confined to only part of New York. Although in proportion to population, the Dutch Reformed were shrinking, they were still vibrant. For Presbyterians, Baptists, and Quakers, the Delaware Valley had become a spiritual and population center. German churches, whether Reformed or Lutheran or sectarian, were growing steadily with immigration. Of all of the European faiths transplanted in the Middle Colonies, only the Huguenots had failed to thrive.

SUGGESTIONS FOR FURTHER READING

Balmer, Randall. *A Perfect Babel of Confusion: Dutch Religion and English Culture in the Middle Colonies.* New York, 1989.

Bonomi, Patricia U. *Under the Cope of Heaven: Religion, Society, and Politics in Colonial America.* New York, 1986.

Bronner, Edwin B. *William Penn's "Holy Experiment": The Founding of Pennsylvania, 1681–1701.* New York, 1962.

Butler, Jon. *The Huguenots in America: A Refugee People in a New World Society.* Cambridge, MA, 1983.

———. *Power, Authority, and the Origins of American Denominational Order: The English Churches in the Delaware Valley, 1680–1730.* Philadelphia, 1978.

Frost, J. William. *A Perfect Freedom: Religious Liberty in Pennsylvania.* New York, 1990.

Hodges, Graham Russell. *Root and Branch: African Americans in New York and East Jersey, 1613–1863.* Chapel Hill, 1999.

Landsman, Ned C. *Scotland and Its First American Colony, 1683–1765.* Princeton, 1985.

Larson, Rebecca. *Daughters of Light: Quaker Women Preaching and Prophesying in the Colonies and Abroad, 1700–1775.* New York, 1999.

Roeber, A. G. "'The Origin of Whatever Is Not English among Us': The Dutch-Speaking and German-Speaking Peoples of Colonial British America," in Bernard Bailyn and Philip D. Morgan, eds., *Strangers within the Realm: Cultural Margins of the First British Empire.* Chapel Hill, 1991.

16

RELIGION IN THE SOUTHERN ENGLISH COLONIES, 1680s–1730s

CHARLES H. LIPPY

When the English set up their first permanent settlement in what became the southern United States, they envisioned transplanting English life and institutions with relative ease. Those who survived the first year at Jamestown, Virginia, after arriving in 1607, knew differently. The struggle to carve a society in what seemed a strange wilderness required extraordinary strength and determination. It also involved fashioning afresh social institutions, including religious ones, for familiar models simply did not transfer readily from the mother country to the colonial enterprise.

The traditional story of religion in the southern colonies focuses on the Church of England, which had legal standing at some point in each of them, and then on the gradual ascendancy of an evangelical style. In reality the picture is more complicated. From the start, religious life included interaction with Native American tribal cultures and their ways of being religious. After 1619, when the first slave ship arrived in Virginia, it also involved intimate association with African tribal modes of religious expression. Although the assumption was that the church in the southern colonies echoed the Church of England as it existed across the Atlantic, the colonial setting as well as the interplay with Native Americans and Africans meant that many religious cultures were transformed, not just transplanted. By the time that the English evangelist George Whitefield made his first tour through English colonial America in the 1740s, religious practice and its institutional expression had taken on many new dimensions, and already a diversity that would become more apparent later had appeared in embryonic form. Throughout the South, then, transformation rather than transplantation characterized the development of colonial religious culture.

EARLY COLONIAL VIRGINIA PAVES THE WAY

The Virginia Company, which spearheaded English settlement in North America, although nominally committed to supporting the Church of

England, bore the imprint of the Puritan wing of Anglicanism. Even if the major intent of the enterprise was economic – some sort of financial gain for investors in the Virginia Company – a religious spirit infused the endeavor. But from the outset, just how to take that spirit and plant a vibrant religious life presented challenges. For about the first three years after the founding of Jamestown, formal religious life and practice were erratic at best. At first, regular prayer was offered twice daily and two sermons preached each Sunday. Yet for most of those first years, there was no Church of England priest, not even one with Puritan leanings, to oversee religious observance and provide religious counsel.

The first efforts to stabilize the religious situation came after a new charter for Virginia went into effect in 1609. The next year, Thomas Gates arrived as lieutenant governor, bringing with him a set of regulations to guide colonial life that in time became known as Dale's Laws. The new law code addressed religious life directly and strictly.[1] It not only provided for mandatory attendance at worship, but it also specified penalties for speaking against the Trinity and called for the death penalty for those who blasphemed God's name, for those who spoke against the Bible, and even for those who missed three consecutive preaching services. The severity of the code suggests that, left to their own devices, many of the colonists would have readily not engaged in public religious activity, and also that a deep life of personal religious devotion was more an ideal than a lived reality for most of them.

Despite severe challenges, the colony endured. Indeed, by the time Dale's Laws sought to give more formal guidelines to those in Virginia, most believed that the colony would flourish. After a couple of years of negotiation between colonial leaders and representatives of the Virginia Company, on 30 July 1619, the colonial House of Burgesses or lower legislative assembly met for the first time. Within a month, the first ship carrying slaves arrived in Jamestown. Both events were to transform the religious life of the colony in ways no one anticipated at the time, the first leading to the eventual legal establishment of the Church of England in Virginia and corresponding efforts to contain dissent, and the second assuring that colonial religious life would ultimately have a multiracial character.

For white settlers, the Church of England remained the basis for organized religious life, although patterns of settlement made it impossible to duplicate English models in the New World. In Virginia, for example,

---

[1] Dale's Laws are included in Peter Force, ed., *Tracts and Other Papers Relating to the Origin, Settlement, and Progress of the Colonies in North America from the Discovery of the Country to the Year 1776*, 4 vols. (Washington, DC, 1844), 3: 9–19.

settlement along the river ways resulted in the population being dispersed over relatively large areas, rather than concentrated in towns and villages like Jamestown itself. The notion of the parish, a church that served people within a defined geographic area under the authority of a priest subject to the administrative authority of a bishop, early proved impractical. The dispersion of the population meant that parishes could encompass such a large amount of land with such considerable distance separating families that it was impossible for them to gather in a single location for morning prayer on any given Sunday. If there were a priest who could officiate at divine services, he, too, confronted the challenge of having a congregation so scattered as to render problematic effective pastoral leadership. Throughout the colonial period, but especially in the first century or so, these matters of geography and distance worked against the best intentions of setting up vibrant religious institutions and fostering regular religious practice in much of the colony.

In 1624, the House of Burgesses granted legal establishment to Anglicanism, a status in theory identical to what prevailed in England itself. Yet even here there were differences that suggested colonial developments would never merely echo those of the church in England. Establishment had two significant dimensions. First, it tied government to one religious body in a way that not only privileged that church, but gave it unique standing. Technically, no other religious options could have any public standing. In other words, only the established church had the right to exist. Second, establishment also gave the government certain responsibilities for the church. Public funds, for example, could finance the construction of a church building to serve a parish, and public funds could also underwrite the salary and other support for a priest. In colonial Virginia, however, the ideal was seldom realized completely.

For those Anglican priests who came to Virginia and then to other southern colonies, the gap between what establishment meant in the mother country and what it denoted in the colonies proved problematic. In the experience of the clergy, the absence of a colonial bishop symbolized many dimensions of the problem. In theory, colonial parishes and priests served under the jurisdiction of the bishop of London, but having ecclesiastical authority resident on the other side of the Atlantic was another aspect of colonial religious life that made it impossible to duplicate the structures that governed the Church of England in the mother country. Adaptation and transformation followed.

One aspect of that particular transformation came with the increased power that accrued to lay vestries in colonial parishes. Sometimes, if there were no resident rector to serve the parish, the vestry wound up having almost total authority over what went on within the parish. That power began to grow throughout the seventeenth century, and by the early to mid-eighteenth century, parish vestries had basically taken on many of the responsibilities for parish lands and buildings that priests in England exercised. In addition, vestries and the colonial legislative assemblies developed procedures for support of clergy that were quite different from those that prevailed in Britain. In the colonies, land owned by the parish, commonly called glebe lands, would be designated for the support of the priest. That is, income from that land provided salary for parish rectors. By controlling that land and sometimes its use, vestries in essence had far greater power than any lay group in an English parish. Control of salary in this way often became control of both choice and tenure of priests. Because there was no residential bishop to whom to appeal or whose authority could supersede that of the vestry, local priests served at the whim of vestries in a way that did not prevail in England itself.

Another way in which the organizational pattern gave a different cast to colonial Anglicanism came with the ritual duties exercised by bishops. For example, ordination in the Church of England required not only episcopal guidance, but the laying on of hands in a service that signified one had met basic qualifications for priestly ministry. Throughout the colonial period, any Anglican male who sought holy orders had to go to England for study and then for ordination to the priesthood. Many who did so chose not to return to the colonies because of the lower status of priests in both church and society. Beyond the challenges posed by ordination, confirmation and other ritual activity that drew on episcopal spiritual leadership had a makeshift cast in the colonies when compared with the Anglican ideal.

Even in theology, the lay orientation of colonial Anglicanism brought transformation. The absence of bishops and a scarcity of priests did not necessarily mean that southern colonists were theologically illiterate. What does seem to be the case, however, is that a Puritan undercurrent sustained much of the popular understanding of doctrine and belief in the colonies. In England there was a decided difference between a more thoroughgoing Calvinistic Puritan approach and a more rational, catholic Anglican one; in early colonial Virginia, the lines blurred. Evidence for this Puritan influence comes largely from inventories of libraries of colonial planters. If their modest collections had theological titles, they were as likely to be sermons and works by Puritan thinkers as they were to be writings by Anglican divines. In the eighteenth century, however, a more rationalistic, deistic cast developed as an increasingly genteel planter class became more smitten with moderate rationalist thinking associated with English Enlightenment currents. Indeed, by the mid-eighteenth century a moderate Deism was beginning to prevail in Virginia Anglican circles, especially among the planter class.

Little evidence, however, sustains the once-popular belief that those Church of England priests who served in Virginia and then in the other southern colonies, after they were organized, were incompetent and ill-trained. Nor is there evidence that supports the claim that many were noted for their excessive use of alcoholic beverages rather than for their spiritual leadership. On balance, despite the transformations that rendered early colonial Anglicanism a rather different expression of Christianity than the Church of England in Britain, most priests were conscientious spiritual leaders who were often overworked because of the difficulties in ministering to a scattered parish membership, who struggled to exercise their priestly prerogatives despite the de facto power of lay vestries, and who called for increasing assistance from the church at home in their efforts to spread the Anglican gospel among Native American Indians and then among Africans forced to migrate to the southern colonies as slaves.

NATIVE AMERICANS AND AFRICAN AMERICAN SLAVES

For nearly a century after English colonial settlement began in the Southeast, little attention was directed to missions targeting Native Americans. The arrival of the first slaves in Virginia in 1619 also yielded few sustained efforts at conversion. Indeed, early missions among Native Americans in areas later part of the southeastern United States, such as Florida and Louisiana, were almost exclusively the domain of Catholic settlers from Spain and then France. English neglect did not mean that Anglicans appreciated the integrity of Native American cultures, especially the way religious sensibilities undergirded virtually every aspect of Native American life. Ambivalence marked most English interactions with native peoples, even though the southeastern tribes, whose presence was strongest in areas where the English settled, were themselves already becoming semisedentary, agricultural producers with an increasingly organized social structure and thus appeared more like the English than did some other native tribes.

English misunderstanding of the richness of native culture stemmed in part from linguistic barriers and differences. When the English established their first colonial outposts in the Southeast, they – as all Europeans on their arrival in North America – confronted peoples who had no written language. But at the heart of English Christianity lay the written word, from the sacred text of the Bible to the liturgies of the Book of Common Prayer. At the same time, none of the native peoples had a separate word for religion in their oral vocabularies. Looking back, it is clear that a religious cast permeated tribal life, even if there was no word that could be translated as religion. Europeans often did not understand what they observed as having religious character because of these layers of linguistic difference. The green corn dance, prominent among the Cherokee and the Choctaw, came across more as an agricultural festival celebration, for example, than as a profoundly religious event that helped to sustain the identity of the tribe.

What interaction occurred also made English efforts to proselytize difficult. On the one hand, the English benefited from learning what crops might best be cultivated, although in retrospect the fascination with tobacco cultivation that quickly consumed the English was a mixed blessing, as was the later addiction to cotton cultivation. On the other hand, interplay with native peoples that could result in their conversion to Christianity and identification with the Church of England risked collapsing the boundaries that separated colonists from those they regarded as "other." It also complicated relationships when native folk became regarded as enemies to be vanquished by force. After all, the English colonists were encroaching on native land, had rather different notions of landownership than native peoples, and came to fear Native Americans when contests for control of land led to violence. With their innate sense of superiority, colonists dubbed natives as savages prone to hostility and were thus able to overlook their own recourse to violence, which stood in contrast to the message of the Christian gospel, when dealing with them.

Even those who sought to share the Anglican gospel with indigenous peoples faced difficulties. Many of those difficulties were similar to challenges facing Anglicans who hoped to build a strong church presence among the colonists themselves – there were too few clergy to spare any to work among natives, distance made sustained missionary efforts difficult, and there was precious little financial support for such endeavors. Not until an English clergyman named Thomas Bray (1656–1730) accepted appointment in Maryland in 1696 as commissary or representative of the bishop of London did serious interest turn to missions. Bray did not remain long in the colonies, but he was a vital force behind the founding of both the Society for the Promotion of Christian Knowledge (1699) and then the Society for the Propagation of the Gospel in Foreign Parts (1701).

The latter agency, often known simply as the SPG, did support some missionaries. But these men often combined pastoral and educational roles with missionary tasks, instructing colonial youth and providing some spiritual leadership for Anglo colonists while hoping to reach out to Native Americans. At least until the mid-eighteenth century, those who came as missionaries found their zeal muted when they confronted the needs for religious leadership within the struggling parishes; many actually labored more with English colonists than with those they had hoped to convert. This diverting of attention from missions to focus on ministry with other colonists undermined the hope of organizing evangelistic endeavors among both Native Americans and slaves. Nonetheless, the few natives who did convert to Anglican Christianity and submit to baptism, the rite of initiation into the faith, could on occasion be found at worship in a colonial parish. The presence of SPG missionaries also whittled away at the power of lay vestries, for the missionaries served as symbolic reminders of Anglican church order. So as with the embryonic Church of England in the colonies, the reality of missions to Native Americans was vastly different from the idealized hope that inspired such efforts; transformation brought unintended consequences.

Far greater ambivalence marked attitudes toward African American slaves. Native Americans remained "other" but were accepted as human beings, albeit inferior ones from inferior cultures. Slaves, however, were property, and their humanity was denigrated at every opportunity. Simply put, acknowledging as human any African forced to migrate as a slave would be to challenge the compatibility of slavery and Christianity. English colonists understood the religious issue, even if they refrained from articulating it carefully. Justifying slavery in moral terms required a denial of the innate humanity of the slave; otherwise the potential slave was an equal, a child of God created in the image of God. Greater denial followed if a slave became a baptized Christian. Prior to entering the covenant of baptism, popular theological thinking went, all were equal as unregenerate sinners; after baptism, all were equal in the eyes of God as those justified by God's gracious work in Christ. If baptized African converts were thus equal to their white English owners, could they still be held as chattel?

At the same time, English colonists proved even more unaware of the expressions of tribal religiosity that endured among slaves than they were of the religious life of Native American peoples. On the one hand, in order to solidify their power over Africans forced into slavery, those who engaged in the slave trade attempted to separate Africans thought to be able to communicate with one another, thus supposedly eroding whatever strains of tribal culture might be shared with others. In retrospect, those efforts were far less successful than slave owners thought, with countless customs and practices enduring despite the inhuman horrors of slavery.

In addition, because much traditional African tribal ritual centered on song and dance – some of which became known in the American context as the "ring shout" – white colonists assumed that slaves were merely enjoying a few moments of leisure, when in reality they were entering into a realm of higher sacred power. Within slave communities, rituals marked birth, marriage, and death, although none was recognized by whites as a religious ceremony that had significance for cultural and/or group identity. Practices associated with divination and conjure, also never fully understood by white colonists, flourished and helped link African Americans to a realm of sacred power. From the outset, the invocation of a realm of power not only enabled slaves to endure the rigors of the system to which they were tied, but it also held out hope for a future when tribal integrity would experience revitalization and restoration and the horrors of slavery would dissipate.

Not all forced to migrate as slaves practiced tribal religious ways. Among African Americans were the South's first Muslim settlers. By the age of colonial empire, Islam had long been a growing and dynamic tradition in much of Africa, including areas that constituted the source of those sold into slavery. However, it was harder for Islam to withstand the conditions of slavery than for traditional tribal practice, even though for a time diaries and journals of slave owners did make mention of providing small rations of beef (rather than pork) to some slaves – one indication that there were Muslims present whose religious dietary code forbade eating pork.

In the traditional telling of the story of southern religion, brackets surround Native American and African American religious life, as if these varied tribal expressions were curiosities and somehow peripheral to the story of "real" religion. Yet it is clear that from the outset the Christianity of the English, even as expressed in the colonial religious establishment of the Church of England, bore the imprint of interaction with Native American religious expression, even if the primary mode of interaction was to ignore and denigrate Native American spirituality. The same holds with African American tribal religious life. From the moment the slaves were brought on shore from the first slave ship in 1619, southern religion had a multiracial cast to it. The conditions of slavery may have brought modifications and transformation to tribal life, but those same conditions also brought modifications and transformation to the Christianity of the colonists, who now had to form a theology and create institutions that sanctioned humans holding other humans as property. In essence, slowly evolving were slave religious expressions that were neither identical to what flourished in Africa nor offshoots of the religion of the oppressor. Similarly, white colonial religious expression was not a mirror of the European Christian tradition, but instead a new form of Christianity, one forged in the context of slave culture. That complex interaction would endure long after the colonies had severed ties with Britain and, indeed, long after the Civil War in the nineteenth century finally ended the system of slavery.

Once the Church of England received legal establishment in Virginia, that colony moved more consistently to suppress religious dissent and diversity than was the case elsewhere in North America, even in other southern settlements that favored the Anglican way. That effort to enforce conformity endured despite the parliamentary Act of Toleration in 1689 that supposedly guaranteed some minimal rights to worship for Protestant dissenters throughout the British Empire. Although some of the patterns in Virginia extended to Maryland after colonial settlement there got under way in the 1630s, a rather unanticipated religious diversity transformed the religious landscape of the Maryland proprietary enterprise to an extent that never happened in Virginia. In time, Virginia stood apart for trying to contain diversity and sustain a single establishment, even when across its borders both to the north and eventually to the south it faced an ever-expanding religious pluralism, one that would eventually become a hallmark of the American nation.

MARYLAND MOVES IN NEW DIRECTIONS

In 1634, thanks to the efforts of the aristocratic Calvert family in gaining a grant of land in colonial America from the king, Maryland became the first English colonial settlement in North America to grant Roman Catholics the right to practice their religion without any social or political disability. Maryland, however, was a proprietary colony; that is, it was in a sense the property of the Calvert family, who hoped to reap financial gain from those who settled there. The number of Catholics willing to embark on a hazardous transatlantic journey and build a new society in Maryland remained relatively small, indeed too small to assure the financial success of the colony. Consequently, Maryland from the start welcomed non-Catholics within its borders, with the colony's leaders well aware that many of them harbored hostile, antagonistic attitudes toward Catholics.

One result, hailed as a landmark in the American journey toward religious freedom, was the Act of Toleration promulgated for Maryland in 1649.[2] Toleration is rather different from openly accepting a wide diversity of religious options. In this case, Maryland extended what at the time folk generally called "liberty of conscience" to all who affirmed belief in Christian Trinitarian doctrine. That is, Trinitarian Christians were technically at liberty to worship as they chose without governmental interference; others were not. Lack of interference did not mean that there was an acceptance of the legitimacy of multiple forms of Christian expression. Truth was still truth, even if one could not prohibit misguided expressions of Christianity from existing. The Calverts demonstrated their pragmatic approach, for example, when they urged their fellow Catholics to refrain from making great public display of their faith, lest non-Catholics take offense.

---

[2] The text may be found in William B. Browne, ed., *Archives of Maryland: Proceedings and Acts of the General Assembly of Maryland* (Baltimore, 1883), 244–7.

Indeed, Protestants inclined toward a Calvinistic Puritanism outnumbered Catholics in Maryland within a few years of colonial settlement.

The Act of Toleration had something of an ambiguous history in terms of when and to what extent it was actually accepted. Because the act was promulgated just as the English Civil War brought Puritans into political power in the mother country, Calvert may have thought it would impress the nation's new leaders by assuring that their religious compatriots would have liberty of conscience in Maryland. Moreover, because the act offered such liberty only to those who affirmed belief in Christian Trinitarian doctrine, it tacitly acknowledged that the government retained coercive power to protect authentic belief. In theory, the government could act against non-Trinitarian belief and practice.

Nor did toleration preclude factional politics and upheaval. Within the colony, there was resistance to proprietary power spearheaded by folk of Puritan inclination who came to Maryland after having been driven out of Virginia. In 1654 Calvert and his associates lost control. The rebel leaders repealed the Act of Toleration and forced Jesuits, for example, into exile. Calvert regained power in 1657, reinstating the act, which remained technically in force until new arrangements for all the colonies went into effect after the Glorious Revolution of 1688. But some prosecution of Quakers the year after Calvert regained control suggests that not all who were identified as Christian found a welcome home in Maryland.

Yet in retrospect, the Maryland experiment is noteworthy. Catholics had remained in Britain even after the establishment of the Church of England in the sixteenth century, and the continuing imposition of legal disabilities on those who practiced Catholicism kept the faith marginalized socially and politically. Hence English Catholicism was largely an underground movement. Maryland became the first venue in the English world where Protestants and Catholics lived openly side by side. For the most part, they did so in relative harmony. Thus Maryland helped dismantle the longstanding conviction that there could be no social cohesion where both Catholics and Protestants were on equal legal footing. Indeed, by the middle of the 1670s, the then-current Lord Baltimore noted that alongside Catholics and independents (those of Puritan inclination), Maryland was home to Presbyterians, Lutherans, Anglicans, Anabaptists, and even Quakers.

The restructuring of all colonies following the Glorious Revolution signaled the end of Calvert family control in Maryland. One consequence was the legal establishment of the Church of England there in 1700. That legislation appeared at first to require conformity, but a modified law two years later extended to Maryland colonists the same broad liberty of conscience guaranteed in the mother country. This arrangement meant that not all groups had equal standing, although for the most part adherents could worship as they chose. Hence budding pluralism continued to prevail, even if full religious equality did not.

In Maryland, then, transformation altered the original vision for the religious life of the colony, albeit a different sort of transformation than marked early colonial Virginia. In Maryland a pragmatic toleration redirected the hope that the colony would be a bastion for English Catholic colonists, a place where a minority would be the majority. Yet when religious establishment came to Maryland, it was markedly different from what Virginia attempted. The vitality of dissent, from Puritans to Catholics, meant that Maryland would nurture greater diversity than Virginia – or at least greater diversity than Virginia's political leaders condoned.

RELIGIOUS DIVERSITY IN CAROLINA

By the time Anglicanism received legal establishment in Maryland, an even greater diversity had already come to mark religious life further south, in the area known first simply as Carolina. (The division into two colonies, North Carolina and South Carolina, did not become finalized until 1729.) Here, too, myth and reality are intertwined in terms of how pluralism came to the fore in Charleston, the first hub of Carolina life. Popular perception over time has attached ever greater importance to a document known as the Fundamental Constitutions of Carolina, one version of which – the one issued in 1669 – the English philosopher and political theorist John Locke may have helped craft, although historians still debate the nature and extent of Locke's involvement. But the colony's proprietors issued four somewhat different "fundamental constitutions" between 1669 and 1698. The first, however, is the one revered in popular memory.[3] It is also the one that sanctioned the broadest religious toleration and liberty; the second, promulgated in 1670, called for the establishment of the Church of England as soon as local circumstances allowed, although a rather broad toleration remained in place as well.

Unlike the Maryland approach that restricted religious liberty to Christian Trinitarians, the Carolina arrangements permitted all who professed belief in God to settle, although from time to time additional religious requirements applied to eligibility to hold public office. This latitude meant that Jewish settlers, for example, could make a home for themselves in Carolina, as could non-Trinitarian Christians. Dissenters would also find Carolina inviting, especially in the early years before those ambiguous

---

[3] The 24-page text is reprinted in *The Fundamental Constitutions of Carolina, 1669* (Boston, 1906).

local circumstances made Anglican establishment feasible. Even then, non-Anglicans would not face the opposition that they did in Virginia to the north. The result was that within a few decades of its founding, Carolina had what for its time was an extraordinarily diverse mix of religions.

But that diversity grew also because the 1669 document forbade residents to molest or persecute others for "speculative opinions" in matters of religious belief or worship practice. Even if the Fundamental Constitutions had tenuous legal standing, its intent to provide a wider latitude of religious liberty and to allow adherents of many traditions and denominations to settle within its borders provided for a greater degree of religious pluralism in Carolina than in any other southern English colony.

At first clustered around Charleston and outlying settlements along the Ashley and Cooper Rivers, Carolina's Anglicans moved toward forming the parish that became St. Philip's in 1681. That same year, however, a dissenters' society organized, a clear signal that the Church of England would not enjoy unchallenged dominance in the colony. By then Charleston had a small but growing Jewish population, with the first Jews arriving in 1679. The present-day Congregation Beth Elohim, although not formally organized until 1749, had its roots in a Jewish community already in place by 1695. A few decades later, when the colonization of Georgia began, Jewish settlers also came early to Savannah. By the era of independence, the spirit of toleration allowed South Carolina to claim the largest Jewish population of any state, and Charleston may well have had the most solidly functioning Jewish community of any city.

Events in Europe added to Carolina's diversity. In 1685, the revocation of the Edict of Nantes that had granted limited privileges to French Calvinists spurred a widespread movement of those known as Huguenots to other areas of Europe and also to the New World. More than a century earlier, some French Reformed had a short-lived outpost on Parris Island off the Carolina coast, but the main migration came when, in anticipation of the revocation, Huguenots began to emigrate from France before the actual end of their limited toleration. Carolina's proprietors actively recruited among those who settled temporarily in England, hoping that Huguenot settlers would help get the anticipated colonial silk industry off the ground. Some five hundred came to Carolina and remained, with some arriving in 1679–80 and the rest a few years later. Charleston was the hub for the Huguenot community, but outlying settlements formed as well. A Huguenot church in Charleston, the ancestor of a twenty-first-century congregation that still uses a translation of an eighteenth-century French liturgy, first held services in 1680. Four others outside Charleston more quickly assimilated into the dominant English culture, with all soon aligning with the more influential Anglicans.

Diversity in Carolina also benefited in 1694, when John Archdale, who had a personal proprietary interest in the colony, became governor. He assumed his administrative duties after he arrived in Charleston the following year. Archdale had become a Quaker in the 1670s while still in England, and the first Quakers actually arrived in Carolina during that decade. But Archdale's position as colonial governor served to signal to Quakers, who encountered fierce opposition in colonial Boston and elsewhere, that they too would continue to be welcome in Carolina. Yet Archdale was not entirely committed to the pluralistic cast that Carolina religious life was taking. During his year as governor, for example, Archdale refused to allow Huguenot settlers to serve in the lower house of the colonial legislature. But his apparent hostility toward Huguenots may have been motivated more by politics than by religion. At the time, England was in conflict with France, and Huguenots after all were French and therefore suspect, even if the proprietors themselves had recruited the French Calvinists to settle in Carolina.

Others came to Carolina as well. Proprietary policy encouraged some who were of Puritan persuasion to migrate from New England to this new colony in the South. Like the Huguenots, these folk brought with them a lively Calvinist theological heritage. For several years, those inclined to both Presbyterian and Congregationalist approaches worshipped together in the White Meeting House in Charleston, the precursor to the architecturally well-known Circular Congregational Church of a later date. Not until 1731 did those inclined to more distinctively Presbyterian ways leave the Congregational fold and form the First (Scots) Presbyterian Church. Other Presbyterian enclaves also appeared on the coastal islands near Charleston, where they reaped some success in drawing African American slaves into the Presbyterian fold. The Reformed family also received some growth from a modest immigration from both Scotland and Ireland, although the major impact of Scots-Irish settlement was to come in the eighteenth century.

Other religious and ethnic communities augmented Carolina's growing diversity. Before the end of the seventeenth century, a modest Baptist presence was evident in Charleston, thanks to William Screven, who moved there from Massachusetts Bay. Baptist numbers remained small, however, until well into the eighteenth century. By the third decade of the eighteenth century, largely because of waves of Swiss and German immigration, South Carolina also became home to enclaves of Lutherans. Some remained in and around Charleston, but many found their way to communities that began to develop in the midlands as far as present-day Columbia. In addition, Africans forced to migrate as slaves added not only a stratum of tribal religiosity to Carolina's overall landscape, but also another dimension of diversity. As noted earlier, they introduced Islam to the colony. The conditions of slavery, however, were not conducive to sustaining Muslim practice. Until well into the eighteenth century, white Carolinians, as their Virginia counterparts, did not actively seek to engage slaves with any form of the Christian tradition, but as elsewhere, African tribal religion and the religions of the white colonists interacted, with each influencing the other. That interaction was especially striking in Carolina, because by the end of the 1730s, if not earlier, Africans constituted a majority of the colony's population. These slaves added to the ethnic mix of South Carolina as well as to the diverse religious complexion of the colony.

Not all were happy with these arrangements, however, and Carolina toleration had its limits. Despite Governor Archdale's serving as a symbol for the acceptance of Quakers in Carolina, some of the contention concerned Quakers. Early in the eighteenth century, the Quaker refusal to take oaths aroused suspicion, as did their openness to living amicably with nearby Native Americans, who were increasingly regarded as a threat to colonial growth and expansion. Consequently, efforts got under way to limit the rights of Quakers in Carolina; they expanded to include a proposal to prohibit most dissenters from holding public office. Local legislation in 1704 moved in this direction, but opponents successfully lobbied Parliament and the Privy Council, which in 1706 overturned these attempts to end the rather wide religious liberty enjoyed by Carolinians. Repeated but unsuccessful attempts at similar kinds of restriction occurred until South Carolina became a royal colony in 1719.

But the episode did help formalize some of the religious arrangements in the colony. New legislation introduced in 1706, some of which remained basically intact throughout the rest of the colonial period, led to the nominal establishment of the Church of England in Carolina. How that establishment worked, though, was different from the way establishment operated in Virginia, and the Carolina approach signals yet another way that the colonial context transformed religious patterns. In Carolina, the Church of England received only modest financial support that came from revenue generated by taxes on exports and imports, not from taxes paid by individuals, from taxes on property, or from income generated by land reserved exclusively for church support. At different times, initiatives allowed dissenting groups to have access to some of these public funds, although it seems that allocation to non-Anglican groups was more of a theoretical possibility than a reality. In essence, the Carolina experiment represented an effort to acknowledge diversity and permit liberty of conscience in matters of religion while at the same time trying to reap whatever benefits civil society received from a religious establishment. However one construes this arrangement, the result was what one historian described as a "robust" religious pluralism.[4]

The Carolinas thus illustrate yet a different sort of transformation of colonial religious life in the South than that in Virginia or in Maryland. Although in time the Church of England received legal establishment, the apparatus of that establishment was quite different from what establishment denoted in England or even in Virginia. The basis for financial support was different, and Carolina establishment recognized the presence of diverse religious groups. Indeed, the Church of England may have actually been a minority tradition in terms of numbers of adherents. The openness to diversity meant that South Carolina foreshadowed – more so even than Maryland – the pluralism that later became a hallmark of American religious life. But both Carolina and Maryland demonstrated that forced adherence to a single religion was not a necessary precondition for political stability or for relative social harmony. That awareness, too, represented a transformation in the assumptions that undergirded much of the larger colonial enterprise.

AT THE DAWN OF THE EIGHTEENTH CENTURY

By the early years of the eighteenth century, other currents of diversity were coming into much of the South, through Maryland and Virginia and on into North and South Carolina. Much resulted from a steady increase in the number of Scots-Irish immigrants arriving in the English colonies and from the new patterns of settlement that followed. These newer immigrants initially swelled the population of northern cities, such as Philadelphia, but many soon began to migrate southward along the eastern slopes of the Appalachian mountain chain, through Maryland into the Shenandoah Valley of Virginia and then into the Carolinas. Some also made their way to more urban low-country areas like Charleston and, in time, Georgia, the last of the southern English colonies in terms of founding.

The bulk of the Scots-Irish had an evangelical Calvinistic bent. That is, although they shared the conviction integral to Calvinist theology that God alone determined who was elected to salvation, they also valued some sort of affective experience that enabled individuals to sense that they were among those chosen by God. Although they were not as starkly Calvinistic as the first Scots, for example, those who came to Carolina when the colony initially opened for settlement, they made a particular style of the Reformed tradition integral to local life wherever they settled, a style that fused a powerful sense of the pervasiveness of divine

---

[4] James H. Hutson, *Church and State in America: The First Two Centuries* (New York, 2008), 30.

providence with an equally powerful sensibility of God's presence within. In South Carolina, the numbers were large indeed. By the time of independence, Presbyterians – most of them of Scots-Irish descent – may well have accounted for the largest single religious group in the colony, despite the nominal establishment of the Church of England, with its base in Charleston and the low country.

Even so, there was a rough-hewn quality to the religious culture in the backcountry. Presbyterians, for example, had long insisted on an educated clergy, but only a handful of the pastors who were part of this early migration had the standard formal education expected of clergy. Some surviving records indicate that, by the later 1730s, even those who had received formal education did so at places like the "log college" established by William Tennent in the 1730s that was a precursor to the College of New Jersey (now Princeton). Little wonder, then, that historian Stephen Longenecker, in describing Virginia in the early eighteenth century, observed that "religion on the Shenandoah frontier was as raw as the rest of the new society."[5]

As time went on, the up-country proved fertile ground for other strands of evangelical Protestantism, although much of that surge occurred after 1730. Among the more significant would be German pietists, particularly Moravians, who were there in very small numbers in the first years of the new century. In time, they would lend a quiet evangelical presence to areas of North Carolina especially. Regardless of their theological tradition or denominational identification, up-country evangelicals provided the earliest seeds that led to the South's becoming known not for any vestiges of a colonial religious establishment or even for openness to religious diversity, but as a bastion of evangelical Protestantism. By emphasizing personal religious experience, evangelicalism empowered individuals – especially those who might lack power in the social order, such as women or African Americans. It gave them an access to status in a transcendent realm that they lacked in empirical reality. Nor did one necessarily need clergy or the apparatus of religious institutions in order to foster a deep spirituality. If the inner life is what mattered, then external religious authorities of whatever sort were superfluous. Over decades, those seeds took deep root in the southern religious consciousness.

At the same time, those who came through Maryland to settle in the up-country of Virginia and the Carolinas gradually whittled away the dominance of the low country in ways that went beyond religion. The roots of such challenges are evident by the 1730s. Those in the Tidewater region of

---

[5] Stephen L. Longenecker, *Shenandoah Religion: Outsiders and the Mainstream, 1716–1865* (Waco, 2002), 20.

Virginia and the coastal settlements of the Carolina low country had long exercised almost unchallenged dominion over colonial political and economic life. In particular, throughout the older southern colonies, folk from the coastal regions controlled the legislative assemblies, assuring that they would remain overrepresented as the population elsewhere grew more rapidly. Low country influence far exceeded the proportion of the population resident there once up-country settlement began to boom. In one sense, the Scots-Irish and others who were bringing a more vital evangelical style to southern religious life were often marginalized, as defined by a later age, but they increasingly refused to be deprived of equal representation in the legislatures and often rightly believed they were subject to a colonial tax system that favored plantation and coastal economic interests. In particular, the topography that made plantation life increasingly difficult the closer one was to the mountains joined with a natural evangelical aversion to slavery; as a result, the up-country never had as large an African American population as other areas or a vested interest in promoting an economy based on slave labor. That difference also promoted change. The evangelical movement of the early eighteenth century ultimately transformed southern life at every level.

TRANSFORMATION SUPERSEDES TRANSPLANTATION

When permanent English settlement began in the southern colonies, the intent was to transplant religious structures and institutions from the mother country. In Virginia, those overseeing colonial development expected to grant the Church of England legal establishment, assuming it would function there much the same as it did in England itself. Legal establishment did come, but the church was anything but the same as the Anglican tradition in England. With parishes and people so geographically diffuse, it proved impossible to replicate the English parish system neatly. Then, too, the perpetual shortage of clergy and the absence of a bishop meant that lay control took on great importance. And always in the background were two religious cultures that were not part of the tapestry of English religious life: the tribal traditions of those indigenous to the area and the tribal traditions of those forced to migrate from Africa as slaves. Those who thought that the Virginia Company and its colony would transplant English life instead found transformation, particularly in the religious sector.

For Maryland and Carolina, both initially proprietary ventures, somewhat different visions inspired the first colonists. Maryland was to have been a place where the Catholic faithful could transplant their own way of being religious within the context of English culture. But there, too, transformation became the order of the day, for the number of Catholics willing to migrate never reached the critical mass necessary to sustain the colonial enterprise. Survival and pragmatics required toleration. Even if the vision for Maryland was different from that which inspired the Virginia enterprise, transformation followed, and religious diversity became the norm.

In Carolina, religious diversity existed alongside a token religious establishment. Both shaped the early effort to form a colonial settlement, although the arrangements for establishing the Church of England differed significantly from those at home. That difference in arrangements joined with a pragmatic willingness to welcome any who believed in God to bring a greater pluralism than any anticipated. Hence, Anglican establishment in Carolina remained modest, and the broad toleration of dissent assured that a rich religious diversity would prevail. In Maryland and Carolina, as in Virginia, interplay with Native Americans and African slaves added layers of complexity to ways of being religious. Slowly that interplay transformed the Christianity of the white colonists especially as it adjusted to support and sustain chattel slavery, and slowly that interplay also transformed the various tribal traditions as they absorbed some features of white colonial religious life.

Throughout the region, those who migrated southward along the eastern slopes of the Appalachians brought even more transformation, for they planted styles of evangelical Protestantism that would in time come to dominate southern religious life. In retrospect, then, the story of religion everywhere in the South, from the settlement of Jamestown through the first three decades of the eighteenth century, is a story of constant transformation. Yet that process itself serves as a reminder that the larger cultural ethos is always a prism through which religious developments are refracted.

SUGGESTIONS FOR FURTHER READING

Bolton, S. Charles. *Southern Anglicanism: The Church of England in Colonial South Carolina*. Westport, 1982.

Bond, Edward L. *Damned Souls in a Tobacco Colony: Religion in Seventeenth-Century Virginia*. Macon, GA, 2000.

Butler, Jon. *The Huguenots in America: A Refugee People in a New World Society*. Cambridge, MA, 1983.

Ellis, John Tracy. *Catholics in Colonial America*. Baltimore, 1965.

Hutson, James H. *Church and State in America: The First Two Centuries*. New York, 2008.

Lippy, Charles H. "Slave Christianity," in Amanda Porterfield, ed. *Modern Christianity to 1900: A People's History of Christianity*. Minneapolis, 2007, 6: 291–316.

Marcus, Jacob Rader. *Early American Jewry*, vol. 2, *The Jews of Pennsylvania and the South, 1655–1790*. Philadelphia, 1953.

Raboteau, Albert J. *Slave Religion: The "Invisible Institution" in the Antebellum South*. New York, 1978.

Section IV

RELIGIOUS DIVERSITY IN BRITISH AMERICA – 1730s–1790

17

RELIGIOUS FERMENT AMONG EASTERN ALGONQUIANS AND THEIR NEIGHBORS IN THE EIGHTEENTH CENTURY

AMY C. SCHUTT AND CHRISTOPHER VECSEY

Riding together along the road between Philadelphia and Bethlehem, Pennsylvania, in 1760, two men – one a Euro-American Quaker and the other a Munsee Indian – had an opportunity to discuss religion, a topic of great interest to both individuals. The Quaker thought he could use the occasion "to say something" to the other man "about our Savior's words and good examples, when on earth." The Munsee Indian, named Papoonahoal, listened as the Quaker, through an interpreter, inquired whether Papoonahoal "was disposed to hear such things." Papoonahoal seemed interested in Quakerism; however, now was not the time for such talk. Papoonahoal's response indicates how Native Americans valued ceremony and honored the power of words. Rituals of preparation, he implied, were needed before broaching sacred matters. "Such words are very good," Papoonahoal said,

> and would be very acceptable at a fit time; such things are awful, and should be spoken of at a solemn time, for then the heart is soft, and they would enter into it, and not be lost. But when the heart is hard, they will not go into it, but fall off from the heart, and so are lost, and such words should not be lost; but at a fit time I would be glad to hear of those things.[1]

The era from the 1730s to the 1790s was one of religious ferment within areas that were, or had been, part of the British North American colonies. The exchange on the Philadelphia road was just one of a multitude

---

[1] *An Account of the Behavior and Sentiments of Some Well-Disposed Indians, Mostly of the Minusing Tribe* (Stanford, 1803), Early American Imprints, 2nd ser., no. 3623, filmed (Worcester, 1965), 3, 9, 11, 12. Papoonahoal (or Papunhank) later joined the Moravians. Zeisberger to Seidel, 18 June 1763, item 2, folder 2, box 229, reel 32 (hereafter written as 2:2:229:32), *Records of the Moravian Mission among the Indians of North America* (hereafter *RMM*; these records are in German unless otherwise noted), photographed from original materials at the Archives of the Moravian Church, Bethlehem, PA, microfilm, 40 reels (New Haven, 1970).

of encounters in an increasingly diverse world in which religion was often part of a "trade in culture."² This was a period of tumultuous change, and Native Americans drew on deep-seated spiritual resources as they asserted their place in a complex world. Indians' societies were under assault, with Europeans seeking to transform indigenous cultures and acquire Indians' lands, with epidemic diseases decimating Indian populations, and with international warfare entangling Indians and Europeans. Although this encounter was respectful, Papoonahoal indicated that such was often not the case. "Concerning people reasoning about religion," Papoonahoal said,

> when people speak of these things, they are apt to stand up in opposition one against another, as though they strove to throw each other down, or to see which is the wisest; now these things should not be, but whilst one is speaking, the other should hold his head down till the first has done, and then speak without being in a heat or angry.³

Papoonahoal's statement underscores that this era had its share of conflicts over religious beliefs and practices. Longstanding conflicts between Protestants and Catholics continued, inextricably linked to British power struggles with the French and, to a lesser degree, with the Spanish. Disputes erupted among Protestants – for example, over theology, over attitudes toward evangelical revivals, and over approaches toward missions. Indigenous religious leaders and Euro-American missionaries vehemently criticized each other. Nevertheless, there was a contrary trend in this century – the crossing of religious boundaries. Some Protestant evangelicals revealed latitudinarian tendencies as they shared in revival experiences and sometimes missionary support that spanned denominations.⁴ Native Americans in British North America in the eighteenth century sought spiritual renewal and cultural survival. They were willing to cross boundaries if it allowed them to achieve these goals.

From this time of religious ferment came a spirit of reform within Native American communities that had been profoundly impacted by British colonization by the mid-eighteenth century. Native peoples pushed for reform within their own communities and in the actions of Euro-American neighbors. This era saw Indians advocating one or more of the following: temperance, pacifism, alphabetic literacy, and new religious rituals. As they advocated reforms, some Indians placed themselves in closer alignment

---

² Rachel Wheeler, *To Live upon Hope: Mohicans and Missionaries in the Eighteenth-Century Northeast* (Ithaca, 2008), 33.
³ *Account of the Minusing*, 11–12.
⁴ Katherine Carté Engel, *Religion and Profit: Moravians in Early America* (Philadelphia, 2009), 22–3; Thomas S. Kidd, *The Great Awakening: The Roots of Evangelical Christianity in Colonial America* (New Haven, 2007), 43.

with Euro-American missionaries, whereas others argued that Christian missions were the problem, not the solution. Nevertheless, the situation was more complex than this contrast suggests, given the tendencies toward religious synthesis in this era.[5]

Eastern Algonquians from the New England and mid-Atlantic riverine and coastal areas particularly experienced the religious ferment of the eighteenth century. They were among the Indian peoples who felt the greatest impact of British colonial expansion at the time, and their history shows how this expansion coincided with a flowering of indigenous movements for spiritual renewal. Eastern Algonquians also especially felt the impact of a surge in Protestant missions in the eighteenth century. As a result, there is more documentation on the religious life of Eastern Algonquians than of many other Indian peoples in the same era. For these reasons, this essay focuses on their history, although placing it in a larger context of religious developments among other Native American groups, including Iroquoian peoples, in the region of the British colonies.

Eastern Algonquians of the New England and the mid-Atlantic region included, among other groups, Mohegans, Mohicans (or Mahicans), Montauks, Shinnecocks, Narragansetts, Pequots, Wampanoags, and Delawares (both Munsee and Unami speakers). Some Delawares, Mohicans, and other Eastern Algonquians moved into the Ohio Country as Euro-Americans encroached on their lands. Although the missionaries who worked among these peoples were overwhelmingly Protestant, Indian peoples on the peripheries of the Eastern Algonquians' homelands had relatively more experience with Catholic missionaries. These peoples included Abenakis of Acadia; Algonquins, Montagnais, and Iroquois along the St. Lawrence; Ottawas, Ojibwas, Potawatomis, and Wendats (Hurons) of the Great Lakes; and Choctaws, Creeks, and Houmas to the south.[6]

Catholic influence among Native Americans east of the Mississippi was weaker in the eighteenth century than in the seventeenth century. Jesuit missionary influence, where it existed, was intermittent or limited to a relatively small number of communities in Canada by the mid-1700s. The English worked to undermine Jesuit missions – for example, by destroying a Jesuit mission to the Abenakis on the Kennebec River in 1724. After the peace treaty of 1763 ended the Seven Years' War, the British

---

[5] Jane T. Merritt, *At the Crossroads: Indians and Empires on a Mid-Atlantic Frontier, 1700–1763* (Chapel Hill, 2003), 92 (on reform).

[6] Ives Goddard, "Eastern Algonquian Languages," and "Central Algonquian Languages," in William C. Sturtevant, ed., *Handbook of North American Indians*, vol. 15, *Northeast*, ed. Bruce G. Trigger (Washington, DC, 1978), 70–7, 583–7; James Axtell, *The Invasion Within: The Contest of Cultures in Colonial North America* (New York, 1985), 247–8, 43–70; Christopher Vecsey, *The Paths of Kateri's Kin* (Notre Dame, 1997), 173–203, 2.

victors expelled most of the Jesuits from former New France. Nonetheless, even after Britain's acquisition of Canada, Kahnawake remained as a Mohawk Catholic community, as did Oka (Mission du Lac-des-Deux-Montagnes), and St. Regis (established by Kahnawakes in 1755). Other remaining Catholic missions, dating from the 1600s, were Lorette among the Wendats, St. Frances de Sales among the Abenakis, and La Présentation among the Onondagas and Cayugas. The English destroyed Spanish Catholic missions in Florida near the beginning of the century. An attempt in 1718 to revive Catholic missions in Florida failed. Despite contacts with Catholic missionaries as early as the sixteenth century, southeastern Indians of the 1700s, such as Creeks and Choctaws, largely maintained their traditional religious culture and showed little impact from Catholicism. French Catholics had made inroads among Central Algonquians – Ojibwas, Ottawas, Potawatomis, Kaskaskias, and Miamis, for example – in the 1600s; however, the Jesuits' role also diminished among them in the eighteenth century, and traditional religion remained largely intact, beyond the reach of colonial direction. The Midewiwin, an Ojibwa religious organization first documented in 1804, indicated that Catholic influence, although weakened, had not died out during the eighteenth century. It revealed a blending of traditional Ojibwa religion with Christian elements, such as the symbol of the cross and an ethical code similar to the Ten Commandments.[7]

A belief in manitou, a term used to signify a spirit force suffusing the world, was a vital element of Algonquian traditional religion. Iroquois (or Haudenosaunee) peoples referred to this mysterious power as *orenda*. In an apparent reference to manitou, a missionary found Algonquians had a "notion of a certain *body* or *fountain* of *deity* ... diffusing itself to various animals, and even to inanimate things." Manitou was expressed through multiple spirits. "They believe in numerous spirits or subordinate deities," one observer noted. "Almost all animals and the elements are looked upon as spirits." The Mohegan Christian minister Samson Occom depicted the many spirits (or "gods") in the pantheon of the Montauks of Long Island.

---

[7] Vecsey, *Kateri's Kin*, 7, 22, 53, 92–3, 143–4; Christopher, Vecsey, *On the Padre's Trail* (Notre Dame, 1996), 42–5; David J. Weber, *The Spanish Frontier in North America* (New Haven, 1992), 144; Caleb Swan, "Position and State of Manners and Arts in the Creek, or Muscogee Nation in 1791," in Henry Rowe Schoolcraft, ed., *Historical and Statistical Information Respecting the History, Condition, and Prospects of the Indian Tribes of the United States* (Philadelphia, 1855), 5: 267; Benjamin Hawkins, *A Sketch of the Creek Country in the Years 1798 and 1799* (New York, 1971 [1848]), 78, 19; Louis Le Clerc Milfort, *Memoirs or a Quick Glance at My Travels and My Sojourn in the Creek Nation*, trans. and ed. Ben C. McCary (Savannah, 1972), 37, 54, 102–13; Christopher Vecsey, *Traditional Ojibwa Religion and Its Historical Changes* (Philadelphia, 1983), 174–6.

> There were the gods of the four corners of the earth ... a god over their corn, another over their beans, another over their pumpkins, and squashes ... [and] over their wigwams, another of the fire, another over the sea, another of the wind, one of the day, and another of the night; and there were four gods over the four parts of the year.[8]

Eastern Algonquians had a concept of a being "who is the origin of all," referred to, variously, as Cauhluntoowut (Montauk), Cautantouwwit (Narragansett), Kiehtan (Wampanoag), or Kickeron (Munsee). A Hudson Valley Algonquian stated that "Kickeron made the tortoise" on whose back the earth formed and a tree sprouted, out of which the first man and the first woman came. Wampanoags believed that after creating the first people, Kiehtan used a crow to deliver corn to humans. New England Algonquian traditions also included a powerful spirit of death, Hobbomock or Cheepi, who was revealed through dreams.[9]

Typical among Algonquians and many other Native peoples was a belief in guardian spirits, who also appeared in dreams and visions. "There is scarcely an Indian who does not believe that one or more of these spirits has not been particularly given him to assist him," one missionary explained. "This, they claim, has been made known to them in a dream.... One has, in a dream," he continued, "received a serpent or a buffalo, another the sun or the moon, another an owl or some other bird, another a fish."[10] Maintaining a proper relationship with one's guardian spirit required suitable expressions of thankfulness. Another observer stated that

> there are even some animals, which ... are believed to be placed as guardians over their lives; and of course entitled to some notice and to some tokens of gratitude. Thus, when in the night, an owl is heard sounding its note ... some person in the camp will rise, and taking some *Glicanican*, or Indian tobacco, will strew it on the fire, thinking that the ascending smoke

---

[8] Kathleen J. Bragdon, *Native People of Southern New England, 1500–1650* (Norman, OK, 1996), 184; Arthur C. Parker, *Seneca Myths and Folk Tales* (Lincoln, 1989 [1923]), 3; Sereno Edwards Dwight, *Memoirs of the Rev. David Brainerd* ... (St. Clair Shores, OH, 1970 [1822]), 345 (first quotation); Archer Butler Hulbert and William Nathaniel Schwarze, ed., *David Zeisberger's History of the North American Indians* (Columbus, 1910), 132 (second quotation; hereafter *Zeisberger's History*); Joanna Brooks, ed., *The Collected Writings of Samson Occom, Mohegan: Leadership and Literature in Eighteenth-Century Native America* (Oxford, 2006), 49. Emphasis in the original, here and throughout.

[9] Brooks, *Occom*, 49; William S. Simmons, *Spirit of the New England Tribes: Indian History and Folklore* (Hanover, NH, 1986), 38, 41; David J. Silverman, *Faith and Boundaries: Colonists, Christianity, and Community among the Wampanoag Indians of Martha's Vineyard, 1600–1871* (New York, 2005), 32, 30; Barlett Burleigh James and J. Franklin Jameson, eds., *Journal of Jasper Danckaerts, 1679–1680* (New York, 1913), 78, 174–5 (quotations); Bragdon, *Native People*, 188–9.

[10] Bragdon, *Native People*, 185–6; *Zeisberger's History*, 132 (quotation).

will reach the bird, and that he will see that they are not unmindful of his services, and of his kindness to them and their ancestors.[11]

Certain animals were said to have "invisible powers" and were viewed as "the immediate authors of good to certain persons" – in other words, their guardians, who had the power to make things happen.[12]

Native peoples feared bad results if rituals were not correctly maintained. Spiritual power or manitou could turn from being beneficial to becoming dangerous when ceremonies were neglected. Eastern Algonquians used "roots and herbs or ... the seeds of a certain plant" to make a substance called *beson*, which was believed to contain supernatural powers. Hunters ingested one type of *beson* in order to be able "to shoot deer in considerable numbers"; however, it could have "a contrary effect unless every ceremony connected with its use is attended to with the most scrupulous exactness." It was assumed that spirits that gave "corn, pumpkins, squashes, beans and other vegetables" expected the proper religious acknowledgments of gratitude, as did the spirit providers of game and fish. "Corn is said to be the wife of the Indian and to it they sacrifice bear's flesh," David Zeisberger, a missionary to the Delawares, wrote. "To the deer and bear they offer corn," he added, and "to the fishes they bring an offering of small pieces of bread shaped in the form of fishes."[13]

A Mohican ceremony, held in early November 1734, included an offering of a deer "laid" out in "four quarters upon a bark in the middle of the house" with the prayer, "O Great God, pity us, grant us food to eat, afford us good and comfortable sleep, preserve us from being devoured by the fowls that fly in the air." This last request probably reflected an Algonquian legend of a giant bird that stole children. Included with the ritual was a presentation "to an old Widow woman" of the deer's "skin with the feet, and some of the inwards." Mohicans recounted the origins of this deer ceremony. "Once," they said, there "liv'd a Man among them who was seen to come down from Heaven.... He clear'd their country of monsters that infested their roads." "Esteem'd a Hero and Prophet," this man introduced the ritual, revealing "that this was a religious custom in the country above from whence he came." Unfortunately, the man grew lax in that "sometimes he omitted praying." After a reminder from his wife, he returned to using the ritual's required prayer. Perhaps the deer ceremony's presentation to the "old Widow woman" symbolized gratitude to the hero's wife for not letting this prayer lapse. Other marvelous developments occurred in the

---

[11] John Heckewelder, *History, Manners, and Customs of the Indian Nations* ... (Salem, 1991 [1876]), 212–13.
[12] Dwight, *Brainerd Memoirs*, 345.
[13] *Zeisberger's History*, 83, 84, 139; Heckewelder, *History*, 114.

story; soon the man and one of his children floated up into the heavens, while a remaining child grew into "an Extraordinary man."[14]

Successful performance of these rituals not only reinforced relationships within the human community, but also depended on strong relationships between older and younger generations. Aged persons were repositories of knowledge about ceremonies. Documentary evidence indicates how Eastern Algonquians inculcated in children "a strong sentiment of respect for their elders" and an appreciation for the role that old people played to ensure successful performance of rituals. Significantly, the woman receiving the deer's "skin with the feet, and some of the inwards" during the Mohican ceremony was elderly. Zeisberger described a hunting ceremony that showed the prominent role of the older generation. "Occasionally," he wrote,

> when an Indian would go hunting for a season, he will by way of preparation shoot a deer or two, bring home the flesh and prepare a feast, which is at the same time a sacrifice, to which the aged are invited. The latter pray for him that he may be fortunate and then he departs to stay away some time.[15]

Preserving health or curing sickness was often the focus of rituals. When a chief's wife became "very sick" in 1750 at the Iroquois town of Onondaga, "9 to 14 old women" gathered and "offered a sacrifice." Certain individuals became shamans or powwows, known for an unusual "power of *foretelling future events*, or *recovering the sick*." Some southern New England Algonquians learned of their shamanic powers through dreams and visions in which Cheepi visited them. Shamans also used sweat houses, small buildings heated with stones to produce steam, as part of healing rituals. Southeastern Indians, such as Creeks, maintained traditional curative sweat house rituals during the 1700s. Rituals aimed at purification of pollution were especially prevalent within the Native American religious culture of the Southeast.[16]

Some healing rituals centered on particular families, such as matrilineages. Certain Delaware families handed carefully tended dolls down through the generations and maintained ceremonies to the doll spirit. Such dolls were carefully dressed and maintained. One, in Ohio in 1798, appeared in silk and silver ornamentation. Another had been part of a

---

[14] Samuel Hopkins, "Historical Memoirs Relating to the Housatonic Indians" (1753), *Magazine of History with Notes and Queries* 5:17 (1911): 25–6; Simmons, *Spirit*, 70.

[15] Heckewelder, *History*, 114; *Zeisberger's History*, 84.

[16] William M. Beauchamp, ed., *Moravian Journals Relating to Central New York, 1745–66* (Syracuse, 1916), 60 ("very sick"); Dwight, *Brainerd Memoirs*, 348 ("power"); Silverman, *Faith*, 31; Bragdon, *Native People*, 201; *Zeisberger's History*, 25–6; Heckewelder, *History*, 225; Milfort, *Memoirs*, 59; Swan, "Position," 267; Hawkins, *Sketch*, 78.

family for four generations by the 1830s and was referred to as "mother." This doll was attired in "silver broaches" and "was kept wrapped up in some twenty envelopments of broad-cloth trimmed with scarlet ribbon." A ceremony for this doll spirit was held "in the fall" to prevent "some dreadful sickness."[17]

Continuity but not stasis characterized Native American religion in the eighteenth century, as in times past. Various Indian peoples experienced revelations through visions that caused them to change the way they worshipped or to stress different aspects of their traditional worship. Shamans could gain or lose status based on their success in performing healing rituals or in predicting whether a person would live or die. The prevalence of sickness among Native American populations after contact with Europeans probably caused a renewed emphasis on the roles of some shamans, but also a questioning of the efficacy of others. Traditional stories told to explain the origins of ceremonies and their proper maintenance took on new dimensions as peoples' lives changed. For example, traditional New England Algonquian images of a layered world, including an underwater sea serpent and a thunderbird above, may have been adapted to incorporate experiences with shipborne Europeans. Seventeenth-century narratives told of a ship that could both travel under water and fly, and in later Algonquian narratives the giant bird that stole children could have been a metaphor for a European vessel.[18]

In the midst of this dynamic situation, a rise in Protestant missionary activity, aimed particularly at Eastern Algonquians and at some Iroquois, called forth a variety of Native American responses. Recent scholarship eschews reducing these responses to clear-cut dualities. Rather than merely accommodation or resistance, Indians' approaches toward Christianity were multifaceted and complex. Depending on their location, Native Americans in the eighteenth century might weigh different forms of Christianity and different mission communities as they pondered conversion. Those who overtly opposed one Christian group, such as the Presbyterians, might have a different view of Christianity when they interacted with other types of missionaries, such as the Moravians. Even those who did not declare

---

[17] *Zeisberger's History*, 136; Gnadenhütten/Schönbrunn diary, 14 Jan. 1773, 1:3:141:8, *RMM*; Goshen diary, 9 Dec. 1798, 3:2:171:19, *RMM*; Reuben Gold Thwaites, ed., *Collections of the State Historical Society of Wisconsin* (Madison, 1900), 15: 164–5 (1830s example); Amy C. Schutt, *Peoples of the River Valleys: The Odyssey of the Delaware Indians* (Philadelphia, 2007), 27–8; M. R. Harrington, *Religion and Ceremonies of the Lenape* (New York, 1921), 162–71.

[18] Douglas L. Winiarski, "Native American Popular Religion in New England's Old Colony, 1670–1770," *Religion and American Culture* 15 (2005): 150; Simmons, *Spirit*, 261, 76–7, 177–8, 69–70; Bragdon, *Native People*, 187–8.

themselves Christians might borrow some aspects of Christianity as they fashioned their own responses to their tumultuous era.[19]

By the mid-eighteenth century, Eastern Algonquians, from New England to the mid-Atlantic and beyond, had considerable experience with British expansion into their homelands. Especially after the Treaty of Utrecht in 1713, colonists pushed into interior New England. In the first half of the eighteenth century, European immigrants were increasingly moving through the Delaware River valley and west into the Susquehanna watershed. These and other European migrations onto Indians' lands preceded and then converged with a growth in Protestant mission activity around the 1740s. Scholars have shown that despite the constraints Indians faced in colonial settings, Indians found creative ways to be "both Native *and* Christian." They were likely to respond more favorably to Christianity when it seemed to offer them a "key to their survival as a people." This survival was urgent for Eastern Algonquians confronting the consequences of colonization.[20]

Establishing Protestant Indian missions was certainly not a new idea by the mid-eighteenth century. The seventeenth-century Puritan John Eliot had set up "praying towns," where he attempted to instill English notions of "civility" among Massachusett, Nipmuc, and Pennacook Indians. During King Philip's War (1675–76), English colonists persecuted "praying Indians," with devastating results for Eliot's mission program. On the island of Martha's Vineyard, Puritan Thomas Mayhew, Jr., started a mission among Wampanoag Indians in the 1640s. The Vineyard mission escaped destruction during King Philip's War, and Wampanoag Christianity continued on among future generations on the island. After founding the Society for the Propagation of the Gospel in Foreign Parts in 1701, Anglicans launched missions to southeastern Indians as well as to Mohawks.[21]

---

[19] Wheeler, *Hope*, 229; Merritt, *Crossroads*, 1–2, 2n; Winiarski, "Popular Religion," 151.

[20] Daniel Mandell, "'To Live More Like My Christian English Neighbors': Natick Indians in the Eighteenth Century," *William and Mary Quarterly* 3rd ser., 48 (1991): 553; Schutt, *Peoples*, 62–93; Winiarski, "Popular Religion," 150 (first quotation); James P. Ronda, "Generations of Faith: The Christian Indians of Martha's Vineyard," *William and Mary Quarterly* 3rd ser., 38 (1981): 369–94; Wheeler, *Hope*, 11, 2 (second quotation).

[21] Daniel R. Mandell, *Behind the Frontier: Indians in Eighteenth-Century Eastern Massachusetts* (Lincoln, 1996), 14–17; R. Pierce Beaver, "Protestant Churches and the Indians," in William C. Sturtevant, ed., *Handbook of North American Indians*, vol. 4, *History of Indian-White Relations*, ed. Wilcomb E. Washburn (Washington, DC, 1988), 431; Mandell, "To Live," 555; E. Jennifer Monaghan, *Learning to Read and Write in Colonial America* (Amherst, 2005), 64, 143, 154–5, 169–81; Silverman, *Faith*, 165; Margaret Connell Szasz, *Indian Education in the American Colonies, 1607–1783* (Albuquerque, 1988), 140–1, 132–3; William Bryan Hart, "For the Good of Our Souls: Mohawk Authority,

Often, Protestant missions that attracted Eastern Algonquians in the mid-eighteenth century stressed an emotional response to the divine, a "religion of the heart," in the language of continental Pietism, a movement that influenced missionary activity. A number of missions were started during "the *long* First Great Awakening," as Thomas Kidd calls the period from "before Jonathan Edwards' 1734–35 Northampton revival ... roughly through the end of the American Revolution." Native peoples of Long Island and southern Connecticut were among the first Algonquians to hear from revival preachers. The Presbyterian itinerant James Davenport, whose preaching left English in the Stonington area *"pricked to the heart,"* also influenced conversions among Mohegan Indians. Mohegan preacher Samson Occom wrote that, when he was a teenager, evangelical preachers and lay exhorters arrived among his people. This contact resulted in "the Conviction and Saving Conversion of a Number of us," he wrote, "Amongst which, I was one that was Imprest with the things, we had heard." "These Preachers did not only come to us," Occom explained, "but we frequently went to their meetings and Churches." In 1743, Connecticut Indians spread the revival to Narragansetts in Rhode Island, where Rev. Joseph Park reported on Indians' emotional reaction (or "Outcry") to his preaching. On Long Island, Azariah Horton, a Yale graduate, served as a Presbyterian missionary to the Shinnecock and Montauk Indians. Horton's preaching aroused strong feelings, as in the case of one Montauk woman who exclaimed, "Lord Jesus, take away my stony Heart."[22]

Sponsored by the Society in Scotland for Propagating Christian Knowledge, Presbyterian David Brainerd worked briefly as a missionary to Mohicans in New York and then among Delawares in New Jersey and Pennsylvania. He brought to Algonquians a New Light message of "the wonderful effusion of the holy Spirit" and of having one's heart "pierced with the tender and melting invitations of the gospel." A revival broke out among Delawares at Crosswicks, New Jersey, in 1745, but Brainerd would certainly not have been their only New Light influence. Delawares traveled extensively throughout the region and would have heard, or heard of, other evangelical preachers, such as Gilbert and William Tennent, Jr. The latter promoted revivalism at Crosswicks when Brainerd was absent on a trip. Of the Crosswicks Delawares, Brainerd wrote, "convictions of their sinful and

---

Accommodation, and Resistance to Protestant Evangelism, 1700–1780" (Ph.D. diss., Brown University, 1988).

[22] Frank Lambert, *Inventing the 'Great Awakening'* (Princeton, 1999), 49; Kidd, *Great Awakening*, 24–39, 24 ("religion of the heart"), xix ("*long* First Great Awakening"), 191 (Montauk woman quotation); Engel, *Religion and Profit*, 14–29; Thomas Prince, *The Christian History* (Boston, 27 Aug. 1743), 26, 205 ("*pricked*"), 208 ("Outcry"); Brooks, *Occom*, 53.

perishing state were ... much promoted by the labours and endeavours of Rev. WILLIAM TENNENT ... whose house they frequented much while I was gone."²³

Emotional language of the heart was not confined to the heated atmosphere of the 1740s. Decades later, in 1770, Samuel Kirkland, a Presbyterian missionary to the Oneidas and Tuscaroras, wrote that one Indian reacted to a communion service by saying, "I thought my heart would have broken & fell in pieces." This service came several weeks after a meeting that Kirkland described as "a very considerable assembly," where "many were seen to weep abundantly." On this occasion a "singing meeting" was part of the evening's events. Music's emotional impact should not be underestimated. Occom's journals reveal how music was embedded in Native Americans' experiences of Christianity, helping to strengthen communal bonds. As he neared the home of a fellow Indian Christian in 1785, Occom "heard a Melodious Sin[g]ing." He found that "a number were together Sin[g]ing Psalms hymns and Spiritual Songs." This occurred at the end of a long journey for Occom, and music represented both welcome and unity among the Christians. "We went in amongst them," Occom wrote, "and they all took hold of my Hand one by one with Joy and Gladness from the Greatest to the least, and we Sot [sic] down a While, and then they began to Sing again."²⁴

Of the missionaries from the Great Awakening era, "heart religion" reached its fullest expression among the Moravians, a predominantly German-speaking group that sent missionaries to Mohicans and Delawares beginning in the 1740s. New Light English and Scots-Irish Protestants advocated an "experimental religion," one that stressed the individual's own felt encounter with Christ. Moravians agreed with this but took heart religion several steps farther in their antirationalism and deemphasis on doctrine. References to the heart filled Moravian writings as missionaries tried to discern the work of the Holy Spirit. Using sentences such as "He had a soft heart" and "He was very much struck in his heart," Euro-American Moravians attempted to describe what they believed Native American Christians experienced inwardly. Moravians evoked an emotional response through powerful imagery of Christ's suffering, particularly the blood and wounds at the Crucifixion. They were especially known for their use of music and art, which appealed directly to the senses.²⁵

---

[23] Dwight, *Brainerd Memoirs*, 172, 217, 216; Kidd, *Great Awakening*, 195–6, 34–35; Schutt, *Peoples*, 101–2.

[24] Walter Pilkington, ed., *The Journals of Samuel Kirkland: Eighteenth-Century Missionary to the Iroquois, Government Agent, Father of Hamilton College* (Clinton, NY, 1980), 64, 61; Brooks, *Occom*, 306.

[25] Kidd, *Great Awakening*, 106; Lambert, *Inventing*, 49–50; Craig D. Atwood, *Community of the Cross: Moravian Piety in Colonial Bethlehem* (University Park, PA, 2004), 43–58,

Compared to the Moravians, eighteenth-century missionaries from the Puritan tradition – Presbyterians and Congregationalists – paid stricter attention to doctrine and theological knowledge, even those who were revivalists. Because Euro-Americans wrote so many of the available records, it is difficult to know precisely how Indians viewed these teachings. "The method[s] which I am taking to instruct the Indians in the principles of our holy religion," Brainerd wrote, "are, to preach, or open and improve some particular points of doctrine; to expound particular paragraphs, or sometimes whole chapters of God's word to them; to give historical relations from scripture of the most material and remarkable occurrences relating to the church of God from the beginning; and frequently to catechise them upon the principles of Christianity." Brainerd had received some training under missionary John Sergeant at the Mohican town Stockbridge, Massachusetts, a mission started in the mid-1730s before the surge in revivalism. Sergeant, a Congregationalist, wanted the Stockbridge Indians to have a thorough knowledge of the Bible, as indicated by the range of his translations into the Mohican language, which included "the account of the Creation, of the fall of our first parents, of God's calling Abraham, of his dealings with the patriarchs and the Children of Israel, of the prophecies concerning the coming of Christ, &c. The four Evangelists, the Acts of the Apostles and all the Epistles." Eastern Algonquian and Iroquois pupils who studied under the New Light preacher and teacher Eleazar Wheelock received a heavy dose of Calvinist teachings about their sinfulness and need for redemption. "I am made to see the power and dominion of sin and what a weak and frail thing man is when left to him Self," wrote Nathan Clap, one of Wheelock's Indian pupils.[26]

For those Algonquians who joined Christian missions, correspondences between Christian and traditional indigenous practices could ease their transition and help place new rituals in an understandable context. Dreams and visions offered one such area of correspondence. Traditionally, Native Americans looked to dreams as messages from spirits who pointed out a path for them to follow in life. It appears that dreams and visions functioned in a similar way for Christian Indians. Joshua, a Mohican in a Pennsylvania Moravian mission, had a dream about preaching to "many Indians ... about salvation in Jesus' wounds," seeing this as a sign that he

6; Wheeler, *Hope*, 101, 98–9; Gnadenhütten, PA, diary, 3 Jan. ("Er hatte ein weiches Herz"), 16 Jan. ("Er war sehr geschlagen in seinem Herzen"), 1 Feb., 7 May 1747, 1:1:116:4, *RMM*; Friedenshütten diary, 22 Sept. 1769, 1:6:131:7, *RMM*; Gnadenhütten, OH, diary, 23 Jan. and 16 July 1774, 1:2 and 3:144:9, *RMM*.

[26] Dwight, *Brainerd Memoirs*, 338 (quotation), 119; Hopkins, "Memoirs," 168 (quotation on Sergeant); James Dow McCallum, ed., *The Letters of Eleazar Wheelock's Indians* (Hanover, NH, 1932), 68; Patrick Frazier, *The Mohicans of Stockbridge* (Lincoln, 1992), 18–19, 59; Wheeler, *Hope*, 4–5.

should convert his Delaware neighbors. In 1786, Samson Occom wrote of "a remarkable Dream," which "put me much upon thinking of the End of my Journey." After a long wait, Occom and fellow Christian Indians from around New England were finally moving to a new community, called Brothertown, far off in Iroquoia. The "End of my Journey" could have referred both to this destination and to Occom's sense of his own mortality. In this dream, the late George Whitefield appeared to Occom. If Occom was feeling doubtful about his future course, Whitefield's message offered reassurance. "I thought he was preaching as he use[d] to, when he was alive," wrote Occom of Whitefield.

> I thought he was at a certain place where there was a great Number of Indians and Some White People – and I had been Preaching, and he came to me, and took hold of my wright Hand and he put his face to my face, and rub'd his face to mine and Said, – I am glad that you preach the Excellency of Jesus Christ yet, and [he] Said, go on and the Lord be with thee, we Shall now Soon [be] done.[27]

This era of evangelical revivals saw the flourishing of dreams and visions among people undergoing spiritual struggles. A Narragansett man, Samuel Niles, was a visionary preacher whose Separate Baptist congregation formed after a split with Joseph Park's church at Westerly, Rhode Island. A Euro-American minister, albeit one critical of Niles, revealed the visionary aspects of the Narragansett man's preaching. Niles, he said, was "in imminent danger of leaving *The Word*, for the Guidance of *Feelings, Impressions, Visions, Appearances* and *Directions* of Angels and of Christ himself in a Visionary Way." An identification with Moses, who led his people, experienced God's glory, and received the law, infused the visions of William Tennent, Jr., and George Whitefield. In one of his visions, Tennent perceived that "his spirit seemed to be caught up to the heavens" and "he felt as though he saw God, as Moses did on the Mount, face to face." Having his dream as a teenager, Whitefield was less confident about the prophetic role suggested to him by the dream. He sensed in this dream that he "was to see God on Mount Sinai, but was afraid to meet Him." Like these white evangelicals, Tunda Tatamy, Delaware interpreter for Brainerd, seemed to identify with Moses and the climb to Mount Sinai. Indeed, Brainerd revealed that Tatamy's Christian name was Moses. The account of Tunda Tatamy's vision suggests the influence of evangelical – and in this case Calvinist – teachings about the helplessness of humans and the sovereignty of God. "There seemed to be *an impassible mountain* before him," Brainerd reported of Tatamy's vision.

[27] Merritt, *Crossroads*, 89–90, 106–7; Wheeler, *Hope*, 103–4; Richard W. Pointer, *Encounters of the Spirit: Native Americans and European Colonial Religion* (Bloomington, 2007), 139–40; Gnadenhütten, PA, diary, 1 Jan. 1748 ("viele Indianer ... von der Seeligkeit in Wunden Jesu"), 1:3:116:4, *RMM*; Brooks, *Occom*, 334 (material in brackets added).

He was pressing towards heaven, as he thought; but "his way was hedged up with thorns, so that he could not stir an inch further." He looked this way, and that way, but could find no way at all. He thought if he could but make his way through these thorns and briers, and climb up the first *steep pitch* of the mountain, that then there might be hope for him.[28]

Christian conversions involved recognition of the futility of one's own efforts, as Tunda Tatamy's dream indicated. Here, again, Indian peoples could have found at least a partial correspondence with their past experiences of seeking spiritual aid. Making oneself pitiful and needy was traditionally one way for Algonquians to attract supernatural help. "O poor me!" began a song to the "Great Spirit" by Delaware men going off to war. "O! take pity on me! Give me strength and courage to meet my enemy." Other parts of this song-prayer asked for help for the warrior's wife, who was called a "poor creature," and the warrior begged the spirit to "take pity on my children." The repeated prayers for God's mercy at revivals may have seemed a variation on this traditional model. During the Crosswicks revival, Delawares "were almost universally praying and crying for mercy in every part of the house, and many out of doors." Brainerd said, "*Have mercy upon me; have mercy upon me*; was the common cry." Moravian teachings downplayed the need for a terrible struggle in the conversion process; nevertheless, even in Moravian missions, Indians told of feeling "poor" and in need of God's mercy.[29]

The Moravians were in many ways outliers among evangelical Protestants of the eighteenth century. They were distinct from other Protestants in that their missions were often more successful, at least until near the end of the Revolutionary War, when more than ninety Christian Moravian Indians were massacred by American militia in Ohio. In addition, Moravians received much criticism, including from other Protestant missionaries. At a time when Protestant missions were seen as a way to bolster the British colonies against the French, Moravians faced accusations that they were pro-French and secretly Roman Catholic. Given their

---

[28] William S. Simmons and Cheryl L. Simmons, eds., *Old Light on Separate Ways: The Narragansett Diary of Joseph Fish, 1765–1776* (Hanover, NH, 1982), 5; William S. Simmons, "Red Yankees: Narragansett Conversion in the Great Awakening," *American Ethnologist* 10 (1983): 261–2; Tennent and Whitefield quoted in Kidd, *Great Awakening*, 34, 42; Dwight, *Brainerd Memoirs*, 211–12, 214; William A. Hunter, "Moses (Tunda) Tatamy, Delaware Indian Diplomat," in Herbert C. Kraft, ed., *A Delaware Indian Symposium* (Harrisburg, PA, 1974), 71–88.

[29] Heckewelder, *History*, 211 (Delaware song); Dwight, *Brainerd Memoir*, 219, 221; Atwood, *Community*, 48–50; Engel, *Religion and Profit*, 24–5; Wyalusing diary, 22 Dec. 1765 and 3 Mar. 1766, 1:2 and 3:131:7, *RMM*; Amy C. Schutt, "'What Will Become of Our Young People?' Goals for Indian Children in Moravian Missions," *History of Education Quarterly* (1998): 276–8.

conscientious objections to swearing oaths and bearing arms, Moravians had trouble proving their loyalty to the British after King George's War began in 1744, and their missionaries were barred from preaching in New York. From this outcast position, they turned their attention to converting Delawares in Pennsylvania with the help of Christian Mohicans.[30]

Moravians' relative success among Native Americans can be attributed to various factors. Their use of both female and male missionaries, especially in the 1740s and 1750s, widened their appeal. A Moravian focus on children and their upbringing helped answer concerns of worried Indian parents in times of social crisis. Moravians' deemphasis on doctrinal requirements eased Indians' access to Christianity, and Moravian ceremonialism fit with the Algonquian notion that "ritual brought transformative power." Moravians had a range of rituals, often keyed to specific holidays. Children sang and held candles at Christmas Eve services. Commemorating the manifestation of Christ to the "heathen," Epiphany was used as a special opportunity to welcome Indian visitors. Pentecost highlighted the action of a motherly Holy Spirit, an image that the matrilineal Mohicans and Delawares probably found especially appealing. On St. John's Day in June, young boys were instructed to devote themselves to Jesus. Easter week included vocal reading of the crucifixion story and worship in the cemetery, which was "a celebration of the community of the living and the dead." Moravian ritual life also included love feasts and foot washings; some ceremonies focused on subgroups in the community – called "choirs" – consisting of people at the same stage of life and of the same sex.[31] In addition, Algonquians may have been able to steer their own course to a greater extent in Moravian missions than in many other Protestant settings. Eighteenth-century Moravian missions had strong male and female Indian leaders, who translated, preached, provided hospitality to visitors, and acted as spiritual counselors. At a mission conference in 1753, for example, Indian leaders of both sexes deliberated over several topics, including whether to readmit a former member to their conference and whether a Mohican woman, named Marie, would be able to travel to Europe.[32]

---

[30] Schutt, "Indian Children," 271; Schutt, *Peoples*, 98, ch. 6; Wheeler, *Hope*, 200–6; Axtell, *Invasion Within*, 201–2.

[31] Wheeler, *Hope*, 105 (first quotation), 118–21, 122 (cemetery quotation); Schutt, "Indian Children," 268–86; Amy C. Schutt, "Female Relationships and Intercultural Bonds in Moravian Indian Missions," in William A. Pencak and Daniel K. Richter, eds., *Friends and Enemies in Penn's Woods: Indians, Colonists, and the Racial Construction of Pennsylvania* (University Park, PA, 2004), 87–103; Friedenshütten diary, 7 June 1767, 6 Jan. 1768 and 1769, 20–26 Mar. 1769, 1:4:5, and 6:131:7, *RMM*.

[32] Wheeler, *Hope*, 124–7; Schutt, *Peoples*, 100–1; Schutt, "Female Relationships," 96–101; Gnadenhütten, PA, conference, 24 Jan. 1753, 1:4:117:5, *RMM*; Seidel to Spangenberg, 19 Oct. 1755, 15:6:118:5, *RMM*.

Spiritual and practical concerns merged as Indians considered whether or not to join missions. Typically, missions needed to offer practical benefits for survival in order to draw in new members. Against the backdrop of whites' shady land dealings with them, the acquisition of alphabetic literacy was a skill that could give Indians hope of fairer treatment in the future; often they associated this skill with mission instruction. For many Indian Christians, alliances with missionaries probably seemed a practical way to gain Euro-American support for securing Native American lands. Delawares, for example, tried to strengthen their claim to Ohio Country lands, in part by forming relationships with Moravians and, to a lesser extent, Quakers. Identification with the Moravians and friendships with the Quakers also helped some Delawares promote a message of pacifism after the Seven Years' War.[33] Some Indians saw Christianity as useful in halting the ravages of alcohol among them, and they sought reform in its sale and consumption. Even though certain colonies passed legislation restricting these sales to Indians, regulations were often ignored. Various Indians decried results of heavy drinking, particularly violence and poverty, and criticized Euro-Americans for promoting alcohol consumption. Some Indians decided that Christian missionaries could be allies in temperance reform. In their early contacts with Sergeant, two Mohican leaders, Konkapot and Umpachenee, revealed this orientation. "He is very much griev'd at the intemperance of his people," Sergeant wrote of Konkapot, whom he called "a temperate man himself." For his part, Umpachenee had "entirely left off drinking to excess" by early 1735 and was urging others to do so as well.[34]

Many Indians could not be convinced, however, that becoming Christian ensured their people's survival. Native resentment over a long history of injustices made many highly suspicious of missionaries. Sergeant wrote of "the *Jealousies and Suspicions* the *Indians* entertain'd of us and of our Designs." When Brainerd sought Christian converts, some Indians argued "that the white people have come among them, have cheated them out of their lands, and driven them back to the mountains, from the pleasant places they used to enjoy by the sea-side; that therefore they have no reason to think the white people are now seeking their welfare." Also expressed was the fear that missionaries were preparing Indians for enslavement. One Delaware opponent of the Moravians averred that the Europeans wanted

---

[33] Hopkins, "Memoirs," 23, 29, 78; Wheeler, *Hope*, 51, 1–2; Monaghan, *Learning to Read*, 77–80; Schutt, "Indian Children," 282–5; Schutt, *Peoples*, 74–90, 96–100, 122–3, and chs. 5 and 6.

[34] Peter C. Mancall, *Deadly Medicine: Indians and Alcohol in Early America* (Ithaca, 1995), 103–10, 67, 70, 64–6; Guy Soulliard Klett, ed., *Journals of Charles Beatty, 1762–1769* (University Park, PA, 1962), 66–7; Brooks, *Occom*, 192, 218–19; Hopkins, "Memoirs," 29 ("He is"), 47 ("entirely"), 43, 28, 32.

to use Indians to pull their plows. A common Native American argument against Christianity in the eighteenth century was that of the separate creation of Indians and whites. "It is a notion pretty generally prevailing among them," Brainerd wrote, "that it was not the *same God* made them, who made us.... They suppose our religion will do well enough for us, because prescribed by *our* God; yet it is no way proper for them." A Seneca man spoke out against Kirkland, saying that the Bible "was never made for *Indians*" and that "Our great Superintendent Thaonghyawagon *i.e. Upholder of the Skies* gave us a *book*. He wrote it in our heads & in our minds & gave us rules about worshipping him." Should the Senecas "receive this *white man* & attend to the Book which was made solely for White people, we shall become a *miserable abject people.*" Disagreements over how to respond to Christianity and to different types of Christian missionaries created rifts in Indian communities.[35]

Missionaries often hurt their own cause. English missionaries such as Sergeant and Wheelock promoted a philosophy of "civilization before Christianization" that showed disdain for indigenous cultures. Wheelock manipulated his pupils and former students, sometimes to their great resentment. For good reason, Mohicans worried that Sergeant promoted English encroachment on their lands. Although Moravians were probably viewed as less greedy for Indians' lands, some Delawares had reason to resent them as well. The Moravians' North American headquarters, the town of Bethlehem, Pennsylvania, lay within the bounds of the infamous "Walking Purchase," which Delawares had protested as fraudulent.[36]

As Native Americans faced dispossession and other troubles of the eighteenth century, they continued to seek answers through visions. Native visionaries expressed the religious ferment of the time. A couple of accounts suggest how visions came to troubled individuals who went off alone to pray, and perhaps fast – methods used in a traditional vision quest. Sometime before 1760, Papoonahoal underwent a spiritual crisis during which "he forsook the town, and went to the woods in great bitterness of spirit." "At the end of five days," he said, "it pleased God to appear to him to his comfort, and to give him a sight not only of his own inward state, but [also] an acquaintance into the works of nature." Papoonahoal seemed to gain secret knowledge at this time, for "a sense was given him," he said, "of the virtues and nature of several herbs, roots, plants and trees." In 1766,

---

[35] Prince, *Christian History*, 9 July 1743, no. 19, 151 (first quotation); Dwight, *Brainerd Memoirs*, 343 (second quotation), 176, 345–6 (third quotation); Pilkington, *Journals of Kirkland*, 24; Hopkins, "Memoirs," 28; Langundo Utenünk diary, 17 May 1771, 1:2:137:8, *RMM*; Axtell, *Invasion Within*, 284.

[36] Axtell, *Invasion Within*, 208, 204–13; Brooks, *Occom*, 6, 63; Wheeler, *Hope*, 56–61, 52–3; Schönbrunn diary, 7 Oct. 1772, 1:1:1411:9, *RMM*; Schutt, *Peoples*, 81–93, 98.

Neolin, a "young man," told the missionary Charles Beatty that "he had some thing like a vision about 6 years agoe while he was alone by himself musing & greatly conc[e]rned about the evil ways he saw prevailing among the Indians." Various Indians recounted their mystical journeys to heaven. A Delaware prophet, often assumed to be Neolin, had a vision of going on a journey "to see the Master of Life." In an interesting parallel to Tunda Tatamy's vision, his trip included an arduous climb up a "mountain which was perpendicular, pathless, and smooth as ice."[37]

The answers that Algonquian prophets obtained from visions varied, but reform was one common theme. Alcohol was an issue for these visionaries, just as it was among the Christian Indian reformers. "Do not drink more than once, or at most twice in a day," the Delaware prophet said that he learned from the Master of Life, and Papoonahoal tried to prevent "strong liquor" from entering his town. New rituals, or revivals of old ones, were begun. "In all things I command thee to repeat every morning and night the prayer which I have given thee" were the Delaware prophet's instructions from the Master of Life. At Assinisink (Corning, New York), Indians started "to revive an Old quarterly Meeting which had been many Years laid aside, in which they related to each other their Dreams and Revelations every one had from his Infancy, & what Strength & Power they had received thereby." In Ohio it was said that the Delawares had a "new Plan of Religion" by which "Boys are to be Train'd to ye use of the Bow & Arrow," to follow a special diet, and to consume a "Bitter Drink." Furthermore, according to this plan, after seven years, they would "quit all Commerce with ye White People & Clothe themselves with Skins."[38]

These teachings were a dynamic blend of Delaware and Christian influences. They probably also reflected influences from non-Delaware indigenous sources. By the mid-eighteenth century, Delawares had many contacts with other Indian peoples, including Shawnees, Cherokees, Iroquois, Conoys, and Nanticokes. Neolin's teachings indicated use of an emetic, which may have shown the influence of southeastern Indians' black drink

---

[37] *Account of the Minusing*, 13–14; Szasz, *Indian Education*, 16–17; Klett, *Beatty*, 65; *Zeisberger's History*, 134, 147; Minutes of the Provincial Council of Pennsylvania ... (Harrisburg, PA, 1851–52), 9: 252, 254; Milo Milton Quaife, ed., *The Siege of Detroit in 1763* ... (Chicago, 1958), 12 (last quotation); Gregory Evans Dowd, *A Spirited Resistance: The North American Indian Struggle for Unity, 1745–1815* (Baltimore, 1992), 33–5; Lee Irwin, *Coming Down from Above: Prophecy, Resistance, and Renewal in Native American Religions* (Norman, OK, 2008), 129–32.

[38] Quaife, *Siege*, 16; *Account of the Minusing*, 5; Robert S. Grumet, ed., *Journey on the Forbidden Path* ... (Philadelphia, 1999), 8, 56 ("quarterly Meeting"); John W. Jordon, ed., "Journal of James Kenny, 1761–1763," *Pennsylvania Magazine of History and Biography* 37 (1913): 188 (last set of quotations).

purification ritual. The Delaware prophet, whose teachings inspired the Ottawa Pontiac to strike back at continued British expansion, drew on indigenous traditions about the rituals of war making. "There will be Two or Three Good Talks & then War," he predicted. This comment, filtered through the writings of a Quaker trader, may reflect a tradition Delawares shared with the Iroquois, that "the Great Being ... ordered us to send three Messages of Peace before we make War." Delaware prophecies also pointed to past exposures to missionaries' teachings. Using a map drawn on deerskin, the prophet showed "a straight Line" to heaven and "Hapiness," but "many Strokes" indicating "all ye Sins & Vices which ye Indians have learned from ye White people," which blocked the way. An alternate route took Indians to a hell-like place of "extreme poverty." In these accounts are echoes of Brainerd's earlier preaching of the gospel message "enter in at the strait gate," and of the words of a Delaware woman moved by this message. This woman had a vision of "*two paths*," Brainerd wrote,

> one appeared very broad and crooked; and that turned to the left hand. The other appeared straight and very narrow; and that went up the hill to the right hand. She travelled, she said, *for some time up the narrow right hand path, till at length something seemed to obstruct her journey. She sometimes called it darkness, and then described it otherwise, and seemed to compare it to a block or bar.*[39]

Assessing the impacts of various religious workers and leaders raises questions about numbers. We have no way of knowing how many Indians considered themselves followers of the Delaware prophet, but his and similar Native American teachings clearly had a sizeable audience. The Long Island preacher Horton was said to have baptized 79 Indians, including 44 children. By sometime in 1746, David Brainerd had baptized 77 Indians, of whom 39 were children. Brainerd died in 1747, and his brother John carried on the work, sending a few pupils to Wheelock's school. Between 1734 and 1749, Sergeant baptized 182 Indians. Moravians provided a range of statistics, indicating how many people had been accepted into a mission town, how many of these were baptized, and how many were communicants. At Lichtenau, one of the larger Moravian mission towns in eastern Ohio, the total number of Indian residents was 328 at the end of 1778.[40]

---

[39] Schutt, *Peoples*, 62–72, 119, 146–7; Dowd, *Spirited*, 33; Jordan, "Kenny," 171 ("Two or Three Good Talks," "straight Line"); Alden T. Vaughan, ed., *Early American Indian Documents: Treaties and Laws, 1607–1789*, vol. 2, *Pennsylvania and Delaware Treaties, 1737–1756*, ed. Donald H. Kent (Washington, DC, 1984), 285 ("the Great Being"); Heckewelder, *History*, 292 ("extreme poverty"); Dwight, *Brainerd Memoirs*, 263.

[40] Dwight, *Brainerd Memoirs*, 4, 328; Thomas Brainerd, *The Life of John Brainerd ...* (Philadelphia, 1865), 97–8, 278–80, http://name.umdl.umich.edu/abb4262.0001.001; Hopkins, "Memoirs," 11–12; Lichtenau diary, 31 Dec. 1778, 1:8:147:9, *RMM*.

Missionaries' statistics reflect tendencies toward boundary drawing that can be misleading. Christian Indians continued to be shaped by traditional indigenous beliefs. Some Indians who did not fall under the classifications of baptized or mission resident were still influenced by past contacts with Christian teachings. Such may have been the case for a tiny, nearly all-female Munsee community in present-day western Pennsylvania in 1770. Its residents, who had decided not to marry, may have been influenced by teachings about celibacy from a French priest formerly in the area. The impact of past encounters with Quakers also surfaced in 1768, when some Ohio Indians planned to use "a large meeting house" for preaching that showed Quaker influence. In New England, Indian shamans interacted with Euro-Americans in ways that shaped the latter's experience of "supernatural lore" and "popular magical practices." Religious influences moved along complex and diverse paths. These and many other examples are part of the ferment of the era, which resulted in fevered religious argumentation, heartfelt spiritual exchange, and religious synthesis.[41]

SUGGESTIONS FOR FURTHER READING

Brooks, Joanna, ed. *The Collected Writings of Samson Occom, Mohegan: Leadership and Literature in Eighteenth-Century Native America.* Oxford, 2006.

Dally-Starna, Corinna, and William A. Starna, trans. and ed. *Gideon's People: Being a Chronicle of an American Indian Community in Colonial Connecticut and the Moravian Missionaries Who Served There.* 2 vols. Lincoln, 2009.

Merritt, Jane T. *At the Crossroads: Indians and Empires on a Mid-Atlantic Frontier, 1700–1763.* Chapel Hill, 2003.

Murray, Laura J., ed., *To Do Good to My Indian Brethren: The Writings of Joseph Johnson, 1751–1776.* Amherst, 1998.

Schutt, Amy C. *Peoples of the River Valleys: The Odyssey of the Delaware Indians.* Philadelphia, 2007.

Silverman, David J. *Faith and Boundaries: Colonists, Christianity, and Community among the Wampanoag Indians of Martha's Vineyard, 1600–1871.* New York, 2005.

Simmons, William S. *Spirit of the New England Tribes: Indian History and Folklore.* Hanover, NH, 1986.

Wheeler, Rachel. *To Live upon Hope: Mohicans and Missionaries in the Eighteenth-Century Northeast.* Ithaca, 2008.

---

[41] Langundo Utenünk diary, 23 Apr., 3 and 13 May, and 3 June 1770, 1:3:137:8, *RMM*; Goschgoschunk diary, 13–14 June 1768, 1:1:135:8, *RMM*; Winiarski, "Popular Religion," 166–8, 169 (last two quotations).

18

AFRICAN SLAVE RELIGIONS, 1400–1790

SYLVESTER A. JOHNSON

African slave religions were rooted in the cultural forms of western and central African religions. The paradigmatic features of these religions included central concern with powerful beings of the extraordinary realm who were related to the phenomenal world of experience through African ideas of matter and spirit. African religions had established a tradition of incorporating elements of theology and ritual from cultures other than that of the devotee. This history of refashioning and blending continued in the religion of African slaves that resulted from the dispersion of the transatlantic slave trade.

PRE-COLUMBIAN ERA TO 1600

The nature of African slave religions is discernible from the major patterns of theology and culture that had defined African societies for centuries. The oldest stratum of religion in western and central Africa is Orisha religion, which mutually obligated humans and members of the extraordinary realm of divine and ancestral beings.[1] Beginning in the ninth century of the Common Era, varieties of Islam would become familiar to the region. And by the early 1500s, the Kongo state, followed by the Ndongo kingdom, would establish an African form of Christianity as its official religion. Orisha religion, nevertheless, by far and away dominated the numerous states of West Africa. The theological interpretations of matter, commerce, and governance throughout West Africa were deliberately shaped and continually refashioned to conform to Orisha philosophical norms.[2]

---

[1] This essay employs the Yoruba-derived term "Orisha(s)" instead of the Latin-derived "spirit(s)" to denote the extraordinary beings honored in the variety of cults that constituted African indigenous religion. This use is meant to connote the African philosophies of spirit and matter that differed substantially from that of the Latin Christian tradition, because Orishas could often manifest as part of the material world.

[2] Mervyn Hiskett, *The Development of Islam in West Africa* (London, 1984), 19.

Important parallels existed across the varieties of Islam, Christianity, and Orisha religion in West Africa. With few exceptions, the professional leaders or specialists within these traditions provided clients with the important service of manufacturing sacred objects known as gris-gris, which found wide use as amulets.[3] West Africans, for example, used the gris-gris as a legitimate embodiment of the spiritual power to ward off evil and to ensure health and success. A gris-gris frequently took the form of prayers written in Arabic or brief excerpts from the Qur'an perhaps sealed in a leather pouch and worn about the neck. White observers often called them "fetishes." Their production and use was rooted in an African theory of materiality that viewed matter as one possible manifestation of spiritual power (*ashe* in Yoruba) or of the powerful beings of the divine community. These objects offered protection from harm and success in worldly ventures. They also might be sworn on to bind parties in mutually obligatory oaths, and they became a standard means of ensuring that the terms of economic exchange among African and European merchants were honored.[4]

Healing was also pervasive in African religions. Healing practices combined medicinal and spiritual methods to restore health and were rooted in complex traditions of botanical knowledge. This approach to treating disease and promoting health was integral to the successful mastery of religion that exemplified African religion as a system that bridged the realms of matter and spirit. Slaves in western and central Africa who followed the traditions of Orisha, Christianity (largely Kongolese), and Islam regularly sought out religious experts – often across religious boundaries – to restore physical health and to address social rifts (e.g., within families or larger communities). The redress of physical and social problems involved petitioning and sacrificing to the powerful Orishas and ancestors, which marked an important intersection of Orisha religion and Christianity. More than one observer, for this reason, has noted that Christianity under Portuguese missionaries and the pre-Christian religion of the Kongo state were, in a fundamental sense, religions of the "powerful dead," commanding cultic attention to favorably obligate the deceased in reciprocal service to the living.[5]

The religion of African slaves of the pre-Columbian era, like that of free Africans, was also guided by enduring theological themes of ancestral veneration, spirit possession, sacrifice, and divination. This framework had

---

[3] Walter Rodney, *A History of the Upper Guinea Coast, 1545–1800* (New York, 1982), 230–1.

[4] William Pietz, "The Problem of the Fetish, II," *Res* 13 (Spring 1987): 23–45.

[5] See the description of early Atlantic religion by Albert J. Raboteau and David Wills in their introduction to the African American Religious Documentary Project. http://www3.amherst.edu/~aardoc/Atlantic_World.html (accessed 1 Feb. 2010).

been shaped in the earlier history of African religion and would continually inform the paradigmatic structures of African slave religions.[6] Religion in western and central Africa had for centuries promoted belief in a vast hierarchy of divine beings, the most important of whom was often credited with creating lower-ranking deities, who in turn were responsible for creating the phenomenal world of matter and spirit. The lower-ranking deities were also credited with introducing cultural and technological knowledge to humankind. So distant was the supreme God from the world of spiritual communication and material interests that this being was typically without a cult. With few exceptions, direct homage to the supreme God was not required. The reign of the supreme deity was passive rule whose social meaning and force were constituted through the agency and discretion of a community of Orishas. In this sense, the highest God was a figurehead who brought coherence to a pluralistic field of divine agents. Even the supreme status of a high God invites careful scrutiny because this often depended on the particular theme of concern. Among the Yoruba, for instance, Orunmila (Ifa) was certainly supreme in matters of knowledge and wisdom, rather than the "supreme" Olodumare. The divine beings who populated the spiritual realm, moreover, did so because of their agency, not their moral status; these extraordinary beings were powerful, not good or evil. The binary system of ontological good versus ontological evil that played a central role in European religion never defined this African cosmos.[7]

Divination was a means of identifying the underlying cause of misfortune, illness, or social conflict using material objects, such as cowry shells or kola nuts, that could be interpreted by trained priests. This indicates one way that matter was understood to be a manifestation of spiritual essences. Orishas communicated via material objects and could thereby reveal knowledge to devotees.[8] The significance of human relations with the Orishas revolved around the principle of obligation. West African religions of the fourteenth and fifteenth centuries attest to an expansive means of obligating humans to the Orishas. This meant Africans were required to offer sacrifice, nourishment, pilgrimage, and quotidian communications to petition assistance for virtually every kind of human endeavor. The major points of passage from birth to puberty to marriage to eldership, and so on, were passable only with permission and assistance from the Orishas.[9] And the rites of passage reconstituted the nature and identity of initiates

---

[6] Dianne M. Stewart, *Three Eyes for the Journey: African Dimensions of the Jamaican Religious Experience* (New York, 2004), 24–7.
[7] Kólá Abímbólá, *Yoruba Culture: A Philosophical Account* (Birmingham, 2006), 29.
[8] *Ibid.*, 126–7.
[9] Benjamin Ray, "African Religions: Overview of," in Lindsay Jones, ed., *Encyclopedia of Religion* (Detroit, 2005), 2: 85.

by taking them through sites of liminality to a stable category of existence (children became adults, men became husbands, etc.). Ties were mutually obligatory, of course, and the rituals that were performed in service to the Orishas established evidence that ancestors and Orishas were bound to serve humankind by offering protection, ensuring prosperity, bringing physical well-being, or ending affliction.

After the religion of Orisha veneration, Islam was the next most important component of African slave religions in western and central Africa. By the tenth century the Saharan city of Tadmakkat, rooted in the Ibadiyya sect, was the key source of Islamicizing influences on West Africa. This was an old trading city, pre-Christian in legacy and well established, linking multiple trade routes. By the eleventh century, the kingdom of Ghana had become a massive empire and began to employ Muslims as state scribes. Their religious influence only increased as Islam began to spread through the trade activities of Muslim merchants. The Almoravid Dynasty, meanwhile, was commanding greater sway, often convincing state officials to convert to Islam, hoping this would trickle down to the local populace. As early as 1076, the Ghanaian court had converted to Sunni Islam, although the royal cult of the Orishas continued alongside this adoption of Islam. This pattern of officials converting to Islam but also continuing the historical cult of the Orishas became the norm throughout the Islamic regions of western and central Africa. It meant that West African Islam could thrive because its devotees continued to shape it to local culture in the way earlier Muslim communities had done.[10]

Sharia law strictly regulated trade among Muslims, and conversion to Islam helped to promote the growth of West African trade networks with Muslim states and Muslim merchants, because Muslims were more likely to engage in fiduciary trust with other Muslims. This situation clearly spurred the growth of Islam in West Africa, and it is one reason the Islamic Empire of Mali became a powerful polity in trade relations with Egypt, the Maghreb, and northern Africa in the fourteenth century. Islam never dominated West Africa in the ensuing centuries. Nevertheless, by the time Afro-European trade relations were sending African slaves to Europe (1400s) and the Americas (1500s), a significant minority of African slaves were taking with them a historically developed tradition of Islam acquired through upbringing or conversion. And free and enslaved African Muslims were among the first who would encounter Portuguese merchants along Africa's Atlantic coast.[11]

---

[10] Hiskett, *Development of Islam*, 22–35; Michael Gomez, *Exchanging Our Country Marks: The Transformation of African Identities in the Colonial and Antebellum South* (Chapel Hill, 1998), 61–5.

[11] Hiskett, *Development of Islam*, 2900IE30.

Until the 1440s, African slaves were sold to Europeans by Arab merchants. This long-established practice soon changed, however, as the Portuguese Prince Henry "the navigator" promoted exploration of the West African coast in hopes of establishing new, profitable commercial relations.[12] In 1441, the Portuguese succeeded in navigating further south along coastal West Africa than any other Europeans previously, and they purchased the first African slaves to be used as forced labor in Europe. By 1448, more than nine hundred would be acquired and sent to Portugal.[13] Spain soon followed Portugal's rapidly growing trade in African slaves, such that Iberia would easily have the greatest population of Africans (almost all of whom were slaves) in all of Europe. In 1519, the first African slaves would be transported to the Americas, as Spain sought a substitute for Indian slavery in Puerto Rico. The Dutch, English, and French followed. By the end of the slave trade, more than fifteen million Africans had been enslaved for this transatlantic slave trade, and roughly twelve million of these survived the journey to the seaports of West Africa for transport out of Africa to the Americas (mostly) and to Europe. Of this number, 90 percent would be transported to Portuguese and Spanish colonies in South America and the Caribbean. North America would be the destination of the others, who numbered more than one million.[14]

Although the extant data about African slave religions in Iberia is scant, it is clear that some Africans were proselytized by their white Christian slave masters. In Granada, Africans who were most assimilated (e.g., fluent in Castilian and embracing a Christian ethos) were referred to as *ladinos*. Among the most famous perhaps is Juan Latino, an African slave eventually manumitted by his white Christian owner. Juan Latino became a Latin scholar and authored several books before his death in 1590. He even distinguished himself from other Africans who were not Christians, justifying the enslavement of other blacks on this basis and representing his own enslavement as an accident.[15] Among the Moors persecuted in Granada were African slaves whose religion was Islam. Some Africans were converted to Islam under the influence of Muslim slave masters. Others, however, were reared in Islam from childhood. Both patterns were common and resulted from the centuries-long history of Islam in West Africa.[16]

---

[12] Sergio Tognetti, "The Trade in Black African Slaves in Fifteenth-Century Florence," in T. F. Earle and K. J. P. Lowe, eds., *Black Africans in Renaissance Europe* (Cambridge, UK, 2005), 215–16.

[13] *Ibid.*, 214, 215; Albert J. Raboteau, *Slave Religion: The "Invisible Institution" in the Antebellum South* (New York, 1978), 5.

[14] Marcus Rediker, *The Slave Ship: A Human History* (New York, 2007), 5.

[15] Jonathan Schorsch, *Swimming the Christian Atlantic: Judeoconversos, Afroiberians and Amerindians in the Seventeenth Century* (Leiden, 2009), 35.

[16] *Ibid.*, 35; Hiskett, *Development of Islam*, 20–35.

By contrast, Africans who resisted assimilation and adhered most closely to their native African culture were derisively described as "uncivilized" or "bush." There is every reason to suspect this latter group remained devotees of the Orishas. Furthermore, because Granada had two confraternities (mutual aid societies), one for blacks and the other for mulattoes, it is also evident that African slaves in Granada, like those of Valencia, had a formal social network that would have reinforced their continued participation in Orisha cults.[17]

Most of the early slave purchases transacted by Portuguese merchants to other Europeans were for luxury purchases. And it was very common for white slavers in Iberia to have sex with their African female slaves. In Florence, the offspring of these forced sexual unions were often reared by European orphanages that impressed on the children a life of Christian devotion.[18] In Valencia, free and enslaved Africans formed a confraternity, a pattern that would be replicated in New World slavery as well. This formal community of slaves was granted a charter in 1472, although the group was active before that date. The charter allowed them certain limited freedoms such as assembling without a permit, purchasing homes, and creating a coat of arms. The confraternity functioned as a hospice and as a charitable institution. And slaves could even serve as elected officials in the confraternity. The confraternity often functioned to appeal on behalf of slaves to magistrates and owners for redemption, that is, the opportunity to purchase one's freedom.[19]

By the early 1500s African slave religions were undergoing further change due to the momentous wave of new trade relations the numerous African states were establishing with the Portuguese. Along the coastal regions of West Africa and further inland in the central region of the Kongo and Ndongo states, a new demographic arose of Africans who were fluent in Portuguese and in multiple African languages. Portuguese Christian missions to the region arose in this context during the 1490s. In 1491, the Kongolese monarch Nzinga a Nkuwu converted to Catholicism, which subsequently became the state religion. Whereas Iberian Christians made prayers to saints and maintained altars in honor of particular divine, extraordinary beings – saints, angels, the highly exalted redeemer-figure Jesus, and Mary his mother – in exchange for protection from evil, success at war, prosperous health, and other quotidian successes, so also did the

---

[17] Aurelia Martín Casares, "Free and Freed Black Africans in Granada in the Time of the Spanish Renaissance," in Earle and Lowe, *Black Africans*, 250–8.
[18] Tognetti, "Black African Slaves," 220.
[19] Debra Blumenthal, "'*La Casa dels Negres*': Black African Solidarity in Late Medieval Valencia," in Earle and Lowe, *Black Africans*, 233–6.

Kongolese make devotion to their own venerated dead – the ancestors of individual families and of larger kinship groups, patron defenders of towns or larger polities, powerful divine spirits, and so on. Both Iberian and Kongolese religions had cultivated extensive traditions of spiritual warfare against malevolent beings, whether human "witches" or dangerous spirits. Most important was the fact that the state-sponsored Catholicism of the Kongo state was thoroughly defined by the autonomy of the Kongolese and was not imperially administered by Europeans, to the constant chagrin of Portugal. Thus, rather than cultivating a contempt for the historically deeper traditions of Kongolese religion among converts, Catholicism in Kongo characteristically became incorporated into the phenomenal structures of an African sacred cosmos and local regimes of Kongolese authority.[20] Kongolese Christians had not rejected the historical religion of their ancestors; instead, they introduced into their religion of continuous revelation the revelatory knowledge of Christianity. This meant that in addition to making devotion to African ancestors and African gods, they could also obligate Christian saints and the Christian divinities to work in their interest and to defend them from the chaotic whim of evil through the ritual language of sacrifice and veneration.[21]

Because Africans of the Kongo state accepted the claims of Iberian missionaries to the extent that the revealed knowledge of Iberian Catholics conformed to Kongolese revealed religion, the Catholic Church of the Kongo state understood their affiliation with the Catholic officials of Portugal to be affirming religious claims that were already attested in the history of their own religion. This approach was helped along by the fact that Iberian missionaries to the Kongolese used the names of African gods to explain divinities in Catholicism. Rather than thinking of Kongolese Christianity as the product of conversion to a European religion (it was not), it is more helpful to interpret this as expanding somewhat a complex system of African revealed religion that presumed continuous emanations or revelations from the realm of the gods and the powerful dead.[22]

1600 TO 1700

Spanish and Portuguese ambitions to colonize the Americas had long since been under way by the early 1600s. Spain's adoption of the agricultural

---

[20] John Thornton, "The Development of an African Catholic Church in the Kingdom of Kongo, 1491–1750," *Journal of African History* 25 (1984): 147–67.
[21] John Thornton, *Africa and Africans in the Making of the Atlantic World, 1400–1680* (New York, 2007), 257–65.
[22] *Ibid.*, 255–6.

plantation model of economy in Hispaniola and in other New World colonies rapidly increased the demand for African slaves in the face of a remnant population of Taino almost entirely exterminated by the Spanish. In 1518, the Spanish monarch Charles V granted permission for four thousand slaves to be imported from Africa to the Caribbean; half of these went to the Spanish governors of Hispaniola, and even more would follow in the decades ensuing. African slaves were also forcefully introduced into Florida, the Mississippi River valley, the lands of Mexico, and throughout the southwestern region of North America, extending to the Pacific Ocean.[23]

In the 1600s England began in earnest to compete with the Catholic nations of France, Portugal, and Spain for conquest and converts in the New World. In terms of religious ideology, slavery and empire were to be the secular means of achieving religious ends of a global Protestant empire. The English Council for Foreign Plantations received a direct mandate from Charles II himself in 1660 to prioritize Christian conversion in the Americas. And colonial governors in the English colonies of Virginia and New York were likewise instructed to Christianize African slaves and native peoples. In the minds of English secular and religious leaders, African slaves were to be "reduced" to Christian devotion and thereby rescued from their "bestial" and "heathen" habitudes. In 1693, the New England minister Cotton Mather established the Society of Negroes, a Sunday meeting devoted exclusively to sermonizing and catechizing African slaves. Those few slaves who attended also learned prayers and Christian songs. John Eliot, renowned for his efforts to Christianize the native nations of New England, offered to preach to Africans once per week, if their white owners would but allow them to attend meetings.[24]

In sharp contrast to the Anglo-American colonies of the Chesapeake and southern regions, New England was characterized by a strong presence of clergy; its parishes were well supplied with trained theologians and established churches that ensured the urban population was provided with Christian instruction. This was especially the case in Puritan-dominated regions of New England. By 1636, New England's white settlers had established their "New College" (Harvard University) to ensure a ready supply of highly trained ministers. Slavery, furthermore, was an integral part of Puritan life. And so it is telling that with an optimal environment for Christianizing a local population of slaves, the vast majority of

---

[23] Irving Rouse, *The Tainos: Rise and Decline of the People Who Greeted Columbus* (New Haven, 1992), 7–10; Antonio Benitez Rojo, *The Repeating Island: The Caribbean and the Postmodern Perspective* (Durham, 1996), 93; Schorsch, *Swimming the Christian Atlantic*, 13–14.

[24] Raboteau, *Slave Religion*, 97, 109.

New England's slaves in the seventeenth century were not converted to Christianity. In fact, not until 1641 was the first African slave converted to Christianity there, in Dorchester, Massachusetts. As late as 1706, Cotton Mather would complain that New England's white Christian population generally refused to attempt converting their African slaves, some on the grounds that Africans were subhuman, others viewing slave conversion as an unnecessary distraction from extracting labor from their African chattel.[25]

Despite official mandates to convert African slaves, the fact remained that the transatlantic slave trade was a *business*, and owning slaves was a *capitalist* enterprise made worthwhile only with the promise of financial profit. Thus, there was little incentive for slave masters to convert African slaves to Christianity and far greater reason not to do so. White slavers feared Christian conversion might create a legal basis for Africans to challenge their enslavement. Add to this Christianity's theological emphasis on freedom, which slaves took literally, and it is a small wonder that individual slaveholders largely viewed the Christian missionary enterprise as a troublesome sore that was best removed from proximity to their slaves.[26] In an effort to assuage the concerns of slave masters and encourage them to convert their African chattel, several colonial legislatures formulated legal codes that stipulated that the status of African slaves was a permanent condition unaltered by Christian salvation. In 1664, Maryland formally legislated that Christian baptism marked a strictly spiritual salvation that by no means altered the physical plight of African slaves. The Virginia House of Burgesses followed with its own version of this law in 1667. By 1706, no fewer than six colonial legislatures had incorporated a legal buffer between Christian salvation and the physical enslavement of Africans.[27]

In the low country of South Carolina and Georgia, Christianization was minimally promoted, despite mandates from the British crown and from church officials in England and the American colonies. The "plantations" of the South Carolina and Georgia low country during the early 1600s were not the vast complexes of massive African labor gangs directed by overseers that would characterize the region in the late 1700s. Rather, white slaveholders typically owned at most a few African slaves (fewer than twelve) and also employed white indentured servants and Indian slaves; all labored

---

[25] Michael O. Emerson and Christian Smith, *Divided by Faith: Evangelical Religion and the Problem of Race in America* (New York, 2001), 23; Raboteau, *Slave Religion*, 101–2, 108.

[26] Jon Butler, *Awash in a Sea of Faith: Christianizing the American People* (Cambridge, MA, 1990), 133; Raboteau, *Slave Religion*, 96–8, 133–4; Emerson and Smith, *Divided by Faith*, 23–5.

[27] Butler, *Awash in a Sea of Faith*, 133; Raboteau, *Slave Religion*, 99.

side by side on farms of modest size to raise crops, fell trees, and construct buildings. Moreover, because the livestock of white slaveholders roamed freely to graze and fatten before being sold at market, the African slaves who tended them also moved about with relative autonomy, one condition that created opportunities for maroonage, to the continuing despair of slaveholders.

In addition, the normative reticence of white slaveholders to provide food and clothing for slaves (a financial difficulty) meant that African slaves were expected – even required – to spend one day per week (typically Sunday) working to ensure their own physical provisions. This included gardening, hunting, fishing, and raising domesticated fowl; this economic activity precluded attending meetings for religious instruction that Christian missionaries sought to promote. African slaves also hired out their own labor and sold their goods at market in Charleston. These conditions did not result from any goodwill of white colonial settlers; they were demanded by the rigorous exigencies that defined the terms of survival and thrift for the early waves of English migrants to the colonies along the Atlantic seaboard. The South Carolina legislature passed multiple legal codes intended to quell the relatively autonomous movement of African slaves, to deny them independent economic activity, and to stem the tide of maroonage. But white slaveholders continued to permit these African laborers to do what was necessary for the survival of this phase of an agrarian slave economy.[28]

Throughout the 1600s, then, ahead of the plantation revolution that would define the character of the latter decades of slavery in the American South, African slave religion in the low country, as in the Chesapeake region, was conditioned by an overwhelming lack of any institutional and cultural support for Christian conversion. Instead, African slaves met with a relatively loosely organized system of labor and surveillance. This allowed for frequent gatherings in the small urban space of Charleston that afforded opportunities to exchange news of Atlantic events, meet newly arrived blacks from throughout the Atlantic, pursue romantic liaisons, and plan maroonage or armed resistance to free other slaves. As a result, the religious traditions of Africans were able to continue among South Carolina's African slaves. The difficult conditions of life in English settlements, for instance, demanded recourse to the herbally based medicinal practices that were central to religious knowledge in Orisha traditions. Throughout the history of American slavery, English efforts to convert to Christianity those

---

[28] Charles Johnson and Patricia Smith, *Africans in America: America's Journey Through Slavery* (New York, 1998), 89; Ira Berlin, *Many Thousands Gone: The First Two Centuries of Slavery in North America* (Cambridge, MA, 1998), 68–9.

Africans who were not born in America came to naught, with one important exception. A significant number of the Africans who arrived at the slave ship port of Charleston brought with them a historically deep tradition of Kongolese Catholicism that had thrived in central Africa for almost two centuries.[29]

During the late 1600s, the Spanish would invest more concertedly in defending their trade routes that carried mineral wealth from Mexico to Spain, an issue of growing concern throughout the seventeenth century as the British Empire quickly began to compete with both Spain and France in colonizing the Americas. The proximity of white English settlers to Spain's lucrative territories demanded a new order of defense that relied on Spanish garrisons. Both free and enslaved Africans were integral to arming and defending the garrisons. Unlike the English, Spanish governors enlisted African slaves (along with free Africans) to constitute a standing militia to thwart English settlers from the north, especially from Charleston (originally Charles Town) in the low-country region that would become South Carolina. The Africans arriving in Florida included populations from Europe, the interior of West Africa, the coastal cities in the vicinity of Angola, the Atlantic seaboard of the Chesapeake, the Caribbean, and even Mexico. The vast majority were rooted in the African religion of obligatory patronage to Orishas. These Africans combined strategies of maroonage with an enterprising legacy of being cultural brokers in the Atlantic world context of the seventeenth century, which combined African, native, and European languages; exchange economies; kinship through intermarriage; and religions. A minority of these Africans was already familiar with Christianity in either its Catholic or Protestant forms.[30]

In 1686, Spanish forces invaded the white English settler town of Edisto Island and captured about a dozen slaves, whom the Spanish employed as wage laborers and trained in Christianity. Sensing a pivotal change in conditions as more English settlers poured into the Carolina region north of Florida, the Spanish monarch mandated in 1693 that all fugitive African slaves arriving in St. Augustine who converted to Catholicism be granted their freedom. Although the Spanish at times ignored this mandate and sold some fugitives into Caribbean slavery, South Carolina's African slaves could usually count on manumission on their avowal to fight for Catholicism and

---

[29] Berlin, *Many Thousands Gone*, 73.
[30] Robin D. G. Kelley and Earl Lewis, *To Make Our World Anew: A History of African Americans* (Oxford, 2000), 20–33, 70–93; Kai Wright, *The African American Experience: Black History and Culture Through Speeches, Letters, Editorials, Poems, Songs, and Stories* (New York, 2009), 43; Jane Landers, *Black Society in Spanish Florida* (Urbana, 1999), 29–40; Berlin, *Many Thousands Gone*, 64–5, 71.

the Spanish Empire. The simple reason for this development was that the English were becoming too numerous for Florida's relatively small population of Spanish settlers to thwart; and Spain could ill afford to lose its strategic garrison city to the English settler militia.[31]

By the early decades of the 1700s, Spanish officials were becoming almost ecstatic in their delight over the increasing surge of Africans fleeing Charleston and the surrounding English region to join the Catholic Empire to the south. For these Africans, devotion to Catholicism literally meant being redeemed from a life of physical slavery and taking up arms – sometimes almost immediately – to return to the Carolina low country as African Christian soldiers whose mission was to liberate even more African slaves, who subsequently further strengthened the ranks of St. Augustine's African Catholic militia. This led to the creation of an African military-religious settlement just 2 miles north of the Spanish colonial garrison city of St. Augustine. Named Gracia Real de Santa Teresa de Mose (Fort Mose), the fort was built by Africans in 1738, was appointed a Catholic priest, and was governed by the Mandinga African soldier Francisco Menéndez. Africans enslaved and free lived there and served the Spanish governor of Florida in its defense.[32]

1700 TO 1790

When the Virginia colony's governor, Francis Nicholson, told the legislature, the House of Burgesses, to Christianize slaves and attend to their instruction, the legislature replied in 1699 that Africans were too unintelligent, too culturally foreign, and too bestial to be converted to the elevated religion of white Europeans.[33] Despite nearly one century of British settlement employing African slaves, the religion of these slaves was largely unaffected by the missionary efforts of English Christianity. The determination of British officials to change this led to the most important religious development of Anglo-American efforts to alter the religious condition of African slaves: the creation of the Society for Propagation of the Gospel (SPG) in 1701. This global missionary society of the Anglican Church targeted both Native Americans and African slaves in the British colonies. The society entered what was largely a vacuum of Christian clergy in most of Anglo-America. It was advantaged by its financial independence and

---

[31] G. S. Boritt et al., *Slavery, Resistance, Freedom* (New York, 2007), 11–13; Wright, *African American Experience*, 43; Berlin, *Many Thousands Gone*, 71.

[32] Kelley and Lewis, *To Make Our World Anew*, 92–3.

[33] Raboteau, *Slave Religion*, 100.

was able to circumvent local politics and strangleholds. With more than three hundred missionaries, its presence was more robust than the parish clergy in much of colonial Anglo-America.[34]

The SPG soon became the primary means of promoting Anglicanism throughout the colonies, and it was Anglo-Christianity's best effort at Christianizing the African population. At the time the SPG was founded, half of Virginia's forty-six parishes, containing forty thousand white settlers, were without a single minister. Churches and Christian clergy were even more scant in South Carolina, where only a single church existed in Charleston. The majority of South Carolina's seven thousand white settlers were themselves unchurched. By 1769 the Georgia colony had a total of only two churches, 150 miles apart. SPG missionaries reported that white settlers living inland knew little more of Christianity than Native Americans. The well-trained, highly educated clergy serving as SPG missionaries typically looked askance at local whites, who were nominal Christians, were laid-back in disposition, and often lacked sufficient knowledge of Christian theology to adequately instruct their African slaves even if they had possessed the will to do so (although most did not). Given that the majority of the rural white settlers were isolated from institutional Christianity, it is easy to grasp why African slaves remained largely insulated from the efforts of white Christians to effect the erasure of African religion.[35]

For all the ambition of its vision of converting the "heathen races," the SPG was only minimally successful in converting a few Africans at a time to Christianity. The vast majority of African slaves in eighteenth-century Anglo-America lived and died apart from Christianity. Virtually all of the slaves arriving from Africa continued to follow Orisha religion. Their adherence to an African view of sacred cosmology enjoined a routine, intuitive association of the material world with spiritual power and extraordinary beings. Just as Africans in central and western Africa had employed the gris-gris, so also did those African slaves of the Chesapeake and southern colonies craft items for the same purpose, referring to them with the same terminology. During the 1700s in North America, African slaves recognized as religious specialists also crafted objects to gain power over enemies or potential lovers, using hair, clothing, or other personal items. The strategy lay in implementing sympathetic rituals conceived to control events and influence the behavior of others through spiritual power.

---

[34] Mechal Sobel, *Trabelin' On: The Slave Journey to an Afro-Baptist Faith* (Westport, 1979), 64–5.
[35] Raboteau, *Slave Religion*, 105.

The theory of matter that guided the interpretation of the cosmos among Africans demonstrated an intimate association between spiritual power and the material world.[36]

The Anglican view of materiality and religion could scarcely have been more at odds with the cosmological assumptions of African slaves. Europe's Reformation had stringently expunged from Protestantism any legitimate close association between spirit and matter. European occultism in the wake of the Enlightenment was robust and widespread, and the popular religion of white settlers in the Americas was almost feverish in its concern with portents, signs, and material strategies for exercising spiritual power.[37] But white Christians viewed this as an illegitimate means of accessing religious power, a view brutally demonstrated in the Christian execution of white European settlers accused of witchcraft in New England during the late seventeenth century. In official terms, Anglicanism interpreted religion within the moral-ethical sphere, which seemed to bear no relation to material substances. In addition to this, the SPG clergy were characteristically stoic and condemned emotionalism. Anglican Christians, for instance, were only beginning to introduce the innovation of group singing in North America (this was discouraged in Britain), and even this was restrained by the overwhelming tendency to associate a highly tempered disposition with dignified piety.[38]

The collective liturgical practices of West African religion, on the other hand, employed thunderous drumming to communicate with and to invite the experience of spirit possession or trance; communicants danced vigorously, sang boisterously, and patterned their physical participation along the order of what seemed to white observers an athletically intensive event. By comparison, African slaves viewed the more sedate atmosphere of Anglican worship and the mechanical nature of catechism as banal and bewildering. Christianity, in this guise, seemed not to meet the criteria for being a spiritual technology; the religion of the SPG, instead, seemed designed to confound the very receptive modes that would otherwise have created a channel of exchange between African subjects and the Orisha and ancestors. Given this context, most African slaves found that Christian conversion made little sense. This African slave view of Christianity is evidenced by the experience of the Anglican minister William Tibbs of

---

[36] Philip D. Morgan, *Slave Counterpoint: Black Culture in the Eighteenth-Century Chesapeake and Lowcountry* (Chapel Hill, 1998), 420; Sobel, *Trabelin' On*, 13, 67–8, 70, 73.

[37] David D. Hall, *Worlds of Wonder, Days of Judgment: Popular Religious Belief in Early New England* (Cambridge, MA, 1990); Leigh Eric Schmidt, *Hearing Things: Religion, Illusion, and the American Enlightenment* (Cambridge, MA, 2000); Sobel, *Trabelin' On*, 80.

[38] Sobel, *Trabelin' On*, 70–3.

St. Paul's Parish in Maryland in 1724. Tibbs expressed grave disappointment as he found that the majority of Africans he confronted with the prospect of Christian conversion simply refused to be catechized and balked at participating in Christian meetings.[39]

The dismal outcome of efforts to convert Africans inspired several new strategies, however. In 1773, the white New England minister Samuel Hopkins, who would become famous for opposing the transatlantic slave trade, first promoted using African slaves as missionaries and catechists, which he believed to be a more effective means. Bristol Yamma and John Quamino, two Africans who attended his church, were trained for this task. But the outbreak of the Revolutionary War and Quamino's death in 1789 meant little came of this initiative. Among the nominally successful efforts of SPG missionaries were two schools that Christianized Africans through educating them. The first missionary school was opened in 1704 in New York City. The school's teacher, Elias Neau, went from household to household, asking white slave owners to allow their African slaves to meet at the school at four o'clock every Monday, Wednesday, and Friday afternoon. By decade's end, more than two hundred African slaves were attending. These slaves learned the Lord's Prayer, the Anglican catechism, and Bible stories such as the narratives of Creation and the Flood. This African Christian school continued to function until the Revolutionary War.[40]

The SPG attempted another school in Charleston, South Carolina, in 1742. The society purchased two teenage African slaves in hope of utilizing them to convert other slaves to Christianity. After more than a year of training, the two were deemed ready to serve as teachers at the school, which opened in 1743. Within three years, the Charleston school had graduated twenty-eight Africans and had enrolled seventy more (mostly children) in day and evening classes. Until the school's closing in 1764, African slaves could, with their owner's permission, attend and gain basic literacy by reading a primer and the Bible. Students also read the Book of Common Prayer, memorized catechisms, and learned the basic structure of the Christian salvation myth.[41]

From 1722 to 1728 the Anglican minister of All Hallows Parish in Maryland converted and baptized more than 100 African slaves. From 1724 to 1732, more than 350 African slaves were persuaded to convert and were baptized by the minister at North Farnham in Richmond County Virginia. As the 1700s progressed, there were even more counts of success by the SPG, although never more than a small portion of the total

---

[39] Ibid., 58, 63.
[40] Raboteau, *Slave Religion*, 109.
[41] Ibid., 116–18.

African slave population. It was generally the case that African slaves of the Chesapeake colonies were more readily converted than those of the Carolina and Georgia low country. In fact, the most heavily proselytized slaves of eighteenth-century Anglo-America seem to have been in Virginia, particularly in Richmond County. Close to 1,000 were baptized there between 1750 and 1775. But promising beginnings often dwindled into the faintest presence of Christianization among African slaves. In the 1720s the SPG received a missionary report indicating that 10 percent of the 1,300 slaves in one Virginia parish had turned to Christianity. By 1741 that proportion had decreased to 3 percent of the then 3,347 slaves. By 1750 the same missionary reported there were almost no African Christians in that parish. By comparison, in 1762 fewer than 500 of South Carolina's African slaves were Christians, out of a slave population exceeding 50,000.[42]

Throughout the eighteenth century, the SPG continued to meet with formidable opposition from not only slaveholders, but also African slaves themselves. For instance, Africans who were instructed in Christianity and underwent conversion did not necessarily absorb or accept the rudiments of the religion. The Methodist founder John Wesley himself was struck with numbing disappointment after conversing with an older enslaved African woman who had received numerous lessons on the tenets of the Christian faith but seemed to have missed entirely the whole point of the Christian myth of redemption. In addition, African slaves continued to interpret the freedom offered by Christian salvation in terms of physical manumission. During what was perhaps the earliest sustained revival among the African slaves of Virginia in 1751, a Presbyterian minister named Samuel Davies reported more than 100 slaves attending his revival meetings. Over a seven-year period he baptized 140. But he continually found that many African slaves took Christian conversion to be either a popular ritual of social status or else a rite for effecting manumission. The frustrated Davies adamantly refused to baptize the Africans who embraced such an understanding of conversion.[43] Once it became clear to African slaves that Christian conversion would not bring manumission from slavery, many were outspoken in their refusal to convert and refused to participate in baptism and catechesis. And the Africans who did were subject to ridicule by their fellow slaves for joining the religion of their masters.[44]

Among the exceptional cases of Christianization of African slaves is that of the Moravian Christians. This piedmont community of North

---

[42] Robert Olwell, *Masters, Slaves, and Subjects: The Culture of Power in the South Carolina Lowcountry, 1740–1790* (Ithaca, 1998), 132–6; Morgan, *Slave Counterpoint*, 421–2.

[43] Morgan, *Slave Counterpoint*, 422, 426.

[44] *Ibid.*, 420; Raboteau, *Slave Religion*, 121–3.

Carolina was home to an interracial movement comprising a small but significant number of African slaves. The first of these black Moravians was "Sam," renamed Johannes Samuel and baptized in 1771. About twenty other Africans joined him and his wife Maria in the Moravian church. At most maybe one-fourth of the piedmont African population was Moravian. These Moravians washed each other's feet, sat together (in unsegregated pews), held communal love feasts, prayed in German, were accountable to the same system of discipline, and were buried together. White Moravians sponsored Africans as godparents and gave them the kiss of peace. The white parishioners even blew the conch shell to call members to assemble at the church, a practice they had learned from their African slaves. This was in sharp contrast to the hostility most whites displayed toward Africans. The Christian brotherhood and sisterhood of this interracial Moravian community did not, however, disintegrate the bonds and boundaries of a veritable slavocracy, nor did it erase the socially meaningful boundaries of race. The same white Christian slave masters who joined their slaves in Christian fellowship often meted out physical brutality to these same slaves. Indeed, incorporating African slaves into the church increased the ability of slave masters to control them.[45]

Although English officials were fond of citing the gains of their Spanish nemesis to the south in winning African converts to incite greater zeal among Anglo-American Protestants, some African slaves among the relatively few Catholics of Anglo-America were minimally converted as well. In 1785, about three thousand of Maryland's fifteen thousand Catholics were African slaves. In Pennsylvania, however, which had a Catholic population of more than seven thousand, very few Africans were to be found.[46]

Just as African slave religions among the British and Spanish were devolving in a distinctive pattern, those among the French colonial settlers and Mississippi Indians were taking their own course in the eighteenth century. France had finally aspired to develop a distinct plantation society. In previous decades, the French had restrained the import of Africans into the Mississippi River valley in favor of making New France primarily a military buffer populated by French settlers against Spanish and English imperial expansion. But by 1719, the French crown relented in concession to the lucrative aspirations of would-be planters. Over the next twelve years, France forced more than six thousand African slaves into the

---

[45] John F. Sensbach, *A Separate Canaan: The Making of an Afro-Moravian World in North Carolina 1763–1840* (Chapel Hill, 1998), 107–8, 151–4; Jon F. Sensbach, *Rebecca's Revival: Creating Black Christianity in the Atlantic World* (Cambridge, MA, 2006); Morgan, *Slave Counterpoint*, 432.

[46] Raboteau, *Slave Religion*, 112.

Mississippi River valley region. About two-thirds of these African slaves were from Senegambia and were mostly Bambaras. The recent history of this ethnic group in West Africa was marked by intensive warfare against the Mandinga and other Islamic states; as a result, they had cultivated exceptional military skill. New France had unwittingly imported some of the most highly skilled military professionals in West Africa as the core of their labor force.[47]

The rise of an African slave population in the Mississippi River valley under French colonialism had a slow, difficult beginning. The brutal conditions of the Middle Passage not only killed up to 20 percent of those Africans embarking, but also ensured that many of the newly arriving slaves who survived were severely weakened and susceptible to disease and the challenges of adjusting to the New World climate. The cargohold of a slave ship, in which hundreds of Africans were crowded amid their own human waste, held barely enough oxygen to support a candle flame. The level of sickness among survivors was brutal. Two-thirds of the first two thousand African slaves arriving in the French-dominated Mississippi River valley died within one year. Over the next decade, their numbers would stabilize. During this same period of the 1720s, however, the white population declined by two-thirds. By 1728, the French governor had demanded that Indians no longer be enslaved, further solidifying a well-developed commitment to making Africans the most exploited and severely dominated source of slave labor. Because France had abandoned its original plan of making New France a white settler buffer colony without African labor, African slaves soon outnumbered whites.[48]

Meanwhile, the Chickasaw nation had cultivated alliances with the British and was an adversary of the smaller native nations. These less populous nations – Choctaws, Apalachees, Mobilians, Tunicas, Arkansas, Houmas, Natchez, and Yazoo – at first allied with the French against the Chickasaw-British alliance. But as the French continued to make forays into native territory, particularly that of the Natchez, the African slave population became a more decisive presence. Over the next several decades, African slaves with typically exceptional experience in military combat established maroon societies with astounding frequency, surpassing the rates of maroonage in both the Chesapeake and in the Carolina low country. These maroon societies were either entirely African or comprised African and native families, the latter pattern building on the initial practice of the

---

[47] Rodney, *History of Upper Guinea*, 232; Gwendolyn Midlo Hall, *Africans in Colonial Louisiana: The Development of Afro-Creole Culture in the Eighteenth Century* (Baton Rouge, 1992), 101–12; Berlin, *Many Thousands Gone*, 81–2.

[48] Hall, *Africans in Colonial Louisiana*, 57–87, 177; Berlin, *Many Thousands Gone*, 81–3.

predominantly male population of African slaves of establishing families with native women.[49]

When African slaves first began to arrive in the French colony, most whites were indentured servants. Only a tiny minority of the French in the lower Mississippi River valley could afford to own slaves, yet they wielded the greatest social power of any group of whites, as would their aristocratic successors in the century that followed. And they bid the whites who owned no slaves to join in raids against the native nations and maroon societies to protect a common interest – endlessly arrogating to themselves more Native American territory. In this context, African maroons became famous for leading successful military campaigns against the French settlers in strategic alliance with the Natchez nation. Despite the French Code Noir's mandate that African slaves be baptized by force if necessary and instructed in Christian doctrine, it was extremely rare for slaveholders to devote time or effort to this task. A small, elite community of free Africans in New Orleans managed to stake claims to a modest existence and had easy access to Christian instruction under the auspices of the parish clergy. Beyond the urban reaches of New Orleans, however, as one Capuchin missionary noted, African slaves typically lived and died without hearing of Christianity.[50]

Most of New France's African slaves were born in Africa and had grown up steeped in the religious knowledge of the cultures in West Africa's interior. As more Africans continued to arrive from across the Atlantic throughout the 1700s, there was little opportunity for African Christianization. On the contrary, the African slaves in the lower Mississippi River valley formed a creolized world of African spiritual knowledge that introduced the rituals of Orisha veneration and African theories of matter and spirit into the territories that the French were ever seeking to usurp from the numerous native nations. During the eighteenth century it was Native American religion, not Christianity, that most altered the sacred cosmos of African slave religion in this region. The medicinal practice grounded in knowledge of the botanical properties of western and central African flora was synthesized with that of native nations like the Natchez so that African slaves could support their health, treat New World diseases, and heal the numerous injuries incurred in the seemingly endless fighting that was shaking the social foundations of the Mississippi River valley.[51]

---

[49] Daniel H. Usner, *Indians, Settlers and Slaves in a Frontier Exchange Economy: The Lower Mississippi Valley Before 1783* (Chapel Hill, 1992), 58–9, 72–5, 86–7; Berlin, *Many Thousands Gone*, 79–81.

[50] Hall, *Africans in Colonial Louisiana*, 156–200.

[51] *Ibid.*; Usner, *Indians, Settlers and Slaves*, 72–80; Berlin, *Many Thousands Gone*, 87.

A few African slaves were offered freedom by French slave masters in exchange for hunting down fugitives, raiding maroon societies, and joining military campaigns against Native American towns. But this tactic never remotely approached the scale of St. Augustine's African Catholic militia. And it never produced the large-scale symbolic alignment of Christianity with manumission that characterized the African slave religion of Spanish Florida. Instead, the little that African slaves gleaned of Christianity in the lower Mississippi River valley began to alter the meaning of the Orisha religion of African slaves by politicizing African material and spiritual exercises of power. African slave religion, far more than before, became increasingly associated with maroonage and freedom wars. African slaves venerated and served the divine and ancestral beings to petition their aid in making war against French slaveholders. The alliances between nations like the Natchez and maroon or fugitive African soldiers only increased under the expanding pressure of unrelenting French settler colonialism.[52]

By 1729, the Natchez nation reached a new level of desperation after years of losing land to the French Empire and being forced into more concentrated quarters. They united with experienced African slave soldiers in a reprisal that succeeded in killing 10 percent of the French population, which totaled about two thousand at the time. As a result, hundreds of Africans were liberated from slavery and joined the maroon and Afro-native societies. The French, at a severe military disadvantage, formed their own alliance with the Choctaw nation and subsequently retaliated with unprecedented vengeance in the wake of this major loss. They defeated the Natchez-African alliance. In a striking display of brutality, they opted to forgo reenslaving some of their African captives and instead offered them up to the Choctaw soldiers to be burned alive.[53]

At this point, Samba Bambara, a multilingual African slave of the West African Bambara nation, abandoned his employ as an official interpreter for the French in New Orleans and lived his remaining life as a fugitive African solder. He revived the African alliance with the Natchez to help lead further wars against the French. Bambara was eventually captured and dismembered by his French enemies, but his militarism and that of other African slave soldiers continued in alliance with the Mississippi River valley's native nations. In this way, African slave religion created an overwhelming resistance that crippled France's efforts to create an authentic plantation society in the region, one in which a totalizing master-slave relationship would have structured every aspect of society.[54]

---

[52] Hall, *Africans in Colonial Louisiana*, 97–118; Berlin, *Many Thousands Gone*, 88–9.
[53] *Ibid.*
[54] Berlin, *Generations of Captivity: A History of African-American Slaves* (Cambridge, MA, 2004), 42; Berlin, *Many Thousands Gone*, 77–8.

The style of tension between African slave religion and French imperialism in the Mississippi River valley was even more pronounced in the prized colony of Haiti (French St. Domingue), which passed from Spanish to French rule in 1697.[55] The unusually high profit margins garnered by coffee, tobacco, cocoa, indigo, and especially sugar cane made it France's most lucrative colony. African slaves were imported into French-controlled Haiti in record numbers, increasing from 3,500 in 1687 to 450,000 in 1791. By the last decade of the eighteenth century, whites numbered only about 30,000. With an 11:1 ratio of African slaves to whites, the island had one of the highest concentrations of African slaves in the New World, a demographic condition that directly shaped the nature of African slave religion in the region.[56]

France's Code Noir required that African slaves be forcibly Christianized, and Catholic officials attempted to do so, legally banning the African religion of slaves and creating catechisms exclusively for these slaves that described African religious specialists as servants of Satan. St. Domingue's African slaves, nevertheless, continued to serve the extraordinary beings they called *loas*, continually reshaping the African sacred cosmos that had developed in West Africa and even incorporating into their religion the altars, incense, and votive candles of Christianity. The divine community of Christian cosmology (Jesus, Mary, the saints, and angels), moreover, was reinterpreted to correspond to members of the African divine community – for example, the spirit Legba was associated with Peter, Agbe (Agwe) with St. Ulrich, and Aziri (Ezili) with Mary. Most importantly, St. Domingue's African slave population would respond with theological innovation to the especially murderous labor regime of the sugar plantations, which reduced the life expectancy of newly arriving slaves to at most a few years or even months. Very aggressive rituals of the Petro tradition – in contrast to the milder Rada rituals – emerged in Haiti and supported violent attacks against slave masters; they became an essential part of the eventual war that African slaves would wage to create an independent republic. In the decades following Haiti's revolution, both Petro and Rada traditions would significantly shape religion among free and enslaved Africans in the American South. Throughout the 1700s, Haiti's African slaves would establish maroon societies in the hills extending beyond the plantation lands, and they forged lasting alliances with the surviving native communities as a basis for making continuing raids against the plantations.[57]

By the 1760s, the British succeeded in toppling Spanish imperial dominance in the lands of Florida. As a result, Anglo-American settlers in the

---

[55] Joan Dayan, *Haiti, History, and the Gods* (Berkeley, 1996), 205.
[56] Steeve Copeau, *The History of Haiti* (Westport, 2008), 17–19.
[57] Anthony Pinn, *Varieties of African American Religious Experience* (Minneapolis, 1998), 29.

Carolina and Georgia low country could relax their previous dependence on armed slaves to thwart Native American militias and help defend the region against the freedom wars of African soldiers and Spanish troops from the south. Since the 1690s, the cultivation of rice and indigo had garnered record profits for the white slaveholding aristocracy, and the southern colonies were steadily developing as plantation societies in which massive labor gangs of African slaves were more stringently dominated and surveilled. By the 1740s, when New France was reeling under the impact of Afro-native freedom wars and New Spain was pitting its resistance to Anglo-American expansion with waning efficacy, African slave religion in the Anglo-American colonies began to experience the impact of a new brand of Christianization throughout the eastern seaboard – evangelical revivalism.

The earliest period of revivalism, the Great Awakening, staged by Anglo-American evangelicals in the 1740s, had attracted some African slaves. White itinerants repeatedly claimed African slaves were more devout and open to workings of the spirit than were whites, in light of their propensity for shouting, dancing, and otherwise participating in a vigorously embodied liturgical paradigm. Such praise from white Christians problematically derived from racial condescension that demeaned Africans as pedantic and naturally given to emotional display, but it nevertheless attests to the influence of Africans on revival meetings from their earliest point. Because the awakenings promoted workings of the spirit; sought to evoke actions like dancing, shouting, and jumping; and were affectively centered in order to connect emotionally with the audience, these meetings resonated with African religion. This was in sharp contrast to the relatively dispirited Anglican formula for conceiving of religion. The focus of the evangelist was to simplify Christian theology by instilling a sense of deep shame, humility, and guilt in the prospective convert and then effecting a desire for intense devotionalism. In light of this, revivalist Christianity made its mark on a significant minority of African slaves, far more than did Anglicanism.[58]

In the Chesapeake, Methodists and Baptists produced their most numerous converts during the 1780s and 1790s, immediately following the Revolutionary War years. By the 1770s sufficient numbers of Africans were converting to revivalist Christianity to form the first independent churches. Strictly speaking, independent churches were not operated by America's slaves. Independent black Christian congregations, rather, were organized by free Africans who could legally incorporate and own real estate. These churches usually included in their membership a modicum of slaves whose

---

[58] Sobel, *Trabelin' On*, 98; Morgan, *Slave Counterpoint*, 428–9.

owners permitted them to attend religious meetings; white slaveholders were typically reluctant to do so. Most popular in the South was the First African Church of Savannah, Georgia, begun by Andrew Bryan. Bryan was born a slave and was baptized by a freed African named George Liele. In 1790 Bryan purchased his own freedom. He started the First African Church in 1794 as a small building on his own property. By 1800, his congregation (strongly attended by local slaves) had grown to more than seven hundred members, and it was able to sponsor smaller independent black churches in the region.[59] By that time, Bryan had become a wealthy real estate investor and landowner; he even became a slaveholder, owning eight slaves by the turn of the century.[60] It was not typical for so many hundreds of slaves to congregate in churches; therefore Bryan's Savannah church is not paradigmatic. Moreover, theirs was not an antislavery gospel, because Bryan and George Liele made their start preaching to other slaves under the watchful aegis of their slave masters. Nevertheless, Bryan's congregation spawned the earliest separate black churches by sponsoring smaller communities of African Christians. As a significant minority of African slaves continued to convert to Christianity, it was evident that this limited success was largely due to the evangelical institution of revivalism.

SUGGESTIONS FOR FURTHER READING

Bennett, Herman L. *Africans in Colonial Mexico: Absolutism, Christianity, and Afro-Creole Consciousness, 1570–1640*. Bloomington, 2003.

Earle, T. F., and K. J. P. Lowe, eds. *Black Africans in Renaissance Europe*. Cambridge, UK, 2005.

Gomez, Michael. *Black Crescent: The Experience and Legacy of African Muslims in the Americas*. New York, 2005.

Heywood, Linda, and John K. Thornton. *Central Africans, Atlantic Creoles, and the Foundation of the Americas, 1585–1660*. Cambridge, UK, 2007.

Morgan, Philip D. *Slave Counterpoint: Black Culture in the Eighteenth-Century Chesapeake and Lowcountry*. Chapel Hill, 1998.

Raboteau, Albert J. *Slave Religion: The "Invisible Institution" in the Antebellum South*. New York, 1978.

Sobel, Mechal. *Trabelin' On: The Slave Journey to an Afro-Baptist Faith*. Westport, 1979.

Stewart, Dianne M. *Three Eyes for the Journey: African Dimensions of the Jamaican Religious Experience*. New York, 2004.

---

[59] Milton Sernett, *Black Religion and American Evangelicalism: White Protestants, Plantation Missions, and the Flowering of Negro Christianity, 1787–1865* (Metuchen, NJ, 1975), 111–13.

[60] Sernett, *Black Religion and American Evangelicalism*, 113.

19

COLONIAL JUDAISM

JONATHAN D. SARNA

BEGINNINGS

The first known individual of Jewish origin to arrive in the New World was Luis de Torres, the interpreter who accompanied Christopher Columbus in 1492. Baptized shortly before the expedition sailed, de Torres settled in Cuba. Although many have claimed that Christopher Columbus himself was of Jewish origin, the *Encyclopedia Judaica* properly concludes that "it is equally impossible to exclude or to confirm" this hypothesis. Columbus concealed much about his origins.[1]

Whether or not Columbus himself was Jewish, his discovery made an enormous impact on Jews and Jewish history. Just before his voyage commenced, Spain's King Ferdinand and Queen Isabella had expelled "all Jews and Jewesses of whatever age they may be" from their "kingdoms and seignories," warning them never to return. Five years later, in 1497, Jews were likewise expelled from Portugal. Only those who converted to Catholicism – voluntarily or forcibly – were allowed to remain on the Iberian Peninsula. Because the Holy Inquisition targeted these conversos if it suspected them of practicing Judaism in secret, hundreds of them traveled to the New World to seek haven. In time, the New World would likewise provide haven for millions of persecuted Jews from other places.[2]

Enough sixteenth-century New World conversos practiced Jewish rituals clandestinely that the Inquisition soon took notice. Beginning in 1569, it began pursuing "Judaizing heretics" – real and imagined – in the Americas. Some Catholics of Jewish origin continued to practice selected Jewish rituals secretly, notwithstanding the rising danger of discovery. But

[1] Cecil Roth and Roni Weinstein, "Columbus, Christopher," in Fred Skolnik, ed., *Encyclopaedia Judaica*, 2nd. ed., 5:70; Jonathan D. Sarna, "The Mythical Jewish Columbus and the History of America's Jews," in Bryan F. Le Beau and Menahem Mor, eds., *Religion in the Age of Exploration* (Omaha, 1996), 81–95.
[2] Jane S. Gerber, *The Jews of Spain* (New York, 1992), 115–44, 285–9.

well into the nineteenth century no synagogue or overt Jewish presence was tolerated anywhere in Spanish America. The expulsion of Jews from Spain and Portugal applied to their New World colonies as well.[3]

In 1630, Holland captured Pernambuco, Brazil, from Portugal and sought to develop it for the benefit of the mother country. Holland was Calvinist rather than Catholic and was home to a significant Jewish community, the bulk of which consisted of conversos who had returned to Judaism and practiced their faith openly under comparatively tolerant conditions. Thanks to this and subsequent Dutch colonies, Jewish communal life became possible for the first time in the New World.[4]

The Dutch West India Company, which governed Dutch Brazil as a profit-making venture for its investors, actively sought to attract enterprising Jews to its new dominion. It considered Jews to be stimulators of industry and trade and knew that many Jews spoke Portuguese and maintained ties with Catholics of Jewish descent living in Brazil who had emigrated there from Portugal. To lure Jews across the ocean, the company granted them liberty on par with Roman Catholics: "No one will be permitted to molest them or subject them to inquiries in matters of conscience or in their private homes." Subsequently, the States General of the United Netherlands granted Jews rights unmatched by any other seventeenth-century Jewish community in the world. "Treat and cause to be treated the Jewish nation on a basis of equality with all other residents and subjects in all treaties, negotiations and actions in and out of war without discrimination."[5]

Jews soon flocked to Pernambuco, establishing in the city of Recife and its environs a community that, at its peak in the 1640s, amounted to between 1,000 and 1,450 Jews – between a third and a half of Dutch Brazil's total civilian white population. The community included ordained rabbis, an active synagogue, and two Jewish schools – more than any North American Jewish community would be able to claim for another two hundred years. But the community did not last. Portuguese troops recaptured the area on 26 January 1654, and gave Jews and other non-Catholics three months to leave.[6]

---

[3] Yosef Kaplan, "The Sephardim in North-Western Europe and the New World," in Haim Beinart, ed., *Moreshet Sepharad: The Sephardi Legacy* (Jerusalem, 1992), 2: 240–87.

[4] Miriam Bodian, *Hebrews of the Portuguese Nation: Conversos and Community in Early Modern Amsterdam* (Bloomington, 1997); Daniel Swestschinski, *Reluctant Cosmopolitans: The Portuguese Jews of Seventeenth-Century Amsterdam* (London, 2000).

[5] Arnold Wiznitzer, *Jews in Colonial Brazil* (New York, 1960), 57, 128–30; Isaac S. Emmanuel, "Seventeenth-Century Brazilian Jewry: A Critical Review," *American Jewish Archives* 14 (Apr. 1962): 41; Jacob Rader Marcus, *The Colonial American Jew, 1492–1776*, 3 vols. (Detroit, 1970), 1: 67–84.

[6] Egon and Frieda Wolff, *A odisséia dos judeus de Recife* (São Paulo, 1979); Tania Kaufmann, *Passos perdidos, história recuperada: a presença judaica em Pernambuco* (Recife, 2001).

ARRIVAL OF JEWS IN NEW AMSTERDAM

Many of those expelled from Recife returned to Holland. Others started life anew in one of the Caribbean colonies where Jews were welcomed, such as Curacao, Suriname, or Jamaica.[7] A small number of Jews, perhaps twenty-three, sailed to the furthest reaches of the Dutch Empire in North America.[8] Their boat, apparently known as the *Sint Catrina*, sailed into the port of New Amsterdam in September 1654. Unlike earlier Jewish visitors to North America who came for short periods of time, the refugees from Brazil sought to settle down and form a permanent Jewish community in North America, to "navigate and trade near and in New Netherland, and to live and reside there."[9]

The clergy of the dominant Dutch Reformed Church in New Amsterdam opposed the Jews' request. Not for the first time, given the other faiths already in town, they feared that their legal prerogatives as the colony's only recognized faith were being usurped. Peter Stuyvesant, the dictatorial director-general of New Netherland, sympathized with these views. His mission was to establish order among the citizenry, to combat "drinking to excess, quarreling, fighting and smiting." He sought to root out Nonconformity and promote social cohesion by enforcing Calvinist orthodoxy in his domain; he therefore forced Lutherans to worship in private and outlawed Quakers. When the Jews arrived, he tried to bar them altogether, calling them "deceitful," "very repugnant," and "hateful enemies and blasphemers of the name of Christ." He asked the directors of the Dutch West India Company to "require them in a friendly way to depart" lest they "infect and trouble this new colony." His most revealing line about Jews was this: "giving them liberty we cannot refuse the Lutherans and

---

[7] Marcus, *Colonial American Jew*, 95–208; Paolo Bernardini and Norman Fiering, eds., *The Jews and the Expansion of Europe to the West, 1450–1800* (New York, 2001); Yosef H. Yerushalmi, "Between Amsterdam and New Amsterdam: The Place of Curacao and the Caribbean in Early Modern Jewish History," *American Jewish History* 72 (Dec. 1982): 172–92; Mordehay Arbell, *The Jewish Nation of the Caribbean: The Spanish-Portuguese Jewish Settlements in the Caribbean and the Guianas* (Jerusalem, 2002).

[8] The basic surveys of colonial American Jewish life are Marcus, *Colonial American Jew*; Eli Faber, *A Time for Planting: The First Migration* (Baltimore, 1992); and William Pencak, *Jews and Gentiles in Early America* (Ann Arbor, 2005). For a brief survey focusing on religion, see Jonathan D. Sarna, *American Judaism: A History* (New Haven, 2004), 1–30.

[9] Arnold Wiznitzer, "The Exodus from Brazil and Arrival in New Amsterdam of the Jewish Pilgrim Fathers, 1654," *Publications of the American Jewish Historical Society* 44 (1954): 80–98. Leo Hershkowitz, "By Chance or Choice: Jews in New Amsterdam 1654," *American Jewish Archives Journal* 57 (2005): 1–13. Quote from "Request of the Jewish Merchants of Amsterdam to the Mayors of Amsterdam to the Mayors of Amsterdam in Behalf of the Jews of New Netherland," *American Jewish Archives* 7 (Jan. 1955): 51.

Papists." Decisions made concerning the Jews, he understood, would serve as precedents, determining the colony's religious character forever after.[10]

The directors of the Dutch West India Company in Amsterdam, influenced in part by a petition from the city's Jewish merchants, some of whom were also stockholders in the company, ordered Stuyvesant to permit Jews to "travel," "trade," "live," and "remain" in New Netherland, provided they took care of their own poor. Subsequently, Jews also secured the right to trade throughout the colony, serve guard duty, own real estate, and worship in the privacy of their homes. In admonishing Stuyvesant over his treatment of Quakers, the Dutch West India Company articulated the ideology that underlay its treatment of Jews as well: "allow every one to have his own belief, as long as he behaves quietly and legally, gives no offense to his neighbor and does not oppose the government."[11]

The bulk of the Jews who settled in New Amsterdam (renamed New York following the British takeover in 1664), identified as Sephardim or Sephardic Jews, meaning Jews with roots in the Iberian Peninsula, known in Hebrew as Sepharad (Obadiah 1:20). They distinguished themselves from the Jews of the Germanic lands, known as Ashkenazic Jews or Ashkenazim, based on the biblical name Ashkenaz (Jeremiah 51:27), associated with Germany. In colonial America, unlike in much of Europe, the two groups of Jews lived side by side, socialized, and married each other. The Sephardic rite predominated in synagogues, because it came first, held higher status, and linked Jews to wealthier Sephardic communities in the Caribbean. But both Sephardic and Ashkenazic Jews assumed positions of communal leadership in these Sephardic synagogues.[12]

---

[10] Oliver A. Rink, "Private Interest and Godly Gain: The West India Company and the Dutch Reformed Church in New Netherland, 1624–1664," *New York History* 75 (1994): 245–64; Samuel Oppenheim, "The Early History of the Jews in New York, 1654–1664: Some New Matter on the Subject," *Publications of the American Jewish Historical Society* 18 (1909): 4, 5, 20. For context, see Joyce Goodfriend, *"Before the Melting Pot": Society and Culture in Colonial New York City, 1664–1730* (Princeton, 1992); and Patricia U. Bonomi, *Under the Cope of Heaven: Religion, Society and Politics in Colonial New York,* 2nd ed. (New York, 2003).

[11] Oppenheim, "Early History of the Jews in New York," 8–37; E. T. Corwin, ed., *Ecclesiastical Records of the State of New York* (Albany, 1901), 1: 530; James Homer William, "An Atlantic Perspective on the Jewish Struggle for Rights and Opportunities in Brazil, New Netherland, and New York," in Bernardini and Fiering, *Jews and the Expansion of Europe to the West,* 369–93.

[12] Sarna, *American Judaism,* 5, 18–19; H. J. Zimmels, *Ashkenazim and Sephardim* (London, 1976); Martin A. Cohen, "The Sephardic Phenomenon: A Reappraisal," in Martin A. Cohen and Abraham J. Peck, eds., *Sephardim in the Americas: Studies in Culture and History* (Tuscaloosa, AL, 1993); Malcolm H. Stern and Marc D. Angel, *New York's Early Jews: Some Myths and Misconceptions* (New York, 1976).

PORT JEWS

The identical pattern prevailed in other colonial cities where Jews settled and established communities: Savannah, Charleston, Philadelphia, Newport, and Richmond, the last established during the American Revolution.[13] Colonial Jews resided, for the most part, in port cities: they lived in heterogeneous communities that placed a premium on commerce and trade, and they shared much in common with the so-called port Jews of Europe. As historian David Sorkin has observed, these port Jews pioneered aspects of Judaism that we associate with modernity.

> Virtually all those developments thought to be characteristic of the modern Jew can be found among the port Jews a century or two earlier: the reduction of Judaism to a synagogue-based religion with a growing emphasis on faith as opposed to practice; immersion in the larger Christian culture; the emergence of various forms and degrees of assimilation; and, as a consequence of all of these, the development of a segmental Jewish life and identity.[14]

HOPE OF ISRAEL

Incipient modernity, however, marched hand in hand with the hope of messianic redemption. Menasseh Ben Israel, the Dutch rabbi who did more than anybody else of his day to promote Jewish settlement in the New World and to underscore its religious significance, wrote in 1656 that he "conceived, that our universall dispersion was a necessary circumstance, to be fulfilled, before all that shall be accomplished which the Lord hath promised to the people of the Jewes, concerning their restauration, and their returning again into their own land." According to this assessment,

---

[13] Marcus, *Colonial American Jew*, and Pencak, *Jews and Gentiles*, survey the development of Jewish life in these colonies. Individual studies include Malcolm H. Stern, "New Light on the Jewish Settlement of Savannah," *American Jewish Historical Quarterly* 54 (Mar. 1963), 163–99; Holly Snyder, "We Have the World to Begin Againe: Jewish Life in Colonial Savannah 1733–1783," *Proceedings of the Middle Atlantic Historical Association of Catholic Colleges and Universities* 6 (1991): 122–32; James W. Hagy, *This Happy Land: The Jews of Colonial and Antebellum Charleston* (Tuscaloosa, AL, 1993); Edwin Wolf II and Maxwell Whiteman, *The History of the Jews of Philadelphia from Colonial Times to the Age of Jackson* (Philadelphia, 1975); Hyman B. Grinstein, *The Rise of the Jewish Community of New York* (Philadelphia, 1945); Morris A. Gutstein, *The Story of the Jews of Newport* (New York, 1936); George M. Goodwin and Ellen Smith, eds., *The Jews of Rhode Island* (Waltham, MA, 2004); and Myron Berman, *Richmond's Jewry, 1769–1976: Shabbat in Shockoe* (Charlottesville, 1979).

[14] David Sorkin, "The Port Jew: Notes Toward a Social Type," *Journal of Jewish Studies* 50 (Spring 1999): 96–7; Jonathan D. Sarna, "Port Jews in the Atlantic: Further Thoughts," *Jewish History* 20 (2006), 213–19.

the Jewish dispersion, furthered by the expulsion from Spain, presaged Jews' imminent ingathering. In his *Hope of Israel,* the rabbi argued that the colonization of Jews in the New World was both a harbinger and an instrument of messianic redemption. The names of early New World synagogues – at least four of which were actually named Mikveh Israel, meaning "hope of Israel" – as well as scattered other evidence from Christians who knew Jews make it clear that messianism played a significant role in the lives of colonial American Jews.[15]

SYNAGOGUE COMMUNITY

The precise dating of colonial Jewish communities remains problematic. Should it be based on the arrival of the first Jew? The establishment of the first cemetery? The formation of the first synagogue? Or, as has more recently been suggested, the arrival of a Torah scroll, the handwritten parchment text of the Pentateuch, which is a defining symbol of Jewish communal life and culture and a marker of sacred space? Savannah's first Jews, who arrived as a group from England in 1733, brought a Torah scroll with them and established a community at once. The other communities may have had a Jewish presence early on but only developed as full-fledged communities, with a minyan (prayer quorum) of at least ten Jewish males over the age of thirteen and regular worship services, from the middle of the eighteenth century. In smaller eighteenth-century colonial Jewish settlements such as Lancaster and Reading, where there was no regular minyan, Judaism was maintained for years by dedicated laymen without a salaried officiant or formal synagogue. The Torah would be read on special occasions when a prayer quorum could be assembled.[16]

Jews initially worshipped quietly in private homes. Public worship, as late as 1685 in New York, was "tolerated ... but to those that professe faith in Christ." This changed around the turn of the century, at which time the community drew up a constitution, commenced to keep records, and began worshipping in rented quarters. From then until at least the end of the eighteenth century, the synagogue dominated Jewish religious life in all of America's Jewish communities. Indeed, the synagogue and the organized Jewish community became one and the same – a synagogue

---

[15] Menasseh Ben Israel, *Vindiciae Judaeorum* (1656), 37, reprinted in Lucien Wolf, *Menasseh ben Israel's Mission to Oliver Cromwell* (London, 1901), 143; Jonathan D. Sarna, "The Mystical World of Colonial American Jews," in Lauren B. Strauss and Michael Brenner, eds., *Mediating Modernity: Essays in Honor of Michael A. Meyer* (Detroit, 2008), 185–94.

[16] On the role of the Torah scroll in early America, see Jonathan D. Sarna, "Torah," in Peter Williams, ed., *Encyclopedia of American Religion* (forthcoming).

community – and as such it assumed primary responsibility for preserving and maintaining local Jewish life.[17]

Communal worship, dietary laws, life-cycle events, education, philanthropy, ties to Jews around the world, oversight of the cemetery and the ritual bath, the baking of Passover matzah, and more all fell within the province of the synagogue. It saw itself and was seen by others as the representative body of the Jewish community. It promoted group solidarity and discipline, evoked a feeling of kinship toward similarly organized synagogue communities throughout the Jewish world, and improved the chances that even small clusters of Jews, remote from the wellsprings of Jewish learning, could survive from one generation to the next. It also acted in the name of all area Jews and proved to be an efficient means of meeting the needs of an outpost Jewish community.[18]

The laity dominated colonial synagogue communities. Power was generally vested in men of means. As in Sephardic synagogues elsewhere, governing authority was held by the *parnas* (president or warden), assisted by a small number of officers and elders who constituted the *mahamad* or *adjunta* (standing committee). *Yehidim* (first-class members), men of status who materially supported the congregation, made most of the important decisions; they were the equivalent of "communicants" in colonial Protestant churches. The rest of the worshippers, including all women, occupied seats at services but held no authority whatsoever.[19]

No rabbi, or what the Sephardic Jews would have called a *haham*, held any permanent pulpit in colonial America. The first permanent rabbi only arrived in 1840. This distinguishes North American synagogues of the day from those in Holland, London, and the Caribbean, where rabbis did officiate for periods of time. The small size, diversity, and impecunious character of colonial synagogues partly explain this anomaly. In addition, synagogues felt under no social compulsion to hire a rabbi because the majority of local churches often lacked ordained ministers. The absence of a professional religious authority did not demean Jews in the eyes of their neighbors.[20]

To compensate for the lack of a rabbi, the officiating hazan (cantor-reader) assumed many of the ceremonial functions that a *haham* might otherwise

---

[17] Morris U. Schappes, *A Documentary History of the Jews in the United States, 1654–1875* (New York, 1950), 19; Sarna, *American Judaism*, 12–20; Holly Snyder, "Rethinking the Definition of 'Community' for a Migratory Age 1654–1830," in Jack Wertheimer, ed., *Imagining the American Jewish Community* (Waltham, MA, 2007), 3–27.

[18] Marcus, *Colonial American Jew*, 855–1110; David de Sola Pool and Tamar de Sola Pool, *An Old Faith in the New World: Portrait of Shearith Israel, 1654–1954* (New York, 1952).

[19] Marcus, *Colonial American Jew*, 899–911.

[20] Sarna, *American Judaism*, 15.

have performed, including on rare occasions public speaking. Non-Jews came to respect the hazan as "reader and notary," "rector," "minister," "reverend," "pastor," "Jew priest," and even "doctor." To insiders, however, he remained a religious functionary, subject to the whims of the lay governing authorities.[21]

Colonial synagogue authorities could not rely on the state to buttress their power when conflicts developed. Nor did fear of the state lead synagogue authorities to closely supervise their members, as sometimes happened in Europe. In America, local governments (at least in the eighteenth century) extended a great deal of autonomy to churches and synagogues and rarely intervened in their internal affairs. Occasionally, synagogue leaders threatened *herem,* or excommunication, against recalcitrant members, but they seldom invoked it. The effectiveness of this traditional sanction in a society in which Jews and Christians mixed freely was highly dubious, and there was always the danger that it would backfire and bring the whole Jewish community into disrepute. More commonly, therefore, punishments consisted of fines, denial of synagogue honors, and, most effective of all, threatened exclusion from the Jewish cemetery – punishments limited to the religious sphere and thus parallel to church forms of discipline.[22]

SYNAGOGUES IN NEW YORK AND NEWPORT

Jews built two synagogues in the colonial period: the so-called Mill Street (today South William Street) Synagogue of Congregation Shearith Israel in New York (1730) and Jeshuat Israel (renamed in the nineteenth century the Touro Synagogue) in Newport (1763). The latter was designed by the famous Newport architect Peter Harrison and is today the oldest extant synagogue in North America. Both synagogues, on the outside, looked modest in comparison to neighboring churches, favoring tradition over external display. On the inside, they resembled classic Sephardic synagogues in Amsterdam and London. Both synagogues, like most of their counterparts in Western Europe and the Americas, eschewed spires and towers, in part to visually distinguish themselves from established churches and avoid offending the majority faith. They projected an image of deference, offering neighbors the reassurance that Jews kept to themselves. In so doing, they reinforced for local Jews an important cultural lesson that centuries of diaspora experience had repeatedly taught them: to practice

---

[21] *Ibid.*
[22] Cf. Yosef Kaplan, "Deviance and Excommunication in the Eighteenth Century: A Chapter in the Social History of the Sephardic Community of Amsterdam," *Dutch Jewish History* 3 (1993): 103–15; Marcus, *Colonial American Jew,* 924–6.

great discretion on the outside, not drawing excessive attention to themselves, while glorying in their faith on the inside, where tradition reigned supreme.[23]

Seating arrangements in the new synagogue underscored this message. They mirrored social and gender inequalities within the community and reinforced religious discipline. The congregation assigned a "proper" place to every worshipper, and each seat was assessed a certain membership tax in advance. Members of the wealthy Gomez family thus enjoyed the most prestigious seats and paid the highest assessments. Others paid less and sat much farther away from the Holy Ark. Women, in accordance with Jewish tradition, worshipped upstairs in the gallery, removed from the center of ritual action below. In Amsterdam, Recife, and London, few women attended synagogue services, so there was little need for designated seating. In New York, however, where Protestant women frequented church, Jewish women attended synagogue much more punctiliously, and seats had to be assigned to them. Because the women's section was small, disputes over status and deference abounded – so much so that a special area was eventually reserved just for the elite women of the Gomez clan.[24]

JEWISH AND WORLDLY DOMAINS

Synagogue communities, as they developed in the major cities of colonial America, bespoke the growing compartmentalization of eighteenth-century American Jewish life into Jewish and worldly domains. This distinction was unknown to medieval Jews or for that matter to most European Jews of the day, but it was characteristic of American Judaism almost from the beginning. Colonial synagogue communities did not tax commercial transactions, censor what Jews wrote on the outside, or punish members for lapses in individual or business morality, unlike synagogues in Amsterdam, London, and Recife. Instead, like the neighboring churches,

---

[23] David de Sola Pool, *The Mill Street Synagogue of the Congregation Shearith Israel* (New York, 1930); Leo Hershkowitz, "The Mill Street Synagogue Reconsidered," *American Jewish Historical Quarterly* 53 (1964): 404–10; Theodore Lewis, "Touro Synagogue, Newport, RI," *Newport History* 48 (Summer 1975): 281–320; Nancy H. Schless, "Peter Harrison, the Touro Synagogue, and the Wren City Church," *Winterthur Portfolio* 8 (1973): 187–200; on American synagogue architecture, see Rachel Wischnitzer, *Synagogue Architecture in the United States* (Philadelphia, 1955).

[24] Jonathan D. Sarna, "Seating and the American Synagogue," in Philip R. Vandermeer and Robert P. Swierenga, eds., *Belief and Behavior: Essays in the New Religious History* (New Brunswick, 1991), 189–206; Sarna, "The Debate Over Mixed Seating in the American Synagogue," in Jack Wertheimer, ed., *The American Synagogue: A Sanctuary Transformed* (New York, 1987), 363–94.

they confined their activities to their own sphere, disciplining some religiously wayward congregants with fines and loss of religious privileges, but leaving commercial and civil disputes, even those that pitted one Jew against another, to the municipal authorities. Some Sephardic Jews went so far as to employ different names in each realm, recalling their former double identities as crypto-Jews.[25]

Central Jewish observances, such as maintaining the Sabbath on Saturday, celebrating Jewish holidays in the fall and the spring, and observing Jewish dietary laws, blurred the boundaries that the separation of realms sought to uphold. They created sometimes agonizing conflicts between the demands of Jewish law and the norms of the larger society in which Jews moved. Refusing to work on the Jewish Sabbath effectively meant working five days instead of six, because local "blue laws" prohibited work on Sunday, the Christian Sabbath. Jewish holidays, amounting to as many as thirteen days a year, similarly conflicted with the workaday world of early America. As for Jewish dietary laws – a complex system of forbidden foods, separation of milk and meat, and special laws for slaughtering and preparing ritually acceptable animals – they made travel away from home, as well as social interactions outside of Jewish homes, both difficult and awkward.[26]

Early American Jews found no easy solutions to these dilemmas. Religious laxity there was aplenty, just as historians have found among English Jews of the time, but there were also those who managed to weave Judaism into the fabric of their daily existence. Indeed, the most striking feature of Jewish life in the colonial period was its diversity. Within every community, even within many individual families, a full gamut of religious observances and attitudes could be found, a spectrum ranging all the way from deep piety to total indifference.[27]

THE JEWISH PEOPLE AND THE JEWISH GOD

For all this, at least two bedrock principles continued to unite colonial American Jews: their commitment to the Jewish people and their belief in one God. Commitment to the Jewish people reflected deep-seated feelings of kinship that linked Jews one to another, obligated them to assist Jews around the world, and set them apart from everybody else. These bonds were essentially tribal in nature, rooted in faith, history, and ties

---

[25] Sarna, *American Judaism*, 20–2. The Newport merchant Aaron Lopez illustrates the phenomenon of living in two worlds. See Stanley F. Chyet, *Lopez of Newport* (Detroit, 1980), esp. 173.

[26] Sarna, *American Judaism*, 20–5.

[27] Marcus, *Colonial American Jew*, 955–60; for the English comparison, see Todd Endelman, *The Jews of Georgian England 1714–1830* (Philadelphia, 1979), 132–65.

of blood. They began for males with circumcision, a rite of religious initiation that colonial Jews scrupulously maintained (if not necessarily on the traditional eighth day of life). Surviving ritual circumcision records demonstrate that even Jews far removed from major settlements and other traditional Jewish rituals continued to circumcise their sons – and when necessary adult males too. In 1767, when Aaron Lopez spirited his half brother and family out of Portugal, saving them "from the reach of Barbarous Inquisition," he arranged for them to obtain what he called, significantly, "the Covenant which happily Characterize us a peculiar Flock." Circumcision, he understood, defined Jews as "peculiar" by permanently distinguishing them from their uncircumcised neighbors. It reminded even Jews remote from the wellsprings of Jewish life that they belonged to a worldwide community.[28]

The other bedrock principle that underlay colonial Jewish life was even more fundamental than the first: belief in one supernatural God – no Jesus, no Holy Spirit. References to the divine power alone abound in colonial Jewish correspondence, from stock phrases like "whom God protect," to heartfelt prayers for life, health, and prosperity. We have it on the authority of Jonathan Edwards, the distinguished Protestant theologian, that some Jews prayed to God with special devotion. In a remarkable passage, he recalled that in 1722/23, while in New York City, he

> lived for many months next to a Jew (the houses adjoining one to another), and had much opportunity daily to observe him; who appeared to me the devoutest person that ever I saw in my life; great part of his time being spent in acts of devotion, at his eastern window, which opened next to mine, seeming to be most earnestly engaged, not only in the daytime, but sometimes whole nights.[29]

Some American Jews, to be sure, were less spiritually inclined. "I cant help Condemning the Many Supersti[ti]ons wee are Clog'd with & heartily wish a Calvin or Luther would rise amongst Us," Abigaill Franks, the highly intelligent wife of one of New York's foremost Jewish merchants, famously wrote in a 1739 letter to her son, Naphtali. But she remained a believing and observant woman. Eight years later, she consoled Naphtali

---

[28] Sarna, *American Judaism*, 25–6; Malcolm H. Stern, "Two Jewish Functionaries in Colonial Pennsylvania," *American Jewish Historical Quarterly* 57 (1967): 24–51; Samuel Broches, *Jews in New England: Six Monographs* (New York, 1942), 2: 61–2; Barbara Kirshenblatt-Gimblett, "The Cut that Binds: The Western Torah Binder as Nexus Between Circumcision and Torah," in Victor Turner, ed., *Celebration: Studies in Festivity and Ritual* (Washington, DC, 1982).

[29] George M. Marsden, *Jonathan Edwards: A Life* (New Haven, 2003), 47–8; Sarna, *American Judaism*, 26.

on the death of his firstborn child, terming it "the Will of that Divine Power to wich all must submit."[30]

THE FAMILIARITY OF STRANGERS

Even as their private beliefs and practices defined colonial Jews religiously and set them apart from their Christian neighbors, social interactions in trade, on the street, and wherever else Jews and Christians gathered inevitably drew them together. Theirs was the "familiarity of strangers," a paradox well familiar to Jews from other port cities such as Livorno. We know of Jews and Christians who joined forces in business, witnessed each other's documents, and socialized in each other's homes. Nevertheless, the bulk of Jews lived in close proximity to one another and to the synagogue and maintained primary ties with members of their own faith.[31]

Familiarity explains how it was that on occasion colonial Jews and Christians fell in love and married. This was an alarming development from the point of view of the Jewish community, which for religious and social reasons considered intermarriage anathema. But it was also a sure sign of Jewish acceptance – particularly because only a small number of the Jews who intermarried converted to Christianity in order to do so. Estimates of Jewish intermarriage in the colonial period range from 10 to 15 percent of all marriages. Men intermarried more frequently than women, and those living far from their fellow Jews were more likely to marry out than those whose primary relationships were with Jews. In one famous case from 1742, Phila Franks, daughter of the aforementioned Abigaill, married a wealthy Huguenot merchant named Oliver DeLancey. Abigaill, feeling deeply ashamed, withdrew from the city and in traditional Jewish fashion resolved to turn her daughter into a stranger: never to see her again, "nor Lett none of the Family Goe near her." But her more politic husband, Jacob, demurred: "Wee live in a Small place & he is Related to the best family in the place," he explained, and he tried to promote reconciliation.[32]

---

[30] Edith B. Gelles, ed., *The Letters of Abigaill Levy Franks 1733–1748* (New Haven, 2004), 68, 147–8.

[31] Francesca Trivellato, *The Familiarity of Strangers: The Sephardic Diaspora, Livorno, and Cross-Cultural Trade in the Early Modern Period* (New Haven, 2009); Pencak, *Jews and Gentiles*; Marcus, *Colonial American Jew*, 397–515, 1113–248.

[32] Malcolm H. Stern, "The Function of Genealogy in American Jewish History," in Jacob Rader Marcus, ed., *Essays in American Jewish History* (Cincinnati, 1958), 85; Gelles, *Letters of Abigaill Levy Franks*, 123–8, 134; Jonathan D. Sarna, "Intermarriage in America: The Jewish Experience in Historical Context," in Stuart Cohen and Bernard Susser, eds., *Ambivalent Jew: Charles Liebman in Memoriam* (New York, 2007), 125–33.

JEWISH RIGHTS IN COLONIAL AMERICA

As a matter of law, Jews were second-class citizens in all of the American colonies prior to the American Revolution. The earliest charter of an English settlement in America, the First Charter of Virginia (1606), granted by King James I, associated the settlement with missionary work, the "propagating of Christian religion." Connecticut's Fundamental Orders (1639), the first to be drawn up by the colonists themselves, pledged to "maintain and preserve the liberty and purity of the gospell of our Lord Jesus which we now profess." Maryland, in a special act concerning religion that actually became known as the Toleration Act (1649) owing to its path-breaking effort to guarantee tolerance for minority Catholics, forbade blasphemy, religious epithets, and profaning of the Sabbath and explicitly promised freedom of religion without fear of molestation or disrespect – but, again, only to those "professing to believe in Jesus Christ." Most colonial constitutions, down to the Revolution, denied Jews the right to vote, demanded Christian test oaths of those in public office, and linked the state to Christianity. Although Jews still enjoyed more rights in colonial America than they did most anywhere in the world, they did not stand on an equal footing with Protestants.[33]

COLONIAL JEWISH CULTURE

When it came to culture, Jews also did not stand on an equal footing with Protestants. Colonial Jews published very little and contributed nothing of significance to scholarship or literature. A few colonial Jews had studied traditional Jewish texts prior to immigrating, but none is known to have possessed even a rudimentary Jewish library. Hebrew, the language of the Bible and the Prayer Book, was "imperfectly understood by many, by some not at all," according to Shearith Israel's Isaac Pinto. This prompted him to produce a translation of the Sabbath and High Holiday prayers into English.[34]

The most original colonial Jewish publication was a sermon delivered in Newport on the holiday of Shavuot (Feast of Weeks, seven weeks after Passover) in 1773 by the visiting itinerant Sephardic scholar Rabbi Haim

---

[33] Jonathan D. Sarna and David G. Dalin, *Religion and State in the American Jewish Experience* (Notre Dame, 1997), 47, 48, 50; Abraham V. Goodman, *American Overture: Jewish Rights in Colonial Times* (Philadelphia, 1947); Stanley F. Chyet, "The Political Rights of the Jews in the United States, 1776–1840," *American Jewish Archives* 10 (1958): 14–75; Milton Borden, *Jews, Turks and Infidels* (Chapel Hill, 1984).

[34] Isaac Pinto, trans., *Prayers for Shabbath, Rosh Hashanah and Kippur* (New York, 1765–66), iii.

Isaac Carigal of Hebron. The goal of the sermon, Laura Leibman persuasively argues, was not just to raise funds, but also to "reiterate the rabbinic covenant that tied *conversos* in the colonies both to God and to other centers of Sephardic life." The sermon directly responded to threats that Christianity and modernity posed to Judaism, and it sought to reinforce "rabbinic privilege" in a region where no permanent rabbis resided. It was the only American Jewish sermon from the colonial era to be published.[35]

EVE OF REVOLUTION

Partly because Jews published so little, Judaism was all but invisible to most Americans on the eve of the American Revolution. No more than one in two hundred Americans was Jewish, and Jews were concentrated in a small number of port cities. There were no Jews in North Carolina at all.[36]

The fact that Jews were present in the American colonies was nevertheless significant. Judaism was the only organized non-Christian religious community in America aside from Native American religions. Its presence helped to ensure that the boundaries of religious pluralism extended beyond Christendom. In addition to contributing to the pluralistic character of American religious life, Jews, along with minority religious groups like the Huguenots, Quakers, and Baptists, helped to legitimate religious dissent.

The Jewish community itself was increasingly diverse on the eve of the Revolution. The 1790 United States Census recorded Jews who had been born in England, France, Germany, Holland, Poland, Portugal, and the West Indies, as well as in the American colonies, a mix that mirrored the composition of the late colonial Jewish community. The Sephardic form of Judaism predominated, as it always had in North America, but the preponderance of colonial Jews was actually of Ashkenazi or mixed background; "pure" Sephardim represented a vanishing breed. As a result, the synagogue community functioned as something of a melting pot, its diversity echoing that of many a colonial city.[37]

New York was the oldest and largest colonial Jewish community, but it exercised no authority over its more recent counterparts. Even fledgling congregations, like Newport and Philadelphia, jealously guarded

---

[35] Laura Leibman, "From Holy Land to New England Canaan: Rabbi Haim Carigal and Sephardic Itinerant Preaching in the Eighteenth Century," *Early American Literature* 44 (Mar. 2009): 87.

[36] Jacob R. Marcus, *To Count a People: American Jewish Population Data 1585–1984* (Lanham, MD, 1990).

[37] Ira Rosenwaike, "An Estimate and Analysis of the Jewish Population of the United States in 1790," *Publications of the American Jewish Historical Society* 50 (1960): 23–67.

their prerogatives. American Judaism thus developed along staunchly congregationalist lines, characterized by increasing multiformity, with each synagogue functioning as an autonomous entity.

Finally, Judaism on the eve of the Revolution was largely confined to two settings, the synagogue and the home, leaving a large public space in between in which Jews and Christians interacted. The kind of communal discipline that the synagogue community exercised elsewhere was no longer possible in the latter decades of the eighteenth century; the reach of its leadership was severely limited.

JEWS AND THE AMERICAN REVOLUTION

The American Revolution pitted Jews, and even individual families, against one another. New York's approximately 400 Jews were reputedly "sharply divided on the lines of Tory and Patriot," and elsewhere, particularly in Newport, "a substantial minority ... remained loyal to the mother country." Many Jews vacillated and pledged allegiance to both sides in the dispute for as long as they could. Jews scarcely differed from their neighbors in this regard. Nativity, ties to Europe, and economic factors determined the loyalties of many colonists. When finally forced to choose, however, most – but by no means all – of America's 1,000 to 2,500 Jews cast their lot for independence.[38]

Individual Jews fought in the Revolution, and Haym Salomon famously served as "Broker to the Office of Finance" during the Revolution. Jews who themselves lived through the Revolution, however, tended to portray their experience more in personal and religious terms. They saw the divine hand working behind the scenes on the field of battle. This helped them to make sense of the events transpiring around them and imbued their struggle with transcendent meaning. Without going so far as some of their Protestant neighbors who read scripture typologically, comparing King George to Pharoah and themselves to Israel, Revolutionary-era Jews did evoke such themes as exile, loss, destruction, and redemption. Linking their experience to these classic Jewish religious motifs consecrated their wartime experience. It cast them as travelers on a sacred road to liberty.[39]

---

[38] Sarna, *American Judaism*, 31; Richard Morris, "The Jews, Minorities and Dissent in the American Revolution," in Aubrey Newman, ed., *Migration and Settlement: Papers on Anglo-American Jewish History* (London, 1971).

[39] Sarna, *American Judaism*, 31–6; Jacob R. Marcus, *United States Jewry 1776–1985* (Detroit, 1989), I: 48–77; Samuel Rezneck, *Unrecognized Patriots: The Jews in the American Revolution* (Westport, 1975).

The Revolution effected changes in law and in the relationship of religion to the state that transformed American Jewish life forever after. Already in the first decade and a half of American independence, the parameters of religious liberty in the new nation steadily widened. New York, with its long tradition of de facto religious pluralism, became in 1777 the first state to extend the boundaries of "free exercise and enjoyment of religious profession and worship" to "all mankind," whether Christian or not, although it required those born abroad to subscribe to an anti-Catholic test oath. Virginia, in its 1785 Act for Religious Freedom originally drafted by Thomas Jefferson in 1779, went even further, with a ringing declaration "that no man shall be compelled to frequent or support any religious worship, place or ministry whatsoever ... but that all men shall be free to profess and by argument to maintain, their opinions in matters of religion, and that the same shall in no wise diminish, enlarge or affect their civil capacities." The Northwest Ordinance, adopted by the Continental Congress in 1787, extended guarantees of freedom of worship and belief into the territories north of the Ohio River. Finally, the Federal Constitution (1787) and the Bill of Rights (1791) outlawed religious tests "as a qualification to any office or public trust under the United States" and forbade Congress from making any law "respecting an establishment of religion, or prohibiting the free exercise thereof."[40]

America's Jews played no significant role in bringing these epochal developments about. On a few occasions, however, Jews did speak up on their own behalf, justifying such extraordinary exceptions to their customary "quietness" by their contribution to the Revolutionary cause. For example, in a petition by the German-Jewish immigrant merchant Jonas Phillips to the 1787 Federal Constitutional Convention meeting in Philadelphia, the only significant petition that it received concerning religious liberty, Phillips complained that Jews had "bravely fought and bled for liberty which they can not Enjoy." He promised that "the Israelites will think themself happy to live under a government where all Religious societies are on an Equal footing."[41]

In the end, the Constitutional Convention and most state discussions concerning the place of religion in American life did not mention Jews even once. Jews gained their religious rights in the United States, and in most but not all of the separate states, as individuals along with everybody else – not, as so often the case in Europe and the Caribbean, through a special privilege or "Jew bill" that set them apart as a group. It did require a controversial Jew bill to win Jews the right to hold public office in Maryland

---

[40] Sarna and Dalin, *Religion and State*, 2–3, 63–71.
[41] Schappes, *Documentary History of the Jews in the United States*, 68–9.

in 1826, and it took another fifty-one years before Jews achieved full legal equality in New Hampshire. Issues like Sunday laws, school prayer, and religious celebrations in the public square reminded Jews of their minority status long after that. Nevertheless, on the national level and in most of the American communities where Jews actually lived, they had achieved an unprecedented degree of "equal footing" by the end of the eighteenth century.[42]

The famed correspondence between Jews and George Washington went even further in defining Judaism's place in the new nation. The address of the "Hebrew Congregation in Newport" to the president, composed for his visit to that city on 17 August 1790, following Rhode Island's ratification of the Constitution, paralleled other letters that Washington received from religious bodies of different denominations and followed a long-established custom associated with the ascension of kings. Redolent with biblical and liturgical language, the address noted past discrimination against Jews, praised the new government for "generously affording to all liberty of conscience and immunities of citizenship," and thanked God "for all of the blessings of civil and religious liberty" that Jews now enjoyed under the Constitution. Washington, in his oft-quoted reply, reassured the Jewish community about what he correctly saw as its central concern – religious liberty. Appropriating a phrase contained in the Hebrew congregation's original letter, he characterized the United States government as one that "gives to bigotry no sanction, to persecution no assistance." He described religious liberty, following Thomas Jefferson, as an inherent natural right, distinct from the indulgent religious "toleration" practiced by the British and much of enlightened Europe, where Jewish emancipation was so often linked with demands for Jewish "improvement." Finally, echoing the language of the prophet Micah (4:4), he hinted that America might itself prove something of a promised land for Jews, a place where they would "merit and enjoy the good will of the other inhabitants; while every one shall sit in safety under his own vine and fig tree and there shall be none to make him afraid."[43]

As the eighteenth century ended, Washington's hope seemed almost within reach. The burgeoning pluralism of American religion, the impact of new federal and state laws, and liberal pronouncements from political leaders all reassured Jews of their rights under the new regime and gave

---

[42] Sarna, *American Judaism*, 37–8 and works noted above, n. 33; on the Maryland Jew Bill, see Edward Eitches, "Maryland's 'Jew Bill,'" *American Jewish Historical Quarterly* 60 (Mar. 1971), 258–80.

[43] Joseph L. Blau and Salo W. Baron, eds., *The Jews of the United States: A Documentary History 1790–1840* (New York, 1963), 8–11.

them a heightened sense of legitimacy. Judaism too was slowly changing in response to the Revolution. Liberty, freedom, and especially democracy were beginning to profoundly affect Jewish life. In the first quarter of the nineteenth century, before masses of Central and Eastern European Jews arrived, a more democratic and more openly pluralistic American Judaism would take shape.

SUGGESTIONS FOR FURTHER READING

Bernardini, Paolo, and Norman Fiering, eds. *The Jews and the Expansion of Europe to the West, 1450–1800*. New York, 2001.

Faber, Eli. *A Time for Planting: The First Migration*. Baltimore, 1992.

Grinstein, Hyman B. *The Rise of the Jewish Community of New York*. Philadelphia, 1945.

Marcus, Jacob Rader. *The Colonial American Jew, 1492–1776*. 3 vols. Detroit, 1970.

———. *United States Jewry, 1776–1985*. 4 vols. Detroit, 1989–93.

Pencak, William. *Jews and Gentiles in Early America*. Ann Arbor, 2005.

Sarna, Jonathan D. *American Judaism: A History*. New Haven, 2004.

Schappes, Morris U. *A Documentary History of the Jews in the United States, 1654–1875*. New York, 1950.

Snyder, Holly. "A Sense of Place: Jews, Identity and Social Status in Colonial British America 1654–1831." Ph.D. diss., Brandeis University, 2000.

20

ROMAN CATHOLICISM IN THE ENGLISH NORTH AMERICAN COLONIES, 1634–1776

TRICIA T. PYNE

The English Province of the Society of Jesus was responsible for the Catholic mission to the English North American colonies. The first missionaries were sent to Maryland (established 1634) at the invitation of the proprietor, the Catholic Lord Baltimore Cecil Calvert (1605/6–75), where they maintained a presence for the entire colonial period. Maryland served as their headquarters for a mission that encompassed the territory between New York and Virginia at the time of the American Revolution. In all, more than 150 priests and brothers were sent to labor in the colonies between 1634 and 1776.[1] The Jesuits financed the mission with the support of the English Province, the profits generated by the plantations and properties they owned in Maryland and Pennsylvania, bequests they received from the laity, and two endowed funds. They operated independently of the Sacred Congregation of the Propaganda Fide, the Vatican agency created in 1622 to oversee missions, which expressed little interest in the activities of these missionaries. When the Jesuits were suppressed as a religious order by Pope Clement XIV in 1773, the missionaries in the American colonies submitted to the authority of the vicar apostolic of the London district and continued on in their labors as secular (diocesan) priests. The suppression sent home to the colonies several native-born Jesuits who had remained in Europe after being ordained, most significantly, John Carroll (1735–1815), who emerged as a leader among the clergy and Catholic community after the American Revolution and was appointed the United States Catholic Church's first bishop in 1789.

---

[1] Extracts from the Catalogues of the Society kept at Rome in the Gesù, box 5, fol. 10, Archives of the Maryland Province of the Society of Jesus, Special Collections Research Center, Lauinger Library, Georgetown University, Washington, DC (hereafter cited as MPA, SCGU); and Beatriz Betancourt Hardy, "Papists in a Protestant Age: The Catholic Gentry and Community in Colonial Maryland, 1689–1776" (Ph.D. diss. University of Maryland, 1993), 576–630.

The Jesuits were assisted by a small number of other priests, including four English secular priests, whose expenses had been paid by the second Lord Baltimore, and at least seven Franciscan friars. The English Province of the Franciscans sponsored a mission to Maryland for nearly fifty years (1672–1718). The Franciscans had come in response to an appeal made by Lord Baltimore for more clergy and worked closely with their Jesuit counterparts. Their presence ended with the death of the last friar laboring in the colony, James Haddock.[2]

Unlike their French and Spanish counterparts, the Jesuits sent to evangelize English North America did not have the support of the state or a mandate to establish a Christian empire. The first missionaries instead had to board secretly the ships that would carry them to Maryland, for Great Britain was a Protestant nation. In the years after King Henry VIII had broken with Rome and declared himself head of the Church of England, the Catholic Church had been suppressed and its members persecuted for not abandoning the faith of their ancestors. This was, after all, an age of religious uniformity, when subjects were expected to profess the religion of their monarch. Efforts to induce conformity culminated in the Elizabethan Acts of Supremacy and Uniformity (1559) and the enactment of a series of penal laws that stripped dissenters of their political rights and imposed fines, imprisonment, and even death for nonconformity. Catholics, because of their obedience to the pope, were deemed subjects of a foreign power and were portrayed as conspirators who sought to undermine the political stability of the state. The fear that Catholics would stop at nothing to seize power and force their religion on the country fueled a rampant anti-Catholicism that became inextricably bound to English national identity.

This anti-Catholic feeling was brought to North America, and by the end of the colonial period all of the colonies under English control had laws on the books that either discriminated against Catholics or forbade them from entering the colonies altogether. Only two colonies, Pennsylvania and Delaware, allowed Catholics to worship freely, but even there they were barred from holding public office and entering the legal and teaching professions. With such a pervasive anti-Catholicism, it is not surprising that so few Catholics immigrated to the colonies and that they represented, as a group, less than 1 percent (less than 25,000) of the total population at the time of the American Revolution. Maryland was home to nearly two-thirds of the total Catholic population, of which 20 percent were slaves. Another one-third was settled in Pennsylvania, with small numbers found in Delaware, New Jersey, New York, and Virginia. There were no organized

---

[2] Dominic V. Monti, "Franciscan Friars" in Michael Glazier and Thomas J. Shelley, eds., *The Encyclopedia of American Catholic History* (Collegeville, MN, 1997), 534–5.

Catholic communities in the remaining colonies, despite the presence of an unknown number of Irish that had arrived as indentured servants or convicts. Spanish missionaries had attempted to evangelize the native peoples in present-day Georgia, South Carolina, and Virginia but had withdrawn by the time the English began to colonize the region, as had the French missionaries who labored among the native peoples in present-day Maine, Vermont, New York, and Pennsylvania. The French territory brought under English control as a result of the treaties of Utrecht (1713) and Paris (1763) in present-day Canada did not become the responsibility of the English Jesuits but remained part of the Diocese of Quebec.[3]

MARYLAND AND VIRGINIA

The Maryland Catholic community was ethnically and economically diverse. Members were largely of English heritage with significant minorities of Irish and Africans and small numbers of Dutch, French, Acadians, and Germans, who ranged from prosperous merchant-planters to slaves. In between were middling planters, tenant farmers, and laborers and their families, the majority of whom earned their living from tobacco, a plant that brought great wealth to a few and unspeakable suffering to many thousands of others. The Catholic community represented 10 percent of Maryland's total population at the end of the colonial period, with the majority of Catholics living in the three southern counties of St. Mary's, Charles, and Prince George's. The five plantations owned by the Jesuits in the colony served as bases for their missionary activities.[4] The missionaries dressed not in religious garb but as gentlemen and farmers and were addressed as "Mister" instead of "Reverend" or "Brother".

Across the Potomac River in Virginia was the Brent family, who had left Maryland in 1651. Their wealth and political connections protected them from the colony's penal laws, and the plantations they owned on

---

[3] In 1785 Rev. John Carroll, then superior of the U.S. missions, estimated the number of Catholics in Maryland at 15,800, in Pennsylvania at 7,000, and in the other former colonies at not more than 2,000, in his "Report to His Eminence Cardinal Antonelli on the Condition of Religion in the Sections of the United States of America," in Thomas O'Brien Hanley, ed., *The John Carroll Papers* (Notre Dame, 1976), I: 179 (hereafter cited as *JCP*); and Kerby Miller, *Emigrants and Exiles: Ireland and the Irish Exodus to North America* (New York, 1985), 139–44.

[4] The five plantations were St. Inigoes Manor, 1,837 acres, and Newtown Manor, 700 acres, both in St. Mary's County; St. Thomas Manor, 923 acres, later incorporated into the larger plantation of Cedar Point Neck, 3,500 acres, Charles County; White Marsh Manor, 1,600 acres, Prince George's County; and Bohemia Plantation, 943 acres, Cecil County.

the northern neck became the principal center of Catholic activity in the colony. They remained tied to the Maryland Catholic community socially through marriage and pastorally through annual visits by the Jesuits. After the Revolution, the future bishop John Carroll estimated there to have been two hundred Catholics in Virginia, who were visited by a priest four to five times a year.[5]

The initial scope of the Jesuits' mission had included evangelizing the Indian population, and they devoted considerable resources to working with members of the Piscataway, Patuxent, and Anacostan tribes. Hampered initially by the language barrier, Rev. Andrew White, the Apostle of Maryland, and Rev. Roger Rigbie became fluent enough by 1640 to translate a catechism and traditional prayers into the Piscataway dialect and baptize the *tayac* (king) of the Piscataway tribe and his family. Political instability during the colony's early years disrupted their efforts and forced them to withdraw from this ministry by 1655. At the end of the seventeenth century there were few Indians left in the colony, the majority having been driven out.

The colony of Maryland had been founded as an experiment in religious toleration. It had been the first Lord Baltimore, George Calvert (c. 1579–1632), who had conceived of a society in which people of different faiths could live together peacefully. The model of church-state relations he proposed was simple but radical, perhaps too radical for the times in which he lived. Church and state were to be separate, religious groups were to fund their activities independently of the state, members of the clergy were not to receive any of the traditional immunities and privileges they were usually accorded, and liberty of conscience was guaranteed to all inhabitants who professed belief in Christ. The penal laws that discriminated against dissenters in England were disallowed in Maryland, freeing them to participate fully in the state. In this form of government, religion became a private matter, and the state limited its role to civil matters.

The first Lord Baltimore did not live long enough to see the "Calvert vision" implemented. This was left to his son, Cecil, who proved himself a faithful steward of his father's plan. Unfortunately, he never visited his colony. Attacks of political enemies who sought to overturn his charter by exploiting anti-Catholic feeling kept him at home. In Maryland, challenges to his authority took the form of armed uprisings. Twice in the first twenty years of the colony's history the local government was toppled under the banner of the Protestant cause. It was a third rebellion led by the Protestant Associators in 1689 and inspired by the

---

[5] Gerald P. Fogarty, *Commonwealth Catholicism: A History of the Catholic Church in Virginia* (Notre Dame, 2001), 14, 21–2.

Glorious Revolution of 1688, however, that finally brought an end to their "Maryland designe."[6]

While the colony remained under the protection of the Lords Baltimore and the original charter, Catholics worshipped openly and freely. The community constructed at least eight freestanding chapels prior to 1689 and appears to have engaged in a number of activities that had been prohibited in England, such as the opening of schools and the proselytizing of Protestant settlers.[7] The great brick chapel (1667–1705) at St. Mary's City, the colony's first capital, perhaps best symbolized the confidence Catholics had attained in the colony during this period. Built on the highest point in the town, the chapel was visible to all who entered the city by way of its principal land entrance. Only the State House rivaled its grandeur.[8]

Maryland became a royal colony in 1690, when rebel leaders appealed to the English crown for legitimacy and support of their actions. This period in Maryland's history (1690–1715) was characterized by the crown's efforts to centralize its authority over the colony, the most visible symbol of which was the establishment of the Anglican Church in 1702. It was also during this period that the colony's first penal laws were enacted. In the fall of 1704, the Act to Prevent the Growth of Popery in This Province was passed by the Maryland Assembly. It had been submitted by the royal governor, John Seymour, and was clearly modeled on the English Parliament's Act to Further Prevent the Growth of Popery (1700). The legislation was directed largely at the proselytizing activities of the Jesuits and prohibited priests from performing any pastoral duties in the colony. In 1707 a compromise that had been achieved with the approbation of Queen Anne I permitted priests to celebrate Mass within "a private family of the Roman Communion" and characterized religious conditions for the remainder of the colonial period. Other penal laws stripped Catholics of their political rights, prohibited Catholic schools, and forbade the baptism of any but the children of Catholics. Catholics were also subject to a number of taxes, including one to support the Anglican Church, but were never required to attend Anglican services or have their marriages and baptisms performed in the Anglican Church as they were in England.[9]

---

[6] John D. Krugler, "The Calvert Vision: A New Model for Church-State Relations," *Maryland Historical Magazine* 99:3 (Fall 2004): 269–86, passim.

[7] Governor Francis Nicholson requested information on the Jesuits' activities in 1697. The report was reprinted in William S. Perry, ed., *Historical Collections Relating to the American Colonial Church*, vol. IV, *Maryland* (repr.; New York, 1969), 19–20.

[8] John D. Krugler and Timothy B. Riordan, "'Scandalous and Offensive to the Government': The 'Popish Chappel' at St. Mary's City, Maryland, and the Society of Jesus, 1634–1705," *Mid-America: An Historical Review* 73:3 (Oct. 1991): 193–9.

[9] William Hand Browne et al., eds., *Archives of Maryland*, 72 vols. (Baltimore, 1883–1972), http://aomol.net/html/index.html, 24: 265–73; 26: 340–1; 27: 146–8; 33:

The restrictions placed on religious practices led to Catholic public chapels being closed. The great brick chapel was dismantled and the materials transported to St. Inigoes, a farm owned by the Jesuits outside of St. Mary's City, where a new residence with an attached chapel was constructed. Others fell into disrepair. Chapels were eventually built on all of the Jesuits' plantations, which became important centers of Catholic life in the colony. A number of the Catholic gentry also maintained chapels in their homes, which were opened to the larger community, a practice that explains the common reference to this period as "manor house Catholicism." These chapels were modest in size and frequently had separate entrances to provide worshippers direct access. Decoration was simple, usually a crucifix displayed on the altar, along with freshly cut flowers. Paintings, stained glass windows, and statues were conspicuously absent, but religious-themed prints were displayed and used by the Jesuits for catechetical and devotional purposes. The design and interior of these chapels were kept plain intentionally to accommodate the tastes of the larger Protestant society.[10]

Neighborhoods without a chapel designated a private home to serve as a Mass house. The celebration of Mass and other church-related activities were conducted in a room that had been prepared for the priest, or, weather permitting, out of doors to accommodate larger crowds. Families from the surrounding area, some traveling ten or more miles, gathered at the appointed house when a missionary was scheduled to visit. The exact number of chapels and Mass houses and their locations remain unknown, but it is believed that fifty had been established throughout the colony by the 1770s, with the greatest number located in those counties with the largest concentration of Catholics and others appearing in areas as they were being settled.[11]

The Jesuits divided the colony into circuits, or territories comprised of neighborhoods where stations (private chapels or Mass houses) were located, that could cover a distance of thirty or more miles. Each of the Jesuit farms was responsible for specific circuits, which were visited regularly over the course of the year. The missionary stayed up to a week in each neighborhood and traveled the circuit on horseback or by boat. He brought with him everything he needed to perform his pastoral duties: an altar

---

287–9. Hereafter cited as *AOM*. Catholics, however, were required to have baptisms and marriages recorded in Anglican registers.

[10] Henry S. Spalding, *Catholic Colonial Maryland* (Milwaukee, 1931), 113; and Tricia T. Pyne, "Ritual and Practice in the Maryland Catholic Community, 1634–1776," *U.S. Catholic Historian* 26:2 (Spring 2008): 22.

[11] Mary Xavier Queen, *Grandma's Stories and Anecdotes of ye Olden Times* (Boston, 1899), 40; and Hardy, "Papists in a Protestant Age," 534–75.

stone, altar cloths, chalice, stole, holy oils, missal, hosts, and catechisms. It was the custom for the priest to lodge with the family whose home was designated as the station and for other families from the neighborhood to prepare his meals and provide corn for his horse during his stay.[12] Beyond celebrating Mass and the sacraments, duties of the priest included offering religious instruction and spiritual direction, preparing individuals to receive the sacraments, training catechists, and making home visits. Catholics who lived near one of the Jesuit farms were able to attend Mass on two Sundays each month and on holy days of obligation. Those who lived at a distance were limited to when a priest visited their neighborhood, which could range anywhere from once a month to once a year.[13]

Although Catholics adapted to conditions under the penal laws, they never accepted the loss of their religious and political rights. Their opposition coalesced into a coherent political dissent that rejected the changes wrought by the Glorious Revolution and, instead, adhered to the ideals on which the colony was founded. Out of this experience emerged the Maryland tradition that embraced such principles as the separation of church and state, religious freedom, ecumenism, and public service. After the American Revolution, when Catholics were accepted on equal terms with their fellow citizens, they drew on this tradition to show the compatibility between Catholicism and the principles of the new nation and to ease the community's integration into the larger society.[14]

The Carroll family had been at the center of the Catholic community's struggle for political and religious rights in Maryland since the overthrow of Lord Baltimore in 1689. Charles Carroll the Settler (1660–1720) had immigrated to Maryland in 1688. Born in Ireland to a wealthy Catholic family, Carroll had been sent to the continent to receive his education. On completing his studies, he went to London, where he entered the Inner Temple. It was there that he was introduced to the third Lord Baltimore, Charles Calvert (1637–1715). Impressed with Carroll's self-assured style, Calvert commissioned him to act as his attorney general in Maryland. It would be the first of several lucrative commissions Carroll held under the proprietor, and he soon amassed one of the colony's greatest fortunes. It

---

[12] Spalding, *Catholic Colonial Maryland*, 119, 123–4; and John LaFarge, "The Survival of the Catholic Faith in Southern Maryland," *Catholic Historical Review* 21 (April 1935): 10–11.

[13] Official Report from the Superior, Father G. Hunter, to the Provincial, Father Dennett, 23 July 1765, reprinted in Thomas Hughes, *History of the Society of Jesus in North America: Colonial and Federal* (New York, 1908), documents, 1: 1, 337.

[14] Thomas O'Brien Hanley, *Charles Carroll of Carrollton: The Making of a Revolutionary Gentleman* (Chicago, 1982), 16–18; and Thomas W. Spalding, *The Premier See: A History of the Archdiocese of Baltimore, 1789–1989* (Baltimore, 1989), 17–20.

was Carroll's outspokenness and political maneuvering on the community's behalf during the royal period, when the first penal laws were enacted, that thrust him into a leadership role.

Carroll's namesake and heir, Charles Carroll of Annapolis (1702–82), inherited not only his father's wealth, but the mantle of political leadership for the community. Ties to Lord Baltimore, who had been restored as proprietor with the conversion of Benedict Leonard Calvert (1679–1715) in 1713, remained close and were reinforced through an alliance with the proprietary party in Maryland. Although Carroll lacked the irascible nature of his father, he found himself at the center of a fight against the enactment of stricter penal laws during the 1750s, which was the most contentious period for Maryland's Catholics in more than thirty years. The failure of Lord Baltimore to support the community during this struggle left members of the Catholic leadership disillusioned, called the proprietor's loyalty into question, and provided an opening for the political argument advanced by Carroll's son nearly twenty years later.

Charles Carroll of Carrollton (1737–1832) was to play the most significant role in the struggle for Catholic political and religious rights. Following in the tradition of his father and grandfather, Carroll was sent to Europe for his education. It was during his years abroad that Carroll developed a political thought that led him to conclude that the Maryland Catholic community's future no longer lay in alliance with Lord Baltimore or as subjects under English law, but as citizens of a free and independent America. He chose to assume a public role in the heated debate regarding the taxation privileges of the proprietor within the colony, where he articulated the arguments that would be at the heart of the movement for American independence in the much-acclaimed 1773 *Maryland Gazette* editorial debate with Daniel Dulaney. From that moment on he cast his future and fortune with the Patriot cause and, in doing such, brought about a sea change of opinion within the Catholic community to support the Revolution.[15]

NEW YORK AND NEW JERSEY

Before New York and New Jersey came under English control, they had been included in the Dutch province of New Netherland (1625–64). The Dutch did not have a policy of religious toleration, and few Catholics were found within the territory. The only significant Catholic presence was found on the western frontier, where French Jesuit missionaries labored

---

[15] See Ronald Hoffman, *Princes of Ireland, Planters of Maryland: A Carroll Saga, 1500–1782* (Chapel Hill, 2000), 91–7, 270–302.

among the Iroquois (1642–1709). When the English seized control of New Netherland in 1664, King Charles II gave the territory to his brother the Duke of York (later King James II). The duke maintained control over what became the province of New York and gave New Jersey to his close friends Sir George Carteret and Lord Berkeley of Stratton. This period in New York's history is noted for the policy of liberty of conscience that was extended to colonists. In 1683 this policy was codified in the Charter of Liberties and Privileges, which granted religious freedom to all Christians and was enacted during the colony's first representative assembly. Governor Thomas Dongan had introduced the bill at the Duke of York's request. The Irish Catholic Dongan had arrived in the colony that year with Rev. Thomas Harvey, an English Jesuit sent to establish a mission in New York. Over the next three years Harvey was joined by Rev. Henry Harrison, Rev. Charles Gage, and two lay brothers. Together they staffed a chapel at Fort James and operated a Latin school in present-day Manhattan. It had been Dongan's intention to transfer control of the Iroquois mission from the French Jesuits to the English, and he had even acquired land outside of Albany to build a church for their use, but the Glorious Revolution of 1688 disrupted his plans. The overthrow of James II inspired an armed rebellion led by the anti-Catholic Jacob Leisler that overthrew the colony's sitting government in 1689. The Charter of Liberties and Privileges was revoked two years later, and in 1700 the Act against Jesuits and Popish Priests was enacted to suppress the Catholic Church in the colony. The Jesuit mission had been closed at the time of the rebellion, when the priests fled New York. Rev. Harvey, who had made his way to Maryland, returned in 1690 and remained until 1693, when he departed for good. While traveling between the two colonies, he ministered to Catholics in Delaware, Pennsylvania, and New Jersey under the assumed name of Rev. John Smyth. The Jesuits would not return to New York until the 1770s, when German-born Rev. Ferdinand Farmer (alias for Steinmeyer) was assigned to attend the Catholics settled in the Hudson Valley from Pennsylvania. Few records have survived to detail his secret visits to New York, but tradition identifies the Manhattan home of Joseph Idley as a mission station. Here Farmer celebrated Mass for a faith community whose members were of German, Irish, French, and African descent. Mr. Idley later served as sexton at St. Peter's (1785), the first Catholic Church built in New York.[16]

---

[16] James Hennesey, "Catholicism in the English Colonies" in Charles H. Lippy and Peter W. Williams, eds., *The Encyclopedia of the American Religious Experience: Studies of Traditions and Movements* (New York, 1988), I: 352; Thomas J. Shelley, *The History of the Archdiocese of New York* (Strasbourg, 1999), 7–11; Governor Dongan to the Committee of Trade on the Province of New York, 22 Feb. 1687, reprinted in *American Catholic Historical Researches* 12:1 (Jan. 1895): 64 (hereafter cited as *ACHR*); Leo R. Ryan, *Old St. Peter's:*

In the provinces of East and West Jersey, the two proprietors drew up a charter (Concession and Agreement, 1664) that listed religious freedom as one of the privileges extended to colonists. This charter remained in effect until 1702, when the Jerseys were placed under royal control and Catholics lost the privilege to worship freely. The Catholic community at that time included French and Irish laborers employed in the clay pits and salt mines near Woodbridge and Elizabethtown, as well as Sir John Tatham (alias for Gray), an English gentleman with extensive land grants in West Jersey and Pennsylvania, and William Douglas of Bergen County, who in 1668 was prevented from taking office in the East Jersey Assembly because of his faith. The Jesuits of the New York mission visited the colony until they withdrew from the region in 1693. They did not return until 1743, when Rev. Theodore Schneider began making clandestine visits from Pennsylvania to the growing numbers of Irish and German immigrants arriving to labor in the colony's emerging glass industry. Matthew Geiger's home served as a Mass house and became a center of Catholic activity in Salem County. Within three years Rev. Schneider's circuit covered a distance of 100 miles that took him as far north as Bound Brook, Somerset County. He was succeeded in 1758 by Rev. Farmer, the Apostle of New Jersey, who established the first mission stations in the northern part of the colony. The discovery of iron ore brought German immigrants to work in the mines and forges established at Ringwood, Charlottenburg, and Mount Hope. Farmer traveled the length of the colony biannually for the next eighteen years.[17]

PENNSYLVANIA AND DELAWARE

A Catholic presence in William Penn's colonies of Pennsylvania (1681) and Delaware (placed under Penn's authority in 1682) dates to the end of the seventeenth century, with the arrival of such individuals as Peter Dubuc, a wealthy Frenchman who lived in Philadelphia, and Jacobus Seth, a Dutch sea captain, who settled with his family near Lewes, Delaware. In 1704 the Jesuits established a permanent presence in the region with the acquisition of Bohemia Plantation at the head of the Chesapeake Bay in Cecil County, Maryland. From there they were positioned to attend Catholics

---

The Mother Church of Catholic New York, 1785–1935 (New York, 1935), 34; and Jason K. Duncan, *Citizens or Papists: The Politics of Anti-Catholicism in New York, 1685–1821* (New York, 2005), 28–9, 54.

[17] Joseph Kirlin, *Catholicity in Philadelphia from the Earliest Missionaries Down to the Present Time* (Philadelphia, 1909), 17; Lambert Schrott, *Pioneer German Catholics in the American Colonies, 1734–1784* (New York, 1933), 35–71; and Raymond J. Kupke, *Living Stones: A History of the Catholic Church in the Diocese of Paterson* (Clifton, NJ, 1987), 7–13.

in these two colonies. Within ten years they were visiting families regularly between Concord (now Ivy Mills), Delaware, and Philadelphia. A 1693 bequest made by Mr. Dubuc to a Father Smyth suggests that the Jesuits had been preceded there by one of their colleagues. Growing numbers of German and Irish immigrants who labored as skilled and unskilled workers led to the establishment of a mission in Pennsylvania, which was supported by funds established by Sir John James and Rev. Gilbert Talbot, S.J., thirteenth earl of Shrewsbury. In 1729 Rev. Joseph Greaton, the Apostle of Pennsylvania, was appointed the mission's superior and became the colony's first resident priest. Headquartered in Philadelphia, he set out from his residence on Walnut Street to identify the colony's Catholics and was soon responsible for a territory that stretched from the Delaware River to the Conewago Valley. With no legal proscriptions on the practice of their religion, Catholics were able to engage in activities banned in other colonies, most significantly worshipping in public and printing Catholic books. Decoration of their chapels was more elaborate, as were their liturgies. In 1734 the colony's first Catholic church was constructed in Philadelphia. Dedicated to St. Joseph, it was supported by voluntary contributions. Thirty years later a second church was needed, and St. Mary's (1763) was opened. Parishioners reflected the growing affluence of both the port city and the Catholic community, with such prosperous merchants as Thomas Fitzsimons, Stephen Moylan, and George Meade counted among its members. In 1741 Rev. Theodore Schneider and Rev. William Wappeler arrived, the first of nine German-speaking Jesuits to labor in the colonies.

Rev. Robert Molyneux, a former Jesuit who was superior of the Pennsylvania mission during the 1770s, prepared the first Catholic books published in English North America, *A Manual of Catholic Prayers* (Philadelphia: Robert Bell, 1774) and an American edition of Bishop Richard Challoner's *The Garden of the Soul: Or, a Manual of Spiritual Exercises and Instructions for Christians who (Living in the World) Aspire to Devotion* (7th ed., corrected; Philadelphia: Joseph Crukshank, 1774). He later oversaw the publication of the country's first Catholic hymnbook, John Aitken's *A Compilation of the Litanies and Vespers Hymns and Anthems as They Are Sung in the Catholic Church* (1787). Prior to their publication, religious and devotional books had to be imported from Europe. These works were used extensively in their pastoral labors by the Jesuits, who, as a religious order, had recognized from an early date the power of the printed word to evangelize and catechize.

The Conewago Valley, located 125 miles west of Philadelphia, was the other center of Catholic life in the colony. Catholics who had relocated from Maryland (many unwittingly after a lengthy border dispute transferred land previously claimed by Maryland to Pennsylvania) and Germans, largely from the Palatinate, composed this rural community of poor farmers. The Jesuits had visited the region in the early 1700s, but the first mission was not established until 1730 at Conewago (now Hanover) by Rev. Greaton. Mass was celebrated at the Owings' family home until the first church, St. Mary of the Assumption, was built in 1741. Over the next fifty years, missions were founded throughout the valley, reaching as far north as Reading. As colonists pushed further into the interior, so too did the Jesuits, traveling as far west as Northumberland.

Pennsylvania failed to attract many Catholics, however. A 1757 census identified fewer than 1,500 adult Catholics in the colony out of a total population of 500,000. Emigration spurred by wars in Europe would subsequently swell the Catholic population to 6,000 by 1765, more than half of whom were German.[18]

Catholics were less numerous in Delaware. The community was made up largely of former Marylanders (the result of another border dispute), such as Joseph Weldon and his family, who had settled on Duck Creek in 1701, and immigrants from Ireland, including Cornelius "Con" Hollahan, who had arrived by 1747. Prior to the Jesuits' arrival at Bohemia Plantation in 1704, the colony's Catholics rarely saw a priest and had to travel to Maryland to attend Mass and receive the sacraments. By the 1720s the Jesuits began to visit the colony regularly, establishing missions at such places as present-day Willow Grove and Smyrna, Kent County, and Hockessin, New Castle County, where the colony's first church, St. Mary of the Assumption, was constructed by 1788. The faith community there dated back forty years when Mass was first performed at the home of the Con Hollahan family.[19]

ACADIAN REFUGEES

During the Seven Years' War (1754–63), the English deported between 8,000 and 10,000 French neutrals from the Acadia region of Nova Scotia. A number were returned to Europe, and others were confined to English

---

[18] Hennesey, "Catholicism," 351–2; see the transcription of Peter Dubuc's will dated 14 Oct. 1693, in which he gives "ffather Smyth now or late of Talbott County in the Province of Maryland" fifty pounds silver, reprinted in *ACHR* 14:4 (Oct. 1897): 177–9; Kirlin, *Catholicity in Philadelphia*, 14–20, 39; John W. O'Malley, *The First Jesuits* (Cambridge, MA, 1993), 114–15; and Linda V. Itzoe, *Highway of Missionaries: An Illustrated History of the Diocese of Harrisburg* (Strasbourg, 2006), 6–7.

[19] Donn Devine, "Beginnings of the Catholic Church of Wilmington, Delaware," *Delaware History* 28:4 (2000): 329; and Thomas J. Peterman, *Bohemia, 1704–2004: A History of St. Francis Xavier Catholic Shrine in Cecil County, Maryland* (Devon, PA, 2004), 22–7.

prison ships, but the overwhelming majority was sent for resettlement in nine of the thirteen English North American colonies (Massachusetts, Connecticut, New York, Pennsylvania, Maryland, Virginia, North Carolina, South Carolina, and Georgia). Not all welcomed these French-speaking Catholic refugees. North Carolina and Virginia refused to accept the 1,500 they had been asked to take in. In Maryland, where an approximate 600 Acadians were sent, the exiles were divided among the counties. Acadians sent to southern Maryland were integrated into existing Catholic communities. In Baltimore, they received shelter and aid from local Catholics and settled in what became known as the Frenchtown neighborhood of the city. In 1770 they founded St. Peter's, the city's first parish, which later served as the pro-cathedral for Bishop John Carroll. Those sent to Pennsylvania were not as fortunate. The ships with 450 of the exiles also carried smallpox. They were placed into quarantine on arrival in Philadelphia, where many soon died. Survivors were aided by the city's Catholic and Quaker communities. Anti-Catholic fears stirred up by the governor, however, made their presence in the colony difficult. When the war ended in 1763, many of the refugees deported to the colonies returned to Nova Scotia, whereas others made their way to French-controlled Louisiana.[20]

RELIGIOUS PRACTICES

As the only clergy to minister continuously to the Catholics of English North America, the Jesuits had a tremendous influence on the development of the Church there. The defining feature of the Jesuits' pastoral plan was the Spiritual Exercises, which, as historian John W. O'Malley observes, contains "in embryo the basic design for Jesuit spirituality and ministry."[21] The Exercises were authored by the order's founder, St. Ignatius of Loyola (1491–1556). Influenced by *devotio moderna*, a spiritual movement of the late Middle Ages that adapted the monastic method of meditative prayer for popular use, St. Ignatius further refined this method by systematizing it into a set program of spiritual direction that became known as the retreat and was used by the Jesuits in their work with the laity. Individuals typically made the Exercises for the first time after receiving spiritual direction and catechetical instruction and thereafter as part of their ongoing

[20] Natasha Dubé, "Le Grand Dérangement," Centre for Constitutional Studies, University of Alberta, http://www.law.ualberta.ca/centres/ccs/issues/legrandderangement.php; Arthur G. Doughty, *The Acadian Exiles: A Chronicle of the Land of Evangeline* (Toronto, 1916), 138–61; and Spalding, *Premier See*, 6.
[21] John W. O'Malley, "Some Distinctive Characteristics of Jesuit Spirituality in the Sixteenth Century," in John W. O'Malley et al., contribs., *Jesuit Spirituality: A Now and Future Resource* (Chicago, 1990), 2.

spiritual formation. The Exercises promoted a Christocentric spirituality that employed prayer, imagination, and meditation to lead the individual through a process that culminated in the decision to commit one's life to Christ. Herein lay the defining mission of the Jesuits as a religious order: conversion of the individual. The pastoral plan they developed flowed out of this mission, which was implemented through a program of catechesis and spiritual direction and reinforced by the Tridentine reforms, which placed emphasis on frequenting the sacraments; doctrinal orthodoxy; development of an interior, affective spirituality; and the performance of good works.

In ministering to the laity, the Jesuits blended traditional methods with new ideas, as seen in the remaking of confraternities and popular devotions. In the colonies, confraternities for the Adoration of the Blessed Sacrament, Bona Mors (preparation for a good death), and Sacred Heart of Jesus were founded. Devotions that encouraged the frequenting of the sacraments and veneration of the saints who personified the Catholic Reformation, such as St. Ignatius of Loyola and St. Francis Xavier, were promoted through the granting of indulgences and distribution of sacramentals that had been approved by the Holy See, including religious medals, rosaries, *agnus dei* (a wax disc with an imprint of the Lamb of God), and religious prints.[22]

The Jesuits also promoted two practices that had long been associated with the English Catholic community: the rosary and spiritual reading. By remaking them to incorporate the Tridentine reforms, they became two of the most effective means for sustaining the communities in England and the colonies.[23] The rosary is a meditation on the lives of Jesus and Mary. The devotee is to reflect on each of the fifteen mysteries while reciting the prescribed prayers. It can be said individually or in a group, in the privacy of the home or in the communal setting of a church. When introduced by the Jesuits through membership in a confraternity, the format and prayers of the rosary were systematized to bring about uniformity in practice and to

---

[22] Subscribers List, Perpetual Adoration of the Blessed Sacrament, Aug. 1768, box 57, fol. 2, MPA, SCGU; see sodality membership lists recorded in Rev. James Walton's Diary, 3, box 4, fol. 2 [photocopy], *ibid.*; Fr. George Hunter's Manual, c. 1747–49, 7–8, box 3, fol. 15, *ibid.*; *Liber continens ... facultates, indulgentias, et privilegia a Summnis Pontificus Societate concessa*, 1759–1855, 1–2, 6–10, box 12, fol. 9, *ibid.*; and Geoffrey Holt, ed., *The Letter Book of Lewis Sabran, SJ, Rector of St. Omers College, Oct. 1713 to Oct. 1715* (London, 1971), 281.

[23] See Alexandra Walsham, "'Domme Preachers'? Post-Reformation English Catholicism and the Culture of Print," *Past and Present* 168 (Aug. 2000): 72–123; and Anne Dillon, "Praying by Numbers: The Confraternity of the Rosary and the English Catholic Community, c. 1580–1700," *History* 87 (2003): 451–71.

ensure that the teachings examined in each of the mysteries were doctrinally correct. The rosary's flexibility and simplicity made it adaptable to the difficult conditions that characterized the penal years and gave Catholics of all backgrounds and abilities a way to practice their faith during those periods when a priest could not be with a community.[24]

Recognizing the role that spiritual reading played in the pastoral plan of the Jesuits casts new light on the significance of the libraries they maintained at all of their residences, which contained Bibles, devotional works, catechisms, lives of the saints, Church histories, sermon collections, and spiritual retreats.[25] The libraries were made available to both the missionaries, who could consult their contents when writing sermons or preparing for other pastoral duties, and the laity, who had borrowing privileges. Access to these works provided the laity with opportunities to continue their spiritual development and religious education, while reinforcing the teachings and practices introduced by the Jesuits through preaching and catechesis.

The existence of these libraries begs the question as to how the children of the Catholic community were educated in light of the penal laws and anti-Catholic feeling in the colonies. The short-lived schools founded by the Jesuits in Maryland (Newtown, c. 1677–1704, and Bohemia Plantation, 1745–49) and New York (c. 1683–89) are the most noted, but the Jesuits also acted as tutors and operated small schools at several of their residences in Maryland and Pennsylvania. The laity made significant contributions as well through the informal network of schools they supported, which ranged from home schooling to country schoolmasters. Evidence of these schools was passed down through personal recollections, bequests, and civil records. The first Catholic school in English North America was opened in 1640 by the layman Ralph Crouch at St. Mary's City and operated intermittently for nineteen years. Jane Matthews Doyne of St. Mary's County instructed girls in her home in the early 1700s, and Patrick Cavanagh opened a school near the head of Deer Creek in Baltimore County in the 1750s, after having taught in York, Pennsylvania. A complaint made to the Maryland Assembly in 1753 claimed that there were so many Catholic schoolmasters in St. Mary's County that Protestant children had to be sent abroad for their education. In Pennsylvania, Irish schoolmasters advertised in the local newspapers, and Catholic schools were founded at Haycock, Bally, and Reading. In Delaware, the school staffed by lay teachers at

---

[24] Dillon, "Praying by Numbers," 456, 464.
[25] Rev. James Walton's Diary, 2, 23, MPA, SCGU; Newtown Memoranda, 13–15, box 3, fol. 8, *ibid.*; and Accounts, 1764–1767, St. Joseph's Church, Talbot County, box 47, fol. 2, *ibid.*

Appoquinimink (now Odessa-Middletown) served one of the colony's largest Catholic communities.[26]

The gentry also had the resources to import tutors (principally Irish) to instruct their children at home or to send them to Europe, where sons were educated by the Jesuits and daughters placed in convent schools. A number of these children chose to remain in Europe to pursue religious vocations, for there were neither seminaries nor convents in the colonies, despite the short-lived novitiate operated by the Jesuits at St. Mary's City (c. 1674–90). Of the young men who sought holy orders, forty-nine were ordained. Forty-three of that number entered the Society of Jesus, with twenty-one returning to serve in Maryland. Thirty-three young women from Maryland took the veil, three of whom (Anne Matthews and her two nieces, Susanna and Ann Teresa Matthews) returned in 1790 to establish the first community of women religious in this country, the Discalced Carmelites, at Port Tobacco in southern Maryland. For those young men and women who were unable to pursue a vocation, for either financial or family reasons, there is evidence that a number devoted their lives to the Church in North America, serving as *donnés* (lay co-workers) or adopting a religious-like rule and receiving spiritual direction from the Jesuits.[27]

There are few details on how Catholics practiced their religion during the colonial period. When Catholics were able to attend Mass, they were encouraged to bring manuals, such as Bishop Richard Challoner's *Garden of the Soul* (1740) and *Catholick Christian Instructed* (1737), which included a vernacular translation of the service. Members of the community who were unable to read were encouraged to engage in private devotions, such as the rosary.[28] It is believed that free and enslaved worshiped as one community during the colonial period and that slaves were included in all aspects of the liturgical and sacramental life of the Church. Slaves, however, were separated from their white coreligionists during services by being required

---

[26] W. C. Repetti, "Catholic Schools in Colonial Maryland," *Woodstock Letters* 81 (1952): 130; R. Emmett Curran et al., *The Maryland Jesuits* (Baltimore, 1976), 1634–1833, 15–17; Beatriz Betancort Hardy, "Women and the Catholic Church in Maryland, 1689–1776," *Maryland Historical Magazine* 94:4 (Winter 1999): 402; Robert Barnes, School Teachers of Early Maryland, MSA SC 5300, entry for Patrick Cavanagh, Maryland State Archives, http://www.msa.md.gov/msa/speccol/sc5300/sc5300/html/main.html; Testimony of Thomas Reader, St. Mary's County, 26 Oct. 1753, *AOM*, 50: 304; Schrott, *Pioneer Germans*, 91; Kirlin, *Catholicity in Philadelphia*, 30; and Peterman, *Bohemia*, 24, 37.

[27] Hennesey, "Catholicism," 350; James Hennesey, "Several Youth Sent from Here: Native Born Priests and Religious of English America, 1634–1776," in Nelson H. Minnich et al., eds., *Studies in Catholic History in Honor of John Tracy Ellis* (Wilmington, DE, 1985), 2–3; Hughes, *History of the Society*, documents, 1:1, 64–5, 135–8; and LaFarge, "Survival of the Catholic Faith," 12.

[28] John Bossy, *The English Catholic Community, 1570–1850* (repr.; London, 1979), 131.

to stand at the back or along the sides of the church.[29] A typical Sunday schedule began with families arriving early in the morning at the appointed place, where confessions were heard until 11:00 a.m. Mass was celebrated at midday, with Holy Communion distributed afterward. The gospel was read in Latin, followed by announcements, including the reading of marriage banns. The gospel was then read in the vernacular, followed by a sermon. Hymns, sung in both Latin and the vernacular, were also a part of church services. Before dismissing the congregation, the Our Father, Hail Mary, Apostles' Creed, and the acts of faith, hope, and charity were recited by the congregation in the vernacular. It was then the custom to break for a meal and allow for socializing among the families before concluding the day with religious instruction. Couples who wished to be married or have their children baptized could do so on Sunday, although there is evidence the Jesuits regularly performed these sacraments in private ceremonies for families in their homes.[30]

For many Catholics, however, most Sundays and holy days were observed without a priest. The Jesuits responded to this situation by implementing a pastoral plan they had first developed in England, where conditions in the post-Reformation Church had persuaded them to shift from a parish-based model to one that was directed toward the family and meeting the needs of the domestic church. In this program of home ministry, families were provided with instructions on how to fulfill their religious obligations and nurture their spiritual development in the absence of a priest. It reinforced the principal role that parents, and especially mothers, played in the formation of their children's faith by maintaining a Christian home, where through word and example they lived out the teachings and practices of the Catholic Church. Families were expected to fulfill their religious obligations by gathering together as a household to recite their prayers, engage in private devotions or spiritual reading, and conduct catechism lessons.[31] Instructions for how the laity could hear the Mass "spiritually" were included in manuals such as Challoner's *Garden of the Soul*, which

---

[29] LaFarge, "Survival of the Catholic Faith," 14.

[30] Petition of John Baptist Mattingly, 6 Sept. 1773, excerpt translated and published in R. Emmett Curran, ed., *American Jesuit Spirituality: The Maryland Tradition, 1634–1900* (New York, 1988), 12; "Concerning Arrangements for Divine Service and the Observance of Feasts" in the Report of the First Diocesan Synod, 1791, *JCP*, I: 531–2; John Grassi, "The Catholic Religion in the United States in 1818," translated and published in *ACHR* 8:3 (1891): 105, 108; "Ecclesiastical Discipline," Baltimore, 15 Nov. 1810, transcribed and published in *ACHR* 11:1 (1894): 32; and William Treacy, "Historical Points Connected with Newtown Manor and Church, St. Mary's County, Maryland," *Woodstock Letters* 13:1 (1884): 71.

[31] Curran, *Maryland Jesuits*, 18.

recommended that its readers designate a specific room in the house to serve as the family's oratory, thus helping to create a sacred space within the home that would be associated with the performance of the family's religious duties.[32]

Outside of the Sunday schedule, the laity was encouraged to observe a daily routine of morning and evening prayers, spiritual reading, and an examination of conscience. They were also to follow the religious obligations and dietary restrictions of the feast and fast schedule that structured the liturgical year. The latter was another area in which women could exercise particular influence as the person who set the household schedule and maintained the kitchen. In the middle of the eighteenth century, the English Catholic Church observed thirty-six feasts or holy days. The laity was to observe a Sunday schedule, which required attending Mass or engaging in private devotions and refraining from any form of manual labor or socializing. The sanctity of the day was to be upheld by carrying out a routine of quiet reflection and solitude. The Jesuits held the position that servants and slaves were not to be exempted from their holy day obligations, excepting absolute necessity, and were to be included in the household's religious observances.

The colonies were also subject to the fasting regulations of the English Catholic Church, which during the post-Reformation period were characterized as rigorous. Required days of fasting and abstinence, when individuals were to eat only one full meal a day and to abstain from flesh meat, which at times included white meats (eggs and cheese), numbered close to one hundred, including all forty days of Lent (excepting Saturdays). Added to this were another forty days of abstinence, which together represented more than one-third of the calendar year.[33]

There is evidence that the demands of fulfilling these obligations, especially the regulation that forbade engaging in manual labor, had become increasingly burdensome for Maryland Catholics by the first decades of the eighteenth century. The source of their discontent can be expressed in one word: tobacco, a crop that required intensive labor during the months that it was being harvested and prepared for market (May–September). Another contributing factor was the changing socioeconomic makeup of the community. Initially associated with its wealthy and influential members,

---

[32] Richard Challoner, *Garden of the Soul: Or a Manual of Spiritual Exercises and Instructions for Christians, who Living in the World Aspire to Devotion* (Philadelphia, 1792), Early American Imprints, first series; no. 24184; 46712, 103–4.

[33] John A. Gurrieri, "Holy Days in America," *Worship* 54:5 (Sept. 1908): 422, 426; Richard Challoner, *The Garden of the Soul: Or, a Manual of Spiritual Exercises and Instructions for Christians who (Living in the World) Aspire to Devotion*, 7th ed. (corrected; Philadelphia, 1774), 1–5; Curran, *Maryland Jesuits*, 18; and Bossy, *English Catholic Community*, 110.

over time this group was vastly outnumbered by white immigrants from the middling to lower classes and Africans who had been brought over to the colony as slaves. Unlike the gentry, these latter groups, either by force or necessity, had to work in the fields to bring in the crop. In the 1720s the Jesuits requested and received dispensations from holy day and fasting obligations for those Catholics employed in the growing of tobacco. The superior of the mission was eventually given the authority to grant dispensations "as he shall judge proper, to lessen the number or to add thereunto."[34] A schedule published at the end of the colonial period revealed that the Jesuits had reduced days of fasting by one-third to sixty-three. Days of abstinence, however, were little altered and only two feast days had been dropped from the calendar.[35]

CONCLUSION

The Catholic community in English North America was able to sustain itself through a joint recognition among the laity and the Jesuits of their unique circumstances in the colonies. An examination of this history reveals the centrality of family and the domestic church to its survival. The pastoral program of the Jesuits reflected this reality and was directed to providing families with the support they needed to maintain their practices and pass the faith from one generation to the next.

SUGGESTIONS FOR FURTHER READING

Curran, R. Emmett, ed. *American Jesuit Spirituality: The Maryland Tradition, 1634–1900*. New York, 1988.

Hardy, Beatriz Betancourt. "Papists in a Protestant Age: The Catholic Gentry and Community in Colonial Maryland, 1689–1776." Ph.D. diss., University of Maryland, 1993.

Hennesey, James. "Catholicism in the English Colonies," in Charles H. Lippy and Peter W. Williams, eds., *The Encyclopedia of the American Religious Experience: Studies of Traditions and Movements*. New York, 1988, I: 345–55.

Hughes, Thomas, ed. *History of the Society of Jesus in North America: Colonial and Federal documents*. New York, 1908, vol. 1, part 1.

Krugler, John D. "The Calvert Vision: A New Model for Church-State Relations." *Maryland Historical Magazine* 99:3 (Fall 2004): 269–86.

Pyne, Tricia T. "Ritual and Practice in the Maryland Catholic Community, 1634–1776." *U.S. Catholic Historian* 26:2 (Spring 2008): 17–46.

---

[34] An Abstract of Fr. Thomas Lawson to Fr. George Thorold, S.J., 6 Mar. 1724/5, transcribed in Old Record Book, box 3, fol. 8, MPA, SCGU.

[35] Challoner, *Garden of the Soul* (1774), 4–5.

21

ANGLICANISM AND ITS DISCONTENTS: PROTESTANT DIVERSITY AND DISESTABLISHMENT IN BRITISH AMERICA

DANIEL VACA AND RANDALL BALMER

About fifteen years after embarking in April 1759 on a one-and-a-half-year tour of North America's "middle settlements," the Anglican minister Andrew Burnaby published an account of his travels. By 1775, political unrest in North America had led the English to wonder if their North American colonies would claim independence, and Burnaby's book attempted to ease anxieties. In his account, Burnaby insisted that his time spent traveling between Virginia and New Hampshire had shown him that England's colonies could not cohere independently of Britain. They simply were too diverse. Noting that the colonies "are composed of people of different nations, different manners, different religions, and different languages," Burnaby pointed out that "religious zeal too, like a smothered fire, is secretly burning in the hearts of the different sectaries that inhabit them."

Burnaby was largely right. The peoples of British North America were diverse, and religious differences provided flash points of discord. Immigration to England's colonies had exploded in the decades preceding Burnaby's visit, with large waves of immigrants coming from Scotland, Ireland, and Germany. As Burnaby indicated, "different nations" and "different manners" brought with them "different religions," which almost invariably were strains of Protestantism. With different Protestant loyalties serving as ciphers for other forms of difference, Protestant identities were more distinct and more discordant in eighteenth-century North America than at any time before or after.

Reflecting the prevailing wisdom of eighteenth-century political theorists, Burnaby assumed that this religious and ethnic diversity fostered crippling social tension. Without English oversight, Burnaby predicted, "such is the difference of character, of manners, of religion, of interest, ... there would soon be a civil war, from one end of the continent to the other."[1] Although the Civil War of the 1860s may have substantiated Burnaby's prophecy, it did not materialize in the short term.

Nevertheless, Burnaby's failed prophecy sheds light on Britain's approach to empire. Although the complexity of British imperial policy defies easy distillation, Britain generally treated ethnic and religious diversity as an obstacle to imperial unity and mutual self-interest. Britain accordingly used its Anglican Church as a tool with which to undermine diversity and strengthen attachment to the empire.[2] But the diverse social origins, contexts, goals, and relationships of North America's Protestant communities consistently engendered contestation with England and its church.

VIRGINIA'S ANGLICAN ESTABLISHMENT

Burnaby began his tour in Virginia, Britain's first and most economically significant colony. Virginia also was the colonial heart of the Church of England, also known as the Anglican Church. Through the middle of the eighteenth century, Virginia's established church not only maintained unusually high levels of religious conformity, but also served as an effective instrument of imperial power. English authorities regularly attempted to wield that tool elsewhere, but Virginia's situation proved an exception to Britain's desired rule.

Virginia's Anglican establishment was a carryover from England. The Church of England and the Anglican tradition emerged in the sixteenth century when King Henry VIII repudiated Rome's authority over Christianity in England. As "supreme head" of the church, Henry and subsequent monarchs instituted oaths of allegiance to the church, funded the church through taxes, and legally protected it from religious dissent. Religious groups whose views conflicted with the establishment became known as "dissenters." Describing Virginia's religious landscape in 1759, Burnaby noted that "the established religion is that of the Church of England; and there are very few Dissenters of any denomination in this province."[3] Anglican triumphalism may have led Burnaby to underestimate dissenters' standing in Virginia, but the Church of England was undeniably dominant.

The parish stood at the center of Virginia's ecclesiastical inheritance. Deriving from the Greek word for "district," the "parish" served as the local territorial unit into which the Church of England divided its labors.

---

[1] Andrew Burnaby, *Burnaby's Travels through North America* (New York, 1904), 7–9, 151–2, 198–203. Hereafter *Burnaby's Travels*.
[2] Rowan Strong, *Anglicanism and the British Empire c. 1700–1850* (Oxford, 2007), 104–5.
[3] *Burnaby's Travels*, 48.

But the colonial context made Virginia's parishes dissimilar to England's. In Virginia, the population grew not just within established parishes, but also west of the frontier, as settlers ventured farther from the coast in search of agricultural opportunities. To serve the expanding populace and to organize expanding territories, provincial authorities tried to establish parishes relatively regularly. In some cases, authorities assigned western borders to parishes only when new parishes were organized even farther west. Between 1740 and 1770, a steady influx of settlers caused the number of parishes to expand from 53 to 92, serving collectively an average of 2,820 white Virginians. The colony contained 107 parishes in 1784.

As an administrative unit, Virginia's parish system was far more flexible, multifunctional, and altogether essential than in England. This gave the Church of England in Virginia significant control over the Commonwealth's affairs. With local civic governance existing mostly on paper in more remote regions, the church served functions ranging from disciplining crime, to inspecting tobacco production, to keeping track of population figures, to administering what functioned as parish-centered welfare systems.[4] Virginia's parish churches therefore stood both figuratively and literally at the center of the Commonwealth's diffuse communities. Because Virginia's parishes were as much as twenty times larger than typical English parishes, however, Virginia generally bucked the English convention of assigning one church to every parish. Multiple parish churches made Sunday morning services more convenient for diffuse parish residents, allowing services to function as opportunities for community assembly and sharing of public notices.

In general, priests presided over services.[5] But partly because priests served multiple churches, laypeople regularly handled those tasks.[6] Laypeople also managed the majority of parish affairs. The twelve members of a parish's vestry made the vast majority of its decisions. In addition to hiring and firing ministers, for example, vestries organized and administrated the parish's social services and reported parishioners' moral infractions to civil authorities. Socially selective, Virginian vestries comprised the congregation's "more able men," which generally meant the wealthiest or most influential white men. Unusually, Virginia's vestries filled their own vacancies when they became available. Burnaby himself noted this

---

[4] David L. Holmes, *A Brief History of the Episcopal Church* (Valley Forge, PA, 1993), 21.
[5] John K. Nelson, *A Blessed Company: Parishes, Parsons, and Parishioners in Anglican Virginia, 1690–1776* (Chapel Hill, 2001), 14–20, 190–1.
[6] Paul K. Longmore, "From Supplicants to Constituents: Petitioning by Virginia Parishioners, 1701–1775," *Virginia Magazine of History and Biography* 103:4 (Oct. 1995): 411.

curiosity, remarking that vestries "were originally elected by the people of several parishes; but now fill up vacancies themselves."[7]

Virginia's church became entwined so closely with the Commonwealth's social structure precisely because the Commonwealth's gentry families essentially ran both church and state. In South Carolina, where Anglicanism was established in 1706, ecclesiastical and political power was more diffused. In Maryland, where Anglicanism was established in 1702, the proxies of the crown retained much of the authority that lay Virginians had taken for themselves.[8] Those colonies never saw Anglicanism possess the kind of authority that it enjoyed in Virginia. Yet even Virginia's vestries did not possess unchecked power, and squabbling over vestry composition provides an illuminating example of how Anglicans, dissenters, and provincial authorities each made use of the establishment's machinery.[9] Although the House of Burgesses had given vestries the power to select their own members, the House also had retained the ability to dissolve vestries and force parishes to elect new ones. The burgesses typically invoked that privilege in response to requests from parishioners.

Until the middle of the 1750s, requests to dissolve vestries usually came from middle-class parishioners who disagreed with their vestry's tax or spending policies. As immigration increased to Virginia's backcountry in the 1750s, however, dissenters began attempting to co-opt vestry power. They regularly requested, for example, that authorities form new parishes, which would require new vestries. With appointments to newly established vestries typically open to parish elections, vestries in frontier areas sometimes included dissenters. In some places, dissenters held a majority of vestry seats.[10]

How did dissenters attain and retain power over Anglican affairs? The nature of the establishment made all parish residents de facto members of the church. All dissenters paid parish taxes, meaning not only that they helped fund Anglican activities, but also that they could pay their own ministers and build their own buildings only on the basis of voluntary contributions from members already burdened by parish taxes. Particularly in the first half of the eighteenth century, these logistical limitations often made differences between Anglicans and Baptists or Presbyterians more theoretical than practical. Occasionally Virginia's Protestants did not know what label to apply to themselves.[11]

---

[7] *Burnaby's Travels*, 48.
[8] Nelson, *A Blessed Company*, 344n27.
[9] J. R. Gundersen, "The Myth of the Independent Virginia Vestry," *Historical Magazine of the Protestant Episcopal Church* 44 (June 1975): 133–41.
[10] Longmore, "From Supplicants to Constituents," 414–20, 435–6.
[11] Rhys Isaac, *The Transformation of Virginia, 1740–1790* (Chapel Hill, 1982), 148.

If the case of vestry appointments helps explain dissenters' ability to navigate the religious and political pathways of an oppressive establishment, provincial authorities' use of vestry seats as a political tool also illuminates England's approach to governance.[12] When Anglicans complained about the large proportion of dissenters on Anglican vestries, for example, authorities instituted a 1759 statute that banned dissenters from vestries with Anglican majorities. This legislation partially appeased Anglicans, but it meanwhile attempted to secure the loyalty of the dissenters who populated Virginia's strategically important frontier by letting them rest easy in the knowledge that their communities would not develop Anglican majorities quickly and that they always could petition for a new parish, with a new vestry.

Because the church provided a handy instrument of imperial rule, England accordingly attempted either to establish or to strengthen Anglicanism in other colonies. Between its founding in 1701 and the Revolution, the Society for the Propagation of the Gospel in Foreign Parts worked toward those goals by sending approximately six hundred ministers and founding nearly three hundred churches in areas of North America where Anglicanism lacked strength.[13] But at least three problems kept Virginia's model of political and religious governance from working elsewhere. One problem was that Anglicanism's long history in Virginia could not be duplicated elsewhere. The other problems, which plagued Virginia no less than other colonies, came in the form of evangelical and immigrant dissent.

NEW ENGLAND'S CONGREGATIONAL ESTABLISHMENT

Throughout the eighteenth century, Anglicans strengthened their presence in New England, but they constantly found opposition from the region's Congregational Church. The institutional manifestation of the seventeenth-century Puritan movement, the Congregational Church functioned as New England's established church well into the nineteenth century. More than immigrant dissent, Anglican advances and evangelical dissent provided the most significant threats to the Congregational establishment.

The Puritan movement began in England following the Marian Exile, when many of the Protestants who had fled to the continent during the

---

[12] John A. Ragosta, *Wellspring of Liberty: How Virginia's Religious Dissenters Helped Win the American Revolution and Secured Religious Liberty* (New York, 2010), 4–11.
[13] Boyd Stanley Schlenther, "Religious Faith and Commercial Empire," in P. J. Marshall, ed., *Oxford History of the British Empire: The Eighteenth Century*, vol. 2, *The Oxford History of the British Empire* (Oxford, 1998), 131.

reign of Mary Tutor returned to England impatient to purge all vestiges of Roman Catholicism from the Church of England. Elizabeth I, however, battled the Puritans to a draw, and they fared only marginally better during the reign of James I, who acceded to Puritan demands for an "authorized" translation of the Bible, better known as the King James Version. Charles I, however, whose wife was Roman Catholic, evinced little sympathy for the Puritans. Charles's 1629 appointment of William Laud, who loathed the Puritans, as archbishop of Canterbury persuaded a small band of Puritans that the Church of England would never be reformed or "purified" according to the norms of biblical godliness – at least not in England.

Yet Puritans continued to see themselves as members of the Church of England. New England's Puritans embodied just one of several competing visions of a pure English church. On the matter of church polity, for instance, Puritans emphasized the biblical justification for autonomous "congregationalist" governance. Others in England and especially Scotland, however, had championed "presbyterian" governance, wherein individual churches appoint elders or "presbyters" who collectively govern the churches that they represent. Baptists generally subscribed to congregationalist polity but insisted that only adult believers should undergo baptism. Each of these approaches to Anglican reform ultimately traveled to North America, but Congregationalist reformers claimed the wilderness setting of New England as their religious laboratory.

Far more than in Virginia, the Puritans of Massachusetts sought to intertwine religion with the social order in hopes of creating a religiously homogeneous society. By 1645, however, the confidence of the Puritans themselves had been shaken. The experiment had struggled initially, with too few ministers to serve the rapidly expanding population; and the gap between ministerial supply and demand created space for such dissidents as Anne Hutchinson and Roger Williams. Although both were banished from the colony – Hutchison for questioning the Calvinist credentials of the clergy, and Williams for resisting the conflation of church and state – it became clear that a homogeneous society might never materialize in Massachusetts. The onset of the English Revolution diverted attention to the capture of the king and the archbishop of Canterbury by the Puritans back in England, and the "eyes of the world" no longer were trained on New England. Some Puritans in Massachusetts effected a reverse migration in the 1640s, whereas the majority who stayed were, in Perry Miller's haunting phrase, "left alone with America."[14]

By the 1690s, the rise of the merchant class and continued immigration had diffused the piety and doctrinal rigor of the initial Puritan generation and reordered New England's priorities toward commerce, especially

---

[14] Perry Miller, *Errand into the Wilderness* (Cambridge, MA, 1956), 15.

in Boston. By the turn of the eighteenth century, Puritan dreams of a homogeneous religious culture were fading. In 1685 the royal governor, Edmund Andros, had insisted that the dreaded Church of England be allowed a foothold in the colony; and by 1698, Thomas Brattle donated land for the formation of an alternative Congregational church in Boston, one that departed from the strict Calvinism of the city's Puritan churches and embraced a more liberal form of Protestantism.

Early in the eighteenth century, Congregationalist ministers sought to strengthen control over their churches. Enduring commitments to congregational polity forestalled many of these initiatives, but some associations were established with such duties as screening ministers. The establishment of these sorts of associations helps explain how Burnaby could describe Congregationalism in the early 1760s as "a religion, different in some trifling articles, though none very material, from Presbyterian."[15] The Congregationalist strongholds of Harvard and Yale provided a steady flow of ministers.

Although Massachusetts' 1691 charter theoretically opened up New England to other Protestant groups, Congregationalists rebuffed the dissenters' advances for decades. Even the Church of England gained ground slowly. Only in 1727, for example, did Anglicans escape taxes that supported the established church; most other dissenters waited until 1740 for that privilege. Before 1740, dissenters were relatively scarce in New England, and Congregational leaders attempted to retain members by introducing more convenient meeting times, offering better heating in church buildings, delivering better sermons, and – in some cases – allowing music during worship.

Despite these efforts, the 1720s and 1730s saw cracks in the Congregational establishment developing from at least two directions. First, England continued its attempts to strengthen Anglican authority. Anglicans performed much of this work subtly, nurturing Congregationalists' curiosity instead of mandating allegiance. John Murrin gives this subtle work credit for the so-called Anglican Apostasy of 1722, when two Yale tutors, four local Congregationalist ministers, and Timothy Cutler, Yale's rector, announced during Yale's commencement festivities their intention to convert to Anglicanism. Although Cutler and his confreres were dismissed, the event reverberated throughout New England.[16]

Anglicanism's status rose discernibly by midcentury. Testifying to this pattern, Burnaby remarked in the 1760s that "the religion of the Church of England ... seems to gain ground, and to become more fashionable

---

[15] *Burnaby's Travels*, 138.
[16] John M. Murrin, "Anglicizing an American Colony: The Transformation of Provincial Massachusetts" (Ph.D. diss., Yale University, 1966), 27–32.

every day."[17] More than half of Connecticut's ninety-two clergymen were Congregational converts, and, like Cutler, their conversions generally reflected a high view of the church's authority. Such high churchmen traced Anglicanism's preeminence to its sacramental traditions and the apostolic succession of episcopal authority; Yale's 1716 book collection had emphasized those very themes. Northern high churchmen accordingly clamored for authorities in England to appoint a North American bishop on the twin logic that the episcopacy was apostolic in origin and that a lack of hierarchical organization had limited the ability of Anglicans to assert colonial dominance. Virginia's Anglicans, by comparison, were relatively content both with their establishment and with the extraordinary power of laity within that establishment. They generally opposed the appointment of an American bishop.[18]

Tensions between high-church northern Anglicans and defensive Congregationalists continued to grow throughout the middle of the eighteenth century, escalating still further after the Seven Years' War ended in 1763. Before then, France had remained a threat, and close cooperation between England and its colonies had been a commonsense necessity. With the French threat nullified, however, the question of the American episcopate transformed from a debate regarding the merits of Anglican self-governance to a debate over the merits of colonial self-governance.

The episcopacy debate was contracted precisely because all sides of the debate believed that the stakes were high: Congregationalists feared that England would impose Anglican faith; Anglicans hoped that an episcopacy would keep Congregationalists from clawing back Anglicans' hard-earned advances; and English authorities feared alienating both sides. To be sure, authorities in both London and Canterbury generally favored an American episcopacy. But as in Virginia, they recognized that the practicalities of governance depended on cultivating a broad base of loyalty.[19]

EVANGELICAL DISSENT

In Virginia, New England, and elsewhere, evangelical dissent undermined religious establishments in general and Anglican authority in particular. Etymologically, the term "evangelical" refers to the Greek word *evangel*, the "good news" of the New Testament. Historians tend to use the term as a way of linking together Protestants who share such characteristics as

---

[17] *Burnaby's Travels*, 139.
[18] Peter M. Doll, *Revolution, Religion, and National Identity: Imperial Anglicanism in British North America, 1745–1795* (Madison, NJ, 2000), 205.
[19] *Ibid.*, 156–221.

fidelity to the Bible, an emphasis on a warm-hearted conversion, and the impulse to evangelize, or bring others into the fold. Although historians sometimes disagree over which individuals and movements to count as part of the evangelical tradition, the usefulness of the term lies not in its precise inclusions and exclusions, but rather in its broad gesture toward a particular approach to Protestantism. Historically, that approach has been marked not just by the characteristics listed previously, but principally by evangelicals' tendency to criticize prevailing Protestant traditions they have found wanting. Consistently championing their own interpretations of Christianity as the most true to the gospel, evangelicals in virtually all of their manifestations have functioned as dissenters among dissenters.

If the rise of Anglican authority represented the first challenge to the Congregational establishment, the rise of evangelical revivalism represented the second. Anglicans themselves feared this threat, although in New England Anglicans ultimately benefited from the confusion that evangelical dissent produced among Congregationalists.[20] As early as the 1690s, Congregational minister Solomon Stoddard had reported religious "harvests" among his parishioners. Known for opening communion to members of the community rather than restricting it to the elect, Stoddard is better known for anticipating the ministrations of his grandson, Jonathan Edwards, who assisted his grandfather at Northampton, Massachusetts, beginning in 1725.

In the 1730s, after Edwards took over at Northampton, it became a center of the so-called Great Awakening, a religious revival that swept through the Atlantic colonies. Although some historians have questioned whether any such phenomenon as a great awakening actually occurred, contemporaries themselves referred to a "great and general awakening" in the middle decades of the eighteenth century. The movement may not have been as chronologically or geographically coherent as a single label implies, but it does gesture toward a period in the eighteenth century when a revivalistic style of Protestantism became "great" in both its impact and geographic diffusion.[21]

In New England, the revival generally is traced to Northampton during the winter of 1734–35. There, under Edwards' preaching, many of the town's denizens experienced the evangelical "new birth." As with all revivals, the fervor eventually abated, but the fires of religious enthusiasm were rekindled by the peregrinations of the Englishman George Whitefield, an

---

[20] John Frederick Woolverton, *Colonial Anglicanism in North America* (Detroit, 1984), 189.
[21] Jon Butler, "Enthusiasm Described and Decried: The Great Awakening as Interpretative Fiction," *Journal of American History* 69:2 (Sept. 1982): 305–25; Frank Lambert, *Inventing the "Great Awakening"* (Princeton, 1999).

extraordinarily talented preacher. Trained in the London theater, Whitefield used his stentorian voice and dramatic techniques to lure colonists to the faith; and the Great Awakening benefited from the ability of its proponents to promote and publicize the faith.[22]

The Great Awakening had a paradoxical effect in New England. On the one hand, it shattered whatever vestiges of religious consensus had survived the seventeenth century. In many places, congregations divided between New Lights (evangelicals) and Old Lights (opponents of the revival); and in other places the revival prompted the rise of dissenter groups, which sought to distinguish themselves from the "standing order" of Congregationalism. On the other hand, the Great Awakening created new grounds for consensus. With the Congregationalists divided and, to some degree, turning against one another, the new organizing principle became a disposition toward the Great Awakening itself. Whereas previous historians have drawn a neat demarcation between New Lights and Old Lights, Thomas Kidd sees a continuum of attitudes toward revival. The *antirevivalists*, at one extreme, derided the Great Awakening as frenzy and mere "enthusiasm"; *moderate evangelicals* supported the revival but became concerned about its excesses; and *radical evangelicals*, in Kidd's words, "eagerly embraced the Spirit's movements, even if social conventions had to be sacrificed."[23]

In important ways, the real contestation arising from the Great Awakening was the dispute not so much between the proponents and opponents of the revival as between the moderate evangelicals and the radical evangelicals. The radical evangelicals, as epitomized by itinerant preachers and by the Shepherd's Tent school in New London, Connecticut, sought to reorder society by attacking its conventions and its institutions, including religious institutions.[24] Moderate evangelicals prevailed, by and large; the social radicalism emanating from the Great Awakening never approached that of, for example, the Levelers during the English Revolution.

These new evangelical alliances spawned a variety of new religious organizations. Evangelical groups provided such a challenge to religious establishments in places like Virginia largely because new organizations and alliances allowed evangelicals to manage their ecclesiastical affairs

---

[22] Harry S. Stout, *The Divine Dramatist: George Whitefield and the Rise of Modern Evangelicalism* (Grand Rapids, 1991).
[23] Thomas S. Kidd, *The Great Awakening: The Roots of Evangelical Christianity in Colonial America* (New Haven, 2007), xiv.
[24] Richard Warch, "The Shepherd's Tent: Education and Enthusiasm in the Great Awakening," *American Quarterly* 30 (Summer 1978), 177–98.

domestically, a situation that seems innovative only by comparison with the Anglicans, Dutch Reformed, and Quakers, who relied on overseas authorities.[25] New evangelical organizations included the Presbyterian Synod of New York, a 1745 evangelical breakaway from the Old Light Synod of Philadelphia, and the Separate Baptists. Downplaying the Calvinist theology of the antirevivalist "Regular" Baptists and emphasizing emotional religious conversion and strict moral discipline, Separate Baptists insisted that true Christians should be "separate" from the less dedicated.

Although the Separate Baptists established a presence in Virginia and the Carolinas only in the late 1750s, evangelical groups had an impact in the South almost immediately. Such New Light Presbyterians as Samuel Davies, for example, came to Virginia in 1747. Based in Hanover County, he organized as many as twenty Presbyterian churches in Virginia by the time he left in 1758 to become president of the College of New Jersey. Preaching a Presbyterianism that emphasized themes of sin and repentance, that enforced rigorous congregational discipline, and that preceded seasonal communion festivals with periods of reflection, fasting, and prayer, Davies also converted as many as three hundred slaves.[26]

IMMIGRANT DISSENT

Even more than evangelical dissent, the dissent of Protestant immigrant groups both constrained and drew the ire of England's imperial authority. Immigrant dissent was most diverse in three broad regions: Pennsylvania, New York and New Jersey, and the Southern backcountry. Both Protestant diversity and English authority operated differently in each of those regions.

Pennsylvania

After leaving the Anglican strongholds of Virginia and Maryland, Andrew Burnaby had made his way to Pennsylvania, a colony known for its diverse religious population. While touring the capital of Philadelphia, Burnaby counted "eight or ten places of worship; viz. two [Anglican] churches, three Quaker meeting-houses, two Presbyterian ditto, one Lutheran church,

---

[25] Schlenther, "Religious Faith and Commercial Empire," 135.
[26] Jewel I. Spangler, *Virginians Reborn: Anglican Monopoly, Evangelical Dissent, and the Rise of the Baptists in the Late Eighteenth Century* (Charlottesville, 2008), 44, 63, 80–3; Charles F. Irons, *The Origins of Proslavery Christianity: White and Black Evangelicals in Colonial and Antebellum Virginia* (Chapel Hill, 2008), 36.

one Dutch Calvinist ditto, one Swedish ditto, one Romish chapel, one Anabaptist meeting-house, one Moravian ditto."[27]

The Swedes settled the region first, founding New Sweden along the Delaware River in 1638. Like Sweden itself, New Sweden was distinctly Lutheran. Relatively secure in their establishment, the Swedes tolerated Dutch Reformed worship – but only the Dutch Reformed. When the Dutch West India Company conquered the Swedes in 1655, the Dutch returned the favor and tolerated Swedish Lutheranism. But the Dutch limited the number of Lutheran ministers to just one and initially tolerated no other faiths.[28]

When the English conquered the territory in 1664, they offered toleration to such groups as Lutherans, Quakers, Presbyterians, Baptists, the Dutch Reformed, and even Catholics and Jews – but not primarily out of principle. Anglicans simply had not yet settled the region. When the Quakers became the first group of English people to settle the area in any significant numbers, English authorities welcomed their own kind despite Quakers' unorthodoxy.

Emerging in England during the mid-seventeenth century's political and religious turmoil, the Quaker movement or the "Religious Society of Friends" focused on the notion that the "Inner Light" or "Inward Light" of the Christ lives within each individual. Known later for meekness and a charitable disposition, the first generation of Friends was countercultural, refusing to serve in the military, to take oaths in court, to financially support the established church, or to doff their hats in deference to superiors. These unorthodoxies earned Quakers persecution in England, and Quakers accordingly took advantage of emigration opportunities early, establishing settlements by the mid-1660s in most British colonies, including the Caribbean and New England, where Quakers settled as early as 1656.[29]

Given a wide berth by the English in West Jersey, located along the Delaware River, more than a thousand Quakers settled the territory in the 1670s, overrunning the Dutch Reformed. When Quaker William Penn received a proprietary land grant from Charles II in 1681, he continued that welcoming policy. By virtue of their early settlement and Penn's religious convictions, Quakers dominated Pennsylvania up through the 1720s. But that dominance waned by the 1750s, as other immigrant groups flooded the

---

[27] *Burnaby's Travels*, 90, 95.

[28] Evan Haefeli, "The Pennsylvania Difference: Religious Diversity on the Delaware before 1683," *Early American Studies* 1:1 (2003): 32–47.

[29] Carla Gardina Pestana, *Quakers and Baptists in Colonial Massachusetts* (Cambridge, UK, 1991), 29; Pestana, *Protestant Empire: Religion and the Making of the British Atlantic World* (Philadelphia, 2009), 109–11.

area and as Quakers themselves sought to impose greater spiritual discipline within their ranks.[30] Burnaby likely understated the situation when he commented that "the Quakers have much the greatest influence in the assembly.... Their power, however, at present seems rather on the decline."[31]

The other principal group of British immigrants to Pennsylvania was the Scots-Irish, who became the most widespread and arguably most influential non-English group in North America. The Scots-Irish (or "Ulster Scots") were linguistically, culturally, and religiously distinct from the Scots who had sent them to Ireland in the early seventeenth century, but both the Scots and Scots-Irish arrived in the colonies in the first decades of the eighteenth century. Scots came first to the colonies, arriving in large numbers after the 1707 Act of Union made Scotland part of the British Empire. By 1730, Scots had settled throughout the colonies, but especially in the Middle Colonies.[32] A large proportion of Scots-Irish settled in Pennsylvania from 1720 on, largely because they found other northern colonies less hospitable than William Penn's "holy experiment." Settling first around Philadelphia, they spread west to Pittsburgh and then south. Reaching northwestern Virginia by the 1730s, they established a 700-mile-long chain of backcountry settlements by the 1750s that stretched from Pennsylvania to Georgia. Those communities soon established direct channels of immigration from Ulster.[33] For both Scots and Ulster Scots, who shared an agrarian orientation, a desire for cheap land determined their initial settlement patterns.

Wherever they settled, both kinds of Scots generally adhered to forms of Presbyterianism. Scots-Irish often worshipped with Scottish and English Presbyterians, but disagreements always festered over such issues as governing styles and approaches to creeds. With the onset of the Great Awakening, Scots-Irish laity generally hewed to Old Light positions in the 1740s, but evangelical groups ultimately appealed for at least two reasons. First, the practice of holding revivals resonated with traditional Scottish "holy fairs."[34] Second, evangelical groups typically had lower requirements

---

[30] Jack D. Marietta, *The Reformation of American Quakerism, 1748–1783* (Philadelphia, 1984).
[31] *Burnaby's Travels*, 99.
[32] Eric Richards, "Scotland and the Uses of Empire," in Bernard Bailyn and Philip D. Morgan, eds., *Strangers Within the Realm: Cultural Margins of the First British Empire* (Chapel Hill, 1991), 68–9.
[33] Maldwyn A. Jones, "The Scotch-Irish in British America," in Bailyn and Morgan, *Strangers Within the Realm,* 294; Warren R. Hofstra, "Land, Ethnicity, and Community at the Opequon Settlement, Virginia, 1730–1800," *Virginia Magazine of History and Biography* 98:3 (July 1990): 423.
[34] Leigh Eric Schmidt, *Holy Fairs: Scottish Communions and American Revivals in the Early Modern Period* (Princeton, 1989).

for clergy.[35] Like most groups on the frontier, the Scots-Irish always had found clergy difficult to draw to their frontier settlements.

For much of the eighteenth century, German Lutherans, the largest of the German groups to settle in the colonies, also struggled with ministerial supply. Part of the problem for both German Lutherans and the Calvinist German Reformed was their incredibly high numbers. In most of Germany, either the Lutheran Church or the Reformed Church was the established church, which meant that everyone living within its territories belonged by default. Lutheran and Reformed ranks therefore boomed after 1710, when German immigration began in earnest. By the Revolution, 84,500 Germans had come to the colonies; among whites, only the Scots-Irish came close to these numbers, with 66,100.[36]

But single ethnic identifiers always imply more cohesion than actually exists, and "Germans" displayed a wide range of religious affiliations and points of origin. That diversity in turn reflected a variety of push and pull factors. Factors that pushed Germans to emigrate included economic and political turmoil in their home territories. Factors that pulled Germans to Britain's colonies included extensive promotional literature. North America's regions of robust immigration all had extensive recruitment operations in Germany. Print advertisements, for example, regularly promised cheap land, religious toleration, and relative freedom from state control.[37] However they arrived and whenever they settled, several German groups stood out. Anabaptist groups, for example, established settlements at Germantown, Pennsylvania, as early as 1683. Classed as members of the "radical" Reformation, Anabaptists emphasized what they saw as the biblical mandates to rebaptize (thus "ana-baptist") believing adults, to practice a commemorative version of the eucharist, and to forswear alliances between church and state. Viewed by Protestant authorities in Europe as unorthodox, Anabaptists suffered persecution that included regular imprisonment and indentured servitude.[38]

The principal Anabaptist groups were the Mennonites and the Amish. Named after their founders, the Mennonites descend from the Dutch leader Menno Simons, and the Amish from the Swiss Mennonite Jacob Amman,

---

[35] Spangler, *Virginians Reborn*, 49.

[36] Aaron Fogleman, "Migrations to the Thirteen British North American Colonies, 1700–1775: New Estimates," *Journal of Interdisciplinary History* 22:4 (Spring 1992): 698.

[37] Marianne Wokeck, "The Flow and the Composition of German Immigration to Philadelphia, 1727–1775," *Pennsylvania Magazine of History and Biography* 105:3 (July 1981): 249–78; Hope Frances Kane, "Notes on Early Pennsylvania Promotion Literature," *Pennsylvania Magazine of History and Biography* 63:2 (Apr. 1939): 144–68.

[38] Rosalind J. Beiler, "German-Speaking Immigrants in the British Atlantic World, 1680–1730," *OAH Magazine of History* 18:3 (Apr. 2004): 21.

who taught followers to "ban and shun" those Amish who persisted in violating community norms. Although the Amish community generally kept to itself in Pennsylvania, Mennonites tended to be more open, often settling on individual farmsteads rather than walled-in communities. Also known as Brethren or Dunkers because they dunked those they baptized not once but thrice, German Baptists had relatively close ties with the Mennonites.[39] In addition to emigrating from similar regions of Germany during the 1720s, the Brethren tended to draw Mennonites who participated in the Great Awakening. As a result, Brethren sometimes were referred to as New Mennonites.[40] But Brethren also could be described as "pietistic" Mennonites.

An approach to Protestantism that placed the heart before the head, colonial-era pietism is associated above all with the Moravians. Championing what founder Nikolaus Ludwig, or Count von Zinzendorf, termed the "theology of the heart," Moravians emphasized emotion and experience as the path to knowledge of God (literally "theo–logy"). Beginning in 1742, Moravians settled in Bethlehem, Pennsylvania, where they lived communally and developed an array of small manufacturing industries. That lifestyle funded extensive missionary work, an outgrowth of their desire to cultivate spiritually renewed pan-Protestant unity.[41]

As the Moravian community illustrates, Pennsylvania's ethnic and religious groups possessed diverse styles of belonging and community self-imagination. Germans, for instance, tended to immigrate as families, whereas other ethnic groups displayed high proportions of young, ambitious, single men.[42] On account of family density, language barriers, and extensive networks of communication among German groups in the colonies and abroad, many German communities tended to remain more cohesive and insular than other immigrant groups. They accordingly dealt with English authority by retreating from it more than opposing it.[43] With their communities' openness dependent on local circumstances, by comparison, the Scots-Irish often became relatively involved in local affairs.

---

[39] Donald F. Durnbaugh, "Relationships of the Brethren with the Mennonites and Quakers, 1708–1865," *Church History* 35:1 (Mar. 1966): 35–59.

[40] Theron F. Schlabach, "Mennonites, Revivalism, Modernity: 1683–1850," *Church History* 48:4 (Dec. 1979): 398–9.

[41] Craig D. Atwood, *Community of the Cross: Moravian Piety in Colonial Bethlehem* (University Park, PA, 2004); Katherine Carté Engel, *Religion and Profit: Moravians in Early America* (Philadelphia, 2009).

[42] Jon Butler, *Becoming America: The Revolution Before 1776* (Cambridge, MA, 2000), 30.

[43] A. G. Roeber, "'The Origin of Whatever Is Not English among us': The Dutch-Speaking and German-Speaking Peoples of Colonial British America," in Bailyn and Morgan, *Strangers Within the Realm*, 281.

Most infamously, they established their own order in the Carolinas when English authorities did not.

For German groups and the Scots-Irish alike, religious affiliation largely served as a proxy for ethnic and cultural difference. Religious language accordingly provided the means by which ethnic groups articulated agreements and disagreements – both between themselves and with English authorities. This use of religious identity was clearest not in Pennsylvania, where English authorities never imposed their authority very strongly, but rather in the southern backcountry and New York and New Jersey.

New York and New Jersey

From its earliest days, New York and New Jersey presaged the religious pluralism that emerged elsewhere in the eighteenth century. Burnaby remarked that "besides the religion of the Church of England, there is a variety of others: dissenters of all denominations, particularly the Presbyterians, abound in great numbers."[44] In the 1770s, no less than eleven Protestant denominations competed for the patronage of Protestants in New York County.

New Netherland had been founded in the 1620s as an entrepôt for the Dutch West India Company, but the Dutch Reformed Church's attempts to establish a foothold in the Middle Colonies met both internal and external challenges. Beginning in 1664, when the English conquered New Netherland and established New York, the English became the principal external obstacle. Governor Benjamin Fletcher's Ministry Act of 1693 attempted to establish Anglicanism in New York City and the surrounding counties, but the Dutch frustrated Fletcher's efforts. A succeeding governor, Edward Hyde, or Viscount Cornbury, sought, albeit with limited success, to advance the Church of England by placing Anglican priests in the vacant pulpits of Presbyterian and Dutch Reformed congregations.

The Society for the Propagation of the Gospel in Foreign Parts abetted Cornbury's efforts, and Anglicans soon reported success in the Middle Colonies. "The French, the Dutch, and what Dissenters we have," an Anglican missionary on Staten Island wrote in 1711, "allow their children to be taught the Church Catechism."[45] William Vesey, rector of Trinity Church in lower Manhattan, sometimes supplied Dutch congregations on

---

[44] *Burnaby's Travels*, 116.
[45] Francis Mackenzie to S.P.G., 8 Nov. 1705, S.P.G. Records, Letterbook Series A, Vol. 2, no. CXVI; Mackenzie to S.P.G., 4 May 1711, S.P.G. Records, Vol. 6, no. LXXIV.

Long Island, where he found "all of the English and some of the Dutch well affected to the Church of England."[46]

For the Dutch Reformed Church, however, internal divisions proved more vexing than external circumstances. Lower-class Dutch resented the merchants and the clergy for assimilating to English rule and customs following the English conquest. Their simmering rage had boiled to the surface in Leisler's Rebellion in 1689, when colonial and ecclesiastical authorities, in the view of the Leislerlians, failed to respond with sufficient glee to news of the Glorious Revolution in England. Stark divisions among the Dutch persisted throughout the eighteenth century, frustrating British attempts to consolidate imperial authority in the Middle Colonies. A division among the churches on Long Island festered for years, with two ministers – one a traditionalist and the other a pietist – each laying claim to the congregations. More significantly, these divisions spilled into New Jersey. There, under the preaching of pietists like Guiliam Bertholf and Theodorus Jacobus Frelinghuysen, the Dutch became full participants in the Great Awakening. Frelinghuysen and Presbyterian revivalist Gilbert Tennent preached in each other's pulpits in New Brunswick, and Frelinghuysen's ministry among the Dutch caught the eye of George Whitefield.

By 1747, the ecclesiastical disruption among the Dutch took institutional form when the Coetus, an indigenous Dutch Reformed entity independent of the Netherlands, was gaveled to order. The antirevivalists called themselves the Conferentie Party, and so the Coetus-Conferentie dispute mirrored the New Light–Old Light divisions in New England. Members of the Conferentie, paradoxically, sought to hold on to Dutch language and customs, whereas the Coetus embraced their status as Americans. Although these divisions reflected theological conviction, they also reflected generational change, as the older generation tended to uphold denominational traditions and the authority of religious leaders in their home countries. The younger generation of leaders, by comparison, accommodated their groups to the American context by transforming their groups from overseas branches of European churches into more flexible and dynamic domestic denominations.

But the English consistently undermined those efforts. As in Virginia, they saw the Anglican establishment as a means of solidifying their authority. Because Protestant diversity complicated that endeavor, Anglicans challenged the social structures that sustained diversity. Anglicans denied dissenting groups the right to own property, for example. When Lutheran, Presbyterian, Huguenot, and Dutch Reformed congregations began challenging that policy

---

[46] E. B. O'Callaghan, ed., *Documentary History of the State of New-York* [quarto ed.], 4 vols. (Albany, 1850–51), III: 75.

in 1759, Anglicans held firm, fearing that granting charters would establish an unsavory precedent. On other occasions, Anglicans enforced their rules of establishment and attempted to either replace or remove dissenting ministers.[47]

Other examples are more positive. Because colonial Protestant groups always struggled to produce enough clergy to suit population growth, clerical education became a priority. Both Anglicans and the Coetus had taken note, for instance, of the ministerial success that New Light Presbyterians achieved by investing early in ministerial education. The Presbyterian revivalist William Tennent had operated the "Log College" in rural Pennsylvania between 1726 and 1745; seeking a larger institution to suit their rising respectability, New Light Presbyterians founded the College of New Jersey (Princeton) in 1746. Thus in the 1750s Anglicans and dissenters alike welcomed talk of establishing a nonsectarian college in New York. But Anglicans moved to make it an Anglican college, with an Anglican board of governors and a charter that offered the vague promise of "toleration" to dissenters. Anglicans founded King's College (later renamed Columbia) in 1754; the Dutch would found Queen's College (Rutgers) in 1766.

In the 1760s, New York Anglicans also joined New England Anglicans in calling for the appointment of an American bishop. In response to critics, such leaders as Samuel Johnson insisted that Anglicans desired a bishop more for spiritual leadership than for administrative authority. Whatever the reason, Anglicans' desire for a bishop betrayed their conviction that Anglicanism could and should spread. Dissenters responded to increased Anglican assertiveness in two principal ways. First, some ethnic Protestants reinforced their insularity, establishing schools, for example, to rival Anglican alternatives.[48] Second and more important, some Protestants began linking English religious authority to English political authority, casting both as threats to freedom. Many dissenters saw an Anglican bishop as little better than a resident monarch.

The Southern Backcountry

By the 1760s, New York's dissenters began linking English religious power to English political power; around the same time, South Carolina's dissenters made similar connections. As in Pennsylvania, South Carolina historically had not harbored high levels of tension between dissenters and

---

[47] Richard W. Pointer, *Protestant Pluralism and the New York Experience: A Study of Eighteenth-Century Religious Diversity* (Bloomington, 1988), 40–51, 61–2.
[48] Ibid., 30–60.

the Anglican Church. That apparent peace stemmed from the colony's high concentration of dissenters, which had kept England from imposing its authority in a way that provoked much outrage. Founded as a proprietary venture in 1663, South Carolina lured its initial settlers partly through promises of religious toleration. By 1700 the colony's 4,000 white citizens accordingly included 1,300 Presbyterians, 400 Baptists, 100 Quakers, 500 Huguenots, and 1,700 Anglicans.[49]

Most of these settlers came to the backcountry, which contained 50 percent of the population in 1760, but as much as three-quarters by 1770. In addition to using settlers as a buffer between eastern settlements and Indian populations, South Carolina's authorities hoped that white settlers would balance a population dominated by slaves. Scots and Scots-Irish together made up as much as 30 percent of the settler population, with smaller percentages of German, French, and Welsh immigrants. Religious diversity came along with ethnic diversity. Earlier in the century, English Anglicans and Presbyterians made up most of the population. After 1750, however, the denominational landscape shifted, with Scots-Irish expanding the Presbyterian and Baptist ranks and German and Swiss settlers augmenting Lutheran and Reformed churches.

As the established church since 1706, the Church of England had formed parishes throughout the colony. But neither parishes nor counties encompassed all of South Carolina's territory.[50] Although the Church of England flourished in such lowland cities as Charleston, backcountry parishes offered minimal social and religious services. Particularly after midcentury, Anglican territory closer to the coast became culturally and politically distant from the immigrant backcountry. Until midcentury, South Carolina's authorities took a relatively passive approach to governance, compensating for meager governmental resources by allowing for significant local autonomy. The established church largely allowed local Anglican vestries to appoint their own members, for example, and to decide on local levels of cooperation with dissenters.

This hands-off approach not only reinforced the isolationism of diverse dissenter communities, but also nurtured an unstable social order. Different groups in different regions offered their own solutions to social challenges. In the late 1760s, many of the region's leading men and small planters followed the example of an earlier movement in North Carolina and attempted

[49] Patricia U. Bonomi, *Under the Cope of Heaven: Religion, Society, and Politics in Colonial America* (New York, 1986), 32.
[50] Bradford J. Wood, "'A Constant Attendance on God's Alter': Death, Disease, and the Anglican Church in Colonial South Carolina, 1706–1750," *South Carolina Historical Magazine* 100:3 (July 1999): 208; Robert M. Weir, *Colonial South Carolina: A History* (Columbia, SC, 1997), 209–22.

to "regulate" inland territories for both criminal and moral infractions.[51] They even built their own schools, jails, and courthouses.[52] This so-called Regulator movement alerted English authorities to the extraordinary strength of local authority in South Carolina. In the late 1760s, provincial authorities began attempting to bring Regulators' backcountry social services under English jurisdiction.

But those decisions to tighten English authority came at the same time as the English Parliament drastically changed the economic relationship between England and its colonies, imposing a number of controversial tax measures: the Sugar Act in 1764, the Stamp Act in 1765, and the Townshend Duties in 1767. To dissenting South Carolinians, these actions collectively violated England's previous governing philosophy.[53] Unlike in Virginia, South Carolina's backcountry dissenters generally had not regarded the Anglican Church as a great impediment to their religious lives. England simply had not used the church as a tool of imperial power in the same way it had in Virginia or in New York. By the 1770s, however, dissenters increasingly talked about the Anglican Church as an oppressor, for it had become a visible symbol of imperial authority. In the face of this apparent oppression, dissenters increased their religious activity as a means of competing with and resisting Anglican institutional authority.[54] Baptists in particular thrived under these conditions, advancing a critique of Anglicanism that drew on the distaste for hierarchies enshrined in Baptists' dedication to congregational governance.[55]

BACK TO VIRGINIA: DIVERSITY AND DISESTABLISHMENT

By the time of the Revolution, Presbyterians were the largest dissenting group in Virginia, but Baptists were the fastest-growing group.[56] United in their opposition to the Anglican establishment, both Presbyterians and Baptists saw greatest growth in western and southern Virginia, where Anglicanism was weakest. Both groups achieved some of their advances by converting slaves. Claiming that conversion to Christianity made slaves

---

[51] Durward T. Stokes, "The Presbyterian Clergy in South Carolina and the American Revolution," *South Carolina Historical Magazine* 71:4 (Oct. 1970): 270–82.

[52] George Lloyd Johnson, *The Frontier in the Colonial South: South Carolina Backcountry, 1736–1800* (Westport, 1997), 114, 131.

[53] Weir, *Colonial South Carolina*, 291–319.

[54] Thomas J. Little, "The Origins of Southern Evangelicalism: Revivalism in South Carolina, 1700–1740." *Church History* 75:4 (Dec. 2006): 806.

[55] Johnson, *Frontier in the Colonial South*, 58.

[56] Brent Tarter, "Reflections on the Church of England in Colonial Virginia," *Virginia Magazine of History and Biography* 112:4 (2004): 359–60.

more docile, dissenting preachers converted slaves not out of abolitionist sentiment, but rather as a way of undermining Anglicans, who traditionally had refused to reach out to slaves.[57]

As England had heightened its hold on the colonies in the decade following the end of the Seven Years' War, dissenters in Virginia and elsewhere had increasingly seen Anglican authority as a symbol of England's oppressive rule. Virginia's dissenters had always suffered more under Anglican authority than dissenters in other colonies, and Virginia's Baptists had suffered most. Establishmentarian Anglicans had targeted Baptists most frequently, using establishment laws to arrest, fine, or otherwise penalize them for such infractions as failure to attend an Anglican Church or for presiding over a marriage. Baptists therefore led the calls for religious freedom.

The Revolution ultimately gave those calls a hearing. With military recruiting lagging in 1776, the Anglican leaders of Virginia's legislature and military realized that the Revolution's success hinged on dissenters' support. Sensing an opening, Baptists in particular conditioned their support not on expanded toleration, but rather on full religious freedom. Whereas dissenters in other colonies regularly became Loyalists, this conditional cooperation made Virginia's dissenters almost universally Patriots.[58]

When the end of the war left dissenters without political leverage, Anglicans attempted to revive their establishment. But a great public debate in 1784–85 effectively prohibited direct government funding for religious activity and promoted full religious freedom in Virginia. James Madison vigorously attacked any government aid for religion in his famous 1785 "Memorial and Remonstrance against Religious Assessments." In it he called religion an "unalienable right" that no government could usurp.[59]

By the time the drafters of the Constitution met in 1787, Virginia had become the most religiously progressive state in North America, but other states had followed its lead. South Carolina's 1778 constitution, for example, had authorized government aid to several Protestant groups, but its 1790 constitution abandoned the compromise of "multiple establishment" and guaranteed "the free exercise and enjoyment of religious profession and worship, without discrimination or preference."[60] Modeled largely

---

[57] Irons, *Origins of Proslavery Christianity*, 43–4.
[58] Ragosta, *Wellspring of Liberty*, 87–104.
[59] See Thomas E. Buckley, *Church and State in Revolutionary Virginia, 1776–1787* (Charlottesville, 1977).
[60] Jon Butler, Grant Wacker, and Randall Herbert Balmer, *Religion in American Life: A Short History* (Oxford, 2003), 147.

on Virginia's 1786 Statute for Religious Freedom, the First Amendment settled the matter of religious establishment in 1791, although several erstwhile colonies in New England would cling to religious establishments for several decades.

Before the Revolution, Andrew Burnaby had remarked that Virginians were "impatient of restrains" and "consider[ed] the colonies as independent states, not connected with Great Britain, otherwise than having the same common king."[61] Although different Virginians experienced different restraints, the Revolution bore out Burnaby's observation. Nonetheless, Burnaby failed to predict both the Revolution and disestablishment.

Burnaby's lack of foresight stemmed largely from his misunderstanding of ethnic and religious diversity. Assuming that it would engender division, Burnaby did not recognize that diversity also could exist alongside certain kinds of agreement. In the decades preceding the Revolution, North America's diverse dissenters became increasingly discontent with the way that English political and religious rule impinged on the life of their communities.

SUGGESTIONS FOR FURTHER READING

Balmer, Randall. *A Perfect Babel of Confusion: Dutch Religion and English Culture in the Middle Colonies*. New York, 1989.

Bonomi, Patricia U. *Under the Cope of Heaven: Religion, Society, and Politics in Colonial America*. New York, 1986.

Butler, Jon. *Becoming America: The Revolution Before 1776*. Cambridge, MA, 2000.

Landsman, Ned C. *Scotland and Its First American Colony, 1683–1765*. Princeton, 1985.

Nelson, John K. *A Blessed Company: Parishes, Parsons, and Parishioners in Anglican Virginia, 1690–1776*. Chapel Hill, 2001.

Pointer, Richard W. *Protestant Pluralism and the New York Experience: A Study of Eighteenth-Century Religious Diversity*. Bloomington, 1988.

Ragosta, John A. *Wellspring of Liberty: How Virginia's Religious Dissenters Helped Win the American Revolution and Secured Religious Liberty*. New York, 2010.

Roeber, A. G. *Palatines, Liberty, and Property: German Lutherans in Colonial British America*. Baltimore, 1998.

---

[61] Andrew Burnaby, *Burnaby's Travels through North America* (New York, 1904), 55–6.

22

PROTESTANT EVANGELICALISM IN EIGHTEENTH-CENTURY AMERICA

THOMAS S. KIDD

On the eve of the American Revolution, Mary Cooper was a fifty-four-year-old farm woman living in Oyster Bay, Long Island, in the colony of New York. Her life, as revealed in staccato entries in her diary, was hard. She constantly struggled to manage the demands of farm and domestic life and hopelessly watched as her daughter's marriage disintegrated. Winter was, of course, the hardest season on Long Island. Typical was an entry from March 1769. "Extreeme high wind. Cold. Freezes all day long. O, I am tired almost to death, dirty and distressed." In her dark moments, Cooper found comfort — fleeting though it might have been — in her faith, and in a new congregation of saints she had recently discovered and joined. Although Cooper came from a traditional Anglican background, this church was like none she had ever seen before. African Americans, Native Americans, and women all not only participated actively in her New Light meeting, but often exhorted and preached sermons. Almost the only joy in her diary was associated with the new, exciting church. She often commented that the redeemed, motley community had a "happy meeten." Occasionally in those meetings she even experienced "heavenly tranceports" of spiritual ecstasy herself.[1]

Mary Cooper had become part of evangelical Christianity, a movement that revolutionized colonial American religion. Long Island was one of many epicenters of Anglo-American revivalism, a religious force that had begun to emerge in the early eighteenth century and then appeared fully with the coming of the Great Awakening in the early 1740s. Evangelicalism was not unique to America, as it descended from several pietist strains of European Protestantism, including movements within continental Protestantism, Scots-Irish Presbyterianism, and English Puritanism. Pietists emphasized that true Christianity was a matter not merely of ritual and doctrine, but

---

[1] Field Horne, ed., *The Diary of Mary Cooper: Life on a Long Island Farm, 1768–1773* (Oyster Bay, NY, 1981), 9, 23, 29.

of godly emotions and the heart. True believers knew God personally, and that heart knowledge transformed their desires and behaviors in conformity with God's will.

Historian David Bebbington has developed the most commonly cited definition of evangelicalism, involving four common characteristics: conversionism ("the belief that lives need to be changed"), activism ("the expression of the gospel in effort"), biblicism ("a particular regard for the Bible"), and crucicentrism ("a stress on the sacrifice of Christ on the cross").[2] This is a very good definition for evangelicalism generally, but to distinguish evangelical faith from its immediate antecedents, we might add a couple more characteristics. First, evangelicals put much more emphasis on periodic outpourings of the Holy Spirit – the third person of the Trinity in Christian doctrine – to generate revivals of religion. These revivals featured the renewal of religious commitment among the converted and the mass conversion of those who never knew Jesus Christ personally.

A second and related new development was the emphasis on the discernible and often rapid conversion of individuals. Earlier movements, especially Puritanism, had certainly highlighted the need for conversion, but conversion was normally an uncertain, arduous, and lengthy process. Good Puritans would always hesitate to pronounce someone definitively converted because of the nearly infinite potential for hypocrisy and self-deception. Evangelicals, by contrast, believed that because conversion represented a wrenching transformation of the soul by the Holy Spirit, the convert could not miss it when he or she was "born again," a phrase derived from the Gospel of John, chapter 3. Many evangelicals also believed that the Spirit allowed them to perceive whether others were truly converted – or not.

Conversion represented one of the many issues on which evangelicals disagreed, not only with their opponents, but among themselves. Historians have often presented early evangelicals as a monolithic movement, the New Lights, as opposed to their Old Light opponents. It makes more sense of the Great Awakening, however, to see the variety of opinion about evangelicalism as points on a continuum. On one end was the group one could call the Old Lights, those who fundamentally opposed the revivals as godless frenzy. They believed that all the evangelicals, led by the itinerant preacher George Whitefield, threatened the established churches and ministers with their extreme focus on the new birth.

Among the New Lights there were also bitter divisions that emerged early in the Great Awakening. All evangelicals agreed that the new revivals

---

[2] David Bebbington, *Evangelicalism in Modern Britain: A History from the 1730s to the 1980s* (Grand Rapids, 1992), 3.

of the 1740s were essentially godly, but beyond that, they disagreed about all manner of issues. Moderate evangelicals appreciated the enhanced level of religious commitment and legions of conversions, but they did not anticipate that the Great Awakening would lead to major new social or ecclesiastical changes. Like the Old Lights, they worried that common people – African Americans, Native Americans, women, children, and uneducated white men – might take the experience of the revivals too far by asserting a new kind of religious authority on the basis of the indwelling Holy Spirit alone. They certainly did not want the revivals to threaten the authority of established ministers, because many evangelicals, especially in New England, were beneficiaries of the state churches.

Radical evangelicals, at the other end of the continuum, took a very different approach to the awakenings. They saw the Great Awakening as the inauguration of a new era of the Holy Spirit in which all kinds of conventions were questioned and undermined. For them, the Great Awakening was a religious and social revolution. They gave unprecedented authority to common people because they believed that the Holy Spirit dwelled in all converts. They ordained uneducated whites, African Americans, and Native Americans as preachers and allowed almost anyone to speak as exhorters in chaotic revival meetings. Because of their strong focus on the workings of the Holy Spirit, the radicals were much more comfortable with the mystical and physical manifestations of revival. Dreams, trances, visions, shouting, and trembling were not only tolerated, but often celebrated as signs of the Spirit's presence. Antirevivalists looked on the radicals' "noisy" meetings with disdain, and they argued that the revivals were about self-indulgent emotion, not true godliness. Moderate evangelicals believed that the radicals' excesses would ruin the work of God, whereas the radicals believed that the signs and wonders were essential to the work of God.

Periodic events very similar to revivals had been happening in Europe and America for decades – even centuries – prior to the 1740s, but the Northampton, Massachusetts, revival led by Jonathan Edwards in 1734–35 was the first major episode in the colonies, leading to the Great Awakening. Edwards had deep roots in the Reformed and Puritan pietist traditions, and both his father Timothy and grandfather Solomon Stoddard had led significant revivals in their pastoral careers. Edwards succeeded Stoddard as the pastor of the Northampton church in 1729, and soon he established himself as one of New England's most formidable proponents of Calvinist distinctives such as predestination – namely, the idea that God chose certain people to be saved – and the sovereign grace of God in redeeming sinners.

Edwards' Calvinism hardly hindered his evangelical quest for revivals. Indeed, all the major revivalists on the American side of the Great

Awakening were Calvinists. In 1733–34, Edwards began to notice a new spiritual receptiveness among the young people of his congregation who previously had given the serious young pastor trouble with their joking and carousing. The untimely deaths of a couple of youths in the community sobered the others, and Edwards exploited their new openness to the message of salvation. Young people began converting in droves, followed by many adults. Soon the whole town was swept up into the fervor of revival. By the end of the excitement, Edwards estimated that perhaps 300 people had been converted in six months. The church had grown to 620 members, which represented almost all the adults in the town. Edwards also noted that several of Northampton's household slaves had experienced conversion.

The excitement at Northampton spread throughout the Connecticut River valley, but the news also shot through the growing evangelical network of ministers and devout laypeople when Edwards wrote *A Faithful Narrative of the Surprising Work of God*, first published in London in 1737. Leading Boston minister Benjamin Colman had sent a copy of the narrative to key English evangelicals, John Guyse and Isaac Watts, who arranged for its publication. *A Faithful Narrative* helped to frame many evangelicals' expectations for revival across America and Britain.

One of those in England who learned about the Northampton revival was the young Anglican revivalist George Whitefield, the preaching prodigy who would become the key leader of the Great Awakening in Britain and America. Whitefield had attended Oxford, where he met John and Charles Wesley and their Methodist club. They introduced him to classics of the Puritans and continental Pietists, and Whitefield soon experienced a dramatic conversion. In 1739 Whitefield began preaching the religion of the new birth in open-air field meetings in England and Wales. Whitefield had acted in the theater as a youth, and he brought those acting skills to his sermons, which were delivered emotionally and without notes. By mid-1739 he had become a sensation, drawing tens of thousands to his meetings. Later that year he departed for his first preaching tour of America.

Whitefield met with considerable success in Pennsylvania and New Jersey, and he saw some modest results in the southern colonies. But his tour, and the Great Awakening generally, hit its peak when he came to New England in late 1740. Whitefield mastered the use of media – newspaper coverage and book publishing, in particular – in order to generate the most advance excitement possible. Day after day he preached to huge audiences and saw legions experience conversion. As he journeyed across New England, Whitefield met Jonathan Edwards and preached at the Northampton church. Even the usually staid Edwards cried during Whitefield's sermon.

Spurred by the advance publicity and word of Whitefield's phenomenal personality, crowds followed him wherever he went. One of the best accounts we have of a common person's experience at one of Whitefield's meetings came from Nathan Cole, a farmer from Kensington, Connecticut. In October 1740, word arrived at Cole's house that Whitefield would be in a nearby town that day, and Cole and his wife immediately departed, afraid they would miss their chance to see the British superstar. When he saw Whitefield, Cole wrote, "he Lookt almost angelical; a young, Slim, slender, youth before some thousands of people with a bold undaunted Countenance."[3] Whitefield's preaching began to convince Cole that his good works could do nothing to save him, and he entered a lengthy travail of conversion.

Although Cole's conversion did not transpire as quickly as those of many other evangelicals, the ordeal did end with a stunning visitation from God, which was typical of radical evangelical piety. Cole struggled mightily to believe he was one of the elect, or those chosen by God for salvation. He wondered if he would burn for eternity for his sins, and sometimes he stuck his finger into his smoking pipe to see how fire felt. Then one evening as he lay on his bed, looking morbidly at the fireplace, he came face-to-face with the divine. "God appeared unto me and made me Skringe," he wrote. He was not sure whether he remained in his body or not, but God interrogated him, asking whether he was willing to accept God's sovereign power over his eternal destiny. Then God vanished just as quickly as he had come. Cole found that his spiritual burden had been lifted, and he had assurance that Christ would forgive him.[4]

Even after George Whitefield had returned to Britain, the revivals grew in America, often featuring the kinds of mystical experiences of converts like Nathan Cole. In time, these kinds of experiences, and the behavior of key revivalists like Gilbert Tennent of New Jersey and James Davenport of Long Island, began to elicit opposition from antirevivalists as well as concern from moderate evangelicals. Gilbert Tennent was the oldest son of William Tennent, a Scots-Irish Presbyterian pastor who brought his family to Pennsylvania in 1718. In the late 1720s, William Tennent began training candidates for ministry at his "Log College" seminary, which would become the key school for evangelical ministers in the Middle Colonies.

Gilbert Tennent became the most famous, and notorious, revivalist in the family. Tennent had already begun preaching revival at his church in New Brunswick, New Jersey, before he met George Whitefield in late

---

[3] Michael J. Crawford, ed., "The Spiritual Travels of Nathan Cole," *William and Mary Quarterly* 3rd ser., 33:1 (Jan. 1976): 93.
[4] *Ibid.*, 96.

1739. Then in March 1740, Tennent preached one of the most controversial sermons of the Great Awakening, *The Danger of an Unconverted Ministry*, at a revival meeting in Nottingham, Pennsylvania. In this sermon, Tennent assaulted the established ministers of the colonies who did not support the revivals, portraying them as spiritually dead hypocrites. Whereas most colonists had traditionally been expected to attend their closest parish church, Tennent advocated the right to attend the church of one's choice, preferably the church where the pastor's teaching was the most edifying. This attack on established ministers and parish boundaries was deeply offensive and threatening to many longtime pastors in the colonies.[5] Benjamin Franklin, who also published many of George Whitefield's writings, jumped at the chance to print a copy of Tennent's incendiary sermon in Philadelphia.

As controversial as Tennent was, James Davenport was the person most responsible for wrecking evangelical consensus over the revivals. He also became the antirevivalists' ultimate example of the disorder, and even lawlessness, created by the Great Awakening. Davenport began with fervent revivals on Long Island, where he once reportedly preached for twenty-four hours straight. But he also itinerated in New England and the Middle Colonies, often entering churches without the resident pastor's permission. Occasionally, Davenport told congregations that their own pastor was unconverted. He also led crowds of poor people, African Americans, and Native Americans singing through the streets of New England towns.

Davenport's and other radical itinerants' subversive behavior incurred the wrath of the colonial governments. In 1742, Connecticut passed a law banning itinerants from entering parishes without the resident pastor's permission. Davenport was soon arrested for violating the law, precipitating a wild scene at the Hartford courthouse. Davenport rallied his supporters outside the courthouse, and when the sheriff tried to lead him away, bedlam ensued, with "many of the concourse beginning to sigh, groan, beat their breasts, cry out, and to be put into strange agitations of body," a newspaper reported. The tumult did not end until the Connecticut militia was called in.[6]

Davenport was expelled from Connecticut, but he was hardly chastened, and soon he arrived in Boston, where he was banned from most pulpits. He was relegated to speaking on the Boston Common, where he began naming Boston ministers he regarded as unconverted. The list included several moderate evangelicals, as well as the town's antirevivalist leaders. He was

---

[5] Timothy D. Hall, *Contested Boundaries: Itinerancy and the Reshaping of the Colonial American Religious World* (Durham, 1994), 49.

[6] *Boston News-Letter*, 1 July 1742, in Thomas S. Kidd, ed., *The Great Awakening: A Brief History with Documents* (Boston, 2007), 101.

arrested and charged with slander, but at trial he was declared non compos mentis and released.

Davenport's meteoric career as an itinerant came to an inglorious end when, guided by a vision, he returned to Connecticut in March 1743. In New London, he hosted a book burning, featuring Puritan classics as well as works of antirevivalists and moderate evangelicals. He also tried to turn the conflagration into a clothes burning, telling the audience that they had made idols of their fancy apparel. But when Davenport himself pulled off his pants and cast them into the fire, a woman snatched the pants out, threw them in Davenport's face, and told him to come to his senses. This confrontation instantly sobered the audience, which turned against Davenport. His followers quickly admitted that their zeal had turned to chaos, and Davenport found himself with almost no remaining support and in danger of losing his pastoral career altogether.

To the Old Lights, Davenport was the chief instigator of this frothy, vain religion. Davenport's "enthusiastic wildness has slain its thousands," the chief antirevivalist, Charles Chauncy of Boston, concluded. But it was not simply the Great Awakening's challenge to the established religious system that bothered people like Chauncy. Critics of the revivals also noted that common people and people of color took unusually prominent roles in the evangelical meetings. Among the most disturbing features of the revivals were the exhorters, those converts who informally spoke in the meetings about their experience of grace. Sometimes these exhorters spoke only briefly, but sometimes they spoke for hours on end and took on a pseudo-pastoral role in evangelical congregations. Most shockingly, exhorters crossed all boundaries of authoritative religious speaking, which had traditionally been the privilege of educated white men only. Chauncy expressed a common concern about exhorters when he wrote that among these speakers were "Men who, though they have no Learning, and but small Capacities, yet imagine they are able, and without Study, too, to speak to the spiritual Profit of such as are willing to hear them.... Nay, Women and Girls; yea, Negroes, have taken upon them to do the Business of Preachers."[7]

The advent of the exhorters led to unprecedented scenes in the revival meetings that were unnerving to many like Chauncy. Radical itinerant Daniel Rogers of Ipswich, Massachusetts, repeatedly recorded lengthy exhortations by women, children, and African Americans in his diary. At one meeting, a woman named Lucy Smith was given the "Spirit of Prophecy" by the Holy Spirit, leading her to deliver a two-hour exhortation

---

[7] Charles Chauncy, *Enthusiasm Described and Caution'd Against* (Boston, 1742), 3; and Chauncy, *Seasonable Thoughts on the State of Religion in New England* (Boston, 1743), 226.

in the meeting. When Rogers was challenged by some men in the congregation about the propriety of the women exhorters speaking, Rogers told them that he would let God work in his own way, no matter who was speaking. Radicals like Rogers figured that if the Holy Spirit was being poured out on all ages, races, and genders, then all should have the right to speak in the meetings.[8]

When the major phase of the revivals began in 1740, few religious leaders openly criticized the new evangelical leaders. But over time, doubts and cautionary notes became more common, and by 1742 a full-fledged debate had emerged over the "late revival of religion." Although many weighed in, Jonathan Edwards and Charles Chauncy offered the best-known defense and critique of the revival, respectively. Edwards' defense of the awakenings began with his 1741 commencement address at Yale, soon published as *The Distinguishing Marks of a Work of the Spirit of God*. Edwards then expanded his defense in *Some Thoughts Concerning the Present Revival of Religion* (1742). In that book, Edwards admitted that there were unfortunate excesses happening in the revival meetings, but that in general the awakening was "a very great and wonderful, and exceeding glorious work of God. This is certain that it is a great and wonderful event, a strange revolution, an unexpected, surprising overturning of things, suddenly brought to pass; such as never has been seen in New England, and scarce ever has been heard of in any land." Edwards detailed the wonderful transports and devoted piety of his own wife, Sarah, as clinching evidence of the revival's legitimacy.[9]

To Chauncy, the awakenings had primarily bred enthusiasm and chaos, the opposite of godly piety. He responded to Edwards with *Seasonable Thoughts on the State of Religion in New England* (1743), a compendium of the horrors of radical revivalism. Davenport was Chauncy's key exhibit, but he argued that Davenport's type of behavior ruined and condemned the whole work. "One of the main Ends of the Out-pouring of the Spirit, is to dispose and enable People to behave as Christians, in their various Stations, Relations and Conditions of Life," Chauncy wrote. If a so-called revival produced the opposite results, leading people to challenge their superiors, then it was no outpouring of the Holy Spirit.[10]

The radical awakeners had less prominent advocates than Edwards and Chauncy, and most lacked the connections to publish defenses of their

---

[8] Daniel Rogers diary, 1 Jan. 1742, in Kidd, *Brief History*, 71; Thomas S. Kidd, *The Great Awakening: The Roots of Evangelical Christianity in Colonial America* (New Haven, 2007), 127.

[9] Jonathan Dickinson, *A Display of God's Special Grace* (Philadelphia, 1743), v; Jonathan Edwards, *Some Thoughts Concerning the Present Revival of Religion*, in C. C. Goen, ed., *The Works of Jonathan Edwards*, vol. 4, *The Great Awakening* (New Haven, 1972), 343–4.

[10] Chauncy, *Seasonable Thoughts*, 320.

exuberant style. But their actions signaled that although they totally disagreed with Chauncy's portrayal of the revivals, neither did they find the moderate approach of Edwards satisfying. Edwards warned of the dangers of setting untutored people up as preachers and of establishing unauthorized separate congregations, but the radicals commonly did both in the course of the awakenings.

New England saw the most dramatic revivals of the Great Awakening, and it also experienced the most turmoil related to church separations. Hundreds of them occurred there in the eighteenth century.[11] The separations, innocuous as they might seem today, were generally illegal in the colonies with established churches. The state alone authorized the forming of new churches, so people could not simply decide to establish a new congregation, whatever they might think about the existing parish church or pastor. In the era of the Great Awakening, the most common reasons given for establishing a new church were a lack of purity in the old churches and/or a lack of commitment to the message and tactics of revivalism.

Especially in Connecticut and Massachusetts, the crisis of separatism led to a legal crackdown on dissenters, who faced fines and even imprisonment for illegal meetings or for tax evasion, as they often refused to pay the required tithes to support the established churches. The persecution of separating evangelicals began to generate an evangelical case for the disestablishment of the state churches, a cause that gained a great deal of momentum in the 1770s and 1780s with the coming of the American Revolution.

Some Separates took one step further and became Baptists. The Baptists became the most controversial radical sect emerging from the Great Awakening, because in addition to their refusal to attend the established churches, the Baptists refused to baptize infants, believing that only those old enough to put their faith in Christ were fit candidates for baptism. In a society that almost universally practiced infant baptism, the exclusion of children from this revered sacrament seemed cruel.

Although Baptists had existed in America since the earliest colonial settlements, the Great Awakening essentially began a new Baptist movement in America that emerged from radical evangelicalism. The experiences of the great New England Baptist leader Isaac Backus illustrate well the journey that many evangelicals took from radical evangelical to separating Baptist. Backus, of Norwich, Connecticut, was converted in 1741 under the ministry of several itinerant preachers, including James Davenport. Backus' home church was supportive of the revivals, but not

---

[11] C. C. Goen, *Revivalism and Separatism in New England, 1740–1800: Strict Congregationalists and Separate Baptists in the Great Awakening*, rev. ed. (Middletown, CT, 1987), 327.

the radicals' extremes or the work of lay exhorters. The church practiced relatively easy membership standards, but the new evangelicals wanted membership limited only to the converted. When the minister balked, a small group of radicals withdrew from the church. When challenged about their lack of attendance at the parish church, the Separates accused the minister of failing to support the revivals fully and of indulging unconverted members.

Despite his lack of a college education, Backus began working as an itinerant preacher. In 1748 Backus helped start a new Separate congregation in Titicut, Massachusetts, one of the nearby towns he visited in his preaching tours. In spite of harassment from local church and government authorities, the Titicut Separates made Backus the pastor of their new church. Backus, like many Separates, experienced growing doubts about the legitimacy of infant baptism. He found no basis for the practice in the Bible, which was very troubling because, as Protestants, New England Congregationalists claimed to base their whole religion on the Bible alone. In 1751 Backus announced publicly that he had rejected infant baptism, and he himself received believer's baptism by immersion in water. This development caused bitter contention within the Titicut church, and eventually Backus was forced to separate yet again and start a new Baptist church. Backus and his church continued to experience persecution from the Massachusetts government, and eventually he became one of the most articulate proponents of disestablishment in New England.

Although many of the Separate congregations in New England were short-lived, the Separate Baptists generated a powerful missionary movement that brought their gospel to the South, which until the early nineteenth century was the least religious section of the country. Anglicanism was the official religion in the southern colonies, but evangelical dissenters began to intrude there as a result of the Great Awakening. The Great Awakening's early phase had touched the coastal South but had made little headway in the lonely stretches of the backcountry. In the late 1740s, Presbyterians of Pennsylvania and New Jersey began to send missionaries to Virginia, led most notably by Samuel Davies in Hanover, Virginia. Then in the 1750s, the Separate Baptists began to establish missionary work in the Carolinas. The great Baptist leader Shubal Stearns of Connecticut formed a new congregation at Sandy Creek, North Carolina, in 1755, which became the key base of operations for the Separate Baptists in the South. The evangelicals made great numbers of converts in the Carolinas and Virginia in the 1760s and 1770s. A crabby Anglican itinerant named Charles Woodmason complained about the evangelicals in 1767, saying that the backcountry was "eaten up by Itinerant Teachers, Preachers, and

Imposters from New England and Pennsylvania – Baptists, New Lights, Presbyterians, Independents, and a hundred other Sects."[12]

In the South, white evangelicals had to deal more directly than in the North with the gospel's implications for race relations and slavery. Evangelicals in the northern colonies routinely ministered to African Americans and Native Americans and sometimes allowed them to exhort. In the South, such attention and empowerment were alarming, especially to many slave masters who had often withheld the Christian gospel from slaves because they feared that Christianity might give the slaves ideas about equality and freedom.

Evangelicals would not deprive anyone of the gospel message, and their preaching to slaves resulted in one remarkable episode early in the Great Awakening that confirmed the slave masters' worst fears. The Charleston slave owner Hugh Bryan had been converted under George Whitefield's preaching in 1740, and he and Whitefield discussed opening a school for slaves. But Bryan soon took things to a much more radical level, as he became convinced that God was raising him up as a prophet to lead the slaves out of bondage. In 1742, he sent a book of prophecies to the South Carolina legislature in which he predicted that Charleston would be destroyed by the slaves within a month. The assembly put out a warrant for Bryan's arrest, but when the officers arrived to take him into custody, they found him repentant, apparently sobered by a failed attempt to part the waters of a nearby river.

The humiliated Bryan took a new, more moderate path that was typical of Whitefield and many white evangelicals: he evangelized the slaves but no longer promoted their freedom. Indeed, he never freed his own slaves. Whitefield himself went on to own slaves through the assistance of Bryan's family. Many of the major leaders of the evangelical movement in America, including Jonathan Edwards and James Davenport, owned at least one slave, often as household servants.

The antislavery implications of evangelicalism did not come to naught, however, especially as the movement entered the Revolutionary era. Many second-generation evangelicals, including Jonathan Edwards, Jr., became antislavery advocates. Just as important, many of the earliest African American evangelicals offered trenchant, if quiet, criticisms of American slavery. Among the most fascinating African American evangelicals who spoke out against slavery was Lemuel Haynes, who served in the Massachusetts militia and Continental Army in the American Revolution, and who went on to pastor a biracial Congregational church in Vermont.

---

[12] Richard J. Hooker, ed., *The Carolina Backcountry on the Eve of the Revolution: The Journal and Other Writings of Charles Woodmason, Anglican Itinerant* (Chapel Hill, 1953), 13.

In 1776, shortly after the publication of the Declaration of Independence, Haynes wrote "Liberty Further Extended: Or Free Thoughts on the Illegality of Slave-Keeping." Haynes pointedly quoted the slave owner Thomas Jefferson's assertion that "all men are created equal," and he argued that people's equality by creation made slavery immoral. "Liberty is a Jewel which was handed Down to man from the cabinet of heaven," he wrote. "Even an affrican, has Equally as good a right to his Liberty in common with Englishmen."[13] Although Haynes never published this provocative document, it was likely well known in New England antislavery and evangelical circles.

Haynes' sort of evangelical antislavery thought was one of the most direct political outcomes of the Great Awakening. Of course, not all evangelicals became antislavery activists, but a significant number did, especially in the North. Several of the most influential antislavery evangelicals were disciples of Jonathan Edwards and architects of the so-called New Divinity, an effort to codify and extend Edwards' brilliant Calvinism. Motivated by the Christian ideal of "disinterested benevolence," pastors such as Samuel Hopkins began to attack slavery in the late 1760s. In 1769, Hopkins moved to Newport, Rhode Island, where he confronted the full brutality of the slave trade, which accounted for much of Newport's shipping business. By 1773 Hopkins began to denounce slavery from the pulpit, and in 1776 he wrote a treatise against slavery that, like Haynes' "Liberty Further Extended," used the language of the Declaration to condemn slavery as one of America's greatest sins.[14]

Some evangelicals in the South also pushed fleetingly for restrictions on slave owning, before massive pressure forced them to drop most antislavery activism by about 1800. Following the lead of English Methodist leader John Wesley, many early American Methodist leaders condemned slavery. In 1784 the American Methodists took the remarkable step of calling for slave owners in their churches to free their slaves or face expulsion. The move generated an enormous backlash, and the policy was suspended within months. Some white Baptists similarly expressed strong reservations about slavery, and in 1790 the General Committee of Virginia Baptists characterized slavery as "a violent deprivation of the rights of nature, and inconsistent with a republican government; and therefore recommend it to our Brethren to make use of every legal measure, to extirpate the horrid

---

[13] Ruth Bogin, ed., "'Liberty Further Extended': A 1776 Antislavery Manuscript by Lemuel Haynes," *William and Mary Quarterly* 3rd ser., 40:1 (Jan. 1983): 94.

[14] Kenneth P. Minkema and Harry S. Stout, "The Edwardsean Tradition and the Antislavery Debate, 1740–1865," *The Journal of American History* (June 2005): http://www.history cooperative.org/journals/jah/92.1/minkema.html (accessed 7 July 2009).

evil from the land." Local churches tended not to make slave owning a punishable offense, however. As more slave owners joined southern evangelical churches, radical positions on slavery became less likely. White evangelical antislavery sentiment still existed in Virginia as late as 1825, however, when a Baptist minister in Southampton County refused to serve communion to his congregation because of their toleration of slave owning members. But this brave act only won the minister expulsion from the church.[15]

Aside from antislavery, the other major political movement emerging from evangelicalism was disestablishment. The persecution of the new evangelicals by the state churches and governments resulted in growing pressure for the Revolutionary state governments to end support for specific churches and to stop punishing anyone for their religious views. The campaign for disestablishment had the most disappointing results in the New England states, despite courageous efforts by Isaac Backus and others. Baptists found it galling that although Americans complained about unjust taxes from Britain, they were asked to pay taxes in the colonies to support churches other than their own. Backus wondered in his *Appeal to the Public for Religious Liberty* (1773) how an American union could be sustained when the colonies would not respect the liberty of conscience for all? He asked, "how can any reasonably expect that HE who has the hearts of kings in his hand, will turn the heart of our earthly sovereign to hear the pleas for liberty, of those who will not hear the cries of their fellow-subjects, under their oppressions?" Backus and the Baptists were sorely disappointed when a new Massachusetts state constitution of 1780 still provided tax support for pastors, even though people could choose the recipient. Not until 1833 did Massachusetts finally end tax support for religion.[16]

The greatest triumph for disestablishment came in Virginia, where Enlightenment rationalists, including James Madison and Thomas Jefferson, cooperated with legions of evangelicals to end state funding for religion. At the beginning of the American Revolution, Virginia had stopped funding the Anglican Church, largely as a measure of expediency. But in 1784 the legislature, led by Patrick Henry, considered resuming public funding under a "general assessment" for religion, which would have collected taxes for support of a Christian church of one's choice. Madison

---

[15] *Minutes of the Baptist General Committee* (Richmond, 1790), 7; Donald G. Mathews, *Religion in the Old South* (Chicago, 1977), 69; Randolph Ferguson Scully, *Religion and the Making of Nat Turner's Virginia: Baptist Community and Conflict, 1740–1840* (Charlottesville, 2008), 182–3.
[16] Kidd, *Brief History*, 137.

and the evangelicals organized a reaction against the general assessment. A Baptist petition against the assessment insisted that "the Holy Author of our religion needs no such compulsive measures for the promotion of his cause."[17] In his *Memorial and Remonstrance* (1785), Madison similarly argued that state support for religion hurt the interest of religion because pure Christianity had always thrived without state support. These combined efforts led to the defeat of Henry's general assessment and to the passage in 1786 of Thomas Jefferson's Bill for Establishing Religious Freedom, which banned state support for churches and prohibited civil penalties for anyone's religious beliefs.

The evangelical attacks against slavery and establishment of religion show that the Great Awakening had direct political consequences. But how much did it have to do with the coming of the American Revolution? Historians have hotly debated this question, especially since the 1966 publication of Alan Heimert's *Religion and the American Mind*, which argued that evangelical Calvinism fueled the "radical, even democratic, social and political ideology" behind the Revolution.[18] Many historians have rejected this direct connection because most of the leading Founders were not evangelicals, and because evangelical faith was only one contributing ideological factor in the revolutionaries' constellation of ideas. Most historians today would probably agree, however, that the Great Awakening had some indirect effect on the American Revolution. The celebrated historian of the American Revolution Gordon Wood has written that the Great Awakening, as a "massive defiance of traditional authority" only thirty years before the Revolution, must have had some shaping influence on the revolt against Britain.[19]

Evangelicalism probably made its greatest contribution to the Patriot cause in the form of rhetoric and style. Many evangelical Patriots ardently supported the war in moralistic and even apocalyptic terms. But the Great Awakening had also introduced a style of popular address that had a unique ability to mobilize the common people of America. George Whitefield was the master of this speaking style, speaking directly to the people in biblical language that they could easily understand. The greatest Patriot orator, Patrick Henry, and the polemical writer Tom Paine both had deep familiarity with evangelical revivalism, even though neither was an evangelical

---

[17] *Petition of the Baptist General Committee* (1785), in Charles F. James, ed., *Documentary History of the Struggle for Religious Liberty in Virginia* (Lynchburg, VA, 1900), 138.

[18] Alan Heimert, *Religion and the American Mind: From the Great Awakening to the Revolution* (Cambridge, MA, 1966), viii.

[19] Gordon S. Wood, "Religion and the American Revolution," in Harry S. Stout and D. G. Hart, eds., *New Directions in American Religious History* (New York, 1997), 182.

himself. Paine and Henry both peppered their addresses with biblical references and arguments in a style highly reminiscent of the evangelical preachers.[20]

The majority of American evangelicals did seem to support the Revolution, but many did not. Some became Loyalists, convinced that the Bible permitted protests but not revolution against the legitimate British government. Others tried to maintain neutrality because of pacifism, or a conviction that war would do no good for the kingdom of God. The Mohegan pastor Samson Occom, the most influential Native American evangelical of the eighteenth century, made a case for Christian Indians to remain neutral. He asked that Native Americans "not meddle with the Family Contentions of the English, but will be at peace and quietness. Peace never does any hurt. Peace is from the God of Peace and Love." Occom's neutrality was wise, but the war still proved ruinous to many Native communities, even nonpartisans.[21]

One historian who vehemently denied the connection between the Great Awakening and the American Revolution, Jon Butler, went even further in a 1982 *Journal of American History* article and questioned the concept of the Great Awakening altogether. Butler argued that what historians have uncritically called the Great Awakening was little more than a "short-lived Calvinist revival in New England in the early 1740s." According to Butler, the notion of a (capitalized) "Great Awakening" was invented by nineteenth-century evangelical historians.[22] Most historians probably still accept the idea of the Great Awakening as a discrete event, but Butler's provocative article forced scholars to be much more precise when describing the Great Awakening and its effects. Some, like Frank Lambert, have argued that the Great Awakening was indeed invented, but by pastors and publicists in the 1740s, not the nineteenth century.[23]

In conclusion, the Great Awakening was "great" not because it caused the American Revolution, but because it created the evangelical movement in America. The Great Awakening had remarkable egalitarian potential that was often restricted by opposition from outside and within the evangelical movement. The Great Awakening's height was certainly reached in New England in the early 1740s, but its effects eventually touched most of the English colonies in America (including Nova Scotia) by the 1780s.

---

[20] Harry S. Stout, "Religion, Communications, and the Ideological Origins of the American Revolution," *William and Mary Quarterly* 3rd ser., 34:4 (Oct. 1977): 519–41.

[21] W. DeLoss Love, *Samson Occom and the Christian Indians of New England*, rev. ed. (Syracuse, 2000), 228.

[22] Jon Butler, "Enthusiasm Described and Decried: The Great Awakening as Interpretative Fiction," *Journal of American History* 69:2 (Sept. 1982): 309.

[23] Frank Lambert, *Inventing the "Great Awakening"* (Princeton, 1999).

Related revivals also shook the British Isles and the European continent. Although it has gone through many changes over three centuries, the evangelical movement remains a major force today, not only in America, but increasingly in world regions such as Latin America, Africa, and Southeast Asia. With its strong emphasis on conversions and outpourings of the Holy Spirit, evangelical Christianity transformed colonial American religion, with effects that linger in the contemporary religious world.

SUGGESTIONS FOR FURTHER READING

Bonomi, Patricia. *Under the Cope of Heaven: Religion, Society, and Politics in Colonial America*. New York, 1986.

Frey, Sylvia R., and Betty Wood. *Come Shouting to Zion: African American Protestantism in the American South and British Caribbean to 1830*. Chapel Hill, 1998.

Isaac, Rhys. *The Transformation of Virginia, 1740–1790*. Chapel Hill, 1982.

Kidd, Thomas S. *The Great Awakening: The Roots of Evangelical Christianity in Colonial America*. New Haven, 2007.

Lambert, Frank. *Inventing the "Great Awakening."* Princeton, 1999.

Marsden, George M. *Jonathan Edwards: A Life*. New Haven, 2003.

Noll, Mark A. *The Rise of Evangelicalism: The Age of Edwards, Whitefield and the Wesleys*. Downers Grove, IL, 2003.

Stout, Harry S. *The Divine Dramatist: George Whitefield and the Rise of Modern Evangelicalism*. Grand Rapids, 1991.

23

SECTARIAN COMMUNITIES: RELIGIOUS DIVERSITY IN BRITISH AMERICA, 1730–1790

ETTA M. MADDEN

Jonathan Edwards' *Faithful Narrative of the Surprising Work of God* (1737), a report of religious activities during the preliminary stages of the New England revival known as the Great Awakening, introduces several aspects of sectarianism, or "the appearance of indigenous new religious cultures" that permeated the British colonies between 1730 and 1790.[1] Written to dispel rumors of heresy and to convince Puritan Congregationalist leaders in Boston of the validity of spiritual fervor within his community, Edwards' report explains, "There has been much talk in many parts of the country, as though the people have symbolized with the Quakers, and the Quakers themselves have been moved with such reports; and came here, once and again, hoping to find good waters to fish in; but without the least success, and seemed to be discouraged and have left off coming."[2] Employing a derisive name to label another religious group, namely, the "Quakers"; discussing popular accusations of religious affiliation afloat at the time; and describing itinerant practices of attempted conversion, Edwards' comments present some patterns that recurred throughout the colonies with regard to these numerous "new religious cultures." Not only were many individuals seeking religious and spiritual fulfillment in groups they believed the "true church," but also religious leaders were working diligently to build and sustain such faith communities through their public messages. The pulpit and the press provided popular venues for leaders to defend their distinct doctrines and practices as well as to convert additional followers.

Edwards' commentary elsewhere in the *Narrative* on spiritual behaviors manifested in his geographic region attests to the sometimes fluid boundaries among the sects, for only in periods of flux are such definitions

---

[1] Stephen Marini, *Radical Sects of Revolutionary New England* (Cambridge, MA, 1982), 4.
[2] Jonathan Edwards, *The Works of Jonathan Edwards*, ed. Clarence C. Goen (New Haven, 1972), 4:189, 32–34.

of difference necessary.³ At the time of Edwards' comments, the Quakers had been present in the colonies for decades; yet his reference suggests that their presence was a threat to the well-established Congregationalists. Records of other subsequent religious groups – the Separate Baptists, the Ephrata Cloister, and the Shakers, for example – also demonstrate ways in which members and leaders of those communities freely moved from one community to another, maintaining overarching beliefs in the freedom to find and follow God's way, independent from the strictures of larger, established religious institutions, yet maintaining clear demarcations among themselves.

These "sects" – as the etymological root, *sequi*, "to follow," indicates – often emerged from existing groups, sometimes following a charismatic leader, other times gathering around similar beliefs rather than one particular person. Generally, their zeal for and manifestation of new beliefs overpowered those of the original group from which they departed. Many claims have been made to distinguish sectarian communities from established churches, such as how they emerge, grow, and maintain membership.⁴ Eighteenth-century American communities do reveal some common patterns, although variations existed among them. "Outsider" status depended both on numbers – being in the minority – and on apparent practices – being clearly different from the established, larger religious communities.⁵ With the ability to articulate and persuade others of a vision of a better place, charismatic leaders often drew a following of like-minded individuals. Ann Lee, "Mother" of the Shakers, for example, visualized America as a promised land and brought a handful of followers with her from England to New York in 1774. Reasons for conversion and commitment to a community varied, ranging from sociological and physiological causes such as kinship ties and need for food to theological explanations such as the guidance of the Spirit and the reading of scripture. In distinguishing themselves from others, the sects often diverged from existing establishments with what appear to be only slight differences in theology and praxis. Separate Baptists in New England, for example, emerged from the Separates, or strict Congregationalists, because of differences over infant baptism; Seventh-Day Baptists differed from "mainstream" Baptists

---

³ *Ibid.*, 159–91.
⁴ Sydney E. Ahlstrom, *A Religious History of the American People* (New Haven, 1972), 230; Ernst Troeltsch, *The Social Teachings of the Christian Churches*, 2 vols. (New York, 1931); Bryan R. Wilson, *Religious Sects* (New York, 1970); Marini, *Radical Sects*, 2–3.
⁵ John A. Hostetler, *Amish Society* (Baltimore, 1963), 35–6; Rosabeth Moss Kanter, *Commitment and Community: Communes and Utopias in Sociological Perspective* (Cambridge, MA, 1972); Stephen L. Longenecker, *Shenandoah Religion: Outsiders and the Mainstream, 1716–1865* (Waco, 2002), 10.

in their observance of Saturday as the Sabbath. Within these emerging communities, some fluidity of fellowship existed, especially during formative periods. For example, Separate Congregationalist Isaac Backus began to meet with "open communion" Baptists before assuming Separate Baptists' beliefs and leadership.[6]

Because of differences from the mainstream, the outsider sectarian communities suffered verbal and physical persecution, often glorying in it as a sign of righteousness. Perhaps the most widespread forms of persecution in the British colonies were verbal attacks, including numerous tracts and newspaper articles published about dissenters and the common use of derisive labels rather than formal names, for example, "Dunkers" for the Pennsylvania Anabaptist Church of the Brethren, and "Quakers" for the Society of Friends. Yet more severe physical persecution also occurred, especially in the period surrounding the Revolution. John Murray, a leader of the Universalists, was stoned in Gloucester, Massachusetts; Shaker leader Mother Ann Lee was beaten by mobs in western Massachusetts; Quakers accused of treason were imprisoned during the Revolution; and Baptists were jailed for not paying taxes. Such persecution – or the lack thereof – forced sectarian communities to make decisions about their behavior and theology. To what degree would they remain separate or "peculiar"? A sectarian community sometimes became less of a threat to the mainstream because of changes in size or in locale. Sometimes cultural practices of the mainstream or the sectarian community changed, causing the latter to be less different or better understood. Yet surviving communitarian sects continued to view themselves as different and chose means of maintaining difference, even if mainstream reactions were not so extreme.

TEMPORAL NODES, GEOGRAPHICAL DIFFERENCES, AND MIGRATION

The historical period 1730–90 includes two major events acknowledged as significant for sectarian life and the sectarian spirit within the colonies: the Great Awakening and the Revolutionary War. These two chaotic and disruptive events have been seen as both contributing factors to and reflections of American individualism and enthusiasm in religious life. Rather than being merely causal, the activities associated with revivalism and the rebellion sprang from preexisting conditions; the grounds for dissent

---

[6] William McLoughlin, *Soul Liberty: The Baptists' Struggle in New England, 1630–1833* (Hanover, NH, 1991), 127; Stephanie Grauman Wolf, *Urban Village: Population, Community, and Family Structure in Germantown, Pennsylvania, 1693–1800* (Princeton, 1976), 203–42.

and difference were present already in the seventeenth century.⁷ From its beginning, the British experiment in North America by its very nature welcomed and sustained sectarian groups. Driven by situations in Europe where the Reformation had kindled new religious practices and subsequent persecution, many groups of like-minded individuals migrated to the open space that offered hope of a new beginning. Print technology as well as the spoken word and kinship ties provided the means for circulating these visions of better places. Quaker William Penn's charter from Charles II in 1681 for a "holy experiment" in religious freedom, for example, and the difficulty of life in Germany in the seventeenth and eighteenth centuries brought about a large influx of emigrants with sectarian affiliations to the area now known as Pennsylvania. Once on American soil, these groups were drawn together for not only ideological but also economic and social reasons. Factors such as language separated many German-speaking groups, such as the Mennonites, from their English-speaking neighbors.⁸

Although the terrain and the climate, the need for food and shelter, and language may have caused some groups to be more communal than they perhaps initially visualized, revivalism and the Revolution forced groups to delineate their beliefs in ways that contributed to their flourishing. Although "the Great Awakening" is a phrase constructed by historians and its exact dates are difficult to determine, eighteenth-century documents record enthusiastic revivalism in many regions. Fanned initially by the preaching tours of Gilbert Tennent and George Whitefield, revivalism persisted throughout the century, from before the "awakening" in Northampton, Massachusetts, that Edwards described and through the New Light Stir of the post-Revolutionary period in New England.⁹ Before, during, and after the colonies' revolt against England, sectarians such as the Quakers, Mennonites, and Dunkers collectively identified themselves through concepts of pacifism, whereas others, such as Separate Baptists, responded collectively against taxation that supported a state church.

Historical events influenced locales diversely, depending on the regional composition of the mainstream and the outsiders.¹⁰ Revivals associated with the Great Awakening in New England primarily had an impact on the

---

⁷ Nathan O. Hatch, *The Democratization of American Christianity* (New Haven, 1989); Jon Butler, *Awash in a Sea of Faith: Christianizing the American People* (Cambridge, MA, 1990); Ruth Bloch, *Visionary Republic: Millennial Themes in American Thought, 1756–1800* (New York, 1985).

⁸ Arthur E. Bestor, *Backwoods Utopias: The Sectarian and Owenite Phases of Communitarian Socialism in America, 1663–1829* (Philadelphia, 1950), 24–31.

⁹ Thomas S. Kidd, *The Great Awakening: The Roots of Evangelical Christianity in Colonial America* (New Haven, 2007), xviii–xix.

¹⁰ Longenecker, *Shenandoah Religion*; Marini, *Radical Sects*.

mainstream Congregationalists and the sectarian "Baptists," whereas in the Middle Colonies revivalism flourished in a region where German-speaking communities contributed to the sectarianism, often defining themselves against Lutherans.[11] Whitefield's message and style not only influenced Baptists in Virginia and the Carolinas, but also, during his first visit to the colonies, directly motivated the German-speaking Moravians in Georgia to move north; his final tour influenced Benjamin Randel, a Universalist leader, to migrate from New Jersey to New England later in the century.

Migration occurred not only with itinerant ministers or missionaries looking for fertile fields for their seminal ideas, but also with communities and family clusters. For example, Mennonites, Dunkers, and Sabbatarians from the Middle Colonies migrated west and south, most often motivated by desire for land, spreading the seeds of dissent into the Shenandoah Valley and beyond. Thus the religious diversity that had been present among immigrants first in New England, and soon after in Pennsylvania, existed in the southern colonies as well.[12]

Some sectarian communities are classified "Anabaptists," or rebaptizers, referring to their practice of adult baptism following an earlier infant baptism; others are labeled "Pietists," referring to their radical "efforts to intensify Christian piety and purity of life." Some of these "protest[ed] against intellectualism, churchly formalism, and ethical passivity," whereas others emphasized self-education.[13] Many communities met in members' homes rather than in church buildings, and most selected lay ministers, without formal education or ordination. Some allowed women to teach or preach, a few had female leaders, and still others allowed women little public or authoritative voice. Attempts to categorize such a diverse conglomeration of communities may not be as helpful as examining each group to understand its theology and practice. In spite of labels and sometimes formal associations that linked these communities, differing beliefs and practices existed in different regions and varied over time. Quakers in the mid-Atlantic region differed from those in Salem, Massachusetts; and the Baptists of the Carolinas and Virginia differed from those of Boston and Pennsylvania. Nonetheless, a survey of well-known English-speaking and German-speaking sectarian communities in the British colonies illustrates numerous characteristics they had in common, such as their origins in preexisting establishments, leaders who fostered their growth, and strong reactions to them by the mainstream religious communities.

---

[11] Sally Schwartz, "A Mixed Multitude": The Struggle for Toleration in Colonial Pennsylvania (New York, 1987), 120–58.
[12] Longenecker, Shenandoah Religion.
[13] Ahlstrom, Religious History, 236.

QUAKERS

Among the earliest sects in the colonies was the Society of Friends that began in England as followers of George Fox (1624–91). A few Quakers appeared in the Massachusetts Bay colony as early as 1656. Numerous others settled in the Philadelphia and the Germantown areas after William Penn received his charter ensuring religious toleration, so that by 1730 the sect was relatively well established in New England and in Pennsylvania. Labeled by outsiders as "Quakers" because of their enthusiastic practices, the sect was often persecuted in the colonies for their radical beliefs and practices. Most significantly, they had set aside the ordinances of baptism and the Lord's Supper because of their belief in the Inner Light – a spiritual baptism available to all who allowed this presence of divinity within.

Quakers have been described as inducing less fear and subsequently less persecution in the colonies after 1730, in part due to the circulation of Robert Barclay's *Apology* (1676), a publication said to have moved the sect into a period of more traditional Christian dualism and quietism and of less emphasis on ecstatic behavior. In addition, the sect had gradually become more involved in the civic fabric of political and mercantile culture in Philadelphia and in Boston. Writings by John Woolman (1720–72) and Anthony Benezet (1713–84) are representative of quietism and a humanitarian spirit committed to abolishing slavery and poverty. However, Barclay's tract did not assert that the sect should be considered a part of the mainstream, and records of Quaker meetings (congregations) such as that at Salem, Massachusetts, as well as narratives and diaries of individuals demonstrate that the Friends clearly defined themselves against the mainstream throughout their existence in the eighteenth century.[14] Friends such as Milcah Martha Moore (1740–1829) were expelled for not adhering to the practice of marrying a Friend, and others were persecuted during the Revolution when many were imprisoned for their pacifist beliefs.[15]

Quaker records also demonstrate the powerful role many women had within the Society, because it granted them speaking and teaching

---

[14] *Ibid.*, 3, 211; Frederick B. Tolles, *Meeting House and Counting House, the Quaker Merchants of Colonial Philadelphia, 1682–1763* (New York, 1963); Carla Gardina Pestana, *Quakers and Baptists in Colonial Massachusetts* (New York, 1991), 176–86; Thomas D. Hamm, *The Quakers in America* (New York, 2003).

[15] Karin A. Wulf, "Introduction," in Catherine La Courreye Blecki and Karin A. Wulf, eds., *Milcah Martha Moore's Book: A Commonplace Book from Revolutionary America* (University Park, PA, 1997), 14–15, 37–57; Pestana, *Quakers and Baptists*, 176–86; Elaine Forman Crane, "Introduction," in Elaine Forman Crane, ed., *The Diary of Elizabeth Drinker: The Life Cycle of an Eighteenth-Century Woman* (Boston, 1994), ix–xx.

privileges and emphasized education and literacy.[16] In addition to Moore's *Book*, the writings of Elizabeth Ashbridge (1713–55), Elizabeth Drinker (1735–1807), and Sarah "Sally" Wister (1761–1804), for example, reveal the breadth and diversity of women's experiences. Ashbridge's spiritual autobiography, *Some Account of the Forepart of the Life* (c. 1755), describes her many moves as a religious seeker, beginning in an Anglican family in England, through affiliation with the theater in New York, to enduring verbal and physical abuse by her second husband, who loathed the Quakers. Her later marriage into an established Quaker family and her itinerancy for the faith reveal the choices and support the sect afforded her as a female called to preach.

Membership in the Society of Friends occurred for a variety of reasons, in addition to being born within it. In Salem, Massachusetts, for example, converts were family-connected females who through reading discovered the "truth." (This was also the case with some Baptists in New England).[17] Yet Ashbridge's story presents the picture of a seeker who picked up a Quaker book out of curiosity, "wondering what these people might write about," because she understood they had "given up all the Holy Ordinances." Thus reading in private prompted her conversion; however, social relations sealed her faith. First, a female Friend was sympathetic to Elizabeth's situation as an abused wife; second, her husband's spite provoked Elizabeth to grow stronger in her faith; and finally, the local meeting, where she began to speak, provided her encouragement. Ashbridge's testimony of seeking, finding truth, being persecuted, and enduring provided an example for potential converts.[18]

SEPARATE BAPTISTS

The Separate Baptists provide an illustrative example of sectarian life in the period through the fluidity of their beginnings and boundaries. They did not emerge as much from preexisting Baptist congregations in New England as they did from established Congregationalist churches responding to the Great Awakening. Nonetheless, the theology and existence of the

---

[16] Phyllis Mack, "Religion, Feminism, and the Problem of Agency: Reflections of Eighteenth-Century Quakerism," *Signs* 29:1 (2003): 149–77; Rebecca Larson, *Daughters of Light: Quaker Women Preaching and Prophesying in the Colonies and Abroad, 1700–1775* (New York, 1999); Christine Levenduski, *Peculiar Power: A Quaker Woman Preacher in Eighteenth-Century America* (Washington, DC, 1996).

[17] Pestana, *Quakers and Baptists*, 68–72.

[18] Elizabeth Ashbridge, *Some Account of the Forepart of the Life of Elizabeth Ashbridge 1774*, ed. Daniel B. Shea, in *Journeys in New Worlds: Early American Women's Narratives*, ed. William L. Andrews (Madison, 1990), 147–70, 158.

established Baptists influenced the Separates. Baptists arrived in the colonies in the seventeenth century, labeled as such because of their teachings against infant baptism and in favor of adult baptism as a holy ordinance. They also distinguished themselves from Puritan Congregationalists and from Anglicans in Virginia most clearly by their negative attitudes toward taxes that supported ministers and meetinghouses. These two characteristics – emphasis on adult baptism and the freedom from taxes imposed for support of the state church – were distinguishing features of eighteenth-century Separate Baptists.

Among Baptists in 1730, those who had set aside the Calvinist doctrine of election or predestination to emphasize a broader salvation were referred to as General Baptists for their Arminian belief in a more "general" salvation. Baptists maintaining orthodox Calvinism were known as Particulars, because salvation was available for only a particular few. During the Great Awakening, Congregationalists began to be described as New Light and Old Light, Calvinist and Arminian, supporters and opponents of the Great Awakening, respectively. Many New Lights lost faith in the denomination because ministers lacked sufficient zeal, were too inclusive, or favored ecclesiastical associations over congregational polity. By the late 1740s, many New Lights left congregations in Cumberland, Attleboro, Easton, Norton, and Middleborough, Massachusetts, for example, to become part of the Separates, also called "come-outers" and "strict" Congregationalists. Through increased study of scripture, some Separates decided that one problem among Old Lights was the unscriptural practice of infant baptism; subsequently, a majority of them adopted adult baptism by immersion, becoming the Separate Baptist churches. By 1760 these churches were widespread.[19]

Separate Baptist leaders included Isaac Backus, whose *History* (1777) is a key source on the sect, and Shubal Stearns (1706–71). Backus's writings contributed to the establishment of a college in Warren, Rhode Island (1764), and to a growing association among Baptists throughout the colonies. Although he opposed formal association on the grounds of biblical example, at times Backus employed his persuasive and political skills to lead Separate Baptists to join with other groups or to maintain a distinct status, depending on the goal.[20] Stearns and his brother-in-law Daniel Marshall (1706–84), both originally New England Congregationalists, took their ideas to the South. First arriving on the "southern frontier" of Pennsylvania and West Virginia, they eventually left with family for

[19] McLoughlin, *Soul Liberty*, 6–7, 105–6.
[20] Ibid., 7–8.

the piedmont of North Carolina, where, they had heard, southerners were "hungry for preaching." By 1760 the region included ten churches.[21]

In Virginia, growth of the Separates was fed by the Hanover Awakening of the 1740s, along with the development of the rugged Shenandoah Valley, which encouraged independence among those migrating from the already religiously diverse Pennsylvania colony. By 1765 the Separate Baptists were a threat to the establishment, resulting in verbal and physical persecution. In the 1760s and 1770s, Separatists' beliefs spread "from the peripheral to the longer-settled regions," increasing from seven churches in 1769 to twelve in 1771, thirty-four in 1773, and fifty-four by 1774. Growth also occurred in South Carolina and in Georgia up through 1790.[22] In the South, matters of difference occurred not just in theology, but more vividly in appearance and behavior. The Separates were recognized for more "austere" haircuts and dress, as well as "Sabbath" observance that eschewed the Sunday frivolities of their Anglican neighbors. The familial language of believers as "brothers" and "sisters" extended also to slaves. Indeed, not only slaves but also females were granted more power than they had in mainstream churches, as both disenfranchised groups were given speaking privileges that included testimonies of faith, and women participated some in decision-making meetings.[23]

The Separates in the South joined the Regulars in the 1780s, due to the persuasiveness of John Leland (1754–1841) who went from Massachusetts to Virginia in 1776 and who convinced the Separates to compromise for the sake of the religious liberty that was brought about by Thomas Jefferson's statute in 1786. Nonetheless, concrete differences among Separate Baptists and others continued, exhibited in such issues as congregational autonomy or association and election and free will.[24]

The most significant union and persecution of Separate Baptists arose in relationship to taxes. Although occurring much earlier with individuals, in 1773 in New England Isaac Backus led "a campaign of massive civil disobedience" to fill the jails with those refusing to pay taxes.[25] The results of such actions varied, depending on the sectarian constituency within each town. As long as most citizens were Congregationalists, the taxes were equally spread among everyone; however, if there were too many dissenters, then the taxes would be higher for the mainstream. Thus, sectarians

---

[21] Ahlstrom, *Religious History*, 319.
[22] Longenecker, *Shenandoah Religion*, 13–29; Rhys Isaac, *The Transformation of Virginia, 1740–1790* (Chapel Hill, 1982), 164, 173.
[23] Isaac, *Transformation of Virginia*, 164, 170–1.
[24] Ahlstrom, *Religious History*, 320–1.
[25] McLoughlin, *Soul Liberty*, 8.

and itinerants were viewed negatively as people bringing dissent, disorder, and lower property values. Often itinerants would arrive and meet secretly in people's homes. When enough people had been converted and baptized, then the group could hire their own minister and, soon after, ask for tax exemption. Mob violence against Separate Baptists came "from both the respectable and disreputable members of the community," as a case in Pepperell, Massachusetts, in 1778 demonstrated. Yet four years later, in Attleboro, Massachusetts, when Baptists refused to pay their property taxes and subsequently the town seized and sold members' cows to pay the debt, the Baptists sued, and a local judge ruled in their favor.[26] In Virginia, scorn toward ministers seen as uneducated and ignorant appeared in the extreme 1771 incident of an established parson and other gentlemen violently attacking a Baptist preacher during worship.[27]

Although the Separate Baptists experienced persecution for their beliefs, they were not adverse to persecuting smaller dissenting groups that emerged from within them. Some such groups in New England came to be known as "perfectionists" and "immortalists" who, because of their interpretation of scripture and the embodied Spirit, manifested behaviors that threatened not only the mainstream, but also other outsiders. For example, the followers of Ebenezer Ward and John Finney, Jr., in the area of Easton, Massachusetts, were accused of adultery and polygamy.[28]

SEVENTH-DAY BAPTISTS

Less extreme in their differences from the Separate Baptists were those who understood and observed Saturday as the Sabbath, commonly known as Seventh-Day Baptists, or Sabbatarians. In New England, Samuel Hubbard and his wife, who had left the Congregationalists to become Baptists in 1647, by 1665 had determined through study that they should be setting aside the seventh day as sacred. They and a few others formally withdrew from the First Baptist congregation in 1671 to establish a Seventh-Day Baptist congregation in Rhode Island. Other congregations, which became Baptist through the teachings of former-Presbyterian-turned-Quaker George Keith, had their origins among Quakers in the Philadelphia area. In Pennepek, Abel Noble led a group and later influenced the German Dunkers in the area to adopt Sabbatarianism. New congregations emerged in the early eighteenth century; thus by 1770 in Pennsylvania, according to Morgan Edwards' count, approximately twenty-six families identified

---

[26] *Ibid.*, 196–7, 228.
[27] Isaac, *Transformation of Virginia*, 162–3.
[28] McLoughlin, *Soul Liberty*, 100–23.

with them. A group of persecuted Baptists in Plymouth colony migrated to Piscataway, New Jersey, where Edmund Dunham, through careful study, led a small following to Sabbatarianism. In 1705 they established a congregation that remained prominent in the denomination for 250 years.[29] During the Revolution, Sabbatarians in Pennsylvania took a pacifist stance similar to the Quakers, and they too were often persecuted by fines and imprisonment. The homes of members in Piscataway were looted and burned, and church property was used by the British to house soldiers and horses. After the Revolution and the Treaty of Paris, the opening of new territory led some families to migrate west, taking their beliefs with them into Virginia.[30]

FREEWILL BAPTISTS

Another Baptist splinter group, designated Freewill Baptists, began in New England as reactionaries against Calvinist evangelicals who emphasized atonement limited to the elect. By the end of 1780, there were "a dozen ministers and several whole congregations that had joined the sect," and it had become "the hill country's largest indigenous religion."[31] This development was due primarily to the strong leadership of Benjamin Randel (1749–84), who was first an Old Light Congregationalist in New Castle, New Hampshire. Randel came to some of his later beliefs through direct intervention of the Holy Spirit, but he was first influenced by Whitefield on his final 1770 tour. In 1773 Randel attempted to invigorate the congregation of which he was a member with frequent and regular meetings for song, prayer, and study. By 1775 he and a following had withdrawn from the congregation due to New Light differences. By 1776 he had changed his beliefs about infant and adult baptism; he was himself immersed and joined the Madbury Baptist Church. In 1779, soon after being called to preach at the New Durham Baptist Church, he was rejected by the Madbury Baptists because of his Arminianism. Following this rejection, Randal came to understand more broadly the possibilities of salvation as well as the importance of free will and human attempts at Christian perfection. He soon began to itinerate in Baptist congregations of New Hampshire, meeting both acceptance and rejection. The Randelites, who followed "freewill principles," came to be known as the Freewill Baptists.

---

[29] Don A. Sanford, *A Choosing People: The History of Seventh Day Baptists* (Nashville, 1992), 94–113; Morgan Edwards, *Materials Towards a History of Baptists*, ed. Eve B. Weeks and Mary B. Warren (Danielsville, GA, 1984), 1: 30–31, 134–40.
[30] Sanford, *Choosing People*, 130–4.
[31] Marini, *Radical Sects*, 67.

UNIVERSALISTS

Universalists, like Freewill Baptists, began in New England in the 1770s as reactionaries against Calvinist teachings that emphasized limited atonement. Leaders responsible for their beginnings and growth emerged from diverse religious groups, including followers of Whitefield, Separates, Baptists, and radical evangelicals; they moved among existing communities as they sought and taught spiritual truth. John Murray (1741–1815) and Elhanan Winchester (1751–97), for example, carried the weight of thinking, writing, preaching, and promoting the cause on the coast in urban centers, under the influence of ideas from Europe. Adams Streeter (1735–86), Isaac Davis (c. 1700), and Caleb Rich (1750–1821) spread the word in the rural areas, prompted by their own biblicist backgrounds, study, and direct revelation. The urban and rural movements became affiliated in the 1780s.[32]

John Murray was first a Calvinist and then an Irish Wesleyan preacher before being converted by the Universalist teachings of James Relly. Pulled by personal crises to the colonies, where he hoped to live in "retirement" and "solitude," Murray's account is that he was rescued in New Jersey by radical evangelical Thomas Potter, who believed Murray was the evangelist for whom his congregation had been waiting. Murray immediately became a successful preacher in the Middle Colonies before going to New England in 1773 and 1774, following the route of Whitefield's 1770 tour. His popularity just as quickly diminished, however, when in 1775 he publicly declared for Universalism. Previously, his preaching had been a mixture of "Calvinist doctrine, Whitefieldian New Birth, and Rellyan exegesis," with no specific statements of Universalism.[33] The results in Gloucester, Massachusetts, in 1775 were typical of the period. Murray "was arrested for vagrancy, cursed and stoned by angry crowds, and threatened with deportation" as well as being accused of "Toryism, espionage, and immorality." According to Murray's *Records*, Ezra Stiles accused him of being "a Romanist in disguise, endeavoring to excite confusion in our churches." Nonetheless, Murray established churches in Gloucester by 1779 and in the 1780s in Boston; Salem, Massachusetts; and Portsmouth, New Hampshire. "His forceful leadership and strict moral code" had an appeal to religious seekers, but his strong personality later caused a division with the Universalists of the rural areas.[34]

Elhanan Winchester, born in Brookline, Massachusetts, perhaps inherited religious seeking from his father, who was first an Old Light

---
[32] *Ibid.*, 68–72, 144–8.
[33] *Ibid.*, 68–9.
[34] *Ibid.*, 69.

Congregationalist and then a New Light, a Baptist, and a Universalist, before dying as a Shaker. The younger Winchester was first an open-communion Baptist and then such a strict Calvinist Baptist preacher that he was released from one congregation for his hyper-Calvinism. He became an itinerant and settled in Welsh Neck, South Carolina, where in 1778, on reading *The Everlasting Covenant* (1753), a tract initially written in German by Paul Siegvolck (1710), he began to understand Universalism. Motivated to return to New England, as a successful evangelist among the New Light Stir in 1779 and 1780 he was called to the largest Baptist church in America, the First Baptist Church of Philadelphia. Winchester took the position, but he was already half Universalist. On being influenced by the prevalent ideas afloat in Philadelphia of George de Benneville, who had translated Siegvolck's work, and of Benjamin Rush and Jacob Duché, Winchester ended up being dismissed. Along with one hundred followers, he then created the Society of Christian Baptists; and in the next year, 1781, he formally declared the coming of the "Universal Restoration."[35]

Isaac Davis itinerated from his home in Somers, Connecticut, beginning in the 1770s, and made an impact in the Connecticut River valley, especially Worcester County, Massachusetts. In 1775 some Davisonians withdrew from the Oxford Congregationalist Church, creating a strong Universalist group. Davis most likely influenced the younger Adams Streeter, who converted around 1777 and became a leader for the Oxford group. From 1780 to 1786 Davis served Oxford, Milford, and Providence, Rhode Island, on a circuit, and he was welcomed by Murray in Boston, creating an affiliation that strengthened the scattered Universalist cause.[36]

Caleb Rich, born in Sutton, Massachusetts, into a community of Separates and Baptists, was young and unconverted during a church split there over theology. As a result, he began to look seriously for truth and to have visionary experiences. In 1772, while wrestling with the teachings of his brother Nathaniel, he came to believe that the elect were predestined since Adam's creation and that those who were not elect were not immortal, and therefore they would not have everlasting punishment. His judgment that he should convert the Baptists by sharing these beliefs caused his and his brother's removal from the Warwick Baptist Church. They then organized a new sectarian community in 1773. By 1776 there were additional followers in Sutton, Oxford, and Douglass; by 1777 there was a community around Richmond, New Hampshire. In 1778, visions changed Rich's

---

[35] Ibid., 69–71; Elhanan Winchester, *The Universal Restoration, Exhibited in Four Dialogues between a Minister and His Friend* (Philadelphia, 1792).

[36] Marini, *Radical Sects*, 71–2.

theology so that he began preaching a "message of divine benevolence and universal salvation."[37]

SHAKERS

Sometimes confused with the Quakers because of the similarity of the derisive names given by outsiders, the Shakers flourished in post-Revolutionary New England under the leadership of Ann Lee (1736–84). The United Society of Believers in Christ's Second Appearing, as they called themselves, may be distinguished from other radical sects by their emphasis on the mystical Lee as an embodiment of the Christ Spirit and by their ecstatic worship, which gave rise to their popular name.

Known as Mother Ann to her followers, Ann Lee was born in Manchester, England, the illiterate daughter of a blacksmith. Lee immigrated to America in 1774 with a small group of followers due to religious persecution in England and a vision she had of America as a promised land. Her most important vision, however, was one in which she saw celibacy as God's will. Prior to the vision, Lee had married and given birth to several children, none of whom lived beyond infancy or early childhood, and she had become affiliated with a group of "Shaking Quakers" in England.

Narrative accounts of the early Shakers are scanty, due to Lee's illiteracy and the primacy of orality within the sect's first phase of "gathering." Key sources of the period are newspaper accounts produced by outside observers; narratives provided by disgruntled apostates such as Valentine Rathbun, who was a Baptist elder until he and his entire congregation converted to Shakerism; and documents the sect printed in 1790 and in the following decades.[38] These accounts describe details of Lee's early life and immigration; her settling first in New York with her husband, but without active evangelism; her later travels with a few followers, excluding her husband,

---

[37] Ibid., 74–5.
[38] Valentine Rathbun, *Brief Account of a Religious Scheme, Taught and Propagated by a Number of Europeans, who Lately Lived in a Place Called Nisqueunia, in the State of New-York, but Now Residing in Harvard, Commonwealth of Massachusetts, Commonly called, Shaking Quakers* (Worcester, 1782); Joseph Meacham and James Whittaker, *A Concise Statement of the Principles of the Only True Church, According to the Gospel of the Present Appearance of Christ* (Bennington, VT, 1790); Rufus Bishop and Seth Y. Wells, eds., *Testimonies Concerning the Life, Character, Revelations, and Doctrines of Our Every Blessed Mother Ann Lee, and the Elders with Her* (Hancock, MA, 1816); Glendyne Wergland, ed., *Visiting the Shakers, 1778–1849* (Clinton, 2007), 14–17, 133–8; Stephen J. Stein, *The Shaker Experience in America* (New Haven, 1992), 3–38; Clarke Garrett, *Spirit Possession and Popular Religion: From the Camisards to the Shakers* (Baltimore, 1989), 160–226.

who had given up on the faith, to Niskeyuna in the Albany area; and the "opening the gospel" of celibacy through evangelistic preaching in 1780.

With an itinerancy throughout New England between 1781 and her death in 1784, Ann Lee gathered numerous followers in rural Massachusetts and New York. Lee's message encouraged a sharing of worldly goods, and early believers clustered together in houses owned by prominent converts in towns such as Harvard and Shirley, Massachusetts. Their communalism contributed to survival during the lean years following the Revolution. Beginning in 1787 at Mount Lebanon, New York, communal villages were established in this region as well as later in Connecticut, New Hampshire, and Maine.

Among the numerous accusations hurled at the Shakers were dishonesty, drunkenness, sexual impropriety, and lack of patriotism. Ann Lee herself was accused not only of being a man in woman's clothing, but also of being a British spy; and the physical persecution of mob violence most likely led to her premature death. Both insider and outsider accounts attest to the violence she and her followers endured because of their differences from their neighbors – most notably their female leader and their divergence from the ideals associated with the biological family and private ownership of property. Lee's "gospel" of celibacy was interpreted by some as a message that tore apart families, breaking up marriages and the farms that were essential to the new nation.

JEMIMA WILKINSON AND JERSUALEM

Ann Lee often has been paired with another female sectarian leader of the period, Jemima Wilkinson (1752–1819). As with Lee and the Shakers, much information about Wilkinson and her followers exists in the accounts of observers, although only one publication and some manuscripts are attributed to her. Born in Rhode Island and previously a member of the Society of Friends, Wilkinson left Quakerism, probably influenced by New Light Baptists, and began preaching in southeastern New England and western New York, eventually establishing a community called Jerusalem in central New York in Yates County in 1788.[39]

---

[39] Susan Juster, "To Slay the Beast: Visionary Women in the Early Republic," in *A Mighty Baptism: Race, Gender, and the Creation of American Protestantism* (Ithaca, 1996), 27–32; Abner Brownell, *Enthusiastical Errors Transpired and Detected* (London, CT, 1783); David Hudson, *History of Jemima Wilkinson, a Preacheress of the Eighteenth Century; Containing an Authentic Narrative of Her Life and Character, and of the Rise, Progress, and Conclusion of Her Ministry* (Geneva, 1821); Marquis de Chastellux, *Travels in North America in the Years 1780, 1781, and 1782*, trans. Howard C. Rice, Jr. (Chapel Hill, 1963), 1: 322; Bestor, *Backwoods Utopias*, 33–4.

In 1782 Wilkinson made a notable trip to Philadelphia with six followers. Calling herself the "Public Universal Friend," Wilkinson delivered "appeals for radical reformation" with a "militant rhetoric and apocalyptic message." Wilkinson's message was like Mother Ann's in its call for immediate radical reform. In fact, she and her closest followers also practiced celibacy. Yet she proclaimed herself the reincarnation of Christ and did so with an "authority only possible with an assumption of masculine characteristics."[40] By contrast, Ann Lee, called "Mother" by her followers, appeared enough like a female that persecutors who suspected she was a man stripped her clothing for confirmation of her sexual identity. Lee's followers, rather than Lee herself, spoke and wrote of her as the second incarnation of Christ. Yet Wilkinson, never called "Mother," took on masculine garb and masculine behavior. Her male followers, by contrast, became somewhat feminized, sporting longer hair and a peculiar style of hat.

Wilkinson's departure from Quakerism – a separation from an existing sect – suggests that the Friends were not meeting her spiritual needs. Perhaps the Quakers in post-Revolutionary New England were not active enough in their evangelism. Wilkinson's behavior appears more like the early Quakers, whose radical public actions and speaking brought about imprisonment. Her motivation and message seem more like that of other Universalists, active in Portsmouth and in Philadelphia, calling for immediate moral reform.

MORAVIANS

Similar to followers of Jemima Wilkinson and Ann Lee, the German-speaking Moravians exhibited radical practices associated with their views of the Holy Spirit and of accompanying gender roles, as well as a "general economy" in communal villages such as those in the Bethlehem, Pennsylvania, and Salem, North Carolina, areas. The Renewed Church of the United Brethren, or Unitas Fratrum, began in Moravia; thus their common name. Almost wiped out in the Counter-Reformation, these radical pietists managed to exist through immigration, secrecy, and the support of Count Nicholaus Ludwig Zinzendorf (1700–60) in Saxony, who became their bishop in 1737 and a leading force in the colonies. The first Moravian immigrants to the British colonies, led by Augustus Gottlieb Spangenberg, left for Georgia in 1735 with the goal of evangelizing among the Creek and Cherokee natives. Subsequently, the fervent messages of John Wesley and George Whitefield influenced the struggling group to move from Georgia to Philadelphia in 1740. After settling in nearby Nazareth, where they

---

[40] Juster, "To Slay the Beast," 20, 30–4.

were to build a school for African Americans under Whitefield's direction, the impassioned minister's Calvinism conflicted with their beliefs. The recently arrived Zinzendorf led them to Bethlehem, Pennsylvania, which became a key site for the sect, along with Nazareth, which they later purchased from Whitefield.[41]

Zinzendorf's theology focused on the corporality of Jesus and his suffering, especially the side wound, which was represented in art and hymns as a womb. Through this womb of Jesus, with the assistance of a female Holy Spirit, Moravians were born into their life of union with the divine. The Litany of the Wounds, performed sometimes as often as thirty times a year at Bethlehem from the 1740s through the 1760s, emphasized Christ's wounded nature and privileged divine mystical union above physical marriage. At Bethlehem at midcentury, even married community members were separated into "choirs" for same-sex housing, labor, and worship; however, spousal sexual union was also seen as sacramental and as a form of worship performed at regular intervals within rooms set apart for the sacrament. The Moravians' visual and verbal art as well as their rituals and communal living elicited numerous questions about and accusations against them.[42]

Moravians also experienced persecution for their missionary practices. In addition to supporting female leaders and missionaries, they provided fervent, evangelical preachers for faith communities that had none.[43] Successful at drawing support, they were accused of wearing veils of dishonesty, of not revealing Moravian communal rituals as they preached messages of rebirth and salvation within non-Moravian churches. Among their evangelical efforts was Zinzendorf's attempt to unify German sects of the region in the 1740s through a "Congregation of God in the Spirit." In the process, Moravians established congregations at a handful of additional sites. By midcentury they consisted of thirty-one congregational sites, and they had fifty missionaries among the natives as well as itinerant preachers, with work supported from Maine to the Carolinas. Yet they also provoked outrage among the established Lutheran and Reformed churches. An encounter between Zinzendorf and Heinrich Melchior Mühlenberg in 1742 contributed to the sect's social difficulties, as Zinzendorf lost favor with the Lutheran leader.[44] Economic and social

---

[41] Ahlstrom, *Religious History*, 241–3; Bestor, *Backwoods Utopias*, 23–4; Craig D. Atwood, *Community of the Cross: Moravian Piety in Colonial Bethlehem* (University Park, PA, 2004), 115–39.

[42] Aaron Fogleman, *Jesus Is Female: Moravians and the Challenge of Radical Religion in Early America* (Philadelphia, 2007), 137; Atwood, *Community of the Cross*.

[43] Katherine M. Faull, *Moravian Women's Memoirs: Their Related Lives, 1750–1820* (Syracuse, 1997).

[44] Schwartz, "A Mixed Multitude," 127–47; Fogleman, *Jesus Is Female*, 185–216.

concerns throughout the decade contributed to crisis, as did the French and Indian War. A decree from Europe in 1761 after Zinzendorf's death dissolved the general economy. In the 1780s and 1790s the Moravians "gradually purged their liturgy" of elements that had distinguished it, transforming the sectarian community into a more typical "American evangelical denomination."[45]

SCHWENCKFELDERS

Approximately two hundred followers of Reformation writer Kaspar Schwenckfeld von Ossig (1489–1561) arrived in Pennsylvania in 1734 and established themselves in Lehigh, Montgomery, and Berks counties. Leaders included George Weiss until 1741 and Balzer Hoffman until 1749. Their quiet practices, with an emphasis on the Spirit and ecumenical inclusiveness and unity, did not attract many followers. Their differences, other than perhaps plain clothing, were minimal. Nonetheless, the small group survived, forming the Society of Schwenckfelders in 1782 and erecting their first building in 1789. From the earliest immigration, women played a role in the community's preservation through their letter writing and manuscript copying. Approximately 50 percent of the first immigrants and about 20 percent of the copyists of important religious texts were female. Also, whereas men contributed to the dissolution of religious differences through their social interactions, females tended to remain tightly knit with others in the society.[46]

DUNKERS

The Dunkers (also Tunkers or Taufers), formally the Church of the Brethren, began in 1708 in central Germany near the village of Schwarzenau, where eight adults baptized each other, demonstrating their nonconformity and willingness to defy secular laws. Peter Becker, who led a group to Germantown, Pennsylvania, in 1719, was succeeded as a leader by Alexander Mack (1679–1735), who brought a second group to the area around 1729. Other congregations of the "Harmless Tunkers" were established at Coventry, Conestoga, and elsewhere in the region, and there were

---

[45] Atwood, *Community of the Cross*, 227.
[46] "We Are ... the Schwenkfelders," Central Schwenkfelder Church, http://www.centralschwenkfel.com/history.htm (accessed 7 Feb. 2010); Ahlstrom, *Religious History*, 244; Christine Hücho, "Female Writers, Women's Networks, and the Preservation of Culture: The Schwenkfelder Women of Eighteenth-Century Pennsylvania," *Pennsylvania History* 68:1 (2001): 107, 112, 129.

fifteen churches and four meetinghouses in Pennsylvania, but members primarily met in members' homes. They were also located in New Jersey, Maryland, Virginia, and the Carolinas. The practice of triple immersion, which included the laying on of hands and prayer, gave them their common name. In addition to baptism, other ritualized practices included anointing with oil, foot washing, the holy kiss, and the love feast. Additional differences from the mainstream were plain language and dress, wearing beards, refusal to fight and swear, and not "go[ing] to law" or taking interest for any money loaned. Their stance as separate and resistant included during the Revolution joining with the Mennonites to petition the Pennsylvania Assembly as objectors to violence. The desire to return to primitive Christianity, manifested in a strong sense of community and separation from the world, motivated decisions about religious rituals and daily life.[47]

Conrad Beissel was affiliated with this group prior to leaving it and becoming a leader of the Ephrata Cloister. He added to the Dunker practices celibacy and communal sharing of goods. Christopher Sauer (1693–1758), who arrived in America in 1724 and farmed in Lancaster County before moving to Germantown in 1731, is remembered for literary and educational endeavors. He is credited with a printing press, publication of the *Hoch-Deutsch pensylvanische Geschichts-Screiber* (1739), and "the first Bible in a Western language printed in America," as well as for his involvement with establishing "a papermill, an ink factory, ... a type foundry" and "a high school in Germantown."[48]

The groups gradually moved west and south. Between 1719 and 1740 almost all Dunkers in Germany had left for England or America, with some immigration to Pennsylvania continuing through 1750. By the time of the Revolution, there were no more than a thousand members among twenty congregations in Pennsylvania, New Jersey, and Maryland.

MENNONITES

Followers of the Anabaptist Menno Simons (1496–1561), the Mennonites emerged in and near what is now the Netherlands and first arrived in the American colonies in the seventeenth century, with the first permanent settlement at Germantown, Pennsylvania, in 1683. In the eighteenth century, as more and diverse immigrants arrived, newly arriving Mennonites moved farther west, settling along Skippack Creek and expanding into

---

[47] Edwards, *Materials*, 32–42; 141–2; Carl Bowman, *Brethren Society: The Cultural Transformation of a "Peculiar People"* (Baltimore, 1997), 1–50.
[48] Ahlstrom, *Religious History*, 240–1.

what are now Montgomery, Berks, Bucks, Lehigh, Northampton, Chester, and Lancaster counties. In 1712 there were an estimated two hundred Mennonites in the area; in 1770 there were perhaps only twenty-five members remaining in Germantown. Involved neither in political affairs nor in evangelistic mission work, and with little new immigration from these groups in Europe, the sect saw little growth between 1760 and 1790. The Mennonites moved west and into the Shenandoah Valley throughout the century, with one group going as far south as North Carolina.[49]

Followers of Mennonite Jacob Amman, from Berne, Switzerland, appeared first in the colonies in 1727, settling in Lancaster and Berks counties, and continued in increasing numbers through the 1740s. These Mennonites, called Amish, were stricter in practice than others, refusing to build meetinghouses or any church organization, whereas the less radical Mennonites engaged in practices of affiliation. Mennonites were linked with Quakers through social issues such as a stance against slavery and warfare. As a result of maintaining their outsider status, they were sometimes imprisoned and subject to mob violence.[50]

EPHRATA CLOISTER

The monastic and celibate Ephrata Cloister was led by Johann Conrad Beissel (1691–1768), who was influenced by English Seventh-Day Baptists as well as by German Anabaptist and Pietist groups. Formally known as Der Lager der Einsamen, or Camp of the Solitaries, the name emphasized each member's celibate and hermitic qualities as well as the community's separation from the world. Also recognized as "Besselianer" or "Beisselites" and "Siebentäger" or "Sabbatarians," the sect is known for their music and hymnals, *fraktur* (illuminated manuscripts), architecture, and prodigious printing on one of the colonies' earliest presses. The group flourished from about 1730 to 1770, with a peak of "about three to five hundred members and associates at mid-century." It consisted of celibate orders of both men and women as well as an order of married couples, called "householders." Distinguishing the sect from its neighbors was its emphasis on union with God, a sensual experience that occurred only through penitence and self-denial, often reflected in community art as pairs of turtledoves.[51]

As with other sectarian communities, the founder's early personal experiences seem to have prompted his religious searching, and Beissel's charisma

---

[49] *Ibid.*, 233; Henry C. Smith, *The Story of the Mennonites*, 3rd ed. (Newton, KS, 1950), 529–36, 539, 547.
[50] *Ibid.*, 547–52, 558; Longenecker, *Shenandoah Religion*, 31–43.
[51] Jeff Bach, *Voices of the Turtledoves: The Sacred World of Ephrata* (University Park, PA, 2004), 4.

attracted many followers. A life of poverty as an orphan in war-torn and religiously divided Germany led to his arrival in the colonies in 1720, along with many other Germans and Swiss seeking better economic conditions. Moving from Boston to Philadelphia to Germantown, Beissel settled in an area that included numerous dissenting groups. According to the accounts of his followers, including the history *Chronicon Ephrantense* (1786), he was selected in 1724 as a leader from among the Dunkers with whom he had been meeting.[52] In 1728 he led away a following, and in 1732 he tried to separate himself to live alone. His followers would not allow his isolation, however, and joined him to establish the community. Two teachings distinguished Beissel: Saturday was to be recognized as the Sabbath and celibacy as "superior to marriage." Beissel's personal readings and interpretations fed his beliefs, which he readily shared with others, and he drew support from a variety of sectarian communities and recent immigrants.[53]

Ephrata's practice of celibacy and belief in mystical union with the divine influenced gender roles within the community and appears in its writings. God was seen as androgynous, with Jesus Christ and the spirit Sophia, respectively, seen as male and female elements of the divine. Adam's fall was a division of the divine into the human male and female forms. Male members of the cloister feminized or emasculated themselves through celibacy, preparing themselves for union with the male Christ. Female members, through celibacy, became more masculine, in preparation for union with Sophia, or divine wisdom. The goal for both males and females was mystical union that would return them to divine androgyny. The emphasis on celibacy as superior created an ongoing tension among householders, who refused celibacy, and the more monastic male and female orders.[54]

As in other sectarian groups, Beissel's strong beliefs won him enemies as well as followers. Those closely associated with the group were the most bitter. For example, one internal struggle arose with Ezechial (Georg Heinrich) Sangmeister, a householder who had arrived at Ephrata in 1748. Disagreements centered on decisions regarding the cloister's successful economic ventures, such as their mills, and their daily spiritual rituals, which were thought to be in conflict with the industry. Sangmeister left dissatisfied in 1752, and he established a community in the Shenandoah Valley of Virginia. Many of his followers returned to Ephrata in 1764 because of resistance from locals in the area where they had settled. As Sangmeister presented his life story and his views of theology and praxis at Ephrata in *Leben*

---

[52] *Ibid.*, 17, 4, 30–1.
[53] *Ibid.*, 19, 30–1, 17.
[54] *Ibid.*, 97–114.

und Wandel (1825–26) and *Mystische Theologie* (1820), he accused Beissel of "sexual affairs and financial chicanery." Additional conflicts erupted in the sect's later years "over Beissel's successor" and over property rights. When Beissel died in 1768, Peter Miller became the next "superintendent." The battle over property was not so quickly resolved. It centered on Samuel Eckerlin, a follower of Sangmeister, who contested the community for ownership on returning from Virginia in 1764. The celibates eventually all passed away (1813), and the householders continued in the community, reorganized in 1814 as the German Seventh-Day Baptist Church.[55]

CONCLUSION

The Ephrata Cloister provides a microcosm of the German- and English-speaking sectarian communities in the British colonies between 1730 and 1790. One seeker, emboldened by revivalism in the region, shared his vision of divine will with those around. From a group of immigrants who were drawn together for sociological and theological reasons, a sectarian community emerged. Surrounded by others who differed from them, the community flourished for several decades, but not without trials and struggles about daily life and higher ideals. Following the passing of the first leader, the community was forced into transitions, making decisions that determined their outsider status in the decades to come.

SUGGESTIONS FOR FURTHER READING

Bestor, Arthur E. *Backwoods Utopias: The Sectarian and Owenite Phases of Communitarian Socialism in America, 1663–1829*. Philadelphia, 1950.

Garrett, Clarke. *Spirit Possession and Popular Religion: From the Camisards to the Shakers*. Baltimore, 1989.

Kanter, Rosabeth Moss. *Commitment and Community: Communes and Utopias in Sociological Perspective*. Cambridge, MA, 1972.

Longenecker, Stephen L. *Shenandoah Religion: Outsiders and the Mainstream, 1716–1865*. Waco, 2002.

Marini, Stephen. *Radical Sects of Revolutionary New England*. Cambridge, MA, 1982.

Pestana, Carla Gardina. *Quakers and Baptists in Colonial Massachusetts*. New York, 1991.

Schwartz, Sally. *"A Mixed Multitude": The Struggle for Toleration in Colonial Pennsylvania*. New York, 1987.

Wilson, Bryan R. *Religious Sects*. New York, 1970.

---

[55] *Ibid.*, 61, 193.

24

LIBERAL RELIGIOUS MOVEMENTS AND THE ENLIGHTENMENT

LEIGH E. SCHMIDT

Liberal religion, as a discernible movement, was far more a product of the nineteenth century than of the seventeenth and eighteenth centuries. "Liberalism," like "secularism," was a coinage of the nineteenth century, and the first group, the Unitarians, to self-describe as liberal Christians only took denominational shape in the 1820s and 1830s. Even in the case of the Unitarians, the label of "liberal Christian" was first pinned on them as a tag to mark their departure from the soundness of Calvinist orthodoxy, not as a proud party badge. Only in 1815 did William Ellery Channing formally embrace the appellation as an indicator of the Christian charity, broad-mindedness, and creedal flexibility – the disposition toward liberality – that he thought typified the nascent Unitarian movement.[1] This essay, with British America its primary purview, necessarily details the background, not the foreground, of religious liberalism. It explores the intellectual and political frameworks out of which full-blown liberal religious movements and organizations – from Unitarianism to Reform Judaism to the Ethical Culture Society – subsequently emerged. It highlights the theological, political, cosmopolitan, and colonial roots of religious liberalism: the advent of deism and universalism, the development of church-state separation, and the process of liberal self-definition through conflict with religious opponents and through growing knowledge of the world's manifold religions.

DEISM AND ENLIGHTENMENT THEOLOGY

In matters of religion the Enlightenment represented many things and covered a broad spectrum from moderate Christian reasonableness (whether that

---

[1] William Ellery Channing, *A Letter to the Rev. Samuel C. Thacher on the Aspersions Contained in a Late Number of the Panoplist, on the Ministers of Boston and the Vicinity* (Boston, 1815), 32–3. Channing has in this sermon a two-page appended note explaining his use of the liberal epithet. In turn, "Liberal Christian" was used as the title for a Unitarian periodical that began publication in Jan. 1823.

of John Locke or Benjamin Rush) to out-and-out Freethinking suspicion (whether that of David Hume or Thomas Paine). There were few common denominators across this wide swathe of inquirers, but there were certainly shared conversations and preoccupations, many of them deeply theological. Much of that learned exchange was a debate about the implications of deism, a reconstruction of God as rational architect rather than engaged creator, redeemer, and revealer.

Deism was already disturbing the English theological world of the 1690s, evident in the notoriety of Charles Blount's *The Oracles of Reason* (1693) and John Toland's *Christianity Not Mysterious: Or, a Treatise Shewing that There Is Nothing in the Gospel Contrary to Reason, nor Above It* (1696). Forty years later, a steady downpour of deistic tracts had effectively flooded the Church of England with controversy on everything from miracles to prophecy to Christ's divinity. The freshet included such works as Matthew Tindal's *Christianity as Old as Creation: Or, the Gospel a Republication of the Religion of Nature* (1730) and Thomas Chubb's *Discourse Concerning Reason, with Regard to Religion and Divine Revelation* (1731).[2] By then, too, the deist controversy had spread to the continent where, for example, Voltaire's *Philosophical Letters* (1734) explicitly joined the English ferment to the cause of the French Enlightenment. Over the next two generations deism would become a critical form of learned speculation among America's Revolutionary Founders, including Benjamin Franklin, Thomas Jefferson, James Madison, and John Adams. It would also have homegrown Yankee embodiments such as Ethan Allen's *Reason the Only Oracle of Man* (1784), which paid homage to Charles Blount's work and offered a virtual compendium of English deist attacks on biblical errors and Christian falsehoods. Deist militancy reached its quintessentially distilled form in Tom Paine's *Age of Reason* (1794–96), a work written in the shadow of the French Revolution but aimed too at his previously rapt audience of American Patriots. The Connecticut deist Joel Barlow served as Paine's trusted emissary in getting the first part of his incendiary manuscript into print.

Deism hardly constituted a large-scale movement in England, let alone in early America. A Deistical Society, for instance, was organized in New York City in the 1790s, and that group served as the primary constituency for a short-lived weekly called *The Temple of Reason*, which began circulating

---

[2] The literature on deism in England is extensive. For a recent account that emphasizes its diverse strands – deisms over deism – while at the same time taking stock of the current historiography, see Wayne Hudson, *The English Deists: Studies in Early Enlightenment* (London, 2009). See also J. A. I. Champion, *The Pillars of Priestcraft Shaken: The Church of England and Its Enemies, 1660–1730* (Cambridge, UK, 1992), and Robert E. Sullivan, *John Toland and the Deist Controversy: A Study in Adaptations* (Cambridge, MA, 1982).

after Jefferson's election in 1800. Deism also found a potential network through the burgeoning fraternalism of the eighteenth century. The gentlemanly lodges of Freemasonry regularly served as religious alternatives to Christian orthodoxy – ritualistic refuges that were sometimes occult, sometimes deistic, and often both. The lodge as Freethinking retreat was explicitly the case with one group in Newburgh, New York, that briefly mutated (from 1799 to 1804) into an infidel club known as the Society of Ancient Druids. The isolated peculiarity of the Newburgh example, though, makes evident that "organized deism" rarely took adequate measure of the movement.[3] Instead, the better gauge was how widely dispersed and intensely felt deism's theological critiques of Christian orthodoxy became in the Enlightenment's transatlantic republic of letters. Deism put Christian theologians and preachers on defensive watch and deeply affected the tenor of their apologia. As the resolute Congregational minister Lyman Beecher lamented of his late eighteenth-century youth at Yale, he had grown up in "the day of the infidelity of the Tom Paine school." It was a sorry age – with "a leaven of skepticism all over the world" – and he felt compelled to be on constant guard against that faithlessness.[4]

Deism, as the very name suggests, started with a reconceptualization of God. As supreme creator, God set the world in motion, but that carefully ordered creation hardly required the divinity's continued tinkering. "The Almighty is the great mechanic of the creation, the first philosopher and original teacher of all science," Paine remarked in fine deist fashion. God was not a revealer of biblical scriptures who commanded worship or obedience, but an "Almighty Lecturer" who demonstrated "the principles of science in the structure of the universe" and who invited humanity to study that natural order.[5] Such deistic propositions about God's designs – that

---

[3] For discussion of "organized deism," see G. Adolf Koch, *Religion of the American Enlightenment* (New York, 1968), 74–129. On deistic organizing, see also Herbert M. Morais, *Deism in Eighteenth-Century America* (New York, 1934); on Freemasonry, see Steven C. Bullock, *Revolutionary Brotherhood: Freemasonry and the Transformation of the American Social Order, 1730–1840* (Chapel Hill, 1996); and, on both deists and Freemasons together, see J. A. Leo Lemay, ed., *Deism, Masonry, and the Enlightenment* (Newark, 1987), and Margaret C. Jacob, *The Radical Enlightenment: Pantheists, Freemasons, and Republicans* (London, 1981). For a very helpful compendium and set of commentaries, see Kerry S. Walters, ed., *The American Deists: Voices of Reason and Dissent in the Early Republic* (Lawrence, KS, 1992).

[4] Lyman Beecher, *Autobiography, Correspondence, etc., of Lyman Beecher, D.D.*, ed. Charles Beecher, 2 vols. (New York, 1866), 1: 43, 100. Brooks Holifield makes a good case for the disproportionate impact of deism on Christian theology of the period in his *Theology in America: Christian Thought from the Age of the Puritans to the Civil War* (New Haven, 2003), 159–72.

[5] Thomas Paine, *The Age of Reason*, ed. Philip S. Foner (Secaucus, 1998), 76, 89.

the Creation was like clockwork and that the pursuit of natural philosophy was the primary way to reverence the divine – were often advanced without Paine's axe-in-hand attack on Christian revelation. In order to allow liberal religious reflection to flourish, this was always a first order of business: to make God compatible with – if not reducible to – the advancement of Enlightenment learning. The Great Architect that deism imagined served that purpose well.

In making God more remote and less communicative, deists tried to foreclose a piety of deep affections and dramatic experiences and cultivate instead a religion of civic virtue and moral benevolence. They disdained the excesses of religious feeling, the overboard enthusiasm associated with troublesome upstarts from the Quakers and French Prophets to the evangelical revivalists of the 1730s and 1740s. As a counterweight, they embraced the secular vocabulary of civic virtue and liberal benevolence, disjoining humanity's moral capacities from Christian notions of regeneration and sanctification. "I believe that religious duties consist in doing justice, loving mercy, and endeavoring to make our fellow creatures happy," Paine explained with typical trenchancy.[6] He then went on to be clear about what that meant he did not believe in: original sin, human depravity, and all those other Christian doctrinal formulations that seemed to demean humanity as worms, beggars, or outlaws. John Adams put his alienation from such doctrines more temperately, but he made just as clear his rejection: "I have read many of the Calvinistical Treatises on original sin and they have not convinced me of the total Depravity of human Nature. They go further than to say that human nature is destitute of benevolence. They say it is positively malevolent, altogether malicious and malignant. *Je n'en crois rien*."[7] To render this theological disposition into Franklinesque aphorism: Deists believed in good deeds, not bad seeds, and in civic virtues, not sudden conversions.

Not surprisingly, given how little respect deists showed for Calvinist anthropology, they were not keen on Christian eschatology either, particularly notions of hell and the last judgment. They drastically reworked the afterlife, usually retaining a general sense of future rewards and punishments as well as the immortality of the soul, but with eternal damnation and bodily resurrection nowhere in sight. Any rewards, and they remained nebulous, were to be meted out based on the embodiment of humanistic virtues, not as an outgrowth of justifying faith or sovereign decree. Deists held to this thinned-out afterlife sometimes out of a confrontation

---

[6] *Ibid.*, 50.
[7] "I believe none of it." John Adams to Francis van der Kemp, 9 Mar. 1806, in James H. Hutson, ed., *The Founders on Religion* (Princeton, 2005), 200.

with a more despairing skepticism. As John Adams remarked in a letter to Thomas Jefferson, "I believe in God and in his Wisdom and Benevolence: and I cannot conceive that such a Being could make such a Species as the human merely to live and die on this Earth." Without a belief in "a future State," he thought the universe – in "all its swelling Pomp" – would be no better than "a boyish Fire Work."[8] The nihilistic specter did not necessarily haunt the deists' rather tenuous hold on future rewards and punishments. Sometimes the doctrine was maintained on strictly utilitarian grounds – a necessary incentive for the faint and feeble to practice virtue and avoid vice. Franklin and Jefferson both explored this line of argument, even as they continued to harbor hopes for the continued pursuit of happiness in the hereafter.

Deistic revisions of the afterlife were indicative of much wider reconsiderations of heaven and hell, particularly an assessment of how the latter comported with a liberal sense of divine benevolence: What kind of God, after all, would damn even notorious sinners, let alone virtuous pagans, to an eternity of hellfire? Such theological concerns took root right in the heart of Congregational New England as part of the endemic wrangling over that region's Puritan inheritance. The sounds of cracking were heard around one doctrine after another – from original sin to justification by faith alone – but perhaps nowhere more so than around eternal damnation and limited atonement. The most notorious sign of this was Charles Chauncy's closely guarded manuscript on universal salvation, which he finally saw fit to publish anonymously near the very end of his life, *The Mystery Hid from Ages and Generations, Made Manifest by the Gospel Revelation* (1784).[9] Chauncy's foray into universalism became especially infamous because it issued from the pen of a venerable worthy of the standing order, but others had already moved on to the harvest. John Murray, an English itinerant preacher, had none of Chauncy's caution in spreading universalism's good news. After arriving in New Jersey in 1770, he preached widely in the colonies before helping establish the first independent Universalist congregation in Gloucester, Massachusetts, in 1779. Murrayites and Universalists soon became synonyms for the wholesale expansion of the Christian order of salvation. By the 1790s, Murray's excoriated sect was showing signs

---

[8] John Adams to Thomas Jefferson, 8 Dec. 1818, in Lester J. Cappon, ed., *The Adams-Jefferson Letters* (Chapel Hill, 1959), 530.

[9] On Chauncy's work as part of the long prologue to the Unitarian controversy, see Conrad Wright, *The Beginnings of Unitarianism in America* (Boston, 1955), 185–99. For a complementary history of American Unitarian origins, one that effectively refocuses attention on English Unitarian roots, made notable through Joseph Priestley's arrival in Pennsylvania in 1794, see J. D. Bowers, *Joseph Priestley and English Unitarianism in America* (University Park, PA, 2007).

of denominational coalescence, a full generation ahead of William Ellery Channing's Baltimore manifesto on Unitarian Christianity in 1819 and the founding of the American Unitarian Association in 1825.[10] On most points, Chauncy and Murray remained far removed from deism, but on the questions of universalism and the afterlife they were part of a wider public debate about the divine wisdom and benevolence of an eschatological scheme that included eternal damnation and selective salvation.

Most Enlightenment apostles thought that orthodox Christianity had an unduly low estimate of human capacities and that this had for too long impeded the progress of knowledge and the flourishing of civil society. Many of those same apostles, though, would not have made the next leap with the radical deists – that the churches had inflated Jesus' divinity through cunning and ignorance. Perfecting human nature was one thing, diminishing Jesus' nature quite another. Deists grandly reopened, often with bravado, the ancient Trinitarian and Christological controversies and reaped the whirlwind of the old heretical epithets – Arianism and Socinianism. In 1791 Elihu Palmer, a Presbyterian minister turned deist renegade, announced a lecture in Philadelphia at a local Universalist congregation attacking Christ's divinity, only to have a mob collect to run him out of the city. Perhaps the rabble knew what it was doing, because Palmer went further than most other deists in indicting the "moral merit" and "good character" of Jesus right alongside those other two notorious "imposters," Moses and Muhammad.[11]

Knowing the scandal involved in openly questioning Jesus' divine credentials, Thomas Jefferson was far more circumspect than Palmer and tried to keep his own Christological reflections close to his chest. Within the privacy of his own study, though, he was radically contrarian in his Socinian understanding of Jesus as a moral instructor rather than the incarnation of a triune God. Influenced especially by the English Unitarian and natural philosopher Joseph Priestley, Jefferson wanted to distill the philosophical and ethical principles of Jesus apart from the doctrinal myths with which the Christian church had surrounded him. To that end, Jefferson gathered up a set of New Testaments in Greek, Latin, French, and English; he then literally cut away the scriptural verses that he thought wrongly

---

[10] For these denominational streams, see David Robinson, *The Unitarians and Universalists* (Westport, 1985); Ann Lee Bressler, *The Universalist Movement in America, 1770–1880* (New York, 2001); and Conrad Wright, ed., *A Stream of Light: A Short History of American Unitarianism* (Boston, 1975).

[11] On the Philadelphia incident, see Henry F. May, *The Enlightenment in America* (New York, 1976), 231; on Palmer's view of the three imposters, a trope with deep roots in the most radical strains of Freethought, see Kerry S. Walters, ed., *Elihu Palmer's "Principles of Nature": Text and Commentary* (Wolfeboro, NH, 1990), 231–2.

mystified Jesus. The last verse in Jefferson's scissored New Testament was this: "There laid they Jesus, and rolled a great stone to the door of the sepulcher, and departed."[12] In that sepulchral ending, Jefferson effectively underlined the deistic view of Jesus' nature. The Resurrection itself became one of the defects of Christian theology, a distraction from Jesus as great moral teacher, the exemplar of philosophical insight and sound judgment.

As the clandestine quality of Jefferson's project of biblical extraction makes evident, deists worked under the threat of clerical reprisal for their heterodoxy. Intent on creating the intellectual space for theological autonomy, they often flared with anticlerical invective: there was hardly a greater bugbear than "priestcraft" among deistic critics of Christian ecclesiology. "Let the human mind loose," John Adams proclaimed in a letter to his son John Quincy Adams. "It must be loose. It will be loose. Superstition and Dogmatism cannot confine it."[13] If this debate about the tyranny of religious authority was carried out with high public visibility and volubility, it was also evident that many among the enlightened preferred a private resolution to the question: namely, a view of religion as strictly a matter of individual conscience, not Christian community. As Paine declared, "I do not believe in the creed professed by the Jewish Church, by the Roman Church, by the Greek Church, by the Turkish Church, by the Protestant Church, nor by any church that I know of. My own mind is my own church." To allow room for their theological denials, for the open expression of their disbelief, and for mental freedom, deists frequently argued, often vehemently, that state churches would have to be dismantled. "All national institutions of churches," Paine concluded, "whether Jewish, Christian, or Turkish, appear to me no other than human inventions, set up to terrify and enslave mankind, and monopolize power and profit."[14] In other words, deism's theological dissent from Christian orthodoxy became entwined with a revolutionary political program for reconfiguring the relationship between religion and the state.

CHURCH-STATE SEPARATION

Religious freedom is a sine qua non of liberal religion and liberal politics. When liberalism became a self-conscious platform in the second half of the

---

[12] Dickinson W. Adams, ed., *Jefferson's Extracts from the Gospels* (Princeton, 1983), 297.
[13] John Adams quoted in Edwin S. Gaustad, *Faith of Our Fathers: Religion and the New Nation* (San Francisco, 1987), 88. Gaustad's volume remains an excellent introduction to the religious views of the Founders, but see also David L. Holmes, *The Faiths of the Founding Fathers* (New York, 2006), and Frank Lambert, *The Founding Fathers and the Place of Religion in America* (Princeton, 2003).
[14] Paine, *Age of Reason*, 50.

nineteenth century through the National Liberal League and the American Secular Union, its most visible demands were for stricter church-state separation. That included the elimination of state-supported chaplaincies, Bible reading in the public schools, and tax exemptions on church property, as well as publicly proclaimed days of fasting and thanksgiving. This animating liberal impulse – combating state-established religion as a dangerous tyranny – was grounded in the political and religious developments of the seventeenth and eighteenth centuries. The historical matrices of religious toleration, church disestablishment, and liberty of conscience were absolutely crucial for the subsequent emergence of more codified forms of liberal religion.

"Congress shall make no law respecting an establishment of religion or prohibiting the free exercise thereof." After more than two centuries the very familiarity of this clause in the First Amendment may well have dulled the immediacy of its revolutionary significance, and yet it remains a stunning formulation of bedrock liberal principles about law, governance, and religious freedom. Not that this grand experiment with disestablishment and free exercise owed everything to Jefferson, Madison, and their Enlightenment brethren. Certainly, the prominence of radical Protestantism in the colonial American landscape served as much as a precedent for this formulation as did the precursory reflections of independent Whigs such as Thomas Gordon and John Trenchard in their various essays of the 1720s on religious and civil liberty. Roger Williams had turned Rhode Island into a cauldron of riffraff religious diversity in the seventeenth century, a refuge of tolerance for separatist dissenters who proved intolerable to the rest of New England's Puritan commonwealth. Likewise, William Penn imagined his holy experiment as a colonial outpost where faith, worship, and conscience were set free from state infringement. That Paine's radical anticlericalism drew on resources in his own Quaker background was more than incidental. The liberty of conscience commonly championed among separatist Protestants permeated the air that the subsequent political founders breathed. Madison himself readily acknowledged that "the American Theatre" had already exhibited the benefits of according equal rights to competing sects; whereas "torrents of blood had been spilt in the old world" in efforts to enforce religious uniformity, a remedy had been found (in a tiny handful of American colonies) in the "equal and compleat liberty" of Protestant dissenters.[15]

---

[15] James Madison, "Memorial and Remonstrance," 1785, reprinted as an appendix in Gaustad, *Faith of Our Fathers*, 142–9, at 146. On the dissenting Protestant impact on church-state relations, see, for example, Edwin S. Gaustad, *Liberty of Conscience: Roger Williams in America* (Grand Rapids, 1991); J. William Frost, *A Perfect Freedom: Religious*

The actual formulation of these principles in the nation's founding documents was in the hands not of Baptist separatists or Quaker spiritists, but of those deeply shaped in the classical Enlightenment theorizing of rights and liberties. In 1785 and 1786 Jefferson and Madison foreshadowed the First Amendment in leading the campaign for the formal disestablishment of the Anglican Church in Virginia, which, along with South Carolina, was one of the colonial strongholds of the Church of England. Virginia's "Statute for Establishing Religious Freedom," first penned by Jefferson in 1777 and finally passed in 1786, crystallized the Enlightenment commitment to religious liberty as an unalienable right and sharply curtailed the power of the civil magistrate to interfere with religious ideas. The legal substance of this enactment came in two parts, the first affirming the freedom from religious coercion and the second hailing the freedom for religious expression:

> That no man shall be compelled to frequent or support any religious worship, place, or ministry whatsoever, nor shall be enforced, restrained, molested, or burthened in his body or goods, nor shall otherwise suffer on account of his religious opinions or belief; but that all men shall be free to profess, and by argument to maintain, their opinion in matters of religion, and that the same shall in no wise diminish, enlarge, or affect their civil capacities.[16]

These dual principles of religious freedom – disestablishment and free exercise – were anything but transparent in application and practice. True, Madison and Jefferson sometimes made it sound as if the separation of religion from politics was perfectly clear. "Religion," Madison explained in 1785, "is wholly exempt" from the "cognizance" of civil authorities and legislative bodies. Both Madison and Jefferson were fully convinced of the demonstrated evils of ecclesiastical establishments and rejected the long-standing proposition that the functioning of any government depended on harnessing religion as "an engine of Civil policy."[17] Madison was unambiguous even on the point of federal chaplaincies in the military and in Congress. "Is the appointment of Chaplains to the two Houses of Congress consistent with the Constitution, and with the principles of religious freedom?" he asked. "In strictness the answer to both points must be in the negative." Such state-appointed chaplains inevitably favored one sect above another and allowed the larger religious groups to lord their authority over smaller ones. These common arrangements, in short, were "a palpable violation of equal rights, as well as Constitutional principles."[18]

Liberty in Pennsylvania (New York, 1990); and William Lee Miller, *The First Liberty: America's Foundation in Religious Freedom* (Washington, DC, 2003).

[16] Jefferson's statute is reprinted as an appendix in Gaustad, *Faith of Our Fathers*, 149–51.
[17] Madison, "Memorial and Remonstrance," in Gaustad, *Faith of Our Fathers*, 142–4.
[18] Hutson, *Founders on Religion*, 46–7.

Most Americans, though, lacked such thoroughgoing clarity on the separation of church and state, continuing to favor a more interactive and mutually supportive relationship between Protestant Christianity and republican political institutions. That tenor was set by moderate Christian intellectuals such as Samuel Stanhope Smith at Princeton and physician Benjamin Rush in Philadelphia, those who considered it crucial to anchor the commitment to religious liberty in the underlying codes of Protestant morality as well as the disciplines of Baconian natural philosophy. Historian Henry May has seen this American trajectory as the triumph of a Didactic Enlightenment, whereas historian Mark Noll has depicted it as the victory of a Republican Christian Enlightenment.[19] Whatever the label given this synthesizing impulse, it quickly became evident that religion was not exempt from the cognizance of civil society. Indeed, religious liberty would be closely monitored in order to ensure that Protestant Christianity continued to undergird the American republic and its sound government. Whether through the promulgation of Sabbath laws, the regulation of popular entertainments, the content of public prayers, or the defense of marital norms, Protestant Christianity sought to prevent American liberty from slipping into license.

The continued prosecution of blasphemy, as historian Sarah Barringer Gordon has shown, is a good case in point. When John Ruggles, for example, let fly the insult "*Jesus Christ* was a bastard, and his mother must be a whore," he was hauled before New York's Court of Appeals in 1811. In England, with its Anglican establishment, the common law had long protected Christianity from such ridicule and treated such slanderous religious speech as an enemy of public peace and morals. Ruggles and his lawyer argued that Christianity's federal disestablishment, along with New York's explicit toleration of all religions in its state constitution, made it unacceptable to protect any one faith from such verbal offenses. That proved an utterly ineffective argument, because it was plain, as the judge in the case concluded, that "we are a Christian people, and the morality of the country is deeply engrafted upon Christianity." Free discussion of religion was protected, but not when such debate turned indecent, obscene, and contemptuous – not, in short, when it degenerated into blasphemy. At issue was not simply foul-mouthed cursing, but the right of seething Freethinkers, in the mold of Tom Paine, to give vent to their anti-Christian mockery.

---

[19] See May, *Enlightenment in America*, 307–62; Mark A. Noll, *Princeton and the Republic, 1768–1822* (Princeton, 1989), esp. 185–213; and Mark A. Noll, *America's God: From Jonathan Edwards to Abraham Lincoln* (New York, 2002), esp. 11–13, 94–5, 210–16. For a good example of a temperate Christian version of the American Enlightenment, see John Fea, *The Way of Improvement Leads Home: Philip Vickers Fithian and the Rural Enlightenment in America* (Philadelphia, 2008), esp. 41–2, 212–15.

Only a few in the Revolution's wake thought that church-state separation required tolerating the licentiousness of Freethinkers, deists, and infidels. Christian moral restraints were widely seen as crucial for the fragile republic's very survival, and the courts often rallied to protect the commonweal from such corrosive opinions. At the end of his life Jefferson was simply left shaking his head at how much of the new nation's jurisprudence had come to assume that a common-law Christianity was integral to civil society.[20]

John Adams, too, wondered at the incongruity of American legislators and judges perpetuating these Old World laws on blasphemy. "We think ourselves possessed or at least we boast that we are so of Liberty of conscience on all subjects and of the right of free inquiry and private judgment in all cases," he wrote Jefferson in 1825, "and yet how far are we from these exalted privileges in fact." In most countries of Europe, he lamented, it was still considered blasphemous to question the divine inspiration of any of "the books of the old and new Testaments from Genesis to Revelation." In the United States nobody's tongue was going to be bored through with a red-hot poker for such offenses, he admitted, but it was still "not much better," with fines and imprisonment having taken the place of crueler punishments. For Adams, a scholarly savant, the charge of blasphemy had chilling effects not only on boisterous drunkards like John Ruggles, but also on the whole enterprise of the rational study of religion. "What free inquiry when a writer must surely encounter the risk of fine or imprisonment for adducing any argument for investigation of the divine authority of [the Bible]?" Adams queried, then going on to suggest specific works of the French Enlightenment likely to be impeded. "Who would run the risk of translating [Comte de] Volney's *Recherches Nouvelles?*" he wondered. "Who would run the risk of translating [Charles] Dupuis?"[21] When John Stuart Mill published *On Liberty* (1859), the canonical tract of nineteenth-century liberal political theory, a prominent subtext remained the ways in which freedom of thought, discussion, and speech were limited – legally and socially – for those who scoffed at Christianity or who wanted to examine its foundations critically.[22] Long after the American pronouncement of disestablishment and free expression, blasphemy shadowed liberalism, but that very inhibition also proved crucial to galvanizing some of the most forceful defenses of religious and civil liberties.

---

[20] This paragraph relies on Sarah Barringer Gordon, "Blasphemy and the Law of Religious Liberty in Nineteenth-Century America," *American Quarterly* 52 (Dec. 2000): 682–719, with quotations on pp. 682, 685.

[21] John Adams to Thomas Jefferson, 23 Jan. 1825, in Cappon, *Adams-Jefferson Letters*, 607–8.

[22] See Joseph Hamburger, "Religion and *On Liberty*," in Michael Laine, ed., *A Cultivated Mind: Essays on J. S. Mill* (Toronto, 1991), 139–81.

If Freethinkers and unbelievers were often viewed as being on unequal footing with upstanding Christians, particularly of the Protestant variety, so too were Roman Catholics. Associated in the Anglo-American imagination with popish tyranny and Jesuit treachery, they were regularly viewed with extreme wariness. Was the very presence of the Catholic Church on American soil, Protestants recurrently asked, a danger to hard-won liberties? These deep intra-Christian antagonisms occasioned fierce church-state battles over the next two centuries, particularly evident in innumerable fights over parochial and public schools. Catholic acceptance was often grudging in the face of Protestant privilege, and that hesitancy and hostility shadowed the debates about religious toleration during the Revolution and long afterward. Several of the early state constitutions retained explicit Protestant tests for full participation in civil society. As New Jersey framed its constitutional standard in 1776, "No Protestant inhabitant of this Colony shall be denied the enjoyment of any civil right, merely on account of his religious principles."[23]

The still more groundbreaking challenge during the Revolutionary era involved the rights and liberties of Jews as religious believers and fellow citizens. Had the First Amendment been intended only as a way of moderating Christian rivalries and preventing one form of Christianity from gaining sole governmental favor? Or did the principle of free exercise extend beyond the Christian religion itself and place other religions on the same legal footing? With Freethinkers and infidels largely ruled out of bounds, American Jews proved singularly well positioned to test whether religious liberty and equality reached beyond Christianity.

In the American colonies Jewish immigrants had faced various forms of religious and political disadvantage – from laws protecting the Christian Sabbath to Trinitarian requirements for holding political office to Christian oath-taking in the courts. The dramatic reconfiguration of church-state relations imagined in the Constitution and the Bill of Rights did not erase those burdens overnight, but it nonetheless represented a seachange. It tendered, on Enlightenment terms, an offer of full citizenship and religious freedom after centuries of ghettoization in Europe. To be sure, at the state level, these federal principles were not uniformly embraced or enforced: Pennsylvania, for example, had initially preserved a Christian test for public office, only to shift the rule to a more generic theism – a belief in God as well as future rewards and punishments – after Philadelphia Jews petitioned the legislature for a less exclusive formula. As the petitioners noted,

---

[23] For the early state constitutions, including those with Protestant religious tests (Georgia, New Jersey, North Carolina, and South Carolina), see Gaustad, *Faith of Our Fathers*, 159–74. The quotation is on p. 168.

the Christian test (which required affirmation of the divine inspiration of the New Testament) "deprived the Jews of the most eminent rights of freemen, solemnly ascertained to all men who are not professed Atheists." Not surprisingly, the safest approach to claiming full religious liberty was not to celebrate the creation of a secular state, but to join an alliance of godly believers against dissolute unbelievers in maintaining the public virtues necessary for the well-being of the republic.[24]

Although a tiny minority – only about two thousand in a population of more than three million during the founding period – a number of American Jews nonetheless made clear their community's desire to fulfill the opportunities of the Revolutionary moment. Jonas Phillips, one of the leaders in Philadelphia's Jewish community, appealed for full religious liberty out of a sense of dedicated patriotism: "It is well known among all the Citizens of the 13 united states that the Jews have been true and faithful whigs, & during the late Contest with England they have been foremost in aiding and assisting the states with their lifes & fortunes, they have supported the cause, have bravely fought and bled for liberty which they can not Enjoy." Would the new government have the courage to follow its convictions about liberty and equality to their logical conclusion – with respect to Jews, and also, the same question was asked by others at the time, with respect to African Americans and women? "The Israelites," Phillips concluded, "will think themself happy to live under a government where all religious societies are on an Equal footing." Likewise, when the Jewish community of Newport, Rhode Island, sent a letter of welcome to George Washington as the nation's first President, the community highlighted the new "blessings of civil and religious liberty" the American republic afforded.

> Deprived as we hitherto have been of the invaluable rights of free citizens, we now – with a deep sense of gratitude to the Almighty Disposer of all events – behold a government which to bigotry gives no sanction, to persecution no assistance, but generously affording to all liberty of conscience and immunities of citizenship, deeming every one of whatever nation, tongue, or language, equal parts of the great governmental machine.[25]

Washington replied to this letter from Newport's Hebrew congregation with a warm endorsement of the community's sentiments. He claimed that

---

[24] For excellent analysis of the issues as well as a superb compendium of the relevant documents, see Jonathan D. Sarna and David G. Dalin, eds., *Religion and State in the American Jewish Experience* (South Bend, 1997). The cited petition is reprinted on pp. 70–2. See also Morton Borden, *Jews, Turks, and Infidels* (Chapel Hill, 1984).

[25] Jonas Phillips to the Federal Constitutional Convention, 1787, and *Letter from the Hebrew Congregation of Newport to President Washington*, 1790, in Sarna and Dalin, *Religion and State*, 73, 79.

the new nation should be proud of its achievement of a constitutional order that went beyond mere toleration – as if the position of religious minorities amounted to no more than an "indulgence" on the part of the majority. "The citizens of the United States of America have a right to applaud themselves for having given to mankind examples of an enlarged and liberal policy – a policy worthy of imitation. All possess alike liberty of conscience and immunities of citizenship," the president assured. Washington's use of the word "liberal" in this context was suggestive. A liberality of spirit – to give to bigotry no sanction – was at the heart of liberalism's emergence as a full-blown religious movement.[26]

Sometimes wildly amorphous, sometimes politically sharp, that liberal disposition pushed beyond forbearance into a cosmopolitan sensibility. As Channing would explain in initially defining liberal Christianity in positive terms in 1815, "The word *liberality* expresses the noblest qualities of the human mind, freedom from local prejudices and narrow feelings, the enlargement of the views and affections." Liberals, Channing suggested, were characterized by their ability to transcend "exclusive connexion with any sect" as well as by their cultivation of a more universal sense of human brotherhood. Even so, religious fellowship was for Channing still defined in broadly Christian terms, and the drawing of that line highlighted a quintessential liberal dilemma. "What indeed is liberality, or charity," an orthodox clergyman countered, "without any boundaries?" How then were the bounds of this new Christian charitableness to be understood and specified? Was the ability to transcend sectarianism to be seen as an exclusively Unitarian trait? At what points did such Protestant liberality become particularly illiberal? Did it sometimes, for example, prove little more than the ability to treat with cavalier indifference doctrines that mattered deeply to other Christians? Instituting the nation's "liberal policy" toward religion was saddled with difficulties – among them, preventing "local prejudices and narrow feelings" from simply reappearing in the new guise of liberal Protestant universality. Church-state separation, in other words, hardly solved the problem of liberalism's own exclusions and conceits.[27]

---

[26] George Washington to Hebrew Congregation of Newport, 1790, in Sarna and Dalin, *Religion and State*, 79–80.

[27] Channing, *Letter*, 32–3; Clark Brown, *The Absurdity and Danger of that Liberality, which Looks with Complacency on All Opinions Advocated by Those Calling Themselves Christians* (Boston, 1814), 13; George Washington to Hebrew Congregation of Newport, 1790, in Sarna and Dalin, *Religion and State*, 79–80. On liberalism's exclusionary limits, particularly in its defenses of colonialism, see especially Uday Singh Mehta, *Liberalism and Empire: A Study in Nineteenth-Century British Liberal Thought* (Chicago, 1999); and Uday S. Mehta, "Liberal Strategies of Exclusion," *Politics and Society* 18 (1990): 427–54.

LIBERAL RELIGION AND RELIGIOUS OTHERS

In the founding epoch of liberal political theory John Locke anticipated the dilemmas that would arise for the espousers of toleration as they worked out their principle of "equal and impartial liberty" in the religious realm. His liberal cure for the sectarian discord that plagued early modern civil society would, he knew, leave many questions yet to settle. Toleration might begin as a mutual forbearance among Christians – "presbyterians, independents, anabaptists, Arminians, quakers, and others," all living alongside one another with "the same liberty." But then the principle, Locke realized, would have to be pressed further: "Nay, if we may openly speak the truth, ... neither pagan, nor Mahometan, nor Jew, ought to be excluded from the civil rights of the commonwealth, because of his religion." Pursuing a vision of fair and harmonious inclusion, Locke moved toward a sweeping inference: "No man whatsoever ought therefore to be deprived of his terrestrial enjoyments, upon account of his religion." Indeed, not even those indigenous peoples encountered through the colonization of North America "are to be punished ... for not embracing our faith and worship. If they are persuaded that they please God in observing the rites of their own country, and that they shall obtain happiness by that means, they are to be left unto God and themselves." Locke's liberality was apparent.[28]

Still, the terrain got more hazardous from there. What about Freethinking infidels, blasphemers, and libertines, for example? "Those are not at all to be tolerated who deny the being of God. Promises, covenants, and oaths, which are the bonds of human society, can have no hold upon an atheist. The taking away of God, though but even in thought, dissolves all," Locke warned. Likewise, it was well and good to say that citizens were free to worship as they wished if those rituals were about as orderly as the Anglican liturgy, but what about the seditious conventicles of dissenters? Locke urged as much latitude as was consistent with civil order and public peace, but still history was filled with warnings about the dangerous turns that religious assemblies could take. What about those who "lustfully pollute themselves," make human sacrifices, or harm children in religion's name? The conclusion necessarily followed of no special exemptions: "Those things that are prejudicial to the commonweal of a people in their ordinary use, and are therefore forbidden by laws, those things ought not to be permitted to churches in their sacred rites." There was the problem, too, of all those religious folks who wanted to refuse the terms of the liberal bargain altogether, namely, "those that will not own and teach the duty of tolerating all men in matters of mere religion." Was the enlightened civil

---

[28] John Locke, *A Letter Concerning Toleration* (Amherst, 1990 [1689]), 12, 49–50, 70.

magistrate required to tolerate the intolerant? Locke anticipated many instances in which the answer would have to be in the negative.[29]

Liberalism's liberality was put to the test again and again in the generations that followed Locke's influential theorizing of toleration. That was evident in how much enlightened self-definition took place through the rejection of religious enthusiasm and visionary piety. When Adams, ever curious about religion's manifold expressions, read in succession a biography of the evangelical John Wesley and another about the Swedish seer Emanuel Swedenborg, he hastily borrowed "a very rational exclamation" from his friend Jefferson, "What a bedlamite is man!" Swedenborg, converser with angels, and Wesley, field-preaching Methodist, had "vast memories and imaginations, and great talents," Adams concluded wryly, "for Lunaticks."[30] Evangelicals (and Swedenborgians, too, for that matter) were quick to explain why they were not guilty of enthusiasm – an almost entirely derogatory designation in the seventeenth and eighteenth centuries for the delusion of direct personal inspiration from the divine. Such disavowals left deists, Freethinkers, and other rationalists unconvinced; they knew an enthusiast when they saw one. Wesley and his fervent followers fit the type, and so did Swedenborg's claims to visions of heaven and communication with angels. Charles Chauncy, commonly presented as a precursor of nineteenth-century liberal Christianity for his defense of universalism, was an even more seasoned critic of enthusiasm and evangelical revivalism. Indeed, one of the most consistent markers of American liberal religion would be its disdain for evangelical ecstasies and the revivalists who fed them. To be a charitable, cosmopolitan liberal Christian meant renouncing the provincialism and censoriousness of the evangelical vernacular.[31]

Another location of elemental liberal self-definition was in the polemic over Calvinism and Congregational orthodoxy. Not to be outdone in diagnostic acumen by Adams, when Jefferson received a pamphlet attacking John Calvin and his New England avatar Samuel Hopkins, he rejoiced that "the reveries, not to say insanities of Calvin and Hopkins" had been appropriately blasted. "Mr. Locke defines a madman to be one who has a kink in his head on some particular subject, which neither reason nor fact can untangle," Jefferson elaborated. "This was the real condition of Calvin and Hopkins, on whom reasoning was wasted. The strait jacket

---

[29] *Ibid.*, 47–9, 63–4.
[30] John Adams to Thomas Jefferson, 3 Feb. 1821, in Cappon, *Adams-Jefferson Letters*, 571.
[31] On these contests over enthusiasm and religious experience during the Enlightenment and afterward, see Ann Taves, *Fits, Trances, and Visions: Experiencing Religion and Explaining Experience from Wesley to James* (Princeton, 1999); and Leigh Eric Schmidt, *Hearing Things: Religion, Illusion, and the American Enlightenment* (Cambridge, MA, 2000).

alone was the proper remedy."[32] Creating distance from unreason – in this case, Calvinism – was constitutive of an enlightened, liberal posture.

The boundary-drawing polemic on both sides was heated. As the Unitarian controversy started to rumble in New England in the first decade of the nineteenth century, the staunch Calvinist Jedidiah Morse, for example, claimed that if Harvard liberals carried the day, a new heretical religion – he called it "the Boston religion" – would put the true Christian religion in grave danger. (From Morse to John Henry Newman to J. Gresham Machen, drawing a sharp distinction between Christianity and liberalism would be crucial to delimiting orthodoxy. Liberals were *not* Christians; they were apostates.) Liberals, in turn, asserted their charitableness against that excommunicative impulse, and yet how were liberals to denounce the sectarian narrowness of orthodoxy without sacrificing their own principle of liberality – what one historian of Unitarianism proudly called "the greatest glory of the liberal spirit"? Indeed, how would liberals know they were liberals at all if they did not unashamedly bash Calvinism for everything from human depravity to infant damnation to Trinitarian mathematics to exclusionary fellowship? The liberal representation of its own generous cosmopolitanism was built on specifying a Calvinist other – indeed, on confining Reformed orthodoxy to the domain of unreason, where all those other forms of false religion resided, including enthusiasm, superstition, mysticism, quietism, priestcraft, and creedalism.[33]

Liberal religion took its initial definition from battles within Protestantism and the Enlightenment. A religion of reason, civic virtue, and progress came to know itself through neighboring others, including rapturous evangelicals and strict Calvinists. The alterity of Roman Catholicism was also quite serviceable for liberal self-definition in British America, and Catholic examples always remained near at hand as warnings about the prevalence of tyranny, imposture, credulity, and ignorance. The deistic scholar Conyers Middleton, for example, produced a frequently reprinted embodiment of that line of reasoning in *A Letter from Rome, Shewing an Exact Conformity between Popery and Paganism* (1729). Such rhetorical conventions, in turn, could be creatively combined, as in George Lavington's tract *The Enthusiasm of Methodists and Papists Compared* (1751). In the Anglo-American context the enlightened were more immediately worried about enthusiasts and Reformed scholastics than Catholic relics, images, shrines, processions, or miracles, but that did not mean deistic critics of revealed religion forgot the utility of anti-Catholic polemics. What,

---

[32] Thomas Jefferson to Thomas B. Parker, 15 May 1819, in Adams, *Jefferson's Extracts from the Gospel*, 385–6.
[33] Charles C. Forman, "Elected Now by Time," in Wright, *Stream of Light*, 10–17, 20.

for example, was the Catholic cult of the saints but a prime illustration of euhemerism, the primeval error of apotheosizing and venerating dead heroes? Enlightenment anticlericalism and Whig politics depended, time and again, on a reliably villainous image of priestcraft and superstition.[34]

In the eighteenth century most deists and reasonable Christians cared about other religions primarily as object lessons for the improvement of civil society, the advancement of practical learning, and the pressing of theological critique. Whether it was knowledge of enthusiasm or euhemerism, the point was emancipation from the darkness of religious error and progress toward the light of scientific experiment. That same attitude was also prevalent in the growing Enlightenment curiosity about the religions of the world. Much of this ground was initially tilled by seventeenth-century Anglican compilers – from Samuel Purchas to Alexander Ross – who were interested in maintaining the twin hierarchies of monarchy and episcopacy. To that end, they collated patterns of religiopolitical subordination from the numerous accounts that filtered back through mercantile, missionary, and colonial contact. Enlightenment inquirers, in turn, brought their own theological and political projects to bear on comparing the world's mythologies and ceremonies. Certainly, one use was to sharpen the tools of critical suspicion. David Hume's *Natural History of Religion* (1757) was an exemplar in that regard: all religion, not just false religion or superstition, was taken to be a problem of human nature, particularly the passions of fear and hope. Or, as Charles Dupuis, one of the authors whom Adams wished to favor with translation, concluded in his *Origine de tous les cultes* (1795), "The genius of a man capable of explaining religion seems to me to be of a higher order than that of a founder of religion. And this is the glory to which I aspire."[35]

Americans had their own reasons for joining this enterprise of making dictionaries and histories of religions. Rarely was that because they felt a deep affinity with Hume or Dupuis – or, for that matter, with Samuel Purchas or Alexander Ross. The methods of collection, collation, and comparison often displayed more than a superficial similarity, but the ends were "as modern and as American as possible" – or so claimed David Benedict, a Baptist historian from Rhode Island, who offered an entrant

---

[34] See Peter Harrison, *"Religion" and Religions in the English Enlightenment* (Cambridge, UK, 1990), esp. 9–10, 144–6; Mark Goldie, "Priestcraft and the Birth of Whiggism," in Nicholas Philllipson and Quentin Skinner, eds., *Political Discourse in Early Modern Britain* (Cambridge, UK, 1993), 209–31; and David Pailin, *Attitudes to Other Religions: Comparative Religion in Seventeenth- and Eighteenth-Century Britain* (Manchester, 1984), 124–5.

[35] Charles Dupuis quoted in Frank E. Manuel, *The Eighteenth Century Confronts the Gods* (Cambridge, MA, 1959), 243.

into this domain in 1824.³⁶ In Benedict's case, this meant providing a history of all religions that would underscore the Protestant quality of the new nation and feed evangelical astonishment over the depraved diversity of religions out there in budding mission fields. (The American Board of Commissioners for Foreign Missions had been chartered in 1812, and the American Baptist Foreign Mission Society had been organized shortly thereafter in 1814.) There was one American foray into this area of inquiry, though, that took its orientation more from liberal Christianity and broad Enlightenment learning than from evangelical Protestantism's burgeoning empire. Hannah Adams, a New England Congregationalist on her way to Unitarianism, issued the first edition of her *Alphabetical Compendium of the Various Sects* in 1784 and kept revising and augmenting it up to the fourth edition in 1817. Fittingly, she dedicated the second through fourth editions to her distant relation John Adams, who, long after serving as president, dreamed of having "a Library of a million Volumes" and a lifetime to pursue a universal history of religion.³⁷

Hannah Adams' compendious work was a model of the virtue of liberality. Two early commentators declared her "History of Religions" to be "the best of its kind, eminent for its great impartiality." Using her father's library as her initial base for learning and exploration, she pursued, despite ill-health, an ambitious program of self-cultivation. "The first strong propensity of my mind which I can recollect," she observed in her *Memoir*, "was an ardent curiosity, and desire to acquire knowledge. I remember that my first idea of the happiness of Heaven was, of a place where we should find our thirst for knowledge fully gratified." Finding a tutor for Greek and Latin as a young woman, she learned through him of Thomas Broughton's *Historical Dictionary of All Religions* (1742), an encyclopedic work in the Anglican mold. From there her native inquisitiveness took over; she started her own compilation, motivated by what she saw as "the want of candor" in Broughton and company. These authors provided, she complained, "the most unfavorable descriptions of the denominations they disliked," even applying to them "the names of heretics, fanatics, enthusiasts, &c." By contrast, she claimed a dispassionate curiosity as her impetus – along with a desire to lift herself out of penury and menial labor through "literary pursuits."³⁸

---

[36] David Benedict, *A History of All Religions* (Providence, 1824), 4–5.
[37] John Adams to Thomas Jefferson, 15 July 1817, in Cappon, *Adams-Jefferson Letters*, 518–19. On the relationship between John Adams and Hannah Adams, see Hannah Adams, *A Dictionary of All Religions and Religious Denominations: Jewish, Heathen, Mahometan, Christian, Ancient and Modern*, ed. Thomas A. Tweed (Atlanta, 1992), xi–xiii.
[38] Hannah Adams, *A Memoir of Miss Hannah Adams, Written by Herself, with Additional Notices by a Friend* (Boston, 1832), iv, 3–4, 11, 35, 43, 90.

Adams, to be sure, kept a finger on the scale, weighting it toward liberal Christianity. Her principal patrons came from those ranks, including the Unitarian Joseph Buckminster, and she harbored a special fondness for the preaching of William Ellery Channing. Still, she went a long way toward disengaging her compendious view of religions from subservience to the raging doctrinal debates within Anglo-American Protestantism, including those between Trinitarians and latter-day Arians and Socinians. Her first rule of study was "to avoid giving the least preference of one denomination above another" and to allow the various sects and religions to speak for themselves apart from the weighty divisions of orthodox from heterodox or enlightened from unenlightened. Even as more didactic editors and publishers pushed her to pass judgment on the "quicksands" of other religious systems, she consistently refused that "infringement" of her guiding rule of impartiality. "This liberal principle," she remarked in the preface to her final rendition of the dictionary, "has been adopted in all the editions of my work," and she had no intention of allowing a divisive orthodoxy to creep in at the last. Indeed, she ended that final version of her preface with a paean to the "diversity of sentiment" her broad charity allowed, to the enlargement of soul that the liberal principle of liberality made possible.[39]

In another generation Hannah Adams' impartiality and Channing's liberality would shift, among their Unitarian heirs, to the more affective disposition of sympathy. Broadmindedness and dispassion would not be enough for liberal religion, especially once the leaders of that movement had taken a romantic and Transcendentalist turn. The Unitarian minister and essayist Thomas Wentworth Higginson wrote the manifesto for that shift, "The Sympathy of Religions," a piece he began in the 1850s but only issued after the Civil War. Liberal cosmopolitanism required more than a studied indifference to sectarianism, more than a political recognition of the civil equality of divergent denominations. It required a sensitive appreciation of religious variety, a fellow feeling with people of different faiths.[40] Liberal religious movements of the nineteenth and twentieth centuries would be steeped in such ecumenical attachments and spiritual sympathies. Behind those deep-felt aspirations was the disposition toward liberality that had taken shape in the seventeenth and eighteenth centuries.

---

[39] Adams, *Dictionary of All Religions*, unpaginated "Advertisement" and "Preface."

[40] See Leigh E. Schmidt, "Cosmopolitan Piety: Sympathy, Comparative Religions, and Nineteenth-Century Liberalism," in Laurie Maffly-Kipp, Leigh E. Schmidt, and Mark Valeri, eds., *Practicing Protestants: Histories of the Christian Life in America* (Baltimore, 2006), 199–221.

SUGGESTIONS FOR FURTHER READING

Adams, Dickinson W., ed. *Jefferson's Extracts from the Gospels*. Princeton, 1983.

Gaustad, Edwin S. *Faith of Our Fathers: Religion and the New Nation*. San Francisco, 1987.

Holmes, David L. *The Faiths of the Founding Fathers*. New York, 2006.

Lambert, Frank. *The Founding Fathers and the Place of Religion in America*. Princeton, 2003.

May, Henry F. *The Enlightenment in America*. New York, 1976.

Robinson, David. *The Unitarians and Universalists*. Westport, 1985.

Walters, Kerry S. *Rational Infidels: The American Deists*. Durango, CO, 1992.

Wright, Conrad. *The Beginnings of Unitarianism in America*. Boston, 1955.

25

FOLK MAGIC AND RELIGION IN BRITISH NORTH AMERICA

RICHARD GODBEER

When several girls and young women living in Salem Village, Massachusetts, began to have strange fits in January 1692, their worried families and neighbors wanted to know what was causing the afflictions and how to end them. Two of the girls lived in the household of Samuel Parris, the minister in Salem Village: his daughter, Elizabeth Parris, and his niece, Abigail Williams. Parris responded to the situation by calling in the local physician, William Griggs, so as to establish whether the afflictions had a "natural" cause. But the doctor told Parris that he could do nothing for them: they were, he declared, "under an evil hand." Parris then consulted with fellow ministers from neighboring communities, who agreed with Griggs that the fits were "preternatural." They advised Parris to "sit still and wait upon the Providence of God to see what time might discover; and to be much in prayer for the discovery of what was yet secret."[1]

Yet not all villagers were willing to wait on "the Providence of God" to reveal the cause of the fits. Mary Sibley, a member of the local church and the aunt of another afflicted girl, Mary Walcott, suspected that her niece was bewitched and turned to countermagic in an attempt to cure her. Sibley asked two Indian slaves who lived and worked in the minister's home, Tituba and John, to bake a cake consisting of meal and the afflicted girl's urine, which they then fed to a dog. If the experiment worked, the witch responsible would be revealed. Sure enough, once the cake had been baked, the girls could see "particular persons hurting of them." Tituba, whom Parris had purchased while living in Barbados, had a reputation for occult skill. She later admitted that "her mistress in her own country ... had taught her some means to be used for the discovery of a witch," although the urine cake recipe seems to have been English rather than Caribbean in origin.[2]

---

[1] John Hale, *A Modest Enquiry into the Nature of Witchcraft* (Boston, 1702), 23, 25.
[2] *Ibid.*; and Deodat Lawson, *A Brief and True Narrative of Some Remarkable Passages Relating to Sundry Persons Afflicted by Witchcraft at Salem Village* (Boston, 1692), 9. For references

On both sides of the Atlantic, there survived and flourished alongside Christianity deeply rooted folk beliefs that governed magical experiments such as Sibley arranged in early 1692. Folk magic was based on the assumption that men and women could manipulate the supernatural world for their own ends. Many settlers believed that through the use of simple techniques, passed down from one generation to the next, they could harness occult forces so as to achieve greater knowledge and control over their lives: they could predict the future, heal physical ailments, inflict harm, and defend themselves against occult attack. Most magical techniques were quite straightforward, and so colonists often experimented on their own. But in times of need they also turned to neighbors who were known to have occult skill. These local experts – often called cunning folk – performed an important social service as they told fortunes, claimed to heal the sick, and offered protection against witchcraft.[3]

Magical divination enabled people to locate lost or stolen goods and to predict future events. Cunning folk used a variety of fortune-telling techniques that they sometimes learned from manuals circulating on both sides of the Atlantic. Dorcas Hoar of Beverly, Massachusetts, had "a book of palmistry" in which "there were rules to know what should come to pass." She also claimed that she could predict a neighbor's future by the "veins about her eyes." Samuel Wardwell of Andover, Massachusetts, told people's fortunes by "look[ing] in their hand and then would cast his eyes down upon the ground always before he told anything." In Chester County, Pennsylvania, Robert Roman had a reputation for "practicing geomancy" and "divining by a stick."[4] Some divining techniques required no particular expertise and so could be used independently of cunning folk. One such technique involved balancing a sieve on a pair of shears or scissors and asking a question; if the sieve turned or fell to the floor, the answer was positive.

---

to urine cakes in England, see George L. Kittredge, *Witchcraft in Old and New England* (New York, 1956 [1929]), 435n237.

[3] The following discussion of folk magic and its relationship to religion in British North America draws on Richard Godbeer, *The Devil's Dominion: Magic and Religion in Early New England* (New York, 1992); Jon Butler, *Awash in a Sea of Faith: Christianizing the American People* (Cambridge, MA, 1990), ch. 3; and David D. Hall, *Worlds of Wonder, Days of Judgment: Popular Religious Belief in Early New England* (New York, 1989), ch. 2. This essay does not discuss the use of "learned" or "natural" magic in British North America; for this see Walter W. Woodward, *Prospero's America: John Winthrop, Jr., Alchemy, and the Creation of New England Culture (1606–1676)* (Chapel Hill, 2009); and Herbert Leventhal, *In the Shadow of the Enlightenment: Occultism and Renaissance Science in Eighteenth-Century America* (New York, 1976).

[4] Bernard Rosenthal et al., eds., *Records of the Salem Witch Hunt* (New York, 2008), 593, 595, 645; and *Records of the Courts of Chester County, Pennsylvania, 1681–1697* (Philadelphia, 1910), 363.

At the Salem witch trials, Rebecca Johnson of Andover "acknowledged the turning of the sieve in her house by her daughter" in an attempt to find out "if her brother Moses Haggat was alive or dead."[5]

People also used magic to protect themselves from harm and to heal the sick. When Edward Cole of Northumberland County, Virginia, suspected that a neighbor was bewitching his wife, he hung a horseshoe over their door to ward off evil. When the woman whom he suspected was still able to enter their house, he concluded that his suspicions must have been unfounded.[6] Farther north in New England, Cotton Mather knew a woman "who upon uttering some words over very painful hurts and sores did ... presently cure them." Indeed, Mather had heard that in some New England towns it was "a usual thing for people to cure hurts with spells." Traditional folk medicine often combined the application of plants and minerals with the use of charms or incantations. The verbal formulae used in these "spells" often originated as Catholic prayers, their use for this particular purpose a survival from the medieval belief that sanctioned church rituals could protect against harm and heal the sick. According to Increase Mather, a healer in Boston prescribed as "an effective remedy against the toothache" a "sealed paper" containing the words, "In nomine Patris, Filii, et Spiritus Sancti, Preserve thy servant, such a one."[7]

But magic could be used to harm as well as to heal. Those suspected of deploying magical skill for malevolent ends were distrusted by their neighbors and labeled as witches. From this perspective, witchcraft was the misuse of occult skill, the dangerous underside of an otherwise valued local resource. The most notorious magical technique for inflicting harm was image magic, which operated on the principle that damaging an object taken to represent an enemy would also injure the person represented. At the Salem witch trials, a remarkable number of testimonies mentioned the use of "poppets" to injure enemies. Susannah Sheldon claimed that Job Tookey had "run a great pin into a poppet's heart which killed" Gamaliel Hawkins. Workers who were demolishing a wall in Bridget Bishop's cellar found there several cloth "poppets" with pins stuck into them. Whether or not these accused witches had in fact used image magic in the hope of harming their enemies, residents of Salem Village and the surrounding

---

[5] Rosenthal, *Salem Witch Hunt*, 597.

[6] Northumberland County Record Book, 1666–1672 (Library of Virginia, Richmond, VA), depositions by Edward LeBreton and Thomas Bandmill, 11 April 1671, published in "The Good Luck Horseshoe," *William and Mary Quarterly* 1st ser., 17 (1908–09), 247–8.

[7] Cotton Mather, "Paper on Witchcraft," *Proceedings of Massachusetts Historical Society* 47 (1914): 265–6; Cotton Mather, *Wonders of the Invisible World* (Boston, 1692), 96; and Increase Mather, *An Essay for the Recording of Illustrious Providences* (Boston, 1684), 261.

communities were evidently familiar with this magical technique and its underlying assumptions.[8]

Fortunately for those who feared occult attack, there were straightforward countermagical techniques that could defend them against witchcraft, identify the person responsible, and inflict retribution. When someone used occult means to harm their enemies, a two-way channel of communication was believed to open between the malefactor and victim. By damaging a bewitched object or something associated with the bewitched person, the witchcraft could be undone and the harm translated back on to whoever had caused it. This might involve burning something associated with the bewitched creature or person, such as the tail of an animal or the hair of a human being. If the experiment worked, the person responsible for the witchcraft would be drawn to the fire or would suffer injuries supposedly caused by the countermagic. When Margaret Garrett of Hartford, Connecticut, suspected that one of her cheeses had been bewitched, she flung it into the fire. Elizabeth Seager, who was at the time in Garrett's barn, came into the house and "cried out she was full of pain, and sat wringing of her body and crying out, 'What do I ail? What do I ail?'" Goodwife Garrett concluded that Seager must be the culprit.[9]

The belief that magic could be used for both good and evil purposes placed cunning folk in an ambiguous and vulnerable position. Neighbors who possessed occult powers performed an important service in predicting futures and healing the sick, but they were also potentially deadly enemies. When New Englanders feared that they were bewitched, they often blamed men and women in their local communities who already had a reputation for occult skill and with whom they had quarreled: they might conclude that skills previously used for their own benefit were now being turned against them. Indeed, much of the surviving information about the use of folk magic comes from depositions presented at witch trials. Witnesses would often testify that the defendant had assisted them or their neighbors by divining or healing on their behalf, which proved the defendant to have occult skill; that expertise was apparently serving less benign ends. Healers were especially vulnerable to accusations of witchcraft if they applied their skills to a patient whose condition then worsened.

English colonists in North America encountered and lived alongside non-Europeans whose cultures also included magical beliefs and practices. Yet it is difficult to tell from the surviving documentation whether cunning folk or other colonists of European descent incorporated Indian

---

[8] Rosenthal, *Salem Witch Hunt*, 371, 393.

[9] Willys Papers: Records of Trials for Witchcraft in Connecticut (Brown University Library, Providence, RI), W-4, 17 June 1665, testimony of Margaret Garrett.

and African occult techniques into their own magical repertoire. It is clear that colonists appropriated Indian and African medical knowledge. English accounts of contact with Indians often recognized their skill in the use of indigenous plants to heal a range of illnesses.[10] And when an enslaved African healer in South Carolina known as Doctor Caesar developed a cure for snakebites, he was granted his freedom by the colonial assembly in return for sharing his remedy. But the description of Caesar's cure in the colonial records makes no mention of any charms that Caesar may have used when administering the cure to African patients. Africans and Indians believed, in common with many English settlers, that the successful treatment of illness needed to incorporate both natural and supernatural components, but white colonists may well have been unwilling to adopt occult charms proffered by peoples whom they believed to be pagans and devil worshippers. Or Caesar may have withheld such information.[11]

The records do contain occasional hints of supernatural exchange across racial lines, but they are little more than suggestive. A story circulated in mid-seventeenth-century Fairfield, Connecticut, about an Indian who had apparently visited the home of Mary Staples and offered her "two things brighter than the light of the day ... Indian gods, as the Indian called them." When Staples was later tried for witchcraft, locals resurrected the story as incriminating evidence. Staples admitted having been offered these objects but claimed that she had refused to accept them. Decades later Mary Sibley turned to Tituba, an Indian slave, for occult assistance when her niece became afflicted in 1692.[12] Farther south, a white South Carolinian wrote down a charm for warding off witchcraft that consisted of Christian phrases and crosses on a paper that was then to be put "in a small rag tied round the neck." This bears a close resemblance to Nkisi charms for protecting against evil spirits, although English men and women also carried protective charms in bags hung around their necks; it

---

[10] See, for example, John Lawson, *A New Voyage to Virginia*, ed. Hugh Talmage Lefler (Chapel Hill, 1967), 17–18; and letter from Maurice Mathews in Charleston, 18 May 1680, South Caroliniana Library, published in *South Carolina Historical Magazine* 55:3 (1954): 153–9.

[11] See Mary L. Galvin, "Decoctions for Carolinians: The Creation of a Creole Medicine Chest in Colonial South Carolina," in David Buisseret and Steven G. Reinhardt, eds., *Creolization in the Americas* (College Station, TX, 2000), esp. 82–4, 88–9.

[12] Charles J. Hoadly, ed., *Records of the Colony or Jurisdiction of New Haven*, 2 vols. (New Haven, 1857–58), 2: 80, 86. For more on Tituba, see Elaine G. Breslaw, *Tituba, Reluctant Witch of Salem: Devilish Indians and Puritan Fantasies* (New York, 1996). For tantalizing references to African fortune-tellers in early eighteenth-century Boston, see Butler, *Awash in a Sea of Faith*, 94.

is impossible to tell whether this prescription reflected African influence or shared beliefs.[13]

Evidence of magical belief and examples of magical experimentation survive from each region of British America, but most of the extant documentation comes from seventeenth-century New England. The War of Independence and later the Civil War inflicted disproportionate damage on the southern colonies, destroying lives, property, and also historical records that might otherwise have given us much more detailed information about early southern culture. But even had these wars not taken place, there would most likely survive more information about early New England than colonies farther south for the simple reason that more of those who settled in the northern colonies could read and write. Puritans believed that becoming literate was a crucial part of becoming a person of faith, because it was through reading the Bible that individual men and women would gain access to divine truth.[14] The ability to write was less crucial than learning how to read, yet a significant minority of New Englanders could do both. Literate colonists left behind a remarkable written testimony to their struggles against temptation and the forces of evil – individually and in concert, informally and through institutional channels. One of the dangers that Puritan leaders saw as threatening their spiritual enterprise was the persistence of folk magic among the New England colonists.

The basic assumption underlying folk magic – that people could harness occult powers for their own ends – contrasted sharply with the teachings of Puritan theology, which placed supernatural power firmly in God's hands. Clergymen were horrified by the popularity of magical techniques. They insisted that scripture gave no sanction for such experiments and that human beings could not wield supernatural forces on their own. The Puritan clergy did not doubt that magic worked, but according to them it did so because the devil provided assistance to the person conducting the experiment. Divination served "a vain curiosity to pry into things God ha[d] forbidden and concealed from discovery by lawful means," declared John Hale, the minister at Beverly. People could gain access to "forbidden" knowledge, he warned, only "through the assistance of a familiar spirit." Ministers were particularly shocked by the use of religious words and phrases in protective and healing spells. According to Samuel Willard,

---

[13] Hutson Family Papers, 34/570, Ellison and Mulligan Receipt Book, South Carolina Historical Society. I am grateful to Mary Calvin for bringing this evidence to my attention. For the use of divination, charms, and invocations by African slaves, see Philip D. Morgan, *Slave Counterpoint: Black Culture in the Eighteenth-Century Chesapeake and Lowcountry* (Chapel Hill, 1998), 621, 624.

[14] See Hall, *Worlds of Wonder*, ch. 1.

a minister in Boston, this was "an horrible abusing of the name of God to such purposes as serve egregiously to the establishing of the Devil's kingdom in the hearts of men." From this perspective, countermagic was no less dependent on diabolical intervention than the bewitchments that it sought to undo. Deodat Lawson, who had served as minister in Salem Village prior to Samuel Parris, condemned such techniques as "using the devil's shield against the Devil's sword." Individuals might think that they were successfully harnessing occult powers, but in fact the Devil was doing it for them and so luring them into his service.[15]

Ministers had similar concerns about the use of astrology to predict human affairs. Interest in astrological prognostication was widespread in New England and indeed throughout British America.[16] Puritan theologians accepted that celestial bodies had a direct influence over natural events and had no quarrel with the use of astronomical information to predict the weather, farming conditions, and even physical health, but they would not countenance "judicial" astrology, the application of astronomical information to human affairs. In common with magical divination, they argued, judicial astrology intruded into "things secret" that could not be revealed by "lawful means." Its claim to foreknowledge must, therefore, be false, unless the devil was intervening to provide the information.[17] This was not the only connection between magic and astrology: the latter's assumption of a direct causal linkage between celestial and terrestrial phenomena bore a close resemblance to belief in image magic. Puritans also worried that the signs of the zodiac were potential objects of idolatry; their dominion over different parts of the body was disturbingly reminiscent of Catholic saints' responsibility for the cure of various diseases.[18]

In addition to sanctioning "natural" astrology, Puritan ministers were also interested in the broad providential significance of extraordinary celestial phenomena such as comets and eclipses, which they believed God sent either as "signal of great and notable changes" or as "heralds of wrath."[19] They were just as convinced as other English men and women that the universe was filled with awe-inspiring portents, prodigies, and wonders

---

[15] Hale, *Modest Enquiry*, 165; Samuel Willard, *The Danger of Taking God's Name in Vain* (Boston, 1691), 10; and Deodat Lawson, *Christ's Fidelity the Only Shield Against Satan's Malignity* (Boston, 1692), 62.

[16] For the use of astrology in British North America, see Godbeer, *Devil's Dominion*, ch. 4, and Butler, *Awash in a Sea of Faith*, ch. 3.

[17] Charles Morton, "Compendium Physicae," *Collections of the Colonial Society of Massachusetts* 33 (1940): 29.

[18] See Keith Thomas, *Religion and the Decline of Magic* (New York, 1971), 435–40.

[19] Samuel Danforth, *An Astronomical Description of the Late Comet or Blazing Star* (Cambridge, MA, 1665), 16–17.

that carried supernatural significance. Puritans drew on a wonder lore that derived from folklore, classical meteorology, apocalyptic prophecy, and natural philosophy. But ministers condemned specific interpretations of any such phenomena as "too much boldness" and insisted that heavenly movements were "only signal and not causal" of human events. To think otherwise was a blasphemy against God's omnipotence and an invitation to Satan, who was always ready and eager to exploit human presumption.[20]

Yet many colonists were much less fastidious than their ministers and used astrology as well as divination to foretell human events. They saw no harm in benevolent magic or astrological predictions and branded as witches only those who sought to wield occult forces for malevolent ends. Such distinctions were, from a clerical perspective, either dangerously naïve or disingenuous. Folk magic and judicial astrology were, insisted ministers, dependent on a diabolical agency, regardless of whether the intention was benign or malevolent. Particularly worrisome was the apparent failure of church members to recognize the dangers inherent in magical experimentation, people like Mary Sibley, who responded to her niece's affliction in 1692 by asking the minister's own slave to bake a urine cake in hope of identifying whoever was responsible. When Parris discovered what Sibley had done, he summoned her to his home and reduced her to "tears and sorrowful confession" for what he saw as her "grand error." Two days later, he denounced Sibley from the pulpit of the village meetinghouse for "going to the Devil for help against the Devil." That a member of his own congregation would act in this way was "a great grief" to Parris, yet he did not believe that Sibley had self-consciously forsaken her commitment to obey God's commandments. "I do truly hope and believe," Parris declared, "that this our sister doth truly fear the Lord, and am well satisfied from her that what she did, she did it ignorantly, from what she had heard of this nature from other ignorant, or worse, persons."[21]

According to other ministers serving in New England, there were "manifold sorceries practiced by those that ma[d]e a profession of Christianity." New England's clergymen generally took the view that most of those who turned to magic did so because they failed to understand how dangerous it was. Increase Mather believed that some people "practice[d] such things in their simplicity, not knowing that therein they gratifie[d] the Devil." John Hale believed that such people used magical techniques simply because

---

[20] Increase Mather, *Heaven's Alarm to the World* (Boston, 1682), 16–17; and Increase Mather, *Kometographia* (Boston, 1683), 133. For wonder lore in New England, see Hall, *Worlds of Wonder*, ch. 2.

[21] Paul Boyer and Stephen Nissenbaum, eds., *Salem-Village Witchcraft: A Documentary Record of Local Conflict in Colonial New England* (Boston, 1993 [1972]), 278–9.

they believed that they worked, without considering how they worked. "Such have an implicit faith," he wrote, "that the means used shall produce the effect desired, but consider not how; and so are beguiled by the serpent that lies in the grass unseen."[22] Ministers thus acknowledged that they had been far from entirely successful in communicating their perspective on the workings of the supernatural world and also that even seemingly devout colonists sometimes behaved in ways that were inconsistent with their profession of Puritan faith.

One might perhaps expect that Puritan New England would have been the one cultural venue in British North America where official principles and popular behavior would have coincided quite closely, but such was by no means always the case. Many New England colonists clung to traditional beliefs and assumptions even when these contradicted ideals to which the individuals in question were supposedly committed. Some colonists were doubtless rigorous and exclusive in their commitment to Puritan faith, but others were more inclusive and drew on folk magic as well as astrology and religious faith in combinations that were intellectually inconsistent and yet worked well for them. It may well be that some colonists did not understand why magic was offensive from a Puritan perspective. We cannot assume that most ordinary folk shared the intellectual self-consciousness that prompted ministers to assess the assumptions underlying magical techniques. Nor can we assume that logical consistency was more important to the average colonist than the needs of the moment and the widespread assumption that such techniques did work. Others may have understood that magic was heterodox but quietly ignored clerical injunctions when it suited them. When John Hale berated Dorcas Hoar for using a fortune-telling manual, for example, she promised "to renounce or reject all such practices." Yet several years later it transpired that she still had a fortune-telling book in her possession.[23]

Some individuals seem to have believed that magical power came from God. John Hale met one man who used as medicinal charms words and phrases that he believed to be taken from scripture; he told Hale that God had given him "the gift of healing." This fellow was clearly not unique. Winifred Holman of Cambridge, Massachusetts, offered to cure a neighbor's illness "with the blessing of God." Increase Mather was concerned that laymen and laywomen might think they were drawing on divine power when using magical techniques. He cautioned that people who turned to countermagic should not declare, "The Lord was my healer," because it

---

[22] Cotton Mather, *A Discourse on Witchcraft* (Boston, 1689), 25; Increase Mather, *Illustrious Providences*, 260; and Hale, *Modest Inquiry*, 131.
[23] Rosenthal, *Salem Witch Hunt*, 593–4.

was in fact the Devil who had come to their aid. And Deodat Lawson also found it necessary to remind listeners that divinatory powers came "from the Devil, not from God."[24]

Magic may have appealed to some New Englanders in part because it enabled them to alleviate anxieties created by Puritanism itself. Those anxieties arose from the uncertainty created by predestinarian theology. Even those who believed that they had felt within themselves the transformative power of divine love and mercy were supposed to remain doubtful of their salvation. Ministers warned their congregations that assurance was dangerous because indications of grace were elusive and unreliable. They insisted that recognizing one's own spiritual worthlessness was a crucial part of becoming worthy of God's forgiveness. A growing emphasis on the importance of preparation in Puritan sermons gave believers some sense of agency in their own redemption. Ministers taught that believers should nurture within themselves a desire for grace that would make them fit receptacles for that gift, should it be proffered. Yet preparatory exercises offered no guarantees: just as nobody could be certain that they were elect, so nobody could tell if they were fully prepared. Indeed, the whole purpose of preparation was to cultivate a sense of one's own spiritual inadequacy, so that the more successfully people prepared, the more they would doubt their worthiness of God's mercy.[25]

Some believers accepted doubt and anxiety as normative and desirable, but others sought at least occasional relief from spiritual anxiety. Magic offered one potential outlet, and among those who turned to divination were devout people who yearned for some sense of certainty about the future. Knowing how long one's children would live or who one's future husband would be paled into insignificance when compared with the question of whether one would be saved, but such knowledge did offer some degree of certitude, however limited or short term. Some New Englanders went further and attempted to penetrate the mystery of election itself through divination. Cotton Mather was horrified to discover that some colonists took their Bibles, let them fall open, and then determined "the state of their souls" from the first word that their eyes fell on. Such practices were clearly inconsistent with the religious principles taught by New England's clergy, but the men and women using them may have either not

---

[24] Hale, *Modest Enquiry*, 131–2; Middlesex Court Files, Massachusetts State Archives, Columbia Point, MA, fol. 25, no. 4; Increase Mather, *Illustrious Providences*, 266; and Deodat Lawson, *Christ's Fidelity*, 65.

[25] See Norman Pettit, *The Heart Prepared: Grace and Conversion in Puritan Spiritual Life* (New Haven, 1966); and Charles Hambrick-Stowe, *The Practice of Piety: Puritan Devotional Disciplines in Seventeenth-Century New England* (Chapel Hill, 1982).

fully grasped that inconsistency or ignored it because of the comfort that divination offered.[26]

Folk magic also met needs that had previously been answered by a repertoire of ecclesiastical magic within the Catholic Church but that Protestants in England had abolished. The medieval church had taught that holy water, coins, candles, and relics could offer protection against harm and heal the sick. Theologians stressed that the efficacy of such rituals depended on the spiritual sincerity of those who used them, yet ordinary folk seem to have endowed religious objects and rituals with an automatic power, often treating ecclesiastical magic and folk techniques as all but interchangeable, much to the dismay of church officials.[27] Protestant reformers rejected the notion that performance of specific rituals could bring about a desired effect: they insisted that the only way to achieve safety or release from suffering was to appeal to God's mercy. Thus, it is hardly surprising that ecclesiastical magic had no place in the Church of England or the religious culture that Puritans established in New England. But suppressing folk magic turned out to be much more challenging on both sides of the Atlantic, in large part because the knowledge and control that it offered was so appealing, even among those who identified with a reformed sensibility.

Ambiguities within Puritan theology may also have encouraged New Englanders to use magic. When colonists suspected that a particular affliction had been caused by witchcraft and turned to countermagic in a bid to undo the harm and identify the person responsible, their ministers were horrified and insisted that all suffering should be understood as a providential judgment; looking inward, repenting for one's spiritual failings, and begging God to forgive one's sins was the only acceptable route to recovery. Yet those same ministers delivered through their sermons a very mixed message when it came to responsibility for suffering and sin. On the one hand, any misfortune should be understood as a punishment for sin, which was itself the product of human corruption. The devil was assuredly eager to tempt men and women into sin, but those who entertained wicked thoughts or committed sinful acts were culpable in giving way to the devil's advances. Satan was thus empowered by humanity's own moral depravity. Yet on the other hand, ministers often depicted Satan as a formidable force in his own right and a serious threat to the human soul, luring men and

---

[26] Cotton Mather, *Discourse on Witchcraft*, 27.
[27] See Valerie Flint, *The Rise of Magic in Early Medieval Europe* (Princeton, 1991); Richard Kieckhefer, *Magic in the Middle Ages* (New York, 1990); Gabor Klaniczay, *The Uses of Supernatural Power: The Transformation of Popular Religion in Medieval and Early Modern Europe* (Princeton, 1990); and Thomas, *Religion*, esp. ch. 2.

women away from obedience to God's commandments. At times the devil figured in sermons as an almost invincible force.

Some New Englanders were temperamentally more inclined to blame themselves for their afflictions and sinful impulses, whereas others tended to blame Satan. Samuel Willard condemned the latter for trying "to extenuate [their] own fault by seeking to throw it upon Satan." This was, he lamented, "a thing too frequent among such as profess themselves to be the children of God."[28] Yet the implicit tension in clerical teaching on the subject of liability between diabolical power and human responsibility gave layfolk considerable leeway in deciding whom to blame for their sins and misfortunes. The ministers' portrayal of the world as a dangerous place troubled by an active devil may well have encouraged even devout believers to focus on external sources of evil and to protect themselves against such threats by resorting to countermagic.[29] The likelihood of individuals deciding to blame their troubles on outside forces instead of their own moral failings would have depended on their own psychological inclinations and also those of their minister, their mood at the time of the misfortune, and the broader influences being exerted on them by their cultural environment. Recent scholarship on the underlying causes of the Salem witch hunt reaffirms the crucial link between accusations of witchcraft and a predisposition to blame suffering on external rather than internal causes.

During the last quarter of the seventeenth century, New England faced a series of external threats that created an intense sense of danger among settlers in the region. Native American attacks in 1675–76 and 1689–91, political reforms imposed during the 1680s by the government in London that threatened to undermine the colonists' independence, the increasing visibility of religious dissenters, and the imposition of a new charter in 1691 giving freedom of worship and the vote to previously disfranchised groups such as Quakers and Anglicans all left the colonists feeling imperiled. From a modern perspective these events may seem unconnected to witchcraft, but New Englanders described these threats in much the same language used to characterize witches: as alien, invasive, and malevolent forces. Many colonists believed that Indians were devil worshippers and that Quakers who claimed to access divine truth through inner revelation were actually possessed by the devil. To be attacked by Indians or evangelized by Quakers was thus equivalent to being assaulted by Satan. The accusations in Salem Village unleashed fears of alien, invasive, and diabolical forces that had accumulated during the preceding years. Indeed, the crisis of 1692 struck some contemporaries as the climax of a demonic

---

[28] Samuel Willard, *The Christian's Exercise by Satan's Temptations* (Boston, 1701), 149.
[29] For a more extended version of this argument, see Godbeer, *Devil's Dominion*, ch. 3.

assault on the region. Ministers responding to the outbreak of witch accusations urged their congregations to look inward for the source of their troubles, but in recent years they and their flocks had become increasingly preoccupied with external threats. That preoccupation exploded in 1692 as a deadly witch panic.[30]

The Salem witch trials have often distracted attention away from the many other prosecutions for witchcraft that occurred throughout the seventeenth century in New England. Fear of witches and accusations of witchcraft were part of everyday life in the northern colonies. When people became convinced that a neighbor had used witchcraft against them, they could respond in a number of ways. They could focus on their own spiritual failings as the ultimate reason for God's having unleashed the devil and his minions, in which case they would commit to a regimen of repentance and reformation in the hope that God would withdraw his chastising rod. Or they could seek revenge through the use of countermagic, perhaps burning the hair or urine of the bewitched person in hope of identifying and injuring the witch responsible. Or they could lodge a formal complaint and so initiate a criminal prosecution. The first response treated the situation as a spiritual challenge and placed at least some blame for what was happening on the victims themselves. The second responded to supernatural affliction by blaming someone else and seeking retribution through occult means. A legal response offered victims the possibility of official and public retribution. The penalty for witchcraft throughout the New England colonies was death. While encouraging their flocks to look inward for the causes of misfortune, pastors also sanctioned the prosecution of suspected witches. After all, the Bible declared very clearly, "Thou shalt not suffer a witch to live."

Around four-fifths of those New Englanders tried for witchcraft were women. Cunning women were much more likely to be accused of witchcraft than were their male counterparts. The power wielded by cunning folk was potentially threatening whether in the hands of a man or a woman, but it was especially threatening if the cunning person was female, because the aura of power surrounding cunning folk contradicted gender norms that placed women in subordinate positions. Neither magical beliefs nor magical practices were gender specific: men as well as women resorted to and functioned as cunning folk. Yet suspicions that magical skill had been used

---

[30] See *ibid.*, 179–203, and also Mary Beth Norton, *In the Devil's Snare: The Salem Witchcraft Crisis of 1692* (New York, 2002). During the decades prior to the witch hunt, Salem Village itself had become bitterly divided around a series of issues that paralleled crises in the region at large and created a similar sense of besiegement. See Paul Boyer and Stephen Nissenbaum, *Salem Possessed: The Social Origins of Witchcraft* (Cambridge, MA, 1974).

for malicious ends were much more likely to be directed against female practitioners.

Puritan ministers did not teach that women were by nature more evil than men, but they did see them as weaker and thus more susceptible to sinful impulses. Clergymen reminded New England congregations that it was Eve who first gave way to Satan and then seduced Adam. All women inherited that potential for collusion with the devil from their first mother. Yet some women were much more likely than others to be accused of witchcraft. Throughout the seventeenth century, women in New England became especially vulnerable to such allegations if they were seen as challenging their prescribed place in a gendered hierarchy that Puritans held to be ordained by God. Especially vulnerable were women who had passed menopause and thus no longer served the purpose of procreation, women who were widowed and so neither fulfilled the role of wife nor had a husband to protect them from malicious accusations, and women who had inherited or stood to inherit property in violation of expectations that wealth would be transmitted from man to man. Women who seemed unduly aggressive and contentious were also more likely to be accused. Conduct that would not have struck contemporaries as particularly egregious in men seemed utterly unacceptable in women. Any behavior or circumstance that seemed disorderly could easily become identified as diabolical and associated with witchcraft: the devil had, after all, led a rebellion against God's rule in heaven.[31]

Yet convincing oneself and one's neighbors of an individual's guilt was not the same as convincing a court. Puritan theology depicted witches as heretics who had renounced Christianity and sworn allegiance to the devil. New England laws defined witchcraft in theological terms, demanding proof of diabolical allegiance. Yet ordinary men and women were more inclined to think about witchcraft as a practical problem: having concluded that a particular misfortune was caused by occult attack, they wanted to know who the witch was and they wanted her punished. The evidence presented at most witch trials reflected that practical preoccupation and rarely made any mention of the devil. That deponents did not adapt their testimony to fit legal criteria suggests that ordinary colonists were quite stubbornly focused on practical threats to their safety when thinking about witchcraft and also that at least some people were much less thoroughly schooled in official ideology than persistent stereotypes of early New Englanders would suggest. The disjunction between legal requirements

---

[31] See Carol Karlsen, *The Devil in the Shape of a Woman: Witchcraft in Colonial New England* (New York, 1987); and Elizabeth Reis, *Damned Women: Sinners and Witches in Puritan New England* (Ithaca, 1997).

and the nature of most popular testimony resulted in frequent acquittals. Of the sixty-one known prosecutions for witchcraft in seventeenth-century New England, excluding the Salem witch hunt, sixteen at most (perhaps only fourteen) resulted in conviction and execution, a rate of just more than one-quarter. Four of these individuals confessed, which made the court's job much easier. If they are omitted, the conviction rate falls to just less than one-fifth.[32]

The depositions given against New England's accused witches generally fell into one of four categories. Most frequently, villagers and townsfolk described quarrels with the accused individual that had been followed by misfortune or illness for which they could find no natural explanation; the witnesses claimed that the alleged witch had afflicted them as a direct consequence of these arguments. Second, deponents claimed that the accused had a reputation for skill as a fortune-teller or healer; this established that the accused had occult powers that could also have been used for malign purposes. Third, witnesses described having used countermagic, perhaps cutting off part of a bewitched animal's tail and throwing it in a fire or boiling the urine of a bewitched child; if a neighbor suffered an analogous injury soon afterward or was drawn inexplicably to the house in which the experiment had taken place, that information was offered up to the court as incriminating testimony. And finally, neighbors would describe suspicious behavior or preternatural characteristics, such as extraordinary strength.

These depositions demonstrated beyond any doubt the fear that alleged witches aroused among their neighbors, but they were mostly unconvincing from a legal perspective. Magistrates and the learned ministers whom they consulted during many of these trials dismissed testimony relating "strange accidents" following quarrels as "slender and uncertain grounds" for conviction. Clergymen denounced countermagic as "going to the Devil for help against the Devil" and warned that Satan was a malicious liar, which hardly encouraged magistrates to rely on testimony describing countermagical experiments. They were occasionally willing to conclude that divination or other magical practices that ministers condemned as diabolical proved collusion between the accused witch and the devil, but even here magistrates were mostly reluctant to convict unless there was explicit mention of the devil.[33]

---

[32] Godbeer, *Devil's Dominion*, 158.

[33] David D. Hall, ed., *Witch-Hunting in Seventeenth-Century New England: A Documentary History, 1658–1693*, 2nd ed. (Boston, 1999), 348; and Boyer and Nissenbaum, *Salem-Village Witchcraft*, 278. Accused witches were much less likely to be convicted and executed than their counterparts across the Atlantic. In England the statutes enacted against witchcraft in 1542 and 1563 had defined the crime as a hostile act rather than as heresy; thus the preoccupation of popular depositions with practical harm was less

New England magistrates were ready and willing to convict and execute those accused of capital offenses, should the evidence against them prove convincing. But they insisted that the evidence before them should satisfy rigorous standards of proof: this meant either a voluntary confession or at least two independent witnesses to any incident demonstrating the individual's guilt. It was difficult enough to secure two witnesses for sexual offenses that carried the death penalty, but the challenge was compounded when dealing with an invisible crime involving alleged collusion with supernatural agents. Only in a minority of cases were New England magistrates convinced that the evidence did satisfy the established criteria for conviction. At other trials, their fastidious adherence to evidentiary standards resulted in acquittal. In some instances they overturned jury verdicts, rejecting the instincts of local jurymen who were convinced of the accused person's guilt.

The neighbors and enemies of accused witches who had given what they considered to be damning testimony were often infuriated by the reluctance of magistrates to convict on the basis of their depositions. Sometimes they would confer with each other, gather new evidence against the acquitted individual, and then renew legal charges. Three individuals were each prosecuted on three separate occasions; another five appeared in court twice on charges of witchcraft. All of these cases resulted in acquittal.[34] Repeat prosecutions expressed unshaken belief in an individual's guilt and also dissatisfaction with the court's handling of witchcraft cases. That dissatisfaction sometimes resulted in extralegal retaliation. Mary Webster of Hadley, Massachusetts, was tried and acquitted in 1683; but a year later, when another of her neighbors fell ill and accused her of bewitching him, several young men paid Webster a visit and brutally assaulted her.[35]

As the difficulty of securing a legal conviction for witchcraft became increasingly apparent, New Englanders became less and less inclined to initiate legal prosecutions against suspected witches: there were nineteen witch trials during the 1660s, but only six during the 1670s and eight during the 1680s. That dramatic decline was not due to a lessening fear of

problematic. Continental law generally defined witchcraft in theological terms, but in many European countries the courts could use torture to extract the kinds of evidence that would justify conviction for diabolical heresy. The New England authorities, operating under English jurisdiction, had no legal recourse to torture when questioning defendants in witchcraft cases. The Salem witch hunt was the only occasion on which New England courts gathered extensive evidence of diabolical allegiance; this was also the only occasion on which the authorities used psychological pressure and physical torture, illegally, to extract a large number of confessions.

[34] Godbeer, *Devil's Dominion*, 173.
[35] Samuel Drake, *Annals of Witchcraft in New England* (New York, 1972 [1869]), 179.

witches, as would become clear in 1692, when official encouragement of witchcraft accusations in and around Salem Village unleashed a deluge of allegations. It is perhaps not a coincidence that ministers became much more vociferous in their denunciations of countermagic during the 1680s. As colonists became disillusioned with the court system as a weapon against witches, they may have turned increasingly to countermagic instead.

At first it seemed that the evidentiary problems that had plagued previous witch trials would not thwart the proceedings at Salem. More than fifty of the accused in 1692 confessed, describing in graphic detail their initiation into the devil's service and often naming other individuals who had allegedly joined the satanic confederacy. These confessions lent a horrifying credibility to the accusations pouring in from communities throughout Essex County. The evidence given by witnesses against the accused contained, moreover, countless references to the devil and his involvement with the alleged witches; these also facilitated conviction. By the end of summer, however, a growing number of critics were casting doubt on the court's proceedings. Many of the confessing witches had recanted, claiming that their confessions had been forced from them by overly zealous officials through the use of physical torture and psychological pressure. Some of them had been promised that those who confessed, renounced their allegiance to Satan, and then cooperated with the authorities would be spared from execution. In a ghastly irony, only those who refused to perjure themselves by admitting to crimes that they had not committed went to their deaths.

Other than confessions, almost all of the testimony describing the devil's involvement in the alleged witch conspiracy came from the afflicted girls whose torments had sparked the witch hunt. Most of the information that they provided in their numerous depositions supposedly came from the specters of witches that had appeared to them. Puritan theologians taught that human beings could not themselves turn into or produce specters; instead, devils assumed their form and acted on their behalf. The Salem court assumed that devils could appear in the image of a particular individual only with that person's permission; thus the appearance of a specter could be treated as proof that the individual represented was, in fact, a witch. Yet a growing chorus of ministers and magistrates warned that Satan might represent innocent persons in spectral form so as to incriminate them falsely. The girls suffered terrible agonies in the courtroom whenever accused witches moved or looked at them, but this might also be a trick brought about by the devil rather than a genuine sign of guilt. Because the devil was a liar, critics warned, evidence that originated with him could not be trusted. These critics cast doubt on the spectral testimony presented to the court not because they questioned the existence of witchcraft, but because they feared that the devil might be using the court to attack innocent parties. In other words, their very belief in the devil and his hatred of New Englanders made them doubt the trustworthiness of the evidence before the court.

Once spectral testimony and the confessions came under attack, the court found itself in an extremely difficult position. There were many depositions against the accused from witnesses other than the afflicted girls, but hardly any of that testimony included references to diabolical involvement such as the law demanded. In early October, Governor Phips halted the trials. That accusers were now naming individuals from prominent families, including the governor's own wife, doubtless figured in his decision. But the collapse of the trials was due primarily to controversy over the evidence being used to justify conviction. From the perspective of people who wanted the courts to take decisive actions against witches living among them, the acquittal and release of so many suspects in the weeks and months following the suspension of the trials must have been frustrating and also frightening. Popular disillusionment combined with official embarrassment following the debacle at Salem to bring about an end to witch trials in New England.

By the early eighteenth century, a degree of skepticism about certain kinds of allegedly supernatural phenomena began to take hold among those who embraced Enlightenment ideas. But belief in magic and astrology would prove to be resilient among other Americans. In 1728 the pastor at Medford, Massachusetts, condemned young people for "sieve-turning" and "palmistry." And in 1755 the pastor at Westborough, Massachusetts, had to preach "against the foolish and wicked practice of going to cunning men to inquire for lost things." People continued to blame their misfortunes on witchcraft: countermagic remained a popular weapon against occult attack, and popular fear of witchcraft occasionally erupted into physical violence. In the summer of 1787, as delegates met in Philadelphia to draft the federal constitution, a woman sustained fatal injuries inflicted by a mob in a street nearby because they believed that she was a witch. Meanwhile, treasure-seekers across the newly independent states were using divining rods and peep stones that they scrutinized in the darkness of their hats to locate pirate hoards in the hope of instant enrichment. Belief in the occult as a credible and valuable tool might no longer be intellectually respectable, but the nineteenth century would show just how powerful a force it remained within American culture.[36]

---

[36] Ebenezer Turrell, "Detection of Witchcraft," *Collections of the Massachusetts Historical Society* 2nd ser., 10 (1823): 19–20; Francis Wallett, ed., *The Diary of Ebenezer Parkman, 1703–1782* (Worcester, 1974), 288; *Independent Journal* (New York), 18 July 1787; and Alan Taylor, "The Early Republic's Supernatural Economy: Treasure-Seeking in the American North-East, 1780–1830," *American Quarterly* 38 (1986): 6–34. For nineteenth-century occult practices, see Butler, *Awash in a Sea of Faith*, ch. 8.

SUGGESTIONS FOR FURTHER READING

Butler, Jon. *Awash in a Sea of Faith: Christianizing the American People.* Cambridge, MA, 1990.

Demos, John Putnam. *Entertaining Satan: Witchcraft and the Culture of Early New England.* New York, 1982.

Godbeer, Richard. *The Devil's Dominion: Magic and Religion in Early New England.* New York, 1992.

Hall, David D. *Worlds of Wonder, Days of Judgment: Popular Religious Belief in Early New England.* New York, 1989.

Hansen, Chadwick. *Witchcraft at Salem*, New York, 1969.

Karlsen, Carol F. *The Devil in the Shape of a Woman: Witchcraft in Colonial New England.* New York, 1987.

Leventhal, Herbert. *In the Shadow of the Enlightenment: Occultism and Renaissance Science in Eighteenth-Century America.* New York, 1976.

Reis, Elizabeth. *Damned Women: Sinners and Witches in Puritan New England.* Ithaca, 1997.

Woodward, Walter W. *Prospero's America: John Winthrop, Jr., Alchemy, and the Creation of New England Culture, 1606–1676.* Chapel Hill, 2009.

Section V

AMERICAN RELIGIONS IN THE EIGHTEENTH-CENTURY INTERNATIONAL CONTEXT

26

RELIGION AND IMPERIAL CONFLICT

JON SENSBACH

As war between Britain and France raged around the world in the 1750s, religious writers in colonial British America described the conflict as nothing short of the apocalypse foretold in the Book of Revelation. The battle between Protestant Britain and Catholic France, as they saw it, represented the death struggle between Christ and the Antichrist, and Britain's triumph would deal a mortal blow to the "beast" of Rome. With British victory in the Seven Years' War assured, sealing the ouster of France from North America in 1763, millennialist prophets anticipated Christ's imminent return and the onset of a thousand-year reign of peace. In the short term, however, Britain was suddenly faced with the practical problem of what to do with the Catholic population it inherited in Canada. Should these French and Indian faithful, some seventy thousand of them, be absorbed into the empire, forced to convert to Protestantism, or banished altogether? In the end, the British adopted a relatively lenient policy of religious toleration and recognition of rights for Catholics. The policy was met with anger in the British colonies, especially in New England, where traditional anti-Catholicism ran deep, and the controversy exacerbated the deteriorating relationship between the colonies and Britain in the early 1770s.

The policy dilemma, and Britain's resolution of it, illustrates two dominant, if countervailing, themes in the relationship between religion and empire in America during the eighteenth century. For the three major powers in North America – Britain, France, and Spain – imperial dominion went hand in glove with the advancement of state religion, and as had been the case since the sixteenth century, the cycle of international wars among these competitors was as much about the struggle between Protestantism and Catholicism as about national might. At the same time, the exigencies of imperial rule, compounded by a tenuous movement toward toleration of some religious nonconformists, occasionally dictated a more pragmatic approach to the deployment of religious ideology in political disputes.

The age of revolution disrupted orthodox religious and political alliances among the contestants.

Religion had been an ideological cornerstone of Spanish, British, and French imperial designs in America since the sixteenth century. The bloody wars of the Reformation and Counter-Reformation that left thousands dead across Europe leaped the Atlantic and fueled what would become a longstanding Protestant-Catholic rivalry in the New World. Spain claimed North America in the early sixteenth century in the cause of global Catholicism, a stake it backed up violently with the massacre of several hundred French Huguenot Protestant settlers in Florida in 1565, marking an early victory for the Counter Reformation in America. England responded with aggressive attempts at colonization along the Atlantic seaboard beginning in the 1580s to secure a base for militant Protestantism that would, according to imperial theorist Richard Hakluyt the Younger, "abate the pride of Spaine and of the supporter of the great Antechriste of Rome."[1] France, in turn, claimed the vast interior of the continent in the early seventeenth century, anchoring another bastion of Catholicism in its colony of New France.

In Mexico, the mission system had proven the centerpiece of Spain's attempts to secure North America for Catholicism. Jesuit and Franciscan priests regarded the New World as a sacred space in which to project their providential vision of a redeemed world. To them, Indians were the important players in this divine drama because, in their innocence and purity, they represented mankind before the Fall, through whom God would act to restore paradise and usher in his kingdom in America. Accordingly, church officials built chains of missions along the North American edge of the empire in Florida and New Mexico in an attempt to forcibly assimilate Indians into the realm. Although seventeenth-century Indian rebellions inspired by the friars' harshness in both Florida and New Mexico gave evidence that earthly paradise remained a distant vision, the crown still considered missions the front line of Spain's North American defense network against Protestant heresy and a vital part of Spanish strategy. Jesuit missions among the Hurons, and later the Mohawks in New France, served a similar purpose.

A narrative of Protestant struggle against Catholic tyranny, meanwhile, emerged as a defining feature of English national and imperial identity in the late sixteenth century. Several key events became touchstones in this sense of struggle: the persecution of Protestants during the reign of

---

[1] Richard Hakluyt, *A Discourse Concerning Western Planting* (1584), quoted in Jonathan Locke Hart, *Representing the New World: The English and French Uses of the Example of Spain* (New York, 2000), 148.

Mary Tudor, or Bloody Mary, who had hundreds of dissenters burned at the stake; the St. Bartholomew's massacre of thousands of Huguenots in France in 1572; the assault on England by the Spanish Armada in 1588; and the attempted assassination of King James I and the Protestant-dominated Parliament by Catholic conspirators in the Gunpowder Plot of 1605. The New World also played a fundamental role in this narrative, as tales of Spanish atrocities against native people became the basis for the "black legend" popularized by Protestant propagandists eager to demonstrate that America needed magnanimous English rule and superstition-free Protestant religion. Despite these lofty promises, English colonists could be just as harsh toward natives; and in contrast to the Spanish, who sought to draw Indians into colonial society through religion, the English quickly came to regard Indians as unassimilable, made little effort to convert them to Protestantism, and generally excluded them from society.

The intensity of religious antagonism ebbed and flowed throughout the seventeenth century among the principal combatants in both Europe and America. Monolithic Protestant and Catholic coalitions did not always hold fast, and religious unity sometimes became subordinate to political rivalry. The Thirty Years War, which ravaged continental Europe between 1618 and 1648, began as a religious war between traditional Catholic and Protestant enemies. In the 1630s, however, France, fearful of the power of Habsburg Spain and the Holy Roman Empire, abandoned its Catholic allies and sided with the Protestants. In England, meanwhile, civil war between Royalists and Parliamentarians in the 1640s also embodied a religious conflict between rival groups of Protestants, Church of England supporters against Puritan dissenters; and the beheading of Charles I gave the death knell for the divine right of monarchs in England. The restoration of royal power under Charles II in 1660 did, however, reestablish the Church of England in a nation that had had no state church during Oliver Cromwell's rule.

Despite these schisms among Protestants and Catholics, the larger rivalry between those two branches of Christendom intensified during the final two decades of the seventeenth century, bringing deep repercussions for America during the long eighteenth century. In 1686, France's King Louis XIV revoked the Edict of Nantes, ending limited religious toleration and sending thousands of Huguenot refugees to Britain and America, where thousands settled in New York, New Jersey, and South Carolina. To many Protestants, the migration of these radical Calvinist dissenters confirmed the sense of America as a haven for spiritual fugitives joined in a holy international movement against Catholic aggression. This notion ran particularly deep in Puritan New England, where colonists had long seen their "city on a hill" as the vehicle of providential destiny in the New World and as Protestantism's main line of defense against French Catholicism.

The Huguenot expulsions helped reinvigorate anti-Catholicism among English Protestants fearful their Catholic king, James II, would bring England into an unwelcome alliance with France. The overthrow of James and the installation of a new Protestant king, William III, in the Glorious Revolution of 1688 forged a new relationship between religion and politics in England and her American colonies based on Protestantism as a foundation of empire and hostility toward Catholicism. This moment of national unification was grounded further on limited toleration for Protestant dissenters as a way to overcome decades of crippling social upheaval and promote political consolidation. Religious toleration, wrote John Locke, the Glorious Revolution's chief political philosopher, "is the chief characteristic mark of the true church." Indeed, he added, to dispute that "toleration of those that differ from others in matters of religion is so agreeable to the Gospel of Jesus Christ, and to the genuine reason of mankind" would be "monstrous."[2] Locke took an expansive view of toleration, arguing that it should embrace Catholics and Jews as well as Protestant dissenters. But legislators still considered Catholicism too great a threat to the crown and to national security. Accordingly, the Toleration Act passed by Parliament in 1689 stated that "some ease to scrupulous consciences in the exercise of religion may be an effectual means to unite their Majesties Protestant subjects in interest and affection." The act guaranteed freedom of worship for Protestant dissenters, although they were still denied some political rights. But it also reaffirmed previous statutes against "popish recusants" and banned "Papists from sitting in either house of Parliament."[3] Granted no rights, Catholics were purged from the many government posts they had held under James, and the constitution guaranteed a Protestant succession to the throne. England joined the Dutch Republic in declaring war against France in what Protestant champions hailed as an energized struggle against global Catholicism.

The symbiotic connection between nationalism and anti-Catholicism was tempered by the realpolitik of imperial rivalry. When convenient, Britain sometimes allied with Catholic nations such as Austria, which was considered less of a threat than France to impose worldwide Catholic supremacy. Still, British popular culture reinforced the connection between national glory and providential Protestant victory. John Bunyan's widely sold *The Pilgrim's Progress* (1678–84), for example, which featured cruelties inflicted on Protestant protagonists by Catholic tormentors, portrayed popish tyranny as a trial to be overcome by enlightened Protestants on the way to spiritual and national triumph.

---

[2] John Locke, *A Letter Concerning Toleration* (London, 1689), 1.
[3] Toleration Act (1689), in Andrew Browning, ed., *English Historical Documents, 1660–1714* (London, 1953), 400–3.

In England's American colonies, anti-Catholicism had likewise intensified during the 1680s, overlapping with the Glorious Revolution. The ouster of James II and the new reign of William III were widely viewed in the colonies as a saving triumph for Protestantism. Without it, a New York colonist declared, Catholics would have "fetter'd all Europe."[4] Deep-rooted hostility toward Catholicism was particularly vehement along the northern and southern imperial fringes, where the threat from England's rivals for New World supremacy, France and Spain, was most conspicuous. In New England, colonists bearing raw memories of King Philip's War in 1676 remained wary of a French and Indian alliance on their borders. Militant Puritans in Massachusetts considered the war evidence of divine displeasure with their colony's ungodliness, regarding the Catholic power of New France as an agent of the Antichrist bent on undermining God's work in America. But the Puritan leadership also opposed toleration for Protestant religious dissenters such as Quakers and Baptists, believing that adherence to the congregational order laid out by the colony's founders was part of their collective covenant with God that could not be undermined by alternative religious viewpoints. As late as 1692, the colony's defiant intolerance became increasingly anachronistic in light of official metropolitan recognition of Nonconformity, and even compared with the relative toleration practiced in Restoration-era colonies such as Pennsylvania, New Jersey, and New York. To the south, likewise, the relatively new proprietary colony of Carolina, founded in 1670 on land once claimed by Spain, also saw itself on the frontier of the struggle against the Catholic bastion of Florida, although in somewhat less apocalyptic terms than did New Englanders. The colony excluded Catholics, but unlike Massachusetts, it provided toleration for Protestant dissenters even before the Glorious Revolution and established the Church of England in the early eighteenth century.

As in England, colonial anti-Catholicism reflected fears of political repression by royal authority. Before the Glorious Revolution, this resentment was directed toward Edmund Andros, governor of the unpopular new administrative district called the Dominion of New England, formed by James II in 1686 out of the Puritan colonies as well as New York and New Jersey. James sought to bring these colonies under closer royal control by enforcing the Navigation Acts and revoking colonial charters. Andros was considered in Massachusetts to be the king's Catholic-loving flunky determined to make peace with the French, abrogate colonial liberties, and impose the Church of England. After the Glorious Revolution, a coalition of merchants and ministers raised troops, arrested Andros, and deported

---

[4] Brendan McConville, *The King's Three Faces: The Rise and Fall of Royal America, 1688–1776* (Chapel Hill, 2006), 114.

him to England. Two more popular antiroyalist uprisings in 1689 similarly deposed colonial officials regarded as papist conspirators. In New York, merchant Jacob Leisler denounced Dominion officials as papist lackeys, unseated Governor Francis Nicholson, and seized power. In the Catholic-controlled colony of Maryland, planter John Coode formed "an Association in Arms for the Defense of Protestant Religion," seized control of the colonial government, expelled Catholics from office, and prohibited Catholics from worshipping publicly. In all these cases, King William III reasserted crown control over the rebellious colonies by 1692, installing royal governors and representative assemblies, restoring some liberties, and enforcing grudging religious tolerance of Protestant dissenters. In Massachusetts, resentment over crown interference and tensions produced by a persistent fear of Catholicism, Indians, and dissenters helped feed the Salem witchcraft hysteria of 1692.

By the end of the seventeenth century, therefore, religious intolerance helped reinvigorate the imperial struggle among Britain, France, and Spain that played out on a global theater, including multiple venues in North America and the West Indies. This contest gained new force in 1699 with the French colonization of Louisiana, a move that, by exerting control at the mouth of the Mississippi, sought to open a new front in the containment of Anglo-American Protestant imperialism. The bold French claim to the enormous middle third of the continent was designed to link Canada to the Gulf of Mexico and to France's sugar colonies in the West Indies while securing a Catholic base in the region. The strategy intensified Anglo-American fears of French encirclement and strengthened British colonial resolve to confront the threat aggressively.

Long-simmering contention over territory and religious hegemony in Europe and the New World erupted in 1701 with the War of the Spanish Succession, pitting an alliance of European states against the union of Spain and France. Known in British America as Queen Anne's War, the conflict brought Britain's enduring rivalry with France and Spain into open hostility as a contest over many things – territorial and geopolitical supremacy, trade, Indian allegiances, and even slaves – but fundamental to it as well were competing visions of empire rooted in religious identity. Thus it was seen on both sides as a continuation of the long-running Protestant-Catholic holy war over imperial politics and cosmic hegemony. As during the previous quarter century, the war was waged particularly bitterly in contested borderlands regions. French and Mohawk raids decimated Puritan communities in western Massachusetts, taking hundreds of captives. To the south, combined forces of South Carolina militia and Creek Indians raided the Spanish missions in northern Florida in 1702 and 1704, destroying the mission system that had been the bulwark of Spanish colonization in the

Southeast for more than a century. Hundreds of Catholicized Apalachee and Timucua Indians as well as several Spanish friars were killed in the assault, including many who were burned alive by Creek captors. In one mission, seventeen prisoners were tied to stakes or "stations of the cross" in the town plaza and set alight. Thousands more Indians were taken captive and sold into slavery in Carolina and the West Indies. Spanish reports on the massacres portrayed the victims as martyrs sacrificed in God's holy war against paganism. Religious and political violence thus transformed the southeastern frontier by annihilating the great majority of the region's native Catholic adherents. Although the Treaty of Utrecht ended the War of the Spanish Succession in 1713, essentially resulting in a stalemate in both European and American theaters, it left deep scars on colonial and Indian communities in New England and the deep South.

Although native people controlled much of the Southeast throughout the first half of the eighteenth century, the vast region remained a volatile disputed zone of competing imperial claims triangulated between Spanish Florida, French Louisiana, and Britain's southern colonies. The contested border between Florida and South Carolina, in particular, became for Britain a test case of the mixed political objectives of imperial expansion, anti-Catholic militancy, and religious toleration, leading to the founding of a new colony, Georgia, in 1732 as a buffer against the Spanish threat to Carolina. The colony was meant, among other objectives, to deter escape by enslaved Africans, who were tempted by Spanish promises of freedom to flee Carolina, seek refuge in Florida, and convert to Catholicism. Toleration and religious diversity became weapons in the arsenal of James Oglethorpe, the colony's principal founder, to anchor Georgia as a vital southern link in a transatlantic Protestant chain encompassing northern Europe, the British Isles, and British America. With no established church, Georgia welcomed Protestant dissenters (and even a small number of Jews), such as a group of Lutheran pietist Salzburgers who, after their expulsion from Austria, eagerly embraced the founding vision of tolerance, humanitarian philanthropy, and antislavery that for a time made the colony unique in British America.

In 1739 the long dispute between Britain and Spain again flared, in the War of Jenkins' Ear, which recharged a British sense of global Protestant unity against Catholic aggression. The Anglican bishop Isaac Maddox expressed that sense of struggle by denouncing "all the Methods of Violence, and all the Influence of Persecution" perpetrated by Catholicism. "With other gross Absurdities of Popery," the Church of England "most cordially rejects that cruel Spirit, which spreads Devastation and Misery upon Earth, and calls down Fire from heaven." In contrast to those atrocities, he declared, the Anglican Church was a model of humility and toleration, "*in meekness instructing those that oppose.*"[5] Such noble pronouncements, expressed from the safety of London, furnished a religious justification for an imperial war, but for James Oglethorpe the desperate struggle for Georgia's survival against the Spanish Catholic threat from Florida was much more pressing. His defeat of a Spanish attack on Georgia from St. Augustine in 1742 preserved the fledgling colony as a Protestant stronghold, anchoring Britain's southern mainland claim. An unintended consequence of Oglethorpe's victory was that with the end of the Spanish threat the colony's original humanitarian mission lost its lustre. The Trustees, Georgia's governing board, revoked the ban on slavery in 1750, hastening the colony's embrace of slaveholding.

Hatred of Catholics proved a potent tool for binding disparate elements of the Anglo-American population to the power of the empire, defining Britishness as Protestant. Catholicism became the enemy against which British liberties were defined. Anti-Catholicism instilled fear and suspicion that could be manipulated for purposes of social control, resulting in a desire to root out perceived outsiders; a distrust of ethnic, linguistic, and religious difference; an eagerness to blame misfortune on Catholic subversion; and an enforced social conformity. When, in 1741, a suspected slave revolt was uncovered in New York, officials blamed a shadowy priest for "the most horrible and Detestable" plot "brooded in a Conclave of Devils, and hatcht in the Cabinet of Hell." The blame for the revolt lay on "popish emissaries" who had led the slaves astray – not on the slaves' desire to be free. After the leaders of the plot were executed, city officials searched house by house to uncover "Strangers ... obscure People that have no visible way of Subsistence" who might pose threats to public safety. Anti-Catholicism merged with xenophobia to unite those holding relative social power by rooting out potential foes, deflecting attention away from underlying social tensions.[6]

Mercantilist commercial expansion and shared defensive needs helped draw Britain's North American and West Indian colonies into the empire during the first half of the eighteenth century. Religion played an essential role in this work of imperial integration by providing a shared commitment to Protestant ideals within a loose structure of religious pluralism, limited toleration, and decentralized state religious control. Although the colonies exercised some measure of autonomy through their elected legislatures, their essential relationship to the empire was one of political unity and commitment to British conceptions of liberty. But the colonies themselves

---

[5] Eliga H. Gould, *The Persistence of Empire: British Political Culture in the Age of the American Revolution* (Chapel Hill, 2000), 19. Emphasis in the original, here and throughout.
[6] McConville, *King's Three Faces*, 116–17.

were unruly, contentious places marked by religious traditionalism as well as dissent, social heterogeneity, and rapid growth. These factors produced a weak religious presence by established religion. By the late seventeenth century, the population of colonial British North America had the fastest growth rate in the world, at 3 percent annually, driven by natural increase, the African slave trade, and the voluntary migration of British, Scots-Irish, and Germans. A population of fifty thousand in 1650 rose to more than two million by 1750. There was no consistent pattern of church-state relations. Congregationalism was established in some colonies, the Church of England was established in others, and Pennsylvania had no state church. Georgia established Anglicanism in 1756. But with no American bishops, a chronically underdeveloped infrastructure, and a diverse colonial population from numerous dissenting traditions, Anglicanism remained weak, even in some places where it did have a foothold, as in the Carolinas. Imperial policy, therefore, was predicated more on minimal state religious control than on voluntary or forced adherence to an established church.

The advancement of Protestantism as an imperial aim thus became a crucial ideological glue that bound these competing forces together. The advent of the evangelical revivals during the 1730s that came to be known as the Great Awakening intensified this conviction among evangelicals and more traditional churchgoers alike. Although the era of religious awakening left a powerful imprint on the culture and politics of colonial America – forming a precursor to the American Revolution, as many historians have argued – the revivals in America should also be appreciated as a part of a transatlantic evangelical Protestant series of awakenings in continental Europe, Britain, and America. Much of this revivalist spirit bore the imprint of continental pietism, which, originating within the Lutheran Church in the late seventeenth century, deemphasized the finer points of formal theological doctrine and elevated an emotional religion of the heart and the need for spiritual rebirth in Christ. This influential approach made its way from Britain to the colonies, resurfacing in localized revivals, first in Dutch Reformed congregations in New Jersey and slightly later in western Massachusetts under the auspices of Jonathan Edwards. Across the Atlantic, by the 1730s thousands of Protestants eagerly embraced some version of teaching that encouraged them to bypass orthodox religious authority and take charge of their own salvation through a close relationship with Christ.

The revivals did not begin as explicit attempts to foster social divisions or to redefine the link between religion and politics in colonial British America, but they quickly achieved that effect. Given the weakness of civil and ecclesiastical authority, the Great Awakening generated, or revealed, new layers of religious, social, and political division that established churches had always sought to subsume under their hierarchy. By the late 1730s, itinerant evangelical preachers such as George Whitefield, Gilbert Tennent, and James Davenport took their preaching out of the pulpit and directly to the public, addressing crowds of thousands in town squares, fields, and barns. The evangelicals, or New Lights, portrayed themselves as champions of the people seeking to revive moribund Christianity and undermine the stodginess of church authorities who jealously guarded their prerogative to interpret and control God's Word. Accusing the Old Lights of spiritual lifelessness and insufficient piety, the New Lights urged listeners to make their own choices, to take a greater role in church affairs. Tennent called the established clergy "ungodly ministers" constantly "driving, driving, to duty, duty" as a substitute for real Christian conversion. He and other New Lights cast their attacks as a matter of spiritual freedom, as an "unscriptural infringement on Christian liberty" for false ministers to deny authentic teachers of the gospel at the people's expense. The effect of such language was to encourage ordinary people, especially socially marginal groups such as the laboring poor, slaves, and women of all classes, to begin challenging authority and to participate eagerly in congregational life, even to preach and exhort others.[7]

As the revivals surged up and down the Atlantic seaboard from New England to Georgia, sharply dividing Presbyterian, Baptist, and Congregational churches, factions repeatedly split off from the "spiritual tyranny" of their parent congregations and set themselves up as regenerate new apostolic churches. As the Old Lights feared, religious schism and the questioning of ecclesiastical authority fostered calls for social equality and resentment against civil authority. Some New Lights denounced wealth and social hierarchy as ungodly, and ostentatious luxury as a sign of corruption. Threatened by the breakdown in religious and social deference, the Old Lights responded vigorously, denouncing the "enthusiastic, factious, censorious Spirit" of the evangelicals and accusing itinerants such as Tennent of sowing "the Seeds of all that Discord, Intrusion, Confusion, Separation, hatred, Variance, Emulations, Wrath, Strife, seditions, Heresies, &c that have been springing up in so many of the Towns and Churches thro' the Province." One minister, Charles Chauncy, contended that "Good Order is the Strength and Beauty of the World," which was threatened, wrote Isaac Stiles of Connecticut, when "Contempt is cast upon Authority both Civil and Ecclesiastical."[8]

---

[7] Gilbert Tennent, *The Dangers of an Unconverted Ministry* (Philadelphia, 1740), 10, 21.
[8] Patricia U. Bonomi, *Under the Cope of Heaven: Religion, Society and Politics in Colonial America* (New York, 2003), 150, 151.

Some colonies passed legal restrictions on evangelical preaching, even providing for the expulsion of radicals considered too threatening. In Virginia, New Lights were attacked by mobs, arrested and fined, and forbidden from preaching. As established religion and orthodox political authority became directly implicated in the maintenance of social order, the awakenings forced a dispute over the meaning and limits of religious toleration. Anticipating language that would become famous a generation later, Connecticut cleric Elisha Williams drew on John Locke in *The Essential Rights and Liberties of Protestants* (1744) to argue that the objective of civil government was the "greater Security of Enjoyment of what belongs to everyone," and that *"this Right of private Judgment,* and *worshipping* GOD according to the *Consciences"* was the *"natural and unalienable Right of every Man."*[9] For George Whitefield, likewise, it was a question of liberty – religious, political, and social liberty, bound up together, a British imperial birthright that Americans shared. "We breathe indeed in a free air," he told an audience in Philadelphia in 1746, "as free (if not freer) both as to temporals and spirituals, as any nation under heaven."[10]

For many evangelicals, the question of religious freedom assumed a larger political dimension when they linked the swelling of revivalist fervor with the larger cosmic struggle against the Antichrist. In this radical millennialist outlook, religious enthusiasm presaged the advent of Christ's kingdom and the defeat of the wicked, who might be not only the ungodly in colonial society, but also the traditional and convenient enemy of Catholicism. Elisha Williams' "unalienable right" to freedom of conscience was grounded in the warning of what followed in the absence of toleration: "the clergy through Pride and Ambition assumed the power of prescribing to, imposing on and domineering over the Consciences of men; civil Rulers for their own private Ends helping it forward; which went on 'till it produced the most detestable *Monster* the Earth ever had upon it, the *Pope,* who has deluged the Earth with the Blood of Christians." Thus was revealed the "true Spirit of *Popery,* to impose their Determinations on all with their Power by any Methods" necessary, and any *"civil magistrates* that suffered and helped that *Beast* to invade this Right, did therein *commit Fornication with her, and give her their Strength and Power."*[11] Evangelicals throughout the Protestant world on both sides of the Atlantic saw the new

---

[9] Elisha Williams, *The Essential Rights and Liberties of Protestants* (Boston, 1744), quoted in Alan Heimert and Perry Miller, eds., *The Great Awakening* (Indianapolis, 1967), 324.
[10] Gould, *Persistence of Empire,* 20.
[11] Williams, *Essential Rights and Liberties of Protestants,* in Heimert and Miller, *Great Awakening,* 325.

spiritual fervor as evidence of God's mighty dealings against the Catholic beast. Several British military victories against the French during the 1740s, combined with the British defeat of the Catholic Jacobite claimant to the throne, Charles Edward Stuart (derided as "the Young Pretender" by his opponents), at Culloden, Scotland, in 1746, gave encouraging signs of divine approval for the struggle.

Reinvigorated by the awakenings, conventional Anglo-American antipopery found further reinforcement in the prophetic view, advanced perhaps most forcefully by Jonathan Edwards, that America stood poised to realize its special destiny as the site of Christ's new kingdom on earth. Echoing the providential certainty of the Puritan founders' vision of America as the New Jerusalem, Edwards saw the revivals as God's sign of the approaching millennium, which, unfolding in the New World, would sweep the Antichrist to final doom. From his reading of the Book of Revelation, Edwards construed the likelihood "that this work of God's spirit, that is so extraordinary and wonderful, is the dawning, or at least, a prelude of that glorious work of God, so often foretold in Scripture.... And there are many things that make it probable that this work will begin in America." Noting that the end time was prophesied to begin "in some very remote part of the world" accessible only by sea, he concluded that America must be the site of divine intent, and "it gives more abundant reason to hope that what is now seen in America, and especially in New England, may prove the dawn of that glorious day," the beginning "of something vastly great."[12] Historians have identified Edwards' writings as fundamental to an emerging kind of religious nationalism that, when mixed with Whiggish constitutionalism, marked a potent marriage of religion and politics in the mid-eighteenth century that emphasized the language of American rights and freedom. And the traditional foe of Catholicism provided a convenient target for these sensibilities.

Many New Lights saw the advent of war with France in the 1750s as the culmination of eschatological politics, the moment of God's final reckoning with the Antichrist. Although the war was to be waged on a global scale, evangelicals often saw the American theater of war as the essential struggle for the soul of the continent and the confirmation of American providential destiny. Writers invoked history to remind readers of the implacable awfulness of the Catholic persecutors. A Boston newspaper in 1754 reviewed the history of the St. Bartholomew's Day massacre in France in 1572 and the revocation of the Edict of Nantes in 1686 to illustrate the consequences of Catholic absolutism. During the revocation, the paper explained, "The

---

[12] Jonathan Edwards, *Some Thoughts Concerning the Present Revival of Religion in New England* (Boston, 1742), quoted in Heimert and Miller, *Great Awakening*, 270, 273.

Intendant of each Province, with the Bishop, went from Town to Town, and having summoned the Protestants ... let them know, That it was his most Christian Majesty's Pleasure, that the Roman Catholick Religion only should be professed in his dominions." Those who refused to convert were slaughtered by troops shouting, *"Die, or turn Roman Catholick!"* Protestants were hung "on Hooks in their Chimneys, by their Hair and Feet, and smoaked with Whisps of wet Hay.... Others were thrown into Fires ... and after they were desperately scorched, let down by Ropes into Wells." Protection from these dangers could only be safeguarded by the British Empire and its Protestant – in this case Hanoverian – monarchs.[13]

The onset of war rekindled the hunt for internal Catholic enemies. The governors of Maryland and Virginia expressed concern about the loyalty of Maryland's Catholic population, who, it was feared, would welcome an invasion by French and Indians as a means to "establish their religion."[14] British imperial administrators also turned their focus on Acadia, the former French colony conquered by the British in 1713, where Catholic colonists had been allowed to practice their faith. Now deemed too great a threat to security, some ten thousand Acadians were expelled in 1755, most of them migrating to Louisiana. Fear of an internal Catholic enemy in this case resulted in a thorough ethnic and religious cleansing of virtually an entire colony.

Endorsing violence in a righteous cause, preachers urged their flocks to take up arms in the cosmic battle with the Catholic Whore of Babylon. A successive string of British defeats in the early years of the war was as disheartening to evangelicals as to other Anglo-American colonists, but some reminded downhearted listeners that the righteous must endure God's stern test before claiming prophetic victory. "The Destruction of *Antichrist*, and the End of this Night of *Popish* Darkness, is near at hand," to be followed by God's *"plentiful, outpouring* of the Spirit of all Grace," assured one writer. In Virginia, New Light Presbyterian Samuel Davies wondered in 1756 whether "the present war is the commencement of this grand decisive conflict between the Lamb and the beast, i.e. between the protestant and the popish powers?" He felt certain that it was: "However bloody and desolating this last conflict may be, it will bring about the most glorious and happy revolution that ever was in the world."[15] Davies made a direct connection between the Roman Catholic threat and his own work evangelizing among African slaves in Virginia. "When the *French*

---

[13] McConville, *King's Three Faces*, 85, 118.
[14] *Ibid.*, 118.
[15] Ruth Bloch, *Visionary Republic: Millennial Themes in American Thought, 1756–1800* (New York, 1985), 40.

and *Indians* are invading our country, and perpetrating the most shocking barbarities and depredations upon our frontiers, we have not been without alarming apprehensions of Insurrection and Massacre, from the *numerous Slaves* among ourselves, whom they might seduce to their interest by the delusive promises of Liberty." He saw the war as a chance to steer the slaves away from such delusions and to seek help from their true friends, the Anglo-Americans. "Now I can distribute these books among them as tokens of disinterested benevolence, as helps to understand Christianity, and in the mean time to detect the Impostures, Superstitions and Cruelties of POPERY."[16] Evangelicals like Davies, still considered potentially subversive by the authorities in part because they preached to slaves, might have declared their support for the war in unequivocal religious terms to demonstrate patriotism and mollify their critics. Still, that position was also theologically consistent with their belief in God's mighty Protestant cause. Throughout the Protestant Atlantic, Britain's victory in 1763 was hailed as a glorious defeat of militant Catholicism; for evangelicals and even many mainstream liberal Protestants in British America, the eviction of Britain's great foe from the continent – along with the takeover by the British of Spanish Florida – confirmed God's glorious plan to use America to usher in the millennium.

As the American Revolution just thirteen years later would demonstrate, Anglo-American victory would help drive a wedge almost immediately between Britain and its North American colonies. Without the common enemy of Catholic France to unite them, the imperial partners quickly fell to squabbling. Disputes over Indian rebellions on the Appalachian frontier, the Proclamation Line of 1763, taxes, and the broader relationship of the colonies to the metropole could not be covered over by appeals to a shared Protestant identity. In fact, the changes to early American society and religion wrought by the Great Awakening found ample expression in the emerging disputes with Britain, with the result that the epithets of anti-Catholicism could be quickly turned back on the colonies' imperial protector. In short, whereas religion had once served to keep the empire together, now it helped drive it apart.

As made manifest by the bitter denunciations by evangelicals of perceived British high-handedness during the 1760s, the revivals had sowed in large cross sections of the colonial Anglo-American public a suspicion of power. Religious awakening produced a skeptical and even harshly critical antiauthoritarianism that was easily transferred from church figures to imperial government officials. "The common people now claim as good a

---

[16] Samuel Davies, *Letters from the Rev. Samuel Davies* (London, 1757), quoted in Thomas S. Kidd, *The Great Awakening: A Brief History with Documents* (Boston, 2008), 118–19.

right to judge and act for themselves in matters of religion as civil rulers or the learned clergy," wrote Isaac Backus in 1768. Evangelical religion and classical republican theory, as one historian has written, shared common ground not only in the language of "unalienable rights," but also in "the revolutionary appeals to a virtuous citizenry, the ethic of self-sufficiency and frugality ... [and] the characterization of the royal ministers as greedy, self-interested, dissolute, and even Catholic at heart."[17]

Beyond the dispute over imperial authority and colonial rights, several specific religious issues added to colonists' pique on the eve of permanent political rupture. One was the fear that the Anglican Church would install a bishop over the American colonies in an effort to enforce religious conformity and fasten imperial control all the tighter. Indeed, Anglican officials had discussed the possibility for years without acting on it, but the renewed prospect of a bishop in the context of the political tensions of the 1760s confirmed to many colonists Britain's desire to impose arbitrary rule and religious conformity to a state church established in all the colonies. Perceived British political tyranny now sought to deprive religious freedom. "Let the pulpit resound with the doctrines and sentiments of religious liberty," John Adams wrote in 1765. "There is a direct and formal design on foot to enslave America."[18] Although it was unclear how broadly and inclusively Adams and others defined "religious liberty" – or whether it meant in this case simply the absence of a bishop – some revolutionaries were already framing their arguments partly on the basis of freedom of conscience.

A second grievance was the resurgent fear of Catholicism now represented by Britain's acquisition of Quebec in the Seven Years' War. The British had debated what to do with the seventy thousand Quebecois and natives who now became subjects of the empire. Some imperial administrators were uneasy about absorbing so many Catholics into a realm predicated on Protestant identity. Compounding the problem of assimilation was the presence of several thousand Catholic Indians, about whom one British official said, "These Savages are extremely attached to the Ceremonials of the [Catholic] Church, & have been taught to believe the English have no Knowledge of the Mystery of Man's Redemption by Jesus Christ."[19] Forced conformity to Protestantism for these servants of Rome no doubt seemed the best option to some imperial officials. In the end, however, rather than removal or forced conversion, Britain decided on a policy of lenience. To

---

[17] Bloch, *Visionary Republic*, 15.
[18] John Adams, *A Dissertation on the Canon and Feudal Law* (Boston, 1765), 34.
[19] Carla Pestana, *Protestant Empire: Religion and the Making of the British Atlantic World* (Philadelphia, 2008), 222.

ensure that the French and native Catholics would not join the growing revolutionary movement to the south, Parliament passed the Quebec Act in 1774, which permitted officeholders to practice Catholicism, eliminated references to Protestantism in the imperial oath of loyalty, and allowed state support of Catholic schools. In other parts of Canada that did not have a French Catholic presence, the Church of England would be established in the hope that in time Catholics would convert voluntarily. The Quebec Act was one of a series of punitive measures passed in response to the Boston Tea Party that came to be known in the colonies as the Intolerable Acts, and it was not calculated to win favor with rebellious colonists. Nonetheless, although imperial administrators insisted the act did not represent a softening of their commitment to a state church, the policy reflected a more pragmatic approach to the problem of absorbing large numbers of conquered people under Britain's control. In effect, the problem of maintaining an empire with all its divergent parts forced on them a grudging acknowledgment of a need for religious toleration.

This kind of toleration was not what Anglo-American colonists wanted. The Quebec Act generated backlash on both sides of the Atlantic. Protesters decried what they saw as the incorporation of popery and tyranny into an empire based on British freedom. The City of London protested that the act permitted Catholic worship "without any provision being made for the free exercise of the Protestant religion which may prove greatly injurious and oppressive to his Majesty's Protestant subjects."[20] In New England, the presence of an established Catholic state within British imperial borders only intensified colonial Anglo-American resentment against the crown. Colonists who, according to one memoirist, had been taught "religiously" from birth to "abhor the Pope, Devil and Pretender," were now expected to coexist with their traditional enemies.[21] Rather than quell for good the papist threat on their northern border, as they had hoped, the Seven Years' War had brought their antagonists imperial protection and toleration. Many colonists, conflating their anti-Catholicism with opposition to an Anglican bishop, were now convinced that Parliament and the crown were conspiring to deprive them of liberty and impose on them the absolutism of a high church.

Many American evangelicals redirected their former rage toward the French against their own empire, focusing apocalyptic expectations on the dispute with Britain. The crown now became the Antichrist, coddler of Catholics, destroyer of natural liberties. Preachers urged support for boycotts to purge the sin of luxury and purify the country for the day of

---

[20] *Ibid.*, 223.
[21] McConville, *King's Three Faces*, 119.

reckoning with the Beast. They equated armed resistance to tyranny with godliness and attacked the Anglican Church for an unholy relationship to the state. In pamphlets, broadsides, and sermons, New Light clergy breathed life into Jonathan Edwards' millennial nationalism, comparing America to Israel and Britain to Egypt while proclaiming America the world's last, best hope for freedom. Imagining the eyes of the world on the colonial struggle, evangelicals described the showdown with Britain as a cosmic drama, the chosen moment in divine time that would banish the stain of sin and hasten Christ's kingdom. Anglican officials repeatedly accused New Light clergy of "breathing the spirit of rebellion on the people," and one churchman contended that "religion itself, or rather the Appearance of it, [has been] humbly ministered as an handmaid to Faction and Sedition."[22]

Although the Revolution split religious communities, as it did the general population, evangelical support proved crucial to the cause of independence. But their support came at a price. Evangelicals had directed their critique of the sins of luxury, unholiness, and corruption not only against the crown and its colonial representatives, but also against Anglo-American merchants, planters, lawyers, and other elites, many of them leaders in the revolutionary movement. To court evangelical support for independence, elites promised more electoral representation from ordinary folk as well as a greater degree of toleration and freedom for religious dissenters. With these concessions from influential leaders, many evangelicals backed the revolutionary movement, believing independence offered the best chance for religious and political reform. Theologically, resistance to Britain proved a compatible marriage of their desire for liberty of conscience and their belief that the struggle heralded a call for a new age of godly freedom. Of course, evangelicals and other revolutionaries flinched when the United States forged an alliance with France in 1777, but the pragmatic necessity of bolstering the flagging revolutionary cause overcame their reservations about making common cause with an old Catholic foe.

In its way, the American Revolution signaled an end to two centuries of religious warfare in the cause of imperial expansion in North America. Spain and France had staked their New World claims in the cause of Catholic triumph, Britain the same for Protestantism. The wars of the Reformation that carried over to America were central to the maintenance of transatlantic imperial identities for all three competing powers. Religion patterned the ways the rivals thought about themselves and their mission in America, their relations with native people, their conception of the state and its relationship to the church in America, and their notion of struggle

[22] Gould, *Persistence of Empire*, 189.

against a remorseless adversary. For Anglo-Americans, anti-Catholicism framed their earliest colonization attempts in the sixteenth century, shaped the notion of divine errand in New England, sustained them through the long-running wars with Spain and France during the seventeenth and eighteenth centuries, and carried through the American War of Independence. A shared commitment to Protestant religion helped bind the colonies to Britain, but that commitment was not strong enough to overcome social and political divisions that ultimately rent them apart.

By the end of the Revolution, the ideological and religious terrain had changed. France had been evicted from North America in 1763, never to return, its support for the American Revolution notwithstanding. Although substantial numbers of the Catholics who served as a rallying cry for Anglo-American anger against Britain remained in Quebec, their importance as an alien threat dimmed after the war. Britain retained control over Canada, and although its relations with the United States remained tense for the next 30 years, disputes between the two nations were much less about religion than about economic competition. The only other European power remaining in North America was Spain, which regained Florida in 1783 to accompany its vast claim to the western two-thirds of the continent. As such, it remained a potent Catholic presence in North America and an erstwhile ally during the Revolution of which the young nation remained wary.

In the United States, religious toleration gradually gave way to religious freedom and separation of church and state as codified in the Constitution. A cacophonous pluralism became the signifying marker of American religious liberty and identity, although popular intolerance toward Catholics, Jews, and other religious minorities and perceived outsiders continued. Officially, at least, disestablishment ended in the United States the long Anglo-American entwining of religious ideology and national advancement. Yet, in very different ways, religion remained as central to the sense of the American nation-state as it had to the British Empire whence it emerged. Whereas once the colonies had embraced and expressed the religious nationalism of the British Empire, many religious people, including elected officials and church leaders, now projected on the United States a sense of divine national destiny in spiritual and global affairs. To many, the post-Revolutionary world was simply that much closer to God's kingdom than the pre-Revolutionary one; a new generation of radical apocalyptic prophets urged the nation to purify itself and return to an unadulterated religion of the soul in preparation for the coming millennium.

And it was a Protestant millennium they had in mind. To the west, a seemingly inexhaustible wealth of land stretched to the far reaches of the continent that would guarantee the fulfillment of a divinely ordained rise of American freedom, empire, and global power. In this triumphal vision of what Thomas Jefferson called an "empire for liberty,"[23] the destiny of the nation went hand in hand with religious chosenness, a revitalized sense of America as the new Israel. The Louisiana Purchase in 1803 prepared the way for U.S. expansion, and as revolution swept Spain from the Americas by the 1820s, American conquest of Mexican territory would be characterized by the 1840s as American "manifest destiny." Certainly popular bigotry against native religions and Catholicism played a role in the confrontation with, and often removal of, Indians and Spanish-speaking people. But land as the putative lifeblood of American democracy was the chief objective of western expansion, and religion played a lesser ideological role in justifying conquest. The U.S. government did not advance an official state religion or religious philosophy as a handmaiden of expansion. In that regard, the United States departed from the long-standing link between religion and imperial identity in America.

SUGGESTIONS FOR FURTHER READING

Armitage, David. *The Ideological Origins of the British Empire*. New York, 2000.

Bloch, Ruth. *Visionary Republic: Millennial Themes in American Thought, 1756–1800*. New York, 1985.

Bonomi, Patricia U. *Under the Cope of Heaven: Religion, Society and Politics in Colonial America*. 2nd ed. New York, 2003.

Colley, Linda. *Britons: Forging the Nation 1707–1837*. New Haven, 1992.

Elliott, J. H. *Empires of the Atlantic World: Britain and Spain in America, 1492–1830*. New Haven, 2006.

McConville, Brendan. *The King's Three Faces: The Rise and Fall of Royal America, 1688–1776*. Chapel Hill, 2006.

Miller, Peter N. *Defining the Common Good: Empire, Religion and Philosophy in Eighteenth-Century Britain*. Cambridge, UK, 1994.

Pestana, Carla. *Protestant Empire: Religion and the Making of the British Atlantic World*. Philadelphia, 2008.

---

[23] Thomas Jefferson to James Madison, 27 Apr. 1809, cited in Bernard W. Sheehan, "Jefferson's 'Empire for Liberty,'" *Indiana Magazine of History* 100 (2005): 346.

27

EVANGELICAL AWAKENINGS IN THE ATLANTIC COMMUNITY

RICHARD P. HEITZENRATER

The eighteenth century in British America witnessed the flowering of an evangelical movement, especially within, but not entirely limited to, the Protestant churches. The spiritual phenomenon flourished during the first half of the century in many parts of the eastern colonies in what has often been called the Great Awakening. Many people of the time were certainly aware of a more widespread quickening of the Spirit in the ministries of the churches along the Atlantic seaboard, but the term has become a moniker by which historians now treat the American developments as part of a broader transatlantic spiritual awakening during that period.

Historians have debated such epoch-naming as though such questioning itself was part of their vocation. Is "medieval" an appropriate denominator for a period, seen as a "middle age" between the grandeur of the Greco-Roman world and its renaissance centuries later? Is "renaissance" a fitting term for a multifaceted movement that is difficult to define and date? Is "reformation" a singular term that fits a series of movements with different goals in different places at different times? Is "enlightenment" a useful designation for a movement that manifests itself in so many ways? The didactic usefulness of such terminology provides constant grist for the careful historian's mill, and the debates over such terminology will be endless. So it is also with the topic of this essay, the so-called evangelical awakenings, especially in their American manifestation.[1]

Any treatment of this phenomenon during this period, whatever it is called, thus demands some definitions and delimitations, which should emerge in the following discussion. Several key terms can connote different meanings, such as "evangelical," which here implies any number of approaches to the Christian faith that focus on such transforming

---

[1] Susan O'Brien, "A Transatlantic Community of Saints: The Great Awakening and the First Evangelical Network, 1735–55," *The American Historical Review* 91:4 (Oct. 1986): 811–32.

spiritual events as new birth, holy living, and evangelism, and "Atlantic community," which here means the North Atlantic, primarily Europe and the emerging United States.

EUROPEAN ROOTS

The first whiffs of this movement of the Spirit can be seen in German and English Pietism, many dissenting movements in British Protestantism, and similar holy living movements in Roman Catholicism. Ted Campbell has also argued that these developments have parallel movements in other religions that at times focus on "religion of the heart," such as Judaism.[2] In Europe, this religion of the heart can be seen especially within certain Lutheran groups in Germany, among some Roman Catholic mystics in France, and also among several other religions on the continent. In the British Isles, heartfelt religion flourished especially among the Welsh and Scottish Calvinists, the Wesleyan Methodists, and the followers of Lady Huntingdon.

Many common themes and emphases tie these otherwise disparate movements together, especially their emphasis on personal experience (sometimes called "conversion"), their stress on the direct sensation or inspiration of the Spirit (sometimes seen by opponents as "enthusiasm"), their brand of evangelical preaching (often called "gospel preaching"), and their interest in holy practices and disciplines of the Christian life.

One can never determine the actual origins of such a disparate movement. Without going back to the various strands of the sixteenth-century reformations, however, one can begin seeing the configuration of the defining emphases listed previously in Central Europe in Germany in the seventeenth century. Although it might be difficult to designate the "first" person or group to exemplify such a constellation of characteristics, one can certainly begin to see the important shift in emphasis from doctrine to experience in the writings of Johann Arndt, one of many who tried to recover the religious vitality they thought was essential to being a "true" Christian. Arndt was not so concerned about understanding theological truths as he was about personal application of those maxims to life.[3] One should not simply understand that Christ died for the sins of the world, but more so, one should experience the liberating forgiveness of Christ in one's own transformed life. This *pro mea* focus tries to recenter Christian

---

[2] Ted Campbell, *The Religion of the Heart: A Study of European Religious Life in the Seventeenth and Eighteenth Centuries* (Columbia, SC, 1991), 144–51.
[3] W. Reginald Ward, *Early Evangelicalism: A Global Intellectual History, 1670–1789* (Cambridge, UK, 2006), 8.

kerygma on the heart rather than the mind and recapture the vitality of the gospel of Christianity as a way of life more than a system of beliefs.

Philipp Jakob Spener took this message to heart and, although certainly orthodox Lutheran in his doctrinal concerns, he helped shape the emerging spirit of what W. Reginald Ward called "Church Pietism" in *Pia desideria* (1675), a work that was originally written as a preface to an edition of Arndt's sermons.[4] Spener's suggestions for reform include six specific proposals. These ideas became the basic agenda for German Pietism: (1) a return to *sola scriptura*; (2) a more spiritual priesthood of all believers; (3) a shift from *eruditio* to praxis; (4) a concern for restraint and charity in didactic polemics; (5) a reform of theological training toward more spiritual nurturing; and (6) a move toward edifying preaching that brings conviction and change. The soteriological framework for Spener's reforms was shaped by his concern for regeneration, an organic image, rather than justification, a forensic concept. He was also notable for establishing small groups (*collegia pietatis*) for the devotional study of scripture and the promotion of holy living.

These teachings were promoted at Spener's institution, the University of Halle, where August Hermann Francke joined the faculty in 1692 and essentially became Spener's successor as leader of the Pietist movement. He effectively implemented Pietist ideas by starting a school for the poor, an orphanage that accommodated three thousand persons, a publishing house, a medical clinic, and other institutional means of putting Christian love into practice. He also was instrumental in the development of small groups of laity, *collegium philobiblicum*, for the devotional study of scripture. And Francke produced several books that became central to the holy living tradition, such as *Nicodemus* (1706) and *Pietas Hallensis* (1705), a description of the charitable institutions that he started.

Besides the books that were published to spread this practical divinity, a wealth of correspondence began to reinforce a growing network of Pietists in various places in Europe. Many of the Pietist leaders were widely influential through their correspondence as well as their publications. Francke had some five thousand correspondents and wrote regularly to four or five hundred.[5] Laity discovered that they too could participate beyond their local revivals by means of such correspondence, describing holy lives and holy deaths. These letters often shared the personal Christian experiences of believers in various locations.[6] These materials were increasingly featured

---

[4] *Ibid.*, 2–3, 31–5.
[5] W. Reginald Ward, *The Protestant Evangelical Awakening* (Cambridge, UK, 1992), 2.
[6] D. Bruce Hindmarsh, *The Evangelical Conversion Narrative: Spiritual Autobiography in Early Modern England* (Oxford, 2005), esp. ch. 2, "The Revival of Conversion Narrative: Evangelical Awakening in the Eighteenth Century."

at some of their evangelical gatherings and often flowered into regular meetings known as "letter days."[7]

With a growing network of contacts around the world, Pietist influences began to grow. Nicholas Ludwig von Zinzendorf, Francke's student, provided some of his estate at Herrnhut as a haven for the displaced Moravians, the Unitas Fratrum, who soon spread to England and America. Peter Boehler and August Gottlieb Spangenberg were two of Zinzendorf's most notable protégés. Francke also corresponded with Cotton Mather in New England, who tried to put into practice there some of the Pietist program. Henry Melchior Muhlenberg studied at Halle before going to Pennsylvania to help lead Lutheranism in America. Francke's books and correspondence were instrumental in the spread of Pietist sensibilities in many parts of the world.

GREAT BRITAIN

The British Isles also witnessed an awakened interest in holy living and various movements of the Spirit in the late seventeenth and early eighteenth centuries. Anthony Horneck, born in the Palatinate in Germany, moved to England and began to agitate for a more lively sense of religion. His writings, such as *The Happy Ascetic* (1681), pushed for more scriptural discipline in everyday life. His work helped promote religious societies in the Church of England, small groups under the leadership of the parish priest that met for study, devotion, and the promotion of charitable activities, including schools and religious publications. These societies, led by the Society for Promoting Christian Knowledge (SPCK) and the Society for the Propagation of the Gospel in Foreign Parts, included support and participation from such leaders as Josiah Woodward, Thomas Bray, John and Charles Wesley, George Whitefield, and Anton Boehm (who was also a connection to Hallensian Pietism), and played an important role in the beginnings of the evangelical revival in the British Isles.

The interconnectedness of the movement that we are calling the "evangelical awakening" can be seen in the variety of influences that converge in the Wesleyan revival in eighteenth-century Britain. John Wesley's parents were raised in dissenting families but joined the Church of England as young adults. Samuel Wesley, his father, was a strong supporter of the SPCK and encouraged a religious society to flourish in his parish of Epworth at the turn of the century. The Oxford education of their sons, especially John, featured a reading bibliography that included the fixtures of the Pietist tradition, such as Thomas à Kempis, Jeremy

---

[7] Frank Lambert, *Inventing the "Great Awakening"* (Princeton, 1999), 156–7.

Taylor, A. H. Francke, William Law, and Henry Scougal; mystics such as Pierre Poiret and François de la Mothe Fénelon; Puritans such as Richard Baxter; Anglicans such as Robert Nelson and William Beveridge; American Calvinists such as Jonathan Edwards; British Calvinists such as John Newton and George Whitefield; Arminians such as John Owens; continental reformers such as Martin Luther; early Fathers such as Irenaeus and Clemens Alexandrinus; and the list goes on. The criteria of selection were not based so much on correctness of the truth claims in these volumes, from the viewpoint of systematic theology, as on the usefulness of the material in implementing vital habits of Christian living, from the perspective of practical divinity.

The evangelical revivals in Great Britain during the eighteenth century were much more than the creation of the Wesleys. For instance, the religious fervor at Cambuslang, near Glasgow, in the 1740s was more the result of William McCulloch, the local Scottish evangelical, and George Whitefield, the traveling evangelist. The Wesleyan movement in eighteenth-century Britain, however, is in itself a good example of the complex nature of the evangelical movement. Not only does it reflect the coalescence of a number of background influences in John Wesley himself, but the growth of the Methodist organization through the century is in large part the amalgamation of many small revivals of differing sorts with a variety of theological frameworks and an array of denominational affiliations. Methodism was not simply the result of Wesley's itinerating throughout the British Isles, establishing societies in every remote corner. Rather, it brought together some of the regional eruptions of religious fervor, incorporating the work of local leaders who either knew Wesley previously or knew of his work and wanted to band together in a growing network of evangelical people. What bound them together was their mutual concern for holiness of heart and life – the hope that a life of faith would produce works of mercy as well as works of piety. Wesley encouraged an interesting blend of radical commitment to holy living shaped by primitive Christian practices, tinged by Puritan morality, and grounded in Anglican doctrine.

Revivalists were active in many areas, such as Wales, contemporaneously with the Wesleys' work in England. And local revivals throughout the three kingdoms were prevalent throughout the century. One might find Methodists whose background is Quaker, Moravian, Pietist, Anglican, Presbyterian, or Puritan, drawn together by a common vision of Christianity that entails disciplined holiness of heart and mind. One of the main reasons that Wesley needed to call an annual conference of his preachers was to bring them together on the same page in matters of spiritual and theological discipline. In this yearly endeavor, he had no model to imitate in his own Church of England but rather built on earlier practices of the Welsh evangelicals, including Howell Harris.[8]

The Wesleyan revival has often been seen by English-speaking peoples as the example par excellence of the evangelical revival in Europe. That opinion is not simply the result of the size of the Wesleyan family of denominations that developed in the two centuries after his death. Wesley's reputation at his death was reflected as well as propelled by his obituary in the *Gentleman's Magazine*, which referred to him as "one of the most extraordinary characters that this or any age ever produced."[9] That having been said, one must recognize that the Methodist movement at his death in 1791 numbered only about 75,000 members in Great Britain – less than 1 percent of the population. And during the last three decades of his life, he spent a great deal of effort simply trying to hold his movement together, at one point suggesting that at his death, one third of his people would hold fast to their Anglican heritage, one third would separate off into a Methodist church, and one third would become dissenters. This prediction was a realistic reminder that the Methodist revival, although a recognizable phenomenon on the British scene, was rife with internal tensions throughout its initial century.

The Wesley brothers, John and Charles, were not always on the same page themselves. Charles was always a stauncher Anglican and, especially in his later years, less involved in the leadership of the movement. He looked somewhat askance at John's encouragement of lay preachers, feared his inclination to move toward the brink of separation from the Church of England, and was especially distraught at his brother's irregular ordinations for the American Methodists. Charles desired a minimum level of talent among their preachers, whereas John was more concerned about their vital experience of God's grace. Together, the Wesleys tried to keep the movement supplied with an adequate and somewhat unified leadership, in line with their basic Anglican heritage, unfettered by predestinarians, and free from hymnody that might exhibit petty doggerel rather than pure doctrine.

John Wesley's writings to and about opponents readily display the diversity of the wider revival movement in Britain. He chided John Newton, author of "Amazing Grace," for overuse of the words "Christ" and "faith"; he argued with Augustus Toplady, author of "Rock of Ages," over the doctrine of election; he decried the emphasis of George Whitefield, author

---

[8] Derec Llwyd Morgan, *The Great Awakening in Wales*, trans. Dyfnallt Morgan (London, 1988), 95–6.
[9] *Gentleman's Magazine* 61 (Mar. 1791): 284.

of "Free Grace, Indeed!," on the absolute decrees; he sparred with Caleb Evans, who published as "Americanus," about the revolt of the American colonies; and he sidled up to Lady Huntingdon, head of a Calvinist connection, hoping she would help sway Whitefield to abandon his plans to transform his Georgian orphanage into an academy. Many enthusiasts or radical dissenters of the period found themselves unwittingly burdened with the moniker "Methodist," without actually being associated with Wesley's movement.

Wesley was not hesitant to attack many of the so-called gospel preachers who were part of the enthusiastic revivals of the period. That term designated preachers who, Wesley claimed, just ranted and raved about "having faith" and "being saved by the blood of Jesus" without ever breathing any word of the expectations of the gospel for holy living among the believers. Wesley's own answer to such solafidianism can be found in many places, including his first major apologia, *An Earnest Appeal to Men of Reason and Religion*, in which he musters his considerable grasp of historical theology to defend his movement.[10] His sermon "The Law Established by Faith" points out a common fallacy among revival preachers of his day – that believers who had received the forgiving love of Christ were not held accountable for obedience to the will of God. Wesley felt that the grace of God found in the new covenant did not do away with the law found in the old covenant but rather helped the believer fulfill the law. This expectation was one of the distinctive marks of the Methodist movement, which was characterized by a strong expectation of disciplined holy living.

The various revivals and movements that composed the general sense of widespread spiritual awakening in Great Britain in the eighteenth century, therefore, like those on the continent, were not homogenous by any means. They were grounded in different theological systems, reflected various doctrinal positions, represented diverse ecclesiastical bodies, manifested many approaches to structure, and held divergent views on the practices and methods that were considered useful or even essential to the faith. Although there was a kinship of spirit even in their internecine bickering, they generally were as competitive among their evangelical groupings as they were with the established church.

AMERICA

The earliest leaders of revival in America include Jacobus Frelinghuysen, a Dutch Reformed pastor who brought his hopes for a church of the visible

---

[10] Edited by Gerald Cragg, in the *The Bicentennial Edition of the Works of John Wesley* (Nashville, 1976–), vol. XI.

saints to the immigrants in New York, and Gilbert Tennent, an English dissenter who befriended and teamed with Frelinghuysen to help bring the discipline of holy habits to the Atlantic seaboard colonies. The abrasive style and unrestrained zeal of such leaders led critics to claim that such antics confirmed the worst implications of "enthusiasm" among such revivalists.

Gilbert Tennent had been educated in the Log Cabin academy of his father, William, who had trained a large handful of preachers as practical evangelists. But Gilbert's conversion experience left him more expressively spiritual and focused concerning the need for conversion, especially among the clergy. His sermon *The Danger of an Unconverted Ministry* (1740) became a landmark of the awakening in the colonies. His methods, learned in part from Frelinghuysen, although not disregarding doctrine, focused on the psychology of revival and the practical disciplines of holy living. His friendships in ministry resulted in much of this program being transmitted to many, including George Whitefield, which caused increasing tensions in his Presbyterian synod.

New England has traditionally been seen as the heart of the American Great Awakening, which gives it more attention and credit than it probably deserves. The revival in America was quite limited, both geographically and chronologically, and had its strong critics and counterinfluences. But the flag was carried by men of remarkable intellectual force, such as Cotton Mather and Jonathan Edwards, who were able not only to express a vital theological framework for the revival, but also to provide in published and private form a clear rationale for the movements of spiritual renewal and lively accounts of their progress. James Davenport, who graduated at the top of his class at Yale, was in some ways more notorious, in part because he seems to have had some mental problems. Many of the revivalists were accused of instability by critics who suspected their excessive enthusiasm as being caused by more than spiritual zeal. William Seward, Whitefield's traveling companion to Georgia, for instance, seems to have had some physical problems that may have contributed to his violent temper and attacks on Wesley after his return to England, as well as to his early death following a public stoning, which has given him the title of Methodism's first "martyr."

Cotton Mather was strongly influenced by Francke, as can be seen in his *Bonifacius, or Essays to Do Good* (1710). He also self-consciously presented to the world (including specifically his friends in Halle) a two-volume tome, *Magnalia Christi Americana*, which he felt would put the colonies on the map. Mather's propaganda was effective in its day, largely through the forcefulness of his own personality and intellect. He was convinced that New England religion was on a par with any of the forms of

Franckian Pietism in Europe. Mather, like his father Increase, promoted this American pietism through small religious societies. He also became increasingly emotional in his preaching, and he became the precursor of many later evangelicals who tried to combine sound doctrine and vital practice in a church that was not hesitant to renew its covenant with God. Mather's father had adapted the Puritan concept of covenant such that it would technically allow for half-members in "mixed" families. Other groups during this period adapted the covenant concept to their own theological framework in a variety of ways.[11] Wesleyans also had used a variation on this Puritan approach, using a covenant-renewal service adapted from Richard Alleine first as a watch night service and eventually as the heart of a New Year's vigil.

Jonathan Edwards is often portrayed as the leader par excellence of the Great Awakening, if not its instigator. His tract *A Faithful Narrative of the Surprising Work of God ... in Northhampton* describes the work of his grandfather and predecessor in the parish, Solomon Stoddard, who had earlier started a revival of sorts. However, neither that work nor the efforts of Edwards himself had the contagion that is necessary for the spread of a general awakening. His tract itself, however, was widely circulated and had more impact in far-flung places than Edwards' efforts had in Massachusetts. Reginald Ward makes the argument that even the tract was not so much an inspiring cause of revival as it was a harbinger of hopes and fears that were very widely felt.[12]

Edwards' influence came more from his writings than his local leadership. He presented a theological rationale for evangelical revival that persisted long after his own efforts had waned.[13] His powerful intellect is seen in *A Treatise concerning Religious Affections* and in his book *Freedom of the Will*.[14] These publications not only became the bellwether for American evangelical theology, especially from the Calvinist perspective, but also had an impact abroad.[15] And his sermon *Sinners in the Hands of an Angry God*, which was published in many editions for many years and is still included in anthologies of material from this period, became known as the prime example of powerful preaching in the New England revival. Edwards himself did not have the exuberant preaching style of Tennent, he was not an itinerant like Wesley, he did not start impressive institutions like Spener

---

[11] Mark Noll, *America's God: From Jonathan Edwards to Abraham Lincoln* (Oxford, 2002), 48.
[12] Ward, *Early Evangelicalism*, 96.
[13] Douglas A. Sweeney, "Evangelical Tradition in America," in Stephen J. Stein, ed., *The Cambridge Companion to Jonathan Edwards* (Cambridge, UK, 2007), 218–19.
[14] Jonathan Edwards, *The Works of Jonathan Edwards* (New Haven, 1957–2008).
[15] Mark Noll, "Jonathan Edwards's Freedom of the Will Abroad," in Harry S. Stout et al., eds., *Jonathan Edwards at 300* (Lanham, MD, 2005), 98–110.

and Francke, and his travels were not as widespread as Whitefield. But his direct influence on American religion, as seen in the New Divinity theology, outlasted any of these persons, largely on the strength of his publications.

Nevertheless, at the time, Edwards became a central figure within a coterie of friends, including Tennent and Whitefield, that promoted revivals as generally as possible. After Whitefield's visit to Northhampton in 1740, Edwards seems to have changed his preaching style in a less than successful attempt to imitate Whitefield, even to the point of using manuscripts that would allow his preaching to appear extemporaneous.[16] Whereas Edwards remained close to his home in Massachusetts, Whitefield itinerated along the whole eastern seaboard of America, in addition to his constant trips back and forth to England – thirteen trips across the Atlantic in all. In many ways, Whitefield personifies the transatlantic awakening more than any other person.

A BRIDGE BETWEEN EUROPE AND AMERICA

For nearly the first decade of the erupting Methodist movement, George Whitefield was the "Methodist" most often attacked in British publications. He was born of lowly estate – his parents owned a tavern in Gloucester – which he was quick to point out was not unlike the origins of Jesus. As a servitor at Oxford (a student who worked as a servant) among the gentleman commoner students, he seems to have developed his skills of hyperbole to overcome an inferiority complex. He called himself Wesley's successor at Oxford, and he was quick to follow suit in Georgia, even though the Trustees tried to convince him that such a position required their approval, not simply Wesley's invitation. His early career in America was marked by constant turmoil – criticisms of the SPCK and others over his mishandling of finances; opposition to his requests for more free land in the colony; consternation over his attempts to circumvent the colonial charter's restrictions on slavery and rum trade in Georgia; concern for his continual absenteeism from Savannah, once he received an official appointment there; and tensions with the local population over his reputed mismanagement of Bethesda, the orphanage just outside Savannah.

Whitefield found a greater response to his preaching of the "new birth" in the colonies to the north of Georgia. The revivals in New England had already started, and he felt a kinship of spirit with those Calvinists who were preaching a strongly evangelical message. As a parish priest in

---

[16] Harry S. Stout, "Edwards as Revivalist," in Stein, *Cambridge Companion*, 138.

Savannah, he was criticized for harping on one topic – the necessity of the new birth. As an itinerant preacher along the eastern seaboard of America, he found one receptive audience after another along his pathway. When he decided to give up his Savannah charge (he had actually been dismissed by the Trustees), he told the people of Georgia that he was going to spread the gospel in areas that showed more appreciation for his work – where they actually wept during his sermons and were so moved by his preaching that they followed him to his abode.

Whitefield became the iconic leader of the American revival scene and in some sense helped tie together some of the local revivals. His thespian-like theatrics – he was apparently a frustrated actor – were attractive to some, repulsive to others, and fascinating to most, including Benjamin Franklin, whose stories about Whitefield's oratorical power and fund-raising savvy became part of American folklore. It is not hard to believe that Whitefield himself helped perpetuate the image of one who could make women weep by the way he pronounced "M-e-s-o-p-o-t-a-m-i-a."

When John Wesley began preaching outdoors to the miners at Kingswood, he was following the example of George Whitefield, a younger man who had become acquainted with the Methodists at Oxford University in the last two years before the Wesleys left for America. But as an itinerant preacher in both Britain and America, Whitefield was never known as one who followed his mentor in organizing religious societies, building new churches, exhibiting a substantial theological perspective, or having much effect on the religious institutions as such. During the two decades after the Wesleys left America, Whitefield was the main, if not the sole, Methodist preacher in America, preaching to thousands of people. But there is no evidence of even one Methodist society being formed under his leadership. Yet he was not simply an individual evangelist with a notoriously large ego and a carefully cultivated charismatic presence; he was quick to develop alliances with other leading religious leaders in the colonies, such as Gilbert Tennent and Jonathan Edwards. His own inclination to Calvinism put him in good stead with the Presbyterians in America, especially in New England, with whom he continued to affiliate closely until his death in 1770.

Whitefield's thirteen trips across the Atlantic made him a natural link between the revivals in Great Britain and America. His work demonstrated many of the elements that were common to most Protestant revivals during that period of awakening: an emphasis on conversion and holy living, a free expression of emotionalism as central to religious experience, a lack of concern for denominational loyalty, and a diminution of doctrinal and theological concerns.

OTHER FACTORS IN THE REVIVAL

As apparent as it may sound, prolific publishing became a hallmark of the leading participants in this period of awakening.[17] For instance, a large percentage of the books published in America during the eighteenth century were, in fact, religious publications, and many of them came from the pens of those associated with the evangelical revivals. Throughout much of the eighteenth century, however, London remained the main source of printed works for the American colonies. In England, the lapsing of the Licensing Act just before the turn of the eighteenth century resulted in a dramatic increase of printers and serial publications during the following generation.[18] Wesley poured a large proportion of his resources into a publishing effort that produced more than four hundred items in his last fifty years, many of them multivolume works such as his fifty-volume Christian Library, which included abridged writings of more than eighty divines that represented, in his words, "the choicest pieces of practical divinity which have been published in the English tongue," and many biographies of contemporary "saints," from the French mystic Madame Guyon to the missionary to the Native Americans David Brainard, but no eighteenth-century British Calvinists.[19] Wesley never heard Jonathan Edwards preach and did not even correspond with him, but the Methodist founder was influenced by some of Edwards' publications concerning the revival in New England that, in effect, extended Edwards' revival beyond the "local" scope. Whitefield published many sermons and tracts not only to broaden the reach of his preaching efforts, but also to raise money for some of his charitable projects, such as an orphanage in Georgia. Publications served a number of important functions, from polemics to propaganda, and helped strengthen the transatlantic ties of the religious revival efforts.

The movements of reform and renewal appeared in various corners of the European world, from Silesia to Russia, including Bohemia, Moravia, France, Switzerland, the Low Countries, and other localities, as well as Germany, Great Britain, and America.[20] The cross-fertilization of ideas among evangelical groups in Europe entailed a great deal of linguistic translation. British devotional literature was translated into many languages, perhaps most often into German. And the British also benefited from increasing translation of material from other languages. The national

---

[17] Ward, *Protestant Evangelical Awakening*, 48.
[18] Lambert, *Inventing the "Great Awakening,"* 158–9.
[19] David Hempton, *Methodism: Empire of the Spirit* (New Haven, 2005), 59.
[20] Ward, *Protestant Evangelical Awakening*, 54–240.

religious societies, such as the Society for Promoting Christian Knowledge, contributed immensely to this effort, which reached down to the local level. Part of the stated design of Samuel Wesley's little society in Epworth was to make available religious literature from other countries through translation.[21]

Women played a significant role in many of these spiritual developments. The most radical groups, such as the Quakers, were the quickest to allow women to have leadership roles. Other groups, such as the Methodists, incorporated women into the leadership of certain local groups, such as classes and bands, and expected them to fulfill such roles as visitors of the sick and teachers of children. Their function as preachers was limited by the prejudices of the Church of England, although Mary Bosanquet and other women pressed Wesley into pushing the envelope by accepting their gifts of preaching as "extraordinary prophets" in local situations, without technically naming them as preachers within the Methodist connexion. Broader participation of women in the Methodist revival, however, mirrored the heavy involvement of women in all of the evangelical religious movements of the time.

Children also played an important role in the revivals of the eighteenth century. The orphanage at Halle was an important model for Christian outreach and education, copied (although on a much smaller scale) by many evangelicals, such as Wesley and Whitefield. Traditional methods of preparation for confirmation were resurrected by some German Pietist groups but tended to give way to less institutional forms of religious instruction in many areas of Great Britain. Outbreaks of revival among children became more prevalent in some British localities and raised important questions for many about the validity of religious experiences among children. Wesley had stressed the need for his preachers to spend time working with the children and even produced literature especially for their benefit. But the work of the Spirit among young folks was probably more controversial than some of the rather parentally controlled educational methods promoted by Milton and Locke. Views on the nature and role of children in society were in transition during this period, and many people did not know whether to treat children as miniature adults or as an age group in their own right. Many people began to realize that the future of religion, as they knew and practiced it, rested with the next generation, which for some represented a very real field of struggle with the devil. As with many other issues of this type, however, there was no consensus among "the awakened" as to how one should deal with children. The spread of children's prayer meetings in Silesia in the early eighteenth century was called "the uprising of the children."[22]

---

[21] Richard P. Heitzenrater, *Wesley and the People called Methodists* (Nashville, 1995), 29.
[22] Ward, *Protestant Evangelical Awakening*, 71–2; see also 127, 260.

AFTER 1750

The Quaker colony of Pennsylvania gave comfort to several movements with soft boundaries that shared a sense of heart religion. Martin Boehm and Philip William Otterbein brought together a mixed group of Mennonites, Quakers, Amish, German Reformed, and Lutherans. The lowering of denominational barriers was in part the result of increasing influence by laity on the American religious scene, combined with the lack of state establishment of religion. The pluralism of the society and the increasing proliferation of sects meant that many families exhibited mixed languages and religious traditions. The spiritual kinship of people across denominational lines also reinforced the sense among many of the leaders that religion of the heart especially, in place of religion of the mind, meant that holy habits were more important than firm doctrinal beliefs.

Whitefield, for one, represents something of an enigma to those who expect spiritual urgency to be accompanied by doctrinal stringency. In his later years, Whitefield asked Wesley if his old friend would allow him to preach in the Wesleyan societies. When Wesley balked over having a predestinarian Calvinist preach to his people, Whitefield promised to eliminate any reference to the "decrees" from his preaching, which, understandably, made some of his own people quite mad. The Whitefield followers at his tabernacle in London were equally distressed just a few years later when Wesley preached a funeral sermon for Whitefield at the latter's request in which he pointed out that he and his friend George had spent their lives preaching essentially the same gospel, a somewhat astounding claim that confirms their common stress on transformed lives. Perhaps there was only a hair's breadth difference between Wesley and the Calvinists in that sense.

Those involved in these interrelated movements found that denominational affiliation did not matter so much as alliances of the heart. So Muhlenberg, who as a friend of Francke was as Hallensian as any Pietist, did not hesitate to establish an orthodox sort of Lutheranism in America distinct from any state connection. So also Whitefield, who in England was known as a Methodist (seemingly as *the* Methodist before the mid-1740s), was familiarly affiliated with Presbyterian churches in America. Count Zinzendorf apparently tried to lure people from their congregations in order to join a diverse association of believers in which he would serve as their bishop.[23] And Philip Otterbein, a German pastor in the Evangelical Reformed Church in Pennsylvania who formed the United Brethren denomination in the tradition of the Heidelberg Confession, had no qualms associating with the Wesleyans, whom he viewed as fellow evangelicals. The

[23] *Ibid.*, 273.

eventual institutional union of these latter two traditions in the twentieth century simply reinforces the idea that these ties among "the awakened" were very strong across institutional boundaries.

Increasing communication between Europe and America created a cross-fertilization of ideas and practices that worked in both directions. Just as much of the American mindset grew out of a European heritage, so also the new political and social conditions in which religion was planted in the New World brought about many shifts that raised questions about those traditions. Jonathan Edwards recognized that many parts of America depended on Great Britain for its government, its literature, and its trade, but his own account of the work of the Spirit in the revival in Northhampton had worked its way eastward across the Atlantic and helped shake up the religious scene in Great Britain.

In his later years, Whitefield warned his American friends of the dangers of the British government, which was becoming more and more out of touch with the tied concepts of religious and civil liberties. When Whitefield heard that Wesley was thinking of coming to America in the later 1760s to help with the revival, George sent him a curt note suggesting that he would do well to stay at home – what they needed in the New World were leaders who had experience in the colonies and were familiar with the mindset of the people. His perception of Wesley was probably more accurate than he may have realized, because the Methodist founder's brief experience in Georgia thirty years earlier did not leave a good taste in his mouth or a positive view of the colonists in his mind.

Whitefield's hesitation regarding Wesley in this instance was confirmed in the mid-1770s, when Wesley became outwardly opposed to the Americans' revolutionary tendencies. He abridged Samuel Johnson's *Taxation No Tyranny* under the new title, *A Calm Address to Our American Colonies*. His argument, that the Americans should not resist being taxed in order to help pay for their national security, was not received well by the revolutionary-minded colonists. The Methodists in America were thus all tainted by his views, such that even the pacifist tendencies of their leaders, such as Francis Asbury, were seen as the result of Loyalist sentiments.

The difficulties of the doctrine of God's providence became evident in the various evangelical views of the political situation in the 1770s. Whereas many American religious leaders were propounding a view that "we trust in God," other evangelicals in England were proclaiming that "God is on Britain's side."[24] Many of the Calvinists, such as Augustus Toplady and Caleb Evans, supported the American cause, whereas other evangelicals,

---

[24] See John Fletcher, "The Bible and the Sword" (1776), in Luis Sandoz, ed., *Political Sermons of the American Founding Era, 1730–1805* (Indianapolis, 1998), 559–78.

such as Wesley, opposed the colonists' rebellious actions. Both sides saw God as active in the events. Wesley's sermon "The Late Work of God in North America" proclaimed that the Americans' greedy miscalculations on the matter of gaining worldwide economic trading partners would result in their eventual economic isolation and necessary reentry into the British colonial enterprise.[25]

Evangelical religion became associated with the Revolution in a variety of forms, not least of which was through the preaching that took place on special occasions, such as election days, convocation days, and other occasions for civic gathering at the church, such as publically proclaimed days of prayer, fasting, or thanksgiving.

MOVEMENT OR PHENOMENON?

What can generally be said, then, about the evangelical awakenings that broke out around the transatlantic world in the eighteenth century? True, the use of terminology is crucial in this regard. "Great awakening" did not mean quite the same thing to Jonathan Edwards as it did later to Joseph Tracy when he applied it more generally to a broader segment of time and place, nor to later American historians such as William Warren Sweet or Edwin Gaustad when they characterized the century, nor to William McLoughlin when he claimed that it was the key to the coming of the Revolution in America.[26] "Conversion" did not mean the same thing to John Wesley within the Church of England as it meant to Gilbert Tennent in America or to the revivalists in the holiness movement in nineteenth-century America. The term "born again" did not include the same nuances for Arminians such as John Fletcher as it did for Calvinists such as Jonathan Edwards. The phrase "works of mercy" did not bear the same soteriological connotation for an Arminian Wesleyan as it did for a Calvinistic Puritan. "Assurance of faith" could mean something quite different for a Moravian as compared with a Methodist.

But beyond the disputes over theological perspectives, terminological idiosyncrasies, or even political implications, many people during this period experienced a spiritual transformation that they understood to be the beginning of a new life in Christ. Many of them considered themselves to be "awakened" or "reborn." The people thus affected did not generally quibble over the theological or anthropological differences between being awakened or reborn. Is there an internal latent spiritual dimension

---

[25] John Wesley, Sermon 113 (1778), in *Bicentennial Works*, III: 594–608.
[26] Jon Butler, "Enthusiasm Described and Decried: The Great Awakening as Interpretative Fiction," *The Journal of American History* 69:2 (Sept. 1982): 305–6.

that needs to be awakened by the Holy Spirit, or does one need to be completely renovated by the presence and power of God? More often than not, they probably had no sense that they were in a long historical tradition that went back to early Christianity; had different manifestations in the Eastern and Western medieval churches; and was experienced by some French Catholic mystics, many German Lutheran Pietists, several strains of English Puritans and Scottish Presbyterians, and a variety of faithful Christians in different places in their own day. Tying these events together is the task not so much of the preacher as of the historian.

Therefore, when we use such didactic terms to interpret related movements during a certain period or place, we are not trying to say that everybody experienced the same thing, had the same theological perspective, or considered themselves as part of a larger uniform movement. But the eighteenth century did witness a remarkable number of regional revivals that resulted in thousands of people experiencing what might be called an "awakening" or "rebirth" or "conversion." These revivals were, by and large, not necessarily correlated movements, and any connection between many of them should be seen as more coincidental than coordinated. They did not all exhibit the same characteristics; they did not happen at the same time; they did not share the same causative factors. The various forms were complicated by local variations in theology and practice. Any list of combined characteristics of these movements would not accurately describe any particular one of them. In fact, each major characteristic exhibits a variety of forms within itself. Such a combined list of characteristic marks of these evangelical revivals and the range of their variations might look something like this.

Conversion – instantaneous or gradual transformation,
    but also an emphasis on schools and teaching
Prayer-centered worship – devotional piety,
    but also often social outreach
Biblical orientation – *sola scriptura* or *analogia fides* interpretation of scripture,
    but also a broad publishing enterprise
Small groups of pious laity – Christian fellowship (social holiness),
    but also individual piety
Itinerant preaching – field preaching, traveling the countryside,
    but also local institutional forms and sacraments
Extemporaneous preaching – spirit-filled, affective rhetoric, without notes,
    but also use of manuscripts by many individuals
Revival meetings – traditional evangelism through preaching,
    but also witness through society meetings

Sectarian flavor – dissenting tendencies,
>   but also many people from established church
Emotional manifestations – groaning and weeping,
>   but also use of closely reasoned theology by some
Gifts of the Spirit – frequent emphasis on extraordinary gifts,
>   but also focus on ordinary gifts
Required ordination – traditional ministry,
>   but also lay preachers, extraordinary prophets, even women
Visible saints – "true" Christians,
>   but also an allowance for searching, "almost" Christians
Covenant renewal – frequent incorporation of renewal into worship practices,
>   but some practices without renewal or with different connotations

The awakenings on both sides of the Atlantic, then, although not by any means a unified movement, did display in their various forms an emphasis on holy living and religion of the heart that resulted in outcroppings of revival and renewal in many places during the eighteenth century. Many of these revivals were distinctly regional phenomena, such as the Welsh revival, the Cambuslang revival, and the Northhampton revival. Certainly there were many areas that were not strongly affected, because of either active opposition or benign disinterest. And the activity flared up in different places at different times. The Wesleyan movement in England at midcentury, for instance, was concentrated in nine or ten areas that were served by preachers in circuits that covered a relatively small proportion of the countryside at that point.[27] The revivals in Virginia began about five years after a decade of revival fires in New England had begun dying down in 1745, and those in the Carolinas were even later. But the limited nature of these movements can be overstressed by selective overuse of heavily Calvinistic sources and limiting the chronology to the period before 1750.

The theological roots of these movements were also diverse. One can trace some relationships among certain manifestations of revival, but there were also great tension and competition between different groups. Pietism, Puritanism, Mysticism, Calvinism, Arminianism – each had some effect on various regional segments of the awakenings, and the revivals did not always bring them into closer contact or cooperation.

The practical effects of these regional movements were probably quite a bit less imposing than subsequent historians have argued. Certainly

---

[27] See map in Heitzenrater, *Wesley and the People*, 180.

they did have important local consequences, although some preachers like Whitefield had more or less transient effects on the permanent religious scene of the areas that he traveled through. Wesley would have considered Whitefield's work a "rope of sand."[28] Whether or not Edwards' concept of the will or Wesley's concept of freedom from sin had a direct effect on the development of national self-identity in America, even as an unintended consequence, is left for the historians to debate.[29] The Wesleyan revival in Britain probably was not the major preventative of a popular revolution in the three kingdoms, any more than the American awakening had a direct link to the coming of the Revolution there. Latter-day analysts can surmise these connections, but the evidence for contemporary consciousness of such causations is less than conclusive.

One of the unifying forces among these variegated movements, as well as one of the unintended results of their presence, may have been the growth of the opposition that they drew. Following the unleashing of religious fanaticism in England during the Cromwellian period in the seventeenth century, for instance, the English establishment was so skittish about exhibitions of spiritual zeal that anything like a revival became suspect and was outwardly opposed by many clergy. In America, the skeptics toward the revivals, such as Charles Chauncy and the Old Lights, were not simply irreligious folks who detested outward display of religious fervor. There was a strain of tradition, if not rationalism, that would support ideas such as religious toleration and freedom of expression without having to like everything they saw and heard in that regard. The growth of deism and Unitarianism, especially during the last half of the eighteenth century, seems to have been, in part, a reaction to many of the more exuberant forms of religion that persisted in some evangelical movements.

Having been appropriately cautious in making grandiose claims for these revival movements and the awakenings that they brought, however, we can still assert that there developed early a sense of comradeship among the leaders of many of these revivals and a feeling that divine providence was at the root of a global resurgence of religious experience among many people. This concept of a transatlantic movement of the Spirit, which might be considered "global" in that day, was self-consciously expressed, if not promoted, in many of the letters and publications that circulated among evangelical leaders in the middle of the eighteenth century. The poem that was read at Whitefield's tabernacle in Moorfields in 1742

---

[28] Wesley, *Plain Account of the Methodists* (1749), in *Bicentennial Works*, IX: 259; and letter to Charles Wesley (21 Apr. 1741), *ibid.*, XXVI: 55.

[29] See, e.g., Noll, *America's God*, 13–14.

expresses the excitement generated by the sense of the Spirit's moving among them.

> Great Things in England, Wales, and Scotland wrought,
> And in America to pass are brought:
> Awak'ned souls, warn'd of the Wrath to come
> In Numbers flee to JESUS as their Home![30]

SUGGESTIONS FOR FURTHER READING

Butler, Jon. "Enthusiasm Described and Decried: The Great Awakening as Interpretative Fiction." *The Journal of American History* 69:2 (Sept. 1982): 305–25.

Hempton, David. *Methodism: Empire of the Spirit*. New Haven, 2005.

Hindmarsh, D. Bruce. *The Evangelical Conversion Narrative: Spiritual Autobiography in Early Modern England*. Oxford, 2005.

Maddox, Randy L., and Jason E. Vickers. *The Cambridge Companion to John Wesley*. Cambridge, UK, 2009.

Noll, Mark A. *The Rise of Evangelicalism: The Age of Edwards, Whitefield, and the Wesleys*. Leicester, 2004.

O'Brien, Susan. "A Transatlantic Community of Saints: The Great Awakening and the First Evangelical Network, 1735–55." *The American Historical Review* 91:4 (Oct. 1986): 811–32.

Stein, Stephen J. *The Cambridge Companion to Jonathan Edwards*. Cambridge, UK, 2007.

Ward, W. Reginald. *Early Evangelicalism; A Global Intellectual History, 1670–1789*. Cambridge, UK, 2006.

---

[30] From "A Call to the Sleeping Virgins," *The Weekly History, or, An Account of the Most Remarkable Particulars Relating to the Present Progress of the Gospel* 84 (13 Nov. 1742): 2.

28

RELIGION AND THE AMERICAN REVOLUTION

FRANK LAMBERT

Religion played only a supporting role in the American Revolution. As the new republic's founding documents attest, secular matters were paramount. The Declaration of Independence sets forth a rationale for revolution that closely follows John Locke's liberal conception of the relationship between the governed and the government, and it includes a long list of grievances against George III for his alleged violation of the colonists' constitutional rights. The offenses listed relate to such issues as taxation, representation, standing armies, and markets; they do not include religious issues.

Similarly, the U.S. Constitution is a secular document with scant mention of religion. Records of the Federal Convention that deliberated in Philadelphia for four months in 1787 include only a smattering of religious language. The name of Jesus or Christ does not appear at all, and the framers invoked the name of God just twelve times. Even then several of the phrases were such popular expressions as "Good God, Sir ..." and "God knows how many more ..." rather than reverent invocations of the deity's name.[1] The Constitution itself contains only one reference to religion and that a negative one: "no religious Test shall ever be required as a Qualification to any Office or public Trust under the United States." The Constitution granted no power whatever to Congress pertaining to religion. Although applied only to the federal government, the removal of religion from government jurisdiction soon led the states to adopt similar measures. Indeed, one of the most revolutionary consequences of the American Revolution was the separation of church and state, which meant that the support of religion in the new republic was left primarily to individuals and voluntary associations.

Although the American Revolution was a secular event, religion nonetheless played an important supporting role. On some of the Revolution's most dramatic occasions, churches provided sanctuaries for protest and

---

[1] Frank Lambert, *Religion in American Politics: A Short History* (Princeton, 2008), 27.

continue to sanctify the Revolution as sites of public memory. After the so-called Boston Massacre on 5 March 1770, Boston Patriots gathered at the Old South Meeting House to remember those killed and to protest the continued presence of British troops. In December 1773, a reported crowd of five thousand gathered at Old South to plan resistance to Parliament's Tea Tax. The church provided more than a place to meet; it also justified the rebellious acts hatched therein. Whereas Parliament considered the destruction of the tea as unlawful, the Patriots deemed their actions to be not only consistent with Christian teachings but prescribed by scriptural admonitions to obey God and resist tyrants. Then, on the night of 18 April 1775, Paul Revere began his historic and immortalized ride toward Lexington when he spotted the prearranged signal from the tower of Christ Church (Old North Church).

Sometimes religion and revolution intersected in dramatic fashion, such as on 25 July 1775, at St. Barnabas Church in Upper Marlboro, Maryland. As he rose to deliver his sermon, Pastor Jonathan Boucher climbed the stairs of the pulpit with a pistol in his hand. Although normally armed only with the Word of God, he had reason to believe that he needed more immediate ammunition on this day. Some of Boucher's parishioners were angry with the rector's words and deeds in the growing confrontation between the colonies and Whitehall. He first met with disfavor when, after Parliament closed the port of Boston in 1774 following the tea party, he refused to denounce the British. He saw the matter as a political issue, not the subject for a sermon. Then he became openly critical of Patriots, contending that "when Christians are disobedient to human ordinances, they are also disobedient to God." So on 25 July, a fast day, an angry group of men attended services ready to spring into action at the first hint of anything from Boucher that was less than full support of the Patriots. Having been forewarned by one of his supporters that an insurgent by the name of Osborne Sprigg led the opposition, Boucher made a preemptive strike by seizing Sprigg by the collar while aiming his cocked pistol at Sprigg's head. He then told the insurgent leader that if there were any violence that day by the troublemakers, he, Boucher, would "instantly blow his brains out."[2]

Religion and politics were entwined during the American Revolution, although rarely in such dramatic fashion as that involving Boucher. First, although the colonists' grievances were primarily secular, at least two complaints accused Britain of undermining faith. Second, ministers were effective messengers during the War of Independence, preaching sermons that

---

[2] James Spalding, "Loyalist as Royalist, Puritan as Patriot: The American Revolution as a Repetition of the English Civil Wars," *Church History* 45 (Sept. 1976), 337–8.

both reinforced political positions and elevated the struggle to a spiritual plane. Third, the religious culture that framed the war as a holy war also shaped the postwar millennialist vision of America as God's chosen nation. And, fourth, the Revolution influenced religion in profound ways. On the one hand, specific groups were attacked for their positions on independence and the war, most especially the Church of England and the Quakers. But, more broadly, the political revolution wrought a religious revolution in defining the nature and place of religion in American public life.

Most of the colonists' grievances related to constitutional questions and trade regulations, but two were explicitly religious in nature. One was the real or perceived threat of the Church of England's establishing a resident bishop on the North American mainland. Well before Britain's new imperial policies led to protests against tyranny and oppression among American colonists, the prospects of a resident bishop in America had led to similar outcries. The affairs of the Church of England in America fell under the jurisdiction of the bishop of London, an arrangement that many Anglican priests and missionaries found unsatisfactory. Without a resident bishop, they claimed, there was inadequate oversight of parish life, too lax enforcement of church discipline, and far too much control by lay vestries. But every discussion of a bishopric in the colonies brought warnings from dissenters who connected greater ecclesiastical oversight of the colonies to tighter political control. In his 1750 sermon *A Discourse concerning Unlimited Submission and Non-Resistance to the Higher Powers*, Boston Congregationalist minister Jonathan Mayhew reminded his readers that English history was filled with instances in which civil and ecclesiastical powers combined and crushed the rights of English subjects. Mayhew declared, "People [will] have no security against being unmercifully priest-ridden but by keeping all imperious bishops, and other clergymen ... from getting their foot into the stirrup at all."[3] Throughout the 1760s and 1770s, the prospect of tyranny arising from a colonial bishop fed a number of conspiracies that fueled Patriot protest. With its massive budget and secret proceedings in London, the Society for the Propagation of the Gospel in Foreign Parts (SPG) constituted, dissenters declared, a cabal whose goal was to destroy them. Although the organization claimed that its goal was to extend the gospel where it was not preached, why would it, dissenters asked, open scores of congregations in New England, which was already well served by Congregationalists, Baptists, and Presbyterians? Why not spend their resources out on the frontier and in Indian settlements? The explanation

---

[3] Jonathan Mayhew, *A Discourse Concerning Unlimited Submission and Non-Resistance to the Higher Powers* (Boston, 1750), preface.

could only mean that the members of the SPG were "agents of repression," and with a resident bishop, they could subvert the rights of dissenters.[4]

The second religious grievance was the Quebec Act of 1774, which conjured images of "secret Catholicism." From earliest settlement, anti-Catholicism had been the one position that bound together all colonial Protestants, despite their internecine squabbles. So Parliament's passage of the Quebec Act fueled a furious outcry that linked anti-Catholic sentiments with British tyranny. Intended as a bill to address issues of governance in Quebec, the law came on the heels of the hated Intolerable Acts of 1774 that closed the port of Boston and threatened Massachusetts rights following the Boston Tea Party. Having obtained Quebec just a decade earlier at the end of the French and Indian War, the British faced a population very different from Protestants in the thirteen colonies. First, most Quebecois were Catholic, and, second, they had had little experience in representative government. So, in response to Governor Guy Carleton's plea, Parliament granted religious toleration to Quebec's Catholics and dispensed with an elective assembly. Although the law applied to Quebec, it fueled the belief in the thirteen colonies that Britain was preparing to impose Catholicism as part of a bigger scheme to seize colonial property and subvert colonial rights. Paul Revere played on that fear in an engraving entitled "The Mitred Minuet," showing the devil, Anglican bishops, and British ministers in a cabal plotting the Catholicization of the American colonies.[5]

Even those grievances not directly related to religion were conceived as moral issues and expressed in moral language. When Patrick Henry, for example, delivered his treasonous speech against what he considered to be Parliament's trouncing on the colonists' constitutional rights, he justified his protest as loyalty to the "Majesty of Heaven," a loyalty that he placed higher than that toward "all earthly kings."[6] By 1776, Patriot rhetoric had shifted from a defense of constitutional rights to an assertion of natural rights, which emanated from the Creator.

No greater testimony attests to religion's cultural influence on the American Revolution than British assessments of the war and its causes. Edmund Burke, statesman and pro-American member of Parliament, considered the War of Independence to be primarily one that can be explained by religious differences. The colonists were steeped in a culture of dissent, and "with an emphasis on the heterodoxy of Dissent, the war was truly a war of religion." He pointed out that many Americans, especially

---

[4] Jon Butler, *Awash in a Sea of Faith: Christianizing the American People* (Cambridge, MA, 1990), 198.
[5] *Ibid.*, 198–9.
[6] William Wirt, *Sketches of the Life and Character of Patrick Henry* (Philadelphia, 1817), 120.

those in New England, had fled religious and political persecution in the seventeenth century and had a long tradition of rising up against any threat to their cherished rights. Burke observed that in New England, especially, "the religion most prevalent ... is a refinement of the principle of resistance: it is the dissidence of dissent, and the Protestantism of the protestant religion."[7]

Loyalist Peter Oliver also identified religious dissent as a cause of the American Revolution. From first settlement, Massachusetts Bay colony was, he argued, "an Asylum" for Nonconformists to enjoy "their own tenets," which ran counter to those of the Church of England. He maintained that dissent against the established church led to dissent against established political authority. Moreover, religious dissent led to what Oliver called a "Torrent of Enthusiasm," in which individuals claimed to have direct communication with the divine.[8] The result was the fracturing of religious unity with the creation of myriad sects, each claiming that it had a particular call from God to separate from other Christians. Oliver declared that this spirit of dissent permeated New England culture and accounted in large part for the political dissent that led to independence.

To be sure, religion was not the only cultural prism through which colonists interpreted events, but it offered a set of ideas that reinforced liberal and radical Republican notions. When Thomas Jefferson drafted the Declaration of Independence, he relied heavily on John Locke's thought in setting forth the logic of revolution. At the center was the idea of popular sovereignty grounded in a social contract made between the governed and the governor. The people agreed to live under the rule of their elected officials only so long as the governors protected their rights and property. The idea of a sacred contract binding people together under an agreed-upon set of rights and obligations was central to Protestant theology, especially among those sects that embraced a congregational polity. Congregations drew up covenants, which bound members together as a body of believers. Moreover, those church covenants rested on divine covenants set forth in scripture. In the Mosaic covenant, God agreed to bless the people of Israel and make them his chosen people so long as they obeyed his commandments. Christians believed that Christ introduced a new covenant, whereby his sacrificial death satisfied God's demands for justice. New England Puritans claimed that they were a covenanted people, chosen to establish the "true" faith in the American wilderness. During the American

---

[7] See Elliott Barkan, *Edmund Burke: On the American Revolution, Selected Speeches and Letters* (New York, 1966), 84.

[8] Douglass Adair and John Schutz, eds., *Peter Oliver's Origin and Progress of the American Rebellion: A Tory View* (Stanford, 1961), 15–20.

Revolution, ministers extended that claim to all the American people by declaring that the United States was a new Israel, God's chosen people. Rev. Samuel Sherwood of New York was typical of those who preached that America was the new Israel. In a 1774 sermon, he claimed that "this American quarter of the globe seemed to be reserved in providence, as a fixed and settled habitation for God's church." Moreover, in such a land, government would be "duly regulated by Christian principles and rules."[9]

Politicians saw ministers as useful allies in promoting the Patriot cause. Thomas Jefferson supported fast day sermons because he believed that they would be effective in "arousing our people from the lethargy in which they had fallen."[10] Massachusetts Loyalist Peter Oliver described just how "arousing" a sermon could be in mobilizing parishioners against royal authority. He recalled that Jonathan Mayhew, minister of the West Church of Boston, turned his funeral sermon for Chief Justice Joseph Sewall to political ends. Oliver called Mayhew a "partisan in Politicks" who that day "gave a loose to his Passions." Mayhew preached a "fiery sermon on the text, 'I would they were even cut off which trouble you.'" Following the service, a mob destroyed Governor Thomas Hutchinson's house because the governor supported the Stamp Act. One rioter, when caught, tried to excuse his actions on the grounds that he had been stirred by Mayhew's sermon and "thought that he was doing God service." Others testified that "whilst the Doctor was delivering [the sermon] they could scarce contain themselves from going out of the Assembly & beginning their Work."[11]

Loyalist and Patriot ministers based their messages on biblical foundations. One of Boucher's most powerful sermons declared that government was ordained by God and that attacks on government were attacks on God. "Obedience to Government is every man's duty," he proclaimed, "but it is particularly incumbent on Christians, because ... it is enjoined by the positive commands of God."[12] Jonathan Mayhew read the same scripture differently and came to the opposite conclusion. Mayhew argued that godly rulers are indeed of God, but ungodly rulers are of the devil. Moreover, people should obey rulers who rule justly and in accordance with God's law; but for them to obey unjust rulers is to dishonor God.[13]

Ministers supporting both sides in the War of Independence portrayed the war as a just war. Abraham Keteltas, pastor of the Presbyterian church

---

[9] Samuel Sherwood, *A Sermon Containing Scriptural Instructions to Civil Rulers, and All Freeborn Subjects* (New Haven, 1774), 27.
[10] Spalding, "Loyalist as Royalist," 331.
[11] Adair and Schutz, *Peter Oliver's Origin*, 43–4.
[12] Spalding, "Loyalist as Royalist," 337.
[13] See Jonathan Mayhew, *Concerning Unlimited Submission and Non-Resistance to the Higher Powers* (Boston, 1750).

in Newburyport, Massachusetts, claimed that by "enslaving" the colonies, Britain had lost the support of God. In a 1777 sermon, he cast the war as the "cause of the oppressed against the oppressor." It was "pure and undefiled religion, against bigotry, superstition, and human invention." In short, he argued, the American Revolution was "the cause of heaven, against Hell." Having begun as a constitutional crisis, the war soon became a matter of British "impiety." So the "glorious cause" of the Patriots was also the "cause of God."[14]

Anglican Alexander Carlyle was equally sure that God favored the British cause. He remembered how during the French and Indian War British citizens had supported the American cause, but now the "ungrateful colonies" had engaged in a "foul revolt." He compared the conflict between Britain and the colonies with that of King David and his rebellious son Absalom. Parents ordinarily should not go to war against their children, but rebellion changes everything. Quoting David, Carlyle wrote, "Let us give our captains and our mighty men a charge, that they deal with the young man." He assured his readers that the "event is in the womb of providence" and that the British cause is a "righteous cause." He called for the British to depend on a "pious trust in the Almighty" in order to bring their "rebellious children" back in line.[15]

God's providence was a major interpretative theme of the American Revolution. Nathan Strong, pastor and chaplain from Hartford, Connecticut, was representative of Patriot ministers who saw God's hand directing the war. In 1780, he delivered a sermon contending that it was the "agency and providence of God" that guided the British in the "persecution of the American States." Underlying his sermon was the belief that God directed history; maybe that direction could only be seen in hindsight, but nonetheless it was there. Even actions that one might deem to be ungodly could, under a wise and all-knowing deity, have good results. Strong said that it was the providence of God that led the British in their "froward headlong" assault on the colonists, leading them to adopt measures "which hastened what they meant to prevent." Further, the "astonishing union" of thirteen disparate states could only be explained by the "immediate influence of Jehovah." God's guidance could be seen even in military defeat, such as the chain of setbacks that beset Washington's army in the retreat from Long Island through New Jersey in 1776. In the midst of that and other "gloomy periods," Americans had been lifted by "the arms of the Lord

---

[14] See Abraham Keteltas, *God Arising and Pleading His People's Cause* (Newbury, MA, 1777), 30–1.

[15] Alexander Carlyle, *The Justice and Necessity of the War with Our American Colonies Examined* (Edinburgh, 1777), 3, 49–50.

and the counsel of the Almighty" and the result was "salvation for us." The providential interpretation of the American Revolution persisted after the war. At the Federal Convention at Philadelphia in 1787, Benjamin Franklin admonished the delegates to rely on God's providence in solving such contentious problems as representation and taxation. He declared that Providence had delivered Americans through the War of Independence and would again help them usher in the new republic.[16]

Patriot sermons mirrored radical republican themes. To make sense of how Britain's imperial policies violated colonists' rights, Revolutionary leaders borrowed from radical Whig ideology, an English opposition ideology with roots in the Commonwealth period of the seventeenth century and more recent expression in the revolt against Robert Walpole's administration in the mid-eighteenth century. Patriots argued that when the court garnered too much power, it threatened the liberty of subjects. For example, through patronage, Walpole developed a powerful party that reinforced his influence in the court of George II, but his horde of placemen necessitated higher taxes, which eroded citizens' property. And, because Whigs believed that property was the basis of political independence, rising taxes undermined liberty. Defenders of liberty, therefore, had to be ever vigilant against "vicious" placemen, and above all, they had to be virtuous, that is, above sacrificing the public good for private gain. Many Americans in the 1760s and 1770s saw a parallel. George III's corrupt ministers were once again imposing high taxes on subjects, in this case colonists, and those taxes threatened their liberty. To preserve their liberty, colonists must be virtuous, which meant at least to be industrious and frugal. By refusing to buy tax-burdened English goods and wearing homespun instead, they protected their rights and liberties.

Christian ministers translated republican virtue into Christian morality. Like Whig propagandists, preachers portrayed Britain, and more particularly, the king's ministers and parliament, as being driven by "public vices." Harvard president Samuel Langdon in a 1775 sermon justified the colonists' rebellion on the grounds that Britain had "wage[d] a cruel war with its own children in these colonies, to gratify the lust of power and demands of extravagance."[17] To counter such viciousness, colonists must return to a strict morality. In pulpits across the colonies, ministers thundered against immorality among Americans that, the preachers insisted, had led to God's punishing them with British oppression. Samuel Webster, pastor at Salisbury, Massachusetts, told one fast-day congregation that the

---

[16] See *Notes of Debates in the Federal Convention of 1787 Reported by James Madison*, Bicentennial ed. (New York, 1966), 209–11.

[17] Samuel Langdon, *Government Corrupted by Vice* (Watertown, MA, 1775), 19.

crisis emanated from their own morality: "It is for a people's sins, when God suffers this [evil] to come upon them." Americans should not, he warned, expect a miracle from God to save them from their own immorality. Rather, they must make themselves a "*holier* and *better*" people.[18] So, Americans gathered on fast days as well as Sunday services to confess their sins and return to their moral roots. Only through moral behavior would their opposition to British oppression be truly virtuous.

In addition to preaching sermons, Patriot ministers wrote religious publications that recast the crisis as a moral play. One genre that they used to good advantage was biblical parody. They knew that most Americans were familiar with Old Testament stories, so the authors made parallels between the ancient Hebrews as God's chosen people and present-day Americans as a new chosen people. One such work was *The First Book of the American Chronicles of the Times*, published in Philadelphia in 1774 and attributed to a layman, John Leacock of Philadelphia. Written as a series of six pamphlets, the piece was popular, as evidenced by its being reprinted in such places as Boston, Newbern, Norwich, Providence, and Salem. Following the organization and language of the King James Version of the Old Testament Book of Chronicles, the parody drove home its message from the first page. It opens by calling Britain the evil tyrant. "And behold! When the tidings came to the great city that is afar off, the city that is in the land of Britain, how the men of Boston, even the Bostonites, had arose, a great multitude, and destroyed the TEA, the abominable merchandize of the east, and cast it into the midst of the sea." Royal governors are the oppressive ministers who enable the king to tyrannize God's chosen people: "Thy throne, O King, is encompassed about with lies, and thy servants, the Bernardites and the Hutchinsonians, are full of deceit, for be it known unto thee, O King, they hide the truth from thee, and wrongfully accuse the men of Boston, for behold, these letters in mine hand witnesseth sore against them, O King, if thou art wise, thou understand these things."[19]

The most widely circulated pamphlet espousing the cause of independence draws on the Old Testament to make the radical claim that the crisis is not merely the result of an ineffective king surrounded by vicious ministers, but the result of monarchy itself. Thomas Paine was perhaps the most effective propagandist for the cause of independence because he made the case in clear, commonsense prose. In early 1776, his *Common Sense* was published and instantly became a best-seller. In language readily available

---

[18] Samuel Webster, *The Misery and Duty of an Oppress'd and Enslav'd People* (Boston, 1774), 10 and 29. Emphasis in the original.

[19] John Leacock, *The First Book of the American Chronicles of the Times* (New York, 1774), ch. 1, 1–2.

to most colonists, he argued that "exalting one man so greatly above the rest cannot be justified on the equal rights of nature" or the authority of scripture. He maintained that according to Gideon and Samuel in the Old Testament, God "expressly disapproves of government by kings." Far from being a biblically sanctioned institution, monarchy was the result of a rebellious people who put selfish interests ahead of obedience to God. God had made a covenant with the children of Israel, declaring that they would enjoy his protection so long as they obeyed his commandments. But, during the judgeship of Samuel, disgruntled Israelites, jealous of neighboring kingdoms, begged Samuel to plead their case for a monarch of their own. Although God insisted that he was their king, he granted their plea. The results were disastrous, as Israel became embroiled in wars with other kingdoms and encountered dissension within the kingdom. In the end, the disobedient people asked God's forgiveness for placing their trust in an earthly monarchy. Paine's conclusion was that monarchy, far from being a divine institution, was contrary to the will of God.

Whereas religion helped give the War of Independence a moral foundation, it also sustained the soldiers and militiamen who fought the war. Current estimates are that a total of 25,000 Americans died, perhaps a third on the battlefield and the others from diseases contracted in camps and prisons of war. Chaplains performed many important duties in their ministry to soldiers. First, they instilled in them the glorious cause for which they fought. Abiel Leonard, a Congregational pastor in Woodstock, Connecticut, wrote *A Prayer, Composed for the Benefit of the Soldiery, in the American Army*, which assured those fighting for independence that they were also fighting under God's banner. "I desire now to make a solemn dedication of myself ... through Jesus Christ," the prayer intoned, "presenting myself to thy Divine Majesty to be disposed of by thee to thy glory and the good of America."[20] So as they slogged through cold, wet marches and faced the fury of close-range firing, soldiers could take comfort that they were serving God as well as country. Second, chaplains gave "animating [and] spirited" sermons aimed at bolstering flagging spirits in trying times. In late 1775, when Connecticut troops were eager to leave the battlefield and return home, Leonard gave a powerful plea for reenlistment taken from an address that Joab gave to the chosen men of Israel: "Be of good courage, and let us play the men for our people, and for the cities of our God: and the Lord do that which seemeth him good." Third, chaplains exhorted soldiers to exert themselves against the enemy rather than await God's providence. Addressing the First and Second Virginia Brigades at

---

[20] Abiel Leonard, *A Prayer, Composed for the Benefit of the Soldiery, in the American Army* (Cambridge, MA, 1775), 4.

Valley Forge, Chaplain John Hurt asked for divine assistance in that deadly camp, but he also called on the soldiers to be the "instrument of doing good."[21] The message was clear: God helps soldiers who help themselves.

Although ministers promoted the American Revolution as preachers and chaplains, a few also advocated the cause as politicians, none more prominently than John Witherspoon. A devotee of the Enlightenment and a Scottish Presbyterian minister, Witherspoon in 1768 became president of the College of New Jersey. Under his leadership, the college at Princeton expanded its curriculum and offered a course of studies that focused on the arts and sciences. Three years prior to his arrival, "religion held the dominant place in the minds and hearts of faculty and students." But campus protests against the Stamp Act in 1765 turned the college into a "cradle of liberty." Witherspoon added his fervor to the patriotic cause and soon gained prominence as a champion of liberty. John Adams met Witherspoon on his way to the Continental Congress in 1774 and pronounced him "as high a Son of Liberty, as any Man in America." That same year, Witherspoon defended the central Patriot argument that colonial assemblies are sovereign over internal matters in a political treatise, *Considerations on the Nature and Extent of the Legislative Authority of the British Parliament*. The next year he was elected president of the Somerset County Committee of Correspondence, and then in 1776 he was elected delegate to the Continental Congress. There he became a strong supporter of independence and a signer of the Declaration of Independence. Witherspoon saw the fight for civil liberty as inextricably tied to that for religious liberty. "There is not a single instance in history," he lectured, "in which civil liberty was lost, and religious liberty preserved entire."[22]

Witherspoon was not the only minister who became a politician during the American Revolution. Indeed, one of his fellow delegates at the Continental Congress, John Zubly from Georgia, argued the opposite position on the question of independence. Also a Presbyterian, Zubly agreed that Parliament had overstepped its authority in some of the new imperial measures enacted during the 1760s and 1770s, but he opposed independence as rebellion against God. During the war, he preached a sermon contending that because all rulers are ordained by God, any rebellion against constituted authority was disobedience to God. In Congress, he claimed that Patriot outrage against Parliament was misplaced. He thought it an "extreme absurdity" that Americans would strive for "civil liberty, yet continue slaves to sin and lust." Rather than struggling to make America

---

[21] John Hurt, *The Love of Our Country, a Sermon Preached Before the Virginia Troops in New-Jersey* (Philadelphia, 1777), 11.
[22] See Thomas Wertenbaker, *Princeton, 1746–1890* (Princeton, 1946), 55–6.

independent, the colonists should, Zubly declared, dedicate themselves to making America Christian.[23]

Just as politics found expression in pulpits across America before and during the War of Independence, religion found expression in the halls of Congress. Politicians found religion to be a means to unite Americans in the war's both brightest and darkest hours. By declaring days of Thanksgiving and fast days, politicians were able to infuse the American cause with a higher purpose and emphasize that all Americans were engaged in a great struggle directed by Providence. Near the end of 1776, when Washington's army was in full retreat, Congress passed a resolution calling for a day of fasting. The measure declared that it "becomes all public bodies," as well as individuals, to acknowledge God as the "supreme disposer of all events, and the arbiter of the fate of nations." It followed that if God decided great events such as the War of Independence, then Americans should trust the Almighty for deliverance. In appointing "a day of solemn fasting and humiliation," Congress urged all citizens "to implore of Almighty God the forgiveness of the many sins prevailing among all ranks, and to beg the countenance and assistance of his Providence in the prosecution of the present just and necessary war."[24] Behind the declaration was the conviction that Americans were God's chosen people and that divine favor was conditional, dependent on their obedience to God's commandments.

Similarly, victory on the battlefield inspired politicians to reassert the claim that God favored the Patriots' cause. Following the victory at Saratoga, Congress called for a day of Thanksgiving, or specifically, "to set apart Thursday, the eighteenth day of December next, for solemn thanksgiving and praise; that with one heart and one voice the good people may express the grateful feelings of their hearts, and consecrate themselves to the service of their divine benefactor." So with "one voice" all Patriots would acknowledge God's grace in granting the army a much-needed victory. Congress also tied independence to the higher cause of ushering in the kingdom of God on earth. Not only would independence lead to self-government, but it would "prosper the means of religion for the promotion and enlargement of that kingdom which consisteth 'in righteousness, peace and joy in the Holy Ghost.'"[25]

Religious symbols reminded Americans that theirs was a holy cause. When George Washington sailed into Boston Harbor as the newly

---

[23] Jim Schmidt, "The Reverend John Joachim Zubly's 'The Law of Liberty Sermon': Calvinist Opposition to the American Revolution," *Georgia Historical Quarterly* 82 (Summer 1998): 354.

[24] Worthington Ford, ed., *Journals of the Continental Congress, 1774–1789* (Washington, DC, 1904–37), 6: 1022.

[25] Ford, *Journals of the Continental Congress*, 9: 854–5.

appointed commander of the Continental Army, the ships in his squadron bore the New England pine tree flag, to which were affixed the words, "Appeal to Heaven." Although facing the might of the British navy, Washington and his troops claimed an even mightier power. In addition, many Patriot units carried battle flags linking their cause to that of a higher calling. One bore the inscription, "Resistance to Tyrants is Obedience to God," a slight rephrasing of a sermon delivered by Jonathan Mayhew. In 1782, with the war coming to an end, Congress authorized the creation of a national seal that would symbolize the ideals of the new republic, including that of God's providence directing the nation's affairs. On the obverse side the Eye of Providence is at the zenith of an unfinished pyramid, with the caption *Annuit Coeptis*, "Providence has favored our undertakings."

The American Revolution influenced religion just as religion influenced the Revolution. Some churches were particularly distressed. First, the Church of England's presence in the United States was a casualty of the War of Independence. As the state church of England, it was linked in Patriots' minds to political tyranny. Furthermore, more than 80 percent of the clergymen in the church in New England and the Middle Colonies were Loyalists. In the Chesapeake and southern colonies, only about 20 percent of the clergy were Loyalists. Nonetheless, Virginia moved quickly to disestablish the church, and all the other states where it had been the official religion followed suit. By 1789, an American episcopal church had been established.

The American Revolution confronted Quakers with difficult choices. The Quakers faced heated opposition both from within their own synods and from Patriots who opposed their pacifism. Even before combat began, Quakers had experienced a schism, as a group of Pennsylvania Friends split off and supported the Revolution while rejecting pacifism. Those remaining true to the sect's historical opposition to war were dogged by Patriots who were unsympathetic to citizens who refused to fight for freedom. Quakers were stoned and jailed, and their homes were ransacked because of their refusal to display proper "patriotic" spirit. In 1775 the Philadelphia Yearly Meeting issued a statement explaining why the Friends would not take up arms. The document declared that Quakers disapproved of the Patriot call to arms because the spirit and temper of the bellicose speeches and pamphlets were "contrary to the nature and precepts of the gospel, [and] destructive of the peace and harmony of civil society." Six months later, when Philadelphia Friends refused to obey a congressional call for a fast day, a stone-throwing mob forced the Quakers to comply.

The Revolution's influence on American religion went far beyond institutional changes and realignments. Indeed, one could say that there was a revolution of American religion from 1776 through the end of the eighteenth century. Revolutionary ideals of individual rights, equality, and popular sovereignty found expression in religious circles. Evangelicals emphasized individual conversion, encouraged "egalitarian theology," and promoted a "Christianity of the people." Whereas republicans challenged the authority of political tyrants, dissenters fought against ecclesiastical oppression caused by religious establishments. Dissenters, especially the fast-growing Baptists, Methodists, and Presbyterians, insisted that, before God, all people and sects were on equal footing. There was also the beginning of a theological shift, from strict Calvinism, which gave individuals no say in the drama of salvation, to Arminianism, which emphasized the believing individual who accepted God's grace through faith. Moreover, there was what one historian has called a "crisis of authority" within churches. Evangelicals, in particular, gave primacy to private authority, that is, the testimony of converted individuals, rather than accepting the authority of a learned ministry. The result was the growth of a popular religion that trusted in the "collective will of the church."[26]

The American Revolution also Americanized religion by infusing it with secular ideals. In fact, the boundary between sacred and secular became blurred as politicians borrowed from theologians, and theologians borrowed from politicians. Historian Nathan Hatch sees some "odd mixtures" combined in the "crucible of this new American Christianity." There was a blend of "renewed supernaturalism and Enlightenment rationalism, of mystical experiences and biblical literalism, of evangelical and Jeffersonian rhetoric." The result was an expansion of religious options available to individuals. Armed with the authority of a personal conversion experience, men and women freely interpreted the Bible according to their own lights, chose the religious leaders they were willing to follow, and determined exactly how to express and practice their faith.[27]

The American Revolution contributed to the creation of a civil religion in the United States. Jean Jacque Rousseau coined the term "civil religion" in his 1762 essay on the social contract, meaning by the term those religious beliefs that a society holds in common, apart from sectarian tenets that are beyond the state's jurisdiction. Those beliefs include the idea of a nation's divine origins and of God's providence in its history. Leaders in the early republic laced their speeches and writings with their firm belief that God had guided the United States through the War of Independence and through the creation of a constitution. Moreover, the great ideals of the Revolution – life, liberty, equality – became sanctified in the civil

---

[26] Nathan Hatch, *The Democratization of American Christianity* (New Haven, 1989), ch. 2, "The Crisis of Authority," 17–48, quotations at 45, 46, 22, 182.
[27] *Ibid.*, 35.

religion. The Declaration of Independence, the U.S. Constitution, and the Bill of Rights were canonized as part of "America's scripture," and George Washington, Thomas Jefferson, and Abraham Lincoln were heralded as its major prophets.[28] According to Robert Bellah, who has written at length on the subject, America's civil religion, "while not antithetical to and indeed sharing much in common with Christianity, was neither sectarian nor in any specific sense Christian." It gave religious content to the nation's sense of identity and mission without committing it to a particular religion.[29]

One of the most significant and long-lasting effects of the American Revolution on religion was that it began the process of separating church and state. During the colonial period, ten of the thirteen colonies had some form of a religious establishment, and most tied religious beliefs and practices to civil liberties. With its focus on individual liberty and the eradication of political tyranny, the Revolution undermined establishment laws. All states but Massachusetts and Connecticut disestablished religion, and in 1787 delegates to the Federal Convention separated church and state at the federal level. The effect was to put religion in America on a voluntary basis in which adherents of a particular sect bore their own expenses. Further, separation of church and state meant that no one would be regarded as a dissenter. Without an official state church, the idea of dissent ceased to have meaning.

During and following the War of Independence, former dissenters moved quickly to claim equal rights under the law. Dissenting Protestants, Roman Catholics, and Jews all invoked the Revolutionary rhetoric of natural rights to insist that they should suffer no civil disadvantages because of their faith. Baptists and Presbyterians played leading roles in fighting against establishment in Virginia and demanding unfettered religious liberty. In 1775, Virginia Baptists announced that they were "fast and firm friends of liberty," and that their religious tenets did not forbid their fighting for their country, and that "the pastors of their flocks would animate the young of their persuasion to enlist for our battles." But, a year later, the Baptists made their loyalty to the Patriots conditional. In a memorial to the assembly, they reminded the legislators that although Americans fought against Britain's "enslaving schemes," some Americans faced severe limitations on their freedoms imposed by their own elected representatives. They petitioned the assembly "that they be allowed to worship God in their own way, without interruption; that they be permitted to maintain

---

[28] Pauline Maier discusses the canonization of American civil documents in *American Scripture: Making the Declaration of Independence* (New York, 1997).

[29] Robert N. Bellah, "Civil Religion in America," in "Religion in America," special issue, *Journal of the American Academy of Arts and Sciences*, 96:1 (Winter 1967): 1–21.

their own ministers, and none others; that they be married, buried and the like, without paying the clergy of other denominations." They closed by vowing that if those freedoms were granted, they would "gladly unite and promote the common cause."[30]

Presbyterians also came out early for disestablishment. The Hanover Presbytery, the oldest in Virginia, petitioned the assembly in 1776, stating that Presbyterians sought no ecclesiastical support from the state, nor would they approve of any granted to others. Instead of the state supporting religion, the Presbyterians favored voluntary support of churches. Their preference was that every religious society be left to "voluntary contributions for the maintenance of the gospel." The authority for ministers to preach the gospel derived from "a higher source than any Legislature on earth, however respectable."[31] Thomas Jefferson and James Madison led the fight that culminated in the *Virginia Statute for Religious Freedom* (1785), but they credited dissenters for securing its passage.

After the war, Jews petitioned George Washington, the presumptive president-elect, for the removal of all civil disabilities heretofore placed on Jews. On behalf of the Hebrew congregation in Newport, Rhode Island, Moses Seixas declared that a government by and of the people should be one that "to bigotry gives no sanction, to persecution no assistance, but generously [affords] to all liberty of conscience." Washington replied that all citizens of the United States possessed alike liberty of conscience and civil liberties on the basis of "their inherent natural rights." It was not for the government, he added, to tolerate a particular religion or grant indulgence to one sect or another.[32] All were equal. None were dissenters.

By creating what amounted to a free marketplace of religion, the American Revolution fostered the spawning of new religious groups. Such diverse groups as Unitarians, Shakers, and Freewill Baptists found the new climate of religious freedom conducive to their interests. A blend of rationalism and Christianity, Unitarianism never attracted a large following, but it did provide a religious home for intellectuals who might otherwise have embraced a full-blown secularism. At the other end of the spectrum, visions, dreams, and appearances motivated Shakers, who migrated to America on the eve of the Revolution. Ann Lee, their leader, claimed that Jesus appeared to her and instructed her to build a millennialist church in America that would usher in the kingdom of God. The Revolution sparked evangelical revivals, and Freewill Baptists emerged from that revivalism.

[30] Charles James, *Documentary History of the Struggle for Religious Liberty in Virginia* (New York, 1971), 65.
[31] James, *Documentary History*, 224–5, 233.
[32] See "On the Blessings of Civil and Religious Liberty," *The Annals of America*, 18 vols. (Chicago, 1968), 3: 433–4.

Moreover, the Revolution had profound theological impact on the Freewill Baptists, who rejected the Calvinist notion of predestination and replaced it with the more democratic, liberal idea of free choice. God continued to be the giver of grace, but individuals were free to choose to accept or reject that gift.

In Benjamin Rush's view, the War of Independence represented the beginning, not the end, of the American Revolution. By that, he meant that the real revolutionary challenge was to establish the new republic on the great principles enunciated in the Declaration of Independence. Both secular and religious leaders contributed to a sense of optimism that the United States could not only do that, but also be an example for the rest of the world. Their respective calls for American greatness, however, exposed a gap between how each conceived of the nation and its mission.

Most of the Founders, that is, those who had been most directly involved in shaping the Revolution's public documents, were shaped by Enlightenment ideas. Although they acknowledged God as Creator and believed that ultimately Providence guided events, their emphasis was on humans and human reason. They thought that through rigorous rational endeavor, Americans could make the country great. Congress in 1782 adopted *Novo Ordo Seclorum*, "a new order for the ages," as the nation's motto, a bold conception of what the American Revolution represented. With liberty and self-determination at the center, this new age would transform the way the world did business. There would be free trade. All religious views would be tolerated. Individual rights everywhere would be safeguarded. Science and discovery would bring exciting new inventions. The old artificial restraints on human endeavor would be removed.

Religious leaders exhibited similar optimism but made the vision sacred. Employing millennialist rhetoric, Protestant ministers saw the Revolution as an auspicious moment, not just in human history, but in sacred time. Ebenezer Baldwin, Congregationalist pastor at Danbury, Connecticut, and chaplain during the war, saw the Revolution as the beginning of Christ's thousand-year reign on earth before the Second Coming. That such a propitious moment occurred in the United States reinforced the sense shared by many citizens that the country was indeed God's new chosen people. Millennialist preaching contributed to a new cycle of revivals in America, which, among other things, called on men and women to renew their faith in God. There was a sense that the war had fostered irreligion and immorality, and that if the country were to be great, there must be a revival of true Christianity.[33]

---

[33] For discussion of millennialism and the American Revolution, see Ruth Bloch, *Visionary Republic: Millennial Themes in American Thought, 1756–1800* (New York, 1985).

The presidential election of 1800 was in a sense a clash between secular and sacred conceptions of the new republic. New England Calvinist ministers who supported the Federalist candidate John Adams attacked Thomas Jefferson, the Democratic-Republican candidate, for his religious views. Seizing on Jefferson's few public remarks on religion, the ministers concluded that he was an atheist and, if elected, would lead the country into atheism, just as radical revolutionaries had done in France. In his *Notes on the State of Virginia,* Jefferson had written, in support of his views on religious freedom, that it mattered not to him if his neighbor believed in one, three, twenty, or no gods. In that same work, he rejected the biblical account of a general flood as a scientific impossibility. The ministers concluded that he was an infidel who should not be elected. And yet Jefferson was elected. Although other factors no doubt influenced the outcome, the candidates' putative positions on religion were major factors. Jefferson's supporters had responded to the clergy's charges by depicting Adams as no friend of religious freedom, as one who would be sympathetic to making Calvinism America's established religion. Years later Adams attributed his loss to his portrayal as one who would promote a national establishment of Presbyterianism in America.[34] He knew that although voters held dear their own religious beliefs, they also cherished freedom of religion. Indeed, perhaps the American Revolution's greatest legacy was its considering the free exercise of religion as a natural right, a sacred right beyond the reach of even the most powerful.

SUGGESTIONS FOR FURTHER READING

Bloch, Ruth. *Visionary Republic: Millennial Themes in American Thought, 1756–1800.* New York, 1985.

Butler, Jon. *Awash in a Sea of Faith: Christianizing the American People.* Cambridge, MA, 1990.

Hatch, Nathan. *The Democratization of American Christianity.* New Haven, 1989.

James, Charles. *Documentary History of the Struggle for Religious Liberty in Virginia.* New York, 1971.

Lambert, Frank. *Religion in American Politics: A Short History.* Princeton, 2008.

Maier, Pauline. *American Scripture: Making the Declaration of Independence.* New York, 1997.

Wertenbaker, Thomas. *Princeton, 1746–1890.* Princeton, 1946.

---

[34] See Lambert, *Religion in American Politics,* 34–40.

29

THE RELIGIOUS LANDSCAPE: FROM THE REVOLUTION TO THE NEW NATION

PATRICIA U. BONOMI

During the War of Independence the American clergy fervently solicited divine support for their cause. Yet none was so bold to assert outright that God was on the side of the rebels. Although preachers discerned positive omens in such rare early triumphs as the battles of Trenton and Princeton, any claim to certain knowledge of God's will would have been condemned as blasphemous. Indeed, military setbacks, of which there were many during the early war years, were often perceived as heaven's retribution for the inhabitants' sins of arrogance, avarice, unchaste behavior, and similar vices. And so, in accordance with the understanding of that time, although pulpits throughout the land resounded with pleas for God's favor, the language was always cautiously supplicatory and conditional.

Both preachers and ordinary Americans shaped their case as an "appeal to heaven," imploring God to recognize the righteousness of their cause. The battle flag of the Third Connecticut Regiment bore the motto, "AN APPEAL TO HEAVEN." General George Washington, when awaiting the British attack at New York in 1776, had ordered a day of fasting and prayer by the troops to "incline the Lord, and Giver of Victory, to prosper our arms."[1] The next year he informed soldiers who had emerged victorious from a firefight at the battle of Brandywine that "another Appeal to Heaven with the blessing of providence, which it becomes every officer and soldier to supplicate," might bring further success.[2] Sometimes the troops fell short, as when the chaplains he had assigned to each regiment reported that the men often resorted to profane cursing. Washington admonished that they might jeopardize "the blessing of Heaven on our Arms, if we insult it by our impiety and folly."[3] As the British were eventually worn down, and

---

[1] W. W. Abbot and Dorothy Twohig et al., eds., *The Papers of George Washington, Revolutionary War Series*, 18 vols. (Charlottesville, 1985–2008), General Orders, New York, 15 May 1776, IV: 305.
[2] *Ibid.*, General Orders, near Germantown, [PA], 13 Sept. 1777, XI: 211–12.
[3] *Ibid.*, General Orders, 1778, XV: 13; General Orders, V: 551.

the war turned in the Americans' favor after the Battle of Saratoga and the final triumph at Yorktown, Washington ordered the army to give thanks for the "astonishing interpositions of Providence."[4] Only with the outcome finally settled could the people declare with confidence that God had, indeed, been on their side. Thus both celebratory fireworks and prayers of thanksgiving flew heavenward as victory was proclaimed.

George Washington, raised in the Church of England, was comfortable with religion in both his personal and public life. First as general, and later as statesman, he believed with many of his contemporaries that strong religious institutions supported public morality and promoted political stability. His embrace of Americans of all religions was more generous than that of many of his fellow citizens. Colonial Americans had long harbored anti-Catholic prejudices, owing to the centuries-long rivalry between Catholics and Protestants in both Europe and North America, with the French in Canada being the most proximate threat. Yet in 1778, when France at last aligned itself openly with the revolutionaries, Washington set the tone for the reception of this powerful military, although Catholic, ally. He declared a day of thanksgiving to be observed by the army encamped at Valley Forge, and then he paraded the troops before the assembled dignitaries under orders to shout, "Huzza! Long Live the King of France."[5] Nor when the republic later came into being did Washington's vision of religion and the state narrow. Jews, among others, were to be included as full citizens, as he declared to the Hebrew congregation at Newport, Rhode Island. "It is now no more that toleration is spoken of, as if it was by the indulgence of one class of people, that another enjoyed the exercise of their inherent natural rights. For happily the Government of the United States, which gives to bigotry no sanction, to persecution no assistance requires only that they who live under its protection" offer it their support.[6] That Washington's expansive view of religious inclusion was not shared by all Americans would become apparent in the new state constitutions, written after the casting off of British government. Washington himself, having given the full measure of his strength and devotion as commanding general during the war, did not participate in the framing of these first charters. At the peak of his fame and haled as the Joshua of the day, he was content

---

[4] John C. Fitzpatrick, ed., *The Writings of George Washington*, 39 vols. (Washington, DC, 1931–44), General Orders, 20 Oct. 1781, XXIII: 247.
[5] Abbot and Twohig, *Papers of Washington, Revolutionary War Series*, General Orders, 5 May 1778, XV: 38–9.
[6] W. W. Abbot and Dorothy Twohig et al., eds., *The Papers of George Washington, Presidential Series* (Charlottesville, 1987–), To the Hebrew Congregation in Newport, RI, 18 Aug. 1790, VI: 284–6 (quotation, p. 285).

to relinquish power like his Roman hero Cincinnatus and to retire to his farm at Mount Vernon.

Those who took up the task of constitution writing were, nonetheless, like Washington, drawn largely from the old provincial elite, and thus most were associated with the traditional colonial churches. Many were adherents of the Congregational communion and the rapidly growing Presbyterian denomination, who as prime supporters of the Revolution emerged from the war as respected leaders. Adherents of the Church of England were also well represented. That church had divided more or less along a North-South axis, with northerners swelling the ranks of Loyalists and the majority of southerners joining the rebellion. The Society of Friends had also divided during the war: although many Friends had chosen neutrality, a minority of "free Quakers" had supported the Revolution, with some now returned to office in Pennsylvania and southern New Jersey. As members of the state legislatures and Continental Congress, these leaders were principals in forging new constitutions in the years after July 1776. They carried the burden not only of reforming governmental and economic structures, but also of determining the place of religion in the new states. In a society in which observation of the Sabbath was deeply ingrained, local ordinances enforced blue laws, and education was largely a denominational function, religion was not a thing apart for these leaders but was entwined with daily life. They did not question the conventional view that religion was an essential bulwark of government, especially in an infant republic founded on the moral character and consent of its citizens.

Even so, Americans' notion of the relationship between religion and the state had advanced a good distance beyond the Old World conception of church establishments, as a glance at their early history reveals. For more than a century and a half, the English colonies had been peopled first by Anglicans, English Puritans, Dutch Reformed, Swedish Lutherans, and a few Catholics and Jews and later by Quakers, Mennonites, Welsh Baptists, French Huguenots, German Pietists, Scottish Presbyterians, Amish, Schwenckfelders, Moravians – the list goes on. Wherever the first wave of early seventeenth-century colonists had settled in concentrated communities, such as English-Anglicans in the Chesapeake and Anglo-Puritans in New England, official tax-supported churches had been planted: the Church of England in Virginia and later Maryland and the Congregational churches in Massachusetts, New Hampshire, and Connecticut. Dissenters from these sanctioned establishments were grudgingly granted "toleration," which was not the same as true religious liberty. Tolerated sects might be required to conduct services privately or to seek licenses from local officials, and their civil rights could be withheld. Outright persecution, although rare, led to such extreme episodes as the hanging of four Quakers at Boston in 1659–60, and elsewhere to the exclusion of Catholics from civil privileges and the rejection of Jewish and Quaker votes in local elections. Passage of the Toleration Act by the English parliament in 1689 tempered some of these excesses, although resistance to full acceptance of dissenters continued where strong religious majorities prevailed.[7]

As the population continued to diversify, however, new forms of religious practice emerged, first and most notably in the increasingly pluralistic Middle Colonies of New York, New Jersey, and Pennsylvania. Newcomers often coalesced as church congregations on a voluntary basis, initially under lay leadership owing to the shortage of incoming clergy. When these "gathered" congregations outgrew the houses and barns where they first met, the members pooled their resources to build churches and eventually to hire a preacher. Such clergy were then supported by the free gift of their congregations rather than by public taxes. These voluntary churches, contrary to conventional assumptions about church-state interdependence, proved surprisingly resilient, thriving as they did on the leadership, energy, and personal commitment of their adherents. Religious voluntarism continued to gain favor in newly settled areas as the population grew and diversified over the eighteenth century.

In the post-Revolutionary era, the self-sustaining, voluntary church provided a model for opponents of religious establishments. Thomas Jefferson argued that "Pennsylvania and New York ... have long subsisted without any establishment at all.... They flourish infinitely. Religion is well supported." James Madison early discerned that the "rights of conscience" were fully protected in Pennsylvania; and in a later summation he praised "the example of the Colonies ... which rejected religious establishments altogether, [proving] that all Sects might be safely & advantageously put on a footing of equal & entire freedom."[8] This positive experience with voluntary religion was at the heart of Jefferson's and Madison's Virginia proposal that in the mid-1780s led to the comprehensive disestablishment of religion in that state. The Virginia Act for Establishing Religious Freedom (1786) was devised by Jefferson and shepherded through the legislature by Madison after ferocious debate. Arrayed against it was the emotive power of Patrick Henry, who sought a statewide religious tax to

---

[7] Christopher Beneke, *Beyond Toleration: The Religious Origins of American Pluralism* (New York, 2006), chs. 1–2; Patricia U. Bonomi, *Under the Cope of Heaven: Religion, Society, and Politics in Colonial America*, rev. ed. (New York, 2003 [1986]), ch. 2.

[8] Jefferson, *Notes on the State of Virginia* (Torchbook ed., New York, 1964 [1785]), 154; Gaillard Hunt, ed., *The Writings of James Madison*, 9 vols. (New York, 1900–10), Madison to William Bradford, Jr., Orange County, VA, 1 Apr. 1774, I: 23, and see also Madison to Edward Livingston, 10 July 1822, IX: 486; Adrienne Koch, ed., *The American Enlightenment* (New York, 1965), 465–6.

be distributed among all Christian denominations, and such gentry leaders as John Marshall and Richard Henry Lee, who threw their support to the assessment campaign. Even George Washington saw no harm in Henry's plan, which nearly became law in 1784. But as Virginia was no longer peopled exclusively by English Anglicans, Henry's plan generated fierce resistance from Baptists, Presbyterians, and others long shut out by the Anglican establishment. The dissenters organized petition campaigns and rallied opponents in well-attended public meetings until Jefferson's and Madison's bill at last prevailed. Known today as the Virginia Statute for Religious Freedom, it declared that no one should "be compelled to support any religious worship, place, or ministry whatsoever," and that the inhabitants' religious opinions "shall in no wise diminish, enlarge, or affect their civil capacities."[9] Virginia's solution was unique in severing the state from all things religious.

To be sure, most state constitutions paraded their enlightenment bona fides by asserting, as did Massachusetts, for example, that "no subject shall be hurt, molested, or restrained, in his person, liberty, or estate, for worshiping GOD in the manner and season most agreeable to the dictates of his own conscience." Yet often a number of caveats followed. The Massachusetts Constitution went on to remind its still-overwhelmingly Congregational citizens of their duty "to worship the SUPREME BEING," leaving to local communities the provision of support to churches and "public Protestant teachers" by local tax or, in the case of dissenters from the Congregational churches, by "voluntary gift." A clause stating that attendance at public services could be enforced by the legislature erased any doubt that this was a religious establishment.[10] The arrangement lasted until 1833. New Hampshire, long accustomed to local control of religious taxes, made no statement about religion in its hastily written constitution of 1776. But the revised charter of 1784 authorized local governments to support "public protestant teachers of piety, religion, and morality," although inhabitants were obliged to support none but their own denomination, and Quakers were exempt altogether. Enforcement seems to have been haphazard, although it was only in 1819 that all ties between church and state were ended.[11]

---

[9] John A. Ragosta, *Wellspring of Liberty: How Virginia's Religious Dissenters Helped Win the American Revolution and Secured Religious Liberty* (New York, 2010). The bill (Broadside Collection, Rare Book and Special Collections Division, Library of Congress) is reproduced in James H. Hutson, *Religion and the Founding of the American Republic* (Washington, DC, 1998), 73.

[10] Francis Newton Thorpe [comp.], *The Federal and State Constitutions*, 7 vols. (Washington, DC, 1909), III: 1889–90.

[11] *Ibid.*, IV: 2454; Thomas J. Curry, *The First Freedoms: Church and State in America to the Passage of the First Amendment* (New York, 1986), 185–8.

Elsewhere in New England, Rhode Island continued its singularly liberal path by simply adopting as its state constitution the colonial charter of 1663, which had granted to its inhabitants "full libertie in religious concernments," a promise that had been amply fulfilled throughout Rhode Island's colonial history.[12] The young state explicitly included Catholics within its church family after French troops landed with Rochambeau in 1780 to support the Revolution. Connecticut also incorporated as its first constitution the colonial charter of 1662, in which there was no comment whatsoever on religion. But after more than a century of fervent religious practice supported by a predominantly Congregational population and firm legal scaffolding, it was clear that the new state had no intention of abandoning its establishment. As the Rev. Judah Champion proclaimed in his election sermon to the General Assembly in 1776, "Civil rulers are God's ministers for good" and government should promote religion and virtue. Resistance to Congregational dominance came from minority Anglicans (now Episcopalians), Baptists, Quakers, and especially Separatists, who had broken from the orthodox Congregational churches during the Great Awakening of the 1740s. A statute of 1777 laid taxes to maintain the establishment but forgave Separatists who could provide certificates proving financial support for their own congregations. This arrangement was extended to all "Protestant" dissenters in 1784 and continued until Congregationalism was disestablished in 1818.[13]

Outside of New England a single official church was no longer tenable, owing to the diversity of religious opinion, although in at least one case it was not for lack of trying. Maryland, which along with Virginia had in colonial times supported an Anglican establishment, granted freedom of conscience in its constitution of 1776 to "all professing the Christian religion." Nonetheless, the accompanying Declaration of Rights gave the legislature power to "lay a general and equal tax" to support Christian churches, which in the eyes of many seemed a ruse to favor the Episcopalians, who held key offices in the first state government. After the war ended a general assessment bill, which exempted all who declared themselves to be Jews, Muslims, or other than Christians, was promulgated by the legislature, but a number of Protestant groups as well as leading Catholics protested and petitioned against it. Anti-assessment forces heralded the example of colonial Pennsylvania to show that voluntary support of churches worked best, and after gaining strength in the election of 1785, they defeated the bill

---

[12] Sydney V. James, *The Colonial Metamorphoses in Rhode Island: A Study of Institutions in Change*, ed. Sheila L. Skemp and Bruce Daniels (Hanover, NH, 2000), 50.
[13] Champion, *A Sermon Delivered before the General Assembly* (Hartford, 1776), 11; *The Public Records of the State of Connecticut, 1776–1792* (Hartford, 1894–), I: 232.

by a margin of two to one. The religious tax allowed in the Declaration of Rights, never implemented, was specifically repealed in 1810.[14]

South Carolina also toyed with the notion of an establishment, but in its haste to write a constitution in 1776 no mention at all was made of religion. As if to compensate for that lapse, a new charter in 1778 devoted almost half of its text to religious issues. It established "the Christian Protestant religion" although with no tax assessment, mandated public worship, and declared that all who acknowledged "one God" and a future state of rewards and punishments "shall be freely tolerated" and granted equal civil rights. But, in fact, such rights were curtailed, for only Protestants could serve in the state senate, and electors were required to affirm "the being of God, and ... [an afterlife] of rewards and punishments." Apparently these clauses were never enforced, and when the constitution was revised in 1790, they were dropped entirely.[15]

New Yorkers had the most prolonged experience resisting church establishments, as Reformed, Lutherans, Quakers, Anglicans, Baptists, and Presbyterians schemed and battled to a stalemate over the 150-year span of their colonial history. Given that background, the state constitution of 1777 decisively "abrogated and rejected" all prior laws that might be construed as favoring any particular denomination, upholding instead "the free exercise and enjoyment of religious profession and worship without discrimination or preference." Yet it did so not only from the high ground of principle, but also, as the constitution declared, to guard against the ambitions of "wicked priests and princes" – a clear reference to the Roman Catholic Church, which had been outlawed for much of colonial New York's history. John Jay, long considered the father of the state's first constitution, was probably responsible for this rather startling passage. For Jay had also attempted – unsuccessfully – to insert a section barring adherents of "the church of Rome" from landholding and civil rights until they foreswore all submission to "pope, priest or foreign authority" and "the dangerous and damnable doctrine, that the pope, or any other earthly authority, have power to absolve men from sins or their obligation to the state of New York." The constitutional convention softened Jay's language, requiring only that liberty of conscience should not endanger the state. The usually mild-mannered Jay's uncharacteristic passion regarding the Church of Rome can likely be attributed to persecution of his Huguenot ancestors by French Catholics following the revocation of the Edict of Nantes in 1685,

---

[14] Thorpe, *Federal and State Constitutions*, III: 1689–90; Curry, *First Freedoms*, 153–7.
[15] Thorpe, *Federal and State Constitutions*, VI: 3247, 3250, 3253, 3255–6; Curry, *First Freedoms*, 150–1.

which family history he never forgot.[16] But Jay, as we have seen, was not alone in resisting equal rights for those who did not meet the religious preferences of local legislators.

As it turned out, Delaware, Georgia, New Jersey, Virginia, and North Carolina were the only states, beside Rhode Island, of course, whose constitutions placed no restrictions whatsoever on religious liberty, granting to their citizens, in language similar to that of the North Carolina Constitution of 1776, the worship of "Almighty God according to the dictates of their own consciences."[17] One might expect to find Pennsylvania in this group, given its founding by William Penn and the salubrious religious climate of the Quaker colony. Penn's view that in religion "force makes hypocrites, it is persuasion only that makes converts," had long set the tone for devotional life in the colony.[18] But with Quakers and other easterners divided over the Revolution, and with the more radical western counties pressing for greater representation, Pennsylvania became the one state in which newcomers rather than the colonial elite gained a dominant voice in writing the first state constitution. To be sure, liberty of conscience as well as freedom from religious taxes were never in dispute in that multisectarian state. But the constitution's assertion that no man "who acknowledges the being of a God" could be deprived of civil rights was immediately compromised further by the requirement that members of the legislature subscribe to the following declaration: "I do believe in one God, the creator and governor of the universe, the rewarder of the good and the punisher of the wicked. And I do acknowledge the Scriptures of the Old and New Testament to be given by Divine inspiration." Clearly legislators had to affirm belief not only in God, but in a Christian God, which although admitting Catholics would exclude Jews, who protested the document's language until it was modified in the amended constitution of 1790.[19]

Were these religious exclusions a consequence of oversight or design? Some constitution writers who granted religious liberty specifically to

---

[16] Thorpe, *Federal and State Constitutions*, V: 2636–7; Patricia U. Bonomi, "John Jay, Religion, and the State," *New York History* LXXXI:1 (Jan. 2000): 9–18.

[17] Thorpe, *Federal and State Constitutions*, I: 567 (Delaware); II: 784 (Georgia); V: 2597 (New Jersey); VII: 3814 (Virginia); V: 2788, 2793 (North Carolina). For statutory qualifications of religious practice, see the following.

[18] *The Select Works of William Penn*, ed. James Phillips, 3rd ed., 5 vols. (London, 1782), III: 242.

[19] Thorpe, *Federal and State Constitutions*, V: 3082, 3085, 3100; Willi Paul Adams, *The First American Constitutions: Republican Ideology and the Making of the State Constitutions in the Revolutionary Era*, expanded ed. (Lanham, MD, 2001 [1980]), 76 and n 52; Jonathan D. Sarna and David G. Dalin, *Religion and the State in the American Jewish Experience* (Notre Dame, 1997), 70–2; Curry, *First Freedoms*, 160–1.

"Protestants," in their overwhelmingly Protestant states, might conceivably have simply forgot about their few Jewish, Catholic, or Muslim residents. But in other instances the exclusionary language was deliberate, as was the case regarding Catholics in New York. This fencing of religious rights can be seen as an effort to concentrate power in the "right" hands, as is particularly evident in the requirements laid down for officeholders in a number of state constitutions. Even in states offering the broadest support for unfettered religious worship, some leaders were not prepared to open governance of their new republics to individuals of questionable religious character. New Jersey and North Carolina reserved state offices for Protestants only, and North Carolina further required a belief in God and the Old and New Testaments. Indeed, as late as 1808 a Jew elected to the North Carolina legislature was ousted from his seat as unfit to serve. Delaware, despite its liberal constitution, required a belief in the Bible and also showed its Trinitarian hand: all officers of the state had to pledge their faith in God, Jesus Christ, and the Holy Ghost. Georgia came closest to the Enlightenment ideal by requiring only that its oath of office conclude "so help me God."[20]

South Carolina's oath of office also asked for God's help, and the oath takers were restricted to Protestants. Electors, moreover, had to swear to their belief in God and a future state of rewards and punishments. Maryland required officeholders to declare "a belief in the Christian religion," which while easing previous restrictions against Catholics did nothing for Jews, who would only gain full civil rights in the nineteenth century. All government officers in the state of Massachusetts not only had to renounce foreign princes and prelates, but were obliged to swear, "I believe the Christian religion, and have a firm persuasion of its truth."[21]

That the state constitutions proclaimed religious liberty while hedging it with qualifications deemed compatible with each state's religious demography may in part explain the absence of any specific reference to religion in the Articles of Confederation, the new nation's first constitution, proposed by the Continental Congress in 1777 and finally ratified by all the states in 1781. The Continental Congress had struggled with the religious diversity of its members from the first meeting in 1774, when John Jay objected to opening the session with prayer (although by a cleric of his own church) because of the wide variety of members'

---

[20] Thorpe, *Federal and State Constitutions*, V: 2597 (New Jersey), 2793 (North Carolina); I: 566 (Delaware); II: 760 (Georgia). Jon Meacham, *American Gospel: God, the Founding Fathers, and the Making of a Nation,* (New York, 2007), 108 (North Carolina Jew).

[21] Thorpe, *Federal and State Constitutions*, VI: 3247, 3250–1 (South Carolina); *ibid.*, III: 1690; Curry, *First Freedoms*, 157–8 (Maryland); Thorpe, *ibid.*, III: 1908 (Massachusetts).

denominational affiliations.[22] If prayers were, nonetheless, offered and chaplains subsequently appointed, the chosen celebrants were carefully distributed among a variety of Protestant clergy. And although the articles avoided all mention of God (only the closing paragraph allowed one chaste reference to "the Great Governor of the World"), the Confederation Congress itself was not so reticent. Appeals for divine intervention, especially during the war years, took the form each spring and fall of proclamations of days of fast and thanksgiving, with some specifically addressed to the Holy Ghost or Jesus Christ. The congress enjoined the army and navy to provide church services and urged all troops to attend. It also approved, indeed promoted, the first English-language Bible published in the United States, that of Philadelphia printer Robert Aitken, in 1781. That all but a very few Americans were Christian apparently gave sanction to these legislative actions, so long as they did not narrow the language to specific denominations.[23] After the war ended in 1783, congressional declarations in support of religion were muted.

In the years of transition from colonies to nation, many Americans displayed a kind of double consciousness regarding state support for religion. They believed in one sense that they had moved beyond mere toleration to full liberty of conscience, while at the same time they imposed specific restrictions on religious freedom and limited political privileges to favored groups – a contradiction that may not always have been apparent to many inhabitants of the new republic. Americans' understanding of the place religion held in their society was framed by two major influences: their memories of the Old World and their experiences in the New World. It is easy to forget that from the perspective of eighteenth-century Americans, the upheavals of the Protestant Reformation in the sixteenth century were not remote but had inflicted wounds still palpable to the inhabitants and thus formed the context of their religious understanding. The sundering of Protestant from Catholic had been followed by a century and a half of religious wars and forced migrations that had uprooted and thinned entire communities in Europe, some more than once. Many of those dislocated by these dolorous times had made their way over the seventeenth and eighteenth centuries to the British colonies, where they sought refuge from the sanguinary struggles of their former homelands and the opportunity to practice unmolested their own version of the truth. Even in the later

---

[22] Derek H. Davis, *Religion and the Continental Congress* (New York, 2000), 74.
[23] Hutson, *Religion and the Founding*, 51–8. The single exception was the grant of lands in Ohio to the Moravians in 1787 to encourage Christianity among the Indians (p. 57).

eighteenth century, memories of these events, as we saw with John Jay, remained vivid from stories told by parents and grandparents.

A further consequence of the Reformation that shaped the American religious experience was the unprecedented diversity of peoples and sects arriving in North America. Although pluralism was most evident in the middle region, it also increasingly affected the religious sociology in newly settled parts of the South and even New England. Combined with an initial scarcity of clergy, this phenomenon gave rise, as we have seen, to the voluntary, or gathered, church, a development whose importance is central to the history of American religion. Gathered churches had from the beginning of Christianity been viewed by those in power as a potential threat, because their strength came from the many below rather than from the anointed few at the top. In the eighteenth century this voluntary impulse had posed a particularly unsettling challenge to orthodox church leaders, as many newcomers embraced pietistic or evangelical practices, which were seen as unduly passionate and disorderly. As a wave of revivals struck in the 1740s, these "enthusiasts," in the vocabulary of that time, opened the church to all manner of innovation and potential chaos. As the Rev. Charles Chauncy of Boston had thundered, even "FEMALE EXHORTERS" were encouraged to speak in meeting.[24] The awakenings eventually subsided, of course, and power gradually returned to more conventional precincts.

Nonetheless, the established elite who held most authority in the late eighteenth-century era of constitution writing were often uneasy as they embarked on an unprecedented and perilous political experiment. Their republic would place in the people's hands more power than they had ever before known, making selflessness and moral integrity essential to its success. To remove religion – historically associated with building moral character and an ethical society – as a buttress of the state was, not surprisingly, beyond the intellectual horizon of many Americans.

And, indeed, the separation of church and state is a highly sophisticated idea, one with which Americans continue to wrestle to this day. Was it possible that both states and churches could survive and prosper without an enforced religious scaffolding? Like their European counterparts, Americans were long familiar with statutes forbidding nonessential travel or frivolity on the Sabbath, civic declarations assigning days of fasting and prayer, and laws regulating both public and private behavior. Punishments, at least potentially, could be severe, as a late eighteenth-century Vermont statute illustrates in the extreme: "if any person ... shall blaspheme the

---

[24] Charles Chauncy, *Enthusiasm Described and Caution'd Against* (Boston, 1742), 13. Emphasis in original.

name of God, the Father, Son, or HOLY GHOST ... ; or shall curse in the like manner; such person shall be put to death."[25] To have achieved the leap of imagination and policy required to fully separate state and church while founding the first popularly based republic in modern history, and this during the harrowing years of war against Britain, was probably too much to ask of any people.

That was true except, perhaps, for the likes of Thomas Jefferson, James Madison, and some few others long designated as the nation's Founders. These leaders possessed a remarkably prescient understanding of the compatibility of a secular state with a voluntary church. Although often dismissed as deists or mere nominal church adherents, they too were shaped by their own time, and their religious beliefs are best understood when framed accordingly. Jefferson, especially, has been caricatured as both viscerally anticlerical and contemptuous of traditional Christianity, a view that fails to place him within the context of the rationalist religious philosophy that formed his sense of the supernatural. Because not only Jefferson and Madison but also Washington, Franklin, Adams, Hamilton, and Jay have so often been rousted from the grave to support modern assumptions about "original intent" and other notions of church and state, their religious ideals and principles take on heightened importance and thus bear closer scrutiny.

The Virginians, Jefferson, Madison, and Washington, were born into families affiliated with the Church of England, and they continued as lifelong members of that communion. For many years Anglicanism in the southern colonies was depicted as a low-energy sort of religion: a cool, deistic faith whose success in reconciling reason with Christianity led to a shallow belief and religious practice. This perception first gained traction in the 1840s and 1850s, when the initial histories of American religion were written by authors in the grip of the Second Great Awakening. To evangelicals and their historians, "real" religion involved camp meetings, dramatic preaching, emotional displays on both sides of the pulpit, and waves of conversions. When compared with this colorful populist religion, the cerebral Episcopalians and other rationalists of moderate mien seemed dull indeed. As revivalism expanded in the nineteenth century, with its frontier circuit riders and association with the westward thrust of American history, the evangelical interpretation gained control of the narrative. Recently, a more balanced appreciation of the Enlightenment-influenced religious mentality has restored a fuller picture of the early national religious spectrum,

---

[25] William Slade, comp., *Vermont State Papers ... and the Laws ... 1779 to 1786* (Middlebury, VT, 1823), 355.

including the thinkers and rationalist theologians who helped shape the understanding of many leaders in the founding generation.[26]

The assumption that the Virginians and other Founders would have taken their religious beliefs lightly, or considered them less sincere and worthy than those of their contemporaries, is simply not tenable. True, their religious understanding included such worldly goals as moral behavior in one's earthly passage, service to one's fellows, and public virtue. But they too looked to the life hereafter – in which all of the Founders believed. Their afterlife, like that of the evangelicals, would reward good and punish evil. Confidence in the enlightened superiority of their faith grew from an understanding, propelled by such thinkers as John Locke and the Scottish common sense school, that reason as well as one's senses revealed the existence of God. Having embraced the scientific revolution, they rejected the miraculous explanations for natural phenomena that still held so many in thrall.

Thomas Jefferson's views are of special interest because in later life, having overcome a reluctance to discuss religion publicly or privately, he probably wrote more on the subject than any other of the Founders. Jefferson had little patience for those who unthinkingly embraced a religion disfigured, in his view, by centuries of doctrinal accretions. Priest-made miracles and rituals that obscured the simple message of Jesus were particular anathema. The doctrine of the Trinity was "mere Abracadabra," invented in the fourth century. Jefferson's scorn might be directed at contemporary clergy of any denomination, including the Episcopalian, but it was especially aimed at old-school Calvinists, as when he denounced "pious young monks from Harvard and Yale" who continued to promulgate the "absurdities" of Calvin.[27] At the same time Jefferson had close friends among the moderate Anglican clergy, whose acuteness of mind and elegance of expression he admired. He recommended young men for ordination and helped finance their education and travel to London. When the Revolution disrupted the Church of England, including public funding of its clergy,

---

[26] Edwin S. Gaustad, *Faith of Our Fathers: Religion and the New Nation* (San Francisco, 1987), provides a balanced and insightful discussion of the Founders' religious views; esp. ch. 5. For a sensitive consideration of the colonial Church of England, see John K. Nelson, *A Blessed Company: Parishes, Parsons, and Parishioners in Anglican Virginia, 1690–1776* (Chapel Hill, 2001), esp. part III. For influences on Jefferson's religious thought, see Dickinson W. Adams et al., eds., *Jefferson's Extracts from the Gospels*, in Charles T. Cullen, ed., *Papers of Thomas Jefferson*, 2nd ser. (Princeton, 1983), introduction.

[27] Adams et al., *Jefferson's Extracts*, Jefferson to Francis Adrian Van der Kemp, Monticello, 30 July 1816, p. 375 (mere Abracadabra); Paul L. Ford, ed., *The Works of Thomas Jefferson*, 12 vols. (New York, 1905), Jefferson to Horatio Gates Spafford, 10 Jan. 1816, with enclosure to Thomas Ritchie, Monticello, 21 Jan. 1816, XI, in the Online Library of Liberty, http://oll.libertyfund.org (monks); Gaustad, *Faith of Our Fathers*, 106 (absurdities).

Jefferson organized among his neighbors a voluntary subscription, to which he contributed by far the largest sum. In other words, his anticlericalism was reserved for clergy he described as "impious dogmatists ... [and] false shepherds."[28] In support of these opinions, Jefferson, an intense student of the Bible, undertook to purge the Gospels of their excesses. By stripping away the layers of priestly augmentation, his objective was to return Christian teachings to the simple version of the primitive church, for Jefferson regarded the moral system of Jesus as the most "sublime ... ever fallen from the lips of man." And although he denied the Trinity and moved closer to Unitarianism in later life, Jefferson specifically declared that he was neither atheist nor deist. As he wrote in 1816: "*I am a real Christian*, that is to say, a disciple of the doctrines of Jesus."[29]

He was not alone. Others in his elite group prided themselves on having risen above the superstitions of priest-made religion to reach a higher plane of spiritual truth. Benjamin Franklin, often depicted as the supreme rationalist, found the Calvinist church of his youth too doctrinaire. In Philadelphia he bought a pew for his family at Anglican Christ Church, where two of his children were baptized. Although his personal connection to that church beyond financial support cannot be documented, he chose its churchyard as his final resting place. Franklin had some doubts about the divinity of Jesus, disparaged church dogma, emphasized good works — both in his fictional character, Silence Dogood, and in his own life — and embraced the moderate views of his fellow Episcopalians. He, like Jefferson, admired the moral and religious principles taught by Jesus: they were "the best the World ever saw or is likely to see," although they had received "corrupting Changes." As he wrote to Ezra Stiles in 1790, he believed in "one God, Creator of the Universe," the hereafter, and the efficacy of prayer. He supported public fasts, and it was Franklin who proposed that the Constitutional Convention of 1787 open with prayer.[30]

---

[28] Julian P. Boyd et al., eds., *The Papers of Thomas Jefferson* (Princeton, 1950–), Jefferson to William Preston, Staunton [VA], 18 Aug. 1768, I: 23; *ibid.*, Jefferson to Thomas Adams, Charlottesville, 11 July 1770, I: 48–9; *ibid.*, Jefferson to Peyton Randolph, 23 July 1770, I: 49–51 (clergy); *ibid.*, Subscription to Support a Clergyman in Charlottesville, Feb. 1777, II: 6–9. Thomas Jefferson Randolph, ed., *The Writings of Thomas Jefferson*, 4 vols. (Boston, 1830), Jefferson to Benjamin Waterhouse, 26 June 1822, IV: 349 (impious dogmatists ...).

[29] Adams et al., *Jefferson's Extracts*, Jefferson to William Short, Monticello, 31 Oct. 1819, p. 388 (sublime); Jefferson to John Adams, 11 Apr. 1823, p. 410 (no atheist); Jefferson to Charles Thompson, Monticello, 9 Jan. 1816, p. 365 (real Christian); Gaustad, *Faith of Our Fathers*, 108 (no deist).

[30] Albert Henry Smyth, ed., *The Writings of Benjamin Franklin*, 10 vols. (New York, 1905–07), Franklin to Ezra Stiles, 9 Mar. 1790, X: 84; Davis, *Religion*, 207.

John Adams' Congregational upbringing left its mark on his later religious practice. He declared himself a lifelong churchgoing animal and, although acknowledging the legitimacy of all faiths, never fully disavowed the Congregational establishment in his native state of Massachusetts. Adams believed in the joys of heaven and the punishments of hell. But he rejected the Calvinist doctrine of predestination as arbitrary and a discouragement to industry; instead, he had a "high notion of the efficacy of human endeavours in all cases." As early as 1761, at age twenty-six, he had expressed opinions that marked him as a moderate rationalist, and his late-life correspondence with Thomas Jefferson reveals the similarity of their reading about and perception of the supernatural. As president, Adams displayed no qualms, however, about issuing thanksgiving proclamations.[31]

George Washington, as seen previously, regularly invoked the aid of God in his military life, and as president he ordered days of thanksgiving "to acknowledge the providence of Almighty God."[32] Like his fellow Virginians, Washington kept his beliefs to himself, considering it inappropriate to parade one's religion for public consumption. What little can be known of his private beliefs is based primarily on Washington's behavior. He actively supported his church by regular attendance, diligent membership on the Truro parish vestry, and three terms as churchwarden. He stood rather than kneeled to pray (perhaps because of his unusual height), and he was not known to take communion. At meals he either requested a prayer from a visiting cleric or said a brief grace himself; he called no clergyman to his deathbed. Nonetheless, in a rare private comment on religion to fellow Virginian Landon Carter, he specifically acknowledged Providence's "protection & direction of me."[33] Still, it was in his public role that Washington made the greatest contribution to his country's religious happiness, for his benign and very public embrace of all faiths – non-Christian as well as Christian – as equally deserving the protection of the state served as a model for more pinched and timid souls in the new nation.[34]

Perhaps the most reticent of all the Founders regarding his faith was James Madison, for he considered his personal beliefs an entirely private matter. Madison was a lifelong member of the Anglican-Episcopal Church,

---

[31] Charles Francis Adams, ed., *The Works of John Adams,* repr. ed., 9 vols. (Freeport, 1969 [1850–56]), Adams to Samuel Quincy, 22 Apr. 1761, I: 646; Gaustad, *Faith of Our Fathers,* 91ff, 108.

[32] Abbot and Twohig, *Papers of Washington, Presidential Series,* 3 Oct. 1789, IV: 129–30.

[33] Abbot and Twohig, *Papers of Washington, Revolutionary War Series,* Washington to Landon Carter, Valley Forge, 30 May 1778, XV: 267.

[34] For a discussion of Washington's views on religious inclusion, see Paul F. Boller, Jr., "George Washington and Religious Liberty," in James Morton Smith, ed., *George Washington: A Profile* (New York, 1969), 168–79.

was known to be a steady church attender, and regularly conducted family worship at home. Yet perhaps the most we can say of his personal religious views is that they were likely similar to those of Thomas Jefferson.[35] There can be no doubt, however, that in the public arena robust religious liberty was dear to his heart. Such was evident in Madison's dedicated effort to assure freedom of conscience in the Virginia Statute for Religious Freedom, and it would culminate in his role as a leading author of the religion clause in the Bill of Rights.

Among the most prominent leaders of the early nation were two New Yorkers, Alexander Hamilton and John Jay. Hamilton has recently been described as a zealous Anglican during his youth and college years whose observance then lagged until the death of his son, Philip, in a duel in 1801, after which he returned to the faith. In fact, little is know about Hamilton's private beliefs or religious practice in the period from 1776 through the 1790s, when he was engaged in the Revolution and service to the early nation, although biographers often fill the gap by assuming a religious hiatus. During those middle years Hamilton married Eliza Schuyler, a devout member of the Dutch Reformed Church; their children were baptized in the Episcopal Church; and the family purchased a pew at Trinity Church in Manhattan, which involved a financial commitment and formal tie between the Hamiltons and Trinity. Was Alexander Hamilton an irregular church attender, as is often suggested? This question cannot be answered, because individual attendance at Trinity was not recorded. Did he take communion? Possibly not. It is known that at the height of the tension with France in 1797, Hamilton proposed "a day of humiliation and prayer" to impress the seriousness of the times on the citizens and "to strengthen their religious ideas." Three weeks later he urged "a national appeal to Heaven for protection ... [against the] Atheistical tenets of their enemies."[36]

Best documented is the scene at Hamilton's deathbed, following his duel with Aaron Burr in 1804. Hamilton asked to take communion, which was initially refused by the bishop of New York, Benjamin Moore. The Anglican Church had over the entire eighteenth century worked to eradicate dueling among its members, a reform Bishop Moore firmly supported. Although he wished to offer Hamilton solace, Moore believed he must "unequivocally condemn the practice which had brought [Hamilton]

---

[35] Gaustad, *Faith of Our Fathers*, 56–7, 63.
[36] Harold C. Syrett et al., eds., *The Papers of Alexander Hamilton*, 27 vols. (New York, 1961–87), Hamilton to Timothy Pickering, New York, 22 Mar. 1797, XX: 545; Hamilton to William Loughton Smith, New York, 10 Apr. 1797, XXI: 41. The most recent biography is Ron Chernow, *Alexander Hamilton* (New York, 2004); on religion see pp. 53, 132, 205, 659–60.

to his present unhappy condition." Yet Hamilton was so determined to receive the sacrament that he next turned to his neighbor John Mason, a Presbyterian minister. But Mason's church would not allow him to give communion "privately," no doubt because it veered perilously close to the Roman Catholic rite of extreme unction. Bishop Moore subsequently returned to Hamilton's bedside, obtained his promise never to duel again should he survive, heard him affirm his Christian belief, and shortly before he died granted him communion.[37]

The other New Yorker, John Jay, was the most outspokenly religious member of the founding group surveyed here. Whereas Jay was a rationalist in worldly affairs, his embrace of God's mysteries led him to declare publicly that "mere human reason" was insufficient ground for religious belief. Although Jay was a communicating member of the Episcopal Church, his Huguenot heritage had left a mark, giving a Calvinist, faith-based edge to his worship. He believed in the Trinity, did not flinch at acknowledging sin, and once described salvation as "the free gift and grace of God, not of our deserving, nor in our power to deserve" – words that would have brought comfort to traditional predestinarians. Jay was instrumental in founding the Protestant Episcopal Church as an entity independent of its English parent. He also smoothed the way for consecration of the first American bishops. As he confided at the time to John Adams, although he personally could do without bishops, if others wanted them he would acquiesce. Jay was a devout student of the Bible, and from 1822 to 1828 he served as president of the American Bible Society.[38]

Looking at the founding generation as a whole, it is apparent that their religious views were more complex than is often acknowledged. Although the Founders' perspective on the supernatural reflected the progressive rationalism of the Enlightenment, which itself energized their search for eternal truths, in many respects their outlook remained grounded in the eighteenth century. All embraced Christianity's moral system, and some found solace in its more mystical teachings. Although Jefferson, Adams, and Franklin specifically labored to strip Christianity of nonessentials, they did so in order to reveal its internal beauty. The Founders were neither atheists nor deists, labels explicitly rejected by Jefferson and Franklin, but believed that they had constructed a religious philosophy as valid spiritually as that of any of their fellow Americans.

---

[37] Syrett et al., *Papers of Hamilton*, Benjamin Moore to William Coleman [New York], 12 July 1804, XXVI: 315–16; see also pp. 278, 308. Donna T. Andrew, "The Code of Honour and Its Critics: The Opposition to Duelling in England, 1700–1850," *Social History* V (1980): 409–34; Chernow, *Alexander Hamilton*, 706–8.

[38] Bonomi, "John Jay," 10–11, 16–17.

This mental landscape shaped the perspective of those who either influenced or directly undertook the task of forming a new government at the national level. Whereas by the opening of the Constitutional Convention in May 1787 a number of state charters and statutes still included clauses that narrowed religious freedom in their localities, the document the delegates met in Philadelphia to amend – the Articles of Confederation – said nothing about religion. That the articles were silent on this subject when composed in 1777 was most likely owing to Congress's long-ripening awareness of the multisectarian character of the national population. Ten years later, the United States contained an ever more dense sacramental web, as Methodists, splintering Baptist factions, and other sectarian communities continued to proliferate, including newly forming African American churches under black leadership.[39] Although the new Constitution would address itself no longer to "we the ... States," but instead to "We the people," in fact the people had already expressed their religious preferences at the state level and expected no meddling from a body even more remote from their daily lives. Eighty-one-year-old Benjamin Franklin, nonetheless, urged the convention to open its deliberations with morning prayers, noting "the longer I live, the more convincing proofs I see of this Truth – *that God governs in the Affairs of Men*."[40] Even so revered a figure as Franklin could not prevail with the religiously diverse delegates, however, who apparently saw no reason to complicate their already delicate task. The result was that the U.S. Constitution produced by the convention in September 1787 made only a single reference to religion: "no religious test shall ever be required as a qualification to any office or public trust under the United States" (Article VI, Section 3).

Such pronounced secularism aroused consternation among some delegates to the conventions called by each state in 1788 to ratify the Constitution. A North Carolinian protested that without a religious test, "pagans, deists, and Mahometans might obtain offices among us, and ... the senators and representatives might all be pagans."[41] Although not widely articulated, this fear contributed to the demand that a bill of rights be added to the Constitution. In the Pennsylvania ratifying convention, a sizeable minority called for the rights of conscience to be secured at the federal level; and the states of New York, North Carolina, Rhode Island, and Virginia proposed

---

[39] Sylvia R. Frey, "'The Year of Jubilee Is Come': Black Christianity in the Plantation South in Post-Revolutionary America," in Ronald Hoffman and Peter J. Albert, eds., *Religion in a Revolutionary Age* (Charlottesville, 1994), 87–124.

[40] Max Farrand, ed., *The Records of the Federal Constitution of 1787*, 4 vols. (New Haven, 1937), I: 451–2.

[41] Jonathan Elliot, ed., *The Debates in the Several State Conventions on the Adoption of the Federal Constitution*, repr. ed. (Salem, 1987 [1901]), IV: 192.

specific amendments guaranteeing nonestablishment and the free exercise of religion.[42] Not surprisingly, the calls for religious liberty issued most loudly from states that had long experienced religious diversity within their own borders.

Ratification of the Constitution won approval in divided states only with the promise that a bill of rights would be appended to the document when the first Congress met in 1789. James Madison was the most illustrious member of that Congress, having been elected to the House of Representatives from Virginia after his cantankerous political rival, Patrick Henry, blocked his path to the Senate.[43] And although Madison had originally believed that parchment barriers, as he called them, were insufficient to secure rights, he now grudgingly accepted the benefit of a declaration of rights toward reconciling public doubters to the new Constitution. As the leading philosopher and architect of that document as well as the premier member of the House, Madison was the logical choice to draw the amendments suggested by the ratifying conventions into a coherent whole.[44]

No one had been more consistent than Madison regarding the core principle of religious liberty. From at least his early twenties Madison was persuaded that "ecclesiastical establishments tend to great ignorance and corruption." He had amplified this view in his *Memorial and Remonstrance* (1784), which opposed Patrick Henry's plan for a general assessment of Virginians in support of the Christian religion. "Who does not see that the same authority which can establish Christianity, in exclusion to all other Religions," he asked, "may establish with the same ease any particular sect of Christians, in exclusion of all other Sects?"[45] His thinking matured further when he took up his pen to defend the federal Constitution during the ratification debates of 1788. In *Federalist 51,* Madison made a compelling case that the clash of rival interests provided the most reliable guarantee of individual and minority rights. It was the very "multiplicity of sects" spread over a large territory, he wrote, that shielded "one part of society against the injustice of the other part."[46] That is, religious diversity itself, and the consequent competition among sects for adherents, provided a

---

[42] Cecelia M. Kenyon, ed., *The Antifederalists* (New York, 1966), 35, 431; Noah Feldman, *Divided by God: America's Church-State Problem – And What We Should Do About It* (New York, 2006 [2005]), 43.

[43] Trevor Colbourn, ed., *Fame and the Founding Fathers: Essays by Douglass Adair* (New York, 1974), 136.

[44] Jack N. Rakove, *Original Meanings: Politics and Ideas in the Making of the Constitution* (New York, 1996), 330–6.

[45] Gaillard Hunt, ed., *The Writings of James Madison*, 9 vols. (New York, 1900–10), Madison to William Bradford, 24 Jan. 1774, I: 19; William Lee Miller, *The First Liberty: Religion and the American Republic* (New York, 1986), appx. II (*Memorial and Remonstrance*), 360.

[46] Jacob E. Cooke, ed., *The Federalist* (Middletown, CT, 1961), 351–2.

kind of check and balance that guarded each person's or group's right to religious freedom from a potentially tyrannical majority, a gift that flowed from both the sectarian pluralism and the broad geographic expanse of the American republic.

When the House of Representatives took up debate on the amendments that would become the Bill of Rights, the language proposed by Madison and a select committee was agreed on with relative ease once it was determined that the national government only, not the states, was the object of the guaranteed rights. By 1791 the necessary two-thirds of the states had ratified the amendments, which thus became the law of the land. The first of the ten amendments that comprised the Bill of Rights opened with the religion clause, "Congress shall make no law respecting an establishment of religion, or prohibiting the free exercise thereof."[47]

Even so, the separation of church and state enunciated in the religion clause remained enmeshed in a web of longstanding practices and public observances that affected the way it would be implemented. Thus neither President George Washington nor President John Adams shrank from issuing proclamations ordering days of public prayer and thanksgiving. Thomas Jefferson proved the greater purist, refraining from all religious proclamations during his presidency because he considered them a violation of the government's authority. James Madison also made clear his thinking about such presidential actions when he looked back on the subject some years after he left office. Not only should one fear the state trespassing on the churches; there was also the "danger of silent accumulations & encroachments by Ecclesiastical Bodies" on the state. On the question of whether the office of chaplain for the houses of Congress was consistent with the Constitution, his answer was unequivocal: because tax-supported appointment of a chaplain from one denomination "shut the door of worship against the members whose creeds & consciences forbid a participation in that of the majority," such chaplainships were "a palpable violation of equal rights, as well as of Constitutional principles." The same prohibition applied to military chaplains, to which Madison added that nonvoluntary religious observance was unlikely in any case to make the troops more devout. Proclamations of fast and thanksgiving were similarly to be avoided because "they imply a religious agency ... [not] part of the trust delegated to political rulers." They also "nourish the erroneous idea of a *national* religion."[48] But if Madison's actions hewed close to these

---

[47] Leonard W. Levy, *The Establishment Clause: Religion and the First Amendment*, 2nd rev. ed. (Chapel Hill, 1994 [1986]), ch. 5.

[48] Elizabeth Fleet, "Madison's 'Detached Memoranda,'" *William and Mary Quarterly*, 3rd ser., III, no. 4 (Oct. 1946): 554, 558–60; Hutson, *Religion and the Founding,* 79–82.

principles during his first term as president, he deviated from them during the second term, possibly owing to public pressure at critical junctures of the War of 1812. At the recommendation of Congress in 1814 for a proclamation of thanksgiving and supplication of a peaceful end to the war, he designated a day of "voluntary" repentance and "humble adoration to the Great Sovereign of the Universe." When word of the peace treaty arrived in March 1815, he again proclaimed a day of public thanksgiving "in a freewill offering to their Heavenly Benefactor." Madison later justified these acts as "merely recommendatory," while reconfirming his general opposition to thanksgiving proclamations.[49]

Congress, of course, continued the longstanding practice of appointing chaplains, although members were careful to choose them from among a number of denominations, including the Roman Catholic Church. Indeed, during the opening decades of the nineteenth century, when the capital city of Washington was no more than a raw and muddy outpost, the House of Representatives turned itself into a church on Sundays, with a variety of speakers, including the first female – Dorothy Ripley, an English evangelist – preaching to the assembled congregants. It is of some interest that one of the most constant attenders at these services was President Thomas Jefferson, who also allowed the War and Treasury Departments to hold religious worship at their headquarters.[50] During Jefferson's presidential years, it would seem that his famous "wall of separation" between church and state took on the more fluid contours of the serpentine wall he had built at Monticello.

Still, the ideal and practice of religious liberty, as well as the separation of church from state, achieved a widening acceptance and more elevated standing in the public mind in the years from the Revolution to the founding of the nation. The relative ease with which this transition occurred, given centuries of contrary tradition, was no doubt owing in large part to Americans' physical distance from Old World establishments as well as to the unprecedented religious diversity of their communities. But another significant although less visible element was the immanent reinforcement such ideas received in that Bible-reading society, for the New Testament portrays an inclusive spirituality in a heaven of "many mansions." And one of the most often-quoted biblical passages of that day, Matthew 22:21, asserts a clear division between the secular and the spiritual worlds: "Render therefore unto Caesar the things which are Caesar's; and unto God the things that are God's."

---

[49] www.presidency.ucsb.edu/ws/index.php?pid=65981 and 65984 (proclamations); *Letters and Other Writings of James Madison* (New York, 1884), Madison to Edward Livingston, 10 July 1822, III: 274–5.

[50] Hutson, *Religion and the Founding*, 84–93.

SUGGESTIONS FOR FURTHER READING

Adams, Dickinson W., et al., eds. *Jefferson's Extracts from the Gospels,* in Charles T. Cullen, ed., *Papers of Thomas Jefferson.* 2nd ser. Princeton, 1983.

Bonomi, Patricia U. *Under the Cope of Heaven: Religion, Society, and Politics in Colonial America.* Rev. ed. New York, 2003 [1986].

Curry, Thomas J. *The First Freedoms: Church and State in America to the Passage of the First Amendment.* New York, 1986.

Gaustad, Edwin S. *Faith of Our Fathers: Religion and the New Nation.* San Francisco, 1987.

Hutson, James H. *Religion and the Founding of the American Republic.* Washington, DC, 1998.

Levy, Leonard W. *The Establishment Clause: Religion and the First Amendment.* 2nd rev. ed. Chapel Hill, 1994 [1986].

McLoughlin, William G. *New England Dissent, 1630–1833: The Baptists and the Separation of Church and State.* Cambridge, MA, 1971.

Miller, William Lee. *The First Liberty: Religion and the American Republic.* New York, 1986.

Ragosta, John A. *Wellspring of Liberty: How Virginia's Religious Dissenters Helped Win the American Revolution and Secured Religious Liberty.* New York, 2010.

30

RELIGION IN CANADA, 1759–1815

MARK A. NOLL

The history of British North America from 1759 to 1815 set Canada on a religious course that would differ significantly from what transpired in the United States. To be sure, much in early Canadian religious history is familiar to Americans because of circumstances, heritages, and events shared by all North Americans. These common experiences included historic tensions between Roman Catholics and Protestants, a large measure of Protestant pluralism, the presence of evangelical revival, consistent disregard of native religion, internal conflict over the wisdom of revolution, strong commitment to liberty, full exposure to Enlightenment thinking, and deep divisions created by ethnicity or race. Yet because of the distinctive unfolding of Canadian history, religion in Canada has never simply replicated American experience.

The kind of national comparison offered by Seymour Martin Lipset describes much that has been distinctive in religion as in other spheres. In Lipset's account, Canadian society "has been and is a more class-aware, elitist, law-abiding, statist, collectivity-oriented, and particularistic (group-oriented) society than the United States."[1] The antistatism, individualism, populism, violence, and egalitarianism that have often characterized American history have been decidedly less prominent in Canada. Some explanations for these systematic differences are geographical. Canada's vast space and sparse population have required a more active government and have placed a premium on cooperation in the churches. But an even broader explanation is historical. For religion in Canada, it meant a very great deal that Quebec began as (and remains) a distinct society, that Canadians rejected the American Revolution, and that Canadian Loyalism was reaffirmed during the War of 1812. These seemingly secular events and circumstances gave shape to Canadian religious life and account

---

[1] Seymour Martin Lipset, *Continental Divide: The Values and Institutions of the United States and Canada* (New York, 1990), 8.

for some of the deep differences that have always accompanied the many similarities that also exist between religion in the United States and religion in Canada.

BRITAIN IN COMMAND

Parts of what would much later become the Dominion of Canada began as scattered European colonies. By far the most important was New France, with its main settlements concentrated along the St. Lawrence River, but with tendrils of exploration and Indian trading stretching far to the west and southwest into what is now the Mississippi River valley. By 1760, this colony enjoyed a population of 60,000 to 70,000 inhabitants, almost all of whom were French-speaking Roman Catholics mostly living in a traditional agricultural society. (For comparison, New England had a population of about 450,000 at the time.) Quebec, the seat of the one Catholic bishop for almost all areas of French and English colonization, was the main city, with smaller settlements at Trois-Rivières and Montreal further up the St. Lawrence.

Acadia, or Nova Scotia (the present-day provinces of Nova Scotia and New Brunswick), was settled lightly with less than ten thousand inhabitants. Although this area was also first colonized by the French, it had been administered by the British since the Treaty of Utrecht in 1713 ceded French control. In 1754, at the start of Europe's Seven Years' War (in America, the French and Indian War), the British had removed a large portion of the French-speaking and Catholic Acadian population as a war measure. Only shortly before the Acadian removal, imperial competition had also stimulated the first British efforts to colonize Nova Scotia, with several thousand settlers lured from Germany and Switzerland (mostly Lutherans and Reformed) and from New England (mostly Congregationalists) to settle the port of Halifax and nearby areas.

Unlike the situation for the American colonies, Canada came into the British Empire by conquest. When in September 1759 the British triumphed over the French on the Plains of Abraham outside the city of Quebec, the way lay open to the British takeover of all North American French possessions, which was formalized by the Treaty of Paris in 1763.

Immediately the British faced the question of how they would incorporate a nearly all-Catholic colony into an empire that had become increasingly militant about its Protestant character because of warfare with Catholic France. The Treaty of Paris (Article IV) contained conciliatory language, but with accommodations to Quebec's Catholics firmly hedged:

> His Britannick Majesty ... agrees to grant the liberty of the Catholick religion to the inhabitants of Canada: he will, in consequence, give the most

precise and most effectual orders, that his new Roman Catholic subjects may profess the worship of their religion according to the rites of the Romish church, as far as the laws of Great Britain permit.[2]

The last clause was significant because "the laws of Great Britain" prohibited Catholics from holding public office, excluded them from the universities, and forbade any Catholic hierarchy.

Moreover, from London came a directive to pursue all possible means to Anglicize the French-speaking population and promote the Church of England. In Quebec itself, however, one of the British military governors, James Murray, filed an extensive early report that urged a different approach: because, he said, the Canadians were "extremely tenacious of their Religion, nothing can contribute so much to make them staunch subjects of his Majesty as the new Government giving them every reason to imagine no alteration is to be attempted in that point."[3] The same report singled out Quebec's communities of women religious as being especially valued by the population. The conciliatory policy of Murray, who was soon named the first governor of the new colony, set a course that most of his successors followed. While patiently listening to imperial directives, Murray went out of his way to let Catholics carry on as much as possible as they had before.

The first difficulty concerned leadership, because the bishopric of Quebec had been vacant since the incumbent's death in 1760. The problem was how to name a replacement without compromising Britain's victory over France, where Quebec's earlier bishops had all been consecrated. Overcoming this difficulty required a complicated set of maneuvers and considerable cooperation from General Murray, but it was accomplished. As their new bishop, the cathedral chapter in Quebec City nominated Jean-Olivier Briand, who had come to New France as a young priest in 1741 and who was the only local candidate whom Governor Murray would support. Briand traveled to London, where he sought permission to go to France for the consecration, which was finally granted after a long delay. Briand was then ordained without fanfare by three French bishops in a quiet ceremony outside of Paris. When he finally returned to Quebec in June 1766 after an absence of two years, he was greeted with great joy. In addition, Briand returned to North America with papal permission to name a coadjutor bishop, with right of succession, so that Britain and France would no longer have to intercede in order for Quebec to enjoy a permanent succession of bishops.

---

[2] John S. Moir, ed., *Church and State in Canada, 1627–1867: Basic Documents* (Toronto, 1967), 77.
[3] *Ibid.*, 75.

Great difficulties still confronted Canadian Catholics. The war had damaged more than 30 of the 140 churches along the St. Lawrence and ended the annual subsidy provided to the Church by the king of France. The shortage of clergy remained severe, because Britain prohibited fresh clerical recruits from France, and the preparation of Canadiens for the priesthood at local seminaries moved slowly. ("Canadien" refers specifically to the French-speaking Quebeckers who at that time made up most of "Canada.") Shutting off the supply of Jesuits and Recollets from France took a special toll on missions to the Indians. Moreover, when Briand returned to Quebec he was recognized by the British not as a bishop, but only as "Superintendent of the Romish Church." And intense anti-Catholic sentiment continued to be expressed by some Protestant settlers in Canada as well as by Protestants in Britain's colonies further south. When in the late 1760s Britain authorized funds to support a Catholic priest working among the Acadians in Nova Scotia, he reported to Bishop Briand, "Two Presbyterian ministers have preached against me in public.... It is said that if the king is allowed to put a priest in Nova Scotia, he will have to allow one in Boston. The appointment of a priest in Nova Scotia is a disgrace: that summarize their objections."[4] A last difficulty was the wide expanse of Bishop Briand's official responsibilities – all of North America except Newfoundland and Louisiana – which meant that he was never able to provide proper oversight for all aspects of his charge.

Nonetheless, the all-out assault on Quebec Catholicism that many Canadiens feared after the British took control did not take place. Briand, an individual of unusual diligence and rare self-effacement, succeeded in restoring Catholic morale while holding at bay the forces working against the Church. When Briand's friend, Governor Murray, was replaced by another military man, Sir Guy Carleton – provisionally in 1766, permanently in 1768 – relations with the British improved still more.

Carleton, an Anglo-Irish Protestant, received orders similar to those that had been given to his predecessor; he was to hasten the Anglicization of Quebec linguistically, religiously, and politically. To that end he did cooperate with a scheme of the archbishop of Canterbury to provide three French-speaking Huguenot ministers for Quebec, Trois-Rivières, and Montreal. He also provided support to the Anglican and Presbyterian military chaplains who ministered to the small English-speaking population of the colony (less than one thousand until the American Revolution). Yet like Governor Murray before him, Carleton realized that efforts to convert

[4] Giles Chaussé, "French Canada from the Conquest to 1840," trans. James MacLean, in Terrence Murphy and Roberto Perin, eds., *A Concise History of Christianity in Canada* (Toronto, 1996), 69.

the local population would be counterproductive. He, therefore, pulled the strings that in 1772 gained British permission for Briand to consecrate a coadjutor bishop, Louis-Philippe d'Esgly, who was Quebec's first Canadian-born prelate. With this step, the Catholics of Quebec secured the ability to perpetuate their own hierarchy, and Carleton succeeded in pulling Quebec even more firmly out of the French orbit.

Even more important was Carleton's persistent efforts to rework the provisions of the 1763 Treaty of Paris dealing with Quebec. His goal was legal protection for the functioning status quo. After several years of intense lobbying at a distance and then in London, Carleton finally won out in Parliament. The Quebec Act, which received George III's royal assent in June 1774, did prohibit direct communication from Canada's bishops to Rome and did give the royal governors official supervision over ordinations to the priesthood and the consecration of bishops. (In practice, the governors simply signed off on the names provided by the bishop and also allowed communications to France that could be forwarded to Rome). Yet the most important clauses of the act gave formal British sanction to much of what had defined Quebec life before the conquest.

Canadiens were exempt from the Test Act, which required an oath to uphold the Anglican Church in order to participate in public life, gave official recognition to French civil law, and permitted the Church to collect tithes for its maintenance. The net effect was to restore the establishment privileges of the Catholic Church.

Given the timing of this legislation – just as Parliament was passing a series of acts known as the Intolerable Acts to punish Massachusetts for the Boston Tea Party of December 1773 – many in the thirteen colonies interpreted it as part of a massive British assault on colonial liberty. In a typical response, Alexander Hamilton asked, "Does not your blood run cold, to think an English parliament should pass an act for the establishment of arbitrary power and popery in such an extensive country?" And he went on to affirm that if the British "had any regard to the freedom and happiness of mankind, ... they would not have given such encouragement to popery.... They may as well establish popery in New-York and the other colonies as they did in Canada."[5]

Just as predictably, the act confirmed the confidence that Bishop Briand, the Catholic clergy, and most of the seigneurs (or landowners) had placed in the goodwill of first Governor Murray and then Governor Carleton. In letters of the time, Briand spoke glowingly of the result. "Here we enjoy perfect peace under the government of one of the most amiable of men.

---

[5] Alexander Hamilton, *A Full Vindication of the Measures of the Congress* (Dec. 1774), in H. C. Syrett, ed., *The Papers of Alexander Hamilton* (New York, 1961), I: 68–9.

Religion is practised here in complete freedom, and in many cases more fervently than ever.... We hardly notice that we are under a Protestant prince. It must be admitted that no nation is as humane as the English one."[6]

The unexpected outcome of the British conquest was to transform Quebec's leaders into staunch supporters of a Protestant monarchy. It also led to the Catholic Church becoming the defining center of Canadien identity. With ties to France cut, local government and trade dominated by the British, and political leadership in the hands of the conquerors, the Church was the one institution in which Quebeckers controlled their own lives. The Catholic situation in postconquest Quebec was analogous to Ireland under British rule, Poland under Nazis and Communists, or African Americans in the United States during segregation and Jim Crow. Because the churches were all that remained in control of the people themselves, they became centers for culture, language, learning, and social organization, as well as for religion narrowly construed. The intense identification with the Catholic Church that would be so important in Quebec life until the 1960s took shape in the years immediately following Britain's triumph over France.

At the time a few Canadiens protested that too much deference was being given to Church officials, especially Bishop Briand. Michel Chartier de Lotbinière spoke for a small class of French-speaking merchants and urban professionals in complaining about the secretive means by which Briand, Carleton, and Parliament arranged local affairs. Protests in favor of democracy, representative government, and liberalism more generally would remain an ongoing theme in Quebec life, but until the middle of the twentieth century they were subordinate to a much larger reality: British and Canadian leaders gave Quebec Catholics control over their own lives, Quebeckers defined themselves by the practice of conservative Catholicism, and Quebec Catholics remained loyal to the political system that guaranteed their French-Catholic identity.

AGAINST REVOLUTION

During the War of Independence, American Patriots used diplomacy and military invasion to seek Canadian support for the struggle against Britain. But in decisions with immense consequence for their religious future, Canadians remained loyal to Britain.

Leaders of the Continental Congress held out great hope that Quebec would respond favorably to their appeal to join the independence movement. When in 1775 Congress authorized an invasion of Quebec, George

[6] Chaussé, "French Canada," 71.

Washington wrote a circular letter that was distributed throughout the province in French and English. He described the British menace as "the Hand of Tyranny" and, without mentioning Catholicism by name, nonetheless offered reassurance that the thirteen colonies' traditional anti-French and anti-Catholic attitudes would be set aside entirely. "The Cause of America, and of Liberty, is the Cause of every virtuous American Citizen; whatever may be his Religion or his Descent, the United Colonies know no Distinction but such as Slavery, Corruption, and arbitrary Domination, may create."[7] Washington also ensured that the invading American armies under Philip Schuyler and Benedict Arnold would not celebrate Pope's Day, the traditional anti-Catholic festival on November fifth that marked the foiled Gunpowder Plot against the English Parliament in 1605. As military action unfolded, the invaders did receive some support from local habitants (the agricultural workers on seigniorial estates) and a few English merchants in Montreal. Although the invading Americans arrested some priests to prevent them from obstructing their march, most of the strongly Protestant Continental Army treated Catholic churches with respect and allowed Catholic practice to continue.

Yet led by Bishop Briand, the colony remained loyal to Britain. As the invasion was getting under way, Briand sent a letter to be read in his churches that staked his position in unmistakable terms.

> The remarkable goodness with which we have been governed by his very gracious Majesty, King George the Third, ... the recent favours with which he has loaded us, in restoring to us the use of our laws and the free exercise of our religion ... would no doubt be enough to excite your gratitude and zeal in support of the interests of the British Crown.

And Briand reminded his flocks that "your oaths, your religion, lay upon you the unavoidable duty of defending your country and your King with all the strength you possess."[8] Later when some Quebeckers did offer support to the Americans, he threatened them with excommunication. In April 1776, after Benedict Arnold had been defeated at Quebec but while the Americans still held Montreal, Congress dispatched a delegation to Canada to promote the American cause. It included Benjamin Franklin and the Rev. John Carroll, a former Jesuit who had become a secular priest and would later serve as the first Catholic bishop in the United States. When Carroll was allowed to say Mass in Montreal at a Jesuit church that

---

[7] George Washington, "Address to the Inhabitants of Canada" (Sept. 1775), in W. W. Abbot, ed., *The Papers of George Washington, Revolutionary War Series: June–September 1775*, ed. P. C. Chase (Charlottesville, 1985), I: 461–2.

[8] Bishop Briand, "The Authority of the Church" (1775), in George A. Rawlyk, ed., *Revolution Rejected, 1775–1776* (Scarborough, ON, 1968), 63.

had been taken over by the British to use as a prison, Briand responded by excommunicating the American.

The Quebec Act of 1774, which by its concessions to Quebec Catholicism convinced American Patriots that Britain supported tyranny, by contrast convinced most Canadiens of Britain's magnanimity and so maintained their loyalty during the war. Because of that expression of loyalty, Britain remained unusually accommodating to the province's Catholics. For their part, leading Quebec Catholics came to see the hand of Providence in preserving their loyalty to Britain during the American war. That conviction grew stronger after the beginning of the French Revolution in 1789. Loyalty to Britain was now protecting Quebec from the ravages sweeping over France, even as it already had protected them against the strongly anti-Catholic sentiments at loose in the new United States. Quebec's conservative Catholicism was strengthened in 1793 when twenty-two priests exiled from France during the Revolution arrived in the province.

In Nova Scotia, there were different reasons for not supporting the American Revolution. Even though a majority of that colony's still small population had come from New England — and bringing New England's strong Protestant affiliations tinged with republican ideology — Nova Scotia remained neutral during the war. Some of the neutrality came from the fact that Halifax was a major garrison for the British army and navy. In addition, Loyalists, whom the Americans labeled "Tories," began to arrive in the Maritimes shortly after warfare broke out. But another factor was religious, namely the spread of intense revivalism that absorbed so much energy during the war years that little was left over for political insubordination. The revival was led by Henry Alline, a peripatetic preacher who imitated the style of George Whitefield with some of Whitefield's remarkable effects. Yet unlike Whitefield's converts, numbers of whom became strongly republican, Alline's converts remained politically neutral. Alline's message stressed especially the new birth that made it possible for believers to be "ravished with a divine ecstasy beyond any doubts or fears" and enjoy a mystical union with God.[9] This preaching won a particular hearing in the scattered rural communities largely populated by immigrant New Englanders like himself. The New Light Stir resulted from Alline's work, and also from the early itinerations of Methodists, who were active in the region before the end of the Revolutionary War. Alline's intense spirituality left little room for political engagement. Once, when international tensions were rising and he was asked to accept a militia commission, he

---

[9] "Alline's Journal," in George A. Rawlyk, ed., *Henry Alline: Selected Writings* (New York, 1987), 88.

was tempted briefly but then resolved that he would allow only "a commission from heaven to go forth, and enlist my fellow-mortals to fight under the banners of King Jesus."[10] For the future of Canadian religion – in the Maritimes as also in Quebec, the decision against independence was as momentous as was the choice for independence in the United States.

POLITICAL COMPLICATION, ANGLICAN ASPIRATION, PROTESTANT PLURALISM

The American Revolution was a crucial event in Canadian religious history because it secured loyalty to Britain. In turn, loyalty encouraged trust in centralized institutions of church and state instead of preoccupation with abuses of centralized power, it countered enthusiasm for democracy with reliance on tradition, and it set a trajectory of evolutionary rather than revolutionary social and political change. But the war was also important for greatly expanding the Protestant population and the diversity of Protestant denominations in Canada. That Protestant impetus came first from Loyalists fleeing the newly founded United States, but then soon from new waves of British and American immigration.

With the Patriots triumphant in the war, upwards of one hundred thousand residents of the thirteen colonies voted with their feet against the new order by departing. Something like fifty thousand of these Loyalists came to Canada. More than thirty thousand arrived in Nova Scotia, where, however, they received a less than cordial welcome. As a result, the fourteen thousand Loyalists who settled along the Saint John River asked Britain to create a separate province where Loyalist interests could dominate. Britain agreed and in 1784 carved out the separate colony of New Brunswick. Included among Loyalists who arrived in the Atlantic region were nearly two thousand African Americans from Georgia, South Carolina, and elsewhere who had been released from slavery when they went over to the British side. Into the former New France eventually came as many as thirteen thousand Loyalists of European ancestry as well as several thousand Native Americans of the Iroquois Six Nations who had fought for the British during the war. Most of these United Empire Loyalists settled in Montreal and places further west.

The presence of the former American colonists soon led to difficulties from the effort to merge the large existing French and Catholic population with the smaller number of English and largely Protestant newcomers. Agitation by the Loyalists for the traditional rights of Englishmen, as well as solicitude for the Canadiens who wanted to preserve a distinct

[10] *Ibid.*, 96.

French-speaking Catholic sphere, led Parliament in 1791 to pass a constitutional act that divided mainland British North America into two separate colonies, Lower Canada (roughly modern Quebec) and Upper Canada (modern Ontario).

The Protestant history of the period 1780 to 1815 was defined by strong population expansion and complicated by countervailing tectonic forces. The growth came from the Loyalist influx, but even more from large numbers of Irish, Scottish, English, and especially American immigrants. The scale of population increase is indicated by the fact that in 1776 the Atlantic region counted only a dozen Protestant clergymen, while all of what would become Quebec and Ontario had far fewer. By 1812, the population of Maritime Canada had risen to more than one hundred thousand (a large majority Protestant and fairly well supplied with ministers), the English-speaking Protestants in Lower Canada numbered thirty thousand (out of the colony's three hundred thousand total), and the almost entirely Protestant population of Upper Canada stood at just less than one hundred thousand. Population growth also created an almost instant religious pluralism, because the immigrants brought with them a wide variety of faiths – Congregational, Lutheran, Baptist, Methodist, Quaker, Mennonite, and Moravian, as well as Anglican and Catholic (and a large number with no functioning religion).

In this welter of rapid change, Canadian Protestants were pushed along two opposite trajectories. One, which worked against the American grain, was a partially successful effort to re-create the values of traditional religious establishments in the New World. This effort was formally similar to what Catholics achieved in Lower Canada (Quebec), but with a distinctly Protestant flavor. By contrast, the other was quite similar to parallel developments in the United States that witnessed denominational pluralization, evangelical revival, democratic voluntarism, and the separation of church and state. The formal, establishmentarian trajectory has been better documented than the antiformal, voluntaristic trajectory, but until the War of 1812 the tide of rampant evangelicalism seemed every bit as strong as the bulwark of established tradition.

The move toward a traditional order was supported by many Loyalists and some of the new immigrants from England and Scotland who wanted to create a distinctly Christian society, but with Christianity differing significantly from what was taking shape in the United States. This vision came mostly from Anglican leaders, who were influential beyond their numbers in all regions. In contrast to the "Christian republicanism" of the United States, this conception of order was hierarchical and aristocratic; freedom meant positive liberty to enjoy a good life, not negative liberty to do what individuals pleased; prosperity was not to be pursued heedlessly in the American fashion; and civilization was grounded in the union of church and state rather than their separation.

In pursuit of such goals, Anglicans could count on some support from colonial governments, namely, a 1758 act that established the Church of England in Nova Scotia, the 1786 Act for Preserving the Church of England in New Brunswick, and the Clergy Reserves stipulation of the 1791 Constitutional Act for the two Canadas. This last provision specified that up to one-seventh of the land in both provinces would be set aside "for the Support and Maintenance of a Protestant clergy."[11] Yet if the goal of an English-style establishment of the Anglican Church was the end in view, that goal never came close to realization. The very broad toleration granted to other Protestants, the presence of very strong non-Anglican forces (Catholics in Lower Canada and diverse Protestants elsewhere), and the small number of Anglican ministers on the ground all meant that the materials for a full Anglican establishment were never adequate for the task.

Nonetheless, the ideal remained strong. Its leading advocates were Charles Inglis of Nova Scotia, Jacob Mountain of both Canadas, and John Strachan of Upper Canada. Inglis was named the Anglican bishop of Nova Scotia in 1787, the first bishop appointed for the colonial New World. Earlier he had served as rector of Trinity Church in New York City, until he was forced into exile at the end of British rule, which Inglis had supported with sermons, practical services, and a well-reasoned but futile response to Tom Paine's *Common Sense*. In his new charge, Inglis was competent but not particularly aggressive in pursuing an establishment, because, as he put it, "Being the first Bishop sent to the British Colonies in America, & aware of the prejudice that prevailed against that measure, I deemed it prudent on my arrival to go through my duty with as little noise, or offence as possible."[12]

Jacob Mountain became the second Canadian Anglican prelate when in 1792 he was appointed the "Lord Bishop" of Quebec with jurisdiction over both Lower and Upper Canada. Even though the huge expanse of Mountain's diocese was being served by only nine clergy in three working parishes and four mission stations, this former tutor of Prime Minister William Pitt the Younger was determined to advance the Anglican cause in both Catholic Lower Canada and rapidly settling Upper Canada. Mountain's efforts to fund Anglican expansion with income from the Clergy Reserves, to defend Anglicans in his position as a lord who sat on the executive councils of both Canadas (a position Inglis had not enjoyed), and to recruit new Anglican

[11] Moir, *Church and State*, 108.
[12] John S. Moir, *The Church in the British Era: From the British Conquest to Confederation* (Toronto, 1972), 65.

clergy succeeded partially but never came close to a fully functioning establishment.

Scottish-born John Strachan arrived in Upper Canada on the last day of 1799 after study in his native land with Thomas Chalmers, Scotland's leading Presbyterian and a strong advocate of church-state cooperation of the sort that Strachan pursued as an Anglican in Canada. Strachan rapidly became a pacesetter in Canadian Anglican education, an influential voice in government, a stout defender of Canada against American invasion during the War of 1812, a promoter of education at all levels, and much later (1839) the first Anglican bishop of Toronto when it was separated from the Diocese of Quebec.

In their conception of a Christian society, Inglis, Mountain, and Strachan promoted what was, in effect, a Christendom for the New World. Inglis once described this ideal as the cooperation of "Government and Religion ... the pillars on which society rests, and by which it is upheld; ... Whoever is sincerely religious towards God ... will also ... be loyal to his earthly Sovereign, obedient to the laws, and faithful to the government which God has placed over him." By contrast, his career in New York had taught him that "Fanatics are impatient under civil restraint, and run into the democratic system. They are for Leveling every thing both sacred and civil."[13] In 1810 Strachan reiterated this vision when he published a flattering account of the aging George III, which was meant to strengthen the loyalty of Canadiens and recent immigrants from the United States for what Strachan feared might soon be an invasion from south of the border: "Were we to model our lives by the conduct of our sovereign, corruption and venality would hide their heads, and all would be cheerfully obedient to the laws. Instead of pride, cruelty, and oppression, Christian charity would reign, each would embrace his fellow subject as a brother deserving of his confidence and friendship."[14] The evils against which Strachan warned were similar to ones that American Christian republicans attacked; his antidote, in contrast to what Americans proposed, was tradition, history, and deference to proper authority.

Although never successful in gaining unqualified acceptance, this conservative conception of Christian social order, nonetheless, took root in the first decades of the nineteenth century. Surprisingly, American immigrants in Upper Canada, who made up 60 percent of the population by 1812, seemed to follow this path. Significantly, most of the new Canadians were

---

[13] *Ibid.*, 23.
[14] John Strachan, *A Discourse on the Character of King George the Third, Addressed to the Inhabitants of British America* (1810), in J. L. H. Henderson, ed., *John Strachan: Documents and Opinions* (Toronto, 1969), 29.

New Yorkers or New Englanders of a Federalist bent – that is, Americans who occupied the most traditional and least democratic segment of the new nation's political spectrum and who were influenced by the establishmentarian Congregationalism that survived in Massachusetts, Connecticut, and New Hampshire. For this kind of immigrant, it was relatively easy to absorb conservative Federalist culture into the monarchical and loyal conception of Christian social order taking shape in Upper Canada.

The other side of the early Protestant story was defined by the reality of denominational pluralism and an aggressive evangelicalism that matched efforts at work in the United States. The mere presence of many other religious traditions stymied Anglican aspirations for an orderly establishment. Small numbers of Presbyterians, for instance, were present in Nova Scotia from the 1750s and in Quebec from the 1780s. After the Presbyterians of Nova Scotia remained staunchly loyal during the Revolutionary War, further migration – from Scotland (including Highland Gaelic speakers), the north of Ireland, and America – was more than welcome. Settlers and ministers from the established Church of Scotland, who might have provided support for an establishmentarian regime in Canada, were outnumbered by American Presbyterians and secessionists along with other dissenting Presbyterians from Scotland. These groups worked much harder to create their own strong institutions than to support the Anglicans. For example, shortly after Bishop Mountain arrived in Lower Canada, he faced a stiff challenge from Presbyterian John Bethune, who vociferously protested the monopoly on marriages that had been given to the Anglicans. A few years later, Thomas McCulloch in Pictou, Nova Scotia, established a successful academy alongside his church in a secession synod, which eventually contributed significantly to the region's educational history. Before long, even more Scottish and American immigrants made Presbyterians the largest Protestant denomination in the Maritimes and a substantial presence in Upper Canada as well. Later, a few Presbyterians did try to draw on funds from the Clergy Reserves, but for the most part they encouraged a Protestant ethos rather than a Protestant establishment.

Others among the proliferating tide of Protestant newcomers were even more indifferent to Anglican hegemony than the Presbyterians. A main reason for that indifference was the active evangelical voluntarism that emerged with a vengeance in many Canadian regions from the late 1770s. New Lights, Baptists, and Methodists in the Maritimes as well as a rapidly emerging Methodist movement in Upper Canada zealously pursued personal religious goals with religious means very similar to what democratic evangelicals sought in the United States.

The New Light Stir sparked by Henry Alline's itinerant preaching continued to expand for about a decade after his death in 1784. New Light preachers like Alline's brother-in-law, John Payzant, and Edward Manning, whose dramatic conversion in 1789 set him on a decades-long course of evangelical leadership in the Maritimes, actively propagated a message of world-denying piety. A hymn that Manning composed sometime after his conversion communicated the intense New Light vision.

> Within one theres A fire / That burns with Rapid flame
> And with A Pure Desire / Cries worthy is the Lamb –
> Yea Worthy Thou art forever / For thou wast slain for me
> And I obtain the favour / To know thy Love is free.[15]

Over time, however, the intensely personal, mystical, and anti-sacramental passions of New Light revivalism evolved into the more orderly, education- and church-centered faith of the region's Baptist churches. Manning, for instance, pastored a New Light Congregational church for several years before helping to found the Nova Scotia Baptist Association in 1800; he himself was ordained as a Baptist minister in 1807. With a growing number of his fellows, Manning came to emphasize adult believer's baptism as an important institution for Christian identity and church stability. Although an impetus from New Light revivalism continued to mark his career, Manning also became a leader in civilizing projects involving temperance, education, and missions. The main comparative point about these Maritimes New Lights and Baptists is that they followed more an American pattern of charismatic religion becoming more organized and restrained, rather than a European establishment pattern of church-state integration and authority exercised from on high.

Evangelical ferment in Nova Scotia received a boost in 1782 with the arrival of David George, a Loyalist who had been liberated from slavery by the British. Almost immediately George began to organize blacks into Baptist congregations, as he had already done in Georgia and South Carolina. His first church was in Shelbourne, Nova Scotia, where about 1,500 black Loyalists were living. Soon he was itinerating to the other areas where blacks had settled. His impassioned preaching won many hearers among whites as well as blacks but provided special reassurance to the freed slaves who were objects of continual discrimination in their new land. Opponents of George and the black Baptists objected when whites attended his services or asked him to baptize them, they criticized him for undercutting the work of other churches, and they ignored his complaints asking for economic fair play. Yet despite vigorous opposition, within less than a decade, perseverance by George and his associates resulted in

---

[15] George A. Rawlyk, *The Canada Fire: Radical Evangelicalism in British North America, 1775–1812* (Kingston/Montreal, 1994), 83–4.

well-established black chapels in Preston and Shelbourne, Nova Scotia, as well as in Saint John and Fredericton, New Brunswick. When, in the early 1790s, the promise of land and full British citizenship was extended to black Loyalists who would emigrate to Sierre Leone, George led a third of the Maritimes' black population, which had risen to more than 3,500, in taking up the British offer.

By that time, Methodists had already begun their work in all Canadian regions. William Black, who came with his family from York to Nova Scotia in 1775, experienced an evangelical conversion in 1779 at a class meeting organized by some of the region's earliest Methodists. Two years later, at the age of twenty-one, he began to itinerate and for several years preached sin, redemption, and the new birth as passionately as his contemporary Henry Alline. Maritime Methodism received a further boost in the mid-1780s, when Freeborn Garretson, an early leader of the American church, answered a call to Nova Scotia. For two years, Garretson preached powerfully, even as he reached out to leaders of other denominations. When he left, Black and a small number of regularly ordained pastors assumed control of the work.

Methodist progress in the Maritimes remained slow, however, in part because of Black's reputation as a radical, which he carried from his early preaching, and in part because of Garretson's American connections, which were no asset in post-Revolutionary Nova Scotia. In addition, neither Black nor any of the missionaries sent out from England ever exercised the effective authority over itinerants and the general Methodist scheme that their contemporary, Francis Asbury, wielded so successfully in the United States.

The story of Methodism in Upper Canada was quite different. There a more consistently vigorous evangelism combined readily with organization guided from the United States to produce a vibrant, expanding movement. By contrast to minimal Methodist advance in Lower Canada, as soon as the very first Loyalists appeared, Methodist cell meetings flourished in Upper Canada at scattered points along the St. Lawrence River and in the Niagara Peninsula. The families of Barbara Heck and Philip Embry, who were among the first lay Methodist organizers in the thirteen colonies, had joined the Loyalist migration and reestablished class meetings by 1785. Contiguity to upstate New York, where Methodists steadily expanded after the war, meant an easy flow of itinerants across the new national border. William Losee came as the first American missionary in 1789–90, when he worked around the Cornwall area just across the St. Lawrence from Massena, New York. Francis Asbury himself took charge of assigning itinerant circuits and organizing districts. By 1806, in this still lightly populated colony, there were more than two thousand regular members, several times more adherents, seven preaching circuits, and sixteen itinerants at work. Distances for travel by horseback and on foot were immense and conditions were harsh, but with preaching from effective itinerants like William Case and Henry Ryan, the Methodist message of grace with discipline took hold. Case represented the accommodating side of Methodism, for he was diligent, kindly, and tolerant; Ryan provided backbone, with a more demanding, harsher, and authoritarian style.

Upper Canadian Methodism resembled its American counterpart of the period by stressing the need for rebirth, personal growth in holiness, and faithful participation in class meetings, love feasts, and communion celebrations. Emotion-driven revival also played a major part. A first memorable Canadian revival took place at Hay Bay on the Bay of Quinte circuit in September 1805. Its moving force was Nathan Bangs, a young preacher from Connecticut who had been itinerating in Canada since 1799. This four-day event attended by about 2,500 people experienced the same overwhelming "cloud of divine glory" that was witnessed at several locations in the United States at the same time.[16] Also similar to the United States was the stimulation that revivals gave to the regular work of preaching, praying, and organizing that itinerants like Bangs carried out with telling effect, as he would continue to do for nearly sixty more years as one of the great leaders of the American Methodist Church.

Yet for all their partnership with Americans, the Upper Canadian churches maintained a distinctive character. The move from white-hot revivalism to evangelical order proceeded somewhat faster, the concern for educational advance began somewhat sooner, and the aspiration for respectable civilization was a little stronger. These contrasting tendencies between American and Canadian Methodism might have remained barely perceptible had not violent politics once more altered the course of Canadian religious history.

REJECTING AMERICA AGAIN: THE WAR OF 1812

For Canadian religion, the War of 1812 marked a decisive break between the American course defined by democracy, voluntarism, and evangelical democracy and a Canadian course that moderated these characteristics with strong elements of tradition, authority, and communalism. The war was especially disruptive for Methodists. In the Maritimes, the ties that had already been established with Britain grew much stronger, whereas in Upper Canada it took longer for the division to take place. The start of

---

[16] Neil Semple, *The Lord's Dominion: The History of Canadian Methodism* (Montreal/Kingston, 1996), 130.

the war in 1812 disrupted plans for the Genesee Conference, which took in much of Upper Canada as well as upstate New York, to hold its annual meeting in Niagara. Some of the American itinerants serving in Canada felt compelled to return to the United States because they could not swear the required oath of loyalty to George III. The American invasions of the Niagara Peninsula and of York (later Toronto) confirmed most Canadian Methodists in their loyalty to Britain, even as it made them suspect in the eyes of other Canadians because of their links south of the border. During the war itself, extensive American raids led to a severe decline in Methodist membership. Leaders of the church responded by speeding up training for Canadian-born itinerants, even as they looked to forge closer ties with the British Wesleyan church. It would be some years after the end of the war until a final organizational break took place between American and Upper Canadian Methodists, but the foundations for a self-standing Canadian Methodist denomination were securely laid during the conflict.

Egerton Ryerson, the leading Canadian Methodist of the middle decades of the nineteenth century, experienced the war as a child, but it made him as fiercely loyal as any high-church Anglican. Years later he wrote in highly romantic terms about what the war had done to create Canadian identity over against the American neighbor: "In the extremity of this contest, the democratic President of the United States combined with the tyrant despot of Europe to seduce and sever the Canadians from their British connection; but the Canadians nobly maintained their fidelity and triumphantly vindicated their honour and independence." Although the war wrecked havoc in many areas, Ryerson felt that it "did much good to Canada" by cementing

> the people together as one family; English, French, Scotch, Irish, and Americans had forgotten former distinctions and jealousies, and had all become Canadians, with increased devotion not only to the land of their nativity or adoption, but to the glorious mother country which had become the victorious champion of the liberties of Europe and leader in the civilization of mankind.[17]

The war confirmed Anglican loyalty to Britain just as much as it established it for Canadian Methodists. John Strachan moved to York in the summer of 1812 shortly before active fighting began. From his new post as rector of St. James Church and chaplain of the local garrison, he quickly became a mainstay. During the American attacks on York in 1813, Strachan organized defenses, cared for the sick and wounded, and was the principal negotiator with American commanders. This experience earned Strachan lasting renown as a Canadian Patriot; even more, it

---

[17] Egerton Ryerson, *The Loyalists of America and Their Times: From 1620 to 1816*, 2 vols. (New York, 1970 [1880]), II: 471.

confirmed his own commitment to the traditional, establishmentarian, and loyal Anglicanism that proved such a bulwark against what he considered destructive democratic aggression. A parallel account concerns the Rev. Alexander Macdonell, a Gaelic-speaking Catholic priest who had earlier led a contingent of his fellow Highlanders to Glengarry County in the Cornwall region (the southeast of Upper Canada). During the war he organized a regiment of Highlanders, led them into battle, and won renown for his distinctly Catholic patriotism.

For Catholics in Lower Canada, the War of 1812 offered the hierarchy a dramatic stage on which to reaffirm its loyalty to Britain. Joseph-Octave Plessis, another in the long line of adept Quebec bishops, had been required to argue forcefully for customary Catholic privileges when a new governor general arrived in 1807 who supported Jacob Mountain's plan to Anglicanize the colony. Plessis, nonetheless, guided his clergy and the faithful as a whole in rallying support for Britain while discouraging sympathy for the Americans. After British troops and Canadian militia defeated an invading American force at Queenston Heights near Niagara, Bishop Plessis responded to the request of the governor general by urging his priests to thank God that their government protected security, religion, and economic livelihood. Several times during the war he called for masses and other special observances to support the British cause. At a service in April 1815 to celebrate the Treaty of Ghent, which ended hostilities, Plessis preached a sermon that identified impiety and ambition as the causes of the French Revolution, the Napoleonic war, and the two American wars. He went on with this strong commendation: "In addition, if in the midst of a whirlwind that disturbed everything, the United Kingdom is the only place where the throne remains unshakable, its possessions intact, its commerce trusted, its manufacturers flourishing, does one not have the right to regard these advantages as recompense granted by heaven to British generosity?"[18]

Catholic loyalty during the war was amply rewarded. Later there would be further plans from London for Anglicizing and converting the Canadiens, but not for the next quarter century. Instead, the stipend provided by colonial officials to the church was increased; in 1818 Britain for the first time publicly recognized Plessis as the *bishop* of the Roman Catholic Church in Quebec with the right to sit on the province's legislative council; and colonial officials finally agreed to the reorganization of Plessis' vast domain – with separate dioceses created for Montreal, the northwest, and Maritime regions – that Catholics had desired for a long time.

[18] Lucien Lemieux, *Histoire du catholicisme québécois*, ed. Nive Voisine, vol. I, *Les années difficiles (1760–1839)* (Montreal, 1989), 47.

In general, the War of 1812 fortified the Old World tendencies in Canadian religion while weakening American tendencies. For Quebec, it was a straightforward matter of continuing on the path marked out during the Revolution. For Protestants throughout Canada, it was not quite as simple, because the fact of pluralism and the force of evangelicalism remained strongly influential. Yet in contrast to the United States, pluralism and revivalism were being drawn into a church movement that also affirmed the necessity of tradition, the benefits of authority, and the advantage of slower change. The distinguished historian John Webster Grant underscored another important result of the conflict when he defined its effects with specific reference to the Protestants of Upper Canada: "The War of 1812 ... left an indelible mark on the Upper Canadian mentality. Most immediately, it changed colonists' perceptions of the United States and thereby – by a peculiar but well-understood Canadian logic – their perceptions of themselves."[19]

THE FIRST NATIONS

Generalizations are risky for Native Canadian religion during this period because of the great variety of native peoples and the vastly different levels of engagement with Europeans and their religions. Nonetheless, three general patterns can be discerned.

First was the continuation of traditional native religions in many forms and combinations. Indian tribes that came latest to European contact, like the Cree around Hudson Bay and the Ojibwa north of Lake Superior, were most likely to maintain ancestral faiths, but many traditional beliefs and practices also continued among those who had been in contact the longest, like the Six Nation Iroquois of upper New York State and the Micmacs (or Mi'kmaqs) of the Atlantic region. The Native Canadian cosmos was animist in the sense of picturing the world as filled with spiritual forces. In many groups, shamans, sometimes referred to as medicine men (or medicine women), mediated between the human and spirit worlds. They also passed along origin myths that described spiritual forces in the sun, moon, and other celestial bodies; in lakes and mountains; or even more frequently in animal spirits. For many tribes, the bear was the most important spirit to appear in animal form; to the bear was ascribed much power over health, hunting, and community harmony. Dreams, personal vision quests that usually involved vigils with fasting, and use of the sweat lodge for spiritual purification helped

---

[19] John Webster Grant, *A Profusion of Spires: Religion in Nineteenth-Century Ontario* (Toronto, 1988), 68.

maintain personal religion. Drums, dancing, and sometimes mild hallucinogens expressed corresponding values for communities. Europeans in the early nineteenth century were less adept than the Catholic missionaries of the seventeenth century in building bridges between Christianity and these traditional practices, but by that time the mixture of native and Christian practices had made it difficult to isolate pure types of indigenous religion.

The second pattern, from the other end of the spectrum, involved wholehearted embrace of different strands of Christianity. The Micmacs, Abenakis (at the juncture of New England, Quebec, and the Maritimes), and the Maliseets (northern New England and across the border) were bands that had become firmly Catholic. Among the Micmacs, a series of effective missionaries culminated in the work of Abbé Pierre Maillard, who came from France in 1735 and served until his death in 1762. Maillard, an expert in the Micmac language and culture, secured the Micmacs' attachment to Catholicism, although he was frank about how long it was taking for the Indians to differentiate God from the sun, and also about how destructively the alcohol provided by European traders worked among his flock. At the conquest, when Britain shut off the supply of priests from France, Catholic work among the Indians suffered greatly across all of Canada and down into the Mississippi River valley. Maillard, for example, was not replaced until 1768, when the British allowed Abbé Charles-François Bailly de Messein to take over his work. But then, in one of the anomalies that peppered imperial practice, Britain helped fund the new abbé's mission in order to ensure the loyalty of Micmacs against overtures from France and American Patriots. Catholic Indian work would revive, but not until well into the nineteenth century, with the reconstitution of the Jesuits and the formation of new religious orders.

Protestant footholds among the First Nations came much later. The Anglican Society for the Propagation of the Gospel in Foreign Parts tried to start Indian work in Nova Scotia after serious British colonization began in the late 1750s, but Protestant missionaries did not accomplish much until after the turn of the century and the general upsurge of evangelical voluntary mobilization. From these efforts some tribal groups, like the Ojibwas, would become staunch Christian adherents. Before that later time, however, German-speaking Moravians had made some progress among Inuits in Labrador; they were also responsible for one of the earliest Protestant First Nations settlements in Upper Canada. This settlement was of Delaware Indians who had been won over by Moravian missionaries in Pennsylvania in the 1750s. Particularly poignant is the story of how the peace-loving Delawares were violently expelled by land-hungry whites from one supposed place of refuge after another – around Philadelphia, further west in Pennsylvania, and then in Ohio. It was not until the Delawares crossed the border into Fairfield (also called Moraviantown) on the Thames River that they found a settlement that could become permanent. Unfortunately, the violence that had dogged them since they first turned to Christianity was not at an end, for during the War of 1812 an invading American army burned Fairfield to the ground.

Significant numbers among the Six Nations Iroquois of upper New York State also became Christian through their contact with British missionaries and chaplains. When Iroquois who had sided with the British joined the Loyalist migration to Canada in the early 1780s, they brought along loyalty to Anglican Christianity as well. The Rev. John Stuart, who had worked among the Mohawks as a missionary in New York, helped them resettle on the Bay of Quinte as he took up a post as an Anglican rector in Kingston. A larger body of Mohawks settled along the Grand River west of Buffalo, New York, on the Niagara Peninsula. They were led by Chief Joseph Brant, who had been educated by missionaries in the colonies and who was one of the most skilful leaders in the borderlands that lay between first the British and French, and then the Canadians and Americans. With a grant from the British, Brant in 1785 oversaw construction of the first Protestant church in what would later be Ontario. Regular Anglican services were long held in this structure, but usually under the direction of native lay readers, because it did not enjoy the presence of a regular Anglican clergyman.

The third native pattern involved mingling traditional religion with the forms and beliefs of Christianity. That synergy of faiths may have been the most common pattern, although it is rarely acknowledged as such. One amalgamation, however, did take definite shape. In response to the demoralization of the Iroquois after the American Revolution as well as to the toll of alcohol in his own life, a Seneca of the western New York Allegheny tribe, Ganiodaio (or Handsome Lake) offered an alternative. After experiencing a deep trance in 1799, Ganiodaio announced a program of renewal for the Iroquois. It promoted agriculture, rejected religious practices that whites called sorcery, called for renunciation of drink, and depicted a cosmos defined by heaven and hell. Yet it also supported traditional rituals like the strawberry festival and encouraged communal rites associated with the longhouse. Ganiodaio's further visions spelled out in greater detail how elements of old and new faiths could be joined together. His "good message" spread rapidly among the Iroquois, including Canadians along the Grand River, where it established a presence that remains to this day.

CONCLUSION

Religious practice during this period mirrored much that was taking place elsewhere in the Atlantic world and in France, with local variation. In Newfoundland, which became a residential colony only after the mid-eighteenth century, Anglican, Catholic, and Methodist workers encountered extreme frontier conditions in ministering to the ten thousand scattered residents that inhabited the province in 1780. Elsewhere perpetual complaints arose about conditions nearly as primitive or about the slow pace of movement toward responsible Christian civilization. In Quebec early in the nineteenth century, Bishop Plessis acknowledged the very high rate of regular Mass attendance but bemoaned excessive drinking, widespread immorality, and the tendency to transform religious celebrations into mere revelry. As in earlier periods, Plessis exempted women's religious orders from his indictments, because their work especially in hospitals and schools earned them nearly universal respect. Similar complaints about laxity were uttered by Anglican bishops in visits to their parishes and by ministers of other denominations as well. For their part, Indians sometimes complained that few whites upheld the high moral standards that missionaries demanded of them. And every organized religious body consistently bewailed the paucity of workers available for spreading the gospel and taming the wilderness.

On the other side of the equation, evidence for religious seriousness was not hard to find. Respect and actual reading of the Bible were as widespread as elsewhere in the Christian West, with one particular flashpoint indicating the depth of that attachment. When, in 1795, British officials in Lower Canada tried to use the King James Version in the courts, they met with strong (and successful) protests against replacing the Catholic Douay-Rheims version. The strength of both Christian traditions and Enlightenment ideas was manifest whenever forward-thinkers sparked controversy by publishing advanced ideas or organizing societies to spread the newer thought. Such controversies were a regular feature of public life in French Canada, especially as first the *Quebec Gazette* and then the *Montreal Gazette* opened their pages to radical and anticlerical opinions coming from France. Except for a few years immediately after 1797, when Catholic officials joined British authorities in silencing opinions favorable to the French Revolution, such public debates were continuous, as they would also become in Upper Canada with the growth of York (Toronto) and other urban centers.

Overtly pious practices advanced steadily, although never as rapidly as leaders desired. Veneration of the sacrament was well established in many Catholic parishes by the early nineteenth century. Outbursts of Protestant piety, like the early Methodist revivals, drew on latent Christian convictions even as they stimulated them. In Lower Canada, the *croix du chemin* (roadside crosses) provided regularly spaced occasions to pray for the travelers who made their way along the roads bordering the St. Lawrence.[20]

If only local variations distinguished Canadian religious practice from what was taking place in Europe and the United States, the events of the era did establish deeply grounded patterns that would differentiate Canadian religious history from American religious history. Whereas the most critical U.S. social tension of the era involved blacks and whites, Canada's was between speakers of French and speakers of English. Whereas the Catholic church was a late force in American development, it existed from the start in Canada. Most importantly, whereas Americans aligned religious practice with social and political axioms driven by the American Revolution, Canadians aligned their religion with the practice of loyalty and a commitment to peaceful, evolutionary change.

Much else affected the later religious history of Canada, but events from the British conquest through the War of 1812 made a determinative beginning. Thus, over the course of the nineteenth century, the main Protestant denominations in Canada amalgamated; in the United States they divided. In Canada, the early elimination of slavery (by a decree in 1793) removed a source of perennial American conflict. Compared to what happened in the United States, Canadians experienced a softer clash between traditional confessions on the one side and the newer sciences and approaches to scripture on the other. In Canada, evangelicals participated more naturally in the Social Gospel, and those who emphasized social outreach remained more clearly evangelical. The situation for Canadian Catholics was different in most particulars from the Protestant story, except that the path forged in the crucible of war, revolution, and war once again defined the future – in their case, the path of traditional religion aligned with conservative social order that remained substantially in place until it was finally dissolved in Quebec's Quiet Revolution a century and a half after the War of 1812 came to an end.

SUGGESTIONS FOR FURTHER READING

Chaussé, Giles. "French Canada from the Conquest to 1840," trans. James MacLean, in Terrence Murphy and Roberto Perin, eds. *A Concise History of Christianity in Canada*. Toronto, 1996.

---

[20] Lemieux, *Histoire*, 307–9 (with illustrations).

Christie, Nancy. "'In These Times of Democratic Rage and Delusion': Popular Religion and the Challenge to the Established Order, 1760–1815," in George A. Rawlyk, ed. *The Canadian Protestant Experience*. Burlington, ON, 1990.

Goodwin, Daniel. *Into Deep Waters: Evangelical Spirituality and Maritime Calvinistic Baptist Ministers, 1790–1855*. Kingston, 2010.

Grant, John Webster. *Moon of Wintertime: Missionaries and the Indians of Canada in Encounter*. Toronto, 1984.

———. *A Profusion of Spires: Religion in Nineteenth-Century Ontario*. Toronto, 1988.

Lemieux, Lucien. *Histoire du catholicisme québécois*, ed. Nive Voisine, vol. I, *Les années difficiles (1760–1839)*. Montreal, 1989.

Little, J. I. *Borderland Religion: The Emergence of an English-Canadian Identity, 1792–1852*. Toronto, 2004.

Murphy, Terrence. "The English-Speaking Colonies to 1854," in Terrence Murphy and Roberto Perin, eds. *A Concise History of Christianity in Canada*. Toronto, 1996.

Rawlyk, George A. *The Canada Fire: Radical Evangelicalism in British North America, 1775–1812*. Kingston/Montreal, 1994.

31

FROM RELIGIOUS NATIONALISM TO POLITICAL CONSCIOUSNESS: THE BOURBON REFORMS IN SPANISH AMERICA, 1750–1790

ANA MARÍA DÍAZ-STEVENS AND ANTHONY
M. STEVENS-ARROYO

The historical half century in Spanish America (1750–99) that overlapped the War of Independence by the English colonies of North America can be characterized as a period of gestation. Beginning with the implementation in 1750 of the first in a series of rigorous reforms in the spirit of the Enlightenment and ending in 1799 with the ascension to power of Napoleon in France, this period marked the development of a new and revolutionary religious, cultural, and political awareness that would create independent Latin American republics.

Religion played an important role during this process in Spain's colonies. America's Christianity had been planted by the Spanish as early as 1493 and had set down firm roots for a flowering of Spanish American Catholic identity during the seventeenth-century baroque era. And although the cold rationalism of the Enlightenment pruned back religious growth during a winter of repression that began in 1750, it left behind "seeds of nationalism"[1] that would begin to gestate the new national identities that appeared at the dawn of the nineteenth century with complete political independence for Spanish America.

GEOPOLITICAL BACKGROUND

Religion does not operate in a vacuum but responds to political and social forces that shape particular historical circumstances. The context of Spanish American societies differed notably from the North American experience. For instance, the English colonies' population was crowded along the Atlantic coast, and – except for Pennsylvania's German population and the South's many plantation slaves – was relatively homogeneous. In contrast, Spanish America covered two continents, expanded to two coasts, and

---

[1] Mabel Moraña, "Barroco y conciencia criolla en Hispanoamérica," *Revista de crítica literaria latinoamericana* 28 (1988): 238.

stretched through diverse temperate and tropical climate zones. Moreover, the Native Americans, African slaves, and mixed-race peoples greatly outnumbered European whites in the population.

But if the colonial context was dissimilar, the imperial designs of both British and Spanish monarchies ran in parallel. The third Bourbon king of Spain, Carlos III (regnum 1759–88), made presumptions like those of the British George III (regnum 1760–1820), whose increased taxation provoked the loss of his thirteen colonies. Moreover, the same world events forced equal and opposite reactions. Much like dance partners taking synchronized steps in mirror opposite, Spain and England countered each other in European politics.

When this period began, Spanish foreign policy was straightforward: avoid entanglement in the conflict between France and England that became the Seven Years' War (1756–63). It was wise to avoid alliance with a prospective loser because British troops had captured Quebec in 1759, auguring the eventual loss of all of French Canada. Spain, however, was unable to maintain its policy of neutrality. Continued English aggressions against the Spanish colonies in the Caribbean motivated Carlos III to sign a series of treaties called Agreements of the Family between the French and Spanish Bourbons in what constituted a mutual defense pact. Beginning in 1761, these treaties were intended to convince England to sue for peace because of the threat of Spain's participation on the side of France. Instead, this French-Spanish alliance gave Great Britain cause to attack key Spanish colonies.

Late in the hostilities, France recognized an inevitable British victory. The French Bourbons ceded the Louisiana Territory to their cousins in Spain with the Treaty of Fontainebleau, which was signed in secret 30 November 1762 to prevent England from absorbing French colonies along the Mississippi River and south to the Gulf of Mexico. There were cities in the ceded territory, most notably New Orleans, but the claims extended to all the rivers flowing into the Mississippi. Thus, Louisiana was both a cluster of riverbank and coastal settlements and thousands of miles of unexplored regions populated by Native Americans as far west as the Pacific.

Jolted by the rising power of England that had swallowed whole all of New France, Spain's Bourbon monarchy envisioned the newly acquired Louisiana as a buffer from future English aggressions, even at the cost of surrendering claim to Florida as peace settlement. Carlos III believed that his own colonial empire could survive only by reorganizing governance according to the rationalist principles of the Enlightenment. New policies were imposed under Madrid's Enlightened Despotism to reshape military organization, ecclesiastical operations, and social institutions throughout the empire.

The results were more immediate in Spain than in its colonies. Carlos III remade Madrid into a fitting capitol: wide boulevards and celebratory circles with statuary adorning stately public buildings. New national agencies regulated standards for products like porcelain and crystal; botanists developed seed for organized crop production; a national lottery was begun along with a postal service, while a network of royal highways made all roads lead to Madrid. Carlos III banned regional languages like Catalan from all schools in 1768, confirming Castilian, the Spanish spoken in Castile, as the official language of his realm. A national anthem was chosen, and a national red-and-yellow flag replaced the white banner of the Bourbons. Such measures credit Carlos III with making Spain a unified and modern nation.

The colonies reflected more complex results. On the positive side of the reforms, the integration of Spanish Americans into the empire's armed forces strengthened Spanish support in 1776 for the rebellious thirteen English colonies. Spain's troops in North America fought on the colonists' side and forced England to restore Florida to Spanish rule when the U.S. independence was formally recognized. By 1783, Spanish North America extended from the Florida Peninsula, through the entire coast of the Gulf of Mexico, and westward from the lower Mississippi to the Pacific Ocean. Moreover, Spain controlled the Caribbean islands of Cuba and Puerto Rico. Much like England's expectation for its colonies at the end of the French and Indian War, Mother Spain anticipated growing richer from its far-flung empire and entertained the prospect of the Gulf of Mexico becoming a Spanish lake.

But taxation of his colonies by George III of England had sparked resistance and then rebellion, and similarly, the Bourbons' reforms in Spanish America provided more grief than relief. The Enlightenment effort to eradicate the Church's institutional influence and the people's practice of religion was counterproductive in the colonies. Madrid's reforms were made more difficult when the death in 1788 of Spain's capable Carlos III brought to the throne the bumbling Carlos IV. The French Revolution followed immediately, concluding with rising nationalisms during the Napoleonic era. The cataclysmic disintegration of Spanish control after 1808, however, was not created ex nihilo, but resulted rather from thirty-five years of unachievable policies forced on its colonies after 1763.

RELIGION, RACE, AND NATIONHOOD

Just as medieval Europe had practiced feudal incorporation of Hungarians, Prussians, and Lithuanians by baptism of those peoples' rulers, Hapsburg Spain (1516–1700) had allowed converted Native American chiefs to retain elements of social rank. Urged on by evangelizers such as Bartolomé de Las Casas (1484–1566), Spanish law recognized the authority of rulers professing feudal loyalty. Aztecs, Incans, and others were "nations" boasting of collective sovereign rights within the Spanish Empire more or less like the Catalans and Basques who had been incorporated under the rule of medieval Castile. The Hapsburg dynasty had extended nationhood to all its dominions, in Asia as well as the Americas. In practical terms, it meant that the empire was constituted by many nations, each identified by region, language, and distinct legal customs in matters such as marriage, inheritance, and military organization.

Hapsburg policy also reflected lessons of social diversity learned during Iberia's tense medieval coexistence with the Moors. Colonial Spanish America used native languages and dress in everyday life and had permeable racial boundaries regularly trespassed by racial intermarriage. Without completely avoiding prejudices, Spanish American societies were characterized by *mestizaje,* the biological mixture of Native American and European races. Consider, as an example, that the early eighteenth-century viceroy of New Spain was José Sarmiento y Valladares, Conde de Moctezuma y de Tula (1696–1701), who had married into Aztec royalty. Rather than bringing stigmatization as a half-breed, racial intermarriage in Spanish America often opened the doors of power and influence.

In addition to this physical result of mixed racial heritage, there was a pervasive cultural *mestizaje* that had created hybrid forms of religion, culture, and language. Cultural hybridity, it needs be emphasized, was the heritage of all colonial Spanish America and not just its conquered indigenous peoples. The *mestizaje* culture included white criollos[2] as well as persons of mixed race. In different ways, but with general coherence, Spain's subjects in the Americas had developed cultures different from those of Spaniards in Europe. The glue for these diverse nationalities was a Catholic religious identity that utilized Marian devotionalism to theologically affirm the political equality of diverse peoples within the empire.[3]

Thus, when the Enlightenment reforms of the Bourbons attacked the privileges of the Church, the impact reverberated into racial identity, regional culture, and local commerce. For instance, reorganization of military defenses eliminated the post of alcaide, or manager of the fortress,

---

[2] Because the criollo of Latin America was white, the Spanish term ought not to be translated as "creole," a word with a meaning in English of "racial mixture." We prefer translation as the noun "colonial."

[3] Anthony M. Stevens-Arroyo, "The Evolution of Marian Devotionalism within Christianity and the Ibero-Mediterranean Polity," *Journal for the Scientific Study of Religion* 37:1 (1998): 50–73.

an hereditary title colonial elites had jealously guarded, because it usually bestowed membership in the governance apparatus of the *cabildo*, or town council, made up of leading citizens who could control sales taxes, licensing, city contracts, and who thereby enjoyed significant prominence in public ceremonies like religious processions. Eliminating an alcaide, likely a colonial, and replacing him with a military official, likely a Spaniard, made the defense apparatus more efficient, but it simultaneously undermined established patterns of self-government and social prestige.

The combined effect of attacking both established religious customs and dismantling existing governance would so weaken loyalties in Spanish America that the empire imploded once shaken by revolution and Bonaparte. As Henry Kamen notes, Enlightened Despotism's effort to impose imperial uniformity succeeded neither in Europe nor on the American continents.[4]

CATHOLICISM, POPULAR AND OTHERWISE

Spain's failures as a reluctant imperialist power, however, had not impeded its effective establishment of Catholicism in Latin America. In 1750, Enlightened Despotism encountered Catholicism as the established religion throughout the realm. However, it would be a mistake to translate universal Catholic hegemony into monolithic conformity.

Rather than the confessional or doctrinal Protestant differences like those among Methodists, Baptists, and Congregationalists, Catholic diversity was manifested in differing spiritualities or ways of living out the Catholic faith. Although unified by the same Catholic set of beliefs, the clergy and nuns of religious orders follow a particular rule of life approved by ecclesiastical authority. Each rule establishes standard practices of piety, prayer, and ministry; and these regimens specify the time allotted for prayer, learning, and good works. A teaching order like the Dominicans, for instance, would schedule more time to book study than the Carmelite nuns dedicated to prayer in the cloister. Thus, the rule of each order or congregation produces a distinctive spirituality.

Catholic laypersons were able to choose among spiritualities by joining any of several types of religious organizations such as Third Orders, *cofradías,* and sodalities pledged to a particular spiritual mission.[5] These

---

[4] Henry Kamen, *Empires: How Spain Became a World Power: 1492–1763* (New York, 2003), 488ff.

[5] The English cognate "confraternities" has more narrow functions, and accordingly, "*cofradía*" is used throughout. Third Orders were for the laity, whereas the First (for men) and Second (for women) Orders required solemn vows.

voluntary pious organizations also met social needs by renting buildings for wedding receptions, guaranteeing mourners at funerals, and providing mechanisms of credit and networks for employment, apprenticeship, and skill acquisition. Somewhat like medieval guilds, freewill donations from these lay organizations supported hospitals and orphanages, and they sometimes pursued public commissions to fund such operations.

Social influence was often measured by the size of processions and public celebrations in honor of their patron saints. The feast days were social affairs usually lasting eight days, during which civic leaders left behind everyday drudgery to dress in ceremonial regalia and enjoy public adulation. "Fiesta" meant not only public prayers, but also celebratory eating, drinking, and dancing. Ironically, by selling candles, medals, and the like, or auctioning the space for merchant booths, the less spiritual aspects of the feast often brought needed income to local churches. During such holy days, workers had "holidays" from their labors. In Peru in this period, Cuzco's holidays covered seven months of the year. Just like Catholic Europe, in parts of Spanish America there were "more days of fiesta than days of work."[6]

In 1767, Carlos III ordered the secularization of underfinanced monasteries and convents everywhere in his realm. His ministers also forced each *cofradía* into a complicated accounting process to justify continued existence. Besides assaulting the traditional privileges that popular religious practice had bestowed on local leaders, Enlightened Despotism's reforms added work days. Whereas the attack on religious practices in Spain had generally mild results, in Spanish America popular anger was red hot, because the policies uprooted established customs that had long borne the burden of colonial linkage with the ruler. Ultimately, the radical dislocation of religious traditions by the monarchy became a factor in the later emergence of popular support for revolutions against Spain, largely because the religious customs had deeper roots than political loyalties.

THEOLOGY AS IDEOLOGY

Enlightened Despotism may have won its eighteenth-century clash with the institutional privileges of the Catholic Church, but it lost on the Spanish American battleground of "popular religion." We use the term as equivalent with "lived religion" or "grassroots religious experience." The term "appropriation"[7] fits here because each racial and class grouping

---

[6] David Cahill, "Popular Religion and Appropriation: The Example of Corpus Christi in Eighteenth-Century Cuzco," *Latin American Research Review* 31:2 (1996): 95ff.

[7] Ana María Díaz-Stevens, "Analyzing Popular Religiosity for Socio-Religious Meaning," in Anthony M. Stevens-Arroyo and Ana María Díaz-Stevens, eds., *An Enduring Flame:*

interpreted shared religious symbols in accord with its own social location. For instance, annual mock battles between revelers dressed as Spaniards and others representing Moors or Indians were alternately either vindication for the vanquished people's culture or reassurance of ruling class hegemony based on past military triumphs.[8] These competing, multilayered interpretations of how the faith should be lived, nonetheless, used the public rituals to create a communitarian spirituality that linked all groups within universal Catholicism.[9]

The Protestant Reformation had denounced many aspects of Catholicism's lived religion in the sixteenth century, especially because some appropriated meanings of religion had strayed into superstition. Determined not to discard the statues, medals, and prayers to the saints by which spiritualities had flourished, the Council of Trent created mechanisms to control popular religion rather than extinguish it. Trent's purification of popular Catholicism likely made it stronger.

Trent's reforms featured hugely in the mission of the Society of Jesus. Organized after Columbus' American voyages, the Jesuits served within a global Catholicism replete with substantial cultural differences. Rather than considering non-European nations and cultures in need of extermination before conversion, Jesuit missionaries promoted a Catholic humanist approach, making cultural diversity into a glory for universal Catholicism. Their theological interpretation of non-Christian religion fostered a brand of Catholic providentialism.[10] Finding notions like a "mother of god" and symbols in the native religions that resembled Christian crosses, Jesuits considered these prefigurements or anticipations of the Catholic faith, needing not suppression, but redefinition.

Consider, for instance, the development of the idea launched in 1607 by Gregorio García, who had argued that the natives of the Americas were descended from the ten lost tribes of Israel, thus explaining Aztec ability

---

Studies on Latino Popular Religiosity (New York, 1994), 17–36. See also Gustavo Benavides, "Resistance and Accommodation in Latin American Popular Religiosity," 37–68; and Jaime R. Vidal, "Towards an Understanding of Synthesis in Iberian and Hispanic American Popular Religiosity," 69–96, both in Stevens-Arroyo and Díaz-Stevens, *Enduring Flame*.

[8] Max Harris, *Aztecs, Moors and Christians: Festivals of Reconquest in Mexico and Spain* (Austin, 2000).

[9] For description of the most common practices, see Anthony M. Stevens-Arroyo and Ana María Díaz-Stevens, "Religious Faith and Institutions in the Forging of Latino Identities," in Felix Padilla, ed., *Handbook for Hispanic Cultures in the United States* (Houston, 1993), 257–91.

[10] Anthony M. Stevens-Arroyo, "A Marriage Made in America: Trent and the Baroque," in Raymond F. Bulman and Frederick J. Parrella, eds., *From Trent to Vatican II: Historical and Theological Investigations* (New York, 2006), 39–59.

to construct pyramids. Antonio Vieira (1608–97), a Brazil-born mulatto Jesuit priest, added navigational science about early transatlantic voyages to introduce Christianity. Because Cabral had landed in Brazil by sailing westward to overcome the African currents, Vieira attributed the same route for St. Thomas the Apostle. Thus, the Jesuit connected a passage in Origen that Thomas had sailed "beyond Hispania," to pre-Portuguese Brazil. Not to be outdone, the Mexican priest and eventual Jesuit Carlos de Sigüenza y Góngora (1645–1700) speculated that the apostolic landing was actually in Mexico, based on Aztec beliefs in a returning ruler named Quetzalcoatl.

The science invoked by these findings may be suspect by today's standards, but such reasoning was warmly accepted in Spanish America. Believing that Catholicism was glorified with historical proofs of the incorporation of the world's nations into a single Church, eighteenth-century Jesuits compiled histories of indigenous American peoples, translated native codices, and examined archaeological remains. A typical Jesuit college curriculum in Spanish America included chronicles such as those of the mestizo Incan prince Garcilaso de la Vega (1539–1616), who had promoted the nobility of the Native Americans in his 1609 publication, *Comentarios Reales de los Incas*. The Jesuits' global vision of Catholicism was part of the spirituality they shared with Spanish American laypersons through their retreats, sodalities, colleges, and universities. Many Jesuit-educated colonials were thus intellectually prepared by 1750 to affirm the cultural and religious legacy of the Native American nations as equal to their European counterparts.

Jesuits were not the only ecclesiastics fostering scholarship that was at once scientific and faith filled. The erudite Galician Benedictine Benito Jerónimo Feijóo y Montenegro (1674–1764) ridiculed Catholicism's religious excesses as a means of demonstrating that these were not essential to the Catholic faith. Feijóo was much read in the Americas by clergy pursuing Enlightenment modernity. They imitated his skewering of European superstitions because it helped make the case that Old World religion was no less beset with ignorant superstitions than the New World version. As believers, these clerics attacked popular religion's superstitions and implausible miracles in defense of a purified Catholic faith that would withstand Protestant criticisms. Ultimately, they would be at odds with the Freethinkers who intended to discredit religion altogether.

EXPULSION OF THE SOCIETY OF JESUS FROM SPANISH AMERICA

The Jesuits could not have anticipated their undoing when Portugal and Spain signed a treaty in 1750 to establish a clear boundary between

Portuguese Brazil and the Spanish viceroyalty of La Plata. In the spirit of the Enlightenment, the Europeans treated the Plata River as a line of demarcation. However, the seven Jesuit missions to the Guaraní people lay on both sides of the waterway. Appealing to the common sense that rivers unite rather than separate settlements, the Society sought to nullify some terms of the treaty, because otherwise the missions would be dismantled.

The Guaraní missions represented the wedding of native language, dress, and customs with European technology for self-sufficient economic production. The Jesuit missions manufactured products and, in bypassing European trade monopolies in the marketing process, the missions produced considerable profits. These were shared by the entire population, approximating today's community cooperatives. Montesquieu, no friend of religion, called the Jesuit missions an example of Plato's Republic, whereas Voltaire composed *Candide,* a journal of a fictitious visit to missions where "savages" lived in societies unburdened by European pretensions.[11]

Because the treaty's border involved both Portugal and Spain, Jesuit resistance incurred the wrath of the Enlightened Despotism of both countries. Moreover, the Guaraní, who had demonstrated their military capacity earlier against marauding tribes, posed the threat of armed resistance. Sebastião José de Carvalho e Melo (1699–1782), Marquis de Pombal and Portuguese prime minister with virtual dictatorial powers, viewed Jesuit power over education and Brazil's economy as an impediment to progress. Although he can be credited with rebuilding Lisbon as the world's first earthquake-proof city because of his use of seismology, Pombal was also a master of conspiracy theory as a political tool. When a Jesuit missionary, Father Gabriel de Malagrida, published a tract suggesting that the 1755 earthquake had been divine punishment on Portugal, Pombal had him arrested. Efforts of the Society to support Malagrida or the Guaraní were reported to the king as conspiracies. Finally, in 1759, all Jesuits were forced to leave the realm under pain of death. Indeed, the eighty-year-old Father Malagrida was strangled in 1761, and his body burned as a heretic.

In Spain, enemies of the Jesuits employed a similar strategy. Seeking to rebuild Madrid much as Pombal had Lisbon, King Carlos III had given the task to the Marquís de Esquilache. In an example of governmental overreach, Esquilache outlawed the popular wide-brimmed hat or *chambergo* within city limits, ordering male residents to dress in French fashion with three-cornered hats. On Palm Sunday, 10 March 1766, citywide riots

[11] Germán Arciniegas, *Latin America: A Cultural History* (London, 1969), 230–63.

began days of defiance against the unpopular orders. Persuaded that popular protest was fostered by conspiratorial Jesuits, on 2 April 1767 Carlos III decreed the expulsion of every Jesuit from Spain's dominions. Secrecy allowed the arrests to preempt popular resistance, synchronizing compliance worldwide in overnight raids on the Society.

Some 2,200 Jesuits were forced to leave Spanish America. The impact on religion was incalculable, stripping away the faculties of the leading schools and universities of the Spanish colonies. If, as suggested previously, the Spanish Empire depended on Catholicism to hold together disparate peoples, why weaken religion by expulsion of a most influential order? The answer lies in the radical opposition between the philosophy of a centralized state held by Enlightened Despotism and the Catholic teachings of the Jesuits about national sovereignty.

The ten-volume *Tractatus de legibus ac deo legislatore* (1612) by the Jesuit Francisco Suárez (1548–1614) relativized state authority. The organic laws of tradition, even if unwritten, took precedence over positive laws formulated by a monarch in this theory. If a king's orders violated natural law, wrote Suárez a century before Montesquieu and Rousseau, a people could revoke the social contract. Another Jesuit, Juan de Mariana (1536–1624), invoked the just war theory to justify armed revolt or assassination of a tyrant when it was necessary to break the social contract.

Whereas most books from confiscated Jesuit libraries were distributed to other institutions in 1767, the works by Suárez and Mariana with these theories of national rights were burned.[12] Ironically, dispersing Spanish American Jesuits spread their teachings that placed sovereignty with the people. Exiled Jesuits not only upheld the philosophical principles of resistance to royal decrees, but also voiced increasingly nationalistic stirrings. From Italy, the Mexican Jesuit Francisco Javier Clavijero (1731–87) extolled the ancient Aztecs. Another Jesuit exile, the Peruvian Juan Bautista Vizcardo y Guzmán (1748–98), met with Benjamin Franklin in France and later published in Philadelphia in 1791 a letter that linked the independence of colonies everywhere as humanity striving "to recapture possession of the natural rights we owe to our Creator, precious rights that we do not have the power to transfer, and of which we may not be deprived."[13] Thus by the 1790s, the suppression of the Jesuits had not only undermined imperial rule in Spanish America, but also popularized principles for future revolutions.

---

[12] Guillermo Furlong, "The Jesuit Heralds of Democracy and the New Despotism," in Magnus Mörner, ed., *The Expulsion of the Jesuits from Latin America* (New York, 1965), 41–6.
[13] "Letter to the American Spaniards," cited in Arciniegas, *Latin America*, 305.

PATTERNS OF REFORM AND RESISTANCE IN SPANISH AMERICA

To formulate policy according to rationalist principles, Madrid sent officials sharing Enlightenment views to conduct a census and to issue detailed reports on commerce and social organization in each region. The principal architect of Spain's new colonial policy was José de Gálvez y Gallardo (1720–87). As royal visitor to New Spain from 1761 to 1772, Gálvez had gained firsthand knowledge of the provinces, eagerly enforcing the 1767 decree that expelled the Jesuits. In the aftermath, Gálvez recommended a new viceroyalty of Nueva Viscaya to separate administratively what are now Texas, New Mexico, Arizona, and California from the viceroyalty of Nueva España (Mexico). His recommendation was embraced by King Carlos III, who eventually made him minister of the Indies in 1775. Distrusting the capacity of local officials, Gálvez appointed his brother Matías (c. 1725–1784) viceroy of Nueva España, and he made his nephew Bernardo (1746–86), military governor of Louisiana. What follows provides a profile attentive to religion in each of the islands and territories contiguous with the United States.

SANTO DOMINGO

The city of Santo Domingo had flourished as the seat of Columbus' brief rule with the prestige of a primatial see and the first colonial appellate court (Audiencia). By 1750, however, these functions had been surrendered to more prosperous continental jurisdictions, especially because Española (Hispaniola) had been divided by the 1697 Treaty of Ryswick to accommodate a French colony, today's Haiti, on the western third of the island.

The population of the two colonies was hugely disproportionate. The French colony in 1761 had more than half a million inhabitants, with nine out of ten persons either black or mulatto. The 1769 census of the Spanish side showed only 73,319 inhabitants, and in 1783, some 25,000 of the colony's total 80,000 residents lived in the single city of Santo Domingo.

Ironically, the open range of the underdeveloped Spanish colony allowed it to be a supplier of meat on the hoof to the French side, where mercantilist policies had turned its colony into a rich sugar producer. The French planters found it cheaper to import food for their slaves rather than subtract valuable acres from their cash crop. In 1777, the Treaty of Aranjuez accepted careful survey work that had placed pyramidal markers along the border; and in a climate of Bourbon coexistence, Spain decided pragmatically to cede military defense of all of Española to French troops while encouraging intra-island free trade between the two island colonies.

Cultural differences between French Catholicism and Spanish-speaking Española remained, however. Because the Spanish side of the island lacked a substantial sugar industry, most of the settlers were freemen, and even the nonwhites among them considered the Catholic faith a badge of status. On the other hand, there were so many slaves in the French colony that religious practices of African origin survived as cloaked defiance of the cruelty of slavery under Catholic masters. As described by Terry Rey in his study of the Haitian Revolution, feeling no compulsion to reject such elements of popular religion, several notable French Catholic priests in Haiti allied Catholicism with the struggles of slaves for Haitian freedom.[14] This example of religious support for rebellious blacks in the Caribbean echoes the earlier Jesuit defense of the Guaraní in Brazil against the impositions of the European Enlightenment.

The exploding violence of the French Revolution in 1789 had immediate effects on the island. Without resources to staunch turmoil in Haiti among a population of more than a half million or even to protect sparsely populated Española, Spain ceded its entire colony to France on 22 July 1795 through the Treaty of Basilea. The island's Spanish-speaking population was invited to resettle elsewhere, although this course was adopted mostly by people of means. On 20 December 1795, Bishop Fernando Portillo y Torres carried what was thought to be the remains of Christopher Columbus out of Santo Domingo's cathedral and placed them on a ship bound for Cuba. But Spanish Catholicism was too deep to be so easily transferred.

The Spanish speakers of Española treasured devotion to Our Lady of Altagracia, whose shrine at Higüey in the eastern portion of the island had been established in 1517. A military victory against French marauders on 21 January 1691 had been attributed to her intercession, and the next year the battle's anniversary became her feast day in Higüey's parish, instead of the traditional 15 August. Nearly a century later in troubled revolutionary times, the archbishop of Santo Domingo, Isidoro Rodríguez y Lorenzo (1767–88), formally transferred Our Lady of Altagracia's feast day for everyone in the Santo Domingo colony. Similarly, Pope Pius VI granted in 1791 papal blessings on the faithful who prayed in honor of Our Lady of Altagracia on the January feast day, elevating this local Marian devotion to the status of national patron of the Spanish-speaking Catholics there.

---

[14] "Catholic Religious Capital and the Haitian Revolution: The Priest and the Prophetess," American Academy of Religion Conference, 2010.

PUERTO RICO

For its role during the Thirty Years War, Puerto Rico had been designated as the bastion of the Spanish Empire in the Americas, largely because of its strategic position at the entrance to the Caribbean Sea. A hundred years later, in 1750, military defenses had added security to commercial trade and had positioned the island colony for rapid commercial growth, including a postal service. Between 1751 and 1799, twenty-four new towns were incorporated, nearly doubling the existing fourteen.

The Enlightenment gathered systematic and reliable demographic data. In 1765, the total population was recorded at 44,883; a generation later in 1795, it had nearly tripled to 129,758. The new approach to census taking adopted categories of race and slavery, reflecting the Enlightenment's heightened racial anxieties. On trial in 1761 for hosting scandalous dances with mulatta women, Puerto Rico's Captain General Ambrosio de Benavides defended himself by saying it was "impossible" in Puerto Rico to tell who was or was not mulatto.[15]

In 1765, Dublin-born Field Marshall Alejandro O'Reilly (1722–94) arrived in Puerto Rico as royal visitor. One of the Irish "wild geese" in the employ of an increasingly anti-English Madrid, O'Reilly's recommendations followed an Enlightenment formula for promoting an agriculture based on cash crops; a financial *sociedad anónima* approximating a stock exchange; infrastructure, principally roads and harbor facilities; and military preparedness by building fortifications and training local men with regular army standards.

As a result of O'Reilly's report, engineer Thomas O'Daly began in 1766 to construct Fort San Cristobal at the eastern end of San Juan's city walls. The well-designed fortifications would repulse the 1797 attack by a considerable force of 14,100 redcoats under Sir Ralph Abercrombie, thus meriting a 1799 Spanish royal decree that named San Juan the "most noble and most loyal" of Spanish American cities.

O'Reilly's recommendations also brought land reform (1778), the establishment of a fire company, the paving of San Juan's streets, the issuance of paper money (1780), the end of the *carimbo* – the branding of slaves (1784) – and the founding of a local trading company to handle the island's tobacco commerce with Holland (1786). Most of the reforms of commercial privileges benefited Europeans who had migrated to Puerto Rico and not the islanders. For instance, James O'Daly, the Irish brother of the army engineer building the castle, was made head of Puerto Rico's newly founded trading company.

---

[15] Salvador Brau, *Historia de Puerto Rico* (San Juan, 1956), 180–1.

The state of religion in Puerto Rico was described by a Benedictine, Agustín Iñigo Abbad y Lasierra, who was on the island (1771–78) as secretary to the bishop. Abbad y Lasierra's comprehensive *Historia geográfica civil y natural* of Puerto Rico was composed in the style of the encyclopedists of the day, notably Reynal and Montesquieu.[16] The book was published in 1788, and although dependent on secondary sources in recording the earlier history of Puerto Rico, it supplies invaluable eyewitness descriptions based on notes taken during the bishop's pastoral visitations. The Benedictine describes native fruits, insects, and animals, providing a capsule description of the rural culture of the time. His observation that the native islanders called white Europeans *de la otra banda* (from the other side) confirms the rise of racial and class consciousness.

Abbad y Lasierra's perspective about the Puerto Rican natives was filtered through the optic of Montesquieu's theory of climatically determined behavior. Because the Puerto Ricans live in a tropical climate and have inherited the biological characteristics of Africans through frequent intermarriage, it was reasoned, they became naturally "indolent and shiftless" when compared to Europeans. Nonetheless, the cleric admires the Catholic faith of the Puerto Ricans, who, he wrote, "are much devoted to Our Lady," wearing her rosary around their necks and reciting it "three times a day." He blames the rural remoteness for the lack of doctrinal understanding of the faith and calls for education.[17] His work is a reliable example of the adoption of elements of the Enlightenment by ecclesiastics in Spanish America.

CUBA

The largest Spanish island in the Caribbean, Cuba, at thirteen times the size of Puerto Rico, was the early target for economic reforms of the tobacco trade. But because the profits were destined only for Madrid, the Bourbons' new policy initially resulted in sporadic protests, beginning in 1717 and extending to 1723, often including violence. In 1731, copper miners near Santiago protested against longer work hours and fewer religious holidays. Settling the dispute in favor of the workers was a colonial clergyman, Pablo Agustín Morell de Santa Cruz (1694–1768), born in Santo Domingo, but then serving as vicar general in Santiago for the Spanish bishop, Jerónimo

---

[16] Guillaume Thomas François Raynal, *Histoire Philosophique et Politique Des Établissements et du Commerce des Européens Dans les Deux Indes*, 6 vols. (Amsterdam, 1770); Charles de Secondat, Baron du Montesquieu, *L'Esprit Des Loix*, 3 vols. (Geneva, 1750).

[17] Agustín Iñigo Abbad y Lasierra, *Historia geográfica, civil y natural de la isla de San Juan Bautista de Puerto Rico*, 3rd ed. (Río Piedras, 1970), 193.

Valdés (1705–29). Morell de Santa Cruz was to prove the exception to the rule that American-born clergy were to be assigned rural, less affluent posts. Promoted bishop of Nicaragua in 1749, he would return as Cuba's bishop in 1753.

Havana had been occupied during the Seven Years' War from June 1762 until 1763. After the evacuation by the British, Field Marshall O'Reilly arrived in 1764 to evaluate defenses and make recommendations for governance. Much as he was to do in Puerto Rico the next year, O'Reilly urged development of agriculture by intensifying cash crop production and by expanding Cuba's infrastructure. The census taken in 1774 showed that sugar mills had tripled since 1750, and the population stood at more than 172,000, with seven whites to five persons of color, and three black slaves to each two free blacks. Havana alone had some 75,000 residents. New prosperity came from direct trade with the United States and an increased international demand for sugar due to troubles in Haiti. The island population rose rapidly to more than 272,000 by 1791; and by the end of the century, Cuba had acquired Enlightenment-inspired institutions, from vigilant custom houses to paved streets and postal service, such as described previously for Puerto Rico.

The career of the American-born Bishop Morell gives witness to the rise of a newly assertive generation of colonials, especially among the clergy, who would passionately defy dictatorial officials coldly imposing Enlightenment mandates on Americans. During the occupation of Havana, the English governor George Keppel, Count of Albemarle, summoned Bishop Morell, informing him that a Catholic church had to be turned over to the invaders for Anglican services. The bishop adamantly refused to subordinate the faith to rationalist pragmatism and was deported to St. Augustine, Florida, by the invaders.

Morell's postwar return brought beekeeping to Cuba, a skill the cleric had learned while in exile. He also wrote a history of Cuba and its cathedral, reproducing *Espejo de Paciencia*, a patriotic poem written in 1608 by Silvestre de Balboa praising resistance to French corsairs. Preserved only in the bishop's history, it is considered the first literary work by a Cuban, one of the seeds of nationalism and a sign of the bishop's love of Cuba. Morell also fostered devotion to Our Lady of Charity, whose shrine near Santiago dated back to 1609, and whose popularity he had witnessed while serving Bishop Valdés. The year before his death, he received a doctoral degree from the University of Havana, giving him educational titles equal to bishops from Spain.

Bishop Valdés had opened Cuba's first diocesan seminary (1722) in Santiago on the eastern end of Cuba, inviting Jesuits as faculty. When it came to founding a new university for Cuba, however, he chose the western port city of Havana as its site. The University of Havana and its affiliated seminary signaled the eclipse of Santiago as the island's chief city, a fact ecclesiastically confirmed with the creation of the Diocese of Havana in 1789 at Morell's petition. Seminaries for diocesan priests did a great deal to elevate the academic formation of native Cuban clergy, and the university initiated the formation of a class of colonial professionals.

The impact of education on fostering the study of local history and instilling pride among Americans was not limited to Cuba, although that island offered special examples of the process. With the expulsion of the Society of Jesus in 1767, the curriculum of the Seminary of St. Charles and St. Ambrose in Havana shifted away from Scholasticism. Father José Agustín Caballero (1765–1835) published in 1797 his *Philosophia electiva* in Latin. The textbook cited Descartes, Locke, and Bacon, thus opening the door to Enlightenment, shrinking the intellectual distance of the Americas from Europe.

In the aftermath of the Napoleonic invasion of Spain, Caballero would be elected a delegate to the Spanish Cortes, as later would be one of the priest's students, the saintly Father Félix Varela. Neither occupied as important a post in Spain's national assembly as had the Puerto Rican naval officer Ramón Power y Giralt, who had been vice president (1810–13) when the Constitution of 1812 crafted a short-lived limited monarchy for Spain. Caballero, Father Varela, and like-minded American clerics would turn the arguments of the Enlightenment against European rule. By insisting that true enlightenment meant equal rights for everyone, including Americans and persons of color, these Catholic colonials laid down the intellectual arguments for independence from a recalcitrant Spain and made the case for the simultaneous abolition of slavery.

FLORIDA

The Spanish colony of Florida was originally intended to check French entry into the region when it began with the 1565 settlement of St. Augustine on Florida's Atlantic coast. But religion was never absent from Spanish colonization. Citing the charge to evangelize Native Americans, Spanish Florida's claims extended northward to contemporary South Carolina and westward to the Mississippi. This Spanish province remained sparsely settled for the next century and a half and barely survived English aggressions under Georgia's Governor Oglethorpe, who in 1740 brought English troops within two miles of St. Augustine. When Spain consequently encouraged settlement by recruiting white Canary Islanders, evangelization lost importance, and by 1759 only ten friars remained for missionary work.

When Florida was briefly transferred to English rule in 1763, virtually all 3,000 Spanish colonists of St. Augustine boarded ships for Cuba, along with 83 Christian Yamassee Indians and 350 black slaves. The western Florida settlement at Pensacola Bay, founded in 1699 as Fort San Carlos de Austria, was similarly dismantled to transfer its residents to Mexico. Of the 700 residents, including 108 Christian Native Americans, only one Spanish settler chose to remain in Florida under British rule.

Spanish rule was restored to Florida twenty years later by the Treaty of Paris, and St. Augustine and Pensacola were designated military installations, which meant civilian residents' needs were to be subordinated to those of soldiers. The new classification did not close down St. Augustine's historic church or disband the *cabildo,* but local governance was curtailed. Madrid had determined that Florida's usefulness was in its fur trade and not the evangelization of natives. North American Protestants were allowed to settle in trappers' villages in present-day Mississippi and Alabama, and Madrid even authorized the construction of Protestant churches. Although this policy deflected violent incursions into Florida's Spanish towns from the new United States, it unleashed English settlement patterns that quickly decimated the Native Americans. All of Florida would be lost to Spain in 1821.

LOUISIANA

The transfer of the Louisiana Territory from France to "cousin" Spain in 1762 did not occasion mass relocation of the French-speaking residents, partly because it represented a temporizing effort from both Bourbon monarchies to oppose English expansion in the Americas. The appointed Spanish governor, Antonio de Ulloa, arrived in March 1766 in New Orleans, promising not to upset the established order; in fact, he did not even lower the flag with the French fleur-de-lis. He focused Spanish control over customs taxes on furs brought downriver from Illinois for export and on wine being imported. But the three thousand inhabitants of New Orleans perceived the governor's conciliatory nature as weakness and petitioned the French king for outright reannexation. In October 1768, Ulloa was forced to ship out to Havana, against cries from the angry populace with epicurean as well as political goals, shouting, "*Vive le roi, vive le bon vin de Bordeaux.*" (Long live the King! Long live good Bordeaux wine!)

Reprisal of the French colonists' recalcitrance was swift. A fleet of twenty-one ships and two thousand Spanish troops arrived in New Orleans under O'Reilly in August 1769. The no-nonsense Irishman hung five key leaders of the protest that had driven Ulloa from the city. Before he left six months later in February 1770, O'Reilly had installed a Spanish-style *cabildo,* outlawed the enslavement of Indians, and utilized the existing boundaries of twenty-two ecclesiastical parishes to organize civil governance. He also raised the Spanish flag, declared Castilian the official language, and convinced the king to send Spanish settlers to counterbalance the French populace. Nearly two thousand Canarians arrived over the years, and one band of settlers from Málaga founded New Iberia in 1779.

Bernardo de Gálvez was named governor of Louisiana in 1777 by the minister of the Indies, who was also his uncle, José. During the revolt of England's American colonies, the nephew organized military expeditions against the British. He marched troops, including some from Cuba and Puerto Rico, through the former French settlements of East Louisiana in Baton Rouge and Mobile, eventually retaking Pensacola. Spanish military successes on behalf of American independence won back Florida at the treaty table in 1783.

Louisiana remained French-speaking, however, and its brand of Catholicism resisted assimilation to Spanish America. The parishes in the rural areas outside New Orleans endured as pillars for governance, despite general indifference to religion from officials. With the cession of most of Upper Louisiana (Missouri and Illinois) to the United States in 1783, French settlers from those areas migrated southward, strengthening French Catholicism. Like other colonials, lived religion was more important to them than Enlightenment philosophizing. The troubles in Haiti after 1790 made Louisiana a home for exiles, whereas the forced deportation from Acadia in Nova Scotia brought an additional three thousand French speakers to the colony. Moreover, the marriage of two governors, including Gálvez, into prominent French families of New Orleans' high society pointed assimilation toward French dominance and not a Spanish identity. By 1799, when Napoleon took power in Paris, most of Lousiana's ten thousand inhabitants were more French than Spanish in culture, language, and religious style of Catholic worship.

THE BORDERLANDS

The settlement of the territories north of the Rio Grande had begun in 1598 among the Pueblo people of New Mexico. Contrasted with the organized empires of the Aztecs and Incas, most of the native peoples there were hunters and gatherers in subsistence economies. The introduction of the horse by Europeans made the nomadic economy of the buffalo hunt far more attractive than laborious farming. Well into the eighteenth century, Native Americans on horseback were more inclined to plunder sedentary missions rather than live in them.

A missionary premise derived from medieval Europe held that evangelization was impossible without the permanent settlement brought by agriculture. However, efforts to impose this social change on the existing native culture were complicated by Spanish abuses, resulting in the bloody Pueblo uprising in 1680 led by Popé, whose rule replaced that of Europeans for more than a decade. When Spanish rule was restored after 1693, the policy employed was to protect the missions with military forces stationed in a presidium, that is, in a fort that also housed resident colonials. Most of the areas in the present-day southwestern United States were placed under the 1729 issuance of regulations that pushed aside clerical jurisdiction and subordinated missionary activity to civil concerns.

Carlos III ordered a major report on all his colonies north of New Spain, and the Marqués de Rubí arrived in 1764 to inspect the northern territories or "borderlands" between Mexico and Indian territories. Rubí found that the hostilities and cruelties on both sides had rendered future colonization problematic. Reaching the presidium of El Paso in July 1766, the marqués met fifty beleaguered soldiers hopelessly charged with guarding wide swatches of outlying territory. On 19 August 1766, the party marched eastward to Santa Fe, which had been the base of governance after the 1693 reentry of Spanish power. On leaving this settlement, the officials set the next leg of their expedition east and southward toward the border of Texas and Louisiana at Los Adaes, which had only sixty-one soldiers, lacking uniforms and shoes. The garrison had survived by selling its best horses to the French. Marching westward along the Gulf Coast, the marqués and his men returned to Mexico City on 23 February 1768.

The expedition's report produced regulations issued in 1772. Force was given preference over diplomacy among the natives. An impregnable cordon of presidios was planned to stretch from the Louisiana border to the California coast, each set at a moderate distance apart from others. Stone, not adobe, was to be the construction material, and the garrisons were raised from forty-three to a minimum of seventy-six defenders. The soldiers were to be local residents, trained in military and cavalry tactics, and were to don defensive leather coats as protection from arrows.

Implementation of this plan was given to a cousin of O'Reilly's, the Dublin-born Hugo O'Conor, nicknamed Capitán colorado (Red Captain) for his hair. O'Conor shrank the line of the presidios in the present-day United States to Santa Fe, San Antonio, and La Bahía on the Gulf Coast near present-day Corpus Christi, Texas. The presidium at Tubac in Arizona was also moved to Tucson among the Pima people, where wood and water were in better supply.

In 1776, Madrid ordered a new administrative post, the Comandancia General of the Interior Provinces, to pair with the defensive measures already taken. But the idea that Spain could erect a line of impregnable forts along a 1,800-mile border with less than 2,000 troops was a bureaucratic illusion. Rather than bastions stopping aggressions, the forts became targets of intensified attacks with 243 deaths in the decade, higher than the previous ten years.

On promotion by his uncle to the viceroyalty of New Spain in 1782, Lousiana's former governor Bernardo de Gálvez used his experience as background for new instructions to the Comandancia. Abandoning evangelization as a goal of colonization, the 1786 policy imitated English and French strategies with the native peoples. Sale of alcohol to the natives was encouraged, even though the same had been prohibited for nearly two centuries. The native peoples were to be sold firearms, but of the worst possible quality, so that they would be dependent on the Spaniards for repairs and munitions. The objective of the policy was to vanquish "the heathens" by "obliging them to destroy one another." This set a policy of "peace by deceit," so named by the youngest Gálvez,[18] and this was how Enlightened Despotism utilized rationalism to undercut the two centuries of missionary work that had generally respected native rights.

Despite the hard line of the Instructions of 1786, pragmatism prevailed as local officials found it easier to bribe prospective native marauders than capture and punish them. Moreover, the beginnings of trade along trails linking Santa Fe, San Antonio, and Tucson with Mexico and the U.S. frontiers to the east of the Mississippi brought in goods that were used in exchanges with native peoples, and a modest prosperity was enjoyed by the 1790s.

RELIGION IN TEXAS, NEW MEXICO, AND ARIZONA

The most striking feature of the borderlands under the Comandancia General was the sparse population. Of course, there were hundreds of thousands of Native Americans living free from Spanish rule, but of those considered to be colonists of Texas in 1763, there were little more than 2,000. The population of the San Antonio presidium that became the seat of provincial government in 1773 harbored almost half the Texas population, surpassing in size all of the surrounding missions with Christian Indians. New Mexico as a province counted only 9,580 colonials total, with slightly more than 3,000 in the El Paso region. Santa Fe had a population of 2,324, and neighboring villages like Taos to the north did not amount to more than a few hundred residents each. There were only 600 colonials and Hispanicized Indians living at Tubac in present-day Arizona.

---

[18] Cited in David Weber, *The Spanish Frontier in North America* (New Haven, 1992), 229.

In comparison, Puerto Rico had more than 100,000 inhabitants living compactly on an island scarcely 115 miles long and 30 miles wide, meaning there were more Spanish subjects on that small island than in all the settlements of the continent's borderlands.

Although the policies of Enlightened Despotism had frozen missionary activity to focus on protection of towns, the frontier settlements did not abandon religion. Rather, traditional feast day celebrations with attendant processions of *cofradías* became signs of normalcy and traditional prestige. Officials had the luxury of Enlightenment principles, but ordinary people preferred popular religion. Thus, the practice of religion in borderland towns withstood the secularizing intentions of Enlightened Despotism.

CALIFORNIA

Although California had been explored by Fortún Jiménez in 1533, it was only late in the seventeenth century that Spain considered building a harbor there in support of the maritime trade between Mexico and the Philippines. The Jesuits established missions in the Lower (Baja) California peninsula beginning in 1697, but the arid soil was barely capable of subsistence farming. Conditions northward in what is now the state of California promised greater prosperity, and the scholarly Jesuit Eusebio Kino had established the Mission of San Xavier del Bac (1700) in present-day Arizona as the way station of proposed overland travel from Mexico to Upper California.

The proposal to establish new settlements in California north of the barren Baja was greatly motivated by Spain's fear of losing still more of its American territories. Urgency had come from a 1757 book written – ironically – by a Jesuit, warning of encroachment by Russians from Alaska and from English explorers seeking the Northwest Passage. José de Gálvez, who had served Spain as a civil servant reporting on the colonies, drafted a plan with detailed specifics that caught the king's eye. As a son of the Enlightenment, José de Gálvez had little affection for the Church; yet he realized that there would never be enough colonials from Mexico or settlers from Spain to populate the area. Conversion of the natives, however, would quickly create towns where Spanish rule was recognized.

Gálvez turned missionary responsibilities over to Franciscans, considering them less likely to interfere in civil matters than the Jesuits, who had just been expelled. He proposed combining the religious functions of the mission with those of the military presidium, leaving power over the settlements to civil authority. Gálvez placed Gaspar de Portolá, a nobleman from Catalonia, in charge of the expedition; Fray Junípero Serra (1713–84), a zealous Franciscan from Mallorca, was to be religious superior in California.

Basing themselves on maps and descriptions from the 1602–03 voyage of Sebastián Vizcaíno, three ships bearing soldiers, settlers, livestock, and equipment sailed northward in January 1769 from Mexico, while soldiers were sent overland from Mexico. Fray Junípero chose a penitential journey on foot with the Franciscans from the Lower California missions. All the contingents were to converge at San Diego Bay before sending some settlers northward to Monterey Bay, near present-day Santa Cruz. With seaport garrisons protecting both limits of the colony, the missionaries would evangelize the natives, setting up missions along a coast-hugging royal road, the Camino Real.

Of the three ships, one was lost at sea, and the other two were so delayed by bad weather and treacherous currents that their crews were sick with scurvy by the time they arrived at San Diego Bay in April 1769. Despite the sad state of his sixty soldiers, Portolá marched onward to secure the northern end of the California settlements. However, faulty maps betrayed the commander's search for Monterey Bay, and, despite grumbling from his men, they reached instead an uncharted but unexpectedly magnificent bay in November 1769. Fray Juan Crespí, one of those with the Portolá expedition, wrote back, "doubtless not only all the navies of our Catholic Monarch, but those of all Europe might lie within the harbor."[19] Thereafter, the key port for northern California was San Francisco Bay, the best harbor on North America's Pacific coast.

Franciscans established twenty-one missions along the California coast, beginning with San Diego in 1769, and ending with San Francisco de Solano near present-day Sonoma in 1823. The proximity of the missions to white settlers and soldiers invited abuses of rights and sexual predations on the natives. Moreover, the corruption came from Mexican colonials whose vices proved as disruptive to the missions in the eighteenth century as the greed of the Spanish conquistadors had in the sixteenth century. The 1781 Yuma revolt made it clear that overland access to California through Arizona was not dependable. Also working against missionary success was the grinding mortality of European diseases that had a fatal impact on many Native Americans. It has been estimated that from a population of some three hundred thousand when the colonization began, their numbers had been reduced to about two hundred thousand in 1821.

However, natives did join the missions. By the end of the century, eighteen missions held a combined resident population of 13,500. The Hispanicized natives of California greatly outnumbered the white colonials, who were less than 1,000 in 1790. Although these white Mexican and Spanish settlers were to grow in numbers during the decade to about

[19] *Ibid.*, 245n36.

1,800, they were concentrated in the four secular presidios and generally did not live among the Christianized natives.

The political turmoil in Europe after the French Revolution of 1789 diminished Madrid's influence, enabling the Franciscans to maintain the integrity of a religious regimen. The fertility of the land and the introduction of European crops along with a systematic use of knowledge of botany and animal husbandry bestowed prosperity. Cut off from overland commerce with the rest of the continent by unexplored terrain, mountains, and deserts, only maritime trade penetrated New California's isolation. Mercifully, and in contrast to the Caribbean, there were few pirates and less smuggling. A 1795 accord with England, during a brief break with Spain's traditional alliance with France, settled a conflict over rights to settlement at Neah Bay in present-day Washington State. The agreement did not fix a permanent northern boundary with Canada at that time, but it did relieve the governor of New California from preoccupation with Russian incursions.

The California missions succeeded in establishing permanent Spanish settlements; indeed, many contemporary California cities carry the original mission names. The religious legacy of the California missions endured even after Mexican independence in 1810. Franciscan spirituality characterized life in the missions among the Christianized natives, who were a majority of the population and would remain so until secularization of the missions in 1833 by the Mexican Republic. The Franciscans did not afford as much importance to Christian humanism as had the Jesuits, nor did they share the Jesuits' benign view of pre-Christian religion. Since its founding by Francis of Assisi, the Order of Friars Minor had measured God's grandeur by emphasizing the magnitude of divine love that embraced a lowly human condition. The effect of God's grace was to make all human distinctions meaningless. Franciscan piety leveled all creation to a radical equality in which everyone was "Brother" or "Sister" – titles the saintly founder had also extended to God's animal creatures. Impulses that ran counter to gospel norms were attributed to weak human nature or to temptations from the devil. The human body was considered an "ass," and its waywardness merited scourging and physical punishment.

Junípero Serra, superior of California's Franciscans, was fervent in his embrace of a Franciscan spirituality that minimized the value of this world. Penances in the form of fasting and self-inflicted pain by hair shirts, hooks, and scourging were the spiritual tools of Serra to overcome the attractions of the world and grow closer to the divine. To some, they represented sainthood; to others, excess. Contemporary criticism of the Franciscan missions in California sometimes condemns corporal punishment of the natives, but Franciscan piety imposed the same sort of corporal punishment on the friars themselves. The practices may have been excessive, but they were not discriminatory.

The lasting effects of this spirituality are manifest. Franciscan devotions such as the Christmas *creché* and the *via crucis* inserted the believer into the life of Christ by recreating the key moments of his incarnation. Ironically, Enlightened Despotism's efforts from 1750 to 1799 to weaken American religion by imposing rationalist policies produced the greatest success in California, where the opposite occurred.

THE TUPAC AMARU REVOLT, REACTION, AND THE END OF THE ERA

The Tupac Amaru II Revolt of 1780 in Peru took place far from the northern colonial borderlands and the Spanish Caribbean. Restrictions in Cuzco against the traditional feast of Corpus Christi were the catalysts, because Madrid's heavy hand suspended long-standing privileges enjoyed by the people. The Enlightenment viewed the local celebration as superstitious, a judgment based on vestiges of native religion within the festive ceremonies. The Incans had celebrated Inti Raimi to the sun spirit during the winter solstice (June in the southern hemisphere), coinciding on the Christian calendar with the post-Easter feast of Corpus Christi. Multilayered appropriation had enabled baroque Catholicism to view the hybrid of the two festivals as a popular religious celebration that incorporated the Incan nation into Christianity.

José Gabriel Condorcanqui (1738–81), a descendant of Incan rulers and graduate of a Jesuit college, had studied Garcilaso de la Vega's accounts of the Incan rituals. This inclusion into the standard college curriculum would be denounced later as Jesuitical subversion by Juan Manuel Moscoso y Peralta, the bishop of Cuzco. The initial target of the revolt was not royal authority, but reforms of taxation and work patterns. As hostilities escalated, however, José claimed the title "Tupac Amaru II," successor to the first Tupac, the last Incan ruler before the Spaniards, and appropriated symbols used in the feast days as evidence of a never-surrendered Incan sovereignty.[20]

Pleading for a peaceful end to the revolt in a letter read in all churches, Bishop Martínez y Compañón of Trujillo cited principles from Rousseau's 1750 book about the nature of the social compact, an implicit presumption that ordinary churchgoers would understand his argument. When Tupac

---

[20] This appropriation is discussed by David Cahill, "Popular Religion and Appropriation: The Example of Corpus Christi in Eighteenth-Century Cuzco," *Latin American Research Review* 31:2 (1996): 67–110.

was captured in 1781, the Enlightenment officials brutally executed his wife, Micaela, before his eyes. He was sentenced to death by draw and quarter, and when that failed to rip apart his limbs, they cut off his head, exhibiting it as a trophy. Moreover, every fifth male was executed in towns that had supported the revolt, the hated *quintado* ordered by Gálvez from Madrid as the "reconquest" of the Americas.

The terror used by Spanish officials failed to deter revolt. Moreover, the purposeful exclusion of people of color and even of white colonials from influence under the Enlightenment had instead strengthened demands for autonomy, even from those who rejected armed revolt. Despite a pragmatism that dictated a softening of penalties, Tupac's rebellion had produced an irreversible popular mindset that hastened the empire's dissolution.

King Carlos' advisor, the Count of Aranda (1719–98), saw the impossibility of Spain continuing its rule by force. In 1783, he counseled Carlos III to add new kingdoms of Mexico and Peru for the royal princes. Without monarchs closely identified with and living among their American subjects, revolt was inevitable, he thought. The plan was not implemented, but with Mexican independence in 1821, monarchists proposed the Plan of Iguala, which would have allowed the deposed Spanish king, Fernando VII, to rule Mexico instead. This ill-fated resurrection of Aranda's proposal, nonetheless, reaffirmed his earlier judgment that single rule for Spanish America and Spain was impossible.

Spanish America's racial differences figured in the thinking of the Venezuelan revolutionary Francisco de Miranda (1750–1816), of whom Napoleon wrote, "He is a Don Quixote, except that this one isn't crazy."[21] Miranda wanted to implement Montesquieu's separation of powers by creating a senate for all of Latin America, composed of descendants of Native American rulers, to pair with an elected lower body of ordinary citizens. His formula would have separated republicanism from racism.

Spanish America strove to reconcile Enlightenment science with the traditional religious practices that had protected American rights to their national identities. Consider the sermon delivered in Mexico on 12 December 1794 by the Dominican friar and Mexican colonial José Servando Teresa de Mier (1765–1827). He spoke on the feast day of Our Lady of Guadalupe in the church built in Tepeyac held sacred as the site of the apparition. The preacher began by citing José Ignacio Borunda, a Jesuit-trained Mexican lawyer, about excavations at Mexico City's square (*zócalo*) that proved St. Thomas the Apostle had preached in the Americas. Servando added that the Madonna's image in Guadalupe's church was not the result

---

[21] Cited in Miguel Jorrín and John D. Martz, *Latin-American Political Thought and Ideology* (Chapel Hill, 1970), 59n7.

of a miracle. It was, rather, the human effort by an anonymous artist to reproduce the original picture painted by St. Luke on the apostle's cape and blessed by the Blessed Virgin Mary herself when she bade him farewell on his missionary voyage. The overstretched theorizing in Servando's sermon retained the Mexican devotion to Our Lady of Guadalupe while submitting to mounting scientific evidence that the image had been painted by native artists. But simultaneously, the preacher placed the origins of Catholicism among the Aztecs in the apostolic age and long before the Spanish arrival a millennium and a half later.

The Dominican's sermon's political meaning was clear: the papal donation conferring dominion to Spain had been based on the falsehood that the gospel had never been preached in the Americas. Because Mexican Christianity had been founded instead in apostolic days, said Servando, it was not merely an "offshoot of Spain," but rather its equal. Calling the Spanish ministers of Enlightened Despotism "Philistines of France," Servando closed with a prayer for Guadalupe to protect Mexicans from attacks and insults and reportedly addressed Mary as "Teotenantzin entirely Virgin, trustworthy Tonacayona ... Flowery Coyolxauhqui, true Coatlicue de Mingó."[22]

The friar's challenge to both civil and ecclesiastical orders soon won him many years in jail and the life of a political exile, including a sojourn in Philadelphia (1820–22). Servando, however, provides evidence that the European Enlightenment did not transfer easily to the Americas, especially when a rationalistic racialism attacked long-held Catholic concepts of equality for people of color as distinct nations united under a single polity. David Brading states that Spanish Americans had "succeeded in creating an intellectual tradition that, by reason of its engagements with the historical experience and contemporary reality of America, was original, idiosyncratic, complex, and quite distinct from any European model."[23] Servando's 1794 sermon anticipated the idealization of nationality, culture, and an imagined past that would become the pillars of the Romantic movement – and he wrapped them all in religion.

CONCLUSION

The history of Spanish American religion during this period cannot be understood as merely a reflection of trends in Europe or imitation of a

---

[22] For analysis of the sermon, see David A. Brading, *Mexican Phoenix: Our Lady of Guadalupe: Image and Tradition across Five Centuries* (Cambridge, UK, 2001), 203ff.

[23] David A. Brading, *The First America: The Spanish Monarchy, Creole Patriots, and the Liberal State, 1492–1867* (Cambridge, UK, 1993), 5.

newly independent United States of America. Through the half century, the legacy of the expelled Jesuits, extinguished Native American revolts, claims for equality from mixed-race peoples, and protests from exasperated colonials had shaped a complex religious and racial identity. Religion in Latin America in 1799 anticipated what Hegel would describe in 1820, namely, how an historical era comes to its end: "History thus corroborates the teaching of the conception that only in the maturity of reality does the ideal appear as counterpart to the real, apprehends the real world in its substance, and shapes it into an intellectual kingdom.... The owl of Minerva, takes its flight only when the shades of night are gathering."[24]

SUGGESTIONS FOR FURTHER READING

Caraman, Philip. *The Lost Paradise: The Jesuit Republic in South America.* New York, 1976.

Hargreaves-Mawdsley, W. N. *Eighteenth-Century Spain: 1700–1788 – A Political, Diplomatic and Institutional History.* London, 1979.

Jorrín, Miguel, and John D. Martz. *Latin-American Political Thought and Ideology.* Chapel Hill, 1970.

Lafaye, Jacques. *Quetzalcoatl and Guadalupe: The Formation of Mexican National Consciousness, 1531–1813.* Trans. Benjamin Keen. Chicago, 1976.

Mörner, Magnus, ed. *The Expulsion of the Jesuits from Latin America.* New York, 1965.

---

[24] Georg Wilhelm Fredrich Hegel, *Elements of the Philosophy of Right,* ed. Allen W. Wood, trans. H. B. Nisbet (Cambridge, UK, 1991), 23.

Section VI

THEMATIC ESSAYS

32

RELIGIOUS THOUGHT: THE PRE-COLUMBIAN ERA TO 1790

E. BROOKS HOLIFIELD

A large number of early Americans thought often about religion. Until the 1770s, the most frequently published and reprinted books in the American colonies were sermons and religious treatises. But the colonists – and the Native Americans who preceded them – also differed about religion. It divided them. The most prolific producers of formal theology were the Calvinist clergy of New England, but Christian alternatives could be found among Catholics, Anglicans, Swedish and German Lutherans, Presbyterians, Methodists, Moravians, Baptists, Dutch Reformed, Quakers, Mennonites, Amish, Universalists, Gortonites, Rogerines, Shakers, and an assortment of even smaller groups like the Ephrata utopians or the Society of the Woman in the Wilderness. But Christian thought was far from the sole option. Sephardic and Ashkenazic Jews, although lacking rabbis, preserved ancient traditions and practices along with many of the ideas embedded within them. Deists dispensed with notions of a special biblical revelation. Africans, most enslaved, some free, imported not only African traditional religions but also Christian and Muslim ideas; and more than 250 Native American societies interpreted their ritual practices and ethical injunctions with a vast collection of narratives and beliefs. Americans could also be eclectic, combining inherited traditions with strands of esoteric and metaphysical ideas that had different origins. The realm of religious thought was turbulent.

The diversity registered conflicting interpretations of scripture, opposing assessments of the authority of tradition, differing views about the value of primitive precedents, controversies about ritual, disputes over ethics, and incompatible attitudes toward the broader culture. Not only did the Christian communities view with suspicion any group outside Christianity, but they also battled within their own traditions. Not only did Native Americans defend their rituals and beliefs from Christian missionaries, but they also used ritual practices and narratives to contrast themselves to other native groups. The story of religious thought in colonial America is therefore a story of conflict. Although religion also supported group unity, serving as a bond of mutuality, legitimating their enterprises, giving them a common vocabulary, and encouraging concern for one another, the contrasting ideas divided people. One way to give an account of colonial religious thought, therefore, is to note the issues that generated conflict.

RELIGIOUS THOUGHT, THE SOCIETY, AND THE STATE

The most obvious sites of conflict developed out of the relation between religious thought and state power. French and Spanish missionaries represented not only the church, but also the interests of the European monarchs. They depended on government support even while they often criticized colonial governors for hindering their mission, so they supported their states in competition with other imperial powers. Religious ideas legitimated the aims of the state particularly in times of warfare. The New England clergy interpreted wars with Native American groups as divine crusades of righteous governments against infidel savages. Protestants justified English opposition to Spanish intrusions into Georgia from Florida as a defense of Protestant truth against Catholic error, while Spanish Catholics viewed such incursions as a battle not only for territory but also against heretics. During the French and Indian Wars, Protestants gave older religious views of the Antichrist a political interpretation; and in the years leading up to the American Revolution, struggles over the appointment of an Anglican bishop, resentment of British laxity toward Catholics in Quebec, and religiously grounded convictions about British immorality exacerbated hostility. Especially in New England, the clergy used religious ideas to generate opposition to the British king, whereas many of the clergy of the Anglican Church in the colonies departed for England after reminding the revolutionaries that scripture required obedience to authority.

Religious ideas also amplified political struggles within the colonies. In nine of the thirteen colonies that would constitute the early United States, state-supported clergy tried to ensure that their religions – especially the Congregationalists in New England, the Anglicans in the South, the Dutch Reformed in New Netherland, and the Lutherans in New Sweden – would have a monopoly on religious thought, a policy that produced conflict with Baptists, Quakers, and other dissenters, who rejected the religious establishments. After the English conquered New Netherland in 1664, the colony became an arena for religious competition. Protestants in Maryland justified their rebellion against the colony's authorities on the grounds that Catholic influence was too strong. In four colonies individual churches enjoyed no special privileges, but many found the diversity and competition troubling. The Great Awakening of the 1730s and 1740s produced religious skirmishes, dividing Congregationalists into Old Light and New Light factions and Presbyterians into Old Side and New Side parties. In Connecticut in the eighteenth century, disputes between New Lights and Old Lights formed the background for divisions in the political regime. By the time of the Revolution, the divisions between Patriots and Loyalists within each colony frequently had religious parallels. Countless Anglican clergy left the colonies, and the intrusion of pronounced forms of religious liberalism, including deism, separated Americans who otherwise joined politically.

Theology also justified the social distinctions that separated the upper and lower levels of the colonial hierarchy. John Norton of New England spoke for most in the seventeenth century when he said that God had established "superior and inferior relations" by "distributing to each one respectively, what is due thereunto." Sometimes disputes between the common people and their superiors – which was how political leaders interpreted Bacon's rebellion in Virginia in 1676 – exposed fractures between backcountry dissenters and eastern members of the established church. In the seventeenth century, ministers and magistrates denounced the idea of democracy, and restrictions on the franchise seemed to accord with the hierarchical ordering that God had preordained. But changing political ideals brought new interpretations, and by the eighteenth century colonial clergy used religious ideas to honor the sovereignty of the people against the "aristocratic" pretensions of the British ruling class.

GENDER

The majority of the colonial authors who published religious sermons and treatises were male, and religious thought justified their privileged position in colonial society. They used scriptural passages to prove female inferiority, to insist on wives' subjection to their husbands, and to prevent them from teaching men in the church. When Anne Hutchinson in Boston presumed to teach males, her audacity, as well as her doctrines, led to her banishment. Puritan preachers taught that men and women were equal in the eyes of God, but that spiritual equality had no implications for women's participation in state or church governance. By the end of the seventeenth century, New England clergy praised women for displaying a piety and virtue that exceeded that of men, but the witchcraft episodes in New England – in which almost all the victims were women – illustrated the way in which religious ideas cast women into occasional peril. When women ventured to "prophesy" publicly during the Great Awakening, they drew contemptuous and fearful comment from respectable clergy. By the end of the colonial period, Americans had backed away from the killing of witches, but religious ideas still justified a subordinate place for women.

It is only part of the story, however, albeit the larger part, to recall that religious thought justified women's subordination. After all, women constituted the majority of church members throughout most of the colonial period, and they made their own uses of religious ideas. Sometimes they used genres that allowed them to teach without openly challenging religious taboos. Anne Dudley Bradstreet (c. 1612–72) in Ipswich and North Andover was able to write of the conflict between flesh and spirit, the joys of grace, and the assurance of salvation by embedding the ideas in poetic forms. The African American writer Phillis Wheatley (c. 1753–84) in Boston published poems on the works of Providence, the mysteries of God, the evils of slavery, and divine love. Other women discovered that it was perfectly acceptable for them to express religious ideas in certain narratives. Mary Rowlandson (c. 1647–1710) in Lancaster published in 1682 *The Sovereignty and Goodness of God*, describing her captivity at the hands of the Narragansetts but interspersing her descriptions with biblical interpretations and theological assertions. Marie de l'Incarnation (1599–1672), superior of the Ursuline monastery in Quebec, used her *Explication* to explain doctrine for young religious women and her *Lettres* (1677–81) to describe not only the mission to New France, but also the theological ideas that stood behind it. Hannah Adams (1755–1831) in New England wrote a two-volume *View of Religious Opinions* (1784) in which she described the religious views of Americans in ways that promoted her own liberal religious perspective.

Still other women found that the diary form became a way to engage religious ideas. Sarah Osborn (1714–96) in Newport, Rhode Island, wrote not only a fifty-volume diary, but also a theological treatise in which she defended Calvinist teaching and explored the intricacies of her own religious experience. Fully conversant with the details of Edwardsean theology, she used her diaries – and public teaching in her home – to warn against the dangers of liberalism and the errors of antinomianism. Judith Sargent Stevens Murray (1751–1820) was even more venturesome than Osborn, not only defending women's rights, but also publishing in 1782 a theological treatise – one of many that she wrote – defending the doctrine of universal salvation. She was one of the few women of the period to publish, in addition to her books, articles on theology in such journals as the *Massachusetts Magazine*. By that time, Quaker women had long testified in fields and meetinghouses, for after facing persecution and even execution (as in the case of Mary Dyer) in the seventeenth century, they prospered with the emergence of women's monthly meetings in 1681 and the expansion of the movement in the eighteenth century. Women like Grace

Lloyd and Jane Hoskins in Pennsylvania typified the scores of Quaker women who explained their doctrine both to converts and to outsiders in the colonies. And by the eighteenth century, prophetic figures like Jemima Wilkinson (1751–1820), who styled herself the Universal Publick Friend, and Ann Lee (1736–84) were drawing on their own visionary religious experiences to proclaim versions of the gospel that stepped outside the mainstream. Wilkinson combined evangelicalism and Quakerism into a religious vision that called for pacifism and the abolition of slavery; Lee, who came to America only ten years before her death, preached a demanding message of celibacy as a way of salvation.

By their insistence on preaching and teaching publicly, most of these women found that their ideas produced division in a male-dominated culture. Women who found alternative forums – the poem, the letter, the diary – aroused the least resistance; women who insisted on both public teaching and deviation from doctrinal norms elicited the most. But the public teaching of religious ideas was an act of assertion that collided with tenacious adherence to traditional views of gender relations.

RACE

Already in the seventeenth century, the institution of slavery ensured that religious ideas would color the relations between Europeans and Africans. Many Europeans resisted the introduction of Christian theological notions to the enslaved African population. A Dutch Reformed pastor in New York refused baptism to slaves because he feared that they connected it with temporal freedom for their children. The Anglican preacher Morgan Godwin in Virginia complained in 1680 that slaveholders forbade missions to the slaves for fear that conversion would render the slaves ungovernable, but the masters also used the biblical story of the curse of Canaan to argue against conversion, and some said that Africans were not fully human and so neither capable nor suited for inclusion in the church. The rise of abolitionist sentiments in New England as early as 1700 with the publication of Samuel Sewall's (1652–1730) *The Selling of Joseph* meant that race would become a divisive issue not only politically and socially but also theologically. The reply to Sewall by the Boston lawyer John Saffin laid out biblical arguments for slavery that would become standard in the nineteenth century. The antislavery activities of the Quakers, especially of John Woolman (1720–72), who wrote on slavery, poverty, and peace, countered a proslavery position that was already attracting theological defenders. Anglican missionaries used catechisms to teach the enslaved their duty to obey their masters.

Largely excluded from Christian churches, at least in the South, until the revivals of the 1750s, the Africans relied on memories of rituals and practices from their homelands. Coming from different cultures and speaking different languages, the Africans brought no singular religious tradition. Some West Africans had a conception of a high god associated with the sky while also sharing a devotion to lesser spirits associated with water and forests and mountains. Many had a shared sense of respect for ancestors who had founded villages or kin groups, and some practiced rituals to procure mundane benefits, used charms or amulets for protection, and practiced divination to foresee the future. African traditional religions often taught conceptions of existence after death, although the emphasis could also be this-worldly. But other slaves were adherents of Islam, whereas evidence continues to accumulate that some were Catholic descendants of ancestors converted by Portuguese missionaries.

By the late eighteenth century, however, African American preachers were promoting the theologies of colonial Christian traditions. Jupiter Hammon (1711–1806), a Long Island slave preacher, proclaimed an evangelical Anglican theology with Calvinist overtones. Hammon wrote three essays before 1790 that combined a moderate Anglican Calvinism with ideas of "holy living." The New England Congregationalist Lemuel Haynes (1753–1833) preached the doctrines of Jonathan Edwards and George Whitefield. The Georgia Baptist preacher George Liele (b. 1750) wrote a short Calvinist creedal statement, and one of his converts, Andrew Bryan (1737–1812), spread moderate Calvinist ideas when he founded the First African Church in Savannah in 1788. The Methodist Richard Allen (1760–1831) preached Methodist notions of conversion and sanctification to both black and white listeners as he traveled as an exhorter, before settling down in Philadelphia in 1786. After 1750, the slaves turned in growing numbers to Christian belief.

A few black preachers used Christian ideas to advance the abolitionist cause. Lemuel Haynes' "Liberty Further Extended" (1776) urged that disinterested benevolence should mean the end of enslavement; and although Hammon told his African hearers that they were obliged to obey their masters and that slavery had served purposes of Christianization, he also managed to communicate the thought that freedom was "a great thing." For the most part, however, whites carefully monitored black religious expression, and religious ideas about freedom had to be carefully encoded, as they seemingly were in some of the African spirituals that conveyed religious ideas in musical form.

NATIVE AMERICAN RELIGIONS

No single account can capture the complexity that marked the religious practices, attitudes, and beliefs of the more than 250 Native American groups who occupied the continent before the Europeans came, but they exemplified the diversity that would become characteristic of American religion. Interwoven into their everyday lives, their rituals and narratives helped form the sense of distinctiveness that separated them from one another. Although certain motifs, such as reverence for the natural world and the animals that provided food and clothing, could be found in many Native American societies, the details of their religious worlds differed so greatly that one can only hint at the variety by giving three examples.

The Pueblos of the upper Rio Grande valley practiced rituals in ceremonial kivas (holy rooms connecting the surface of the earth to the mysterious underworld) that honored the spirits of the water, the mountains, the hunt, and the crops who had emerged in primeval time to show the Pueblo people how to flourish as a group, for it was the group, not separated individuals, who would eventually return to the underworld place of origin. In the meantime, Pueblo caciques, ceremonial specialists bearing the wisdom of the ancient ones, led the rites that ensured the group's success in the natural cycles of planting, irrigating, harvesting, and hunting. The Pueblos cherished ceremony and dance in which dolls and kachina masks embodied corporate hopes and memories. The kachinas honored the ancient ones, who continued to ensure ample harvests and successful hunts.

The Hurons of southern Ontario and upper New York erected no sacred shrines like the Pueblo kivas. They viewed the sky as an overarching spirit and saw in every natural object, every hill and rock, every lake and river, a spirit – an *oki* – that could be friendly or unfriendly. The Huron creation story told about the first woman, Aataentsic, who had fallen from the sky onto the back of a great tortoise. Aataentsic's grandson Iouskeha, sometimes identified with the sun, not only created the lakes and rivers, but also filled nature with wild game and caused the crops to grow. Unlike his grandmother, who brought disease and death and reigned over the dead, he made the earth flourish. Huron rituals were designed to maintain harmony with this natural and yet supernatural world. They included a winter festival that symbolized their return to a chaotic primeval time that produced a flurry of dreams that could be narrated in ways that aided the sick and the weak, and similar rituals also sanctified every hunting expedition, fishing trip, or battle, events that the Hurons believed would continue in a life following death. The Hurons thought that occasional reburial of the dead in large ossuaries would ensure that the entire group would eventually rejoin in this afterlife; and their notion of dual souls – one animating the body and one transcending it – gave them a way to think of themselves as both traveling westward to join those who had died earlier and remaining in the ossuary as part of the larger community of souls awaiting rebirth.

The southern New England Wampanoags, the Massachusetts, and the Narragansetts had a mental world rooted in the soil, tradition, and the authority of ceremonial specialists. By the seventeenth century, they were farmers as well as hunters, and they expanded their symbolic world in the quest for harmony with the land. They had a creator deity, Cautantowwit, residing in the southwest, who had created from a tree the ancestors of all Indians and then sent to his followers corn and beans from his field in the southwest. To that warm and fruitful region, the souls of good men and women would one day return. Other spirits, however, dwelt within the sun and the moon, fire and water, and animals. These Algonkian speaking societies used the word manitou to designate spirits of the sky, the wind, the directions, corn, colors, and human beings; and they used ceremonies to acknowledge and control land that they co-owned with the spirits and with one another. Harvest and winter festivals distributed gifts ritually to the poor, especially at the time of planting, the appearance of green corn, and the harvest. These festivals followed the wisdom of their ancestors, who had handed down the rituals and transmitted knowledge about Cautantowwit. Gifted powwows, part-time religious specialists, extended this knowledge into the present and acted as healers, interpreted dreams, communed with spirits, and interpreted the future. These leaders derived their authority in part from their access, through dreams, to the Manitou Hommamock, or Chepi, and other spirits who conveyed knowledge and power.

Such beliefs enhanced unity within the groups, although there could be conflicts among contestants for religious leadership, and religion also marked lines of demarcation with other Native American societies. Conflicts among groups, which in some regions were frequent, had ritual dimensions. In addition, converts to Christianity often found themselves as objects of opprobrium from other groups. But conversion was relatively rare; the *Jesuit Relations* in New France reported an Indian claim that the French God was adequate for the French, but the God who created the world of the French did not create the world of the Indians. They had their own creator. The Pueblos who revolted against the Spanish in 1680 acted after Franciscans persuaded the Spanish state to abolish the Pueblo sacred sites. The differences in religious thought encapsulated the wide scope of cultural differences that complicated Native American and European relationships.

ROMAN CATHOLICS

The first European religious groups to appear in America were the Catholic missionaries who began to arrive in the sixteenth century and eventually spread out over the continent, from the Atlantic to the Pacific coasts. The

Catholics shared a common allegiance to the doctrines of the Council of Trent (1545–63), which declared, in opposition to the Protestant reformers, that justification (God's favor) came not solely from grace through faith, but also from God's prevenient grace that enabled the will to choose the good, from the administration of sacraments (especially baptism, the Holy Eucharist, and penance), from true belief (understood mainly as assent to church teachings), and from works of love and charity. Trent confirmed a sacramental system that accompanied the Christian from infant baptism to extreme unction at the time of death. The council also insisted that scripture and tradition were coequal authorities and that bishops, especially the bishop of Rome, had the special duty of defining doctrine and preserving the deposit of faith that Jesus conveyed to the apostles. Catholic theologians therefore opposed the Protestant ideology of "private judgment," which asserted that anyone could properly interpret the Bible. John Carroll (1735–1815), the first American bishop, observed that most men and women lacked the training or ability to "judge for themselves" in religious matters. Yet Carroll also wrote in 1784 that "rational investigation" was as open to Catholics as to anyone else, and the Catholic Church in colonial America was no site of monolithic consensus.

The sixteenth- and seventeenth-century Catholic missionaries to America represented different religious orders, and the Franciscans who led the mission in New Spain often worked with fervent millennial expectations that distinguished them from the Jesuits.

They also did not share the suspicions of Roman control that sometimes marked the Jesuit mission, especially in Maryland, where Jesuits arrived in 1634. Jesuits like Isaac Jogues (1607–46) in New France, moreover, urged the missionaries to adapt themselves to Native American cultures as much as possible; Franciscans in New Spain were more wary of cultural adaptation.

Moreover, the seventeenth- and early eighteenth-century baroque devotionalism of Catholics like Alonso de Benavides (1588–1635) in New Spain, with its emphasis on penitence, sin, relics, and indulgences, differed significantly in tone from the later, more humanistic, more republican form of Catholicism represented by Carroll at the end of the colonial era. The leader of the seventeenth-century Jesuit mission to Maryland, Andrew White (1579–1656), had suffered expulsion from his teaching post in Belgium because of his conservatism and the fervor of his defense of Thomas Aquinas' theology. The sermons of eighteenth-century Jesuits in Maryland, however, avoided both the predestinarian theology of the Thomists, the rigor of the French Jansenists, and the mystical piety of the French Quietists, promoting instead a humanistic tradition that saw virtuous living as the best sign of piety.

ANGLICANS

The Anglican Christians who came to Virginia in 1607 knew from the outset that they were members of a divided communion. The first minister, Robert Hunt, once remarked that reformers back in England who objected to the use of traditional vestments should come to Virginia, where Hunt inaugurated a "low church" tradition that ignored such disputes. Located mainly in the southern and Middle Colonies but also present in New England, Anglicans irritated other traditions by questioning the validity of their churches and ministers. The most learned colonial Anglican theologian, for example, Samuel Johnson (1696–1772), rector in Stratford, Connecticut, and the first president of King's College in New York, argued, after his defection from New England Congregationalism, that a true church required the authority of bishops and the threefold order of bishops, priests, and deacons. He also contended that salvation normally required the sacraments. Along with the Anglican polemicist John Checkley (1680–1753) in Boston, Johnson made forays against the Calvinist doctrine of predestination, using mainly biblical exegesis, but supplementing it with an idealist philosophy closely related to the thought of George Berkeley (1685–1753), who spent two years in Rhode Island. Johnson's *Ethices Elementa* (1746) exemplified the influence of British moral philosophy on Anglican theology.

Colonial Anglicans, however, had their own internal tensions, and Johnson represented some of them. An admirer of Archbishop William Laud in England, he espoused a "high church" theology that can be contrasted to Virginia's "low church" style and the revivalist forms of Anglicanism promoted by the revivalist George Whitefield (1715–70), whose seven trips to America kept him in the colonies for twelve years. Whitefield's Calvinism, as well as his revivalist style, also drew rebukes from Anglican theologians in the South, who followed in the tradition of Thomas Bray (1656–1730), a commissary (bishop's representative) who stressed the importance of baptism and attributed salvation to both faith and ethical obedience. Alexander Garden (1685–1756) in South Carolina also opposed Whitefield's "Calvinistical scheme," insisting on good works, along with faith, as a condition of salvation. The South Carolina Anglican Samuel Quincy carried the Anglican emphasis on virtue to its logical conclusion in his *Twenty Sermons* (1750), which presented Christianity as a rational religion consisting "principally" in moral goodness. Devereux Jarratt (1733–1801) in Virginia found such views widespread among Anglican clergy, although he tried to work out a compromise that rejected predestination but held on to notions of human inability and sinfulness.

A lofty regard for reason led Anglican theologians like Quincy to adopt a "latitudinarian" (or relaxed) view of doctrinal correctness. Bishop James Madison in Virginia (1749–1812) and William Smith (1727–1803) in Philadelphia even tried during the 1780s to omit the ancient Nicene and Athanasian creeds from the Prayer Book. Their chief antagonists were the high church theologians in the North – such men as Thomas Bradbury Chandler (1726–90) and Samuel Seabury (1729–96) – who claimed that creedal allegiance, a properly ordained ministry, and the apostolic succession of bishops were necessary for a true church. The most influential Anglican theologian of the period, William White (1748–1836) of Philadelphia, tried to hold these feuding parties together, and his 1782 defense of episcopal theology and polity guided much of the thinking behind the forming of the Protestant Episcopal Church in 1789. White's opposition to Calvinism helped ensure that it would have little appeal within the new denomination. But divisions among latitudinarians like Quincy, revivalists like Jarratt, Calvinists like Whitefield, traditionalists like White, and high church theologians like Johnson and Seabury created divisions within Anglicanism that would prove to be long lived.

CONGREGATIONAL CALVINISTS

The most extensive body of religious thought that endures in printed form came from the Calvinist theologians of New England, who began arriving in 1620. In the early seventeenth century, six Puritan clerics – John Cotton (1584–1652) in Boston, Thomas Hooker (c. 1586–1647) in Hartford, Thomas Shepard (1604–49) in Cambridge, John Norton (1603–63) in Ipswich, Peter Bulkeley (1583–1659) in Concord, and Richard Mather (1596–1669) in Dorchester – laid out the essentials of the Calvinist covenant theology. Later in the century, Increase Mather (1639–1723), Cotton Mather (1663–1728), and Samuel Willard (1640–1707) in Boston defended the older orthodoxy in the face of emerging Enlightenment criticisms. In the early eighteenth century, Jonathan Edwards (1703–58) in Northampton – the most sophisticated of the colonial Christian theologians – elaborated a synthesis of Calvinist and Enlightenment themes that attracted disciples long after the colonial period had ended.

At the center of religious thought in New England was the traditional Christian idea of a transcendent Trinitarian God. In sermons and technical theological treatises, New England Puritans either spoke of God using the language of the Bible or they referred to him as the Being who was "increated" rather than a creature, "infinite" rather than finite, or the "First Being," or "Being itself," rather than a derivative being. This Calvinist

God exercised absolute control over both the natural and social worlds as well as the dominions of angels, whether good or fallen. Nothing occurred outside the scope of divine providence. Fortunately, this God, who could be wrathful, was essentially gracious and loving; and he therefore accommodated himself to human finitude, first through his incarnation in Jesus, then through such "means of grace" as biblical revelation, sermons and sacraments, and the gift of a covenantal relationship.

The covenant provided the dominant image of New England Calvinist theology. According to the covenant theology, God initially offered Adam and Eve a covenant of works, through which their obedience might be saving. When they failed to obey God's law and fell into a sinfulness that marked all their posterity, God responded with a covenant of grace, requiring only faith in the saving efficacy of Jesus' death on the cross. Through that sacrifice, the elect – those chosen from eternity to enjoy eternal life – could hope for ultimate rescue from the perils of death and the sorrows of earthly existence. Calvinists assured themselves that God promised, at least to the faithful elect, ultimate and eternal protection from the terrors of hell.

Puritan theologians could agree on several implications of covenantal thought. They agreed that the covenant of grace meant that salvation required no more than true faith. They agreed that the two Protestant sacraments, baptism and the Lord's Supper, functioned as seals of the covenant. And they agreed that they should ground their churches on explicit covenants among the members. They also agreed that this covenantal view was in accord with the thinking of the primitive church described in the New Testament, which they had an obligation to restore. But on a host of other issues, the New Englanders could not agree.

In the seventeenth century, New England religious thinkers debated dozens of issues. Did God prepare the heart for conversion by driving the soul to contrition and humiliation, and did Puritan preachers therefore have the obligation to preach in ways that evoked terror? Or would such sermons only cast people into despair and distraction? Did a sense of "legal humiliation" – a sorrowful awareness that one flouted God's law – constitute a saving work in the soul, as Thomas Hooker for a time thought? Or, as most other ministers believed, was this humiliation merely a work of "common grace" that did not signal a true faith? When Christians looked to their sanctified lives for assurance that they stood among the elect, were they implicitly relying on the "covenant of works" and thus abandoning the central Protestant conviction of justification by grace alone? Anne Hutchinson in Boston thought that most of the preachers, John Cotton apart, had fallen away from this Protestant core. But the ministers replied that she and other similar antinomians had ignored the distinction between a habit of faith infused into the soul by the Holy Spirit and an act of faith that realized and perfected the habit, and they also insisted that the New Testament described love and obedience as the fruits of a genuine faith. The dispute tore Boston apart.

Puritans also disagreed about the church. Roger Williams wanted a statement of separation from the Church of England; most preferred not to define themselves as separatists. Williams also called for religious liberty; most found the idea too threatening. A tiny minority concluded that infant baptism was unbiblical; the majority used covenantal ideas to oppose these Baptists, although for a time the colony also used physical force against some of them. Many of the clergy argued that church membership should be limited only to apparently genuine "saints" who had undergone spiritual rebirth, although they also included the children of the saints within the church covenant; others concluded in a 1662 synod that a specified group of the unconverted could enjoy what amounted to a partial membership. By the end of the century, Solomon Stoddard in Northampton offered full membership rights to all believing and moral Christians; Increase and Cotton Mather led the opposition to Stoddardeanism, but the controversy continued into the following century. Finally, the Puritans disagreed about the end of the world. Some argued that the world stood on the brink of a millennial era – a thousand years of peace and righteousness – whereas others were suspicious of millennial ideas. The millenarians themselves disagreed about the timing of the millennial period and whether Christ's return would precede or follow it.

In the eighteenth century, the debates proliferated. Some clergy felt safe in accenting "the light of reason"; others viewed them as dangerous rationalists. Some concluded that moral effort could make salvation more likely; most others accused them of Arminianism, the denial of the doctrine of election. During the revivals of the Great Awakening, some of the revivalists accused more lukewarm clergy of abandoning justification by faith, forgetting that God prepared the soul by humiliating it, and denying that the Spirit offered immediate assurance of faith. Their opponents accused the revivalists of unnecessarily preaching terror, imposing a rigid preparatory scheme on the doctrine of conversion, and subverting Christian morality.

The disputes over revivalism drew the attention of Jonathan Edwards, who defended the revivals in his *Treatise on Religious Affections* (1746), but who also opposed extreme revivalists who seemed to forget that the best sign of true religion was a "disinterested benevolence," or a selfless love of the neighbor and of a God who was to be loved for his intrinsic beauty rather than for selfish ends. Edwards engaged most of the issues of his time: he opposed British deists who denied the necessity for a special biblical revelation, defended the doctrine of original sin against its Enlightenment opponents, elaborated a Calvinist view of the freedom of the will over against more expansive Arminian conceptions of freedom, took a millenarian position in the debates over the end-times, laid out a Christian view of true virtue in opposition to British moralists who downplayed the necessity of divine grace in the moral life, and argued against the ecclesiology of his grandfather Stoddard. His struggle to tighten membership standards helped cost him his pulpit in Northampton, but his use of idealist philosophy and an enlightened theory of beauty to define the nature of God continued to draw scholarly attention.

Edwards' disciples, the theologians of the New Divinity, especially Joseph Bellamy (1719–90) and Samuel Hopkins (1721–1803), expanded on the Edwardsean theme of disinterested benevolence. Hopkins even insisted that the best sign of election was a willingness to be damned for the glory of God. The New Divinity theologians capitalized on an older distinction between moral inability and natural ability to justify a revivalist theology that would limit church membership to the truly faithful. The unconverted had the natural ability to repent; they simply lacked the moral will to do it. Such declarations incurred the opposition of both New England "liberals" like Jonathan Mayhew (1720–66) and Charles Chauncy (1705–87) and the self-appointed Old Calvinists like Moses Hemmenway (1735–1811) and William Hart (1713–84), who insisted that the Edwardsean position failed to recognize the positive side of self-regard and unduly minimized the means of grace in the church, which could nurture true faith in nominal members. The liberals had begun to doubt the Calvinism that Edwards represented; the Old Calvinists disliked Edwardsean metaphysics and the New Divinity restrictions on church membership. The argument would continue through the first half of the nineteenth century.

PRESBYTERIANS

Colonial Presbyterians shared in the Calvinist tradition, but that did not prevent conflict among them. One faction expanded on English Puritan perspectives, whereas another looked to Scottish and Scotch-Irish precedents, although the ethnic division was not airtight. Both groups of Presbyterians differed from their Congregationalist competitors mainly by virtue of the greater authority they gave to presbyteries and synods to regulate congregations. Like the Congregationalists, they were prone to internal debate that split the denomination. In 1706, seven Presbyterian ministers, led by the Scottish itinerant Francis Makemie, created the Presbytery of Philadelphia as an agency of solidarity, but by 1741 the denomination divided into Old Side and New Side factions, separated by disputes that emerged chiefly during the Great Awakening.

The ablest Presbyterian theologian was a Yale graduate, Jonathan Dickinson (1688–1747), who settled in Elizabethtown, New Jersey. The author of the 1732 treatise *The Reasonableness of Christianity* and an advocate of both natural and revealed theology, Dickinson also defended, in his *Five Points: The True Scripture-Doctrine Concerning Some Important Points of Christian Faith* (1741), the essentials of Calvinism. At least one theologian ranked it as one of the three outstanding treatises on Calvinist thought published in eighteenth-century America, fully equal to the earlier defenses of John Norton and Samuel Willard in the seventeenth century. But Dickinson felt alarmed by what he saw as excesses by some Calvinist revivalists, and he tried to take a moderate position in the Presbyterian disputes.

In those disputes, the New Side clergy defended the revival, whereas the Old Side raised questions about it. Both sides believed that true doctrine was at stake. The New Side theologians found in the opposition to the revival dangerous errors about original sin, the new birth, and justification by faith alone. Gilbert Tennent (1703–64) of New Brunswick, New Jersey, spoke for the New Side when he said that the purpose of theology was to promote an "experimental" knowledge that embraced the will and affections, and he therefore urged that preachers attend to the stages of regeneration, an emphasis he might have derived from the Dutch Reformed pastor Theodore Frelinghuysen. But John Thomson (c. 1690–1753) in Delaware spoke for the Old Side when he denied that regeneration occurred in a set manner. Tennent believed that conviction of sin invariably preceded regeneration; Thomson argued that the preaching of "the law's terrors" should remain secondary to the encouraging promises of the gospel. Tennent worried about overemphasis on happiness and self-love in Old Side preaching; Thomson said that a proper self-love was natural and acceptable. Tennent insisted on an immediate witness of the Spirit to the regenerate; Thomson thought that assurance of regeneration normally came through holiness and humility. The New Side wanted ministers to be examined on their religious experience; the Old Side was more interested in their doctrine. The division of the church over such issues lasted for seventeen years.

BAPTISTS AND ANABAPTISTS

With their main origins in the British Puritan tradition, the Baptists, who insisted on pure churches of faithful adults, appeared in New England even before Roger Williams (1603–83) helped establish the first Baptist congregation at Providence, Rhode Island, around 1638. Ten years later John

Clarke (1609–76) in Newport, Rhode Island, was representing a Particular Baptist tradition known for its Calvinist insistence that Christ died only for particular persons (the elect), that salvation was entirely a divine gift, and that men and women lacked the free will to choose for Christ without special saving grace. But no singular form of Calvinist theology dominated the early Baptist movement. By the 1740s, Isaac Backus (1724–1806) of Norwich, Connecticut, was defending a form of Calvinism that insisted on a limited atonement (Christ died only for the elect) and gave covenantal thought a Baptist interpretation, but he also employed the Edwardsean distinction between natural ability and moral inability, repeated Edwardsean theories of free will, and opposed any antinomian impulse to disregard the law. Backus also became widely known for his defense of religious liberty. In 1742, the Philadelphia Baptist Association adopted the Second London Confession (1667) of English Calvinistic Baptists, and this document remained authoritative for many colonial Baptists.

From an early period, however, Baptists also taught an anti-Calvinist theology that had roots in the writings of the founder of the movement, John Smyth (c. 1544–1612) in Holland, who had eventually denied original sin and insisted that Christ died for all. Smyth taught that the preventing grace of the Spirit gave every adult the ability to believe, but that the will could resist the Spirit's prompting. The belief that Christ died for everyone, or that the atonement had a general or universal scope, marked the General Baptist movement in England that grew out of Smyth's congregation, and by 1652 the General Baptists were spreading in Rhode Island, from where they eventually reached the South. Similar anti-Calvinist impulses emerged by the mid-eighteenth century, and in 1778 Benjamin Randall, a lay exhorter, preached in Durham, New Hampshire, that God offered "assisting grace" freely to everyone. The church that emerged from Randall's teachings, the Free Will Baptists, found inspiration in the writings of Henry Alline (1748–84) from Nova Scotia, whose *Two Mites Cast into the Offering of God, for the Benefit of Mankind* (1781) taught an eclectic mixture of themes from the English Methodist John Wesley, the Anglican William Law, and the poet John Milton and also promoted a speculative mysticism combined with esoteric ideas popular in English occult circles.

For some Baptists, however, neither a Calvinist nor an Arminian version of theology proved sufficient. The self-educated John Leland (1754–1841), who battled against the Anglican establishment in Virginia and the Congregational establishment in Massachusetts, not only found the Edwardseans unappealing, but also claimed that he was able to combine "sovereign grace" and "a little of what is called Arminianism." He thought of sinners as laboring under a natural, not merely a moral, necessity to sin and as lacking both the desire and the power to repent, but he saw no need to affirm a rigorous Calvinism.

Baptists also disagreed about the authority of confessional statements. Especially the Separate Baptists, some of whom moved southward after breaking away from Congregational churches in the 1740s, refused to subscribe to the Philadelphia confession, insisting that the Bible was their sole source of authority. This created tensions with the Regular Baptists, who favored subscription, although by 1787 the two groups were reaching compromises that permitted the Separates to subscribe "in substance."

John Smyth's theology had developed during his discussion with Dutch Anabaptists, but the Anabaptist movement differed in substantial ways from the British and American Baptists. Like the Baptists, the continental Anabaptists saw the church as a community of faithful believers separate from the state and from the world. Beginning in 1683, Dutch and Swiss Mennonites, followers of the Dutch Anabaptist leader Menno Simons (c. 1496–1561), migrated to Germantown, Pennsylvania, under the leadership of Francis Daniel Pastorius and then spread into Lancaster County and beyond. What distinguished them from the Baptists was their rejection of violence and legal oaths. Calling for conversion as a "new creature," intent on enduring peaceful suffering, hoping for a restoration of the fallen creation, and celebrating the Supper of the Lord as its symbolic foreshadowing, the Mennonites made a mild use of the "ban," or excommunication of the apostate, in order to maintain the purity of the church.

Even the Mennonites, however, could not avoid conflict with other Anabaptist groups. In particular, the Amish – the Swiss and Alsatian French followers of Jakob Amman – separated from Mennonites in those regions and called for an even more rigorous mode of living the Christian life. Arriving in Pennsylvania shortly after 1710, the Amish emphasized self-denial and submission to the authority of the church. They practiced an uncompromising observance of the ban through strict shunning of sinful church members. Distinguished also by their ritual of foot washing, the untrimmed beards of their men, and the starkly simple attire of their women, the group maintained a suspicious distance from the main body of Mennonites.

LUTHERANS AND MORAVIANS

The Swedish Lutherans who came to New Sweden on the Delaware River in 1638 followed the teachings of Martin Luther, including his doctrine of justification by faith alone, the sole authority of scripture in religious matters, and the saving efficacy of baptism and the Lord's Supper, in which the body of Christ was corporeally present. They shared also Luther's tolerance for traditional ceremonies, and their services had a medieval coloration, with vestments and church decoration that Reformed, or Calvinist, groups found objectionable. Among colonial Lutherans, however, the main divisions appeared in the tension between the Pietists and the Orthodox. The Pietist traditions associated with Philipp Jakob Spener and August Hermann Francke in Germany found theological expression in the colonies as early as 1708, when Justus Falckner (1672–1723), a graduate of the pietistic Halle University, published his *Fundamental Instruction*, exalting the truth of "scripture alone" and the need for "rebirth." The arrival in 1742 of Henry Melchior Muhlenberg (1711–87) set the Pietist tone for colonial Lutheranism. He defended the Pietist emphasis on conviction of sin, repentance, the experience of rebirth, and good works as the necessary fruits of faith. In alliance with Muhlenberg, the Philadelphia and Germantown pastor Peter Brunnholtz prepared in 1749 an edition of Martin Luther's *Small Catechism* to which he affixed an "order of salvation," which outlined the typical Pietist stages of saving experience, from conviction of sin to sanctification. John C. Kuntze (1744–1807) treated the whole of the catechism as if it were an order of salvation, moving from knowledge of the law to faith in the gospel. Colonial Lutheran theology by 1708 was deeply Pietist.

Yet Pietism had no monopoly. On the one side were Orthodox theologians like William Berkmeyer and Peter Sommer in New York, who suspected the Pietists of indifference to purity of doctrine. The Orthodox wanted to preserve not only the essentials of Luther's theology but also the positions taken in such documents as the Formula of Concord (1577), which opposed any form of doctrinal compromise. On the other side were more rationalistic Lutherans like Frederick Henry Quitman (1760–1832), a pastor in Rhinebeck, New York, who sought to justify Christianity with arguments from reason, history, and experience. For the rationalists it was important that the teachings of Jesus coincided with the evidence of design and order in nature, and they sought rational proofs for the validity of biblical revelation. To them, it was the "liberal and catholic spirit" of the gospel that commended it, and Quitman did not hesitate to depart from Luther's theology on such issues as moral depravity, absolute divine decrees, and the idea that the atonement of Christ satisfied God's wrath.

Muhlenberg faced not only tensions within Lutheranism, but also strife with the Moravian leader Nikolaus Ludwig Graf von Zinzendorf (1700–60), who also had roots in Lutheran Pietism. Traveling in America in 1741–43, Zinzendorf and a number of other missionaries, including women like Anna Nitschmann, tried to convince German Protestants to join in a union that transcended confessional differences and grounded itself in a "religion of the heart" that came from intimate association with Christ. Proclaiming an emotional "blood and wounds" theology, the Moravian missionaries saw the crucified Christ as the sole means of knowing God and added that the incarnation made every human experience potentially sanctified. The purpose of the Moravian missions was to prepare the way for the second coming of Christ by spreading the gospel throughout the world. Zinzendorf and other Moravians influenced the Methodist founder John Wesley, but to Muhlenberg the Moravians appeared as seducers, and their churches in America remained separate from Lutheran groups.

FRIENDS AND SHAKERS

Two missionaries from the Society of Friends, or the Quakers, Mary Fisher and Ann Austin, arrived in Boston as early as 1656 and spent five weeks in prison before being shipped out of the colony; but scores of Quaker missionaries – with a large majority of women among them – made their way into New England and elsewhere, spreading out along the East Coast. Despite persecution and even hangings, they became, for a time, one of the largest religious groups in the colonies. The Quaker founder George Fox (1624–91) toured America in 1672–73, preaching the movement's central ideas: the Inner Light of Christ within the soul, the claim that scripture could be understood only with the help of this Inner Light, the necessity of both faith and strenuous inner effort to reach salvation, the need for humility, and the importance of pacifism. But by the time William Penn (1644–1718) arrived in America for a short stay in 1682, it was already clear that the Quakers shared no doctrinal consensus. Already in the seventeenth century, some Quakers – especially the followers of the Englishman Robert Barclay (1648–90) – stood closer to the older Protestantism, whereas those who followed the tradition of Mary Dyer's (d. 1660) speech to the General Court of Massachusetts before her execution relied more on the light of Christ within as a source of authority. Penn stood somewhere in between.

Despite a universal rejection of the Calvinist doctrine of predestination, early Quaker thought churned with inner tensions. Some Quakers cited the Bible as an authority; others joined them while insisting that it remain subordinate to the light within; and still others seemed to deprecate the "outward letter." Penn thought that the Inner Light could enlighten even men and women who had never read scripture. Some Quakers sought external evidences of revelation; others insisted on relying solely on the inward apprehension of the Spirit. Some emphasized the eternal Christ dwelling within the faithful; others took care to note that the Christ within and Christ without were "one and the same." Some dwelt on human sinfulness and attributed salvation to a grace passively received; others could see no possibility of salvation apart from a sanctification of the heart that occurred gradually through spiritual discipline. In the eighteenth century, they moved toward a quietist style in worship that encouraged them to wait in silence for divine inspirations, although they also moved in this period toward the social activism of John Woolman and others who had a yearning for holiness that sparked activism against slavery and for peace. After the colonial period, these tensions reappeared in forms that split the Quaker movement.

Even more confident than the Quakers in the possibilities of inner revelation were the Shakers, who followed the teachings of Ann Lee (1736–84) after she arrived in America in 1774 and soon formed a small community in Niskeyuna, New York. The creative period came after 1790, but in that year Joseph Meacham began to outline the dispensations that led to "the second appearance of Christ" in Ann Lee's movement, and soon her insistence on celibacy, self-denial, and obedience to her teachings set the foundation for a nineteenth-century flowering. For the Shakers, the immediate revelations of God to Ann Lee eventually provided justification for setting her alongside Jesus as one "anointed" by the Spirit. Despite some internal tensions, the Shakers maintained their unity, but they later drew opposition when they tried to attract adherents from the southern revivals.

METHODISTS AND UNIVERSALISTS

Between 1764 and 1766, Irish lay preachers formed local Methodist societies in Maryland and New York; and in 1784 the Methodists became a denomination separate from the Anglicans, presenting themselves as a church for the common people. A revivalist movement, the Methodists pressed on their hearers three special doctrines: the necessity of a new birth, the inner assuring witness of the Spirit, and "holiness of heart and life." Following the teachings of their Anglican founder John Wesley, they proclaimed justification by faith but also insisted on a process of sanctification that could lead to "entire sanctification" or "Christian perfection," which they defined as wholehearted love of God and the neighbor. They published little theology during the colonial period, but it quickly became evident that their arch opponents would be the Calvinists on the one side and the Universalists on the other. Methodists taught a doctrine of general atonement – Christ died for all – but they did not want their hearers to confuse it with universal salvation.

Universalist teaching emerged in New England as early as the seventeenth century. Samuel Gorton (c. 1592–1677) in Rhode Island and John Rogers (1648–1721) in Connecticut, the members of the Ephrata Society under Conrad Beissel (1691–1768) in Pennsylvania, and George de

Benneville (1703–93) in Germantown preached universalist doctrines. The liberal Charles Chauncy (1705–87) in Boston also reached the conclusion that all would eventually know salvation. But it was not until John Murray (1741–1815) and Judith Sargent Stevens Murray (1751–1820) in Boston began spreading universalist ideas after 1770 that a Universalist denomination began to emerge. The Murrays taught that God beheld all humanity "in Christ" from the beginning of creation and that his death on the cross therefore saved everyone. The universalists argued by weaving together biblical texts, often read allegorically, but divisions surfaced as soon as Elhanan Winchester (1751–97), a Universalist preacher in Philadelphia, criticized Murray's notion of universal election and substituted for it a doctrine of universal grace that would enable a free decision from every person. Everyone would accept the offer of salvation, either in this life or the next, even if some would undergo years of punishment after death before they finally agreed. Murray accused Winchester of teaching a "purgatorial satisfaction" that detracted from the "finished redemption" of Christ, although Murray also believed that the sinful would suffer for a time after they died. Universalists battled among themselves at the same time as they took on Methodists and Calvinists.

SEPHARDIC AND ASHKENAZIC JEWS

Standing apart from the majority forms of religious thought in America, colonial Jews also could not entirely escape the centrifugal force of conflict. The first Jews to form a synagogue arrived in 1654 in New Netherland. They were Sephardic Jews who traced their origins to earlier expulsions from the Iberian Peninsula, and they arrived without a rabbi, but they soon did have a Torah scroll, at least for a while; and despite Dutch reluctance, they attained permission to worship, initially in private homes but by the beginning of the eighteenth century in public synagogues. Their observance consisted of the traditional prayers on the Sabbath, adherence to the dietary laws, oversight of a cemetery and ritual bath, and celebration of at least some of the traditional holidays, but they lacked the resources that would permit full conformity to Jewish law and custom. By the mid-eighteenth century, moreover, the Sephardim were joined by Ashkenazic Jews from Central and Eastern Europe, whose growing numbers brought them enhanced authority in the five synagogues that existed in coastal cities and Philadelphia by the 1750s. Jews were committed to Jewish peoplehood and to the worship of one God, but diverse Jewish origins – and the absence of authoritative rabbis – entailed differences over the details of dietary law, the language of worship, and even the precise hours of the Sabbath. The need to avoid offending the Christian majority also created worries about relations to the larger society, a problem that required constant decisions about the degree of compromise that should be allowed.

ECLECTICISM

An indeterminate number of colonists had no reluctance to draw on multiple traditions and place them in new combinations. Groups like the Society of the Woman in the Wilderness (1697ff.) in Pennsylvania blended pagan and Christian ideas by incorporating astrological amulets, alchemy, and hermetic traditions into their religious routines. Beissel's Ephrata community combined Baptist practice with esoteric traditions that included notions of an androgynous God. Even earnest Lutherans could also make use of folk magic without seeing themselves as departing from Lutheran orthodoxy. The eclectic impulse could sometimes be modest, consisting of isolated practices that did not alter adherence to the traditional Christian system, or it could sometimes produce combinations that stood on the margins, or outside the circle, of more conventional communities. When these eclectics diverged too far from the convictions of their neighbors, they sometimes fell into conflict with them.

ENLIGHTENMENT

Historians have long debated about the influence of the European Enlightenment on religious Americans. It is clear that enlightened ideas contributed to an American deism. As early as 1700, Cotton Mather in Boston was attempting to refute English deists, and by 1712 he feared that deism might be rampant in the colonies. It was not, but the deist position – which at its core was the denial of any supernatural biblical revelation – did gain adherents during the colonial period, including some of the founding figures who led the Revolution. But even deists in America were a diverse lot, ranging from Benjamin Franklin (1706–90) and Thomas Jefferson (1743–1826), who excoriated dogma but attended church and admired the morality of Jesus, to Ethan Allen (1738–89) and Elihu Palmer (1764–1806), who decried "Christian superstition."

The American Enlightenment, moreover, often assumed moderate forms that proved to be compatible with both liberal and evangelical forms of Christianity. Liberal New England clergy in the mid-eighteenth century drew on Enlightenment philosophers to question Calvinist dogmas; Calvinists like Jonathan Edwards made creative adaptations of Enlightenment thought; and even evangelical Protestants, with their emphasis on experience and the evidences of Christianity, showed the influence of the new spirit in European intellectual life. Yet it remains true that the Enlightenment intensified the religious conflicts in America. The Enlightenment sought universals – universal truth and universal harmony – but colonial Americans were far too diverse and set in their opinions to abandon their differences. The theme of conflict does not tell the whole story, but it clarifies a substantial portion of it.[1]

SUGGESTIONS FOR FURTHER READING

Bozeman, Theodore Dwight. *To Live Ancient Lives: The Primitivist Dimension in Puritanism*. Chapel Hill, 1988.

Guelzo, Allen C. *Edwards on the Will: A Century of American Theological Debate*. Middletown, CT, 1989.

Holifield, E. Brooks. *Theology in America: Christian Thought from the Age of the Puritans to the Civil War*. New Haven, 2003.

Hultkranz, Ake. *The Religion of the American Indians*. Berkeley, 1979.

Noll, Mark A. *America's God: From Jonathan Edwards to Abraham Lincoln*. Oxford, UK, 2002.

Sarna, Jonathan. *American Judaism: A History*. New Haven, 2004.

Sernett, Milton C., ed. *African American Religious History*. New Haven, 2004.

Walters, Kerry S., ed. *The American Deists*. Lawrence, KS, 1992.

---

[1] To see most of the primary sources on which this essay is based, see E. Brooks Holifield, *Theology in America: Christian Thought from the Age of the Puritans to the Civil War* (New Haven, 2003).

33

PIETY AND PRACTICE IN NORTH AMERICA TO 1800

ERIK R. SEEMAN

A Narragansett woman beseeches the spirits of her ancestors to protect her newborn son. A Puritan carpenter prays to his God to help him avoid the temptation of sin after a long day of work. An Anglican couple in Virginia celebrates the baptism of their daughter within their humble home. African slaves in South Carolina solemnize the funeral of one of their companions by praying that her soul will return to Africa.

These imagined scenes illustrate the range of piety and religious practices in colonial North America, yet none of them takes place within a church. For the ordinary men and women of this period, the church represented only one landmark in a religious geography marked by numerous sites of engagement with the supernatural world. Yet this was not a changeless religious landscape. Over time many groups in colonial North America became increasingly influenced by Christianity.

This judgment draws on changes within the field of American religious history. At one time, many understood colonial America as synonymous with New England and Puritanism. More recently, historians of religion in early America have employed a broader geographical focus and have included laypeople as significant actors, drawing American Indians, Africans, and others into the narratives. This essay's analysis of the religious practices of ordinary men and women reflects this expanded scholarly agenda. Even among the groups examined here, however, the coverage is not encyclopedic. Four groups are described in detail: Algonquians in southern New England, Puritans in New England, Anglicans in the southern British colonies, and Africans in the plantation colonies.

This essay analyzes daily religious practices, occasional worship, calendrical rituals, and life-cycle rituals, including deathways: beliefs and practices associated with death, such as deathbed scenes, burials, funerals, and mourning customs. Deathways are an effective way to gauge the religious practices of the nonliterate majority, who did not leave written records, but who left behind material remains that hint at some of their deepest beliefs.

Overall, religious practices and rituals reveal the intimate connections between piety and everyday life. For all residents of the early modern world, there was no sharp division between sacred and secular such as we find today in the industrialized West. Religious belief emerged from and was shaped by the quotidian practices of childrearing, engaging with the natural world, laboring in fields or the home, and attending to the sick and the dead.

ALGONQUIANS OF SOUTHERN NEW ENGLAND

In the early seventeenth century, the Algonquians of southern New England – including Narragansetts, Wampanoags, Pequots, and Massachusetts – embraced a religion that centered on the concept of manitou or spiritual power. In this they were similar to other Algonquian peoples who ranged from present-day North Carolina to Nova Scotia to Michigan and beyond. Manitou imbued with power both the natural and the supernatural, including humans, animals, prominent topographical features, and spirits. Thus, individuals encountered manitou on a daily basis. Manitou, however, was not evenly distributed; some things had more manitou than others. As English colonist and ethnographer Roger Williams described the Narragansetts in 1643, "there is a generall Custome amongst them, at the apprehension of any Excellency in Men, Women, Birds, Beasts, Fish, &c. to cry out Manittóo, that is, it is a God," or more precisely, it contains spiritual power.[1] This "excellency" was the key to understanding the variability in the amount of manitou: the more extraordinary something was, the more manitou it contained.

The most extraordinary other-than-human beings were the spirits Cautantouwit and Hobbomok. Cautantouwit was a benign god who lived to the southwest. Not only had he created the world, but he also had given a kernel of corn to a crow, who then brought it to the Algonquians of southern New England, thereby establishing life-sustaining maize agriculture. The souls of the dead, when attended with the proper ritual treatment, journeyed to Cautantouwit's house in the southwest, a land of plenty and ease. More fearsome was Hobbomok. This was the god of the underworld, usually figured as an eel or a snake. A few English informants claimed that when bad Algonquians died their souls went to Hobbomok's realm, although some scholars wonder if this parallel with the Christian hell was a figment of colonists' imaginations. Either way, Hobbomok was associated with darkness and night, but he was not entirely or even largely malevolent. According to Plymouth Colony Governor Edward Winslow,

---

[1] Roger Williams, *A Key into the Language of America* (London, 1643), 126.

Hobbomok "as farre as wee can conceive is the Devill," yet "him they call upon to cure their wounds and diseases."[2]

Algonquian religious practice therefore focused on establishing positive reciprocal relationships with those beings and objects that contained the most manitou. Adolescent males used vision quests to seek out Hobbomok. A more frequent practice was the soul wandering that occurred during dreaming. Algonquians believed that each person had two souls: one that was located in the heart, and another – the "dream soul" – that was located in the head. The dream soul wandered in the spirit world while a person lay sleeping, returning with information gleaned about the forces of manitou. An important aspect of Algonquian religious practice was deciphering the meaning of dreams. From dreams individuals learned what might happen in the future, where lost objects lay hidden, and whether their religious rituals needed modification. Algonquians therefore had regular encounters with manitou through the act of dreaming.

Certain individuals gained renown for the frequency, vividness, or prescience of their dreams, which others believed demonstrated their power to interact with the supernatural world. These religious adepts fell into two categories: *pniesok* (the plural of *pniese*) and powwows. *Pniesok* directed their spiritual prowess toward preparation for and bold leadership in warfare. Their communication with the spirit world caused them to claim invulnerability to attack. Thus it was especially demoralizing when a *pniese* was killed in battle, as occasionally happened in wars against English colonists.

Powwows, by contrast, were not associated primarily with warfare. Instead, their supernatural power led them more into the realms of divination and healing. These men and women conjured great fear among the English colonists: one described them as "wizards and witches, holding familiarity with Satan, the evil one."[3] In one respect this contemptuous description was correct: powwows gained their powers by communicating with the supernatural world. They had especially powerful visions during which Hobbomok and other supernatural beings informed them of the source of a person's illness. This allowed the powwow to prescribe the appropriate curing rituals and herbal treatments. For the Algonquians of southern New England, as with native people elsewhere, the everyday experiences of sickness and healing were intimately bound up with the supernatural world.

Calendrical rituals were another class of religious practices. Unsurprising for an agricultural people, Algonquians performed many

---

[2] Edward Winslow, *Good Newes from New England* (London, 1624), 53.
[3] Quoted in Kathleen J. Bragdon, *Native People of Southern New England, 1500–1650* (Norman, OK, 1996), 201.

rituals that were closely tied to the rhythm of planting and harvest. Algonquians had annual feasts marking the first fruit in late spring, the first green corn in midsummer, and the harvest in autumn, as well as a two-week-long winter ritual that may have been associated with the lengthening of days after the shortest day of the year. Of this last, Roger Williams observed that "they run mad once a yeare in their kind of Christmas feasting."[4] English observers reported that nearly a thousand individuals would attend these calendrical feasts, where rituals offered thanks to the spirit world and helped ensure continued good harvests in the future. Nor should one imagine that these events were all solemnity simply because they involved invocations of other-than-human beings. At the harvest festivals there were ball games, dances, and the communal sharing of good food.

If calendrical rituals marked the cyclical progression from planting to harvest to replanting, life-cycle rituals likewise marked the progression from birth to death to rebirth. We know less about Algonquian childbirth rituals than other life-cycle traditions due to Englishmen's lack of interest in topics associated with women. Nonetheless, it is clear that newborn babies were first washed and then smeared with ashes. Although the exact meaning of these practices remains unclear, it is possible that both were associated with transitions between life stages, in this case between death and life. Likewise, both male and female adolescents underwent puberty rituals to mark the transition to adulthood. Again, little evidence for the female rite of passage exists, save for a mention of sequestration at first and subsequent menstruations. Boys, on the other hand, endured painful deprivations to offer evidence of their transition to adulthood. They were sent off into the forest, where they fasted and drank emetics in order to spur visions. During these vomit-induced visions, boys encountered other-than-human beings who served thenceforth as guardian spirits. Men would invoke these spirits throughout their lives when they needed assistance in hunting or warfare. Thus the once-in-a-lifetime experience of a puberty ritual led to a lifetime of daily encounters with one's guardian spirit.

The life-cycle rituals about which we know the most are those related to death. When an Algonquian person lay dying, his or her friends and relatives paid careful attention to the deathbed scene. Because of the highly charged nature of the event, with the individual on the boundary between this world and the next, encounters with the spirit world were common for both the dying and the observers. During deathbed scenes the dying person's loved ones made "loud lamentations" and were fond of "calling

---

[4] Williams, *Key into the Language*, 127.

to mind" the "good fortune" of the dying person.[5] These loud lamenters were usually women who had blackened their faces with soot. When the person died, the corpse was treated with respect by ritual specialists in order to help the soul enter the spirit world. The body was rubbed with red ochre and adorned with jewelry – more lavishly supplied, in fact, when the deceased was a youngster. Among the Narragansetts there was a person who was in charge of wrapping the corpse in mats made out of grasses and reeds.

The corpse was then placed into a shallow oval grave within a designated burial ground. The body was placed on its side, with its knees tightly flexed and pulled up to the chest, and the head pointed toward the southwest, in the direction of Cautantouwit's house. Mourners usually placed goods into the grave, not a great many, but with important symbolic associations. Some of these items were sex specific: women received hoes to symbolize their work tilling the earth, whereas men were more likely to receive tobacco pipes. The grave was then marked with some more of the deceased's personal items, sometimes placed underneath a small structure that looked like a miniature unthatched wigwam. A period of mourning then commenced. One colonist asserted that "to behold and hear their throbbing sobs and deep-fetcht sighs ... would draw tears from adamantine eyes."[6] Loved ones blackened their faces with soot to symbolize their grief. This period of mourning could last weeks or months.

In a village of five hundred persons, Algonquians enacted these deathways roughly twenty times a year. Factoring in the length of deathbed scenes, funerals, and mourning periods, this represented a nearly continual way – in addition to the manifold other ways in which Algonquians encountered manitou in their daily lives – that the Indians of southern New England experienced the powerful connections between this world and the spirit world.

NEW ENGLAND PURITANS

Like their Algonquian neighbors, the Puritans of seventeenth-century New England embraced a religion that was intertwined with the experience of daily life. Unlike Indians, Puritans left behind libraries full of their writings, so we have better evidence of their practices.

Puritans divided their experience of the divine into two broad categories: public ordinances and private devotions. In contrast to Algonquians,

---

[5] George Parker Winship, ed., *Sailors Narratives of Voyages along the New England Coast, 1524–1624* (Boston, 1905), 19.

[6] William Wood, *New Englands Prospect* (London, 1634), 104.

whose religious calendar was dictated by the yearly transition through the four seasons, Puritan public religious practice was structured by the weekly Sabbath. Puritans did have calendrical rituals, but in their eagerness to distance themselves from Catholicism they dispensed with virtually all of the holy days that had given the early modern European calendar its distinctive rhythms of feast and fast. For Puritans the Sabbath became the centerpiece of their public ordinances.

The Sabbath began with the ringing of the church bell to alert parishioners that worship was about to begin. Even though only those who had narrated a conversion experience could be full church members with the privilege of participating in the Lord's Supper (and, for men, voting in church affairs), the law required all community residents to attend weekly services or face a fine for nonattendance. But this did not happen frequently. Even though there were many "horse-shed" Christians – David D. Hall's term for those who spent the time between morning and afternoon services in the stable, talking about worldly rather than holy topics – there were very few New Englanders who avoided the religious and social offerings Sabbath services provided.

The service started at about 9:00 in the morning. The minister began the proceedings with a prayer that commonly lasted fifteen to thirty minutes, but could last much longer. Rev. Peter Thacher once wrote in his journal, "God was pleased graciously to assist mee much beyond my Expectation.... I was near an hour and halfe in my first prayer and my heart much drawne out in it."[7] It may seem incredible that a minister could pray for ninety minutes at a stretch, or that his parishioners would stay awake during that time. But the key to Puritan prayer was its extemporaneous nature. Puritans hated the set liturgy of the Church of England, arguing that the Book of Common Prayer had, as Thomas Shepard indelicately put it in 1653, "stunke above ground twice 40 yeeres, in the nostrills of many godly."[8] As a result, Puritan ministers made up their prayers as they went along, and when their hearts were "drawne out" it could be a powerful invocation of the divine.

After prayer the minister read a biblical passage and then expounded on it, "giving the sence, and applying the use" of it, according to Puritan minister John Cotton.[9] Next came the singing of a psalm or two. Then

---

[7] Charles E. Hambrick-Stowe, *The Practice of Piety: Puritan Devotional Disciplines in Seventeenth-Century New England* (Chapel Hill, 1982), 104–5.

[8] Thomas Shepard, *A Treatise of Liturgies, Power of the Keyes, and of Matter of the Visible Church* (London, 1653), 60–1.

[9] John Cotton, *The True Constitution of a Particular Visible Church, Proved by Scripture* (London, 1642), 6.

the minister delivered a lengthy sermon. Clergymen often wrote out their words in advance because a sermon ordinarily took the form of an argument, which benefitted from careful phrasing and multiple references to scripture. As a result, the sermon sometimes lacked the extemporaneous flair of the opening prayer. Nonetheless, pious laypeople paid close attention to the sermons, with some bringing small notebooks to church so they could jot down ideas for future study and edification.

Once a month the end of the sermon signaled the imminent approach of the Puritan saint's most profound moment of worship: the Lord's Supper. On Sabbaths when the Lord's Supper was scheduled, most of the congregation departed after the sermon. Remaining were only those full members who had offered a conversion narrative that testified that they believed they were among the elect or "visible saints." The minister blessed bread and broke it, offering it to the saints as a symbol of Christ's body. He then poured wine into a cup, said a prayer, and again offered it to the full members, this time as a symbol of Christ's blood. It is hard to exaggerate the importance of this ritual for lay Puritans. They approached the Lord's Table warily, frightened by Paul's admonition to the Corinthians that "he that eateth and drinketh unworthily, eateth and drinketh damnation to himself" (I Corinthians 11:29). Yet when laypeople conquered their fears, they were rewarded with an intense encounter with the "real presence" of Christ, not in the actual bread and wine, as Catholics believed, but in their own hearts.

This marked the end of the morning service. At 2:00 the congregation reconvened. Once again the minister offered a long prayer, the elder led a psalm, and the minister delivered another sermon. If there were candidates for baptism, the parents brought them forward. Next there was the collection for needy individuals, as the deacon stood up and said, "Brethren of the congregation, now there is time left for contribution, wherefore as God hath prospered you, so freely offer."[10] If there was church business to attend to, such as disciplinary matters, this was dealt with, and then the minister offered a final prayer and dismissed the congregation.

The weekly rhythm of Sabbath structured but did not delimit Puritan religious practice. For pious laypeople, what happened the other six days of the week was just as important. Prayer was the centerpiece of their religious practice. In private or with their families, pious men and women beseeched their God to forgive them, to prevent misfortune, and to heal themselves or their loved ones. As Captain Roger Clap wrote to his children shortly before his death in 1691, "Our Lord and Saviour bids us, 'Enter in our Closets, and shut the Door, and Pray to our Father in Secret.'

---

[10] Thomas Lechford, *Plain Dealing; or, Newes from New-England* (London, 1642), 18.

There you may tell God your very Hearts, and lay open to Him your worst Plague-Sore, your vilest Sins, which no Man knoweth, neither is it meet they should know."[11]

For some New Englanders who faced sickness and other troubles, however, prayer was not enough. Some individuals sought the aid of healers or diviners who offered an alternate path to the supernatural world. Most "cunning men" and "cunning women" practiced white magic, the benign arts of finding lost objects, telling fortunes, and offering magical cures. Ministers opposed such practices but did not get overly exercised about them. Black magic, on the other hand, involved invoking the devil in order to gain the power to harm others, and this was a capital offense in the colonies as it had been in England. That clergymen and magistrates took seriously the threat of black magic is evidenced not only by the hysteria that gripped Salem in 1692, but also by the roughly sixteen other executions for witchcraft that occurred before then.[12]

But most New Englanders did not, it seems, resort to black magic, Nathaniel Hawthorne's short stories notwithstanding. Instead, they opened their "worst Plague-Sores" to God through prayer and, for an especially devoted minority, through journal keeping. The number of extant spiritual journals is greater for the eighteenth than the seventeenth century, which likely reflects the increased prosperity of the society and the resultant greater availability of paper. Still, as the seventeenth century progressed, greater numbers of men and women used spiritual journals to record their daily hopes and fears, to mark notable occurrences such as births and deaths, and to write down key ideas from pious books they read. Another form of religious practice increased as New England became wealthier: reading devotional manuals, printed sermons, and biographies of especially devout Protestant saints.

These daily practices were punctuated by occasional calendrical rituals, which were of much less importance than in Catholic and Algonquian societies but still connected religious practice with seasonality. Puritans rejected Christmas and other Catholic holidays as profane inventions; Samuel Sewall cheerfully noted in his diary when shops were open as usual on 25 December. Yet New Englanders were willing to tie religious practice to the rhythms of the agricultural calendar. They appointed a day of fasting and humiliation every spring planting time, when they were pinched by low food supplies and at the mercy of their God to provide them with

---

[11] *Memoirs of Capt. Roger Clap: Relating Some of God's Remarkable Providences to Him* (Boston, 1731), 31–2.
[12] John Putnam Demos, *Entertaining Satan: Witchcraft and the Culture of Early New England* (New York, 1982), 402–9.

sustenance. Then in early November, with the harvest completed and larders well stocked, Puritans celebrated a day of thanksgiving. This was marked not by turkey and cranberry sauce, but by solemn prayers of thanks in public and private.

Of even greater significance were life-cycle rituals. Baptism shows how laypeople, women in particular, used church rituals to negotiate their own spiritual needs. Women were the parent who most commonly brought children to the sacrament of baptism. Even though no minister claimed that baptism could help a child get into heaven, women acted as if it did: they rushed their newborn infants to the font, with half of all children baptized within their first seven days of life.[13]

At the other end of the life course, funeral rituals became increasingly central to religious practice in early New England. The first Puritans who came to New England brought with them the radically simplified burial practices of the first generations of Reformed Protestants. As Martin Luther argued, because God had predestined the final estate of all humans, postmortem prayers and ceremonies made not a whit of difference in whether the deceased's soul went to heaven or hell. Thus did early Protestant reformers advocate simplified funerals, with Luther famously saying that his body could be tossed into the woods for all he cared. First-generation Puritans followed these principles and did not condone funeral sermons, nor did they mark their burials with headstones. Soon, however, these extraordinarily simple burials began to leave many Puritans cold. By the end of the seventeenth century, Puritan funerals had come to be elaborate affairs, with the greatest pomp reserved for those at the top of the social hierarchy.

Regardless of social station, all Puritans could expect to be surrounded by loved ones during their final moments. Watchers ensured that the dying person was never left alone. Ministers encouraged the dying to accept with Christian resignation their impending death, something ordinary people sometimes had trouble doing. When the person finally died, female family members (or female servants if the family was well-off) washed the body and shrouded it in linen. The body was then placed into a wooden coffin and laid in the main room of the house. This was, from the clergy's perspective, the moment with the greatest potential for wicked quasi-papist actions. Ministers encouraged mourners to pray for forgiveness of their sins as they prepared for their own inevitable death, but under no circumstances were they to engage in the Catholic practice of praying for the soul of the

---

[13] Anne S. Brown and David D. Hall, "Family Strategies and Religious Practice: Baptism and the Lord's Supper in Early New England," in David D. Hall ed., *Lived Religion in America: Toward a History of Practice* (Princeton, 1997), 41–68, esp. 53.

deceased to get into heaven. Whether laypeople always followed this ministerial dictum is impossible to know.

Then began the funeral proper. Underbearers hoisted the coffin; if the family was wealthy enough to afford a pall, this was draped over the coffin (and the underbearers!) and held up by the pallbearers. A procession accompanied the coffined body from the house to the churchyard. There the minister offered some consoling words and a few reminders to the assembled to use this example of human mortality to prepare for their own deaths. If a funeral sermon was to be expounded, this occurred after the burial in the meetinghouse, not in the churchyard. Finally, most members of the community made their way back to the house of mourning for a feast well supplied with food and drink. Indeed, alcohol was such a central component of the funeral that it was even supplied by towns for pauper funerals. When indigent Ruth Bloss died in 1711, the town of Watertown supplied "four gallonds of Wine allso Sugar and spice."[14] Ministers grumbled about laypeople's penchant for overimbibing at funeral feasts, but here their concerns were more behavioral than theological. Clergymen also complained because mourners sometimes did not accept with proper Christian resignation the deaths of their loved ones. Excessive tears could suggest an unorthodox questioning of God's will.

Although Anglo-New Englanders had longer life spans than their disease-ravaged Algonquian neighbors, larger English villages meant that colonists likewise frequently found their pattern of daily interactions with the supernatural world interrupted by deathbed scenes, funerals, and mourning. Ministers instructed their parishioners to prepare daily for death. For most laypeople this stricture was likely observed in the breach, but many times a year even a "horse-shed" Puritan had to confront the mortality of her friend, family member, or fellow village resident and had to wrestle with what this meant for her own relationship with the supernatural world.

ANGLICANS IN SOUTHERN MAINLAND COLONIES

Until recently, scholars have portrayed Anglicans in the southern British colonies as nearly devoid of religious expression. In fact, few scholars refer to them as Anglicans at all, instead using terms that focus on social status: planter, plantation mistress, yeoman farmer, slave, and so on. Historian Dell Upton, in his masterful account of Anglican church architecture in eighteenth-century Virginia, concludes that "the activity of churchgoing

---

[14] Gordon E. Geddes, *Welcome Joy: Death in Puritan New England* (Ann Arbor, 1981), 124.

was predominantly secular."¹⁵ This assertion may, however, simply be an artifact of the sources, or rather the lack thereof. Almost nothing survives to document the piety and practice of seventeenth-century Anglicans; even for the eighteenth century, sources such as diaries and letters are extant only for the most elite members of the gentry. As a result, our understanding of lay piety is sketchy at best.

In recent years, however, a few scholars have begun to assert that lay piety among Anglicans in the plantation colonies (Virginia, the Carolinas, Georgia, and the British West Indies) was more vibrant than previously recognized.¹⁶ Their analyses rely on creative readings of membership and attendance rolls, church rituals, and the divine service. It is too early to tell whether this newer emphasis on a lively Anglican piety will overturn the older historiography.

Even if one accepts that Anglicanism was not as moribund as traditionally assumed to be, it was, among the four religions examined in this essay, the one least intertwined with everyday life. Sunday service was the focus of Anglican religious practice, not to the exclusion of daily piety, but as its culmination. And because Anglicanism was (and is) a liturgical religion, with a series of set prayers, psalms, and responses repeated every week, it has fared poorly in the scholarly imagination. Many historians have unwittingly inherited the Puritan antiliturgical bias, and thus Anglican worship has been seen as repetitive and mind-numbing rather than the powerful encounter with the supernatural world that it likely was for many lay Anglicans.

As with Puritans, the rhythm of Anglican piety was shaped by the movement from Sunday to Sunday. Unlike Puritans, however, Anglicans experienced Sabbaths that differed little from week to week, aside from variations in biblical texts read aloud by the parson, due to the repetitions insisted on by the Book of Common Prayer. Indeed, the law required clergymen to follow the service exactly as written. This did not lead to an insincere parroting of empty phrases, as Puritans insisted, but rather, in the words of an eighteenth-century English bishop, to "a grave, serious, and regular worship." According to historian John K. Nelson, "the entire drama of the faith, an explanation of the meaning of existence, a rule of conduct, and an apprehension of the spiritual were laid out for worshipers" in the weekly repetition of confession, creed, and psalms.¹⁷

---

[15] Dell Upton, *Holy Things and Profane: Anglican Parish Churches in Colonial Virginia* (Cambridge, MA, 1986), 205.

[16] John K. Nelson, *A Blessed Company: Parishes, Parsons, and Parishioners in Anglican Virginia, 1690–1776* (Chapel Hill, 2001); Nicholas M. Beasley, *Christian Ritual and the Creation of British Slave Societies, 1650–1780* (Athens, 2009).

[17] Nelson, *Blessed Company*, 190–1.

Divine service ordinarily began at 11:00 a.m. in the southern colonies. Immediately on entering the church, parishioners came face-to-face with the intersection of sacred and secular that marked Anglican worship. Seating was by rank, so members of the gentry had the best seats, usually near the pulpit. Indeed, elite families were the only ones whose male and female members could sit together, because they enjoyed the comfort of family pews, with benches with backs and sometimes even upholstered seats for greater comfort. Less exalted parishioners made do with backless benches, men on one side of the church, women on another. The few slaves who were interested in divine service and other marginal members of society occupied a bench around the back wall. An Anglican church was not a place to escape the daily realities of society's power structure.

Dell Upton brilliantly captures this mix of sacred and secular in two pieces of communion silver, a silver chalice and a paten used to hold the wine and bread during the Lord's Supper, that were donated to the James City Parish Church in 1661. The pieces are each inscribed "Mixe not holy thinges with profane." Yet they were also marked "Ex dono Francisci Morrison" (gift of Francis Morrison), suggesting that the church and all future partakers of Holy Communion should thank this wealthy man for his kind generosity in supplying the beautiful silver.[18] Thus were the holy things of Christ's symbolic blood and body mixed with the profane reality that the affluent had more sway in these churches than did the poor.

This does not mean that ordinary men and women did not gain spiritual sustenance from divine service. Those who entered the church and took their socially dictated places did so in impressive numbers. Although it is impossible to reconstruct attendance figures with any certainty, even for the eighteenth century, there is evidence that church attendance was higher than some historians have allowed. In a 1724 survey, most clergymen reported full churches, which might be dismissed as a self-serving exaggeration except that vestries (the boards of twelve laymen that ran church affairs) frequently voted to build new churches and enlarge existing ones at great expense to taxpayers. Were churches empty, it is hard to imagine there being any support for such improvements to the region's religious infrastructure.

Within their churches – drafty wooden structures in the seventeenth century that were increasingly replaced by handsome brick buildings in the eighteenth – Anglicans turned their attention to the enormous three-tiered pulpit that dominated the visual field. At the floor level was the clerk's desk, from which the lay reader led hymns and readings. The middle level was where the parson, clothed in his white gown, called a surplice,

[18] Upton, *Holy Things and Profane*, 162.

offered prayers and scripture readings. The top level was reserved for delivering the sermon, after the parson had removed his surplice and donned a black gown.

As parishioners settled in, the clerk called the people to order, and the service of Morning Prayer began. This liturgy was medieval in origin, part of the Catholic monastic ritual of Matins, which helps explain the Puritan antipathy toward it. First, the minister led the congregation in a general confession. For this the congregation kneeled, as the Prayer Book insisted on distinct bodily positions for different aspects of worship: parishioners kneeled to pray, sat to be instructed, and stood to offer praise. "Almighty and most merciful Father," they began, "we have erred and strayed from thy ways like lost sheep."[19] The minister then pronounced the absolution, emphasizing that sinners are forgiven through the blood of Christ. Next, the clerk or parson read scriptures to the parishioners. These texts were read on a set calendar included in the Prayer Book, so throughout the plantation colonies Anglicans heard the same biblical passage on a given Sunday. After this the congregation joined in singing psalms, one of which was Psalm 95, "O Come Let Us Sing unto the Lord." Remaining standing, the minister and parishioners recited the Apostles' Creed, a summary of the Christian faith. This short statement built toward its famous climax: "I believe in the holy Ghost; The holy Catholick Church; The Communion of Saints; The forgiveness of sins; The resurrection of the body, And the life everlasting. Amen."[20] If there was to be a sermon, the parson delivered it after the Apostle's Creed. Anglican ministers did not ordinarily preach weekly, as the most important aspect of divine worship was the unity of the congregation expressed through the repetition of set prayers: thus the "common" in "Common Prayer." Finally, the parson dismissed the congregation with more prayers.

When Anglicans returned home they were expected to engage in private devotions – not to the same extent or with the same intense self-examination as Puritans, but they were supposed to pray daily. Here is where the sources are least satisfactory. The diaries left by the most elite planters such as William Byrd II and Landon Carter include evidence of daily prayers and examinations of faith. Whether the Anglo-Americans below these individuals on the social scale also incorporated their faith into their daily lives remains an open question. As in New England, there is scattered evidence of magical practice as an alternate or complementary means of interaction with the supernatural world. Some elites eagerly read occult books, whereas some middling farmers consulted healers and diviners.

---

[19] *The Book of Common-Prayer, and Administration of the Sacraments* (London, 1662), B4r.
[20] *Ibid.*, B5v.

Compared to their Puritan counterparts, Anglicans experienced the passage of a year as more closely tied to the sacred calendar. Although Anglicans purged the calendar of many Catholic feasts, numerous holy days remained. The church year began with Advent and progressed through Christmas, Epiphany, Shrove Tuesday, Ash Wednesday, Lent, Good Friday, Easter, Ascension, and Whitsunday. Anglicans annually experienced the central story of their faith – the birth, crucifixion, and resurrection of their savior – via the passage through these calendrical rituals. The scriptural readings in divine service were keyed to this sacred calendar.

Along with this annual cycle, Anglicans partook in religious rites of passage at several crucial moments in the life cycle. Historians have been skeptical about whether very many southern Anglicans received baptism, but there is persuasive evidence of widespread participation in the ritual in the eighteenth century. In several parishes ministers baptized more than 80 percent of all white infants whose birth was recorded. In Albemarle Parish, Virginia, between 1740 and 1775, 99 percent of white infants and 48 percent of black infants received baptism.[21] Some of these baptisms occurred in the home, although probably a smaller percentage than has been imagined. Home baptisms may indicate that "secular" concerns "overshadowed" religious aspects of the ritual, although there is precious little evidence either way.[22]

In the plantation colonies, matrimony was a religious ritual performed by the parson. This contrasts with Puritan New England, where marriage was a civil affair. All Anglican adults were expected to marry, and once again the Prayer Book provided memorable phrases to solemnize the occasion. As the man placed the ring on the woman's finger, he said, "With this ring I thee wed, with my body I thee worship, and with all my worldly goods I thee endow: In the Name of the Father, and of the Son, and of the Holy Ghost. Amen."[23] Even though the Prayer Book was explicit that this ritual was supposed to take place in a church, home weddings were common in the plantation colonies.

For too many young Anglican men and women, death arrived not long after matrimony. Because of the semitropical climate, the southern colonies experienced a much higher mortality rate than did New England. As Anglicans prepared for death, they drew on many of the same cultural scripts as did Puritans, although arguably with a more humane emphasis. The comforting tradition of Anglican deathways is best represented by Jeremy Taylor's *Rule and Exercises of Holy Dying* (1662), a work that was a

---

[21] Nelson, *Blessed Company*, 212.
[22] Rhys Isaac, *The Transformation of Virginia, 1740–1790* (Chapel Hill, 1982), 70.
[23] *Book of Common-Prayer*, D6r.

staple on the shelves of pious Anglicans on both sides of the Atlantic for more than a century. Unlike the Puritan minister Cotton Mather, whose writings displayed little sympathy with the struggles of ordinary men and women as they lay dying, Taylor advised Anglicans on how to have a good death despite their pains and fears. For example, in a section on how to avoid the sin of impatience on the deathbed, Taylor acknowledged that the stoic acceptance of impending death was frequently not possible: "sighs and groans, sorrow and prayers, humble complaints and dolorous expressions, are the sad accents of a sick man's language: for it is not to be expected that a sick man should act [the] part of Patience with a countenance like an Orator."[24]

When the sick person died, perhaps comforted by having read or listened to *Holy Dying*, she was given a funeral that differed in some important respects from those in New England. There was, of course, the Anglican burial liturgy, with its famous words as mourners cast earth onto the coffin: "we therefore commit her body to the ground; earth to earth, ashes to ashes, dust to dust; in sure and certain Hope of the resurrection to eternal life, through our Lord Jesus Christ."[25] But there were other distinctive elements as well. There is evidence that at the postfuneral feast, gunfire into the air was common. This suggests a degree of revelry at the feast, as the 1656 law in question forbade colonists to "shoot any guns at drinking (marriages and funerals only excepted)."[26] Finally, the location of the burial sometimes differed from that found in New England. Some, to be sure, were buried in the churchyard, just like their Puritan counterparts. Wealthy members of the gentry, however, sometimes paid more to be buried within the church, a practice that originated in the Catholic desire for burial *ad sanctos*, or near the relics of the saints. Other planters – whether they were less pious is unknown – opted for burial in tidy family cemeteries located on the plantation grounds. With all parishioners eligible for churchyard burial, the humble plot surrounding the church came to be associated by the eighteenth century with the poor. In death as in life, social hierarchy shaped one's position in the religious world of the plantation colonies.

AFRICANS IN THE PLANTATION COLONIES

Southern planters had an insatiable thirst for labor. When indentured English servants could no longer slake that thirst, planters turned to

---

[24] Jeremy Taylor, *The Rule and Exercises of Holy Dying* (London, 1847 [1662]), 78.
[25] *Book of Common-Prayer*, E2r.
[26] William Walter Hening, ed., *The Statutes at Large: Being a Collection of All the Laws of Virginia*, 13 vols. (New York, 1820–23), 1: 401–2.

enslaved Africans to generate profits on their tobacco and rice plantations. Those Africans who survived the terrible Middle Passage and arrived in the Americas in chains brought with them memories of the religious practices of their homelands. However, they faced numerous obstacles in their attempts to re-create African religious systems in the Americas. On each plantation, slaves spoke a variety of African languages, making communication difficult. Finding a religious specialist from one's homeland could be next to impossible. And slaves had to adjust to a new geographical reality, without the religious sites and ritual accoutrements of home. As a result, African religious systems did not survive the Middle Passage unchanged. Instead, new practices emerged that blended the rituals and beliefs of various African regions. Unfortunately, sources describing slave religion before 1800 (and therefore before widespread Christianization) are extremely thin. This section will therefore draw on sources from the British West Indies to complement the nearly nonexistent evidence from the mainland southern colonies.

Given that sickness and death were omnipresent for slaves forced to toil in the blazing sun, it is no surprise that slave religious practices centered on healing. Ordinary men and women wore beads and talismans of various sorts in an effort to ward off disease. It is almost certain that they prayed to gods who had protected them in Africa, even if they were uprooted from the geographic contexts in which their religious systems were embedded. When these efforts were not enough and slaves became ill, they sought the services of obeah men and women. *Obaye* was an Ashanti term for practices that engaged the supernatural world for healing and divining. Practitioners of obeah served as "Physicians and Conjurers," according to Griffith Hughes of Barbados.[27] Yet their skill at manipulating the spirit world led them to perform a range of other functions as well. Obeah men and women not only treated diseases, but also predicted the future, uncovered the identities of those who committed breaches of communal norms, and sometimes even exacted supernatural revenge.

The ritual accoutrements of obeah men and women are not well attested in the documentary record, but an archaeological finding suggests the kinds of magical objects some used. A man, probably a healer, was buried at Newton Plantation in Barbados around 1700. He was roughly fifty years old and interred on his back with his head facing east in a shallow grave in the plantation's slave burial ground. He was buried with an unmatched array of goods: three rings on his left-hand middle finger, a copper bracelet on his right forearm, and two brass bracelets on his left

---

[27] Quoted in Sylvia R. Frey and Betty Wood, *Come Shouting to Zion: African American Protestantism in the American South and British Caribbean to 1830* (Chapel Hill, 1998), 46.

arm; a buff-colored, short-stemmed earthenware pipe of a kind found along Africa's Gold Coast; and, most remarkably, a necklace strung with seven Indian Ocean cowrie shells, five vertebrae from a large fish, twenty-one dog teeth, fourteen glass beads made in Europe, and a large (4.2 cm long) reddish-orange carnelian bead made in Khambhat, southern India.[28] This necklace almost certainly had magical properties that helped the healer interact with the spirit world. Yet the fact that his fellow slaves buried the necklace with him suggests that it was powerless without the gestures and words that he employed.

Those gestures likely included dance, because in Africa healing and religious expression were inextricably entwined with music and dance. Even though African religious systems were not transported whole to the Americas, slaves undeniably brought with them discrete practices of dancing and singing. Englishmen turned up their noses at the "barbarity" of these "Idolatrous Dances and Revels."[29] But even though Englishmen were crassly judgmental in their description of these rituals, which they declared to be "false Worship," they were correct on one score: the dances were indeed worship.[30] People of African descent used music and dance to interact with the spirit world in a variety of ways.

In addition, Africans in the Americas also celebrated some calendrical rituals, even though these were difficult to establish due to the ever-present labor demands of the plantation system. The best-known calendrical ritual was called John Canoe or Jonkonnu. This seems to have been a variation of West African yam festivals, which were harvest celebrations known both for revelry and for thanking the gods for a plentiful crop. Jonkonnu festivals included singing, dancing, and drumming of both a religious and a secular nature. The ritual was most widespread in the Caribbean, but it was also described in parts of the mainland colonies. The celebration of Jonkonnu took place in the period between Christmas and New Year's Day, during which many plantations allowed their slaves a week free from labor.

Aside from deathways, there is not a great deal of evidence about the life-cycle rituals in which slaves participated. Whether slaves practiced birth rituals is an open question. Among some women of African descent there seems to have been a nine-day period at the start of an infant's life when the

---

[28] Jerome S. Handler, "An African-Type Healer/Diviner and His Grave Goods: A Burial from a Plantation Slave Cemetery in Barbados, West Indies," *International Journal of Historical Archaeology* 1:2 (June 1997): 91–130.

[29] Morgan Godwyn, *The Negro's and Indian's Advocate, Suing for Their Admission into the Church* (London, 1680), 144.

[30] Ibid., 34.

baby received little attention. This drew on West African beliefs that an individual did not achieve true personhood until nine days old. Yet some scholars wonder whether in the Americas this may also have dovetailed with a kind of passive infanticide: given the harsh conditions of plantation life, might some mothers have hoped that their children would not survive the nine-day period of ritual neglect? Likewise, our understanding of slave marriages leaves many questions unanswered. Weddings, although not recognized by law, were times of celebration for slaves. It is unknown whether those celebrations contained a spiritual dimension.

Deathways, on the other hand, left more evidence in the documentary and material record. Before widespread Christianization, through at least the middle of the eighteenth century, slave deathways were strongly marked by African precedents. When a slave died, rapid interment was necessary, given the heat of the plantation colonies. Even though many West African groups shrouded their dead, especially their esteemed dead, the poverty of slaves meant that unshrouded and uncoffined burials were the norm through the eighteenth century. Nonetheless, slaves made sure to give their departed friend a respectful burial. They carried the deceased person on a plank or other improvised bier to the burial ground, a marginal plot of land set aside by the plantation owner. As in Africa, the procession to the cemetery was noisy, at least to European ears. A Barbadian minister wrote, "most young people sing and dance, and make a loud noise with rattles, as they attend the corpse to its interment."[31]

When they reached the burial ground, if members of the slave community believed that the deceased's death was owing to witchcraft, those who carried the corpse participated in one of the most distinctively African practices in the entire mortuary program, what one scholar calls the "supernatural inquest."[32] This procedure was a direct carryover from West African practices. According to a Jamaican planter, "they who bear [the corpse] on their shoulders make a feint of stopping at every door they pass, and pretend, that if the deceased person had received any injury, the corpse moves toward that house, and that they can't avoid letting it fall to the ground when before the door."[33] The procession would then demand that the "guilty" person either pay a fine, if the injury was monetary, or offer other restitution for injuries caused by magical powers. The supernatural inquest demonstrates the continued reliance on supernatural categories developed in Africa.

---

[31] Griffith Hughes, *The Natural History of Barbados* (London, 1750), 15.
[32] Vincent Brown, *The Reaper's Garden: Death and Power in the World of Atlantic Slavery* (Cambridge, MA, 2008), 66–9.
[33] Charles Leslie, *A New and Exact Account of Jamaica*, 3rd ed. (Edinburgh, 1740), 325.

Whether or not an inquest occurred, slaves then placed the deceased person into a shallow grave, usually dug along an east-west axis. Into the grave they placed goods, more likely to be food and drink than the magical necklace of the Newton Plantation healer. Finally, everyone returned to the slave quarters for a raucous celebration that included dancing, drumming, and drinking. This was a festive occasion: even though many were sad to lose the company of their friend or loved one, they rejoiced that this person's soul was headed back to Africa. This belief in the transmigration of souls had African roots but took on a poignant new meaning in the Americas, as slaves believed that death released them from their earthly shackles and allowed them to return to their homelands.

CHANGING DEATHWAYS

But people of African descent did not cling to a set of unchanging beliefs. Transmigration of the soul, for example, made sense for individuals who had been born in Africa, but what about those who were one, two, or three generations removed from their ancestral homeland? And what about those who, toward the end of the eighteenth century, began to embrace Christianity? This final section considers how changing deathways offer a window onto the evolution of religious practice in the eighteenth century.

Slave deathways first began to change by adopting aspects of Anglo-American material culture. Plantation owners started to acquiesce to slaves' demands for greater material respect for their burials, and so began to supply shrouds and even coffins. By the end of the eighteenth century, some slaves also became interested in the spiritual dimensions of Anglo-American deathways. When a man named Will was dying on Thomas Thistlewood's Jamaica plantation in 1758, his final wishes were significant: "he desires to be buried at Salt River at his mother (Dianah's) right hand, and that no Negroes should sing, etc."[34] Will did not want the traditional African funeral drumming and dancing and singing, which may indicate that he was a Christian. Other slaves were unquestionably Christians by this time, and their deathways reflect this. On Newton Plantation in Barbados, several slaves received Christian burials that were administered by the Christ Church Parish. The clerk recorded the death, the sexton dug the grave, and the minister performed the burial liturgy. Although we do not know how Anglican piety infused these slaves' daily lives, it seems fair to assume that they prayed to the Christian God in a fashion not unlike their Anglo-American neighbors.

---

[34] Douglas Hall, ed., *In Miserable Slavery: Thomas Thistlewood in Jamaica, 1750–86* (London, 1989), 83.

In the mainland colonies, by contrast, people of African descent were more likely to be attracted to the emergent evangelical movement. Baptists and later Methodists appealed to African Americans with their energetic preaching and message of spiritual equality. The deathways of mainland slaves reflect these changes, with Christian prayers offered on the deathbed and Christian funerals to send the soul of the deceased to the afterlife. Yet some African practices continued in the South. Many slaves continued to decorate the graves of their loved ones with shells, broken pottery, and food offerings.

American Indians, likewise, began to change their religious practices, although at a slightly earlier time than African Americans. The Algonquians of southern New England were much diminished in number by 1700, due to the effects of disease and conflicts such as King Philip's War. Those who survived, especially the Wampanoags of Martha's Vineyard and the Narragansetts of Rhode Island, crafted a new spiritual life that drew on both traditional and innovative practices. For example, around 1700 some Indians began to abandon their longtime practice of flexed burials in favor of the Christian model of supine extended burials. Yet many of these supine burials continued to include grave goods, a practice that was sharply criticized by Anglo-American missionaries. Even grave goods, however, were not unchanged links with the past. In addition to the stone arrowpoints and shell beads that were similar to items used in burials two centuries earlier, Algonquians now furnished their dead with long-stemmed kaolin pipes, iron hoes, and copper finger rings, all items unknown before European colonization, yet all of which contained manitou due to their usefulness and beauty. Burials around 1700 therefore reveal Indians gaining spiritual power from a variety of sources.

Whereas syncretism marked the burial practices and spiritual lives of Indians and African Americans, Anglo-American deathways changed less dramatically over the course of the colonial period. This reveals the power differential between these groups. Africans arrived in the Americas in chains; Indians suffered extraordinary population losses due to virgin soil epidemics. Anglo-Americans were in a position to dominate both groups, despite the best efforts of Africans and Indians at resistance. What all groups – including Anglo-American Protestants – shared was the increasing influence of Christianity. As a result, the eastern third of North America was largely Christianized by 1800.

Anglo-American Protestants in New England experienced important religious developments over the course of the colonial period, including the geographical spread of hundreds of Congregationalist churches across all parts of New England. An even greater change was the rise of evangelical denominations associated with the Great Awakening. In the 1740s moderate revivalists such as Jonathan Edwards and radical preachers such as Gilbert Tennant attracted thousands of New Englanders with passionate extemporaneous preaching. They inspired conversion experiences that were more intense than those of the seventeenth century. But even important changes such as this did not lead to wholesale revisions of mortuary practices. For example, the shift from glowering death's heads to smiling cherubs on New England gravestones used to be attributed to the Great Awakening's supposedly optimistic theology.[35] But, in fact, revivalists sought to recapture the strict Calvinism of the first generation of Puritans. A better explanation for the shift in gravestone iconography is the transatlantic rise of Romanticism. Ordinary men and women began to use Romantic language in their spiritual journals and conversion narratives toward the end of the eighteenth century.

Yet even though expressive styles had grown more elaborate and flowery, the practice of piety remained remarkably constant over time for New England's Congregationalists, with Sabbath services (including baptism and the Lord's Supper), family and secret prayer, journal keeping, and the reading of pious books at the center of religious practice. Deathways likewise retained their core practices despite some superficial changes in form. The American Revolution led to a brief vogue for simple funerals. This was not so much a return to the stripped-down practices of early Reformed Protestants as it was a consumer statement, akin to wearing homespun, which showed that colonists could live without fancy manufactured goods from Great Britain, in this case coffin hardware. But overall deathbed scenes, burials, funeral sermons, and mourning practices continued to emphasize the key theme of Christian resignation in the face of loss.

Anglo-American Anglicans in the southern colonies faced a stronger evangelical challenge than did the Congregationalists of New England. By the time of the American Revolution, Baptists were making strong inroads, especially among poorer whites and free and enslaved blacks. By the end of the eighteenth century, Methodists also began to compete for adherents. Even within Anglicanism there were important changes when the Revolution severed the link with the Church of England. The independence of the new nation necessitated a new American Episcopal Prayer Book in 1789. There were, to be sure, some minor changes of wording in the new Prayer Book. But the structure of the burial liturgy remained the same, as did the Morning Prayer that formed the basis for divine service on Sundays. Psalm singing, prayer, scripture readings, and recitation

---

[35] David E. Stannard, *The Puritan Way of Death: A Study in Religion, Culture, and Social Change* (New York, 1977), 154–5.

of the Apostle's Creed and Lord's Prayer – all these remained the focus of Episcopalian parishioners on the Sabbath.

Thus, significant continuities marked the religious piety and practice of ordinary Anglo-American men and women in British North America from 1600 to 1800. By contrast, the religious practices of Indians and African Americans witnessed much more profound changes. All, however, were more deeply influenced by the institutions of Christian religion in 1800 than they had been two centuries earlier.

SUGGESTIONS FOR FURTHER READING

Axtell, James. *The Invasion Within: The Contest of Cultures in Colonial North America*. New York, 1985.

Butler, Jon. *Awash in a Sea of Faith: Christianizing the American People*. Cambridge, MA, 1990.

Frey, Sylvia R., and Betty Wood. *Come Shouting to Zion: African American Protestantism in the American South and British Caribbean to 1830*. Chapel Hill, 1998.

Hall, David D. *Worlds of Wonder, Days of Judgment: Popular Religious Belief in Early New England*. New York, 1989.

Hambrick-Stowe, Charles E. *The Practice of Piety: Puritan Devotional Disciplines in Seventeenth-Century New England*. Chapel Hill, 1982.

Nelson, John K. *A Blessed Company: Parishes, Parsons, and Parishioners in Anglican Virginia, 1690–1776*. Chapel Hill, 2001.

Seeman, Erik R. *Death in the New World: Cross-Cultural Encounters, 1492–1800*. Philadelphia, 2010.

Silverman, David J. *Faith and Boundaries: Colonists, Christianity, and Community among the Wampanoag Indians of Martha's Vineyard, 1600–1871*. New York, 2005.

34

SACRED MUSIC IN COLONIAL AMERICA

STEPHEN A. MARINI

Sacred music played a complex and crucial role in the development of colonial American religious cultures from the earliest encounters of Europeans and indigenous peoples to the Revolution of 1776. The ritual singing of sacred texts is a constituent part of most religious cultures, and colonial religions produced a rich diversity of such sacred music. This multiplicity, however, developed within the broader context of colonialism that imposed processes of transmission, assimilation, and hybridization on every religious community in the New World. Understanding sacred music in colonial America therefore demands attention both to its variety and to the common cultural processes that shaped it.

MUSIC AND MISSIONS

The original sacred music of North America was that of indigenous peoples. Hundreds of First Nations occupied the continent at the time of European encounter. Their cultures were grounded in traditional religious worldviews whose principal means of expression were singing and dancing. From shamanistic healing chants to calendric festival dances, the religions of Native Americans were filled with musical vocalization, typically accompanied by rhythm instruments like drums and rattles.

Indigenous religions understood humans to live in a sacred cosmos in which all natural forces and things were personified in spirit beings. The religious task of humans was to live in balance with these beings by honoring them in celebrative or sacrificial rituals and invoking them for aid in times of famine or disease. On those occasions singing and dancing, sometimes mimetic in form, became the spirit voice of the people whereby they communicated with the cosmos. Their songs rehearsed and renewed sacred myths; their dances brought spiritual energies to the people and their land.

The encounter of Native Americans with colonizers from Western Europe brought profound changes to their societies and the religious worldviews that supported them. Many indigenous communities were destroyed by military conquest and epidemic disease, but the largest of them survived sufficiently to engage in a complex process of religious and musical transmission, reception, and adaptation. An important example of musical assimilation occurred in New Spain. Within two years of Hernán Cortés' military conquest of the Aztecs, a Franciscan brother named Pedro de Gante (c. 1480–1572) arrived in Mexico City to set up a school for training boy choristers to sing the Catholic liturgy in Latin. They proved apt pupils, and in a matter of months de Gante sent them out to sing and preach Christianity to the newly subjected Aztecs.

De Gante's superiors reined in the experiment because there were not enough priests to supervise the choristers, but his judgment that music would help to evangelize Mesoamerican peoples proved to be correct. Later Franciscan missionaries reported rapt attention to their singing of hymns and liturgical texts, and de Gante's experience with avid native choristers was repeated often in mission parishes. The assimilation of Spanish Catholic liturgical music and popular hymns was greatly enhanced by the biological mingling of indigenous peoples and colonizers that created a huge Catholic mestizo (mixed-race) class by the end of the sixteenth century.

For many indigenous Mesoamericans, however, preconquest hymns still remained powerful reminders of their old religions. Missionaries developed a second strategy to counter this attraction by writing new Christian lyrics for the old songs. The Dominican missionary Bartolomé de Las Casas (1484–1566) was the first to use this approach successfully. In *The Only Method of Attracting All People to the True Faith* (1536), Las Casas argued that Christianity should be spread to New Spain by singing and preaching alone and not by the sword. A year later he used indigenous melodies and original Christian lyrics to help convert the Tuzulutlan people of central Guatemala, for which he named the region Vera Paz, "True Peace."

The Franciscan Bernardino de Sahagùn (1499–1590) carried this strategy of hybridized sacred music forward in Mexico City by composing *Psalmodia Christiana* (Christian Psalms), a book of Christian canticles in the Nahuatl language of the Aztecs published in 1583 but used earlier in manuscript form. Written for converts to sing while they danced, these "psalms" appropriated traditional Aztec melodies and movement in a syncretistic mix. Sahagùn probably also supervised the compilation of *Cantares Mexicanos* (Mexican Songs) (1585–97), a collection of Nahua-Christian song texts for indigenous melodies that blended Catholic and Aztec sacred symbolism.

In at least one major case, however, the Catholic strategies of musical assimilation and hybridization failed dramatically. As the colonization of New Spain expanded northward, Franciscan missionaries brought simple, two-line hymns of popular origin called *alabados* (praises) from Mexico to Santa Fe and the upper Rio Grande valley of New Mexico around 1600. They became staples of colonial worship and popular piety. At first the Spanish authorities permitted the indigenous Pueblo peoples to continue the traditional katsina dances through which they maintained contact with their ancient spirit beings. But during the 1670s Spanish authorities attempted to eradicate Pueblo sacred rites. In 1680 the Pueblo rebelled, driving Spanish colonizers out of New Mexico for a decade. Peace was restored only when the Spanish conceded that the missions would be voluntary and the Pueblo could continue their katsina dances and other sacred rituals. With the restoration of Spanish colonial rule in 1690, the *Guadalupanas* and *alabados* returned as the vernacular sacred songs of Catholic New Mexico.

The defining synthesis of indigenous and Catholic sacred music in New Spain, however, occurred through the figure of Our Lady of Guadalupe, a 1531 apparition of the Virgin Mary revealed to the Aztec convert Juan Diego at Guadalupe near Mexico City. The Virgin's miraculous image attracted throngs of pilgrims seeking her aid, singing new hymns and pilgrimage songs and performing indigenous dances in her honor. By the mid-seventeenth century, she had become the preeminent symbol of Mesoamerican religion. Her official apparition narrative, or *legenda*, written by Luis Laso de la Vega in 1649, contained traditional Christian imagery deeply interwoven with Aztec sacred symbols, including birds, flowers, and the rising sun. These same symbols appeared in her popular pilgrimage songs, called *Guadalupanas*. The most popular of these pilgrimage songs was "Las Mananitas a la Virgén de Guadalupe" (Birthday Song to the Virgin of Guadalupe), a song in which the singer gently awakens the young Virgin and calls her to appear to the pilgrims as she did to Juan Diego.

The processes of sacred music assimilation and hybridization that characterized missions in New Spain were attenuated by violence elsewhere in colonial North America. In seventeenth-century New France, Jesuit missionaries took painstaking efforts to understand Eastern Woodland peoples before evangelizing them. They attended their feasts and sacred dances and tolerated them even after conversion had taken place. Before any significant effort could be made to create indigenized forms of Catholic hymns, however, the French mission was overwhelmed by the defeat of the Huron, the most successfully Christianized Algonquian nation, by the Iroquois in 1648.

Early English colonists did not make systematic efforts to evangelize First Nations, but individual New England Puritan ministers did pursue successful missions. John Eliot (1604–90) and Thomas Mayhew (1593–1682) established "praying towns" among the Naticks of eastern Massachusetts and the Wampanoags of Martha's Vineyard Island, respectively, where they promoted singing of the psalms translated into the indigenous languages. By the early 1670s, fourteen praying towns had been set up in New England. Almost all of them were destroyed in the carnage of King Philip's War of 1675–76.

Protestant missions to First Nations reappeared later in the colonial period. During the 1740s and 1750s, Congregational and Presbyterian ministers, including Jonathan Edwards, David and John Brainerd, and Eleazar Wheelock, served as Indian missionaries in New England and the Middle Colonies. In 1774 a Mohegan convert and Presbyterian minister named Samson Occom (1723–92) published *A Choice Collection of Hymns and Spiritual Songs*, the first hymnal compiled by a Native American. Occom's *Collection*, however, was an assimilationist effort, making no mention of his Native American identity and containing no indigenous hymn texts or tunes.

The Moravian Brethren conducted more successful missions in Pennsylvania and the trans-Appalachian West in which music also played a prominent role. Moravian devotional hymns with instrumental accompaniment attracted Lenni Lenape and Tuscarawas peoples to Moravian mission stations in Pennsylvania and Ohio, both of which were named Gnadenhütten, or "Tents of Blessing." Tragically, Americans destroyed both settlements in time of war. The Pennsylvania community was ravaged in 1755 during the French and Indian War, and the Ohio settlement was massacred at the end of the American Revolution in 1782.

THE AGE OF PSALTERS: BRITISH NORTH AMERICA IN THE SEVENTEENTH CENTURY

The first century of colonization in British North America created a mosaic of Old World sacred musics, the principal element of which was metrical psalmody embodied in Protestant psalters. Psalters are sets of the biblical psalms translated into vernacular poetic meters and furnished with tunes appropriate for congregational singing. The tunes may or may not be harmonized, and psalters may also contain additional materials such as festival hymns and liturgical texts. For the main varieties of English Protestantism in early colonial America, the psalter stood alongside the confession of faith and the catechism as foundational standards for religious belief and practice.

The three earliest English colonies, Virginia, Plymouth, and Massachusetts Bay, used different psalters. The settlers of Virginia were

Anglicans who established the Church of England as the colony's legal religion. Anglicans observed John Calvin's teaching that only biblical songs were appropriate for Christian worship. In 1562 the Church of England authorized *The Whole Booke of Psalmes Collected into English Metre* (1562) by Thomas Sternhold and John Hopkins. Sternhold, a courtier to King Edward IV, composed the first of these metrical psalms in 1549, but exiled ministers produced most of them in Calvin's Geneva during the late 1550s, set to a mixture of English and French tunes. Around 1560 the Anglican minister John Hopkins added a group of his own psalms to these earlier ones to create the complete psalter authorized by Queen Elizabeth I.

Psalms were a central element in Anglican worship. The Book of Common Prayer included a calendar by which nearly all of the psalms were used throughout the year at morning and evening prayer. It also mandated psalms before and after the sermon in Sunday worship. But nowhere did it require the singing of metrical psalms. They were allowed to be sung or said in either metrical or prose translation. Psalmody practice therefore varied from parish to parish. During the early decades of Elizabeth's reign, however, psalm singing became hugely popular both during worship and afterwards in the streets. The new metrical psalms, with their popular tunes, became a badge of Protestant identity for England and a religious bulwark that secured the reign of its new queen.

Sternhold and Hopkins wrote most of their psalms in alternating lines of eight and six syllables. They used two of these pairs for each psalm verse, creating a basic poetic stanza of 8-6-8-6. This metrical form matched the musical structure of many traditional English folk songs and Elizabethan art songs. So popular were Sternhold and Hopkins' metrical psalms and their tunes that the 8-6-8-6 stanza came to be called "common meter" in English psalmody. Their collection also included some psalms in short meter (6-6-8-6) and long meter (8-8-8-8), as well as a scattering of unusual "particular meters." Sternhold and Hopkins assigned tunes for each psalm. Early editions contained a number of French tunes from Geneva, but gradually the *Whole Booke of Psalmes* became musically more English, relegating the French tunes primarily to the rare particular meter psalm texts.

By 1607 the *Whole Booke of Psalmes* was entrenched as an essential part of Anglican worship and English identity. The settlers of Virginia took Sternhold and Hopkins with them and sang it as part of Anglican worship mandated by law. The colony's first law code, *Lawes Divine, Moral, and Martiall* (1611), required daily attendance at morning and evening prayer and at two services each Sunday. Later legislation reduced the Draconian sanctions of the *Lawes* against those who did not attend, but the Church of England continued to maintain a powerful religious establishment in the rich Virginia Tidewater plantation country through the entire colonial period and with it the use of Sternhold and Hopkins in local congregations.

The *Whole Booke of Psalmes* was also the first sung Christian text heard by African slaves. Most masters on the sprawling tobacco plantations of the seventeenth-century Virginia Tidewater kept their field slaves away from Anglican worship, but domestic servants heard the psalms read or sung in the manor house during family worship, pastoral visits, and singing lessons. Whether such exposure made any direct impact on the complex religious culture of the slave quarters is unclear, but it is certain that the psalms of Sternhold and Hopkins were heard, if not sung, by the earliest generations of African Americans in Virginia. Over the course of the next century these Virginian patterns of Anglican sacred music transmission and use gradually spread to the plantations and market towns of the South from the Chesapeake Bay to the Carolina low country.

The Pilgrims who founded the Plymouth Colony in 1620 sang from a different psalter, Henry Ainsworth's *The Book of Psalmes: Englished Both in Prose and Metre* (1612). The Pilgrims were Separatists, early Puritans who wanted the Church of England to reform further along Genevan lines and who were willing to separate from the Anglican communion and suffer exile in the Netherlands for their religious radicalism. They also followed Calvin's theology of praise, but Ainsworth (1571–1622), a minister of the Separatist congregation in Amsterdam after 1596, questioned the accuracy of Sternhold and Hopkins' translations. He prepared a new psalter using their meters as well as a new one, 10-10-10-10, that better accommodated some of the original Hebrew texts and fit well with some of the popular Genevan and Dutch tunes his congregation sang.

In 1609 John Robinson's Pilgrim congregation fled from Scrooby to Leiden, where they maintained close ties to Ainsworth's community in Amsterdam. When Ainsworth published the *Book of Psalms Englished* three years later, they adopted it. Pilgrim Elder William Brewster carried Ainsworth's psalter to Plymouth Colony in 1620 and made it the worship standard for the new settlements there. It provided music and texts for worship in Plymouth Colony from 1620 until 1692, when the Pilgrim settlements were incorporated into Massachusetts Bay.

The founders of the Bay Colony were Puritans of a different kind. Although they also disagreed strongly with the ecclesiastical organization and liturgy of the Church of England, they did not separate, and the strongly Genevan character of Sternhold and Hopkins' psalmody made the *Whole Booke of Psalmes* acceptable to them. Soon after establishing their new colony in 1630, however, several Puritan ministers, including John Cotton, John Eliot, Richard Mather, and Thomas Weld, set about making a new translation. Their 1640 psalter, *The Whole Book of Psalms Faithfully*

Translated into English Meter, was the first book published in British North America. Cotton's preface cited the archaic expressions and erroneous translations of Sternhold and Hopkins as reasons for undertaking a new psalter, but the Bay Colony's ministers also took a principled stand on plainness of style as a theological imperative for psalmody. Literary art, Cotton said, must always give way to textual accuracy when offering praise from God's Word.

Such plainness had its cost, however, and the New England Puritans paid it with the awkward poetic grammar, unreliable meter, and inconsistent rhyme of their "Bay Psalm Book." The new psalter also did not contain any tunes because there was no means to print music in the colony. Ministers and parish clerks relied on Sternhold and Hopkins or Thomas Ravenscroft's *The Whole Booke of Psalmes Composed into 4 Parts* (1621) for tunes. Nonetheless, first-generation Puritan congregations seem to have established a high level of psalmodic performance, possibly even including part singing.

They learned their tunes by a scale system published in 1597 by the Anglican church composer Thomas Morley (1557/58–1602) called the Lancashire Solfa. Instead of the ut-re-mi syllables – ancestor of today's do-re-mi – formulated in the tenth century by Guido of Arezzo, Morley's scale read fa-so-la-fa-so-la-mi-fa. The Puritans used this Solfa scheme to sound out their parts, but without printed scores they soon began to sing from memory, with the attendant loss of accuracy and pace.

The Puritans lost still more musical ground to the practice of "lining-out." Endorsed in 1645 by the Westminster Assembly's *Directory for the Publique Worship of God*, lining-out was an antiphonal form of psalmody in which the minister or clerk pitched the tune and read a line or two of text, which the congregation sang back in unison. The *Directory* justified lining-out as a technique for assuring that all worshippers understood what they were singing to God during an era when printed psalters and tune books were still scarce. But lining-out had dire effects on the ritual performance of psalmody. Reading continually stopped the melodic flow of psalm tunes, making it difficult for the congregation to resume singing accurately and defeating the emotional effect of the tunes. Such interrupted singing inevitably lost tempo and pitch and invited spontaneous ornamentation that further altered the tunes. By the late seventeenth century the "usual singing" of many congregations had contracted to a handful of tunes that suffered increasingly from the combined effects of rote learning and lining-out.

As New England psalmody staggered under these adverse conditions, John Cotton defended it in his 1647 treatise, *The Singing of Psalms a Gospel Ordinance*, one of the most important Puritan treatments of praise from either side of the Atlantic. His colleague Henry Dunster, however, saw inadequacies in the Bay Psalm Book and undertook to revise it in the late 1640s. Dunster (1609–59), the first president of Harvard College, and his assistant Richard Lyon made careful changes that preserved the overall contours of the 1640 texts but improved their metrical cadences and rhymes. They also introduced subtle modifications of theological and literal meanings that reshaped the original collection. Dunster published the work in 1651 as *The Psalms, Hymnes, and Spiritual Songs of the Old and New Testaments.* Known as the New England Psalm Book, it enjoyed more than a century of use as colonial Congregationalism's canonical psalter.

The Anglican and Separatist psalters used in Virginia and Plymouth were colonial artifacts in the passive sense that they were elements of Old World religious culture carried by emigrants to America. Transatlantic traditions and institutions also determined the psalters and hymnals of Swedish and German Lutherans, the psalters of Dutch and German Reformed and Scots Presbyterians, the Latin liturgy of Catholics, and the Hebrew synagogue songs of Sephardic Jews in the early colonies. These forms of sacred music did not change, even after decades of colonial settlement.

The New England psalters, by contrast, were expressions of colonial culture in the active sense that the colonists created them. Like the *alabados* and *Guadalupanas* of New Mexico, the metrical psalms of seventeenth-century New England expressed cultural situations that had already become irrevocably changed from their European societies of origin. Although the New England Puritans were employing models of praise formulated in Geneva and England, their execution of those models produced the first expressions of sacred music by communities resident in British North America.

THE REGULAR SINGING CONTROVERSY AND THE NEW ENGLAND SINGING SCHOOL, 1698–1730

Widespread acceptance of the New England Psalm Book, however, did not stem the decline of psalm singing in Congregational parishes. An initial step toward musical reform was taken in 1698 with the printing of a small pamphlet of thirteen commonly used psalm tunes that was appended to the ninth edition of the New England Psalm Book. *Tunes to the Psalms* was the first printed music in the colonies. It presented popular two-part tunes with an underlay of letters beneath each melody note that indicated which syllable should be used when sounding it out in Lancashire Solfa.

Intended as an aid for ministers, parish clerks, and lay singing leaders or precentors, the tune supplement also provided brief instructions on selecting and pitching tunes for the most spiritually effective singing. *Tunes to the Psalms*, however, had only limited effect in halting the decline of Congregational praise. Even after 1700 the congregation of Boston's elite Old South Church could not follow the lead of its precentor, Judge Samuel Sewall, who reported its "falling in" from one tune to another while lining-out.

Anglicans took more decisive steps to improve their psalmody. In 1696 William III authorized *A New Version of the Psalms Fitted to the Tunes Used in Churches* by Poet Laureate Nahum Tate (1652–1715) and Royal Chaplain Nicholas Brady (1659–1726). Tate and Brady tempered the Calvinism and literalism of Sternhold and Hopkins' psalms with Enlightenment doctrinal moderation and the poetic rhetoric of Augustan lyric as developed by John Dryden, Joseph Addison, and Alexander Pope. In 1702 Tate and Brady published *A Supplement to the New Version*, with new renderings of the biblical canticles, festival hymns, and particular-meter psalms, along with a group of tunes drawn primarily from John Playford's 1677 collection *The Whole Book of Psalms ... Compos'd in Three Parts*. Among the new festival hymns was the Nativity lyric "While Shepherds Watch'd Their Flocks by Night." It became an instant favorite throughout Anglo-America. The definitive 1708 edition of the *Supplement* added a group of more emotively expressive tunes.

By 1710 the *New Version* and *Supplement* had become so popular in Boston that several Congregational parishes began to use them in worship. In 1713 King's Chapel, the city's only Anglican church, installed the first organ used for worship in America. In response to these challenges, Cotton Mather, minister of Boston's Second Church, rallied Congregationalists to reform their psalmody. Mather (1663–1728) tried to provide a new textual foundation by composing *Psalterium Americanum* (1718), a psalter in blank verse each of whose texts could be adapted to common-, short-, or long-meter tunes. Mather's concept was brilliant, but his poetry lacked the genius of John Milton's, on which it was modeled.

Fortunately for the Congregationalists, an English poet of their communion was also hard at work on a psalter. He was Isaac Watts, minister of the Mark Lane Independent congregation in London and author of *Hymns and Spiritual Songs* (1707), a revolutionary collection of original poems on scripture, doctrine, and the Lord's Supper. Watts' long-awaited "Christianized" psalter, *The Psalms of David Imitated in the Language of the New Testament*, appeared in 1719. It supplied New England Congregationalists with the kind of metrical psalms Mather knew they needed but could not write.

Mather, however, did find ministers able to reform the performance of singing. His nephew Thomas Walter and his cousin-by-marriage John Tufts were part of a younger generation of ministers trained in psalmody at Harvard and eager to restore "regular singing," or singing by rule (*regula* in Latin), as practiced by New England's Puritan founders. When one of their colleagues, Thomas Symmes, reported stiff resistance to singing reform by "usual singers" in his congregation at Bradford, Massachusetts, Mather, Tufts (1689–1750), and Walter (1696–1725) leapt to his aid in print and in practice. Mather's 1721 sermon *The Accomplished Singer* depicted psalm singing as a means to heighten devotion in worship and prescribed a technique to offer a prayer as each line was sung. A year later Walter's sermon *The Sweet Psalmist of Israel* extolled the virtues of the psalms and described how music and praise convey prayers to heaven.

Walter and Tufts took practical action to promote regular singing by publishing the first American tune books in 1721. Walter's *Grounds and Rules of Musick Explain'd* and Tuft's *Introduction to the Art of Psalm-Singing* included basic instruction in music as well as several dozen common psalm tunes. Walter positioned his tune book as an explicit corrective and denounced usual singing as a confused and cacaphonous jumble of notes. Tufts devised a system of music notation for his tune book that placed the letters of the Lancashire Solfa scale on ledger lines to assist beginners in reading music. Tuft's *Introduction* also included his "Anthem on Psalm 100," the first original tune published by an American.

Most importantly, the new tune books provided the means for Walter, Tufts, and other ministers to conduct singing schools to introduce regular singing into their parishes. Walter led the first documented American singing school in early 1723, using *Grounds and Rules* as a textbook. Over several weeks he taught the "rudiments" of music theory, notation, rhythm, keys, and vocal production with illustrative psalm tunes to members of the newly organized Boston Society for Promoting Regular and Good Singing. Itinerant singing masters soon codified this curriculum into one- or two-month singing schools that became the staple of early American music education. The schools spread steadily through New England during the rest of the colonial period, but not without occasionally fierce resistance from usual singers. Boycotts, walkouts, and even leaps from church windows by usual singers continued to accompany the introduction of regular singing in rural parishes up to the Revolution.

The development of the singing school established regular singing as the standard for Congregationalist praise, but at the same time it laicized psalmody as the liturgical specialty of itinerant singing masters, who taught the schools and parish clerks or precentors who led singing in local congregations. Regular singing also eliminated lining-out and introduced new tune repertory as singers developed musical skills. These complex effects emerged unevenly between the 1720s and the Revolution. In some parishes, core singers simply assisted congregational singing; in others they demanded choice gallery seats opposite the pulpit from which they dominated singing; and in still others they developed into organized musical societies and choirs that performed anthems as well as congregational psalmody. Slowly but surely, colonial processes of cultural change created yet another sacred music hybrid in the New England singing school.

EVANGELICAL AND PIETIST HYMNODY, 1735–1760

Shortly after the regular singing reform movement, a wave of religious renewal known as the Great Awakening swept through British North America. During the 1730s and 1740s advocates of the Awakening, called Evangelicals, created a new ritual modality known as revivalism that gave a prominent place to sacred music. The heart of revivalism was the preaching of the necessity of the new birth, the teaching that true religion could be attained only through a conscious experience of spiritual regeneration. Evangelical leaders like John Wesley, George Whitefield, and Jonathan Edwards believed that singing fostered the "holy affections" or emotions necessary to facilitate the new birth. All of them used singing in their revival ministries.

The Anglican ministers John and Charles Wesley, founders of Methodism, came to Georgia as missionaries in 1736–38 seeking to promote piety and strict moral discipline in the raw settlement of Savannah. As part of this campaign John Wesley (1703–91) published *A Collection of Psalms and Hymns* (1737) in Charleston. He used these hymns, which included the first published poems written by his brother Charles (1707–88), in "social worship," a term that referred to small meetings for prayer, bible study, and spiritual sharing that he conducted outside of Sunday service. After the Wesleys returned to England, their protégé George Whitefield took the Great Awakening in America to its zenith between 1738 and 1744 with his incendiary preaching. Whitefield (1714–70) took revivalism out of the churches and into the streets and public venues. As great crowds thronged to hear him during his tours of the Atlantic seaboard, he devised a simple revival service that began and ended with extended hymn singing. To support this service of song, Whitefield published his own hymn collection, called *The Divine Melody, or a Help to Devotion* in 1739.

The revivalism of Wesley and Whitefield illustrated the rise of the hymn, as opposed to the metrical psalm, as the preferred lyrical form for Evangelicals. They endorsed the views of Isaac Watts, who had argued in *Hymns and Spiritual Songs* that many of the psalms were inappropriate for Christian worship and that original hymns of religious experience were better suited to heighten singing and express regenerate faith. So it proved in the Great Awakening. Jonathan Edwards (1703–58), for example, sponsored parish singing schools in his Northampton, Massachusetts, parish during the mid-1730s. He then reported in *A Faithful Narrative of the*

Surprising Work of God (1737) that at the peak of the Awakening his congregation sang with exceptional musical intensity and spiritual elevation, carrying four parts, three for the men and one for the women. By 1742 his congregation had begun to sing Watts' hymns at the conclusion of Sunday afternoon worship.

Edwards even drew analogies between music and regenerate spirituality in his sermons and writings. He called singing a means of spiritual understanding, described authentic religious affection as the apprehension of God's perfect beauty and symmetry, and envisioned the kingdom of God as the harmony of a complex tune. From these musical, textual, and theological beginnings in the Awakening, hymn singing by the mid-1750s had become a hallmark of praise among New Light Congregationalists, New Side Presbyterians, and Regular Baptists, the dominant Evangelical factions of the three major colonial Calvinist denominations.

An important aspect of this development was the inclusion of African American slaves in Evangelical hymn singing. Some converted planters took the evangelization of their slaves as a moral obligation and began to include them in church attendance and social worship. Contemporary accounts document the slaves' embrace of hymn singing. More significant perhaps was the gradual synthesis of biblical imagery with the African musical heritage of gapped scales and call-and-response chant that created the slave spiritual. No spirituals survive from the colonial period, but the process that produced them began with the mutual engagement of white masters and African slaves with Evangelicalism during the Great Awakening.

The large population of German Protestants in colonial Pennsylvania followed an analogous pattern of musical tradition and innovation between 1735 and 1760. During this period they experienced a powerful resurgence of Pietism, a seventeenth-century precursor of Evangelicalism that bore many similarities to the Great Awakening. Like Evangelicals, Pietists considered hymn singing to be the quintessential ritual vehicle for experiencing the Holy Spirit and sharing regenerate beliefs and practices. By 1730 an enormous body of Pietist hymns had been published in Germany. The most popular of them were written by Lutherans Paul Gerhardt (1607–76) and Gottfried Arnold (1666–1714) and the Reformed preacher Gerhard Tersteegen (1697–1769) and set to chorale tunes by German baroque composers.

German Reformed congregations sang from psalters designed along the same Genevan lines as the various English ones, whereas Lutherans sang hymns along with psalms as mandated by Martin Luther. Both denominations incorporated Pietist hymns into the collections they began publishing in Pennsylvania during the 1750s. The German Reformed Church published *Kern alter und neuer* (Seeds Old and New) in 1753, a composite volume consisting of reprints of Ambrosius Lobwasser's 1573 psalter and a large collection of "new" Pietist hymns. The Lutherans followed in 1757 with *Vollständiges Marburger Gesang-Buch* (Complete Marburg Song Book), a collection of 615 psalms and hymns by Luther and later Pietist writers. It was reprinted four more times before 1778.

Radical German sects also flourished during the Pietist renewal in colonial Pennsylvania. Among them the Ephratans, Mennonites, Schwenkfelders, and Moravians made the most original contributions to sacred music. In 1732, Seventh-Day Baptist Johann Conrad Beissel set up a celibate, communal regime for men and women at Ephrata, near Reading, Pennsylvania. Beissel (1691–1768) gave music a prominent place in his esoteric and gendered mystical theology, identifying it with Sophia, the supreme expression of divine knowledge and harmony.

Beissel, a violinist, wrote lyrics and chorales in four to seven parts for Ephrata's frequent worship services. The community's singers performed with a distinctive closed falsetto head-tone that Beissel cultivated through a prescribed diet of wheat bread, root vegetables, and cold water. Ephrata's press produced six major hymn collections beginning in the mid-1730s, the most important of which was *Das Gesäng der einsamen und verlassenen Turtel-Taube* (The Song of the Lonely and Lost Turtle-Dove) published in 1747. Although Conrad Beissel's works were esoteric in style, eccentric in performance, and limited in influence, he nonetheless earned the distinction, generally unacknowledged, of being the first major American colonial composer of sacred music.

Two sects from the Radical Reformation also produced colonial hymnals of note. First were the Mennonites, a large Anabaptist sect who published an edition of their *Ausbund: Etliche schone christliche Gesang* (Paragon: Some Beautiful Christian Songs) in 1742. This collection, also used by the Amish, was the earliest collection of Radical Reformation hymnody, dating to 1533–36. The Schwenkfelders, followers of the anti-sacramental radical reformer Caspar Schwenkfeld von Ossig (1489–1561), had gathered enough members by 1762 to publish a massive collection of 917 hymns titled *Neu-eingerichtites Gesang Buch* (Newly Arranged Song Book) edited by their leader Christopher Schulz (1718–89). This obscure sectarian hymnal contained not only Schulz's discourse on sacred song, matched only by Beissel's musical writings among colonial Germans, but also dozens of hymns by members of the Pennsylvania community, including Balthasar Hoffman, Abraham Wagner, and Georg Weiss. Aside from Beissel himself, no other colonial American poet in any language approached the published hymn output of these Schwenkfelders.

The most accomplished radical Pietist sacred music came from the Moravian Brethren, who first appeared in the colonies during the early 1730s and founded large communitarian settlements in Pennsylvania and North Carolina over the next few decades. Moravians sang at work, daily community prayer, watch-night services, and love feasts. Their hymnody combined fifteenth-century Hussite songs with their own new lyrics, especially those of their leader, Nikolaus Count von Zinzendorf (1700–60), who wrote two thousand hymns. The Moravians used instruments in their worship and organized a *collegium musicum* at each of their major centers to perform sacred and secular instrumental music of German composers including Franz Joseph Haydn, Carl Stamitz, and Christian Friedrich Bach. Late in the colonial period Pennsylvania Moravians John Antes (1740–1811) and Johann Friedrich Peter (1746–1813) composed sacred choral music for the Brethren.

Like their Evangelical counterparts, the major colonial German communions preserved their traditional sacred music while also singing a newer body of deeply emotive hymnody during the mid-eighteenth century. German colonists also produced greater musical and textual diversity than the English denominations, thanks to the original texts and music of Pennsylvania's Radical Reformation and Pietist sects. The Evangelical and Pietist movements together, moreover, had greater influence in colonial America than in their respective homelands during the spiritual quickening of the 1740s and 1750s. Their dominance across most colonial denominations brought a decisive shift away from the scriptural praise of psalmody to the hymnody of religious experience that marked the first major differentiation of colonial American sacred music from its Old World origins.

PARISH-STYLE TUNES AND WATTS' TEXTS

After the Great Awakening, the pace of tune book and hymnal production increased rapidly in Anglophone America. A new generation of editors began to replace the singing school manuals of Walter and Tufts with anthologies that reflected the development of parish-style music in England. After the Glorious Revolution of 1688, some Anglican composers turned their attention to country parishes that lacked the resources to perform the cathedral-style music of the Anglican Reformation. During the early decades of the eighteenth century, they began writing psalm tunes that achieved intense harmonic effects and deep emotional expression, yet were easy to perform. William Croft's "St. Anne's" (1724), set to Isaac Watts' psalm text "Our God, Our Help in Ages Past," is perhaps the best-known example.

In the 1730s and 1740s, self-trained composers like William Tans'ur (1700–83) and parish clerks like John Arnold (c. 1720–92) published large sacred music collections specifically designed for country parishes. By the 1750s the parish style included three major musical genres: plain tunes – harmonized psalm tunes like "St. Anne's" in three or four parts; anthems – extended sectional compositions that set verses of scripture; and fuging tunes – a compound form that began with a plain tune "head" and ended with a fugue-like section in which the different parts entered separately, repeating lines of text before reuniting in a final cadence. As the parish style matured, its composers ornamented the melodies of their plain tunes, elaborated the counterpoint of their fuging tunes, and dramatized the choral effects of their anthems.

In the early 1760s, Philadelphia emerged as the earliest colonial American center of the parish style. Francis Hopkinson (1737–91), an Anglican organist, composer, poet, lawyer, and judge, published *A Collection of Psalm Tunes . . . for the Use of the United Churches of Christ Church and St. Peter's in Philadelphia* in 1763. Hopkinson's *Collection* was the first American tune book to provide a figured bass for each piece, signaling the arrival of organs – an essential element of English parish-style performance – in the elite Anglican churches of colonial America. Hopkinson also edited the *New Version* for the Collegiate Church (Dutch Reformed) of New York City in 1767. His commission was to fit Tate and Brady's lyrics to the Dutch and Genevan tunes that were still markers of the congregation's ethnic identity. His *Psalms of David . . . for the Use of the Reformed Protestant Dutch Church in the City of New-York* echoed Ainsworth's 1612 Separatist psalter in its adaptation of English psalm texts to tunes written in the meters of other languages.

James Lyon (1735–94), Hopkinson's Philadelphia colleague, was a singing master, composer, and Presbyterian minister who published *Urania, or a Choice Collection of Psalm-Tunes, Anthems, and Hymns from the Most Approv'd Authors* in 1761. This landmark collection contained fifty-nine parish-style works previously unpublished in America, as well as ten of Lyon's own fluent compositions. *Urania* was well received, passing through at least six printings from 1761 to 1773. Flushed with this success, Lyon created a furor with his 1763 treatise *The Lawfulness, Excellency, and Advantage of Instrumental Musick in the Publick Worship of God Urg'd and Enforc'd*. He directly challenged the unaccompanied Calvinist praise of Presbyterians and Baptists by urging them to employ organs and other instruments to strengthen congregational singing. *Lawfulness* touched off a decades-long controversy among American Presbyterians over the propriety of instruments in worship and the use of original hymns instead of Francis Rous' 1643 *Psalms of David*, the approved psalter of the Church of Scotland.

Lyon's *Urania* introduced the fully developed parish-style to colonial praise. New England compilers quickly followed his lead. In 1764 Daniel Bayley (1729–92), a potter, printer, and Anglican parish clerk from Newburyport, Massachusetts, began publishing a series of tune books that popularized the works of William Tans'ur and Aaron Williams (1731–76), two of the most celebrated parish-style composers and compilers. Bayley reprinted Tans'ur's *Royal Melody Complete*, a 1755 collection of original compositions, and later bound it with Williams' popular 1763 tune book, *The Universal Psalmodist,* under the title *The American Harmony*. By combining works by Williams, clerk of the Scots Presbyterian Church in London, and Tans'ur, a fervent Anglican, Bayley brought together New England's Reformed and Anglican traditions of sacred song in one publication. He successfully pursued this combination strategy in a succession of reprints and new compilations over the next two decades.

By the time the Boston jeweler, engraver, and musician Josiah Flagg (1737–95) published *A Collection of the Best Psalm Tunes* in 1764, he felt the need to explain in print why a new tune book was necessary. His *Collection* was fully justified, however, by providing sixty parish-style tunes published in America for the first time. Flagg's other musical publication, *Sixteen Anthems* (1766), presented complex and difficult compositions by Handel, Tans'ur, Williams, Joseph Stephenson, Caleb Ashworth, and William Knapp. The collections of Lyon, Bayley, and Flagg supported the rapid growth of colonial choirs during the 1760s and 1770s. Whether organized as a cappella musical societies in Congregational and Presbyterian churches or as choirs directed by organists in urban Anglican parishes, these ensembles gained the ability to perform at a high level of musical excellence. In the major cities, their singers occasionally performed sacred oratorios, especially those by Handel, in public concerts.

By 1770, local congregations in colonial America drew their sacred music from a combination of traditional psalters, tune supplements, and singing school tune books. The overlapping preferences of Congregationalists, Presbyterians, and Anglicans had established tunes like "Old Hundred" and "Wells" as perennial favorites. A smattering of parish-style tunes also gained interdenominational popularity late in the colonial period. Compositions such as Tans'ur's "St. Martin's" and Joseph Stephenson's "Psalm 34" took hold, especially in congregations that supported choirs or musical societies. On the eve of the Revolution, however, the specific group of tunes a particular congregation sang continued to vary significantly according to its denomination, region, singing master, and level of musical talent.

If colonial psalmody developed impressive musical diversity, however, its textual dimension became increasingly the domain of one writer, Isaac

Watts. Tate and Brady's *New Version* enjoyed substantial popularity, especially in the Anglican South, but its influence paled in comparison to the impact of Watts' metrical psalms and hymns on Anglophone Protestants everywhere in the colonies. George Whitefield featured Watts' lyrics in his 1753 *Collection of Hymns for Social Worship*, reprinted at Philadelphia in 1768, and even Wesley included them in his Methodist hymnals.

Surprisingly, many Evangelical Congregationalist leaders in New England were slow to embrace Watts' sacred lyrics, despite their endorsement by Jonathan Edwards. For example Thomas Prince, Boston's leading Evangelical minister, issued a revised version of the *New England Psalm Book* in 1758 rather than embrace Watts' psalms or hymns. Not until Samson Occom's *Choice Collection of Hymns and Spiritual Songs* (1774) did a New England hymn compiler endorse Watts unambiguously. The same pattern prevailed among Baptists, who were one of the earliest Reformed communions to embrace hymns in worship. Benjamin Wallin of Boston included Watts' sermon hymns in his 1762 *Evangelical Hymns and Songs*, but Samuel Hall of Newport placed none of Watts' texts in his 1766 *Hymns and Spiritual Songs*.

Yet Watts had become the poetic voice of most American Protestants, and especially Evangelicals, by the early 1770s. The publication of his poetical works and their appropriation by colonial tune book compilers accomplished this transformation. Watts was the most widely published author in eighteenth-century America. Benjamin Franklin printed the first American edition of *The Psalms of David Imitated* in 1729 and one of the first editions of *Hymns and Spiritual Songs* in 1742. Boston printers were not far behind. From these beginnings, forty editions of *Psalms* and fourteen editions of *Hymns* appeared in America before 1776, along with eight editions of the widely circulated 1760 Boston *Appendix, Containing a Number of Hymns Taken Chiefly from Dr. Watts's Scriptural Collection*.

Watts' sacred poems were also eminently suitable for singing. His carefully crafted stanzas and emotionally heightened rhetoric drew the attention of parish-style composers in England. Colonial compilers, in turn, highlighted those compositions in their collections. Eight of the ten most frequently printed hymn texts in colonial tune books were written by Watts, including "The God of Glory Sends His Summons Forth," "And Am I Born to Die?" and "Hark! From the Tombs a Doleful Sound." By the Revolution, the singing school had become a principal agent through which Watts' powerful synthesis of biblical imagery, homely metaphors, and emotive spiritual rhetoric articulated the shared Evangelical beliefs of colonial American Protestants. His words, set to parish-style tunes, taught in singing schools, and sung in Sunday services and social worship, reached merchants, farmers, artisans, laborers, and even slaves whose

Evangelical masters included them in plantation devotions and congregational worship.

WILLIAM BILLINGS AND THE AMERICAN REVOLUTION IN PRAISE

As the Revolutionary era began, colonial American psalmody was well on its way to appropriating English parish-style music and a canon of psalm and hymn texts drawn primarily from Watts and the *New Version*. This development may properly be called Anglicization, another example of passive colonial culture, in the sense that the musical theory, compositional genres, and textual resources for American tune books were taken directly from English sources. Americans had written very few tunes or texts for the service of praise. Even James Lyon's *Urania* represented colonial mastery of the parish style more than American originality.

This trajectory changed dramatically in 1770 with the publication of an original tune book by William Billings of Boston called *The New-England Psalm-Singer*. Billings (1746–1800) was a tanner by trade who associated with Samuel Adams and the Sons of Liberty at the city's White Horse Tavern. He attended the independently minded Brattle Street Church. Unlike earlier colonial singing masters, Billings aspired to be a parish-style composer of the first rank like William Tans'ur. *The New-England Psalm-Singer* delivered 127 of his compositions in all of the parish-style genres, including powerful plain tunes, spirited fuging tunes, and difficult and idiosyncratic anthems. The size of Billings' collection rivaled anything Tans'ur had published. The young Boston composer also imitated the English master's works by providing extensive musical instructions, poetic encomiums to music, and a learned essay on the properties of sound. *The New-England Psalm-Singer* even included a frontispiece illustration of singers around a table, modeled on Tans'ur's *Royal Melody Complete* and engraved by Paul Revere.

Despite these many gestures toward parish-style precedents, however, Billings also delivered an unprecedented declaration of musical independence in his prefatory remarks "To all Musical Practitioners" in *The New-England Psalm-Singer*. Billings proclaimed himself unconfined by any established rules of composition and accordingly laid down none of his own for others to follow. His music embodied his principles. Although his compositions were clearly grounded in conventions of the parish style, they moved in dramatically innovative melodic, harmonic, and rhythmic directions. Billings' plain tunes "Amherst," "Brookfield," and "Lebanon" from *The New-England Psalm-Singer* became instantly popular and gained enduring fame in the early republic. "Majesty" and "Maryland," two fuging tunes from Billings' 1778 collection *The Singing-Master's Assistant* (1778), enjoyed similar notoriety, and his late "Anthem for Easter" (1787/1800) was perhaps the most influential choral composition written in early America.

Billings also experimented with texts. The *New-England Psalm-Singer* balanced Watts and the *New Version* against original sacred lyrics by Billings himself and Boston poets Mather Byles and Perez Morton. His small 1786 collection, *The Suffolk Harmony*, highlighted the hymns of James Relly (c. 1722–78), a Whitefieldian Universalist whose theology was briefly popular in Boston. But over time Watts became Billings' favorite lyricist, his poems taking a larger proportion of settings in each new collection. Billings also composed important music for the Revolutionary cause. He wrote the tune and lyrics to "Chester" ("Let tyrants shake their iron rod"), the leading Patriot battle hymn.[1] Two of his anthems with original lyrics from *The Singing-Master's Assistant* – "Lamentation over Boston" ("By the Rivers of Watertown we sat down and wept"), an adaptation of Psalm 137,[2] and "Independence" ("The States, O Lord, with Songs of Praise shall in thy Strength rejoice")[3] – initiated a tradition of nationalist music that flourished through the post-Revolutionary decades.

In addition to producing a steady stream of compositions that eventually filled five major collections, Billings was a tireless singing master, itinerating across eastern and central Massachusetts for more than three decades. Ever attentive to young talent in his singing schools, he helped to gather a generation of younger Massachusetts composers, including Supply Belcher (1751–1836), Jacob French (1754–1817), and Abraham Wood (1752–1804). Billings' career also inspired singing masters elsewhere in New England. As early as the mid-1770s, the young New Haven composer Daniel Read (1757–1836) was studying Billings' music. A few towns away in Cheshire, Connecticut, composer-compiler Andrew Law (1749–1821) began a long and successful career with the publication of his *Select Harmony* in 1778.

With the achievement of American independence, the emerging New England singing school style quickly blossomed into the republic's first national form of artistic expression. New tune books, including original collections by French, Read, and Wood, poured from New England presses during the 1780s. Philadelphia and Baltimore soon joined this expansion of tune book publication and the network of singing masters it supported. With the Second Great Awakening (1799–1805), the singing

---

[1] Karl Kroeger, ed., *The Complete Works of William Billings*, 4 vols. (Boston, 1977–90), I: 321.
[2] *Ibid.*, II: 136.
[3] *Ibid.*, 244.

school expanded into the South and the trans-Appalachian West, where it acquired new stylistic elements from camp meeting songs, fiddle tunes, folk ballads, and emergent African American spirituals.

On the eve of political revolution, the development of singing school music as the canonical praise of the new nation was still years away. But by 1776 William Billings and his followers had already broken free from the constraints of colonial sacred music culture and were embarked on a new synthesis of traditional psalmody, revival hymnody, English parish-style music, and Evangelical lyrics that would soon bring an American revolution in praise.

SUGGESTIONS FOR FURTHER READING

Bach, Jeff. *Voices of the Turtledoves: The Sacred World of Ephrata*. University Park, PA, 2003.

Benson, Louis F. *The English Hymn: Its Development and Use*. Richmond, 1962 [1915].

Buechner, Alan Clark. *Yankee Singing Schools and the Golden Age of Choral Music in New England, 1760–1800*. Boston, 2003.

Crawford, Richard, ed. *The Core Repertory of Early American Psalmody*. Madison, 1984.

Haraszti, Zoltan. *The Enigma of the Bay Psalm Book*. Chicago, 1958.

Lara, Jaime. *City, Temple, Stage: Eschatological Architecture and Liturgical Theatrics in New Spain*. Notre Dame, 2004.

Marini, Stephen A. *Sacred Song in America: Religion, Music, and Public Culture*. Urbana, 2003.

McKay, David P., and Richard Crawford. *William Billings of Boston: Eighteenth-Century Composer*. Princeton, 1975.

Pointer, Richard. "The Sounds of Worship: Nahua Music Making and Colonial Catholicism in Sixteenth-Century Mexico." *Fides et Historia* 34:2 (2002): 25–44.

Spencer, Jon Michael. *Protest and Praise: Sacred Music of Black Religion*. Minneapolis, 1990.

Temperley, Nicholas. *The Music of the English Parish Church*. 2 vols. Cambridge, UK, 1979.

Watson, J. R. *The English Hymn: A Critical and Historical Study*. Oxford, UK, 1997.

35

RELIGIOUS ARCHITECTURE

PETER W. WILLIAMS

The peoples whom European explorers, conquerors, and colonists found in North America were as diverse as the newcomers would eventually become, and their built environment, including their sacred structures, was equally diverse. One of the determining factors was their natural environment and the lifestyle it dictated. Northern peoples, who depended on hunting for much of their sustenance, followed a semi-nomadic course, and the buildings they constructed were often impermanent. Those further south, where the land conduced to agriculture, were able to erect more elaborate and permanent structures, such as the sun temple in the "grand village" of the mound-building Natchez near today's Mississippi city of that name. Still further south, in what is now Mexico, imperial powers such as the Aztecs arose, which were able to command the resources to build vast temple complexes such as that at Tenochtitlán near present-day Mexico City.

For most of the aboriginal peoples of present-day Canada and the United States, sacrality was not confined to buildings set apart for ritual use, although the latter certainly existed. The lines that separate public and private as well as sacred and secular were blurry or absent among native peoples. The longhouse of the Iroquois in upstate New York, for example, served as a general center both for family residence and for communal activity, whether in the form of ritual or public discussions. Like many native structures, it was modeled on a legendary prototype. Early longhouses were constructed from poles covered with bark, whereas contemporary examples are generally made with Euro-American materials such as stud frames, clapboard siding, and shake roofs. This pattern of continuity of form and function with continual adaptation of materials is a common theme, as exemplified in present-day sweat lodges among the Omaha made from brightly colored plastic sheets.

For the Plains Indians, their seminomadic lifeways dictated more ad hoc building techniques. For the performance of their Sun Dance, they would erect a temporary enclosure with a forked cottonwood tree at the center, from which rafters made of saplings would radiate to join an encircling fence. The tree at the center, adorned with the head of a buffalo, constituted an axis mundi, or center of the world, which was reproduced in microcosm in this ritual structure and served as a means through which prayers and sacrifices could be directed to the supernatural powers. As with most such constructions, this ritual ground was modeled on a mythic prototype, in this case the story of a vision quest that resulted in the salvation of the people from starvation through the receipt of vital information of supernatural origin.

The Pueblo peoples of the Southwest have always been easily recognizable through their distinctive apartment house-like complexes made of stone and adobe bricks. Amidst the residential units are public plazas in which are located kivas, or underground ceremonial chambers, where members of the kiva societies reenact creation stories dressed as kachinas, or supernatural figures. As with most native structures, the kiva was oriented according to cardinal directions – in this case on a north-south axis – and underwent annual rituals of renewal. A ladder projected outward, symbolizing the cosmic axis, and a ceremonial altar, firepit, and *sipapu* – a small, round hole symbolizing the point of entry of the first people onto the earth from the realm below – were located on the floor. The kiva thus provided a symbolic and ritual center for the entire complex, which in turn was framed by the four holy mountains that delineated the Pueblo cosmos.

For the nearby Navajo, or Dineh, whose settlement patterns were as dispersed as the Pueblos' were concentrated, the primary building unit was the hogan, or single-family house. Hogans, which can still be seen frequently throughout northern Arizona, are single-room circular structures with a hole in the center of the roof for smoke. Their doors face eastward, toward the rising sun, and their poles are aligned with the four cardinal directions. Like many Native American structures, hogans are not freestyle creations but imitations of an archetype – in this case, mountains – provided at the creation of the world and retold in the Blessingway ritual complex of songs and prayers dealing with creation and harmony, which were recited at their dedications. Hogans are considered to be living beings and must be periodically purified and fed after their initial consecration. To live in a hogan is not simply to exist, but to dwell in the sacred manner of the Dineh people.

The coming of Europeans to North America beginning in the late fifteenth century came not through the immigration of individuals, but rather through the extension of empires – in particular, those of Britain, France, and Spain. In each of these cases the establishment of European hegemony involved not only military conquest and the settlement of productive colonists, but also the importation of an established church – Anglican or

Roman – that aided in the imposition of an alien culture on the aboriginal peoples. These church representatives sent over or brought with them the archetypes for church construction that, often in drastically adapted fashion, would provide the material infrastructure for Christian worship in the New World for generations to come.

The French colonial presence left the least enduring impact on the North American built environment; what little can still be found lies, unsurprisingly, in such areas of French settlement as the Canadian province of Quebec and the Mississippi Valley culminating in New Orleans. Only a few such structures survive more or less intact, such as the Sulpician *seminaire* in Montreal (1685) and the Ursuline convent in New Orleans (1749–53). Both reflect the late Renaissance classicism dominant in the mother country. St. Louis Cathedral in New Orleans was originally built in 1789–94 but extensively remodeled in 1849–51, resulting in an architectural hodgepodge composed of elements from a variety of period styles. It fronts present-day Jackson Square (formerly the Place d'Armes and Plaza de Armas) and is surrounded by the Cabildo (1795–99), which housed the city's Spanish administration, and the Presbytère (1791–1813), the cathedral's rectory. The juxtaposition of styles, functions, and languages represented in these structures is amply suggestive of the relationship between church and state in this most cosmopolitan of early American cities.

What is now the southwestern portion of the United States was previously the northernmost outpost of Nueva España, or New Spain, a section remote from the colonial capital in Mexico City and consequently neglected in the course of imperial affairs. Most of the religious presence was in the form of missions to the native peoples by the Jesuit and Franciscan religious orders. Many of these fell into neglect after independence from Spain and subsequent acquisition by the United States until later generations sought to restore them for historic, religious, or commercial reasons. The best known of these missions is the chain of twenty-one missions founded by the Franciscan missionaries Junípero Serra and Fermín Lasuen along the Camino Real (royal road), which leads from San Diego north to San Francisco, at the time of the American Revolution and the final days of the Spanish Empire. Franciscans also established a number of missions in Arizona, New Mexico, and Texas, including the Misíon San Antonio de Valera, better known as the Alamo (1724; secularized 1793). All were part of the imperial plan to bring civilization to the region in the form of a Spanish Christian hegemony to be achieved not only by Christianizing the native peoples, but by resettling them in mission complexes in which they would become resocialized into a European lifestyle.

The Spanish missions in what is now the American Southwest differ somewhat in style – the mission at Santa Barbara, for instance, is an unusual example of classicism – but most are consistent in their reflection of modes of building developed in Iberia, brought across the Atlantic to Mexico, imported northward by missionaries who were not trained architects, and erected by native laborers unfamiliar with European building techniques and materials. The result was a creative hybridity, which had begun with the Spanish, who had incorporated elements of Mudéjar (Moorish) elements from their Muslim neighbors in Andalusia. In Mexico an elaborate Spanish baroque decorative style known as the churrigueresque flourished in the eighteenth century but required far too much in the way of technical knowledge and financial resources to be replicated in the remote north. The Spanish mission churches in what is now the United States range in sophistication from the elegantly baroque San José and San Miguel de Aguayo (1720–31) in San Antonio to the vernacular San Francisco de Asís (1772–1816) in Ranchos de Taos, New Mexico, whose dramatic tamped-earth masses and stark forms have inspired such painters of the southwestern landscape as Georgia O'Keefe.

Whereas the French and Spanish imperial presences were monolithically Catholic, the British were much more complicated religiously. Although Maryland was established by English Catholics as a place where they and others could find religious freedom absent in the mother country, successive actions by Puritans, who burned the Catholics' churches, and later by Anglicans forced them into minority status, and they were obliged to worship in private homes. The main religious forces in the Atlantic colonies were those that were also prominent in Britain: Puritan Congregationalists in New England, their Presbyterian and other Reformed coreligionists in the Middle Colonies, and Anglicans in the New York City area and most of the South. Their disagreements over theology, liturgy, and polity were materially reflected in their conflicting ideas over the proper public setting for worship. The conflict can be summarized briefly: church versus meetinghouse.

"Church" is a word of multiple meanings. As a designation for a house of worship, it today is a broadly inclusive term for almost any such Christian site. For the religious antagonists of the Reformation era, however, it strongly implied a place for worship that was also thought to be a sacred place. This latter position had long been held by Roman Catholics, who had elaborate rituals for consecrating a church, which had to contain a relic of a saint in its altar stone to possess full sacral efficacy. Opinion in the Church of England under the Tudors varied greatly about this and other issues, but by the time of the Stuarts in the early seventeenth century, Church of England opinion had swung definitely in the Catholic direction. Anglicans had churches, whereas their Puritan opponents had meetinghouses (or meeting-houses) as buildings for worship. According to chapter XXI of the Westminster Confession, a creedal statement drawn up by an assembly of Puritan divines summoned by Parliament during the English Civil War,

> Neither prayer, nor any other part of religious worship, is now, under the gospel, either tied unto, or made more acceptable to, any place in which it is performed, or towards which it is directed: but God is to be worshipped everywhere in spirit and in truth; as in private families daily, and in secret each one by himself, so more solemnly in the public assemblies, which are not carelessly or willfully to be neglected or forsaken, when God, by his Word or providence, calleth thereunto.[1]

Anglican churches in seventeenth-century New England were unknown under Puritan rule, and few from that era in the southern colonies have survived. After England's Glorious Revolution of 1688, however, the imperial government began to cast a harder eye on what was going on across the Atlantic. This resulted in the establishment of Anglican churches in Boston (e.g., King's Chapel, already organized in 1686) as well as the more rapid dissemination of English fashion in its overseas dominions. London had been devastated by fire in 1666, and the remarkable Sir Christopher Wren had received a commission to design dozens of new churches in what is sometimes called the Wren baroque style. Notable among them are the great domed St. Paul's Cathedral (1677–1708) and St. Bride's Parish Church (1675), whose steeple has been cited as the prototype of the modern wedding cake. He and his successor, Sir James Gibbs, the architect for the iconic St. Martin-in-the-Fields (1721) at Trafalgar Square, collectively produced the ecclesiastical archetype that became known as the Wren-Gibbs style, characterized by classical form and detail, multitiered steeples, and massive porticoes.

It was this style, popularized in Gibbs' widely circulated 1728 *Book of Architecture*, that set the tone for American church design throughout the eighteenth century and far beyond. Christ Church in Boston (1721) attained iconic status for its role in Paul Revere's legendary ride ("one if by land ..."). It is at least as important, however, for its introduction of the Wren-Gibbs mode into the northern colonies, albeit in a much simpler provincial version than its London prototypes. In the southern colonies, especially Virginia and South Carolina, the design was extremely popular among the Anglican grandees who controlled the colonial governments and the established church that accompanied it. Charleston in the latter colony boasts two grand urban churches in this style, St. Philip's (1727; rebuilt 1835) and St. Michael's (1752–61). In Virginia, a colony in which the plantation was the primary unit of settlement, churches were scattered

---

[1] John H. Leith, ed., *Creeds of the Churches* (Garden City, NY, 1963), 217–18.

throughout the countryside. Many of these were built and dominated by local planters, such as Christ Church, Lancaster County (1730), commissioned by Robert "King" Carter.

Most central was Bruton Parish Church in Williamsburg, the colonial capital. The current church, the third on the site, was built in 1715 and is situated on the Duke of Gloucester Street, more or less midway between the College of William and Mary and the House of Burgesses. Built of red brick and flanked by a burying ground, it has an entry tower with a modest two-stage steeple capped by a spire, and a transept (crossing) that provides extra seating, giving the structure a cruciform shape. Inside are an ornate pew near the altar reserved for the governor, galleries for the college students, box pews (as opposed to the "slip pews" of modern-day churches), and the four "liturgical stations" that had become mandatory for Anglican churches. These latter included the altar (referred to as the "table" by those of the Puritan persuasion), the reading desk for the proclamation of scripture, the pulpit, and the baptismal font. Bruton, like most Anglican churches of this era, had clear rather than stained glass, reflecting the Enlightenment propensity for rationality and clarity. Colonial Anglican churches were also required to post the Ten Commandments and the royal arms, reminders of the cooperative relationship of church and state in exerting divinely legitimated authority.

The counterpoint to the church model of religious design was the Puritan meetinghouse, which dominated the New England built environment during the seventeenth century. The name is an overt repudiation of the idea of church as a holy place in material form. One of the few surviving examples of the early colonial meetinghouse is the Old Ship Church (1681; now Unitarian Universalist) in Hingham, Massachusetts, on Boston's south shore. When stripped of its later embellishments, Old Ship resembles not a church but rather a large private home. The main entry is on one of the long sides, and inside, a towering pulpit is axially aligned with that entrance, emphasizing that worship was focused on the preached Word. The walls have no ornament, in keeping with the Puritan embracing of the ancient Hebrew prohibition of graven images and resulting in a distinctive aesthetic known as the "plain style." As in most contemporary houses of worship, there are box pews, which were made available to family units by sale or rent according to that family's status in the covenanted community. Meetinghouses were supposed to be treated with respect but not reverence and could be used for appropriate civic functions such as town meetings and education – even defense against hostile natives.

Despite the growing aversion of many colonists to both king and bishop in the decades leading up to the Revolution, the Wren-Gibbs church, nevertheless, prevailed as the defining prototype of a house of worship as the eighteenth century progressed. Instructive is the design of the Old South Meetinghouse, built in what is now downtown Boston in 1729. In general proportions and design, Old South bears a distinct resemblance to its Anglican counterpart, Old North. The difference becomes apparent when one seeks the main entrance, which is not in the central tower but rather on one of the long sides, in meetinghouse fashion. The interior is elegantly decorated in neoclassical fashion, with a dominant pulpit, but lacks any representational art. By the time of the Revolution, such meetinghouses – which would soon be referred to commonly as churches – approximated even more the Anglican norm, retaining the central pulpit but shifting the main axis so that entry was now, in churchly fashion, on one of the short sides. By this time other churches in the Reformed tradition, such as First Baptist (1771–75) in Providence, Rhode Island, had come on board as well. As New Englanders began to emigrate westward, the Wren-Gibbs prototype, which had morphed into the more elegant Federal style, accompanied them. The style is strikingly exemplified in the Congregational church in Tallmadge, Ohio (1822–25), near Akron, which graced the 1944 Thanksgiving issue of *Life* magazine as an icon of traditional American values in a time of war. Translated from London to Boston and then across the westward trajectory of the "Yankee exodus," it eventually manifested itself in the Central Union Church (1922–23) in Honolulu, surrounded by palm trees. In the form of the "colonial revival," the style has persisted into the twenty-first century, and it has been especially popular among conservative denominations in the South.

By the beginning of the nineteenth century, neoclassicism took on new forms, influenced less by the Renaissance than by that historicizing cultural movement's own prototypes, the architecture of ancient Greece and Rome. Thomas Jefferson himself popularized the Roman revival as ideologically appropriate for the new republic, although the "lawn" of his University of Virginia is anchored not by a chapel but by a library. The power of the symbolism is exemplified in the story of the design of the first American Roman Catholic cathedral. When in 1804 then bishop John Carroll was presented with two plans by the architect of the national capitol, Benjamin Henry Latrobe – one Roman, the other Gothic – Carroll selected the former as more appropriate for Catholics living in a republic.

By the 1820s, the national vogue had shifted to the Greek revival – like the Roman, a suitable expression of republican values – and manifested itself in every sort of structure from private homes to the U.S. Treasury (Robert Mills, 1836–42). By this time religious communities outside the Protestant spectrum had begun to acquire sufficient numbers and resources to mount substantial building projects. Thus, in addition to such iconic structures as the Congregational church (1838) in Madison, Connecticut,

Catholics in Cincinnati built St. Peter in Chains Cathedral (1845) in the Greek mode, as did the Jews of Charleston, South Carolina, with their Reform-leaning Temple Beth Elohim in 1840.

By the 1840s, the Enlightenment rationalism associated with neoclassicism had begun to yield to Romanticism as a broad cultural force. This trend manifested itself in part in a new enthusiasm for the Middle Ages, which heretofore had been scorned by Protestants as the domain of superstition and popery. The medieval cause in the realm of ecclesiastical architecture was particularly promoted in England by the Cambridge Camden (or Ecclesiological) Society as a liturgical counterpart of the contemporaneous Oxford movement, which advocated a new respect for tradition and the institutional church within Anglican circles. The Ecclesiologists undertook the scholarly study of medieval religious architecture and used it as the basis for promoting Gothic revival churches, a style they believed to be the only one truly appropriate for Christian worship. In addition to its elaborate symbolism – some of which may have been post hoc imaginings by later scholars – the Gothic was deemed singularly appropriate because it did, in fact, house the very sort of sacred space rejected out of hand by the Westminster Confession and its Puritan advocates. Essential here was the recessed chancel, which elevated and distinguished the part of the church that held the altar from the nave, to which laypeople were consigned.

Soon ecclesiological societies were founded by American Episcopalians, especially in New York and New Jersey, and the "pure" Gothic style – as opposed to earlier ornamented boxes such as Trinity Church, New Haven (1814) – made an early appearance in what is now Philadelphia in the form of St. James the Less (1846–48). A Gothic vision on a grander scale was Richard Upjohn's Trinity Church (1839–46) at the corner of Broadway and Wall Street in Manhattan, although financial problems led the designer to forego traditional medieval vaulting techniques. For the next several decades Upjohn, a transplanted Englishman, would be the nation's premier Gothic revival architect, specializing in Episcopal churches but serving other denominations as well, as illustrated in the First Congregational Church in Brunswick, Maine (1845–46). A particular contribution of Upjohn to the American "churchscape" was the vernacular style known as "carpenter Gothic," easily made by local builders with "board and batten" construction – alternating wider and narrower vertical strips of wood – and rapidly adopted by virtually all denominations as their adherents settled the Great Plains and the prairies.

Gothic was also an obvious choice for Roman Catholic church building as immigrants from Ireland, Germany, and, later, Central and southern Europe began to swell the great cities of the Northeast and Great Lakes regions. Where Anglicans and British Protestants favored the English mode, however, American Catholics – especially those of Irish origin, who had no love for the English – opted for continental versions of the style. St. Patrick's Cathedral (1858–79) was designed by Smithsonian architect James Renwick, Jr., on the model of the Kölner Dom, Cologne's grand medieval cathedral, which was only completed during the nineteenth-century Romantic revival. Built through the small contributions of countless poor New York Irish faithful under the leadership of Archbishop "Dagger John" Hughes, the imposing presence of St. Patrick's was a powerful statement of the immigrant Catholic presence in the American metropolis. Hundreds of other Gothic-revival Catholic churches on various scales were also designed during the second half of the nineteenth century by Irish immigrant architect Patrick Keeley.

Another medieval theme was struck in the 1870s when the great H. H. Richardson designed the new Trinity Church (Episcopal) in Boston's Copley Square for that "prince of the pulpit," Phillips Brooks. Based on French and Spanish prototypes and characterized by the use of massive arches, polychromy, rough stone, and a dominant tower, Trinity reflects a Protestant preference for the Christian style that predated Gothic and thus seemed more harmonious with the spirit of pre-Roman Christianity. Trinity's lush interior was assembled through the coming together of several prominent contemporary British and American artists and artisans working in a variety of media, including mural painting, wood carving, and stained glass. As such, it embodied the ideas of the arts and crafts movement, inspired by the English artists and critics John Ruskin and William Morris, who mounted a critique of modern industrial society as betraying the religious, ethical, and aesthetic values exemplified by the handwork of medieval craftsmen. One of its most influential American advocates was the Anglo-Catholic Boston architect Ralph Adams Cram, who with his partner Bertram Grosvenor Goodhue became the center of a new phase of the Gothic revival that lasted from the 1890s until the Great Depression. Cram's designs, exemplified in Manhattan's St. Thomas Church (1913), combined a deep knowledge of medieval Gothic rendered in a modern, somewhat streamlined form and accompanied by liturgical art – glass, wood and metal work, embroidery, statuary, and so on – by the finest craftsmen of the day.

The vogue of the cathedral – a church that housed the cathedra, or chair, that symbolized the bishop's office – among Episcopalians correlated with the Gothic enthusiasms of the day. Cram himself was the principal architect of the enormous (and still unfinished) Cathedral Church of St. John the Divine (1892–) in Manhattan's Morningside Heights. (Its size was possibly a response to that of St. Patrick's.) The Cathedral Church of SS. Peter and Paul (1907–90) in the nation's capital – better known as the Washington

National Cathedral – dominates the city from its highest point. It was the creation of Episcopal bishop Henry Yates Satterlee, who envisioned an Anglican but ecumenical Christian symbolic presence at the nation's political center dedicated to urban ministry. Designed by a series of English and American architects with considerable input from Satterlee himself, it has, in fact, functioned as a national pulpit for everyone from Martin Luther King, Jr., to George W. Bush, to the fictional president Jedidiah Bartlett of television's *West Wing*. Its stained glass, in a variety of styles, includes the "space window," which contains a piece of rock from the moon. In a similar gesture of comprehensiveness, San Francisco's Grace Cathedral (1928–64) has windows that depict, among others, Albert Einstein and astronaut John Glenn.

Cathedrals were, in fact, markers of denominational presence and power but were also intended to be centers for urban ministry in cities beset by the interconnected problems brought about by immigration and industrialization. Eastern Orthodox Christians from Eastern Europe and the Balkans brought with them their own tradition of churches arrayed with icons on the interiors and bedecked with domes outside – one central dome for Greeks, a myriad of onion-shaped ones for the Russians. Roman Catholic leadership responded to the problems of immigrant workers, many of them coreligionists, through the creation of a vast network of institutions to provide an infrastructure for sacramental worship and social service while at the same time developing a cultural and social "ghetto" that would insulate Catholics from the pressures of Protestantism and the temptations of secularity. This network included parish churches and their accompanying parochial schools, social halls, rectories, and convents, as well as cathedrals, orphanages, hospitals, youth hostels, high schools and colleges, seminaries, motherhouses for sisterhoods, monasteries, and cemeteries, many designed as large-scale "total institutions" in which their inhabitants lived in a completely Catholic atmosphere.

Protestants devised the institutional church, exemplified in Fourth Presbyterian (Ralph Adams Cram, 1914) on Chicago's Michigan Avenue. Built in the then-fashionable Gothic mode, "Fourth Pres" occupies an entire block of valuable commercial land, and it consists not only of an elaborate facility for worship but also offices, a library, and recreational, social, and educational facilities in a cloister-like arrangement. This and many similar mainline Protestant complexes, which sometimes boasted basketball courts and bowling alleys, were designed to attract young inmigrants from small towns and farms who might otherwise be seduced by the city's many secular amusements and snares. Wealthy Protestant congregations also opened mission churches offering services in the languages of immigrant communities, while keeping the newcomers at a safe distance from the main congregation. The "Akron plan" was yet another short-lived Protestant innovation of the 1920s that featured a large worship space, areas of which could be partitioned into smaller modules for Sunday school instruction and then mechanically reunited for common worship. Many of these urban churches conducted their services in auditorium spaces similar to contemporary theaters, with tiered rows of curved seating that provide the congregation with good views of the preacher and musical performers on the central platform.

Christian Science churches, typified by Mary Baker Eddy's Boston Mother Church, were built in a variety of revival styles, in this case Romanesque for the original building (1894) and the domed Byzantine-Renaissance "extension" of 1906. These churches were built on an auditorium plan, with twin desks on a frontal platform from which passages from scripture and Eddy's *Science and Health* could be read to the congregation. The Mother Church is augmented by administrative and publishing facilities that include a plaza and reflecting pool designed by I. M. Pei's firm in the 1970s. Christian Science "reading rooms" in urban downtowns and suburbs provide another distinctive venue for the promotion of denominational literature.

Two major forces, one religious and one aesthetic, converged during the twentieth century to bring about major shifts in religious architectural design: modernism and the liturgical movement. Modernism is an architectural philosophy that arose in reaction to Victorian-era ornamental excesses and stressed instead a simplicity of line and integrity of materials that emphasized the building's function. Modernism's best-known American exponent was Frank Lloyd Wright, who began his iconic career with the design of Unity Temple (1905–08) in Oak Park, Illinois, a suburb of Chicago. Rejecting its Unitarian minister's request for a New England-style church, Wright instead produced a low-lying meetinghouse-style structure of reinforced concrete. The church drew on a wide variety of design sources and maximized interior space through tiered balconies to create an effect of light, intimacy, and unity with the earth. Later architects emulated this spirit in different ways, such as the Finnish-born Eliel Saarinen in his First Christian Church (1942) in Columbus, Indiana, which reduces traditional forms of basilican church and campanile to highly stylized rectangular solids. Chapels at the Massachusetts and Illinois Institutes of Technology (1955, 1952) by, respectively, Saarinen's son Eero and German-born Mies van der Rohe are similar testaments to the minimalist geometric imagination. (It was van der Rohe who coined the modernist slogan, *wenig ist mehr*: "less is more.") The contrast of these latter chapels with their colonial and Gothic revival counterparts at Harvard and Yale respectively is instructive.

Although very different in motivation, the liturgical movement shared with architectural modernists a concern with simplicity as a reaction and antidote to excessive ornamentation. The Benedictine order of the Catholic Church, first in Europe and then at their abbey in Collegeville, Minnesota, advocated reforms in worship that were at once modernizing and firmly rooted in historical scholarship on liturgical practice in the early and medieval eras of church history. These ideas were highly influential on the reforms that emerged from Vatican II (1961–65), as well as worship in Anglican and Protestant denominations. The abbey church at Collegeville (1954–61) designed by Hungarian-born Marcel Breuer is notable for its sculptural banner-like bell tower and a façade in a honeycomb pattern of glass and concrete. The interior of this square-plan building, however, is particularly notable for its centralized altar, flanked by seating for monks on one side and laity on the other. This model, which facilitated an interaction between clergy and laity during Eucharistic celebrations, became the basis for many post-Vatican II churches among Catholics and other liturgically oriented denominations such as Episcopalians and Lutherans, and for the retrofitting of many pre-Vatican II structures as well. Lutheran architect Edward Sövik designed many "nonchurches" based on his theological assumption that Christian worship should not recognize a sacred-secular dichotomy; thus church interiors should be domestic in ambience and not include structural distinctions between clergy and laity. His designs, commissioned by a variety of denominations, include St. Leo's Roman Catholic Church (1969) in Pipestone, Minnesota.

A distinctive product of late twentieth-century American evangelicalism is the megachurch, which designates congregations raging from two thousand into the high five figures. Usually located in suburbs or exurbs near interstates or other major traffic arteries, they feature large parking lots and sprawling physical plans sometimes likened to shopping malls. Their prototype, Willow Creek Community Church (1977–81) in South Barrington, Illinois, was designed through consumer research methods that indicated its potential clientele was indifferent to typical "churchly" imagery and worship. The outcome is that, in the meetinghouse tradition, there is little or no overtly Christian iconography, and services are held in auditorium spaces similar to those that characterized many urban Protestant churches in Victorian America. The rest of the megachurch campus may contain a variety of facilities including a childcare unit, a food court, a bookstore, and any number of rooms for the extensive educational and recreational programming designed for different segments of their often huge congregations.

The long series of new religious movements lying at the edges of traditional Christianity that have characterized American religious history has produced a variety of approaches to religious design and appropriation of space. The Quakers who settled Pennsylvania under William Penn's leadership beginning in 1682 established Philadelphia – "the city of brotherly love" – according to Penn's plan for a "green country town," laid out on a rectilinear grid with broad avenues and large lots conducive to amicable coexistence. Worship was held in meetinghouses on the Puritan model, in the secular domestic styles of the day; their interiors, however, lacked the massive pulpits that indicated a distinction in authority between laity and the clergy, an institution the Friends rejected. The Shakers, who arrived from England under the leadership of "Mother" Ann Lee in the 1770s, had some of their roots in English Quaker practice and erected in the new American nation a series of nineteen (or more, if one includes offshoots) communities from Sabbathday Lake, Maine, to Lexington, Kentucky. Their meetinghouses, along with their residential and work buildings, reflected an aesthetic of American rural functionality and simplicity elevated into a religious principle.

The Latter-day Saints (LDS) under Joseph Smith, whose theology included elements of biblical restorationism, created a new religious architectural form, the Mormon temple, in which they performed not weekly worship, but rather the distinctive ceremonies that Smith claimed to have learned of through divine revelation. The first such temple, the exterior of which resembled a New England meetinghouse with some Gothic and Renaissance design elements, was erected in Kirtland, Ohio, between 1833 and 1836. After the great trek to Salt Lake City that followed Smith's assassination in 1844, a "great basin kingdom" was laid out in Utah – called Deseret by the Mormons – under the leadership of Brigham Young and resulted in massive-scale planned colonization and the emergence of a distinctive LDS landscape. The Salt Lake Temple, designed by Young himself, now anchors a complex of Mormon structures in Temple Square at the center of the city's grid. Begun in 1853 and not completed for several decades, it is reminiscent in general outline of a Gothic cathedral but follows no single style and displays a distinctive array of LDS iconography on its exterior. In the early twenty-first century, there were about 130 LDS temples throughout the world, plus several under construction.

The Jews who came to North America – first the Sephardim from Iberia, later the German- and Yiddish-speaking Ashkenazim from northern Europe – had a long history of experience in adapting their buildings to the styles of their host cultures over centuries of diaspora. After the destruction of the Second Temple in Jerusalem by the Romans in 70 C.E., the synagogue – a place of public assembly rather than the site of the altar of sacrifice – became the norm. The oldest surviving Jewish house of worship in the American colonies is the Touro Synagogue in Newport, Rhode Island, designed in 1763 by Peter Harrison, often cited as the incipient nation's first professional architect. Still in use by the local community, it contains the three features essential for Orthodox worship: a bimah, or platform for the worship leaders; an ark of the covenant in which the Torah scrolls are kept; and a gallery or balcony, in which women and children sit during services. The synagogue is in the neoclassical style popular at the time and resembles more the home of a prosperous merchant than a house of worship, an understandable strategy for a community not wishing to draw the attention of often-hostile gentiles.

The arrival of the Reform movement in America in the nineteenth century brought about accompanying changes in architecture. Synagogue design tended to follow the fashions of the broader society, including the Greek revival exemplified in Beth Elohim in Charleston, South Carolina (1841), sometimes characterized as the nation's first Reform congregation; the Egyptian revival, an exotic architectural strain with Middle Eastern associations; and the *Rundbogenstil*, a contemporary German adaptation of the Romanesque favored by Jews of such background, who often espoused the Reform movement that had originated in that area of Europe. Reform interiors did away with much of the traditional apparatus for worship, exhibiting stained glass, organs, pulpits, and family pews on the Protestant model and substituting a reading desk for the bimah. During the second half of the nineteenth century, prosperous urban congregations began to assert a distinctive identity by embracing a style best described as Jewish Victorian, in which Gothic and Romanesque design components were combined with Moorish domes and minaret-like towers, exemplified in Isaac Mayer Wise's Bene Yeshurun in Cincinnati (1866). Reform Jews also abandoned the use of the term "synagogue" in favor of "temple," a way of asserting that the Jerusalem temple would never be rebuilt and that diaspora was the normative state for the Jewish people.

Orthodox Jews, especially in Manhattan's Lower East Side, began to arrive in vast numbers after the Civil War and often retrofitted former Christian churches and Reform temples for their traditional worship. More prosperous congregations, often sponsored by *landsmanschaften* – mutual benefit associations formed by immigrants from the same locale – built shuls (Yiddish for synagogues) to their own specifications in the interstices between tenement houses, and eventually grander structures such as the Eldridge Street Synagogue (1887), rehabilitated between 1991 and 2007 into an elegantly restored house of worship and museum.

The main contribution of Conservative Judaism to synagogue design was the synagogue-center, nicknamed the "shul with a pool." Like the urban Protestant institutional church, it combined facilities for recreation – gyms and swimming pools – with educational and recreational facilities and stayed in vogue mainly during the interwar years. Postwar synagogue growth followed the movement of the general population to the suburbs and expressed itself in flexible modernist design, often by signature architects. Later in the century the *havurah* movement of small, lay-led gatherings resembling Christian "house churches" favored domestic settings for communal worship, and synagogues or temples often incorporated facilities for more intimate gatherings.

Prior to 1965, the vast majority of structures for worship in North America were built in the various traditions of Christianity and, to a lesser extent, Judaism. The Hart-Cellar Immigration Reform Act of that year marked a dramatic change in that pattern, because it opened the door for large numbers of new immigrants. Many of these came from Asia and the Middle East, and they brought with them their ancestral religions of Buddhism, Hinduism, and Islam, as well as Jainism, Sikhism, and other traditions only sparsely represented previously in the United States. Prior to the later twentieth century, these communities were not only small but rarely possessed the financial resources to do anything more than adapt already-extant structures, religious or otherwise, for the purpose of worship.

After these immigrants began to acquire critical mass in both numbers and wealth, they found themselves able to build temples and mosques in abundance but discovered that such structures in the New World existed in dramatically changed contexts from those of the Old. In Muslim countries, for example, mosques were simply part of the landscape, supported by the state, and largely taken for granted as part of the established faith of that society. Although India is more religiously pluralistic, Hinduism is nevertheless the dominant religion of that nation, and its temples similarly are regarded as givens. In the United States or Canada, however, there was no official status or state support for religion, a cultural area open to entrepreneurship. Hindus and Muslims were free to build temples or mosques, but they had to raise their own funding as well as conform to zoning restrictions and be sensitive to the sensibilities of communities in which they were a small, if often well-to-do, minority. This led to innovations in design and function never anticipated in Asia, exemplified in entirely new institutions such as the Islamic Center. Buddhists, Hindus, and Muslims, in short, had to recapitulate the lessons that earlier immigrants – such as American Jews with their synagogue-centers – had learned successfully in previous generations.

The first authentic Hindu temples in the United States – Sri Ganesha in Flushing, Long Island, and Sri Venkateswara in Pittsburgh – were not built until 1976, eleven years after Hart-Cellar. The notion of authenticity is central here, because Hindu temples in India bear a special relationship to the Indian landscape itself. A Hindu temple is a mandala, or microcosmic diagram used as an aid to meditation, and as such partakes of sacred power. That power is derived from rituals of consecration that involve proper alignment with both the land on which temples sit as well as nearby rivers. To build a temple in North America thus requires the expertise of ritual specialists imported from India, knowledge of temple architectural and iconographic traditions, and symbolic homologization of the North American landscape with that of India, for example, through the equation of an American river with one in the mother country.

The core of a Hindu temple is the *garbha griha*, or "wombhouse," a sanctuary set apart in the larger structure for the display of images of the deities (frequently referred to as "idols" by North American Hindus) to whom puja food offerings are ceremonially rendered. In India, each temple is usually dedicated to a single deity held in particular reverence by the local populace. In the United States and Canada, however, one temple often serves an entire metropolitan area, which may be populated by immigrants from various parts of the subcontinent. This results in the temple's containing images of a variety of deities, at times including the Jain founder-figure Mahavira for followers of that historically related tradition. (The Cincinnati temple diplomatically resolves this issue of theistic pluralism by featuring a representation of the sacred syllable "Om" in its center.) Temples also usually have a tower representing the sacred Mount Meru, either a north Indian-style *shikhara* with a beehive-like shape or a pyramidal *gopuram* more typical of south India. Also, whereas Indian temples are mainly houses of worship, American-style temples usually are part of a complex that includes assembly halls, cafeterias, and other educational and cultural facilities necessary for perpetuating the tradition in a culture in which it will not be automatically sustained by the broader society.

Jains, as noted, often share worship facilities with Hindus; when they have sufficient means to construct their own temples, they are often in the Hindu styles of northern and western India. North American Sikhs established their first *gurdwara* in 1912 in Stockton, California. Sikhism is textually oriented, and a *gurdwara* – "doorway to the guru," in Punjabi – is a room that houses a canopied platform for that tradition's sacred scripture, the Guru Granth Sahib, from which passages are publicly read and devotional hymns sung, followed by a meal and community discussion. *Gurdwaras* in recent years have been designed in an Indo-Persian style. The oldest United States *gurdwara* was established in Richmond Hill in Queens, New York, in 1972, originally in a school basement. After the congregation had grown in size and wealth, it was able to build a much more elaborate worship and cultural center.

The material setting for Buddhist worship in North America reflects a sea change from Asian tradition as well. The earliest Buddhists settled in Hawaii and along the west coast of the continent in the late nineteenth century and, like other Asian groups, were unable to legally replenish their numbers through immigration during the first two-thirds of the twentieth century. Many early American Buddhists were Japanese followers of the Jodo Shinshu branch of Pure Land Mahayana tradition, and they Americanized themselves into the Buddhist Churches of America. Their earliest houses of worship, such as the Buddhist Church of San Francisco on Pine Street (1905; remodeled 1935), are based in many ways, both inside and out, on a Christian church, with slip pews, an organ, and a sanctuary area on the interior. The Buddhist character is revealed mainly in the contents of the sanctuary and in a few exterior ornamental touches, such a domed roof with a pagoda finial. On the Christian model, the worship space is enclosed in a larger complex with administrative and recreational facilities.

Early North American Chinese Buddhists often practiced a folk religion in which Buddhist elements were intermixed with Confucian and Daoist features. Their "joss houses" (a corruption of the Portuguese *deus*, "god") housed no professional staff or structured worship but rather were rooms with altars, tables for offerings, gongs, and traditional ornaments, contained within buildings, such as are still found in San Francisco's and other cities' Chinatowns, in the distinctively American hybrid Chinese Renaissance style.

More sophisticated Buddhist temples of various origins have been modeled more strictly on traditional Asian prototypes, such as the Byodo-In Temple near Honolulu, which is a re-creation of its namesake in Uji, Japan. Zen Buddhism, which is practiced in North America more by Euro-American converts than by Asians, focuses on meditation, and its main material need is an open hall in which practitioners can practice *zazen* (seated meditation). The San Francisco Zen Center, established in 1962, is one of the best-known institutes for the teaching of Zen and is housed in a large converted Mediterranean Romanesque building. In addition to this City Center on Page Street, it also maintains Green Gulch Farm in Marin County, at which organic vegetables are raised, as well as the Tassajara Zen Mountain Center near Big Sur, the first Zen training monastery in North America. The latter complex consists of buildings in the Japanese tradition adapted to California circumstances, with landscaping that is as much a part of the Zen built environment as the buildings themselves. These finely designed structures differ considerably from the majority of

American Buddhist centers, which are as likely as not to be converted houses or other secular buildings adapted for ritual or meditative practice through economic necessity, but nevertheless laid out according to traditional principles of geomancy and directional orientation.

Muslims worship in structures called mosques (from the Arabic *masjid*, through Spanish), a term that evokes the concept of prayer through prostration. A mosque is simply a place where devout Muslims can fulfill the requirement of prayer five times daily, an act that can be carried out anywhere but that, on Fridays especially, can best be done in a mosque designed for the purpose. Intentionally designed mosques often embody traditional Middle Eastern and Mediterranean historic forms, such as domes and minarets, or prayer towers, but these latter are optional, as are Qur'anic verses rendered in Arabic calligraphy on the walls of more elaborate examples. A mosque is essentially an unfurnished prayer hall where men and women can prostrate themselves in spaces separated by gender. The *qiblah* wall, opposite the main entrance, is supposed to be parallel to a line leading to Mecca. The mihrab is a niche in the center of the *qiblah* wall that indicates the direction of Mecca, the point in the mosque from which the imam leads the five daily prayers. To its side may be a pulpit, called the *minbar*. Mosques may also have facilities for performing ritual ablutions before entering the prayer space.

Although Muslims have lived in the United States at least since colonial times, the first permanent structure designed specifically for their worship is the Mother Mosque of America (1934) in Cedar Rapids, Iowa, a small rectangular structure with a dome – a nod in the direction of Islamic tradition – over the front door. Since Hart-Cellar, the number of North American Muslims has increased greatly, with a concomitant surge in the construction of mosques, which numbered more than two thousand in the United States alone at the turn of the twenty-first century. The majority of these were houses or storefronts adapted for the purpose. However, beginning with the opening of the Islamic Center in Washington, D.C., in 1957, a small but significant number of intentionally designed mosques have opened in the United States and Canada as well.

The Washington Islamic Center, although larger and more ornate than most, illustrates some significant aspects of this proliferation. As its name suggests, this is not simply a mosque – that is, a prayer hall – but rather a distinctively North American innovation, an "Islamic center," a complex of structures for education, recreation, and communal activity that provides a venue for American Muslims to reinvent themselves as a religious community outside the ethnically homogeneous contexts of traditional Islamic societies. To do this involves negotiation, for example, over which style among those historically available should be chosen for that particular community, which may include among its members Muslims from Algeria to Indonesia. In the case of the national capital's community, much of the financing was provided by the governments of Islamic nations – the Center is sited on Massachusetts Avenue, or Embassy Row – which made possible not only a structure of considerable size and opulence, but one designed by Mario Rossi, a "signature architect" from Italy. Its design is firmly situated in the tradition of Mamluk architecture from Cairo with hints of Ottoman Turkish and Andalusian provenance as well.

Omar Khalidi, of the Aga Khan Program in Islamic Architecture at MIT, cites the Washington Islamic Center as a prime example of imported Islamic design in the United States. In contrast, the Islamic Cultural Center in Manhattan (Skidmore, Owings and Merrill, 1991) pays homage to Islamic tradition, but only in a highly stylized manner through geometrical forms that include a dome and minaret. Even more radical is Gulzar Haidar's Islamic Society of North America headquarters in Plainfield, Indiana (1979), which omits any iconic references to tradition except, perhaps, its cubical form's allusion to the Ka'aba, the cubic structure in Mecca that is the ultimate geographical center of Muslim reference and the destination of all Muslim pilgrims. Khalidi terms these latter two as examples respectively of adaptation and innovation, in contrast with importation, in North American high-style mosque design.[2] Like all American religious groups, Muslims have come to terms in innovative ways with uniquely American circumstances.

SUGGESTIONS FOR FURTHER READING

Buggeln, Gretchen T. *Temples of Grace: The Material Transformation of Connecticut's Churches, 1790–1840.* Hanover, NH, 2003.

Goldman, Karla. *Beyond the Synagogue Gallery: Finding a Place for Women in American Judaism.* Cambridge, MA, 2000.

Kilde, Jeanne Halgren. *When Church Became Theatre: The Transformation of Evangelical Architecture and Worship in Nineteenth-Century America.* New York, 2002.

Lippy, Charles H., and Peter W. Williams, eds. *Encyclopedia of Religion in America.* 4 vols. Washington, DC, 2010.

Nabokov, Peter, and Robert Easton. *Native American Architecture.* New York, 1989.

Nelson, Louis, ed. *American Sanctuary: Understanding Sacred Spaces.* Bloomington, 2006.

———. *The Beauty of Holiness: Anglicanism and Architecture in Colonial South Carolina.* Chapel Hill, 2009.

---

[2] Omar Khalidi, "Mosque Design in the United States," *Saudi Aramco World* (Nov./Dec. 2001): 24–33.

Roth, John D., ed. "Anabaptist-Mennonite Spaces and Places of Worship." Special issue, *Mennonite Quarterly Review* 73:2 (1999).

White, James F. *Protestant Worship and Church Architecture*. New York, 1964.

Williams, Peter W. *Houses of God: Region, Religion and Architecture in the United States*. Urbana, 1997.

36

RELIGION AND VISUALITY IN AMERICA: MATERIAL ECONOMIES OF THE SACRED

DAVID MORGAN

Virtually anything human beings use to live their lives must be manufactured or harvested, wrought from raw materials by skill and labor. This may seem obvious, but consider the rows of hand-crafted thimbles, needles, hand tools, footwear, images, and amulets displayed in museums. The ingenuity and careful fabrication they exhibit demonstrate in the most material way the fact that human beings build their worlds and expend incessant effort to keep them in good working order. The plentiful availability of goods to which members of modern, industrialized societies are accustomed is easily taken for granted.

Things matter precisely because of the work they do. This essay will survey the visual and material cultures of religions in America with an eye to understanding how religious peoples of many different kinds have relied on things. "Material culture" refers not only to objects and images, but also to what they do and the power they have in performing the cultural work of organizing the world, cultivating and maintaining relations with sacred realities, and imagining the communities, places, pasts, and futures that compose one's sense of reality. By producing, collecting, revering, and exchanging their sacred objects, people are able to secure vital relationships among themselves, their ancestors, and the divine. It will become evident that this applies to modern as well as ancient peoples. Moderns cling to photographs, monuments, plastic statuary, and mass-produced lithographs no less emotionally than ancient peoples gripped stone effigies or medicine bags.

Sketching the history of many centuries of the material life of religions in America requires moving from Neolithic cultures to the world of skyscrapers and the Internet. There is perhaps nothing in human history comparable to the degree of material change that has taken place in the short span of the last few millennia. And this dramatic transformation is reflected in the bewildering array of religions – from nomadic Stone Age peoples to Protestant book-worshippers to New Age spiritualists. But the project is useful, for it is able to underscore the importance of materiality in understanding religions. For a long time religions have been framed in terms of their beliefs, philosophical systems, or mythologies. Ideas and texts (verbal or printed) have received far more attention than practices and things. But scholarship over the past few decades has seen a significant shift toward including material culture and ritual practice as primary evidence in the study of religions. Objects and images, I wish to suggest, may be studied as operating within economies of exchange that also engage humans and spiritual realities such as ancestors and gods. Far from reducing religion to economics, this approach allows us to scrutinize the constructive activity of material culture. Sacred systems of exchange organize time and space in a variety of ways by allowing human beings to thread divine power into the fabric of everyday life, in which time and space are ordered in the form of rites, stories, images, and places.

THE FIRST PEOPLES

About fifteen thousand years before the Common Era, as the glaciation of the last Ice Age began to subside, a few thousand human beings began a southern migration from the region of the Bering land bridge, where they had lived for several millennia, to what are now called the Americas. These were the first Americans, and it is to them, so far as we know, rather than the much later European arrivals, that the narrative of discovering a "virgin" wilderness actually belongs.[1] The Paleo-Indians who eventually arose in regions from the Northwest Pacific coast to the Southwest desert are known largely for their stone projectiles, suggesting they were nomadic hunters living on the edge of the last glacial period, feeding on the large mammals that had thrived during the Ice Age – mammoth, camels, and giant bison. As these mammals became extinct around 8,000 B.C.E., archeological records reflect a subsequent shift to other foods, changes in hunting technology, and the emergence of farming and fishing cultures. Beginning around 6,000 B.C.E., large and permanent architectural structures begin to be built in the Ohio and Mississippi River valleys. The rich soil, regular rainfall, and steady flow of the Mississippi provided ideal conditions for the development of agriculture. A major center of life and trade developed in what is today southwestern Illinois, known as Cahokia after a much later Indian group. By the year 1,000 C.E. as many as fourteen thousand inhabitants may have resided at the site. Like groups throughout central North America, the Mississippians built vast earthen mounds as means of burial, protection, religious ceremony, and celestial correspondence. In a

---

[1] See, for instance, James D. Keyser, *Indian Rock Art of the Columbia Plateau* (Seattle, 1992), 24.

FIGURE 36.1. Lloyd K. Townsend, *Reconstruction of Cahokia Mounds*, 3 x 7 feet, acrylic. Courtesy of Cahokia Mounds State Historic Site.

6-square-mile area at Cahokia, scores of mounds were raised. The largest rose to more than 100 feet above the central plaza of the district (Fig. 36.1). Circular and square plazas marked the cardinal directions, and the largest mound was nestled within an array of axes that registered sunrise and sunset at summer and winter solstice and the vernal and autumnal equinox.[2] The towering summit of the chief mound likely served as the point at which sun and moon and other astral bodies were ritually addressed in a sacred calendar keyed to the fecundity of the land. Stabilizing seasonal change and duration by ritual intervention was a fundamental aspect of a sacred economy that was grounded in the earthworks of this massive city.

In the American Northwest, on the Columbia Plateau, where cliffs and boulders were dominant and enduring features of the landscape, a wide range of petroglyphs (engravings in rock) and pictographs (paintings on rock) survive today, even though they were produced as long ago as the seventh millennium before the Common Era and as recently as the early twentieth century. Little evidence survives to tell us in any detail what these markings and figures meant to those who made them. Yet it is possible to date many of them, to associate them with known populations, and to combine rudimentary information with what has been gathered by ethnographers from latter-day Indians who continued to create and use such imagery.[3] Naturally, it is presumptuous to believe that modern Indians and their ancestors six or seven thousand years ago shared the same thoughts and rites. But ethnography can provide a useful framework for thinking

---

[2] See Roger G. Kennedy, *Hidden Cities: The Discovery and Loss of Ancient North American Civilization* (New York, 1994), 12; and Sally A. Kitt Chappell, *Cahokia: Mirror of the Cosmos* (Chicago, 2002), 51–3.

[3] See Carling I. Malouf and Thain White, *Recollections of Lasso Stasso*. Anthropology and Sociology Papers, no. 12 (Missoula, MT, 1952).

in new ways about ancient imagery. There is also some provocative internal evidence to be gleaned from the thousands and thousands of scattered figures and from their groupings at particular sites. And the visual evidence may be combined with other archeological information regarding diet, technology, weather, terrain, migration, ritual, and trade to sketch out some notion of the peoples who inhabited the region and what their lives were like.[4]

Rock imagery may have been used for a broad range of purposes, much of which is lost to us. But some of it seems to answer to purposes that were still in use in the historical period, two of which had considerable importance as religious practices. James Keyser has tabulated the incidence of rock art subject matter across the Columbia Plateau and has found that animal imagery counts for approximately a fifth of all rock art; human figures, just more than a fourth; geometrical designs, from a tenth to more than a third; and tally marks, from less than 5 percent to nearly 40 percent, depending on region.[5] Animal imagery is clearly important as a depiction of the source of food and also as shamanic and totemic symbols. Keyser suggests a common interpretation regarding animals as food: humans and animals alike existed within a spiritual economy. "As did many hunting groups around the world, Columbian Plateau tribes thought that animals had spirits controlling their behavior."[6] To take the life of an animal meant risking offense to the spiritual reality to which the species belonged. Compensation was owed to that reality in the form of recognition or thanks. The tribal member chosen to organize and conduct the hunt may have been charged with offering a ritualistic recompense for what the group took. The powers that be had to be placated, lest they take offense. Rock imagery portraying hunting scenes (Fig. 36.2) was installed at points of power, where certain spirits were accessible and where it memorialized hunts of ages past and may have served as the place where petitions or offerings were made. "Thus," Keyser contends, "hunting-related pictographs are likely to be the result of such ceremonies led by the hunt chief either before or after the hunt."[7] The use of tallies with animals, especially in western Montana, may indicate quantities of time, people, or animals. Thus, the images are both ritually efficacious artifacts and ways of storing information.

---

[4] See Grant Campbell, *The Rock Art of the North American Indian* (Cambridge, UK, 1983); Beth Hill and Ray Hill, *Indian Petroglyphs of the Pacific Northwest* (Seattle, 1974); and Verne F. Ray, *Cultural Relations in the Plateau of Northwestern America* (Los Angeles, Frederick Webb Hodge Anniversary Publication Fund, Publication no. 3, 1939).
[5] Keyser, *Indian Rock Art*, 37, 51, 66, 84, and 105.
[6] *Ibid.*, 46.
[7] *Ibid.*

FIGURE 36.2. Hunting scene, prehistoric Native American rock painting, Big Petroglyph Canyon, California, United States. Photo: Art Resource, NY.

Around five thousand years before the Common Era, the Anasazi, whose name derives from a Navajo word for "ancient ones," emerged in the four corners region. By 500 C.E. the first permanent villages appeared, suggesting that the Anasazi had successfully changed from the nomadic life of the hunter-gatherer to the stationary culture of agriculture. The Anasazi are remembered for developing essential technologies for farming, such as irrigation and basket weaving. Whereas earlier Anasazi lived in natural caves and mud-and-log kivas, around 700 C.E. they began building pueblos from stacked stone and mud mortar. About this time the Pueblo Indian groups, including the Hopi and Zuni, appeared, having either evolved from or defeated the Anasazi. The Pueblo Indians dominated the region until 1540, when Coronado arrived to subjugate the territory he dubbed New Mexico, after the capital city of New Spain, which Cortés had captured in his military conquest of the Aztec Empire in 1521. Franciscan missionaries had accompanied Coronado northward. Although Coronado was disappointed not to find the gold and silver that had lured him there, it was useful to the empire to establish a northern provincial limit to Spain's holdings in the New World, and that is what the remote reaches of New Mexico came to mean.[8] As the principal means of rooting Spanish culture in the frontier, the Franciscan fathers wasted no time in the work of conversion.

NEW SPAIN

Colonial farmers from New Spain followed, and life along the Rio Grande and its tributaries was organized around the mission and village church. Whether painted or sculpted, the santos, or holy images, produced by artisans, at first by priests themselves, evince a familiar structure and formula. The sculpted figures, known as *bultos*, were carved from local cottonwood, sanded with stones, and then covered with gesso and painted. They were created as discrete parts and then pieced together with dowels. Some, especially those used in processions, were fitted with leather joints; for example, the figure of Jesus could be built such that he might be taken from his cross and laid to rest during Easter rites. The figures are shown alone, unless accompanied by their identifying iconographical attendants, such as angels or soldiers. The *santeros* followed precedent very carefully, because identifying the figure was essential for purposes of devotion. The power of the figures resided in recognizing who they were, because each saint possessed a special potency for the problems faced by the people. St. Anthony was known for help in finding lost things; St. Isidro, for help with rain and farming; and St. Roc, for protection against disease and plague. The different versions of the Holy Virgin were powerful in overcoming the menace of Satan, as were various archangels. Every aspect of life was overseen by a patron saint, which accounts for the large number of their images that survive. The images themselves were linked to their sacred prototypes in powerful ways. There is evidence of santos being charred or burned to obtain

[8] Instructive overviews of the history and material culture of the region are Mitchell A. Wilder with Edgar Breitenbach, *Santos: The Religious Folk Art of New Mexico* (New York, 1976), and Robin Farwell Gavin, *Traditional Arts of Spanish New Mexico: The Hispanic Heritage Wing at the Museum of International Folk Art* (Santa Fe, 1994).

ash for medicinal purposes and to be used for blessing on Ash Wednesday, the first day of Lent, when the priest rubbed the shape of a cross on the foreheads of the devout.[9]

People were especially attached to images of the saints, offering to them petitions for assistance and then thanking the saint afterward by gifting him or her a new garment, a string of beads, votive medals, or paper flowers.[10] And when a saint was slow in responding to the petition, he might find himself suffering the abuse of the frustrated admirer. St. Anthony might be turned to face a wall or have the infant Christ plucked from his adoring arms. (Perhaps unwittingly, this same practice occurs today among Catholic homeowners who bury a statue of St. Joseph in their yard in order to expedite the sale of their homes.) The logic is perfectly clear: if the saint can be induced by favors, when recalcitrant he might be prompted by stern reproof. In both instances, the saint's relation to the devout was bodily mediated by the image. The entire community experienced this collectively on occasions when *bultos* or *retablos* were carried in procession to the homes of the ill or to the fields, when rain was implored, or when the harvest was blessed.[11]

Sacred imagery circulated in several domains in the New Mexican provinces. Domestic altars to saints provided family members a private shrine for approaching and thanking the saint. Penitential lay brotherhoods presented images of the suffering Jesus to inspire flagellation among members as penance, the benefit of which was directed toward the community as compensation for its sin. Elaborately painted *retablos* and altar screens in the churches could array programs of iconography that were a map of the social world of the parish: one might find saints dedicated to the agriculture sustaining the community; saints who were patrons of the religious orders at work there; or saints who were the patrons of the colonial governor, guilds, or brotherhoods.[12]

Some imagery, such as Guadalupe and decorative elements in altars, could also address Indians by integrating indigenous, ethnic features into the iconographic program. Locating the sacred in the landscape was a fundamental aspect of Catholicism in New Spain. Around 1810, for example, in the Chimayo Valley of New Mexico, a friar discovered on a hillside what was quickly called the miraculous crucifix of Our Lord of Esquipulas. The

[9] Wilder, *Santos*, 35.
[10] *Ibid.*, 32.
[11] Gavin, *Traditional Arts*, 48.
[12] See Thomas J. Steele, S.J., *Santos and Saints: The Religious Folk Art of Hispanic New Mexico* (Santa Fe, 1994), 24; Elizabeth Boyd, *Popular Arts of Spanish New Mexico* (Santa Fe, 1974), 155–63; and William Wroth, *Images of Penance, Images of Mercy: Southwestern Santos in the Late Nineteenth Century* (Norman, OK, 1991).

FIGURE 36.3. Main altar of the Chimayo shrine, New Mexico, built circa 1816, Chimayo, New Mexico. Photo: Isabel Silva/Art Resource, NY.

crucifix refused to leave its original site, returning miraculously each time it was taken away. So a chapel was dedicated on site, where an altar was devoted to the object, which served to usher in a spate of healings. In 1816, the chapel was replaced by a mission, whose main altar (Fig. 36.3) registers the regional aesthetic, marked by fluid coloration and dense texture.

A variety of religious practices certainly drew from Pueblo traditions that predated the Spanish arrival. Yet the santos were part of a visual piety that belonged principally to a baroque Hispanic Catholicism. The images were engaged via pilgrimage to holy sites such as Chimayo or addressed in local churches or the home.[13] This visual practice of piety drew from the penitential tradition of late medieval Europe and was paralleled by devotion to the Sacred Heart of Jesus, the suffering of Mary, and the power of holy images to establish a visceral participation in a sacred economy of exchange. The divine was understood to operate in the world through the intercessions of the saints, the angels, and the Mother of God, all of whom responded to the petitions and pledges of the pious with favors that were repaid by devotion and ritual forms of gratitude.

CALVINISM IN NEW ENGLAND

A very different notion of divine-human relations fired the Puritan imagination, and the implications for visual culture were considerable. Reformed Protestants also thought of their relationship with God in overtly economic terms. In his catechetical "First Principles of the Oracles of God," composed for his congregation in Cambridge, Massachusetts, in 1655, the Rev. Thomas Shepard answered the question "what is redemption?" with the terse prose of the typical catechism: "The satisfaction made, or the price paid, to the justice of God for the life and deliverance of man out of the captivity of sin, Satan, and death, by a Redeemer, according to the covenant made between him and the Father."[14] Christ paid the price of human transgression demanded by God's insulted honor, the encroachment on his sovereignty and the besmirching of his majesty undertaken by the disobedience of the first parents, Adam and Eve. Human beings were not equal to the demand because they were incapable of the perfection and infinite redress that it required. Not so God himself, in the form of the second person of the Trinity. Jesus' sacrifice fully and exclusively compensated humanity's debt to God. Yet there must be a human portion – not in effecting salvation, but in striving to respond to Christ's call. Shepard distinguished between justification (entirely the work of Christ) and sanctification, which is "imperfect, being begun in this life," but not completed. He defined this as a "benefit" or fruit of justification, and as something that required time, the rest of one's life. Sanctification was the slow process by which "the sons of God are renewed in the whole man, unto the image of their heavenly Father in Christ Jesus, by mortification, or their daily dying to sin by virtue of Christ's death; and by vivification, their daily rising to

---

[13] Stephen F. de Borhegyi, "The Miraculous Shrines of Our Lord of Esquipulas in Guatemala and Chimayo, New Mexico," *El Palacio* 60 (1953): 83–111.

[14] Thomas Shepard, "First Principles of the Oracles of God," in David D. Hall, ed., *Puritans in the New World: A Critical Anthology* (Princeton, 2004), 73.

newness of life, by Christ's resurrection."¹⁵ The consequence of this daily dying and rising is "a continual war and combat" in the human being between the power of God and the power of Satan.

This ongoing psychomachia, or struggle for the soul, shifted Puritan consciousness to the theatre of the psyche, accounting for the voluminous biographical and autobiographical writing that became both a personal therapy and a steadfast devotional exercise. Self-scrutiny was exacerbated by the necessity of never knowing for a fact that one's soul was included among the truly redeemed. Sanctification was a slow work that led toward the recovery of the image of God in the soul, an image that was never to be fully achieved in this life, but one that introspection impelled the devout to seek through ongoing discernment. Puritan spirituality is often regarded as inimical toward visuality, but in fact it pivoted on seeing, understood in the register of time. Puritans in Europe and America alike made use of images in this search, and their imagery consistently reflects the dimension of temporality. Be they carved gravestones marking the end of a life's span, funerary imagery illustrating sermons and tracts to urge the reader or viewer to remember death (*memento mori!*), or broadsides charting the "road to heaven," such as the many illustrated editions of Bunyan's *A Pilgrim's Progress* (Fig. 36.4) – one finds time marked by images throughout Puritan life. Plotting time as the course of the soul toward the heavenly Jerusalem allowed the Puritan imagination to trace the soul's response to grace and to organize its efforts into a moral progression toward an eventual accomplishment of divine work on the soul. Figure 36.4 may even indicate a new recognition of the imagination as a devotional faculty for envisioning allegorically the soul's struggle and eventual progress toward the heavenly city, which appears as the frontispiece in the second part of Bunyan's book. We see the allegory taking shape as the author's dream (he is pictured in sleep at the bottom of the image): Christiana, wife of Christian, the protagonist of part one, is accompanied by her neighbor, Mercy, and followed by her four sons. They leave the city of Destruction, the worldly domain of sin and satanic influence, and set out for the Celestial City, unveiled in clouds above. Along the way they encounter all the tests and distractions of mortal life, their narrative path buffeted by the vicissitudes of a Christian's struggle here below. Narrative made sense to evangelicals because it captured the temporal nature of moving from loss to gain, from ignorance of sin through conviction to conversion, and the long trek of the sanctified life that ensued. Images that marked time were not idols but way-markers, signs pointing away from the present toward the eventual goal above, beyond time.

¹⁵ *Ibid.*, 75.

FIGURE 36.4. Frontispiece, "Road to Celestial City," from John Bunyan, *A Pilgrim's Progress*, Part 2. Boston: John Draper, 1744. Courtesy of Library Company of Philadelphia.

Such imagery therefore avoided the "idolatry" that Calvinists never tired of denouncing: static images spawned by the human imagination, which take the place of divine transcendence.[16] Temporal imagery stressed the lack of perfection, the unfinished state of the saint's moral progress. Even portraits and self-portraits were fashionable among many Puritans as memorials of those who had engaged in the soul-struggle of spiritual growth.[17]

Calvinists were not the only Christian subculture in the Anglophone regions of the continent. Anglicans in the South evinced a range of material culture that reflects a keen interest in time. Louis Nelson has documented a fascinating shift in South Carolina gravestones over the course of the eighteenth century. By the 1770s the formulaic inscription "Here lies the body of" was clearly being replaced by "In Memory of" and was completely eclipsed in the 1790s by "In Memory of" and "Sacred to the Memory of."[18] The earlier formula remembered the body as the physical trace of the now-absent soul, awaiting reunification on the last day, when judgment will occur. The later formula remembered the person and omitted from mention the humiliated body turned to dust. Nelson parallels this development with the iconographical change from depictions of death's head or a skull to a winged soul's head. During the mid-eighteenth century, gravestone portraiture emerged, and during the second half of the century mourning miniatures become a favorite form of American commemoration. Portraits celebrated the individual person, shown in effigies exquisitely painted on ivory.[19]

HEART RELIGION IN EARLY NATIONAL AND ANTEBELLUM AMERICA

Pietism thrived among German immigrants in the colony and later state of Pennsylvania. German-speaking Lutherans made use of imagery more

---

[16] See John Calvin, *Institutes of the Christian Religion*, trans. Henry Beveridge (Grand Rapids, 1989), book 1, chs. 11 and 12, pp. 90–107.

[17] See Sally M. Promey, "Seeing the Self 'in Frame': Early New England Material Practice and Puritan Piety," *Material Religion* 1:1 (March 2005): 10–46; Barbara E. Lacey, *From Sacred to Secular: Visual Images in Early American Publications* (Newark, 2007), 31–9. For discussion of the portraiture of Reformed figures see Mary G. Winkler, "Calvin's Portrait: Representation, Image, or Icon?" and Paul Corby Finney, "A Note of Bèze's Icones," in Paul Corby Finney, ed., *Seeing Beyond the Word: Visual Art and the Calvinist Tradition* (Grand Rapids, 1999), 243–51 and 253–63.

[18] Louis P. Nelson, *The Beauty of Holiness: Anglicanism and Architecture in Colonial South Carolina* (Chapel Hill, 2008), 241.

[19] Robin Jaffee Frank, *Love and Loss: American Portrait and Mourning Miniatures* (New Haven, 2000). For further consideration of the culture of memory, see Susan M. Stabile, *Memory's Daughters: The Material Culture of Remembrance in Eighteenth-Century America* (Ithaca, 2000), esp. 178–227.

freely than Calvinists, because Luther had endorsed the use of illustrations from the very beginning of the Reformation. An allegorical frontispiece appeared in an American edition of Johann Arndt's widely reprinted *True Christianity*, which was published in 1751 by Benjamin Franklin. The image (Fig. 36.5) recalls the daily rhythm of dying and living articulated by Thomas Shepard, mortification and vivification, which formed the spiritual calisthenics of sanctification. The interior struggle of and with the self so prized by Pietism is evident in the imagery of the heart that constitutes the chest of each female figure in the engraving. "I kill him each day," reads the text over the woman on the left, which she proceeds to do by thrusting a knife into her heart-medallion, in which Adam reclines beside the Tree of Knowledge. "Yet I do not live, but Christ lives in me," announces the figure on the right, quoting St. Paul and referring visually to the resurrection of Jesus, who emerges victoriously from the grave. Death and life join hands as complements, Old and New Adam.[20]

Pietist heart iconography continued to be of importance to Lutheran immigrants and the German-speaking community in Pennsylvania well into the nineteenth century. Among the most widely reproduced booklets was Johannes Gossner's *The Heart of Man* (Fig. 36.6). The original German text from 1812 was translated into English and published in Pennsylvania in 1822 and then issued in a steady stream of editions that reached as late as the 1870s. Gossner had been a Catholic priest who converted to Lutheranism and became an advocate of missions. His book drew from Catholic as well as Protestant sources; in fact, he derived the illustrations from an eighteenth-century Catholic work entitled *Spiritual Mirror of Morality* (1732), although the emblematic tradition of the heart was much older.[21] The imagery (Fig. 36.6) applied a theology of conversion and the sanctified life to a series of images and brief explanatory texts. The book comprised ten plates, which charted the trajectory of the soul (heart) from the natural state of sin to rebirth, through an occasion of backsliding, and culminated in the death of a redeemed man and an unredeemed man. It is a visually driven narrative that was directly applicable to children and to illiterate or semi-literate adults.

---

[20] Heart imagery was fundamental to Puritan devotionalism. Its iconography draws from both Protestant and Catholic emblem traditions in the early seventeenth century in Germany and England. See David Morgan, "Iconography," in Hans Hillerbrand, ed., *Encyclopedia of Protestantism*, 4 vols. (New York, 2003), 2: 926–32; Don Yoder, *The Pennsylvania German Broadside: A History and Guide* (University Park, PA 2005), 199–203; and Promey, "Seeing the Self 'in Frame,'" 28–31.

[21] See Ingetraut Ludolphy's biographical entry on Gossner, "Gossner, Johannes Evangelista," in Julius Bodensieck, ed., *The Encyclopedia of the Lutheran Church*, 3 vols. (Minneapolis, 1965), 2: 944–5.

FIGURE 36.5. Allegorical frontispiece from Johann Arndt, *Der wahren Christenthum*. Philadelphia: Benjamin Franklin and Johann Böhm, 1751. Courtesy of the Historical Society of Pennsylvania.

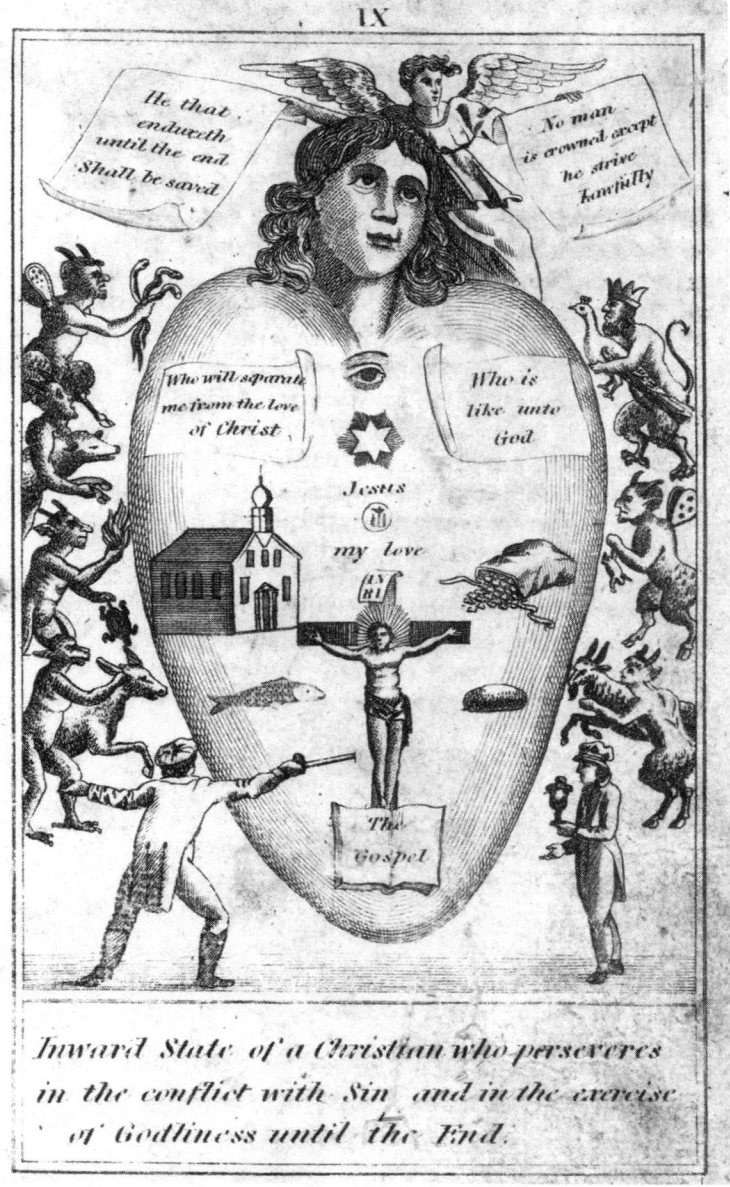

FIGURE 36.6. Heart emblem, "Inward State of a Christian who perseveres in the conflict with Sin and the exercise of Godliness until the End," plate IX from Johannes Gossner, *The Heart of Man*. Reading, PA, 1822. Courtesy of Library Company of Philadelphia.

The heart image that came to dominate Catholic devotionalism in the nineteenth and twentieth centuries was the Sacred Heart of Jesus (Fig. 36.7). The devotion to the heart of Jesus may be traced to late medieval spirituality, but the distinctive imagery comes from the visions and ecstatic experience of Margaret Mary Alocoque, a seventeenth-century French Visitationist nun to whom Jesus appeared in 1675 and several times thereafter.[22] Jesuits took up the cause during her lifetime and after, seeing in the devotion a strong form of traditional Catholic piety that resisted the rationalism of liberal reformers in the Church. The devotion was especially dear to French nuns and was brought to North America in the nineteenth century by the Daughters of the Sacred Heart, a new order passionately dedicated to the Heart and to the care for and education of children. Image producers such as Currier & Ives recognized the commercial opportunity of inexpensive Catholic devotional imagery among immigrants to Canada and the United States and issued hundreds of different Catholic themes in lithographs beginning in the mid-1840s. Lithographs were especially well received by devotees to the Sacred Heart because the devotion came to focus during the second half of the nineteenth century on installation in the Catholic home, where an image like Fig. 36.7 would be "enthroned," that is, ritually blessed by a priest; presented with the vows of the *pater familias*, head of the domestic cult of the Sacred Heart; and established thereafter as a domestic shrine for the family's prayer and devotion.[23]

For nineteenth-century Protestants, imagery tended to be much more about teaching and evangelism than devotion, though that would begin to change by the end of the century. Before then, however, the range and frequency of the visual means of teaching and evangelism broadened dramatically, especially in the context of the Second Great Awakening, a period of revivalism that produced modern Evangelicalism, Adventism, and Mormonism and saw the climax of Shakerism during the first several decades of the century. Although Mormonism did not make use of visual media in a significant way until the early twentieth century, groups such as the Shakers and the Adventists used charts and emblematic imagery during the early 1840s to promote their interpretation of the disclosure of a radically countercultural conception of time. The Shakers envisioned the New Jerusalem on a hand-colored map consisting of a circular grid that was an archetype for Shaker society to emulate. Those in the community of New Lebanon even regarded their city as the latter-day likeness

---

[22] See David Morgan, *The Sacred Heart of Jesus: The Visual Evolution of a Devotion*. Meertens Ethnology Cahier 4 monograph (Amsterdam, 2008).
[23] *Ibid.*, 33–6.

FIGURE 36.7. Nathaniel Currier, *Sacred Heart of Jesus*, 1848, hand-tinted lithograph. Courtesy of Library of Congress.

of the celestial city.[24] For contemporary Adventists, the imminent time of revelation held the return of Jesus.[25] The most well-known such chart was a large lithograph on cloth created by followers of William Miller,

---

[24] See Sally M. Promey, *Spiritual Spectacles: Vision and Image in Mid-Nineteenth-Century Shakerism* (Bloomington, 1993), 66–9, and plate I for a reproduction of the drawing of the Holy City.

[25] For a history of twentieth-century visual uses among Latter-day Saints, see Noel A. Carmack, "Images of Christ in Latter-day Saint Visual Culture, 1900–1990," *BYU Studies* 39:3 (2000): 18–76.

FIGURE 36.8. Millerite chart, 1842, lithograph. Courtesy of American Antiquarian Society.

who developed an elaborate reading of the Bible in predicting the Second Coming in 1843 (Fig. 36.8). As we have noted several times with other Protestant images, this one also bears a striking preoccupation with time, visualizing in a mix of graphic, numerological, and textual devices the course of prophetic events from ancient Babylon to the present, decoding biblical symbols as marking events in world history, and composing a kind of calendar for determining the appearance of Jesus. Millerite preachers and teachers carried charts like this one around the country and abroad, unrolling them on steamships and in dining rooms for the purpose of illustrating their lectures.[26]

EVANGELICALISM AND IMAGES

Mainstream Protestant groups like Presbyterians and Congregationalists also made extensive use of illustrational imagery in the thousands and thousands of books and tracts issued from the first decade of the century and aimed at Christian education, evangelism, and moral reform (Figs. 36.9 and 36.10). The two largest national organizations were the American Tract Society, founded in New York in 1825, and the American Sunday School Union, founded in Philadelphia in 1824. Tracts were believed especially useful for distribution among those deemed in need of spiritual attention – children, immigrants, the urban poor, prostitutes, drunkards, and infidels, but also anyone to whom Providence might direct the tract as an instrument for reviving evangelical religion in a young nation in which religion was undergoing rapid privatization in the process of disestablishment. Cheap mass-print was also responsible for helping to construct a new imagination of the distant world. As European empires opened up the Asian and Middle Eastern world to Western missionaries, religious societies formed to support them, relying on tracts, books, and magazines to do so. Illustrations like Figure 36.9 accompanied these publications and likely supplied the popular American imagination with charged images of Muslims and Hindus, and of Chinese "idol worship." The image reproduced here illustrated a Baptist mission history of Asia published in 1840. The image documents the artifice of Christian propaganda: a colossal and oversized caricature of Budai (a widely varying figure in Buddhist and Taoist lore who is sometimes identified in China with Maitreya, the Buddha of the next age of history). A jovial and generous figure in popular Buddhism, Budai is traditionally shown in laughter. But in this illustration he appears with a dark leer and is flanked by monstrous demons from Western Christianity. The linkage of Buddhist popular devotion with Christian demonology apparently made sense to pious Baptists, whose interest in the illustration and the account it accompanied was not ethnographic accuracy but the lure of a Christian Orientalism. The gaze the image conjured of the East presented Asian religions such as Buddhism and Hinduism as lurid instances of demonic delusion.[27]

---

[26] For a much fuller discussion of Millerite imagery and its interpretation, see David Morgan, *Protestants and Pictures: Religion, Visual Culture, and the Age of Mass Production* (New York, 1999), 123–58.

[27] For a study of twentieth-century media and representations of Asian religions in America, see Jane Iwamura, *Virtual Orientalism: Asian Religions and American Popular Culture* (New York, 2011).

Chinese god.

FIGURE 36.9. "Chinese god," from *The Baptist Mission in India*. Worcester: Spooner and Howland, 1840, p. 201. Courtesy of Library Company of Philadelphia.

The Tract Society produced its several hundred tracts with particular readers in mind, devising themes and illustrating most of its tracts with wood engravings designed to catch the eye.[28] One of the principal strategies of the Tract Society was to reissue heavily edited versions of "classic" texts such as the work of Jonathan Edwards and a host of earlier British evangelical writers such as John Flavel and Philip Doddridge. Tracts were understood to be brief, accessibly written, lively texts that would make a quick and enduring appeal to modern readers. The images that accompanied them, such as Figure 36.10, were intended to convey the essence of the message in fetching visual terms. The images were always placed on the cover so that they were the first thing a potential reader noticed. Having snagged one's attention, tract producers hoped the image would lead the viewer to become a reader, and thereby inaugurate the process of conviction and contrition that would lead to the regeneration so clearly visualized in Gossner's series of plates.

In 1827 the American Tract Society issued a sixteen-page, illustrated tract entitled "Conversion of President Edwards," an autobiographical account written in 1740 (Fig. 36.10). The narrative relates the prolonged

[28] Morgan, *Protestants and Pictures*, 43–120.

FIGURE 36.10. "Conversion of President Edwards," tract illustration. New York: American Tract Society, 1827. Photo by author.

process of self-examination and eventual conversion during the precocious youth's early teenage years. On the cover of the tract appears a small wood engraving, presumably by Alexander Anderson, who had been hired in 1825 by the Tract Society to oversee its iconographical program and produce wood engravings for its publications. The illustration shows the young Edwards at a particular moment in his spiritual awakening. The line quoted beneath the image refers the reader to the very moment narrated in the tract. Aroused by a New Testament passage praising the honor and glory of God, the young Edwards became inwardly moved and convinced of God's excellence. From this time, he related, a new understanding of Jesus possessed him, and he found "an inward sweetness that would carry me away in my contemplations."[29] He compared the experience to "being alone in the mountains, or some solitary wilderness, far from all mankind, sweetly conversing with Christ, and rapt and swallowed up in God."[30] The only son of a stern Calvinist minister actively engaged in revival work in his East Windsor, Connecticut, congregation, Edwards wasted little time in speaking to his father about these new affections. The conversation was deeply significant for him. He wrote that he "walked abroad alone, in a solitary place in my father's pasture, for contemplation."

> And as I was walking there, and looking up on the sky and clouds, there came into my mind a sweet sense of the glorious majesty and grace of God, that I know not how to express. I seemed to see them both in a sweet conjunction; majesty and meekness joined together; it was a gentle and holy majesty; and also a majestic meekness; a high, great, and holy gentleness.[31]

Anderson's small vignette portrays the moment when Edwards' introspection led to a spiritual effervescence, a reconciliation of two typically opposite aspects: God's majesty and God's meekness, that is, God's radical transcendence of human being and God's very humanity. The reconciliation also parallels the sickly, earnest, bookish boy and his stern, authoritarian clergyman father. And it takes place in the romantic solitude of nature, where the beauty of the landscape performs as a medium or theatrical stage for revelation. Nature and the boy's own tender frame host what on other occasions were the terrifying otherness of an angry, paternal deity, one who holds himself aloof from the frail human soul. But Edwards was very explicit: his devotional life was passionately grounded in the affections,

---

[29] *Conversion of President Edwards: From an Account Written by Himself* (New York, 1827), 4; Edwards, "Personal Narrative," in Jonathan Edwards, *Letters and Personal Writings*, ed. George S. Claghorn, in *Works* (New Haven, 1998), 16: 790–804.
[30] *Conversion*, 5.
[31] Ibid.

in the intense feelings pulsing in his heart and amplified in the landscape before him.

Despite its small stature, Anderson's scene recalls a contemporary tradition in European and American landscape painting. The placement of the figure with his back to the viewer, facing into the scene, is a familiar technique used by Romantic landscape painters at this time. The landscape was a pastoral matrix configured to receive the infusion of the human imagination. The pictorial practice of empathy became a dominant aesthetic modality in Romanticism on both sides of the Atlantic. One finds it powerfully at work in the images of the painter Thomas Cole (1801–48). During a brief stay in New York City in 1723, Edwards had recalled that he "frequently used to retire into a solitary place, on the bank of the Hudson's river, at some distance from the city, for contemplation on divine things, and secret converse with God."[32] A century later Thomas Cole joined the young divine there to paint spiritual musings on the moral edification of the American landscape. In an essay published in 1836, Cole proclaimed his theological aesthetics of the natural scene as the meeting of a "loving eye" with the beautiful handiwork of the Almighty:

> He who looks on nature with a "loving eye," cannot move from his dwelling without the salutation of beauty.... The delight such a man experiences is not merely sensual, or selfish, that passes with the occasion leaving no trace behind; but in gazing on the pure creations of the Almighty, he feels a calm religious tone steal through his mind, and when he has turned to mingle with his fellow men, the chords which have been struck in that sweet communion cease not to vibrate.[33]

This beauty was not purely objective but also subjective, ringing in the soul of the sympathetic viewer, whence it bridged the gulf separating interior from exterior just as meekness and majesty touched one another in Edwards' experience of the landscape. And Cole registered the Calvinist gloom that could also occupy Edwards' soul. One sees the expansive theatre of divine judgment unfold in the five canvases of *The Course of Empire* (1834–6), in which meekness succumbs to retribution as humanity sinks from Arcadian calm to apocalyptic frenzy. Cole's series preached an alarming sermon, not so very different than the tone of Edwards' famous homily, "Sinners in the Hands of an Angry God." Cole directed his Whiggish remarks to his nation, which was in the midst of metamorphosis in the new age of Jacksonian democracy.[34]

---

[32] *Ibid.*, 9.
[33] Thomas Cole, "Essay on American Scenery," *American Monthly Magazine* 1 (Jan. 1836): 2.
[34] For further discussion and very fine reproductions of the series, see Allan Wallach, "Thomas Cole: Landscape and the Course of American Empire," in William H. Truettner and Allan Wallach, eds., *Thomas Cole: Landscape into History* (New Haven, 1994), 90–8.

TIME, NARRATIVE, AND IMAGE

Once again, the element of time was a leitmotif. Cole limned the descent, or moral decline of the republic, as a way of warning his countrymen of the danger of losing virtue and submitting to the pursuit of luxury in the rise of urban civilization, a development he believed threatened to overwhelm the proper relationship between humanity and nature. At the same moment Adventists and other millennialists urged Americans to read "the signs of the times." In an age of rapid and cataclysmic change, the theme of temporality appealed to many different Americans. One thinks, for example of the winter counts of Plains Indians such as the Lakota, which recorded in pictographic symbols the history of a group over a century and longer (Fig. 36.11). Painted on a robe made from buffalo hides, the winter counts accorded one year to each visual device, which registered the most important event of that year. As a visual archive, winter counts depended on extensive supporting information in the possession of tribal elders and the keeper of the count, information that was ritually shared with members of the community by the exhibition of the robe.[35]

Epic journeys from bondage to liberation have been a powerful trope in art by African American artists. Jacob Lawrence created a very large body of work, much of it organized in series that plotted the careers of African American leaders of powerful moral example. Influenced by the importance of stories and the biographies of iconic figures, Lawrence developed a narrative art that naturally gravitated toward such heroic personalities as Toussaint L'Overture, Frederick Douglass, Harriet Tubman, and John Brown. In another early work, he painted in sixty panels the great exodus of his own lifetime, *The Migration of the Negro* (1941), following the epochal transit of African Americans from the South to northern urban centers such as Chicago and New York in the early twentieth century.[36] The year before this major work, Lawrence painted *The Life of Harriet Tubman* in thirty-one panels, the second of which is a solemn icon of suffering and injustice (Fig. 36.12). Seen from behind, an African American man hangs from an unseen tree in a gesture that immediately suggests the Crucifixion. Seeing the lynched African American as a latter-day image of the crucified Jesus had become a trope among African American writers and artists. In *Darkwater* (1920), W.E.B. DuBois described the cruciform body of an African American man swaying from the tree in which he was hung, and

---

[35] As discussed by Evan M. Maurer, *Visions of the People: A Pictorial History of Plains Indian Life* (Minneapolis, 1993), 274–5.
[36] See Peter T. Nesbett and Michelle DuBois, *Jacob Lawrence: Paintings, Drawings, and Murals (1935–1999), A Catalogue Raisonné* (Seattle, 2000), 47–55.

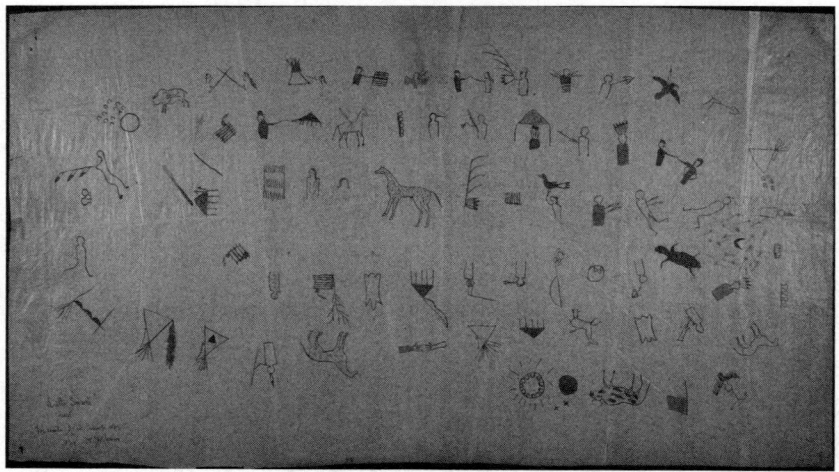

FIGURE 36.11. Tracing of the Swan winter count, 1870. Courtesy of Smithsonian National Museum of Natural History, National Anthropological Archives.

in 1929 Charles Cullen produced a frontispiece juxtaposing a lynched man and the crucified Christ for Countee Cullen's *The Black Christ and Other Poems*. In Lawrence's picture, three violent gashes streak across his back, flattening the form of his body into a dark silhouette. The austere scene, stark symmetry, and the cropping of hands and feet of the figure stretched from top to bottom endow the image with an iconicity that is visually searing. The figure overlooks a blank distance from what appears to be a hilltop, once again referring to Jesus on Calvary. His head is fallen, in death or unconsciousness, disposing the viewer to see the man as a symbol of a larger cultural economy, a brutal transaction in flesh between two races over the fate of a nation.[37]

Lawrence selected captions to accompany each image in the Tubman series and the one for panel two (Fig. 36.12) underscores the broadly symbolic nature of the figure. The caption ("I am no friend of slavery, but I prefer the liberty of my own country to that of another people, and the liberty of my own race to that of another race. The liberty of the descendants of Africa in the United States is incompatible with the safety and liberty of the European descendents")[38] was a passage from a speech against abolitionism

---

[37] Caroline Goeser, *Picturing the New Negro: Harlem Renaissance Print Culture and Modern Black Identity* (Lawrence, KS, 2007), 207–45, has discussed the portrayal of crucified black Christ figures in Harlem during the generation preceding Lawrence.

[38] Ellen Harkins Wheat, *Jacob Lawrence: The Frederick Douglass and Harriet Tubman Series of 1938–40* (Hampton, VA, 1991), 82. The speech was delivered on 7 Feb. 1839 and inspired a sharp response from Thomas Morris, antislavery senator from Ohio.

FIGURE 36.12. Jacob Lawrence, *The Life of Harriet Tubman*, plate 2, Harriet Tubman series, 1939–40. Photo: The Jacob and Gwendolyn Lawrence Foundation/Art Resource, NY; Artist's Rights Society (ARS), New York.

delivered before the U.S. Senate in 1839 by Kentucky Senator Henry Clay. An advocate of the colonization of Liberia, where he and others urged free American blacks to emigrate, Clay believed that blacks could not thrive in the United States. Indeed, he considered white and black fundamentally at odds. Free blacks (as Tubman would become on escaping slavery in Maryland), he claimed in a speech before the American Colonization Society in 1827, were a menace: "Of all classes of our population, the most vicious is that of the free coloured. It is the inevitable result of their moral, political and civil degradation. Contaminated themselves, they extend their vices to all around them, to the slaves and to the whites."[39] The problem, Clay argued, was that there were many African Americans "who never can amalgamate with the great body of our population."[40] This view makes very clear what lay behind Clay's remark quoted by Lawrence. In that portion of the 1839 speech quoted by Lawrence, Clay racialized allegiance to the nation: "I prefer the liberty of my own country to that of another people, and the liberty of my own race to that of another race." Lawrence suggests that the legacy of Clay's racial imagination of nationhood contributed to the violence committed against the African American body: lynching was a brutally racist act of declaring blacks a threat to America conceived as a white nation. Lynching was therefore an extreme expression of the oppositional logic of colonization. Yet by invoking the Crucifixion in the execution of the lynched man, Lawrence pitted Christianity against race-nationalism, implying that, as Martin Luther King, Jr., would later put it standing on the steps of the Lincoln Memorial, one hundred years after the signing of the Emancipation Proclamation, "unearned suffering is redemptive."[41]

The Christian understanding of Jesus as sacrificial atonement for sin was itself modeled on the ancient Hebrew practice of sacrificial offering. Indeed, the crucifixion of Jesus was described in the Gospels as occurring after the Passover meal that Jesus held with his disciples. Whereas Christians celebrate Easter in formal eucharistic services in churches, the observance of Passover by Jews is an annual liturgical event that, although associated with a synagogue service, has long centered in the home. A familiar aspect of the seder or ritual meal is the Haggadah (Fig. 36.13), an inexpensive pamphlet consisting of narrative, instruction, scripture, and prayer that unfold as the meal progresses. The content of the Haggadah varies, especially during the modern period. American publication of Haggadoth began in the second half of the nineteenth century. These were often illustrated with engravings and lithographic imagery drawn from a variety of sources, including much older Haggadoth produced in Europe and the Middle East, but also Christian Bible illustrations such as Gustave Dore's images of the Old Testament, and illustrations based on or drawing from iconographical aspects of other Christian art. Haggadoth production has never been regulated by Jewish religious authorities and has

---

[39] Henry Clay, "'On the Colonization of the Negroes,' speech before the American Colonization Society ... January 20, 1827," in Clay, *The Speeches of Henry Clay* (Philadelphia, 1827), 327.

[40] *Ibid.*, 319.

[41] King delivered his so-called "I Have a Dream" speech in Washington, DC, on 28 Aug. 1963, as the culminating event in a march he helped organize on the national Mall to promote economic justice and civil rights.

FIGURE 36.13. "The family at the Seder," from Haggadah, J. D. Eisenstein, ed. New York: Hebrew Publishing Company, 1928, p. 7. Photo by author.

been undertaken by independent producers. In the present, families and individuals even create their own.[42]

The Haggadah provides a flexible, yet revered structure to the experience of the Pesach seder. The task is an annual ritual remembrance that grounds collective identity in the family gathered about its patriarch. Jewish fathers are assigned the ritual role of instructing their sons, which is commended by Moses in the book of Exodus. "And Moses said to the people: 'Remember this day in which you went out of Egypt.... And you shall tell your son in that day, saying, This is done because of what the

---

[42] See Vanessa L. Ochs, "The Homemade Passover Haggadah," in Colleen McDannell, ed., *Religions of the United States in Practice*, 2 vols. (Princeton, 2001), 2: 53–66; Yosef Hayim Yerushalmi, *Haggadah and History: A Panorama in Facsimile of Five Centuries of the Printed Haggadah from the Collections of Harvard University and the Jewish Theological Seminary of America* (Philadelphia, 1974); and David Morgan, *The Lure of Images: A History of Religion and Visual Media in America* (London, 2007), 121–34.

Lord did for me when I came up from Egypt.... You shall therefore keep this ordinance in its season from year to year'" (Exodus 13:3, 8, 10). The seder meal reenacts this personal address in a domestic theater of symbolic action. The elements of the meal – wine, herbs dipped in salt water and horseradish, unleavened bread, and lamb – are all intended to invoke by sensation events in the exodus of Israel from bondage in Egypt. The meal is an embodied form of memory, an evocation of a long-distant event that is annually reenacted in the bodies of participants.

Time is fundamental to the meaning of the seder as the Haggadah presents it. The present is laid over the past by recalling it. And the future is projected from that past through the present. Repeatedly, God is called on to rebuild Jerusalem "speedily in our days."[43] And participants pray that they might celebrate Passover next year in a reconstituted Israel. Situating the meal in the home rather than a public space accents the central importance of the family as the locus of religious identity, as the principle of transmission, and as the lived medium of temporality that shapes Jewish identity. Traditionally, this emphasis on family has made the structure of time patriarchal. The father traces his authority back to the Mosaic mandate to teach his sons and thereby ensure the transmission of community through the channel of the family, centered in paternal authority.

The importance of the home for many religions in the United States cannot be overemphasized. American Muslims, for example, use the home as an important place for daily prayer as well as ritual meals such as breaking fast (iftar) during the holy month of Ramadan. These practices usually rely on the inherent flexibility of space, that is, a refusal to dedicate it to one purpose. The sacred is not identical with a place but happens there as the devout direct their petitions and praise to the divine. Thus, a family room will serve as a prayer space, an eating space, and a place for conversation. Puritans and later Calvinists in colonial America observed this ambivalence, using churches as meeting halls for secular matters such as community or municipal functions. But the Muslim use of domestic space is not quite the same. Some Muslims display tapestries of the Ka'ba or other scenes of Mecca, images associated with the hajj, perhaps purchased on the pilgrimage and displayed as souvenirs, or perhaps to mark the direction of Mecca for daily prayer. This is particularly the case among immigrants in Western nations.[44] Living at a distance from their homelands and from

---

[43] *Form of Service for the Two First Nights of the Feast of Passover*, new illustrated edition (New York, 1886), 36; also 55.

[44] See Moustapha Diop and Laurence Michalak, "'Refuge' and 'Prison': Islam, Ethnicity, and the Adaptation of Space in Workers' Housing in France," in Barbara Daly Metcalf, ed., *Making Muslim Space in North America and Europe* (Berkeley, 1996), 74–91.

Mecca and Medina, they may find such imagery and objects able to evoke the sacred spaces whence Islam entered the world. But the more common use of domestic space involves no special signage. Domestic sites for prayer are to be clean, plain, and uncluttered, especially by anything that might distract the prayerful mind. The site is not intrinsically sacred. The sacred space is imagined, addressed as distant, yet alluring. The strong devotional aspect of Islam, the longing to venerate the saint or revere the Prophet, infuses Muslim practice with the need to evoke the distant other through prayer, chant, reading, and meditation. Pilgrimage is more imagined than actual for most Muslims. Envisioning the principal pilgrimage destinations may be assisted by calendar imagery, posters, tapestries, souvenirs, or other forms of graphic or textile art. Each of these forms of beholding leads toward an imagined holding or touch. And yet none of them is necessary. Chant and prayer are able to evoke the sacred in the unadorned space. The plain site of the home hosts the family gathering as a domestic architecture of bodies and sensations. Sound and the meal are the sensation of the sacred. The plain style of dress, architecture, imagery, or gathering space becomes the vehicle of sacred imagination. Downplaying one sensory modality allows one to evoke another. By subduing optical vision, hearing and taste may be accented.

The use of the past as encoded in imagery and objects is a common strategy. Images, for example, carry with them the past from which they are drawn, acting like a kind of bridge to bygone days, the ritually invoked formative moments that founded a faith or people. Haggadot combine imagery from other Haggadoth, but also from Christian illustration and sacred art. Christian image makers have used secular popular culture to sacred ends; take for example the commercial artist Thomas Kinkade, whose pious landscapes draw from nineteenth-century fine art, Christian symbols, and iconography but also rely on such popular imagery as calendar landscapes, advertising photography, and tourist postcards to create images of the rural landscape, mountain ranges, and coastline that American viewers find especially appealing. In fact, images are a medium that facilitates this heterogeneity or hybridity. But whereas Jewish and Christian image makers have often (successfully or unsuccessfully) sought to integrate the many sources into a single, unified product, other religious image producers want the diversity of their sources to remain manifest. In the case of Neopagans in the United States as well as practitioners of New Age spirituality, the range of sources serves to underscore the perennial nature of an ancient and ultimately universal religious sensibility, variously called Wiccan, Neo-Pagan, or shamanistic, but now come to be widely known as earth-centered spirituality. In fact, the differences can be many and sharp. Wiccans do not wish to be confused with New Agers; Native American shamans and practitioners of traditional native ways often sharply distinguish themselves from either group, regarding New Age Spirituality in particular as nothing less than a form of white (re)colonization.

Yet many advocates of witchcraft insist on its ancient and universal presence in human history and commonly draw on a wide array of practices and symbols to explain and enrich their views and rituals. *The Witches' Almanac* for 1974–75, for example, asserted that "witchcraft is part of the human experience" and that "there has never been a time in history, nor any culture within that time that lacked occult wisdom."[45] This ubiquity of the craft urges practitioners and adepts to seek its wisdom everywhere and to regard the human past as a vast storehouse of occult wisdom whose inventory moderns would do well to discover. *The Witches' Almanac* and any number of how-to and self-help books available in specialty shops or commercial bookstores avidly undertake the task. One of the *Almanac*'s writers, Paul Huson, doubtless spoke for many of his readers when he described "all ancient things" as possessing "a power which flows from their very oldness itself."[46] For Huson, this power was acknowledged by Carl Jung's theory of the unconscious, was named "numen" or "mana" by anthropologists, was recognized as "inspiration" by poets, but was best called "magic" by witches. Huson found it at work in lore and legend, in tarot cards, in mythology, and in the Middle Earth of J. R. R. Tolkien's fiction. Jung's notion of universal archetypes served the writer well as a way of discerning in the plurality of symbols an underlying unity: "Whether we care to call them ... Pan and Diana, Lucifer and Aradia ... or even, yes, Sweet Jesus and Mary ... the archetypes are the same." It did not matter, Huson insisted, if the practices people observe are traditional or invented, cloaked in secrecy or found "in the pages of a book or within the fabric of a dream," only that they "elicit the deep response, that unmistakable shiver of wonder and awe, [for] then they are of the Old Ways."[47]

In the following year's edition of the *Almanac*, Huson contributed an article on the Fool card of the tarot deck. There he modeled the pervasive tendency among occultists as well as other modern religious people to employ imagery and lore as tools for self-therapy. Portraying the Fool as the "night side of nature," Huson regarded the figure as access to "that hidden part of our personalities where not only the roots of creativity and inspiration lie, but also our deepest links with one another and the world

---

[45] Elizabeth Pepper and John Wilcock, ed., *The Witches' Almanac, Aries 1974 to Pisces 1975* (New York, 1974), 5.
[46] Paul Huson, "The Old Ways," in Pepper and Wilcock, *Witches' Almanac*, 6.
[47] Ibid., 7.

FIGURE 36.14. Indiana labyrinth, 2003. Photo by author.

about us."[48] Witchcraft consists of divinatory and other practices that lay hold of the forces that direct and propel the world and its inhabitants. The traces of these forces and the technology for their application are images, which for Huson and for many others remain especially accessible in the visual archive of tarot. "Lay out a deck of tarot cards," Huson wrote, "and you will feel [magic] breathing out from behind the pale hands and faces of the actors in the tarot play, once gods and goddesses, now funny puppets, quaint and hieratic, but still very potent."[49] The image as trace or fossil implied a distance from the sacred, but also the promise of access to it. And so visitors to a labyrinth in the Midwest are fond of leaving a variety of objects keyed to lore and legendry at the center (Fig. 36.14). Celtic scrollwork, crystals, and faux gems are symbols whose deposit marks the end of a self-narrative, the ritual event of walking the maze and finding its center, which, in the therapeutic ethos of New Age spirituality, means the center of self aligned with larger spheres. Left as testimony, the object may act as coin in an occult economy of the sacred, as payment for knowledge gained,

---

[48] Paul Huson, "The Wise Fool of Tarot: Spirit of the Rising Sun," in Elizabeth Pepper and John Wilcock, eds., *The Witches' Almanac* (New York, 1975), 7.
[49] Huson, "Old Ways," 6.

or as a gift to those who come after, paid forward and limning in the process a dim but encompassing order whose intuition provides the encouragement that lures the seeker into the gentle vortex of the labyrinth.

SUGGESTIONS FOR FURTHER READING

Carmack, Noel A. "Images of Christ in Latter-day Saint Visual Culture, 1900–1990." *BYU Studies* 39:3 (2000): 18–76.

Iwamura, Jane. *Virtual Orientalism: Asian Religions and American Popular Culture*. New York, 2011.

Maurer, Evan M. *Visions of the People: A Pictorial History of Plains Indian Life*. Minneapolis, 1993.

Metcalf, Barbara Daly, ed. *Making Muslim Space in North America and Europe*. Berkeley, 1996.

Morgan, David. *Protestants and Pictures: Religion, Visual Culture, and the Age of Mass Production*. New York, 1999.

Nesbett, Peter T., and Michelle DuBois. *Jacob Lawrence: Paintings, Drawings, and Murals (1935–1999), A Catalogue Raisonné*. Seattle, 2000.

Wroth, William, *Images of Penance, Images of Mercy: Southwestern Santos in the Late Nineteenth Century*. Norman, OK, 1991.

Yoder, Don. *The Pennsylvania German Broadside: A History and Guide*. University Park, PA, 2005.

37

RELIGION AND RACE

PAUL HARVEY

There are no "red," "white," or "black" people as such. The specific ways in which we understand these terms have some roots in antiquity, but as full-blown categories they are relatively recent inventions. Once the categories emerged, however, they took on lives of their own, so much so that "race" became deeply inscribed in Western thought, permeating its religious beliefs, fables, and mythologies. Historically, Christianity in England, Europe, and America mythically grounded, and later frequently regrounded and revised, modern notions of race. This essay explores the lengthy history of how religion helped to create and later to deconstruct race through the colonial, antebellum, post–Civil War, and civil rights eras. In addition, the essay suggests how groups who were seen as ethnic rather than racial groupings – especially Jews – or who came late to the history of American religio-racial history – namely, Asians and Asian Americans – encountered ideas and practices of race that were foreign to their own histories. Some of these groups were thought of in racial categories because of their presumed religions, namely, Asians; others, namely Jews, usually were not. Finally, the essay examines how a more contemporary project of pluralism claims to efface this historic confluence of religion and race, even as race still fundamentally informs how religious groupings conceptualize and organize themselves.

A complex of historical factors, such as the gigantic global enterprise of colonizing the New World and then populating it with Europeans and African slaves, and mythic groundings, such as stories from the Old Testament and diverse indigenous American and African traditions, influenced the construction of modern racial categories. Euro-American Christianity was hardly the sole or even primary force in this process. Yet religious myth, originating from interpretations of biblical stories as well as speculations about God's providence, played an important role in the formation, revision, and reconstruction of racial categories in the modern world. In short, *religion* played a significant part in creating *race*. More specifically, Christianity necessarily was central to the process of *racializing* peoples, that is, imposing categories of racial hierarchies on groups of humanity or other societies.

If Christianity fostered racialization, it also undermined it. Biblical passages were powerful but ambiguous, and arguments about God's providence in colonization, proselytization, the slave trade, and slavery were contentious. Christian myths and stories were central to the project of creating racial categories in the modern world; but the central text of Christianity, the Bible, was also amenable to more universalist visions and in that sense could never be a fully reliable ally for theorists of racial hierarchy.

For much of the eighteenth and even more so nineteenth centuries, race and religion were joined in the project of civilization. Christianizing others involved civilizing them. Sometimes this involved brutally stripping colonial subjects, especially Native Americans, of the garments of their own civilizations. This included language, religious belief, and cultural practice. "Kill the Indian, Save the Man," went the motto of the Friends of the Indian, a philanthropic group devoted to Indian education in the late nineteenth century. At other times, the joining of Christianization and civilization underwrote idealistic crusades of bringing formerly enslaved peoples into American civilization, as in the abolitionist movement, and later in the creation of black schools and colleges during the Reconstruction. In other instances, the intertwining of Christianity, civilization, and whiteness justified the complete exclusion of peoples from the American republic, notably in legislation such as the Chinese Exclusion Act of 1882. Progressive Christian writers such as Josiah Strong articulated a strong sense of Christian nativism, warning against the dilution of the Protestantism that had been instrumental in forming American democracy. In short, the connections between religion and race were complicated; idealism and brutality often went hand in hand, as did notions of inclusion together with the instruments of exclusion. Idealism and imperialism often joined in projects both inspiring and ignoble.

In the twentieth century, Christian thought helped to undermine the racial system that it had been instrumental in creating. In the 1950s and 1960s, black civil rights activists in the Congress of Racial Equality (CORE), Southern Christian Leadership Conference (SCLC), and Student Nonviolent Coordinating Committee (SNCC) emerged from black churches and finally penetrated the walls of segregation, still guarded by conservative white churchmen and opportunistic politicians. The civil rights revolution in American history was, to a considerable degree, a religious revolution, one whose social and spiritual impact inspired numerous other movements around the world.

To some degree, this had always been implicit in biblical texts that envisioned a Christian community that broke bonds of male and female, Jew and Gentile. It took considerable intellectual convolution to read the Bible as advocating something other than the universal humanity of mankind, all born of Adam and potentially redeemed through the salvific work of Jesus. And yet theology played a central role in justifying social hierarchies based on race as well as on other distinctions, including class. In the twentieth century, ideas of cultural pluralism that percolated through the progressive intellectual world of the early twentieth century eventually found their way into an American discourse of religious pluralism. This pluralism was never all-inclusive. For groups whose spiritual practices did not constitute a discernible religion and thus did not enjoy the benefits of First Amendment protection, religious freedom remained a more distant ideal. Yet for many others, including those who were excluded by the legacy of racist immigration legislation and others who historically had been dishonored, the emergence of religious pluralism as an ideal in public discourse constituted a true revolution.

When challenged, the power of the state does not recognize all "religion" equally; the implicit, de facto Protestantism of the American republic historically has defined public discourse, shaped public ceremonies, and dominated public life in the personage of political officials. Moreover, racial profiling as applied to Latino Catholics, African Pentecostals, or Middle Eastern Muslims affects lives and individual liberties in a way that is simply unthinkable for the dominant Protestant majority. In this way, the nexus between religion and race has never died. But it undeniably exerts a relatively smaller influence in comparison to the power of that dualism in earlier centuries. Religious pluralism requires an official rhetoric of respect and neutrality. However imperfectly practiced, religious pluralism has opened up spaces for ethnic groups and minority religions that were formerly surveilled and suppressed.

Religion and race remain tied together in the public mind. Well past the civil rights movement and the end of officially sanctioned apartheid, religious institutions have remained largely and voluntarily separated by race, the legacy of centuries of tradition as briefly outlined in this essay. Even while scholars dispute the singular notion of "the black church," the term remains widely used in public discourse, including by members of black churches themselves. Latino Catholics have moved into and taken over numerous parishes formerly controlled by various European ethnic groups; Asian Buddhists have built temples in which Thais, Cambodians, Vietnamese, and others congregate; and Korean Christians bring an especially fervent style of evangelical Christianity to congregations denominated by the Korean script that often is painted onto buildings formerly used for other purposes. In short, if religion is no longer racialized in the ways it was in previous centuries, religious congregations tend to be racially separated, a simple reality of how Americans of diverse ethnic backgrounds have ordered their lives. Race still has a color and a religion, even while the public rhetoric of American religion is ostensibly raceless and colorless. Thus, in a society sometimes said to be moving into a postracial era, ethnic and racial constructions remain a central ordering fact of religious life. Given the history of race and religion in America, it is hard to see how it could be otherwise.

RELIGION AND RACE IN THE ERA OF THE SLAVE TRADE AND COLONIZATION, 1500–1800

Europeans brought diverse religious and racial ideas to exploring and colonizing the New World, and to searching for laborers in Europe, America, and Africa to do the necessary labor to make the new colonies economically successful. The basic question they faced was whether or not the Christian message was to be universal. Could Africans, Indians, and others be brought into the Christian fold? For the colonized and enslaved groups, the questions were very different. Generally, these groups practiced religious beliefs that relativized human culture – as in one Indian's response to a Jesuit priest that "your God has not come to my country" – and as such, religions were to be respected but not to be proselytized. In other words, when the universalizing messages of Protestantism and Catholicism, which competed avidly and sometimes violently for souls, met the localized practices of Native North Americans and Africans, the historic roots of misunderstanding and conflict quickly emerged.

In the sixteenth and early seventeenth centuries, Spanish, French, and English colonizers, settlers, priests, and soldiers encountered native groups as diverse as the hunting Innu, called Montagnais by the French in the Great Lakes region of Canada; the highly complex civilizations of the Powhatan Confederacy in Virginia; and the deeply settled agricultural peoples of the southwestern Pueblos – and any myriad of others. Meanwhile, Portuguese, Dutch, and English slave traders encountered a bewilderingly diverse variety of human groupings from West and central Africa, including numerous converts to Islam and Christianity as well as those who practiced widely divergent native religious traditions. Native North Americans did not think of themselves, religiously or racially, as "Indians" or as "red men." The same held true for diverse groupings of people in the western and central part of the African continent, who thought of themselves in categories of designation derived from locales or kingdoms rather than as

"Africans" or as "Negroes" or "black." The process of racializing people into these kinds of categories, of "Indian" and "African" and of "red" and "Negro," would take centuries. To a considerable degree, even the early Europeans did not do so. Hence, European slave traders were careful to distinguish ethnic groupings of people forced onto ships for the Middle Passage. Slaves sometimes were marketed based on the alleged "character" of the people from whom they came. Those who were considered ethnically to be naturally harder workers fetched higher prices; those believed to be more naturally inclined to rebel or run away yielded lower value.

Most importantly for our discussion here, none of these groups were considered to have religion, or at least not a religion that required respect. Instead, they had "pagan" or "barbaric" customs. In a few cases, such as with the Jesuits in New France, relatively sensitive priests, set down in locales where there were few Europeans and cooperation with native peoples was a condition of survival, produced volumes such as the *Jesuit Relations*, which closely described and sometimes implicitly respected native religious ritual. In other cases, even Europeans who dealt in regions of Africa heavily influenced by Islamic and Catholic missionaries generally could not see their subjects as possessing religion. Indeed, the very process of enslavement virtually required Europeans to place the victims outside the category of possessing religion, for slavery could be practiced on others but not on Christians. In short, the earliest process of racializing diverse peoples involved ignoring, denying, or denigrating their religions, for a religionless or a soulless people could be enslaved in a way that a believing or ensouled people could not. This held true for both Christian and Islamic enslavers.

The slave trade took off during a great age of religious ferment and expansion following the Protestant Reformation and Catholic Counter-Reformation. Thus, although the trade was fundamentally economic, the European participants sought some religious sanction for what was obviously a coercive and necessarily brutal activity. Judeo-Christian stories were not necessarily, immediately, or inherently amenable to providing a religious basis for modern racial slavery. Biblical characters lived in an ancient Semitic, Mediterranean, and North African world, one in which modern understandings of white and black people would have been meaningless.

Once slavery took root in the Americas, it was easy enough for religious authorities simply to decree that, if slavery existed, God must have a reason for it – and that reason must be in the Bible. But slavery in the Americas was specifically a *racial* form of bondage. This stood in contrast to traditional forms of slavery found throughout the world, which were not racial in the modern sense, although they were sometimes ethnic. Thus the religious justification of slavery would have to clarify God's providence particularly in having one race of people enslave another. In this way, Euro-Americans worked out some of the meanings of race itself in the modern sense. They began to define what constituted whiteness and blackness, categories that would long outlive slavery itself. And those categories were, at least initially, fundamentally religious ones as well.

In his classic work *White over Black*, the historian Winthrop Jordan demonstrated how white supremacist racial thought emerged early in the modern world. It fundamentally and fatally shaped interactions between whites and others, especially Africans, from the fifteenth century forward. Other scholars have traced early European thought toward native peoples of the New World, showing again the European roots of the colonialism and racism that emerged fully formed later. Religious divisions drawn by Europeans between Christians and others, between those of Christ and those in the heathen world, became part of defining what race meant. "European" or "English" meant "Christian," and in future centuries that came also to mean "white"; "African" meant "heathen," despite the fact that many Africans had been Christianized, especially by Portuguese Catholic missionaries, and that large swaths of the African continent had fallen under the sway of Islam. Regardless, African came to denominate heathen, and in future centuries that came also to mean "black." In the New World, Indians were, variously, pagan, heathen, or "sons of the forest," and over time these congeries of earlier attitudes coalesced into the category "red man." In short, the categories of religion and race intertwined throughout American history, each helping to delimit and define the other. Religion helped to create and solidify modern notions of redness, whiteness, and blackness; in that sense, religion helped to create common understandings of red, white, and black people.

Early colonizers in the Americas faced first the question of whether Christianity would apply to Indians and black slaves at all. The answer required, in part, deciding on whether native peoples in North America, Africans, and African Americans were fully human – a debate that raged for several centuries and indeed continued on into the post–Civil War era of scientific racism. If only Christians were truly men – and Christians were white – then where did that leave Negroes? And what was the status of Indians, people who never appeared in the biblical texts and whose origins were unclear? Were they heathen? Were they potential Christians? Or might they be the remnants of the lost tribe of Israel, whose discovery and reconversion would set the stage for the coming millennium? English and Anglo-American theologians grappled with such quandaries.

The rise of slavery made such queries especially urgent for black people. Was there a separate category, apart from "man," into which blackness could be fit? The Virginia House of Burgesses in 1699 noted that "the negroes born in this country are generally baptized and brought up in the Christian religion; but for negroes imported hither, the gross bestiality and rudeness of their manners, the variety and strangeness of their languages, and the weakness and shallowness of their minds, render it in a manner impossible to make any progress in their conversion." The English Christians in particular, it seemed, were relatively indifferent to Christian duty. But at least in part, this indifference might have come about because so many white settlers remained unconvinced about whether blackness ultimately was compatible with the state of being Christian. For many, blackness conjured images of savagery even in the practice of religion itself. The Rev. Morgan Goodwin, who ministered in seventeenth-century Virginia, charged that "nothing is more barbarous and contrary to Christianity, than their ... *Idolatrous Dances*, and *Revels*."[1]

As some slaves converted to Christianity, however, reality once again confuted ideology and theology. Anglo-Americans faced this question: would baptism require freedom? That is, did baptism into the Christian religion make men white? The early advocates of slave Christianization, accordingly, had to dissociate Christianity from whiteness – from freedom – precisely for the purpose of defining blackness as a state of perpetual servitude continuing beyond one's potential baptism into the Christian faith, and indeed beyond one's own life into the lives of one's children, grandchildren, to perpetuity. In the late seventeenth century, as slavery took hold in the Chesapeake, Virginians defined further the status of free and Christian by enumerating precisely what constituted its opposite: unfree heathen. By the early eighteenth century, Christians were legally and explicitly defined by a physical distinction; the same act condemned non-Christians to slavery. The law stated that "all servants imported and brought into this country ... who were not Christians in their native country ... before they were shipped ... shall be accounted and be slaves, and as such be here bought and sold notwithstanding a conversion to Christianity afterwards." In the act, the English defined their own Protestant identity further by differentiating it from the inalienable status of heathen. It was part, of course, of the larger project of defining freedom by enumerating what constituted the status of unfreedom. On baptism, the act stated "that the conferring of baptisme doth not alter the condition of the person as to his bondage or freedome; that diverse masters, [freed] from this doubt, may more carefully endeavour the propagation of Christianity by permitting children, though slaves, or those of

---

[1] Rebecca Goetz, "From Potential Christians to Hereditary Heathens: Race and Religion in the Early Chesapeake, 1590–1740" (Ph.D. diss., Harvard University, 2006), 186–7. Emphasis in the original.

greater growth if capable to be admitted to the sacrament." Virginia's law provided a model for later legislation.[2]

Anglican missionaries complained that planters resisted slave Christianization because, as one put it, "it often makes them proud, and not so good servants." There were substantial reasons for this suspicion, for Christianized slaves sued for freedom and pointed out the contradiction of Christianity and slaveholding. In one case in 1723, a group of Christian slaves, of mixed-race parentage, pled their case for freedom in a letter to a newly installed bishop who oversaw Anglican affairs in the colonies. They were, they wrote, "Baptised and brouaht up in a way of the Christian faith and followes the wayes and Rulles of the chrch of England." They complained about laws "which keeps and makes them and there seed Slaves forever." The hardness of their masters kept them from following the Sabbath: "wee doo hardly know when it comes for our task mastrs are has hard with us as the Egyptians was with the Chilldann of Issarall." Their letter concluded with an explanation of why they did not sign their names, "for freare of our masters for if they knew that wee have Sent home to your honour wee Should goo neare to Swing upon the Gallass tree." These slaves retained an older, more radical view of Christian conversion: their religious status gave them rights to freedom and respect, for which they were willing to fight. They spoke the language of power precisely because they knew the language of power – in courtrooms, in letters to imperial officials, and, as a last resort, in rebellions.[3]

Over the decades of the evangelical revolution of the mid-to-late eighteenth century, planter resistance to Christianization lessened in the face of the rise of the proselytizing power of the evangelicals. This suggested that planters came to see a Christian obligation, that African American slaves pressed for recognition of their Christianity within the church, and that rising generations of planters were more willing to support baptism and creole slaves whose parents had been baptized or had baptized their own children. Still, the ambiguity of slave Christianization remained troubling. If blackness was (by definition) unfreedom, and Christianity was (by natural law) freedom, then how could the two be commingled? Christianity and whiteness were both states of freedom, making it easy for many to essentially equate the two: white equaled free and Christian; black, Indian, or other equaled unfree and un-christian. For many Christians, whiteness simply became woven into the very fabric of Christianity itself.

---

[2] Ibid., 142–5.
[3] Thomas Ingersoll, ed., "'Releese Us out of This Cruell Bondegg': An Appeal from Virginia in 1723," *William and Mary Quarterly* 3rd ser., 51:4 (Oct. 1994): 781–2.

Yet the inescapable fact remained that white Christians somehow had to fit black people into God's providence. Passages from the Old Testament, especially Genesis 9:18–27, outlined the curse on Canaan, son of Ham, who had originally espied Noah's naked drunkenness and thereafter was consigned to slavery. "A servant of servants shall he be," the verse proclaimed. Once exegeted properly, it provided at least a start at a religio-mythical grounding for modern racial meanings, and a long-lived one. The passage was still cited in segregationist literature of the 1950s, and it remains an ideological part of certain fringe groups, such as the Christian Identity movement, down to the present day. Respectable theologians often skirted the son of Ham story, as it smacked more of folklore than "high" theology. Moreover, as the historian Colin Kidd has argued, the major thrust of Christian theology weighed in against the varieties of racism that cast particular groups out of the category of humanity. Passages such as, "Of one blood hath God made all nations," provided the basis for a universal message and tended to marginalize Christian thought that questioned the full humanity of Africans and Native Americans. That being said, the fable of Ham deeply penetrated the religious consciousness of white southerners, who were for the most part biblical literalists.

The son of Ham saga served well in the sense that it seemed to explain how black people could be free Christians and unfree slaves at the same time. But the curse on Ham was at best a shaky foundation for religio-racial mythologizing, for the passage invoked was simply too short, mysterious, and fable-like to bear up under the full weight of the interpretations imposed on it. Once again, the Bible proved a powerful but somewhat troubling and unreliable guide in the formation of mytho-racial ideologies.

ANTEBELLUM ERA (1800–1860): CHRISTIANIZATION AND DEGRADATION

As Africans, African Americans, and Native Americans adopted Christianity in particular times and places, Christianity could no longer be synonymous with whiteness. Even still, nineteenth-century notions of whiteness encompassed Christianity and civilization, so much so that even those who might be Christianized might not be considered civilized. This powerful confluence of Christianity, civilization, and whiteness fundamentally shaped American notions of religion and race for centuries.

Proslavery theologians worked feverishly through the antebellum era (1800–60) to enunciate a Christian proslavery apologetic, one that would preserve boundaries of whiteness-blackness while also supporting their efforts to Christianize the slaves. By the nineteenth century, white southern clergymen repeatedly insisted that Christianization would make blacks more secure in their enslavedness because it would render them content in obedience. With such reasoning at hand, white southerners supported a substantial missionary enterprise to the slaves. Although it remained controversial in some quarters through the antebellum era, white southern denominations accepted that such activity was part of spreading the word of God even to the poorest and most miserable of God's creatures. Contrary to views in the seventeenth and eighteenth centuries, which often set in dichotomous relief whiteness and Christian freedom versus blackness and un-Christian unfreedom, by the nineteenth century the missions to the slaves had been successful enough that many whites came to see black religion as peculiarly fervent and reassuringly orthodox. Blackness now signified a particular type of Christian fervor, one with occasional fits of menace, such as in Nat Turner's rebellion in 1831, but one largely consonant with the white southern version of paternalism. White Americans, formerly skeptical that barbaric Negroes could understand or accept the Christian faith of whites, now reassured themselves that the Negro, in his religion, was "simple" and "orthodox," if a bit "emotional" and "frenzied" in his religious expressions.

Later in these years, the development and full-fledged exposition of a proslavery argument explained away the obvious contradictions of slaveholding in a free republic and justified the daily repression required to enforce enslavement even in the midst of the rapid Christian evangelization of the South. As black abolitionists such as Frederick Douglass tirelessly pointed out, American Christianity and American slavery spread in a kind of dark lockstep pattern through the early republic and antebellum era, creating the bewildering and tragic paradox of the United States, the Christian slaveholding free republic. But enslaved people refused to allow their Christianization to enforce their subjugation in the way that white slaveholding proselytizers had hoped.

As Anglo-Americans developed their own particular ideas of Christianity and freedom in the New World, they were involved at the same time in the process of racializing themselves and others – and the "others" were reciprocal agents in this process. Native Americans had a tortured relationship with Christianity. On the one hand, Christianity was the religion of the colonizers. Often the religion of Jesus rendered as holy the brutal displacement and genocide of Indian peoples. On the other hand, Christian missionaries – from the Franciscans in New Mexico and the Protestant missionary John Eliot in New England forward – made significant inroads among Native Americans, both by coercion and by enticement. The natives they encountered, at the same time, struggled to fit the foreign religious ideas of Christianity into their own religious context, a process made even more complex within a historical context of disease, death, colonialism, and intermittent warfare. In other cases, notably including missionaries to the Cherokees in the 1820s and 1830s, Anglo Christians defended Native American rights against the encroachments of the U.S. government.

In responding to the coming of the colonizers, and later to the rise of the Anglo-American nation-state, Native American groups chose various courses of accommodation, resistance, acculturation, and revitalization, according to their very different and contradictory geopolitical realities. In no way could the Christian tradition become their ally in the way it eventually did for African Americans. Yet in no way could it be rejected either, for it had become too much a part of Indian life: both internally, in the evolution of native religious customs, and externally, in the dominant world of the nation-state.

For Native Americans, the era of democratic Christianity and the so-called Second Great Awakening also witnessed the apogee of state-sanctioned ethnic cleansing. Most famously, of course, was the tragic Trail of Tears episode. The relationship between Christianity, freedom, and sovereignty also was played out with a variety of Indian groups throughout the South and newly opening regions of the "Great West." Democratic Christianity, the market revolution, the rapid expansion westward and southward, and a populist faith in self-determination joined together in destroying precarious balances of power on the frontier and making America a white man's country. For the Indian Free Methodist convert William Apess, who preached for the church in the 1820s and 1830s while publishing prolifically, the melancholy results of white Christian ethnic cleansing appeared all too evidently since the time of the arrival of whites to New England. What was then in the process of being transformed, by Daniel Webster and other great orators and nationalists of the era, into the mythical story of heroic Pilgrims and pioneers conquering the wilderness and spreading civilization westward through empty lands appeared to Indians such as Apess as a virtually untrammeled history of conquest, violence, and repression. For Apess' generation, race was a yawning gulf separating religion from American ideas of freedom.

William Apess' *Eulogy* in honor of King Philip – or Metacom, the leader of the brutal conflict later known as King Philip's War of 1676 – made clear the native conception of the history of religion and American ideas of freedom. What were the weapons of this vaunted Christian civilization, Apess asked. And what had become of Indians under this Christian civilization? "Had the inspiration of Isaiah been there," Apess averred, "he could not have been more correct. Our groves and hunting grounds are gone, our dead are dug up, our council-fires are put out, and a foundation was laid in the first Legislature to enslave our people, by taking from them all rights."

The Pilgrims had created a "fire, a canker" designed to "destroy my poor unfortunate brethren," and even to the time of Apess himself the president "tells the Indians they cannot live among civilized people, and we want your lands and must have them and will have them."[4]

Throughout America and in the newly created United States, Native Americans were compelled to respond to Anglo-American power in the new republic. Religious awakenings involving the revival of native customs periodically swept through beleaguered native communities. From the visions of the Delaware Neolin in the mid-eighteenth century, to the Shawnee prophet Tenskwatawa in the early nineteenth century, to Handsome Lake's teachings among the Iroquois, and to the Red Sticks and militant nativists among the Creeks and Seminoles in the Southeast, religiously inspired prophetic resistance ran through Indian communities from the Great Awakening forward. American observers among the tribes in the early nineteenth century noted the differing and contested theologies at play. Nativists and prophets insisted on the separate creation of peoples and the notion that the "Great Spirit did not mean that the white and red people should live near each other." After all, whites had "poison'd the land."[5]

Native Americans of the Southeast could do little in the face of aggressive expansion. Whether they chose to Christianize and Anglicize, or whether they chose to engage in limited economic commerce with Europeans but otherwise maintain their own cultural practices, or whether they resisted violently under the leadership of messianic individuals, the outcome for most was more or less the same – forcible removal from their lands, repression of religious practices, and exile far westward out of the way of white settlers. Along the way, Creeks, Cherokees, and others in Georgia and elsewhere picked up white allies, namely missionaries intent on using the force of the Americans' own legal codes to provide some degree of protection for besieged natives. In Georgia, state legislators employed every means necessary to clear out areas for land-hungry settlers and for the coffles of slaves being transported overland to the newly opening regions. When missionaries among the Cherokees were ordered to clear out as well, they refused to obey, were arrested, and eventually took their case to the Supreme Court. In *Worcester v. Georgia*, the famous case that arose from this incident, Chief Justice John Marshall ruled in the Cherokees' favor. He found that the state of Georgia did not have legal authority to enforce laws within the bounds

---

[4] Barry O'Connell, ed., *On Our Own Ground: The Complete Writings of William Apess, a Pequot* (Amherst, 1992), 246–50.

[5] Gregory Dowd, *A Spirited Resistance: The North American Indian Struggle for Unity, 1745–1815* (Baltimore, 1991), 142.

of the Cherokee lands. President Andrew Jackson was just as famously contemptuous of the court's edicts, as he knew it would be military force, not Supreme Court doctrine, that would carry the day. And so it did.

Democratic politics and the rapid rise of populist Christian sects created a new context for American ideas of freedom, a kind of Methodist millennium. From the underside of that millennium, however, American ideas of freedom promised universalist visions but delivered a republic that was based on universalist premises but was, in practice, racially exclusivist and white supremacist. That paradox lay at the heart of Native and African American thought and practice. Just as the Declaration of Independence became a touchstone for African American thought, as both a positive and a negative reference point, and as white idealists and missionaries took their Christianity to Indian tribes whom they defended against governmentally imposed removal and repression schemes, the universalist language of democratic Christianity provided a base for alternative visions.

Northern black thinkers in particular enthusiastically participated in the rhetoric, language, and concepts of their place and time, including ideas of America's chosen mission. At the same time, nationalism fused with religio-messianic ideals increasingly informed black thought as the antebellum era progressed. Enlightenment universalism and black nationalism often merged, for both spoke to profound and deep aspirations of African Americans as a people, and both were also consonant with Afro-American religious traditions. Forms of rhetoric often understood to be antithetical, or competing brands of black thought, merged into one another. On the one hand, African American writers and orators repeated many of the same phrases about the divinely appointed destiny of America as did their white contemporaries. This did not mean they spared America of biting critiques for its racist oppression, but they saw the true American ideals as within the ultimate design of God. Using the familiar arguments drawn from American Christian theodicy, African Americans understood the African fall into slavery as a form of evil that God permitted in order to bring about a greater good. Slavery "has been your curse, but it shall become your rejoicing," as former slave Austin Steward said, for slavery had placed black Americans "in the midst of the path of progress." Black thinkers and writers trusted in God's providence but warned Americans of their ultimate fate for ignoring the course of history. As David Walker put it, "Unless you speedily alter your course, *you* and your *Country are gone!!!!!* For God Almighty will tear up the very face of the earth!!!"[6]

---

[6] Patrick Rael et al., eds., *Pamphlets of Protest: An Anthology of Early African American Protest Literature, 1790–1860* (New York, 2001), 271. Emphasis in the original.

Whereas the monumental figure of Frederick Douglass consistently articulated universalist ideals of black integration into the American republic and resistance to all forms of separatism or colonization, black nationalists such as the well-known antebellum black ministers Henry Highland Garnet and Martin Delany pressed the case for resistance and separate black institutions. As Delany put it, the "determined aim of the whites" was to "crush the colored races wherever found," with the Anglo-Saxon taking the lead in "this work of universal subjugation."[7] Delany and others came from a generation as inspired by the possibilities of the spread of civilization worldwide as they were resistant to American racism. Their answer was a sort of intellectualized form of what became a mass movement in the twentieth century with the advent of Marcus Garvey and the African Orthodox Church. Delany and Alexander Crummell were two of the best-known spokesmen for black nationalist thought in the nineteenth century. Both placed African Americans within the movement of history – not as a people without history, as Hegel said of Africa, but as a people who would carry history forward on their shoulders. Twentieth-century black prophets and thinkers, from W.E.B. DuBois to Elijah Muhammad, Malcolm X, and James Cone, carried forward diverse varieties of black nationalism that arose from this nineteenth-century context.[8]

RACE AND RELIGION AFTER 1865

After the Civil War, many self-proclaimed race theologians and scientists, both crackpots and serious thinkers, challenged older religious notions of the unity of races by fantasizing instead about the separately created origins of races. They reread African Americans back out of the category of humanity, just as many of their seventeenth-century forebears had done. By mixing biblical and scientific reasoning, they took "scientific" studies of Negro inferiority (including those from phrenology, the pseudoscience of measuring the brain skeleton and inferring intelligence from such measurements) and found in scripture explanations (such as fables in Genesis) that allegedly supported the science. Many of these writers fiddled with the curse of Ham legend, struggling to fit the Genesis myths with the findings of the racially biased science of that era. The late nineteenth century witnessed the apogee of the polygenesis and scientific racism. A combination of close biblical exegesis and the twentieth-century reliance on science produced truly miscegenated offspring, including mytho-scientific racism – that is, a blending of racism, Darwinian ideas, and biblical exegesis.

---

[7] *Ibid.*, 235.
[8] Edward Blum, *W.E.B. Du Bois: American Prophet* (Philadelphia, 2007).

These pseudoscientific mythologies, drawn from race and religion, figured heavily in white fears of miscegenation, that is, the sexual intermixture or marrying of white and black people. The fear of race mixing most particularly between white women and black men, the symbol of virginal purity encountering the "black beast rapist" so feared in southern folklore, was used to justify the entire system of segregation that separated the races. "Race purity" was at stake – and that, ultimately, meant the honor of white women.

Nowhere was the violence enforcing white supremacy more gruesomely displayed than in the often horrific acts by which white men claimed to preserve the honor of the white woman – that is, in lynching black men. Of the nearly five thousand lynchings in America from 1880 to 1950, many of the best known were what one historian has called "spectacle lynchings." These were purposeful, solemn events – *rituals* – in which dozens, hundreds, or even thousands engaged in acts of purification, hence the frequency with which lynching victims were burned, and the invocations pronounced at such events by clergymen or other religious leaders. For centuries, Anglo-Americans had identified blackness with impurity and found biblical sanction for this connection. This image also had pernicious consequences within the post-Civil War Bible Belt South.[9]

Against centuries of onslaught of such deeply rooted myths and religiously sanctioned degradation, black Americans stood little chance of mounting an effective defense. But they tried. In the nineteenth century, particularly when a small but significant set of educated black Americans encountered the romantic and racialist ideas of their era, many of them responded by trying to write the black man *into* the reigning mythologies and categories. It was the destiny of black Americans, some of them believed, to bring civilization back to their home continent. It was biblically prophesied that it should be so. George Wilson Brent, a black Methodist minister and race man, took the biblical stories as evidence for the black man's indispensable role in furthering human history. "Africa, our fatherland, the home of the Hamitic race," he wrote, "is the only country on earth whose past, present, and future so concerned the Lord." Even the son of Ham himself, Canaan, was blessed, for he "invested and built up a country and settled a nation bearing his name, whose glory ... remains today the typical ensign of the Christian's hope, concerning Africa's future glory." The biblical prophecy that "Ethiopia shall soon stretch forth her hand to God" arose from this Old Testament history. Brent dated the origin of the white man to *after* Noah's flood, meaning (in this view) that the

---

[9] Grace Hale, *Making Whiteness: The Culture of Segregation in the South, 1890–1940* (New York, 1997).

black man could claim the more ancient pedigree than the white man, no matter what their current state of power relations.[10] Other black commentators also produced race histories that explained the origins and destiny of black people to African American readers. Whether to accept the biblical mythologies but to invert the stories (as did George Wilson Brent), or to put on display entirely new mythological constructs (as did the black leader Marcus Garvey in Harlem in the 1920s), or to insist that blackness and whiteness were simply not biblical categories because "of one blood hath God made all nations," black Americans responded vigorously to the creation of blackness as a category of inferiority and shame. Until later in the twentieth century, however, few white Americans listened.[11]

Native peoples, now clearly subjugated and colonized in the American republic, faced two alternatives: assimilation or extermination. Or so went the dominant thought of many Protestant leaders in the decades after the Civil War. Idealists and abolitionists who had led the fight against slavery and in support of black rights after the Civil War increasingly turned their attention to "the Indian" in the 1880s and 1890s. Forming groups such as the Friends of the Indian, they created Indian boarding schools, intending to train up a younger generation of Indian youngsters and teach them the arts of civilization. They also persuaded Congress to pass the Dawes Act of 1883, which broke up communal property on Indian reservations, allotted plots of land to Indian families for purposes of farming, and sold off or leased the remainder of the land, the proceeds going to fund those same Indian boarding schools. Protestant and Catholic organizations divided up Indian tribes for purposes of mission work; and those with the best reputations for dealing fairly with Indians in the past, the Quakers, took charge of the national missionizing endeavor.

The result was disaster and scandal, mocking the idealism that had motivated Protestant philanthropists. The successes of bringing freedom and Christianity to the Afro-American simply were not transferrable as a model to Indians. African Americans found ways to turn Christianity into a force for liberation, regardless of the motives of the white Christianizers. For native peoples, the idealistic motives of many of the Christianizing groups turned out to have disastrous consequences, so much so that the 1890s probably represented the nadir of Native American life and population for all of American history since colonization. The Ghost Dance

---

[10] George Wilson Brent, "The Ancient Glory of the Hamitic Race," *A.M.E. Church Review* 12 (Oct. 1895): 272–5; and George Wilson Brent, "Origin of the White Race," *A.M.E. Church Review* 10 (Jan. 1893): 287–8.

[11] Laurie Maffly-Kipp, *Setting Down the Sacred Past: African American Race Histories* (Cambridge, MA, 2010).

episode at Wounded Knee, South Dakota, in 1890, resulting in the massacre of more than two hundred Lakotas at the hands of U.S. army personnel baffled and frightened by Indian religious ritual, is often seen as the low point of white-Indian relations.

RELIGION AND RACE THROUGH THE CIVIL RIGHTS ERA: 1860S–1960S

From the Civil War through the civil rights era of the 1960s, racialized religious communities sanctified their quests for freedom. The Christian mythic grounding for ideas of whiteness, blackness, and redness was powerful but unstable, subject to constant argument and revision. In the twentieth century, this grounding was radically overturned in part through a reimagination of the same Christian thought that was part of creating it in the first place. Black Christians who formed the rank and file of the civil rights movement demolished the political structures of segregation, and with them some of the folklore of blackness as inferiority that had enslaved so many Americans for so many centuries. After the Civil War, newly organized black churches and independent black denominations, freed from the constraints of slavery, organized vigorously among the freed people. Even as black Christians created institutional forms to celebrate religious and temporal freedom, white southern (and sometimes northern) believers elaborated a theology of apartheid that sanctified temporal racial strictures.

It is sometimes said that the civil rights movement emerged from "the black church," a falsely singular term for what was, in fact, a multifarious set of beliefs and institutions. Historians cite evidence such as the number of ministers in the struggle and churches that served as gathering points for mass meetings. At the same time, movement leaders constantly contended with the fact that the black church actually was not, by and large, behind the movement. Whether because of indifference, fear, theological conservatism, or coercion and terrorism, many congregations simply avoided involvement. Thus the relationship between religion, race, and rights during the 1960s is considerably more complicated than often portrayed, particularly in the recent deification and consequent oversimplification of Martin Luther King's life and work. Still, a movement based on secular ends – the extension of citizenship rights in the American nation-state – drew its sustenance from spiritual understandings, language, and motivations. It was a fundamentally Protestant imagery – of exodus, redemption, and salvation – that inspired the revivalistic fervor of the movement. And it was ministers and church activists who lent their moral passion and steely commitment to the quest for freedom.

Meanwhile, white believers throughout the civil rights–era South connected the preservation of race purity with the fear of miscegenation and defense of southern social customs. Most arguments employed some form of received wisdom and familiar folklore – the immutable "nature" of the Negro, the "impurity" that would inevitably accompany integration, or time-honored scriptural staples such as the Old Testament story of Noah and his progeny. Denominational ethicists and theologians consistently showed how the ancient and cryptic Old Testament stories in no way buttressed the specific twentieth-century social system of segregation. But this biblical jousting was beside the point, for the theoreticians of Jim Crow were by definition suspicious of officially sanctioned modes of scriptural interpretation. Christian desegregationists quoted Acts 17:26, "Of one blood has God made all nations." Segregationists, in response, explicated the second half of the verse, which referred to God assigning to his creatures the "bounds of their habitation."[12]

Native Americans were kept within the bounds of their habitations, usually on reservations, but the results were unsatisfactory for those who believed they should be assimilated into the dominant society. For Native Americans in the post–Civil War era, religious resistance appeared increasingly futile, but controversies over religious assimilation tore apart many communities. The Bureau of Indian Affairs repressed native religious practices in Indian boarding schools. There children were punished for "talking Indian," appealing to "medicine men," or otherwise practicing parts of their cultural heritage. Adult ceremonies were also repressed. Thus, regulations in the 1920s attempted to delegitimize or stamp out native dances held at Indian pueblos in New Mexico and Arizona. In the Indian New Deal of the 1930s, John Collier and other Indian reformers reversed these practices, and for the first time in decades gave Indian peoples some hope that they might be able to practice openly their religious ceremonies. Here religion and race were still connected, but in a way that could be valorized rather than condemned.

In the contemporary United States, more Native Americans claim Christianity than any other religion as their belief. Deliberately modeling his work on James Cone's notion that "God is Black," Vine Deloria, a scholar of Native American history and religions, produced his classic work, *God Is Red*, in 1973. The work appeared during a standoff between the American Indian Movement and federal authorities at Wounded Knee, South Dakota. United States army personnel had butchered hundreds of Indian ghost dancers at that very site in 1890, a massacre sometimes referred to as the last of the "Indian wars." In his work, Deloria

---

[12] Paul Harvey, *Freedom's Coming: Religious Culture and the Shaping of the South from the Civil War through the Civil Rights Era* (Chapel Hill, 2005), ch. 5.

thoughtfully explored what it means for Indian people to look for meaning in their tribal religions, given their Christian educations and the seculariztion and techno-rationalizm of the modern world. He found an "amazing resilience in restoring the old ceremonies" and noted that even among Native American Christian clergy who sought a merger of the two traditions, the effect was to "bring attention to traditional ways to the detriment of the particular Christian denomination." Meanwhile, whites unsettled by the social revolution of the 1960s were seeking spiritual wholeness outside of Christianity, including their own (sometimes fumbling) attempts to connect with Indian traditions of reverence for sacred spaces rather than a rational religion of "doctrine" and "belief."[13] Native American attempts to exercise religious freedom have compelled a rethinking of the First Amendment, as well as a revitalization of Indian religious traditions. In a sense, New Age practitioners have reracialized (and appropriated) Native American beliefs, although this racialization resulted from romanticism rather than condemnation.

ASIANS, JEWS, AND MUSLIMS: RELIGIONS OR ETHNICITIES IN THE NINETEENTH AND TWENTIETH CENTURIES

In the colonial era, religious "diversity" referred to diverse varieties of Protestants who populated the American landscape, along with a handful of others. In the nineteenth century, Catholics entered the picture of diversity in a much more major way, requiring American Protestants to reconsider whether this was to be a specifically Protestant, or more generally Christian, republic. Catholic immigrants inserted themselves into that picture in part through their sheer numbers, while Catholic theologians placed themselves on the American intellectual landscape.

In the late nineteenth century, much the same happened for Jews during their period of massive immigration. Jews had been accepted in colonial America, so much so that George Washington famously wrote to a Jewish congregation in Rhode Island that

> happily, the Government of the United States, which gives to bigotry no sanction, to persecution no assistance, requires only that they who live under its protection should demean themselves as good citizens.... May the children of the stock of Abraham who dwell in this land continue to merit and enjoy the good will of the other inhabitants while every one shall sit in safety under his own vine and fig tree and there shall be none to make him afraid.[14]

---

[13] Vine DeLoria, *God Is Red: A Native View of Religion* (Golden, CO, 1994), 253.
[14] George Washington, "Letter to the Hebrew Congregation at Newport," Aug. 1790, reprinted at "Teaching American History," http://www.teachingamericanhistory.org/library/index.asp?document=21 (accessed 4 July 2011).

A relatively small number of Jews, largely of German origin and highly assimilated into Western culture, arrived through the first two-thirds of the nineteenth century. The latter decades of the nineteenth century, and going forward to World War I, witnessed a far more massive migration, fueled by pogroms and economic decline in Eastern Europe and Russia. American Jews invented Reform Judaism as a religious mechanism by which Jewish people could maintain some traditions while participating fully in the modern world and in American democracy. Late nineteenth-century Jewish immigration challenged this pact, for Russian and Eastern European Jews brought with them an orthodoxy and a "foreignness" that concerned the same kinds of nativists and Protestant thinkers who decried the transformative immigration patterns of that era.

Jews were not blacks, Native Americans, or Asians, however. Judaism was a religion, one respected by Christians who understood themselves to be in the same religious universe as Jews – as opposed, for example, to Asian Buddhists. Thus, although Judaism as practiced might pose some challenges to a Protestant or Christian Republic, it could be incorporated, for Jews were not racialized in the way other groups were. As an ethnoreligion that provided the historic basis for the Christian story, Judaism gradually found its way into the American language of religious tolerance and pluralism – the so-called Judeo-Christian tradition, a term that took hold in the 1950s but can be traced back conceptually to earlier decades.

If Jews could be understood to be at least partially white and with a religious narrative that spoke to deep American understandings, such as the Exodus story, the same could not hold true for Asians and Pacific Islanders. Never eligible for assimilation into the category of white, and racialized in a way that left them unassimilable, Asian immigrants practiced diverse varieties of religious traditions but none that counted as deserving full respect. And yet, the Asian religious presence was ambiguous in one sense: "Oriental" religious thought had long since drawn the intense interest of American intellectuals and seekers, most especially the Transcendentalists, who translated "Eastern" religious texts into English. Moreover, spectacular religious events, such as the World's Parliament of Religions at the Chicago's World Fair of 1893, introduced certain strands of Eastern Indian thought, in the personage of Swami Vivekananda, to Americans who were already participating in alternative, metaphysical, New Thought, and other movements that self-consciously drew from the Eastern traditions. Thus, although Asian immigrants and their everyday religious practices met discrimination, harassment, and outright exclusion, Eastern religious thought drew respect, fascination, and imitation on the part of Americans from Ralph Waldo Emerson and Henry Steel Olcott, called America's first "white Buddhist"; to the followers of the New Thought and Unity movements; and later to Beat writers and poets such as Allen Ginsberg and Gary Snyder.[15]

Regardless of the intellectual and cultural fascination, Asians and their religions were racialized in a way that made it impossible to claim the privileges of whiteness. Starting with anti-Chinese riots through the late nineteenth century, and with legislation such as the Chinese Exclusion Act of 1882, which remained in force until the 1940s, white Americans could not conceive a place for Asians in the republic. Part of this resistance and hostility derived from economic factors, such as working-class men's attacks on Chinese railroad workers and Japanese farmers in some of the richest regions of California; but a considerable part, too, came from the sense of religious unassimilability. Aside from those who might have been Christian converts, Asian immigrants simply had no historic religions that could fit them into dominant notions of American religio-cultural nationalism.

Nor could Asian immigrants stake any claim to whiteness. The case of Bhagat Singh Thind in 1923 made this abundantly clear. In 1920, Thind, a Sikh from northern India, sued for citizenship under the claim that he was scientifically classified as a Caucasian and was therefore white, only to be met with a unanimous Supreme Court decision that ruled against him on the grounds that whiteness was equivalent to assimilability, and that therefore a "Hindoo" (never mind that he was a Sikh) was not in anyone's actual working definition of whiteness. Like obscenity, apparently, the justices could not define whiteness, but they knew it when they saw it – and it did not include anyone wearing a mysterious headdress. Not a citizen but a legal resident, Thind married a white woman and later became well-known as a sort of proto-New Age author of books about the ancient wisdom of the East, playing off the very stereotypes that had defeated him in court.[16]

Following closely on the heels of Thind, the National Origins Act of 1924 and two subsequent amendments in the next few years instituted a new immigration regime that tilted the balance of European immigration decisively back toward northern and western Europeans and away from southern and eastern ones. The 1924 law also classed Europeans ethnically – as Italians and Germans, for example – in the process of setting quotas for the various European ethnic groups. The law forbade Asian immigration entirely. In other words, the common sense of white Americans about who might be fully assimilable, who were of dubious origin but nonetheless

[15] Stephen Prothero, *The White Buddhist: The Asian Odyssey of Henry Steel Olcott* (Bloomington, 1996).
[16] Jennifer Snow, "The Civilization of White Men: The Race of the Hindu in *United States V. Bhagat Singh Thind*," in Henry Goldschmidt and Elizabeth McAlister, eds., *Race, Nation, and Religion in the Americas* (New York, 2004), 259–82.

ultimately eligible for whiteness and therefore citizenship, and who would be permanently foreign became clear. From 1924 to 1965, this immigration regime defined the contours of citizenship.[17]

In 1965, a revised immigration law altered the rules of the quota system and set the stage for a new era of immigration from the Caribbean, Africa, South America, and diverse parts of Asia. For the first time in history, America's potential as a center of cultural pluralism and its promise as a land where religious freedom could be extended to all came closer to a reality than ever before. The language of religious intolerance, once widely accepted and practically mandatory, has fallen into opprobrium, such that, to cite one example, attacks of certain members of the evangelical Right in recent years classifying Islam as a "terrorist religion" have been met by rebukes even from other members of the evangelical consensus. Such an acceptance of religious pluralism was simply unthinkable in any previous era of American history. At the same time, a resurgence of conservative rhetoric about America's history and legacy as a Christian nation, and the continued predominance of the white Protestant and Catholic elite in positions of political power suggest that the legacy of race and religion in American history remains contested and that the project of pluralism is far from complete.

The United States is now the most religiously diverse country in the world, with, for example, more Muslims than Episcopalians and more Buddhists in California than Baptists. The religiously neutral American polity is increasingly challenged by the diversity of practice, ranging from Somali girls attending ethnically separate public schools in order to be able to wear their headscarves without persecution to Afro-Caribbeans seeking permission for animal sacrifice in their rituals. Religious thought, from both the Right and the Left, vitally influences national politics, as has been clearly in evidence in recent presidential elections. The tension between religious neutrality at the level of the state, spiritual passion in everyday practice, and the continued struggle for ethnic understanding and racial equality set a compelling project for contemporary American life. Race and religion remain implicitly connected in American religious practice, even if the intellectual and ideological links between them largely have been deconstructed.

SUGGESTIONS FOR FURTHER READING

Blum, Edward. *W E. B. Du Bois, American Prophet*. Philadelphia, 2007.

Brooks, Joanna. *American Lazarus: Religion and the Rise of African American and Native American Literatures*. New York, 2003.

---

[17] Mae Ngai, *Impossible Subjects: Illegal Immigrants and the Making of Modern America, 1924–1965* (Chicago, 2005).

Cone, James, and Gayraud Wilmore, eds. *Black Theology: A Documentary History*. Maryknoll, NY, 1993.

Frey, Sylvia, and Betty Wood. *Come Shouting to Zion: African American Protestantism in the American South and British Caribbean to 1830*. Chapel Hill, 1998.

Harvey, Paul. *Freedom's Coming: Religious Culture and the Shaping of the South from the Civil War through the Civil Rights Era*. Chapel Hill, 2005.

O'Connell, Barry, ed. *On Our Own Ground: The Complete Writings of William Apess, a Pequot*. Amherst, 1992.

Rael, Patrick, Richard Newman, and Phillip Lapsansky, eds. *Pamphlets of Protest: An Anthology of Early African American Protest Literature, 1790–1860*. New York, 2001.

38

RELIGIONS AND FAMILIES IN AMERICA: HISTORICAL TRADITIONS AND PRESENT POSITIONS

KEVIN J. CHRISTIANO

As fundamental and even venerable social institutions, religion and the family for centuries have enjoyed a close association. Both families and religions are approached with a special reverence; both offer to their members the possibility of merging selves and souls within a larger group; each harbors settings for important rituals of unity and continuity. Involvement in religions and in families can spawn similarly intense emotions; each can subdue or smother individual feelings and instead deposit the follower squarely in the swirl of ceremony – be it for a bar mitzvah or a betrothal, a baptism or a burial.

More than sixty years ago, Margaret Park Redfield insisted that, historically, families (and, she could have easily added, religions) provide for people

> a sense of security derived from status in a group of which they are permanent members, initiate into a consistent mode of procedure so that there may be some standards for action and principles of right and wrong, and create an attachment to certain rituals which not only give color to life but also supply in certain areas of existence sacred rather than secular values.[1]

The reasons for such close relations are as obvious as they are numerous. Religion and the family occupy adjacent and overlapping spaces in the private realm of modern existence. Yet neither is totally isolated in that sphere.

> Religion – despite being officially excluded from modern public affairs – achieves a complex mediation between public and private life due to its simultaneously intimate and ecclesiastical, subjective and institutional nature. The same applies to the family, since, despite being confined to the walls of the household, it constitutes a legally recognized institution, valued

---

[1] Margaret Park Redfield, "The American Family: Consensus and Freedom," *American Journal of Sociology* 52 (Nov. 1946): 178.

as a minimal instance of sociopolitical organization and attributed with responsibilities and rights carefully safeguarded by the State.[2]

As a practical matter, families furnish the venue in which persons are initially socialized into religious norms and values and are taught the rudiments of their faith. Families are the unit of membership in most religious organizations, and they gravitate to the churches to mark significant interludes in the human life cycle: birth, maturity, marriage, and death.

In return, religions frequently apply their theologies to upholding the earthly family: numerous faiths explicitly cast familial roles as religious duties and impose other obligations as well. The Bible, for instance, requires that faithful believers honor their fathers and mothers, and not only provide for their own spouses and children, but additionally furnish support to the widowed and protection to the orphaned or abandoned.[3] Indeed, the promotion of the family in religious thought has helped to spawn an ideology known as *familism*, which holds that the family is the key institution of organized society, and so, for civilization to continue, it must be protected and preserved in a normatively acceptable form. "In a fundamental sense," the prominent sociologist Carle C. Zimmerman once declared, "there is no such thing as a basic relation between man and man uncolored by family guidance."[4]

Because the ties between religions and the family seem so basic and natural, they predictably have received a great deal of attention in the research of social scientists.[5] In fact, a cross-national study on the institutions of religion and the family in forty-one countries represented in the 1990 World Values Survey suggests that a strong family structure (with relatively few divorces and nonmarital births) is close to being a necessary, but not sufficient, condition for establishing a robust and resilient religious environment (with high rates of prayer and attendance at religious services).[6] This finding ought not to surprise, for, as William V. D'Antonio

---

[2] Luiz Fernando Dias Duarte, "The Home Sanctuary: Personhood, Family and Religiosity," trans. David Rodgers, *Revista Religião e Sociedade* (Rio de Janeiro) (*Nova Série*) 26:2 (2006): 2–3.

[3] Robert H. Bremner, "Other People's Children," *Journal of Social History* 16 (Spring 1983): 83.

[4] Carle C. Zimmerman, "The Family and Social Change," *Annals of the American Academy of Political and Social Science* 272 (Nov. 1950): 27.

[5] Comprehensive summaries of the recent social-scientific literature on religions and families include W. Bradford Wilcox, "Family," in Helen Rose Ebaugh, ed., *The Handbook of Religion and Social Institutions* (New York, 2005), 97–120; and Patricia A. Wittberg, "Families and Religions," in Marvin B. Sussman, Suzanne K. Steinmetz, and Gary W. Peterson, eds., *The Handbook of Marriage and the Family*, 2nd ed. (New York, 1999), 503–23.

[6] Kristen R. Heimdal and Sharon K. Houseknecht, "Does a Strong Institution of Religion Require a Strong Family Institution?" *Comparative Sociology* 2:4 (2003): 631–66.

has put it simply, the family may be regarded as "the cross-generational life blood for most religious organizations."[7]

This essay charts salient points of contact between families and religions through American history, beginning with the colonial period and moving forward to the present day. Included in this selective survey are treatments of the Puritan or, more generally, the Calvinist family in the seventeenth and eighteenth centuries; the cultivation of the Christian home in the nineteenth century; and the dominant changes in religious and family forms (not to mention the politicization of the family) in the twentieth century. Also presented are examinations of the family in non-Western religions, in new religious movements, and in native religions in America, as well as summaries of contemporary research on religion's influence over marriage, childbearing, and child rearing.

THE FAMILY IN THE COLONIAL ERA

The Puritans who colonized New England, note Gerald F. Moran and Maris A. Vinovskis, "not only clothed piety with ideas taken from household experience but also invested family life with religious values. Each sphere supplied codes for interpreting acts played out in the other sphere."[8] This free mixing of interpretive language can be identified in the frequent assertion by Puritan clergy that the heavenly status of the faithful elect was akin to that of "brides of Christ."[9] So common was such usage that the historian of Puritanism Edmund S. Morgan could not but suspect "that the Puritans' religious experiences in some way duplicated their domestic experiences."[10]

This tendency became a problem, however, when congregations tied to the Calvinist doctrine of predestination set to work devising standards of admission for coming generations of unsanctified followers of Christ. What to do with (that is, how to keep in the pews) the children of the visible saints was a question that consumed "an inordinate amount of attention ...

The United States, perhaps only for the time being, is a glaring exception to this generalization.

[7] William V. D'Antonio, "The American Catholic Family: Signs of Cohesion and Polarization," *Journal of Marriage and the Family* 47 (May 1985): 395.

[8] Gerald F. Moran and Maris A. Vinovskis, "The Puritan Family and Religion: A Critical Reappraisal," *William and Mary Quarterly* 3rd. ser., 39 (Jan. 1982): 32.

[9] Edmund S. Morgan, *The Puritan Family: Religion and Domestic Relations in Seventeenth-Century New England,* 2nd ed. (New York, 1966), 161–8. See also Ben Barker-Benfield, "Anne Hutchinson and the Puritan Attitude Toward Women," *Feminist Studies* 1 (Autumn 1972): 72–3, 82, and 85–7.

[10] Morgan, *Puritan Family*, 166.

often at the expense of the religious needs of the unchurched."[11] Of course, church membership could not be inherited, although children, until they matured, could be accepted by virtue of their parents' membership. Yet, many thought, did it not make sense that God would seed liberally among the children of the elect his younger choices for salvation?[12] The risk in this idea, Morgan feared, was realized when the Puritans "allowed their children to usurp a higher place than God in their affections," and "theology became the handmaid of genealogy."[13] Or, as Moran and Vinovskis put it, "in late seventeenth-century New England the church was the established kin group writ large."[14]

Still, this situation featured a positive side. Parents did much to bring their children into the church, enabling Christian tradition to be transmitted across multiple generations. Mothers especially were assigned the responsibility of tutoring their offspring in religion, and, from all indications, their efforts were unusually vigorous and effective. These new adherents in turn were sustenance to the churches in often-trying secular times.

HOME AND HEAVEN IN NINETEENTH-CENTURY AMERICA

By the nineteenth century the family in America had largely lost its economic function. For those with enough wealth, the household was transformed from being a center of production to one of consumption. The rise of the middle class led to the creation of a "cult of domesticity" that consolidated consumer spending and child rearing in the home.[15] The home and not the broader community thus became the place where primary child care and moral instruction, economic choice, and emotional exchange all occurred.

The numerous affluent families of the age could still navigate community living in a manner that preserved the home as "an enclave of morality and repose." Yet dangers to the family lay just beyond its front door. The nation's rapidly expanding cities, after all, "were not only crowded, dirty, noisy, and populated by the poor and immigrants, but they were also filled with the temptations of saloons, gambling dens, dance halls, and other amusements considered immoral to the proper nineteenth-century white, middle-class Christian."[16]

[11] Moran and Vinovskis, "Puritan Family and Religion," 32.
[12] Douglas L. Winiarski, "Native American Popular Religion in New England's Old Colony, 1670–1770," *Religion and American Culture* 15 (Summer 2005): 155–6.
[13] Morgan, *Puritan Family*, 185 and 186.
[14] Moran and Vinovskis, "Puritan Family and Religion," 38.
[15] Melanie Archer and Judith R. Blau, "Class Formation in Nineteenth-Century America: The Case of the Middle Class," *Annual Review of Sociology* 19 (1993): 34–5.
[16] Laura J. Miller, "Family Togetherness and the Suburban Ideal," *Sociological Forum* 10 (Sept. 1995): 399.

Consequently, the family home increasingly took on the character of a retreat from the larger world.[17] For that reason, too, the earliest suburbs in the United States promised to would-be residents a refuge not only from the chaos and filth of the city, but from its spiritual pollution as well. These new habitations on the suburban outskirts, accordingly, were designed from the start so that family life could be conducted without resort to the shared public spaces of the community, where possibly lurked corrupting pastimes and carnal indulgences.

The cult of domesticity readily joined itself to the moral and religious functions of the family. "The sacredness of the Victorian home," remarks the historian John R. Gillis, "was more than just a metaphor."[18] The Puritan strain in Protestant thinking reasoned that "every family became a potential Holy Family. The roles of husband and wife, father and mother, were sanctified. The Puritans reinterpreted pilgrimage to be a lifelong journey in the world, with the result that coming home replaced leaving home as an act of spiritual significance."[19]

Protestant homes functioned, then, as unconsecrated churches where family members gathered regularly for reading and recitation of the Bible, group prayer, and pious exhortation. Home-based religious observances and family devotions became common, whereas domestic rituals that were less formal in style schooled the young and the uninitiated in middle-class propriety, if not in Christian duty. A comparable process unfolded among Catholic families in American society. For them, too, the model of life in the home was the Holy Family of Jesus, Mary, and Joseph. Veneration of the biblical Holy Family permitted "various divine or semi-divine personae" to "maintain mythical kinship relationships" that enabled "a continual elaboration of the correlations between the sacred and the earthly family."[20]

Over time women learned how to "keep" a home (a "sanctuary" in more senses than one), and those who were mothers trained their sons to aspire to a virtuous or "godly" manhood.[21] While family living withdrew behind the protective walls of the home, the capacity of newly introduced techniques of mass production to churn out domestic kitsch meant that the

---

[17] Tamara K. Hareven, "The Home and the Family in Historical Perspective," *Social Research* 58 (Spring 1991): 254, 258–9, 262–3, and 269–71.

[18] John R. Gillis, "Ritualization of Middle-Class Family Life in Nineteenth Century Britain," *International Journal of Politics, Culture, and Society* 3 (Winter 1989): 214.

[19] *Ibid.*, 217.

[20] Duarte, "Home Sanctuary," 28.

[21] See E. Anthony Rotundo, "Body and Soul: Changing Ideals of American Middle-Class Manhood, 1770–1920," *Journal of Social History* 16 (Summer 1983): 23–38. Also see Gillis, "Ritualization of Middle-Class Family Life," 227.

ever-more-spacious houses of Victorian America soon filled to the rafters with religious images and objects.[22]

CHANGES IN FAITHS AND FAMILIES

For most of the twentieth century, visible and measurable religious and family-oriented behavior in the United States appeared not to change much in character or frequency. The famous Middletown III project, for instance, compared statistics of religious activity and family strength for a bellwether Midwestern community (Muncie, Indiana) in 1976–78 with previous studies executed during the roaring 1920s and again in the depressed 1930s. Overall, the team of latter-day researchers in Muncie concluded that, in the words of two of its members, "the myths that American families are mere shadows of their former selves, and that organized religion in America is an anachronistic hulk shambling into oblivion, are demonstrably false." Instead, "Americans remain religious," they wrote, and "their family ties are surprisingly strong." These findings, they speculated modestly, "may be related."[23]

But by the 1960s and 1970s numerous changes in both families and religions were either under way or in the offing. On the side of religion, theorists such as Thomas Luckmann posited that "church-centered religion has become a marginal phenomenon in modern society" – not because modern Americans would no longer join a congregation or attend religious services, but because "churches have accommodated themselves to cultural, social and psychological functions in the context of the American Dream," and these "secular" functions had crowded out the more purely "religious" ones of the past. The churches had become, in a phrase, "internally secularized"; and religious practice had degenerated into "a set of performances devoid of religious meaning, motivated by social pressure, respectability and prestige-considerations, aesthetical-sentimental reasons, sociability and the like."[24] Religion thus survives, according to Luckmann, but like the family, it largely dwells in a far corner of individual consciousness, there robbed of its coherent sense-giving function.

---

[22] Hareven, "The Home and the Family," 264. See also Colleen McDannell, *The Christian Home in Victorian America, 1840–1900* (Bloomington, 1986).
[23] Howard M. Bahr and Bruce A. Chadwick, "Religion and Family in Middletown, USA," *Journal of Marriage and the Family* 47 (May 1985): 408 and 410.
[24] Thomas Luckmann, "On Religion in Modern Society: Individual Consciousness, World View, Institution," *Journal for the Scientific Study of Religion* 2 (Spring 1963): 150 and 157. See also Luckmann, *The Invisible Religion: The Problem of Religion in Modern Society* (New York, 1967).

At the same time that organized religion in America was undergoing sweeping changes, so was the American family. The latter half of the twentieth century, and particularly the period from the decade of the 1950s through the 1970s, saw enormous change in social attitudes toward the family. In only fifteen years, from the early 1960s to the late 1970s, disapproval of premarital sex, cohabitation in lieu of marriage, and divorce all had weakened, as had criticism of voluntary childlessness among the married. Negative attitudes about singlehood declined, undermining the imperative to marry. Insistence on a gender-based division of spousal roles and household labor within marriage softened, whereas conformity to norms of equality grew more pronounced.[25]

Opinions about sexual behavior of nearly all sorts were liberalized. For example, 69 percent of young women and 65 percent of young men in 1965 took the position that sex before marriage was "always or almost always wrong." Less than a decade later, in 1972, the corresponding proportions were about two-thirds smaller, at 24 and 21 percent, respectively.[26] Such trends were found to signify "the relaxation of the social prescriptions for family behavior and the expansion of the range of individual choice."[27] In this respect, changes in the American family seemed to mirror those in religion: "the overall similarity between trends in religious beliefs and participation," on the one hand, "and trends in family norms," on the other, reflected a leading demographer, "is striking."[28]

POLITICAL FAMILISM AND LIVED RELIGION

"Marriage is no stranger to the national debate in the United States," wrote sociologist Steven L. Nock in 2005. "It has been at the center of a variety of American social, religious, and political movements over the nation's history."[29] The same, in fact, could be said for an entire range of issues surrounding family life, in which sharp rhetoric has traced clear lines of division in an ongoing cultural conflict. Referring to rifts in the Catholic

---

[25] Arland Thornton and Linda Young-DeMarco, "Four Decades of Trends in Attitudes Toward Family Issues in the United States: The 1960s Through the 1990s," *Journal of Marriage and the Family* 63 (Nov. 2001): 1009–37.
[26] Arland Thornton, "Changing Attitudes Toward Family Issues in the United States," *Journal of Marriage and the Family* 51 (Nov. 1989): 875–85; and Thornton, "The Developmental Paradigm, Reading History Sideways, and Family Change," *Demography* 38 (Nov. 2001): 457.
[27] Thornton, "Changing Attitudes," 887. See also Thornton and Young-DeMarco, "Four Decades of Trends," 1010–11 and 1031–2.
[28] Thornton, "Changing Attitudes," 890.
[29] Steven L. Nock, "Marriage as a Public Issue," *The Future of Children* 15 (Autumn 2005): 14.

Church, sociologist William D'Antonio concluded, "For conservatives God's laws are known and need only be applied; for the progressives life is a developmental and unfolding process."[30] The struggle between these two points of view in recent decades has taken political form.[31] Since at least 1992, it has been argued, there has existed a "family gap" in the national electorate: in that year, married parents aged eighteen to thirty-four preferred the Republican presidential candidate, incumbent George H. W. Bush, 48 to 39 percent, whereas singles in the same age category, whether or not they were parents, voted 20 percent for the Republican and fully 58 percent for the Democrat and eventual winner, Governor Bill Clinton.[32]

Cultural progressives have sought to render familial relationships less restrictive and family obligations more equally shared. They have campaigned for more autonomy for women, greater reproductive freedom, easier dissolution of unsatisfying marital unions, recognition of rights for sexual minorities, and the possibility of intimate relations without demanding of the participants a formal, not to say enduring, commitment. Traditionalists, on the other hand, seek to reinforce historical norms that include sexual abstinence before marriage and nuptials between partners of opposite genders in a lifelong monogamous bond. They advocate sexual exclusivity between spouses during marriage, openness to parenthood, the male headship of families, the formative role of mothers, and strict but loving child rearing.[33] As lengthy as this list of goals may be, other values are also at stake in the conflict. The feminist scholar Judith Stacey confidently reaches the heart of the matter when she observes that "'the family' has become a voracious floating signifier for all manner of social ties, as 'family breakdown' is for all manner of social disarray."[34]

Despite the starkness with which the rhetoric of leaders on opposing sides of this struggle has been framed, and despite the clarity with which the battle lines have been drawn, empirical research has demonstrated repeatedly that average believers are not as polarized. Instead, ambivalence and contradiction often mark the living-and-breathing families of our everyday world. In particular, Americans who espouse highly traditional

---

[30] D'Antonio, "American Catholic Family," 401.
[31] Contrast, for example, Daniel Patrick Moynihan, "Defining Deviancy Down," *The American Scholar* (Winter 1993): 17–30; with Judith Stacey, "Scents, Scholars, and Stigma: The Revisionist Campaign for Family Values," *Social Text* 40 (Autumn 1994): 51–75.
[32] Findings of a postelection poll in *The Washington Post*, cited by Stacey, "Scents, Scholars, and Stigma," 74n74.
[33] See, for a discussion, Dorothy E. Smith, "The Standard North American Family: SNAF as an Ideological Code," *Journal of Family Issues* 14 (Mar. 1993): 50–65.
[34] Stacey, "Scents, Scholars, and Stigma," 67.

and religiously based norms for family life nevertheless actually live, it seems, in ways that suggest adaptation and compromise of those values.[35] Indeed, as a thorough survey-based analysis by Melinda Lundquist Denton concluded,

> If in fact belief in the headship of the husband had the practical consequences of creating male dominance and patriarchal marriage patterns, we should expect the religious groups who adhere to this ideology also to report more male-dominated decision-making patterns. Instead, it appears that they are not significantly more traditional in their decision-making practices than the respondents from other, more liberal, religious categories.[36]

This style of adaptation can be witnessed also in conservative religious organizations for men, like the Promise Keepers (PK). John P. Bartkowski's participant-observational studies of the group help to highlight how "elite PK discourses of godly manhood," which dwell on "innate, categorical, and largely immutable gender differences," end up being "negotiated, or even recrafted, in the crucible of its members' actual social relationships."[37] The result, he says, is "a melange masculinity" that incorporates pieces of both the "instrumentalist" and "expressive" notions of manhood.[38]

Certainly this is not to assert that those who advocate religious values for their families are being insincere or cynical. Denton maintains that religious conservatives are managing "*a spiritually symbolic interpretation* of the meaning" of certain of their traditional values.[39] Family scientist Kerry Daly agrees, contending that these commitments "serve as a kind of moral anchor for the way things are supposed to be."[40] Their symbolic power is simultaneously descriptive in nature and prescriptive in direction. Moreover, this dual valence of family symbolism is useful: "For while our public and private lives are now radically separated," John Gillis has argued, "the symbolic family serves to mediate this chasm, to mask its contradictions, and

---

[35] John P. Bartkowski, "Changing of the Gods: The Gender and Family Discourse of American Evangelicalism in Historical Perspective," *The History of the Family* 3 (Mar. 1998): 95–116; and Sally K. Gallagher, *Evangelical Identity and Gendered Family Life* (New Brunswick, 2003), 65–151.

[36] Melinda Lundquist Denton, "Gender and Marital Decision Making: Negotiating Religious Ideology and Practice," *Social Forces* 82 (Mar. 2004): 1173.

[37] John P. Bartkowski, "Breaking Walls, Raising Fences: Masculinity, Intimacy, and Accountability Among the Promise Keepers," *Sociology of Religion* 61 (Spring 2000): 34 and 35.

[38] *Ibid.*, 38.

[39] Denton, "Gender and Marital Decision Making," 1173. (The emphasis appears in the original.)

[40] Kerry Daly, "Family Theory Versus the Theories Families Live By," *Journal of Marriage and the Family* 65 (Nov. 2003): 778.

thus to sustain what otherwise might be unsupportable."[41] Conservative family standards in some respects are unrealistic in their strictness, yet they gain in significance precisely *because* they describe few families literally. Explains Daly,

> The persistence and tenacity of these images suggests that they play a very important role in shaping how families live through the messiness and disorder of their everyday routines. This nostalgic construction of family stability, strength, and cohesiveness plays a very important role in managing the tensions, conflicts, and disappointments that arise in the course of living *with* a family.[42]

As long as standards for family life do not succumb to a sinking relativism, many in the churches – in both the laity and the clergy – seem content to muddle through. For example, the local churches in one small-scale study engage in "considerable symbolic affirmation" of received traditions concerning gender and the family, Penny Edgell and Danielle Docka report. Yet they also found that the congregations adapted their ideals flexibly to the situations that life presented to their members. "The variation is greater than we might have believed," they concede.[43]

FAMILIES AND FAITHS FROM AFAR

Today there is burgeoning interest in studying non-Western religions, in some cases the faiths that are brought to America with the immigrants who are admitted to this land, often with their families.[44] Currently, more than one million persons per year come legally to our shores. However, the overwhelming majority of these "new" immigrants derive from sources that are very different from those that supplied previous flows of newcomers to America. As a single example, fewer than one in seven (13 percent) of the five million immigrants who entered the United States between 1985 and 1990 listed Canada, Australia, New Zealand, or any of the nations of Europe as his or her native country. "The new immigration," remarks R. Stephen Warner, "is more truly global than ever before."[45]

---

[41] Gillis, "Ritualization of Middle-Class Family Life," 213–14.
[42] Daly, "Family Theory," 778. (The emphasis appears in the original.)
[43] Penny Edgell and Danielle Docka, "Beyond the Nuclear Family? Familism and Gender Ideology in Diverse Religious Communities," *Sociological Forum* 22 (Mar. 2007): 26 and 49.
[44] For surveys of this research, see Kevin J. Christiano, "The Church and the New Immigrants," in Helen Rose Ebaugh, ed., *Vatican II and U. S. Catholicism* (Greenwich, CT, 1991), 169–86; and Peter Kivisto, "Religion and the New Immigrants," in William H. Swatos, Jr., ed., *A Future for Religion? New Paradigms for Social Analysis* (Newbury Park, CA, 1993), 92–108.
[45] R. Stephen Warner, "Religion and New (Post-1965) Immigrants: Some Principles Drawn from Field Research," *American Studies* 41 (Summer/Fall 2000): 268. Although

Chinese religions (and the religions of Chinese immigrants to the United States – whether or not they are Christians) are deeply infused with values that uphold the family. This is in keeping with the four-thousand-year tradition of Confucianism that underlies much of Chinese social ethics.[46] Confucius taught an unerring respect for, deference toward, and obedience to parents; by their every action children were to serve their parents and to bring credit to their families. Devotion to father and mother was to last during their lives and extend to honoring them after their deaths. Confucius answered one student with the direction, "When the parents are alive, serve them with propriety; when they die, bury them according to propriety; and sacrifice to them according to propriety."[47]

Confucianism also preached commitment to one another by partners in a marriage. Married men were to behave lovingly toward their wives and affectionately toward their children. The married woman, it was said, could no more reasonably estrange herself from her husband than the earth could detach itself from the heavens. Early texts "emphasized chastity, submissiveness, frugality, and faithfulness as indispensable qualities" for wives to possess. In turn, wives who became mothers could expect placement at "the center of Chinese domestic life." In life, her children were obliged to install a mother in "a very exalted position" in the family; after her death, they were to conduct a full range of mourning rituals for her.[48]

Ancestors likewise receive the caring attention of the living through their descendants' maintenance of personal virtue (which, despite having departed from this world, the dead can monitor), the erection of a home worship space or ancestral temple, and seasonal and annual patterns of sacrifice to their hovering spirits. These practices contribute to solidarity by making the Chinese family "self-contained, self-perpetuating, and self-sufficient." Another Confucian text, in the form of advice from a governmental minister to a young king, reads: "To set up love, it is for you to love your elders; to set up respect, it is for you to respect your relatives. The commencement is the family."[49] Interestingly, the Confucian influence has not been confined only to non-Christians. In the nondenominational churches that claim the commitment of many Chinese converts to Christianity, the

---

several varieties of world religions are represented among these immigrants, the majority of them are at least nominally Christian (*ibid.*, 273–5).

[46] See Duarte, "Home Sanctuary," 11; and Max Weber, *The Religion of China: Confucianism and Taoism*, trans. and ed. Hans H. Gerth, introduced by C. K. Yang (New York, 1968).

[47] Quoted in Cheng Ch'Eng-K'Un, "Familism, the Foundation of Chinese Social Organization," *Social Forces* 23 (Oct. 1944): 51.

[48] *Ibid.*, 52 and 54.

[49] *Ibid.*, 56 and 57.

generic Protestant evangelicalism that predominates is welcome for its emphasis on "family values" that conform to Confucian ethics.[50]

Confucianism mixed with elements of Buddhism, especially the veneration of ancestors, when the latter came to China approximately one thousand years ago. The first Buddhist presence in America arrived in the nineteenth century with immigrants from East Asia. In 1853, Chinese immigrants to San Francisco constructed the first temple in the United States to house Buddhist devotions.[51]

Coupled with native-born converts, Buddhism for the last half century has been one of the fastest-growing religions in the nation.[52] Among its attractions for Asian Americans and migrants from Asia is that Buddhism, like many immigrant religious traditions, "reaffirms their sense of traditional identity by locating them within a particular community defined by family, ethnicity, culture, and national origin." For Asians, as opposed to non-Asian practitioners, "expressions of Buddhism tend to be more integrated into family life within a community.... Asian American religious life tends to be multigenerational, and Buddhism is often practiced in a context in which the family, both living and dead, has a greater importance, and different meaning, than it typically has in the life of Americans of European ancestry."[53]

However, Chinese Americans have lagged behind the Japanese, both immigrants (Issei) and the first native-born generation (Nisei or Bussei [youth]), in building lasting Buddhist institutions in this country.[54] Japanese Americans anchored their families in the Buddhist temple, where they could hold weddings and funerals and undertake rituals for the ancestral dead (*obon*).[55] Indeed, temple membership was not an individual but a family status.[56] More broadly, religious officials in the home country encouraged Buddhist priests to minister to their congregations as a family: "the priest should help them to realize the American idea of 'Home Sweet Home' with the Lord Buddha as universal parent."[57]

---

[50] Warner, "Religion and New (Post-1965) Immigrants," 275–6.
[51] Peter N. Gregory, "Describing the Elephant: Buddhism in America," *Religion and American Culture* 11 (Summer 2001): 255n14.
[52] For a critical examination of some relevant statistics of growth, see Gregory, "Describing the Elephant," 236–39 and 257–8nn31, 33–5.
[53] Ibid., 244.
[54] Ibid., 243.
[55] David Yoo, "Enlightened Identities: Buddhism and Japanese Americans of California, 1924–1941," *The Western Historical Quarterly* 27 (Autumn 1996): 287.
[56] Robert F. Spencer, "Social Structure of a Contemporary Japanese-American Buddhist Church," *Social Forces* 26 (Mar. 1948): 284.
[57] Quoted in Yoo, "Enlightened Identities," 291.

These continuities did not prevent Japanese Buddhism, with understandable defensiveness, from adopting more and more an American style of organization and worship.[58] Buddhist temples took on the outer appearance and internal structure of American Protestant churches. Gathering spaces hosted more purely social events than devotional events. Priests came to perform many of the same functions as Christian ministers, and singing hymns replaced reciting sutras. These changes notwithstanding, one area in which the values of the two cultures coincided was in endowing families with a special importance in religion. Buddhism, with its frequent memorials, it was said, is a "religion of the home" and "a family affair."[59]

Similar assessments could be rendered about another world faith tradition that is adapting itself to America: Islam. Muslims from some sixty nations around the world have settled in the United States, and for them, "family, religion, and ethnic identity are intertwined."[60] "The Muslim communities," according to another scholar, believe that "the family unit is the basis for any society."[61] This conviction can be witnessed clearly in Arab communities. Although only a minority of Arabs in the United States are Muslim, the common ethnic culture of Christians and Muslims alike locates the family at its root. "The family is considered the foundation of the Arab community," notes Jen'nan Ghazal Read, "and there is a strong emphasis on traditional gender roles."[62] In the latter regard, Muslim Arab women are more conservative than their non-Muslim peers, she finds.

For Hindus in America, collective religious life is situated primarily before a shrine in the family home, and only secondarily at a local temple. In the home, religion endures because "both fathers and mothers are religious specialists for the family." Moreover, the "life-cycle and other family-based rituals" over which they preside "are fundamental to personal identity."[63] That identity mainly emerges from relations between and among family members; conversely, many Hindu Americans distrust the normative

---

[58] Tetsuden Kashima, *Buddhism in America: The Social Organization of an Ethnic Religious Institution* (Westport, 1977), 167–96; Warner, "Religion and New (Post-1965) Immigrants," 278; and Yoo, "Enlightened Identities," 288–91.

[59] Spencer, "Social Structure," 281 and 287.

[60] Raymond Brady Williams, "Asian Indian and Pakistani Religions in the United States," *Annals of the American Academy of Political and Social Science* 558 (July 1998): 185; and M. Arif Ghayur, "Muslims in the United States: Settlers and Visitors," *Annals of the American Academy of Political and Social Science* 454 (Mar. 1981): 154–5 and 160.

[61] Aminah B. McCloud, "American Muslim Women and U.S. Society," *Journal of Law and Religion* 12 (1995–96): 57n18.

[62] Jen'nan Ghazal Read, "The Sources of Gender Role Attitudes Among Christian and Muslim Arab-American Women," *Sociology of Religion* 64 (Summer 2003): 210.

[63] Williams, "Asian Indian and Pakistani Religions," 182.

American family as too liberal to impart a morality that is derived from religion and too weak to enforce intergenerational obligations.[64]

THE NEW AND THE NATIVE

Some other modern-day religious groups are so adept at duplicating the traditional functions of the family that they not so much compete with as substitute for that institution. Through them are formed attachments to fictive kin who compose an idealized church family that members view as more real than their flawed families of origin.[65] Sociologist Kathleen E. Jenkins lists some samples: "The Oneida community, the Shakers, the Bruderhof 'Society of Brothers,' 'sisters' in Catholic convents, and new religious movements founded during the countercultural revolution like the Family, Hare Krishna, and the Peoples Temple," she writes, "offer just a few examples from hundreds of religious groups where members were constructed as 'real' family."[66]

Among the new religions in which images of family figure most centrally is the Unification Church, founded in Korea by the Rev. Sun Myung Moon and brought from there to the United States in 1959.[67] (The media often refer to the movement's followers using the shorthand label "Moonies," after the organization's founder, but many in the church regard this designation as offensive.) Of the multitude of religious groups that were spawned in the cultural ferment of midcentury, the Unification Church, in the estimation of one trio of researchers, "has developed and legitimated an alternative family structure most fully."[68]

Like the adherents of many other religions, members of the Unification Church address their peers as "brothers" and "sisters." The highest leaders of their church, however, are more than merely ministers or lay executives. The Rev. Moon and his wife are regarded as "True Spiritual Father and Mother" to their flock. Unification doctrine holds that the Jesus of the New Testament was indeed the Son of God. But the church further teaches that the salvific mission of Jesus on earth was stymied when he was crucified

---

[64] Ibid., 189–90.
[65] See, e.g., Kathleen E. Jenkins, *Awesome Families: The Promise of Healing Relationships in the International Churches of Christ* (New Brunswick, 2005), 196–7 and 200.
[66] Ibid., 196. See also Duarte, "Home Sanctuary," 12 and 12n9.
[67] For background, see Eileen Barker, "Unificationism," reprinted in Kevin J. Christiano, William H. Swatos, Jr., and Peter Kivisto, *Sociology of Religion: Contemporary Developments*, 2nd ed. (Lanham, MD, 2008), 313–19.
[68] David G. Bromley, Anson D. Shupe, and Donna L. Oliver, "Perfect Families: Visions of the Future in a New Religious Movement," *Marriage and Family Review* 4:3–4 (1982): 120.

before he could marry and create a family of his own. Hence, Unificationists believe in the theological necessity of a "Lord of the Second Advent" whom the majority think is the Rev. Moon himself. This successor-savior has as his purpose to usher in a new era of fellowship throughout the world by the establishment of spiritually "perfect" families, all of which will be merged one day into a sole "universal personalized family."[69]

The natural product of this heavy emphasis on families as instruments of a divine plan is the normative mandate in the Unification Church that members marry and become parents. Indeed, a source of nearly constant public relations discomfort for the movement has been the spectacle of mass weddings ("Blessings") at which the Rev. Moon officiates. During these events, which are held in sports arenas and similarly cavernous venues, hundreds of young devotées are joined by arrangement of the church's leaders to other members whom they may have met only hours before the ceremony.

Nevertheless, if the Unification Church can be categorized as strange or exotic, its deviance lies mostly in the outsized degree of its adhesion to ideals of family life that much of the rest of society has tried, tested, and eventually consigned to inert tradition. "While such movements directly challenge the legitimacy of the social arrangements of their host societies," a scholar of Unificationism has commented, "they also tend to imitate the cultural ideals and practices of the very societies they so enthusiastically condemn." Ultimately, he writes, "at the core of innovative movements, in their fundamental moral principles and in their most ritualized social practices, we find components of secular society that have not been rejected but elaborated and intensified."[70]

For example, an early survey of students enrolled in the church's main seminary revealed that all aimed to marry, even though one third expected the church to choose their future spouse. Eighty-one percent thought that the husband would be the principal or exclusive source of income for the family, a difficult position to take when almost one third (32 percent) looked forward to having seven or more children![71] Unificationists thus are peculiar not because they repudiate the normative elements of American family life, but primarily by virtue of their hyperconventional commitment to precisely those principles.[72]

---

[69] Arthur S. Parsons, "The Secular Contribution to Religious Innovation: A Case Study of the Unification Church," *Sociological Analysis* 50 (Autumn 1989): 216; and Bromley et al., "Perfect Families," 121–2.

[70] Parsons, "Secular Contribution," 211 and 223.

[71] Bromley et al., "Perfect Families," 123–5.

[72] See Eileen Barker, "Free to Choose? Some Thoughts on the Unification Church and Other Religious Movements, II," *Clergy Review* (London) 65 (Nov. 1980): 392–8; and

Just as the faiths that are newest to North America routinely emphasize their connections to the family, so do some of the oldest religious systems on the continent, those of its numerous native peoples. The tribal cultures of the American Southwest offer vivid examples of how central the family can be to the maintenance and transmission of a communal religious heritage.

In present-day New Mexico, for instance, the symbolically dense ritual drama of the people of the Zuni Pueblo is situated partly in the ceremonial chambers (kivas) of the community and premised partly on a cult of familial ancestors. The ancestors, who hold a deified status, are enshrined in the homes, and masked male dancers impersonate them in seasonal ceremonies. The six kin-based dance groups themselves share a relationship that is described as like that of siblings.[73] Sacred clowns, simultaneously as childlike as grandchildren and as knowing as grandfathers, circulate among the homes that host interior dances in the winter.[74]

The religious roles for Zuni women are confined to grinding the cornmeal that the masked actors eat, and also feeding those who conduct the sacred ceremonies. Despite the fact that women in Zuni society, as well as those in the neighboring pueblo of Hopi, seldom participate directly in the performance of religious ritual, "they are central to the ideological basis of this religion," writes one expert. Again, the answer to how this pertains lies in the family bond. Eschewing individual and communal aggression, the cultures of the Zuni and the Hopi stress life and its production in the process of motherhood. "This centrality of women is underscored," the expert continues, "by the fact that much of the ritual behavior of the men is imitative of the reproductive power of the women."[75]

Rather than in doctrines or creeds, Zuni belief inheres in a set of symbols surrounding the natural and material worlds. Prayersticks made of willow serve as tangible implements that tie "all Zunis together into the common root stock of Zuni society, which is matrilineal and matrilocal," meaning that descent and clan membership (and thus inheritance) are traced through the mother's line, and homes are established in the mother's place of residence.[76]

Kevin J. Christiano, "Religion and the Family in Modern American Culture," in Sharon K. Houseknecht and Jerry G. Pankhurst, eds., *Family, Religion, and Social Change in Diverse Societies* (New York, 2000), 61–4.

[73] Barbara Tedlock, "Zuni Sacred Theater," *American Indian Quarterly* 7 (Summer 1983): 97.

[74] *Ibid.*, 103–4.

[75] M. Jane Young, "Women, Reproduction, and Religion in Western Puebloan Society," *Journal of American Folklore* 100 (Dec. 1987): 436 and 438.

[76] Tedlock, "Zuni Sacred Theater," 94; and Young, "Women, Reproduction, and Religion," 441.

The Navajo people of Arizona, New Mexico, and Utah, who compose the largest tribe in the United States, also sustain a culture that is matrilineal and matrilocal. Indeed, as one anthropologist has observed, "the mother/child bond is what binds Navajo people together. In less abstract terms, the mother/child bond forms the basis of clan relations, social obligations, residence, and probably anything else you could think of in Navajo culture."[77]

Traditionally, Navajo life revolved around the extended family, whose members lived close together in small, kin-specific settlements of homes (hogans) and practiced herding and small-scale farming. When intrusions, disruptions, or death summoned the need for a ritual cure, the arrangements were secured through clan networks. In some more recent cases, Christian denominations and the Native American Church (once termed the "peyote cult")[78] have supplanted family-based rituals as religious options, although some Navajo combine features of several practices in their personal devotions.[79]

This close relationship between religion and the family is especially apparent when Navajo cope with illness. Navajo spirituality emphasizes that people must strive to remain in a balanced and harmonious posture toward others and toward the natural world: one is expected to accept and to cooperate with each. A healthy person is one who can achieve and remain in this state and thus live to an advanced age; a good person, further, is one who honors tradition and discharges family obligations without falling out of balance.[80] In the Navajo worldview, then, illness is not purely a biological or physical matter. Instead, infirmities can occur for any number of reasons: obsessions or addictions of the individual, tensions in a marriage or the family, discordant social interactions, or exposure to some polluting taint – even misdeeds of forebears for which responsibility carries through to the present moment.[81]

CONTINUING INFLUENCES

The latest evidence from surveys of American public opinion and analyses of national demographic data testifies to the continuing influence of religion

---

[77] Gilbert A. Quintero, "Gender, Discord, and Illness: Navajo Philosophy and Healing in the Native American Church," *Journal of Anthropological Research* 51 (Spring 1995): 79.

[78] See Weston La Barre, *The Peyote Cult* (Norman, OK, 1938).

[79] Mary Shepardson, "Changes in Navajo Mortuary Practices and Beliefs," *American Indian Quarterly* 4 (Nov. 1978): 391.

[80] Quintero, "Gender, Discord, and Illness," 73–5 and 77.

[81] David H. Begay and Nancy Cottrell Maryboy, "'The Whole Universe Is My Cathedral': A Contemporary Navajo Spiritual Synthesis," *Medical Anthropology Quarterly* (New Series) 14 (Dec. 2000): 498–520.

on the timing, structure, and conditions of marriages; on the incidence of marital fertility; and on practices of child rearing.[82] Most Americans marry at some point in their lives, and those whose marriages end in divorce or death of the other partner are inclined to marry again. For their part, religious institutions in the United States remain unabashedly pronuptial. They consider marriage to be more than a civil contract; many churches maintain that the marital bond is a covenant linking the spouses in a special relationship to God and in the eyes of the assembled congregation. Accordingly, many denominations encourage marriage among their members, and sometimes expect it at the very brink of adulthood.

Among religious couples, individuals who identify as members of the Church of Jesus Christ of Latter-day Saints (Mormons), or as members of one of several conservative Protestant churches, tend to marry earlier in life than members of other faiths. To generalize further, American Jews and Protestants from liberal denominations, as well as persons who claim no religious affiliation, marry somewhat later than others. Marriages by Roman Catholics assume an intermediate spot – earlier than Jews and liberal Christians, but later than evangelical or Fundamentalist Protestants and Mormons.[83]

Approximately 40 percent of married Americans are wed to someone from their own religious background. In recent decades, moderate-to-liberal (i.e., mainline) Protestants, who for some time have tolerated "mixed" marriages, have shown an increasing willingness to marry outside their own churches. Catholics, for their part, have displayed only a middling degree of this behavior; their rates of homogamy (in-group marriage) have fallen, but just slightly, from about two in three (66 percent) to about three in five (59 percent). Along with Mormons and Jews, Catholics retain a strong religious attachment to in-marriage.[84] Similarly, a pattern of sharply growing intermarriage has not arisen among Protestants from conservative denominations, where such occasions are more common only among members with high levels of education. When conservative Protestants do marry across religious boundaries, they often locate a mate in a church that is not far from their point of origin on the left-to-right denominational spectrum.

---

[82] W. Bradford Wilcox, *Soft Patriarchs, New Men: How Christianity Shapes Fathers and Husbands* (Chicago, 2004).

[83] Xiaohe Xu, Clark D. Hudspeth, and John P. Bartkowski, "The Timing of First Marriage: Are There Religious Variations?" *Journal of Family Issues* 26 (July 2005): 584–618.

[84] Samuel C. Heilman, "The Sociology of American Jewry: The Last Ten Years," *Annual Review of Sociology* 8 (1982): 141–2 and 152; Evelyn L. Lehrer, "Religious Intermarriage in the United States: Determinants and Trends," *Social Science Research* 27 (Sept. 1998): 245–63; and Darren E. Sherkat, "Religious Intermarriage in the United States: Trends, Patterns, and Predictors," *Social Science Research* 33 (Dec. 2004): 606–25.

Turning to the partners themselves, research among urban women who have born a child out of wedlock suggests that those new mothers who attend church on a frequent basis (more than monthly) are significantly more likely to marry within one year of giving birth than those whose rate of participation is lower.[85] Specifically, urban mothers who participate in religious services at least several times per month are as much as 63 percent more likely to marry before the first birthdays of their children. In addition, an active religious life appears to enhance the qualities of strength and stability in a marriage – and again, especially among parents who are situated at the low end of income distribution. Couples whose marital bond entails a shared religious interpretation of their relationship, involvement in joint prayer, and attendance together at religious services experience more satisfaction in their married state than others and are plagued less by episodes of marital discord.[86] Moreover, other research has demonstrated that regular church attendance yields lower levels of spousal abuse in marriages,[87] even considering the independent effects of social isolation, drugs and alcohol, and mental distress.[88]

Religion maintains an effect not only on when and whom one chooses to marry, but also on a couple's decision to have children. Churches in America often preach a pronatalist theology, one in which motherhood is honored and children are welcomed and cherished as a blessing from God, entrusted to parents for guidance to salvation. "Being a housewife is a noble profession," contended the Christian television host Pat Robertson in 1982. "My father was a senator, but my mother stayed home to tell me about Jesus Christ."[89] Not surprisingly, then, women who deem religion "very important" to themselves (a dominant trait among Fundamentalist and evangelical Protestants) hold more traditional values concerning gender and family than their less religious peers. As a consequence, the more devout both plan larger families and actually bear more children. This

---

[85] W. Bradford Wilcox and Nicholas H. Wolfinger, "Then Comes Marriage? Religion, Race, and Marriage in Urban America," *Social Science Research* 36 (June, 2007): 569–89.

[86] Consult, among others, Daniel T. Lichter and Julie H. Carmalt, "Religion and Marital Quality Among Low-Income Couples," *Social Science Research* 38 (Mar. 2009): 168–87; and W. Bradford Wilcox and Nicholas H. Wolfinger, "Living and Loving 'Decent': Religion and Relationship Quality Among Urban Parents," *Social Science Research* 37 (Sept. 2008): 828–43.

[87] Christopher G. Ellison, John P. Bartkowski, and Kristin L. Anderson, "Are There Religious Variations in Domestic Violence?" *Journal of Family Issues* 20 (Jan. 1999): 87–113.

[88] Christopher G. Ellison and Kristin L. Anderson, "Religious Involvement and Domestic Violence Among U.S. Couples," *Journal for the Scientific Study of Religion* 40 (June 2001): 269–86.

[89] M. G. "Pat" Robertson, quoted in Bremner, "Other People's Children," 93.

relation applies even when age, delays in childbearing, and unwanted fertility are discounted.[90]

In contrast, Roman Catholic women, who in the middle part of the twentieth century exceeded Jews and Protestant Christians in intended and actual fertility, no longer greatly surpass other religious Americans in the sizes of their families. Whereas total marital fertility for Catholic wives at midcentury was 3.54 births (as opposed to 3.15 births for non-Catholics), by 1975 the fertility gap had closed, with a rate of 2.27 births for Catholics and 2.17 for their counterparts in other categories. In 2000, the mean number of children ever born to Catholic women aged eighteen to forty-four in the United States was 1.50; for Protestant women, the rate was nearly the same: 1.46. Indeed, starting in the 1980s, total fertility was higher for Protestants as a group in America than it was for Catholics. Much of this difference is attributable to more frequent and earlier marriage by Protestants, presumably ones with more conservative affiliations.[91]

At one time, members of different American denominations sought to inspire different commitments and habits in their children. Now much of this distinctiveness has diminished. However, mothers and fathers who are theologically conservative Protestants persist in a greater preference for correcting their children with corporal punishment.[92] Finally, although denominational differences in patterns of child rearing may have declined in recent decades,[93] there remains a pronounced effect of religion in general. Parents who attend religious services on a regular basis tend more than their nonattending counterparts to value obedience over other traits, like independence and autonomy, in their children.[94]

SUGGESTIONS FOR FURTHER READING

Bartkowski, John P. *Remaking the Godly Marriage: Gender Negotiation in Evangelical Families*. New Brunswick, 2001.

---

[90] Sarah R. Hayford and S. Philip Morgan, "Religiosity and Fertility in the United States: The Role of Fertility Intentions," *Social Forces* 86 (Mar. 2008): 1163–88. See also Bahr and Chadwick, "Religion and Family in Middletown," 412–13. On Jewish Americans especially, see Heilman, "Sociology of American Jewry," 140 and 152.

[91] Tomas Frejka and Charles F. Westoff, "Religion, Religiousness and Fertility in the US and in Europe," *European Journal of Population* 24 (2008): 5–31.

[92] Christopher G. Ellison, John P. Bartkowski, and Michelle L. Segal, "Conservative Protestantism and the Parental Use of Corporal Punishment," *Social Forces* 74 (Mar. 1996): 1003–28; and Ellison and Darren E. Sherkat, "Conservative Protestantism and Support for Corporal Punishment," *American Sociological Review* 58 (Feb. 1993): 131–44.

[93] D'Antonio, "American Catholic Family," 398.

[94] Duane F. Alwin, "Religion and Parental Child-Rearing Orientations: Evidence of a Catholic–Protestant Convergence," *American Journal of Sociology* 92 (Sept. 1986): 412–40; and Thornton, "Changing Attitudes," 88.

Edgell, Penny. *Religion and Family in a Changing Society*. Princeton, 2005.

Houseknecht, Sharon K., and Jerry G. Pankhurst, eds. *Family, Religion, and Social Change in Diverse Societies*. New York, 2000.

McDannell, Colleen. *The Christian Home in Victorian America, 1840–1900*. Bloomington, 1986.

Moran, Gerald F., and Maris A. Vinovskis. *Religion, Family, and the Life Course: Explorations in the Social History of Early America*. Ann Arbor, 1992.

Morgan, Edmund S. *The Puritan Family: Religion and Domestic Relations in Seventeenth-Century New England*. 2nd ed. New York, 1966.

Wilcox, W. Bradford. *Soft Patriarchs, New Men: How Christianity Shapes Fathers and Husbands*. Chicago, 2004.

39

RELIGIOUS HISTORY

EUAN KERR CAMERON

Christianity is a religion rooted in historical claims and historical narratives, as is the Judaism from which it emerged and whose scriptures it shares. On the one hand, their linear narratives of salvation history locate cosmic and essential significance in particular highly specific events, people, places, and times. Yet on the other hand, Christianity has been from its earliest centuries a highly philosophical system. Great weight has been attached to metaphysical propositions about the relationship of the divine and the human that are claimed to be absolute and timeless. The history of religion, therefore, embraces both the history of peoples and the history of beliefs and teachings – teachings that, to some extent, claim to defy the flow of historical change. The business of doing religious history intrinsically threatens some aspects of traditional belief. It challenges the claim of certain doctrines to be timeless, or to be rooted in the universal consent of the faithful. It illuminates the context-driven character of so many of the church's decisions and pronouncements. Finally, it analyzes the often highly mixed and often discreditable motives and behaviors of key players in the messy business of religious politics.

Like its subject matter, religious history has evolved considerably across two millennia. In part, the evolution simply reflects the changing intellectual cultures of different epochs, the constant and inevitable dialogue between a world faith and the particular cultural matrices in which it grows and finds expression. History is written against the background of philosophies of history, whether or not they are consciously articulated. However, the major fractures of the early modern period required a whole adjustment to the perspectives of the discipline. For those who embraced the Reformation in one or another of its forms, history had to be rewritten so as to demonstrate that the breach with the Roman papacy and hierarchy did not amount to a breach of continuity with the historical church. A Reformed historiography had to provide a rationale for linking the Reformed churches to the ancient, primitive church, while somehow explaining the several centuries of profoundly mistaken worship, theology, and polity that stretched from the Gregorian reform (at least) until the sixteenth century. It had to frame in historical terms the basic premise of Protestant anthropology that human beings – and the churches that they constitute – are at one and the same time the saved elect of God and sinners in profound need of redemption. Moreover, the impulse to institutional and self-criticism that arrived with the Reformation continued to generate new modes of historical critique. By the eighteenth century at least, reformed church histories themselves began to subject their own historical-doctrinal claims to analysis and investigation.

Some two centuries ago reformed theology retreated from its more grandiose claims to arbitrate over other disciplines and areas of knowledge. This strategic retreat in the Romantic era generated a more restricted sense of the proper business of the theologian. The disciplines of history and theology underwent a long, gradual process of divergence, despite the interest of many theologians in the more specific areas of doctrinal history or historicist speculation. Since the mid-nineteenth century church history acquired certain critical methods, collections of sources, and literary conventions that progressively distinguished it from previous historical approaches to theology. Moreover, the relationship between religious identity and historical analysis has grown more and more problematic. It is no longer assumed that historians of a given religious movement will embrace the values or objectives of that movement. This discontinuity has made it progressively more difficult to agree on the agenda, the preferred sources, or the methods of religious history: it has created a fruitful but occasionally puzzling diversity in which works are written from a range of radically different perspectives.

Traditionally, the genre of historical writing in the Christian tradition has been held to originate with the work of Eusebius of Caesarea in the late third and early fourth century. Eusebius wrote a distinct form of history, differing in its techniques from the classical models that he might otherwise have imitated. He avoided the rhetorical tradition of constructing imaginary speeches for his participants. Because the subjects of his history were the bishops and martyrs of the early church, he had no room for the moralizing condemnation of the character flaws of political leaders found in Suetonius, except perhaps for assassinating the character of heresiarchs. Although Eusebius did draw on some aspects of the classical tradition, notably the annalistic style of arranging the book around the reigns of the emperors, his work chiefly showed a certain kind of deliberate restraint. The first seven books of his history assembled materials with little stylistic unity, but with great passion for the collection of lists and the presentation of original transcriptions of source documents.[1] Even in his later works Eusebius worked as much in the manner of a compiler as of a narrator.

Nevertheless, Eusebius founded a distinct approach to church history. Christianity was really the one, most ancient, and true monotheism. Doctrine never developed or evolved but only survived the threats and challenges of heretics. The authenticity of church teaching depended on the continuous succession of diocesan bishops and the churches that they served. A cosmic gulf separated the true orthodox faith from the ravings of heretics (usually described more in terms of their moral depravities than their teachings). The apocryphal New Testament texts were not merely doubtful, but thoroughly heretical. Nearly all of these claims fly in the face of the conclusions of more recent scholarship. As a pupil and admirer of Origen of Alexandria, Eusebius must have realized that the line between heresy and orthodoxy was often marked only with hindsight. To draw sharp distinctions between canonical and "heretical" scriptures before the canon of the New Testament was agreed entailed a positivist rereading of the past.

The Eusebian model of the continuity of timeless true doctrine and apostolic succession proved to be enormously influential. The history of the church became the history of its bishops and charismatic leaders, just as the history of secular society focused on its leaders and heroic worthies. For centuries after Eusebius, there was no assumption that Christian doctrine evolved or developed in any way. The true church preserved the apostolic teaching; and heretics, morally depraved as well as theologically misguided, assailed it unsuccessfully. In many histories of the church written during the Western Middle Ages, doctrinal issues were almost entirely absent. Before the Reformation one did not write the history of Christian doctrine. Critical judgment was reserved for individuals. The church might be perfect, but its human representatives were often far from perfect.

Writers committed to the absolute truth of medieval Christianity could freely admit that its individual servants might often be at fault. Bede's *Ecclesiastical History*, written circa 730, generally showed itself more sparing of the vices or failings of clergy than some of his occasional pieces, especially the *Letter to Egbert*.[2] However, even in the *Ecclesiastical History*, Bede could present the encounter between Augustine of Canterbury and Welsh bishops in terms unflattering to the former. He described rather sardonically the aura of suspicion of heresy that hung around Wilfrid of

---

[1] Eusebius, of Caesarea, *The History of the Church from Christ to Constantine*, trans. G. A. Williamson, revised and ed. with new introduction Andrew Louth (London, 1989).

[2] Bede, *The Ecclesiastical History of the English People*, trans. Bertram Colgrave, ed. with introduction Judith McClure and Roger Collins (Oxford, UK, 1994).

Hexham. He did not spare the nuns of Coldingham from moral criticism when describing the fire that consumed their monastery.[3] The same tendency to depict an ideal church staffed by less than ideal people persisted through the Middle Ages. The celebrated chronicle of the Abbey of Bury St. Edmunds written by the learned monk Jocelin of Brakelond (c. 1210) portrayed the political machinations of a wealthy and prestigious Benedictine house in complex shades of grey.[4] The insular, efficient, politically savvy abbot and his jockeying lesser officials would be completely recognizable to any biographer of a small community at any age. A far more graphic image of clerical malfeasance emerged in one of the most disarmingly frank clergy memoirs of the early Renaissance, the *Commentaries* of Enea Silvio Piccolomini (1405–64), Pope Pius II from 1458.[5] He subjected fellow prelates like Guillaume d'Estouteville of Rouen or Dieter von Isenburg of Mainz to merciless character assassination. He showed sardonic skepticism about the holiness of supposed models of piety such as Giovanni Capistrano.[6] Bartolomeo Platina, in the same era, charted the lives of the popes in a similarly Suetonian mode, leaving his sixteenth-century editors with the complex task of expurgating his text and saving the papacy's reputation.[7] In these shaded and sometimes highly colored portraits of individual church people, historical writers usually took for granted that the church continued to teach as it had always taught and to worship as it had always worshipped.

At the opposite extreme, much medieval historical writing more properly belonged to hagiography. In the lives of saints, wholly exceptional sanctity sparkled against the dull background of everyday church events. Hagiographers treated the presence of sanctity as an exceptional personal charism. Hagiography developed its own conventions and tropes: the life, conversion, and ministry of the saint were described, followed often in formulaic fashion by his or her sufferings and persecutions, martyrdom if applicable, and miracles pre- and postmortem. The most famous collection

---

[3] *Ibid.*, book II.2, 72–3; book V.19, 271–2; book IV.25, 218–21.

[4] Jocelin of Brakelond, *The Chronicle of Jocelin of Brakelond Concerning the Acts of Samson, Abbot of the Monastery of St. Edmund*, trans. from the Latin with introduction, notes, and appendices H. E. Butler (London, 1949).

[5] The modern scholarly edition is Pius II, *Pii II Commentarii rerum memorabilium que temporibus suis contigerunt ad codicum fidem nunc primum editi*, ed. Adrian van Heck, Studie testi della Biblioteca apostolica vaticana, 2 vols. (Vatican City, 1984), 312–13.

[6] For convenience, reference is made here to the translation and abridgement, *Secret Memoirs of a Renaissance Pope: The Commentaries of Aeneas Sylvius Piccolomini, Pius II*, trans. Florence A. Gragg, ed. with an introduction Leona C. Gabel (London, 1988), 51–2, 74–81, 118, 174–5, 191–3.

[7] Stefan Bauer, *The Censorship and Fortuna of Platina's Lives of the Popes in the Sixteenth Century*, Late Medieval and Early Modern Studies 9 (Turnhout, 2006).

of this type, the *Golden Legend* of Jacobus de Voragine, acquired vast dissemination and inspired many imitators.[8] The rhetorical tactic of isolating the exemplary narrative from the wider flow of events generated numerous collections of exempla and model sermons, from Caesarius of Heisterbach's *Dialogue of Miracles* (c. 1220) to John Mirk's *Festiall* (possibly of the later 1380s) and Johannes Nider's *Formicarius* (1430s).[9]

The same strategy of fragmenting the records of the past may be observed in one of the largest, most compendious and massive works of the later medieval encyclopedic tradition. Vincent de Beauvais' *Speculum Historiale*, compiled in various versions between the 1240s and 1250s, encompassed world history through the biblical creation narratives, ancient and classical history, and the full flow of world events in the Christian era from canonical, apocryphal, and traditional sources.[10] Crusader narratives and saints' lives appeared in the mix. Recent miracles formed part of the continuing ministry of saints even long since departed. The account of the apostles' Council of Jerusalem could provoke a long theological discourse on the cessation of the rites of the Mosaic law and the institution of the Christian sacraments.[11] Narrative of the early Christian persecutions dissolved into a great sequence of lives (and deaths) of saints; in one book the lives of some saints could not even be assigned to a secure period and were presented undated.[12] As the chronology reached key figures in the life of the church such as Augustine, Gregory the Great, or Bernard of Clairvaux, short chapters described their teachings and writings. Rhetorical or explanatory structure entirely disappeared in the policy of collecting material and disposing it according to a rough chronological scheme determined by the lives of the Holy Roman emperors.

In historical writing as in so much else, the Reformation of the sixteenth century marked a tectonic shift. Previous "reforms" in the history

---

[8] A translation and abridgment is Jacobus de Voragine, *The Golden Legend: Readings on the Saints*, trans. William Granger Ryan, 2 vols. (Princeton, 1993). A fuller translation is available online at http://www.ccel.org/ccel/voragine/goldleg1.html through http://www.ccel.org/ccel/voragine/goldleg7.html.

[9] Caesarius, of Heisterbach, *Dialogus miraculorum / Dialog über die Wunder*, ed. and trans. Horst Schneider and Nikolaus Nösges, 5 vols. (Turnhout, 2009); *Mirk's Festial: A Collection of Homilies*, ed. Theodor Erbe, Early English Text Society, extra ser., 96 (London, 1905); Johannes Nider, *De visionibus ac revelationibus* (Helmstedt, 1692) (edition of Formicarius).

[10] The *Speculum Historiale* forms the fourth part of Vincent of Beauvais' *Speculum Quadruplex, sive Speculum Maius*. The standard early modern edition is in 4 vols: John Jones, ed. (Douai, 1624; repr. Graz, 1964–65); an online critical edition based on manuscript sources is in preparation at http://atilf.atilf.fr/bichard/.

[11] Vincent, *Speculum Historiale*, book 9, chs. 11–89.

[12] *Ibid.*, book 16 passim.

of the Western church had presupposed that, whatever political strife might arise, the ideals and objectives of Western Christianity were not in dispute. In the Protestant Reformation that consensus collapsed. The reformers argued that for several centuries theologians had been asking the wrong question about human salvation. Medieval thinkers had analyzed minutely how God might cleanse and purify a sinful human soul sufficiently to make it fit to be saved. For Martin Luther and those who followed his arguments, the whole point was that God did not purify the soul in order to accept it. God chose out of pure grace and for Christ's sake to accept the soul in spite of its continuing and fatal impurities.[13] Righteousness before God came through trust in a divine gift of grace, apprehended in knowing, conscious faith. The duty of the church was to proclaim grace, not to mediate purification. Theologically deep instruction and worship in the common tongue replaced ceremonies performed mysteriously in an arcane language.

The church was no longer a single organic entity linked mysteriously to the heavenly economy; therefore it needed neither a single centralized organization on earth nor a separate caste of clergy governed by distinct laws. The individual churches of each effective political entity were local manifestations of the one universal and invisible church. Their ministers were specialist servants drawn from the community, not somehow separate from it.[14] This theological reenvisioning entailed liturgical, political, social, and economic change on a scale not seen since the end of the Roman Empire. It diametrically reversed the most definitive achievements of the medieval papacy and Latin Catholicism more generally. The ritual and legal separation of clergy from laity, derived from the Gregorian movement and the canonists, was replaced by a conviction that clergy were full members of the community. The crucial role of sacramental absolution and penance in the life of the Christian, made definitive by Innocent III, yielded to a new theology of grace. The claims of the papacy to supranational authority, vigorously promoted by Boniface VIII, although not original to him, came to be denounced as anti-Christian.

The implications of this reversal of direction for the churches' understanding of their own past were profound. How had the leadership of the churches managed for so many centuries to be egregiously in error about the fundamental truths of salvation and the proper means to approach God? What was the relationship between the visible hierarchy, where such error and political pride had reigned, and the eternal, unfailing, but

---

[13] See the discussion of this point in my *The European Reformation* (Oxford, 1991), 121–3 and references.

[14] *Ibid.*, 144–55 and references.

also invisible congregation of the faithful? Theological error now was no longer external to the church; it was the foe that had reigned in the citadel of Christendom for centuries. The true church had to be sought somewhere other than in the papacy. Posing these questions in the first instance remained the task of the Protestant churches. Catholic historical scholarship could and did continue to represent itself as the one true tradition. However, in time Protestant lessons about the fragility of the traditions of religious institutions would spread to other branches of church history. Even in the East one finds increasingly subtle reflection on the evolving character of a religious tradition.

In the first decades of Reformed religious history, the northern European Renaissance modified the dogmatic perspective in critical ways. Two emblematic exponents of the Renaissance approach to religious history were Johannes Sleidan (1507–66) of Strasbourg and Joachim von Watt (1484–1551), better known as Joachim Vadian of St. Gallen in the Swiss Confederation. Sleidan's Reformation history, correctly entitled *Commentaries on the State of Religion and the Commonwealth under Emperor Charles V*, began as a commissioned history of the military-political league of Schmalkalden. His narrative presented religious politics first, and theological ideas only secondarily. Sleidan notoriously avoided writing a history of doctrine.[15] He adopted what others found an infuriatingly evenhanded approach to the history of controversy and conflict. A Strasbourg Protestant pulled between Wittenberg and Zürich, he stressed the agreement between reformers and minimized the tensions between the different magisterial traditions. Even the bitter sacramental strife between Wittenberg and Zürich was played down in his account. However, Sleidan did not extend this evenhandedness to those movements that eschewed any alliance with secular authority. The Zwickau Prophets, Thomas Müntzer, and the Anabaptists earned his scorn and sarcasm. Their claims to direct inspiration, their social subversiveness, and their alleged proneness to acts of violence all provoked hostility and condescension from this highly educated bourgeois.[16] Nevertheless, and with that important qualification, Sleidan wrote political history of religious events rather than confessional, dogmatic history. Neither the criteria for right action nor the marks of a genuinely Christian community were defined exclusively in doctrinal terms.

---

[15] Eduard Fueter, *Geschichte des neueren Historiographie* (Munich, 1911), 201ff.; Ingeborg Berlin Vogelstein, *Johann Sleidan's Commentaries: Vantage Point of a Second Generation Lutheran* (Lanham, MD, 1986), 64ff., 69ff.; compare Alexandra Kess, *Johann Sleidan and the Protestant Vision of History* (Aldershot, 2008).

[16] See E. Bohun, trans., *The General History of the Reformation of the Church, Written in Latin by John Sleidan, L.L.D., Faithfully Englished* (London, 1689), 52, 83ff., 97ff., 110, 141.

Independently of Sleidan, another humanist Protestant in Switzerland developed a similarly restrained approach to church history. Joachim Vadian converted to the Reformation after a career as a prolific and polymathic scholar and poet laureate at Vienna.[17] On his return home to promote humanistic studies in St. Gallen, he joined the cause of religious reform. He led the Reformation movement in his town as its Bürgermeister and physician rather than as its preacher.[18] Vadian wrote a history of the abbots of the great Benedictine abbey of St. Gallen, the abbey that he attempted, ultimately without success, to secularize and take over for the city.[19] He published with Johann Stumpf (1500–76) a history of Switzerland and Germany in 1547–48,[20] and in 1534 a work of biblical geography, the *Epitome of the Three Parts of the World, Asia, Africa and Europe, Containing Descriptions ... Especially of Those Places Which the Evangelists and Apostles Related.*[21] This work stood, even in 1534, closer to the skepticism and reserve of the Renaissance than to the dogmatism of the developed Reformation. Vadian warned against excessive claims to certainty, whether over historical or doctrinal claims.[22] Persecution of a colleague because of a minor disagreement over doctrine was always wrong.[23] Some institutions that later Protestantism would see as entirely pernicious, such as monasticism, he envisaged as a good idea in the primitive church: monasteries had provided for spiritual education and discipline without superfluous ritual.[24] Only afterwards did monasticism become corrupted into a fastidious and vainglorious pursuit of foolish regulations.[25]

In the Lutheran no less than the Swiss Reformation, Protestant religious history began as humanistic and only subsequently became dogmatic.

---

[17] For a mere handful of Vadian's copious output as an editor of Latin classical and later texts in humanist mode, see his editions of *Strabi Fuldensis ... Hortulus* (Nuremberg, 1512); *P. Ovidii Nasonis artis amandi libri tres* (Vienna, 1512); *C. Plinii Secundi praefatio in historiam mundi, ad Vespasianum* (Vienna, 1513).

[18] Bruce Gordon, *The Swiss Reformation* (Manchester, 2002), 89–92, 326–7; Gordon Rupp, *Frontiers of Reformation* (London, 1969), 357–78. See also Friedrich Wilhelm Bautz and Traugott Bautz, eds., *Biographisch-bibliographisches Kirchenlexikon* (Hamm, 1970–), article "Vadian, Joachim."

[19] Joachim v. Watt (Vadian), *Deutsche historische Schriften*, ed. Ernst Götzinger, 3 vols. (St. Gallen, 1875–97).

[20] Johann Stumpf and Joachim Vadian, *Gemeiner loblicher Eydgnoschafft Stetten, Landen vnd Völckeren Chronick ...* (Getruckt Zürych, 1547–48). The "Swiss Chronicle" was republished several times in the sixteenth century.

[21] [Joachim Vadian], *Epitome Trium Terrae Partium, Asiae, Africae et Europae compendiarum locorum descriptionem continens* (Zürich, 1534).

[22] *Ibid.,*. 122–5, 145.

[23] *Ibid.*, 194–6, 417, 422–7.

[24] *Ibid.*, 187–9, 433ff.

[25] Compare *The Judgment of Martin Luther on Monastic Vows* in Martin Luther, *Luther's Works*, ed. Jaroslav Pelikan and H. T. Lehmann, 55 vols. (St. Louis, 1955–86), 44: 243–400.

Philipp Melanchthon (1497–1560), the Renaissance philosopher and pedagogue of the Reformation, insisted on retaining classical scholarship, literature, philosophy, and above all history in the reformed curricula. He edited successive revisions and continuations of the humanist world chronicle of Johannes Carion.[26] Melanchthon's pupils developed over succeeding decades a philosophy of religious history that stressed its humane and improving qualities. Viktorin Strigel (1524–69) argued in the 1540s that church history was the history of the soul as secular history was the history of the body: it had a separate kind of sources and separate priorities.[27] As the sixteenth century progressed, however, even the Philippists in the Lutheran camp began to identify the history of religion as the history of doctrine and its preservation, corruption, and restoration. As Christoph Pezel (1539–1604) wrote toward the end of his life in his *Mellificium Historicum*, or "the historical beehive":

> Histories show the series of divine revelations, the origin of true religion, its propagation, and the rise and growth of superstition and idolatry. We need to know this, to know what is the first and most ancient doctrine of God; when, where, and by what testimonies it was handed down, and how it can be discerned from other false religions.... Therefore histories are useful for deciding in controversies regarding doctrine.[28]

A theological principle became dominant: the reformed church should and could claim to follow the practices of the primitive church in the fullest way possible. The elaboration of institutional and liturgical practices – for instance, in the rituals of the Eucharist, the cult of saints, or the customs of monastic devotion – therefore represented a falling away from primitive simplicity that the historian could observe, track, and document. An early example of the appeal to the primitive church appeared in the Zürich reformer Heinrich Bullinger's two-part work *On the Origin of Error*, published in 1539, although based on work done some years earlier. Historical Christianity, Bullinger argued, tended to lapse from better to worse.[29] Even in pagan religions people had once recognized and worshipped the one

---

[26] J. Carion, *Chronica durch Magistrum Johan Carion fleisig zusamen gezogen, menigklich nützlich zu lesen* (Wittenberg, [1532]); the Melanchthon recension appeared as *Chronicon Carionis, latine expositum et auctum multis et veteribus et recentibus historiis* (Wittenberg, 1558; second part, *ibid.*, 1560); see also *Philippi Melanthonis Opera quae supersunt omnia*, ed. C. G. Bretschneider, Corpus Reformatorum, vols. 1–28 (Halle, 1834–60), XII, cols. 712–1094; Fueter, *Geschichte*, 186 ff.

[27] Emil Clemens Scherer, *Geschichte und Kirchengeschichte an den deutschen Universitäten: Ihre Anfänge im Zeitalter des Humanismus und ihre Ausbildung zu sebständigen Disziplinen* (Freiburg im Breisgau, 1927), 49–51.

[28] Christoph Pezel, *Mellificium Historicum integrum*, ed. Johannes Lampadius (Marburg, 1617), sigs **4v-***1v.

[29] Heinrich Bullinger, *De Origine Erroris Libri Duo ...* (Zürich, 1539), fols. 3v–4v.

God; over time their primitive monotheism lapsed into polytheism, and from polytheism arose idolatry and the cult of images.[30] This narrative of primitive simplicity and subsequent decline informed Bullinger's analysis of the Mass. Jesus must have blessed the Last Supper in the simplest possible way. Subsequently the apostles gathered together, preached the gospel, offered prayers, and broke bread. Cyprian and other fathers preserved and transmitted an extremely brief and simple responsorial Eucharistic prayer, which Bullinger believed was widely used up to the time of Augustine.[31] Images of martyrs in the early church served as memorials only, like the "icons" of the reformers published by Protestant printers. With the passage of time and especially with the need to make converts from paganism feel at home, the saints deteriorated into surrogates for the pagan gods, with many of the same responsibilities for the affairs of the living.[32] Martin Luther himself argued in his controversial pamphlet, *On Councils and the Churches* (1539), that all of Christian history demonstrated the leaders of the church trying and often failing to "prune the vines," to restrain the always pernicious growth of heretical doctrines such as those rejected in the early councils, or the elaboration of apocryphal and unnecessary practices, such as monasticism.[33] Unlike the Swiss humanists, however, Luther made doctrinal considerations his criterion for approval right from the start.

In hard-line Lutheranism, especially after Luther's death, dogmatically informed religious history identified the "true" succession of the Christian church in those dissenters oppressed as heretical by the ever more corrupt and illegitimate Catholic hierarchy. Matthias Flacius Illyricus (1520–75), a Croat from Albona in Istria, converted to Lutheranism at the age of nineteen and became professor of Hebrew at Wittenberg.[34] His enthusiastic collecting of manuscripts of antiquarian theology bore fruit in a monumental first work, *A Catalogue of Witnesses to the Truth, Who before Our Time Cried out Against the Pope*.[35] Opponents ("heretics") had proliferated following the age of Innocent III. The "heresies" in the *Catalogue* formed disembodied lists of doctrines rather than religious biographies. The cumulative effect conjured up centuries of antipapal and anti-Roman sentiment across history. During the era of papal error the visible Church was not the church of Jesus Christ

---

[30] *Ibid.*, fols. 33r–45r.
[31] *Ibid.*, fols. 202r–205r.
[32] Bullinger, *De Origine Erroris*, fols. 160vff., 164v–167r, 167vff.
[33] Luther, *Luther's Works*; *On Councils and the Churches* is found in vol. 41, 5–177.
[34] Fueter, *Geschichte*, 249; on Flacius see Oliver K. Olson, *Matthias Flacius and the Survival of Luther's Reform*, Wolfenbütteler Abhandlungen zur Renaissanceforschung; Bd. 20 (Wiesbaden, 2002).
[35] Matthias Flacius Illyricus, *Catalogus testium veritatis: qui ante nostram ætatem reclamarunt papæ* (Basel, 1556).

at all. The same claims about the history of the "true" (minority) church of the Middle Ages appeared in the multivolume work edited by Flacius and his colleagues, usually known as the *Magdeburg Centuries*.³⁶ Adapted versions of the *Catalogue* and the *Centuries* were published in the early seventeenth century for the Calvinist market.³⁷

The same theological-historical argument then found echoes in the English-speaking world in the highly influential *Acts and Monuments* of the English Reformed martyrologist John Foxe (1516/17–87). From the time of Innocent III to the Reformation

> the true Church of Christ, although it durst not openly appear in the face of the world, oppressed by tyranny; yet neither was it so invisible or unknown, but, by the providence of the Lord, some remnant always remained from time to time, which not only showed secret good affection to sincere doctrine, but also stood in open defense of truth against the disordered Church of Rome.³⁸

The history of the protests and the sufferings of medieval heretics – not, be it noted, the heretics of the early church, who at this period were still outcasts even in Protestant historical writing – told the true narrative of the continuing life of the church. In the hands of Foxe and his ilk, this narrative took on an apocalyptic character. In Revelation 20 it was prophesied that an angel would seize the "dragon," Satan, and chain him up for a thousand years, after which he would be released for "a short while."³⁹ Foxe interpreted this to mean that for about a thousand years after the coming of Christ "Satan was chained," that is, the church was allowed to grow more or less unmolested. When that time was over, the enemy was progressively let loose to seduce the church into error. In the time of Reformation, the devil was definitively cast out of the church.⁴⁰

Confessional conflict revived a specialized genre of writing about the recent past. Religious martyrs had been relatively rare in the Middle Ages, outside crusading and Mediterranean conflicts. In the Reformation era unprecedented numbers of people from Reformed (Calvinist) minority churches and from Anabaptist movements defied their prosecutors when tried, leading to their own execution. Fewer Lutherans took the same

---

³⁶ *Ecclesiastica historia, integram Ecclesiae Christi ideam, ... secundum singulas centurias, perspicuo ordine complectens*, 13 vols. (Basel, 1559–74).

³⁷ See S. Goulart, ed., *Catalogus Testium Veritatis, qui ante nostram aetatem Pontifici Romano atque Papismi erroribus reclamarunt*, 2 vols. (Lyon, 1597; later ed. Geneva, 1608); Ludovicus Lucius, ed., *Historiae Ecclesiasticae*, 3 vols. (Basel, 1624).

³⁸ John Foxe, *The Acts and Monuments*, ed. Joseph Pratt, 8 vols. (London, 1877), 1: xxi.

³⁹ Rev. 20:1–3, 7–8.

⁴⁰ Foxe, *Acts and Monuments*, 2: 724–6.

route; Catholic priests accused of treason under the Draconian secular laws of Elizabethan England could be represented as martyrs for their faith. All the major sixteenth-century religious traditions developed martyrologies.[41] These accounts typically presented compendious but not particularly orderly collections of individual stories of evangelism, detection, capture, trial, and execution. Sometimes the accounts related to whole communities or movements that suffered mass attacks.[42] This genre of writing returned to the roots of church history in Eusebius: martyrologies presented narratives and primary documents with minimal interpretation. The polemical atmosphere provoked great care in the accurate presentation of evidence, because none of the parties wished to be detected in falsehood or forgery. Interpretation was predictable: the barbarous cruelty of the persecutors demonstrated their anti-Christian character; the constancy and endurance of the victims showed divine grace at work.

The sixteenth-century Protestant reformers laid down the basic lines of historical thinking and rhetoric for their seventeenth-century successors. However, the process known as confessionalization worked its often perverse effects in historiography as in other areas of religious culture. Not only did Protestant historians critique Catholic history, and vice versa; different varieties of Protestants engaged in internecine strife through their historical writings. Two examples can illustrate the schools of religious history associated with the iron age of confessional orthodoxy. Lucas Osiander the Elder (1534–1604) published his *Epitome of Church History* in multiple volumes between 1592 and the author's death. This truly monumental work of controversy and scholarship divided church history into centuries, with a colossal final volume of 1,158 pages devoted solely to the era of the Reformation.[43] Like earlier polemical histories, Osiander claimed that the history of the church up to the Reformation was of the loss of innocence, the gradual decline from apostolic purity and simplicity to medieval corruption. He argued that Catholic writers had misrepresented the early church, and he gleefully dissected the pseudo-Isidorian or "false decretals," spurious ninth-century forgeries purporting to prove the claims of a centralizing papacy.[44]

In the medieval period "the leaders of the Church more and more departed from the Word of God, and admired works-laden ceremonies,

---

[41] On the martyrologies, see Brad S. Gregory, *Salvation at Stake: Christian Martyrdom in Early Modern Europe* (Cambridge, MA, 1999).

[42] See, e.g., the martyologists' accounts of the attacks on the Waldensian communities in Provence and the southwestern Alps.

[43] Lucas Osiander, the Elder, *Epitomes Historiae Ecclesiasticae, Centuriae I.–XVI.*, 10 vols. (Tubingæ, 1592–1604).

[44] *Ibid.*, cent. 3, 69; cent. 4, 21–2, 28, 132–3.

nowhere prescribed by God. While they were absorbed in these things, they meanwhile neglected to conserve the purity of heavenly doctrine." Miracles attributed to saints were either false or the result of demonic illusions "to erect and confirm superstitious and idolatrous cults, by which the true worship of God might be largely oppressed. God permitted this, in order that superstitious people, by his just judgment, should be punished by darkness, because they preferred lies rather than heavenly truths handed down in the word of God."[45] After such decline the Reformation represented a providential rescuing of the Christian community, through the heroic witness and epoch-changing insights of Martin Luther. Tragically, the churches did not remain united and disciplined under the standard of Lutheran orthodoxy. Sacramentarian "heretics" like Zwingli and his followers corrupted the evangelical insights with disputes over the Eucharist. Calvin was worse, because he presented the same errors in language more learned, more polished, and more apt to deceive the educated.[46] Ironically, Osiander often grafted his vitriolic asides on to his text as marginal annotations, because much of his text came from neutral (Sleidan) or even from Reformed sources, such as the history attributed to Philippe de Marnix van St-Aldegonde, the Dutch Calvinist.[47]

Roman Catholic historiography received as potent a stimulus to critical precision from the exigencies of controversy. If Protestants argued for the discontinuity of institutional church history, Catholics claimed that the continuing tradition of the Church preserved perfect continuity with its remote apostolic origins. These opposed objectives inspired similar deployments of carefully edited sources. Cesare Baronio (known as Caesar Baronius, 1538–1607) drafted a reply to the Lutheran *Magdeburg Centuries*. He began publishing the *Ecclesiastical Annals* in 1588, and by 1607 he brought the story up to 1198.[48] Baronius announced his own scholarly and critical superiority to those who had gone before him. "Nothing in the Church seems so far to have been so much neglected, as a true, certain, exact and diligently researched narration of Ecclesiastical history." Medieval chroniclers copied down "old wives' tales [*aniles fabulas*], the ravings of old men, the rumors of the common herd." Their credulity had discredited truths.[49] Baronius disposed of old legends, such as the legend that Adam was buried

---

[45] *Ibid.*, cent. 6, 3–4.

[46] *Ibid.*, cent. 16, sigs.): (3v-4v; pp. 68–9, 85, 89, 98, 118–21, 123, 144ff., 184f.

[47] Osiander repeatedly cited "A. Henricpetri," *General Historien: Der aller namhafftigsten ... Geschichten, Thaten und Handlungen ...* (Basel, 1577), attributed by some to P. de Marnix.

[48] Caesar Baronius, *Annales Ecclesiastici*, 12 vols. (Rome, 1588–1607).

[49] References here are to Caesar Baronius, *Annales Ecclesiastici auctore C. B. Sorano, ex congregat{ione} oratorii ... Tomi duodecim*, "Edition novissima" (Cologne, 1624), i, sig †† 4v.

at Golgotha, or that the wedding at Cana was the wedding of St. John the Evangelist.[50] He suppressed the texts of the so-called false decretals, but insisted on the single character of Mary of Magdala, a conflation in medieval tradition of several women called Mary and others unnamed. He insisted on the authenticity of the letters attributed to Ignatius of Antioch, many of which contained spurious affirmations of the principle of episcopal sovereignty.[51] Most obviously, Baronius selected his sources to prove the uninterrupted succession of the papacy, the continuous unfolding of liturgical tradition and theological expression. Baronius' history received a series of continuations until a massive collected edition in three volumes by Augustin Theiner completed the work in 1856.[52]

In Protestantism rare exceptions to this partisan and confessionally driven approach appeared. The pietist and mystic Gottfried Arnold (1666–1714), in *An Impartial History of the Church and Heresies* (1699–1700),[53] declined to adhere conventionally to the doctrinal orthodoxy of late antiquity. Many "orthodox" theologians were uncharitable; many "heretics" led exemplary lives. He almost anticipated Adolf von Harnack in seeing the profusion of dogmatic statements as proof of decline.[54] There was good in the mystics, and mystics were to be found in many different traditions, even those that were antithetical to one another. If the true church was defined by the witness to the love of God, then the true church might be dispersed throughout many churches, rather than being the exclusive preserve of one.[55] Arnold's critique of dogmatic partisanship aroused the furious ire of traditional orthodox Lutherans. Ernst Salomon Cyprian wrote one of the most energetic rejoinders against the work. He issued his *General Remarks on Gottfried Arnold's History of the Church and Heresies* in 1700 and continued to oppose the work long after Arnold had withdrawn from the controversy.[56]

---

[50] *Ibid.*, i. cols. 112, 200.

[51] *Ibid.*, i. col. 137; ii. cols. 33ff., 40. For the Mary Magdalenes in the sixteenth century, see Richard Rex, *The Theology of John Fisher* (Cambridge, UK, 1991), 65–77. For the letters of Ignatius, compare James Ussher, ed., *Polycarpi et Ignatii Epistolae* (Oxford, UK, 1644).

[52] Augustin Theiner, *Annales Ecclesiastici quos post ... Card. Baronium, O. Raynaldum ac J. Laderchium ... ab an. MDLXXII. ad nostra usque tempora ...*, 3 vols. (Rome, 1856).

[53] Gottfried Arnold, *Unparteyische Kirchen- und Ketzer-Historie, von Anfang des Neuen Testaments biß auff das Jahr Christi 1688*, 2 vols. (Frankfurt am Main, 1699–1700).

[54] References here are to Gottfried Arnold, *Unpartheyische Kirchen- und Ketzer-Historien ... an vielen Orten, nach dem Sinn und Verlagen, des Seel. Auctoris, vebessert ...*, 3 vols. (Schaffhausen, 1740–42), i. 165, 243–4, 256–7.

[55] *Ibid.*, i. 25–30.

[56] C. Scott Dixon, "Faith and History on the Eve of Enlightenment: Ernst Salomon Cyprian, Gottfried Arnold, and the History of Heretics," *The Journal of Ecclesiastical History* 57 (2006): 33–54.

In the eighteenth century a different challenge came from Johann Lorenz von Mosheim (c. 1694/5–1755).[57] Mosheim lamented the proneness of historians to import into their work their prejudices and partis pris.[58] He saw misfortune and misdirection in many of the same things that the philosophes rejected: priestcraft and the artificial mysteries of ritual, monasticism and "holy indolence," and above all the credulity of popular belief that the Enlightenment casually dismissed as "superstition," including the taste for the spectacular and miraculous instances of divine power.[59] Mosheim's work was far more influential and more widely disseminated than Arnold's. However, the presages of modernity in his work derived largely from his humane and critical attitudes toward the psychology of the human actors in the historical drama. He relied on basically the same methods and approaches as earlier historians; many of his critical tools, especially the sense of a progressive fall from grace through the elaboration both of beliefs and of rituals, drew heavily on earlier Reformation examples. Only during the nineteenth and twentieth centuries would one see a radical change in the method and techniques of religious history.

During the nineteenth century, in Protestant Christian circles one witnesses a progressive and intentional separation between the disciplines of theology and history, as theologians retreated from their previous claims to regulate and make comprehensible every aspect of human affairs. In addition, the century produced increasing professionalism and specialization in the tools, techniques, and sources of religious history. That specialization fragmented the discipline and discouraged grand narratives: historians aspired only to resolve issues within a few centuries or so in one tradition. Finally, in the twentieth century historians – and theologians – sought to align their work with a range of ideological movements, whether secular or ecclesiastical in nature. Consciously or unconsciously they absorbed and reflected the values of their own era.

In a context shaped by Kantianism, Hegelianism, and Romanticism, theological statements no longer transparently described objects that existed independent of the observer or believer. They represented in a communicable way the responses that the divine evoked in the theologically oriented mind. Friedrich Schleiermacher (1768–1834) divorced theological

---

[57] Johann Lorenz Mosheim, *Institutionum historiae ecclesiasticae antiquae et recentioris libri quatuor* (Helmstedt, 1755); trans. as *An Ecclesiastical History, Antient and Modern, from the Birth of Christ, to the Beginning of the Present Century*, trans. Archibald Maclaine, 2 vols. (London, 1765).

[58] References are here to Johann Lorenz Mosheim, *An Ecclesiastical History ...*, trans. Maclaine, 4 vols. (New York, 1824), i. 17, 19, 21–4.

[59] See, e.g., *ibid.*, i. 264, 281–2, 289–90, 424, 428ff.

reflection from scientific or other attempts to make sense of the universe. He remarked that "metaphysicians and moralists in religion ... confuse all points of view and bring religion into the disrepute of encroaching upon the totality of scientific and empirical judgments.... [R]eligion ... leaves you, your physics, and, may it please God, your psychology inviolate."[60] Romantic theorists of culture stressed the historically conditioned quality of religious experience. J. G. Herder observed that medieval Christianity "[was] invaluable as the rude envelope of tradition which could endure the storms of the barbarians ... but it could scarcely have constant value for all times. When the fruit becomes ripe, the shell breaks."[61] Protestant historians could freely treat their discipline as a narrative of human actors on a stage designed by the dialectical progression of cultural evolution. In the age of G. W. Hegel, dogmatic certainty would subside more and more below the flow of world-historical events.

Post-Romantic church history was most famously developed by Leopold von Ranke (1795–1886). To take one instance, Ranke's *History of the Popes* argued that Roman paganism and imperial Roman political structures shaped the early form of the clerical hierarchy. Under the Germanic barbarians, "the old Teutonic superstition, by which the Gods were described as nearer to some spots of the earth than others, and more readily to be propitiated in places thus favored," helped to foster belief in holy places and shrines.[62] Papal monarchy was useful for Europe's cultural growth in the high medieval centuries; by the late Middle Ages it had become a hindrance, so it was eroded by ecclesiastical nationalism.[63] Ranke was also an incurable gossip. He loved the inner story, the narrative behind the narrative, the psychological complexity of the actors in the often conflicted and troubling dramas of ecclesiastical politics. His work drew copiously on letter collections, memoirs, archives, and other manuscript sources that previous generations of historians had not found useful. Indifferent to most doctrinal issues, he could return to a much earlier model in which the moral performance of the principal actors seemed of more interest and relevance than their ideological positions. The Rankean approach did not entirely displace the dogmatic or confessional models, but it helped to provoke the production of standard editions of the literature and correspondence of the primary actors in church history. A whole series of definitive editions

---

[60] Friedrich Schleiermacher, *On Religion: Speeches to Its Cultured Despisers*, ed. and trans. Richard Crouter (Cambridge, UK, 1988), 48 (quotation).

[61] Quoted in Rudolf Bultmann, *History and Eschatology: The Gifford Lectures 1955* (Edinburgh, 1957), 82–3.

[62] Leopold von Ranke, *History of the Popes: Their Church and State*, trans. E. Fowler (New York, 1901), i. 7–12.

[63] *Ibid.*, i. 24–8.

of primary texts appeared: the *Monumenta Germaniae Historica* from 1826, the *Corpus Reformatorum* from 1834 onward, J.-P. Migne's *Patrologia Latina* from 1844 and *Patrologia Graeca* from 1857, and the standard editions of the works of reformers such as Calvin (1859–) and Luther (1883–).

Despite the increasing difficulty of writing comprehensive church histories, the Swiss-born Mercersburg theologian and church historian of Union Theological Seminary in New York, Philipp Schaff (1819–93), issued what became the eight-volume *History of the Christian Church* from the apostolic age to the end of the sixteenth century. The first three volumes covering the first six centuries appeared between 1859 and 1868, followed by the volumes on the Reformation. The Middle Ages were described by Schaff's son, David Schley Schaff, and the resulting composite history appeared in 1910.[64] Schaff was predominantly a patristic scholar, the editor of the standard series of English translations of the Nicene and post-Nicene fathers.[65] The limitations of the work were as obvious as its scholarly base. The early centuries were represented as the story of doctrines, heresies, councils, and emerging structures, although Schaff also heeded archaeological and art-historical discoveries of early Christianity. The elaboration of ritual and worship in the post-Constantinian age elicited the same sort of hostile commentary that it had among post-Reformation historians. The final clause of the *Ave Maria* was an "unscriptural addition ... offensive to the Protestant and all sound Christian feeling" and mistakenly attributed to the early church.[66] The volumes on the Reformation majestically focused on Protestantism alone. They left Catholics and Anabaptists largely unrepresented, except as the foils for Protestant controversial and polemical writings.

Early twentieth-century Protestant theology debated historical readings of the past. Adolf von Harnack, the doyen of German liberal Protestants, wrote prolific scholarly theological histories of the early church.[67] This historical work convinced him, and others, that philosophical and dogmatic elaboration had been one of the original sins of Christianity that required repentance and redirection. A more daring liberal, Ernst Troeltsch, developed his vision of religious sociology and social history through an exhaustive metanarrative.[68] Harnack's rebellious student Karl

---

[64] Philip Schaff, *History of the Christian Church*, new ed., 8 vols. in 7 (New York, 1882–1910).

[65] P. Schaff et al., eds., *A Select Library of the Nicene and Post-Nicene Fathers*, 2nd ser. (Grand Rapids, 1956).

[66] Schaff, *History*, III, ch. 7, sect. 82.

[67] Adolf von Harnack, *Lehrbuch der Dogmengeschichte*, 4th ed., 3 vols. (Tübingen, 1909–10).

[68] Ernst Troeltsch, *The Social Teaching of the Christian Churches*, trans. Olive Wyon, 2 vols. (New York, 1931).

Barth read the significance of history differently. Theologians ought to recognize the everyday life of the church as the shadowy zone in which corruptible human nature reigns, but into that zone bursts the timeless, irreducible, and explosive fact of revelation.[69] All three theologians were gifted historians; however, as theological debates intensified, the content of history receded further and further from the minds of practicing theologians.

From the second quarter of the twentieth century onward, historians of society and politics in Britain and Europe wrote about religion as a branch of social history. Sometimes this kind of history came close to denying religious or theological motives altogether: religious ideas were proxy arguments to cover or justify some earthier or more fundamental ambition in the spheres of class rivalry, political faction, or economic self-advancement. The impact of intellectual Marxism in mid-twentieth-century Europe trained a group of social historians to seek to "unearth" the "real" motives behind apparently religious movements. Rebellions against the religious policies of rulers could be attributed to political or economic motives, provincial separatism, cultural difference, or a range of other alibis. Historians of the urban Reformation used to argue that if one looked closely enough, reformed agitators "really" wanted the removal of clerical economic immunities, greater access to communal resources, or more political say in their towns. It took the robust common sense of an older historian to point out that "few people embrace martyrdom or even exile merely in the expectation that a new creed may lighten their taxes or give some of their friends seats on a city council."[70] Recently the proxy factors have shifted from economics or class politics narrowly conceived to more elusive factors associated with culture, gender, and beliefs about the supernatural. Social historians interpret religious events through cultural motifs that mark their subjects as different and definitely premodern. This trend reverses the old teleological history in which past religious movements mattered because they were "our" antecedents.

By the end of the twentieth century, several distinct strands in historical writing about religion had emerged. A few theologians developed historicist modes of theology.[71] Writers of *Dogmengeschichte* continued to explore

---

[69] Karl Barth, *The Epistle to the Romans*, trans. from the 6th ed. Edwyn C. Hoskyns (London, 1933), e.g., 29, 36, 65.

[70] A. G. Dickens, "Intellectual and Social Forces in the German Reformation," in Wolfgang J. Mommsen, Peter Alter, and Robert W. Scribner, eds., *Stadtbürgertum und Adel in der Reformation: Studien zur Sozialgeschichte d. Reformation in England u. Deutschland* (Stuttgart, 1979), 22.

[71] Gordon D. Kaufman, *Systematic Theology: A Historicist Perspective* (New York, 1968); Sheila Greeve Davaney, *Historicism: The Once and Future Challenge for Theology* (Minneapolis, 2006).

the history of theology in traditional terms.[72] Other historians wrote with empathy, even with explicit partisanship, for a particular tradition or branch of the Christian church or another faith. These historians' empathy was often detached from present-day faith commitment. Those who wrote passionately about medieval Catholicism, Anabaptism, or Pietism might not belong to, or believe in, the movements that they wrote about: their partisanship has grown out of scholarly fascination rather than belief.[73] Finally, cultural historians analyze the history of religion as a cultural artifact, as the economic, sociopolitical, artistic, and sensory expression of a particular way of viewing the world. The diversity and complexity of the ways of conducting religious history reflect the complexity and diversity of the present climate in regard to religious thought and practice more generally.

For this volume, it is vital to bring the history of religion – and especially Western Christianity in Europe – into conversation with that written about the churches and religious communities of North America, and more especially of the United States. The religious history of the United States is quite unique: it generated its own historiography, separate from the rest of the British possessions west of the Atlantic, long before the American colonies became independent. Since independence, American religious historiography has set its own questions. Many reasons for that exceptionality are obvious. First, in contrast to the uniformity sought back in England, each colony of what later became the United States came into being in a separate process and gave a distinct religious character to the community that grew up there. Religion became patriarchally and uniformly Puritan in Massachusetts, diversely and disobediently so in Connecticut and Rhode Island, diffusely and almost invisibly Anglican in Virginia, multitraditional and multiethnic from the start in New Netherland/New York and Pennsylvania, and weakly Catholic in Maryland. Second, the nascent republic embodied in the First Amendment to the Constitution the principle that no federal law should require or prohibit the free exercise of any religion. Legal protections of established churches and sanctions against dissenters were moribund in the West soon after 1800, but the United States raised the nonestablishment of religion into a fundamental principle. Third, the American colonies and the United States, especially but not only in the

---

[72] For examples of thoughtful but traditional historical theologians, see the work of Oswald Bayer and Mark C. Mattes on Luther, and Richard Muller and Paul Helm on Calvin.

[73] In the preface to his *English Reformations: Religion, Politics, and Society under the Tudors* (Oxford, UK, 1993), Christopher Haigh pointed out firmly that he was not a Roman Catholic, despite his spirited arguments for the popularity and durability of Catholicism in sixteenth-century England.

South, shaped their society and their culture around the slave trade and slavery. The terrible dynamics of systematic oppression, humiliation, and disempowerment of African Americans shaped the common culture of the colonies and later the United States for most of their existence.[74]

The fragmented and complex structure of American society had important results for its religious history. The narrative of secularism and of the professionalization of the historical profession sketched out earlier does not describe the American situation as well as the European. West of the Atlantic each religious tradition could develop separately amid a dizzying diversity of proliferating denominations and movements, whether determined by confessional allegiance, formed by the ethnic memory of an immigrant demographic, or shaped by racial selection and/or segregation. The members of each tradition could write their own histories; but only the most ancient, influential, or self-confident would try to write an overall narrative. The winds of secularization that blew so fiercely through Europe in the twentieth century exerted a much weaker effect on American culture in the same period. Although some historians have remarked on "the American religious depression" of the second quarter of the twentieth century, it tends to be assigned to a relatively short period in the 1920s and 1930s. It was then followed by a massive revival in the fortunes of the main church traditions.[75] Structurally as well as temperamentally, American intellectual life has given more support to the intellectual study of religion. Apart from the at times stridently secular atmosphere of university departments of religion, the United States sustains a large and often intellectually distinguished cohort of seminaries and schools of divinity. In such schools academics are under no pressure to explain away religious ideas and spiritual imperatives. They engage in a complex dialogue between critical reflection and confessional commitment that plays out in the histories that they produce. The American context leads historians to write, at least in recent decades, of "religious history" rather than "church history," even when it is predominantly the history of Christianity that is under discussion. Something of an allergy to institutional history, an awareness that religious life is a story of movements as well as structures, may lie behind this semantic trait.

With appropriate caveats, one can construct a provisional trajectory for the prevailing genres of religious history practiced in America. The proto-history of the New England church appeared in 1702 from the hands

[74] David W. Wills, "The Central Themes of American Religious History: Pluralism, Puritanism, and the Encounter of Black and White," *Religion and Intellectual Life* 5:1 (1987): 30–41.

[75] Robert T. Handy, "The American Religious Depression, 1925–1935," *Church History* XXIX (Mar. 1960): 3–16.

of Cotton Mather. *Magnalia Christi Americana* presented a compendious review of the first eighty or so years of the churches in the New England colonies from Plymouth to Connecticut and New Haven.[76] Mather's approach combined the administrative with the providential. On the one hand, in Eusebian manner he supplied sequences of secular governors and prominent religious leaders, synodical structures and rules, and the early history of Harvard College.[77] On the other hand, spectacular providences, remarkable conversions, and "wonders of the invisible world," including possessions, poltergeists, and other marvels, received a whole book.[78] In one sense Mather set some of the standards for those who followed. Although the early New England colonies embraced significantly different attitudes to discipline and ecclesiology, Mather conveyed the impression that the authoritative leaders of the various colonies represented an acceptable Presbyterian-Congregationalist amalgam. Heretics, sectaries, and troublemakers – Familists and Quakers, to name but two – disrupted community life and polity by fomenting internal strife. Again echoing Eusebius' logic, Mather argued that the true church was more or less united, even if dispersed geographically; only heretics and heathens threatened it from outside.[79]

To the extent that Mather constructed the image of a doctrinally and even structurally near-homogeneous entity called Puritan New England, that image proved extraordinarily durable and influential, perhaps beyond even its author's intentions. In succeeding centuries the story of Puritan New England became the master narrative for most Protestant general histories of American religion. Successive great awakenings and the ensuing revivalism unified the culture and spirit of Protestant piety across denominational boundaries. Revivalist Protestantism generated its historian in the form of Robert Baird (1798–1863). Baird, a Presbyterian missionary to Roman Catholics in Europe, published *Religion in America* in 1844. This work treated evangelical, missionary Protestantism as the norm and gave only brief coverage of any other forms of Christianity.[80] Subsequent Protestant church historiography witnessed the gradual expansion and

---

[76] Cotton Mather, *Magnalia Christi Americana: Or, the Ecclesiastical History of New-England, from Its First Planting in the Year 1620 unto the Year of Our Lord, 1698* (London, 1702).
[77] *Ibid.*, books I–V.
[78] *Ibid.*, book VI.
[79] *Ibid.*, book VII.
[80] Robert Baird, *Religion in America: Or an Account of the Origin, Relation to the State, and Present Condition of the Evangelical Churches in the United States: With Notices of the Unevangelical Denominations* (New York, 1844). See discussion in Sydney E. Ahlstrom, "The Problem of the History of Religion in America," *Church History* 39:2 (June 1970): 224–35, esp. 228–9.

broadening of this providentialist Protestant vision to include others outside the fold, while the architecture that made the Puritan story the dominant narrative theme was largely preserved. A follower of Baird, the Methodist Daniel Dorchester (1827–1907) published an eight-hundred-page history entitled *Christianity in the United States* in 1888; although far more compendious and inclusive than its predecessor, it retained many of Baird's preferences.[81]

The classic histories of the twentieth century continued this basic approach with greater subtlety and breadth of vision. At the behest of Philip Schaff (1819–93), a significant pioneer in ecumenical thought, Leonard Woolsey Bacon (1830–1907) published *A History of American Christianity* in 1897.[82] Bacon espoused a version of the providentialist approach, but with a twist. God had kept the Americas concealed for centuries until European Christianity was restored to vigor – but not just in its Protestant forms. The Catholic Reformation, as represented by the Spain of Ferdinand and Isabella, represented as providential a recovery from "decadence" as Protestantism.[83] In some contrast to the older orthodoxies, Bacon could see the hand of Providence even in theological controversy.

> How great is the debt which the church owes to its heretics is frequently illustrated in the progress of Christianity in America. If it had not been for the Unitarian defection in New England, and for the attacks from Germany upon the historicity of the gospels, the theologians of America might to this day have been engrossed in "threshing old straw" in endless debates on "fixed fate, free will, foreknowledge absolute." The exigencies of controversy forced the study of the original documents of the church.[84]

Nevertheless, Bacon's expressed preference for the Congregational-Presbyterian nexus of the Reformed tradition manifested itself, even as he believed he detected signs of growing unity in American Protestantism. All other traditions came in for their measure of critique and censure.

This ecumenically generous but Protestant-centered style of historical writing may have proved especially durable precisely because it did not display vehement sectarian hostility to other traditions and attempted to bring as many of the actors in the story as possible under one tent. Important versions of this narrative appeared in the work of William Warren Sweet (1881–1958), whose *Story of Religion in America* first appeared in 1930. Most influentially in recent decades, Winthrop S. Hudson's *Religion in*

---

[81] Daniel Dorchester, *Christianity in the United States from the First Settlement down to the Present Time* (New York, 1888).

[82] Leonard Woolsey Bacon, *A History of American Christianity* (New York, 1897).

[83] Bacon, *History of American Christianity*, chs. I–II.

[84] *Ibid.*, ch. XXI, p. 378.

America, originally published in 1965, continues to appear in revised editions. Hudson (d. 2001) was a Baptist, and some denominational loyalty and commitment continued to show through in his work.[85] Numerous recent scholars have further revised the general narrative: either they have attenuated or eliminated its theological and providential attributes, or they have broadened the scope of their coverage. Martin E. Marty, in a sequence of works, has presented an ever more encyclopedic and inclusive coverage. Sydney E. Ahlstrom (1919–84) proved to be fully aware that the age of the confessionally Protestant-centered church history was ending, although he himself was one of its last and most subtle practitioners.[86] Robert T. Handy (1918–2009), in a particularly inclusive and ambitious contribution to the Oxford History of the Christian Church series entitled *A History of the Churches in the United States and Canada*, willingly embraced and applauded the end of Protestant hegemony in the United States. He demonstrated how the apparently unassailable position of "mainstream" American Protestantism in the 1950s and early 1960s was to some extent an optical illusion, created by the religious revival of the post–Second World War era, and in any case a transient phenomenon.[87]

As representatives of the Protestant mainstream approach were voluntarily distancing themselves more and more from what had been the standard model for American religious history, new waves of more radical revisionists proposed approaches that stood on its head either the thematic or the confessional focus of the old history. There had already been histories of individual elements of American religion, of Roman Catholicism, of the African American Church, or of American Judaism; but these had generally confined themselves to one particular tradition and did not aspire to shape a broader narrative around their own experience. In reaction against the standard Protestant model, a number of collections of essays appeared that privileged much smaller and hitherto "marginal" groups.[88] Other historians sought to refocus the total narrative, whether toward histories of popular

---

[85] William Warren Sweet, *The Story of Religion in America* (New York, 1930); John Corrigan and Winthrop S. Hudson, *Religion in America: An Historical Account of the Development of American Religious Life*, 8th ed. (Upper Saddle River, NJ, 2010). See observations by Stephen J. Stein, "'Something Old, Something New, Something Borrowed, Something Left to Do': Choosing a Textbook for Religion in America," *Religion and American Culture: A Journal of Interpretation*, 3:2 (Summer 1993): 217–27.

[86] Among many works, see, e.g., Martin E. Marty, *Pilgrims in Their Own Land: 500 Years of Religion in America* (Boston, 1984); Sydney E. Ahlstrom, *A Religious History of the American People*, 2nd ed. (New Haven, 2004); note also Ahlstrom's comments in "Problem of the History of Religion," n80.

[87] Robert T. Handy, *A History of the Churches in the United States and Canada* (Oxford, UK, 1976).

[88] Especially Thomas A. Tweed, ed., *Retelling U.S. Religious History* (Berkeley, 1997).

religious practice or by redistributing coverage more toward smaller, more marginal, and more fragmented movements. The immigration of large numbers from Asia, increasing the numbers of Americans from outside the Judaeo-Christian traditions, gave further urgency to this task.[89]

The recent historiography of American religion manifests an unusual but potentially fruitful level of controversy and debate over methods and approaches. Historians of American Protestantism argue over whether the most important story to tell in the late nineteenth and early twentieth century is the divide between doctrinal conservatives, on one hand, and higher-critical social liberals, on the other.[90] Responses to the Puritan story – still an unavoidable theme even if no longer the dominant narrative – range from the disapproval of multiculturalists to the neoconservative lament for the loss of old certainties.[91] Radical revisionist approaches raise the methodological concern that moving the center of religious history away from the old narratives may simply mean substituting one unreasonable focus on an unrepresentative group for another. Too much stress on reading the documents of the past through the modern lenses of race, class, and gender invites the challenge that many of these documents had all too little to say on those topics. At an even deeper level, historians have yet to resolve whether and in what sense a viable central theme for American religious history can ever be identified again.[92] The disciplinary divide between the secular historian and the theologically informed, seminary-based scholar continues to shape the rhetoric of the discipline in a way almost unimaginable outside the United States. Statements such as these, highly charged with faith commitment, appeared in works published in the last fifteen years.

> To understand how to treasure what was right and good in that complex past, and how to abandon what was wrong or outdated, will take all the wisdom and guidance which Christians seek in their worship of God as known in Jesus Christ.[93]
>
> Perhaps if Christians evaluate the history of recent decades honestly, they might find it easier to concede their need for the Great Physician.[94]

---

[89] Catherine L. Albanese, *America: Religions and Religion*, 2nd ed. (Belmont, 1992); Peter W. Williams, *America's Religions: Traditions and Cultures* (New York, 1990).

[90] See the essays in Douglas Jacobsen and William Vance Trollinger, Jr., eds., *Re-Forming the Center: American Protestantism, 1900 to the Present* (Grand Rapids, 1998).

[91] See the remarks of Amanda Porterfield in "Forum: Is There a Center to American Religious History?" *Church History* 71:2 (June 2002): 369–73.

[92] See, in general, *ibid.*, 368–90.

[93] Handy, *History of the Churches*, 427.

[94] Mark A. Noll, *A History of Christianity in the United States and Canada* (Grand Rapids, 1992), 552.

Religious history remains, as it has always been, in a tense, sensitive, but often productive dialogue with the faith commitments that it studies and recounts. It continues to challenge those same claims by its testimony to the complexity of human motives, and to the profound uncertainty of why human events unfold as they do.

SUGGESTIONS FOR FURTHER READING

Ahlstrom, Sydney E. *A Religious History of the American People.* 2nd ed. New Haven, 2004.

Cameron, Euan. *Interpreting Christian History: The Challenge of the Churches' Past.* Oxford, UK, 2005.

Corrigan, John, and Winthrop S. Hudson. *Religion in America: An Historical Account of the Development of American Religious Life.* 8th ed. Upper Saddle River, NJ, 2010.

Dickens, A. G., and John Tonkin, with Kenneth Powell. *The Reformation in Historical Thought.* Cambridge, MA, 1985.

Handy, Robert T. *A History of the Churches in the United States and Canada.* Oxford, UK, 1976.

Marty, Martin E. *Pilgrims in Their Own Land: 500 Years of Religion in America.* Boston, 1984.

Scherer, Emil Clemens. *Geschichte und Kirchengeschichte an den deutschen Universitäten: Ihre Anfänge im Zeitalter des Humanismus und ihre Ausbildung zu sebständigen Disziplinen.* Freiburg im Breisgau, 1927.

Williams, Peter W. *America's Religions: Traditions and Cultures.* New York, 1990.

INDEX

Abbad y Lasierra, Agustin Iñigo, 647
Abbott, George, 89, 90
Aboriginals of Australia, 10, 15
above world (Mississippian tradition), 142–3, 144, 147, 148–9, 153
The Accomplished Singer sermon (Cotton), 717
Acosta, José de, 185
Act for Preserving the Church of England in New Brunswick (Canada) (1786), 620
Act of Toleration (1649), xvi, 225, 335, 337
Acts and Monuments (Foxe), 77, 835
Adams, Hannah, 507, 666
Adams, John, 490
  concerns about religious blasphemy charges, 499
  fasting days ordered by, 607
  letter to son (John Quincy Adams), 495
  meeting with Witherspoon, 580
  religious beliefs of, 492, 493, 504, 602
  viewpoint of church-state separation, 599
  views of religious liberty, 545
Adams, John Quincy (son of John Adams), 495
Addison, Joseph, 716
Africa and Africans in the Making of the Atlantic World (Thornton), 106
African Orthodox Church, 794
African religious traditions, 96–109. *See also* African slave religions; slavery (slave trade)

ancestor veneration, 100
archaeological information, 96–7
"black veiled nuns," 193
burial rituals, 702, 703–4
calendrical rituals, 702
in the Carolinas, 340–1
Christian conversions, 107
Christian traditions, 106–8
Church of England and, 335
class-/race-based religious hierarchy, 193
confraternities, 198
cosmogonist myths, 97, 98
divinatory methods, 101–2, 701
ethnic group specificity, 99
healing practices, 370
influence in the Caribbean, 190
Islam/Muslim traditions, 96, 103–5, 335
in the Middle Colonies, 325–6
missionaries in, 33, 96
New World origins, xv
"Obaye" (supernatural healing) practices, 701
oral traditions, 97, 98
passive infanticide, 703
plantation colonies (to 1800), 700–4
religious preachers, 668
"ring shout" song and dance rituals, 334
rituals/rites of passage, 102–3
sacred authority, 100–1
sorcery, 99–100
Supreme Being, 97–8, 102

851

African slave religions (pre-Columbian
    era to 1600), 369–75
  Catholicism/Iberian Christians, 374–5
  divination practices, 371
  healing practices, 370
  Islam component, 372
  origins/diversity of, xvii
African slave religions (1600 to 1700),
    375–80
  anti-Christianization slaveholder
    attitude, 377–9
  Catholic conversions, 379–80
  Christianization of slaves, 376
  laws governing slaves, 377
  New England, 376–7
African slave religions (1700 to 1900),
    380–91
  Anglican revivalism, 390
  Capuchin missionary activity, 387
  Catholicism, 385
  drumming, dancing rituals, 382
  forcible Christianization attempts, 389
  Moravian Christian missionaries, 384–5
  Orisha religion, 388
  revivalist Christianity, 384, 390, 453
  rituals for influencing others, 381
  SPG Anglican missionaries, 380–2, 384
Age of Reason (Paine), 490
"Agreements of the Family" (France-
    Spanish Bourbons), 635
Ahlstrom, Sydney E., 847
Ainsworth, Henry, 713, 722
Aitken, John, 420
Aitken, Robert, 597
Alexander VI (Pope, 1492–1513), 35, 177
Alexandrinus, Clemens, 554
Algonquian Native Americans.
    See also Eastern Algonquians,
    Eighteenth Century
  absorption into Haudenosaunee/Iroquois
    confederacy, 114
  burial practices, 7
  calendrical rituals, 688–9
  Cautantouwit and Hobbomok (spirits),
    687–8
  dreams, vision quests, soul-wanderings,
    688
  life-cycle rituals, 689–90

manitou (notion of power), xvi, 11, 123,
    352, 354
  powwows, 688
  religious/spiritual practices (southern
    New England), 687–90
  trees, inanimate/animate states of, 12
Alleine, Richard, 558
Allen, Ethan, 490, 684
Allen, Richard, 668
Alline, Henry, 617, 622–3, 678
Alocoque, Margaret Mary, 763
Alphabetical Compendium of the Various Sects
    (Hannah Adams), 507
Alta California Franciscan missions, 251,
    258–9, 262
Althusius, Johannes, 59
Alva Ixtlilxochitl, Fernando de, 188
America, post-American Revolution
    transition
  changing religion-state relationship,
    590–1
  full citizenship for RI Jews, 589
  George Washington's religious
    background, 589–90, 602
  influence of Protestant Reformation, 598
  Middle Colonies religious
    diversity, 591
  Second Great Awakening (1799–1805),
    599, 726, 763, 791
  self-sustaining voluntary church, 591–2
American Baptist Foreign Mission Society
    (1814), 507
American Board of Commissioners for
    Foreign Missions (1812), 507
American Colonization Society, 773
American Episcopal Prayer Book
    (1789), 706
American Revolution, 59, 70,
    433, 570–87. *See also* America,
    post-American Revolution transition
  "America as chosen people" theme, 578
  Battle of Brandywine (1777), 588
  Boucher's suicide threat to
    congregation, 571
  Burke's explanation for, 573–4
  Canada's rejection of, 610, 615–18
  as "the cause of heaven against Hell"
    (Keteltas), 576

Church of England threats to America,
572–3
civil religion created by, 583–4
clash of secular vs. sacred conceptions
(post-war), 587
confrontation of Quakers, 582
Days of Thanksgiving, 581
Enlightenment ideas, 586
evangelicals and, 464–5, 583
Fast Days, 575, 578, 581, 582
"God's providence" theme, 576–7
Great Awakening, influence of, 464
Henry's treasonous speech, 573
influences on religion, 582–4, 588
Jews and, 406–9, 585
ministerial support for, 575–6, 588
ministers as politicians, 580–1
obedience to government as obedience
to God, 575
Old Testament and, 578–9
Oliver's observation of religious
dissent, 574
onset of church-state separation, 584
optimism of religious leaders
(post-war), 586
patriot sermons, 577
post-war dissent, 584–5
"public vices" portrayal of Britain, 577–8
Quebec Act (1774), 546, 573
religion Americanized by, 583
religion in the halls of Congress, 581
religious groups spawned by, 585–6
religious symbols, 581–2
sacred music in praise of, 725–7
soldiers' supported by religion, 579–80
Stamp Act (1765), 448, 575
Sugar Act (1764), 448
Townshend Duties (1767), 448
transition to the New Nation, 588–608
United States declared as
"New Israel," 575
American Secular Union, 496
American Southeast, 259–60
American Southwest, 257–9.
See also Anasazi culture; Arizona;
Hopi Native Americans; Navajo
Native Americans; New Mexico;
Pueblo Native Americans; Texas

Alta California Franciscan missions,
251, 258–9, 262
Jesuit missionaries, 252
Spanish missions, 251, 730
Texas, 257–8
tribal cultures, 819–20
American Sunday School Union
(1824), 766
American Tract Society (1825), 766,
767–70
American Unitarian Association, 494
"America's Scripture." See Bill of Rights;
Constitution (U.S.); Washington,
George
Amerindian Church, 209
Amerindians. See also French Catholicism
assimilation of French rituals, 204
baptism of, 200, 210
Capuchin missionary work with, 208
Champlain's *petun* smoking with, 201
epidemics, 202, 210, 215
Iroquois raids against, 201–2
Jesuit missionary work with, 208–9
obstacles in dealing with, 209
Recollet missionary work with, 207–8
segregation from the French, 213
Amish, 65, 442
formal theology produced by, 663
Pennsylvania presence, 442
Quaker interaction with, 563
Radical Reformation hymnody
used by, 720
separation from the Mennonites, 679
strict practices of, 486
Amman, Jacob, 442, 486
Amrinians/Arminianism, 554, 565.
See also Fletcher, John; Owens, John
described, 92, 583, 676
ministerial curiosity about, 290
rise of, 91
Synopd of Dort condemnation, 89
Anabaptists (re-baptizers), 52, 62–6.
See also Amish; Mennonites (Dutch
Anabaptists)
adult baptism practice, 316, 471
contributions to the New World, 70–1
Pennsylvania presence, 442–3
Pietism relation to, 67, 322

Anabaptists (re-baptizers) (*cont.*)
  pre-Columbian era religious thought, 677–9
  Roman Catholics comparison, 64
  Simons' restoration of, 63–4
  Swiss-German roots, 63
Anasazi America (Stuart), 167
Anasazi culture, 156–75
  archaeological/oral background, 156–7, 158
  astronomical knowledge, 159–60
  Basketmaker II, Basketmaker III periods, 157, 159
  dwellings/living spaces, xiii–xiv, 157–8, 163, 752–3
  identity background, 157
  katsina religion, 161–2, 164, 168–72
  Kokopelli (rain/fertility) deity, 160–2
  Maasaw (guardian deity), 173–4
  Mexico, importance of contact with, 158–9
  name derivation, 156
  oral transmission of ideas, 162
  planting/harvesting rituals, 159
  Tanama ("The Trembling God") deity, 164–7
  Tlaloc (rain/fertility) deity, 160–2, 180
ancestor veneration
  African religious traditions, 100, 102, 107, 370, 375
  Andean culture, 190
  Chinese culture, 814
  Mississippian culture, 138
  Native American culture, 4, 13, 353–4, 670, 819
Ancestral Puebloans. *See* Anasazi culture
"And am I born to die?" hymn (Watts), 724
Andean customs/religions, 190–1
Anderson, Alexander, 769
Andrewes, Lancelot, 88, 89
Andros, Edmund, 235, 283, 435, 535. *See also* Glorious Revolution
  dictatorial powers in New England, 283
  overthrow of (1689), 283
An Earnest Appeal to Men of Reason and Religion (Wesley), 556
"Anglican Apostasy" (1722), 435

Anglicans/Anglicanism. *See also* Berkeley, William; Burnaby, Andrew; Society for the Propagation of the Gospel (SPG)
  African slaves (1700 to 1900), 390
  antirevivalists, 438, 445
  belief in America's special destiny, 542
  in Boston, MA, 284, 300
  burial rituals, 700
  calendrical rituals, 699
  Calvin/Calvinism and, 56
  Carleton's efforts in Canada, 613–14
  Carolina presence, 338, 339, 381, 383–4, 432, 446–8
  Delaware presence, 309
  development of Christian ideas, 790–1
  Divine Service practice, 697
  domestic private devotional practices, 698
  English Presbyterians and, 288
  folk magic and, 521
  formal theology produced by, 663
  life-cycle rites of passage, 699
  Maryland presence, 337, 338
  Middle Colonies presence, 308–10
  Native American conversions, 332, 334, 380
  New England church architecture, 732–3
  New England Congregationalists vs., 436
  New Netherland presence, 220–4
  Pennsylvania presence, 439–44
  pre-Columbian era religious thought, 672–3
  priesthood ordination, 331
  psalms used in worship, 712
  Puritanism and, 82, 301, 328–9, 331
  Quakers and, 222
  Queen Elizabeth and, 202
  religious/spiritual practices (to 1800), 695–700
  resistance to slave Christianization, 788
  Rhode Island presence, 300
  royalist type of, 221–2
  sabbath practices, 696
  sacred music (psalters), 715
  Southern colony depiction of, 599–600

Virginia presence, 204, 221–2, 226, 328–9, 330, 381, 430–3, 436, 448–50
animatism (Marett), 10
animism theory (Tylor), 9–10, 11, 123, 124–6
antebellum era (1800–1860)
    Christianization and degradation, 789–94
    heart religion beliefs and practices, 759–66
Antes, John, 721
antinomianism, 232, 234
Antonio Abad (Saint), 245
Apache culture, 168
    ancestral rites, 4
    corpse disposal, 7
    oral traditions, 157
Apess, William, 791
Apology (Barclay), 472
archaeological evidence of Native American religion/spirituality, 22–3
Archaic Period (c. 3,500 years ago), 22
architecture (religious architecture), 728–46
    American evangelism "megachurch" style, 739
    Anglican New England churches, 732–3
    Arts and Crafts movement–inspired theme, 736
    Buddhist temples, 744–5
    cathedrals, 736–7
    Christian Science/"Mother Church" revival style, 738
    Gothic style revival churches, 735–6
    Greek revival style, 734–5
    Hindu temples, 742–4
    Jewish synagogues, 740–2
    Liturgical Movement style, 739
    Modernism style, 734–5, 738
    Mormon temples, 740
    Muslim/Islamic architecture, 745–6
    Navajo single-family dwellings, 729
    neoclassic style, 734
    New France/late Renaissance themes, 730
    Northern impermanent vs. Southern permanent structures, 728
    Plains Indians ad hoc building techniques, 728–9
    Protestant institutional churches, 737–8
    Pueblo stone/adobe brick houses, 729
    Puritan meetinghouses, 733–4
    Quaker meetinghouses, 740
    Shaker meetinghouses, 740
    Spanish mission churches, 731
    Wren-Gibbs baroque style, 732, 733–4
arendiouwane (Iroquois shamanic practitioners), 123
Arizona. *See also* Anasazi culture; Hopi Native Americans; Navajo Native Americans; Pueblo Native Americans
    Bourbon reforms, 653–4
    Franciscan missions, 730
    hogan living units, 729
    Jesuit missionary presence, 252
    Mission of San Xavier del Bac, 654
    Mogollon culture, 161
Arminians/Arminianism, 554, 565. *See also* Fletcher, John; Owens, John
    described, 92, 583, 676
    ministerial curiosity about, 290
    rise of, 91
    Synod of Dort condemnation, 89
Arndt, Johann, 551–2, 760
Arnold, Benedict, 616
Arnold, Gottfried, 719, 838
Arnold, John, 722
Articles of Confederation (1977), 596–7, 605
Asbury, Francis, 624
Ashbridge, Elizabeth, 473
Ashkenazic Jews, xvii, 395, 663, 683–4. *See also* Jews/Judaism
astrology practices
    New England, 516, 517, 518
    Society of the Woman in the Wilderness, 322
Athabaskan Navajo, 157
Atlantic community evangelical awakenings, 550–69
    bridge between Europe and America, 559–60
    characteristic marks of revivals, 566–7
    European roots, 551–3
    Great Britain movements, 553–6
    post-1750 movements, 563–5

Augsburg Confession (1530), 55, 224
Augustines Hospitalières de la Miséricorde-de-Jésus of the Hôtel-Dieu of Québec, 266, 269
Augustinians (mendicant order), 33, 179–81, 192
Ausbund: Etliche schone christliche Gesang [Paragon: Some Beautiful Christian Songs], 720
Austin, Ann, 681
Aztec peoples, 651
   learning of sacred music, 709
   religious conversions, 33
   temple complexes (Tenochtitlán), 728

Babylonian Captivity (1303–78), 35
Bach, Christian Friedrich, 721
Backus, Isaac, 459–60, 469, 474–6, 545, 678
Bacon, Leonard Woolsey, 846
Bagwell, Beth, 163
Baird, Robert, 845
BaKongo people (Africa), 99
Bakweri ethnic group (Africa), 99
Bambara, Samba, 388
Bancroft, Richard (Bishop of London), 83, 88
Bangs, Nathan, 625
baptisms
   of adults, by Baptists/Anabaptists, 316, 471
   of African slaves, 297–8, 383–4
   of Amerindians, 200, 210
   of Eastern Algonquians, 367
   infant baptism, 468
   of Native Americans, 334, 367, 380
   rules for children, 285, 286–7
Baptists. *See also* Backus, Isaac; New Light evangelicals; Old Lights (anti-evangelicals); Stearns, Shubal
   adult baptism as rite of entry, 316
   in the Carolinas, 340
   early American settlements, 56
   formal theology produced by, 663
   Freewill Baptists, 477
   General/Particular Baptists, 230
   German Baptist Brethren, 67
   imprisonment for tax evasion, 469
   infant baptism, 468
   in the Middle Colonies (1680–1730), 315–17
   Native American converts, 297
   Particular Baptists, 230, 474
   pre-Columbian era religious thought, 677–9
   problems faced by, 316
   Puritan opposition to, 535
   Rhode Island congregations, 230, 298
   Separate Baptists, 439, 460–1, 468, 470, 473–6
   Seventh-Day Baptists, 468–9, 476–7
Barclay, Robert, 313, 472, 681
Barlow, Joel, 490
bar mitzvah tradition (Judaism), 804
Baro, Peter, 88
Baronio, Cesare ("Caesar Baronius"), 837
Barrett, William, 88
Barth, Karl, 841–2
Bartkowski, John P., 812
Basketmaker II, Basketmaker III (Anasazi periods), 157, 159
Baxter, Richard, 554
Bayley, Daniel, 723
Bear Ceremonialism, 18
beatas (women hermits, visionaries, spiritual guides), 194
beaterios (saintly houses) for women, 192–3
Beatty, Charles, 366
Beauvais, Vincent de, 829
Becker, Peter, 322, 484
Beguine/Beghard monastic communities, 34
Beissel, Conrad, 485, 486–8, 682, 684, 720
Bellamy, Joseph, 676
Benavides, Ambrosio de, 646, 671
Beneath World (Mississippian tradition), 142–3, 144, 146, 147–8, 153
Benedectine monastic tradition (Catholic Church), 34, 641, 739, 832. *See also* Abbad y Lasierra, Agustin Iñigo
Benedict, David, 506–7
Benedict XIV (Pope), 250

Benezet, Anthony, 472
Benneville, George de, 479, 682–3
Berkeley, George, 672
Berkeley, William, 221–2, 226
Berkmeyer, William, 680
Bernardo (Saint), 245
Bertholf, Guiliam, 445
Bethune, John, 622
Beveridge, William, 554
Beza, Theodore, 59
Bible, New Testament
    Anabaptists and, 64
    Book of Revelation, 43, 531, 542, 835
    Catholic teaching origins, 42
    Christ's teachings vs. Seven Deadly Sins, 44
    Luther's recovery of teachings, 54
    promise of salvation, 56
    use of against Puritans by Protestants, 86
Bible, Old Testament
    American Revolution and, 578–9
    biblical jousting/segregation issue, 798
    Book of Chronicles (King James version), 578
    Calvinism and, 56–7
    Catholic teaching origins, 42
    Genesis verses related to slavery, 789
    images of Gustave Dore, 774
    prophecy regarding Ethiopia, 795
Bibles
    first U.S. printing, 597
    justification for slavery, 785–6
    promotion of family values, 805
Bigot, Jacques, 271
Bigot, Vincent, 276
"Bill for Establishing Religious Freedom" (Jefferson), 464
Billings, William, 725–7
Bill of Rights, 407, 500, 584
Birdman (Mississippian tradition), 144, 148–50
Black, William, 624–5
The Black Christ and Other Poems (Countee Cullen), 772
"black drink" (in corn ceremony), 26
Blair, James, 222

The Bloody Tenent of Persecution for the Cause of Conscience Discussed (Williams), 227
The Bloody Tenent Yet More Bloudy (Williams), 227
Blount, Charles, 490
body of Christ (*corpus christianorum*), 39, 46, 679
Boehler, Peter, 553
Boehm, Anton, 553
Boehm, Martin, 563
Bogardus, Everardus, 223
Bohemian Brothers (Unity of the Brethren/*Unitas Fratrum*), 67–8
Bonaparte, Napoleon, 634, 636
Bonifacius, or Essays To Do Good (Cotton Mather), 557–8
Book (Moore), 473
Book of Architecture (Gibbs), 732
The Book of Common Prayer (Anglican worship psalms), 712
"Book of Martyrs." *See Acts and Monuments* (Foxe)
The Book of Psalmes: Englished both in Prose and Metre (Ainsworth), 713
Book of Revelation (New Testament), 43, 531, 542, 835
Borda, José de la, 243
"born again" Christians, 54, 64, 452
Bosa ethnic group (Africa), 100–1
Bosanquet, Mary, 562
Boston, MA
    Anglican presence, 284, 300
    arrival of Quakers (1656), 229
    baptism of slaves, 297–8
    Baptist Church (1718), 298
    Boston Association (1690), 291–2
    Chauncy's antirevival sentiments, 457
    Christ Church, 732
    Christian Science "Mother Church," 738
    Congregational/other churches, 284, 435
    Davenport's move to First Church, 234
    persecution/hanging of Quakers, 590–1
Boston Massacre (1770), 571
Boston Tea Party (1773), 546, 571, 578, 614
Boucher, Jonathan, 571, 575

Bourbon reforms in Spanish America
  (1750–1790), 634–60
  "Agreements of the Family"
    (France-Spanish Bourbons), 635
  Borderlands, 651–3
  California, 654–7
  Carlos III (King of Spain), 635–6, 639,
    642, 644, 652
  Carlos IV (King of Spain), 636
  Catholicism (popular and/or otherwise),
    638–9
  Cuba, 636, 647–9
  Enlightenment Despotism, 637–8, 639
  expulsion of Society of Jesus, 641–3, 649
  fiestas (feast days), 639
  Florida, 636, 649–50
  geopolitical background, 634–6
  influence of George III (of England),
    635, 636
  Louisiana, 635, 650–1
  mestizaje culture, 637
  patterns of reform and resistance, 644
  Puerto Rico, 636, 646–7
  religion, race, and nationhood, 636–8
  Santo Domingo, 644–5
  Texas, New Mexico, Arizona, 653–4
  theology as ideology, 639–41
  Treaty of Fountainbleau (1762), 635
  Treaty of Ryswick (1697), 644
  Tupac Amaru II Revolt (1780), 657–9
Bourbons (French Bourbons), 241,
  256–7, 262
Boyl, Bernal (Apostolic Vicar to the New
  World), 178
Bradley, Bruce, 172
Bradshaw, William, 89
Bradstreet, Anne Dudley, 666
Brady, Nicholas, 716
Brainerd, David, 358, 360, 361, 365, 367
Brandywine, Battle of (1777), 588
Brant, Joseph (Native American chief), 630
Brattle, Thomas, 435
Brattle Street Church (Massachusetts), 290
Bray, Thomas, 333, 553, 672
Breda, Treaty of (1667), 271
Brent, George Wilson, 795
Breuer, Marcel, 739
Brewster, William, 713

Briand, Jean-Olivier, 612, 615, 616–17
Briefe and true Report (Harriot), 204
Brooks, Phillips, 736
Broughton, Thomas, 507
Brown, John, 771
Brunnholtz, Peter, 680
Bryan, Andrew, 668
Bryan, Hugh, 461
Buchanan, George, 59
Buckminster, Joseph, 508
Buddhism, 29, 742, 744–5, 815–16
Bulkeley, Peter, 673
Bullinger, Heinrich, 833
bultos (sculpted figures) of New Spain,
  753–6
burial traditions. *See also* death
  African religious traditions, 702
  burial mounds, 6, 117
  double burials, 6, 7
  gravesites, Archaic Period (ca. 3,500
    years ago), 22
  Native Americans, 6–7, 22, 116–17, 705
  of slaves, 702, 703–4
Burke, Edmund, 573–4
Burnaby, Andrew
  comments on his travels, 429
  Congregationalism description, 435
  Pennsylvania visit, 439–40
  remarks on the Church of England, 435
  Virginia visit, 430–2, 450
burning at the stake, 185, 196
Bush, George H. W., 811
Bush, George W., 737
Butler, Jon, 465
Byles, Mather, 726

Caballero, José Agustin, 649
Cabrera, Miguel, 243
Cadillac, Lamothe (Antoine Laumet), 276
Caesarius of Heisterbach, 829
calendrical rituals
  African religions, 101, 702
  Algonquian Native Americans, 688–9
  Anglicans, 699
  Puritans, 691, 693–4
California
  Alta California Franciscan missions,
    251, 258–9, 262

Bourbon reforms, 654–7
  mission system architecture, 730
  Native American shamans, 22
A Calm Address to Our American Colonies (Johnson), 564
Calusa chiefdom (southwestern Florida), 23–5
Calvert, Benedict Leonard, 417
Calvert, George (Lord Baltimore), 225, 410, 413
Calvin, John
  economic contributions, 59–62
  Institutes of the Christian Religion, 56
  Luther's friendship with, 55
  political contributions, 58–9
  and the role of the will, 42
Calvinists/Calvinism (Calvinist Reformation), 55–62.
    See also Edwards, Jonathan; Evans, Caleb; Newton, John; Toplady, Augustus; Whitefield, George
  Adam's rejection of predestination doctrine, 602
  beliefs of John Adams about, 492
  in the Carolinas, 342–3
  Congregational Calvinists, 673–6
  contributions to the New World, 70–1
  covenant theology of, 56–8
  Eastern Algonquian missions, 360
  educational contributions, 62
  evangelical Calvinism, 89, 90
  formal theology produced by, 663
  Jefferson's anti-Calvinist views, 504
  New England material culture developments, 756–9
  political legacy, 58–9
  predestinarianism, 88, 92, 222
  reformed covenant theology of, 57
  resistance to established authority (concept), 59
  Scottish Calvinists as heartfelt religion, 551
  secular covenant theology of, 57
Cambridge Camden (or Ecclesiological) Society, 735
Cambridge Platform (1648), 293
Campbell, Ted, 551

Canada (1759–1815), 610–32.
    See also New France colonies (in North America)
  Acadia/Nova Scotia settlements, 611, 617, 618, 623–4
  Algonquian Native American presence, 687
  Alline/revivalism, 617
  American invasion of Niagara Peninsula/ Toronto, 626
  American Revolution, rejection of, 610, 615–18
  anti-Catholic sentiments, 613, 617
  architectural themes, 730
  Briand's priesthood, 612, 615, 616–17
  British command of, 611–15
  British Wesleyan church, 626
  Carleton's governorship, 613–14
  Christian society leadership by Inglis, Mountain, and Strachan, 620–1
  Church of England establishment, 612, 620
  Franklin/Carroll's visit (1776), 616
  Genesee Conference, 626
  influence of American Revolution, 618
  Lipset's comparison with United States, 610–11
  Loyalist agitation/creation of separate colonies, 618–19
  Macdonell's Catholic priesthood, 627
  Methodist expansion, 624–5
  Murray's governorship, 612, 614
  Native American conversions, 629
  Native religions, 628–30
  Newfoundland religious workers, 631
  New Light revivalism, 622–3
  onset of religious pluralism, 619
  Plessis/Catholic Quebec bishop, 627, 631
  Presbyterian expansion, 622
  Presbyterians vs. Catholics, 613
  Protestant expansionism, 618, 619, 622, 629–30
  Quebec Act (1774), 546, 573, 614, 617
  rejection of America, 610, 615–18, 625–8
  religious origins, xviii
  Roman Catholics, 611

Canada (1759–1815) (cont.)
  SPG work in, 629
  Strachan's leadership, 620–1, 626
  support for Protestant monarchy, 615
  Test Act exemption, 614
  U.S. Congress authorization of Quebec invasion, 615–16
  War of 1812, 628
cannibalism, 127, 184
canon law judicial system, 36, 86, 181
Cantares Mexicanos [Mexican Songs] (Sahagùn), 709
Capistrano, Giovanni, 828
Capuchins (mendicant order, Italy), 34
  Indies missionary work, 179–81, 192
  New France missionary work, 206, 207, 208, 266, 277
Carillo de Mendoza y Pimentel, Diego, 247
Carion, Johannes, 833
Carleton, Guy, 613–14
Carlos III (Bourbon King of Spain), 635–6, 639, 642, 644, 652
Carlos IV (King of Spain), 636
Carlyle, David, 576
Carmelites (mendicant order)
  Discalced (Barefoot) Carmelites, 193
  importance of formation, 33
  Indies missionary work, 192
Carolina (North/South Carolina) religious diversity (1680s–1730s)
  African traditions, 340–1
  Algonquian Native American presence, 687
  Anglican presence, 338, 339, 381, 383–4, 432, 446–8, 696
  baptism of African slaves, 383–4
  Baptist/Lutheran presence, 340
  Calvinists/Huguenot presence, 339, 342–3
  church architectural style, 732
  Church of England, 341
  Dunker presence, 485
  eighteenth century, early years, 342–4
  Florida–South Carolina border issue, 537
  folk magic, 514
  Huguenots migration to, 533
  Jewish presence, 338–9
  Moravian Christian missionaries, 384–5
  post-Revolution religious tolerance, 593
  Presbyterian presence, 342–3
  Protestant only state offices, 596
  Puritan/Presbyterian presence, 340
  Quaker presence, 340, 341
  religious diversity, xvi
  religious toleration in, 595
  Separate Baptist missionary work, 460
  SPG school opening attempts, 383
Carrasco, David, 160
Carroll, Charles "of Annapolis" (1702–82), 416
Carroll, Charles "of Carrollton" (1737–1832), 417
Carroll, Charles "the Settler" (1660–1720), 416
Carroll, John, 410, 413, 422, 616, 671, 734
Carter, Robert "King," 733
Cartier, Jacques, 120, 131, 203, 204
Cartwright, Thomas, 83
Case, William, 625
castas (people of mixed ancestry), in New Spain, 244
A Catalogue of Witnesses to the Truth, who before our time cried out against the Pope (Illyricus), 834
Cathar *perfecti* (medieval French monks), 31
Catholic Church. See English Catholicism; French Catholicism; Roman Catholicism; Spanish Catholicism; Tridentine Catholicism
Catholick Christian Instructed (Challoner), 425
Cautantouwit and Hobbomok (Algonquian spirits), 687–8
Cayuga nation, 113
celibacy
  Beissel/Dunkers and, 485
  Ephrata Cloister and, 487
  Jemima Wilkinson and, 482
  Mother Ann Lee and, 480, 481
  Munsee all-female community, 368
Central Africans, Atlantic Creoles, and the Foundation of the Americas, 1585–1660 (Thornton & Heywood), 108

Chaderton, Laurence, 88
Challoner, Richard, 420, 425
Champion, Judah, 593
Champlain, Samuel de, xiv, 201–2, 207–8
Chandler, Thomas Bradbury, 673
Channing, William Ellery, 489, 494, 508
Charles I (King of England), 433–4
Charles II (King of England), 229, 418, 440, 470
"Charter of Liberties and Privileges" (1683), 418
Chartier de Lotbinière, Michel, 615
Chauncy, Charles, 457, 458, 493, 504, 540, 676, 683
Checkley, John, 672
Chesapeake colonies. See Maryland; Virginia
children
    baptism rules for, 285, 286–7
    role in revival movement, 562
Children of the Twilight: Folk-Tales of Indian Tribes (Squier), 164
Childs, Craig, 161, 162, 164
Chinese Exclusion Act (1882), 782, 801
Chinese religions/Confucianism, 744, 814–15
Chinook Native Americans, 11
A Choice Collection of Hymns and Spiritual Songs (Occom), 711
Christ. See Jesus Christ
Christian historical writing genre, 826–8
Christian Humanism, 37
Christianity
    African traditions, 96, 106–8
    Anglican resistance to slave Christianization, 788
    "born again" Christians, 54, 64, 452
    Eastern Orthodox Christians, 737
    Eastern/Western medieval church manifestations, 566
    Eucharist/confession participation, 31
    functions of priests, 31
    historical background, 825
    historical writing genre, 826–8
    incarnate Christ as model of virtue, 44–5
    Indian Christianity, 3, 294–5, 296, 297–8
    indigenous population fears of, 182
    "Kill the Indian, Save the Man" motto, 782
    legalization of (313 C.E.), 29
    loss of "whiteness," 789–94
    post-1520 fragmentation, 41
    post-romantic church history, 840–1
    racialization fostered/undermined by, 782–3
    Radical Reformation, 62
    rationale for slavery, 214–15
    reach of (ca. 1500), 29
    Rogel/Calusa chiefdom and, 23–5
    Ten Commandments (moral code), 44
    Trinitarian Christians, 225
Christianity as Old as Creation: Or, The Gospel a Republication of the Religion of Nature (Tindal), 490
Christianity in the United States (Dorchester), 846
Christianity not Mysterious: Or, A Treatise Shewing that There is Nothing in the Gospel Contrary to Reason, Nor Above It (Toland), 490
Christian Scientists, 738
Chubb, Thomas, 490
Church (Roman Catholic Church). See Roman Catholicism
Church of England, 62, 77, 79, 289, 338. See also Tillotson, John
    in the Carolinas, 341
    as casualty of American Revolution, 582
    challenges to Congregationalism hegemony, 300–1
    disowned, by New England "Separatists," 226
    establishment in Canada, 612, 620
    Horneck's promotion of, 553
    John Wesley's connection to, 553
    Laudinism reform movement, 91–5
    obstacles in New England, 301
    persecution of believers, 86
    prejudices against women, 562
    Protestant tradition relation to, 85
    psalters authorized by, 712
    Puritan break from, 230–1, 691
    relation to Church of Rome, 93
    stance against magic, 520
    threats to New World, 572–3
    Virginia settlements, 328–9, 330, 335, 430–3

Church of Nuestra Señora de los Remedios
  (sacred site), 190
Church of Rome, 53, 77, 93, 594, 835
Church of the Brethren (aka Dunkers/
  Dunkards and German Baptist
  Brethren), xviii, 65, 67, 322, 469,
  470, 476, 484–5
"Church Pietism" (Ward), 552
church-state separation, 495–502
  differing views about, 498, 598–9
  National Liberal League/American
    Secular union demands for, 496
  onset during American Revolution, 584
  Paine's religious beliefs, 492, 495
  religious liberty/equality tested by Jews,
    500–2
  viewpoints of Jefferson and Madison,
    497, 599
Cistercian monastic tradition, 34
civil rights era (1860s–1960s), 782, 797
Civil War
  Native American post-war treatment,
    796, 798
  post-war era of scientific racism, 786
  post-war Native American changes, 154
  post-war race and religion, 794–7
  slavery ended by, 335
Clap, Nathan, 360
Clap, Roger, 692
Clarke, John, 677–8
Claviero, Javier de, 242
Clavijero, Francisco Javier, 643
Clay, Henry, 772–3
Clement XIV (Pope), 410
Clinton, Bill, 811
Coahuiltecan Indians, peyote rituals, 25
Coddington, William, 227
Codrington, Bishop R. H., 10
Coetus-Conferentie dispute, 445
cofradías (religious confraternities), 49,
  244, 249, 374, 638
Colbert, Jean-Baptists, 272
Cole, Edward, 512
Cole, Nathan, 455
Cole, Thomas, 770
Coletian mendicant community (Italy), 34
*Collapse: How Societies Choose to Fail to
  Succeed* (Diamond), 170–1

Collection of Hymns for Social Worship
  (Whitefield), 724
A Collection of Psalms and Hymns
  (Wesley), 718
*A Collection of Psalm Tunes ... for the
  Use of the United Churches of Christ
  Church and St. Peter's in Philadelphia*
  (Hopkinson), 722
A Collection of the Best Psalm Tunes
  (Flagg), 723
collective solidarity notion
  (Durkheimian), 4
College of Cardinals, 36
College of William and Mary, 222
Colman, Benjamin, 454
Columbus, Christopher, 26, 41, 47,
  202–3, 392
Comentarios Reales de los Incas (Garcilaso de
  la Vega), 641
Commentaries (Piccolomini), 828
*Commentaries on the State of Religion and
  the Commonwealth under Emperor
  Charles V,* 831
Common Sense (Paine), 578–9, 620
Company of the Hundred Associates
  (1627), 200–1, 212
*A Compilation of the Litanies and Vespers
  Hymns and Anthems as They are Sung in
  the Catholic Church* (Aitken), 420
conciliarism, 37
Cone, James, 794, 798
Conferentie Party, 445
confraternities (Catholic communities), 49
  in Africa (slaves), 374
  in New Spain, 244, 249
Confucianism, 744, 814–15
Congregational Calvinists, 673–6
Congregationalism. *See* New England
  Congregationalism
Congrégation de Notre-Dame (New
  France), 269, 270, 271
Connecticut
  abrogation of charters, 235
  Baptist congregations, 230
  Congregationalist churches, 283
  Davenport's expulsion, 456–7
  evangelical revivals, 438, 459
  folk magic, 514–15

Fundamental Orders (1639), 404
leadership of Hooker, 232–3
Middle Colony Congregationalism, 318
"Presbygationalism" (ecclesiastical situation), 292
Presbyterian presence, 292
Puritan settlements, xv, 220
revival preachers, 358
Consejo de Indias (Council of the Indies, 1524), 178
Considerations on the Nature and Extent of the Legislative Authority of the British Parliament (Witherspoon), 580
Constitution (U.S.). *See also* Articles of Confederation
 First Amendment, 71, 408, 450, 496, 500
 limited mention of religion, 570
 ratification by the states, 605–6
 religious background of writers, 590
Constitutional Convention (1787), 407, 577, 601, 605
Continental Congress (1977), 596–7
Continental Protestant Churches, 70
"Conversion of President Edwards" illustrated tract (American Tract Society), 767
conversions (religious conversions), 47
 Africans to Christianity, 106, 108
 Catholic clerics to Protestantism, 40
 competition for converts, 376
 Indians to Catholicism/Christianity, 23, 25, 33, 136, 177–9
 Jewish converts (*converso*), 50
 Muslim elites to Islam, 103
Coode, John, 536
CORE (Congress of Racial Equality), 782
corn ceremonies
 "black drink" inclusion in, 26
 Eastern Algonquians, 354
 green corn ceremonies, 26, 141, 154, 333
 Southeast//Southwest Native Americans, 26
corpus christianorum (body of Christ), 39
Corpus Reformatorum, 841
Cortes, Hernán, 47, 190
Cosin, John, 92–3

cosmogenic narratives. *See* shamans/shamansm
cosmology
 Africa, 97–8, 101, 102
 Mississippian religious traditions, 142–4
Cotton, John, 90, 673, 674, 691, 714–15
Council of Constance (1415), 32
Council of the Indies (*Consejo de Indias*, 1524), 178
Council of Trent (1545–63)
 baroque art influenced by, 246
 canonization process and, 195
 conversion/"Frenchification" and, 206
 importance/impact of, 37, 245–6
 Omnimoda bull (of Hadrian VI) and, 181
 Society of Jesus and, 640
Counter Reformation Church, 193
The Course of the Empire painting (Cole), 770
covenant theology (of Calvinism), 56–8
Cram, Ralph Adams, 736
Creek rituals, 4
Crisafy, Antoine de, 273
Cromwell, Oliver, 221, 228, 533
Crow Native Americans, 10
Crummell, Alexander, 794
Crypto-Jews, 247, 401
Cuba
 missionary presence, 241–2, 261
 Spanish control of, 636, 647–9
Cullen, Charles, 772
Cullen, Countee, 772
Cutler, Timothy, 301–2, 435
Cyprian, Ernst Salomon, 838

Dablon, Claude, 213
Dale, Thomas, 221
Dale's Laws (of Thomas Gates), 329
Daly, Kerry, 812
dance
 African "ring shout" rituals, 334
 fasting preparations, 131
 Ghost Dances (of Native Americans), 10
 Iroquois practices, 130–1
 Mississippian traditions, 142
 Sun Dances, 5

Daneau, Lambert, 59
"The Danger of an Unconverted Ministry" sermon (Gilbert Tennent), 455–6, 557
D'Antonio, William V., 805–6, 810–11
Daoism, 744, 766
Darkwater (Du Bois), 771
Daughters of the Sacred Heart religious order, 763
Davenant, John, 90
Davenport, James, 455, 456–7, 540
Davenport, John, 232–3, 234
Davies, Samuel, 439, 543
Davis, Isaac, 478, 479
Davis, William, 317
Dawes Act (1883), 796
death. *See also* diseases, epidemics, pandemics
 African rituals, 702, 703–4
 Algonquian rituals, 689–90
 Anglican rituals, 700
 Catholic vs. Protestant beliefs, 48
 corpse disposal, 7
 Luther on postmortem prayers, 694
 Mississippian traditions, 151
 Native American burial traditions, 6–7, 18, 22, 116–17, 705
 Puritan rituals, 694–5
Declaration of Independence, 59, 462, 570, 574
de Gante, Pedro, 709
Deistical Society (New York City), 490
Deists/Deism (and Enlightenment theology), 489–95
 Calvinist anthropology/Christian eschatology, disrespect for, 492–3
 described, xviii, 491–2
 formal theology produced by, 663
 revisions of the afterlife, 493–4
 Trinitarian, Christological, Arianism, Socinianism controversies, 494
deities, 4, 11
 African traditions, 97, 98, 101, 102, 370–2
 Anasazi culture, 158, 160–2, 164–7
 Mississippian traditions, 140, 144–7
 Sri Ganesha Hindu temple, 742–3
DeLancey, Oliver, 403
Delany, Martin, 794

Delaware
 Anglican presence, 309
 Baptist presence, 317
 Dutch Reformed congregations, 305
 Lutheran presence, 53, 224, 320
 Penn's control of (1682), 320, 419
 Quaker settlements, 312, 315
 religious liberty granted in, 595
 religious requirements in, 596
 Roman Catholicism (1634–1776), 411, 418, 419–21
 SPG in, 309
Dellius, Godfrey, 326
Deloria, Vine, Jr., 5
Delumeau, Jean, 44
Denton, Melinda Lundquist, 812
d'Esgly, Louis-Philippe, 614
d'Estouteville, Guillaume, 828
Dialogue of Miracles (Caesarius), 829
Diamond, Jared, 170–1
Díaz, Manuel, 253
Diaz, Porfirio, 262
Dickinson, Jonathan, 677
Didactic Enlightenment (Henry May), 498
"diocese" (defined), 30
Di Peso, Charles, 163
Directory for the Publique Worship of God (sacred music), 714
Discalced (Barefoot) Carmelites, 193, 266, 267, 277, 425
Discourse Concerning Reason, with Regard to Religion and Divine Revelation (Chubb), 490
A Discourse concerning Unlimited Submission and Non-Resistance to the Higher Powers (Mayhew), 572
diseases, epidemics, pandemics
 African slaves and, 386
 measles, smallpox, typhus, 121
 in Native American communities, 120, 121, 131, 135, 208, 215, 350, 705
 in New France colonies, 202, 205
 seventeenth century, 152
 smallpox, 121
 virgin soil pandemic diseases, 154
The Distinguishing Marks of a Work of the Spirit of God (Edwards), 458
divinatory methods (Africa), 101–2, 371

The Divine Melody, or a Help to Devotion
    (Whitefield), 718
doctrinal beliefs of the Catholic Church, 42
Dod, John, 90
Doddridge, Philip, 767
Dominicans (mendicant order)
    book study preferences, 638
    Capuchins' quarrels with, 208
    educational work in Cuba, 241–2
    importance of formation, 33
    Indies access (1500–1542), 179–81
    opposition to indigenous clergy, 180
Dongan, Thomas, 225, 323, 418
Donnacona (Iroquois leader), 203
Dorchester, Daniel, 846
Dosquet, Pierre-Herman, 267
double burials (Native Americans), 6, 7
Douglass, Frederick, 771, 790, 794
Dow, Christopher, 92–3
dream catchers (Native Americans), 5
dreams
    about the deceased (in animism), 9
    in African customs, 97
    at evangelical revivals, 361, 453
    in Mississippian customs, 151
    in Native American customs, xvi, 15,
        20, 114, 129–30, 132, 139, 141,
        165, 353, 360, 366, 688
Drinker, Elizabeth, 473
Dryden, John, 716
DuBois, W.E.B., 771, 794
Duché, Jacob, 479
Duchesneau de La Doussinière et
    d'Ambault, Jacques, 275
Duffy, Eamonn, 74
Dummer's War (1722–27), 276
Dungan, Thomas, 316
Dunham, Edmund, 477
Dunkers (Pennsylvania Anabaptist Church
    of the Brethren), xviii, 65, 67, 322,
    469, 470, 471, 476, 484–5
Dunster, Henry, 715
Dupuis, Charles, 506
Durkheim, Emile, 4, 10, 17
Dutch Reformed Church, 222
    challenges of, 304–5
    Classis of Amsterdam and, 223, 306
    description/beliefs, 304
    doctrinal/theological controversies, 306–7
    ecclesiastical governance problems, 306
    formal theology produced by, 663
    Frelinghuysen and, 307
    Jews and, 394
    in New Amsterdam, 60
    New York/New Jersey presence, 305,
        445, 539
    Pennsylvania toleration of, 440
Dutch Reformed Pietism, 67
Dutch West India Company, 60, 222, 223,
    393, 395
Dyer, Mary, 666, 681

Earth Diver mythic motif (shamanism),
    18, 19
Earth Mother (Mississippian tradition),
    144, 145–7
Easter/Lent tradition, 31, 38, 280, 363,
    657, 699, 753
Eastern Algonquians, Eighteenth Century
    (1730s–1790s), 349–68
    baptisms, 367
    being "who is the origin of all"
        concept, 353
    Congregationalist missionary work, 360
    deer ceremony, 354–5
    guardian spirits/dreams and visions,
        353–4
    intergenerational rituals, 355
    "invisible powers" of certain
        animals, 354
    manitou (Algonquian notion of power),
        11, 123, 352, 354
    Moravian missionary work, 359, 360,
        362–3, 365
    New Light/Calvinist teachings, 360
    Niles/Separate Baptist missionary
        work, 361
    Presbyterian missionary work, 358, 360
    Protestant missionary work, 351, 356–8
    purification rituals, 366–7
    Puritan missions, 360
    Quaker influence, 368
    rituals for preserving health/curing
        sickness, 355
    shamanism/visions, 356
    vision quest practices, 365–6

Eastern Cherokee (Native Americans), 5–6
Eastern Orthodox Christians, 737
Ecclesiastical Annals (Baronio), 837
Ecclesiastical History (Bede), 827
Ecclesiologists, 735–6
Eckerlin, Samuel, 488
Eclecticism, 684
Eddy, Mary Baker, 738
Edict of Nantes, revocation (1685), 205, 339, 533, 542, 594
education
   Anglican contributions, 621
   Calvinism contributions, 62
   Catholic Church contributions, 212, 261
   Dominican contributions, 241–2, 261
   Dutch Reformed Church contributions, 304
   evangelical model, 562
   Franciscan contributions, 180
   Jesuit contributions, 241–2, 261, 424, 642
   in Jewish communities, 398
   Moravian contributions, 69
   in New France, 269, 270, 280
   NYC missionary school (1704), 383
   Pietism's contributions, 66–7, 471
   post-Civil War Native boarding schools, 796
   Quaker contributions, 590
   SPG contributions, 333
Edwards, Jonathan, 288, 539, 554, 767
   antislavery advocacy, 461
   comments about Quakers, 467
   influence on Tennent and Whitefield, 559
   influence on Wesley, 561
   interpretation of Book of Revelation, 542
   meaning of Great Awakening to, 565
   "New Divinity" disciples of, 676
   Northampton, MA revival and, 286, 287, 358, 437, 453–4
   observations on Jewish prayer, 402
   quest for evangelical revivals, 453–4
   "Sinners in the Hands of an Angry God" sermon, 558
   synthesis of Calvinist-Enlightenment themes, 673
   written work of, 454, 458, 467–8, 558, 718–19
Edward VI (King of England), 76, 88
Eliot, John, 357, 711, 790–1
Elizabeth (Queen of England), 73–4, 77, 79, 231
Elizabethan church, 78, 79
Elizabethan Puritan movement, 79, 81
Embry, Philip, 624
Emerson, Ralph Waldo, 800
The Encyclopedia of Native American Religions (Hirschfelder and Molin), 173
England. *See also* Church of England
   Anglicanism, 221
   Baptist return to (1612), 66
   Moravian ministry of Zinzendorf, 69
   North American Empire/thirteen colonies, 219
   restoration of monarchy (1660), 226
   Roman Catholic bishops, 32
   Westminster Assembly, 233
English Catholicism, 73–7
   as defined by Eamonn Duffy, 74
   mid-Elizabethan period, 73–4
   recusant vs. church papist route, 74–5, 91
   relation to English Catholic Christian path, 75–6
English Council for Foreign Plantations (1660), 376
English Presbyterianism, 83, 288, 289, 318. *See also* Morton, Charles
English Province of the Society of Jesus, 410
Enlightened Despotism (1750), 638, 639
the Enlightenment. *See* liberal religious movements and the Enlightenment
The Enthusiasm of Methodists and Papists Compared (Lavington), 505
Ephrata Cloister, 468, 485, 486–8, 663, 682, 684, 720. *See also* Beissel, Conrad
Episcopalism/Episcopalians, 54, 80, 706, 735
Epitome of Church History (Osiander), 836
Epitome of the Three Parts of the World, Asia, Africa and Europe, containing descriptions ... especially of those places which the Evangelists and Apostles related (Stumpf and Vadian), 832

Erasmus, Desiderius, 35
*The Essential Rights and Liberties of
    Protestants* (Locke), 541
Estates-General medieval governance
    (France), 32
Ethical Culture Society, 489
Ethices Elementa (Johnson), 672
Eusebius of Caesarea, 826–8
evangelical Calvinism, 89, 90.
    See also Abbott, George; Davenant,
    John; Hall, Joseph; King, John
Evangelical Hymns and Songs (Wallin), 724
evangelical Protestantism, 81, 343, 350
Evangelical Reformed Church
    (Pennsylvania), 563
Evangelicals/Evangelicalism.
    See also Abbott, George; Atlantic
    community evangelical awakenings;
    Davenport, James; Great Awakening;
    Moravian Church; New Light
    evangelicals; Protestant Evangelicism
    (eighteenth-century America);
    revivals/revivalism; Tennent, Gilbert;
    Tennent, William, Jr.; Whitefield,
    George
  in Alta California, 258–9
  Anglican efforts, 325
  antirevivalist sentiment, 438, 445,
    456–7
  antislavery implications, 461–3
  background/definitions, 451–2
  as branch of Brethren, 68
  Capuchin missionary efforts, 277
  dissent in the colonies, 436–9
  dreams, trances, visions, 361, 453
  "evangel" (def.), 53
  Franciscan missionary efforts, 178,
    186, 251
  Great Britain traditions, 553–6
  Jesuit missionary efforts, 411, 413
  katsina religion comparison, 172
  megachurch style architecture, 739
  missionary work (1500–1542), 179–81
  Native Americans and, 25, 178, 201–2,
    207–8, 210, 326, 358
  in New Mexico, 255
  outcomes in the New World, 190
  Pietism roots, 451–2, 551

post-*reconquista* (1692) violence, 174
Quaker efforts, 299
religious freedom and, 541–2
resistance to slave Christianization, 788
sacred imagery, 766–70
sacred music (Pietist hymnody,
    1735–1760), 718–21
Scots-Irish Calvinist efforts, 342–3
Sulpican efforts (Canada), 277
Evans, Caleb, 564
The Everlasting Covenant (Siegvolck), 479
Exercises (Saint Ignatius of Loyola), 422
Explicitation (de l'Incarnation), 666

*A Faithful Narrative of the Surprising Work of
    God* (Edwards), 454, 467–8, 718–19
Falckner, Justus, 320, 680
families and religion, 804–23
  bar mitzvah tradition (Judaism), 804
  Buddhism, 815–16
  Catholic traditions, 48
  changes of faith, 809–10
  Chinese religions/Confucianism,
    814–15
  Colonial era, 806–7
  cultural progressives vs. traditionalists,
    810–13
  "fictive kin"/"church families," 817
  Hinduism, 816–17
  home and heaven (nineteenth century),
    807–9
  marriage and fertility, 821–3
  Middletown III project studies, 809
  modern religion family figures, 817–18
  Muslim religions, 816
  Puritan/Protestant homes, 808
  sexual behavior issues, 810, 811
  Southwest tribal cultures, 819–20
  World Values Survey (1990), 805–6
the Family religious group, 817
Fast Days (American Revolution), 575,
    578, 581, 582, 588
fasting
  black face painting and, 134
  Calusa beliefs, 24
  as ceremonial dance preparation, 131
  in shamanic practices, 124
  as vision quest preparation, 13, 141

Federalist 51 (Madison), 606
Feijóo y Montenegro, Benito Jerónimo, 641
Fénelon, François de la Mothe, 553–4
Filles Séculières de la Congrégation de Notre-Dame, 266
Finney, John, Jr., 476
First Amendment (U.S. Constitution), 71, 408, 450, 500
The First Book of the American Chronicles of the Times (Leacock), 578
First Charter of Virginia (1606), 404
Fisher, Mary, 681
Five Points: The True Scripture-Doctrine Concerning Some Important Points of Christian Faith (Dickinson), 677
Flagg, Josiah, 723
Flavel, John, 767
Fleché, Jessé, 206
Fletcher, Benjamin, 444
Fletcher, John, 565
Florida, 259–60
  border issue with South Carolina, 537
  Bourbon reforms, 649–50
  French Huguenot Protestant settlers, 532
  mission system, 532, 536–7
  Native American presence, 332
Folger, Peter, 297
folk magic and religion (British North America), 510–27. *See also* Salem Village (Massachusetts) witch craze
  appeal of magic, 519–20
  assumptions of folk magic, 511
  astrology practices, 516
  counter-magical protection techniques, 513, 516, 524
  fortune-telling, 511, 518
  magic divination, 511–12
  malevolent purposes, 512–13
  Native American practices, 514–15
  Native Americans and, 514–15, 521
  needs met by, 520
  for protection and healing, 512
  Puritan concerns about, 515–17, 518, 520–1
  Salem Village (MA) witch craze, 229, 510
  self-blame for illness vs. blaming Satan, 521
  sorcery practices, 517–18
Fon creation myth (Africa), 98
Formula of Concord (1580), 55
fortune-telling (in New England), 511, 518
Foster, Stephen, 294
Fountainbleau, Treaty of (1762), 635
Fox, George, 222, 229, 472, 681
Foxe, John, 77, 835
France. *See also* French Catholicism; New France colonies
  Cathar *perfecti,* 31
  church control of land, 29
  Coletian mendicant community, 34
  colonization attempts (sixteenth century), 201–2, 205
  expulsion of Huguenots, 533
  French Enlightenment, 490
  religious property tax exemptions, 40
  Roman Catholic bishops, 32
  St. Bartholomew's massacre of Huguenots, 533
Franciscans/Franciscan missionaries. *See also* Capuchins
  Alta California missionary work, 251, 258–9, 262
  American southeast missionary work, 259–60
  efforts with evangelicals, 178, 186, 251
  importance of formation, 33
  Indies missionary work, 179–81
  missionary work with evangelicals, 178, 186, 251
  mission system chain establishment, 730
  New Mexico missionary work, 255, 262
  New Spain missionary work, 246, 251, 254, 710
  sacred music two-line hymns, 710
  Texas missionary work, 257–8
Francis I (King of France), 203, 204–5
Francke, August Hermann, 66–7, 552, 553–4, 680
Franckian Pietism, 558
Franklin, Benjamin
  admonition to rely on God's providence, 577

Constitutional Convention opening
prayer recommendation, 605
deism and, 490
meeting with Vizcardo y Guzmán, 643
publication of *True Christianity*
(Arndt), 760
relationship with Whitefield/Tennent,
456, 560
religious beliefs of, 601, 684
viewpoint of church-state
separation, 599
visit to Canada (1776), 616
Franks, Phila, 403
Freedom of the Will (Edwards), 558
Freewill Baptists, 477. *See also* Randel,
Benjamin
Frelinghuysen, Theodore J., 67, 307, 445.
See also Pietism
French and Indian Wars, 484, 664
French Catholicism, 200–17. *See also* New
France colonies
Church of the colonists, 215–16
colonization attempts (sixteenth
century), 201–2
Company of the Hundred Associates,
200–1, 212
conversion/"Frenchification" policy,
206–8, 210–11
Great Peace of Montréal, 202
obstacles faced by missionaries, 207
pre-Counter Reformation
Catholicism, 203
religion of the colonists, 217
religious pragmatism (sixteenth
century), 202–5
and slavery, 214–15
welfare system, 211–14
French Enlightenment, 490
French Reformed Church (Huguenots), 56,
61–2, 202, 205
French Revolution (1789), 260, 617, 627,
631, 645
Frères Hospitalières de la Croix et de
Saint-Joseph of Montréal, 268
Freud, Sigmund, 10
"Friends of the Indian" philanthropic
group (late nineteenth century),
782, 796

Fundamental Instruction (Falckner), 680
Fundamental Orders of Connecticut
(1639), 57

Gage, Charles, 418
Gálvez y Gallardo, José de, 644
Ganiodaio (Iroquois leader), 630
García, Gregorio, 640–1
García Icazbalceta, Joaquin, 251
Garcilaso de la Vega, 188, 641, 657
Garden, Alexander, 672
*The Garden of the Soul: or, a manual of
spiritual exercises and Instructions for
Christians who (living in the World)
aspire to Devotion* (Challoner), 420, 425
Garnet, Henry Highland, 794
Garretson, Freeborn, 624
Garrett, Margaret, 513
Garvey, Marcus, 794, 796
Gates, Thomas, 329
Gaustad, Edwin, 565
Gayanashagowa ("great law of peace")
principles (Iroquois), 113
General Baptists, 230
*General Remarks on Gottfried Arnold's
History of the Church and Heresies*
(Cyprian), 838
geomancy (in Pennsylvania), 511
George, David, 623–4
George II (King of England), 577
George III (King of England), 570, 577,
614, 635, 636
Gerhardt, Paul, 719
German Pietism, 67, 68, 552, 562
German Reformed churches, 55, 56, 61,
67, 319–23, 715, 719–20
Gerson, Jean, 32
*Das Gesäng der einsamen und verlassenen
Turtel-Taube* [The Song of the Lonely
and Lost Turtle-Dove] (Beissel), 720
Ghent, Treaty of (1815), 627
ghost dances (of Native Americans), 10
ghosts (in Native American beliefs), 8
Gibbs, James, 732
Gillis, John R., 808, 812
Ginés de Sepúlveda, Juan, 184
Ginsberg, Allen, 801
Gloria Dei Lutheran church, 320

Glorious Revolution (1688), 225, 235, 283, 337–8, 414, 416, 418, 445, 534, 535–6, 732
God. *See also* Jesus Christ
  in African Christian traditions, 106–8
  beliefs of Benjamin Franklin, 601
  beliefs of Thomas Jefferson, 494–5
  Calvinist beliefs (*See* Calvinists/Calvinism)
  deism beliefs, 491–2
  English Catholic beliefs, 73–7
  English Protestant beliefs, 77–9
  good/evil and, 43–4
  Jewish beliefs, 402–3
  Lutheran beliefs (*See* Lutherans/Lutheranism)
  Native American beliefs, 24
  Protestant beliefs (*See* Protestants/Protestantism)
  Puritan beliefs, 57
  Roman Catholic beliefs (*See* Roman Catholicism)
  Salem witch trials and, 522
  Scottish Common Sense School beliefs, 600
  Seven Deadly Sins and, 44–5
  as source of magical powers, 518–19
"God is Black" notion (of James Cone), 798
God is Red (Deloria), 798–9
"The God of Glory sends His Summons forth" hymn (Watts), 724
Golden Legend (Voragine), 829
Goldenweiser, Alexander, 15
Good and Evil teachings (Catholic Church), 43–4
Goodhue, Bertram Grosvenor, 736
Goodman, Christopher, 59
Good Newes from Virginia sermon (Whitaker), 221
Goodwin, Morgan, 787
Gordon, Sarah Barringer, 498
Gordon, Thomas, 496
Gorton, Samuel, 227, 682
Gortonites, 663
Gossner, Johannes, 760
Gravé du Pont, François, 201–2

Great Abandonment (Ancestral Pueblo civilization collapse), 168, 170, 172, 173, 174
Great Awakening
  Anglo-American evangelicals and, 390, 451, 539
  Baptists and, 459–60
  Butler's viewpoint, 465
  Dutch Reformed Church and, 305, 445
  Edwards' revivals and, 453–4
  Evangelicalism and, 452, 453
  First Great Awakening, 55, 358
  Frelinghuysen and, 307
  influence on American Revolution, 464
  New England Congregationalism and, 294
  Northampton, MA presence, 437
  Protestant Evangelicism and, 451
  religious skirmishes produced by, 664–5
  revivals/revivalism and, 470–1
  Separatists break from orthodox Congregational churches, 593
  varied meanings of, 565
Great Britain, 73–95. *See also* Church of England; expanded entries for individual religions
  anti-Puritanism discourse, 83–4
  arguments in favor of episcopacy, 86
  Arminianism, 92
  command of Canada, 611–15
  Elizabethan church, 78, 79
  English Catholicism, 73–7, 89–91
  English Presbyterianism, 83
  English Protestantism, 77–9, 87, 88
  Episcopal palaces, 80
  evangelical awakenings, 81, 553–6
  Hooker's role, 88
  Laudinism reform movement, 91–5
  Marprelate tracts, 83–4
  Montague's vision of the English church, 91
  Puritanism, 79–82, 85–91
  reign of Henry VIII, 73, 76, 79, 411, 430
  reign of James VI and I, 77, 81, 84, 89
  reign of Queen Elizabeth, 73–4, 77, 79, 231

Wesleyan movement (eighteenth century), 554–6
Great Migration (1629–1642), 231
Greaton, Joseph, 323
Great Peace of Montréal, 202
Great Serpent (Mississippian tradition), 147–8, 153
green corn ceremonies, 26, 141, 154, 333
"Greeting the Sun" ceremony (Mississippian tradition), 147
Gregory XIII (Pope), 181
Gregory XV (Pope), 177–8, 192
Griggs, William, 510
gris-gris (sacred objects), Orisha religion, 370, 381
Grounds and Rules of Musick Explain'd (Walter), 717
Guamán Poma de Ayala, Felipe, 188
Gunpowder Plot (England, 1605), 89, 533, 616
Guyse, John, 454

Hadrian VI (Pope), 181
Haidar, Gulzar, 746
Haitian Revolution, 645
Hakluyt, Richard, 532
Hale, John, 515, 517–18
Hall, Joseph, 90
Hallensian Pietism, 553
hallucinogens, 18, 26, 185, 629
Hamilton, Alexander, 599, 603–4, 614
Hammon, Jupiter, 668
Handy, Robert T., 847
The Happy Ascetic (Horneck), 553
Hapsburg Spain (1516–1700), 636–7
Hare Krishna spiritual organization, 817
"Hark! From the Tombs a doleful Sound" hymn (Watts), 724
Harnack, Adolf von, 841
Harriot, Thomas, 204
Harrison, Henry, 418
Harsnet, Samuel, 88, 89
Hart, William, 676
Hart-Cellar Immigration Reform Act (1965), 742, 745
Hartley, L. P., 175
Harvey, Thomas, 418

Hatch, Nathan, 583
Haudenosaunee Iroquois, 114, 118, 122
Hawkins, Gamaliel, 512
Hawley, Joseph, 288
Haydn, Franz Joseph, 721
Haynes, Lemuel, 461, 668
The Heart of Man (Gossner), 760
Heck, Barbara, 624
Hegel, G. W., 840
Heidelberg Confession, 563
Heimert, Alan, 464
Hemmenway, Moses, 676
Henri IV (King of France), 201–2
Henry, Patrick, 463, 573, 606
Henry VIII (King of England), 73, 76, 79, 411, 430
Herder, J. G., 840
Hermeticism, 323, 684
Hertz, Robert, 6
Hewitt, J. N. B., 10
Heylin, Peter, 92–3
Heywood, Linda, 108
Higginson, Thomas Wentworth, 508
Hildersham, Arthur, 90
Hinduism/Hindu temples, 742, 816–17
Hipólito (Saint), 245
Hirschfelder, Arlene, 173
Historia antigua de México (Claviero), 242
Historia geográfica civil y natural (Abbad y Lasierra), 647
Historical Dictionary of All Religions (Broughton), 507
historical religious writing
  American religious depression (1920s and 1930s), 844
  Britain/Europe (twentieth century), 842
  Bullinger, Heinrich, 833
  Christian historical genre, 826–8
  classic histories (twentieth century), 846
  debates about Protestant theology, 841–2
  Foxe, John, 835
  historicist modes of theology, 842–3
  humanist Protestant genre, 832
  Lutheran genre, 832–3, 834–5
  Mather, Cotton, 845
  medieval historical genre, 828–9, 836–7

historical religious writing (*cont.*)
  Mosheim, Lorenz von, 839
  Northern European Renaissance
    genre, 831
  post-Romantic church history, 840–1
  Protestantism genre, 836, 838, 846–7
  proto-history of the New England
    church, 844–5
  Reformation (sixteenth century) genre,
    829–30
  Revivalist Protestant genre, 845–6
  Roman Catholic historiography, 837–8
  Schaff, Phillip, 841, 846
  Sleidan, Johannes, 831
  Stumpf, Johann, 832
  Swiss Reformation, 832–3
  Watt, Joachim von, 831
  Western Christianity (in Europe), 843–4
History (Backus), 474–5
History (Eusebius), 826
A History of All Religions (Benedict), 506–7
A History of American Christianity
  (Bacon), 846
History of the Christian Church (Schaff), 841
*A History of the Churches in the United States
  and Canada* (Handy), 847
History of the Popes (Ranke), 840
Hoar, Dorcas, 511, 518
Hoffman, Balthasar, 720
Hoffman, Balzer, 484
Holman, Winifred, 518
holy apparitions, 197
Holy Trinity Lutheran church, 320
Hooker, Richard, 87–9
Hooker, Thomas, 232–3, 673, 674
Hope of Israel (Menasseh Ben Israel), 396–7
Hopi Native Americans, 16, 156
  Kokopelli and, 160
  Tanama and, 164, 167
  T-shape doorway explanation, 163
Hopkins, John, 712, 713
Hopkins, Samuel, 383, 504, 676
Hopkinson, Francis, 722
Horneck, Anthony, 553
Horton, Azariah, 358
Hoskins, Jane, 666–7
Hotman, François, 59
House of Lords (England), 32

House of Rain (Childs), 161, 162
Howson, John, 88
Hubbard, Samuel, 476
Hudson, Henry, 222
Hudson, Winthrop S., 846–7
Huguenots (French Reformed Church), 56,
  61–2, 202. *See also* Neau, Elias
  class lines/conflicts, 310–11
  massacre of, in France (1572), 533
  migration to the New World, 533
human sacrifice practice, 24, 184, 503
Hume, David, 490, 506
Hunt, Robert, 672
Hupa Native Americans (California), 22
Hurt, John, 580
Huson, Paul, 778
Hutchinson, Anne, 227, 228, 231, 665,
  674
Hutchinson, Thomas, 575
Hutterites, 65
Hyde, Edward, 444
Hymns and Spiritual Songs (Watts), 716,
  718, 724

"The Idea of Covenant and American
  Democracy" (Niebuhr), 58
Ignatius of Loyola (Saint), 422, 423
Illyricus, Matthias Flacius, 834
*Image of the Virgin Mary, Mother of God of
  Guadalupe* (Sánchez), 250–1
*An Impartial History of the Church and
  Heresies* (Arnold), 838
imperial conflict and religion, 531–49
  Anglican accusations vs. New Light
    clergy, 547
  anti-Catholic sentiment in New
    England, 531, 535–6
  concerns about Anglican Church in the
    colonies, 545
  expulsion of Huguenots from France, 533
  fears of Catholicism, 545–6
  Florida-South Carolina border issue, 537
  French Huguenots/Florida
    settlements, 532
  King William III's reassertion of
    colonial control, 536
  Maryland/Virginia's concerns about
    Catholic loyalty, 543

massacre of French Huguenots (1572), 533, 542
mission system, 532
Protestant advancement as "ideological glue," 539
Protestant-Catholic rivalry, 531–3, 536, 537–8
Quebec Act (1774), 546
raids on Puritan communities, 536
raids on Spanish missions, 536–7
revivalism/evangelical preachers, 539–40, 544–5
role of mercantilist commercial expansion, 538–9
Spanish atrocities vs. native peoples, 533
viewpoint of New Lights, 542–3
War of Jenkin's Ear (Britain vs. Spain) (1739), 537–8
War of the Spanish Succession, 536–7
Inca empire, 33, 178, 179, 188, 637, 651, 657
Index of Prohibited Books, 52, 196
Indian Free Methodists, 791
Inés de la Cruz, Sor Juana, 194
Inglis, Charles, 620–1
Innocent III (Pope, 1198–1216), 35, 834, 835
Innocent XIII (Pope), 242
Institutes of the Christian Religion (Calvin), 56
Intolerable Acts. *See* Quebec Act (1774)
Introduction to the Art of Psalm-Singing (Tufts), 717
Irenaeus (Father Irenaeus), 554
Iroquois
  artistic expression, 133–6
  ceremonial practices, xiii, 129–31
  conflicts in New Netherlands, 224
  cosmogenic narrative of, 18–19
  disease epidemics, 115, 121
  Donnacona (Iroquois leader), 203
  etymology of "Iroquois," 115
  Ganiodaio (Iroquois leader), 630
  Jesuit missionary work, 276
  Longhouse religion, 4
  nations of, 113
  oral traditions, 117, 122, 124
  political struggles for domination, 121–2
  raids in Quebec City, 201–2
  religious leadership/healers (*Arendiouane*), 132–3
  Six Nation Iroquois, 628, 630
  united indigenous nations of, 113–14
Iroquois, pre-contact situation
  Adena-Hopewell artworks/imagery, 117
  Easter Woodlands residential regions, 114–15
  fishing, importance of, 119
  Haudenosaunee Iroquois, 114, 118
  long-distance networks, 115–16
  oral traditions, 117
  owachira (kinship)-based mode of production, 118–19, 122
  political leagues/confederacies, 118
  red paint mortuary ceremonialism, 116–17
  shamanic paradigm, 115
  spread of cultigens, 117–18, 119
Iroquois ontology, 122–9
  of bodies and persons, 123–5
  creation epic, 126–7
  Gayanashagowa principles, 113, 129
  Great League of Peace, 127–8
  Hiawatha (Aionwatha), 128
  multinatural perspective, 124–6
  orenda (power), 10–12, 123, 124, 127, 128, 129, 352
  shamanic paradigm, 115, 123, 132
Isenburg, Dieter von, 828
Islam religion, 29, 742
  in Africa, 96, 103–5, 372, 373–4
  influence of slave trade, 105, 372
  in Spain, 41, 50
Italy
  Capuchin/*Riformati* mendicant orders, 34
  Gonzaga family rulership, 32

Jackson, Andrew, 793
Jackson, Thomas, 92–3
Jacobean Episcopals, 89
Jainism, 742, 743
James, Thomas, 326
James, William, 10

James I (Archbishop of Canterbury), 83, 85, 91, 231, 433–4, 533
James II (Duke of York), 225, 235, 305, 323, 418, 534, 535–6
James VI and I (King of Scots/King of England), 77, 81, 84, 89
Jarratt, Devereux, 672
Jay, John, 594, 596–7, 598, 599, 604
Jedin, Hubert, 37
Jefferson, Thomas
  Adams' letter about God to, 493
  anti-Calvinist views, 504
  assertion about equality of men, 462
  "Bill for Establishing Religious Freedom," 464
  on church-state separation, 497, 599
  deism and, 490
  drafting of Declaration of Independence, 574
  end-of-life views on Christianity, 499
  Fast Day sermons supported by, 575
  Notes on the State of Virginia, 587
  as prophet of "America's Scripture," 584
  religious beliefs of, 494–5, 600–1, 603, 684
  views of human nature, xviii
Jenkins, Kathleen E., 817
Jenkins, Leigh, 171, 173, 174
Jerusalén, Ignacio de, 242
Jesuit Relations (French Jesuit missionaries), 113, 122–3, 124–5
Jesuits/Jesuit missionaries, 23, 52
  American Southwest presence, 252
  Capuchins' quarrels with, 208
  Cuban presence, 241–2
  denunciation of indigenous religions, 113, 122–3, 129
  division of colonies into circuits (territories), 415–16
  English North American Colonies influence, 422–7
  global vision of Catholicism, 641
  identification of indigenous ceremonial dances, 131
  Indies missionary work, 179–81
  Jogues, Isaac (missionary), 223
  Maryland presence, 413, 424
  to Native Americans, 351, 413

New France presence, 202, 206, 208–9, 216, 266, 275
New Spain presence, 246, 251, 252–3, 532
  in Quebec City (New France), 201–2
  in Virginia colony, 226
  work with the Iroquois, 276
Jesus Christ
  Alocoque's visions of, 763
  Anglican beliefs, 700
  anticipated return of, 531
  Arndt on forgiveness of, 551–2
  battles with the Antichrist, 531, 535, 541–2, 543, 546–7
  beliefs of Benjamin Franklin, 601
  beliefs of Thomas Jefferson, 494–5
  body of Christ (*corpus christianorum*), 39, 46, 679
  Calvinist beliefs, 55–62
  Catholic Church theology and, 42–3
  colonial Jews and, 404
  good and evil teachings and, 43–4
  intimate piety centered on, 45–7
  Jefferson's beliefs, 494–5, 600–1
  Last Supper celebration, 31
  Lutheran beliefs, 53–4
  Mennonite beliefs, 64–6
  Moravian beliefs, 68–9
  Pietism/Lutheran Pietism beliefs, 539
  Quaker beliefs, 311, 440
  Renaissance culture representation, 39
  Revolutionary soldiers comforted by, 579
  Ruggles blasphemy about, 498
  Sacred Heart imagery, 763
  Seven Deadly Sins teaching and, 44
Jewel, John (Bishop Jewel), 80
Jews/Judaism, 29. *See also* Phillips, Jonas
  American Revolution and, 406–9, 585
  Ashkenazic Jews, 395, 405, 663
  bar mitzvah tradition, 804
  belief in one supernatural God, 402–3
  beliefs of Paine, 495
  in the Carolinas, 338–9
  circumcision rites, 402
  conversions to Catholicism, 392
  Crypto-Jews, 247, 401
  culture, 404–5

dietary laws, 401
Dutch Reformed Church and, 394
Edwards observations about, 402
eighteenth-century compartmentalization of life, 400–1
eve of American Revolution and, 405–6
expulsion from Spain, Portugal, 392, 393
"familiarity of strangers" of, 403
George Washington's relationship with, 408, 501–2, 585, 589, 799
in Holland, 393
"Jew Bill," 407
Middle Colonies (1680–1730), 308
Mikveh Israel synagogues, 396–7
New Amsterdam presence, 308, 394–5
New Netherlands presence, 223
Newport, Rhode Island Congregation, 501–2
New World origins, xvii, 392–3
nineteenth/twentieth-century assimilation, 800
Passover haggadah illustrations, 774–6
Philadelphia Jewish community, 500–1
"port" Jews, 396
pre-Columbian era religious thought, 683–4
public vs. private worship, 397–8
as "religion of the heart," 551
religious liberty/equality tested by, 500–2
Rhode Island presence, 298
rights of, 404
sacred music (psalters), 715
Sephardic Jews, 395, 398, 404–5, 663
settlement in New Netherlands, 223
in Spain, 41, 50
synagogue architectural style, 740–2
synagogue communities, 397–9
synagogues in New York/Newport, RI, 399–400
Jocelin of Brakelond, 828
Jogues, Isaac, 223, 671
John Paul II (Pope), 259
Johnson, George, 172
Johnson, Rebecca, 512
Johnson, Samuel, 301–2, 564, 672
Jordan, Winthrop, 786

Juana Inés de la Cruz, Sor ("The Tenth Muse"), 242
Julius Excluded from Heaven (Erasmus), 35
Julius II (Pope, 1503–13), 35, 177
Julius III (Pope, 1550–55), 35
Jung, Carl, 778
Just War Theory, 643
Juzgado general de indios (general Indian court), in New Spain, 244

Kabbalism, 323
Kafa ethnic group (Africa), 100–1
Kantorowicz, Ernst, 39
Karuk Native Americans (California), 22
Katchinas (used by Pueblo Native Americans), 8
katsina religion, 161–2, 164, 168–72
Keeley, Patrick, 736
Keith, George, 313–15, 317, 476
Keithian Quakerism, 313–15, 317
Kelpius, Johann, 322
Kempis, Thomas à, 553–4
Kern alter und neuer [Seeds Old and New] (Pietist hymns), 719–20
Keteltas, Abraham, 575
Kgaga ethnic group (Africa), 99
Khalidi, Omar, 746
Khoi Khoi people (early Africa), 96
Kidd, Thomas, 358, 438
King, John, 89, 90
King, Martin Luther, Jr., 737, 774, 797
King Philip's War (1675–76), 283, 294, 357, 535, 791
Kino, Eusebio, 252–3, 256
Kirkland, Samuel, 359
Knox, John, 59
Kohler, Timothy, 172
Kokopelli (Puebloan fertility/creation deity), 160
Kuntze, John C., 680

ladinos (assimilated slaves), 373
Ladurie, Emmanuel Le Roy, 31
Lakota (Native Americans), 5–6, 10–11, 771, 797
Lancashire Solfa (sacred music scale system), 714
Landa, Diego de, 181

Langdon, Samuel, 577
Lankford, George, 175
Large Congregationalists. *See* New England Congregationalism
Larios, Juan (Founder of Coahuila), 254, 256
La Salle, René-Robert Cavelier de, 276
Las Casas, Bartolomé de, 184, 637, 709
Laso de la Vega, Luis, 251
Lateran Council (of 1215), 31, 33, 42
"The Late Work of God in North America" sermon (Wesley), 565
Latino, Juan, 373
Latter-day Saints, 740
Laud, William (Abbott of Canterbury), 91–5, 433–4
Laudinism (Church of England) reform movement, 91–5. *See also* Cosin, John; Dow, Christopher; Heylin, Peter; Jackson, Thomas; Skinner, Robert
Laumet, Antoine, 276
Laval, François de, 264–7
Lavington, George, 505
Law, Andrew, 726
Law, William, 553–4, 678
"The Lawes Divine, Morall and Martiall" government (Virginia), 221
"The Law Established by Faith" sermon (Wesley), 556
The Lawfulness, Excellency, and Advantage of Instrumental Musick in the Publick Worship of God urg'd and enforc'd (Lyon), 722
Law of Contradiction (Lévy-Bruhl), 10
Law of Participation (Lévy-Bruhl), 10
Lawrence, Jacob, 771–4
Lawson, Deodat, 516, 519
Leacock, John, 578
Lee, Ann ("Mother of the Shakers"), xviii, 468, 469, 480–1, 667, 682, 740
Leisler, Jacob, 305, 310, 418, 536
Leisler's Rebellion (1689, England), 445
Leland, John, 475, 678
Le Moyne, Simon, 210
Lent/Easter tradition, 31, 38, 280, 363, 657, 699, 753
Leonard, Abiel, 579

A Letter from Rome, Shewing an Exact Conformity between Popery and Paganism (Middleton), 505
Letter to Egbert (Bede), 827
Lévi-Strauss, Claude, 15
Lévy-Bruhl, Lucien, 10
Leyden, Jan van, 63
liberal religious movements and the Enlightenment, 489–508
  church-state separation, 495–502
  deism and Enlightenment theology, 489–95
  and religious others, 503–8
"Liberty Further Extended: Or Free Thoughts on the Illegality of Slave-Keeping" (Haynes), 462
Liele, George, 668
The Life of Harriet Tubman painting (Lawrence), 771
l'Incarnation, Marie de, 666
Lincoln, Abraham, 584
Lipe, William, 171, 172
Liturgical movement architectural style, 739
Lloyd, Grace, 666–7
Lobwasser, Ambrosius, 719–20
Lock, Lars, 224
Locke, John, 338, 490, 504, 534, 570, 600
Longhouse religion (of the Iroquois), 4
Long Island (New York), 305
  Anglo-American revivalism, 451, 456, 668
  Davenport's revivals, 456–7
  Dutch congregations, 444–5
  ethnic/religious pluralism, 223, 232–3
  Montauk Indians, 352–3
  Native American baptisms, conversions, 326, 367
  Presbyterian presence, 358
  Protestant evangelical presence, 451
  Puritan presence, 318
  Quaker presence, 228, 312
  revival preachers, 358
  Sri Ganesha Hindu temple, 742–3
Looking for Lost Lore: Studies in Folklore, Ethnology, and Iconography (Lankford), 175

Lord Baltimore. *See* Calvert, George (Lord Baltimore)
The Lord's Supper
   Congregationalists and, 285, 286
   Luther/Lutheranism and, 53, 55, 290
   Puritan monthly worship of, 692
   Stoddard and, 290
Losee, William, 624–5
Lost Tribes of Israel, 640–1
Louisiana (New France), 269–72
   Bourbon reforms, 634
   ceding by French Bourbons (1762), 635
   free African community (New Orleans), 387
   French colonization, 536
   Native American presence, 332
   plantation slave labor, 214
Louis XIV (King of France), 272–5, 533
L'Overture, Toussaint, 771
Lozi ethnic group (Africa), 99
Luther, Martin, 28, 554, 679, 834.
   See also Lutherans/Lutheranism
   belief in the devil, 43
   Calvin's friendship with, 55
   criticism of Catholic Church, 31, 37, 53, 74
   on postmortem prayers, 694
   recovery of New Testament teachings, 54
   and the role of the will, 42
Lutheran Pietism, 66–7, 539
Lutherans/Lutheranism, 53–5
   arrival in America from Sweden, 53
   Augsburg Confession/Formula of Concord, 55
   Carolina presence, 340
   contributions to the New World, 70–1
   doctrine, 53–4
   formal theology produced by, 663
   governance of state churches, 54
   as heartfelt religion, 551
   Holy Trinity/Gloria Dei churches, 320
   Middle Colonies (1680–1730) presence, 319–23
   Pennsylvania presence, 442
   pre-Columbian era religious thought, 679–81
   sacred music (psalters), 715

lynching of black men, 774, 795
Lyon, Richard, 715

Macdonell, Alexander, 627
Mack, Alexander, 67, 322, 484
Maddox, Isaac, 537
Madison, James, 449, 464, 490, 496
   on church-state separation, 497, 599
   description of religion by, 497
   Federalist 51, 606
   Henry's conflict with, 606
   Memorial and Remonstrance, 464, 606–7
   religious beliefs of, 602–3
   views of human nature, xviii
Magdeburg Centuries (ed. Flacius), 835
Magnalia Christi Americana (Cotton Mather), 291, 557–8, 845
Malagrida, Gabriel de, 642
Maliki Islam tradition, 104
Malokti, Ekkehart, 173–4
mana (disembodied power), 10, 12
"*Las Mananitas a la Virgén de Guadalupe*" ("Birthday Song to the Virgin of Guadalupe") pilgrimage song, 710
manitou (Algonquian notion of power), xvi, 11, 123, 352, 354
Manning, Edward, 623
Mansa Musa (Mali empire ruler), 104
A Manual of Catholic Prayers (Bell), 420
Marett, R. R., 10
Mariana, Juan de, 643
Marian Exiles (of English Calvinist Protestants), 433–4
Marie-Arouet, François. *See* Voltaire (François Marie-Arouet)
Marnix, Phillipe de, 837
marriage
   arranged, 248
   Calusa customs, 25
   Iroquois customs, 128
   mixed marriages, 55, 91, 206, 211, 278
   Mohawk customs, 119
   New France customs, 206, 211
Marshall, Daniel, 474
Marshall, John, 792
Marty, Martin E., 847
Mary (Queen of England), 73, 76, 78, 79

Maryland
　Act of Toleration (1649), xvi, 337
　African slave Catholicism, 385
　Anglican presence, 338, 432
　baptism of African slaves, 383–4
　Bray's appointment to, 333
　concerns about Catholic loyalty, 543
　Discalced Carmelite community, 425
　Dunker presence, 485
　English Catholic presence, 337
　granting freedom of conscience, post-Revolution, 593
　Jesuit missionaries, 413, 424
　"Jew Bill," 407
　penal laws (1704), 414
　Protestants vs. Catholics, 536
　religious directions (1680s–1730s), 336–8
　religious diversity in, 337
　religious requirements for office holders, 596
　Roman Catholicism (1634–1776), 412–17
　success of Catholicism, 225–6
　Trinitarian Christians, 336
Mary Tudor (Queen of England), 533
Massachusetts. *See also* Boston, Massachusetts; Plymouth colony
　abrogation of charters, 235
　anti-Catholic sentiment, 535, 536
　beating of Mother Ann Lee, 469
　Cambridge Platform (1648), 293
　compromises of the colonists, 282–3
　French Huguenot settlements, 61–2, 205
　growth of religious toleration, post-Revolution, 592
　Mayflower Compact (1620), 57
　Northampton revival/Jonathan Edwards, 453–4
　Praying Indian towns, 294, 295
　"praying towns" (Martha's Vineyard), 711
　Presbyterianism influence, 290–1
　psalters (biblical psalms) used in, 711–12
　Puritan meetinghouses, 733–4
　Puritan settlements, xv, 220, 434
　Quaker presence, 229, 472
　raids on Puritan settlements, 536
　religious requirements for officeholders, 596
　resentment of imperial interference, 536
　synod meetings (1648, 1662), 233–4
　Universalist presence, 478, 493
"The Master of Breath" (Muskogean-speaking Native Americans), 4
Mather, Cotton, 291, 298, 376, 512, 553, 557–8, 673, 684, 700, 716, 717
Mather, Increase, 235, 290, 292, 512, 518
Mather, Richard, 673
Matins for the Feast of Our Lady of Guadalupe (Jerusalén), 242
Mattys, Jan, 63
maxpe (Crow notion of power), 10
May, Henry, 498
Mayan culture and religion, 181, 191
Mayflower Compact (1620), 57, 227
Mayhew, Jonathan, 572, 575, 676, 711
Mayhew, Thomas, Jr., 357
McCulloch, Thomas, 622
McCulloch, William, 554
McLoughlin, William, 565
medieval historical writing genre, 828–9
mediumistic divination (Africa), 102
meetinghouse church architecture (Puritans), 733–4
megachurch style architecture, 739
Megapolensis, Johannes (Jan van Mekelenburg), 223
Melanchthon, Philipp, 833
Mellificium historicum (Pezel), 833
Memorial and Remonstrance (Madison), 464, 606–7
"Memorial and Remonstrance against Religious Assessments" (Madison), 449
Mennonites (Dutch Anabaptists), 63, 64–6, 563
　Amish separation from, 679
　arrival/establishment of, 485–6
　comparison with Protestantism, 65
　description, 321
　formal theology produced by, 663
　language considerations, 470
　migration patterns, 471

pacifist beliefs, 470
peace witness of, 65
Pennsylvania presence, 442
prominent place of women, 66
sacred music, 720
"singing their faith" heritage, 66
strict practices of, 486
Mercedarians missionary work, 179
Mercier, François Le, 211
Methodists. *See also* Wesley, John
  Canada/War of 1812 and, 625–7
  circuit-riding practice, 226
  condemnation of slavery, 462
  conversions of slaves, 384, 390
  expansion in Canada, 624–5
  formal theology produced by, 663
  Indian Free Methodists, 791
  pre-Columbian era religious thought, 682–3
  women's leadership roles, 562
Mexico
  Anasazi culture, 158–9
  ancestral Pueblo culture, 158–9
  archbishop-viceroy conflicts, 246
  Aztec culture, 166, 178, 641
  convents (*convento*), 248
  European-Indian segregation, 243
  Franciscan presence, 180, 193, 254
  Holy Office of the Inquisition tribunals, 196
  Inca culture, 178
  mission system, 532, 731
  mission system establishment, 532
  Tlaloc (rain/fertility) deity, 160–2
  Virgin of Guadalupe and, 250
Michaelius, Jonas, 222–3
Middle Ages
  growth of mysticism and piety, 46
  growth of Virgin Mary shrines, 47
  promotion of monarchical authority, 39
  Seven Deadly Sins teachings, 44
Middle Colonies (1680–1730), 303–27
  African presence, 325–6
  Anglican presence, 308–10
  Baptist presence, 315–17
  Congregationalism presence, 317–18
  Dutch Reformed Church, 304–7. *See also* Dutch Reformed Church

ethnic diversity, xv–xvi
Euro-Americans/Native Americans in, 326–7
Huguenot presence, 310–11
Jewish presence, 308
Quaker presence, 311–15
revivals/revivalism, 470–1
Roman Catholic presence, 323
women in the churches, 324
Middleton, Conyers, 505
middle world (Mississippian tradition), 142–3, 147
Mies van der Rohe, Ludwig, 738
Migne, J.-P., 841
The Migration of the Negro painting (Lawrence), 771
Mikveh Israel (New World) Jewish synagogues, 396–7
Mill, John Stuart, 499
millenarians, 63
Miller, William, 764
Ministry Act (1693), 444
Mirk, John, 829
missionaries (missionary work).
  See also Capuchins; Franciscans/Franciscan missionaries; Jesuits/Jesuit missionaries
  in African religious traditions, 33, 96, 380–2, 384–5, 387
  Carmelites, 192
  Discalced Carmelites, 266, 267, 277
  in English Catholic community, 73
  in the Indies (1500–42), 179–81
  mendicant orders as, 33, 47, 50, 179–81
  Moravians, 359, 360, 362–3, 365
  to Native Americans, 5, 8, 69, 332, 351, 352, 711
  in New France, 275–9
  Pope Gregory XV and, 177–8
  Presbyterians in New Jersey/Virginia, 460
  rationale for slavery, 214–15
  Recollet missionary work, 201–2, 206, 207–8, 266, 271, 275, 277
  Separate Baptists, 439, 460–1
  Zinzendorf's missions, 69

mission system
  Alta California Franciscan missions, 251, 258–9, 262
  establishment in Mexico, 532
  music and, 708–11
  in New France, 201
  in New Spain by Franciscans, 730
  raids on Spanish missions, 536–7
Mississippian religious traditions, 137–54
  Above World, 142–3, 144, 147, 148–9, 153
  basis of leadership, 138
  beneath world, 142–3, 144, 146, 147–8, 153
  Birdman, 144, 148–50
  cosmology, xiii, 142–4
  deities, 144–5
  earthen mounds, 749–50
  Earth Mother, xiii, 144, 145–7
  free soul/life soul belief, 141
  Great Serpent, 147–8, 153
  green corn ceremony, 141, 154
  middle world, 142–3, 147
  oral traditions, 153
  period commencing 700 C.E., 22
  priesthood membership/roles, 139–40, 141
  religious and cultural changes, 151–4
  ritual plants, 139
  shamanism, 139
  tenets of religion, 140–1
  the Twins, 150–1
  visions through deprivations, 141
Mississippi Choctaw (Native Americans), 5–6
"The Mitred Minuet" engraving (Paul Revere), 573
Modernism style architecture, 738
Mohawk nation, 113, 630
Molin, Paulette, 173
Molyneux, Robert, 420
monastics/monasticism, xiv, 32–4.
  See also Dominicans; Ephrata Cloister; Franciscans/Franciscan missionaries; Jesuits/Jesuit missionaries; nuns
  Beguine/Beghard communities, 34
  Catholic monastic rituals of Matins, 698
  desired lifestyle, 32

lay holy people (*beatas*) participation, 194
  in Mexico, 192
  relocation to urban centers, 33
  Santiago order (Spain), 33–4
  St. Ignatius spiritual movement, 422
  travels/conversions of indigenous cultures, 33
  vows taken by nuns, 193
Montague, James, 89
Montague, Richard, 91
Montmorency-Laval, François de, 216
Monumenta Germaniae Historica, 841
Moore, Milcah Martha, 472
Moravian Church, 67–9, 359, 360, 362–3, 365, 384–5, 443–4, 470–1.
  See also Zinzendorf, Ludwig von
  contributions to the New World, 70–1
  formal theology produced by, 663
  practices of, 482–4
  pre-Columbian era religious thought, 679–81
  sacred music of, 711, 720, 721
Morell de Santa Cruz, Pablo Agustín, 647–8
Morely, Jean, 59
Morgan, Edmund S., 806
Morley, Thomas, 714
Mormon temples, 740
Mornay, Louis-François Duplessis de, 267
Morris, William, 736
Morse, Jedidiah, 505
Morton, Charles, 289, 291–2
Morton, Perez, 726
Mosheim, Johann Lorenz von, 839
Mother Ann Lee. *See* Lee, Ann ("Mother of the Shakers")
Mother Church architecture (Christian Science churches), 738
Mountain, Jacob, 620–1
Moya de Contreras, Pedro, 247
Muhammad, Elijah, 794
Mühlenberg, Heinrich Melchior, 320, 483, 553, 680
Munday, Anthony, 83
Muñoz, Juan Bautista, 251
Müntzer, Thomas, 63, 831
Mupun ethnic group (Africa), 101
Murray, James, 612, 614

Murray, John, 469, 478, 493, 683.
    See also Universalists
Murray, Judith Sargent Stevens, 666, 683
Murrin, John, 435
Muskogean Native Americans, 4, 20
Muslims
    and African slaves/slave rebellions, 105,
        325, 335
    communities (*morisco*), 50
    family religious beliefs, 816
    Mansa Musa and, 104
    mosque architecture, 745–6
    sacred imagery, 776–7
    in West African/Sudanese towns, 103
Mwaghavul ethnic group (Africa), 101
The Mystery Hid from Ages and Generations,
    Made Manifest by the Gospel Revelation
    (Chauncy), 493

Nahua culture/religion, 180–1, 190
Nandi people (Africa), 99
Narragansett Native Americans.
    See Algonquian Native Americans
Nashe, Thomas, 83
National Liberal League, 496
National Origins Act (1924), 801
Native Americans, 3–26. *See also* individual
        tribes throughout the index
    aboriginals of Australia, 10
    ancestor veneration, 4, 13, 353–4,
        670, 819
    archaeological data, 22–3
    baptisms of, 334, 367, 380
    Baptist beliefs, 297
    belief in ghosts, 8, 10
    beliefs about death, 6
    burial traditions, 6–7, 18, 22,
        116–17, 705
    calendrical rituals, 688–9
    choice for Christianity made by, 792–3
    Christian beliefs, 3, 294–5
    Church of England and, 335
    Congregationalist beliefs, 294–5, 296
    corn ceremonies, 26, 141, 154,
        333, 354
    corpse disposal tradition, 7
    deities, 4, 11, 140, 144–7, 158, 160–2,
        164–7

diseases/epidemics, 120, 121, 131, 135,
    208, 215, 350, 705
"divine crusades" of New England clergy
    with, 664
dreams as part of religion, xvi, 15, 20,
    114, 129–30, 132, 139, 141, 165,
    353, 360, 366
English lack of knowledge about, 332–3
evangelicals and, 25, 178, 201–2,
    207–8, 326, 358
folk magic and, 514–15, 521
green corn ceremonies, 26, 141, 154, 333
and Hapsburg Spain (1516–1700),
    636–7
King Philip's war vs., 294
"The Master of Breath," 4
Middle Colonies (1680–1730), 326–7
missions/missionaries for, 5, 8, 69,
    208–10, 275–9, 332, 351, 352, 532,
    629, 711
music traditions and rituals, 708–11
New Ager appropriation of features, 5
New England assault (1675), 235
"passage of time" visual theme, 771
post-Civil War treatment of, 796, 798
potlatches, 4, 5
Praying Indian towns (Massachusetts),
    294, 295
"praying towns" (New England), 711
pre-Columbian era religious thought,
    668–70
pre-Socratic ideas vs. Christian
    notions, 7
prophets/shamans, near-death
    experiences, 5
race/religion questions related to, 786
raids on Puritan communities, 536
raids on Spanish missions, 536–7
religions in Canada, 628–30
religious institutions, 4–5
religious origins, xiii
revivalism and, 453
rituals for drought alleviation, 99–100
rocks, powers of (Ojibwa beliefs), 11–12
Rogel/Calusa chiefdoms and
    Christianity, 23–5
Second Great Awakening and, 791
shamans/shamanism, 6, 8, 17–22

Native Americans (*cont.*)
  skeletal material/bones, representation by, 8–9
  Southern English colonies (1680s–1730s), 332–6
  Spanish atrocities against, 533
  Sun Dances, 5
  sweat bathing ritual, 5
  totemism, 12–13, 14–16
  trees, inanimate/animate states of, 12
  tribal notions of power, 10–12, 124, 127, 128, 129
  trickster figures, 139, 144–5, 166, 173
  use of hallucinogens, peyote, 18, 25
  vision quest practices, 4, 13–14, 365–6, 628–9
  winter spirit dancing ceremonies, 14
  witches and sorcery, 16–17
Natural History of Religion (Hume), 506
Navajo Native Americans
  ancestral rites, 4
  corpse disposal, 7
  dwellings, 167–8
  family culture, 819, 820
  hogans/single-family dwellings, 729
  oral traditions, 157, 167
  Tlaloc ("Trembling God") deity, 164
near-death experiences, 8, 21
Neau, Elias, 325, 383
Neile, Richard, 89
Nelson, Robert, 554
Neopagans, 5, 777–8
Netherlands Reformed Church, 56
Neu-eingerichtites Gesang Buch [Newly Arranged Song Book] (ed. Schultz), 720
New Age spiritual movements, 5, 748, 777–8, 799
New Amsterdam. *See also* New York
  Dutch Reformed presence, 60
  Jewish presence, 308, 394–5
  Mennonite presence, 321
"New Divinity" disciples of Jonathan Edwards, 676
New England. *See also* Boston, Massachusetts; Connecticut; Great Awakening; Massachusetts; New England Congregationalism; Rhode Island; Salem Village (Massachusetts) witch craze
abolitionist sentiment, 667
African slave religions, 376–7
Algonquian religious/spiritual practices (to 1800), 687–90
Andros' dictatorial powers, 283
Anglican church architecture, 732–3
anti-Catholic sentiment, 531, 535–6
astrology practices, 516, 517, 518
background of ministers, 291
beliefs, 288
Calvinist material culture developments, 756–9
Congregational establishment, xv, 433–6
"divine crusades" with Native Americans, 664
Dominion of New England (administrative district), 535
Eastern Algonquin settlements, 351, 357
evangelical dissent, 436–9
evangelical revivals, 437–8
folk magic and superstition, 510–27
fortune-telling, 511, 518
Freewill Baptists, 477
growth of religious toleration, post-Revolution, 592
Indian military assault (1675), 235
Jesuit missionaries, 208–9
King Philip's War, 283, 294, 357, 535
Mayflower Compact (1620), 57, 227
Native American "praying towns," 711
Native American religions, 670
New Light–Old Light divisions, 445, 665
Protestant Evangelicism, 286, 287, 358, 437, 453–4, 459
psalters (biblical psalms) used in, 711–12
Puritan meetinghouse architecture, 733–4
Puritan settlements, xv, 57, 58, 79–80, 220, 230–5, 574
Puritan view of women, 523

Quakers presence, 228–9, 298, 299–300
religion's importance to settlement
  process, 219, 574
revivals/revivalism, 286, 287, 358, 437,
  453–4, 459
Salem witch craze, 229, 510
Separate Baptists, xviii, 439,
  460–1, 468
Shaker presence, 481
singing school (sacred music), 715–18
transatlantic slave trade, 383
Universalists, 470–1, 478–80
Whitefield's successes in, 454
witchcraft in, 382
New England Congregationalism
  (1680s–1730s), xv, 54, 282–302.
  See also Edwards, Jonathan
  agenda of founders, 282
  alarmist rhetoric, 284–5
  Anglicans vs., 436
  baptism of children rules, 285, 286–7
  beliefs, 282
  church disputes, 293
  Church of England vs. hegemony of,
    300–1
  in the Colonies, 70
  cracks in (1720s–1730s), 435
  English-Scottish Presbyterianism vs,
    288–9
  establishment of, 433–6
  hegemonic operativeness of, 294
  Increase Mather/Brattle Street Church
    and, 290
  Indian Christianity, 294–5, 296
  male-female church ratio, 287
  male-female shared traits, 287–8
  Middle Colonies (1680–1730),
    317–18
  overthrow of Andros, 283
  Praying Indian towns, 294, 295
  "Proposals" of, 292–3
  relaxation of strictness, 288–9
  rules of attendance, 284
  Saybrook Platform, 292
  terms of membership, 285–6, 288
  "Yale Apostasy" (1722), 301–2
New England Psalm Book (Prince), 724

The New England Psalm-Singer (Billings),
  725, 726
New France colonies (in North America)
  activities of women, 212–13
  alliance of church and crown, 272–5
  architectural themes, 730
  Capuchin missionary work, 206, 207,
    208, 266, 275, 277
  Church of the colonists, 215–16
  colonization/colonization attempts,
    201–2, 205, 536
  Discalced Carmelite missionary work,
    266, 267, 277
  diseases, epidemics, pandemics,
    202, 205
  educational opportunities, 270
  employment of African slaves, 271–2
  explorations of Cartier, 203–4
  fishing industry, 202–3
  imperial dominion issues, 531–2
  Indian missions, 275–9
  Jesuit missionary work, 202, 206,
    208–9, 216, 266, 275
  Laval/Saint-Vallier and church
    continuity, 264–7
  Louis XIV and, 272–5
  nun growth rates, 268–9
  priest growth rates/shortages, 267–8
  raids on Puritans in Massachusetts, 536
  Recollet missionary work, 201–2, 206,
    207–8, 266, 271, 275, 277
  religion of the colonists, 217
  religious standards, 279–80
  rural population, Acadia, the West,
    Louisiana, 269–72
  Séminaire de Québec missionary work,
    264, 266, 275
  slavery in, 214–15
  Société de Saint-Sulpice (secular priests),
    264
  Sulpician missionary work, 266, 268,
    275, 276–7
New Hampshire
  Congregationalist churches, 283
  Jewish settlement, 408
  Wheelright/Hutchinson banishment
    to, 232

New Israel, U.S. as, 575
New Jersey
  Anglican presence, 444–6
  Dunker presence, 485
  Dutch Reformed Church presence, 305, 445, 539
  framing of constitutional standard, 500
  Huguenots migration to, 533
  immigrant group dissent, 439
  post-Revolution religious diversity, 591
  Presbyterian missionary work in, 460
  Protestant only state offices, 596
  religious toleration in, 535, 595
  Roman Catholicism (1634–1776), 417–19
  SPG in, 309
  Whitefield's successes in, 454
New Light evangelicals, 360, 438, 445, 452–3, 474, 481, 540, 542–3, 547, 665. *See also* Old Lights (anti-evangelicals)
New Light Presbyterians, 439, 446, 543
New Mexico, 254–6, 262
  Bourbon reforms, 653–4
  Franciscan missions, 730
  mission system, 532
New Netherland. *See also* New Jersey; New York
  Dutch Reformed Church, 304
  England's seizure of control, 418
  establishment of, 222–5, 444
  fall of, 225
New Spain
  bultos (sculpted figures), 753–6
  castas (people of mixed ancestry), 244
  church and state, 246–7
  cofradias (religious confraternities), 244, 249
  Council of Trent, impact of, 245–6
  culture and society, 242–3
  financial support, 243, 247
  the Inquisition, 244, 247–8
  Juzgado general de indios (general Indian court), 244
  literary figures (colonial period), 242–3
  missionary work in, 246, 251–3, 254, 532

  mission system chain (of Franciscans), 730
  nuns and convents, 194, 198, 242, 248–9
  Our Lady of Guadalupe apparition (1531), 249–51, 710
  Our Lord of Esquipulas crucifix, 754–5
  painters (colonial period), 243
  religious practice (1680s–1713), 245
  retablos (devotional paintings), 754
  sacred music/musical composers (colonial period), 242, 709, 710
  Spanish/indigenous peoples divisions, 243–5
New Testament
  Anabaptists and, 64
  Book of Revelation, 43, 531, 542, 835
  Catholic teaching origins, 42
  Christ's teachings vs. Seven Deadly Sins, 44
  Luther's recovery of teachings, 54
  promise of salvation, 56
  use of against Puritans by Protestants, 86
Newton, John, 554
A New Version of the Psalms fitted to the Tunes used in Churches (Tate and Brady), 716
New York, 222, 305
  "Act Against Jesuits and Popish Priests" (1700), 418
  American Tract Society (1825), 766
  Anglican presence, 444–6
  "Charter of Liberties and Privileges" (1683), 418
  Deistical Society, 490
  Dutch Reformed Church presence, 305, 445
  first missionary school (1704), 383
  German Reformed churches, 321
  Huguenots migration to, 533
  immigrant group dissent, 439
  Jesuit's education work, 424
  Jewish settlements, 223, 399–400
  religious diversity, post-Revolution, 591
  religious toleration in, 535
  resistance to church establishments, 594–5

Roman Catholic presence, 323, 417–19
Shaker presence, 481
slave revolt (1712), 325
Ngas ethnic group (Africa), 101
Nicene/Post-Nicene Fathers, 841
Nicholson, Francis, 536
Nicodemus (Francke), 552
Nicolas de Tolentino (Saint), 245
Nider, Johannes, 829
Niebuhr, H. Richard, 58
Niles, Samuel, 361
Nitschmann, Anna, 680
Noble, Abel, 476
Nock, Steven L., 810
Noll, Mark, 498
Nordenskiöld, Gustaf, 163
Northern Plains, burial traditions, 6
Northwest coast Native Americans
burial traditions, 6
potlatches of, 4, 5
tamanous (notion of power), 11
vision quest practices, 14
Norton, John, 665, 673, 677
Notes on the State of Virginia (Jefferson), 587
Novo Ordo Seclorum (America's motto), 586
nuns, 32, 33
Augustine nuns, 213
"black veiled nuns," 193
Counter-Reformation Church vow requirements, 193
New France growth rates, 268–9
in New Spain, 194, 198, 242, 248–9
Nupe people (Africa), 99
Nyamwezi ethnic group (Africa), 100
Nyole ethnic group (Africa), 102

"Obaye" (supernatural healing/divining) practices, 701
Occom, Samson, 352–3, 359, 361, 711, 724
Oglethorpe, James, 537
Ojibwa Native Americans, 11–13, 352, 628
Olcott, Henry Steel, 800
Old Lights (anti-evangelicals), 438, 441, 445, 452, 474, 540, 665.
See also Chauncy, Charles; New Light evangelicals

Old Light Synod (Philadelphia), 439
Old Testament
American Revolution and, 578–9
biblical jousting/segregation issue, 798
Book of Chronicles, 578
Book of Chronicles (King James version), 578
Calvinism and, 56–7
Catholic teaching origins, 42
images of Gustave Dore, 774
Oliver, Peter, 574, 575
O'Malley, John, 28, 37
Omnimoda (papal bull, Hadrian VI), 181
Oñate, Juan de, 254
On Councils and the Churches (Luther), 834
Oneida nation, 113, 276, 359, 817
On Liberty (Mill), 499
The Only Method of Attracting All People to the True Faith (Las Casas), 709
Onondaga nation, 113, 126, 128, 352
On the Origin of Error (Bullinger), 833
The Oracles of Reason (Blount), 490
oral traditions
African religious traditions, 97, 98
Native North America, 7, 117, 122, 126–7, 153
Oratory of Divine Love, 52
Ordenanza del patronazgo (1574, issued by King Phillip II), 191–2
Order of Friars Minor, 266
"orders" (dependent societal structures), 39
O'Reilly, Alejandro, 646, 648
orenda (Iroquois concept of power), 10–12, 124, 127, 128, 129, 352
Origen of Alexandria, 827
Origine de tous les cultes (Dupuis), 506
Orisha religion (central/western Africa), of African slaves, 381–2, 387
Christian/Islam parallels, 370
described, 369, 370–2
gris-gris (sacred objects), 370, 381
herbal medicinal practices, 378
Islam worship with, 372, 374
Osborn, Sarah, 666
Osiander, Lucas (the Elder), 836
Ossig, Kaspar Schwenckfeld von, 484
Otterbein, Philip William, 563

Ottoman empire, 28
"Our God, Our Help in Ages Past" psalm (Watts), 721
Our Lady of Altagracia (shrine), 645
Our Lady of Guadalupe
  apparition (New Spain, 1531), 710
  Mexican devotion to, 659
Our Lord of Esquipulas crucifix (New Mexico), 754–5
Overall, John, 89
owachira (kinship)-based mode of production (Iroquois), 118–19, 122
Owens, John, 554

Pachak, Joe, 163
Paine, Thomas
  Age of Reason, 490
  Common Sense, 578–9, 620
  familiarity with evangelical revivalism, 464
  influence of Quaker background, 496
  religious beliefs of, 490, 492, 495, 496, 578–9
Palafox y Mendoza, Juan, 246
Palmer, Elihu, 494, 684
palmistry (in Beverly, MA), 511
pan-Boreal complex, 18
papal administration, popes
  Alexander VI, 35, 177
  Benedict XIV, 250
  Clement XIV, 410
  Gregory XIII, 181
  Gregory XV, 177–8, 192
  Hadrian VI, 181
  History of the Popes (Ranke), 840
  Innocent III, 35, 834, 835
  Innocent XIII, 242
  John Paul II, 259
  Julius II, 35, 177
  Julius III, 35
  Pius II, 828
  Sixtus IV, 247
papal administration (Roman Catholicism), 34–6
  canon law judicial system, 36
  centrality of College of Cardinals, 36
  challenges to authority of, 35
  insistence on supreme authority, 39
  transformation of Rome, 35
Papoonahoal (Munsee Indian) 349, 350, 365
Paris, Treaty of (1763), 260, 611–12, 614
Parris, Elizabeth (daughter of Samuel), 510
Parris, Samuel, 510, 517
Parsons, Robert, 75–6
Partenope opera (Zumaya), 242
Particular Baptists, 230, 474
Pastorius, Francis Daniel, 679
Patrologia Graeca (Migne), 841
Patrologia Latina (Migne), 841
Patronato Real (Royal Patronage, 1508), 177, 183
Paulmier de Courtonne, Jean-Pierre, 200
Payzant, John, 623
peace witness (of Mennonites), 65
Peasant Wars of Reformation Saxony (1524–25), 31, 63
Pei, I. M., 738
Penn, William
  arrival in Philadelphia, 219, 681–2
  control of Delaware colony (1682), 320, 419
  focus on Pennsylvania for Quakers, 312
  land grant from Charles II (1681), 440, 470
  leadership of Quaker consortium, 229
  religious toleration charter, 472
  view on forcing religious beliefs, 595
Pennsylvania. *See also* Philadelphia, Pennsylvania
  Anabaptist presence, 442–3
  Anglican presence, 439–44
  Baptist presence, 316
  Church of the Brethren, 67
  Evangelical Reformed Church, 563
  founding by William Penn, 229, 312
  German churches, 55, 56, 319–23
  German Lutheran presence, 442
  immigrant group dissent, 439
  Jesuit's education work in, 424
  Mennonite presence, 63, 321–2
  Moravian presence, 443–4
  Old Light Synod (Philadelphia), 439
  post-Revolution religious diversity, 591
  Presbytery of Philadelphia, 318

Protestant sacred music, 719
Quaker presence, 440–1
religious toleration in, 535
Roman Catholic presence, 323, 411, 418, 419–21
Schwenckfelders presence, 484
Scots-Irish presence, 441–2
SPG in, 309
Whitefield's successes in, 454
Pennsylvania Anapabtist Church of the Brethren ("Dunkers"), 469
people of reason (*gente de razón*), in New Spain, 243
People's Temple, 817
Pequot Native Americans. *See* Algonquian Native Americans
Peralta, Pedro de, 254
Pérez de la Serna, Juan, 247
Perkins, William, 88
Peter, Johann Friedrich, 721
Petit, Louis, 271
Petit Séminaire (New France), 268, 270
peyote rituals, 25, 147, 820
Pezel, Christoph, 833
Philadelphia, Pennsylvania
   American Sunday School Union (1824), 766
   Baptist Association, 317, 678
   Jewish community, 500–1
   Old Light Synod, 439
Philip II (of Spain), 47, 191–2
Philip V (King of Spain), 242
Phillips, Jonas, 407, 501
Philosophia electiva (Caballero), 649
Philosophical Letters (Voltaire), 490
Pia desideria (Ward), 552
Piccolomini, Enea Silvio, 828
Pierson, Abraham, 234
Pietas Hallensis (Francke), 552
Pietism, 66–9. *See also* Bertholf, Guiliam; Francke, August Hermann; Frelinghuysen, Theodore J.; Spener, Philipp Jakob; Tennant, William, Sr. (and sons)
   Anabaptists relation to, 67, 322
   aspects of living, 471
   description, 307

evangelical component, 451–2, 551
founders, 66–7
Franckian Pietism, 558
German Pietism, 68, 552, 562
Hallensian Pietism, 553
heart imagery, 759–60
origins/basic tenets, 66
pre-Columbian era religious thought, 680
revivalist spirit of, 539
sacred music hymnody (1735–1760), 718–21
piety and practice in North America (to 1800), 686–707
   Africans in the plantation colonies, 700–4
   Algonquians of Southern New England, 687–90
   Anglicans in southern mainland colonies, 695–700
   New England Puritans, 690–5
   Protestants, 705–6
The Pilgrim's Progress (Bunyan), 534
Pinto, Isaac, 404
Pius II (Pope), 828
Pius VI (Pope), 645
Pizarro, Francisco, 179
Plateau Native Americans, 14
Platina, Bartolomeo, 828
Playford, John, 716
Plessis, Joseph-Octave, 627, 631
Plymouth colony
   Ainsworth's psalters as settlement standard, 713
   Baptist persecutions, 477
   comparison to Maryland, 226–7
   hymnal of the founding Pilgrims, 713
   Indian assault (1675), 235
   preaching to Native Americans, 294
Poiret, Pierre, 553–4
Ponet, John, 59
Pontbriand, Henri-Marie Dubreil de, 267
Pope, Alexander, 716
Popes. *See* papal administration, popes
"poppets" for injuring enemies, 512
potlatches (ancestral rights), 4, 5
Pourroy de Lauberivière, François-Louis de, 267

A Prayer, Composed For the Benefit of Soldiery, in the American Army (Leonard), 579
pre-Columbian era (to 1790) religious thought. *See* religious thought, pre-Columbian era (to 1790)
predestinarianism (Calvinist predestinarianism), 88, 92, 222
Presbygationalism (Connecticut ecclesiastical situation), 292
Presbyterians/Presbyterianism (ecclesiastical system), 54, 56, 70. *See also* Occom, Samson; Tennent, William
  in the Carolinas, 340, 342–3
  Connecticut presence, 292
  elective political process, 58
  English Presbyterianism, 288
  evangelical component, 451–2
  formal theology produced by, 663
  Long Island missions, 358
  Massachusetts presence, 290–1
  New Jersey/Virginia missionary work, 460
  New Light Presbyterians, 439, 446
  pre-Columbian era religious thought, 676–7
  revivalists, 446
  Scottish Presbyterianism, 288–9
Primavera Indiana (Sigüenza y Góngora), 242
Primitive Culture (Tylor), 9
Prince, Thomas, 724
Prodi, Paolo, 35
Promise Keepers (PK), conservative men's group, 812
Protestant Associators (1689), 413
Protestant Evangelicism (eighteenth-century America), 81, 451–66
  antirevival sentiments, 438, 445, 453, 455, 456–7
  antislavery implications, 461–3, 464
  background/definitions, 451–2
  Baptist conversions, 459–60
  Connecticut evangelical revivals, 438
  conversion issue/conflicts, 452
  disestablishment movement, 463–4
  Edwards' quest for revivals, 453–4
  evangelical Patriots, 464–5
  Gilbert Tennent's preaching, 455–6
  Long Island (NY) presence, 451
  New England revivals/revivalism, 286, 287, 358, 437, 453–4, 459
  New Light evangelicals, 452–3
  Southern white evangelicals, 461
  Whitefield's leadership, 454–5
Protestant Reformation, 28, 35, 52, 597, 640. *See also* Calvinists/Calvinism; Lutherans/Lutheranism
Protestants/Protestantism, 28. *See also* Anabaptists; Calvinists/Calvinism; Luther, Martin; Lutherans/Lutheranism
  belief in the devil, 43
  beliefs of Paine, 495
  vs. Catholic Church, 31, 37, 53, 74
  church-state separation and, 498
  Continental Protestant Churches, 70
  disputes with Catholicism, 350
  English Protestantism, 77–9
  expansion in Canada, 618, 619
  family values, 808
  folk magic and, 520
  French and Indian Wars and, 664
  immigrant group dissent, 439
  institutional church architecture, 737–8
  Maryland, Plymouth, Rhode Island, 225–8
  Mennonite comparison, 65
  missions to Native Americans, 356–8, 711
  New World origins, xiv–xv
  relation to Church of England, 85
  religious development (to 1800), 705–6
  religious liberties granted to, 595–6
  revivalistic styles, 437
  rivalry with Catholicism, 531–3, 536, 537–8
  sacred music in Pennsylvania, 719
  teaching/evangelical imagery, 763
  Toleration Act and, 534
  traditions of, 52
  view of death, 48
  Virginia and New Netherlands, 220–4
  War of 1812 and, 628
Psalmodia Christiana [Christian Psalms] (Sahagùin), 709

The Psalms, Hymns, and Spiritual Songs of the Old and New Testaments (Dunster), 715
Psalms of David ... for the use of the Reformed Protestant Dutch Church in the City of New-York (Hopkinson), 722
The Psalms of David Imitated in the Language of the New Testament (Watts), 716, 724
Psalterium Americanum (Cotton Mather), 716
psalters (biblical psalms) in British North America (seventeenth century). *See* sacred music in colonial America
Pueblo Native Americans
    building tools/farming technologies, 752–3
    ceremonialism of, 4
    family culture, 819
    pre-Columbia era religious thought, 669
    shamanic practices, 21
    stone/adobe brick houses, 729, 752–3
    use of katchinas, 8
Pueblo Revolt (1680), 174
Puerto Rico
    Bourbon reforms, 636, 646–7
    early church establishment, 178
    Indian slavery in, 373
Purchas, Samuel, 506
Pure Land Mahayana Buddhism, 744
Puritans/Puritanism, 56. *See also* Baxter, Richard; Beveridge, William; Chaderton, Laurence; Nelson, Robert; Perkins, William; Willett, Andrew
    Anglicans/Anglicanism and, 82, 301, 328–9, 331
    anti-Puritan discourse, 83–4
    beliefs on God, 57
    break from Church of England, 230–1
    calendrical rituals, 691, 693–4
    Carolina presence, 340
    church meetinghouse architecture, 733–4
    Church of England self-view of, 434
    claims of being a "covenanted people," 574
    concerns about folk magic, 515–17, 518, 520–1
    Connecticut settlements, 220
    conversions, 452
    death/funeral rituals, 694–5
    depiction of witches, 523
    Elizabethan Puritan movement, 79, 81
    evangelical component, 451–2
    family values, 806–7, 808
    Hooker's assault on, 88
    James VI and I, rising hopes for, 89–91
    Long Island presence, 318
    Massachusetts presence, 220, 434
    meetinghouse architecture, 733–4
    missions to Native Americans, 360
    monthly worship of The Lord's Supper, 692
    Native American raids on, 536
    New England settlements, 57, 58, 79–80, 220, 230–5, 690–5
    ongoing development of, 85–9
    opposition to Baptists and Quakers, 535
    origins, 79–80, 433–4
    Quaker rejection of, 227
    radicalization of, 80–2
    Sabbath practices, 691–3
    self- vs. outside-view, 85
    takeover in Maryland (1655), 226
    term ("Puritan") derivation, 82
    Virginia presence, 221, 328–9
    white magic practices, 693
    women as viewed by, 523
    worship of Lord's Supper, 692

Quakers (Society of Friends). *See also* Fox, George; Penn, William
    American Revolution confrontation of, 582
    antislavery activities, 667
    beliefs of, 311, 440, 470
    Carolina presence, 340, 341
    congregation (description), 313
    control of West Jersey, 229
    disciplinary structures, 315
    divisions during American Revolution, 590
    Edwards' commentary about, 467
    First Amendment (Constitution) and, 71
    folk magic and, 521
    formal theology produced by, 663
    historical background, 229, 312, 472–3
    imprisonment for treason, 469

Quakers (Society of Friends) (cont.)
  Keithian Quakerism, 313–15, 317
  Middle Colonies presence, 311–15
  name ("Quakers") derivation, 472
  New England presence, 228–9, 298, 299–300
  Papoonahoal's interest in, 349, 350
  peace witness of, 65
  Pennsylvania presence, 440–1
  persecution/hanging of (1659–60), 590–1
  pre-Columbian era religious thought, 681–2
  Puritan opposition to, 535
  Quietism of, 222
  rejection of Puritanism, 227
  revival movements, 563
  schism (1690s), 313–15
  Stuyvesant and, 395
  Virginia presence, 222
  women's roles, 324, 472–3, 562
Quamino, John, 383
Quebec Act (1774), 546, 573, 614, 617
Quietism of Quakers, 222, 472
Quincy, Samuel, 672
Quitman, Frederick Henry, 680

race and religion, 781–802. *See also* African religious traditions
  antebellum era (1800–60), 789–94
  Asians, Jews, Muslims (nineteenth and twentieth centuries), 799–802
  "black church" term discussion, 783
  Caribbean, African, South American, Asian immigration, 802
  Chinese Exclusion Act (1882), 782, 801
  civil rights era (1860s–1960s), 782, 797
  influence of Christianity, 782–3
  Jewish assimilation (nineteenth/twentieth century), 800
  lynching of black men, 774, 795
  names given to native groups, 784–5
  post-1865 era, 794–7
  racialization of Asians, 800–2
  racial profiling, 783
  slave trade/colonization era (1500–1800), 784–9
  white supremacist racial thought, 786

Radical Reformation, 62.
  See also Anabaptists; Millenarians; rationalists/rationalistic thinking; Spiritualists; Unitarians
Râle, Sébastien, 276
Randall, Benjamin, 678
Randel, Benjamin, 470–1, 477
Ranke, Leopold von, 840
rationalists/rationalistic thinking, 9, 63, 331, 463, 504, 599. *See also* Adams, John; Carlos III; Franklin, Benjamin; Jefferson, Thomas; Madison, James; Quitman, Frederick Henry
Ravenscroft, Thomas, 714
The Reasonableness of Christianity (Dickinson), 677
Reason the Only Oracle of Man (Allen), 490
recogimientos (refuges) for women, 192–3
Recollet mendicant community (Spain), 34, 275
  New France missionary work, 201–2, 206, 207–8, 266, 271, 277
reconquista (Muslim invaders), 177
Redfield, Margaret Park, 804
reducciones (ad hoc communities), 178
Reed, Paul, 174
Reform Judaism, 489
Reinburg, Virginia, 46
Religieuses Hospitalières de Saint-Joseph, 266, 269
Religion and the American Mind (Heimert), 464
Religion in America (Baird), 845
Religion in America (Hudson), 846–7
Religious and Ceremonial Life in the Kongo and Mbundu Areas, 1500–1700 (Thornton), 107
religious thought, pre-Columbian era (to 1790), 663–85
  Anglican Christians, 672–3
  Ashkenazic and Sephardic Jews, 683–4
  Baptists/Anabaptists, 677–9
  Congregationalist Calvinists, 673–6
  Eclecticism, 684
  European Enlightenment, 684–5
  Friends (Quakers) and Shakers, 681–2
  gender considerations, 665–7
  Lutherans and Moravians, 679–81

Methodists and Universalists, 682–3
Native American religions, 668–70
Presbyterians, 676–7
racial considerations, 667–8
Roman Catholics, 670–1
society, the state and, 664–5
Relly, James, 726
Renewed Church of the United Brethren (*Unitas Fratrum*). *See* Moravian Church
Renwick, James, Jr., 736
República de Indios/República de Españoles, 182–4
Republican Christian Enlightenment (Mark Knoll), 498
retablos (devotional paintings) of New Spain, 754
Revelation, Book of (New Testament), 43, 531, 542, 835
Revere, Paul, 571, 573
revivals/revivalism, 222, 361, 390, 437–8. *See also* Evangelicals/Evangelicalism; Frelinghuysen, Theodore J.; Mather, Cotton; Tennent, Gilbert
  American roots, 556–9
  Anglican/African slaves, 384, 390, 453
  antirevival sentiments, 438, 445, 453, 455, 456–7
  in Canada (Henry Alline), 617, 622–3
  characteristic marks of, 566–7
  children's roles, 562
  Connecticut evangelical revivals, 358, 438, 459
  divisions/conflicts caused by, 540
  dreams during, 361, 453
  Edwards/Northampton, MA, 286, 287, 358, 437, 453–4
  Great Awakening and, 470–1
  Great Britain movements, 553–6
  Long Island, Anglo-American revivalism, 451, 456, 668
  Long Island revival preachers, 358
  in the Middle Colonies, 470–1
  in New England, 286, 287, 358, 437, 453–4, 459
  New World origins, 539–40
  post-1750 movements, 563–5
  Protestant styles, 437
  Quakers, revival movements, 563
  Virginia slave revival meetings, 384
  Whitefield's revival preaching tours, 470, 559–60
  women and, 453, 457–8
Revolutionary War. *See* American Revolution
Rhode Island
  abrogation of charters, 235
  Baptist presence, 316
  founding of, 57, 227–8
  General Baptist congregations, 230, 298
  harboring of dissenters, 227
  Jewish presence, 298, 408, 501–2, 585, 589, 799
  limited religious constraints, 228
  Newport Hebrew Congregation, 501–2
  Quaker presence, 228–9
  religious liberty in, 298, 593, 595
  revival preachers, 358
  Seventh Day Baptist congregation, 476
  Wheelright/Hutchinson banishment to, 232
  Wren-Gibbs baroque architectural style, 734
Rich, Caleb, 478, 479
Richardson, H. H., 736
Richelieu, Armand Jean du Plessis de (Cardinal Richelieu), 200, 205, 207
Riformati mendicant order (Italy), 34
Ripley, Dorothy, 608
Robertson-Smith, William, 4
Roberval, Jean-François de La Rocque de, 204–5
rocks, powers of (Ojibwa beliefs), 11–12
Rodriguez y Lorenzo, Isidoro, 645
Rogel, Juan, 23–5
Rogerine theology, 663
Rogers, Daniel, 457–8
Rogers, John, 682
Roman, Robert, 511
Roman Catholicism. *See also* English Catholicism; French Catholicism; papal administration; papal administration, popes; Roman Catholicism, English North American Colonies; Spanish Catholicism
  Anabaptist comparison, 64
  beliefs and practice, 41–2

Roman Catholicism (cont.)
  beliefs of Paine, 495
  bishops, 31–2
  Bourbon reforms/Spanish America, 638–9
  "Church" (defined), 29
  Church reform, rejuvenation, restoration, 37–8
  conciliarism, 37
  Daughters of the Sacred Heart religious order, 763
  devotion and community, 47–9
  "diocese" (defined), 30
  disputes with Protestantism, 350
  diversity (1750–1790), xix
  doctrinal beliefs, 42
  events leading to renewal, 52
  formal theology produced by, 663
  Good and Evil teachings, 43–4
  Gothic style church buildings, 735
  heart (devotional) imagery, 763
  holy living movements, 551
  intimate piety, 45–7
  Jesuits' global vision of, 641
  Latin culture of the Church, 41
  Latin liturgy learned by Native Americans, 709
  liberalism and, 505
  Luther's criticism of, 31, 37, 53
  magic and, 520
  in the Middle Colonies (1680–1730), 323
  monasticism, 32–4
  Native American conversions (Canada), 629
  New World Spanish Catholicism, xiv, 177–99
  organization of, 29–30
  papal administration (papacy), 34–6
  parishes/distribution of priests, 30–1
  pre-Columbian era religious thought, 670–1
  punishment of clerics, 40
  relation to society, 38–41
  religious syncretism and expansion of, 49–50
  rivalry with Protestants, 531–3, 536, 537–8
  secular Church, 30–1
  self-defense vs. Protestant advances, 52
  sentiment against in New England, 531, 535–6
  Seven Deadly Sins, 44–5
  theology, 42–3
  ubiquitousness of, 38
  view of death, 48
  War of 1812 and, 627
Roman Catholicism, English North American Colonies (1634–1776), 410–28
  Acadian refugees, 421–2
  anti-Catholic sentiment, 422
  Jesuit influence, 422–7
  Maryland and Virginia, 412–17
  New York and New Jersey, 417–19
  Pennsylvania and Delaware, 419–21
  religious practices, 422–8
Roman Inquisition, 52
Rose of Lima ("Patron of the Indies"), 196
Rose of Lima (Saint, "Patron of the Indies"), 196
Rosicrucianism, 323
Ross, Alexander, 506
Rousseau, Jean Jacques, 583
Rowlandson, Mary, 666
Royal and Pontifical University of San Jerónimo (colonial Cuba), 242
Royal Melody Complete (Tans'ur), 723, 725
Ruggles, John, 498
Ruiz de Alarcón, Hernando, 185
Rule and Exercises of Holy Dying (Taylor), 699
Rush, Benjamin, 479, 490, 498
Ruskin, John, 736
Rutherford, Samuel, 59
Ryan, Henry, 625
Ryerson, Egerton, 626
Ryswick, Treaty of (1697), 644

Saarinen, Eero (son of Eliel), 738
Saarinen, Eliel, 738
Sabbatarians, 471, 476, 486
Sabbath practices
  Anglicans, 696
  Baptists, 468–9
  beliefs of Beissel, 487

Episcopalians, 707
Jacobeans, 89
Jews, 401, 404, 683
New England Congregational churches, 284
Protestants, 498
punishments for violations of, 598
Puritans, xix, 94, 691–3
Separates, 475
Sacra Congregatio de Propaganda Fide (1622), 177–8
Sacred Heart of Jesus (heart imagery), 763
sacred music in colonial America, 708–27
    Billings/American Revolution in praise, 725–7
    music and missions, 708–11
    parish style tunes/Watts' texts, 716, 718, 721–5
    Pietist hymnody (1735–60), 718–21
    psalters (biblical psalms), 711–15
    singing controversy/New England singing school, 715–18
    slaves inclusion in evangelical hymn singing, 719
Saffin, John, 667
Sagard, Gabriel, 126
Sahagúin, Bernardino de, 180–1, 709
Saint Bartholomew's massacre of French Huguenots (1572), 533, 542
Saint-Vallier, Jean-Baptiste, 264–7, 270, 274
Salem Village (MA) witch craze, xvi, 229, 510
    attack of spectral testimony/confessions, 526–7
    conviction difficulties, 525–6
    convictions/executions, 524
    counter-magic measures against, 524
    Puritan depiction of witches, 523
    spreading influence of, 521
    standard of proof requirements, 525
    trials, 512, 522
    women as witches, 522–3
Salvatierra, Juan Maria, 253, 256
Sánchez, Miguel, 242–3, 250–1
Sander, Nicholas, 75–6
San Francisco de Asis mission church (New Mexico), 731
Sangmeister, Ezechial (Georg Heinrich), 487

San José, María de, 195
San José mission church (Texas), 731
San Miguel de Aguayo mission church (Texas), 731
San people (early Africa), 96
Santiago monastic order (Spain), 33–4
Sarmiento y Valladares, José, 637
Satterlee, Henry Yates, 737
Sauer, Christopher, 485
Schaafsma, Polly, 174
Schaats, Gideon, 224
Schaff, David Schley, 841
Schaff, Phillip, 841, 846
Schleiermacher, Friedrich, 839
Schoolcraft, Henry Rowe, 11
Schuyler, Philip, 616
Schwenckfelders, 484, 720
Science and Health (Eddy), 738
SCLC (Southern Christian Leadership Conference), 782
Scottish Common Sense School, 600
Scougal, Henry, 553–4
Seabury, Samuel, 673
Seager, Elizabeth, 513
Seasonable Thoughts on the State of Religion in New England (Chauncy), 458
Second Great Awakening (1799–1805), 599, 726, 763, 791
Second London Confession (1667) of English Calvinistic Baptists, 678
sectarian communities, religious diversity in British America (1730–90). *See also* American Revolution; Great Awakening; Mennonites; Moravian Church; Quakers; Separate Baptists; Shakers
    Dunkers, 65, 67, 322, 469, 470, 476, 484–5
    Ephrata Cloister, 468, 485, 486–8, 663, 682, 684, 720
    Freewill Baptists, 477
    Jemima Wilkinson/Jerusalem, 481–2
    "Outsider" status, 468
    physical persecutions for beliefs, 469
    Schwenckfelders, 484, 720
    Seventh-Day Baptists, 468–9, 476–7, 720
    Universalists, 470–1, 478–80, 493

Seka ethnic group (Africa), 100–1
Select Harmony (Law), 726
The Selling of Joseph (Sewall), 667
Séminaire de Québec, 264–7, 270, 271, 275
Seneca nation, 113
Separate Baptists, 439, 460–1, 468, 470, 473–6
  austere physical appearance, 475
  beliefs of, 474
  departure from Congregationalism, xviii
  persecution of, 475–6
  persecutions by, 476
Sephardic Jews, xvii, 395, 398, 404–5, 663, 683–4. *See also* Jews/Judaism
Sergeant, John, 360, 364
Seven Deadly Sins, 44–5
Seventh-Day Baptists, 468–9, 720
Seven Years' War (1754–63), 260, 351, 421, 436, 531, 545, 611, 635, 648
Sewall, Joseph, 575
Sewall, Samuel, 667, 693
Seymour, John, 414
Shakers, xviii, 113, 468, 480–1, 817.
  See also Lee, Ann ("Mother of the Shakers")
  charts and emblematic imagery, 763–5
  family values, 817
  formal theology produced by, 663
  meetinghouse architecture, 740
  pre-Columbian era religious thought, 681–2
shamans/shamanism, 17–22
  disease diagnosis role, 21
  Eastern Algonquians, eighteenth century, 356
  in Iroquoian religion, 115
  macrocosmic features, 20
  in Mississippian religious traditions, 139
  near-death experiences of, 8
  orientation of graves of, 6
  origins, 18
  personal calling to shamanism, 21
  premises/worldview of, 18–19
  word derivation, 17–18
Shasta Native Americans (California), 22
Sheldon, Susannah, 512
Shepard, Thomas, 232, 673, 760

Sherwood, Samuel, 575
Shuswap Native Americans (British Columbia), 7
Sibley, Mary, 510, 514, 517
Siegvolck, Paul, 479
Sigüenza y Góngora, Carlos de, 242, 641
Sikhism, 742, 743
Simons, Menno, 63–4, 485, 679
The Singing-Master's Assistant (Billings), 726
The Singing of Psalms a Gospel Ordinance (Cotton), 714–15
"Sinners in the Hands of an Angry God" sermon (Edwards), 558
Sisters of the Hôpital-Général, 269
Six Nation Iroquois (upper New York state), 628, 630
Sixteen Anthems (Flagg), 723
Sixtus IV (Pope), 247
Skinner, Robert, 92–3
slavery (slave trade)
  African American preachers, 668
  baptism of, 297–8, 334
  burial rituals, 702, 703–4
  calendrical rituals, 702
  Clay's abolitionism speech, 772–3
  confraternities in Africa, 374
  Edwards' antislavery advocacy, 461
  Europe (1400s)/Americas (1500s), 372
  expeditions, seventeenth/eighteenth centuries, 152
  folk magic, 514
  French Catholicism and, 214–15
  growth in New England, 219
  Haynes' antislavery stance, 462
  Iberia, 373–4
  inclusion in evangelical hymn singing, 719
  influence of Islam, 105
  Islam conversions, 372, 373–4
  ladinos (assimilated slaves), 373
  in New France, 271–2
  post-Civil War era changes, 794–7
  racial considerations, pre-Columbian era religious thought, 667–8
  religion and race (1500–1800), 784–9
  Southern English colonies (1680s–1730s), 332–6

Spain's demand for slaves, 375–6
trans-Saharan vs. Atlantic, 105
West Africa as source, 103
Sleidan, Johannes (of Strasbourg), 831
Small Catechism (Luther), 680
Smith, Joseph, 740
Smith, Samuel Stanhope, 498
Smyth, John, 678, 679
SNCC (Student Nonviolent Coordinating Committee), 782
Snyder, Gary, 801
Société de Saint-Sulpice (secular priests), 264
society and Roman Catholicism (c. 1500), 38–41
  consecrated spaces, spiritual markers, 38
  feast days, Easter/Lent, 38
  "orders" (dependent societal structures), 39
  property tax exemptions (France), 40
Society for the Promotion of Christian Knowledge (SPCK), 333, 553, 562
Society for the Propagation of the Gospel (SPG), 309, 326, 333, 357, 380–2, 384, 433, 444, 553, 572, 629
Society in Scotland for Propagating Christian Knowledge, 358
Society of Ancient Druids, 491
Society of Brothers (of the Bruderhof), 817
Society of Friends. *See* Quakers
Society of Jesus
  Council of Trent and, 640
  in English North American Colonies, 410, 425
  Eusebio Kino's membership, 252
  expulsion from Spanish America, xix, 641–3, 649
  in New France, 264
Society of Negroes, 376
Society of the Priests of Saint-Sulpice, 267
Society of the Woman in the Wilderness (Kelpius), 322, 663, 684
sodalities (Catholic religious organization), 139, 197–8, 638
sodomy practices, 24, 184
sola fides/sola scriptura (doctrine of justification by faith alone based on Scripture alone), 53

Some Account of the Forepart of the Life (Ashbridge), 473
Some Thoughts Concerning the Present Revival of Religion (Edwards), 458
Sommer, Peter, 680
soul-wandering (Algonquian practice), 688
South Carolina
  religious requirements for officeholders, 596
"Southeastern Ceremonial Complex," 23
Southern Christian Leadership Conference (SCLC), 782
"Southern Cult," 23
Southern English Colonies (1680s–1730s), 328–45
  Anglican settlements, xvi
  Calvinists/Presbyterian presence, 342–3
  Carolina (North/South Carolina) religious diversity, 338–42
  colonial Virginia, 328–32
  evangelical Protestantism, 343
  Maryland religious diversity, 336–8
  Native Americans/African American slaves, 332–6
southwestern United States. *See* American Southwest
The Sovereignty and Goodness of God (Rowlandson), 666
Spain. *See also* New Spain
  assault on England (1588), 533
  atrocities vs. Native Americans, 533
  Columbus/Cortes, conversion of "heathens" by, 47
  demand for slaves, 375–6
  evangelization efforts, 177–9
  expulsion of Jews, 392, 393
  Holy Office of the Inquisition, 196
  Islam communities, 41, 50
  Jewish communities, 41, 50, 196
  Ordenanza del patronazgo (1574), 191–2
  Phillip II, 47
  Recollet mendicant community, 34
  Santiago monastic order, 33–4
  War of the Spanish Succession, 256–7
Spangenberg, August Gottlieb, 553
Spanish America. *See* Bourbon reforms in Spanish America (1750–1790)

Spanish Catholicism, 177–99. *See also* New Spain
  act of consolidation, 260
  American Southeast, 259–60
  American Southwest, 257–9
  Bourbon reforms, 638–9
  community-religious life integration, 197–9
  conquests and conversions, 177–9
  conversion/assimilation issues, 185–9
  evangelical enterprises, 179–81
  holy apparitions, 197
  limits of spiritual life, 195–7
  Nahua culture/religion, 180–1, 190
  in New Mexico, 254–6
  obstacles to establishment, 182
  Patronato Real (Royal Patronage), 177, 183
  post-Tridentine Church, 195
  pre-Hispanic religious structures, 186–8
  reducciones (ad hoc communities), 178
  religious establishment consolidation, 191–5
  religious festival strategy, 188
  saintly houses (*beaterios*) for women, 192–3
  segregation/subjugation policies, 182–4
  syncretism and autonomy, 189–91
  women *beatas*, 194
  women's religious institutions, 192–3
Spanish Inquisition, 244, 247–8
Speculum Historiale (Beauvais), 829
Spener, Philipp Jakob, 66–7, 552, 680
SPG. *See* Society for the Propagation of the Gospel
Spiritualists, 63, 748
spirituality
  continuities/discontinuities of, 6–9
  etymology of term, 3
spiritus (Latin root of spirituality), 4
Sprigg, Osborne, 571
Squier, Emma-Lindsay, 164–7
Sri Ganesha Hindu temple (Long Island, NY), 742–3
Stamitz, Carl, 721
Stamp Act (1765), 575
"Statute for Establishing Religious Freedom" (Jefferson), 450, 497, 585

Stearns, Shubal, 460, 474–5
Stephenson, Joseph, 723
Sternhold, Thomas, 712, 713
Stoddard, Solomon, 290, 558, 675
Story of Religion in America (Sweet), 846
Strachan, John, 620–1, 626
Streeter, Adams, 478, 479
Strigel, Viktorin, 833
Strong, Josiah, 782
Stuart, David, 167
Stuart, John, 630
Student Nonviolent Coordinating Committee (SNCC), 782
Stumpf, Johann, 832
Stuyvesant, Peter, 223–4, 394
The Suffolk Harmony (Relly), 726
Sulpicians (order of priests), 211, 216, 266, 268, 275, 276–7
Sun Myung Moon, 817–18
Supreme Being
  in African cosmology, 97–8, 102
  in Native North America, 4
Suwarian Islam tradition, 104
sweat bathing ritual, 5
Swedenborg, Emanuel, 504
Sweet, William Warren, 565, 846
The Sweet Psalmist of Israel (Walter), 717
Swintzell, Rina, 172
Swiss Reformation, 832
"The Sympathy of Religions" (Higginson), 508
Synod of Dort (1618), 89, 222, 304
Synod of Massachusetts Bay (1662), 234

tamanous (Northwest/Chinookan peoples notion of power), 11
Tanama (Anasazi culture, "The Trembling God"), 164–7
Tans'ur, William, 722, 723, 725
Taoism, 744, 766
tarot card imagery, 778–9
Tatamy, Tunda, 361–2, 366
Tate, Nahum, 716
Taxation No Tyranny (Johnson), 564
Taylor, Jeremy, 553–4, 699
The Temple of Reason (deism circular), 490
Ten Commandments, 44, 279, 325, 352, 733

Tennant, William, Sr. (and sons), 67
Tennent, Gilbert, 358, 445
   antirevivalist opposition to, 455
   "The Danger of an Unconverted Ministry" sermon, 455–6, 557
   influence of Edwards on, 559
   preaching to crowds, 540
   revival preaching tours of, 470
Tennent, William, 343, 359, 446, 455
   "Log College" (Pennsylvania), 446
Tennent, William, Jr., 361
Teresa of Avila (Saint), 193
Tersteegen, Gerhard, 719
Texas, 257–8, 653–4, 730
Theiner, Augustinus, 838
Third Mexican Provincial Council (1585), 244, 245
Third Orders (Catholic religious organization), 638
Thirty Years' War (1618–48), 68, 224, 533, 646
Thomas à Kempis, 45
Thomson, John, 677
Thornton, John K., 106, 108
Tillotson, John, 289
Tindal, Matthew, 490
Tlaloc (rain/fertility deity), 160–2, 180
Tlaxcalan Indians, 251, 254
tobacco (*Nicotiana rustica*)
   cultivation by Native Americans, 117, 138
   use in indigenous rituals, 5, 17, 20, 125, 135, 139
Toland, John, 490
Toleration Act (1649), 404, 534, 591
Tolkien, J. R. R., 778
Tookey, Job, 512
Toplady, Augustus, 564
Torquemada, Juan de, 185
totemism, 12–13, 14–16
totem poles, 6
Tractatus de legibus ac deo legislatore (Suárez), 643
Tracy, Joseph, 565
A Treatise concerning Religious Affections (Edwards), 558
Treatise on Religious Affections (Edwards), 675
trees, inanimate/animate states of (Algonkians), 12

"The Trembling God" (Tanama, Anasazi culture), 164–7
Trenchard, John, 496
trickster figures
   Anasazi tradition, 166, 173
   Mississippian tradition, 139, 144–5
Tridentine Catholicism, 192, 246
Trinitarian Christians, 225, 336, 500, 673
Troeltsch, Ernst, 841
True Christianity (Arndt), 760
Tubman, Harriet, 771, 773
Tufts, John, 717
Tuleo Native American adoption ceremony, 8
Tunes to the Psalms (New England Psalm Book), 715–16
Tupac Amaru Revolt, 657–9
"Turtle Island" expression (shamanism), 18
Tuscarora nation, 113
Twenty Sermons (Quincy), 672
twins
   Fon creation myth, 98
   Iroquois creation myth, 128
   Mississippian tradition, 150–1
Two Mites Cast Into the Offering of God, for the Benefit of Mankind (Alline), 678
Tylor, Sir Edward, 8–10, 11, 123, 124–6. *See also* animism theory

Unam Sanctam (1302), 39
Unification Church (Rev. Sun Myung Moon), 817–18
Unitarians (Unitarian Christianity), 63, 489, 494, 738
United Society of Believers in Christ's Second Appearing. *See* Shakers
Unity of the Brethren (*Unitas Fratrum*/Bohemian Brothers), 67–8, 482, 553
Universalists, 470–1, 478–80, 493, 682–3. *See also* Murray, John
The Universal Psalmodist (Williams), 723
Upjohn, Richard, 735
Urania, or a Choice Collection of Psalm-Tunes, Anthems, and Hymns from the Most Approv'd Authors (Lyon), 722
Urdiñola, Francisco, 254
Ursulines (religious order), 213–14, 269, 270, 730

Utrecht, Treaty of (1713), 271, 276, 357, 537, 611. *See also* War of the Spanish Succession (1701–13)

Vadian, Joachim, 832
Valdéz, Jerónimo, 647–9
Valverde, Vicente de, 179
Vargas, Diego de, 255
Vega, Garcilaso de la, 188
Verrazano, Florentine Giovanni da, 203
Vesey, William, 444–5
Vieira, Antonio, 641
View of Religious Opinions (Adams), 666
Vindiciae Contra Tyrannos (Daneau), 59
Viret, Pierre, 58–9
Virginia, 220–4
  Anglican presence, 221–2, 226, 328–9, 330, 381, 430–3, 436, 448–50, 696
  church architectural style, 732
  Church of England in, 328–9, 330, 335
  concerns about Catholic loyalty, 543
  defunding of Anglican Church, 463
  Dunker presence, 485
  evangelical dissent, 436–9
  First Charter of Virginia (1606), 404
  folk magic, 512
  "Lawes Divine, Morall and Martiall" government, 221
  Native American presence, 332
  New Light Presbyterians, 439
  Presbyterian missionary work in, 460
  psalters (biblical psalms) used in, 711–12
  Puritan presence, 221, 328–9
  Quaker presence, 222
  religious toleration in, 595, 600
  Roman Catholicism (1634–1776), 412–17
  Separate Baptist presence, 475
  slave revival meetings, 384
  "Statute for Establishing Religious Freedom," 450, 497, 585
  Whitaker's *Good Newes from Virginia* sermon, 221
La Virgin Madre de Guadalupe (Sánchez), 242–3
Virgin Mary
  apparitions of, 197, 250, 710
  condemnation for using in prayers, 106
  cults of, 47, 217
  sculptures, shrines, statues of, 38, 47, 190
  veneration in New Spain, 245
Virgin Mary shrines, 47
Virgin of Guadalupe, xiv, 245, 250
vision quest practices, 4, 13–14, 365–6, 628–9, 688
visuality in New America
  American Muslim imagery, 776–7
  American Tract Society illustrated tracts, 766, 767–70
  Buddhist illustrations, 766
  Catholic heart imagery, 763
  evangelical illustrations, 766–70
  Jewish Passover haggadah illustrations, 774–6
  Lawrence/African American-centric art, 771–4
  Neopagan/shamanistic imagery, 777–8
  Our Lord of Esquipulas crucifix (New Mexico), 754–5
  "passage of time" leitmotif, 771–80
  Pietist heart imagery, 759–60
  Protestant teaching/evangelical imagery, 763
  retablos (devotional paintings) of New Spain, 754
  Shaker/Adventist charts, emblematic imagery, 763–5
  witchcraft/tarot imagery, 778–9
Vizcardo y Guzmán, Juan Bautista, 643
Vollständiges Marburger Gesang-Buch [Complete Marburg Song Book] (Luther), 720
Voltaire (François Marie-Arouet), 490
Voragine, Jacobus de, 829

Wagner, Abraham, 720
wakan (Lakota notion of power), 10–11
Walcott, Mary, 510
Walker, David, 793
Wallin, Benjamin, 724
Walloons, settlement in New Netherlands, 223
Walpole, Horace, 59
Walpole, Robert, 577

Walter, Thomas, 717
Wampanoag Native Americans.
    See Algonquian Native Americans
Ward, Ebenezer, 476
Ward, W. Reginald, 552
Wardwell, Samuel, 511
War of 1812, 607–8, 610, 625–8
War of Jenkin's Ear (Britain vs. Spain) (1739), 537–8
War of the Spanish Succession (1701–13), 256–7, 536–7
Washington, George
    fasting/prayer days ordered by, 588, 607
    letter about invasion of Quebec (1775), 615–16
    as prophet of "America's Scripture," 584
    relationship with Rhode Island Jews, 408, 501–2, 585, 589, 799
    religious beliefs of, 589–90, 602
    religious symbol used by squadron of, 581–2
    viewpoint of church-state separation, 599
Watt, Joachim von (Joachim Vadian of St-Gallen), 831
Watts, Isaac, 454, 716, 718, 724
Webster, Daniel, 791
Webster, Mary, 525
Webster, Samuel, 577
Weiss, George, 484, 720
Wesley, Charles, 454
Wesley, John, 454, 462, 482, 560, 678, 718
    Adams' interest in, 504
    Edwards' influence on, 561
    friendship with Whitefield, 560, 563
    "The Late Work of God in North America" sermon, 565
Wesleyan Methodists, 551
Wesleyan movement (Great Britain, eighteenth century), 554–6
Westminster Assembly (England), 233
Wet'suwet'en Native Americans (British Columbia), 7
Wheatley, Phillis, 666
Wheelock, Eleazar, 360, 367
Wheelwright, John, 231
Whitaker, Alexander, 221
Whitaker, William, 221

White, Andrew, 226, 671
White, William, 673
Whitefield, George, 290, 541, 553, 554
    association with Hugh Bryan, 461
    background of, 559
    Collection of Hymns for Social Worship, 724
    in dream of Samson Occom, 361
    friendship with Gilbert Tennent, 557
    friendship with John Wesley, 560, 563, 564
    hymn collection published by, 718
    influence of Edwards on, 559
    influence on other groups, 470–1
    preaching to crowds, 540
    religious enthusiasm inspired by, 437, 482, 540, 554
    revival preaching tours of, 470, 559–60
    tour of colonial America (1740s), 328
    warnings against Great Britain by, 564
white magic practices of Puritans, 693
White Over Black (Jordan), 786
Whitgift, John (Archbishop of Canterbury), 83, 88
Whittingham, William, 59
The Whole Booke of Psalmes Collected into English Metre (Sternhold and Hopkins), 712, 713
The Whole Booke of Psalmes Composed into 4 Parts (Ravenscroft), 714
The Whole Book of Psalms ... Compos'd in Three Parts (Playford), 716
Wicca/Wiccans, 777
Wilfrid of Hexham, 827–8
Wilkinson, Jemima, 481–2, 667
Willard, Samuel, 515, 673, 677
Willett, Andrew, 88
William and Mary (English co-monarchs), 283, 305
William III (King of England), 534, 535–6
William of Orange (King of England), 59, 235
Williams, Aaron, 723
Williams, Abigail (niece of Samuel Parris), 510
Williams, Elisha, 541
Williams, John, 90

Williams, Roger
  banishment of, 231
  description of the Naragansetts, 687
  establishment of Rhode Island, 57, 227
  Native feasting rituals comments, 689
  rejection of Quaker positions, 228
  religious diversity created by, 496
Winchester, Elhanan, 478–9, 683
winter spirit dancing ceremonies, 14
Winthrop, John, 57, 232
Wister, Sarah "Sally," 473
The Witches Almanac, 778
witches/witchcraft and sorcery, xvi, 778–9. *See also* Salem Village (MA) witch craze
Witherspoon, John, 59, 580
women. *See also* nuns
  activities in New France, 212–13
  beatas (hermits, visionaries, spiritual guides), 194
  beaterios (saintly houses) for, 192–3
  Calvinist beliefs, 62
  Christian participation, 41, 45
  Church of England prejudice against, 562
  cloistered/monastic orders, 33–4, 192
  Counter Reformation Church and, 193
  Earth Mother symbol, 145–7
  growth of mysticism, 46
  Iroquois, agricultural production, 119
  Kokopelli and, 160
  Mennonite beliefs, 66
  in Middle Colony churches, 324
  Native vision quests and, 14
  New England Congregationalism data, 287
  pre-Columbian era thought, 665–7
  Puritan view of, 523
  religious institutions for, 192–3
  revivalism and, 453, 457–8
  role of, in Quakers, 324, 472–3
  Rose of Lima, 196
  as shamans, 22
  as slaves/concubines, 105
  spiritual leadership roles, 562
  witches, 43, 99
Woodmason, Charles, 460
Woodward, Josiah, 553
Woolman, John, 472, 667, 682
Worcester v. Georgia Supreme Court case, 792
World's Parliament of Religions (Chicago, 1893), 800
Wren, Christopher, 732
Wren-Gibbs baroque architectural style, 732, 733–4
Wright, Frank Lloyd, 738
writing. *See* historical religious writing

X, Malcolm, 794
Xavier, Francis (Saint), 423

Yaka ethnic group (Africa), 102
Yamma, Bristol, 383
Yoruba cosmology (Africa), 98, 101
Young, Brigham, 740
Yurok Native Americans (California), 14, 22

Zen Buddhism, 744
Zimmerman, Carle C., 805
Zinzendorf, Ludwig von, 68, 69, 482–3, 553, 563, 680. *See also* Boehler, Peter; Spangenberg, August Gottlieb
Zubly, John, 580
Zumárraga, Juan de, 196, 249
Zumaya, Manuel de, 242
Zwickau Prophets, 831
Zwingli, Ulrich, 63